INDEX OF SPREADSHEET APPLICATIONS

QUANTITATIVE DECISION MAKING

with Spreadsheet Applications

QUANTITATIVE DECISION MAKING

7TH EDITION

with Spreadsheet Applications

LAWRENCE L. LAPIN

San Jose State University

WILLIAM D. WHISLER

California State University, Hayward

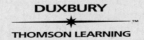

DUXBURY

TM

THOMSON LEARNING

Australia · Canada · Mexico · Singapore · Spain · United Kingdom · United States

DUXBURY

THOMSON LEARNING ™

Sponsoring Editor	Curt Hinrichs
Marketing Manager	Tom Ziolkowski
Marketing Assistant	Mona Weltner
Assistant Editor	Ann Day
Print/Media Buyer	Karen Hunt
Permissions Editor	Bob Kauser
Editorial Assistant	Suzannah Alexander
Production	Summerlight Creative
Text & Cover Designer	Diane Beasley
Cover Photographs	PhotoDisc
Composition & Illustration	G&S Typesetters
Copy Editor	Minda Corners
Text and Cover Printer	Quebecor World Book Services—Versailles

For permission to use material from this text, contact us by
Web: http://www.thomsonrights.com
Fax: 1-800-730-2215
Phone: 1-800-730-2214

Wadsworth/Thomson Learning
10 Davis Drive
Belmont, CA 94002-3098
USA

For more information about our products, contact us:

Thomson Learning Academic Resource Center
1-800-423-0563
http://www.duxbury.com

International Headquarters
Thomson Learning
International Division
290 Harbor Drive, 2nd Floor
Stamford, CT 06902-7477
USA

UK/Europe/Middle East/South Africa
Thomson Learning
Berkshire House
168-173 High Holborn
London WC1V 7AA
United Kingdom

Asia
Thomson Learning
60 Albert Street, #15-01
Albert Complex
Singapore 189969

Canada
Nelson Thomson Learning
1120 Birchmount Road
Toronto, Ontario M1K 5G4
Canada

Library of Congress Cataloging-in-Publication Data

Lapin, Lawrence L.
    Quantitative decision making with spreadsheet applications / Lawrence L. Lapin, William D. Whisler.—7th ed
p.   cm.
    Rev. ed. of: Quantative methods for business decisions. 6th ed. ©1994.
Includes bibliographic references and index.
ISBN 0-534-38024-7 (alk. paper)
1. Decision making—Mathematical models.   2. Operations research.   3. Statistical decision.   I. Whisler, William D.
II. Lapin, Lawrence L. Quantitative methods for business decisions.   III. Title.

HD30.23.L36   2001
658.4′03—dc21

To Lía, Max, and Charlotte

Es intentando lo imposible como se realiza lo posible.

BRIEF CONTENTS

CONTENTS

PREFACE

Our goal in writing *Quantitative Decision Making with Spreadsheet Applications* has been to provide a complete and modern treatment of basic management science methodology. The book is written for college students who have only a limited algebra background. Even more important, it is designed to provide them with a feeling for the variety and power of management science tools, to alleviate their apprehension of the subject, and to enable them to recognize on-the-job situations in which management science methodology can be successfully employed.

Although this is the seventh edition, it is in many ways a new book, due largely to the inclusion of spreadsheet applications. The book's primary software tool is now Microsoft Excel and the add-ins Precision Tree, *@RISK*, BestFit, and RISKView. Those software programs are complemented by the upgraded *QuickQuant 2000* for Windows, which now covers what is not easy to do with Excel or its family of add-ons. All needed software is provided on the CD-ROM that accompanies new copies of this book at no added cost to students.

Although this book embraces several commercial software packages, it keeps the original look and feel. Small problems are still meant to be worked out by hand, and explanations of the underlying models have not been sacrificed to make room for the new. All of the essentials for a first course in quantitative methods are still here, and there is still plenty of choice regarding course topics.

This seventh edition provides a streamlined topical sequence that minimizes jumping back and forth. Its six parts will make it easier for readers to navigate (see the Contents page for a complete listing). The many improvements were motivated by a desire to improve the book's effectiveness while reducing hand computational demands and giving better explanations in those areas where our own students had difficulties. Text revisions appearing in this seventh edition are the most extensive ever in accordance with the dual objectives of making better use of the computer and showing students the relevance of management science to everyday business decision making.

IMPORTANT FEATURES OF THE SEVENTH EDITION

This revision has undergone a complete overhaul, including three drafts, the efforts of many hundreds of students, and countless nights and weekends to get it just right. To this end, the seventh edition of *Quantitative Decision Making* has adopted five major themes to make it modern, practical, and pedagogically effective.

Relevancy

First, we wanted to make the material come alive for students and address their misconception that management science is not relevant. Students must recognize that quantitative concepts and decision-making ability are life skills that will help them immeasurably in their future endeavors. Specifically, we offer the following enhancements:

- The *expanded introduction* substantially broadens exposure to real-life applications.

- *Practical spreadsheet applications appear throughout.* In today's computerized environment, the optimal focus in teaching quantitative methods emphasizes concepts more than hand computations with algorithms, so each chapter contains computer applications that are integrated throughout nearly every chapter, not just at the end of each chapter. The effect of this integration is the inclusion of more realistic illustrations that reflect the types of problems students will face in their future studies and careers.

Concepts Presented with a Student Orientation

In this way, our second theme recognizes that today's students acquire quantitative skills in different ways. We have been careful to fully develop important concepts, often breaking them down into manageable chunks. Specifically:

- *Optimization concepts are reorganized to offer maximum flexibility in course coverage.* Linear programming and its extensions are covered in a more streamlined way. This has been partly achieved by placing the simplex method in an optional section. Those students who seek the simplex details will still be able to find them.

- *Improved topical groupings and simpler presentations are provided.* The linear programming group also has been simplified by combining duality, sensitivity, and postoptimality analysis in a single chapter that emphasizes using the computer and linear programming to strategically improve the business environment. In that same vein, integer and goal programming are combined in one chapter, and transportation problems appear together with assignment problems.

- *Although large problems need computer solutions, small problems are always first solved by hand.* Every topic is explained with concepts, the underlying model, and the solution algorithm. Small problems are used for this—always to be solved first by hand. After those preliminaries, computer tools are described. We strongly believe that skill in using software is just one element to learning quantitative methods.

- *Easy-to-apply algorithms are featured and richly illustrated.* For instance, the complete transportation method is described in such a way that students can work small problems by hand and acquire the flavor of a user-friendly multistep algorithm. They can check themselves with *QuickQuant 2000,* which shows all details as an option, and most will find that package easier than Excel for solving these problem types.

Greater Focus on Decision Analysis

Our third theme was places greater emphasis on this main purpose for studying quantitative methods. To that end, this book:

- *More strongly emphasizes decision making.* The second chapter on probability (Chapter 4) discusses distributions. Its new sections on subjective probability are positioned earlier to reflect its expanding role in decision making.

- *Places decision analysis earlier.* Moving decision analysis up to Chapters 5 and 6 further emphasizes the importance of decision making. The earlier placement of

certainty equivalents, risk premiums, and utility acknowledges of the growing relevance of those topics.

Computing and Spreadsheets

Our fourth theme reflects the latest practice in applying quantitative methods. We have therefore fully embraced spreadsheet modeling techniques and software.

- The new Chapter 2 introduces electronic spreadsheets and Excel. (It may be skipped by students who are already familiar with spreadsheets.)
- Excel add-ins are featured wherever they do a superior job. That is especially true of Monte Carlo simulation, which is applied using *@RISK*.
- *QuickQuant 2000* shows all of the steps taken in reaching a solution, eliminating the need to do messy computations by hand. It can display all iterations of simplex, allowing students to see how linear programming actually works. Those optional details are completely hidden by the Excel Solver, which gives answers only.
- Understanding Excel Solver solutions is easily achieved with *QuickQuant 2000*. Since it will exchange data files with Excel, *QuickQuant* can give detailed evaluations for the same linear programs originally solved with a spreadsheet.
- Software illustrations emphasize ease of use and feature the better approaches. For instance, *QuickQuant 2000* has compelling advantages in applying Program management with PERT/CPM, and it is the featured software for that topic. The package constructs the network on screen using only data about the predecessor activities. Although it can exchange files with Excel, the more capable *QuickQuant* can help perform time–cost tradeoffs and Monte Carlo simulations.

Being Current

Finally, our fifth theme is to have this book be up-to-date. We have tried to make it appealing to today's student in many ways. In addition to the spreadsheets, relevant applications, and careful development, we have taken great care to include new problems and cases that are representative of problems that students may face in the workplace.

- Chapters have minicases and motivating quotes. Each chapter begins with words of wisdom and a realistic business problem that is later solved using the concepts just presented.
- Expanded end-of-chapter cases include more applications and utilize the new software tools.
- The chapters and organized problems have been thoroughly tested in class. This book has been used many times in a variety of courses, which has resulted in the culling, revising, and grading of the problem material. In general, the problems are broken into several distinct parts to make the student's job easier and to permit the instructor added flexibility in making assignments. As an added bonus, brief answers to selected problems are provided in the back of the book so that students can check their own work. They may find detailed answers to those problems in the student solutions manual. Questions for each end-of-chapter case appear with the case, and the cases themselves have been upgraded for this edition.
- Hundreds of new problems, improved cases, and larger data sets have been added. The revised book has a new problem mix that can be tailored to students' capabil-

ities. The problems now reflect greater realism and better represent the various techniques and their nuances. To that end, this edition has new cases based on real applications and involving bigger data sets. The problems and cases make even greater use of the computer, allowing considerable potential for course enrichment.

OUR APPROACH

Quantitative Decision Making seeks to develop students' intuition and their ability to apply quantitative techniques to real business problems. Discussions devoted to difficult topics therefore may be longer than those of other books. We believe our explanations, richly illustrated with relevant and interesting examples, will provide more meaningful and easier learning experiences. The book also highlights the limitations and pitfalls associated with various mathematical models and algorithms. For example, some basic models, such as the EOQ model used in inventory decisions and the simple queuing formulas, are based on assumptions that rarely apply in real life. Wherever practical, alternative approaches such as Monte Carlo simulation are indicated and fully described.

ANCILLARY MATERIALS

The Instructor's Suite for Microsoft Office CD-ROM provides teaching suggestions and detailed solutions to the nearly 800 problems and 37 end-of-chapter cases in the text. It includes test items for each chapter and slides in formats that are compatible with Microsoft Office's PowerPoint application.

The test bank on the Instructor's Suite contains a set of approximately 200 solved problems of slight to moderate difficulty.

A comprehensive bibliography is included in the back of the book for students who wish to pursue a particular topic in greater detail.

The Student CD-ROM will contain data files for the problems and Excel templates.

A Student's Solutions Manual is available for student purchase and includes detailed solution to the answers appearing in the back of the book.

Software. The student's and instructor's CD-ROMs both contain the featured software:

- Palisade's DecisionTools (including Precision Tree, BestFit, @*RISK*, and RISK-View)
- *QuickQuant 2000 for Windows*
- The above are included with every new copy of the text.
- Software guides for Excel and *QuickQuant 2000* are provided on the student and instructors CD-ROMs.
- A Web site—www.duxbury.com—will provide helpful suggestions for instructors and students who use this book.

ACKNOWLEDGMENTS

We wish to thank our colleagues who were instrumental in helping us shape the manuscript and all the users and reviewers of previous editions. We also are grateful for the valuable assistance of our students. Especially helpful were Patricia Axelrod, Roy Reker, Don Ford, Rebecca Richter, Cecilia Mok, Daniel Lorenz, Conrad Tan, and Daryl Watson. Special thanks go to Janet Anaya, who helped find errors and assisted in preparing the Instructor's Manual. Finally, we wish to thank our reviewers: Bruce Anderson, West Virginia University; Barry Blecherman, Brooklyn Polytechnical University; Jan Christopher, Delaware State University; Dinesh Dave, Appalachian State University; Shad Dowlatshaki, University of Missouri–Kansas City; Abe Feinberg, California State University–Northridge; Damodar Golhar, Western Michigan University; Alfred Gomez, Florida Atlantic University; Youngsik Kwak, Delaware State University; Sarah Livingston, Embry-Riddle Aeronautical University; Thomas Pencer, Meredith College; Zinovy Radovilsky, California State University–Hayward; Sunil Sapra, California State University–Los Angeles; and Prakash Shenoy, University of Kansas.

LAWRENCE L. LAPIN
WILLIAM D. WHISLER

PART I

INTRODUCTION

Every journey begins with the first step.

Widespread utilization of quantitative methods in business has caused a decision-making revolution. According to James Crowe, CEO of Level 3 Communications, they give us "a weapon so powerful that it can help transform even fledgling companies into highly efficient optimized organizations capable of competing on any business battle ground in the world."[1]

Chapter 1 uses illustrations involving actual applications to introduce quantitative methods used by modern businesses.

A second revolution over the past decade has been the widespread use of spreadsheets. Chapter 2 introduces the basic spreadsheet concepts to be developed in this book.

---

[1] James Crowe, quoted in "Something to Crowe About," by Peter Horner, *OR/MS Today* (June 2000), p. 38.

CHAPTER 1

INTRODUCTION TO QUANTITATIVE METHODS

Exposure to quantitative methods will teach managers to ask the right questions.

A quiet revolution has taken place in managerial decision making over the past three decades—a revolution that is due largely to the successful implementation of **quantitative methods** and the widespread use of computers. The list of business problems that these procedures can be employed to solve grows daily, and examples of successful applications can be found in every functional area—from marketing to production, from finance to personnel—and in all major industries. Indeed, quantitative methods can be applied to decision making in general and can be used by individuals or groups, in education, in the professions, and in every type of organization, including governments and nonprofit foundations.

Unfortunately, quantitative methods make up one of the least recognized disciplines. Unlike chemistry or history, the term conjures up no images for most people. This is paradoxical, because quantitative methods touch everybody. This may be because their products are less tangible and deal with systems or services so common that we take them for granted. They are in that sense like bridges and roads—part of our society's infrastructure. Usually we do not think much about them, but we expect them always to be there.

A few examples may help us recognize the ubiquitous, although transparent, nature of quantitative methods. When you break your car's plastic light cover or when your television malfunctions, you can order the necessary replacement part. If the item is out of stock, you can expect to get it soon. That is made possible by the infrastructure for controlling inventories, for which quantitative methods play a pivotal role in the necessary planning. Inventory control is discussed in Chapters 15 and 16.

When you place a telephone call, you expect to hear an instantaneous dial tone and your call to be completed. But in some countries, dial tones can take hours to happen, or circuits are so full that calls cannot be completed. Certainly, engineers have a role in telephone system hardware, but so do quantitative methods, even if their role is unrecognized. Telephone capacity planning is done with two main branches of quantitative methods: queuing analysis (waiting lines) and simulation. These are discussed in Chapters 17 and 18.

Who would ever think of quantitative methods while waiting for a ride at Disneyland? Have you ever wondered why some banks, post offices, or fast-food restaurants have switched from having many lines to one line? Over the last twenty years, big im-

provements in waiting in lines have resulted from applying those same quantitative methods.

In the more developed countries, a letter or package only takes a few days to reach its destination, although you may not be aware of the role played by quantitative methods in developing the delivery systems. In some countries, less fortunate people can never be sure the item will arrive; their countries do not have delivery systems optimized by quantitative methods. Such distribution problems are discussed in Chapter 12.

When you book an airline flight, you do not think of using quantitative methods. Yet today's airline industry would not exist without those tools. They are basic to the computerized airline reservation systems we take for granted. Quantitative methods are also vital in setting ticket prices, scheduling flights, maintaining aircraft, and organizing baggage-handling systems. The procedure common to all those areas is linear programming, discussed in Chapters 8–13.

Quantitative methods are all around us and affect our activities in many ways. Even Nobel Prizes have been awarded for work in this field.[2] It is important to know quantitative methods and how they can be used in our daily lives. The list of their improvements to our well-being gets longer each day. The next section gives some concrete examples.

1-1 CONTINUING STORIES OF SUCCESS WITH QUANTITATIVE METHODS

A few short case histories will demonstrate how useful quantitative methods have been in solving a variety of actual problems.

- **Managing Research and Development**   In the late 1950s, the U.S. Navy was faced with the monumental task of equipping its nuclear submarine fleet with Polaris ballistic missiles. A quantitative method called PERT (Program Evaluation and Review Technique) was used to establish schedules and to coordinate and control the efforts of hundreds of contractors.

- **Determining the Number of Bank Tellers**   Banks often use quantitative analysis to decide how many tellers are needed at various times during the week, so employee workloads can be balanced and so customers spend a tolerable amount of time waiting in line.

- **Locating Warehouses**   A chemical company that produces fertilizers and pesticides employed quantitative methods to determine where to locate its warehouses. The resulting sites minimized the combined annual cost of transportation, storage, and handling.

- **Designing an Oil-Tanker Port Facility**   An international oil company committed several hundred million dollars to the construction of a port facility in the Persian Gulf to service oil tankers. Alternative designs were constructed and run "on paper" for a number of years to determine a statistical pattern for future profits. Through this computer simulation, the design was selected that provided the greatest rate of return on invested capital at an acceptable level of risk.

---

[2]T. C. Koopmans and L. V. Kantorovich split the 1975 Nobel Prize for economics. They did pioneering work in one of the earliest quantitative methods techniques, linear programming. H. Markowitz, the winner of the 1992 prize, did much of the original work in quadratic programming and simulation. J. C. Harsanyi, J. F. Nash, and R. Selten shared the 1994 prize for their original work in game theory.

- **Deploying Fire-Fighting Companies**   A study was conducted in New York City to determine how many fire companies the city needed, where they should be located, and how they should be dispatched to alarms.[3] A simulation of the new adaptive procedure indicated that faster response times could be achieved and workloads could be substantially lowered at the same time. Total annual savings to the city exceeded $5 million per year.

- **Improving Investing**   Quantitative methods have been used extensively in the stock market since the 1980s. The following *Business Week* quotation refers to real-world quantitative methods analysts as "quants." They "are extremely competitive and thus reluctant to discuss their Midas Touch methods . . . used . . . to revolutionize the stock market . . . but that's only a 'minor wrinkle' compared with what's possible. . . . The new schemes, based on methods borrowed from the physical sciences, such as pattern recognition, instant data analysis and *linear programming* [discussed in Chapters 8–11], help brokerage [firms] spot trading opportunities faster, construct better portfolios, and invent new financial instruments."[4]

- **Streamlining Distribution, Routing, and Scheduling**   Have you ever waited all day for the delivery of a home appliance or a piece of furniture or for a repair person to fix something in your house such as the TV or the plumbing? If so, the *Wall Street Journal* wrote that the small closely held software company, Lightstone Group, might be the answer to your prayers. The company uses "programs for *routing and scheduling,* a world dominated by . . . United Parcel Service . . . [whose software] allows companies to arrange pickups and drop-offs efficiently and to schedule service calls."[5]

- **Managing Inventory**   The *Wall Street Journal* gave the story of how a maternity shop chain got a jump on its competitors in the summer of 1996 by using inventory management (the topic of Chapters 15 and 16).[6] Another example shows the significant effect quantitative inventory methods have had on the U.S. economy from a macroeconomic perspective. During the delayed recovery of the U.S. economy from the slowdown that started in 1990, the Federal Reserve Bank of San Francisco stated that "*new management techniques* have allowed inventories to be kept under relatively tight control."[7] Those are methods of quantitative inventory management, discussed in Chapters 15 and 16.

- **Scheduling Flights**   An article about major trends in the airline industry mentions quantitative methods.[8] The major airlines sell flights between 50,000 pairs of cities by using "cutting-edge mathematical theorems" such as linear programming

---

[3] Ignall, E. J. et al., "Improving the Deployment of New York City Fire Companies," *Interfaces* (February 1975), pp. 48–61.

[4] John W. Verity, "Street Smarts: The Supercomputer Becomes a Stock Strategist," *Business Week* (June 1, 1987), pp. 84–5.

[5] Raju Narisetti, "Waiting for the Cable Guy? Software Can Save the Day," *Wall Street Journal* (April 4, 1998), p. B1.

[6] Laura Bird, "High-Tech Inventory System Coordinates Retailer's Clothes with Customers' Taste," *Wall Street Journal* (June 12, 1996), p. B1.

[7] Adrian W. Thorpe, "The Slow Recovery," *FRBSF Weekly Letter,* no. 92–93 (September 25, 1992), pp. 2–3.

[8] Thomas Petzinger, Jr., "Four Lessons Our Airlines Need to Learn," *Wall Street Journal* (November 6, 1995), p. B1.

to match crews with flight schedules. Linear programming is discussed in this book in Chapters 8–11. A second article discusses the use of quantitative methods at American Airlines, crediting the methods with helping to establish the SABRE reservation system. More than 600 people became involved in building models for decision support.[9]

- **Optimizing Agriculture** Gary Schneider started a software company in 1996, called AgDecision, based on a course in quantitative methods he took in college. He has used linear programming (Chapters 8–11) to help farmers optimize their crop selection, and he feels that the software he developed would be "the potential breakthrough application—'killer app'—that could cause farmers to buy PCs the way the first spreadsheet program caused the Apple computer to take off."[10]

- **Waiting in Lines** Why are we always waiting in lines? Isn't it possible, with the right planning, to eliminate waiting? Lines are a special concern of fast-food restaurants, although short waits do not happen automatically. One experiment at 70 McDonald's restaurants made hamburger history. The company tested whether to consolidate its multiple waiting lines into just one, like at banks.[11] Waiting lines are discussed in Chapter 17, and simulation is discussed in Chapter 18.

- **Investing in Satellite Communications Systems** Satellites have become an increasingly important element in worldwide communications. Various types of quantitative methods in many different areas of application have been employed to evaluate the various alternatives and to recommend optimal strategies.[12]

- **Planning Political Campaign Strategies** One interesting application of quantitative methods occurred during a U.S. senatorial race. By using quantitative methods to identify the important characteristics of small geographical units throughout the state, one candidate was able to concentrate campaign expenditures on the few that would be most profitable.

1-2 MANAGEMENT SCIENCE AND OPERATIONS RESEARCH

This book is concerned largely with the specific techniques used in the cases just described and in similar situations. These quantitative methods can be broadly categorized as techniques of **management science**— a field melding portions of business, economics, statistics, mathematics, and other disciplines into a pragmatic effort to help managers make decisions. As an area of study, these quantitative methods are often identified as **operations research.** Regardless of the label used, the techniques of management science and operations research are concerned with selecting the best alternative course of action whenever mathematics can be helpful in reaching a decision. Many problem situations can be structured so that the possible choices can be ranked on a numerical scale. Common rankings are *profit* or *cost*. In such cases, an

---

[9]Thomas M. Cook, "SABRE Soars," *OR/MS Today* (June 1998), pp. 27–9.

[10]Thomas Petzinger, Jr., "The Front Lines, Selling a 'Killer App' Is a Far Tougher Job than Dreaming It Up," *Wall Street Journal* (April 4, 1998), p. B1.

[11]Richard Gibson, "Merchants Mull the Long and the Short of Lines," *Wall Street Journal* (September 3, 1998), p. B1.

[12]As an example, see A. K. Nigam, "Analysis for a Satellite Communications System," *Interfaces* (February 1975), pp. 37–47.

optimal solution is the one that yields the maximum profit or minimum cost. Other yardsticks may apply in some applications, so that an optimal solution might be the most effective alternative in terms of time, reliability, or one of many kinds of measures. The particular quantitative method for finding the best solution is sometimes called a **mathematical optimization procedure.**

The beginnings of operations research can be traced to World War II, when the United States and Great Britain employed mathematicians and physicists to analyze military operations. After the war, many of those involved in military operations research retained their interest in analyzing decision making in peacetime endeavors and developed new techniques that could be directly applied to business problems. The availability of digital computers allowed these techniques to be applied quickly to large-scale optimization problems.

1-3   ORGANIZATION AND PURPOSE OF THIS BOOK

This book presents the tools and techniques most commonly associated with quantitative methods as they are used to solve business problems. The discipline incorporates some procedures of management science and operations research and relies heavily on mathematics. Other fields of business have a less-pronounced mathematical foundation, although finance utilizes algebra and calculus to determine rates of return and the cost of capital, and accountants apply mathematics in evaluating businesses. Both the accountant and the financial analyst also use the specialized procedures of quantitative methods, and those tools in turn incorporate methodology from the two older disciplines. Quantitative methods enrich and borrow from all business fields, including marketing, human resources, and organizational behavior.

The procedures, tools, and techniques presented in this book are grouped into six parts:

   I. Introduction
  II. Decision Making and Planning with Uncertainty
 III. Resource Allocation
 IV. Distribution, Routing, and Scheduling
  V. Inventory Management
 VI. Simulation and Waiting Lines

Part I of this book includes this introduction to quantitative methods and includes Chapter 2, which introduces spreadsheets. Part II includes five chapters devoted to uncertainty, beginning with a two-chapter basic review of the probability and statistics needed to analyze real problems. The subsequent three chapters show how these basic tools are used in decision analysis and in making forecasts.

Part III includes four chapters involving resource allocation, always a central problem of everyday life. Since ancient times, managers have strived to best employ scarce resources. Today, that same problem has been studied so extensively that the field has its own vocabulary and special procedures devoted to finding optimal solutions. All chapters in this group are based on linear programming, a mathematical optimization tool for solving a tremendous variety of resource allocation problems. This group includes a related chapter on integer and goal programming.

Part IV begins with a chapter describing the transportation method, which is a specialized form of linear programming for finding the best way to schedule deliveries so that time, distances traveled, and costs are minimized. The same chapter delves into as-

signment problems, for which similar methods are applied in scheduling people to jobs. The second chapter presents network models useful for solving routing and distribution problems. The final chapter addresses project management, presenting procedures of PERT and the CPM (Critical Path Method), tools that help managers complete their projects on time and within budget constraints.

Although inventory is an omnipresent feature of modern life, often unrecognized is the planning needed to ensure appropriate order quantities so that inventories lie within established budgets and meet desired levels of customer service. Part V is concerned with inventory management and control. The first chapter presents procedures for situations when uncertainty may be ignored. The tools developed there are expanded in the second chapter, in which uncertainty is fully explored.

Part VI begins with a chapter devoted to queuing models. Waiting line situations are systematically evaluated and procedures are presented for finding the optimal balance between costs associated with waiting and the expenses of faster service. Those evaluations are based on mathematical models involving uncertainty. The second chapter in this final group presents an omnibus tool, Monte Carlo simulation, for more accurately making queuing evaluations. Simulation can be the tool of last resort in business evaluations. It gives us an alternative way to solve standard problems such as forecasting, scheduling, inventory management, and project planning.

1-4   MODELS AND DECISION MAKING

Every decision-making situation involves **alternatives.** Quantitative methods are used to select the alternative that best satisfies the decision maker's goals. Identifying the possible alternatives and goals is an important task. Once the alternatives are identified, a problem can be quantitatively analyzed by comparing the alternatives in terms of how well they meet the decision maker's objectives. We have already noted that various yardsticks are used for comparison; the classical gauge in business is *profit* or *cost,* although we will encounter other measures as well.

The Mathematical Model: Parameters and Variables

The first step in applying quantitative methods is generally to express the problem mathematically. Such a formulation is called a **mathematical model.** All mathematical models consist of **variables** and constant terms, which are sometimes referred to as **parameters.** The variables and parameters are usually linked by algebraic expressions that reflect the decision maker's goals and any special limitations on the kinds of alternatives to be considered.

As an example, we will consider a simple inventory problem where the decision maker's goal is to determine the quantity of items to order periodically so that total operating cost is minimized. A simple mathematical model takes the form

Total annual cost = Ordering cost + Holding cost + Procurement cost

and the objective can be expressed as

$$\text{Minimize:} \quad \text{Total annual cost} = \left(\frac{A}{Q}\right)k + hc\left(\frac{Q}{2}\right) + Ac$$

where Q is the order quantity and the single decision variable for this particular problem. The variable Q can assume many different alternative values, such as $0, 1, 2, 3, \ldots,$ $100, 101, \ldots.$ The parameters are

A = Annual number of items demanded

k = Cost of placing an order

h = Annual cost per dollar value for holding items in inventory

c = Unit cost of procuring an item

These parameters may be set at any levels that apply to a given situation, so that the same model applies regardless of the levels established for the parameters. This particular model will be explained in further detail in Chapter 15.

Constraints and Feasible Solutions

Sometimes a mathematical model incorporates **constraints** that place special limitations on the problem variables. These constraints are often expressed algebraically. For example, suppose that the storage facilities can accommodate only 300 units at a time. This constraint would be expressed as

$$Q \leq 300$$

which would then become an integral part of the model formulation. This restriction disallows any order quantity greater than 300, such as $Q = 350$ units. In effect, this constraint separates the alternatives into two groups: **feasible solutions** (values of Q not exceeding 300 units) and **infeasible solutions** (values of Q exceeding 300 units).

Optimal Solutions

Quantitative methods are also employed to solve the problem by finding the value of the variable that meets the requirements of the mathematical model. For our inventory model, we must find the optimal value for the variable Q. Here, the **optimal solution** can be found from

$$Q = \sqrt{\frac{2Ak}{hc}}$$

which is derived from mathematical analysis. To illustrate, suppose that each order costs $4 to place, the annual demand is 1,000 units, it costs $.20 per year for each dollar value of items held in inventory, and these items may be procured from the supplier for $1 each. Substituting the values $k = 4$, $A = 1,000$, $h = .20$, and $c = 1$ into the above expression, the minimum-cost order quantity is

$$Q = \sqrt{\frac{2(1,000)4}{.20(1)}} = \sqrt{40,000} = 200 \text{ units}$$

Algorithms and Model Types

The solution procedure we just used to solve our inventory problem is an example of an **algorithm.** Algorithms are often simple formulas, but they can be complex and involve a series of required steps. Sometimes a mathematical model will exhibit certain undesirable features or be so complex or large that it is impractical to arrive at a solution by mathematical reasoning alone. In such cases, it may be impossible to construct an algorithm that results in a truly optimal solution. In such instances, it is still possible to apply quantitative methods to reach a reasonably satisfactory solution.

In this book, we will consider two basic classes of models. The simplest model, like the inventory order-quantity model, involves no uncertainty. These models contain

certain (known and fixed) constants throughout their formulation and are referred to as **deterministic models.** It is more difficult to solve problems that involve one or more uncertain quantities. In these cases, probability must be considered and **stochastic models** may be used.

1-5 COMPUTER SOLUTIONS

Twenty years ago, quantitative methods instructors assumed that all time-consuming calculations were done by hand. Today, computers do routine number crunching, and more time is available for students to see how quantitative methods solve practical business problems. Some hand computations are still essential, although they are done only to solidify understanding. The more realistic business situations are analyzed in this book with computer assistance, employing either Excel spreadsheets or the *QuickQuant* 2000 software package.

Excel Spreadsheets

An Excel spreadsheet solution for the inventory problem discussed previously is shown in Figure 1-1. Cell F10 shows the optimal order quantity of 200 units, as calculated in Section 1-4, and cell F13 shows that the total annual relevant cost is $1,040.00. Using a spreadsheet is not difficult, but it does require some background. Chapter 2 covers the basic concepts of Excel, and details are given with each application encountered throughout the text.

One of the advantages of the spreadsheet approach is that one can see easily how changes in parameter values affect the optimal solution. For example, if the demand doubles to 2,000, then the new $Q = 283$ and the total annual cost is $56.57.

QuickQuant 2000

Excel spreadsheets are not appropriate for some quantitative methods procedures. The *QuickQuant* 2000 software package included with the CD-ROM that accompanies this

	A	B	C	D	E	F
1			INVENTORY ANAYLSIS			
2						
3	Parameter Values:					
4		Fixed Cost per Order: k =				$ 4.00
5		Annual Number of Items Demanded: A =				1,000
6		Unit Cost of Procuring an Item: c =				$ 1.00
7		Annual Holding Cost per Dollar Value: h =				$ 0.20
8						
9		Decision Variables:				
10			Order Quantity: Q =			200.0
11					F	
12		Results:		10	=SQRT((2*F5*F4)/(F7*F6))	
13			Total Annual Cost: TC =			$ 1,040.00
14					F	
15				13	=(F5/F10)*F4+F7*F6*(F10/2)+F5*F6	

FIGURE 1-1

An Excel spreadsheet for the inventory example

FIGURE 1-2
QuickQuant 2000
applications

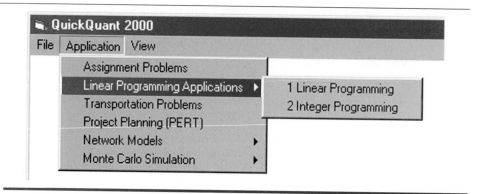

book can be used for these procedures, and it is an alternative to Excel for the others. Figure 1-2 shows the main menu for *QuickQuant* 2000, listing the various quantitative methods applications for which the program can be used: assignment problems, linear programming applications, transportation problems, project planning (PERT), network models, and simulation. Both *QuickQuant* and Excel make use of problem files. The two programs can exchange files. Although simple to do, we wait until Chapter 9 for a detailed discussion.

1-6   THE IMPORTANCE OF STUDYING QUANTITATIVE METHODS

The purpose of this book is not to make you an expert in quantitative methods. Its goal is to familiarize you with the important tools of quantitative methods and to expose you to a variety of successful applications. No great skill in mathematics is required.

Four main advantages can be gained from exposure to quantitative methods. First, it should increase your confidence as a decision maker, largely because you will see how vast and varied the problems are that can be solved through the application of quantitative methods. Second, a study of quantitative methods creates problem-solving skills that will be extremely helpful when you encounter an unsolved problem, whether or not you are directly responsible for finding the answer. The third advantage will be your ability to cope with decisions, as a manager, as an employee, or in your personal life. A final advantage from using this book is that you will learn Excel spreadsheet skills that will be beneficial in any career you pursue.

Some knowledge of quantitative methods is especially crucial to the modern manager. An effective manager must make good choices, and the ability to know where, when, and how to use quantitative methods to make optimal decisions gives managers a definite advantage. This doesn't mean that an effective manager must be mathematically skilled or must personally develop models and solutions. There are a tremendous number of opportunities for the layman to do exactly that, but experts can be hired to perform the more demanding tasks. However, it is important to know enough about this subject to guide those high-powered analysts (who too often stray into a mathematical "never-never land"). As a bare minimum, any exposure to quantitative methods will teach future managers to ask the right questions and to recognize when outside help may be useful.

PROBLEMS

1-1 The subject material of this book is quantitative methods. Name two subjects ordinarily included as part of this discipline.

1-2 What are four advantages to be gained from a study of quantitative methods?

1-3 How are mathematical optimization procedures related to quantitative methods?

1-4 What are two important characteristics of decision-making situations?

1-5 What is the first step in applying quantitative methods?

1-6 What is a mathematical model?

1-7 List the components of a mathematical model.

1-8 (a) What is an algorithm?
(b) Why are algorithms important in the study of quantitative methods?

1-9 Describe the similarities and differences between deterministic models and stochastic models.

1-10 Look for examples of quantitative methods applications in newspapers, magazines, and other material that you use.

1-11 For the inventory model and data in Section 1-4, calculate the total annual cost.

1-12 SuperBuy is a large electronic retailer. One particular model DVD in stock costs $200. Steve Smith, the department manager, estimates that 2,500 will be sold during the coming year, that each order placed to resupply DVDs from the central warehouse costs $45, and that it costs $.20 per year for each dollar value of items held in inventory. Use the formulas in Section 1-4 to help Steve decide how many DVDs should be in each order and what the corresponding total annual cost would be.

CHAPTER 2

INTRODUCTION TO SPREADSHEETS WITH EXCEL

Let the students know that at least 75% of all my work as an analyst is done in Excel. I can be a real-life example for students.

Thomas Wang, quant student

S preadsheets are widely utilized in the business world. Knowing how to use them is a useful career skill. This text employs Microsoft Excel because it appears to be the most widely used spreadsheet software. Other popular spreadsheets such as Lotus 1-2-3 or QuattroPro function in a manner similar to Excel.

This chapter introduces basic spreadsheet concepts. With that background, you will gradually improve your Excel skills as you progress through the text. The *Guide to Excel,* on the CD-ROM that accompanies the text, contains in one place all the material in this chapter. Included there are discussions of all the Excel features used in this book and information about more-advanced Excel functions and options.

DECISION PROBLEM

How Profits Vary with Production Quantities

Swatville Sluggers is a small manufacturer of custom baseball bats. The company may be unfamiliar to the general public because it sells exclusively to professional baseball teams, mainly minor league clubs. Slugger bats are handmade from high-quality 3-by-3-inch blocks of hardwood. The owner, George Herman "Sultan" Swat, wants to know if the company should fill a special order for eighty 30-inch bats. He has asked his nephew, Babe, to analyze the situation. Because the company receives many orders of different quantities for 30-inch bats, Mr. Swat has asked Babe to develop a table showing the profits associated with different order quantities and indicating the minimum profitable amounts. Swat believes such a table will make it easy to analyze future orders.

Babe checks with the production department and learns that many different sizes of bats are produced. For each switch in bat size, the company incurs a $1,000 fixed changeover cost. Marketing advises Babe that although a 30-inch bat normally sells for $22, the market for bats has firmed up and a price of $23 will apply. Accounting informs Babe that each bat will cost the company $9.95 to make, beyond fixed charges.

The following sections of this chapter introduce basic spreadsheet concepts that are useful in answering the above questions and helpful in solving many other common business problems.

2-1   THE FIRST EXCEL WINDOW

Microsoft Excel is launched by clicking its screen icon or by selecting the program from the main pull-down menu. The first Excel window to appear is like the one in Figure 2-1. At the top is the title bar. It gives the file name of the spreadsheet, InitialExcelSpreadsheet.xls in this case. The spreadsheet shown in Figure 2-1 is called a workbook. It is composed of a number of worksheets that have tabs at the bottom of the window. The worksheet names are displayed on the tabs: Sheet 1, Sheet 2, and so forth. The main components of an Excel window are the menu bar, tool bars, the formula bar, the active or selected cell, the fill handle, scroll bars, scroll buttons, and tab scroll buttons.

Each of these components is labeled in Figure 2-1. The menu bar and the tool bars are used to select the various Excel actions, including printing, copying, selecting fonts, centering, changing colors, sorting, solving equations, checking spelling, and doing statistical analyses. The formula bar is used for entering or displaying formulas in the active or selected cell. The fill handle is used in many shortcuts—for example, in copying formulas or in rapidly entering data. Scroll bars and buttons are used for moving around the screen.

Entering Data, Selecting Cells, and Dragging the Mouse

Moving the cursor to a cell (for example, A1) and clicking the left mouse button is *selecting* the cell. The selected cell is the *active cell*. Text or a number is entered into the active cell by typing the desired characters or numbers and pressing the Enter

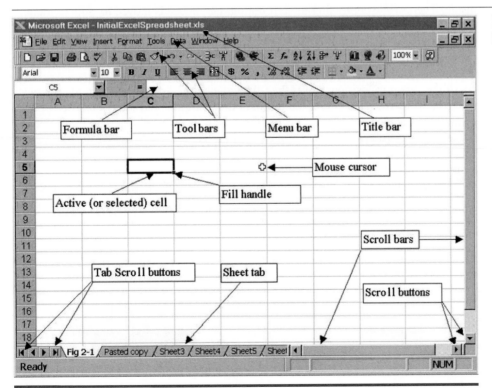

FIGURE 2-1

Initial Excel spreadsheet

FIGURE 2-2

Data in the active cell
and in the formula bar

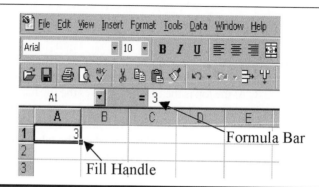

key. Whatever is typed appears in the active cell and in the formula bar. Should that location again become the active cell, data values will reappear in both places. As we shall see, the value in a cell might be governed by a formula; in that case, the answer will appear in the active cell and the originating expression in the formula bar. Figure 2-2 illustrates entering the number 3 in cell A1, the active cell shown with the heavy border.

The small dark square at the lower right-hand corner of the active cell is called the *fill handle*. It is used in quickly copying and deleting cell data from groups of selected cells. It is often convenient to simultaneously select a contiguous group of cells. That is done by selecting the end or corner cell of the desired region and moving the cursor inside. Then, while depressing the left button, the mouse is moved to cells to the left, to the right, above, or below. That is called *dragging*. When the left button is released, the selected region, except for the original cell, will be shaded. Figure 2-3 shows various possibilities using A1 as the starting cell. As we shall see, selected cells may be copied as a group.

If the cursor is positioned over the fill handle before dragging, the number or characters in the active cell are repeated throughout the highlighted selection. The opposite result, deleting the contents in all cells of a region, may be achieved by first selecting the cell group, as above. Then the contents are erased by positioning the cursor over the fill handle of the active corner cell and dragging left or up before releasing the left mouse button; the cross-hatched cells are emptied.

Another method of selecting cells is to hold down the Shift key, use the arrow keys to move the cursor over the area to be selected, and then release the Shift key. In all of these cases, the active cell remains white.

FIGURE 2-3

Selecting cells

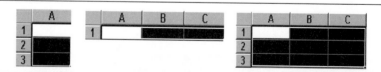

2-2 ENTERING FORMULAS, COPYING, EDITING, AND FORMATTING

We begin with a clear spreadsheet to illustrate entering formulas, copying, editing, and formatting. We select cell A1, type the number 3, and press Enter. The cursor will move to the neighboring cell directly below or to the right, depending on the Excel settings. That will be the new selected cell. In our illustration, cell A2 is selected. There we type the number 5 and press Enter.

Entering Formulas in Excel

We then select cell A3 (if it is not automatically selected), type =SUM(A1:A2), and press Enter. The answer 8 appears in cell A3, as shown in Figure 2-4. Next, we select again cell A3. The formula bar shows the formula, and cell A3 contains the answer. (We can also see the answer inside a cell without first leaving it by clicking the (☑) icon on the tool bar.) That answer will change when new values are assigned to cells A1 and A2.

There is another way to create the formula in cell A3. We could instead select cell A3 and click on the summation icon in the Tool Bar (Σ). That automatically enters the formula into cell A3 without having to type it. SUM is one of the simplest *functions* standard to Excel. Additional functions will be introduced in the following chapters. Formulas need not involve a function and often will be constructed using standard arithmetic operations. For example, we could use the formula =A1+A2 for cell A3 instead of the SUM function.

Copying and Pasting in Excel

Copying with Excel spreadsheets is much like copying with word processing documents. To copy the contents of cells, we select the original cells, click the right mouse button, and then choose Copy from the pop-up menu. That places the contents onto the clipboard (which is invisible). An equivalent way to copy those contents would be to click on Edit on the menu bar and choose Copy. The quickest way to copy the contents of selected cells is to depress the control key while pressing C (Ctrl-C).

The clipboard contents can then be pasted onto the spreadsheet by selecting the upper left corner of the target area. To illustrate, we select cells A1:A3 (i.e., cells A1 through A3) and copy them onto the clipboard. They are pasted onto cells C1:C3 by clicking on cell C1, depressing the right mouse button, and selecting Paste from the pop-up menu. (Alternatively, once cell C1 is active, we may click on Edit on the menu bar and select Paste, or more simply, depress Ctrl-V.) Figure 2-4 presents the results. The contents of cells A1:A3 are duplicated in cells C1:C3. By clicking on cell C3, we may observe =SUM(C1:C2) in the formula bar.

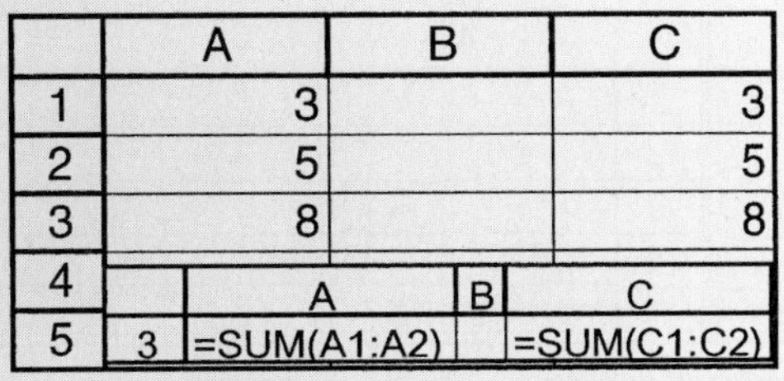

	A	B	C
1	3		3
2	5		5
3	8		8
4	A	B	C
5	3 =SUM(A1:A2)		=SUM(C1:C2)

FIGURE 2-4
Relative references

Absolute and Relative Formula References

Notice that the formula for cell C3 is different from the one for cell A3 (=SUM (A1:A2)). The cell references in a formula, like those for cells A3 and C3, are called *relative* references. When the formula is copied, Excel remembers the cell references relative to the cell governed by the formula. The cell A3 formula sums the numbers in the two cells directly above it, A1:A2. The formula in cell C3 does the same, summing the numbers in the two cells directly above it, C1:C2.

To get a better idea about how a relative reference works, delete the contents of cells C1:C3. (Deleting works like copying. First, we select those cells. Then, we click the right mouse button and choose Clear Contents from the pop-up menu; alternatively, we just press Ctrl-D or the Delete key.) Now, we select just cell A3 and copy its contents to cell C3. A zero results because the formula sums the two blank cells above C3, as shown on the left-hand side of Figure 2-5.

If the formula in cell C3 sums the two numbers in cells A1:A2, then an *absolute* reference must be used. A cell reference is called an absolute cell reference if dollar signs ($) are used before the letter and number. For example, in cell A3 type the formula =SUM($A$1:$A$2), as shown on the right-hand side of Figure 2-5. In this formula, the references to cells $A$1:$A$2 are absolute. When this formula is copied to any other cell, the results will always give the sum of the cells A1:A2. Consequently, with the number 3 in cell A1 and 5 in A2, copying A3 to C3 will give the answer 8 with the absolute references in the formula (instead of 0 with the relative references). This is shown on the right-hand side of Figure 2-5.

Editing Cells and Cutting

To replace the entire contents of a cell, we select the cell and type the new values to go into it. To change a portion of the cell's contents, select the cell and click in the formula bar. (See Figure 2-1 for its location.) Changes are made by inserting or deleting characters inside the formula bar. Another way to edit a cell is to double click on it, which changes the nature of the cell display within the spreadsheet; appearing in the cell will be its underlying formula, if applicable. Insertions or deletions can then be made directly in the cell. Depressing the Enter key ends the editing in both of those cases.

To move data or formulas from one cell to another, we can use Excel's Cut command. It is similar to the Copy command discussed earlier, except that the contents of the selected cell are moved to the new location rather than just copied. The original cell contents are automatically deleted. We do this by selecting a cell, clicking the right mouse button, and choosing Cut. Then we move the cursor to the target cell, click the right mouse button, and choose Paste. The contents of the original cell are emptied and moved to the new cell.

	A	B	C		A	B	C
1	3			1	3		
2	5			2	5		
3	8		0	3	8		8
4		A	B	C	4		A	B	C
5	3	=SUM(A1:A2)	=SUM(C1:C2)	5	3	=SUM($A$1:$A$2)	=SUM($A$1:$A$2)

FIGURE 2-5   Relative versus absolute references

FIGURE 2-6   Tool Bar
icons for font, size, bold,
italics, and underline

Formatting Cells

There are many ways of changing the appearance of a worksheet. Fonts and font sizes
are modified by using the tool bar, just like in word processing. All such changes may
be applied to a selected cell or group of cells or to individually highlighted characters
within cells. Figures 2-6 and 2-7 illustrate using the tool bar to change the font type and
size. Clicking on the left-hand down arrow (▼) displays all the available fonts, as
shown on the left-hand side of Figure 2-7. The other down arrow displays the various
font sizes, as shown on the right-hand side of Figure 2-7. We need only click on a font
type or size to select it. Figure 2-6 shows the icons for bold (**B**), italics (*I*), and underlining (U). Selecting cells or highlighting characters within a cell and clicking on
one of the icons gives the characteristic to the cells or characters selected.

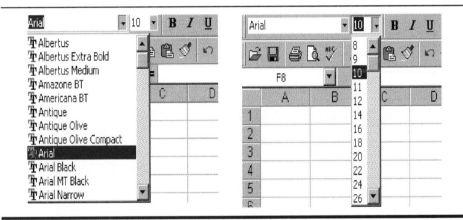

FIGURE 2-7
Changing the font type
and size

Alternatively, we can change any of these font characteristics by choosing Format
on the menu bar, clicking on Cells, and then choosing the Font tab. That will bring to
the screen the Format Cells dialog box, shown in Figure 2-8. In this dialog box, we can

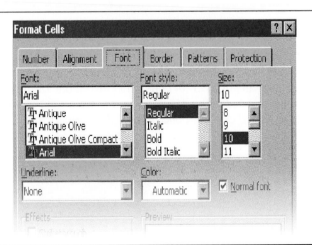

FIGURE 2-8
The Format Cells drop
down menu and the Font
tab of the Format Cells
dialog box

FIGURE 2-9

Tool bar icons for
formatting numbers

select different fonts, sizes, styles (such as italics or bold), types of underlining, and colors. In addition, checking the appropriate boxes under Effects can make characters subscript or superscript.

Figure 2-9 shows how to change the format of numbers by using icons on the tool bar. The first three icons in Figure 2-9 are called the currency, percent, and comma icons. Clicking on one of those icons gives its characteristic to the cell(s) or character(s) selected. That is, a dollar sign ($), a percent sign (%), or commas in a number such as 1,000,000 are inserted. The last two icons adjust the number of decimal places, to increase ( ) and to decrease ( ). We also can use the Number tab of the Format Cells dialog box to change a number's format. Selecting the cells and then choosing the desired characteristic under Category, as shown in Figure 2-10 does that. The Text tab is used to change the number to a text format. (That number cannot then be used to do calculations.) Changing a number to a text format is useful in wrapping formulas. That process will be discussed subsequently.

FIGURE 2-10

The Number tab of the
Format Cells dialog box

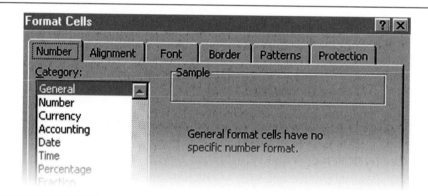

Figure 2-11 shows how to change the alignment of a cell's contents by using icons on the tool bar. The first three icons in Figure 2-11 are to left adjust, center, or right adjust the contents of a cell or cells. Clicking on one of these icons gives its characteristic to the selected cells. The icon on the right ( ) is the merge-and-center icon. It merges selected cells into one cell and then centers the contents in the merged cell.

FIGURE 2-11

Tool bar icons for
aligning cell contents

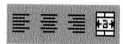

2-3 SPREADSHEET ARITHMETIC

Arithmetic operations are simple to do in Excel. To add the numbers 3 and 2, type =3 + 2 in a cell, press the Enter key, and the result, 5, is displayed in the cell. Subtraction, multiplication, and division are done in a manner analogous to addition using the symbols −, *, and /, respectively. Thus, to subtract 2 from 3, enter =3 − 2 in a cell, and 1 is the result; to multiply 3 and 2, enter =3*2, and 6 is shown in the cell; and to divide 3 by 2, enter =3/2, and 1.5 will be the answer. Notice that to do all arithmetic operations, we must first enter the equal to sign.

Cell references can be used in doing arithmetic. Entering =A1+A2, =A1−A2, =A1*A2, or =A1/A2 in a cell adds the values in A1 and A2, subtracts the value in A2 from the value in A1, multiplies the value in A1 by the value in A2, or divides the value in A1 by the value in A2.

To calculate a power of a number or expression, Excel uses the caret symbol (^). To raise 3 to the second power, enter =3^2 in a cell, and the answer 9 results. Another illustration is =A1^A2, which raises the value in cell A1 to the power in cell A2.

2-4 DISPLAYING EXCEL RESULTS

Several Excel options are essential in displaying printed spreadsheet results. Particularly useful in quantitative methods are those for displaying Greek characters, mathematical signs, formulas, subscripts, gridlines, and spreadsheet row and column numbers.

To display Greek symbols like λ and μ on a spreadsheet, type the letters l and m, highlight them, and change to the Symbol font.

An inequality such as

$$3X_1 + 4X_2 \leq 20$$

contains a less than or equal to sign. To display $\leq$ or $\geq$ in Excel, type < or > and then use the underline icon to underline the character.

A formula used to calculate a result shown in a cell is shown in the formula bar when the cell is selected. A shortcut to displaying the formula in the spreadsheet is to depress the Control and back-tick (or tilde) keys simultaneously. The latter key is just to the left of the one key; it has the symbols ` and ~ on it. Those two keys work like a toggle switch, changing what you see on the screen from the result to the underlying formula and back again.

The inequality constraint given above contains subscripts. To display subscripts in Excel, click Format on the menu bar and select Cells on the drop-down menu. The Format Cells dialog box then appears. Figure 2-12 shows the drop-down menu and the dialog box. Subscripts (or superscripts) are obtained by selecting the appropriate box under the Effects section of the dialog box.

To display an "equal to" sign (=) as text instead of beginning a formula, type '= (the apostrophe plus equal sign keys). The apostrophe will not show (only the equal to sign does). Depressing just the equal key causes Excel to start a formula.

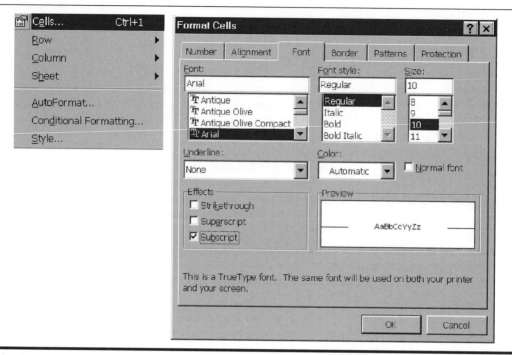

FIGURE 2-12   Displaying subscripts with the Format Cells dialog box

Gridlines and row and column references are essential to following cell references and the logic of calculations done in spreadsheets. They are normally shown on the monitor screen; however, to ensure this shows on printed results, click File on the menu bar and select Page Setup on the drop-down menu. The Page Setup dialog box then appears. See Figure 2-13. Select the Sheet tab and check to make sure that the Gridlines and Row and Column Headings boxes are checked.

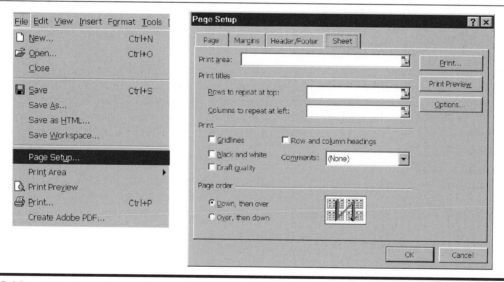

FIGURE 2-13   Displaying gridlines and row and column headings with the Page Setup dialog box

Decision Problem Revisited: Costs, Revenues, and Profits versus Production Quantities (Breakeven Analysis)

To find out if Swatville Sluggers should accept the order for eighty 30-inch bats, Babe prepares the spreadsheet shown in Figure 2-14. This spreadsheet is on the CD-ROM that accompanies this book and can be used as a template for solving other similar problems.

	A	B	C	D	E	F	G	H
1				BREAKEVEN ANALYSIS				
2								
3	PROBLEM:	Swatville Sluggers						
4								
5	Parameter Values:							
6			Unit sales price: p =	$ 22				
7			Fixed cost: k =	$ 1,000				
8			Unit cost: c =	$ 9.95				
9								
10			Breakeven quantity: S	83				

	D
10	=D7/(D6-D8)

Quantity	Cost	Revenue	Profit
0	$ 1,000.00	$ -	$(1,000.00)
20	$ 1,199.00	$ 440.00	$ (759.00)
40	$ 1,398.00	$ 880.00	$ (518.00)
60	$ 1,597.00	$ 1,320.00	$ (277.00)
80	$ 1,796.00	$ 1,760.00	$ (36.00)
82	$ 1,815.90	$ 1,804.00	$ (11.90)
83	$ 1,825.85	$ 1,826.00	$ 0.15
100	$ 1,995.00	$ 2,200.00	$ 205.00
120	$ 2,194.00	$ 2,640.00	$ 446.00
140	$ 2,393.00	$ 3,080.00	$ 687.00
160	$ 2,592.00	$ 3,520.00	$ 928.00
180	$ 2,791.00	$ 3,960.00	$ 1,169.00
200	$ 2,990.00	$ 4,400.00	$ 1,410.00

	B	C	D
12	Cost	Revenue	Profit
13	=$D$7+$D$8*A13	=A13*$D$6	=C13-B13
14	=$D$7+$D$8*A14	=A14*$D$6	=C14-B14
15	=$D$7+$D$8*A15	=A15*$D$6	=C15-B15
16	=$D$7+$D$8*A16	=A16*$D$6	=C16-B16
17	=$D$7+$D$8*A17	=A17*$D$6	=C17-B17
18	=$D$7+$D$8*A18	=A18*$D$6	=C18-B18
19	=$D$7+$D$8*A19	=A19*$D$6	=C19-B19
20	=$D$7+$D$8*A20	=A20*$D$6	=C20-B20
21	=$D$7+$D$8*A21	=A21*$D$6	=C21-B21
22	=$D$7+$D$8*A22	=A22*$D$6	=C22-B22
23	=$D$7+$D$8*A23	=A23*$D$6	=C23-B23
24	=$D$7+$D$8*A24	=A24*$D$6	=C24-B24
25	=$D$7+$D$8*A25	=A25*$D$6	=C25-B25

FIGURE 2-14   Table of costs, revenues, and profits versus quantity produced

The $22 bat price is shown in cell D6, the $1,000 fixed cost is in cell D7, and the $9.95 unit cost is in cell D8. A table giving the results of cost, revenue, and profit computations for different order quantities is in cells A12:D25. Cell D17 shows that the 80-bat order will result in a loss of $36 and, thus, should be rejected. The answer to the other question Mr. Swat asked, about the minimum profitable order quantity, is found in cell A19 to be 83 bats. However, it results in a profit of only $0.15.

The formulas used in the spreadsheet are also shown in Figure 2-14. Column A has the various size orders analyzed in cells A13:D25. The costs associated with each production quantity are in column B.

$$\text{Cost} = k + cS$$

where k is the $1,000 fixed cost, c is the $9.95 unit cost, and S is the size of the order. In Excel, this corresponds to =$D$7+$D$8*A13 in cell B13.

The revenues are in column C:

$$\text{Revenue} = pS$$

where p is the $22 sales price. In cell C13 this yields the Excel formula =A13*$D$6.

Column D contains the profits (the revenues from column C minus the costs from column B). In cell D13 this is $=C13-B13$. The rest of the table is obtained by copying the formulas in cells B13:D13 down to the other cells, B25:D25.

Notice that cell D10 also contains the breakeven quantity, 83. The formula for this result comes from setting the cost equal to the revenue

$$k + cS = pS$$

which, when solved for S, yields

$$S = k/(p - c)$$

In Excel, this is $=D7/(D6-D8)$ and is found in cell D10.

Since the marketing department thought a bat price of $23 might be possible, Babe enters that sales price in cell D6 in Figure 2-14 and finds out that the breakeven quantity drops to 77 bats. In that case, the 80-bat order would be accepted.

2-5 GRAPHING USING EXCEL'S CHART WIZARD

E xcel's Chart Wizard greatly simplifies the task of making graphs and charts. Figure 2-15 shows a breakeven chart for the Swatville Sluggers illustration in Figure 2-14.

To get started making this chart, highlight the cells to be graphed, B12:C25. Note that the first row highlighted includes the names of the data in each column, Cost and Revenue. Excel calls those names *labels*. Click on the Chart Wizard icon located on the toolbar; it looks like a three-dimensional bar chart (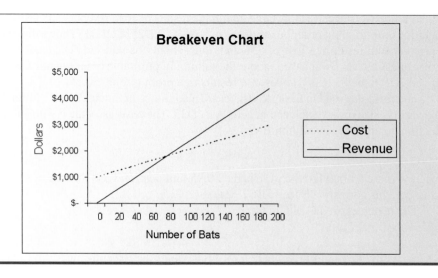). A series of Chart Wizard boxes appears, each of which is described below.

Step 1 of 4—Chart Type (see Figure 2-16). Here we select Line as the *chart type*, pick the first *Chart sub-type* (Line), and click the Next button to bring the second dialog box.

FIGURE 2-15
Breakeven chart for
Swatville Sluggers

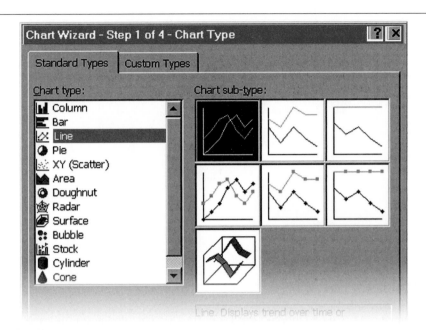

FIGURE 2-16
The first Chart Wizard dialog box

Step 2 of 4 — Chart Source Data (see Figure 2-17). This dialogue box appears showing the Data Range tab. It is shown on the left-hand side of Figure 2-17 and contains a preliminary version of the chart. By clicking the Series Tab, the dialog box on the right-hand side of Figure 2-17 appears. It is used to enter the range of the numbers on the horizontal axis. In our example, type A13:A25 in the *Category (X) axis labels* line. (Instead, you can click in the *Category (X) axis* labels line and then highlight cells A13:A25 directly on the spreadsheet.) Click on the Next button to get the third dialog box.

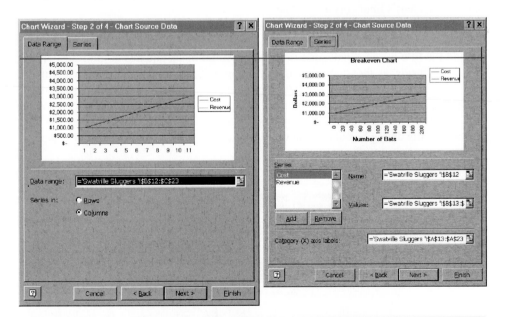

FIGURE 2-17   The second Chart Wizard dialog box, showing the Data Range and Series tabs

FIGURE 2-18

The third Chart Wizard
dialog box

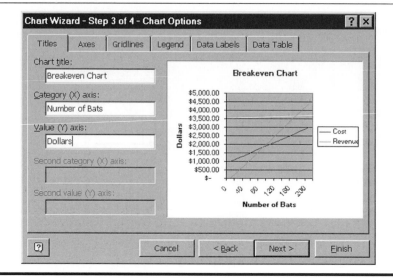

Step 3 of 4 — Chart Options (see Figure 2-18). This dialog box is used to enter titles on the axes or the chart or to change the appearance of the gridlines. In the *Chart title* line, type Breakeven Chart. Then, in the *Category (X) axis* line, type Number of Bats. Finally, in the *Value (Y) axis* line, type Dollars. Click on the Next button to get the last dialog box.

Step 4 of 4 — Chart Location (see Figure 2-19). Here, the chart may be located on the same spreadsheet or on a new one. After selecting one of the options, click on *Finish,* and a chart like that shown in Figure 2-20 appears. Notice that the chart looks a little different from the one in Figure 2-15. This is because several format changes were made to improve the chart's appearance. Such changes depend on individual preferences, so a chart's final appearance can vary.

The normal way to change a chart's appearance is to click on the characteristic to be changed. For example, click on the title of the *X* axis. A dark line will form a box around the title of the *X* axis, and it will have small black squares at the four corners and on each side, as shown on the top left of Figure 2-21. At this point, clicking inside the dark line around the title will permit you to edit the title. To change the title font, right click somewhere in the highlighted *X* axis title, and the drop-down menu shown on the bottom left of Figure 2-21 appears. Selecting Format Axis Title gives the Format Axis Title dialog box shown on the right-hand side of the figure. Font characteristics can be selected here.

FIGURE 2-19

The fourth Chart Wizard
dialog box

Chart Wizard - Step 4 of 4 - Chart Location	? ✕

Place chart:

○ As new sheet: Chart1

● As object in: Swatville Sluggers

Cancel   < Back   Next >   Finish

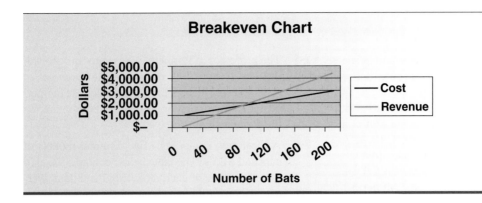

FIGURE 2-20
The initial breakeven chart

To change the format of any characteristic on the chart, follow the procedure described in the above paragraph. First, highlight the characteristic by clicking on it. Second, right click to obtain a drop-down menu with the various options for changing the format. Finally, select one of the options on the drop-down menu to get a dialog box for changing the characteristic.

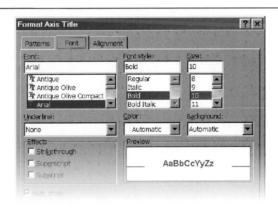

FIGURE 2-21
Changing the X axis font

2-6 USING EXCEL WITH THIS TEXT

The *Guide to Excel* on the CD-ROM accompanying this book describes more detailed procedures for using Excel, including further formatting considerations for displaying spreadsheet information and printing results. Numerous functions are described there and throughout the text. Readers are expected to acquire Excel skills by a process of "osmosis," expanding their capabilities and knowledge in stages as new topics are encountered. Virtually every application in this book involving Excel is illustrated with an example. The spreadsheets may serve as templates for related problems. In many cases, only the spreadsheet numbers will change or only minor cutting and pasting will be needed. The example templates are contained in the CD-ROM accompanying the text.

PROBLEMS

2-1 Karen would like to know how many points she has earned during the quarter in her quantitative methods class. Her midterm exam scores are 84 and 67, and her final exam score is 89. Homework was assigned weekly, and her marks are (out of a total of 10 each week) 8, 9, 10, 7, 10, 8, 10, 7, 7, and 6. Her term project received a grade of 94.

(a) Enter the following into a spreadsheet. Type the word Activity in cell A3, type Midterm 1 in cell A4, Midterm 2 in cell A5, Final Exam in cell A6, Homework 1 in cell A7, and continue down to Homework 10 in cell A16, and Project in cell A17. In cell C3, type the word Points. Enter the corresponding scores in column C next to the appropriate activities; for example, put 84 in cell C4.

(b) In cell C18, calculate Karen's total points using the formula =C4+C5+C6+C7+C8 +C9+C10+C11+C12+C13+C14+C15+ C16+C17.

(c) Calculate Karen's points using Excel's SUM formula.

(d) Karen's professor made a mistake in recording her grades. She actually received 76 on her second midterm. What is her total now?

2-2 In cell A3 of a spreadsheet, type the inequality $X_1 + X_2 \leq 500$ as text.

(a) What is the default font and its size?

(b) Change the font to Courier or Courier New and the size to 16.

2-3 Enter 2000000.1546 in cell A3 of a spreadsheet.

(a) Copy this number to cells A4:A7.

(b) Click on cell A4 and then find the appropriate icon(s) to change the format of the number so that it looks like $2,000,000.

(c) In cell A5, change the format of the number so that it is in bold and shows one decimal. Is the one decimal digit 1 or 2?

(d) In cell A6, change the format so that the font is Times New Roman 12 and all four decimals are shown.

(e) In cell A7, use the merge-and-center icon to center the results between cells A7:E7.

2-4 (a) Copy Figure 1-1 in Section 1-5 on a spreadsheet. Note that cells F10 and F13 contain formulas that are shown in Figure 1-1.

(b) Solve Problem 1-12 with this spreadsheet.

2-5 The professor in Problem 2-1 assigns an A to students who score 90% or more. Will Karen get an A? Use a spreadsheet formula to calculate her percentage. Make sure the format of the result shows the percent sign.

2-6 A local auto dealer sells five different models of cars and SUVs. The table below contains the estimated number of each model sold and their average prices for the next year. Use a spreadsheet to calculate the total estimated dollar sales.

Model	Estimated Sales	Average Sales Price, $
1	60	8,000
2	70	13,000
3	80	19,000
4	58	25,000
5	45	35,000

Make sure that all sales values show dollar signs and that results are rounded to the nearest dollar.

2-7 MartWal's local store is beginning its annual budget cycle. A principal input for this is a monthly sales forecast for the coming year. As a result of a statistical study, the following regression equation has been developed:

$$S = 10,555,000 + 63,445M$$

where S is the monthly sales in dollars, and M is the number of the month: 1 for January, 2 for February, and so forth. In column A of a spreadsheet, list the names of the months of the year, in column C enter the corresponding number of the month, and in column D use the above formula to forecast the monthly sales. What is the total forecast for the year? Use Excel's currency format and round all results to the nearest dollar.

2-8 First National Bank's Trust Department has been named trustee of a $100 million estate. It is required to invest this money in bonds or other fixed-income instruments. The following table summarizes the investments chosen, the amounts to be invested, and the return from each investment.

Bond	Annual Return	Amount Invested, $
A	6%	250,000
B	3%	100,000
C	10%	85,000
D	5.5%	300,000
E	8.3%	265,000

(a) Enter the data in this table in a spreadsheet with the bond names in column A, the annual returns in column B, and the amount invested in column C. That is, in A7:A11 put the letters A to E for bonds, in cells B7:B11 enter the annual returns using a percentage format for the numbers, and in cells C7:C11 enter the amounts invested using a dollar format rounded to the nearest dollar.

(b) In column D, calculate the amount of money earned from each bond, and then in cell D12 compute the total amount earned from all the bonds.

2-9 Swatville Sluggers is a small manufacturer of baseball bats made from high-quality 3-by-3-inch blocks of wood. Once the wood is obtained, it is processed on a lathe, finished, and coated with stain and varnish. The following table provides information about the quantities and costs of each of those steps for a 30-inch bat. The sales price is $22.00, and it has a $3 fixed production cost. For example, each bat requires 30 inches of wood that cost $0.12 per inch, 10 minutes of lathe time at $0.06 per minute, and so forth. In addition, each bat is put in a box that costs $0.50.

Component	Cost $/unit	Amount for 30-inch bat
Wood, ounces	0.12	30
Lathe, minutes	0.06	10
Finishing time, minutes	0.03	25
Stain, ounces	0.25	2
Varnish, ounces	0.20	5

(a) Put the information in the above table in a spreadsheet with the components in column A, the costs per unit in column B, and the amounts in column C. Compute the total cost of each component in column D.

(b) Calculate the profit per 30-inch bat.

(c) An error was made in the above data because the cost per unit for the stain and the varnish were mixed up. Stain costs $.20 per ounce and varnish $0.25 per ounce. How much difference does this make in the profit per unit?

2-10 From Chapter 17, the formula for the probability of waiting at an ATM is λ/μ, and the average time spent waiting in line is $\lambda/[\mu(\mu - \lambda)]$, where λ is the mean number of customers per hour arriving at the ATM and μ is the mean number of cus-

tomers per hour the ATM can service. These formulas are valid only when $\lambda < \mu$. Suppose that customers arrive at a First National Bank ATM at the rate of 18 per hour. From the rate capacity of the ATM, it is known that an average of 60 clients per hour can be served.

(a) In cell A4 enter λ, in cell A5 type in μ, in cell A6 put Probability of Waiting, and in A7 type Average Wait in Line (Seconds). Put the values of λ and μ in cells D4 and D5. The formulas for the probability of waiting and the average time spent waiting in line should be entered in D6 and D7.

(b) What is the probability of having to wait at the ATM?

(c) What is the average time spent waiting in line (in seconds)?

(d) Highlight cells D4:D7 and copy them to columns E through J. Enter arrival rates of 20, 25, 30, 40, 50, and 60 customers per hour in cells E4:J4. What happens to the average waiting time in line when the arrival rate is 60 customers per hour? Why?

(e) The bank's policy is to install a second ATM if customers have to wait too long (defined as two minutes or more on the average). Using the results of (d), at what arrival rate will the bank install a second ATM?

2-11 Reconsider the Swatville Sluggers decision problem and suppose that the company has received an order for eighty 34-inch bats. Each bat sells for $24 and costs $13.19 to make.

(a) Should the order be accepted?

(b) What is the profit or loss associated with this order?

(c) What is the breakeven point for 34-inch bats?

(d) Using Excel's Chart Wizard, draw the breakeven chart.

(e) Re-solve parts (a)–(d) if efficiencies cut the $1,000 fixed changeover cost to $800.

(f) Re-solve parts (a)–(d) if Swatville receives $26 per bat.

2-12 Creative Long Term Capital is a $500 million hedge fund that caters to wealthy individuals. In seeking new clients, it is considering organizing a one-day seminar to discuss its new market neutral strategies. (These strategies have 50% of their portfolio invested in stocks always balanced by 50% in short sales.) The company says that this ensures that the portfolio always earns a few

points more than the current Treasury bill rate. This is because in an up market, the portfolio investments make more than the short sales lose, and in a down market, the profits from the short sales are more than the losses on the investments. Renting a room for the seminar at the local Hilton costs $500. The honorarium for the luncheon guest speakers from Wall Street is $5,000. The luncheon costs $30 for each person attending. Seminar material, including postage, and beverages and snacks during breaks is $25 per attendee. The company does not make money on the seminars, but it does have a policy of breaking even, so it has decided to charge $95 per participant.

(a) How many participants are needed to break even?

(b) Draw the breakeven chart.

(c) Hilton raises its rate to $750. How does this affect the minimum number of participants (that is, the breakeven number)?

(d) A proposal to reduce the price of the seminar to $75 is being considered. The idea is that this may attract more participants. How many more participants must attend to continue to break even?

2-13 Ingrid's Entertainment Company is a medium-sized toy manufacturer. The research and development department has come up with a new doll that can walk, run, sit, sleep, and talk. The marketing department thinks that the doll will be a success with young girls during the approaching Christmas season, and it has set a tentative price of $49.95. However, the production department is concerned because the complicated electronics in the doll will make it expensive to produce. It estimates $1,000,000 to set up the production line, plus an additional variable cost of $25 per doll.

(a) How many dolls must Ingrid's Entertainment Company sell to break even?

(b) Draw the breakeven chart.

(c) If a cost overrun occurs and the doll variable cost increases to $30, what happens to the breakeven level?

2-14 Duplicate the format of the breakeven chart in Figure 2-15 starting with the data in Figure 2-14. (Hint: Delete rows 18 and 19 [corresponding to quantities of 82 and 83] first so that the quantities in column A are all multiples of 20.)

2-15 A company estimates sales for the first six months of next year as shown in the following table.

Month	Sales, millions of dollars
January	5.3
February	5.7
March	5.5
April	5.9
May	6.0
June	6.6
July	6.3

(a) Use Excel's Chart Wizard to draw a clustered column chart.

(b) Format the chart in (a) so that both the X and Y axes' fonts are Arial 10 regular and the chart title is Arial 14 bold. Make sure that the months on the X axis are written horizontally. The legend should be Arial 12 regular.

(c) Format the chart area so that it is not shaded and the border around it does not show.

(d) Format the chart area so that the gridlines do not show.

2-16 Repeat Problem 2-15 with a clustered column chart with a three-dimensional visual effect.

2-17 Outel Chip Corporation expects to sell $20 million worth of computers with Celeron chips in the coming quarter. In addition, sales of Pentium II, Pentium III, and Pentium IV computers are anticipated to be $30 million, $40 million, and $10 million, respectively.

(a) Use Excel's Chart Wizard to draw a pie chart.

(b) Format the pie chart so that the sales of each product show as a percentage of total sales.

(c) Repeat (a) and (b) with a pie chart with a three-dimensional visual effect.

2-18 The data in the following table shows computer sales in the United States in millions of dollars and shows the annual high price of the Dow Jones Industrial Averages from 1982 to 1994.[1] Examine the relationship between the two series using Excel's Chart Wizard.

(a) Do an XY (scatter) chart with the X axis representing the computer sales in millions of dollars and the Y axis representing the Dow Jones Industrial Averages.

---

[1] *The World Almanac and Book of Facts*, 1995, pp. 127, 173. Mahwah, NJ: Funk & Wagnalls.

Year	Computer Sales, millions of dollars	Dow Jones Industrial Average
1982	$1,375	1,071
1983	$2,070	1,287
1984	$2,385	1,287
1985	$2,175	1,553
1986	$3,060	1,956
1987	$3,100	2,722
1988	$3,340	2,184
1989	$3,711	2,791
1990	$4,187	3,000
1991	$4,287	3,169
1992	$5,575	3,413
1993	$6,921	3,794
1994	$8,021	3,978

(b) Format the chart in (a) so that both the X and Y axes' fonts are Arial 10 regular and the chart title is Arial 14 bold. Delete the legend.

(e) Format the chart area so that it is not shaded and the border around it does not show.

(c) Format the chart area so that the gridlines do not show.

(d) What is your conclusion about a relationship between the two series?

2-19 The following table gives Microsoft's daily high, low, and closing prices for 10 days in November 2000.

Date	Price		
	High	Low	Close
11/13	68.125	64.406	66.438
11/14	69.813	66.313	68.813
11/15	70.875	68.688	70.063
11/16	76.500	68.938	68.938
11/17	70.000	67.797	69.063
11/20	68.500	65.563	67.188
11/21	69.250	67.375	67.750
11/22	69.500	66.000	68.250
11/24	70.438	68.500	69.938
11/27	72.250	70.625	70.688

(a) Use Excel's Chart Wizard to draw a high, low, and close stock price chart.

(b) Format the chart in (a) so that both the X and Y axes and legend fonts are Arial 10 regular and the chart title is Arial 14 bold.

(c) Format the chart area so that it is not shaded and the border around it does not show.

(d) Format the chart area so that the gridlines do not show.

PART II

DECISION MAKING AND PLANNING WITH UNCERTAINTY

I am working on planning under uncertainty; that's the big field as far as I'm concerned. That's the future.

George Dantzig[1]

M ost of our daily decisions are reached through intuition and judgment and require no special analysis. But uncertainty often adds confusing complexity that clouds our perspective. This book explores the tools and techniques that are helpful in coping with uncertainty.

Chapters 3 and 4 provide a brief summary of probability and the statistical tools useful for quantifying uncertainty. Subsequent chapters build on that foundation by presenting procedures to aid the decision maker. Chapters 5 and 6 tackle uncertainty head-on, building a structural framework for finding the best choices, and, because the future is the source of most uncertainty, Chapter 7 discusses various forecasting techniques.

[1]Peter Horner, "Planning under Uncertainty," *OR/MS Today* (October 1999), p. 26.

CHAPTER 3

PROBABILITY CONCEPTS: QUANTIFYING UNCERTAINTY

The most important questions of life are, for the most part, really only problems of probability.
—Marquis de LaPlace

P robability plays a special role in our lives, because we use it to measure uncertainty. We are continually faced with decisions that lead to uncertain outcomes, and we rely on probability to help us choose our course of action. In business, probability is a pivotal factor in most significant decisions. A department store buyer will order large quantities of a new style that is predicted to sell well. A company will introduce a new product when the chance of its success seems high enough to outweigh the possibility of losses due to its failure. A new college graduate is hired when the probability for satisfactory performance is judged to be sufficiently high.

A **probability** is a numerical value that measures the uncertainty that a particular event will occur. The probability for an event ordinarily represents the *proportion of times under identical circumstances that the event can be expected to occur.*

DECISION PROBLEM

Employment Screening Test

Debra and George McAdams started a small children's clothing store in 1995 named Whirl-a-Gigs. It was successful from the first day, so they started expanding. By the end of 2000, Debra and George had franchises in 25 cities around the United States.

One of their major problems is finding good employees. In an effort to decrease the number of unsatisfactory employees, they are considering administering a clerical skills test to all job applicants.

The job performance ratings of their current 200 employees are listed below.

Job Performance	Number of Employees
1. Unsatisfactory	30
2. Satisfactory	130
3. Excellent	40

Before trying out the clerical skills test on job applicants, they gave the test to their employees. The following results indicate the number of employees in each job performance category who received high scores on the clerical skills test.

Job Performance Category	Clerical Skills Test Result (Number in Job Performance Category Receiving High Scores)
1. Unsatisfactory	3
2. Satisfactory	91
3. Excellent	34

Debra and George are discussing whether to use the clerical skills test for all job applicants. George thinks the test should not be used, because the above data show that even unsatisfactory employees have high scores. On the other hand, Debra notices that because the percentage of high scores on the test is greatest for the excellent employees, she feels that they cannot lose anything by using the test. Before they make a final decision, they agree to attempt to answer the following questions:

1. How well will the proposed test screen out unsatisfactory employees?

2. How will the screening test improve the overall performance of new hires if only those who score high are hired?

3. Is the test fair? More specifically, will it screen out too many potentially satisfactory employees? Will it accept too many bad employees?

3-1 THE LANGUAGE OF PROBABILITY: BASIC CONCEPTS

Probability theory treats a probability as a number. Such numbers, too, are common. We are all familiar with the weather forecaster's announcement that "there is a 50% chance of rain tomorrow." We may extend our understanding of probability to a family of experiments. The simplest of which is the coin toss, for which there is a 50% chance of obtaining either outcome: head or tail.

Probability as Long-Run Frequency

What does a 50% chance, i.e. a .5 probability, of getting a head really mean? It is an expression of the **long-run relative frequency** with which a head will be obtained in a series of coin tosses. In 10 tosses, we can expect to get five heads (50% of 10). But the exact number is uncertain, and four or six heads are likely possibilities. Fewer or more heads are possible, although most will agree extreme outcomes would be very untypical.

How do we know that .5 is the correct value? Without making some assumptions, the only way to find the long-run frequency would be to toss the coin a very long time and then see how often head occurs. But we may *logically deduce* that .5 is the correct figure by examining a coin and seeing that there are two sides—one designated the head and the other the tail. Then, we assume that weight is distributed evenly, so that we would expect any toss to be just as likely to end head-side up as tail-side up. Finally, we rely on a key property common to all situations having equally likely outcomes.

The Random Experiment and Its Elementary Events

Probability theory focuses on uncertain events, which are generated through a **random experiment.** A coin toss is one example of a random experiment. The most basic outcomes of interest are called **elementary events.** For a coin toss, the usual elementary

events are head and tail. (But we could be interested in other elementary events, such as the number of revolutions, the coin's maximum height, or the angle made by Lincoln's nose with respect to the North Pole.) In a random experiment having *N equally likely* elementary events, the long-run frequency of any one of them must be 1/*N*.

Finding the Probability for an Event   We may use the following expression to calculate the

---

PROBABILITY FOR ONE ELEMENTARY EVENT

(Among Equally Likely Possibilities)

$$\Pr[\text{elementary event}] = \frac{1}{N}$$

For the toss of a perfect coin there are $N = 2$ equally likely sides, and

$$\Pr[\text{head}] = \frac{1}{2} = .5$$

The following gives us a detailed example involving an experiment having equally likely events.

PROBABILITY APPLICATION

Roll of the Die

A die cube has six faces, the first marked with one dot, the second with two dots, and so on, with the sixth face having six dots. Suppose that the die is rolled. One of the following possibilities applies for the up-side face:

If the cube is perfectly shaped and balanced, then each of the above is an equally likely elementary event. What is the probability that the die stops two-face up?

SOLUTION
There are $N = 6$ equally likely elementary events for this random experiment, so that

$$\Pr[2] = \frac{1}{6} = .1667$$

This indicates that the long-run frequency for the two-face is 1/6, so that it occurs 16.67% of the time in repeated rolls of the die. Stated equivalently, there is a 16.67% chance of getting a two on any particular roll.

Complicating Issues

Although many situations involve probabilities that may be computed in the foregoing fashion, complications might arise.

Elementary Events Need Not Be Equally Likely   Some elementary events might be more likely than others. That would be the case if a blob of solder is attached to the head-face or if two opposing die cube faces are shaved. Furthermore, we do not know how much solder might be involved nor where it might be placed; nor do we know how deep into the die the cuts might be made. Under those circumstances, it is impossible to logically deduce probabilities.

We emphasize that the probabilities for head with a lopsided coin and the two-face with a shaved die are *still long-run frequencies.* But their values must be established through observation of actual outcomes. And, they cannot be known with an exactitude until the random experiment has been repeated for a very long time.

Random Experiments May Not Be Repeatable   Consider your grade in quantitative methods. This is strictly a one-shot phenomenon, and only one grade will ever be received. Some uncertainty about the final result undoubtedly exists. But what can we say regarding the probability of getting an A? It is obviously not the long-run frequency of an A; that can happen, if at all, just once. The random experiment of receiving a grade is nonrepeatable.

Objective and Subjective Probabilities

Many statisticians would deny the existence of an A probability. Others hold that it must be a 0 or a 1, we just don't know which. But most would agree, nevertheless, that an A is more likely after hard studying than after no studying. We just have difficulty quantifying such an event. Some might attach a value such as .10 or .20. This number is referred to as a **subjective probability,** reflecting that people might disagree about an appropriate figure. The earlier probability values all arise from repeatable random experiments and are sometimes referred to as **objective probabilities.**

Many important uncertain business events arise from nonrepeatable circumstances. Consider next year's sales of a product, the yearly high of the Dow Jones Average, or your final grade in quantitative methods. Any probabilities given to such events must be based solely on *judgment.*

3-2   PROBABILITIES FOR COMPOSITE EVENTS

To expand our knowledge of probability concepts, let's establish additional important concepts. Consider a deck of playing cards, the contents of which are listed in Figure 3-1. Suppose that the deck is thoroughly shuffled and one card is removed. Each card is an elementary event in this random experiment.

The Sample Space, Composite Events, and Event Sets

What is the probability that the selected card is a queen? In terms of long-run frequency, the desired probability may be determined by the following calculation:

$$\Pr[\text{queen}] = \frac{4}{52} = .077$$

FIGURE 3-1
Sample space for the
card randomly selected
from a deck of 52
playing cards

		SUIT		
DENOMINATION	Spades (black)	Hearts (red)	Clubs (black)	Diamonds (red)
King	♠ K •	♥ K •	♣ K •	♦ K •
Queen	♠ Q •	♥ Q •	♣ Q •	♦ Q •
Jack	♠ J •	♥ J •	♣ J •	♦ J •
10	♠ 10 •	♥ 10 •	♣ 10 •	♦ 10 •
9	♠ 9 •	♥ 9 •	♣ 9 •	♦ 9 •
8	♠ 8 •	♥ 8 •	♣ 8 •	♦ 8 •
7	♠ 7 •	♥ 7 •	♣ 7 •	♦ 7 •
6	♠ 6 •	♥ 6 •	♣ 6 •	♦ 6 •
5	♠ 5 •	♥ 5 •	♣ 5 •	♦ 5 •
4	♠ 4 •	♥ 4 •	♣ 4 •	♦ 4 •
3	♠ 3 •	♥ 3 •	♣ 3 •	♦ 3 •
Deuce	♠ 2 •	♥ 2 •	♣ 2 •	♦ 2 •
Ace	♠ A •	♥ A •	♣ A •	♦ A •

This calculation reflects that 4 out of 52 cards are queens, so in repeated experiments a queen should be obtained about 4/52 of the time. In other words, one of the four queens should be drawn in about 7.7% of all selections. Each queen card constitutes an elementary event for getting a queen. The event "queen" is a **composite event,** because it will occur if any of those elementary events occur.

The following listing of the elementary events may be helpful.

$$\text{Queen} = \{ ♠ \text{ Q}, ♥ \text{ Q}, ♣ \text{ Q}, ♦ \text{ Q} \}$$

Every composite event may be viewed as an **event set** comprising as elements the applicable elementary events. The entire collection of elementary events is an all-inclusive event set sometimes called the **sample space.** Composite events may then be viewed as corresponding to a portion, or *subset,* of the sample space.

The Count-and-Divide Method for Computing Probabilities

In the playing card illustration, all cards have the same chance of being selected. The calculation given for Pr[queen] illustrates the **count-and-divide method** for finding composite event probabilities.

PROBABILITY—COUNT-AND-DIVIDE METHOD

(Equally Likely Elementary Events)

$$\text{Pr}[\text{event}] = \frac{\text{Number of elementary events in the event set}}{\text{Number of possible elementary events}}$$

Consider a second composite event:

Heart = { ♥K, ♥Q, ♥J, ♥10, ♥9, ♥8, ♥7, ♥6, ♥5, ♥4, ♥3, ♥2, ♥A}

Counting the elementary events, we see that there are 13 heart cards, any of which yield the event "heart." The complete deck contains 52 cards, and that is the number of elementary events possible. Thus,

$$\Pr[\text{heart}] = \frac{13}{52} = .25$$

Applying the count-and-divide method, you can verify the following:

$$\Pr[\text{face card}] = \frac{12}{52} \qquad \Pr[\text{red card}] = \frac{26}{52} \qquad \Pr[\text{black jack}] = \frac{2}{52}$$

To further illustrate the count-and-divide method, we will use the sample space in Figure 3-2, which shows the breakdown of the State University business students who hold scholarships. One student is selected at random from the group of 72. The following probabilities apply:

$$\Pr[\text{male}] = \frac{40}{72} = .556 \qquad \Pr[\text{female}] = \frac{32}{72} = .444$$

$$\Pr[\text{accounting}] = \frac{16}{72} = .222 \qquad \Pr[\text{graduate}] = \frac{30}{72} = .417$$

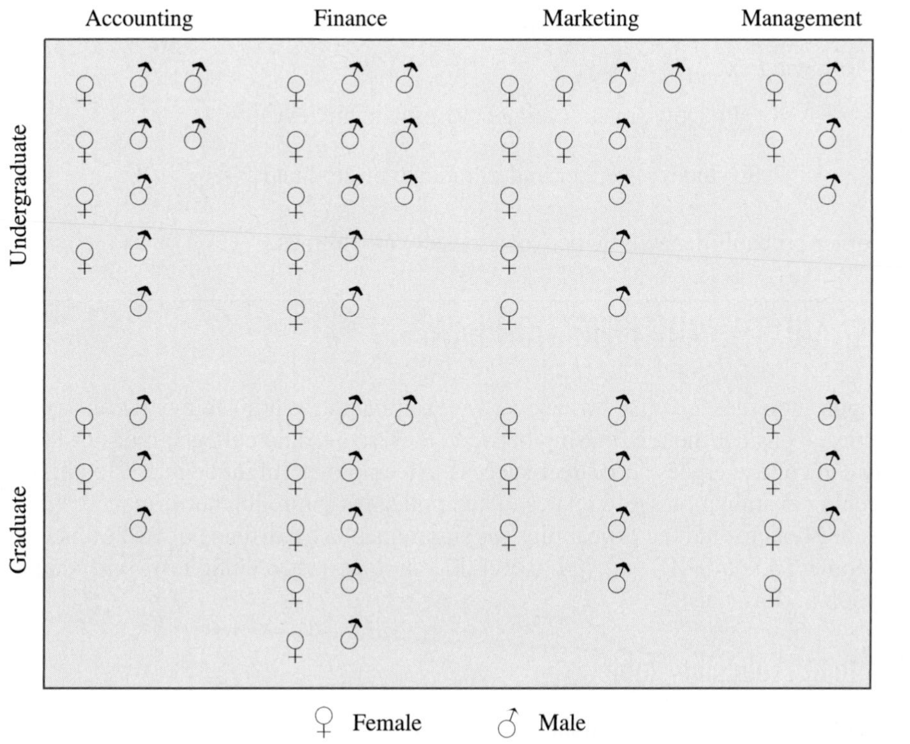

FIGURE 3-2
Sample space for business scholarship students at State University

Probability Estimates

Count-and-divide is one method for determining the long-run frequency at which an event occurs. When we cannot count the possibilities, the count-and-divide approach is unworkable. That is the case for events occurring over time, such as automobile accidents. The true probability for a fatal accident under a given set of circumstances might be .001—the historical frequency. Such a probability value would ordinarily be an *estimate* of the underlying true probability. The count-and-divide method applies only if the elementary events are *equally likely.* What if, for example, a lopsided coin is tossed? The probability for an event in such a random experiment is still a long-run frequency, but it can only be estimated from the actual results experienced by repeating the experiment (tossing the lopsided coin) many times.

Certain and Impossible Events

An event's probability is a fraction or decimal between 0 and 1. You can see this by looking at two extreme probabilities. Because an **impossible event** *never* occurs,

$$\text{Pr[impossible event]} = 0$$

Consider the following examples of impossible events:

$$\text{Pr[Dow Jones Average doubles yesterday's close]} = 0$$

$$\text{Pr[student is both undergraduate and graduate]} = \frac{0}{72} = 0$$

Similarly, a **certain event** (for example, "the selected card has a suit") will *always* occur.

$$\text{Pr[certain event]} = 1$$

The following examples apply:

$$\text{Pr[Dow Jones Average closes at some level]} = 1$$

$$\text{Pr[student is either undergraduate or graduate]} = \frac{72}{72} = 1$$

All other probabilities will lie between these two extremes.

3-3   JOINT PROBABILITY AND THE MULTIPLICATION LAW

Important issues are raised whenever we examine the relationship between two variables. Consider the relationship between SAT scores and college grades or that between college grades and career success. An employer might be interested in how a screening examination score relates to an applicant's future job performance. We now consider how to find the probability for simultaneous occurrence of two events, such as "above 700 on SAT" *and* "GPA of 4.00," or "pass a screening test" *and* "satisfactory job performance."

The Joint Probability Table

Consider the business scholarship students in Figure 3-2. When examining *sex* and *academic level,* the following **cross tabulation** applies:

SEX	LEVEL		
	Undergraduate	Graduate	Total
Male	24	16	40
Female	18	14	32
Total	42	30	72

Suppose that one student is selected at random. We are interested in the sex (*M, F*) and level (*U, G*) for that student, which are now uncertain events. Extending the count-and-divide method to the entire cross tabulation, a complete set of probabilities applies. When arranged in an analogous table, the resulting display in Table 3-1 is called a **joint probability table.**

Mutually Exclusive and Collectively Exhaustive Events

Joint probability tables convey the essential probabilities used in a two-way classification of events. The rows represent for one category **mutually exclusive events** (only one can occur) and **collectively exhaustive events** (at least one must occur). The columns have the same feature.

Joint Events and Probabilities

Each cell in a joint probability table represents an outcome in which the respective row event and column event occur simultaneously. The cell thus signifies a joint event. There are four joint events in Table 3-1:

M and U   *M and G*   *F and U*   *F and G*

The numerical values represent the applicable probabilities. Each cell contains the **joint probability** for the respective row and column event. The top left cell of Table 3-1 contains

$$\Pr[M \text{ and } U] = \frac{24}{72}$$

which expresses the probability that the chosen student is both a male (*M*) and an undergraduate (*U*).

Marginal Probabilities

The margins contain the probability values for the respective row or column event. Because they are located in the *margins* of the table, these are referred to as **marginal probabilities.** The margin of the first row and first column of Table 3-1 contain

TABLE 3-1 Joint Probability Table for Randomly Selected Business Scholarship Students

SEX	LEVEL		
	Undergraduate (*U*)	Graduate (*G*)	Marginal Probability
Male (*M*)	24/72	16/72	40/72
Female (*F*)	18/72	14/72	32/72
Marginal Probability	42/72	30/72	1

$$\Pr[M] = \frac{40}{72} \qquad \Pr[U] = \frac{42}{72}$$

Notice that the joint probabilities within each row sum to the respective marginal probability. (This feature is guaranteed by the nature of the original cross tabulation.) The same fact applies as well to the columns.

The Multiplication Law for Finding "And" Probabilities

As we shall see, the joint probability table is a key element in many probability evaluations. But there may not be a cross tabulation available, and in those cases the count-and-divide method cannot be used in its construction. The needed probabilities must be built using some useful laws provided by probability theory.

The first probability law allows us to compute a joint probability by multiplying the individual probabilities for the component events. This is the *multiplication law.* Before we state that law, it will be helpful to consider an illustration in which the law may be used.

Consider a quarter that has been misshapened on a railroad track:

We want to establish the head and tail probabilities. But there is no reason to believe tosses of this damaged coin will be just as likely to result in a tail as a head. We cannot therefore use 1/2 as the head probability.

A student makes 100 tosses of the bad coin, each time letting it fall free to the floor. She obtains a head on only 35 tosses. The following *estimated* value for the long-run frequency may be used as the approximate head probability:

$$\Pr[\text{head}] = \frac{35}{100} = .35$$

The other 65 tosses result in a tail, and thus a second approximate probability applies for the tail event:

$$\Pr[\text{tail}] = \frac{65}{100} = .65$$

Now consider two later tosses of the bad quarter. Let's denote achieving a head on the first toss as H_1 and use T_1 to represent obtaining a tail. Similarly, for the second toss we use H_2 for a head and T_2 for a tail. We have

$$\Pr[H_1] = \Pr[H_2] = .35 \quad \text{and} \quad \Pr[T_1] = \Pr[T_2] = .65$$

What is the probability that both tosses result in a head?

To answer this question we must use the following:

MULTIPLICATION LAW FOR INDEPENDENT EVENTS

$$\Pr[A \text{ and } B] = \Pr[A] \times \Pr[B]$$

This tells us that when A and B are independent (a relation to be discussed shortly), we may find an unknown joint probability by multiplying the known probabilities for the individual component events. The joint event's set is the **intersection** of the component events, which are logically joined by "and."

We illustrate this law with the two tosses of the damaged quarter. Multiplying the H_1 and H_2 probabilities, we have the probability for getting two successive heads:

$$Pr[H_1 \text{ and } H_2] = Pr[H_1] \times Pr[H_2]$$
$$= .35(.35) = .1225$$

We may use the multiplication law to establish the probability that a randomly selected playing card is both a "heart" and a "queen." Counting and dividing, we first get

$$Pr[\text{heart}] = \frac{13}{52} \qquad Pr[\text{queen}] = \frac{4}{52}$$

Then, multiplying the component event probabilities, we get

$$Pr[\text{heart } and \text{ queen}] = Pr[\text{heart}] \times Pr[\text{queen}]$$
$$= \frac{13}{52} \times \frac{4}{52}$$
$$= \frac{1}{52}$$

Some Advice and Warnings About the Multiplication Law

With the card example, the multiplication law involves a lot of work. If we had first noted that "heart and queen" is the same as drawing the queen of hearts, we could have more easily just counted and divided to establish 1/52 as the probability of getting that card. You should use the multiplication law when it is advantageous to do so. It is definitely *not mandatory* to use this law when you are finding a joint probability.

The foregoing version of the multiplication law only applies when events are *independent,* a relationship we will define in Section 3-5. When events do not have that relationship, the law will not work. Beginners find it perplexing that the multiplication law can give the *wrong answer!*

Joint Probabilities Involving More than Two Events

The multiplication law for independent events extends to any number of component events.

Late Airline Departures

MANAGERIAL APPLICATION

Each noon on weekdays, Unified Airways Flight 22 departs from Centralia. This flight experiences late departures 70% of the time, and the takeoff time on any day has no effect on a future day's experience. What is the probability that a particular week will have late departures every day?

SOLUTION

The probability of a late departure on any particular day is .70. Denoting the respective late-departure events as LMo, LTu, LWe, LTh, and LFr, the multiplication law provides the answer:

Pr[LMo *and* LTu *and* LWe *and* LTh *and* LFr]

$\quad$ = Pr[LMo] $\times$ Pr[LTu] $\times$ Pr[LWe] $\times$ Pr[LTh] $\times$ Pr[LFr]

$\quad$ = .7(.7)(.7)(.7)(.7)

$\quad$ = $(.7)^5$ = .168

This tells us that even though 70% of the daily departures are late, only 16.8% of the weeks involve late takeoffs every day.

3-4   FINDING PROBABILITIES USING THE ADDITION LAW

We have seen that the count-and-divide procedure may be used to determine the probabilities for composite events. That method, however, has limited scope. We now consider a more general approach.

$\quad$ To illustrate, let's return to the damaged coin of the previous section. Again, we will toss it twice. It is easy to see that the sample space comprises these elementary events:

$$H_1H_2 \qquad H_1T_2 \qquad T_1H_2 \qquad T_1T_2$$

What is the probability of exactly one head?

$\quad$ The outcome in question is a composite event with this event set:

$$\text{Exactly one head} = \{H_1T_2, T_1H_2\}$$

The desired probability is *not* equal to 2/4, which is what the count-and-divide method would provide. Counting and dividing works only for equally likely elementary events.

$\quad$ Instead we may get correct values with the following procedure, which uses the probabilities for component events as building blocks.

The Addition Law for Finding "Or" Probabilities

A second probability law allows us to find the probability of composite events whether or not the elementary events are equally likely. This is the **addition law,** which under special circumstances permits us to add the component event probabilities.

ADDITION LAW FOR MUTUALLY EXCLUSIVE EVENTS

$$\text{Pr}[A \ or \ B \ or \ C] = \text{Pr}[A] + \text{Pr}[B] + \text{Pr}[C]$$

This expression may be used in finding the unknown probability for a composite event whose event set is the **union** of two or more *mutually exclusive* component events, only one of which can actually occur. Those individual events are logically connected with "or" and have known probabilities. To illustrate, consider again the business scholarship students in Figure 3-2. The following apply to the major of a randomly selected student:

$$\Pr[\text{accounting}] = \frac{16}{72} \qquad \Pr[\text{marketing}] = \frac{20}{72}$$

$$\Pr[\text{finance}] = \frac{24}{72} \qquad \Pr[\text{management}] = \frac{12}{72}$$

Using the above, we may apply the addition law to establish the probability that a nonmanagement major is selected. Note first the equivalency

$$\Pr[\text{nonmanagement}] = \Pr[\text{accounting } or \text{ finance } or \text{ marketing}]$$

Then, applying the addition law, the correct value is obtained:

$$\Pr[\text{accounting } or \text{ finance } or \text{ marketing}]$$
$$= \Pr[\text{accounting}] + \Pr[\text{finance}] + \Pr[\text{marketing}]$$
$$= \frac{16}{72} + \frac{24}{72} + \frac{20}{72}$$
$$= \frac{60}{72}$$

Some Advice and a Warning About the Addition Law

When the elementary events are equally likely and we can easily count possibilities, a probability for a composite event might be obtained *without* using the addition law. Directly from Figure 3-2, we determine that there are 60 nonmanagement majors (accounting, finance, or marketing) out of 72 business scholarship students, so that a single count-and-divide method more readily provides the same result:

$$\Pr[\text{nonmanagement}] = \frac{60}{72}$$

Like the multiplication law, the addition law does not have to be used every time an "or" joins component events. We should use it only when advantageous to do so. It becomes essential when counting and dividing is impractical or impossible. That is the case in the following example, in which details about the sample space are not provided.

Reasons for Denial of Credit

MANAGERIAL APPLICATION

The credit manager for the Hide-Away Safe Company has several reasons for denying credit to buyers: (1) low income, (2) poor repayment history, (3) high debts, and (4) no collateral. Records of past transactions list one of these as the primary reason for denial of credit. If you assume that past frequencies will apply in the future, you have the following probabilities that the next credit application will be rejected for each primary reason.

$$\Pr[\text{low income}] = .15$$
$$\Pr[\text{poor repayment}] = .20$$
$$\Pr[\text{high debts}] = .25$$
$$\Pr[\text{no collateral}] = .40$$

Reasons (3) and (4) apply to what are called "balance sheet deficiencies." We will determine the probability that a balance sheet deficiency will be the reason for the next credit denial.

SOLUTION

We apply the addition law.

$$\Pr[\text{balance sheet}] = \Pr[\text{high debts } or \text{ no collateral}]$$
$$= \Pr[\text{high debts}] + \Pr[\text{no collateral}]$$
$$= .25 + .40 = .65$$

The addition law can also lead to the *wrong answer*. It requires that the component events be *mutually exclusive,* and it will provide incorrect values if that is not the case.

To illustrate an improper application of the addition law, consider the following calculation for a randomly selected playing card:

$$\Pr[\text{heart}] + \Pr[\text{queen}] = \frac{13}{52} + \frac{4}{52} = \frac{17}{52}$$

This calculation gives an *incorrect* value for Pr[heart *or* queen]. (Go back to Figure 3-1. How many cards fall into the category of being either a heart or a queen?) Adding the two probabilities is fallacious because heart and queen are *not* mutually exclusive events. Both event sets have the queen of hearts in common, and the above calculation accounts for that possibility twice!

Probabilities When Events Are Mutually Exclusive and Collectively Exhaustive

The relevant events from many random experiments are *mutually exclusive*—only one of them can occur—and also *collectively exhaustive,* making it certain that one of the events will occur. Consider the outcomes experienced by SoftWhereHaus, which takes a sample of its program diskettes every hour to determine the quality of its final product. If only 10% of the diskettes are defective, then the following probabilities apply for the number of defectives in a sample of five diskettes.

Number of Defectives	Probability
0	.5905
1	.3280
2	.0729
3	.0081
4	.0005
5	.0000
	1.0000

The events for "number defective" are mutually exclusive and collectively exhaustive, and their probabilities add up to 1.

Application to Complementary Events

When two events are complementary (opposite), their probabilities add up to 1.

$$\Pr[A \text{ } or \text{ not } A] = \Pr[A] + \Pr[\text{not } A] = \Pr[\text{certain event}] = 1$$

Thus,

$$\Pr[A] = 1 - \Pr[\text{not } A]$$

This is helpful when you want to know an event's probability, but the probability for its complementary event is easier to determine. If you want to determine the probability for "at least 1" defective diskette in the above example, you can use the addition law and add the probabilities for "exactly 1," "exactly 2," and so on. But you can determine the answer faster if you recognize that "at least 1" is the opposite of "exactly 0." The probability for "0 defective" is .5905, so that

$$\Pr[\text{at least 1 defective}] = 1 - \Pr[\text{exactly 0 defective}]$$
$$= 1 - .5905 = .4095$$

3-5 STATISTICAL INDEPENDENCE

We have been using the multiplication law to compute various probabilities. That law only works when events are *independent*. We are now ready to formally define this concept.

A Definition of Statistical Independence

The multiplication law stated earlier applies only for independent events.

> **DEFINITION 1**
>
> Two events A and B are **statistically independent** whenever
>
> $$\Pr[A \text{ and } B] = \Pr[A] \times \Pr[B]$$

This indicates that statistical independence is established only by the *probabilities* of two events—not their sequence, cause and effect, timing, or hierarchical ranking.

A Basic Test for Independence Between Events

If the probability data are available, we can establish the independence or nonindependence between two events by comparing probabilities.

To illustrate, consider once more the business scholarship students. The following joint probability table for *sex* versus *major* applies for a randomly selected undergraduate.

SEX	MAJOR				Marginal Probability
	Accounting	Finance	Marketing	Management	
Male	7/42	8/42	6/42	3/42	24/42
Female	4/42	5/42	7/42	2/42	18/42
Marginal Probability	11/42	13/42	13/42	5/42	1

Consider the events "male" and "marketing." The joint probability for these events is

$$\Pr[\text{male } and \text{ marketing}] = \frac{6}{42} = .1429$$

Then, multiplying the respective marginal probabilities, we have

$$\Pr[\text{male}] \times \Pr[\text{marketing}] = \frac{24}{42} \times \frac{13}{42} = .1769$$

Since this product *differs* from the joint probability, the events "male" and "marketing" are *not* statistically independent. Events that are not independent are said to be **dependent events.**

A second comparison using playing card events,

$$\Pr[\text{heart } and \text{ queen}] = \frac{1}{52} = \frac{13}{52} \times \frac{4}{52} = \Pr[\text{heart}] \times \Pr[\text{queen}]$$

establishes that "heart" and "queen" are statistically independent events.

Statistical independence may apply to any number of events. To have independence, the joint probability of any subset of those events, including the whole, must always equal the product of the individual probabilities. Although this test is foolproof, the probability values needed to establish independence or dependence may not be readily available.

In a broad class of random experiments, independence between events may be *assumed,* due to the very nature in which they are generated. This is what we have implicitly been doing all along with coin tosses. To have independence between successive outcomes, a head should be just as likely regardless of whether the preceding toss was a head or a tail. We don't ordinarily need to test for this. (Although a person could sabotage independence by tossing the coin in special ways.)

Independent Events and the Multiplication Law

The multiplication law stated earlier requires independence before it can even be used. We use that law only when independence can be safely *assumed.* (And there obviously is no purpose served in comparing the joint probabilities thereby obtained to establish independence, which had to be known at the outset.)

Finding Joint Probabilities for Dependent Events

When sufficient data are available (as with the business scholarship students), joint probabilities for dependent events may be found by counting and dividing. When no cross tabulation exists, a different procedure must be used. The alternative method works when probabilities are derived from historical frequencies rather than by counting and dividing.

Percentages are common sources of probability data. For instance, a researcher reports that the following apply to Gotham City adults:

5% drive drunk (*D*)

12% are alcoholics (*A*)

40% of all drunk drivers are alcoholics

From that, we can readily establish the following probabilities for a randomly selected Gotham City adult.

$$\text{Pr}[D] = .05 \qquad \text{Pr}[A] = .12$$

Multiplying, we obtain the product

$$\text{Pr}[D] \times \text{Pr}[A] = .05 \times .12 = .006$$

That is *not* the joint probability for the two events.

To find the correct value for the joint probability, we use the fact that 40% of the 5% who are drunk drivers are also alcoholics, so that the product of the respective decimal fractions is

$$.40 \times .05 = .02$$

We see that 2% are *both* drunk drivers *and* alcoholics (*D and A*). That indicates that for a randomly selected adult,

$$\text{Pr}[D \text{ and } A] = .02$$

Note that *D* and *A* are *dependent* events, because

$$\text{Pr}[D \text{ and } A] = .02 \neq .006 = \text{Pr}[D] \times \text{Pr}[A]$$

Constructing a Joint Probability Table Without a Cross Tabulation

We have the essential information for filling in the blanks in the 2-by-2 joint probability table for driver *condition* versus *alcoholism*. We start by inserting the provided probabilities:

CONDITION	ALCOHOLISM		Marginal Probability
	Alcoholic (A)	Nonalcoholic (not A)	
Drunk (D)	.02		.05
Sober (not D)			
Marginal Probability	.12		

The missing marginal probabilities are filled in next. For the right-hand margin, these must sum to 1.00, because the respective events are *complementary*. Thus, .95 applies for Pr[not D]. An analogous condition applies to the bottom margin; Pr[not A] must equal .88. This gives the following (new values in boldface type):

CONDITION	ALCOHOLISM		Marginal Probability
	Alcoholic (A)	Nonalcoholic (not A)	
Drunk (D)	.02		.05
Sober (not D)			**.95** ← 1 − .05
Marginal Probability	.12	**.88**	**1.00**

1 − .12

Next, the cell probabilities are obtained. First, the value .03 is found for the empty cell in the D row, establishing Pr[D and not A]. That gives cell entries in the D row that sum to the marginal probability of .05. In the same way, .10 is found for the empty cell in the A column, establishing the value for Pr[not D and A]. Then, working with the marginal probability for either the not-D row or the not-A column, the entry for the last empty cell must be .85, and Pr[not A and not D] is determined. The completed joint probability table is:

CONDITION	ALCOHOLISM		
	Alcoholic (A)	Nonalcoholic (not A)	Marginal Probability
Drunk (D)	.02	.03	.05
Sober (not D)	.10	.85	.95
Marginal Probability	.12	.88	1.00

.05 − .02

.12 − .02

.88 − .03 or .95 − .10

Had the joint probability in the D and A cell been different, the other joint probabilities would differ too. In effect, there is only one *degree of freedom* in filling the inside of a 2-by-2 joint probability table. The first cell entry always dictates the joint probability values for the other cells.

3-6   CONDITIONAL PROBABILITY AND THE GENERAL MULTIPLICATION LAW

It is useful to have probability values that apply only when a special condition is met. These are called **conditional probabilities,** and they express the chance that one event will occur given that another occurs. We represent symbolically the conditional probability of A given B by

$$Pr[A \mid B] \qquad (Pr[A \ given \ B])$$

The probability value pertains to A, computed under the assumption that B will occur.

The weather provides some examples. Consider the events "rain" and "cloudy," for which the following might be true:

$$Pr[rain \mid cloudy] = .70$$

This equation is read, "The probability that there will be rain *given* that it is cloudy is .70." The event "rain" is listed first, and .70 is the probability for this event. The second event, which appears after the vertical bar, is the **given event,** "cloudy." This event establishes the condition under which .70 applies. Given some other event, "rain" could have a different probability. For example,

$$Pr[rain \mid low \ pressure] = .30$$

In either case, the probability for rain is conditional because it assumes that another event—"cloudy" or "low pressure"—is going to occur. Should no conditions be stipulated for the weather, we might have the value

$$Pr[rain] = .20$$

which is an **unconditional probability.**

Computing Conditional Probabilities

Count-and-Divide Method   The condition, or given event, eliminates extraneous possibilities that would need to be accounted for in establishing unconditional probabilities. For example, consider a randomly selected playing card. You can see that

$$\Pr[\text{jack} \mid \text{face card}] = \frac{4}{12} = \frac{1}{3}$$

because there are only 12 face cards and just 4 cards are jacks. The condition of "face card" effectively reduces the sample space to just 12 cards, and the count-and-divide method can then be applied to the smaller, or restricted, sample space. Without the condition, you would have to consider the entire sample space (all 52 cards), so that

$$\Pr[\text{jack}] = \frac{4}{52} = \frac{1}{13}$$

As another example, consider the student selection experiment in Figure 3-2. You can determine the probability for "finance major given undergraduate" by observing that the condition "undergraduate" eliminates all graduate students. Therefore, the 42 students in the event set "undergraduate" are the restricted sample space. Of those 42 students, 13 are finance majors, so that

$$\Pr[\text{finance} \mid \text{undergraduate}] = \frac{13}{42}$$

Conditional Probability Identity   If the necessary probability values are known, you may find it helpful to use the

CONDITIONAL PROBABILITY IDENTITY

$$\Pr[A \mid B] = \frac{\Pr[A \text{ and } B]}{\Pr[B]}$$

This equation states that the conditional probability for an event can be determined by dividing the joint probability for the two events (if known) by the unconditional probability for the given event (if that value is also known). This calculation provides the long-run relative frequency that A occurs out of all those times that B occurs.

To illustrate, consider the values in the joint probability table found earlier for drunk driving versus alcoholism. The identity equation provides the conditional probability that a randomly selected Gotham City adult is an alcoholic given that he or she is a drunk driver:

$$\Pr[A \mid D] = \frac{\Pr[A \text{ and } D]}{\Pr[D]} = \frac{.02}{.05} = .40$$

This reflects that 40% of the *drunk drivers only* are alcoholics. Do not confuse *A given D* with the joint event *A and D,* which represents *all adults,* 2% of which are both alcoholics and drunk drivers.

Let's now reverse roles, finding the probability that this person is a drunk driver given that he or she is an alcoholic:

$$\Pr[D \mid A] = \frac{\Pr[D \text{ and } A]}{\Pr[A]} = \frac{.02}{.12} = .1667$$

The same value as before appears in the numerator, but a different divisor is used because now alcoholic (A) is the given event. The result tells us that 17% of the alcoholics in Gotham City are drunk drivers. (Be careful when you find conditional probabilities. Reversing the events always gives a different meaning to the result, and the computed value will ordinarily differ as well.)

Although it is always a mathematically correct expression, the conditional probability identity cannot always be used to find conditional probabilities. Consider the following example:

MANAGERIAL APPLICATION

Finding Probabilities for Sample Defectives

The receiving department of SoftWhereHaus is sample testing a small shipment of high-velocity recording heads. Suppose that out of the 10 heads in the shipment, 2 are defective (D) and the rest are satisfactory (S). (Of course, the inspector doesn't know this fact.) Two heads, represented by the subscripts 1 and 2, are randomly selected one at a time and tested just once. We want to find the various probabilities involving D_1 and D_2.

SOLUTION

You can see that

$$\Pr[D_1] = \frac{2}{10}$$

and given that the first head is defective, only 1 defective is among the 9 remaining heads, so that

$$\Pr[D_2 \mid D_1] = \frac{1}{9}$$

Should the first head instead be satisfactory, then 2 defectives are left in the remaining 9, and

$$\Pr[D_2 \mid S_1] = \frac{2}{9}$$

You can't use the conditional probability identity here because you don't know the values for $\Pr[D_1 \text{ and } D_2]$ or $\Pr[S_1 \text{ and } D_2]$.

Conditional Probability and Statistical Independence

Two events are statistically independent if the occurrence of one has no effect on the probability of the other. An alternative definition of independence compares conditional and unconditional probabilities.

DEFINITION 2

Two events A and B are **statistically independent** whenever

$$\Pr[A \mid B] = \Pr[A] \quad \text{or} \quad \Pr[B \mid A] = \Pr[B]$$

Two events are independent whenever the conditional probability of one event given the second is equal to its *unconditional* probability. In effect, the occurrence, nonoccurrence, or lack of knowledge about the other event has no effect on an event's probability value.

An alternative test for independence would therefore be to compare the unconditional probability for either event with its respective conditional probability. To illustrate, "queen" and "face" are dependent, because

$$\Pr[\text{queen}] = \frac{4}{52} \neq \frac{4}{12} = \Pr[\text{queen} \mid \text{face}]$$

When this holds, so must the reverse:

$$\Pr[\text{face}] = \frac{12}{52} \neq \frac{4}{4} = \Pr[\text{face} \mid \text{queen}]$$

And, "queen" and "heart" are independent, because

$$\Pr[\text{queen}] = \frac{4}{52} = \frac{1}{13} = \Pr[\text{queen} \mid \text{heart}]$$

and likewise,

$$\Pr[\text{heart}] = \frac{13}{52} = \frac{1}{4} = \Pr[\text{heart} \mid \text{queen}]$$

The General Multiplication Law

The multiplication law used so far pertains just to *independent* events. That requirement does not apply to the following:

GENERAL MULTIPLICATION LAW

$$\Pr[A \text{ and } B] = \Pr[A] \times \Pr[B \mid A]$$

or

$$\Pr[A \text{ and } B] = \Pr[B] \times \Pr[A \mid B]$$

This law involves the product of an unconditional probability and a conditional probability.

To illustrate, consider the following experience of an accountant. She has established that 60% of all accounts receivable involve incorrect remittances (I), and that 10% of those involve partial payments (P). This history may be expressed as:

$$\Pr[I] = .60$$
$$\Pr[P \mid I] = .10$$

The multiplication law provides the probability that a particular remittance will be both incorrect and a partial payment.

$$\Pr[I \text{ and } P] = \Pr[I] \times \Pr[P \mid I]$$
$$= .60 \times .10$$
$$= .06$$

Thus, 6% of all remittances for accounts receivable will fall into the two categories. (You can verify the result in terms of percentages: 10% of 60% is 6%.)

Illustration: Oil Wildcatting with a Seismic Survey   The owner of the Petroleum Entrepreneurship is a wildcatter who judges that there is a 30% chance of oil (O) beneath his leasehold on Fossil Ridges, with complementary chances that the site is dry (D). That is, the following unconditional probabilities apply:

$$\Pr[O] = .30 \quad \text{and} \quad \Pr[D] = 1 - .30 = .70$$

The wildcatter has the option of drilling now or ordering a seismic survey. Such a test is 90% reliable in predicting a favorable (F) outcome when there is actually oil, but only 70% reliable in providing an unfavorable (U) forecast when a site is dry. The given reliability percentages directly express the conditional probabilities

$$\Pr[F \mid O] = .90 \quad \text{and} \quad \Pr[U \mid D] = .70$$

The general multiplication law may be used to establish the joint probability that Fossil Ridges does indeed contain oil and that the seismic survey will be favorable.

$$\begin{aligned} \Pr[O \text{ and } F] &= \Pr[O] \times \Pr[F \mid O] \\ &= .30 \times .90 = .27 \end{aligned}$$

Similarly, the joint probability for a dry site and an unfavorable seismic survey is

$$\begin{aligned} \Pr[D \text{ and } U] &= \Pr[D] \times \Pr[U \mid D] \\ &= .70 \times .70 = .49 \end{aligned}$$

3-7   PROBABILITY TREES

We have seen how the joint probability table arranges probability information in a convenient display. We are now ready to discuss a second display that is especially useful for decision-making purposes. We then complete our probability introduction by extending the probability laws presented so far and giving some warnings about their misuse.

The Probability Tree Diagram

Business decision makers find the joint probability table cumbersome at times. They prefer to organize their probability calculations using a **probability tree.** The probability tree diagram for the preceding oil wildcatting illustration is shown in Figure 3-3. There, each event is represented as a **branch** in one or more **event forks.** This representation is especially convenient when events occur at different times or stages.

In probability trees, time moves from left to right. Because the geology events precede the seismic events, the branches for oil (O) and dry (D) appear in the event fork on the left. Each is followed by a separate event fork representing the seismic events, with a branch for favorable (F) and another for unfavorable (U). Two seismic-event forks are required because the seismic results can occur under two distinct geological conditions. The complete tree exhibits each outcome as a single **path** from beginning to end. The probability tree in Figure 3-3 has four paths: oil-favorable, oil-unfavorable, dry-favorable, dry-unfavorable. Each path corresponds to a distinct joint event.

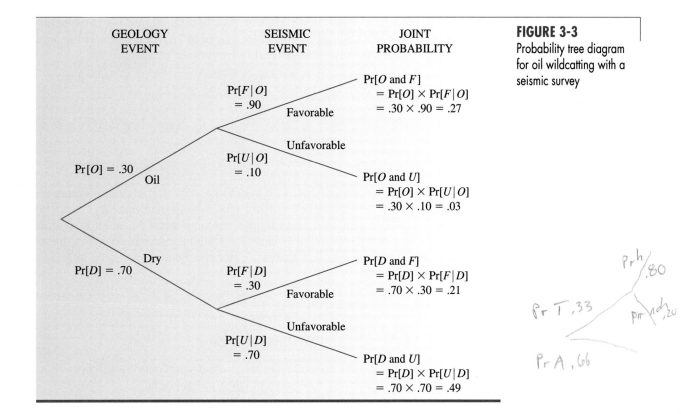

FIGURE 3-3
Probability tree diagram for oil wildcatting with a seismic survey

The probability for each event is placed alongside its branch. The values listed in the left fork, $\Pr[O] = .30$ and $\Pr[D] = .70$, are unconditional because that event fork has no predecessor. Probabilities for later stage events will all be *conditional* probabilities, with the branch or subpath leading to the branching point signifying the given events. The top seismic event fork lists the probabilities $\Pr[F \mid O] = .90$ for favorable and $\Pr[U \mid O] = .10$ for unfavorable. Because that fork is preceded by the oil (O) branch, both conditional probabilities involve O as the given event. A *completely different* set of conditional probabilities, $\Pr[F \mid D] = .30$ and $\Pr[U \mid D] = .70$, apply in the bottom event fork; that branching point is preceded by the dry (D) branch, so that D is the given event.

The events emanating from a single branching point are mutually exclusive and collectively exhaustive, so that exactly one must occur. All the probabilities on branches within the same fork must therefore sum to 1.

The probability tree is very convenient for determining joint probabilities. A joint event is represented by a path through the tree, and its probability is determined by multiplying all the individual branch probabilities for its path. For instance, the topmost path represents the outcome sequence oil-favorable. The corresponding joint probability is

$$\Pr[O \text{ and } F] = \Pr[O] \times \Pr[F \mid O]$$
$$= .30(.90)$$
$$= .27$$

All of the joint probabilities for the oil wildcatter are listed in Figure 3-3 at the terminus of the respective event path. Notice that these sum to 1. That is because the joint events themselves are mutually exclusive and collectively exhaustive.

Multiplication Law for Several Events

The general multiplication law can be expanded to apply to situations involving more than two component events. For three events,

$$\Pr[A \text{ and } B \text{ and } C] = \Pr[A] \times \Pr[B|A] \times \Pr[C|A \text{ and } B]$$

All terms except the first are conditional probabilities, with the preceding events assumed as given events. There may be any number of component events.

To illustrate, in a particular industry it has been found that 80% of all new firms survive (S) past one year. Of those, 40% close (C) within the second year, half due to bankruptcy (B) and the rest for other reasons. This experience provides the following probabilities for a start-up:

$$\Pr[S] = .80$$
$$\Pr[C|S] = .40$$
$$\Pr[B|S \text{ and } C] = .50$$

The multiplication law provides the joint probability that a particular new firm will survive the first year, close during the second, and then go bankrupt.

$$\Pr[S \text{ and } C \text{ and } B] = \Pr[S] \times \Pr[C|S] \times \Pr[B|S \text{ and } C]$$
$$= .80 \times .40 \times .50$$
$$= .16$$

PROBABILITY APPLICATION

The Matching Birthday Problem

Consider the probability that there is at least one matching birthday (day and month) among a group of persons.

SOLUTION

It will be simplest to determine the probability of the complementary event—no matches—by using the general multiplication law. Envision each member of a group of size n being asked in succession to state his or her birthday. We conveniently define our events as follows:

$$A_i = \text{the ith person queried does not share a birthday}$$
$$\text{with the previous } i - 1 \text{ persons}$$

Then $\Pr[\text{no match}] = \Pr[A_1 \text{ and } A_2 \text{ and} \ldots \text{and } A_{n-1} \text{ and } A_n]$, which is the probability of the event that no person shares a birthday with the preceding persons. For simplicity, assume all dates to be equally likely and ignore leap year. Thus,

$$\Pr[A_1] = \frac{365}{365} \qquad \Pr[A_2|A_1] = \frac{364}{365} \qquad \Pr[A_3|A_1 \text{ and } A_2] = \frac{363}{365}$$

so that the nth person cannot have a birthday on the previously cited $n - 1$ dates, $365 - (n - 1) = 365 - n + 1$ days are allowable for his or her birthday. Therefore, we may apply the multiplication law to obtain

$$\Pr[\text{no matches}] = \frac{365}{365} \times \frac{364}{365} \times \frac{363}{365} \times \dots \times \frac{365 - n + 1}{365}$$

The probability for at least one match may be determined from this:

$$\Pr[\text{at least one match}] = 1 - \Pr[\text{no matches}]$$

One interesting issue is finding the size of the group for which the probability exceeds 1/2 that there is at least one match. Knowing this number, you can amaze your less-knowledgeable friends and perhaps win a few bets. The "magical" group size turns out to be 23.

Why such a low group size? If it were physically possible to list all the ways (triples, sextuples, septuples, and so forth) in which 23 birthdays can match (there are several million, and for each a tremendous number of date possibilities), an intuitive appreciation as to why could be attained. Table 3-2 shows the matching probabilities for several group sizes. Note that for groups above 60 there is almost certain to be at least one match.

TABLE 3-2 Probabilities for at Least One Matching Birthday

Group Size	Pr[no matches]	Pr[at least one match]
3	.992	.008
7	.943	.057
10	.883	.117
15	.748	.252
23	.493	.507
40	.109	.891
50	.030	.970
60	.006	.994

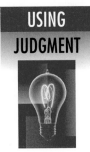

Selecting a Procedure to Find the Probability

Perhaps the most perplexing aspect of probability concepts is determining the proper procedure to get the correct probability value. Often there is more than one way to reach the answer. Sometimes they all work. But often not all approaches apply to a particular situation. Generally, the choice of procedure depends on the *information* structure of the problem. Try the simplest approaches first. When there are lots of data, the count-and-divide procedure may yield quick results. Remember that you do not have to use the multiplication law just because events are joined by "and" nor the addition law because there is an "or."

For many types of problems involving categories, constructing a joint probability table might be an efficient starting point. For some problems, the joint (cell) and marginal probabilities can be found by counting and dividing. In other cases, percentage information must be combined, using multiplication and addition law concepts, to get the table. Once constructed, any conditional probability involving an event for a row given an event in a column, or vice

versa, can be quickly obtained by applying the conditional probability identity with values pulled from the table.

Trees are another useful prop for finding probability values, especially for situations where events occur in stages.

You must exercise some judgment in finding probabilities. All formulas will fail when you do not know the values to plug into them. When you encounter that obstacle, rethink the problem. There must be a more fundamental approach to take, if an answer can be found. (And, in textbook situations, the answers can always be found!)

Unfortunately, we cannot catalog and pigeonhole all problem types and give recipes for finding all answers. You must learn inductively, and the best way is to work lots of probability problems.

3-8   REVISING PROBABILITIES USING BAYES' THEOREM

You may find it valuable to apply the probability revision procedures originally proposed by the Reverend Thomas Bayes more than 200 years ago. These involve changing an initial set of probability values to reflect a particular experimental finding.

Prior and Posterior Probabilities

You often hear a weather forecast such as, "For tomorrow, there is a 50% chance of rain." You may even occasionally come up with your own chance percentage, or **prior probability,** for rain the next day. The adjective *prior* means that the probability value is temporary and might change, depending on what further information develops.

The value 50% for rain is a *subjective probability* because another person might disagree, believing perhaps that there is instead a 40% chance of rain. This subjectivity exists because the underlying random experiment (tomorrow's weather, in this case) is strictly nonrepeatable. Similar uncertainties are common in business. Consider one-shot events such as a new product's reception in the marketplace, a company's sales, or the state of the economy.

If you decide there is a .50 prior probability for rain, you might go to bed planning to dress "for the weather" when you arise. But in the morning you might first look outside at the cloud cover. If it is solid and black, you might revise your probability for rain upward to a value like .90; if the clouds are patchy, you might instead reduce that probability to a number like .20, choosing to leave your umbrella at home. Such a revised value is called a **posterior probability.**

Posterior probabilities are *conditional* probabilities of the form

$$\Pr[\text{event} \mid \text{result}]$$

The given event is the **result** of an experiment (in the preceding example, looking at the sky) upon which the revised probability is based. Thomas Bayes proposed a formal mechanism for determining posterior probabilities by merging prior judgment with empirical results. In doing this, you encounter a third type of probability.

Conditional Result Probabilities

Suppose that for an entire entire year you keep records of a weather forecaster's predictions and the actual next day's weather. Assume that this weatherperson makes one of two forecasts: (1) rain likely and (2) rain unlikely. You may consider your viewing of the 11 P.M. TV weather broadcast as an experiment having those two *results*. Suppose that 60% of the days when rain actually occurred were preceded by an 11 P.M. forecast in which rain was predicted "likely." Suppose further that 80% of the days when no rain fell were preceded by an "unlikely" forecast. Assuming that this pattern continues into the future, the conditional probability is .60 that the forecast will be "likely" given that rain follows and .80 that it will be "unlikely" given that no rain follows. These numbers are referred to as **conditional result probabilities.** They provide a measure of the reliability of predictive information.

Bayes' Theorem

Using the concepts of prior and conditional result probabilities, Bayes arrived at a theorem for determining posterior probabilities.

The posterior probability of event E for a particular result R of an empirical investigation can be found using

BAYES' THEOREM

$$\Pr[E \mid R] = \frac{\Pr[E]\,\Pr[R \mid E]}{\Pr[E]\,\Pr[R \mid E] + \Pr[\text{not } E]\,\Pr[R \mid \text{not } E]}$$

Here E stands for "event" and R stands for "result." The prior probability for the main event of interest E is *specified in advance* as $\Pr[E]$, with $\Pr[\text{not } E] = 1 - \Pr[E]$. The conditional result probabilities must also be stipulated before making calculations.

You can apply Bayes' theorem to the weather illustration to find the posterior probability that it will rain (E) given a likely forecast (R). The prior probability is

$$\Pr[\text{rain}] = .50$$

and the conditional result probabilities are

$$\Pr[\text{likely} \mid \text{rain}] = .60$$
$$\Pr[\text{likely} \mid \text{no rain}] = 1 - \Pr[\text{unlikely} \mid \text{no rain}] = 1 - .80 = .20$$

Plugging these values into Bayes' theorem, you find

$\Pr[\text{rain} \mid \text{likely}]$

$$= \frac{\Pr[\text{rain}] \times \Pr[\text{likely} \mid \text{rain}]}{\Pr[\text{rain}] \times \Pr[\text{likely} \mid \text{rain}] + \Pr[\text{no rain}] \times \Pr[\text{likely} \mid \text{no rain}]}$$

$$= \frac{.50(.60)}{.50(.60) + (1 - .50)(.20)} = \frac{.30}{.30 + .10} = .75$$

A similar calculation provides the posterior probability for rain (E) given an unlikely forecast (different R). The following conditional result probabilities apply:

$$\Pr[\text{unlikely} \mid \text{rain}] = 1 - .60 = .40$$
$$\Pr[\text{unlikely} \mid \text{no rain}] = .80$$

You find that

Pr[rain | unlikely]

$$= \frac{Pr[rain] \times Pr[unlikely \mid rain]}{Pr[rain] \times Pr[unlikely \mid rain] + Pr[no \; rain] \times Pr[unlikely \mid no \; rain]}$$

$$= \frac{.50(.40)}{.50(.40) + (1 - .50)(.80)} = \frac{.20}{.20 + .40} = .333$$

Notice how the posterior probability for rain *increases* to .75 from the prior level of .50 given a likely forecast. This is what we should expect with any reliable experimental result. Similarly the posterior probability for rain *decreases* from .50 to .33 given an unlikely forecast.

PROBABILITY APPLICATION

Posterior Probabilities for Oil Wildcatting with a Seismic Survey

Based on 20 years of wildcatting experience, Lucky Luke assigns a prior probability of .20 for oil (*O*) beneath Crockpot Dome. Thus,

$$Pr[O] = .20 \quad and \quad Pr[not \; O] = 1 - .20 = .80$$

Luke has decided to order a seismic survey. A petroleum engineering consultant has rated this particular test as 90% reliable in confirming oil (*C*) when there is actually oil, but only 70% reliable in denying oil (*D*) when a site has no oil. These figures determine the conditional result probabilities.

$$Pr[C \mid O] = .90 \quad and \quad Pr[D \mid not \; O] = .70$$

Find the posterior probabilities for oil.

SOLUTION

Suppose that the seismic survey confirms the presence of oil. Luke's posterior probability for oil would then be

$$Pr[O \mid C] = \frac{Pr[O] \times Pr[C \mid O]}{Pr[O] \times Pr[C \mid O] + Pr[not \; O] \times Pr[C \mid not \; O]}$$

$$= \frac{.20(.90)}{.20(.90) + .80(1 - .70)} = \frac{.18}{.18 + .24}$$

$$= .429$$

If you assume instead that the seismic survey denies any oil beneath Crockpot Dome, Luke's posterior probability for oil would be different.

$$Pr[O \mid D] = \frac{Pr[O] \times Pr[D \mid O]}{Pr[O] \times Pr[D \mid O] + Pr[not \; O] \times Pr[D \mid not \; O]}$$

$$= \frac{.20(1 - .90)}{.20(1 - .90) + .80(.70)} = \frac{.02}{.02 + .56}$$

$$= .034$$

Notice how a positive experimental result raises the oil probability above its prior level, while a negative result lowers the oil probability below its initial value.

- Remember that a prior probability $\Pr[E]$ is a *known* value (but usually subjective) and is an *unconditional* probability.
- The posterior probability $\Pr[E \mid R]$ must be *computed*. This is a *conditional* probability.
- Don't confuse the posterior probability with the conditional result probabilities $\Pr[R \mid E]$ and $\Pr[R \mid \text{not } E]$. Here E and not E are the given events and are therefore listed last. Conditional result probabilities are *specified in advance*.

Posterior Probabilities Computed from the Joint Probability Table

The fraction used in expressing Bayes' theorem is really nothing more than a detailed rephrasing of the conditional probability identity (page 49).

$$\Pr[E \mid R] = \frac{\Pr[E \text{ and } R]}{\Pr[R]}$$

At times, rather than use Bayes' theorem, you might find it easier to first construct a joint probability table and then apply the identity formula to determine posterior probabilities.

To understand this, continue with the weather illustration. You can construct the following joint probability table using the data originally given.

	RESULT (FORECAST)		Marginal Probability
MAIN EVENT	Likely	Unlikely	
Rain	.30	.20	.50
No Rain	.10	.40	.50
Marginal Probability	.40	.60	1.00

The marginal probabilities for "rain" and "no rain" were given as the prior probability values. You determine the joint probability for "rain" and "likely" by using the general multiplication law (page 51).

$$\Pr[\text{rain and likely}] = \Pr[\text{rain}] \times \Pr[\text{likely} \mid \text{rain}]$$
$$= .50(.60) = .30$$

Subtracting this value from the marginal probability for the first row (.50), you get the second joint probability of .20. You can likewise determine the joint probability for "no rain" and "unlikely."

$$\Pr[\text{no rain and unlikely}] = \Pr[\text{no rain}] \times \Pr[\text{unlikely} \mid \text{no rain}]$$
$$= .50(.80) = .40$$

Now you determine the missing joint probability in the second row by subtracting .40 from the marginal probability for the row (.50). Finally, the marginal probabilities for the columns are determined by adding the joint probabilities in each column.

To determine the posterior probability for rain given a likely weather forecast, you substitute the appropriate values into the identity directly from the joint probability table.

$$\Pr[\text{rain} \mid \text{likely}] = \frac{\Pr[\text{rain } and \text{ likely}]}{\Pr[\text{likely}]} = \frac{.30}{.40} = .75$$

Likewise, the posterior probability for rain given an unlikely forecast is

$$\Pr[\text{rain} \mid \text{unlikely}] = \frac{\Pr[\text{rain } and \text{ unlikely}]}{\Pr[\text{unlikely}]} = \frac{.20}{.60} = .333$$

Posterior Probabilities and Probability Trees

Probability tree diagram (a) in Figure 3-4 depicts the **actual sequence** of events in the Crockpot Dome illustration. The first fork represents the geology events oil or dry. The second-stage forks represent the seismic survey results. This particular arrangement follows the sequence in which the events actually occur: first, nature determined (several million years ago) whether this site would cover an oil field; second, our wildcatter conducts a seismic test today.

Probability tree diagram (b) in Figure 3-4 represents the **information sequence.** This is the sequence in which the decision maker finds out what events occur. First, the wildcatter obtains the result for the seismic survey, which is portrayed by the initial event fork. Then, if he chooses to drill, he ultimately determines whether or not the site covers an oil field. Additional work is required to obtain the probability values shown on tree diagram (b).

We begin by multiplying the branch probabilities on each path in tree diagram (a) to obtain the corresponding joint probability values. The same numbers apply regardless of the sequence so the joint probabilities may be transferred to tree diagram (b). This must be done with care. The in-between joint outcomes are not listed in the same order in (b) as they are in (a), because the analogous paths (event sequences) differ between the diagrams. For example, in diagram (a) we obtain the joint probability for oil and denying seismic result

$$\Pr[O \text{ and } D] = \Pr[O] \times \Pr[D \mid O] = .2 \times .1 = .02$$

This is the second joint probability in diagram (a) and corresponds to the third end position in diagram (b).

Next, we work entirely in diagram (b). First, we compute the **unconditional result probabilities** at the first stage. Here, we use the addition law to obtain

$$\Pr[C] = \Pr[O \text{ and } C] + \Pr[\text{not } O \text{ and } C] = .18 + .24 = .42$$
$$\Pr[D] = \Pr[O \text{ and } D] + \Pr[\text{not } O \text{ and } D] = .02 + .56 = .58$$

These values are placed on the applicable branches at the first stage. Finally, the posterior probabilities for the second-stage events are computed. Thus, we determine the posterior probability for oil, given a confirming seismic survey result, to be

$$\Pr[O \mid C] = \frac{\Pr[O \text{ and } C]}{\Pr[C]} = \frac{.18}{.42} = .429$$

This value is placed on the second-stage branch for oil that is preceded by the earlier branch for a confirming result. Each of the other posterior probabilities shown in diagram (b) is found by dividing the respective end-position joint probability by the probability on the preceding branch.

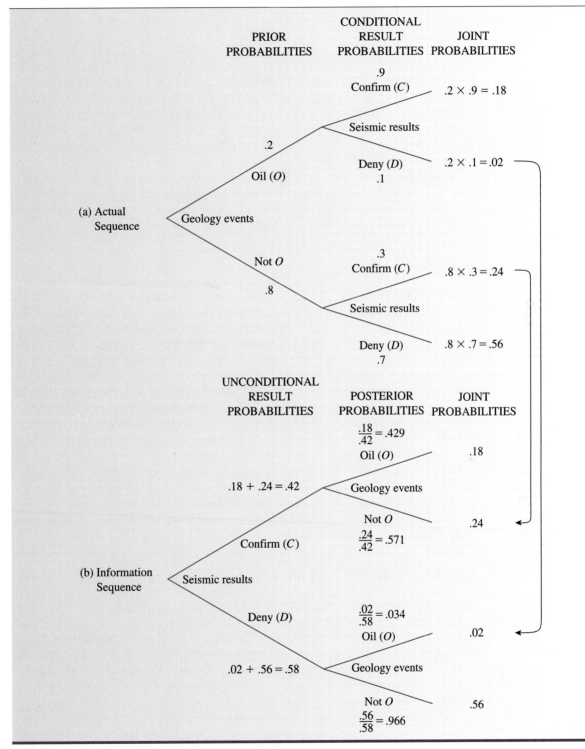

FIGURE 3-4   Using probability trees to find posterior probabilities

3-9   SUBJECTIVE PROBABILITY

Subjective probabilities are applicable to nonrepeatable circumstances, such as introducing a new product or drilling a wildcat oil well, and must be arrived at through *judgment.* This is in contrast to the long-run frequencies used to establish **objective probabilities,** which are valid only when elements of repeatability are present. Because so many business decisions involve one-shot situations that never recur exactly, there is a strong need for subjective probabilities when analyzing decision making under uncertainty.

Subjective probabilities are not tied to a long-run frequency of occurrence, making them helpful in evaluating one-shot situations characterized by nonrepeatable uncertainties. Good *judgment* may be used to transform such uncertainties into a set of probabilities for the various events involved.

Betting Odds

Subjective probabilities can be considered *betting odds;* that is, they can be treated just like the probabilities that the decision maker would desire in a lottery situation of his or her own design. For example, suppose that a contractor assigns a subjective probability of .5 to the event of winning a contract that will increase profits by $50,000 and that losing the contract will cost $10,000. This contractor ought to be indifferent between preparing a bid for the contract and gambling on a coin toss where a head provides a $50,000 win and a tail results in a $10,000 loss. The subjective probability for winning the contract can therefore be transformed directly into an "objective" .5 probability of obtaining a head from a coin toss. Assuming indifference between the real-life gamble and a hypothetical coin toss, we can then substitute the latter into the decision analysis.

One of the practical benefits of substituting a hypothetical gamble for an actual uncertainty is that subjective probabilities can be used in conjunction with the traditional long-run frequencies of occurrence. In effect, apples and oranges may be mixed. A hypothetical gamble or lottery can also help us find the subjective probability value itself. Consider the following example.

Substituting a Hypothetical Lottery for the Real Gamble

A project engineer must choose between two technologies in designing a prototype sonar system. She may use Doppler shift or acoustic ranging. If the Doppler shift is used, time becomes a crucial factor. To analyze this decision, the engineer must determine the probability for completing the project on time. If she is late, the project will be canceled and she will be out of a job. But if she is early or on time, her contract will be extended for two more years. The event fork of concern appears in Figure 3-5(a).

Suppose that the engineer considers the hypothetical lottery shown in Figure 3-5(b) in which one marble is to be randomly selected from a box of 100. Some marbles are labeled *E* (for early); the rest are marked *L* (for late). In this hypothetical gamble, selecting an *E* marble will result in an extended contract, but drawing an *L* marble will result in a canceled contract. Our engineer can determine the mix of *L* and *E* marbles. She is asked what mixture will make her *indifferent* between letting her future be decided by trying the Doppler shift design or by selecting a marble from the box.

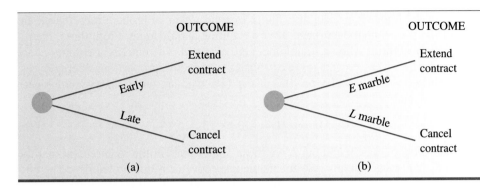

FIGURE 3-5
A project engineer's
actual gamble (a) and a
hypothetical lottery (b)
yielding identical outcomes

Suppose that the engineer determines that 70 E marbles and 30 L marbles would make her indifferent. This means that the probability for selecting an E marble is .70. This value is the engineer's subjective probability that the project will be early or on time if the Doppler shift is used. This number expresses the strength of her conviction that the project will be completed early or on time.

Subjective Probability Expresses Strength of Conviction

Subjective probabilities have been referred to as indexes conveying a person's strength of conviction that a particular event will occur. As such, there are no correct values, and reasonable people will disagree about likely levels for next year's stock prices, the chances for their favorite team winning the Super Bowl, or the odds of a new product's success. There are no "right" values for subjective probabilities.

What really matters is that any choices reached with the help of subjective probabilities employ values that are consistent with the decision maker's judgment. Some object that subjective probabilities are simply numbers "pulled out of thin air." But if the numbers so obtained reflect careful thought by the decision maker or his or her trusted experts, then there is really nothing better.

The unease over the inexactness of the numbers so obtained may be mitigated by limiting their use to preliminary evaluations. In such applications, subjective probabilities would be the starting values and serve only as the prior probabilities for deliberations about whether to pursue more objective information.

Decision Problem Revisited: Screening Test Evaluation

DECISION PROBLEM

The following joint probability table represents job performance and test score events pertaining to a randomly selected Whirl-a-Gigs employee. We will use that table to generate probabilities that may be used to qualify the effectiveness of the test.

	TEST SCORE		
PERFORMANCE	**Low (L)**	**High (H)**	**Marginal Probability**
Unsatisfactory (U)	.135	.015	30/200 = .150
Satisfactory (S)	.195	.455	130/200 = .650
Excellent (E)	.030	.170	40/200 = .200
Marginal Probability	.360	.640	1.000

The historical frequencies establish the right-hand marginal probabilities. These are found from the original data (page 32) by counting and dividing. From these, the remaining probabilities (shown in boldface) are obtained. The entries in column H are found using the given percentages to establish the respective proportions of employees. For instance, just $3/30 = .10$, or 10% of the 15% who are unsatisfactory employees scored high, and

$$\Pr[U \text{ and } H] = .10 \times .15 = .015$$

The joint probabilities in column L are those values that fill the requirement that the sum of the cell values in any row equals the respective marginal probability. The bottom marginal probabilities are the sums of the joint probabilities in the respective columns.

The following probability evaluates how well the test would screen unsatisfactory employees:

$$\Pr[U \mid L] = \frac{\Pr[U \text{ and } L]}{\Pr[L]} = \frac{.135}{.360} = .375$$

This calculation tells Whirl-a-Gigs that, assuming they would be hired regardless of score, and leaving all other personnel policies the same, 37.5% of the low-scoring applicants would be unsatisfactory employees. This percentage is more than twice as high as the percentage of unsatisfactories currently experienced. This suggests that the test will effectively filter potential unsatisfactories.

The following conditional probabilities tell Whirl-a-Gigs how much using the screening test should improve overall employee performance:

$$\Pr[U \mid H] = \frac{\Pr[U \text{ and } H]}{\Pr[H]} = \frac{.015}{.640} = .023$$

$$\Pr[S \mid H] = \frac{\Pr[S \text{ and } H]}{\Pr[H]} = \frac{.455}{.640} = .711$$

$$\Pr[E \mid H] = \frac{\Pr[E \text{ and } H]}{\Pr[H]} = \frac{.170}{.640} = .266$$

Under present hiring policies, if Whirl-a-Gigs were to hire only high-scoring persons, these equations indicate that only 2.3% of future employees would be unsatisfactory, 71.1% would be satisfactory, and 26.6% would be excellent.

The downside to using the screening test is that a lot of low-scoring people, who may otherwise be satisfactory or excellent employees, would never be hired. Consider the probabilities of getting a low-scoring applicant (not hired) who would be satisfactory or excellent:

$$\Pr[(S \text{ and } L) \text{ or } (E \text{ and } L)]$$
$$= \Pr[S \text{ and } L] + \Pr[E \text{ and } L]$$
$$= .195 + .030 = .225$$

PROBLEMS

3-1 Determine the following probabilities:
  (a) A man chosen randomly from a group of 10 men is a lawyer; the group contains two lawyers.
  (b) A particular name will be drawn out of 10,000 persons in a registry.
  (c) A head will be obtained on one toss each of a dime and a penny. (First determine the sample space.)
  (d) A number greater than two will be the value of the showing face from the toss of a six-sided die.

3-2 A roulette wheel has 38 slots. Two are green, numbered 0 and 00. Of the remaining pockets, 18 are red and 18 are black. Assuming that all pockets are equally likely, what is the probability that the ball for a spinning wheel lands in the 00 pocket?

3-3 Besides head and tail, a penny toss may have other types of elementary events, such as the angle made by Lincoln's nose relative to true north. Suggest at least another set of outcomes that might serve as the elementary events.

3-4 A finance student writes 20 important names, including "Bernard Baruch," on separate slips of paper. Each name appears on just one slip. She then draws names one at a time from the box; once selected, a name is not returned to the box.
  (a) What is the probability that Baruch is the first name selected?
  (b) She has selected 10 names already, not including Baruch. What is the probability that Baruch is next?

3-5 In a special study an accountant found the following history for 850 receivables: (a) 119 were paid early, (b) 340 were settled on time, (c) 221 were paid late, and (d) 170 were uncollectible. Assume that this experience is representative of the future. Estimate the probabilities that a particular receivable will fall into each of the four categories.

3-6 The following table shows the number of panelists in each category of a Wee Tees consumer test panel.

| Occupation | Family Income | | | Total |
	Low	Medium	High	
Homemaker	8	26	6	40
Blue-Collar Worker	16	40	14	70
White-Collar Worker	6	62	12	80
Professional	0	2	8	10
Total	30	130	40	200

One person is selected at random. Construct a joint probability table for *occupation* versus *family income*.

3-7 The following joint probability table applies to marital status and job classification of a randomly selected Metropolis worker.

| Marital Status | Job Classification | | | Marginal Probability |
	Blue Collar	White Collar	Management	
Married	.15	.20	.17	.52
Divorced	.12	.02	.04	.18
Widowed	.04	.04	.02	.10
Never Married	.09	.06	.05	.20
Marginal Probability	.40	.32	.28	1.00

  (a) What is the probability that the person has a nonmanagement job?
  (b) What is the probability that the person is presently unmarried?
  (c) What is the probability that the person is a formerly married blue-collar worker?
  (d) What is the probability that he or she is a nonmanagement married person?

3-8 You are asked to toss a pair of six-sided dice, one red and one green. Each side of a die cube has a different number of dots, 1 through 6.
  (a) List the possible sums of the number of dots on the two showing sides.
  (b) For each possible sum, list the corresponding elementary events and determine the sum's probability. (Identify your elementary events using a convenient code, such as 2R-5G for 2 dots showing on the red die and 5 on the green.)

3-9 The following probabilities have been obtained for the lead-time demand for barrels of Boll Toll pesticide.

Number of Barrels	Probability
0	.3
1	.2
2	.1
3	.1
4	.1
5	.1
6	.1
7 or more	0
Total	1.0

Determine the probability for the following number of barrels:

(a) fewer than 4 barrels
(b) between 2 and 6 barrels, inclusively
(c) at least 1 barrel
(d) between 2 and 4 barrels, inclusively
(e) at the most, 2 barrels

3-10 The Helpmaster Employment Agency, specializing in clerical and secretarial help, classifies candidates in terms of primary skills and years of experience. The skills are bookkeeping, reception, and word processing. (We will assume that no candidate is proficient in more than one.) Experience categories are less than one year, one to three years, and more than three years. There are 100 persons currently on file, and their skills and experience are summarized in the following table:

	Skill			
Experience	Book-keeping	Recep-tion	Word Processing	Total
Less than One Year	15	5	30	50
One to Three Years	5	10	5	20
More than Three Years	5	15	10	30
Total	25	30	45	100

One person's file is selected at random. Determine the probability that the selected person will fall into the following categories:
(a) bookkeeping
(b) less than one year of experience
(c) reception
(d) one to three years of experience
(e) word processing
(f) more than three years of experience

3-11 Refer to Problem 3-10.
(a) Assume the selected person has less than one year of experience. What is the probability that his or her skill is bookkeeping?
(b) Does the bookkeeping probability in (a) differ from the one you determined in Problem 3-10? Are "bookkeeping" and "less than one year" of experience statistically independent events?
(c) Determine Pr[bookkeeping *and* less than one year of experience]. Can the multiplication law be used to determine this probability?

3-12 Refer to Problem 3-10. Use the count-and-divide procedure to determine the probabilities for the following composite events:
(a) bookkeeping *or* less than one year of experience
(b) reception *or* more than three years of experience

(c) word processing *or* one to three years of experience

3-13 Refer to the sample space in Figure 3-2 for a randomly selected business scholarship student. Determine the probabilities for the following events:
(a) finance major
(b) undergraduate in management
(c) graduate in finance
(d) female accounting major
(e) female undergraduate in marketing

3-14 There are 100 employees at GizMo Corporation: 40 women and 60 men. Of these, 15 of the women and 35 of the men are married. One employee is selected at random.
(a) Find the probabilities of the following outcomes:
  (1) man   (5) married
  (2) married man   (6) unmarried man
  (3) woman   (7) unmarried
  (4) married woman (8) unmarried woman
(b) Using your answers to (a), apply the addition law to find the probabilities of the following results:
  (1) woman *or* unmarried
  (2) man *or* married
  (3) woman *or* married
  (4) man *or* unmarried

3-15 The following joint probability table applies to the age group and first college degree held by a randomly selected alumnus of State University.

	College Degree				
Age	Science	Liberal Arts	Social Science	Profes-sional	Marginal Probability
Under 23	.01	.01	.01	.00	.03
23–29	.02	.02	.04	.06	.14
30–50	.07	.11	.06	.09	.33
Over 50	.10	.05	.18	.17	.50
Marginal Probability	.20	.19	.29	.32	1.00

(a) What is the probability that he is 23 or older?
(b) What is the probability that he is 30 or older?
(c) What is the probability that he is over 50 and has a science or professional degree?
(d) What is the probability that he is under 23 with a science or social science degree?

3-16 Refer to the sample space in Figure 3-2 for a randomly selected business scholarship student. Construct a joint probability table for *sex* versus *major*.

3-17 Refer to the sample space in Figure 3-2 for a randomly selected business scholarship student. Construct a joint probability table for *academic level* versus *major*.

3-18 Professor Horatio Dull's statistics class has 3 married men and 5 married women; the rest are unmarried. There are 35 people altogether, 20 of whom are men. One student is selected at random.
(a) Construct the joint probability table for *sex* versus *marital status*.
(b) Indicate the probabilities for the following joint events:
  (1) man *and* married
  (2) woman *and* married
  (3) woman *and* unmarried
  (4) man *and* unmarried

3-19 List all the possible side-showing elementary events from three tosses of the damaged coin described on page 40. Find for each the joint probability.

3-20 Refer to the joint probability table in Problem 3-7.
(a) Show that "blue collar" and "widowed" are statistically independent.
(b) Show that "management" and "never married" are statistically dependent.

3-21 Refer to the joint probability table in Problem 3-15.
(a) Show that "over 50" and "science" are statistically independent.
(b) Show that "under 23" and "science" are statistically dependent.

3-22 In conducting a check, an auditor randomly selects 5 accounts receivable out of 10 that are listed as outstanding. Only 4 of the 10 accounts are in error. The following probabilities have been obtained for the number of accounts having incorrect balances.

Number of Incorrect Accounts	Probability
0	1/42
1	10/42
2	20/42
3	10/42
4	1/42

Determine the probability for the following numbers of incorrect balances:
(a) at least 2   (d) greater than 2
(b) at most 3   (e) fewer than 4
(c) 1 or more   (f) 4 or fewer

3-23 The statistics students at Adams College are 60% male. Exactly 20% of the men and 20% of the women are married. Use the multiplication law to find the probability that a randomly selected student will be classified as the following:
(a) man *and* married
(b) man *and* unmarried
(c) woman *and* married
(d) woman *and* unmarried

3-24 Refer to the joint probability Table 3-1. Determine the conditional probabilities for the following:
(a) male *given* undergraduate
(b) undergraduate *given* male
(c) female *given* graduate
(d) graduate *given* female

3-25 Refer to the joint probability table in Problem 3-7 for a randomly selected Metropolis worker. Determine the following conditional probabilities:
(a) $\Pr[\text{blue collar} \mid \text{married}]$
(b) $\Pr[\text{management} \mid \text{widowed}]$
(c) $\Pr[\text{divorced} \mid \text{white collar}]$
(d) $\Pr[\text{widowed} \mid \text{management}]$

3-26 A State University business scholarship student is randomly selected. Figure 3-2 summarizes the sample space. Let U and G denote level; M and Fe, sex; A, accounting major; and Fi, finance major.
(a) Use the count-and-divide method to determine the following probabilities:

(1)	(2)	(3)
$\Pr[U]$	$\Pr[Fi]$	$\Pr[Fe]$
$\Pr[Fe \mid U]$	$\Pr[U \mid Fi]$	$\Pr[A \mid Fe]$
(4)	(5)	(6)
$\Pr[G]$	$\Pr[M]$	$\Pr[Fe]$
$\Pr[M \mid G]$	$\Pr[Fi \mid M]$	$\Pr[U \mid Fe]$

(b) Apply the multiplication law to each pair of probabilities in (a) to determine the following joint probabilities:
  (1) $\Pr[U \text{ and } Fe]$ (4) $\Pr[G \text{ and } M]$
  (2) $\Pr[Fi \text{ and } U]$ (5) $\Pr[M \text{ and } Fi]$
  (3) $\Pr[Fe \text{ and } A]$ (6) $\Pr[Fe \text{ and } U]$

3-27 Forty percent of Natti Nitpicker's students have done their probability homework (H). Eighty percent of all students who do homework will pass (P) the probability quiz. Ninety percent of those who do not do the homework will fail (F). Pick a student at random.

(a) Identify the following: (1) $\Pr[H]$, (2) $\Pr[P\,|\,H]$. Then apply the general multiplication law to find (3) $\Pr[H\ and\ P]$.

(b) Find (1) $\Pr[\text{not}\ H]$, (2) $\Pr[F\,|\,\text{not}\ H]$, (3) $\Pr[\text{not}\ H\ and\ F]$.

3-28 Refer to the joint probability table in Problem 3-15 for a randomly selected State University alumnus. Determine the following conditional probabilities:

(a) $\Pr[\text{over 50}\,|\,\text{professional}]$
(b) $\Pr[\text{professional}\,|\,\text{over 50}]$
(c) $\Pr[\text{social science}\,|\,30-50]$
(d) $\Pr[\text{under 23}\,|\,\text{science}]$

3-29 A *fair* coin is tossed five times. Two possibilities are

(1) $H_1 T_2 H_3 T_4 H_5$
(2) $H_1 H_2 H_3 H_4 H_5$

(a) Without computing any probabilities, which outcome do you think is more likely?
(b) Use the multiplication law to determine the probability for each outcome.

3-30 The Centralia plant of DanDee Assemblers experiences power failures with a probability of .10 during any given month. Assume that power events in successive months are independent. Determine the probability that there will be (a) no power failures during a given 3-month span; (b) exactly 1 month involving a power failure during the next 4 months; (c) at least 1 power failure during the next 5 months.

3-31 For simplicity, suppose that all months of the year are equally likely to be a person's birth month. Several persons are comparing their birth months. Determine the probability for at least one matching birth month when this group consists of (a) two people, (b) three people, and (c) five people.

3-32 The probability is .95 that a GizMo Corporation traveling sales representative will have no automobile accidents in a year. Assuming that accident frequencies in successive years are independent events, find the probability that a particular driver (a) goes five straight years with no accident; (b) has at least one accident in five years.

3-33 The general manager of the Gotham City Hellcats is evaluating an employment screening test for the front office clerical staff. During this experiment all new clerical employees are given the test. Sev-

enty percent pass the test; the rest fail. At a later time, it is determined whether the new clerks are satisfactory or unsatisfactory. Historically, 80% of all clerical hires have been found to be satisfactory, and 75% of the satisfactory clerks in the program have passed the screening test.

Consider the events applicable to a new clerk in the experiment.

(a) From the given information, find the following values:
 (1) $\Pr[\text{pass}]$
 (2) $\Pr[\text{satisfactory}]$
 (3) $\Pr[\text{pass}\,|\,\text{satisfactory}]$

(b) Using your answers to (a), find $\Pr[\text{pass}\ and\ \text{satisfactory}]$.

(c) Construct the joint probability table for test results versus employee performance events.

(d) Using your answers to (c), determine the following conditional probabilities:
 (1) $\Pr[\text{fail}\,|\,\text{unsatisfactory}]$
 (2) $\Pr[\text{fail}\,|\,\text{satisfactory}]$
 (3) $\Pr[\text{pass}\,|\,\text{unsatisfactory}]$
 (4) $\Pr[\text{unsatisfactory}\,|\,\text{fail}]$
 (5) $\Pr[\text{satisfactory}\,|\,\text{pass}]$
 (6) $\Pr[\text{unsatisfactory}\,|\,\text{pass}]$
 (7) $\Pr[\text{satisfactory}\,|\,\text{fail}]$

(e) Using your answers to (d), find the following percentages:
 (1) failing clerks who prove to be unsatisfactory employees
 (2) passing clerks who prove to be satisfactory employees

(f) Government guidelines are that a proper screening test must provide at least 20% for (1) in (e) and at least 60% for (2). Does this test meet those guidelines?

3-34 A new family with two children of different ages has moved into the neighborhood. Suppose that it is equally likely that either child is a boy or girl, so that the following situations are equally likely.

Youngest	Oldest	
boy	boy	(B, B)
boy	girl	(B, G)
girl	boy	(G, B)
girl	girl	(G, G)

(a) Find $\Pr[\text{at least one girl}]$.
(b) If you know there is at least one girl, what is the conditional probability that the family has exactly one boy?

(c) Given that at least one child is a girl, what is the conditional probability that the other child is a girl?

3-35 Waysafe Markets employs two groups of 100 test shoppers to audit store performance. One person is selected at random from each group.

(a) Group A is 50% men and 50% women; 70% of the members are married, and just as many men as women are married. Thus, any two sex and marital status events are independent. Construct a joint probability table by first finding the marginal probabilities and then using the multiplication law to obtain the joint probabilities, which in this case may be expressed as the products of the two respective marginal probabilities.

(b) Group B is also 50% men and 50% women, and 70% of the members are married. However, only 60% of the men are married, whereas 80% of the women are married. Thus, any two sex and marital status events are dependent. This means that the product of the respective marginal probabilities does not equal the corresponding joint probability. Construct a joint probability table using the count-and-divide method.

3-36 A winery superintendent accepts or rejects truckloads of grapes after performing tests on a few sample bunches. She rejects 15% of all the truckloads she inspects. Thus far, she has rejected 95% of all bad truckloads inspected, and 10% of all truckloads have ultimately proved to be bad.

(a) Using this experience as a basis, find the values of the following probabilities regarding the outcome of any particular truckload:
  (1) Pr[reject]
  (2) Pr[bad]
  (3) Pr[reject | bad]

(b) Apply the multiplication law to the appropriate values you found in (a) to find Pr[reject *and* bad].

(c) Construct a joint probability table showing the joint and marginal probabilities for the superintendent's actions (accept or reject) and the quality (good or bad) of the grapes in a truckload.

3-37 Refer to the winery superintendent's situation in Problem 3-36 and to your answers.

(a) What percentage of all good shipments get rejected?

(b) Construct a probability tree diagram representing the disposition of a truckload of grapes. Represent the quality of the grapes (good, bad) in the first fork and the superintendent's actions (accept, reject) as forks in the second stage. Enter all branch probabilities onto your tree and then apply the multiplication law to establish the joint probability for each quality–act combination.

3-38 An experiment is conducted using three boxes, each containing a mixture of 10 (R)ed and (W)hite marbles. The three boxes have following compositions:

BOX A	BOX B	BOX C
6 R	4 R	7 R
4 W	6 W	3 W

Two marbles are selected at random. The first is selected from Box A. If it is red, the second marble is to be taken from Box B; if the first marble is white, the second marble is to be taken from Box C. Use R_1 and W_1 to represent the color of the first marble and R_2 and W_2 to represent the color of the second marble.

(a) Find the following probabilities:
  (1) $\Pr[R_1]$ (3) $\Pr[R_2 | R_1]$ (5) $\Pr[W_2 | R_1]$
  (2) $\Pr[W_1]$ (4) $\Pr[R_2 | W_1]$ (6) $\Pr[W_2 | W_1]$

(b) Apply the multiplication law to your answers to (a) to determine the following joint probabilities:
  (1) $\Pr[R_1 \text{ and } R_2]$ (3) $\Pr[W_1 \text{ and } R_2]$
  (2) $\Pr[R_1 \text{ and } W_2]$ (4) $\Pr[W_1 \text{ and } W_2]$

(c) Determine the following probabilities:
  (1) one red and one white marble will be chosen
  (2) either two red or two white marbles will be chosen

3-39 Felina Wild is an oil wildcatter who decides that the probability for striking gas (G) is .40. Felina orders a seismic survey that confirms (C) gas with a probability of .85 in known gas fields and denies (D) gas with a probability of .60 when there is no gas.

(a) Determine (1) $\Pr[G \text{ and } C]$ and (2) $\Pr[\text{no } G \text{ and } D]$.

(b) Construct the joint probability table for *geology* and *survey* events.

3-40 Refer to Problem 3-39. Construct a probability tree diagram. Determine the joint probability for each geology and seismic outcome.

3-41 Ty Ruth is a switch-hitter for baseball's Gotham Flyers. He bats right-handed (R) on 40% of all trips to the plate. In that direction, Ty's batting average is .320. This means that historically he has achieved a hit (H) on 32% of "official" times at bat. He was out (O) on the remainder. Walks, bases on errors, and sacrifices are categorized separately and are not included as "official" at bats. As a lefty (L), Ty has hit .360. Consider Ty's next time at bat.
   (a) What are the values for the unconditional probabilities (1) $\Pr[L]$ and (2) $\Pr[R]$?
   (b) What are the values for the conditional probabilities (1) $\Pr[H \mid L]$ and (2) $\Pr[H \mid R]$?
   (c) Using your answers to (a) and (b), determine Ty's joint probability table for *"official" hitting result* (H or O) versus *batting direction.*
   (d) Given that Ty makes a hit, what is the probability that he has batted (1) right-handed? (2) left-handed?

3-42 Consider the first three telecommunications queries by Giant Enterprises. Suppose that the system is busy (B) 20% of the time and that a direct connection (D) is achieved the rest of the time. Assume that the status of the system at each query is independent of that for preceding messages.
   (a) Construct a probability tree diagram for the system status encountered by those three queries.
   (b) Identify all elementary events.
   (c) Determine the joint probability for each event.

3-43 Callers to the Midget Motors switchboard encounter busy signals (B) 20% of the time. The remainder of the time calls are connected directly (D). Because of the slow rate at which calls are placed, the connection status of successive calls is dependent. Records show that half of all calls placed after a preceding call encountered a busy signal will also find the switchboard busy. But 90% of calls placed after the preceding call was directly connected will also be directly connected.
   (a) Construct a probability tree diagram for the system status encountered by the first three calls to the Midget Motors switchboard.
   (b) Identify all elementary events.
   (c) Determine the joint probability for each event.

3-44 A phony card deck (P) contains 52 kings. This deck is placed into a sack with four standard decks (S) of 52 playing cards. One deck is selected at random.
   (a) What is the prior probability that the phony deck is selected?
   (b) A king is drawn at random from the selected deck. What is the posterior probability that the phony deck is selected?

3-45 An admissions committee must select students for an MBA program. Past data show that 70% of all admitted students complete (C) the degree program. It is also known that 50% of the graduating students scored above 500 (A) on the Graduate Management Admissions Test (GMAT), while only 20% of the dropouts (D) scored that well. Consider a newly matriculated MBA student.
   (a) What is the prior probability that she will complete the degree?
   (b) Given that she scores 575 on the GMAT, what is the posterior probability that she will complete her MBA?
   (c) Given that she scores 450 on the test, what is the posterior probability that she will graduate?

3-46 A new movie, *Star Struck,* has a prior probability for success of .20. Ruth Grist is going to review the film. She has liked 70% of all the successful films and has disliked 80% of all the unsuccessful films she has reviewed. Find the posterior probability that *Star Struck* will be a success if (a) Grist likes it; (b) Grist dislikes it.

3-47 One student is selected at random from the sample space in Figure 3-2.
   (a) What is the prior probability that the student is male (M)?
   (b) Suppose that the student's major is known. What is the posterior probability that a male is selected given that the student is a finance major (Fi)?

3-48 Wendy Storm makes a daily television forecast indicating the probability that it will rain tomorrow. On one particular evening, she announces an 80% chance of rain (E) the next day. The manager of the city golf courses has established a policy that he will water the greens only if the probability for rain is less than 90%. Using the local TV broadcast as his prior probability, the manager also relies on his mother-in-law's rheuma-

tism. Historically, she gets a rheumatic pain (R) on 90% of all days that are followed by rain, but she also experiences rheumatic pain on 20% of the days that are not followed by rain. The following probabilities therefore apply:

$\Pr[E] = .80$ $\Pr[R|E] = .90$ $\Pr[R|\text{not } E] = .20$

(a) Assuming that the golf course manager's mother-in-law is currently receiving rheumatic signals (R), find the posterior probability that it will rain (E) tomorrow. Should the manager water the greens?
(b) If the manager's mother-in-law does not feel any rheumatic pain, what is the posterior probability for rain (E) tomorrow?

3-49 Felix Wilde has assigned a probability of .50 to striking oil on his property. He orders a seismic survey that has proved to be only 80% reliable in the past. Given oil, it predicts favorably 80% of the time; given no oil, it augurs unfavorably with a frequency of .8.
(a) Given a favorable seismic result, what is the probability for oil?
(b) Given an unfavorable seismic result, what is the probability for oil?

3-50 A marketing researcher wishes to determine whether, given a certain response to a question, a randomly selected person will choose NuScents when next purchasing deodorant. The question is designed to reveal whether or not the selected person recalls the name NuScents—an event we will denote by R. Previous testing has established that 99% of the people who bought NuScents previously recalled the name and that only 10% of the people who did not buy NuScents recalled this particular brand name. Since NuScents has cornered 30% of the deodorant market, the researcher chooses .30 as the prior probability that the person selected will buy NuScents. Denoting this event B gives us the following probabilities:

$\Pr[B] = .30$ $\Pr[R|B] = .99$ $\Pr[R|\text{not } B] = .10$

(a) If the person who is selected remembers NuScents, what is the posterior probability that NuScents will be purchased next?
(b) If the person who is selected does *not* remember NuScents, what is the posterior probability that NuScents will be purchased next?

3-51 Comp-u-Quik is evaluating an employment screening test for possible inclusion in clerical services hiring decisions. Presently, only 50% of the persons hired for these positions perform satisfactorily. The test itself has been evaluated by outside consultants, who have given it an upside reliability of 90% (90% of all satisfactory employees will pass the test) and a downside reliability of only 80% (80% of all unsatisfactory employees will fail the test). One clerical applicant (acceptable in all other screening activities) is chosen at random. Find the following probabilities:
(a) the prior probability for satisfactory on-the-job performance if the applicant is hired
(b) the posterior probability for satisfactory on-the-job performance if the applicant passes the screening test
(c) the posterior probability for satisfactory on-the-job performance if the applicant is hired after failing the screening test

3-52 Discuss whether historical frequencies are meaningful in estimating the probabilities for each of the following cases:
(a) the first-year salary levels of business school graduates
(b) the faces obtained by tossing an asymmetrical die
(c) the deaths during the next year of people in various age, health, sex, and occupational categories

3-53 Use your judgment to assess probabilities for the following events:
(a) The New York Yankees will play in and win the next World Series.
(b) If you are presently single, you will marry within one year. If you are presently married, your spouse will change jobs within one year.
(c) You will replace one of your present automobiles in the coming year.

3-54 Use your judgment to assess the probability that you will receive an A on your next examination. Imagine that your instructor will let you obtain your grade by lottery, so that 100 slips of paper (some labeled A; the rest, not A) will be put into a hat and mixed. You will draw one of these slips at random, and the letter obtained will be the grade you receive. How many A slips must there be to make you indifferent between letting your grade be determined by lottery or earning it?

3-55 Oil wildcatter Rich Wells has assigned a .40 probability to striking oil on his property. He orders a seismic survey that has proved only 80% reliable

in the past. Given oil, it predicts favorably 80% of the time; given no oil, it augurs unfavorably with a frequency of .8.

Construct probability trees for the actual and information sequences, and indicate the appropriate probability values for each branch and end position.

3-56 A box contains two pairs of dice. One pair is a fair one. The other pair consists of one die cube with a three on every side and one die cube with a four on every side. A pair is to be selected at random and tossed. You will only be able to see the top show-

ing faces and not the sides. The main events of interest pertain to the crookedness or fairness of the tossed dice. (Both dice in the tossed pair will fall into the same category.) In each of the following cases, construct probability trees for the actual and information sequences.

(a) The experimental result is finding out whether or not a seven-sum (three and four, two and five, one and six) occurs.

(b) The experimental result is finding out whether or not a three–four combination occurs, which has a greater predictive worth than the result in (a).

CASE 3-1 *Ourman Friday Temporaries*

Ourman Friday Temporaries provides short-term support staff to local businesses. The employees are assigned to various pools. The following persons are in the financial support pool. All persons will be available for assignment next week.

	Specialty	Experience
Bob Browning	Accounting	High
Ted Chavez	Tax	Low
Myra Hansen	Programming	Low
Linda Isaacson	Accounting	Low
Biff Jones	Tax	Low
Jeffry Kennard	Accounting	High
Lisa Kincaid	Accounting	High
Todd Miller	Tax	Low
Yolanda Munro	Programming	High
Mildred Noonan	Programming	Low
Sandra Oynuchi	Tax	Low
Cesar Perez	Programming	High
Oliver Piscwizc	Programming	Low
Donald Quigly	Tax	High
Maureen Raatz	Programming	High
Morris Rabinowitz	Accounting	High
Syl Rutkowski	Accounting	Low
Billy Sol	Accounting	High
Midori Toguchi	Programming	Low
Chinh Tsien	Tax	Low
Ivan Tureg	Programming	Low
Doreen Zurn	Programming	High

The following clients have recently requested temporaries from the Ourman financial pool. The percentages represent the historical frequency at which the various skills have been requested.

		Accounting	Programming	Tax
(a)	Ace Widgets	80%	15%	5%
(b)	BugOff Chemical	20	10	70
(c)	Comp-u-Com	0	100	0
(d)	Dial-a-Pute	10	90	0
(e)	Druid's Drayage	100	0	0
(f)	Kryptonite Corporation	50	0	50
(g)	VBM	10	80	10
(h)	Woody Mills	70	10	20

It may be assumed that the above history applies in establishing probabilities for the requested specialty in any future request for Ourman temporaries.

QUESTIONS

1. One pool employee will be selected at random for the Ourman steering committee.
   (a) Determine the probability that he or she will be (1) an accountant, (2) a tax specialist, (3) a programmer.
   (b) Determine the probability that he or she will have (1) low experience; (2) high experience.

2. Suppose that the first two client requests are each for a tax-qualified person. Ourman will fill these assignments randomly.
   (a) List the employee initials for all possible choices.
   (b) What is the probability that one of the two persons has a high experience level?

3. Suppose that just three companies request people— all tax specialists. Construct a tree showing all the requesting company possibilities.

4. Although they are not equally likely, you can determine how many feasible assignments (person-request with matching skills) are possible. Do this for the first (1) accounting request, (2) tax request, (3) programming request.

5. It is equally likely that a request from any of the eight listed clients will generate the first Ourman employee assignment. Consider the event that this assignment is made to the Kryptonite Corporation.
   (a) What is the prior probability?
   (b) What is the posterior probability, given that the required specialty is:
      (1) accounting?   (2) programming?

6. Consider the characteristics *specialty* versus *experience level*. One Ourman pool employee is selected at random.
   (a) Construct the joint probability table.
   (b) Find the conditional probabilities for each experience level given that the selected person's specialty is (1) accounting, (2) tax, and (3) programming.
   (c) The following prior probabilities apply for the first request: .50 (programmer), .30 (accounting), .20 (tax). Determine the posterior probabilities that each of these skills is actually requested when the selected person happens to have (1) low experience; (2) high experience.

7. All six Ourman tax specialists will be assigned next week as follows: two to BugOff Chemical, two to Kryptonite Corporation, and one each to VBM and Woody Mills. How many distinct assignments of people to companies are possible?

8. During its busy season Ace Widgets gets exactly one Ourman accounting temporary each week. Assuming that a new random selection is made to fill that slot each week, how many distinct assignments are possible when Ace's busy season lasts (1) 2 weeks? (2) 4 weeks? (3) 6 weeks?

CASE 3-2   *The Three Marketeers*

 Dar Tan Yun, president of the Three Marketeers, has formed a consumer test panel to help devise a marketing strategy for a line of microwaveable gourmet meals. The panel would be responsible for choosing promotions, formulating advertising copy, and selecting advertising media.

Table 3-3 (page 74) shows a partial breakdown of the 25 panel members. Dar believes that they are a microcosm of the target market. If true, the probability that a potential customer has various characteristics should coincide with the probability that a randomly selected panel member has them also.

QUESTIONS

1. Various two-way joint probability tables might be constructed for the characteristics of a randomly selected panel member.
   (a) Including a person's sex as a main feature, how many different joint probability tables may be constructed using the demographic groupings in Table 3-3?
   (b) Construct the following joint probability tables:
      (1) marital status versus education
      (2) education versus home
      (3) home versus sibling status
      (4) sex versus marital status
      (5) marital status versus children at home
      (6) sibling status versus education
   (c) Using your answers to (b), identify any event pairs that are statistically independent.
   (d) What might you conclude regarding the incidence of independence among demographic characteristics in target markets?

2. Determine the following conditional probabilities for a randomly selected panel member:
   (a) Pr[bachelor's | married]
   (b) Pr[married | bachelor's]
   (c) Pr[renter | master's]
   (d) Pr[master's | renter]
   (e) Pr[firstborn | owner]
   (f) Pr[owner | firstborn]
   (g) Pr[unmarried | no children at home]
   (h) Pr[no children at home | unmarried]

TABLE 3-3	Demographic Breakdown of Three Marketeers Consumer Test Panel				
Name	**Marital Status**	**Level of Education**	**Home**	**Sibling Status**	**Children at Home**
Ruth Baird	married	high school	renter	firstborn	yes
Ann Schultz	unmarried	some college	renter	youngest	no
Mark Maris	unmarried	bachelor's	renter	firstborn	no
Tom Steel	married	some college	owner	youngest	yes
Bill Adamson	unmarried	master's	renter	only child	yes
Pete Gonzales	unmarried	bachelor's	renter	middle	no
Morris Chin	married	high school	owner	middle	yes
Heidi Gravitz	married	bachelor's	owner	middle	no
Todd Fullmer	unmarried	bachelor's	renter	firstborn	yes
Scott Meadows	unmarried	master's	owner	youngest	no
Harvey Abramovitz	married	bachelor's	owner	firstborn	yes
Andy Pilsner	unmarried	some college	renter	youngest	no
Ann Goldberg	unmarried	some college	renter	only child	yes
Mike O'Hara	married	bachelor's	renter	youngest	yes
Larry Ellington	married	high school	owner	only child	no
Dick Senn	unmarried	bachelor's	renter	firstborn	no
Tom Sellers	married	bachelor's	renter	middle	no
Jack Beringer	unmarried	high school	owner	middle	no
Don McKinsey	unmarried	bachelor's	renter	only child	no
Sally Deerwalker	married	some college	owner	firstborn	yes
Ingrid Folsom	married	bachelor's	owner	only child	yes
Gloria Gravenstein	married	high school	owner	middle	yes
Marsha Markovich	unmarried	some college	renter	middle	yes
Ursula Hernandes	unmarried	bachelor's	renter	only child	no
Tom Fujimoto	unmarried	bachelor's	renter	youngest	no

3. A recent survey showed that 20% of the subscribers to the *Rising Loafer* are college graduates. Another 10% of the subscribers have master's degrees, and only 5% never went beyond high school. Determine the probability that a randomly selected panel member who reads this magazine (a) owns his or her home; (b) is married.

4. Half of the subscribers to *Foodaholics NewScooper* have siblings. Of these, 10% are the firstborn, and 30% are the youngest child. Determine the probability that a panel member who subscribes to this newsletter (a) is a homeowner; (b) has a master's degree.

5. Half of all the people in the target market eat oatmeal. Of these, 30% of the females prefer that dried fruit be added to the premix, whereas only 20% of the men do. Assuming that the same percentages apply to the panel members, determine the probability that a panel member will (a) eat oatmeal; (b) prefer dried fruit in his or her oatmeal.

6. Crunchy-Munchy is a new snack food. Of the children living with a married parent, only 20% will eat the snack. And of the children living with a single parent, 40% will eat it. Crunchy-Munchy will be marketed if at least 5% of all potential buyers have children at home who would eat it. Assuming that the panel matches the market, should Crunchy-Munchy be marketed?

CHAPTER 4

PROBABILITY DISTRIBUTIONS AND EXPECTED VALUE

The curve described by a simple molecule of air vapor is regulated in a manner just as certain as the planetary orbits; the only difference between them is that which comes from our ignorance.

Marquis de LaPlace

O utcomes of business decisions are often uncertain, and any numerical result achieved is usually expressed as a **random variable.** The average level of a random variable is referred to as its **expected value.** In this chapter we introduce those concepts. We will also examine four specific probability distributions: the *binomial distribution,* which is one of the most commonly encountered distributions; the *normal distribution,* which is the most important distribution when sample information is used to help analyze decisions; the *Poisson distribution,* applicable to the number of events occurring randomly over time; and the *exponential distribution,* which provides probabilities for the time between events.

DECISION PROBLEM

A Toll Bridge Evaluation

The operations manager for the New Guernsey Toll Authority is thinking about expanding the toll plaza of the Silver Slate Bridge. This is a difficult problem because expanding means additional costs and staff. On the other hand, not expanding means more traffic congestion and longer waits to pass through the toll plaza. To begin to analyze this situation and to try to balance the expansion costs with the congestion and longer waits, the operations manager has requested her staff to gather data on the arrival of cars at the toll plaza and the time to collect tolls.

The staff's research shows that traffic intensity varies with the time of the day and the day of the week. However, within each of these groups, the arrivals appear to be random with average arrival rates shown below.

	(1) WEEKDAY A.M. RUSH	(2) WEEKDAY P.M. RUSH	(3) SATURDAY AFTERNOON	(4) SUNDAY MORNING
Cars per minute	100	120	50	20

For example, on Sunday mornings, an average of 20 cars per minute arrive at the toll plaza.

One unusual feature uncovered in the study is that the mean time to collect a toll and the corresponding standard deviation both decrease as the traffic becomes heavier. These are shown below.

	(1) **WEEKDAY** A.M. **RUSH**	(2) **WEEKDAY** P.M. **RUSH**	(3) **SATURDAY** **AFTERNOON**	(4) **SUNDAY** **MORNING**
Mean (seconds)	12	10	15	16
Standard deviation	3	2	4	4

For example, on Sunday mornings, the mean time to collect a toll is 16 seconds and its standard deviation is 4 seconds. The number of collections per minute appeared to be random within each of the four time periods.

Before making a decision about whether to expand the toll plaza, the operations manager posed a number of questions to her staff.

1. What are the probabilities that various numbers of cars will arrive at the tollbooths in a given time span?

2. What are the probabilities for the amount of time transpiring between successive arrivals at the tollbooths?

3. What are the probabilities for the amount of time needed to complete the toll-taking task?

This chapter will show how probability distributions can be used to answer those and other similar questions.

4-1 RANDOM VARIABLES AND PROBABILITY DISTRIBUTIONS

A variable whose level is determined by chance is called a **random variable.** When a specific outcome is uncertain, it is treated as a variable. The random variable assumes actual numerical value only *after* all relevant outcomes are known. Many different kinds of random variables can be generated by a single situation.

The Probability Distribution

The relationship between the values of a random variable and their probabilities is summarized by the **probability distribution.** Many probability distributions can be expressed in terms of a table. Table 4-1 lists the possible rates of return from operating a new piece of equipment. Notice that the probabilities sum to 1. When there are too many possibilities to list conveniently in a table, an algebraic expression is used to describe the probability distribution.

TABLE 4-1 Probability Distribution for the Rate of Return

POSSIBLE RATE OF RETURN	PROBABILITY
10%	.05
11	.10
12	.15
13	.17
14	.12
15	.08
16	.09
17	.06
18	.05
19	.05
20	.04
21	.04
Total	1.00

4-2 EXPECTED VALUE

The **expected value** of the random value is found by multiplying every possible value by its probability and summing all the products. The expected value is therefore a weighted average, with the probabilities serving as weights. Table 4-2 shows the calculation of the expected value for the number of dots obtained in tossing a six-sided die.

The Meaning of Expected Value

The expected value has many uses. In a gambling game, it tells us what our long-run average losses per play will be. Roulette provides an example. The winnings from betting $1 on the 7 slot have the following probability distribution:

Winnings	Probability
+$35	1/38
−$1	37/38

TABLE 4-2 Calculation of the Expected Value for a Die Toss

NUMBER OF DOTS	PROBABILITY	NUMBER × PROBABILITY
1	1/6	1/6
2	1/6	2/6
3	1/6	3/6
4	1/6	4/6
5	1/6	5/6
6	1/6	6/6
	1	21/6 = 3.5

Expected value = 3.5 dots

TABLE 4-3   Calculation of the Expected Value for the Rate of Return

POSSIBLE RATE OF RETURN	PROBABILITY	NUMBER × PROBABILITY
10%	.05	.50%
11	.10	1.10
12	.15	1.80
13	.17	2.21
14	.12	1.68
15	.08	1.20
16	.09	1.44
17	.06	1.02
18	.05	.90
19	.05	.95
20	.04	.80
21	.04	.84
	1.00	14.44%

Expected rate of return = 14.44%

Applying the probability weights, the expected value is

$$(+\$35)(1/38) \ + \ (-\$1)(37/38) = -\$2/38 = -\$.053$$

The expected winnings from a single roulette gamble is a loss of 5.3 cents. This means that the gambler who keeps making $1 bets indefinitely will lose an average of 5.3 cents on each bet.

Because any decision that involves uncertainty may be viewed as a gambling situation, knowing the expected value can help us choose among alternative actions. But unlike a casino game, practical business decisions must often be made regarding non-repeatable situations, such as the sales response to an advertising budget. In such cases, there is only one opportunity to "play." Here, uncertainty must be measured in terms of *subjective* probabilities. This is illustrated in Table 4-3, where the expected rate of return is calculated for the equipment discussed in Section 4-1.

What does a 14.44% expected rate of return mean? In this instance, the future conditions that will produce a particular percentage return are not repeatable, and the given probabilities really express the decision maker's convictions that the respective percentages will result. Thus, the expected value calculated from these subjective probabilities expresses the decision maker's "average conviction" as to what the return will be.

Using Spreadsheets to Calculate Expected Values

Figure 4-1 shows an Excel spreadsheet for calculating the expected values for the rate of return example in Table 4-3, where the applicable Excel formulas appear alongside. The number in cell B17 is determined by one of these formulas. That value is the sum of the probabilities in cells B5:B16, computed by the formula =SUM(B5:B16). Another formula finds the value in cell C5, which is the product of the numbers in cells A5 and B5 and is computed by the formula =A5*B5. The formulas in cells C6:C16 are obtained by copying the cell C5 formula down to those locations. The expected value appears in cell C17, which is the sum of values above it (cells C5:C16) and is computed by the formula =SUM(C5:C16).

	A	B	C	D	E
1	**Expected Rate of Return**				
2					
3	Possible		Number x		
4	Rate of Return	Probability	Probability		
5	10%	0.05	0.50%		
6	11%	0.10	1.10%		
7	12%	0.15	1.80%		
8	13%	0.17	2.21%		
9	14%	0.12	1.68%		
10	15%	0.08	1.20%		
11	16%	0.09	1.44%		
12	17%	0.06	1.02%		
13	18%	0.05	0.90%		
14	19%	0.05	0.95%		
15	20%	0.04	0.80%		
16	21%	0.04	0.84%		
17		1.0000	14.44%		
18					
19					

	C
5	=A5*B5
6	=A6*B6
7	=A7*B7
8	=A8*B8
9	=A9*B9
10	=A10*B10
11	=A11*B11
12	=A12*B12
13	=A13*B13
14	=A14*B14
15	=A15*B15
16	=A16*B16
17	=SUM(C5:C16)

	B
17	=SUM(B5:B16)

FIGURE 4-1
Excel spreadsheet for calculating the expected rate of return

The Variance of a Random Variable

The expected value measures the *central tendency* of a probability distribution. A second type of measure —*dispersion or variability*— summarizes the degree to which the possible random-variable values differ among themselves. To determine the dispersion, we use the **variance,** which expresses the average of the squared deviations of the individual values from their expected value. The variance for the number of dots obtained from a die toss is calculated in Table 4-4.

Because the variance expresses dispersion in terms of original units squared (squared dots for a die), its square root is often used to measure dispersion. The resulting value is called the **standard deviation.** The standard deviation for the die toss outcome is

$$\sqrt{2.917} = 1.71 \text{ dots}$$

TABLE 4-4 Calculation of the Variance for a Die Toss

NUMBER OF DOTS	DEVIATION: NUMBER − 3.5	(NUMBER − 3.5)^2	PROBABILITY	(NUMBER − 3.5)^2 × PROBABILITY
1	−2.5	6.25	1/6	6.25/6
2	−1.5	2.25	1/6	2.25/6
3	−.5	.25	1/6	.25/6
4	.5	.25	1/6	.25/6
5	1.5	2.25	1/6	2.25/6
6	2.5	6.25	1/6	6.25/6
				17.50/6

Variance = 17.50/6 = 2.917

Expected Value and Variance in Decision Making

Both the expected value and variance can be useful in evaluating business decisions. To illustrate, consider the simplest investment decision, choosing between two stocks. The probability distributions for year-end prices of ChipMont and Gotham Electric stocks appear in Table 4-5, where the expected value and variance in price for each are computed.

    If the choice is made solely on the basis of expected value, the two stocks are equally attractive, each having an expected price of $30.00. However, many investors would actually prefer Gotham Electric, concurring that it is less risky. Assuming that each stock was bought for the same price, the loss potential for ChipMont is significantly greater. The comparative risks of the two investments can be summarized by the respective *variances*. Notice that the variance for Gotham Electric is 2.00, while the variance for ChipMont is the much higher 130.00.

Using Spreadsheets to Compute the Variance and Standard Deviation

The variance and standard deviation (in addition to the expected value) are calculated in the Excel spreadsheet in Figure 4-2 for the price of ChipMont. The formula for cell C10 shows a shorter way for determining the expected value:

$$= SUMPRODUCT(B4:B8,C4:C8)$$

The above instructs Excel to multiply together the values in columns B and C, and then sum those products.

TABLE 4-5   Expected Value and Variance Calculations for Future Stock Prices

CHIPMONT

Price	Probability	Price × Probability	Deviation	Deviation²	Deviation² × Probability
$10	.10	1.00	−20	400	40.00
20	.25	5.00	−10	100	25.00
30	.30	9.00	0	0	0.00
40	.25	10.00	10	100	25.00
50	.10	5.00	20	400	40.00
	Expected Value	30.00		Variance	130.00

GOTHAM ELECTRIC

Price	Probability	Price × Probability	Deviation	Deviation²	Deviation² × Probability
$28	.20	5.60	−2	4	.80
29	.20	5.80	−1	1	.20
30	.20	6.00	0	0	.00
31	.20	6.20	1	1	.20
32	.20	6.40	2	4	.80
	Expected Value	30.00		Variance	2.00

	A	B	C	D	E	F
1		EXPECTED VALUE, VARIANCE AND STANDARD DEVIATION					
2						
3		Value	Probability			
4		10	0.10			
5		20	0.25			
6		30	0.30			
7		40	0.25			
8		50	0.10			
9						
10	Expected Value =		30			
11	Variance =		130			
12	Standard deviation =		11.40			

	C
10	=SUMPRODUCT(B4:B8,C4:C8)
11	=SUMPRODUCT(C4:C8,(B4:B8-C10)^2)
12	=SQRT(C11)

FIGURE 4-2

The Excel spreadsheet for calculating expected value, variance, and standard deviation for the price of ChipMont

The Excel SUMPRODUCT function is also used in cell C11 to find the variance:

$$= SUMPRODUCT(C4:C8,(B4:B8-C10)\text{^}2)$$

The values (probabilities) in column C are multiplied by the square of the differences of the respective column B values (levels of the random variable) from the expected value in cell C10.

The standard deviation in cell C12 is calculated using the square root function, =SQRT(C11).

4-3 FINDING THE PROBABILITY DISTRIBUTION

There are four primary approaches to establishing a probability distribution.

1. Deduction
2. Historical frequencies
3. Judgment
4. Assumed pattern

When information is conveniently structured, investigators can use the basic laws and procedures to deduce a probability distribution table. But it is far more common to take the second approach and assume that historical patterns will prevail in the future. If neither a suitable structure nor sufficient past data are available, analysts may have to rely totally on judgmental assessments, employing subjective probabilities. Most common is the fourth approach, in which a standard probability distribution is selected and key parameters are set at levels that give a good fit.

Using Deduction to Build the Probability Distribution

When the underlying uncertainties are clearly defined, the basic concepts of probability serve as the building blocks. The following application illustrates the construction of a probability distribution using only the multiplication and addition laws.

MANAGERIAL APPLICATION

Amount Paid for a Personal Computer

Quant Jacques wishes to buy a personal computer made by VBM (Very Big Machines). From past purchases, VBM has established the following breakdown for the percentage of times that a particular component is selected for a system.

COMPUTER AND MEMORY	MODEM	DATA ACCESS
30%—Low ($1500) 70%—High ($2000)	50%—Standard ($500) 50%—High-Speed ($1000)	60%—CD-ROM Only ($200) 40%—Multiple ($400)

Assuming that Quant selects the three components independently and that the probability for each choice agrees with the percentages given in the table, what is the probability distribution for his total system cost?

THE PROBLEM SOLUTION

Begin by listing all the possible combinations. You can determine the probability for each by using the multiplication law.

COMPUTER AND MEMORY	MODEM	DATA ACCESS	COST		PROBABILITY
Low	Standard	CD ROM	1,500 + 500 + 200 =	$2,200	.3(.5)(.6) = .09
Low	Standard	Multiple	1,500 + 500 + 400 =	2,400	.3(.5)(.4) = .06
Low	High Speed	CD ROM	1,500 + 1,000 + 200 =	2,700	.3(.5)(.6) = .09
Low	High Speed	Multiple	1,500 + 1,000 + 400 =	2,900	.3(.5)(.4) = .06
High	Standard	CD ROM	2,000 + 500 + 200 =	2,700	.7(.5)(.6) = .21
High	Standard	Multiple	2,000 + 500 + 400 =	2,900	.7(.5)(.4) = .14
High	High Speed	CD ROM	2,000 + 1,000 + 200 =	3,200	.7(.5)(.6) = .21
High	High Speed	Multiple	2,000 + 1,000 + 400 =	3,400	.7(.5)(.4) = .14

List the possible costs, applying the addition law as needed, to construct the probability distribution table.

COST	PROBABILITY
$2,200	.09
2,400	.06
2,700	.09 + .21 = .30
2,900	.06 + .14 = .20
3,200	.21
3,400	.14
	1.00

The preceding application provides a good exercise for applying probability laws to a useful end. Unfortunately, random variables typically do not have an entire sample space of possibilities that can be so conveniently accounted for.

Using Historical Frequencies

Rich stores of data might be mined to establish historical frequencies for various levels of a variable. The statistical frequency distribution then serves directly as the prob-

TABLE 4-6	Historical Frequency Distribution of FireCo's Fire Insurance Claim Sizes				
(1) FIRE INSURANCE CLAIM SIZE	**(2)** RELATIVE FREQUENCY AS INTERVAL PROBABILITY	**(3)** CUMULATIVE PROBABILITY	**(4)** INTERVAL MIDPOINT AS REPRESENTATIVE VALUE	**(5)** APPROXIMATE EXPECTED VALUE	
$25,000– 75,000	.23	.23	$50,000	50,000 × .23 =	$11,500
75,000–125,000	.41	.64	100,000	100,000 × .41 =	41,000
125,000–175,000	.17	.81	150,000	150,000 × .17 =	25,500
175,000–225,000	.11	.92	200,000	200,000 × .11 =	22,000
225,000–275,000	.07	.99	250,000	250,000 × .07 =	17,500
275,000–325,000	.01	1.00	300,000	300,000 × .01 =	3,000
	1.00				$120,500

ability distribution for a future value. This approach works well with operational quantities such as the size of retail purchases or time to process orders.

To illustrate, consider the data presented in Table 4-6 for FireCo's fire insurance claims for structural damage to three-bedroom houses. Columns (1) and (2) provide the statistical frequency distribution for claim size. The historical relative frequencies serve as the probabilities for future claim sizes.

The probability distribution is sometimes represented using **cumulative probabilities.** These are computed for the fire insurance claims in column (3) of Table 4-6. The cumulative probabilities provide the probability for getting a value of the stated size or less. For instance, the probability that the nearest claim size will be $175,000 or less is the sum of the probabilities for levels $75,000, $125,000, and $175,000:

$$.23 + .41 + .17 = .81$$

Graphical Representations and Fractiles

In Figure 4-3 the cumulative probabilities are plotted as points on a graph. A smoothed curve has been drawn through the points. This curve characterizes the **probability distribution function** that might apply over the entire range of possibilities.

The level of the random variable corresponding to a particular cumulative probability is called a **fractile.** For example, the claim size of $75,000 is the .23-fractile, because $\Pr[\text{Claim} \leq \$75,000] = .23$. Similarly, $125,000 is the .64-fractile and $175,000 is the .81-fractile. The .75-fractile (which alternatively may be called the 75th percentile) is not one of the original points, but may be read from the graph to be approximately $150,000.

The approximate expected claim size is computed in Table 4-6, where each class interval is represented by a single value. These are the midpoints listed in column (4). The products of the midpoints and corresponding interval probabilities are shown in column (5), where the sum of the values obtained approximates the underlying expected claim size, $120,500.

A convenient graphical representation of probability distributions is the **histogram** or bar chart. The histogram for fire insurance claim sizes is shown in Figure 4-4, in which each claim-size class interval is represented by a bar with height equal to the

FIGURE 4-3

Cumulative probability
distribution function for
fire insurance claim sizes

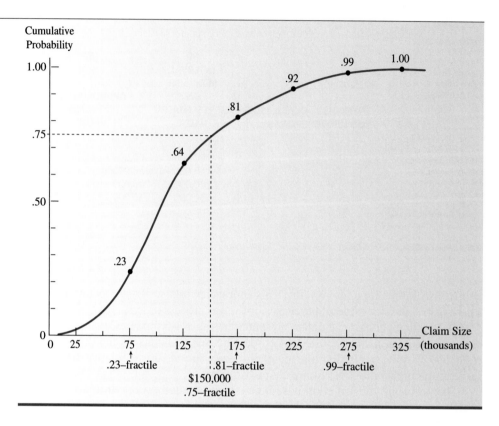

corresponding probability and width spanning the entire interval. Sometimes it is appropriate to graph spikes for individual values, as indicated by the heavy line segments of matching height superimposed above the respective class-interval midpoints.

Another characterization of the probability distribution is the cumulative probability stairway, as shown in Figure 4-5 for the fire insurance claim sizes. That stairway takes one step at the midpoint of each successive class interval of size equal to the interval's probability. The stairway's height above the probability floor equals the corresponding cumulative probability. Superimposed on the graph is the cumulative probability distribution curve shown earlier and whose shape is approximated by the stairway.

There are inherent difficulties in using historical frequencies as probabilities. One is the limited extent of history—the available data may only provide a crude frequency estimate. Unless the number of similar past circumstances is large, statistical estimates of event frequencies can be unreliable. Past history may be suitable for setting fire insurance rates.

Judgmental Assessment of the Probability Distribution

There are no historical data for many uncertain situations encountered in decision making, such as a new product's demand, the size of a future market, or the returns to be achieved from a future project. In these cases, judgment must be substituted for history in arriving at *subjective* probability distributions. A detailed discussion of such a judgmental assessment is given in Section 4-7 at the end of this chapter.

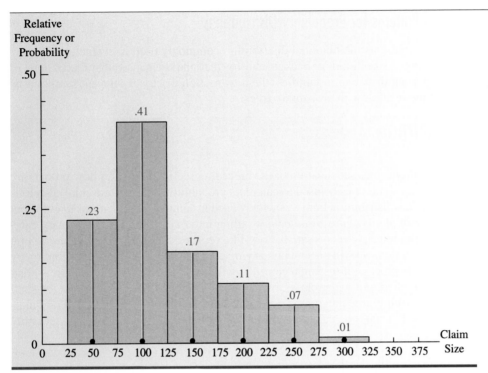

FIGURE 4-4
Histogram showing
probabilities ascribed to
representative values for
fire insurance claims

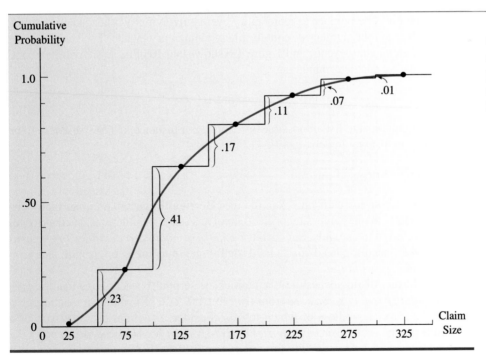

FIGURE 4-5
Cumulative probability
stairway and cumulative
probability distribution
curve fitting original fire
insurance claims data

Assumed Patterns for Probability Distributions

Section 4-4 presents the binomial distribution commonly used in evaluations involving sampling. As preliminary background for that and the subsequent discussions of other important distribution families, the next section discusses relevant sampling issues and the relation with probability trees.

4-4   THE BINOMIAL DISTRIBUTION

The quality-control application of the preceding section illustrates how probability trees can sometimes be used to calculate probabilities for the **binomial distribution.** That distribution family is widely used in sampling applications to represent the *number of observations or outcomes* falling into one of two complementary categories such as defective versus satisfactory, like versus dislike, or success versus failure.

In this section, we will present underlying concepts of the binomial distribution by dissecting the process of tossing a coin. We will then generalize the procedure so that it may be applied to a wider class of situations encountered in business. As we shall see, the probability tree diagram is primarily a conceptual prop, and needed probability values will usually be calculated more directly using formulas or tables, possibly with computer assistance.

A Coin-Tossing Illustration

An evenly balanced coin is tossed fairly five times. The corresponding probability tree diagram appears in Figure 4-6, where the sample space is also listed. Our initial problem is to find the probability for obtaining exactly two heads. Because each of the 32 outcomes is equally likely, the basic definition of probability allows us to find the answer by counting the number of elementary events involving two heads and dividing this result by the total number of equally likely elementary events. The sample space contains 32 elementary events, and Figure 4-6 shows that 10 of these are two-head outcomes. Thus, we can determine that

$$\Pr[\text{exactly two heads}] = \frac{10}{32}$$

It may be impractical to list all possible outcomes. For instance, if 10 tosses were to be considered, the list would contain 1,024 (2^{10}) entries.

The Bernoulli Process

A sequence of coin tosses is one example of a **Bernoulli process.** A great many circumstances fall into the same category: All involve a series of situations (such as tosses of a coin) referred to as **trials.** For each trial, *there are only two possible complementary outcomes,* such as "head" or "tail." Usually one outcome is referred to as a *success;* the other, as a *failure.*

What further distinguishes these situations as Bernoulli processes is that the *success probability remains constant* from trial to trial. The probability for obtaining a head is the same, regardless of which toss is considered. A final characteristic of a Bernoulli process is that *successive trial outcomes must be independent events.* Like a fairly tossed coin, the probability for obtaining a success (head) must be independent of what occurred in previous trials (tosses).

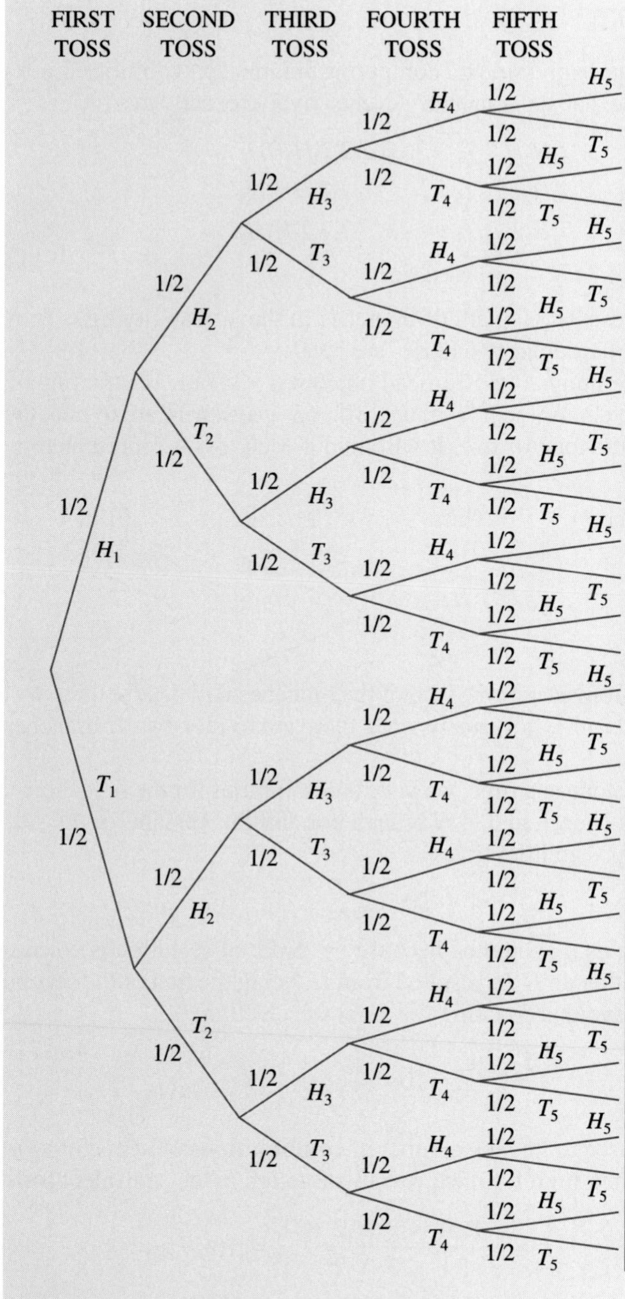

SAMPLE SPACE	PROBABILITY	NO. OF HEADS	TALLY (0 1 2 3 4 5)
$(H_1 H_2 H_3 H_4 H_5)$	1/32	5	* (at 5)
$(H_1 H_2 H_3 H_4 T_5)$	1/32	4	* (at 4)
$(H_1 H_2 H_3 T_4 H_5)$	1/32	4	* (at 4)
$(H_1 H_2 H_3 T_4 T_5)$	1/32	3	* (at 3)
$(H_1 H_2 T_3 H_4 H_5)$	1/32	4	* (at 4)
$(H_1 H_2 T_3 H_4 T_5)$	1/32	3	* (at 3)
$(H_1 H_2 T_3 T_4 H_5)$	1/32	3	* (at 3)
$(H_1 H_2 T_3 T_4 T_5)$	1/32	2	* (at 2)
$(H_1 T_2 H_3 H_4 H_5)$	1/32	4	* (at 4)
$(H_1 T_2 H_3 H_4 T_5)$	1/32	3	* (at 3)
$(H_1 T_2 H_3 T_4 H_5)$	1/32	3	* (at 3)
$(H_1 T_2 H_3 T_4 T_5)$	1/32	2	* (at 2)
$(H_1 T_2 T_3 H_4 H_5)$	1/32	3	* (at 3)
$(H_1 T_2 T_3 H_4 T_5)$	1/32	2	* (at 2)
$(H_1 T_2 T_3 T_4 H_5)$	1/32	2	* (at 2)
$(H_1 T_2 T_3 T_4 T_5)$	1/32	1	* (at 1)
$(T_1 H_2 H_3 H_4 H_5)$	1/32	4	* (at 4)
$(T_1 H_2 H_3 H_4 T_5)$	1/32	3	* (at 3)
$(T_1 H_2 H_3 T_4 H_5)$	1/32	3	* (at 3)
$(T_1 H_2 H_3 T_4 T_5)$	1/32	2	* (at 2)
$(T_1 H_2 T_3 H_4 H_5)$	1/32	3	* (at 3)
$(T_1 H_2 T_3 H_4 T_5)$	1/32	2	* (at 2)
$(T_1 H_2 T_3 T_4 H_5)$	1/32	2	* (at 2)
$(T_1 H_2 T_3 T_4 T_5)$	1/32	1	* (at 1)
$(T_1 T_2 H_3 H_4 H_5)$	1/32	3	* (at 3)
$(T_1 T_2 H_3 H_4 T_5)$	1/32	2	* (at 2)
$(T_1 T_2 H_3 T_4 H_5)$	1/32	2	* (at 2)
$(T_1 T_2 H_3 T_4 T_5)$	1/32	1	* (at 1)
$(T_1 T_2 T_3 H_4 H_5)$	1/32	2	* (at 2)
$(T_1 T_2 T_3 H_4 T_5)$	1/32	1	* (at 1)
$(T_1 T_2 T_3 T_4 H_5)$	1/32	1	* (at 1)
$(T_1 T_2 T_3 T_4 T_5)$	1/32	0	* (at 0)
Totals	**32/32**		**1 5 10 10 5 1**

FIGURE 4-6 Probability tree diagram for five coin tosses

The Number of Combinations

Now we will derive an algebraic expression for computing binomial probabilities. Looking at Figure 4-6 again, we see that 10 elementary events involve exactly two heads.

$H_1H_2T_3T_4T_5$	$T_1H_2H_3T_4T_5$	$T_1T_2H_3H_4T_5$
$H_1T_2H_3T_4T_5$	$T_1H_2T_3H_4T_5$	$T_1T_2H_3T_4H_5$
$H_1T_2T_3H_4T_5$	$T_1H_2T_3T_4H_5$	$T_1T_2T_3H_4H_5$
$H_1T_2T_3T_4H_5$		

Each of these outcomes represents one path of branches in the probability tree. They differ only in terms of which particular two tosses are heads.

If we want to find out the number of two-head outcomes without constructing an entire probability tree we can determine how many different ways there are to pick the two tosses to be heads from the total of five. It will help if each toss is represented by a fork.

First Toss	Second Toss	Third Toss	Fourth Toss	Fifth Toss
H_1	H_2	H_3	H_4	H_5
T_1	T_2	T_3	T_4	T_5

We want to save one branch from each fork. Two of the branches will be H's; three will be T's. Our problem is to determine how many ways there are to pick two H branches to save from the five.

If we pick the H branches one at a time, we have 5 possibilities for the first choice. No matter which H branch is chosen first, 4 H branch possibilities remain for the second choice. Multiplying the possibilities gives

$$5 \times 4 = 20$$

This answer is twice as large as it should be because the order of selection is considered. But we do not care whether an H_3H_5 resulted from H_3 being the first or the second choice, so we divide by 2 to avoid accounting for order of selection.

$$\frac{5 \times 4}{2} = 10$$

This calculation can be used to find the number of **combinations** of items for a variety of situations. It will be helpful if we reexpress this fraction in the equivalent form

$$\frac{5 \times 4}{2} = \frac{5 \times 4}{2 \times 1} = \frac{5 \times 4 \times 3 \times 2 \times 1}{2 \times 1 \times 3 \times 2 \times 1} = 10$$

Multiplying both the numerator and denominator of the middle fraction by 3, then by 2, and finally by 1 leaves the result unchanged. The final fraction contains factorial terms. A **factorial** is the product of successive integer values ending with 1. Such a product is denoted by placing an exclamation point after the highest number.

$$2! = 2 \times 1 \quad (= 2)$$
$$3! = 3 \times 2 \times 1 \quad (= 6)$$
$$5! = 5 \times 4 \times 3 \times 2 \times 1 \quad (= 120)$$

We define

$$1! = 1$$
$$0! = 1$$

In general

$$n! = n \times (n - 1) \times (n - 2) \times \ldots \times 2 \times 1$$

In factorial notation, the number of two-head sequences in five coin tosses is

$$\frac{5 \times 4 \times 3 \times 2 \times 1}{2 \times 1 \times 3 \times 2 \times 1} = \frac{5!}{2!3!} = 10$$

This result suggests the general procedure for finding the number of combinations.

Number of Combinations The number of combinations of r objects taken from n objects may be determined from

$$\frac{n!}{r!(n - r)!}$$

In our illustration, there are $n = 5$ tosses and we are considering exactly $r = 2$ heads occurring in those tosses. Thus, the number of two-head sequence combinations is

$$\frac{5!}{2!(5 - 2)!} = \frac{5!}{2!3!} = 10$$

Using Spreadsheets Ready-to-use Excel formulas allow us to quickly determine factorials and the number of combinations. FACT(n) gives the value of n! and COMBIN(n,r) is the number of combinations of r objects taken from n.

Figure 4-7 shows the spreadsheet for the preceding examples. Cell D4 has the formula =FACT(B4). It gives the value 120 for FACT(5) when the number in cell B4 is 5. The formula =COMBIN(B8,B9) applies to cell D9. It shows the value 10 when cells B8 and B9 contain 5 and 2. We need only change the values in cells B4, B8, or B9 to obtain whatever factorial and combination results are desired.

	A	B	C	D
1	FACTORIALS AND COMBINATIONS			
2				
3				
4	n =	5	n! =	120
5				
6				
7				
8	n =	5	Number of	
9	r =	2	Combinations =	10
10				
11				
12				

	D
4	=FACT(B4)

	D
9	=COMBIN(B8,B9)

FIGURE 4-7
Excel spreadsheet for factorial and the number of combinations

The Binomial Formula

When the trial outcomes result from a Bernoulli process, the number of successes is a random variable with a binomial distribution. The following expression, referred to as the **binomial formula,** can then be used to find the probability values.

BINOMIAL FORMULA

$$\Pr[\text{successes} = r] = \frac{n!}{r!(n - r)!} P^r(1 - P)^{n-r}$$

where n = number of trials achieved
P = trial success probability
$r = 0, 1, \ldots, n$

The binomial formula can be used to determine the probability found earlier for obtaining successes = 2 heads in $n = 5$ tosses of a fair coin. In this case, $P = \Pr[\text{head}] = 1/2$ and $1 - P = \Pr[\text{tail}] = 1/2$, so that

$$\Pr[\text{successes} = 2] = \frac{5!}{2!(5 - 2)!}\left(\frac{1}{2}\right)^2\left(1 - \frac{1}{2}\right)^{5-2} = \frac{5!}{2!3!}\left(\frac{1}{2}\right)^2\left(\frac{1}{2}\right)^3$$

$$= 10\left(\frac{1}{2}\right)^5 = \frac{10}{32}$$

The factorial terms in this product provide the number of outcomes involving exactly 2 heads, which is equal to 10, and represent the number of combinations of 2 particular tosses that may result in heads out of a total of 5 tosses. The product containing 1/2 represents the probability for obtaining any one of the 10 two-head sequences represented by the end positions in the probability tree diagram in Figure 4-6. Each of these positions is reached by traversing a particular path of 2 head and $5 - 2 = 3$ tail branches. Each path probability is an application of the multiplication law. Because a two-head result can occur in any one of 10 equally likely ways, the addition law of probability tells us to add 10 of the identical terms or, more simply, to multiply by 10.

The entire binomial distribution corresponding to the number of heads resulting from $n = 5$ fair coin tosses appears in Table 4-7. There the probability values are found by applying the binomial formula to all possible r values.

We have already noted that different Bernoulli processes will have different probability values. But the number of successes resulting from each process is a random variable belonging to the binomial family. Note that the probabilities for all possible values of r depend on the value of P. Different sizes of n will result in a larger or smaller number of possible r values and will also affect each probability value.

Using the binomial formula to calculate probabilities can be tedious and time consuming. Imagine the effort it would take to determine the probability for 17 successes in $n = 58$ trials when $P = .13$. We can simply find the probabilities we need from a table, but most tables provide only cumulative probabilities.

Using Binomial Probability Tables

Appendix Table A provides the cumulative binomial probability values for various sizes of n (with separate tabulations for several P values). It is possible to use this table to compute probabilities for the number of successes in a variety of situations. To

TABLE 4-7   Binomial Distribution for the Number of Heads Obtained in Five Coin Tosses

POSSIBLE NUMBER OF HEADS r	PR[HEADS = r]
0	$\dfrac{5!}{0!5!}\left(\dfrac{1}{2}\right)^0\left(\dfrac{1}{2}\right)^5 = \dfrac{1}{32} = .03125$
1	$\dfrac{5!}{1!4!}\left(\dfrac{1}{2}\right)^1\left(\dfrac{1}{2}\right)^4 = \dfrac{5}{32} = .15625$
2	$\dfrac{5!}{2!3!}\left(\dfrac{1}{2}\right)^2\left(\dfrac{1}{2}\right)^3 = \dfrac{10}{32} = .31250$
3	$\dfrac{5!}{3!2!}\left(\dfrac{1}{2}\right)^3\left(\dfrac{1}{2}\right)^2 = \dfrac{10}{32} = .31250$
4	$\dfrac{5!}{4!1!}\left(\dfrac{1}{2}\right)^4\left(\dfrac{1}{2}\right)^1 = \dfrac{5}{32} = .15625$
5	$\dfrac{5!}{5!0!}\left(\dfrac{1}{2}\right)^5\left(\dfrac{1}{2}\right)^0 = \dfrac{1}{32} = .03125$
	1.00000

illustrate, suppose we wish to find probabilities regarding the number of $n = 100$ readers who will remember an aspirin advertisement that appears on the back cover of *Time*. We assume that $P = .30$ is the underlying proportion of all readers who will remember the ad. Use the portion of Appendix Table A that begins at $n = 100$.

1. **To obtain a result less than or equal to a particular value.** The probability that 40 or fewer persons in the sample will remember the ad is a cumulative probability value that can be read directly from the table when $r = 40$ successes.

$$\text{Pr[successes} \leq 40] = .9875$$

2. **To obtain a result exactly equal to a single value.** Recall that cumulative probabilities represent the sum of individual probability values and are portrayed graphically as a stairway (see Figure 4-5). A single-value probability may be obtained by determining the size of the step between two neighboring cumulative probabilities. For example, the probability that exactly 32 of the readers will remember the ad is

$$\text{Pr[successes} = 32] = \text{Pr[successes} \leq 32] - \text{Pr[successes} \leq 31]$$
$$= .7107 - .6331$$
$$= .0776$$

3. **To obtain a result strictly less than some value.** The probability that fewer than 30 successes are achieved is the same as the probability that exactly 29 or fewer successes are obtained, or

$$\text{Pr[successes} < 30] = \text{Pr[successes} \leq 29] = .4623$$

4. **To obtain a result greater than or equal to some value.** To find the probability that at least 20 of the readers will remember the ad, we look up the cumulative probability that 19 or less will remember and subtract this value from 1.

$$\Pr[\text{successes} \geq 20] = 1 - \Pr[\text{successes} \leq 19]$$
$$= 1 - .0089 = .9911$$

5. **To obtain a result that lies between two values.** Suppose we want to find the probability that the number of successes will lie somewhere between 25 and 35, inclusively. Thus, we want to determine

$$\Pr[25 \leq \text{successes} \leq 35]$$

In this case, we obtain the difference between two cumulative probabilities.

$$\Pr[\text{successes} \leq 35] - \Pr[\text{successes} \leq 24] = .8839 - .1136 = .7703$$

The Mean of the Binomial Distribution

The expected number of successes can be determined from probabilities obtained by using the binomial formula or a binomial distribution table for a particular n and P. Instead of multiplying these probabilities by the respective number of successes and summing the products, however, a special feature of the binomial distribution enables us to arrive at the answer quickly. The following expression provides the expected number of successes.

$$\text{Expected successes} = nP$$

Thus, the expected number of rememberers when $n = 100$ and $P = .3$ is $100(.3) = 30$.

Using Spreadsheets to Find Binomial Probabilities

The BINOMDIST(r,n,P, cumulative) Excel function calculates binomial probabilities. The first three arguments are the cell locations for the number of successes r, the number of trials n, and the trial success probability P. The argument "cumulative" will be the word TRUE when a cumulative probability is desired and the word FALSE when an individual probability must be calculated from the binomial formula.

    Figure 4-8 shows the Excel spreadsheet for the preceding example with $n = 100$ trials (cell C4) and trial success probability $P = 0.3$ (cell G4). Cell B9 gives $\Pr[R = 25] = .0496$. The Excel formula used to calculate this value is

$$=\text{BINOMDIST(A9,\$C\$4,\$G\$4,FALSE)}$$

The arguments are the respective spreadsheet cells and represent the current cell values. The first argument A9 is the number of successes $r = 25$ when cell A9 has the value 25. (No dollar signs [\$] are used with this designation, because the same formula will be used for other r levels in later rows. The dollar signs in the second and third arguments make those cell references absolute. The copied cell formulas will always refer back to C4 and G4.) The fourth argument FALSE indicates that the individual binomial probability is to be calculated. Copying cell B9 down to cells B10:B19 obtains the remaining binomial probabilities.

    To calculate the cumulative probabilities in cells C9:C19, the same formulas are used as in B9:B19, with TRUE instead as the fourth argument. This is achieved by entering the following formula into cell C9

$$= \text{BINOMDIST(A9,\$C\$4,\$G\$4,TRUE)}$$

and copying it down to cells C10:C19. The cell C9 result is $\Pr[R \leq 25] = .1631$.

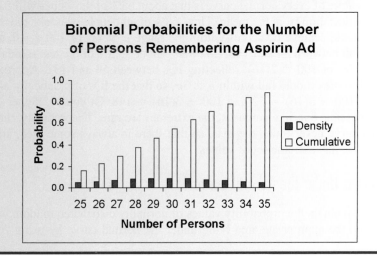

FIGURE 4-8

Excel spreadsheet and graph for finding binomial probabilities for number of persons remembering aspirin ad

	A	B	C	D	E	F	G
1		BINOMIAL PROBABILITY DISTRIBUTION					
2							
3							
4	Number of trials n =		100	Trial success probability P =			0.3
5							
6	Number of	Probability	Cumulative				
7	Successes	Density	Probability				
8	r	$\Pr[R = r]$	$\Pr[R \le r]$				
9	25	0.0496	0.1631				
10	26	0.0613	0.2244				
11	27	0.0720	0.2964				
12	28	0.0804	0.3768				
13	29	0.0856	0.4623				
14	30	0.0868	0.5491				
15	31	0.0840	0.6331				
16	32	0.0776	0.7107				
17	33	0.0685	0.7793				
18	34	0.0579	0.8371				
19	35	0.0468	0.8839				

	B
9	=BINOMDIST(A9,$C$4,$G$4,FALSE)
10	=BINOMDIST(A10,$C$4,$G$4,FALSE)
11	=BINOMDIST(A11,$C$4,$G$4,FALSE)
12	=BINOMDIST(A12,$C$4,$G$4,FALSE)
13	=BINOMDIST(A13,$C$4,$G$4,FALSE)
14	=BINOMDIST(A14,$C$4,$G$4,FALSE)
15	=BINOMDIST(A15,$C$4,$G$4,FALSE)
16	=BINOMDIST(A16,$C$4,$G$4,FALSE)
17	=BINOMDIST(A17,$C$4,$G$4,FALSE)
18	=BINOMDIST(A18,$C$4,$G$4,FALSE)
19	=BINOMDIST(A19,$C$4,$G$4,FALSE)

4-5   THE NORMAL DISTRIBUTION

The **normal distribution** is used to describe frequency patterns for a great many phenomena. It is usually described in terms of a bell-shaped curve, as shown in Figure 4-9. There, x represents the possible values of the random variable, and the height of the curve represents the relative frequency at which the corresponding values occur. A particular normal distribution is specified by only two parameters: the *mean* μ (Greek lowercase *mu*) and the *standard deviation* σ (Greek lowercase *sigma*). The location or center of the corresponding normal curve is determined by the mean, and its shape is established by the standard deviation. Figure 4-10 shows the curves for three different normal distributions.

Because the height of the normal curve above any point expresses its relative frequency, or proportional occurrence, the total area beneath the normal curve is 1. We can find the probabilities for various values of a normally distributed random variable by determining the *areas* under the applicable portions of its normal curve. These areas correspond to the proportion of times that the particular range of values will occur when identical conditions are repeated.

FIGURE 4-9

Frequency curve for the normal distribution

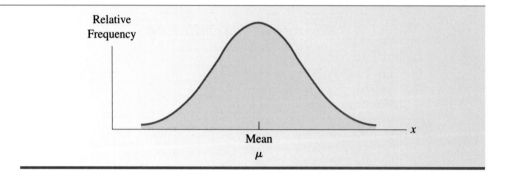

The areas under the normal curve are tied to the distance separating the points of interest from the mean. For example, the Stanford-Binet IQ test was designed so that the scores of persons taking it have a mean of $\mu = 100$ and a standard deviation of $\sigma = 16$. A feature of every normal curve is that about 68% of the values will fall within ± 1 standard deviation from the mean. Thus, 68% of all people who take the Stanford-Binet test should achieve IQ scores within the range $\mu \pm 1\sigma$, or 100 ± 16, and their IQs should fall between 84 and 116. Likewise, about 95.5% of the test scores will fall within $\mu \pm 2\sigma$, or $100 \pm 2(16)$, reflecting IQs between 68 and 132. Approximately 99.7% of all scores should fall within $\mu \pm 3\sigma$, so that the IQs of practically all people lie between $100 - 3(16) = 52$ and $100 + 3(16) = 148$. Of course, higher or lower scores are possible but, like geniuses, the extremes are rare. Theoretically, the tails of the normal curve never touch the axis, so that there is always some area, and hence probability, for any extreme set of values.

Finding Areas Under the Normal Curve

Before we can obtain the probability values of normally distributed random variables, we must find the appropriate area lying under the normal curve by using Appendix Table B.

How would you find the desired areas for the time a particular typesetter takes to compose 500 lines of standard type? We will assume that the population of times

FIGURE 4-10

Three normal distributions graphed on a common axis

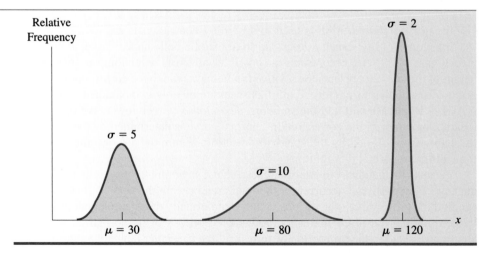

is normally distributed, with a mean of $\mu = 150$ minutes and a standard deviation of $\sigma = 30$ minutes. The time it takes to set any given 500 lines, such as the next 500 to be composed, represents a randomly selected time from this population.

The probability that it takes between 150 and 175 minutes to set 500 lines is represented by the shaded area under the normal curve in Figure 4-11. We know that the area beneath the normal curve between the mean and a certain point depends only on the number of standard deviations separating the two points. We see that 175 minutes is equivalent to a distance above the mean of .83 standard deviation. This figure is determined by observing that 175 minutes minus the mean of 150 minutes is equal to 25 minutes. Because the standard deviation is 30 minutes, 25 minutes is only $25/30 = .83$ of the standard deviation.

Appendix Table B has been constructed for the **standard normal curve,** which provides the area between the mean and a point above the mean at some specified distance measured in standard deviations. Because this distance will vary, it is treated as a variable and denoted by z. Sometimes the value of z is referred to as a **normal deviate.** The distance z that separates a possible normal random variable value x from its mean can be determined from the following expression for the *normal deviate*:

$$z = \frac{x - \mu}{\sigma}$$

A negative value will be obtained for z when x is smaller than μ.

The first column of Appendix Table B lists values of z to the first decimal place. The second decimal place value is located at the head of one of the remaining 10 columns. The area under the curve between the mean and z standard deviations is found at the intersection of the correct row and column. For example, when $z = .83$, we find the area of .2967 by reading the entry in the .8 row and the .03 column. The area under the normal curve for a completion time between 150 and 175 minutes is .2967, which represents the probability that it will take this long to set the next 500 lines of print.

Although Table B provides areas only between the mean and some point above it, we can also use this table to find areas encountered in other common probability situations, such as those shown in Figure 4-12.

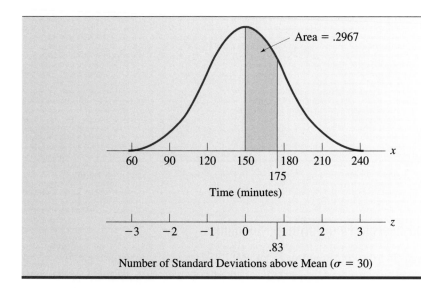

FIGURE 4-11
Determining the area under a normal curve

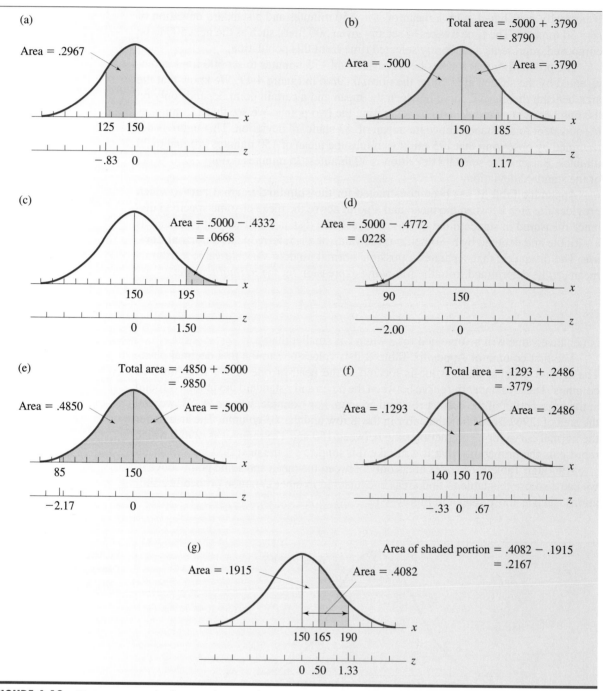

FIGURE 4-12   Various areas under the normal curve, where x = completion time in minutes and z = standard deviations

Using Spreadsheets to Find Normal Probabilities

Excel's normal distribution function is NORMDIST(x, μ, σ, cumulative). The arguments are the cell locations of the variable x under consideration, its mean μ, its standard deviation σ, and the variable "cumulative." The last argument is a word: TRUE

	A	B	C	D	E	F
1			NORMAL DISTRIBUTION			
2						
3	Mean mu =		150			
4	Standard deviation sigma =		30			
5						
6		Frequency	Cumulative			
7	Time	Curve	Distribution			
8	x	f(x)	F(x)			
9	60	0.0001	0.0013		C	
10	85	0.0013	0.0151	9	=NORMDIST(A9,$C$3,$C$4,TRUE)	
11	90	0.0018	0.0228	10	=NORMDIST(A10,$C$3,$C$4,TRUE)	
12	120	0.0081	0.1587	11	=NORMDIST(A11,$C$3,$C$4,TRUE)	
13	125	0.0094	0.2023	12	=NORMDIST(A12,$C$3,$C$4,TRUE)	
14	140	0.0126	0.3694	13	=NORMDIST(A13,$C$3,$C$4,TRUE)	
15	150	0.0133	0.5000	14	=NORMDIST(A14,$C$3,$C$4,TRUE)	
				15	=NORMDIST(A15,$C$3,$C$4,TRUE)	
16	165	0.0117	0.6915	16	=NORMDIST(A16,$C$3,$C$4,TRUE)	
17	170	0.0106	0.7475	17	=NORMDIST(A17,$C$3,$C$4,TRUE)	
18	180	0.0081	0.8413	18	=NORMDIST(A18,$C$3,$C$4,TRUE)	
19	185	0.0067	0.8783	19	=NORMDIST(A19,$C$3,$C$4,TRUE)	
20	190	0.0055	0.9088	20	=NORMDIST(A20,$C$3,$C$4,TRUE)	
21	195	0.0043	0.9332	21	=NORMDIST(A21,$C$3,$C$4,TRUE)	
22	210	0.0018	0.9772	22	=NORMDIST(A22,$C$3,$C$4,TRUE)	
23	240	0.0001	0.9987	23	=NORMDIST(A23,$C$3,$C$4,TRUE)	

FIGURE 4-13
Spreadsheet and graph for typesetting normal distribution

when an area (cumulative probability) is desired or FALSE when the height of the normal frequency curve (density function) is required.

Figure 4-13 shows the spreadsheet for the typesetting example. Cell C9 gives the area under the normal curve up to a time x of 60 minutes, $\Pr[x \leq 60] = .0013$. The formula for that cell is

$$=\text{NORMDIST(A9,\$C\$3,\$C\$4, TRUE)}$$

The first argument is A9, the cell location of the value for x (60, in this case). The next two arguments are the absolute locations C3 and C4 of the mean ($\mu = 150$) and standard deviation ($\sigma = 30$). The last argument is TRUE, because an area under the normal curve (cumulative probability) is required. (Not shown is the formula for cell B9, identical except that the fourth argument is FALSE, because there the *height* of the normal curve is required.)

The formulas for cells in B10:C23 are copied down from B9:C9. Notice that the times for x in the first spreadsheet column have unequal intervals to match those used in the typesetting example. (Excel-generated results may differ slightly from those obtained with Table B, due to rounding.)

Deciding When to Use the Normal Distribution

The normal distribution is a theoretical model possessing many useful properties. It empirically fits well to all sorts of anthropometric data and to many physical measurements. Probability values are easy to establish for ranges of such quantities as human heights and wrist diameters, as well as diameters of ostrich eggs. The normal distribution also applies to sampling situations, allowing us to find probabilities for levels of the sample mean when little is known about the form of the parent population.

Its mathematical description implies that the normal curve's tails will never touch the horizontal axis. No matter, therefore, how far above or below the mean a point falls, there will always be an area in the tail above or below it. Remember, it is the distance separating a point from μ, in units of σ, that determines the tail area (probability). When applied to human heights, the normal distribution allows for the possibility of a man growing to be a mile or more tall. (That would only be an event lying about 40,000 standard deviations above the mean.) Worse yet, there is nonzero probability that a man will be negatively tall.

Like practically any mathematical model, the normal curve only *approximates* reality. We usually do not concern ourselves with the rare events applicable to values lying more than five standard deviations above or below the mean.

In the final analysis, the choice to use the normal distribution for a particular situation is a matter of judgment. It does not give a good fit when data are not unimodal or not symmetrically distributed about a central value.

4-6   POISSON AND EXPONENTIAL DISTRIBUTIONS

Two other probability distributions play very important roles in management-science applications. One of these — the **Poisson distribution** — provides probabilities for the number of events that may occur over time. A related distribution — the **exponential distribution** — provides probabilities for the times between events. Both of these distributions are used extensively in queuing (waiting-line) analysis, where the events of interest are customer *arrivals* to the service facility being evaluated. Both distributions apply to situations in which events occur randomly over time.

As an illustration, consider cars arriving at a tollbooth. Figure 4-14 illustrates this concept. Each dot represents a car and is positioned so that its horizontal distance from the origin (at 9:00 A.M.) indicates when it arrives at the booth. Such a graph could be constructed from an aerial photograph taken at 9:00 A.M. of the two miles of highway leading to the booth. Assuming that all cars are traveling at the speed limit, we could then directly translate each car's distance from the booth into its arrival time. Notice that the dots in Figure 4-14 are scattered with no apparent pattern, as if placed there at random.

The Poisson Process

Even though the cars arrive randomly over time, much detailed information can be gleaned from one key characteristic of the arrival stream (of which our graph is only a small sample). Seemingly without pattern, such an arrival stream is an example of a *Poisson process*, named after the eighteenth-century mathematician and physicist

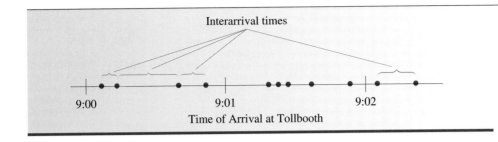

FIGURE 4-14
Random arrival times of cars at a tollbooth

Siméon Poisson. It is the randomness of this pattern that provides the basis for the information it yields. What distinguishes one arrival stream from another — and the only thing that can make any two Poisson processes differ — is the **mean arrival rate.** This parameter, denoted by λ (lowercase Greek *lambda*), tells us the mean number of arrivals occurring per minute (or some other unit of time, such as per second or per hour). A busy tollbooth may experience an arrival rate of $\lambda = 100$ cars per minute, whereas an out-of-the way booth may register a rate of $\lambda = 1/2$ car per minute.

The Exponential and Poisson Distributions

The gaps between the dots in Figure 4-14 represent the interarrival times, or the times between successive arrivals of cars. The exponential distribution is concerned with the *size* of the gap, measured in units of time, that separates successive cars. Although the dots are scattered randomly over time, the relative frequency of interarrival times of various sizes is predictable. Suppose that the cars arriving at the tollbooth are observed for several minutes and the time of each car's arrival is noted. These data would provide a histogram similar to the one in Figure 4-15(a), which approximates the shape of the underlying frequency curve in Figure 4-15(b), the height of which may be determined for any interarrival time t from the expression

$$f(t) = \lambda e^{-\lambda t}$$

This is the probability density function for the exponential distribution and is based on the constant e, which is equal to 2.7183 and serves as the base for natural logarithms. The particular distribution applicable to a specific situation depends only on the level of λ. In our tollbooth illustration, the mean arrival rate is $\lambda = 4$ cars per minute. Notice that the frequency curve intersects the vertical axis at a height of $\lambda = 4$ in Figure 4-15(b). The mean and the standard deviation of the exponential distribution are identical and may be expressed in terms of λ as

$$\text{Mean} = 1/\lambda$$

$$\text{Standard deviation} = 1/\lambda$$

Also notice that the mean time between arrivals is the reciprocal of the mean rate of arrivals. Thus, if $\lambda = 4$ *cars per minute,* then the mean time between arrivals is $1/\lambda = 1/4 = .25$ *minutes per car.*

As is true of the normal curve, probabilities for the exponential random variable can be found by determining the area under the frequency curve. The cumulative probability that the time T between two successive arrivals is t or less may be obtained from

$$\Pr[T \leq t] = 1 - e^{-\lambda t}$$

Figure 4-15(c) shows the applicable cumulative probability graph when $\lambda = 4$. Appendix Table D may be used to find values for $e^{-\lambda t}$.

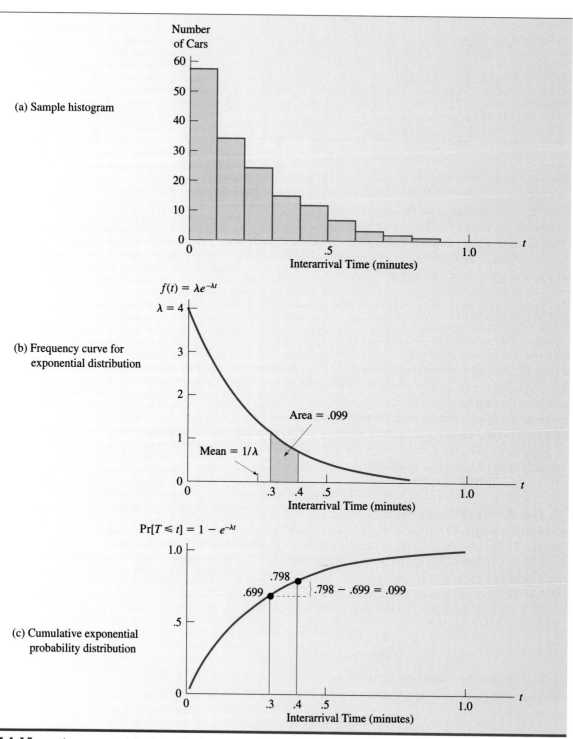

(a) Sample histogram

$f(t) = \lambda e^{-\lambda t}$

(b) Frequency curve for exponential distribution

Area = .099

Mean = $1/\lambda$

$\Pr[T \leq t] = 1 - e^{-\lambda t}$

.798

.699

.798 − .699 = .099

(c) Cumulative exponential probability distribution

FIGURE 4-15   The exponential distribution for the interarrival times of cars at a tollbooth

For example, using $\lambda = 4$ cars per minute, we find that the probability that the interarrival time between any two cars is $t = .4$ minute or less is

$$\Pr[T \le .4] = 1 - e^{-4(.4)} = 1 - e^{-1.6}$$
$$= 1 - .202$$
$$= .798$$

The probability that the time is $t = .3$ minute or less is

$$\Pr[T \le .3] = 1 - e^{-4(.3)} = 1 - e^{-1.2}$$
$$= 1 - .301$$
$$= .699$$

The difference in these two values is

$$\Pr[.3 \le T \le .4] = .798 - .699$$
$$= .099$$

which provides the area under the exponential frequency curve in Figure 4-15(b) between the interarrival times of .3 and .4 minute.

Using Spreadsheets to Find Exponential Probabilities

The Excel function EXPONDIST(t,λ, cumulative) calculates exponential probabilities. The argument t represents the variable under consideration, λ is the mean arrival rate, and "cumulative" is a word variable: TRUE when a cumulative probability is required and FALSE when the height of the frequency curve (probability density function) is needed. The spreadsheet approach is analogous to that for the normal distribution in Figure 4-13. Excel will also graph the exponential frequency curve, as shown in Figure 4-16 for the interarrival times discussed earlier.

The Poisson Distribution

The Poisson distribution expresses the probabilities for the number of arrivals in any given time period, such as the 1 minute between 9:08 and 9:09, the 5 minutes between 9:09 and 9:14, or the 1 hour between 10 A.M. and 11 A.M. Letting X represent the actual number of arrivals in a period of duration t, we can compute the probability that X is equal to one of the possible levels x from

$$\Pr[X = x] = \frac{e^{-\lambda t}(\lambda t)^x}{x!}$$

where

$$x = 0, 1, 2, \ldots$$

Continuing with our illustration, consider any 1-minute interval, so that $t = 1$ minute. Again, given $\lambda = 4$ cars per minute, we find that $\lambda t = 4$ cars. Appendix Table D provides $e^{-4} = .018316$. The probability that exactly 2 cars will arrive is therefore

$$\Pr[X = 2] = \frac{e^{-4}(4)^2}{2!}$$
$$= \frac{.018316(4)^2}{2}$$
$$= .1465$$

FIGURE 4-16

Spreadsheet and graph
for interarrival time
exponential distribution

	A	B	C	D	E	F	G
1	EXPONENTIAL DISTRIBUTION						
2							
3	Mean rate lambda =	4					
4							
5	Interarrival	Frequency	Cumulative				
6	Time	Curve	Distribution				
7	t	f(t)	F(t)				
8	0	4.0000	0.0000				
9	0.1	2.6813	0.3297				
10	0.2	1.7973	0.5507				
11	0.3	1.2048	0.6988				
12	0.4	0.8076	0.7981				
13	0.5	0.5413	0.8647				
14	0.6	0.3629	0.9093				
15	0.7	0.2432	0.9392				
16	0.8	0.1630	0.9592				
17	0.9	0.1093	0.9727				
18	1	0.0733	0.9817				

	C
8	=EXPONDIST(A8,$C$3,TRUE)
9	=EXPONDIST(A9,$C$3,TRUE)
10	=EXPONDIST(A10,$C$3,TRUE)
11	=EXPONDIST(A11,$C$3,TRUE)
12	=EXPONDIST(A12,$C$3,TRUE)
13	=EXPONDIST(A13,$C$3,TRUE)
14	=EXPONDIST(A14,$C$3,TRUE)
15	=EXPONDIST(A15,$C$3,TRUE)
16	=EXPONDIST(A16,$C$3,TRUE)
17	=EXPONDIST(A17,$C$3,TRUE)
18	=EXPONDIST(A18,$C$3,TRUE)

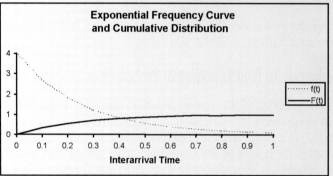

The probability values for other numbers of cars are calculated in Table 4-8.

The Poisson distribution is completely specified by the process rate λ and the period of duration t. Its mean and variance are identical and are expressed in terms of the parameters.

$$\text{mean} = \lambda t$$
$$\text{variance} = \lambda t$$

Using Poisson Probability Tables

Like binomial probabilities, computing Poisson probabilities by hand can be an onerous chore. Cumulative values of the Poisson probabilities are computed in Appendix Table E for levels of λt ranging from 1 to 20. A table of individual probability terms is not provided because, like the binomial probabilities, the Poisson probabilities can be easily obtained from the respective cumulative values.

The table provides values of $\Pr[X \leq x]$. For example, to find the cumulative probability values of the number of cars arriving at a tollbooth during an interval of $t = 10$ minutes when the arrival rate is $\lambda = 2$ per minute, we consult Appendix Table E where $\lambda t = 2(10) = 20$.

The probability that the number of arriving cars is ≤ 15 is

$$\Pr[X \leq 15] = .1565$$

| TABLE 4-8 | Poisson Probability Distribution for the Number of Arrivals at a Tollbooth in 1 Minute ($\lambda = 4, t = 1$) |

NUMBER OF ARRIVALS x	PROBABILITY Pr [X = x]
0	.0183
1	.0733
2	.1465
3	.1953
4	.1953
5	.1563
6	.1042
7	.0596
8	.0297
9	.0133
10	.0053
11	.0019
12	.0006
13	.0002
14	.0001
⋮	⋮
	1.0000

whereas the probability that ≤ 20 cars will arrive during the 10-minute interval is

$$\Pr[X \leq 20] = .5591$$

As with the cumulative binomial table, it is possible to obtain the individual term, the $>, <, \geq$, and interval Poisson probability values from Appendix Table E. For example, the probability that exactly 15 cars will arrive in 10 minutes is

$$\Pr[X = 15] = \Pr[X \leq 15] - \Pr[X \leq 14] = .1565 - .1049 = .0516$$

Similarly, we can obtain the probability that the number of cars arriving lies between two values. Thus, the probability that between 16 and 20 cars inclusively will arrive in 10 minutes is

$$\Pr[16 \leq X \leq 20] = \Pr[X \leq 20] - \Pr[X \leq 15] = .5591 - .1565 = .4026$$

And the probability that >20 cars will arrive is

$$\Pr[X > 20] = 1 - \Pr[X \leq 20] = 1 - .5591 = .4409$$

Using Spreadsheets to Find Poisson Probabilities

Excel uses the POISSON(x, mean, cumulative) function to calculate Poisson probabilities. The argument x stands for the number of events during some time period of duration t. The second argument is the mean number of events (λt). The last is a word variable set to TRUE when a cumulative probability is required and to FALSE when an individual probability (sometimes called the density function) is needed. Those probabilities are computed in a spreadsheet analogous to the one in Figure 4-13 for the normal distribution. Excel can also graph the Poisson probabilities as in Figure 4-17.

FIGURE 4-17

Spreadsheet and graph of the Poisson density function and the cumulative distribution for number of arrivals

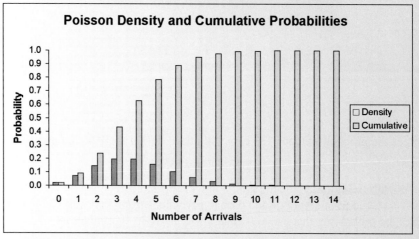

	A	B	C	D	E	F	G
1			**POISSON DISTRIBUTION**				
2							
3	Mean rate lambda =		4				
4	Duration t =		1				
5							
6	Number of	Density	Cumulative				
7	Arrivals	Function	Probability			B	
8	x	Pr[X=x]	Pr[X ≤ x]				
9	0	0.0183	0.0183	=POISSON(A9,$C$3*$C$4,FALSE)			
10	1	0.0733	0.0916	=POISSON(A10,$C$3*$C$4,FALSE)			
11	2	0.1465	0.2381	=POISSON(A11,$C$3*$C$4,FALSE)			
12	3	0.1954	0.4335	=POISSON(A12,$C$3*$C$4,FALSE)			
13	4	0.1954	0.6288	=POISSON(A13,$C$3*$C$4,FALSE)			
14	5	0.1563	0.7851	=POISSON(A14,$C$3*$C$4,FALSE)			
15	6	0.1042	0.8893	=POISSON(A15,$C$3*$C$4,FALSE)			
16	7	0.0595	0.9489	=POISSON(A16,$C$3*$C$4,FALSE)			
17	8	0.0298	0.9786	=POISSON(A17,$C$3*$C$4,FALSE)			
18	9	0.0132	0.9919	=POISSON(A18,$C$3*$C$4,FALSE)			
19	10	0.0053	0.9972	=POISSON(A19,$C$3*$C$4,FALSE)			
20	11	0.0019	0.9991	=POISSON(A20,$C$3*$C$4,FALSE)			
21	12	0.0006	0.9997	=POISSON(A21,$C$3*$C$4,FALSE)			
22	13	0.0002	0.9999	=POISSON(A22,$C$3*$C$4,FALSE)			
23	14	0.0001	1.0000	=POISSON(A23,$C$3*$C$4,FALSE)			

DECISION PROBLEM

Decision Problem Revisited: A Toll Bridge Evaluation

The questions posed earlier are answered below.

1. The following Poisson probabilities apply for the number of cars arriving within any 6-second time span (.1 minute). They are read from Appendix Table E.

	(1) WEEKDAY A.M. RUSH	(2) WEEKDAY P.M. RUSH	(3) SATURDAY AFTERNOON	(4) SUNDAY MORNING
λt	10	12	5	2
(a) Pr[X = 0]	.0000	.0000	.0067	.1353
(b) Pr[X = 1]	.0005	.0001	.0337	.2707
(c) Pr[X = 2]	.0023	.0004	.0843	.2707
(d) Pr[X = 3]	.0075	.0018	.1403	.1804
(e) Pr[X = 4]	.0190	.0053	.1755	.0902
(f) Pr[X ≥ 5]	.9707	.9924	.5595	.0527

2. The following exponential probabilities apply for the amount of time between successive arrivals.

	(1) WEEKDAY A.M. RUSH	(2) WEEKDAY P.M. RUSH	(3) SATURDAY AFTERNOON	(4) SUNDAY MORNING
$\Pr[T < 3 \text{ min.}]$	.9933	.9975	.9179	.6321
$\Pr[.01 \leq T \leq .04 \text{ min.}]$	.1170	.0825	.2325	.2210
$\Pr[T > .03 \text{ min.}]$	.0498	.0273	.2231	.5488

3. The normal distribution is used to obtain the following probabilities for the amount of time to collect a toll.

	(1) WEEKDAY A.M. RUSH	(2) WEEKDAY P.M. RUSH	(3) SATURDAY AFTERNOON	(4) SUNDAY MORNING
$\Pr[X < 10 \text{ sec.}]$	.2514	.5000	.1056	.0668
$\Pr[7 \leq X \leq 15 \text{ sec.}]$	.7938	.9270	.4772	.3891
$\Pr[X > 12 \text{ sec.}]$	.5000	.1587	.7734	.8413

4-7 (OPTIONAL) JUDGMENTAL ASSESSMENT OF THE PROBABILITY DISTRIBUTION*

The following steps apply for getting a subjective probability distribution when no historical frequencies are available:

1. Establish several fractile values based on judgment. This is usually done during an interview in which hypothetical 50-50 gambles are posed.
2. Sketch a curve for the cumulative probability distribution function.
3. Approximate the curve with a cumulative probability stairway having steps of equal width and varying size. The levels of the random variable at each step define the class intervals.
4. Use stairway step sizes as the probabilities for the class intervals.

The following illustration shows how this procedure may be carried out.

The president of a food manufacturing concern wishes to obtain the probability distribution for the demand for a new snack product. This will be used to help the president decide whether or not to market the product. A statistical analyst asks the president a series of questions to obtain answers that will be used to formulate later questions. The interview follows:**

---

*This optional section may be skipped with no loss of continuity.

**This procedure was inspired by Howard Raiffa, *Decision Analysis: Introductory Lectures on Choices under Uncertainty* (Reading, MA: Addison-Wesley, 1968).

Q. What do you think are the largest and smallest possible levels of demand?

A. Certainly demand will exceed 500,000 units. But I would set an upper limit of 3,000,000 units. I don't think that under the most favorable circumstances we could sell more than this amount.

Q. Okay, we have determined the range of possible demand. Now I want you to tell me what level of demand divides the possibilities into two equally likely ranges. For example, do you think demand will be just as likely to fall above 2,000,000 as below?

A. No. I'd rather pick 1,500,000 units as the 50-50 point.
(Aside: This establishes 1,500,000 as the median or .50-fractile. The subjective probability is .50 that demand will fall at or below this amount.)

Q. Very good. Now let's consider the demand levels below 1,500,000. If demand were to fall somewhere between 500,000 units and 1,500,000 units, would you bet that it lies above or below 1,000,000?

A. Above. I would say that a demand of 1,250,000 units would be a realistic dividing point.

Q. We will use that amount as our 50-50 point.
(Aside: Because there is a 50% chance for demand falling below 1,500,000 and a further 50% chance—given that demand lies in that range—for falling below 1,250,000, the subjective probability is $.50 \times .50 = .25$ that demand will be at or below 1,250,000. The .25-fractile is 1,250,000 units.)

Q. Let's do the same thing for the upper range of demand.

A. If I were to pick a number, I would choose 2,000,000 units. I feel that demand is just as likely to fall into the 1,500,000 to 2,000,000 range as into the 2,000,000 to 3,000,000 range.
(Aside: There is a $.50 + .25 = .75$ subjective probability for demand falling at or below 2,000,000 units, making that quantity the .75-fractile.)

Q. Excellent. We're making good progress. To get a finer fix on the points obtained so far, I now want you to tell me whether you think demand is just as likely to fall between 1,250,000 and 2,000,000 units as it is to fall outside that range.

A. No. I think it is more likely to fall inside. I suppose this means I am being inconsistent.

Q. Yes, it does. Let's remedy this. Do you think that we ought to raise the 1,250,000 dividing point or lower the 2,000,000 unit figure?

A. Lower the 2,000,000 figure to 1,900,000.

Q. Let's check to see if this disturbs our other answers. Do you think that 1,500,000 splits demand over the range from 1,250,000 to 1,900,000 into two equally likely regions?

A. Yes, I am satisfied that it does.
(Aside: the .75-fractile was repositioned at 1,900,000.)

Q. Just a few more questions. Suppose demand is above 1,900,000. What level splits this demand range into two equally likely regions?

A. I'd say 2,200,000.

Q. Good. Now if demand is between 2,200,000 and 3,000,000, where would you split?

A. I would guess that 2,450,000 units would be the 50-50 point.

Q. How about when demand is below 1,250,000?

A. Try 1,100,000 units.

TABLE 4-9	Judgmental Assessment of Fractiles for Snack Food Demand	
	FRACTILE	**AMOUNT**
	0	500,000
	.0625	950,000
	.125	1,100,000
	.25	1,250,000
	.50	1,500,000
	.75	1,900,000
	.875	2,200,000
	.9375	2,450,000
	1.000	3,000,000

Q. And when demand is between 500,000 and 1,100,000 units?

A. I think demand is far more likely to be close to the higher figure. I would bet on 950,000 units.

(Aside: The analyst has proceeded to find the medians of the regions by working outward from previously determined 50% points. Thus, the .125 fractile of 1,100,000 units is the median demand for possible levels below the .25 fractile [1,250,000 units], which had to be determined first. The median of demands above 1,900,000 units is the .875 fractile of 2,200,000 units. Similarly, the median of the demands below 1,100,000 is the .0625 fractile of 950,000 units, whereas the median demand level above 2,200,000 is the .9375 fractile of 2,450,000.)

Table 4-9 shows the information obtained from this interview. The fractiles and the corresponding demands are plotted as points in Figure 4-18. The vertical axis represents the cumulative probability for demand. A curve has been smoothed through these points, serving as an approximation of the cumulative probability distribution for the first-year demand for the snack product. The curve has an S shape; its slope increases initially and then decreases over higher levels of demand. The slope changes most rapidly for large and small demands, so that more points in these regions provide

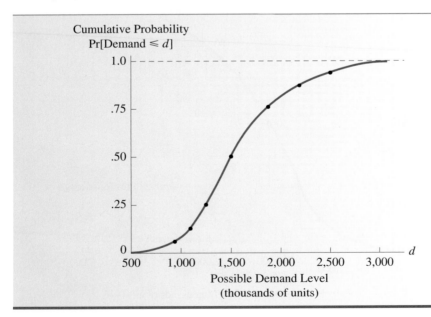

FIGURE 4-18

Cumulative probability distribution for a new snack product

greater accuracy. This is why we work outward from the median in assessing the demand fractiles.

This example illustrates how we can obtain a very detailed measurement of judgment by posing a few 50-50 gambles. As a rule of thumb, the seven fractile values ranging from .0625 to .9375 in Table 4-9 are adequate for this purpose.

Common Shapes of Subjective Probability Curves

Ordinarily, subjective probability distributions obtained by judgmental assessment provide S-shaped graphs that are elongated at either the top or the bottom. Such graphs represent underlying probability distributions that are skewed to the left or to the right. Although **skewed distributions** are most common for business and economic variables, a symmetrical distribution is also possible. Lumpy cumulative probability graphs with two stacked S-shaped curves are to be avoided. The corresponding frequency curve has the two-humped shape that typifies a **bimodal distribution.** Such distributions reflect some underlying nonhomogeneous influence that operates differently for the lower-valued possibilities than it does for the higher-valued possibilities.

Approximating the Subjective Probability Distribution

It is difficult to employ the cumulative S curve directly in decision analysis, where expected values must be determined. Expected values are ordinarily calculated from a table that lists the possible variable values and their probabilities. To obtain such a table, it is necessary to approximate the cumulative probability curve by the method shown in Figure 4-19.

FIGURE 4-19

Approximating the cumulative probability distribution using 10 intervals

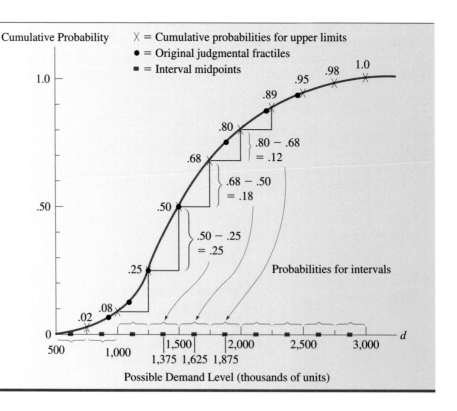

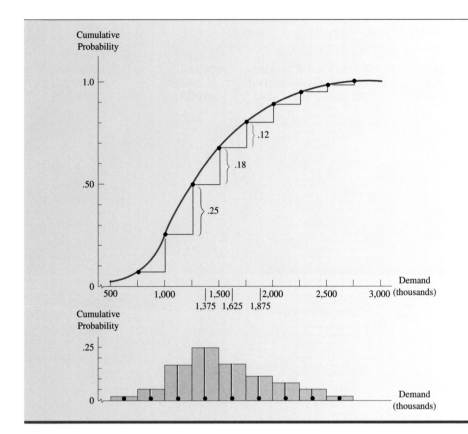

Each possible variable value is represented by an interval. A fairly accurate approximation is obtained with 10 intervals of equal width. The probabilities for each interval are shown as the step sizes at the upper limit for the respective interval. The probabilities for individual intervals are determined by the difference between successive cumulative probability values read directly off the graph. All values in an interval are represented by a typical value. For this purpose, the midpoint is used.

To see how this is done, suppose that the decision maker now wishes to establish subjective probabilities for intervals of demand from 500,000 to 3,000,000 units in increments of 250,000. Beginning with the first class interval (500,000–750,000), the cumulative probability at its upper limit is read to be .02 (marked with a cross). The second reading is .08, and so forth. The difference in successive cumulative probabilities is the probability for the respective class interval, represented by its midpoint.

A second graph in Figure 4-20 shows the cumulative probability stairway, with each step occurring at the representative level. It is not necessary to actually sketch the stairway, which would closely match the original cumulative distribution function curve when the number of steps is large.

Table 4-10 shows the resulting demand probabilities for the snack food demand. The resulting probability distribution can be used in further evaluations. From it, the approximate expected demand is computed to be 1,587,500 units.

The interval probabilities can be used to plot the histogram for demand shown in Figure 4-21. The height of .25 for the bar covering the interval from 1,250,000 to 1,500,000 units represents the probability that demand will fall somewhere between these amounts. Superimposed onto this histogram is a smoothed curve representing the

TABLE 4-10	Subjective Demand Probabilities and Approximating the Expected Demand			
(1) DEMAND INTERVAL (THOUSANDS)	(2) INTERVAL MIDPOINT (THOUSANDS)	(3) PROBABILITY FOR DEMANDS AT OR BELOW UPPER LIMIT (OBTAINED FROM CURVE)	(4) PROBABILITY FOR DEMAND INTERVAL	(5) DEMAND × PROBABILITY (2) × (4)
500 – 750	625	.02	.02	12.50
750 – 1,000	875	.08	.06	52.50
1,000 – 1,250	1,125	.25	.17	191.25
1,250 – 1,500	1,375	.50	.25	343.75
1,500 – 1,750	1,625	.68	.18	292.50
1,750 – 2,000	1,875	.80	.12	225.00
2,000 – 2,250	2,125	.89	.09	191.25
2,250 – 2,500	2,375	.95	.06	142.50
2,500 – 2,750	2,625	.98	.03	78.75
2,750 – 3,000	2,875	1.00	.02	57.50
			Approximate expected demand =	1,587.50

FIGURE 4-21

The frequency curve and the individual interval probabilities for snack food demand

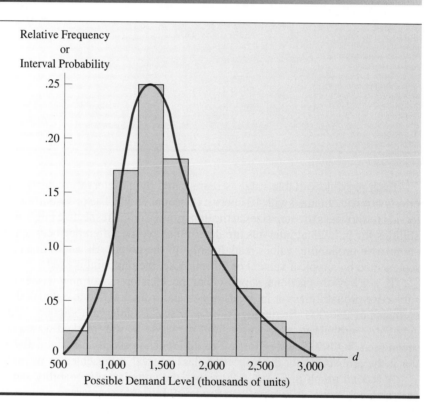

judgmental frequency (density) curve for demand. Note that the curve is positively skewed.

Computer-Assisted Distribution Fits

Chapter 17 discusses statistical tests for comparing data with theoretical probability distributions (in terms of either density functions or cumulative distributions) in order to find the one with the best fit. Software tools, such as RISKview, are useful for estimating probability distributions. RISKview provides a picture of more than thirty dif-

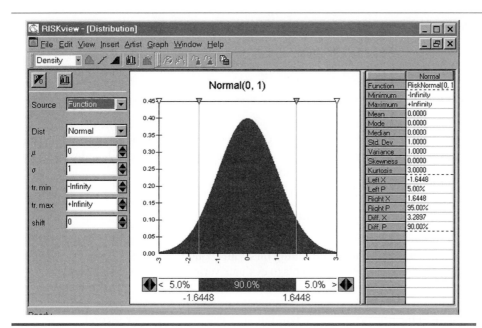

FIGURE 4-22
The standard normal distribution as shown by RISKview 4.0

ferent distributions with any set of parameters: beta, binomial, chi squared, error, Erlang, exponential, gamma, geometric, hypergeometric, logistic, log normal, negative binomial, normal, Pareto, PERT, Poisson, Rayleigh, Student t, triangular, uniform, and Weibull, among others. On opening RISKview (under Palisade Decision Tools on the CD-ROM accompanying the text), click on the RISKview 4.0 icon:

RISKview 4.0

A dialog box like the one in Figure 4-22 appears. Highlighting a distribution in the Distribution line and setting values for the parameters results in a graph of the distribution. Figure 4-22 shows the graph of a normal distribution with mean 0 and standard deviation 1. Clicking on the Graph in Excel icon (▨) exports the graph to an Excel spreadsheet.

Determining a Normal Curve Judgmentally

Any normal distribution is uniquely defined by two parameters—the mean μ and the standard deviation σ. Thus, by using judgment to find those parameters, we establish the entire probability distribution.

We begin with the mean, which is also the median because the normal curve is symmetrical about its center. Therefore, *the subjective mean μ is that point judged to have a 50-50 chance for any value of the variable X to lie at or above it versus below it.*

To illustrate, consider an engineer evaluating a new teleprocessing terminal design, the transmission rate for which is uncertain and assumed to be normally distributed. To get μ, the engineer need only find the 50-50 point for that quantity. After some introspection, she picks 50 lines per second. That establishes that $\mu = 50$.

Similarly, the standard deviation is based on a 50-50 *range,* rather than a single point. From the normal curve table, we find that the area between the mean and a point lying .67 standard deviations above the mean is .25, so that the normal curve area over $\mu \pm .67\sigma$ must be .50. The half-width of that interval, which is specified by the upper limit of that middle 50% region, determines the judgmental standard deviation.

JUDGMENTAL STANDARD DEVIATION

$$\sigma = \frac{\text{Upper limit} - \mu}{.67} = \frac{\text{Half-width}}{.67}$$

The engineer in our illustration is asked to supply that range. She determines it to be equally likely that the true transmission rate will fall somewhere within $\mu \pm 10$ lines per second. That establishes the half-width to be 10 lines per second, and we calculate the judgmental standard deviation to be

$$\sigma = \frac{10}{.67} = 14.9 \text{ lines per second}$$

The subjective probability distribution for the actual printing time of the proposed terminal is now specified. Combining this with economic data, the decision maker can then apply decision-theory concepts to evaluate various alternatives regarding the manufacturing or marketing of the proposed unit.

The engineer used the above parameters to compute the following subjective probability that the true printing rate will fall at or below 45 lines per second.

$$z = \frac{45 - 50}{14.9} = -.34 \text{ (rounded)}$$

$$\Pr[X \le 45] = .5 - .1331 = .3669$$

You may verify the following probabilities:

$$\Pr[45 \le X \le 70] = .5430$$
$$\Pr[X \le 70] = .0901$$

PROBLEMS

4-1 A silver dollar is tossed three times. Use the binomial formula to determine the probability distribution for the number of heads. Then, calculate the expected number of heads.

4-2 In roulette there are 38 slots, of which 18 are red, 18 are black, and 2 are green. A player may bet on red or on black, in which case he will win if the ball drops into a slot of matching color. (Every bettor loses if the ball drops into a green slot.) Determine the probability distribution for the winnings of a player who places a $1 bet on the red field. Then, calculate the expected winnings and state the meaning of your answer in words.

4-3 The following historical frequency distribution applies to dollar amounts for orders received by an Internet retailer.

Dollar Amount	Relative Frequency
$ 0– 20	.17
$20– 40	.13
$40– 60	.39
$60– 80	.25
$80–100	.06

You may assume that this pattern will continue in the future.
(a) Plot a cumulative probability distribution graph for the size of the next order.
(b) Read from your graph the probability that the order amount will be at or below (1) $15, (2) $25, (3) $75, (4) $85.

4-4 Consider the frequency distribution for order amounts in Problem 4-3. Use the class interval

midpoints to answer the following for the size of the next order.
(a) Compute the approximated expected dollar amount.
(b) Construct a cumulative probability stairway graph for dollar amount.

4-5 A pair of six-sided dice, one red and one green, are tossed. The sides of each die cube exhibit the values 1 through 6.
(a) List the elementary events in the sample space.
(b) List the possible sums of the dots showing on the upturned faces of the two cubes.
(c) For each answer to (b), indicate the elementary events that correspond to each possible sum value. Then, determine the probability for each sum.

4-6 Shirley Smart has assigned the following probabilities for her final grades.

	A	B	C
Statistics	.2	.8	0
Finance	0	.4	.6
Accounting	.5	.5	0
Marketing	0	.2	.8

(a) List all possible elementary events for Shirley's grades. Assuming independence between courses, apply the multiplication law to determine the probability for each elementary event.
(b) Assume that the following grade points are assigned:

$$A = 4 \quad B = 3 \quad C = 2$$

Determine Shirley's total grade points for each elementary event identified in (a). Then, for each possibility, compute her grade point average (GPA). Finally, construct a table summarizing her probability distribution for GPA.

4-7 Ty Kune wishes to buy stock to hold for one year in anticipation of capital gain. The choice has been narrowed down to High-Volatility Engineering and Stability Power. Both stocks currently sell for $100 per share and yield $5 dividends. The following probability distributions for next year's price have been judgmentally assessed for each stock.

High-Volatility Engineering		Stability Power	
Price	Probability	Price	Probability
$ 25	.05	$ 95	.10
50	.07	100	.25
75	.10	105	.50
100	.05	110	.15
125	.10		1.00
150	.15		
175	.12		
200	.10		
225	.12		
250	.14		
	1.00		

(a) Determine the expected price of a share of each stock.
(b) Should the investor select the stock with the highest expected value? Explain your answer.

4-8 The point spread for tossing two fair dice is the difference between the number of dots showing on the upturned faces. Determine the probability distribution for this random variable.

4-9 The following probability distribution table has been obtained for the number of persons arriving at Original Joe's during any specified minute between 8 and 9 P.M.

Persons	Probability
0	.4
1	.3
2	.2
3	.1
	1.0

Calculate the expected value and the variance for the number of persons arriving between 8:30 and 8:31 P.M.

4-10 A nervous numismatist tosses an evenly balanced double-eagle $20 gold piece seven times.
(a) Use the binomial formula to determine the probabilities for obtaining (1) exactly 2 heads, (2) exactly 4 heads, (3) no tails, and (4) exactly 3 tails.
(b) What do you notice about your answers to (2) and (4)? Why is this so?

4-11 Suppose that the proportion of product users favoring NuScents is $P = .70$. A random sample of

$n = 5$ users is selected. Use the binomial formula to determine the probabilities for the following number of users favoring NuScents:

(a) exactly five   (b) none   (c) exactly three

4-12 Peppermint Patty randomly selects n wafers from a production process that yields 5% defectives. What is the expected number of defectives when (a) $n = 5$, (b) $n = 10$, and (c) $n = 100$?

4-13 Refer to probability values in Table 4-7 (page 91). Construct the cumulative probability distribution table for the number of heads.

4-14 A fair coin is tossed 20 times in succession. Determine the probabilities for the following number of heads obtained:
(a) less than or equal to 8
(b) equal to 10
(c) less than 15
(d) greater than or equal to 12
(e) greater than 13
(f) between 8 and 14, inclusively

4-15 Bugoff Chemical Company's policy is that five sample vials be drawn from the final stage of a chemical process at random times over a 4-hour period. If one or more vials (20% or more) contain impurities, all the settling tanks are cleaned. Find the probability that the tanks will have to be cleaned when the process is so clean that the following probabilities for a dirty vial apply:
(a) $P = .01$ (c) $P = .20$
(b) $P = .05$ (d) $P = .50$
(*Hint:* Use the fact that Pr[at least 1 dirty vial] = $1 -$ Pr[no dirty vials].)

4-16 A process produces defective parts at the rate of .05. If a random sample of five items is selected, what is the probability that at least 80% of the sample will be defective?

4-17 You are handed a penny with Lincoln's beard filed off. There is now a 60% chance of a head on each toss. If the coin is tossed 20 times, find the probabilities for obtaining the following number of heads:
(a) less than or equal to 8
(b) equal to 9
(c) less than 15
(d) greater than or equal to 12
(e) greater than 13
(f) between 8 and 14, inclusively

4-18 Procrastinator Pete marks an examination consisting of 50 true-or-false questions by tossing a coin. Assuming that one-half of the correct answers should be marked true, find the probability that Pete will pass the examination by marking at least 60% of the answers correctly.

4-19 Errors in the measurement of the height of a weather satellite above a ground station are normally distributed with a mean of $\mu = 0$ and a standard deviation of $\sigma = 1$ mile. These errors will be negative if the measured altitude is too low and positive if the altitude is too high. Find the probability that for the next orbit the error will fall in the following ranges:
(a) between 0 and $+1.55$ miles
(b) between -2.45 and 0 miles
(c) $+.75$ miles or less
(d) greater than $+.75$ miles
(e) -1.25 miles or less
(f) greater than -1.25 miles
(g) between $+.10$ and $+.60$ miles
(h) between $+1$ and $+2$ miles

4-20 The lifetimes of Spinex floppy discs are normally distributed, with a mean of $\mu = 1,000$ hours and a standard deviation of $\sigma = 100$ hours. Find the probability for each of the following lifetime outcomes for one drive unit:
(a) between 1,000 and 1,150 hours
(b) between 950 and 1,000 hours
(c) 930 hours or less
(d) more than 1,250 hours
(e) 870 hours or less
(f) longer than 780 hours
(g) between 700 and 1,200 hours
(h) between 750 and 850 hours

4-21 Creative Robotics recommends that machine shops shut down an automatic lathe for corrective maintenance whenever a sample of the parts it produces has an average diameter greater than 2.01 inches or smaller than 1.99 inches. The lathe is designed to produce parts with a mean diameter of 2.00 inches, and the sample averages have a standard deviation of .005 inch. Assume that the normal distribution applies.
(a) What is the probability that the lathe is shut down when operating as designed, with $\mu = 2.00$ inches?
(b) If the lathe begins to produce parts that on the average are too wide, with $\mu = 2.02$ inches,

what is the probability that the lathe will continue to operate?

(c) If an adjustment error causes the lathe to produce parts that on the average are too narrow, with $\mu = 1.99$ inches, what is the probability that the lathe will be stopped?

4-22 The controller mechanism filling jars of Skater Aid is adjusted whenever the mean of sample jars is more than 1/2 ounce under or over the intended mean of 32 ounces. The filling process has a standard deviation of .2 ounce per jar for means.
(a) What is the probability that the controller will be adjusted when it is operating as intended?
(b) What is the probability that the controller will be adjusted when it overfills each jar by an average of 1 ounce?

4-23 On Tuesday mornings, customers arrive at the Central Valley National Bank at a rate of $\lambda = 1$ per minute. What is the probability that the time between the next two successive arrivals will be (a) shorter than 1 minute; (b) longer than 5 minutes; (c) between 2 and 5 minutes?

4-24 During the late Friday rush at the Central Bank in Problem 4-23, an average of $\lambda = 5$ customers arrive per minute. What is the probability that no customers will arrive during a specified 1-minute interval?

4-25 Soap Opera Updates receives calls between 9 and 10 A.M. during weekdays at the rate of $\lambda = 3$ per minute. Find the probabilities that the number of calls received in any interval of
(a) $t = 2$ minutes will be equal to 3.
(b) $t = 1$ minute will be equal to 0.
(c) $t = 1.5$ minutes will be equal to 4.
(d) $t = 1$ minute will be at least 1.

4-26 In each of the following situations, find the probabilities that the stated number of events occur. Assume a Poisson process with $\lambda = 8$ per hour when the following durations are considered:
(a) $t = 2$ hours; 10 or fewer events
(b) $t = 1.5$ hours; 6 or more events
(c) $t = 1$ hour; exactly 3 events
(d) $t = .125$ hour; between 1 and 5 events

4-27 Sally Strokes commits typing errors at a rate of .01 per word. Assuming that a Poisson process applies, find the probabilities for each of the following numbers of errors made in a 500-word letter:
(a) exactly 5   (c) more than 10
(b) 0   (d) between 3 and 7

4-28 An automobile production manager believes that the time it takes to install a new car bumper is normally distributed. He has established that it is a 50-50 proposition that this task will take more than 60 seconds and that it is "even money" that the required time for any particular car will be between 45 and 75 seconds.
(a) Calculate the mean and the standard deviation of the subjective probability distribution.
(b) Find the probabilities that the installation for a particular car will take
  (1) between 50 and 70 seconds.
  (2) less than 25 seconds.
  (3) more than 1 minute.
  (4) between 20 and 90 seconds.

4-29 The yield of an active ingredient from a chemical process is assumed to be normally distributed. The 50-50 point is 30 grams per liter. The interquartile range (middle 50%) spans 4 grams per liter.
(a) Calculate the mean and the standard deviation of the subjective probability distribution.
(b) Find the probability that the yield falls (1) below 29 grams; (2) between 28.5 and 30.5 grams; (3) above 31.5 grams.

4-30 The dean of The Dover School of Business is assessing the probability distribution for next term's grade point average (GPA) for the entire school. It is "even money" that the GPA will fall at or below 2.75. The dean assigns a 50-50 probability that the low side will be at or below 2.70 and that the high side will be at or above 2.80. If the GPA is lower than 2.70, it is a coin-tossing proposition that it will fall at or below 2.60; similarly, the odds are even that the GPA will fall at or above 2.95, given that it lies above 2.80. Find the subjective probability that the GPA will lie within the following limits:
(a) 2.60 and 2.95   (c) 2.60 and 2.75
(b) 2.70 and 2.80   (d) 2.75 and 2.95

4-31 Establish your own subjective probability distribution for the heights of adult males residing within 50 miles of your campus. Use the normal curve that you obtain to establish the probabili-

ties that a randomly chosen man is (a) less than 6'2"; (b) taller than 5'6"; (c) taller than your father.

4-32   Consider the cumulative probability distribution in Figure 4-23 to determine the following probabilities:
(a) $\Pr[D > 500]$
(b) $\Pr[D \leq 150]$
(c) $\Pr[D \geq 300]$
(d) $\Pr[200 \leq D \leq 800]$

4-33   Consider the cumulative probability distribution in Figure 4-23 to determine the following fractiles:
(a) .10   (b) .50   (c) .125   (d) .75   (e) .37

4-34   The following fractiles apply to the subjective probability distribution for the demand for a new product.

Fractile	Quantity
.0625	10,000
.125	25,000
.25	35,000
.50	40,000
.75	45,000
.875	55,000
.9375	75,000

Determine the probabilities that demand will fall within these limits.
(a) 10,000 to 40,000   (c) 25,000 to 55,000
(b) 35,000 to 75,000   (d) 25,000 to 45,000

4-35   Willy B. Rich is a real estate investor who has established the following judgmental results regarding the rate of return on a proposed project. No value less than -20% or greater than 50% is possible.

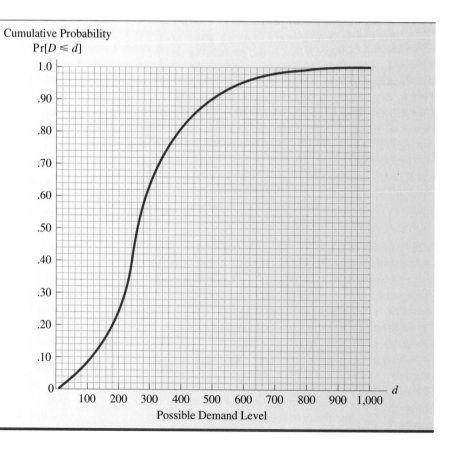

FIGURE 4-23

Cumulative probability distribution for demand

Rate of Return	50-50 Point
all	15%
below 15%	7
above 15%	20
below 7%	3
above 20%	24
below 3%	– 4
above 24%	28

(a) Complete the following table for the investor.

Fractile	Rate of Return
0	
.0625	
.125	
.25	
.50	
.75	
.875	
.9375	
1.000	

(b) Plot the cumulative probability distribution for the investor's rate of return.

(c) From your graph, find the investor's subjective probability that the rate of return is between 20% and 40%.

4-36 Envision your income during the first full calendar year after graduation. Establish your own subjective probability distribution for the adjusted gross income figure that you will report to the IRS. (If applicable, include your spouse's earnings, interest, dividends, and other income.) If your graph has an unusual shape, try to eliminate any inconsistencies or to identify the nonhomogeneous factors (such as pregnancy, unemployment, or divorce) that might explain the shape. Remember, you are the expert about yourself.

4-37 Consider the total size of the U.S. car market (passenger cars are sold — both imported and domestic) from October of the current year to the following October. Establish your subjective probability distribution for this quantity, and plot the results on a cumulative probability graph.

4-38 Consider the cumulative probability distribution for demand in Figure 4-23. Construct the approximate probability distribution for demand, using five intervals in increments of 200. Select the midpoints of these intervals as representative values, and determine the approximate expected demand.

Spreadsheet Problems

4-39 Calculate 100! and 200! using FACT(n) and then find the biggest factorial that Excel can handle (i.e., the largest n possible).

4-40 Use COMBIN (n,r) (the number of combinations of n objects taken r at a time) to find COMBIN (1000,500), COMBIN(2000,500), COMBIN (10000,100), and COMBIN(100000,100) and then find the largest n that Excel can handle for $r = 500$ and for $r = 100$.

4-41 A company has two job openings. Use a spreadsheet formula to find the number of combinations of two individuals who might work for the company if
(a) 3 applicants have applied for the two positions.
(b) 10 applicants have applied for the two positions.
(c) 20 applicants have applied for the two positions.
(d) 100 applicants have applied for the two positions.

4-42 A local shopping mall has five empty sites available to rent to new tenants. Use a spreadsheet formula to find the number of combinations of companies there could be at the mall in these five sites if
(a) 10 companies wish to rent a space.
(b) 30 companies wish to rent a space.
(c) 100 companies wish to rent a space.

4-43 (a) Solve Problem 4-1 using a spreadsheet to find the binomial probabilities (as in Figure 4-8).
(b) Compute expected value, variance, and standard deviation (as in Figure 4-2).
(c) Use a spreadsheet to draw a bar chart representing the binomial probabilities.

4-44 (a) Solve Problem 4-10 using a spreadsheet to find the binomial probabilities (as in Figure 4-8).
(b) Compute expected value, variance, and standard deviation (as in Figure 4-2).
(c) Use a spreadsheet to draw a bar chart representing the binomial probabilities.

4-45 (a) Solve Problem 4-17 using a spreadsheet to find the binomial probabilities (as in Figure 4-8).
(b) Compute expected value, variance, and standard deviation (as in Figure 4-2).
(c) Use a spreadsheet to draw a bar chart representing the binomial probabilities.

4-46 (a) Solve Problem 4-18 using a spreadsheet to find the binomial probabilities (as in Figure 4-8).
(b) Compute expected value, variance, and standard deviation (as in Figure 4-2).
(c) Use a spreadsheet to draw a bar chart representing the binomial probabilities.

4-47 (a) Solve Problem 4-19 using a spreadsheet to find the normal frequency curve and cumulative distribution (as in Figure 4-13).
(b) Use a spreadsheet to draw a graph of the normal frequency curve and cumulative distribution.

4-48 (a) Solve Problem 4-20 using a spreadsheet to find the normal frequency curve and cumulative distribution (as in Figure 4-13).
(b) Use a spreadsheet to draw a graph of the normal frequency curve and cumulative distribution.

4-49 (a) Solve Problem 4-23 using a spreadsheet to find the exponential frequency curve and cumulative distribution.
(b) Use a spreadsheet to draw a graph of the exponential frequency curve and cumulative distribution.

4-50 Bell Computer Corporation sells computers and software via the Internet. It has a Technical Support Department to answer questions and help customers with problems. The length of time a technical support representative spends handling a customer call follows an exponential distribution with a mean of 2 minutes. Use a spreadsheet to find the exponential frequency curve and cumulative distibution and answer the following questions:
(a) What is the probability that a call takes 1 minute or less?
(b) What is the probability that a call takes 3 or more minutes?
(c) What is the probability that a call takes between 1 and 3 minutes?

(d) Use a spreadsheet to draw a graph of the exponential frequency curve and cumulative distribution.

4-51 (a) Solve Problem 4-24 using a spreadsheet to find the Poisson distribution and cumulative Poisson distribution.
(b) What is the probability that two customers will arrive in a 1-minute interval?
(c) What is the probability that three or fewer customers will arrive in a 1-minute interval?
(d) What is the probability that more than three customers will arrive in a 1-minute interval?
(e) Use a spreadsheet to draw a bar chart of the Poisson distribution and the Poisson cumulative distribution.

4-52 In Problem 4-50 calls arrive at Bell Corporation's Technical Support Department at the rate of $\lambda = 10$ per minute. Use a spreadsheet to find the Poisson distribution and cumulative Poisson distribution and answer the following questions:
(a) What is the probability that no customers call during a 1-minute interval?
(b) What is the probability that 10 or fewer customers call in a 1-minute interval?
(c) What is the probability that more than 10 customers call during a 1-minute interval?
(d) Use a spreadsheet to draw a bar chart of the Poisson distribution and the Poisson cumulative distribution.

4-53 Use RISKview to answer the following questions. Suppose a coin is tossed five times.
(a) Find a graph of this distribution.
(b) What are the mean, median, and variance of the distribution?
(c) Find the graphs for six, seven, eight, nine, and ten tosses of a coin.
(d) What is the probability of two or fewer heads?
(e) What is the probability of all heads?

4-54 Use RISKview to answer the following questions for the normal curve in Problem 4-20 (with mean 1,000 and standard deviation of 100).
(a) Find the graph of this distribution.
(b) Answer parts (a)–(h) in Problem 4-20.

4-55 Use RISKview to answer the following questions for the exponential distribution in Figure 4-16 (with $\lambda = 4$ cars per minute).

(a) Find the graph that corresponds to the frequency curve. Note that β in RISKview is equal to $1/\lambda = 1/4$.

(b) What is the probability the interarrival time is 30 seconds or less?

(c) What is the probability that the interarrival time is more than one minute?

(d) What happens to the exponential frequency curve as the arrival rate λ decreases to 1 car per minute?

(e) What happens to the exponential frequency curve as the arrival rate λ increases to 10 cars per minute?

4-56 Use RISKview to answer the following questions for the Poisson distribution in Problem 4-24 (with $\lambda = 5$ customers per hour).

(a) Find the graph that corresponds to the density function.

(b) What is the probability that no customers arrive during a minute?

(c) What is the probability that eight or fewer customers arrive during a minute?

(d) What is the probability that eight or more customers arrive during a minute?

(e) What happens to the Poisson distribution when the arrival rate λ decreases to one customer per minute?

(f) What happens to the Poisson distribution when the arrival rate λ increases to 10 customers per minute?

CASE 4-1 *Brand Nu Soft Drink*

by Gerald J. Maxwell
San Jose State University

The Capital Works Corporation, manufacturer of a variety of soft drinks, including the Brand Nu soft drink, is running a series of market tests in several foreign countries as part of a program to determine whether or not to establish small marketing outlets in these areas. After completing market tests and negotiations, it typically takes 6 to 9 months to establish the marketing outlets and begin selling.

A crucial parameter for determining marketing actions is the proportion P of persons in any country who truly prefer Brand Nu over the competition. The following data are judged to apply for untested countries not now importing Brand Nu.

Country	Expected Value for P	Standard Deviation for P
Albania	.35	.10
Costa Rica	.45	.09
Finland	.40	.10
Nigeria	.55	.15
Sri Lanka	.60	.18
Sudan	.25	.03

The level for P itself is uncertain, and a normal distribution is assumed for the P for any country.

The goal in a series of sample taste tests undertaken is to estimate the extent of population preferences between the Brand Nu soft drink and a drink manufactured by a competitor. Persons participating in the sample testing are asked to state their preference between the two drinks, which are placed in separate containers that bear no indication of brand name. Taste testing has been done in the following countries:

Country	Number of Subjects n	Number Preferring Brand Nu
Algeria	20	3
Botswana	50	28
Cameroon	100	42
Djibouti	50	36
Ethiopia	100	32

Capital Works will enter a small country's market if the probability of breaking even in the first year is sufficiently high. The breakeven level is 450,000 cases per year.

QUESTIONS

1. Capital Works will test a country's soft drink market only if there is at least a 90% chance that the true proportion who prefer the brand is .30 or more. Determine which *untested* countries will be tested with Brand Nu. Substantiate your answers.

2. Determine for each test country the probability of getting the observed number or more to choose Brand Nu when the true proportion who prefer the drink is actually (1) $P = .10$; (2) $P = .20$; (3) $P = .30$; (4) $P = .40$.

3. The exact probability of breaking even in Ethiopia is unknown, but it may be computed using assumed levels for the mean and standard deviation for annual customer demand. Assuming that the normal distribution applies, determine the probability of breaking even in each of the following cases:
(a) $\mu = 500,000$ and $\sigma = 100,000$
(b) $\mu = 600,000$ and $\sigma = 75,000$
(c) $\mu = 650,000$ and $\sigma = 90,000$
(d) $\mu = 400,000$ and $\sigma = 85,000$

4. In one country, the sample proportion of persons who favor Brand Nu drinks is very close to 100%. You have been asked to prepare a report indicating the possible interpretations of these results.

CASE   4-2   *The Permian Plunge*

 Rod Shafter is a geologist who has formed a series of limited partnerships engaging in wildcat drilling for oil and gas. While evaluating a leasehold site in the Permian Basin of West Texas, Shafter employs Cal Crunch as a consultant. Crunch is to provide numbers useful for deciding whether the partnership should take the plunge and sink a wildcat shaft there.

The initial uncertainty pertains to whether a proper structural environment for fossil fuels exists beneath the site. Given the proper structure, there is some probability that the site will contain gas only, oil only, a combination of oil and gas, or neither. Shafter does not feel comfortable about arriving at the correct values for these probabilities. Crunch reassures him that satisfactory numbers can be "pulled out of thin air" using a box of marbles as a prop.

Even if there is oil or gas, Rod is uncertain about the recoverable quantities. Crunch plans to show him how to determine subjective probability distributions for each case. He plans to achieve this by conducting an interview that will "quantify Shafter's judgments."

QUESTIONS

1. With Cal's help, Rod arrives at the following probabilities:

$$\Pr[\text{structure}] = .40$$
$$\Pr[\text{oil only} \mid \text{structure}] = .10$$
$$\Pr[\text{gas only} \mid \text{structure}] = .05$$
$$\Pr[\text{oil } and \text{ gas} \mid \text{structure}] = .20$$
$$\Pr[\text{neither} \mid \text{structure}] = .65$$

Determine the probability that the site contains the following. (Structure must be present in order for oil or gas to have formed.)
(a) oil only   (c) oil and gas
(b) gas only   (d) neither

2. Gas is measured in units of thousand cubic feet (mcf). Rod estimates that given gas (with or without oil), there is a 50–50 chance that the field contains 100 million mcf of recoverable gas reserves. He judges that should the quantity be higher than 100 million mcf, there is an even chance that reserves will be at or below 150 million mcf; should it be lower than 100 million, there is a 50–50 chance that the field will yield at or below 75 million mcf. Above 150 million the median level is 250 million mcf, while below 75 million mcf the median is 60 million mcf. Should there be more than 250 million mcf, it is "even money" that the level of reserves will lie above or below 400 million mcf, and should there be less than 60 million mcf, it is even money again that reserves will be at or below 50 million mcf. Assuming some gas, it is virtually certain that the field will contain more than 25 million mcf and less than 750 million mcf.
(a) Construct a graph showing the cumulative probability distribution.
(b) Starting at 0 as the lower limit and using 8 intervals each at a width of 100 million mcf, construct a table approximating the cumulative probability distribution.
(c) Using your answer to (b), compute the expected level of gas reserves.

3. Oil is measured in barrels. Rod estimates that given oil (with or without gas), there is a 50–50 chance that the field contains 300,000 recoverable barrels of oil. He judges that should the quantity be higher than that level, there is an even chance that reserves are at or below 400,000 barrels; should it be lower than 300,000, there is a 50–50 chance that the field will yield at or below 250,000 barrels. Above 400,000 barrels the median level is 550,000 barrels, while below 250,000 the median is 220,000 barrels. Should there be more than 550,000 barrels, it is even money that the level of reserves will lie above or below 750,000 barrels, and should there be less than 220,000 barrels, it is even money again that reserves will be at or below 200,000 barrels. Assuming some oil, it is virtually certain that the field will contain more than 100,000 and less than 1,000,000 barrels of oil.

(a) Construct a graph showing the cumulative probability distribution.

(b) Starting at 50,000 barrels as the lower limit and using 10 intervals each at a width of 100,000 barrels, construct a table that approximates the cumulative probability distribution.

(c) Using your answer to (b), compute the expected level of oil reserves.

CHAPTER 5

DECISION-MAKING CONCEPTS

There is no more miserable human being than one in whom nothing is habitual but indecision.
William James

T he central focus of this book is on the use of quantitative methods in decision making. This chapter considers the structure of decisions in general. We make a basic distinction between decision making under *certainty,* where no elements are left to chance, and decision making under *uncertainty,* where one or more random factors affect the outcome of a decision.

Modern analysis of decision making under uncertainty has its roots in the area of study called **decision theory.** A primary focus of decision theory is establishing systematic means for choosing an act, which is largely accomplished by using a payoff table. Various **decision-making criteria** may be employed in selecting the best act. The payoff measure itself is a key element in determining rules for decision making, and decision theory encompasses a variety of these measures.

We will begin our discussion of decision theory by examining some of the well-known criteria used in selecting a best act. Then, we will describe **opportunity loss**— a payoff measure that enables us to assess the worth of the *information* that is obtained about uncertain events. The chapter concludes with a discussion of **decision trees.** These analytical tools are especially helpful for evaluating more complex decisions involving a series of choices and intervening uncertainty.

DECISION PROBLEM

Software Copyright Infringement

Klaus DeBugger is the founder of SoftWhereHaus, a start-up software publishing company. The company's major product is the securities evaluation package, *Opt-a-Miser.* Version 1.0 of this program has been a moderate success. A variety of enhancements are contemplated for version 2.0, the release of which could be a vital boost to SoftWhereHaus' future.

Unfortunately, Exploiteers, Inc. has developed a competing package called *Max-a-Myser.* DeBugger claims that this package has the "look and feel" of *Opt-a-Miser,* substantially violating SoftWhereHaus' copyright. He is contemplating retaliatory action.

DeBugger's immediate choices are (1) to negotiate with the help of a mediator (whose fee is $10,000), (2) to litigate (requiring a $20,000 nonrefundable attorney retainer), or (3) to ignore Exploiteers. Ultimately, SoftWhereHaus will either sell the program rights to GrossHaus for an amount dependent on what prior events transpire or

keep the program and develop version 2.0 (at a cost of $20,000). Version 2.0 of *Opt-a-Miser* may be assumed to result in a success (culminating in enhanced profits having a present value of $200,000) or in a weak marketplace reception (yielding only $20,000).

Negotiation may bring about a favorable or unfavorable settlement. With a favorable outcome (50% chance), SoftWhereHaus may sell program ownership for $75,000; releasing instead version 2.0 will provide a 70% chance of success. An unfavorable negotiation result will drastically reduce the selling price to $20,000 and will lower the success probability of version 2.0 to .25.

Litigation may have three results: positive (40% chance), neutral (30% chance), or negative (30% chance). The following data apply in that case.

	LITIGATION RESULT		
	Positive	**Neutral**	**Negative**
V-2.0 success probability	.8	.5	.15
Proceeds from sale	$100,000	$50,000	$15,000

Ignoring Exploiteers will of course involve no unusual cash expenditure. In that case, there would be a 50-50 chance for version 2.0 success versus a weak reception, and GrossHaus will give DeBugger $50,000 to gain ownership of the unrevised *Opt-a-Miser*.

In this chapter, we will develop tools that Klaus DeBugger can use to determine what course of action appears most promising. Later, we will revisit SoftWhereHaus with a concrete analysis.

5-1 CERTAINTY AND UNCERTAINTY IN DECISION MAKING

The least complex applications of decision theory are encountered when conditions are certain. Perhaps the simplest example of *decision making under certainty* is selecting what clothes to wear. Although the possibilities are numerous, we all manage to make this choice quickly and with little effort. But not all decisions are this easy to make. Remember how hard it was to choose from among an assortment of candy bars when you were a child? Not all decisions made under certainty are as trivial as choosing the day's apparel. Consider a Petroleum Company trying to decide whether a gasification or pressurization process is best for making low- and high-sulfur crude oil; or a sporting goods firm choosing how many 30-, 32-, 34-, 36-, 38-, and 40-inch bats to produce in order to maximize profit. Such decision-making situations are encountered in Part II of this book.

This chapter focuses on making decisions in the face of uncertainty. When the outcomes are only partly determined by choice, the decision-making process takes on an added complexity. So that we can see what is involved in structuring a decision under uncertainty, we will consider the choice of whether to carry an umbrella or some other rain protection. Here, we are faced with two alternatives: carrying an ungainly item that can, in the event of rain, help to defer a cleaning bill or a cough, or challenging the elements with hands free and hoping not to be caught in the rain. Because the weather prediction may be inaccurate, we are uncertain about whether it will rain. This illustrates a common decision made under uncertainty: An action must be taken, even though its outcome is unknown and determined by chance.

5-2 ELEMENTS OF DECISIONS

Decisions made under certainty exhibit two elements —**acts** and **outcomes.** The decision maker's choices are the acts. For example, when one must choose among three television programs in the 9 P.M. time slot, each program represents a potential act. The outcomes may be characterized in terms of the enjoyment we derive from each of the programs.

If the decision is made under uncertainty, a third element, **events,** exists. Continuing with our uncertainty about the rain, the acts are "carry an umbrella" and "leave the umbrella home." All decisions involve the selection of an act. But the outcomes resulting from each act are uncertain, because *an outcome is determined partly by choice and partly by chance.* For the act "carry an umbrella" there are two possible outcomes: (1) unnecessarily carting rain paraphernalia and (2) weathering a shower fully protected. For the other act, "leave the umbrella at home," the two outcomes are (1) getting wet unnecessarily and (2) remaining dry and unencumbered. Again, whether the first or second outcome occurs depends solely on the occurrence of rain. The outcome for any particular chosen act depends on which *event,* rain or no rain, occurs.

The Decision Table

To facilitate our analysis, we may summarize a decision problem by constructing a **decision table** that indicates the relationship between pairs of decision elements. The decision table for the umbrella decision is provided in Table 5-1. Each row corresponds to an event, and each column corresponds to an act. The outcomes appear as entries in the table body. There is a specific outcome for each act–event combination, reflecting that the interplay between act and event determines the ultimate result.

Only the acts that the decision maker wants to consider are included in this decision table. "Staying home" is another possible act, which we will exclude because it is not contemplated. The acts in Table 5-1 are mutually exclusive and collectively exhaustive, so that exactly one act will be chosen. The events in the table are also mutually exclusive and collectively exhaustive.

The Decision Tree Diagram

A decision problem may also be conveniently illustrated with a **decision tree diagram** like the one shown in Figure 5-1. The decision tree diagram is similar to the probability tree diagrams we used in Chapters 3 and 4. The choice of acts is shown as a fork with a separate branch for each act. The events are represented by separate branches in other forks. We distinguish between these two types of branching points, using squares for **act-fork nodes** and circles for **event-fork nodes.** A basic guideline for construct-

TABLE 5-1   Decision Table for the Umbrella Decision

EVENT	ACT	
	Carry Umbrella	**Leave Umbrella Home**
Rain	Stay dry	Get wet
No Rain	Carry unnecessary burden	Be dry and free

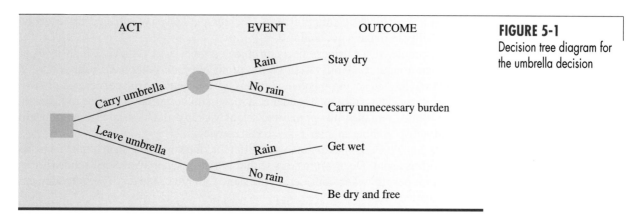

FIGURE 5-1
Decision tree diagram for the umbrella decision

ing a decision tree diagram is that the flow should be chronological from left to right. The acts are shown on the initial fork, because the decision must be made *before* the actual event is known. The events are therefore shown as branches in the second-stage forks. The outcome resulting from each act–event combination is shown as the end position of the corresponding path from the base of the tree.

5-3 RANKING THE ALTERNATIVES AND THE PAYOFF TABLE

In this chapter, we will consider how the choice of an act should be determined. We all cope with rain and manage to make umbrella decisions. But if we analyze the decision-making process, we will be able to make better decisions under more complex circumstances. Our analysis will focus on two measures: one for *uncertainty* and one for the *comparative worth* or **payoff** of the outcomes for the decision maker.

For now, we will consider examples with outcomes that have obvious payoffs, such as dollars. Every outcome — that is, every act–event combination — has a *payoff value*. These values may be conveniently arranged in a **payoff table**, as shown in Table 5-2 for a gambling decision. The decision is to choose one of two acts: "gamble" or "don't gamble." Regardless of the choice made, a coin will be tossed, which will result in one of two possible events: "head" or "tail." The possible outcomes correspond to the four act–event combinations. A wager of $1 will be made if the decision maker chooses to gamble, and net winnings will be the payoff measure.

Objectives and Payoff Values

In determining appropriate payoffs, we will assume that decision makers will choose to take actions that will bring them closest to their objectives. Each outcome must somehow be ranked in terms of how close it is to the decision maker's goal. The payoff

TABLE 5-2 Payoff Table for a Gambling Decision

	ACT	
EVENT	**Gamble**	**Don't Gamble**
Head	$1	$0
Tail	−1	0

table should provide a meaningful basis for comparison and enhance the decision maker's ability to make a good choice.

For example, if a business decision maker's goal is to achieve a high level of profits, then a natural payoff would be the profit for each outcome. Profit is a valid measure for a limited set of objectives, but it is by no means the top concern of all business managers. The goal of the founder of a successful corporation may be to maintain personal control, and the founder may consciously keep profits low so that the firm will not be attractive to other merger-minded entrepreneurs.

In general, decision making involves different kinds of goals, each requiring a distinct payoff measure. Decision makers with different goals may even select dissimilar measures for payoffs when considering the same set of alternatives. The following example illustrates this.

DECISION APPLICATION

Finding the Way to San Francisco

Charles Snyder, Herman Brown, and Sylvia Gold want to choose one of three routes from Los Angeles to San Francisco: (1) Interstate 5, which is a freeway all the way and has a high minimum speed limit; (2) State Highways 118 and 33, which are fairly direct and have no minimum speed limit; and (3) State Highway 1, which winds along the Pacific coast and is slow and long but very beautiful. Mr. Snyder is a salesman who travels to San Francisco regularly; his goal is to reach his destination as quickly as possible. Mr. Brown is an economy "nut"; he wants to reach San Francisco as cheaply as possible. Ms. Gold is on vacation and loves to drive on hilly, winding, scenic roads; she wants to select the route that provides the greatest driving pleasure.

THE PROBLEM SOLUTION

The payoffs that each person would assign to the three routes appear in Table 5-3. Time savings is Mr. Snyder's payoff measure, so he chooses Interstate 5, which yields the greatest payoff of 4 hours. Mr. Brown likes to drive at a moderate speed to obtain maximum gasoline mileage, while taking the shortest route possible. His payoff measure is fuel savings (based on the amount of gasoline required on the most expensive route), so he chooses the back roads, State Highways 118 and 33, to save 7 gallons of gas. Ms. Gold has rated the routes in terms of points of interest, types of scenery, and number of hills and curves. This rating serves as her payoff measure, so her best route is scenic State Highway 1, which rates 10.

TABLE 5-3   Payoffs for the Alternative Routes Relevant to the Goals of Three Decision Makers

	PAYOFF MEASURE		
	MR. SNYDER	MR. BROWN	MS. GOLD
ALTERNATIVE ROUTE	Time Savings (hours)	Fuel Savings (gallons)	Enjoyment (subjective rating)
Interstate 5	4	3	1
Highways 118 & 33	3	7	3
Highway 1	0	0	10

We conclude that *a payoff measure should be selected so that the payoff will rank outcomes by the degree to which they attain the decision maker's goals.* The goal dictates which payoff measures are valid.

Illustration: Choosing a Movement for Tippi-Toes

As a detailed example of a business decision made under uncertainty, we will consider a hypothetical toy manufacturer who must choose among four prototype designs for Tippi-Toes, a dancing ballerina doll that does pirouettes and jetés. Each prototype represents a different technology for the moving parts, all powered by small, battery-operated motors. One prototype is a complete arrangement of gears and levers. The second is similar, with springs instead of levers. Another works on the principle of weights and pulleys. The movement of the fourth design is controlled pneumatically through a system of valves that open and close at the command of a small, solid-state computer housed in the head cavity. The dolls are identical in all functional aspects.

The choice of the movement design will be based solely on a comparison of the contributions to profits made by the four prototypes. The payoff table is provided in Table 5-4. The demand for Tippi-Toes is uncertain, but management feels that one of the following events will occur:

Light demand	(25,000 units)
Moderate demand	(100,000 units)
Heavy demand	(150,000 units)

The toy manufacturer in this example is considering only three possible events — here, levels of demand — which greatly simplifies our analysis. Demand does not have to be precisely 25,000 or 100,000 units, however. The problem could be analyzed at several hundred thousand possible levels of demand — say, from 0 to 500,000 dolls. The techniques we will develop here may be applied to a more detailed situation. Due to the computational requirements, the demand probability distribution could be approximated to the nearest 100, 1,000, or 10,000 units.

Similarly, our example has only four alternatives. In the practical, business decision-making environment, the number of possible acts may be quite large. For instance, deciding what mix of toys to sell could easily involve trillions of alternatives. *The decision analysis should include only the alternatives that the decision maker wants to consider.* When there is no compelling reason for choosing one of the alternatives, "doing nothing" should be an alternative. The search for attractive alternatives is essential to sound decision making. However, decision analysis cannot tell us what factors should and should not be considered, although it may be used to guide our selection.

TABLE 5-4 Payoff Table for the Tippi-Toes Decision

EVENT (level of demand)	ACT (choice of movement)			
	Gears and Levers	Spring Action	Weights and Pulleys	Pneumatic
Light	$ 25,000	−$ 10,000	−$125,000	−$300,000
Moderate	400,000	440,000	400,000	300,000
Heavy	650,000	740,000	750,000	700,000

TABLE 5-5 Modified Payoff Table for the Tippi-Toes Decision

EVENT (level of demand)	ACT (choice of movement)		
	Gears and Levers	Spring Action	Weights and Pulleys
Light	$ 25,000	-$ 10,000	-$125,000
Moderate	400,000	440,000	400,000
Heavy	650,000	740,000	750,000

Reducing the Number of Alternatives: Inadmissible Acts

Regardless of the decision-making process that we ultimately employ to help us make a choice, an initial screening may be made to determine if there are any acts that will never be chosen. To illustrate this, consider the payoffs in Table 5-4. An interesting feature is exhibited by the payoffs of the acts "weights and pulleys" and "pneumatic." No matter which demand event occurs, the weights-and-pulleys act results in a greater payoff. If a light demand occurs, for instance, the payoff for weights and pulleys is -$125,000, which is more favorable than the -$300,000 payoff for the pneumatic movement. A similar finding results if we compare these two acts for the other possible demand events. Because the weights-and-pulleys movement will always be a superior choice to the pneumatic movement, we say that the first act *dominates* the second act. One act dominates another when it achieves a better or an equal payoff, no matter which event occurs, and when it is strictly better for one or more events.

In general, whenever an act is dominated by another one, it is *inadmissible*. Thus, the pneumatic movement is an **inadmissible act.** The toy manufacturer's decision may be simplified by eliminating pneumatic movement from further consideration. Removing the pneumatic act leaves us with the modified payoff table in Table 5-5.

A simple way to determine if an act is inadmissible is to see if every entry in a single column of the payoff table is greater than or equal to the corresponding entry in its column. It is easy to verify that this is not true for entries in Table 5-5, so the remaining movement acts must be retained. The acts that remain are called **admissible acts.**

5-4 MAXIMIZING EXPECTED PAYOFF: THE BAYES DECISION RULE

How does a decision maker choose an act? When there is no uncertainty, the answer is straightforward: Select the act that yields the highest payoff (although finding this particular optimal act may be very difficult when there are many alternatives). But when the events are uncertain, the act that yields the greatest payoff for one event may yield a lower payoff than a competing act for some other event.

Suppose that our toy manufacturer accepts the following probabilities for the demand for Tippi-Toes:

Light demand	.10
Moderate demand	.70
Heavy demand	.20
	1.00

TABLE 5-6 Calculation of Expected Payoffs for the Tippi-Toes Decision

EVENT (level of demand)	PROBABILITY	ACT (choice of movement)					
		Gears and Levers		Spring Action		Weights and Pulleys	
		Payoff	Payoff × Probability	Payoff	Payoff × Probability	Payoff	Payoff × Probability
Light	.10	$ 25,000	$ 2,500	−$ 10,000	−$ 1,000	−$125,000	−$ 12,500
Moderate	.70	400,000	280,000	440,000	308,000	400,000	280,000
Heavy	.20	650,000	130,000	740,000	148,000	750,000	150,000
	Expected payoff:		$412,500		$455,000		$417,500

We calculate the expected payoff for each act in Table 5-6 by multiplying each payoff by the respective event probability and summing the products from each column. We find that the spring-action movement results in the maximum expected payoff of $455,000. Thus, using maximum expected payoff as a decision-making criterion, our toy manufacturer would select the spring-action movement for the Tippi-Toes doll.

The criterion of selecting the act with the **maximum expected payoff** is sometimes referred to as the **Bayes decision rule.** This rule takes into account all the information about the chances for the various payoffs. But we will see that it is not a perfect device and can lead to a choice that is not actually the most desirable. However, we will also see that this criterion is a suitable basis for decision making under uncertainty when the payoff values are selected with great care.

A Software Publisher Decides on a Marketing Strategy

MANAGERIAL APPLICATION

MaxiSoft is a medium-sized software publisher specializing in niche products. It has survived in an industry dominated by large companies through judiciously selecting products in markets not currently exploited by the majors. Hard experience has taught MaxiSoft that early market penetration is the key to success. Having a substantial share of any market gives a software vendor such a strong position that newcomers might never catch up, regardless of product quality or the level of resource commitment.

MaxiSoft's founder and CEO firmly believes that short-term profits are irrelevant in the software business. The name of the game is *market share.* She has stated that profits will follow, no matter how small the market turns out to be, if there is sufficient market share.

She applies this philosophy to *Exchecker,* a novel financial planner for homeowners. She and the marketing vice-president have selected four possible strategies (acts) for launching the product. A slow, deliberate direct mail campaign will result in good market share if the overall product acceptance is mediocre. But if the market for *Exchecker*-type products is a hot one, the majors will swamp the meager start with a splashier one of their own, and *Exchecker* will lose the market share race and end up as an "also ran." A mass marketing campaign at the outset will give MaxiSoft the staying power to exploit success and keep market share; unfortunately, the same heavy marketing will reduce the product's share in a weak market because it will attract competitors. In-between possibilities are targeted advertising and telemarketing.

TABLE 5-7   Payoff Table for MaxiSoft's *Exchecker*

MARKET EVENTS	PROBABILITY	ACTS			
		Direct Mail	Targeted Advertising	Tele-marketing	Mass Marketing
Premature	.10	85%	50%	40%	40%
Lackluster	.30	80	70	65	50
Quick Acceptance	.40	40	50	30	70
Wildly Enthusiastic	.20	25	35	40	60

Table 5-7 shows the payoff table, using percentage market share two years downstream as the payoff measure. Four events are listed for the type of market that will evolve for *Exchecker*-type products.

The CEO wants to determine if all acts are admissible and which one maximizes expected market share.

THE PROBLEM SOLUTION

All of the acts are admissible. The expected payoff from direct mail is computed:

$$\text{Direct Mail}$$
$$85 \times .10 = \quad 8.5\%$$
$$80 \times .30 = 24.0$$
$$40 \times .40 = 16.0$$
$$25 \times .20 = \quad \underline{5.0}$$
$$53.5\%$$

The expected payoffs are similarly calculated for the other acts.

Targeted Advertising	Telemarketing	Mass Marketing
53.0%	43.5%	59%

Mass marketing maximizes expected market share.

Using Spreadsheets to Evaluate Payoff Tables

Computational requirements make spreadsheets particularly attractive for evaluating payoff tables. Figure 5-2 gives the spreadsheet for the *Exchecker* decision. There we see that it is a simple matter to compute the expected payoff using the given probability data in column B and the original payoffs in the respective columns that follow. To calculate the expected payoff for Act 1 (column C) we use a standard Excel function. The result appears in cell C13, where the Excel formula for the expected payoff is

$$=\text{SUMPRODUCT(\$B\$9:\$B\$12,C9:C12)}$$

The other expected payoffs appear in row 13, accomplished by copying the above formula into cells D13:F13.

You may use Figure 5-2 as a template spreadsheet for solving other payoff table problems.

	A	B	C	D	E	F
1	\multicolumn{6}{|c|}{**PAYOFF TABLE EVALUATION**}					
2						
3	PROBLEM:	Exchecker Marketing Strategy				
4						
5			Problem Data			
6						
7			Act 1	Act 2	Act 3	Act 4
8	Events	Probability	Direct Mail	Targ. Ad.	Telemark	Mass Mkt
9	1 Premature	0.1	85.0%	50.0%	40.0%	40.0%
10	2 Lackluster	0.3	80.0%	70.0%	65.0%	50.0%
11	3 Quick Accept.	0.4	40.0%	50.0%	30.0%	70.0%
12	4 Wildly Enthus.	0.2	25.0%	35.0%	40.0%	60.0%
13	Expected Payoff		53.5%	53.0%	43.5%	59.0%
14						

	C
13	=SUMPRODUCT($B$9:$B$12,C9:C12)

FIGURE 5-2
Spreadsheet for payoff table evaluations for the *Exchecker* decision

5-5 OTHER DECISION CRITERIA

Maximizing expected payoff is just one criterion for making choices under uncertainty. **Decision theory** is concerned not only with the ramification of doing that, but also with the potential employment of a host of decision criteria, some of which are described here.

The Maximin Payoff Criterion

We begin with the simplest criterion, the **maximin payoff criterion** — a procedure that guarantees that the decision maker can do no worse than achieve the best of the poorest outcomes possible. As an illustration, we will use the Tippi-Toes payoff table given in Table 5-5.

Suppose that our toy manufacturer wants to choose an act that will ensure a favorable outcome no matter what happens. This may be accomplished by taking a pessimistic viewpoint — that is, by determining the *worst* outcome for each act, regardless of the event. For the gears-and-levers movement, the lowest possible payoff is $25,000 when light demand occurs. The lowest payoff for the spring-action movement is a negative amount, −$10,000, also obtained when demand is light. For the weights-and-pulleys movement, the lowest payoff is −$125,000, again when demand is light. By choosing the act that yields the largest lowest payoff, our decision maker can guarantee a minimum return that is the best of the poorest outcomes possible. In this case, a gears-and-levers movement for the doll will guarantee the toy manufacturer a payoff of at least $25,000.

The gears-and-levers movement is the act with the maximum of the minimum payoffs. A more concise statement would be to say that gears and levers is the **maximin payoff act.** To show how the maximin payoff can be determined in general, we reconstruct the payoff table for the Tippi-Toes decision in Table 5-8.

The suitability of the maximin payoff criterion depends on the nature of the decision to be made. Consider the decision problem in Table 5-9. In this situation, the maximin decision maker chooses A_1 over A_2. Act A_2 may be a better choice if the probability of E_2 is high enough, but the maximin decision maker is giving up an opportunity to gain

TABLE 5-8 Determining the Maximin Payoff Act for the Tippi-Toes Decision

EVENT (level of demand)	ACT (choice of movement)		
	Gears and Levers	Spring Action	Weights and Pulleys
Light	$ 25,000	-$ 10,000	-$125,000
Moderate	400,000	440,000	400,000
Heavy	650,000	740,000	750,000
Column minimums	$ 25,000	-$ 10,000	-$125,000

Maximum of column minimums = $25,000
Maximin payoff act = Gears and levers

$10,000 in order to avoid a possible loss of $1. To avoid losing $1, the decision maker chooses an act that will guarantee the maintenance of the status quo. We may, however, envision circumstances in which A_1 *would* be the better choice. If our decision maker had only $1 and had to use it to pay a debt to a loan shark or lose his life, the payoffs would not realistically represent the true values that the decision maker assigned to them.

Consider the situation represented by the payoffs given in Table 5-10. Here, the maximin payoff act is B_1. This would be the better choice for a decision maker who could not tolerate a loss of $10,000, no matter how unlikely it was. Few people would risk losing their businesses by choosing an act that could lead to bankruptcy unless the odds were extremely small. But an individual who could survive a loss of $10,000 would find B_2 a superior choice if the probability of E_2 were substantially lower than E_1.

Our examples illustrate a key deficiency of maximin payoff: It is an extremely conservative decision criterion and may lead to some very bad decisions. Any alternative with a slightly larger risk is rejected in favor of a comparatively risk-free alternative, which may be far less attractive. Taken to a ludicrous extreme, a maximin payoff policy would force any firm out of business. No inventories would be stocked, because there would always be a possibility of unsold items. No new products would be introduced, because management could never be certain of their success. No credit would be granted, because there would always be some customer who would not pay.

Another major deficiency of the maximin payoff criterion exists if the probabilities of the various events are known. Maximin payoff is primarily suited to decision problems with unknown probabilities that cannot be reasonably assessed. As our illus-

TABLE 5-9 Determining the Maximin Payoff Act for Hypothetical Decision A

EVENT	ACT	
	A_1	A_2
E_1	$0	-$1
E_2	1	10,000
Column minimums	$0	-$1

Maximum of column minimums = $0
Maximin payoff act = A_1

TABLE 5-10 Payoff Table for Hypothetical Decision B

EVENT	ACT	
	B_1	B_2
E_1	$1	$10,000
E_2	−1	−10,000

trations indicate, it is usually in the extreme cases — the person hounded by loan sharks or the business that could go bankrupt — that the maximin payoff criterion leads to the best decision.

The Maximum Likelihood Criterion

Another rule that serves as a model for decision-making behavior is the **maximum likelihood criterion,** which focuses on the most likely event, to the exclusion of all others. Table 5-11 illustrates this criterion for the Tippi-Toes decision.

For this decision, we see that the highest probability is .70 for a moderate demand. The maximum likelihood criterion tells us to ignore the light and heavy demand events completely — in effect, to assume that they will not occur. This rule then tells us to choose the best act assuming that a moderate demand will occur. In this example, the **maximum likelihood act** is to use the spring-action doll movement, which provides the greatest profit of $440,000 for a moderate demand.

How suitable is the maximum likelihood criterion for decision making? Using it in this example does not permit us to consider the range of outcomes for the spring-action movement, from a $10,000 loss if a light demand occurs to a $740,000 profit if demand is heavy. We also ignore most of the other possible outcomes, including the best (selecting weights and pulleys when demand is heavy, which yields a $750,000 profit) and the worst (selecting weights and pulleys when demand is light, which leads to a $125,000 loss). In a sense, the maximum likelihood criterion would have us "play ostrich," ignoring much that might happen. Then why is it discussed here?

We describe this criterion primarily because it seems to be so prevalent in the decision-making behavior of individuals and businesses. It may also be used to explain certain anomalies that would otherwise be hard to rationalize. These quirks are

TABLE 5-11 Determining the Maximum Likelihood Act for the Tippi-Toes Decision

EVENT (level of demand)	PROBABILITY	ACT (choice of movement)		
		Gears and Levers	Spring Action	Weights and Pulleys
Light	.10	$ 25,000	−$ 10,000	−$125,000
Moderate	.70	400,000	440,000	400,000
Heavy	.20	650,000	740,000	750,000

Most likely event = Moderate demand
Maximum row payoff = $440,000
Maximum likelihood act = Spring action

epitomized by the "hog cycle" in the raising and marketing of pigs, which is related to the more or less predictable two-year-long pork price movement from higher to lower levels and back to higher levels again. Hog farmers have been blamed for this because they expand their herds when prices are high, so that one year later the supply of mature hogs is excessive and prices are driven downward; then when prices are low, these same farmers reduce their herds, cutting the supply of marketable hogs, and next year's prices consequently rise.

Why don't the farmers break this cycle? It doesn't seem rational to be consistently wrong in timing hog production. One explanation is that the hog farmers use the maximum likelihood criterion. In their minds, the most likely future market price is the current one — and we know that this has proved to be a very poor judgment. Given such a premise, the maximum likelihood act is to increase herd sizes when current prices are high and to decrease them when prices are low.

The Criterion of Insufficient Reason

Another criterion employed in decision-making problems is the **criterion of insufficient reason.** This criterion may be used when a decision maker has no information about the event probabilities. In this case, no event may be regarded as more likely than any other event, and all events are assigned equal probability values. Since the events are collectively exhaustive and mutually exclusive, the probability of each event must be

$$\frac{1}{\text{Number of events}}$$

Using these event probabilities, the act with the maximum expected payoff is chosen.

A major criticism of the criterion of insufficient reason is that, except in a few situations, some knowledge of the relative chances that events will occur is always available. When more realistic probabilities may be obtained, employing the Bayes decision rule will provide more valid results.

The Preferred Criterion: The Bayes Decision Rule

The three decision-making criteria just discussed have obvious inadequacies. *None of them incorporates all of the information available to the decision maker.* Maximin payoff totally ignores event probabilities. Although it is argued that this is a strength when probabilities cannot be easily determined, judgment may be used to arrive at acceptable probability values in all but a few circumstances.

The maximum likelihood criterion ignores all events but the most likely one, even if that event happens to be a lot less likely than the rest combined. (Out of 20 events, for instance, the most likely event may have a probability of .10, leaving a .90 probability that one of the other 19 events will occur.)

The criterion of insufficient reason essentially asks us to ignore judgments and "willy nilly" assume that all events are equally likely. According to this criterion, even such events as "war" and "peace" and "prosperity" and "depression" have equal probabilities.

The Bayes decision rule (choose the act maximizing expected payoff) has become the central focus of statistical decision theory. This makes the greatest use of all available information. Its major deficiency occurs when alternatives involve different magnitudes of risk. To illustrate this point, we will consider the decision structure in Table 5-12. Acts C_1 and C_2 are equally attractive according to the maximum expected

TABLE 5-12 Payoff Table for Hypothetical Decision C

EVENT	PROBABILITY	ACT C_1 Payoff	ACT C_1 Payoff × Probability	ACT C_2 Payoff	ACT C_2 Payoff × Probability
E_1	.5	−$1,000,000	−$ 500,000	$250,000	$125,000
E_2	.5	2,000,000	1,000,000	750,000	375,000
		Expected payoff	$ 500,000		$500,000

payoff criterion (Bayes decision rule). Yet most decision makers would clearly prefer C_2, because it avoids the rather large risk of a $1,000,000 loss.

The paradox here may be resolved not by choosing another criterion, but by reconsidering the values chosen for the payoffs. The theory of utility presented in Chapter 6 will allow us to establish payoffs at values that express their true worth to the decision maker.

5-6 OPPORTUNITY LOSS AND THE EXPECTED VALUE OF PERFECT INFORMATION

Is it worthwhile to buy information that may help us choose the best act? Information is usually not free. Resources, for example, are required to take a sample or to administer a test. In this section, we will attempt to place a value on such information. To do this, we will introduce the concept of opportunity loss.

Opportunity Loss

Suppose that we view each possible outcome in terms of a measure that expresses the difference between the payoff for the chosen act and the best payoff that could have been achieved. This measure, referred to as an **opportunity loss,** is defined as the amount of payoff that is forgone by not selecting the act that has the greatest payoff for the event that actually occurs.

Table 5-13 shows how the opportunity losses are obtained for the payoffs for the toy manufacturer's decision. To calculate the opportunity losses, the maximum payoff

TABLE 5-13 Determining the Opportunity Losses for the Tippi-Toes Decision

EVENT (level of demand)	PAYOFF Gears and Levers	PAYOFF Spring Action	PAYOFF Weights and Pulleys	ROW MAXIMUM
Light	$ 25,000	−$ 10,000	−$125,000	$ 25,000
Moderate	400,000	440,000	400,000	440,000
Heavy	650,000	740,000	750,000	750,000
	Row maximum − Payoff = Opportunity loss (thousands of dollars)			
Light	25 − 25 = 0	25 − (− 10) = 35	25 − (− 125) = 150	
Moderate	440 − 400 = 40	440 − 440 = 0	440 − 400 = 40	
Heavy	750 − 650 = 100	750 − 740 = 10	750 − 750 = 0	

TABLE 5-14   Opportunity Loss Table for the Tippi-Toes Decision

EVENT (level of demand)	ACT (choice of movement)		
	Gears and Levers	Spring Action	Weights and Pulleys
Light	$ 0	$35,000	$150,000
Moderate	40,000	0	40,000
Heavy	100,000	10,000	0

for each row is determined. Each payoff is then subtracted from its respective row maximum.

The **opportunity loss table** for the Tippi-Toes decision appears in Table 5-14. All opportunity loss values are nonnegative, because they measure how much worse off the decision maker is made by choosing some act other than the best act for the event that occurs. Let us consider the meaning of the opportunity loss values. For example, suppose that the gears-and-levers movement is chosen and that a light demand occurs. The opportunity loss is zero, because we see from Table 5-13 that no better payoff than $25,000 (the row maximum) could have been achieved if another act had been chosen. But if the gears-and-levers movement is chosen and a heavy demand occurs, the opportunity loss is $100,000 because the weights-and-pulleys movement has the greatest payoff for a heavy demand ($750,000). Because the gears-and-levers movement has a payoff of only $650,000, the payoff difference $750,000 − $650,000 = $100,000 represents the additional payoff forgone by not selecting the act with the greatest payoff.

It should be emphasized that the $100,000 opportunity loss is not a loss in the accounting sense because a net positive contribution of $650,000 to profits is obtained. Instead, the opportunity to achieve an additional $100,000 has been missed. We might say that should demand prove to be heavy, the decision maker would have $100,000 worth of *regret* by not choosing weights and pulleys instead of gears and levers.

The Bayes Decision Rule and Opportunity Loss

Expected values can be computed with opportunity losses, and the resulting amounts can be used to choose the act. After calculating the expected opportunity loss for each act, select the act that has the minimum expected loss. This is done in Table 5-15 for the Tippi-Toes decision. The minimum expected opportunity loss is $5,500 for the

TABLE 5-15   Calculation of Expected Opportunity Losses for the Tippi-Toes Decision

EVENT (level of demand)	PROBABILITY	ACT (choice of movement)					
		Gears and Levers		Spring Action		Weights and Pulleys	
		Loss	Loss × Probability	Loss	Loss × Probability	Loss	Loss × Probability
Light	.10	$ 0	$ 0	$35,000	$3,500	$150,000	$15,000
Moderate	.70	40,000	28,000	0	0	40,000	28,000
Heavy	.20	100,000	20,000	10,000	2,000	0	0
Expected opportunity loss:			$48,000		$5,500		$43,000

spring-action movement, which is the **minimum expected opportunity loss act** in this example.

Earlier, we saw that the spring-action movement was also the maximum expected payoff act and was therefore the best choice according to the Bayes decision rule. Our new criterion leads us to the same choice. It can be mathematically established that this will always be so. Because either criterion will always lead to the same choice, we can say that the *Bayes decision rule is to select the act that has the maximum expected payoff or the minimum expected opportunity loss*.

The Expected Value of Perfect Information

Up to this point, our toy manufacturer has selected an act without the benefit of any information except that acquired through experience with other toys. But it is possible to secure better information about next season's demand by test marketing, by taking opinion and attitude surveys, or by obtaining inside information concerning competitors' plans. How much should the decision maker be willing to pay for additional information?

It is helpful to know the payoff that may be expected from securing improved information about the events. We will consider the extreme case when the decision maker may acquire **perfect information,** so that the decision will be made *under certainty*. This is because with perfect information, the decision maker can guarantee the selection of the act that yields the greatest payoff for whatever event actually occurs. Because we want to investigate the worth of such information *before* it is obtained, we will determine the expected payoff once perfect information is obtained. This quantity is called the **expected payoff under certainty** (with perfect information).

To calculate the expected payoff under certainty, we determine the highest payoff for each event. This is illustrated for the Tippi-Toes decision in Table 5-16. The maximum payoff for each demand level is determined by finding the largest payoff in each row. Thus, for a light demand, we find that choosing the gears-and-levers movement yields the largest payoff ($25,000). If perfect information indicated that light demand was certain to occur, our decision maker would choose this movement. Similarly, $440,000 is the maximum payoff possible for moderate demand, and this amount may be achieved only if the spring-action movement is chosen. Likewise, $750,000 is the maximum possible payoff when a heavy demand occurs, and this amount corresponds to a choice of the weights-and-pulleys movement. The last column of Table 5-16 shows the products of the maximum payoffs and their respective event probabilities. Summing these, we obtain $460,500 as the expected payoff under certainty (with perfect information). This figure represents the average payoff if the toy manufacturer were

TABLE 5-16 Calculation of Expected Payoff under Certainty for the Tippi-Toes Decision

EVENT (level of demand)	PROBABILITY	ACT			UNDER CERTAINTY		
		Gears and Levers	Spring Action	Weights and Pulleys	Maximum Payoff	Chosen Act	Payoff × Probability
Light	.10	$ 25,000	-$ 10,000	-$125,000	$ 25,000	G&L	$ 2,500
Moderate	.70	400,000	440,000	400,000	440,000	SA	308,000
Heavy	.20	650,000	740,000	750,000	750,000	W&P	150,000
					Expected payoff under certainty =		$460,500

faced with the same situation repeatedly and always selected the act that yielded the best payoff for the event indicated by the perfect information. Keep in mind that the $460,500 represents the expected payoff viewed from some point in time *before* the information becomes available. *After* the information has been obtained, exactly one of the payoffs, $25,000, $440,000, or $750,000, is bound to occur. When the information is actually obtained, the payoff is a certainty.

We now answer the question regarding the worth of perfect information to the decision maker. As we have seen, the Bayes decision rule leads to the choice of the particular act that maximizes the expected payoff without regard to any additional information. Since this is the best act that our decision maker can select without any new information and since the expected payoff under certainty is the average payoff that may be anticipated with the best possible information, the worth of perfect information to the decision maker is expressed by the difference between these two amounts. We call the resulting number the **expected value of perfect information,** which is conveniently represented by the abbreviation EVPI and may be expressed as

$$\text{EVPI} = \text{Expected payoff under certainty}$$
$$- \text{Maximum expected payoff (with no information)}$$

For the toy manufacturer's decision, we obtain the EVPI by subtracting the maximum expected payoff of $455,000 (calculated in Table 5-6) from the expected payoff under certainty of $460,500:

$$\text{EVPI} = \$460,500 - \$455,000 = \$5,500$$

In this case, the EVPI represents the greatest amount of money that the decision maker would be willing to pay to obtain perfect information about what the demand will be. Stated differently, $5,500 is the increase in the decision maker's expected payoff that may be attributed to perfect knowledge of demand. Both $455,000 and $460,500 are meaningless values *after* the perfect information is obtained. Thus, the EVPI of $5,500 may be interpreted only *before* the perfect information has become known.

EVPI and Opportunity Loss

Note that $5,500 is the same amount as the minimum expected opportunity loss calculated in Table 5-15. Thus, we see that *the expected value of perfect information is equal to the expected opportunity loss for the optimal act.*

Therefore, we calculate the expected value of perfect information by calculating the expected opportunity losses. The minimum expected loss is the EVPI. Table 5-17 summarizes relationships among expected payoff, expected opportunity loss, and expected value of perfect information for the toy manufacturer's decision. Note that for

TABLE 5-17	Relationships among Expected Payoff, Expected Opportunity Loss, and EVPI for the Tippi-Toes Decision		
	Gears and Levers	**Spring Action**	**Weights and Pulleys**
Expected payoff	$412,500	$455,000	$417,500
Expected opportunity loss	48,000	5,500	43,000
Expected payoff under certainty (with perfect information)	$460,500	$460,500	$460,500
Expected value of perfect information (EVPI) = $5,500		Optimal act	

any act, the sum of the expected payoff and the expected opportunity loss is equal to the expected payoff under certainty (with perfect information).

Because perfect information is nonexistent in most real-world decision making, why are we interested in the EVPI? Our answer is that it helps us to establish a limit on the worth of less-than-perfect information. For example, if a marketing research study aimed at predicting demand costs $6,000, which exceeds the EVPI by $500, the study should not be conducted, regardless of its quality.

Using Spreadsheets

As we have seen, spreadsheets can minimize the work in evaluating payoff tables. Figure 5-3 shows another version of the earlier spreadsheet for *Exchecker.* It can be used as a template for similar evaluations.

The expected payoffs are calculated as before and now appear in row 18. The expected opportunity losses are in row 19. The first step in calculating these values is to find the maximum payoff in each row of the payoff table. Those quantities appear in column G, where cell G9 (for the premature event) has the formula

$$=MAX(C9:F9)$$

FIGURE 5-3
New spreadsheet for the *Exchecker* decision

	A	B	C	D	E	F	G
1	PAYOFF TABLE EVALUATION						
2						G	
3	PROBLEM:	Exchecker Marketing Strategy			9	=MAX(C9:F9)	
4					10	=MAX(C10:F10)	
5			Problem Data		11	=MAX(C11:F11)	
6					12	=MAX(C12:F12)	
7			Act 1	Act 2	Act 3	Act 4	Row
8	Events	Probability	Direct Mail	Targ. Ad.	Telemark	Mass Mkt	Maximum
9	1 Premature	0.1	$ 85.00	$ 50.00	$ 40.00	$ 40.00	$ 85.00
10	2 Lackluster	0.3	$ 80.00	$ 70.00	$ 65.00	$ 50.00	$ 80.00
11	3 Quick Accept.	0.4	$ 40.00	$ 50.00	$ 30.00	$ 70.00	$ 70.00
12	4 Wildly Enthus.	0.2	$ 25.00	$ 35.00	$ 40.00	$ 60.00	$ 60.00
13							
14			Act Summary				
15							
16			Act 1	Act 2	Act 3	Act 4	
17			Direct Mail	Targ. Ad.	Telemark	Mass Mkt	
18	Expected Payoff		$53.50	$53.00	$43.50	$59.00	
19	Exp. Opportunity Loss		$19.00	$19.50	$29.00	$13.50	
20							
21			Overall Summary				
22							
23	Maximum Expected Payoff:		$59.00		Act 4	Mass Mkt	
24	Minimum Expected Opportunity Loss:		$13.50		Act 4	Mass Mkt	
25	Expected Value of Perfect Information:		$13.50				

	C
18	=SUMPRODUCT($B$9:$B$12,C9:C12)
19	=SUMPRODUCT($B$9:$B$12,$G$9:$G$12-C9:C12)

	D
23	=MAX(C18:F18)
24	=MIN(C19:F19)
25	=D24

	F
23	=HLOOKUP(E23,$C$16:$F$17,2)
24	=HLOOKUP(E24,$C$16:$F$17,2)

	E
23	=CONCATENATE("Act ",MATCH(D23,C18:F18,0))
24	=CONCATENATE("Act ",MATCH(D24,C19:F19,0))

which was copied for the remaining events into cells G10, G11, and G12. The first expected opportunity loss, applying to Act 1, appears in cell C19 and is computed from the formula

$$=SUMPRODUCT(\$B\$9:\$B\$12,\$G\$9:\$G\$12-C9:C12)$$

The above subtracts from the row maximum to get the opportunity losses, using the argument $G$9:$G$12-C9:C12. (Although it would be easy to include one, a separate listing of the opportunity losses is not included in Figure 5-3.) Those quantities are then multiplied by the respective probabilities. The sum of those products is computed by the above formula. The C19 formula (for Act 1) was copied into cells D19, E19, and F19 to compute the remaining expected opportunity losses for Acts 2–4.

The three Excel formulas for cells D23, D24, and D25 are =MAX(C18:F18), =MIN(C19:F19), and =D24, respectively. The final set of formulas are used to generate the matching labels (which will vary with the problem data). Cell E23 has the formula

$$=CONCATENATE(\text{“Act ”},MATCH(D23,C18:F18,0))$$

which uses the MATCH function to find the identity number of the optimal act and then inserts that value into the text phrase, "Act ". (Notice the blank after the last letter in the phrase "Act ".) Once the identity of the act is known, HLOOKUP functions can find the *name* of the act. Cell F23 has the formula

$$=HLOOKUP(E23,\$C\$16:\$F\$17,2)$$

The above instructs Excel to look for the value in E23 (here, "Act 4") in cells C16:F17 and then return the value in row 2 of the specified range where the match takes place, yielding "Mass Mkt." Cells E24 and F24 have analogous formulas.

5-7   DECISION TREE ANALYSIS

The decisions encountered thus far may be portrayed in terms of a payoff table. But some problems are too complex to be presented in a table. Difficulties arise when the same events do not apply for all acts. For example, a contractor may have to choose between bidding on a construction job for a dam or on one for an airport, not having sufficient resources to bid on both. Regardless of the job chosen, there is some probability (which may differ for the two projects) that the contractor will win the job bid on. Separate sets of events and probabilities are required for each act.

Decisions must often be made at two or more points in time, with uncertain events occurring between decisions. Sometimes these problems may be analyzed in terms of a payoff table, but usually the earlier choice of the act will have a bearing on the type, quantity, and probabilities of later events. At best, this makes it cumbersome to attempt to force the decision into the limited confines of the rectangular arrangement of a payoff table.

The decision tree diagram allows us to meaningfully arrange the elements of a complex decision problem without the restrictions of a tabular format. A further advantage of the decision tree is that it serves as an excellent management communication tool, because the tree clearly delineates every potential course of action and all possible outcomes.

Illustration: Ponderosa Record Company

The president of Ponderosa Record Company, a small independent recording studio, has just signed a contract with a four-person rock group, called the Fluid Mechanics. A tape has been cut, and Ponderosa must decide whether or not to market the recording. If the CD is to be test marketed, then a 5,000-unit run will be made and promoted regionally; this may result in a later decision to distribute an additional 45,000 CDs nationally, for which a second production run will have to be made. If immediate national marketing is chosen, a run of 50,000 CDs will be made. Regardless of the test market results, the president may decide to enter the national market or decide not to enter it.

A Ponderosa CD is either a complete success or a failure in its market. A recording is successful if all manufactured CDs are sold; the sales of a failure are practically nil. Success in a regional market does not guarantee success nationally, but it is a fairly reliable predictor.

The Decision Tree Diagram

The structure of the Ponderosa decision problem is presented in the decision tree diagram in Figure 5-4. Decisions are to be made at two different points in time, or stages. The immediate choice is to select one of two acts: "test market" or "don't test market."

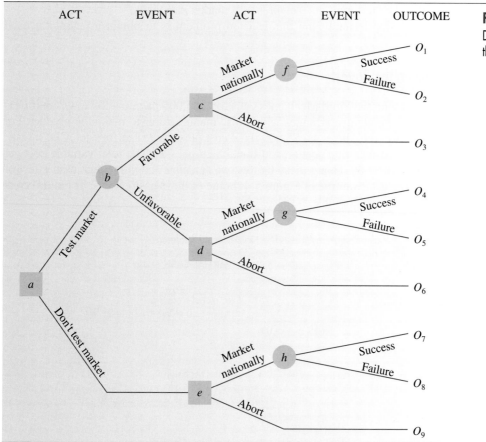

FIGURE 5-4

Decision tree diagram for the Ponderosa decision

These acts are shown as branches on the initial fork at node *a*. If test marketing is chosen, then the result to be achieved in the test marketplace is uncertain. This is reflected by an event fork at node *b*, where the branches represent favorable and unfavorable events. Regardless of which event occurs, a choice must be made between two new acts: "market nationally" or "abort." These acts occur at a later stage and are represented by a pair of act forks. Each fork corresponds to the two different conditions under which this decision may be made: at node *c*, when the test marketing is favorable, and at node *d*, when it is unfavorable. If national marketing is chosen at either node *c* or node *d*, the success or failure of the recording still remains unknown, and the possible events are reflected on the decision tree as branches on the terminal event forks at nodes *f* and *g*.

If the initial choice at decision point *a* is "don't test market," then a further choice must be made at the act fork represented by decision point *e*: "market nationally" or "abort." As before, node *h* reflects the two uncertain events that will arise from the choice to market nationally. The "abort" path leading from node *e* contains a "dummy" branch—a diagrammatical convenience that allows event and act forks of similar form to appear at the same stage of the problem and permits all paths to terminate at a common stage. Thus, all "abort" acts are followed by a dummy branch.

Every path from the base of the decision tree leads to a terminal position corresponding to a decision outcome. Each possible combination of acts and events, or each path, has a distinct outcome. For instance, O_1 represents the following sequence of events and acts: "test market," "favorable," "market nationally," "success."

The first step in analyzing the decision problem is to obtain a payoff for each outcome.

Determining the Payoffs

The contract with the Fluid Mechanics calls for a $5,000 payment to the group if CDs are produced. Ponderosa arranges with a disc manufacturer to make the product. For each production run, there is a $5,000 fixed cost plus a $.75 fee for each CD. Inserts, handling, and distribution cost an additional $.25 per CD. The total variable cost per CD is therefore $1.00. Using these figures, we calculate the immediate cash effect of each act in the decision tree in Figure 5-4. Some of these cash effects, or **partial cash flows,** are computed in Table 5-18.

TABLE 5-18	Some Partial Cash Flows Used to Determine Ponderosa's Payoffs

ACT	PARTIAL CASH FLOW	
Test market	− $ 5,000	(payment to group)
	− 5,000	(fixed cost of production)
	− 5,000	(variable costs of 5,000 CDs at $1.00)
Total	− $15,000	
Don't test market	$0	
Market nationally (without test)	− $ 5,000	(payment to group)
	− 5,000	(fixed cost of production)
	− 50,000	(variable costs of 50,000 CDs at $1.00)
Total	− $60,000	
Abort	$0	

The negative cash flows indicate expenditures. The partial cash flows in Table 5-18 appear on the respective branches extending from decision points a and e of the decision tree in Figure 5-5. In a similar manner, we determine the partial cash flows for the acts at the forks at decision points c and d: −$50,000 to market nationally ($5,000 fixed cost plus $1.00 each in variable costs for 45,000 CDs) and $0 to abort.

Ponderosa receives $2 for each CD it sells through retail outlets. Because the events — "favorable" and "unfavorable" or "success" and "failure" — represent sales of all and no CDs, respectively, the partial cash flows may be obtained by multiplying the number of CDs sold by $2. The partial cash flows for the events at the fork at node b are therefore +$10,000 (for 5,000 CDs sold) and $0 (for no sales). The amounts for the events at nodes f and g are +$90,000 (for 45,000 CDs sold) and $0, whereas the amounts for the events at node h are +$100,000 and $0.

Partial cash flows are combined for each outcome to yield the *net cash flow*. Those amounts serve as the payoffs and are computed by adding the partial cash flows on the branches of the path leading to the outcome. Thus, for O_1, we add the partial cash flows −$15,000, +$10,000, −$50,000, and +$90,000. The payoff for O_1 is therefore +$35,000. The payoffs calculated for each outcome are shown at the respective terminal positions of the decision tree in Figure 5-5.

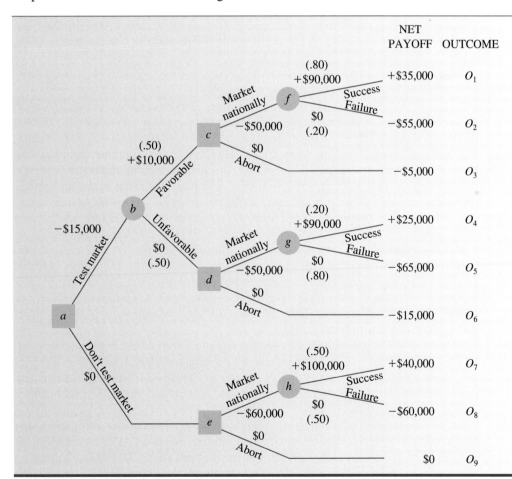

FIGURE 5-5   The Ponderosa decision tree diagram showing partial cash flows and probabilities on the branches, with net cash-flow payoffs at the terminal positions

Assigning Event Probabilities

Ponderosa's management wants to choose the act that will yield the maximum expected payoff. But before this choice can be made, probability values must be assigned to the events in the decision structure. Suppose that Ponderosa's president believes that the chance of favorably test marketing the recording is .50. The probability of unfavorably test marketing the recording is also .50. These probability values are placed in parentheses along the branches at node *b* in Figure 5-5. In assigning probability values to the success and failure events for national marketing, our decision maker is faced with three distinctly different situations. With no test marketing, the chance of national success is judged to be .50. A favorable test marketing indicates that a CD appeals to the regional segment of the market, so the chance of national success in this case is judged to be a much higher .80; this is a *conditional probability*. Similarly, unfavorable test marketing is a likely indication of poor national appeal, so the conditional probability for success is judged to be .20 in this case. The following probability values are placed on the branches for the events at the remaining forks in the decision tree diagram: .80 for success and .20 for failure at node *f*; .20 for success and .80 for failure at node *g*; and .50 for success and .50 for failure at node *h*. (It is just coincidental that the probability for national marketing success after unfavorable test marketing is .20, which is also the probability for national marketing failure after favorable test marketing. Our decision maker could have selected another value, such as .10.)

Folding Back the Tree (Backward Induction)

We are now ready to analyze Ponderosa's decision. Our decision maker wants to select an initial or immediate act at decision point *a*. The first act that we will evaluate is "test market." What is the expected payoff for this act? Figure 5-5 shows us that six outcomes, O_1 through O_6, may result from this choice. How can we translate the corresponding payoffs into an expected value? We cannot do this until we specify the intervening acts that will be chosen at nodes *c* and *d*. In general, *it is impossible to evaluate an immediate act without first considering all later decisions that result from this choice.*

Thus, to find the expected payoff for the "test market" act, our decision maker must first decide whether to market nationally or to abort if (1) test marketing proves favorable or (2) test marketing proves unfavorable. This illustrates an essential feature of analyzing multistage decisions: *Evaluations must be made in reverse of their natural chronological sequence.* Before deciding whether to test market, our decision maker must decide what to do if the test marketing is favorable or if it is unfavorable. The procedure for making such evaluations involves **folding back** the tree. It is sometimes called **backward induction.**

We clarify this point by describing the procedure for our decision-making problem. For simplicity, the Ponderosa president's decision tree diagram is redrawn in Figure 5-6 without the partial cash flows. (Once the outcome payoffs have been computed, the original partial cash flows are no longer needed. To avoid double accounting, they should be ignored while folding back the tree.)

Consider the act fork at decision point *c*. If the decision is to market nationally, then Ponderosa's president is faced with the event fork at node *f*. With a probability of .80 that marketing nationally will be a success, a net payoff of +$35,000 will be achieved. The probability that marketing nationally will be a failure is .20, which leads to a net payoff of −$55,000. The expected payoff for this event fork is calculated as

$$.80(+\$35,000) + .20(-\$55,000) = +\$17,000$$

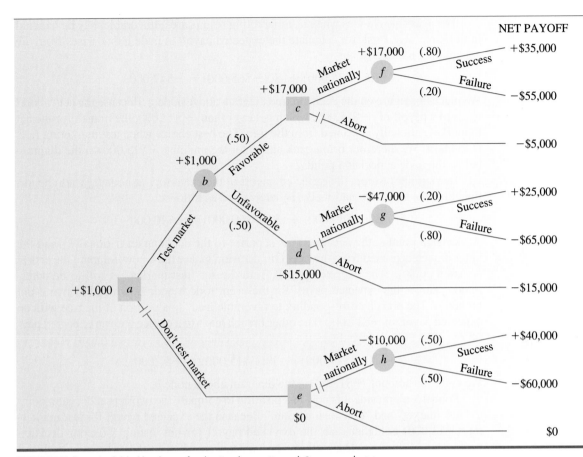

FIGURE 5-6 The folded-back tree for the Ponderosa Record Company decision

The amount +$17,000 is entered on the decision tree at node *f* because this is the expected payoff for the act to market nationally. For convenience, we place the expected payoff for a sequence of acts or events above the applicable node.

The act to abort at decision point *c* will lead to a certain payoff of −$5,000. Because the expected payoff for the act to market nationally (+$17,000) is larger than −$5,000, the choice to market nationally should be made over aborting. We may reflect this future choice by *pruning* the branch from the tree that corresponds to the act "abort" at decision point *c*. This act merits no further consideration because if decision point *c* is reached, the president will choose to market nationally. That is, if the decision maker initially decides to test market and the results turn out to be favorable, the president will choose to market nationally. Thus, +$17,000 is the expected payoff resulting from making the best choice at decision point *c*. We bring back the amount +$17,000 and enter it on the diagram above the node at *c*.

As a rule of thumb in folding back the tree, ultimately all but one act will be eliminated at each decision point (except in the case of ties), so that all branches except those leading to the greatest expected payoff will be pruned. Only the *best single payoff* from the later stage is brought backward to the preceding decision point (square). *Branch pruning takes place only in act forks — never in event forks.* Instead, event forks (circles) involve an expected value calculation, so that an average payoff is always computed from the later stage values.

The available choices when test marketing results are unfavorable may be handled in the same way. First, we calculate the expected payoff at node g that arises from the act "market nationally," or

$$.20(+\$25,000) + .80(-\$65,000) = -\$47,000$$

We place this figure on the decision tree diagram above node g. Because the act "abort" leads to a payoff of $-\$15,000$, which is larger than $-\$47,000$, the branch for the act to market nationally is pruned from the tree. The best choice when test marketing fails is to abort. We therefore bring back and enter the amount $-\$15,000$ on the diagram below the node at decision point d.

In a similar fashion, the expected payoff of the event fork at node h, when the initial choice is to market nationally, is determined as follows:

$$.50(+\$40,000) + .50(-\$60,000) = -\$10,000$$

At decision point e, the act "abort" is superior to the act "market nationally," and the latter branch is pruned from the tree. Our decision maker must now compare the acts at decision point a. The expected payoff from the act "test market" is still to be determined. This is the expected payoff for the event fork at node b, which has two event branches. The branch corresponding to favorable leads to a portion of the tree with an expected payoff of $+\$17,000$. The other branch leads to a choice with an expected payoff of $-\$15,000$. We use these two amounts to calculate the expected payoff at node b.

$$.50(+\$17,000) + .50(-\$15,000) = +\$1,000$$

We enter the amount $+\$1,000$ on the diagram above node b.

Ponderosa's president is now in a position to compare the two acts at decision point a: "test market" and "don't test market." Because the expected payoff for test marketing ($+\$1,000$) is higher than the expected payoff for not testing ($\$0$), our decision maker should choose to test market. The expected payoff of $\$1,000$ is brought back and placed at node a. The branch corresponding to "don't test market" is pruned, and our backward induction is complete.

A decision is indicated. Ponderosa's president should choose to test market the Fluid Mechanics's CD. If the test marketing is favorable, then the president should market nationally; if the test marketing is unfavorable, then the president should abort the recording. This result is illustrated in Figure 5-6 by the unpruned branches that remain on the decision tree. Such a result tells the decision maker what to do under all contingencies and is sometimes referred to as a **policy** or **strategy.**

Decision Tree Evaluation with Excel

PrecisionTree is an Excel Add-In that solves decision tree problems. It is found on the CD-ROM accompanying this text under Palisade Decision Tools. After clicking on the PrecisionTree icon (PrecisionTree 1.0 for Excel), Excel will open that application automatically with the PrecisionTree tool bar shown in Figure 5-7. You may start drawing a decision tree

FIGURE 5-7
The PrecisionTree tool bar

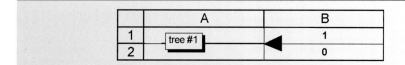

FIGURE 5-8
Initial PrecisionTree decision tree

by clicking on the New Tree icon (🌑) on PrecisionTree's tool bar. Then select the cell where you wish to begin and click on it to start the decision tree. (Alternatively, you may select the cell, click on PrecisionTree on the Excel menu bar, select Create New on the drop-down menu that appears, and then select Tree). For example, clicking in cell A1 results in the initial tree shown in Figure 5-8.

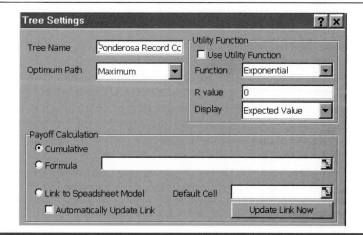

FIGURE 5-9
Tree Settings dialog box for naming a decision tree

The Ponderosa Record Company illustration will show how PrecisionTree works. We begin by clicking on the tree #1 box in Figure 5-8. That brings to screen the Tree Settings dialog box in Figure 5-9. There the name Ponderosa Record is entered in the *Tree Name* line. Clicking on the OK button yields the results in Figure 5-10. The decision tree is built out from the initial node. We begin with the initial decision point, created by moving the cursor over the end node in cells B1:B2 (◀) and clicking. That brings to screen the Node Settings dialog box on the left-hand side of Figure 5-11. Appearing there under *Node Type* are several choice buttons. We click on the decision node icon (▦). That causes the dialog box to change, as shown on the right-hand side of Figure 5-11. There we may enter a name for the node in the Name box. (It is left blank here.) We enter a 2 for the number of act choices in the *# of Branches* line. After clicking OK, the tree grows two decision branches, as shown in Figure 5-12.

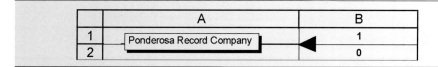

FIGURE 5-10
Initial Ponderosa Record Company decision tree

FIGURE 5-11
Tree Settings dialog box

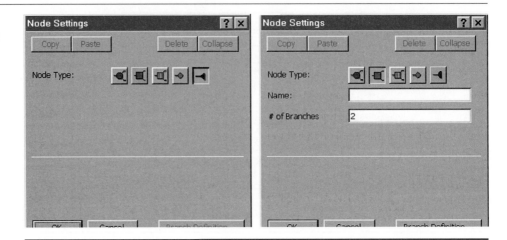

To name the branches, we click inside the boxes containing the word "branch." That will bring to screen the Branch Settings dialog box, as shown in Figure 5-13 for the top branch, where "Test Market" has been entered. The cost of the test market branch is entered directly onto the spreadsheet: 15,000 in cell B2. The format of that cell is then changed to currency with no decimal places. Similarly, the lower decision branch is named "Don't test market" and 0 is entered as the branch cost in cell B6. Figure 5-14 shows the resulting tree at this stage.

FIGURE 5-12
Extended PrecisionTree decision tree for Ponderosa Record Company

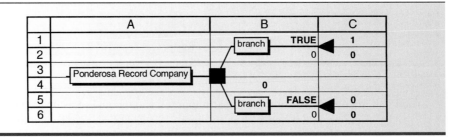

The tree-building process continues for the end node position in cells C1:C2. Clicking there returns the Node Settings dialog box (as in Figure 5-11). This time we click the chance button (◉). The dialog box changes like before, but with the chance button depressed. We leave the *Name* line blank, enter 2 for *# of Branches,* and click OK. The decision tree expands as shown in Figure 5-15, where the two event branches

FIGURE 5-13
Branch Settings dialog box for naming decision branches

Branch Settings	? ×
Branch Name	Test Market	Move Up
		Move Down
OK	Cancel	Delete

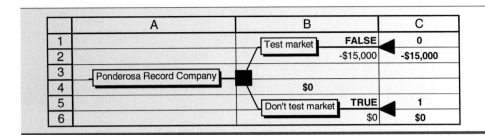

FIGURE 5-14
Extended PrecisionTree decision tree with decisions and partial cash flows

are named "Favorable" and "Unfavorable." Directly onto the spreadsheet probabilities are entered in cells C1 and C5, above the branch lines in percentage format, as 50.0% each. The respective partial cash flows, $10,000 and $0, appear in C2 and C6.

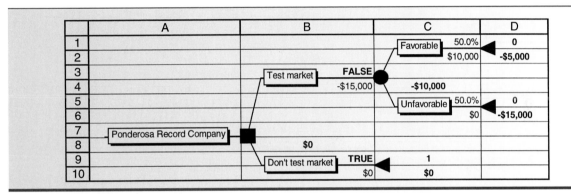

FIGURE 5-15 Second expanded PrecisionTree decision tree

Another decision node is added at the end of the "Favorable" branch. Repeating the process, Figure 5-16 results. There, two act branches, "Market nationally" and "Abort," are created, along with respective partial cash flows −$50,000 and $0 in cells D2 and D6.

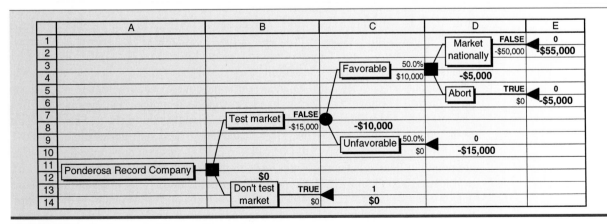

FIGURE 5-16 Third expanded PrecisionTree decision tree

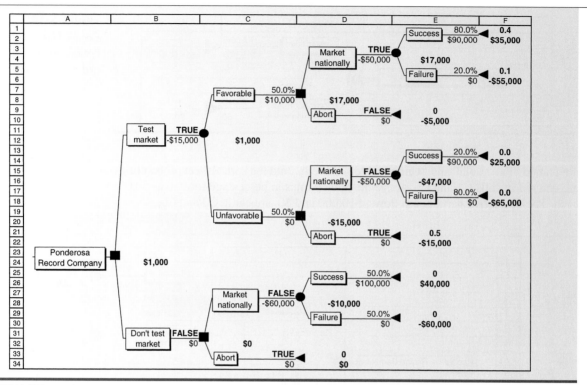

FIGURE 5-17   Final PrecisionTree decision tree for the Ponderosa Record Company decision

We repeat the tree-building process, adding the remaining event and decision nodes, their names, their partial cash flows, and probabilities. The final tree is shown in Figure 5-17. Notice how PrecisionTree folds back the decision tree as new events and acts are added. The numbers in cells E4, E16, D8, D20, D28, C12, C32, and B24 are the expected values resulting from folding back the tree.

PrecisionTree uses the words TRUE and FALSE to indicate whether a branch is selected. For example, in Figure 5-17, the act branch in cells B11:B12 has the word TRUE. This means that this branch, "Test market," would maximize expected payoff instead of "Don't test market," which is indicated as FALSE. Marking a branch FALSE is analogous to pruning it from the complete tree. Some branches, however, are marked with TRUE even though they fall within a pruned portion. (The TRUE in cell C33 means that the "Abort" decision should be chosen if the "Don't test market" decision is selected; but that choice won't be made.) The same course of action for maximizing expected payoff found with the earlier hand-drawn trees is indicated in Figure 5-17: Test market, and if the results are favorable, market nationally; but if the test market result is unfavorable, then abort. The overall expected payoff is $1,000, appearing in cell B24.

If the optimal strategy is followed, Figure 5-17 shows that only three final payoffs are possible: Ponderosa earns a profit of $35,000 (cell F2), it loses $55,000 (cell F6), or it loses $15,000 (cell E22). Figure 5-18 shows the probability distribution of these outcomes as .4, .1, and .5, respectively. PrecisionTree calls this probability distribution the *risk profile*. It is obtained by clicking on the Decision Analysis icon (⌐⌐) on the PrecisionTree tool bar and check marking the Risk Profile box under the Generate section of the Decision Analysis dialog box. (Make sure that the other boxes do not have check marks so that only the Risk Profile is generated.)

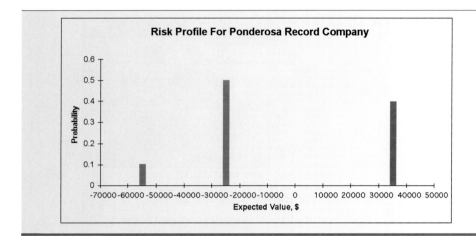

FIGURE 5-18
Risk profile for Ponderosa
Record Company

Sensitivity Analysis with Decision Trees

Because the preceding decision tree was done in Excel, all of its tools are available to analyze the results and to quickly determine how the solution would change as the input data are revised. Such an evaluation is called a *sensitivity analysis.*

Consider the probabilities, which are only assumed quantities. The success probability could be exactly .80, or it might be .75 or .85. Table 5-19 shows how the optimal expected payoff varies for different success probabilities. The original success probability of .8 gives an overall expected payoff of $1,000, from Figure 5-17. Notice that as the success probability decreases, the overall expected payoff decreases until it reaches zero at a probability of .77. Also, larger expected payoffs occur as the success probability increases, peaking at $10,000. (The numbers in Table 5-19 may be verified from the spreadsheet in Figure 5-17 by using trial and error or by using Excel's Data Table option.)

The optimal solution for Ponderosa Record Company depends on many factors. Which is the most important? PrecisionTree has many options to analyze such questions and to do a sensitivity analysis. For example, how does the $1,000 payoff change if the $90,000 partial cash flow in cell E2, the .80 success probability in cell E1, or the $15,000 test marketing cost in cell B12 vary by $\pm 10\%$?

TABLE 5-19	Variations in the expected payoff for various success probabilities
SUCCESS PROBABILITY	**EXPECTED PAYOFF**
0.77	$0
0.78	$100.00
0.79	$550.00
0.80	$1,000.00
0.81	$1,450.00
0.82	$1,900.00
0.83	$2,350.00
0.84	$2,800.00
0.85	$3,250.00
0.90	$5,500.00
0.95	$7,750.00
1.00	$10,000.00

FIGURE 5-19
Sensitivity Analysis
dialog box

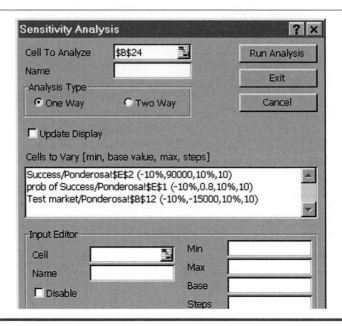

To answer those questions, we click on the Sensitivity Analysis icon (⬇) on the PrecisionTree tool bar, and the Sensitivity Analysis dialog box appears as in Figure 5-19. In the *Cell to Analyze* line, we enter B24 as cell location of the $1,000 payoff. Then, we begin with the first item to vary. Under the Input Editor section at the bottom of the dialog box, we input E2 in the *Cell* line as the location of the $90,000 partial cash flow to vary. Clicking the Suggest Values button, we enter the ±10% variation, then click on the Add button, and Success/Ponderosa!$E$2(−10%,90000,10%,10) appears as the first line in the *Cells to Vary* box. Then we repeat these steps for the other items to vary, the .8 success probability (in E1) and the $15,000 test marketing cost (in B12). Finally, we click on the Run Analysis button, and the bar chart in Figure 5-20 appears.

FIGURE 5-20
Tornado diagram
showing the effect of
10% changes on overall
expected payoff

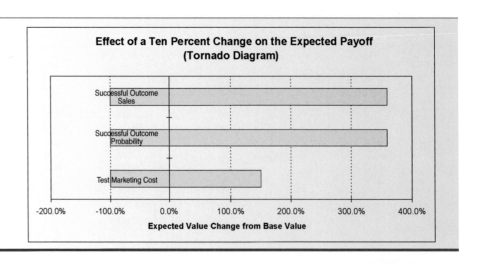

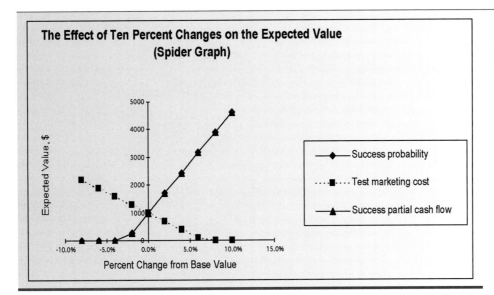

FIGURE 5-21
Spider Graph of the
Ponderosa Record
Company problem

Each horizontal bar shows the effect on overall expected payoff from a 10% change in original levels of (1) partial cash flow from national marketing success ($90,000), (2) success probability (.80), and (3) test marketing cost ($15,000). Notice that a change in the test marketing cost has about half the effect of the other factors. A chart like the one in Figure 5-20 is called a *tornado diagram*.

Figure 5-21 analyzes the effects of the same three factors in a different display called a *spider graph*. It is displayed on another tab in Excel at the same time that PrecisionTree graphs the risk profile. Spider graphs show the change in the expected value for 10% changes in each of the three factors. The steeper the slope of a line in the graph, the larger the effect of that factor on overall expected payoff. We see that a 5% change from the base in test marketing cost has a much smaller effect on overall expected payoff than an equal percentage change in the success probability. The spider graph also shows that changes in success partial cash flow and success probability have identical effects, because each gives a line coinciding with the other.

Although both tornado diagrams and spider graphs are produced automatically with PrecisionTree, they also can be obtained by redoing the decision tree calculations in Excel and then using the Chart Wizard.

Decision Problem Revisited: Software Copyright Infringement

DECISION PROBLEM

Figure 5-22 shows Klaus DeBugger's decision tree diagram, with partial cash flows on the branches. The folded-back tree indicates that SoftWhereHaus will maximize expected payoff by ignoring the competition and proceeding with version 2.0. Neither negotiation nor litigation should be pursued.

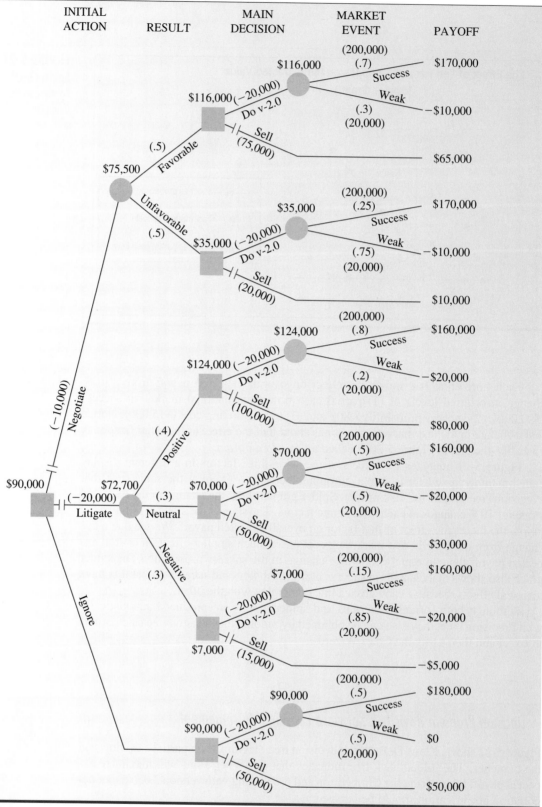

FIGURE 5-22 Decision tree diagram and analysis for SoftWhereHaus decision

PROBLEMS

5-1 Willy B. Rich is deciding whether to spend his Christmas vacation skiing at a resort in Utah or surfing in Hawaii. He must commit himself to one of these alternatives in the early fall because reservations must be made months in advance. He really enjoys skiing more than surfing. Unfortunately, he cannot be certain about December snow conditions, and his ski trip will be ruined if there is poor snow. The trip to Hawaii would be a sure bet. But if he must go there when the snow is good elsewhere, his trip will be somewhat spoiled by regrets that he did not make arrangements to spend his vacation skiing.

(a) Construct Willy's decision table.
(b) Construct his decision tree diagram.

5-2 Peggy Jones, the founder of a computer programming services firm, wants to expand the firm's activities into manufacturing peripheral equipment. Funds must be raised to build and operate the necessary facilities. Three financing alternatives are available: (1) issue additional common stock, (2) sell bonds, and (3) issue nonvoting preferred stock. A common stock issue will provide a strong financial base for future expansion through borrowing, but it will considerably reduce Jones's percentage of ownership and control from its current 100%. New common stock will also divide future earnings into smaller amounts per share to existing shareholders. Bonds will allow existing shareholders to accrue all of the benefits of new earnings, but they will also increase the risk of forced liquidation if the new venture proves unsuccessful. Preferred stock will give its holders no claims on the firm's assets, but it will drastically reduce the rate of earnings participation on the part of existing common stockholders. Table 5-20 summarizes the forecast financial status of the firm if the manufacturing venture is successful.

For each of the following goals, suggest an appropriate payoff measure. Then, use this measure to identify the best and the worst alternative choices for financing in terms of the degree to which each *single* goal is met. Indicate any ties.

(a) Maintain a high percentage of control by Jones.
(b) Maximize the earnings of Jones's shares.
(c) Maximize the availability of short-term credit.
(d) Maximize the potential for cash dividends to Jones.

TABLE 5-20 Payoff Measures and Values for Problem 5-2

Possible Payoff Measure	Financing Alternatives		
	Additional Common Stock	Bonds	Preferred Stock
1. Earnings after taxes and preferred dividends	$5,000,000	$3,500,000	$4,000,000
2. Common shares outstanding	1,000,000	500,000	500,000
3. Earnings per common share	$5	$7	$8
4. Jones's percentage of common ownership	50	100	100
5. Emergency line of credit	$1,000,000	$400,000	$500,000
6. Earnings available for common dividends	$5,000,000	$2,000,000	$4,000,000
7. Maximum possible dividends per share of common stock	$5	$4	$8

5-3 Shirley Smart has final examinations in accounting and finance on Monday and only 10 hours of study time left. The following anticipated grades apply, depending on the exam format:

Study Time (hours)	Multiple-Choice Format		Case Format	
	Accounting	Finance	Accounting	Finance
0	C	B	B	C
5	C	B	A	B
10	B	A	A	A

Shirley plans to allocate her study time in one of the following ways:

Plan	Accounting	Finance
1	0 hours	10 hours
2	5	5
3	10	0

Although a single exam format will apply for any course, Shirley is uncertain which one each professor will pick, so any combination of multiple-choice and case formats is possible.

Using her combined accounting and finance grade point average (GPA) as her payoff measure (A = 4 points, B = 3 points, C = 2 points), construct Shirley's payoff table.

5-4 The Aero Spad plant manager must choose a method for assembling parts. The size of the production run will depend on the number of units ordered, which is an uncertain quantity. The following quantities are believed to be equally likely: 4,000, 6,000, 8,000, and 10,000. The parts will be sold for $200 each, regardless of quantity ordered.

The following data apply to the three methods of production:

	Method A	Method B	Method C
Set-up cost	$200,000	$160,000	$100,000
Unit material cost	20	30	40
Unit labor cost	20	20	30

(a) Using total profit from the parts as the payoff measure, construct the manager's payoff table.

(b) Determine the expected payoff for each act. Which method will maximize expected profit?

5-5 Identify any inadmissible acts in the following payoff table:

	Act				
Event	A_1	A_2	A_3	A_4	A_5
E_1	3	4	4	5	1
E_2	6	2	1	4	2
E_3	1	8	8	7	3

5-6 Consider the following payoff table for a graphical design decision:

Texture Event	Probability	Color Theme Act				
		Brown	Orange	Red	Green	Yellow
Full-tone	.2	100 20	110	50	120	90
Half-tone	.5	80 40	70	80	60	100
Mixed	.3	100 33	90	90	90	110

(a) Identify any inadmissible color choices.

(b) Compute the expected payoff for each admissible act. Which color theme should be chosen?

5-7 Refer to the payoffs for the Tippi-Toes decision in Table 5-5. Suppose that the development cost of the spring-action movement is $40,000 higher than before (regardless of demand) and that revenues generated by the doll when demand is heavy are $50,000 lower than before (regardless of movement chosen).

(a) Construct a new payoff table reflecting these revisions.

(b) Using the payoff table, compute the expected payoff for each act. Which movement should be chosen under the Bayes decision rule?

5-8 Refer to the Tippi-Toes decision in Table 5-5. Suppose that reduction in the development cost of the gears-and-levers movement allows a $50,000 increase in all payoffs for that act. In addition, an upward revision of unit sales when demand is heavy results in a further $100,000 increase in all payoffs for that event. Finally, the following revised probabilities now apply to the demand levels: light, .50; moderate, .30; and heavy, .20.

(a) Construct the new Tippi-Toes payoff table.

(b) Determine the maximin payoff act.

(c) Determine the maximum likelihood act.

(d) Calculate the expected payoffs. According to the Bayes decision rule, which act should be chosen?

5-9 Refer to Problem 5-8.

(a) Calculate the EVPI for the modified Tippi-Toes decision.

(b) Construct the opportunity loss table and compute the expected opportunity losses.

5-10 You have decided to participate in a gamble that offers the following monetary payoffs:

Event	Act	
	Choose Red	Choose Black
Red	$1	−$2
Black	−1	100

(a) Which act is the maximin payoff act?

(b) Supposing that the probability of red is .99, calculate the expected payoffs for each act. Which act is better according to the Bayes decision rule? Which act would you choose?

(c) Supposing that the probability of red is .5, calculate the expected payoffs for each act.

Which act has the maximum expected payoff? Which act would you choose?

(d) In view of your answers to (b) and (c), what is your opinion of the maximin payoff decision criterion in this case?

5-11 Rich Sod is a farmer who intends to sign a contract to provide a cannery with his entire crop. Rich must choose to produce one of the following five vegetables: corn, tomatoes, beets, asparagus, or cauliflower. Rich will plant his entire 1,000 acres with the selected crop. The yields of these vegetables will be affected by the weather to varying degrees. The following table indicates the approximate productivities for each vegetable in dry, moderate, and damp weather and also lists the price per bushel that the cannery has offered for each crop:

Weather	Approximate Yield (bushels per acre)				
	Corn	Tomatoes	Beets	Asparagus	Cauliflower
Dry	20	10	15	30	40
Moderate	35	20	20	25	40
Damp	40	10	30	20	40
Price per bushel	$1.00	$2.00	$1.50	$1.00	$.50

(a) Construct the payoff table for the farmer's decision. For the payoff measure, use the approximate total cash receipts when the crop is sold.

(b) Identify any inadmissible acts and eliminate them from the payoff table.

(c) Which act is the maximin payoff act?

(d) Suppose that the following probabilities have been assigned to the types of weather. Calculate the expected payoff for each act. Then, identify the act that has the maximum expected payoff.

Weather	Probability
Dry	.3
Moderate	.5
Damp	.2

5-12 A news dealer must decide how many copies of *Snappy Almanac* to stock in December. She will not stock less than the lowest possible demand or more than the highest possible demand. Each magazine costs her $.50 and sells for $1.00. At the end of the month, the unsold magazines are thrown away. Three levels of monthly demand are equally likely: 10, 11, and 12. If demand exceeds stock, sales will equal stock.

(a) Using December profit as the payoff measure, construct the news dealer's payoff table.

(b) According to the maximin payoff criterion, how many copies should she stock?

(c) Which number of copies will provide the greatest expected payoff?

5-13 Use the following payoff table to construct an opportunity loss table:

Event	Probability	Act				
		A_1	A_2	A_3	A_4	A_5
E_1	.2	10	20	10	15	20
E_2	.2	-5	10	-5	10	-5
E_3	.6	15	5	10	10	10

Compute the expected opportunity loss for each act. Which act yields the lowest expected opportunity loss?

5-14 Answer the following questions based on the payoff table.

Event	Probability	Act		
		A_1	A_2	A_3
E_1	.3	10	20	30
E_2	.5	40	-10	20
E_3	.2	20	50	20

(a) What is the maximum expected payoff? To which act does this payoff correspond?

(b) What is the expected payoff under certainty (with perfect information)?

(c) Using your answers to (a) and (b), calculate the expected value of perfect information.

(d) What is the minimum expected opportunity loss?

(e) What do you notice about your answers to (c) and (d)?

5-15 A product manager for Gimble and Proctor wants to determine whether or not to market Bri-Dent toothpaste. The present value of all future

profits from a successful toothpaste is $1,000,000, whereas failure of the brand would result in a net loss of $500,000. Not marketing the toothpaste would not affect profits. The manager has judged that BriDent would have a 50-50 chance of success.

(a) Construct the payoff table for this decision.
(b) Which act will maximize the expected payoff?
(c) Compute the decision maker's EVPI. What is the minimum expected opportunity loss?

5-16 B. F. Retread, a tire manufacturer, wants to select one of three feasible prototype designs for a new longer-wearing radial tire. The costs of making the tires follow:

Tire	Fixed Cost	Variable Cost per Unit
A	$ 60,000	$30
B	90,000	20
C	120,000	15

There are three levels of unit sales: 4,000 units, 7,000 units, and 10,000 units; the respective probabilities are .30, .50, and .20. The selling price will be $75 per tire.

(a) Construct the payoff table using total profit as the payoff measure.
(b) Determine the expected payoff for each act. According to the Bayes decision rule, which is the best act?
(c) Calculate the EVPI.
(d) Complete the opportunity loss table and compute the expected opportunity losses.

5-17 Rod Shafter is an oil wildcatter deciding whether to drill on a leased site. His judgment leads him to conclude that there is a 50-50 chance of oil. If Shafter drills and strikes oil, his profit will be $200,000. But if the well turns out to be dry, his net loss will be $100,000.

(a) According to the Bayes decision rule, should the wildcatter drill or abandon the site?
(b) What is the wildcatter's EVPI?
(c) A seismologist offers to conduct a highly reliable seismic survey. The results could help the wildcatter make his decision. What is the most that the wildcatter would consider paying for such seismic information?

5-18 Recompute the expected payoffs for the Tippi-Toes decision in Table 5-5, assuming that the following demand event probabilities now apply:

Light demand	.20
Moderate demand	.50
Heavy demand	.30

According to the Bayes decision rule, which act should the toy manufacturer choose?

5-19 A new product is to be evaluated. The main decision to be made is whether or not to market the product, in which case it will be a success (probability = .40) or a failure. The net payoff for a successful product is $10 million; a failure would result in a − $5 million payoff. Construct a payoff table for the decision, and then compute the expected payoffs. Should the product be marketed?

5-20 Suppose that the president of the Ponderosa Record Company uses the following probability values to analyze the decision about the Fluid Mechanics's recording:

Pr[nat. success | favorable test] = .9
Pr[nat. failure | unfavorable test] = .6
Pr[nat. success] = .7
Pr[favorable test] = .75

Repeat the Ponderosa decision tree analysis to determine the company's optimal marketing strategy. Assume all payoffs remain unchanged.

5-21 The manager of Getting Oil's data processing operations personally interviews applicants for jobs as data-entry operators. Employees who are hired with no previous experience are placed in a 1-month training program on a trial basis. Satisfactory employees are retained; all others are let go at the end of the month. Most of the people who have been let go in the past have been found to be lacking in aptitude. The manager is contemplating contracting the testing services of a personnel agency. For a fee the agency would administer a battery of aptitude tests. The manager has developed the decision tree in Figure 5-23 to help her make her hiring decisions. Perform backward induction analysis to determine the strategy or course of action that will maximize the manager's expected payoff.

FIGURE 5-23
Decision tree for
Problem 5-21

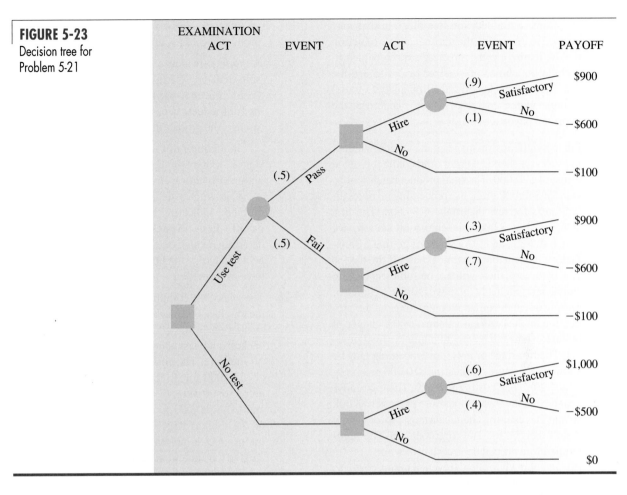

5-22 Buzzy-B Toys must decide the course of action to follow in promoting a new whistling yo-yo. Initially, management must decide whether to market the yo-yo or to conduct a test marketing program. After test marketing the yo-yo, management must decide whether to abandon it or nationally distribute it.

A national success will increase profits by $500,000, and a failure will reduce profits by $100,000. Abandoning the product will not affect profits. The test marketing will cost Buzzy-B a further $10,000.

If no test marketing is conducted, the probability for a national success is judged to be .45. The assumed probability for a favorable test marketing result is .50. The conditional probability for national success given favorable test marketing is .80; for national success given unfavorable test results, it is .10.

Construct the decision tree diagram and perform backward induction analysis to determine the optimal course of action if a net change in profits is the expected payoff.

5-23 Spillsberry Foods must determine whether or not to market a new cake mix. Management must also decide whether to conduct a consumer test marketing program that would cost $25,000. If the mix is successful, Spillsberry's profits will increase by $1,000,000; if the mix fails, the company will lose $250,000. Not marketing the product will not affect profits. The cake mix is considered to have a 60% chance of success without testing. The assumed probability for a favorable test marketing result is 50%. Given a favorable test result, the chance of product success is judged to be 85%. However, if the test results are unfavorable, the probability for the product's success is judged to be only 35%.

Construct a decision tree diagram that may be used to determine the optimal course of action that will provide the greatest expected payoff. Include the choice of whether or not to use the test. Perform backward induction analysis to determine which course of action maximizes the expected payoff.

5-24 Fiber Synthetics' manager must decide whether to process a chemical order or to contract it out at a cost of $20,000. The final product batch will be sold for $40,000. In-house processing involves direct costs for raw materials of $4,000. The first step, costing $2,000, is chlorosulfanation, for which there is an 80% chance of getting a satisfactory intermediate chemical base. If the base is unsatisfactory, there will not be sufficient time to start a new batch, but there will still be a choice of turning down the order or contracting out the production. In the latter case, there is a 60% chance of being too late and having to dump the final product. The last stage of in-house processing may be a low-temperature one costing $10,000 or a high-temperature one costing $16,000. There is a 30% chance that the low-temperature process will fail, so that the resulting chemicals must be dumped; it would then be too late to go outside. The high-temperature procedure is certain to work.
   (a) Using net cash flow (revenue minus costs) as the payoff measure, diagram the manager's decision tree.
   (b) What action maximizes expected payoff?

5-25 Using the new product in Problem 5-19, the following two experiments have been proposed. (Only one experiment can be used.)

Test market at a cost of $1 million. Results will be "favorable" (probability = .48) or "unfavorable." Given a favorable result, the probability for product success is .75. Given

an unfavorable result, the probability for product success is only .08.

Attitude survey at a cost of $.5 million. Results will be "warm" (probability = .40) or "cold." Given a warm response, the probability for product success is .70. Given a cold response, the probability for success is only .20.

In addition to those choices, the main decision to market or not to market may be made without obtaining any further information.

Construct a decision tree diagram for this problem, indicating all of the probabilities and payoffs. Perform backward induction analysis to determine which course of action maximizes expected payoff. (Specify all choices that may then have to be made.)

5-26 The MaxiSoft comptroller is not too happy with the emphasis on marketing used in the *Exchecker* evaluation in the chapter. He hires you to do a backup analysis using first-year profit as the payoff measure. The costs of the product launch are (1) $10,000 for direct mail, (2) $25,000 for targeted advertising, (3) $50,000 for telemarketing, and (4) $200,000 for mass marketing. The size of the market will be 50,000 units per year if the product is premature, 100,000 if lackluster, 250,000 if quick acceptance, and 500,000 if wildly enthusiastic. The post-launch first-year gross profit, on a per-unit basis, for *Exchecker* will be $10 for direct mail, $7 for targeted advertising, $6 for telemarketing, and $5 for mass marketing.
   (a) Using the data on page 130, determine for each act–event combination the first-year net profit. Do this by first finding MaxiSoft's unit *Exchecker* sales, then computing the gross profit, and finally subtracting the launch cost.
   (b) Are there any inadmissible acts? Determine the expected payoff for each act. Which act will the comptroller prefer?

Spreadsheet Problems

5-27 Solve Problem 5-4 with a spreadsheet.

5-28 Solve Problem 5-7 with a spreadsheet.

5-29 Solve Problem 5-18 with a spreadsheet.

5-30 (a) Solve Problem 5-20 with PrecisionTree.
   (b) Draw a risk profile chart for the optimal solution in part (a).

   (c) Draw a tornado chart that shows the effect on the optimal expected payoff of ±10% changes in the $90,000 success partial cash flow, the .9 success probability, and the $15,000 test market cost.
   (d) Draw a spider chart for the conditions in part (c).

5-31 (a) Solve Problem 5-21 with PrecisionTree.
(b) Draw a risk profile chart for the optimal solution in part (a).
(c) Draw a tornado chart that shows the effect on the optimal expected payoff of ±10% changes in the $1,000 satisfactory payoff and the .60 satisfactory probability.
(d) Draw a spider chart for the conditions in part (c).

5-32 (a) Solve Problem 5-22 with PrecisionTree.
(b) Draw a risk profile chart for the optimal solution in part (a).
(c) Draw a tornado chart that shows the effect on the optimal expected payoff of ±10% changes in the $500,000 success profit, the .80 success probability, and the $10,000 test market cost.
(d) Draw a spider chart for the conditions in part (c).

5-33 (a) Solve Problem 5-23 with PrecisionTree.
(b) Draw a risk profile chart for the optimal solution in part (a).
(c) Draw a tornado chart that shows the effect on the optimal expected payoff of ±10% changes in the $1,000,000 success profit, the .85 success probability, and the $25,000 test market cost.
(d) Draw a spider chart for the conditions in part (c).

5-34 (a) Solve Problem 5-24 with PrecisionTree.
(b) Draw a risk profile chart for the optimal solution in part (a).
(c) Draw a tornado chart that shows the effect on the optimal expected payoff of ±10% changes in the .70 low-temperature success probability, the $20,000 contract out net profit ($40,000 sales price of the batch minus $20,000 for the batch cost), and the $40,000 the batch is sold for in the case when the chlorosulfanation is unsatisfactory, the order is contracted out, and it arrives on time.
(d) Draw a spider chart for the conditions in part (c).

5-35 (a) Solve Problem 5-25 with PrecisionTree.
(b) Draw a risk profile chart for the optimal solution in part (a).
(c) Draw a tornado chart that shows the effect on the optimal expected payoff of ±10% changes in the $1 million test market cost, ±100% changes in the $.5 million attitude survey cost, and ±100% changes in 40% success probability with no further information.
(d) Draw a spider chart for the conditions in part (c).

5-36 Determine the course of action that maximizes expected payoff for each of the following versions of the original Ponderosa Record Company decision. In each case, begin with the original data before making the required changes.
(a) Raise the cost of test marketing from $15,000 to $20,000.
(b) Change the variable costs for CDs from $1.00 to $1.25.
(c) Ponderosa is to receive $3 per CD sold instead of $2.
(d) Reduce the probability of national success given favorable test marketing from .8 to .75. Also, given unfavorable test marketing, reduce the probability of national failure from .8 to .75.
(e) Reduce the original tree to eliminate the abort choice after favorable test marketing and to remove the national marketing choice after unfavorable test results.
(f) For the tree in (e), draw a tornado diagram showing the effect of 10% changes in the
  (i) national marketing cost with the test marketing alternative
  (ii) national marketing cost without test marketing alternative
  (iii) success probability with the test marketing alternative
  on the optimal expected payoff.
(g) Draw a spider graph showing the effect of the three changes in (f) on the optimal expected payoff.

CASE   5-1   *Gypsy Moth Eradication*

A government official wants to determine the most effective way to control tree damage from the gypsy moth. There are three methods for attacking the pest: (1) spray with DDT; (2) use a scent to lure and trap males, so that the remaining males must compete for mating with a much larger number of males that have been sterilized in a laboratory and then released; and (3) spray with a juvenile hormone that prevents the larvae from developing into adult moths.

The net improvement in current and future tree losses using DDT is lowest, because it is assumed that DDT will never completely eradicate the moth.

If the scent-lure program is instituted, the probability that it will leave a low number of native males is .5, with a .5 chance that it will leave a high number. Once the scent-lure results are known, a later choice must then be made either to spray with DDT or to release sterile males. The cost of the scent lures is $5 million and the cost of sterilization is an additional $5 million. But if this two-phase program is successful, the worth of present and future trees saved will be $30 million. If scent lures leave a small native male population, there is a 90% chance for success using sterile males; otherwise, there is only a 10% chance for success using sterile males. A failure results in no savings.

The juvenile hormone must be synthesized at a cost of $3 million. There is only a .20 probability that the resulting product will work. If it does, the worth of trees saved would be $50 million, because the gypsy moth would become extinct. If the hormone does not work, savings would be zero.

Should one of the esoteric eradication procedures be chosen and then fail, the official's contingency plan is to spray with DDT. The savings from successful implementation of the sterile male or juvenile hormone procedures reflect the value of environmental damage and other costs avoided by not having to use DDT. To compare outcomes, the official proposes to use the net advantage (crop and environmental savings minus cost) relative to where she would be were she forced to spray with DDT.

QUESTIONS

1. Under the official's proposal, the selection of DDT without even trying the other procedures would lead to an outcome with zero payoff. Discuss the benefits of her proposed payoff measure.

2. Construct the official's decision tree diagram, using the proposed payoff measure.

3. What action will maximize the decision maker's expected payoff?

CASE   5-2   *Warren's Department Stores*

by Gerald J. Maxwell
San Jose State University

Warren's Department Stores, which has 18 retail stores in five states, has sold full lines of men's, women's, and children's clothing for almost 60 years. At various times they have added other lines, including electronic equipment (such as radios, television receivers, and recorders); household goods (such as towels, sheets, bedspreads, and curtains); and grooming products (such as beauty aids, perfumes, and colognes).

Competition from specialty stores and discount stores has increased over the years, especially during the past decade. Conflict of opinion has arisen over what to do. Management has finally decided to determine the maximum expected income from (1) conducting an aggressive advertising campaign; (2) modernizing all fixtures, equipment, and displays; or (3) both advertising and modernizing. An additional part of the determination is whether to add an office line (such as computers, software, calculators, and filing items) or continue the retail department store as is with its existing lines. The specific cost of adding an office line is $170,000. There is, of course, no added specific cost of continuing the retail department store as is with its existing lines. Initial analysis has determined the following three-year projections as they relate to the three main candidate plans:

1. Conduct an aggressive advertising campaign: cost $380,000. Continue the retail department store as is with its existing lines: success $1,430,000 (.55 probability); failure −$110,000. Add office line: success $2,340,000 (.60 probability); failure −$280,000.

2. Modernize all fixtures, equipment, and displays: cost $270,000. Continue the retail department store as is with its existing lines: success $1,440,000 (.50 probability); failure −$110,000. Add office line: success $1,800,000 (.55 probability); failure −$350,000.

3. Conduct an aggressive advertising campaign *and* modernize all fixtures, equipment, and displays. The campaign will have a cost equal to that for the separate components plus an additional 15 percent. If the retail department is then continued as is with its existing lines, success will bring $1,980,000 (.65 probability) and a failure will cause an additional $130,000 in costs. If the office line is added instead, success will bring $2,500,000 (.70 probability) and a failure will further raise costs by $550,000.

QUESTIONS

1. Construct a decision tree for Warren's. Enter the appropriate partial cash flows onto the branches and place the applicable probabilities beside the branches to which they apply. Then determine the net cash flow for each end position.

2. Perform a backward induction to determine what course of action maximizes Warren's expected payoff.

3. What would be the effect on maximum expected payoff and the decision if the probability for success were increased to .80 for continuing the retail department store as is with its existing lines, following an aggressive advertising campaign *and* modernizing all fixtures, equipment, and displays?

4. Suppose that Warren's chooses to do the extensive ad campaign. That will be preceded by a special test at their Centerville store, costing $10,000, to assess the attractiveness of the office line. Test results will either be positive (.62 probability) or negative. The following probabilities apply to adding the office line.

Main Event	Given Positive Result	Given Negative Result
Success	.87	.19
Failure	.13	.81

(a) Construct a new decision tree, incorporating the decision whether or not to use the special test. Determine the net payoff for each end position reflecting the cost of the test for those outcomes where it is used.

(b) Perform a backward induction analysis. What course of action maximizes Warren's expected payoff?

CHAPTER 6

DECISION MAKING AND RISK: CERTAINTY EQUIVALENTS AND UTILITY

It is a truth very certain that when it is not in our power to determine what is true we ought to follow what is probable.

Descartes

R isk is present in any decision situation having possible outcomes that might significantly worsen the status quo. When the possibilities are severe, the best action can literally violate the Bayes decision rule.

Recall that the Bayes decision rule is to select that course of action maximizing expected payoff. As we shall see, a rational decision maker can justify ignoring that rule and choose to reject the act having highest expected payoff, because that choice might lead to huge losses, bankruptcy, or worse. Even though it makes better use of available information than other decision-making criteria such as maximin payoff or maximum likelihood, the Bayes decision rule sometimes fails to select the preferred act.

In this chapter, we will see how to still employ expected payoff in making choices, regardless of risk severity. Two approaches are described for doing this.

One remedy bases choice on **certainty equivalents.** These are hypothetical amounts that the decision maker would be willing to accept in lieu of actually experiencing the uncertain situation. These can be calculated by discounting the expected payoff. Because that discount depends on the magnitude of the risk, it is referred to as the **risk premium.** By maximizing certainty equivalent, a person will always select the preferred actions.

A second fix is to change the payoffs themselves, so that **utility payoffs** replace money. Utility values can even be employed in situations in which there are no natural payoffs. These are predicated on **utility theory,** a special field within the broader context of decision theory.

DECISION PROBLEM

Planning a Career

Wendy Storm is a senior marketing major who must decide whether to go to graduate school for an M.B.A. or to accept a full-time traveling sales position. Her major uncertainty about the M.B.A. is whether she will successfully complete the program; she judges her chances of completion at .70. If she finishes the M.B.A., Wendy will apply for a consulting position, which she believes she will then get with a probability of .80; otherwise, she will take a position in corporate sales. Should Wendy not complete the M.B.A., she will have no recourse but to assume a traveling sales position—a year

later than if she had gone to work immediately after graduation. Wendy believes there is a 50-50 chance she can move from a traveling job to corporate sales within one year after starting.

Listed in decreasing order of preference, the following outcomes apply to Wendy's decision:

> M.B.A. plus consulting
> M.B.A. plus corporate sales
> Corporate sales, no graduate school
> Corporate sales, unfinished M.B.A.
> Traveling sales position, early start
> Traveling sales position, late start

Wendy arbitrarily assigns a utility value of 1,000 to the outcome "M.B.A. plus consulting" and a utility value of 100 to "traveling sales position, late start." She would be indifferent between "M.B.A. plus corporate sales" and a 50-50 gamble yielding those two outcomes. Using this same gamble, she would be indifferent between it and "corporate sales, no graduate school" if the probability for achieving the best outcome were .40. The stigma of failure would so taint the outcome, "corporate sales, unfinished M.B.A," that she would reduce her indifference probability to .20 for winning in exchange. Finally, she would be indifferent between the gamble and "traveling sales position, early start" if the probability of the best outcome were only .10.

In this chapter we will develop methodology that will help us advise Wendy by answering the following questions:

1. How can Wendy quantify her subjective decision by creating useful payoff values?

2. What is the best course of action for Wendy?

6-1   DECISION MAKING USING CERTAINTY EQUIVALENTS

The key issue in evaluating any decision under uncertainty is finding a summary number that clearly indicates for each choice its worth to the decision maker. A little introspection may be all that is required.

Suppose, for example, that you find a lottery ticket selected for a special drawing with a grand prize of $10,000. You may sell your ticket to a broker for cash now or you may wait for tomorrow's drawing; your chance of winning the prize has been judged to be only 1%, and you will get nothing if you lose. Think hard about your answer to this question: What is the minimum amount of money you would take now from the broker for your ticket? Write this amount on a piece of paper.

Of course, there is no "right" answer, because the amount depends upon your attitudes, needs, and preferences. Many people would sell for about $100, although some would want more and a few would settle for less. Your minimum selling price is your **certainty equivalent** for the act of keeping the lottery ticket. Once you have this number, it should be easy to decide what to do with the lottery ticket.

Suppose that the broker offers $75. Your choice would be easy. If your minimum selling price is greater than $75, you should keep the ticket and wait for the drawing; if your minimum selling price is smaller than $75, you should sell; and if your selected

amount is exactly $75, you should be indifferent between selling and keeping the ticket.

This example illustrates how good decision making involves a fundamental valuation of uncertainties. In generalizing this concept, we will make the following definition:

> **DEFINITION**
>
> The **certainty equivalent** is that payoff amount that the decision maker would be willing to receive in exchange for undergoing the actual uncertainty, with its rewards and risks.

A certainty equivalent may be positive or negative. For example, imagine a decision regarding whether or not to insure your luggage against total loss while you make a long airplane trip. You may be willing to pay $5 for complete protection; your certainty equivalent for the act *not* to insure would then be −$5. If such insurance could be bought for $2, you would get it; if the premium were $10, you would forgo it.

The certainty equivalent is a personal valuation, and need not be tied to an actual exchange. There may be no broker willing to buy your lottery ticket at any price, and there may be no luggage insurance available. Nevertheless, your certainty equivalents still exist; they reflect the certain amount you would be willing to exchange, if such an opportunity were to be made available.

Decision Rule: Choose the Greatest Certainty Equivalent

The hypothetical lottery ticket illustrates how we may evaluate a decision using certainty equivalents. Applied to a single-stage decision, with a structure summarized by a payoff table, the first step would be to find a certainty equivalent for each act (column). The optimal choice would be to select that act having the greatest certainty equivalent.

As we have seen, some decisions require a more complex structural representation. These are best represented by a decision tree diagram. To find the best course of action in such decisions, the tree must be pruned at each decision point. This may be accomplished by finding a certainty equivalent for each act in the fork, pruning all branches but the one leading to the greatest certainty equivalent.

The justification for such an approach is compelling. By selecting that act having the greatest certainty equivalent, you are simply picking the biggest certain amount available. This cannot be the wrong thing to do (in the sense of doing what you most prefer). Of course, decision makers will want to establish their certainty equivalents in a *consistent* manner. That is the hard part.

Finding the Certainty Equivalent

You were able to pull "from thin air" your certainty equivalent for keeping the lottery ticket. This may be considerably harder for you to do in deciding what amount you would accept in lieu of the right (or obligation) to participate in a different kind of gamble, one involving the same upside potential (+$10,000, if you win) but with a downside (−$1,000, if you lose). Your certainty equivalent should depend on the probabilities for winning or losing. At a 10% chance of winning, you would value the gamble differently than if the odds were more favorable.

The less clear-cut uncertainties involve a mixture of positive and negative payoffs and probabilities that may be hard to relate to. As we have seen, the expected payoff calculation integrates all available information in a neat package. For uncertain situations with a limited range of payoffs, many people will assign a certainty equivalent that turns out to be close to the expected payoff.

To see how this works, consider the following gambles. The payoff amounts represent your net monetary change, and the lottery probabilities are given in parentheses.

	LOTTERY A		LOTTERY B	COIN GAMBLE C		CARD DRAWING D	
Win	+$10 (80%)	Win	+$100 (60%)	Head	+$100	Face	+$100
Lose	−$10 (20%)	Lose	−$50 (40%)	Tail	−$100	Other	$0

Write on a piece of paper your certainty equivalents for each gamble. Then, compute the respective expected payoffs.*

How do the two sets of amounts compare? You may want to revise some of your certainty equivalents. (Changing your mind is permissible in any evaluation involving these subjective values.)

Discrepancies between certainty equivalents and expected payoffs will ordinarily be substantial when the payoffs are large in magnitude or have great extremes. (To see this, just add a couple of zeros to the payoffs in these gambles, so that the outcomes involve thousands of dollars, and rethink your certainty equivalents.)

Experiments show that it is much easier for a person to arrive at a certainty equivalent for an act by first computing its expected payoff. That amount may then be adjusted up or down until the subject feels comfortable that the resulting figure is a satisfactory certainty equivalent. These experiments show that the most pronounced adjustments arise when there is a mixture of high-valued positive and negative payoffs, with the certainty equivalent for such risky acts ordinarily being smaller than the expected payoff.

This should be no surprise. Consider the amount you are paying for collision and comprehensive insurance for your car. If you have a fairly new car, you undoubtedly have such coverage. Now consider what you may expect to collect in claims against your policy. Whatever that amount is, your insurance company has already figured it out and has priced your insurance accordingly. They must be charging more than they expect to pay in claims, perhaps double or more. (Otherwise, how could they meet operating expenses and earn a profit?) And yet, you still buy that "overpriced" coverage and may continue to buy it even if your rates were suddenly increased. The maximum premium you would be *willing to pay* is your certainty equivalent for that car risk.

Lots of people have no collision or comprehensive coverage. But they drive old cars and have little to lose if their cars are stolen and totaled by wild teenagers. But even they would buy insurance if it were cheap enough.

The Risk Premium

The difference between the expected payoff and the certainty equivalent for any act is the **risk premium** for that act. For example, consider again the lost luggage risk discussed earlier. Suppose that it would cost you $300 to replace your baggage and

---

*These are $6 for *A*, $40 for *B*, $0 for *C*, and $23.08 for *D*.

contents, and that there is a 1% chance that you would lose everything. (For simplicity, we will ignore partial losses.) Your expected payoff from having no insurance would be

$$\text{Expected payoff} = (-\$300)(.01) + (\$0)(.99) = -\$3$$

Suppose that your certainty equivalent is $-\$5$. (That is, the maximum you would be willing to pay for complete replacement insurance is $5.)

Your risk premium for the act of not insuring is computed as follows:

$$\text{Risk premium} = \text{Expected payoff} - \text{Certainty equivalent}$$
$$= -\$3 - (-\$5) = \$2$$

The $2 risk premium represents the amount you are willing to pay for insurance beyond what your expected loss would be. Generally, the more serious the risk, the greater would be the risk premium.

To further illustrate this concept, suppose you win as a door prize the privilege of engaging in a special lottery. If you participate, a fair coin will be tossed. Should a head appear, you will receive $1,000; if a tail appears, you must forfeit $500. (An easy-payment loan will be arranged if you do not have the $500.) One of your friends wants to buy the right to gamble. What would be your asking price (certainty equivalent for gambling)?

The expected payoff from gambling is

$$\text{Expected payoff} = (\$1,000)(.5) + (-\$500)(.5) = \$250$$

Shirley Smart said she would sell for $100, so that for her,

$$\text{Certainty equivalent} = \$100$$

and

$$\text{Risk premium} = \$250 - 100 = \$150 \quad \text{(Shirley Smart)}$$

This indicates that Shirley is considerably risk averse, willing to accept $150 less than her expected payoff to avoid the risk of gambling.

Willy B. Rich said he would take $200 for his rights. For him,

$$\text{Certainty equivalent} = \$200$$

and

$$\text{Risk premium} = \$250 - 200 = \$50 \quad \text{(Willy B. Rich)}$$

Willy has a higher certainty equivalent than Shirley does, and his risk premium is therefore smaller. He is less risk averse than she is.

As a positive quantity, the risk premium may be interpreted as the amount by which the subject would discount the expected payoff in arriving at his or her certainty equivalent.

Discounting Expected Values by the Risk Premiums

For business decision making, the direct approach is a clumsy way to arrive at certainty equivalents. A more workable alternative is to first compute, for each act, the expected value. The certainty equivalent for any act may be viewed as that act's *discounted* expected payoff, so that the certainty equivalent may be found by subtracting the appropriate risk premium from the expected payoff.

$$\text{Certainty equivalent} = \text{Expected payoff} - \text{Risk premium}$$

What makes this approach practical is that risk premiums are easily found. Because a single amount would be appropriate for a wide class of risks, a table of risk premiums may be established ahead of time. These may be applied as required to evaluate a series of decisions. The risk premium table may be periodically updated as circumstances change.

The selection of any act having uncertain payoff and possible loss involves risk. The seriousness of the risk may be gauged by two components: (1) the amount of loss (downside potential) and (2) the probability of loss. Experiments with people show that these two components are the primary determinants of the risk premium used in discounting expected payoff.

The entire adjustment is motivated by the loss and its likelihood. Subjects experiencing two gambles with the same downside will tend to have nearly the same risk premiums for both. For example, consider the following:

COIN TOSS A		COIN TOSS B	
Head	$0	Head	+$1,000
Tail	−$500	Tail	−$500

One subject arrived at a risk premium of $100 each for gambles A and B, even though his certainty equivalents (discounted expected payoffs) of course differed.

	A	B
Expected payoff	−$250	+$250
Less risk premium	100	100
Certainty equivalent	−$350	+$150

Raising the loss probability in any gamble would increase the risk and should therefore result in a higher risk premium. Similarly, a greater downside potential, reflected in a more extreme negative payoff amount, would increase the risk, and, thus, the risk premium.

Not all uncertain situations involve risk. Risk is not present unless there is a downside and some probability of ending there. For example, a coin toss where "head, you win $100" and "tail, you only win $50" has no risk. For most persons, the risk premium would be zero for such an ideal gamble. They would not discount the expected payoff at all, so that it would equal their certainty equivalent.

Illustration: Ponderosa Record Company

The Ponderosa Record Company decision in Chapter 5 illustrates how certainty equivalents, obtained by discounting expected payoffs, may be used in evaluating decisions. A consultant begins this process by obtaining a few risk premiums. These are found by interviewing the president, having him provide assessments for a few relevant risks.

Recording Equipment   Ponderosa's recording equipment has a replacement value of $100,000. The president is asked what he would be willing to pay Lloyd's of London for full coverage against total loss of equipment due to flood, fire, or other natural

disaster. To simplify this assessment, it is assumed that there is a 1% chance of such an occurrence in any given year. Because such a loss could wipe the company out, the president indicates a willingness to pay up to $2,500 for such a policy. The consultant then computes the expected payoff from not having such insurance as

$$\text{Expected payoff} = (\$0)(.99) + (-\$100,000)(.01) = -\$1,000$$

The certainty equivalent is $-\$2,500$, and the difference between these amounts provides the

$$\text{Risk premium} = -\$1,000 - (-\$2,500) = \$1,500 \quad \text{(equipment)}$$

Earthquake Damage   The decision maker owns a home valued at $200,000 that is fully insured against fire and flood, but not earthquake. The consultant brings up the idea of earthquake damage. She presents a scenario in which a high-energy earthquake may cause such severe damage to his home and the neighborhood that its market value would be lost. The president is informed of one geologist who reported that an earthquake of that magnitude may be expected in his region once every thousand or so years. After some introspection, the president reluctantly agreed that he would feel comfortable with earthquake insurance and would pay up to $500 for full coverage. His certainty equivalent for that risk is $-\$500$. Using a probability of .001 for total loss of his home value, the following

$$\text{Expected payoff} = \$0(.999) + (-\$200,000)(.001) = -\$200$$

would apply to not having insurance for the year. The difference in the two amounts gives for this risk the president's

$$\text{Risk premium} = -\$200 - (-\$500) = \$300 \quad \text{(earthquake)}$$

Real Estate Partnership   The president confesses to the consultant the details of a regretted investment involving $50,000 committed to a real estate limited partnership. The partnership has spent its entire capital on an option to buy for resale a piece of land. If the city council approves the buyer's building permit application, the partnership will receive enough proceeds to return the president a profit of $100,000. If the permit is refused, the option will be worthless and the entire commitment will be lost. Both of these monetary amounts are after-tax figures. There has been much anti-growth agitation lately, and there is only a 50-50 chance that the permit will be approved. (These odds are far worse than those that applied when he joined the partnership.)

The consultant suggests that another partner may offer to buy the president's partnership share now for a negotiated amount. The president decides that he would take no less than an after-tax equivalent of $15,000, which becomes his certainty equivalent for staying in the partnership. This act has an expected payoff of

$$(-\$50,000)(.50) + (\$100,000)(.50) = \$25,000$$

and the difference provides his

$$\text{Risk premium} = \$25,000 - 15,000 = \$10,000 \quad \text{(partnership)}$$

Table of Risk Premiums   The amounts obtained are highlighted in Table 6-1, which shows the risk premiums for a variety of losses and probabilities of loss. Because the seriousness of a risk increases as the loss magnitude rises, the risk premiums get larger as you move down each column. Likewise, the risk is higher as the probability for loss increases, so that in each row the risk premiums become progressively larger as you move from left to right.

TABLE 6-1	Risk Premiums for the President of Ponderosa Record Company					
NEAREST POSSIBLE LOSS	**NEAREST PROBABILITY OF LOSS**					
	.001	**.01**	**.10**	**.20**	**.50**	**.75**
$ 5,000	0	0	0	100	200	400
20,000	0	500	800	1,500	3,000	5,000
50,000	0	1,000	2,000	4,000	10,000	15,000
100,000	100	1,500	4,000	8,000	17,000	20,000
200,000	300	4,000	9,000	15,000	30,000	35,000

Only the three "hard" numbers, highlighted in Table 6-1, were directly obtained from the subject. The remaining risk premiums are extrapolations that seem to fit into the president's risk premium "profile." After examining a rough draft of Table 6-1, the president changed only a few values from the consultant's original figures.

Decision Tree Analysis

The consultant reevaluated Ponderosa's decision tree, using certainty equivalents as the basis for selecting acts. Figure 6-1 shows the decision tree diagram. The backward

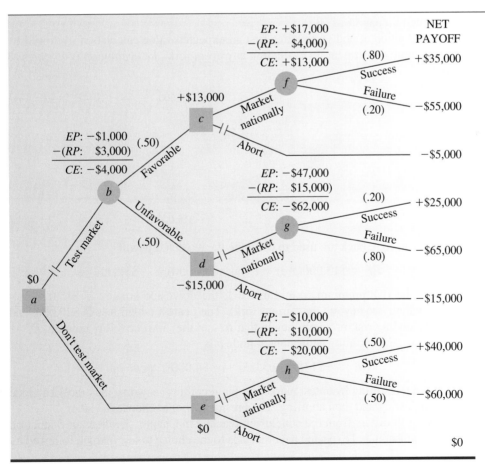

FIGURE 6-1

The Ponderosa decision tree diagram showing backward induction with certainty equivalents computed by discounting expected payoffs

induction begins at nodes f, g, and h. First, the expected payoffs (EP) are computed. Then, from Table 6-1 the respective risk premiums (RP) are read. For node f the loss value is \$55,000 (corresponding to the negative payoff amount); this figure is closest to \$50,000 in the table, and the entry in that row under the .20 probability column gives $RP =$ \$4,000. Thus, at f the certainty equivalent is

$$CE = EP - RP = \$17,000 - 4,000 = \$13,000 \quad \text{(node } f)$$

The event fork at node g represents a huge risk, with the closest tabled risk premium occurring in the \$50,000 loss row and the .75 probability column, $RP =$ \$15,000. For that node, the certainty equivalent is

$$CE = -\$47,000 - 15,000 = -\$62,000 \quad \text{(node } g)$$

The event fork at node h represents a risk with an intensity lying between those of the previous two nodes; from the \$50,000 loss row and the .50 probability column we find $RP =$ \$10,000. The certainty equivalent is

$$CE = -\$10,000 - 10,000 = -\$20,000 \quad \text{(node } h)$$

The act fork at c leads to f ($CE =$ \$13,000) if Ponderosa Records markets nationally and leads to a certain payoff of $-$\$5,000 if the recording is aborted. The latter branch is pruned, and the greater amount is brought back to node c. At that point, marketing nationally has a certainty equivalent to the president of \$13,000, and this figure is the best available valuation for that node. The tree is similarly pruned at node d, where abort is chosen for a certain payoff of $-$\$15,000, and at node e, where abort is also chosen for a certain payoff of \$0.

The valuation at node b requires first an expected value calculation, followed by a risk premium adjustment. In evaluating any event fork, *the evaluation is confined to the fork.*

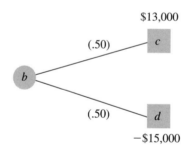

The values brought back are used to compute the expected payoff.

$$EP = \$13,000(.50) + (-\$15,000)(.50) = -\$1,000$$

In finding the risk premium from Table 6-1, the downside amount is \$15,000 (not \$65,000, which lies beyond the current fork). The nearest tabled loss is \$20,000, and the corresponding risk premium lies in that row in the .50 probability column, $RP =$ \$3,000. Thus, the certainty equivalent at node b is

$$CE = -\$1,000 - 3,000 = -\$4,000 \quad \text{(node } b)$$

This amount, resulting from test marketing the recording, is worse than the \$0 at node e from not testing and then aborting. The president should choose the latter.

This result differs from the conclusion reached in Chapter 5, where an evaluation based on undiscounted expected payoffs leads to the choice to test market, followed by

a choice to market nationally only if that proves favorable. Although messier, the analysis here should indicate the action most preferred (which is the best that any decision analysis can possibly do).

6-2 DECISION MAKING WITH UTILITY

In the preceding section, we saw that expected monetary payoffs may not accurately gauge a decision maker's preferences when significant risks are involved. Nevertheless, the preferred choices *always* have the greatest certainty equivalent amounts.

We have seen how to obtain certainty equivalents by discounting the expected payoff by a risk premium. Although that process should ordinarily be workable, proper levels for the risk premiums must be found first. That task can be a daunting one.

In this section, we present an alternative procedure for accommodating attitude toward risk. This is done by replacing monetary payoffs with **utilities.** As we shall see, a decision maker will maximize his or her certainty equivalent whenever he or she maximizes expected utility. This alternative approach has the advantage of avoiding messy computations while still identifying which choices are truly preferred.

As we shall see, utilities may even be found for outcomes that don't involve money. We will begin with decisions involving monetary payoffs, starting with a common dilemma: whether or not to buy insurance.

The Decision to Buy Insurance

The inadequacy of using monetary payoffs is vividly illustrated by the decision whether or not to buy fire insurance. Table 6-2 summarizes Spiro Pyrophobis's decision regarding coverage on his home. The acts are to buy or not to buy an annual policy with a $100 premium charge. If there is a fire, we will assume that Spiro's home and all its contents, valued at $40,000, will be completely destroyed.

Insurance actuaries have established that historically 2 out of every 1,000 homes in the category of Spiro's home burn down each year. The probability that Spiro's home will burn down is therefore set at $2/1,000 = .002$. Thus, the complementary event — no fire — has a probability of $1 - .002 = .998$. We use these probability values to calculate the expected payoffs for each act in Table 6-2. The maximum expected payoff is −$80, which corresponds to the act "don't buy insurance" and is larger than the −$100 payoff from buying fire insurance.

TABLE 6-2 Payoff Table for the Decision to Buy Fire Insurance

		ACT			
		Buy Insurance		**Don't Buy Insurance**	
EVENT	**PROBABILITY**	**Payoff**	**Payoff × Probability**	**Payoff**	**Payoff × Probability**
Fire	.002	−$100	−$ .20	−$40,000	−$80.00
No fire	.998	− 100	− 99.80	0	0
	Expected payoff:		−$100.00		−$80.00
			Preferred act		*"Best" act*

In this example, the Bayes decision rule (maximize expected payoff) indicates that it is optimal for Spiro *not to buy* insurance. That should not be surprising, because policy premiums must be higher than the expected claim size, which is equivalent to the policyholder's expected dollar loss. (Otherwise, the insurance company couldn't pay wages and achieve profits.) Buying insurance may be considered as an *unfair* gamble. Individuals can expect to pay more in casualty insurance premiums than they will collect in claims. Yet most homeowners buy fire insurance. Loss of a home, which composes the major portion of a lifetime's savings for many people, is a dreadful prospect. The expenditure of an annual premium, although not exactly appealing, buys a feeling of security that seems to outweigh the expected payoff disadvantage.

The Bayes decision rule selects the *less preferred act*. Does this mean that it is an invalid criterion? Rather than answer no immediately, let us consider the payoffs used. The true worth of the outcomes is not reflected by the dollar payoffs. A policyholder is willing to pay more than the expected dollar loss to achieve "peace of mind." We say that the policyholder derives greater utility from having insurance.

Numerical Utility Values

We want to obtain *numerical values* that express the true worth of the outcomes. We refer to such numbers as **utilities.** Much investigation has been made of the true worth of monetary payoffs. The early eighteenth-century mathematician Daniel Bernoulli, a pioneer in developing a measure of utility, proposed that *the true worth of an individual's wealth is the logarithm of the amount of money possessed*. Thus, a graphical relationship between utility and money would have the basic shape of the curve in Figure 6-2. Note that although the slope of this curve is always positive, it decreases as the amount of money increases. The person has *decreasing marginal utility for money*.

The Saint Petersburg Paradox   A gambling game called the **Saint Petersburg Paradox** led Bernoulli to his conclusion. In the game, a balanced coin is fairly tossed until the first head appears. The gambler's winnings are based on the number of tosses that are made before the game ends. If a head appears on the first toss, the player wins $2. If not, the "kitty" is doubled to $4 — the reward if a head appears on the second toss. If a tail occurs on the second toss, the kitty is doubled again. The pot is doubled after every coin toss that results in a tail. The winnings are $2 raised to the power of the number of tosses until and including the first head. This procedure will be more interesting

FIGURE 6-2
Bernoulli's utility function for money

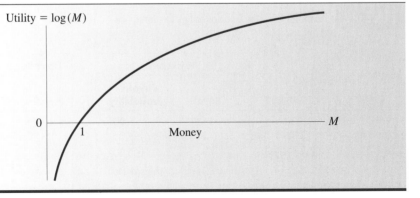

if you pause to think about what amount you would be willing to pay for the privilege of playing this game.

The probability that $n + 1$ tosses will occur before payment is the probability that there is a run of n tails and that the $(n + 1)$st toss is a head, or $(1/2)^{n+1}$. The payoff for $n + 1$ tosses is 2^{n+1}. We calculate the player's expected receipts from the sum

$$\$2(1/2) + \$2^2(1/2)^2 + \$2^3(1/2)^3 + \cdots = \$1 + \$1 + \$1 + \cdots = \$\infty$$

Because the number of \$1's in this sum is unlimited, the *expected receipts from a play of this game are infinite!* Whatever amount you were willing to pay to play must have been a finite amount and therefore less than the expected receipts. Thus, the expected payoff for this gamble is also infinite, no matter what price is paid to play.

Few people are willing to pay more than \$10 to play this game, and even at this price, a player would win only 1 out of 8 games on the average. A player paying \$500 would show a profit in only 1 out of every 256 gambles on the average. The natural reticence of players to pay very much for this gamble led Bernoulli to his conclusion about the utility for money. In general, we say that a person who prefers not to participate in a gamble in which the expected receipts exceed the price to play has a decreasing marginal utility for money.

The Assumptions of Utility Theory

Modern utility theory assumes that a numerical valuation can be found for an individual's preferences. We do this by ranking outcomes by preference and then assigning utility values that convey these preferences. The largest utility number is assigned to the most preferred outcome, the next largest number is assigned to the second most preferred outcome, and so forth. Suppose, for instance, that you are contemplating a menu. If you prefer New York steak to baked halibut and you want to assign utility values to the entrees in accordance with your preferences, the utility for steak will be 5, or $u(\text{steak}) = 5$, and $u(\text{halibut})$ will be some number smaller than 5.

Before we describe how specific utility numbers may be obtained, we will discuss some of the assumptions underlying the theory of utility. All of the assumptions have one feature in common — that the values obtained pertain only to a *single individual* who behaves *consistently* in accordance with his or her own tastes.

Preference Ranking   The first assumption of utility theory is that a person can determine for any pair of outcomes O_1 and O_2 whether he or she prefers O_1 to O_2, prefers O_2 to O_1, or regards both equally. This assumption is particularly advantageous when we consider monetary values, because then we assume that more money is always better than less.

Transitivity of Preference   The second assumption of utility theory is that if A is preferred to B and B is preferred to C, then A must be preferred to C. This property is called **transitivity of preference** and reflects an individual's consistency.

The Assumption of Continuity   The third assumption of utility theory is that of **continuity,** which tells us that the individual considers some *gamble* having the best and worst outcomes as rewards to be equally preferable to some middle or in-between outcome. To illustrate continuity, we will consider the following example:

Homer Briant owns a small hardware store in a deteriorating neighborhood and is contemplating a move. Because Homer is still young and has no special skills, he will

not consider leaving the hardware business. A move cannot be guaranteed to be successful, because relocating will involve the maximum extension of his credit and there will be no time for a gradual buildup of business. Therefore, moving will either improve Homer's present business or be disastrous. Thus, Homer is faced with one of the following outcomes:

Most preferred O_3 Increasing sales (if move is a success)

O_2 Decreasing sales (if Homer stays)

Least preferred O_1 Imminent bankruptcy (if the move is a failure)

Whether a move will be a success depends largely on luck or chance. Our assumption of continuity presumes that there is some probability value for a successful move that will make Homer indifferent between staying and moving. Figure 6-3 presents his decision tree diagram. The fork at node *b* represents a gamble between O_3 and O_1 resulting from the act "move." Continuity may be justified by observing that if Pr[success] is close to 1, Homer will prefer the gamble of moving to staying. But if Pr[success] is close to 0, Homer will prefer to stay in his present location. Thus, there must be a success probability somewhere between 0 and 1 beyond which Homer's preference will pass from O_2 to the gamble. This value for Pr[success] makes the gamble as equally attractive as O_2.

The Assumption of Substitutability   A fourth assumption of utility theory allows us to revise a gamble by *substituting* one outcome or gamble for another that is equally well regarded. The **substitutability** assumption is illustrated by the following example:

A husband and wife cannot agree on how to spend Saturday night. In desperation, they will toss a coin to determine their entertainment. If a head occurs, they will spend the evening at the opera (her preference), and if a tail occurs, they will go to a basketball game (his preference).

The principle of substitutability allows us to replace an outcome by *an equivalent gamble*. For example, suppose that the wife would be happy with a movie instead of the opera. She wants to see a romance story, but he feels that as compensation for being dragged to a movie, they should see an adventure film. Suppose that the husband and wife are indifferent between an opera or a coin toss to determine which of the movies to see. The second coin toss would be an equivalent gamble to the opera outcome. The couple is indifferent between the single- and two-stage gambles in Figure 6-4.

The Assumption of Increasing Preference   The final assumption of utility theory concerns any pair of gambles with identical outcomes. The gamble that has the greater probability for the more desirable outcome must be preferred. Thus, the preference for gambles between the same two outcomes *increases* as the probability for attaining the better outcome increases. The plausibility of **increasing preference** should be apparent. Suppose that when a coin is tossed, you are paid $100 if a head occurs and noth-

FIGURE 6-3
Decision tree diagram for Homer Briant's decision

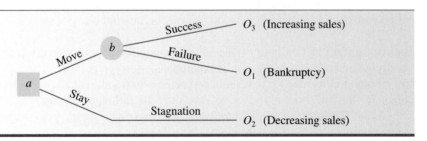

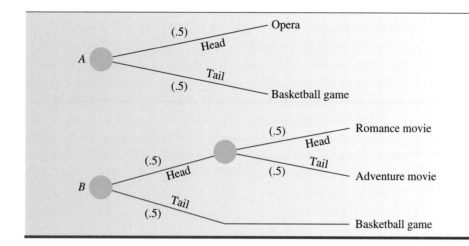

FIGURE 6-4
An illustration of the assumption of substitutability. The single-stage gamble at A and the two-stage gamble at B are equally well regarded.

ing if a tail occurs. The probability for winning $100 is 1/2. It should be obvious that this gamble would be decidedly inferior to a gamble with the same outcomes and a probability for winning greater than 1/2.

Assigning Utility Values

Utility numbers must be assigned to outcomes in such a way that the outcome for which a person has a greater preference receives the greater value. The resulting values gauge that person's relative preferences. Any numbers satisfying these requirements will be suitable as utilities, and their absolute magnitudes may be arbitrarily set.

We are presently concerned with making choices under uncertainty. Thus, the payoffs for decision acts are unknown, and each act may be viewed as a gamble with uncertain rewards. To evaluate such decisions, we must extend the concept of utility to gambles.

Recall that the Bayes decision rule involves comparisons between the expected payoffs of acts, so that the "optimal" choice has the maximum expected payoff. But this can lead to inferior choices (not the most preferred). We want to overcome this obstacle by using utilities in place of dollar payoffs. We therefore require that the expected utility payoffs provide a valid means of comparing alternatives, so that the preferred act will be the one actually having the greatest utility.

But we can go one step further. Suppose that the most preferred action has the greatest expected utility, the next most preferred action has the next greatest utility, and so forth. Then expected utility would express preference ranking, and the *expected utility values would themselves be utilities*. Each utility value would express the worth of a *gamble* between outcomes obtained by averaging the utility values of the outcomes, using their respective probabilities as weights. This may be stated more precisely as a property of utility theory.

PROPERTY

In any gamble between outcome A and outcome B, with probabilities of q for A and $1 - q$ for B

$$u(\text{gamble}) = qu(A) + (1 - q)u(B)$$

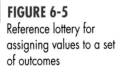

FIGURE 6-5
Reference lottery for assigning values to a set of outcomes

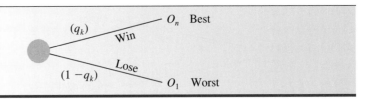

Thus, the utility for a gamble between two outcomes is equal to the expected utility for the gamble. When acts having uncertain outcomes are viewed as gambles, the utility for an act is equal to the expected utility. *When payoffs are measured in terms of utilities, the Bayes decision rule will indicate that the act having the maximum expected utility is optimal*, so that this criterion may always be used to select the most preferred act.

We are now ready to assign utility values to outcomes. The numbers are obtained from a series of gambles between a pair of outcomes, as shown in Figure 6-5.

The Reference Lottery

The process begins with a preference ranking of all the outcomes to be considered. The most preferred and the least preferred outcomes are determined, and a gamble between these outcomes establishes the individual's utilities. We call this a **reference lottery.** It has two events: "win," which corresponds to achieving the best outcome, and "lose," which corresponds to attaining the worst outcome. Such a gamble is purely *hypothetical* and only provides a framework for assessing utility. The events "win" and "lose" do not relate to any events in the actual decision structure and are used to divorce the reference lottery from actual similar gambles. *The probability for winning the hypothetical reference lottery is a variable,* denoted by q, which changes according to the attitudes of the decision maker.

The initial assignment of utility values to the best and worst outcomes is *completely arbitrary*. It does not matter what values are chosen; assigning different values to these arbitrary utilities will result in different utility scales. This is similar to temperature measurement, in which two different and quite arbitrary values are used to define the Fahrenheit and Celsius scales. The choices of 32° Fahrenheit and 0° Celsius for the freezing point of water and of 212°F and 100°C for its boiling point result in quite different values on these two scales for any particular temperature, but either scale can be meaningfully used.

Obtaining Utility Values

Once the extreme utility values are set, the decision maker may use the reference lottery to obtain utilities for the intermediate outcomes. This is accomplished by varying the "win" probability q until the decision maker establishes a value of q that serves as a *point of indifference* between achieving that outcome for certain and letting the reward be determined by the reference lottery. That particular value of q makes the reference lottery a gamble that is equivalent to the intermediate outcome so evaluated.

Once an indifference value of q has been established for an outcome, its utility value may be determined by calculating the expected value of the reference lottery using that value of q. Letting O_1 and O_n represent the least and the most preferred outcomes, we then find the utility of an outcome O_k of intermediate preference from

$$u(O_k) = q_k u(O_n) + (1 - q_k)u(O_1)$$

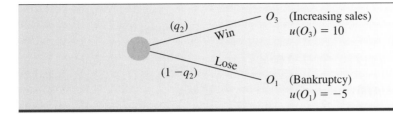

FIGURE 6-6
The reference lottery for
Homer Briant's decision

Here, q_k is the value of q that makes the decision maker *indifferent* between the certain achievement of O_k and taking a chance with the reference lottery. The utility value $u(O_k)$ is analogous to a numerical degree value beside a marking on a thermometer.

To illustrate, we will continue with Homer Briant's contemplated business relocation. Homer has ranked his preferences for the outcomes of increasing sales (O_3), decreasing sales (O_2), and bankruptcy (O_1), and the reference lottery is shown in Figure 6-6. Suppose that the utility values of the extreme outcomes are arbitrarily set at 10 and −5, so that

$$u(O_3) = 10 \qquad u(O_1) = -5$$

Now assume that Homer contemplates the reference lottery in terms of 100 marbles in a box, some labeled W for "win" and the rest labeled L for "lose." A marble is to be selected at random. If it is a W, then Homer will be guaranteed outcome O_3 (increasing sales), but if it is an L, he will go bankrupt for certain, achieving outcome O_1. Homer is then asked what number of W marbles would make him indifferent between facing declining sales (outcome O_2) or taking his chances with the lottery. After considerable thought, Homer replies that 75 W marbles would make him regard O_2 and the reference lottery equally well. This establishes a reference lottery win probability of q_2 that makes it an equivalent gamble to outcome O_2.

$$q_2 = 75/100 = .75$$

This probability may then be used to calculate the utility of declining sales.

$$\begin{aligned} u(O_2) &= q_2 u(O_3) + (1 - q_2) u(O_1) \\ &= .75(10) + .25(-5) \\ &= 6.25 \end{aligned}$$

Attitude Versus Judgment

It must be emphasized that the value $q_2 = .75$ is merely a device used to establish indifference. *The selected probability for winning the lottery has nothing to do with the chance that the most favorable outcome will occur.* In setting $q_2 = .75$, the decision maker is expressing an *attitude* toward one outcome in terms of the rewards of a hypothetical gamble. This value was obtained through introspection in an attempt to balance tastes and aspirations between remaining in a declining business or gambling to improve it. Homer is assumed to be capable of switching from introspection to dispassionate *judgment* when asked later what he thinks the actual chance is that moving his business will be a success. To arrive at the probability of success, our decision maker must use his experience and knowledge of such factors as the history of failures by relocated businesses, prevailing economic conditions, and possible competitor reactions.

Suppose that Homer judges his chance of success after moving to be 1/2. We now analyze his decision problem by applying the Bayes decision rule, using utilities as

FIGURE 6-7
Homer Briant's decision
tree diagram showing
backward induction
analysis with utility
payoffs

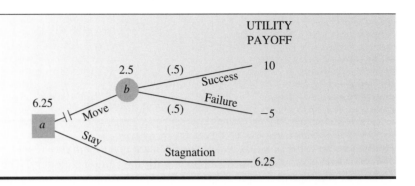

payoff values. The decision tree diagram is shown in Figure 6-7. The expected utility payoff for the event fork at *b* is 2.5, which is the utility achieved by moving. Because this value is smaller than the 6.25 utility achieved by remaining in his present location, Homer Briant should not move. Thus, we prune the branch corresponding to the act "move" and bring the 6.25 utility payoff back to node *a*.

Utility and the Bayes Decision Rule

This example illustrates why the Bayes decision rule is valid when utility payoffs are used. The utility for a gamble is the expected value of the utilities assigned to its rewards. Because any act with uncertain outcomes may be viewed as a gamble, the act that provides the greatest utility — and therefore the one that must be preferred — is the act with the maximum expected utility payoff. The Bayes decision rule may therefore be viewed as an extension of utility theory, and the criterion serves only to translate the decision maker's preferences into a choice of act. Homer Briant decides to stay because this act provides the greater utility — which may only be the case, our theory states, if remaining in the present location is the preferred act. *In arriving at a choice, both the decision maker's attitudes toward the consequences and judgment regarding the chances of the events are considered and integrated.* The choice indicated by the Bayes criterion is optimal because it is preferred above all others.

6-3   THE UTILITY FOR MONEY

Applying the Utility Function in Decision Analysis

The reference lottery may be used to construct a **utility function** for money. Monetary outcomes offer some special advantages. A monetary amount may be measured on a continuous scale, so that the utility function itself will be continuous. This suggests that it may be determined by finding an appropriate smoothed curve relating money values to their utilities. To do this, only a few key dollar amounts and some knowledge of the curve's general shape are required. The curve obtained by connecting the points can then serve as an approximation of the utility function.

Such a curve is shown in Figure 6-8 for the Ponderosa Record Company decision. This utility curve has been derived according to the procedures just described by applying a reference lottery and using a few key monetary amounts as the outcomes. The reference lottery that is used ranges from +$100,000 (win) to −$75,000 (lose), which, for ease of evaluation, are more extreme than any possible payoff. Arbitrary utility values of $u(+\$100,000) = 1$ and $u(-\$75,000) = 0$ have been set for simplicity.

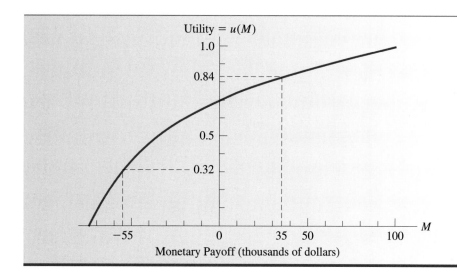

FIGURE 6-8
The utility function for the president of the Ponderosa Record Company

We use the utility curve in Figure 6-8 to analyze the Ponderosa president's decision problem. The original decision tree diagram is reconstructed in Figure 6-9. The utilities corresponding to each monetary payoff have been obtained from the utility curve and added to the tree. For instance, the utilities for the monetary payoffs $35,000 and −$55,000 are .84 and .32, respectively.

Backward induction is then performed using utilities instead of dollars. Here, we find that the optimal choice is "Don't test market" and "Abort." The two alternatives that involve marketing the CD are too risky. (This is the same result found in Figure 6-1 using certainty equivalents directly.)

Certainty Equivalents and Utilities

A tree fold-back using utility payoffs is more streamlined and consistent than one using risk-premium adjustments to arrive at certainty equivalents. And working with expected utilities will accomplish precisely the same thing. That is because any utility amount has a matching dollar amount, found by reading the utility graph in reverse order.

Consider the Ponderosa decision tree in Figure 6-9. Take the utility value of .736 at node f and read the corresponding M from the utility curve in Figure 6-8. This corresponds to about +$13,000 on the monetary scale; that amount may be interpreted as the decision maker's certainty equivalent for node f. Each utility value above the nodes in the decision tree may be converted into a unique certainty equivalent by reading the corresponding monetary value from the utility function graph.

Doing this will provide nearly the same values found earlier in Figure 6-1 (page 171). The utility-generated certainty equivalents may differ slightly from those because of the approximations taken in establishing the risk premiums originally used.

The backward induction itself in Figure 6-9 was conducted wholly with utility values. Here the only role of the certainty equivalent with the already-pruned tree would be to help in communicating the results. (Ponderosa's president would probably relate to $13,000 more easily than to .736, the utility of that amount.) The decision analyst could convert all expected utilities to their certainty equivalent amounts before showing the pruned tree to the decision maker.

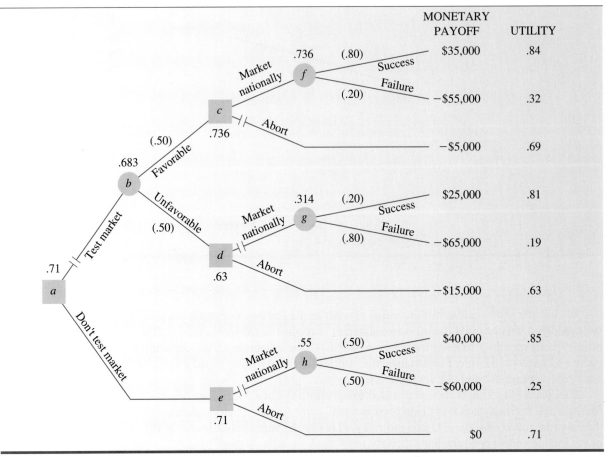

FIGURE 6-9   The Ponderosa decision tree diagram showing folding back with utility payoffs

Constructing the Utility Function

A person's utility function is easily constructed from the information gleaned in a short interview. The following example, involving two M.B.A. students, illustrates how this may be done.

Guy Sharpe asks a few questions of Shirley Smart. Each involves a series of hypothetical win–lose gambles, with various dollar rewards; each time Shirley is asked to establish a win probability that would make her indifferent between the choices of gambling or accepting an intermediate amount. A range of monetary outcomes is used that Shirley, still a student, can relate to; the highest amount is +$10,000, with −$5,000 as lowest. These two amounts are the outcomes of the initial reference lottery. The interview proceeds as follows:

Guy   Suppose that you are offered a gamble in which you receive +$10,000 if you win and must forfeit $5,000 if you lose, so that losing results in a change in your net worth of −$5,000. For simplicity, let's keep this discussion on an "after-tax" basis.

Shirley   That part is easy. I'm presently in the zero tax bracket. But where will I get the $5,000 if I lose?

Guy   A special student loan will be arranged, and you can pay it back for five years after graduation. Interest will be prime plus 2%. Let's begin. You have signed a contract obligating you to participate in the gamble and to take the consequences.

Shirley   Boy, am I glad this is not for real.

Guy   You'll change your mind fast. *You get to pick the win probability!* Before we begin, I want to define the starting utility values. One utility value is arbitrarily given to each outcome of the gamble (reference lottery). These will define your utility scale. Under this scale, a change in your net worth of +$10,000 will have a utility of 100, and your utility for −$5,000 will be 0.

$$u(+\$10,000) = 100 \qquad u(-\$5,000) = 0$$

Shirley   Why don't you use a negative value for the utility of 0?

Guy   We could. But I make mistakes mixing positives and negatives. It really makes no difference. I also like the Fahrenheit temperature scale, which rarely goes negative in our city. It's hard to relate to the Celsius scale, with negatives throughout most of the winter. Our utility scale is totally arbitrary and has nothing to do with how you feel about risk, any more than how our comfort is affected by where the marks are printed on our thermometer. I will be happy to change the utility benchmarks if you want.

Shirley   I like your temperature scale analogy. I'm ready. Let's proceed.

Guy   I'm going to plot the two values defining the "Shirley scale" as two points on a graph (see Figure 6-10). These points will lie on a curve that represents your utility function. We need only a few points to provide a detailed graphical description of your utility function. To help us keep track of things, I am going to designate our first reference lottery as gamble *A* (where you get +$10,000 if you win and −$5,000 if you lose).

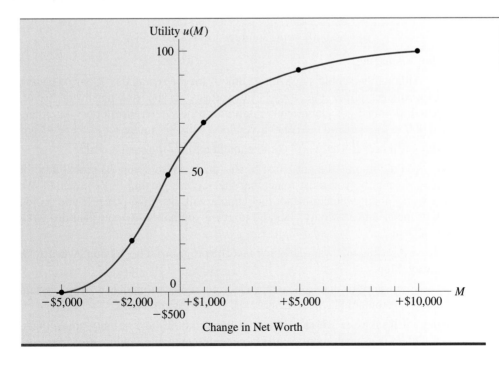

FIGURE 6-10
Shirley Smart's utility function

Shirley   I think I'm going to enjoy this.

Guy   Now, suppose that you may exchange your contract for +$1,000. If the gamble A probabilities were 50-50, would you do it?

Shirley   Of course I would take the $1,000. What have I got to lose by doing that?

Guy   A crack at the $10,000 gain. Let's adjust the odds a bit. Suppose that the probabilities are now .90 for winning and .10 for losing. Would you still take the +$1,000, or would you keep the gamble contract?

Shirley   Oh, I see. Golly, I think I would gamble. My expected payoff would be huge, and if I lose, I'll only have to pay $100 a month for a few years. I'd definitely gamble.

Guy   I hate to shatter the illusion, but I want to change the probabilities. I'm trying to find your point of indifference. Suppose that we reduce the win probability to .60 (increasing the lose probability to .40). How do you feel about the gamble now?

Shirley   Awful! I'll take the $1,000 and run.

Guy   All right, let's raise the odds a bit. Suppose that the win probability is now .70. Would you gamble or take the $1,000?

Shirley   Wow, this is tough! I really would like the $1,000, but the gamble is terribly appealing. I really don't know which I would take.

Guy   Good. We have established your indifference win probability at $q = .70$. We now have a new point for your utility function graph. Your utility for the latest gamble is its expected utility.

$$u(\text{gamble } A \mid q = .70) = .70u(+\$10,000) + .30u(-\$5,000)$$
$$= .70(100) + .30(0) = 70$$

And, since you are indifferent between +$1,000 and the gamble, they must have the same utility. Thus,

$$u(+\$1,000) = u(\text{gamble } A \mid q = .70) = 70$$

Shirley   Amazing.

Guy   Although we could stay with gamble A for the remainder of our interview, things would get a little stale. It will also be easier on you if we narrow the payoff range a little bit. Let's change the gamble to a new reference lottery involving +$10,000 if you win and +$1,000 if you lose. This is gamble B.

Shirley   I'll take it. But who's dumb enough to offer me such a deal?

Guy   You're jumping the gun. First of all, I have not told you the probability for winning. Secondly, you must remember that we are playing "let's pretend." We won't worry about whether or not the gamble will ever take place. If you prefer, think of me as emcee Monty Hall and imagine yourself as a contestant on "Let's Make a Deal."

Shirley   As a kid, that was one of my favorite programs. I hope I don't win a goat. Fire away, Monty.

Guy   Now, suppose that you may trade your rights to gamble B for a certain +$5,000. The outcome will be determined by the toss of a coin.

Shirley   I'll take the $5,000. Although the $10,000 looks mighty appealing, I wouldn't feel that much more comfortable with that than I would with $5,000.

Guy All right, now let's improve the gamble. The win probability is now .70. Do you still prefer not to gamble?

Shirley Yes, but we're close. Raise the win probability to .75 and I'll gamble.

Guy Your indifference win probability here is $q = .75$. We have another data point for your utility function. Using the utility value of 70 established earlier for $+\$1,000$, and using your latest indifference probability of .75, the following applies:

$$u(+\$5,000) = u(\text{gamble } B \mid q = .75)$$
$$= .75u(+\$10,000) + .25u(+\$1,000)$$
$$= .75(100) + .25(70)$$
$$= 92.5$$

Shirley I guess I said that.

Guy Now, Shirley, I'm sure you would prefer a goat to the following reference lottery, which we will label gamble C. If you lose, you end up with $-\$5,000$. If you win, you only get $+\$1,000$ this time. Suppose that you have to pay to get out of this one, and the price for doing so is $500, so that you are looking at a change in your net worth of $-\$500$ if you don't gamble. Furthermore, the outcome will be determined by a coin toss.

Shirley I'll pay to get out of that one.

Guy Let's raise the odds a bit. Suppose that there is a 60% chance of winning. What would you do?

Shirley I would still pay.

Guy Okay, let me raise the win probability to .65.

Shirley I would be indifferent if the probability for winning were .70.

Guy Using $q = .70$, we now add one more point to our graph. Your utility for $-\$500$ is calculated as follows:

$$u(-\$500) = u(\text{gamble } C \mid q = .70) = .70u(+\$1,000) + .30u(-\$5,000)$$
$$= .70(70) + .30(0)$$
$$= 49$$

We need one more point to completely specify your utility function. Consider gamble C one more time, but in comparison to being $2,000 in the hole.

Shirley We've gone from bad to worse. I cannot even fathom such a situation.

Guy Well, you have a well-used car, which I guess would cost you about $2,000 to replace.

Shirley That's right.

Guy Okay. Imagine that you will lose your car if you don't take gamble C.

Shirley I can't imagine how *I* could ever get into such a situation.

Guy Well, you signed a contract to participate in gamble C, and now the ante has been raised.

Shirley This is awful. All right, proceed.

Guy You've already indicated indifference between gamble C and $-\$500$ with a win probability of .70. Suppose that the odds are lowered to 50-50. Would you give up your car or gamble?

Shirley   Being $5,000 down is not much worse than being without a car. I would gamble, hoping to get out of the mess and be $1,000 ahead.

Guy   What if the win probability were only .10?

Shirley   I would give up my car. The chance of getting out of hock would be too low. I think if you split the difference, giving me a win probability halfway between those values, I might be indifferent. But I feel emotionally drained by all of this introspection. I don't think I can do another one of these gambles.

Guy   Relax. We're finished playing "Let's Make a Deal." Using an indifference win probability of $q = .30$, you have established the following utility for $-$2,000$:

$$u(-\$2,000) = u(\text{gamble } C \mid q = .30) = .30u(+\$1,000) + .70u(-\$5,000)$$
$$= .30(70) + .70(0)$$
$$= 21$$

Guy Sharpe completed Shirley Smart's utility graph, as shown in Figure 6-10. Shirley can use this curve in any personal decision analysis in which the payoffs fall between $-$5,000 and $+$10,000. A fresh utility function would be required for evaluating a decision with more extreme payoffs or if Shirley's attitudes change because of a new job or lifestyle change. Utility functions must be revised over time.

Utility functions are totally empirical. Only a few well spread out graphed points (three or four, plus the main reference lottery values) are required. As the interview shows, it can be exasperating to get these points. The interviewer needs some skill, and the subjects must have patience and a willingness to let their minds be probed.

Shirley's curve has an interesting shape. The shape of the utility function reflects the underlying attitude toward risk.

Attitudes Toward Risk and the Shape of the Utility Curve

The utility function for money helps describe an individual's attitudes toward risk. Three basic attitudes have been characterized. The polar cases are the **risk averter**, who will accept only favorable gambles, and the **risk seeker**, who will pay a premium for the privilege of participating in a gamble. Between these two extremes lies the **risk-neutral individual**, who considers the face value of money to be its true worth. The utility functions for each basic attitude appear in Figure 6-11. Each function has a particular shape, corresponding to the decision maker's fundamental outlook. All three utility functions show that utility increases with monetary gains.

Throughout most of their lives, people are typically risk averters. These individuals buy plenty of casualty insurance. They avoid actions that involve high risks. Only gambles with high expected monetary payoffs will be attractive to them. A risk

FIGURE 6-11

Utility functions for basic attitudes toward risk

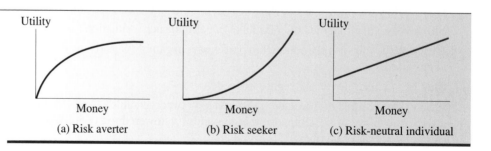

(a) Risk averter   (b) Risk seeker   (c) Risk-neutral individual

averter's utility drops more and more severely as losses become larger, and the utilities for positive amounts do not grow as fast with monetary gains. The risk averter's marginal utility for money diminishes as the rewards increase, so that the risk averter's utility curve, shown in Figure 6-11(a), exhibits a decreasing positive slope as the level of monetary payoff becomes larger. Such a curve is *concave* when viewed from below.

The risk seeker's behavior is the opposite of the risk averter's behavior. Many of us are risk seekers at some stage of our lives. This attitude is epitomized by the "high roller," who may behave recklessly and who is motivated by the possibility of achieving the maximum reward in any gamble. The risk seeker will prefer *some* gambles with negative expected monetary payoffs to maintaining the status quo. The greater the maximum reward, the more the risk seeker's behavior will diverge from the risk averter's behavior. The risk seeker is typically self-insured, believing that the risk is superior to forgoing money spent on premiums. The risk seeker's marginal utility for money is increasing: Each additional dollar provides a disproportionately greater sense of well-being. The loss of one more dollar is felt only slightly more severely for large absolute levels of loss than for small ones. Thus, the slope of the risk seeker's utility curve, shown in Figure 6-11(b), increases as the monetary change improves. This curve is *convex* when viewed from below.

Our third characterization of attitude toward risk is the risk-neutral individual, who prizes money at its face value. The utility function for such an individual is a straight line, as shown in Figure 6-11(c). His or her utility for a gamble is equal to the utility for the expected monetary payoff. Risk-neutral individuals buy no casualty insurance, because the premium charge is greater than the expected loss. Risk-neutral behavior is epitomized by individuals who are enormously wealthy. The decisions of large corporations are often based on the Bayes decision rule applied directly to monetary payoffs, reflecting that increments in dollar assets are valued at their face amount.

In general, risk neutrality holds only over a limited range of money values. For example, many large firms do not carry casualty insurance, but almost all giant corporations will insure against extremely large losses — airlines buy hijacking insurance, for example. The same holds for individuals. That people are risk neutral for small risks is illustrated by their car insurance purchases. Many generally risk-averse people carry deductible comprehensive coverage when they first purchase an automobile, and they usually keep only the liability coverage when their car gets old. Again, this reflects risk neutrality over a limited range of monetary outcomes. This behavior does not contradict the curve shapes in Figure 6-11(a) and (b), because each curve can be approximated by a straight line segment throughout a narrow monetary interval.

Many people may be both risk averters and risk seekers, depending on the range of monetary values being considered. To an entrepreneur founding a business, the risks are very high — a lifetime's savings, plenty of hard work, burned career bridges, a heavy burden of debt, and a significant chance of bankruptcy. Those who embark on the hard road of self-employment may often be viewed as risk seekers. They are motivated primarily by the rewards — monetary and otherwise — of being their own boss. Once entrepreneurs become established and are viewed by peers as future pillars of the community, their attitudes toward risk will have evolved to a point where they may be characterized as risk averters. They are much more conservative (now there is something to conserve), and probably no venture imaginable could persuade them to risk everything they own to further their wealth.

We conceive of an individual's attitudes varying between risk seeking and risk aversion over time. Usually a risk seeker has some definite goal or **aspiration level,** which may be achieved by obtaining a specific amount of money. A young sports enthusiast

might be willing to participate in an unfair gamble if winning would provide sufficient cash for a down payment on a first motorcycle. The young professional may speculate in volatile stocks to try to earn enough money for a down payment on a fashionable home. To these risk seekers, losing is not much worse than maintaining the status quo. But once the goal is achieved, the risk seeker's outlook changes, and with a sated appetite, the risk seeker becomes a risk averter until some new goal enters the horizon.

A hybrid-shaped utility function might also occur for persons having few assets. For them, losing $5,000 may not be materially worse than losing a couple of thousand. Shirley Smart's utility function in Figure 6-12 illustrates this commonly encountered shape. Somewhere around −$1,000, her utility function goes from convex to concave, and she moves from a risk-seeking posture to one of risk aversion for possible changes in her net worth above that level.

Regardless of the shape of a person's utility function, he or she will always find his or her preferred course of action by maximizing expected utility. Two common utility functions are the exponential and the logarithmic

$$u(M) = 1 - e^{-(M/R)}$$
$$u(M) = \ln(M + R)$$

where R is the decision maker's risk tolerance, called the risk coefficient. (For the logarithmic utility function, $R > M$.) An individual who is risk averse has a small risk coefficient. As decision makers become more risk tolerant, their coefficient increases. Graphs of these two utility functions are shown in Figure 6-13.

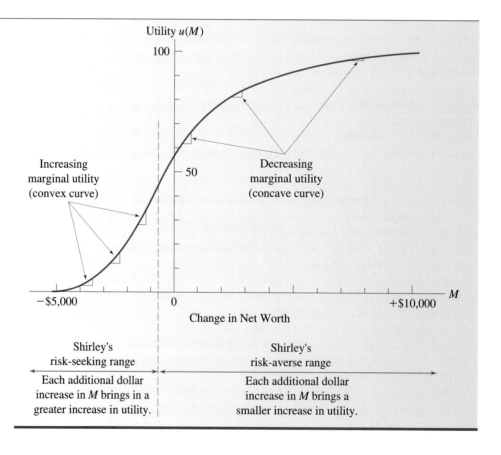

FIGURE 6-12
Shirley Smart's utility function illustrating simultaneous risk- seeking and risk-averse attitudes, depending on ranges of monetary outcomes

Utility $u(M)$

100

Increasing marginal utility (convex curve)

Decreasing marginal utility (concave curve)

50

−$5,000   0   +$10,000 M

Change in Net Worth

Shirley's risk-seeking range

Shirley's risk-averse range

Each additional dollar increase in M brings in a greater increase in utility.

Each additional dollar increase in M brings a smaller increase in utility.

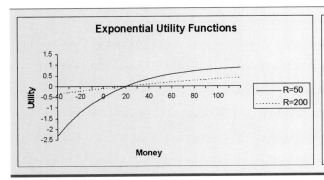 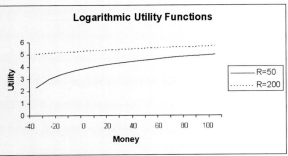

FIGURE 6-13 Exponential and logarithmic utility functions generated by Excel

Using Spreadsheets in Decision Analysis with Utility

The use of utility functions in decision analysis is simplified by using software such as PrecisionTree. They offer various standard utility functions such as exponential or logarithmic. In addition, they permit custom utility functions to be defined. Once utility functions have been selected and answers obtained, all the tools discussed in Chapter 5, such as sensitivity analysis, are available to analyze the results.

Figure 6-15 shows the Ponderosa Record Company problem re-solved using an exponential utility function with a risk coefficient of 10,000. This solution was obtained starting with the final decision tree when using expected values in Figure 5-17. We used the spreadsheet illustrated there and PrecisionTree.

After clicking on the Ponderosa Record Company name box in cells A23:A24, the Tree Settings dialog box in Figure 6-14 came to screen. Under the Utility Function section on the upper right-hand side of the dialog box, we checked the *Use Utility Function* box, selected Exponential in the *Function* line in the menu, entered 10000 in the R value line, and selected Expected Utility in the *Display* line.

FIGURE 6-14

The Tree Settings dialog box for Ponderosa Record Company

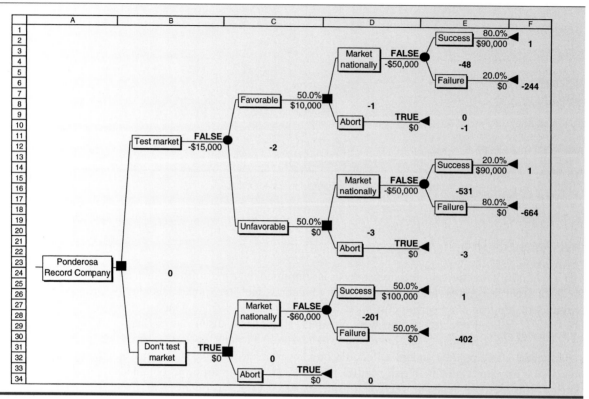

FIGURE 6-15   The Ponderosa Record Company utilizing an exponential utility function with a risk coefficient of 10,000

Clicking on the OK button gives the solution in Figure 6-15. The optimal strategy is to not test market and to abort. Although different utility values are supplied by Excel, this strategy is the same as the one found in Figure 6-9.

DECISION PROBLEM

Decision Problem Revisited: Planning a Career

The questions posed earlier are now answered.

1. Wendy can apply utilities directly to the outcomes of her career-planning decision. Using the indifference equivalencies she established to the gambles posed earlier, the following utilities apply:

$$u(\text{MBA plus corporate sales}) = 1,000(.50) + 100(.50) = 550$$

$$u(\text{corporate sales, no graduate school}) = 1,000(.4) + 100(.6) = 460$$

$$u(\text{corporate sales, unfinished MBA}) = 1,000(.2) + 100(.8) = 280$$

$$u(\text{traveling sales, early start}) = 1,000(.10) + 100(.90) = 190$$

2. Using the above and the original utility values as payoffs, the decision tree diagram in Figure 6-16 applies. There, the backward induction shows that she will maximize her utility by going to graduate school.

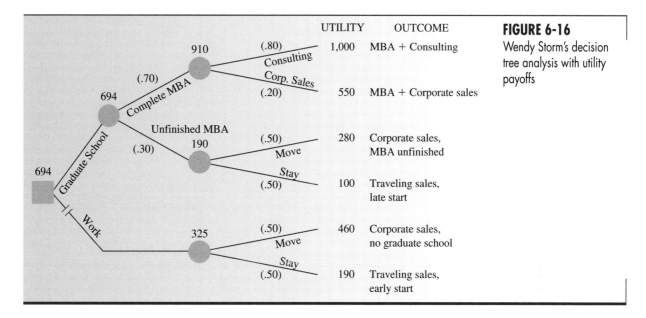

	UTILITY	OUTCOME

910 (.80) Consulting — 1,000 MBA + Consulting

(.70) Complete MBA — Corp. Sales (.20) — 550 MBA + Corporate sales

694

Unfinished MBA 190 (.50) Move — 280 Corporate sales, MBA unfinished

(.30) — Stay (.50) — 100 Traveling sales, late start

694 Graduate School

Work 325 (.50) Move — 460 Corporate sales, no graduate school

— Stay (.50) — 190 Traveling sales, early start

FIGURE 6-16
Wendy Storm's decision tree analysis with utility payoffs

6-4   (OPTIONAL) ATTITUDES TOWARD RISK AND VALUATION IN DECISION MAKING

The shape of a person's utility function fundamentally affects the relationships between utilities, expected payoffs, certainty equivalents, and risk premiums. We are ready to explore in detail those relationships, which are distinctly different, depending on the individual's underlying attitude toward risk.

The Risk Averter

When all possible monetary outcomes fall in the decision maker's range of risk aversion, the following properties hold:

1. Expected payoffs (*EP*) are greater than their counterpart certainty equivalents (*CE*).
2. Expected utilities will be less than the utility of the respective expected monetary payoff.
3. Risk premiums (*RP* = *EP* − *CE*) are *positive*.

Figure 6-17 illustrates these properties for Shirley Smart when evaluating gamble *A* for which there is a 50-50 chance of experiencing a change in her net worth by −$500 or +$2,000. Shirley's expected payoff for this gamble is

$$EP = .50(-\$500) + .50(\$2,000) = \$750 \quad \text{(gamble } A\text{)}$$

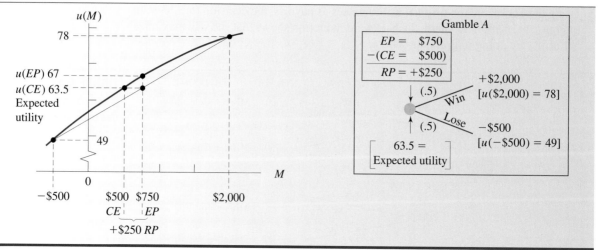

FIGURE 6-17   Illustration of the relationship between expected payoff, expected utility, certainty equivalent, and risk premium when Shirley Smart is *risk averse*

Her utility curve provides respective utilities of 49 and 78 for the gamble payoffs. Her expected utility for the gamble is thus,

$$\text{Expected utility} = .50u(-\$500) + .50u(\$2,000)$$
$$= .50(49) + .50(78)$$
$$= 63.5 \quad (\text{gamble } A)$$

The certainty equivalent for any gamble is that monetary amount such that

$$u(CE) = \text{Expected utility}$$

Shirley Smart's utility curve achieves a height of 63.5 at $M = \$500$, so that

$$u(\$500) = 63.5$$

This establishes her certainty equivalent for the gamble.

$$CE = \$500 \quad (\text{gamble } A)$$

Shirley's risk premium for the gamble is found by subtracting the certainty equivalent from the expected payoff.

$$RP = EP - CE = \$750 - \$500 = \$250$$

We may view Shirley's certainty equivalent valuation of the gamble as the discounted expected payoff,

$$CE = EP - RP = \$750 - \$250 = \$500$$

A similar result would apply to any gamble having outcomes falling in her risk-averse range.

Although the utility curve directly provides CE's, these amounts will always equal that amount reached by discounting an individual's expected payoff by the amount of the risk premium (which will vary with the magnitude of the risk). As long as all monetary payoffs lie within the risk-averse range, the preceding procedure should provide *positive RP*'s — even when all possibilities involve positive monetary payoffs.

To illustrate, consider gamble B, involving a coin toss that determines which of two positive payoffs will occur. A head provides Shirley with $5,000 [$u(\$5,000) = 92.5$] and a tail yields her only $1,000 [$u(\$1000) = 70$]. Her expected utility is 81.25, which corresponds to a certainty equivalent of about $2,500. The expected payoff is $3,000, and Shirley's risk premium is

$$RP = EP - CE = \$3,000 - \$2,500 = \$500 \quad (\text{gamble } B)$$

Even though we would not ordinarily consider such a win–win situation as having risk, Shirley would still be willing to accept a discounted certain amount in lieu of gambling.

The Risk Seeker

When all possible monetary outcomes fall in the decision maker's risk-seeking range, the following properties hold:

1. Expected payoffs (EP) are less than their counterpart certainty equivalents (CE).
2. Expected utilities will be greater than the utility of the respective expected monetary payoff.
3. Risk premiums ($RP = EP - CE$) are *negative.*

Figure 6-18 illustrates these properties for Shirley Smart when evaluating gamble C for which there is a 50-50 chance of experiencing a change in her net worth by $-\$4,000$ or $-\$1,000$. Shirley's expected payoff for this gamble is

$$EP = .50(-\$4,000) + .50(-\$1,000) = -\$2,500 \quad (\text{gamble } C)$$

Her utility curve provides respective utilities of 3 and 37 for the gamble payoffs. Her expected utility for the gamble is thus,

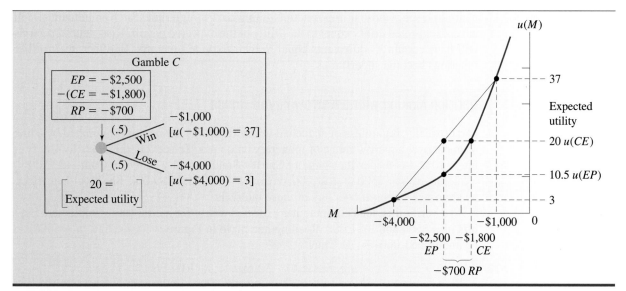

FIGURE 6-18 Illustration of the relationship between expected payoff, expected utility, certainty equivalent, and risk premium when Shirley Smart is *risk seeking*

$$\text{Expected utility} = .50u(-\$4,000) + .50u(-\$1,000)$$
$$= .50(3) + .50(37)$$
$$= 20 \quad \text{(gamble } C\text{)}$$

Shirley's utility curve achieves a height of 20 at about $M = -\$1,800$, so that her certainty equivalent for the gamble is

$$CE = -\$1,800 \quad \text{(gamble } C\text{)}$$

Shirley's risk premium for the gamble is

$$RP = EP - CE = -\$2,500 - (-\$1,800) = -\$700$$

Here, Shirley's certainty equivalent valuation of the gamble implies that she would be indifferent between gambling and paying $1,800 to relieve herself of the obligation to do so. In effect, her CE may be reached by *adding* + $700 to the expected payoff.

$$CE = EP - RP = -\$2,500 - (-\$700) = -\$2,500 + \$700 = -\$1,800$$

Any gamble having monetary payoffs in Shirley's risk-seeking range will involve a similar negative risk premium.

This of course does not mean that Shirley likes gamble C. She would be willing to pay up to $1,800 not to have to undergo it. But that amount is $700 greater than the $-\$2,500$ payoff she would expect by remaining with the gamble. In effect, her *valuation* of terrible gamble C is skewed in the opposite direction (vis-à-vis the expected payoff) to that which applies to favorable gambles A and B.

The Risk-Neutral Individual

The Ponderosa Record Company example shows how the decision maker's course of action can differ tremendously if he maximizes expected monetary payoff (as in Chapter 5) from what he would do by maximizing his expected utility. This is true when the decision maker is risk seeking or risk averse. That is not the case, however, for the risk-neutral person, whose utility function graphs as a straight line. Such an individual will have an expected utility equal to the utility of the expected payoff. Risk-neutral persons will have certainty equivalents equal to their expected payoffs. In effect, their utility functions become superfluous.

Decision Making with a Narrow Payoff Range

Paradoxically, regardless of shape, all utility functions are best approximated by a line segment over a narrow range of monetary outcomes. To see that this is so, look at Figure 6-10 and consider the shape of Shirley Smart's utility function from $-\$2,500$ to $-\$2,000$, from $+\$500$ to $+\$1,000$, or from $+\$8,000$ to $+\$9,000$. She would, in effect, be almost risk neutral over any of these intervals.

To verify this, let's compute her expected utility for a coin-toss gamble with payoffs of $+\$500$ and $+\$1,000$. Reading her curve in Figure 6-10, we have $u(+\$500) = 65$ and $u(+\$1,000) = 70$. Thus,

$$u(\text{coin toss}) = .50(65) + .50(70) = 67.5$$

Next, we find Shirley's expected monetary payoff from the gamble to be

$$.50(+\$500) + .50(+\$1,000) = \$750$$

Shirley's curve provides a utility value very close to 67.5 for getting $750. In effect, the utility of the gamble is nearly equal to the utility of the gamble's expected monetary payoff. She is almost risk neutral over the gamble's range of monetary outcomes.

Because Shirley is nearly risk neutral over the narrow range of payoffs, her utility function would in such cases not really be needed to identify her most preferred course of action. This would be true of any decision where the possible payoffs are all close together. The original Bayes decision rule, maximize expected monetary payoff directly, would nicely find for her what action to take.

But how narrow must the monetary range be before the discrepancies between maximizing expected utility and maximizing expected monetary payoff matter? That depends on the individual and the particular utility function shape. And this partly depends on the individual's overall level of assets.

A teenager might feel comfortable with any gambling situation of ±$5, while a college student's utility function might be linear over ±$100. A young professional person might have a linear utility function over any change in net worth of ±$1,000, while for a small business entrepreneur this might be ±$2,000, and for an established professional, perhaps ±$5,000 might be appropriate. For a corporate officer, we might find that linearity could be assumed over any range of bottom-line impact within ±$10,000. For a chief executive, maybe ±$1 million would work.

Utility theory is important because it permits us to do a better job at decision analysis, by explicitly incorporating risk attitude, but it implies much more than that.

Ratifying the Bayes Decision Rule and the Delegation of Authority

Utility theory implies that an individual always does the preferred thing when he or she maximizes utility. That will be achieved in any decision under uncertainty when *expected* utility is maximized. If we somehow do that, we will end up with a perfect tool for decision making.

Thus, *utility theory ratifies the original Bayes decision rule,* as long as the payoffs are limited to a *narrow range.* We need to know nothing about its shape; it will always be a straight line over a narrow monetary range. Maximizing expected monetary payoff in effect maximizes expected utility. And, since doing that maximizes utility itself, it will also indicate the preferred action. Using the Bayes decision rule would, in those cases with original monetary payoffs, always lead to the best choice.

This allows managers to delegate routine decisions (ones having narrow monetary consequences) to others, with the prescription that expected payoff always be maximized. Only the decisions having extreme outcomes need be evaluated with special care regarding attitude toward risk. Utility theory provides a rationale for delegation of decision-making authority.

PROBLEMS

6-1 Shirley Smart drives a 1987 Toyota Corolla with 147,234 miles and a few major dents. Although she has no comprehensive insurance, she is interested in buying a special theft policy that would give her $1,000 (the replacement value) if her car were stolen. She judges the probability of losing her car to theft in any given year to be 1/200.
  (a) What would be Shirley Smart's expected theft loss by remaining uninsured?
  (b) Shirley would be willing to pay $10 per year for the insurance. According to the strictest interpretation of the Bayes decision rule, should she buy or not buy the insurance at that price?
  (c) Clunkers Insurance Company will sell Shirley a policy for $9 per year. Should she buy the insurance?

6-2 Refer to the risk premiums for the president of Ponderosa Record Company in Table 6-1. For each of the following situations, determine (1) the expected payoff, (2) his risk premium, and (3) his certainty equivalent.

(a)		(b)		(c)		(d)	
Prob.	**Payoff**	**Prob.**	**Payoff**	**Prob.**	**Payoff**	**Prob.**	**Payoff**
.90	+$50,000	.99	+$20,000	.50	+$10,000	.25	+$300,000
.10	−$100,000	.01	−$50,000	.50	−$5,000	.75	−$100,000

6-3 You have been invited to participate in a lottery in which the payoff is determined by a coin toss. If a head is obtained, you receive $10,000. Otherwise, you must forfeit $5,000 (or sign a long-term note at the current interest rate).
  (a) Would you be willing to participate?
  (b) If your answer to (a) is *yes*, what is the least amount for which you would be willing to sell your rights to participate in the gamble? If your answer to (a) is *no*, and supposing that it is mandatory for you to participate, would you then pay $100 for a release from that obligation? What is the most you would be willing to pay?
  (c) What is the expected payoff from the gamble? In view of your response to (b), what can you conclude about blindly applying the Bayes decision rule?

6-4 Refer to Problem 6-3 and your answers. Determine your personal levels of the following for the described hypothetical gamble:
  (a) certainty equivalent
  (b) risk premium

6-5 Refer to Problem 6-1 and your answers. What are Shirley Smart's (a) certainty equivalent and (b) risk premium for remaining uninsured?

6-6 Refer to the Buzzy-B Toys decision in Problem 5-22. Suppose that the following risk premiums apply:

Nearest	Nearest Probability of Loss			
Possible Loss	.10	.20	.50	.90
$ 10,000	$ 100	$ 200	$ 1,000	$ 3,000
50,000	1,000	3,000	10,000	25,000
100,000	3,000	10,000	25,000	50,000

Construct the decision tree diagram and perform backward induction analysis using certainty equivalents obtained by discounting the expected payoffs.

6-7 Refer to the Spillsberry Foods decision in Problem 5-23. Suppose that the following risk premiums apply:

Nearest	Nearest Probability of Loss		
Possible Loss	.10	.40	.60
$ 25,000	$ 1,000	$ 3,000	$ 5,000
100,000	5,000	10,000	15,000
250,000	10,000	25,000	40,000

Construct the decision tree diagram and perform backward induction analysis using certainty equivalents obtained by discounting the expected payoffs.

6-8 Refer to Problem 5-26 and your answers. At the behest of the MaxiSoft comptroller, that problem changes the payoffs from market share to first-year net profit.
  (a) Determine (1) the maximum expected payoff, (2) the best act under the Bayes decision rule, (3) the maximin payoff act, (4) the maximum likelihood act, and (5) the EVPI.

(b) Which act do you believe the comptroller will prefer? Explain.

6-9 Suppose that you are offered a gamble by Ms. I. M. Honest, a representative of a foundation studying human behavior. A fair coin is to be tossed. If a head occurs, you will receive $10,000 from Ms. Honest. But if a tail results, you must pay her foundation $5,000. If you do not *have* $5,000, a loan will be arranged, which must be repaid over a five-year period at $150 per month but may be deferred until you have graduated from school.
 (a) Calculate your expected profit from participating in this gamble.
 (b) Would you be willing to accept Ms. Honest's offer? Does your answer indicate that your marginal utility for money is decreasing?

6-10 Mr. Smith has offered you a gamble similar to that of Ms. Honest in Problem 6-9. If a head occurs, he will hand you $1.00. But if a tail results, you must pay Mr. Smith $.50.
 (a) Calculate your expected profit from participating in this gamble.
 (b) Would you be willing to accept Mr. Smith's offer?

6-11 A homeowner whose cabin is valued at $40,000 is offered tornado insurance at an annual premium of $500. Suppose that there are just two mutually exclusive outcomes—complete damage or no damage from a tornado—and that the probability of damage from a tornado is .0001.
 (a) Construct the homeowner's payoff table for the decision of whether or not to buy tornado insurance.
 (b) Calculate the decision maker's expected monetary payoff for each act. Which act has the maximum expected payoff?
 (c) Suppose that the homeowner decides not to buy tornado insurance. Does this contradict the decreasing marginal utility for money? Explain.

6-12 Actor Nathan Summers enjoys wearing costumes in front of audiences. Nathan likes dressing up like a little old lady the most and hates to dress up like an animal. Somewhere in between lies his preference for wearing a cowboy outfit. Assigning a utility of 10 to playing a lady and a utility of −5 to playing an animal, what is Nathan's utility for playing a cowboy if he is indifferent between

this outcome and a coin toss determining which of the other two roles he will play?

6-13 Ty Kune, a potential entrepreneur, is faced with the following outcomes:
 O_3 Successfully established in his own business
 O_2 Maintaining present employee status
 O_1 Personal bankruptcy

Ty would be indifferent between remaining on his present job and opening a restaurant when the probability is q_2 for success and $1 - q_2$ for bankruptcy.
 (a) At age 22, Ty finds that $q_2 = .50$ makes him indifferent. If he arbitrarily sets $u(O_3) = 200$ and $u(O_1) = -100$, calculate Ty's utility value for keeping his present job (and not going into business for himself).
 (b) At age 30, Ty's outlook has changed drastically, and $q_2 = .90$ now applies. Find $u(O_2)$ again when $u(O_3) = 200$ and $u(O_1) = -100$.
 (c) Undergoing a midlife crisis at age 40, Ty revises his indifference probability to .20. Preferring big numbers, he arbitrarily establishes $u(O_3) = 10,000$ and $u(O_1) = 0$. Calculate Ty's utility for remaining on somebody else's payroll.

6-14 You may achieve the following outcomes (no rights are transferable):
 ▪ 100 new compact discs of your choice
 ▪ A grade of *C* on the next examination covering utility
 ▪ A year's assignment to Timbuktu, Mali
 ▪ Confinement to an airport during a three-day storm
 ▪ A month of free telephone calls to anywhere
 (a) Rank these outcomes in descending order of preference, designating them $O_5, O_4, O_3, O_2,$ and O_1.
 (b) Let the utilities be $u(O_5) = 100$ for the best outcome and $u(O_1) = 0$ for the worst outcome. Consider a box containing 1,000 marbles, some of which are labeled "win" and the remainder of which are labeled "lose." If a "win" marble is selected at random from the box, you will achieve O_5. If a "lose" marble is chosen, you will attain O_1. Determine how many marbles of each type would make you indifferent between gambling or achieving O_2. Determine the same for O_3 and O_4.

(c) The corresponding probabilities for winning q_k may be determined by dividing the respective number of "win" marbles by 1,000. Use these probabilities to calculate $u(O_4)$, $u(O_3)$, and $u(O_2)$.

6-15 Willy B. Rich wants his utility curve constructed for the change M in his net worth over the range from $-\$10,000$ to $+\$20,000$. He arbitrarily sets the respective utilities at 0 and 100. In response to queries regarding hypothetical gambles involving these amounts, Willy establishes the following equivalences:

Equivalent Amount	Probability for Winning $20,000
−$5,000	.60
0	.80
+10,000	.95

(a) Calculate his utilities for these monetary amounts.
(b) On graph paper, sketch Willy's utility function.
(c) From your curve read Willy's utilities for the following changes in net worth:
    (1) −$2,000   (2) +$2,000   (3) +$5,000

6-16 Suppose that Alvin Black's attitude toward risk is generally averse. For each of the following 50-50 gambling propositions, indicate whether Alvin (1) would be willing, (2) might desire, or (3) would be unwilling to participate. Explain.
(a) $10,000 versus $0
(b) $10,000 versus −$1,000
(c) $15,000 versus −$10,000
(d) $500 versus −$600
(e) $20,000 versus $10,000

6-17 Lucille Brown is risk-neutral. Would she buy comprehensive coverage for her automobile if she agreed with company actuaries regarding the probability distribution for future claim sizes? Explain.

6-18 Victor White is a risk seeker. Does this necessarily imply that he will never buy casualty insurance? Explain.

6-19 Refer to Shirley Smart's utility function in Figure 6-10. Shirley is faced with the following gambles:

(1) Gamble V		(2) Gamble W		(3) Gamble Y		(4) Gamble Z	
Probability	Payoff	Probability	Payoff	Probability	Payoff	Probability	Payoff
.90	+$5,000	.50	+$1,000	.75	+$4,000	.20	+$10,000
.10	−$5,000	.50	−$1,000	.25	−$1,000	.80	−$ 2,000

(a) Calculate Shirley's expected utilities for each gamble.
(b) Find Shirley's certainty equivalent for each gamble.
(c) Compute Shirley's expected monetary payoff for each gamble.
(d) For each gamble, subtract your answer to (b) from that for (c), to find Shirley's risk premium.

6-20 Conduct an interview with another person and construct a graph for the individual's utility function. Use changes in net worth ranging from a low of −$5,000 to a high of +$10,000. You may use any arbitrary utility scale. Ignore any tax implications.

6-21 A contractor must determine whether to buy or rent the equipment required to do a job up for bid. Because of lead-time requirements, he must decide whether to obtain the equipment before he knows if he has been awarded the contract. If he buys the equipment, the contract will result in $120,000 net profit after equipment resale returns, but if he loses the job, then the equipment will have to be sold at a $40,000 loss. By renting, his profit from the contract (if he wins it) will be only $50,000, but there will be no loss of money if the job is not won. The contractor's chances of winning are 50-50, and his utility function is $u(M) = \sqrt{M + 40,000}$.
(a) Construct the contractor's payoff table using profit as the payoff measure.
(b) Calculate the expected profit for each act. According to the Bayes decision rule, what act should the contractor select?
(c) Construct the contractor's payoff table using utilities as the payoff measure.
(d) Calculate the expected utility payoff for each act. Which act provides the maximum expected utility?
(e) Which act should the decision maker choose? Explain.

6-22 Refer to the Spillsberry decision in Problem 5-23 (page 159). The decision maker wants to maximize his expected utility. He arbitrarily assigns utilities of 100 to +$1,000,000 and −100 to −$300,000. Using these as the outcomes from his reference lottery, an interviewer found the following indifference probabilities for in-between amounts:

Amount	Indifference Probability
+$500,000	.90
−$100,000	.50
+$200,000	.80

(a) Sketch the manager's utility function.
(b) Construct the manager's decision tree diagram. Then determine the monetary payoff for each end position.
(c) Determine the utility value for each end position. Then perform backward induction analysis to determine which course of action maximizes expected utility.

6-23 Refer to Problem 6-22 and to your answers. Copy a fresh decision tree. Indicate for each node the expected monetary payoff, the certainty equivalent, and the risk premium. Prune your tree to maximize certainty equivalent.

6-24 Suppose that the Ponderosa Record Company's utility function for money is

$$u(M) = [(M + 65,000)/10,000]^2$$

(a) Redraw Figure 6-9 (page 182), and calculate the utility for each end position.
(b) Perform backward induction analysis using the new utilities you have calculated. What strategy is optimal?
(c) On a piece of graph paper, plot the utilities you calculated in (a) as a function of monetary payoffs M. Sketch a curve through the points. Of what attitude toward risk is the shape of your curve indicative?

6-25 An insurance policy would cost Hermie Hawks $1,000 per year to protect his home from tornado damage. Assume that any actual tornado damage to Hermie's house, valued at $100,000, would be totally destructive and that the probability that a tornado will hit his house during the year is .0025.

(a) If Hermie is risk neutral, what would his optimal decision be regarding buying tornado insurance? Show your computations.
(b) How much above its expected claim size is the insurance company charging Hermie for its combined overhead and profit on the proposed policy?
(c) Hermie's utility function for any change in his monetary position for any amount M is

$$u(M) = 10,000 − (M/1,000)^2$$

What action should Hermie take to maximize his expected utility?
(d) What annual insurance premium charge would make Hermie indifferent between buying or not buying tornado insurance?

6-26 J. P. Tidewasser has just undergone the first traumatic phase of determining his utility function for a range of monetary values. By his response to a series of gambles, it has been established that he is indifferent between making the 50-50 gambles on the left and receiving the certain amounts of money shown on the right:

Rewards of Gamble		Equivalent Amount
+$30,000	−$10,000	$ 0
+ 30,000	0	+10,000
0	− 10,000	− 7,000
+ 10,000	− 7,000	1,000

(a) If Tidewasser sets $u(\$30,000) = 1$ and $u(−\$10,000) = 0$, determine his utility for $0.
(b) Calculate J. P.'s utilities for +$10,000 and −$7,000.
(c) Calculate J. P.'s utility for +$1,000. What, if any, inconsistencies do you notice between this and your previous answers?

6-27 Hoopla Hoops is a retail boutique catering to current crazes. The owner must decide whether or not to stock a batch of Water Wheelies. Each item costs $2 and sells for $4. Unsold items cannot be returned to the supplier, who sells them in batches of 500. The following probability distribution is assumed to apply for the anticipated demand for Water Wheelies:

Demand	Probability
100	.05
200	.10
300	.15
400	.20
500	.20
600	.15
700	.10
800	.05
	1.00

Consider demand to mean the potential for sales. No more than what is demanded may be sold; but if demand exceeds on-hand inventory, then not all of the demand may be fulfilled.

(a) Calculate the expected demand. If you assume that the expected demand will actually occur, what profit corresponds to this amount? Use the utility curve shown in Figure 6-19 to determine the corresponding utility value.

(b) Calculate the expected profit from stocking 500 Water Wheelies. Does this differ from the amount you found in (a)? Explain this. Determine the utility for the expected profit.

(c) Calculate the expected utility for stocking 500 Water Wheelies. (First, calculate the profit for each level of possible demand; then, find the utility for each level; finally, apply the probability weights.) Which act — stock-

FIGURE 6-19

Utility function for Problems 6-27 and 6-28

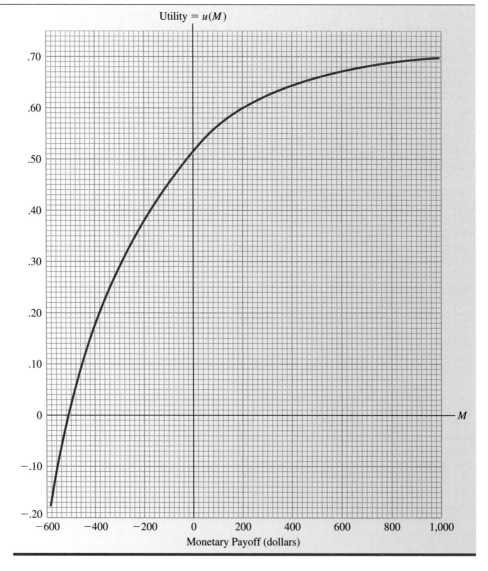

ing or not stocking Water Wheelies — provides the greatest expected utility?

6-28   Consider the plight of the decision maker in Problem 5-21 (page 158). She must interview dozens of candidates annually for data-entry jobs. Losses of her recoverable training expenses may therefore be significant. Suppose that she has constructed the utility function shown in Figure 6-19.

(a) Redraw Figure 5-23 (page 159).
(b) For the monetary payoff value for each end position, determine the decision maker's approximate utility value from the curve in Figure 6-19.
(c) Perform backward induction analysis using utilities as payoffs. Which strategy is optimal?

Spreadsheet Problems

6-29   Solve Problem 6-19 with a spreadsheet.

6-30   Solve Problem 6-21 (a), (b), (c), and (d) with a spreadsheet.

6-31   (a) Solve Problem 6-22 with a spreadsheet using PrecisionTree with an exponential utility function and a risk coefficient of 100,000. Show expected utilities on the decision tree.
(b) Repeat (a) using a logarithmic utility function with a risk coefficient of 300,000. Show expected utilities on the decision tree.

6-32   (a) Re-solve 6-31(a) maximizing the certainty equivalent.

(b) Re-solve 6-31(a) maximizing expected monetary value.
(c) On a decision tree, indicate for each node the expected monetary payoff, the certainty equivalent, and the risk premium. Prune the tree to maximize the certainty equivalent.

6-33   (a) Re-solve 6-31(b) maximizing the certainty equivalent.
(b) Re-solve 6-31(b) maximizing expected monetary value.
(c) On a decision tree, indicate for each node the expected monetary payoff, the certainty equivalent, and the risk premium. Prune the tree to maximize the certainty equivalent.

CASE   6-1   *Arcturus Development Company*

Fritz Dessler is the founder of Arcturus Development Company, a start-up specializing in graphical software tools. The company's major product, an animation sequencer-splicer called Story Board, is used in Hollywood productions and in the making of company training films and fancy presentations. The program has been an artistic success and moderately profitable. Now Mr. Dessler has developed a home entertainment version, called Power Pallet, the release of which could boost Arcturus's future earnings considerably.

Unfortunately, Sherwood Products has developed a competing package, Frame Mover. Mr. Dessler claims that Frame Mover has the look and feel of Power Pallet, substantially violating the Arcturus copyright. He is contemplating retaliatory action.

Mr. Dessler has three immediate options: negotiate with the help of a mediator (whose fee is $10,000); litigate (requiring a $20,000 nonrefundable attorney retainer); or ignore Sherwood. Ultimately, Arcturus will either sell Power Pallet rights to Home Entertainment Software for an amount that depends on what events occur in the meantime or keep it and develop a beta version (at a cost of $20,000), followed by full marketing. At that point, Power Pallet will prove to be either a success (culminating in enhanced profit having a present value of $200,000) or an indifferent entry (yielding only $20,000).

Negotiation might lead to a favorable or an unfavorable settlement. With a favorable outcome (50% chance), Arcturus could sell program ownership for $75,000; releasing Power Pallet under these circumstances would have a 70% chance of yielding a suc-

TABLE 6-3 Data for Litigating Against Sherwood Products

Variable Assessed	Litigation Result		
	Positive	Neutral	Negative
Success Pr[4] of Power Pallet	.80	.5	.15
Proceeds from sale	$100,000	$50,000	$15,000

TABLE 6-4 Fritz Dessler's Risk Premiums (Downside Component)

Greatest Possible Loss	Downside Risk Premium Component Pr[Loss]						
	.15	.20	.25	.30	.50	.70	.85
$10,000	300	400	600	650	800	1,000	2,000
20,000	1,100	1,200	1,400	1,500	2,000	3,000	5,000

TABLE 6-5 Fritz Dessler's Risk Premiums (Upside Component)

Greatest Possible Gain	Upside Risk Premium Component Pr[Gain]						
	.15	.20	.25	.30	.50	.70	.85
$ 25,000	200	100	60	0	0	0	0
50,000	800	500	400	300	200	100	0
75,000	1,100	700	500	400	300	200	100
100,000	1,300	1,100	700	500	300	200	100
125,000	1,500	1,200	900	600	400	300	200
150,000	2,000	1,300	1,100	800	600	400	200
175,000	2,500	1,500	1,300	1,000	800	500	400
200,000	3,000	2,000	1,500	1,200	1,000	700	500

cess. An unfavorable negotiation result would dramatically reduce the selling price to $20,000 and would lower the success probability to .25.

Litigation could have any of three results: positive (40% chance), neutral (30% chance), or negative (30% chance). The data in Table 6-3 apply in that case.

Ignoring Sherwood products would of course involve no unusual cash expenditure. In that case, the program would have a 50-50 chance of success versus a weak reception, and Home Entertainment would give Arcturus $50,000 to acquire ownership of Power Pallet if the company decided to sell rather than develop it for marketing.

QUESTIONS

1. Construct Fritz Dessler's decision tree diagram, placing all partial cash flows and probabilities alongside their respective branches. Then determine for each outcome the net cash flow.

2. Perform backward induction, using the tree in Question 1. What course of action maximizes Dessler's expected net cash flow?

3. Consider the negotiation case only.
   a. Suppose that Dessler chooses to keep Power Pallet. From your decision tree analysis in Question 2, find the net expected payoff (1) when the negotiation is favorable, and (2) when the negotiation is unfavorable.
   b. Using your answers from part (a) as the payoff values for keeping the program, construct Dessler's payoff table applicable under the negotiation case.
   c. Determine each of the following: (1) maximin payoff act, (2) maximum likelihood act, and (3) maximum expected payoff act
   d. Determine Dessler's EVPI. How might this number help him in his evaluations? What kinds of predictive information might Dessler find helpful in evaluating his negotiation choices?

e. Construct Dessler's opportunity loss table. Which act minimizes expected opportunity loss?

4. Although less so than most people, Fritz Dessler is risk averse. This is evidenced by his willingness to buy casualty insurance at various amounts exceeding the expected claim size (see Table 6-4). But Dessler also expresses the need to make upside adjustments by further discounting (see Table 6-5). Dessler's risk premium is the sum of the two components:

   Risk premium = Downside component + Upside component

   Using the nearest applicable values in Tables 6-4 and 6-5, determine (1) Dessler's expected payoff, (2) his risk premium, and (3) his certainty equivalent for each of the following gambles (probabilities in parentheses):

	(a)	(b)	(c)	(d)
Win	$100,000 (.30)	$50,000 (.50)	$200,000 (.30)	$20,000 (.90)
Lose	−$20,000 (.70)	$20,000 (.50)	−$20,000 (.70)	−$20,000 (.10)

5. Fritz Dessler's certainty equivalents are determined by the rules in Question 4. Perform a second backward induction analysis of his decision tree to determine which course of action maximizes his certainty equivalent.

FORECASTING

My interest is in the future because I am going to spend the rest of my life there.—
Charles F. Kettering

F orecasting the future is a fundamental aspect of business decision making. A variety of quantitative techniques have been developed to forecast future values. The underlying models can be classified into three broad categories.

1. **Forecasting Using Past Data**   The historical patterns of a variable are identified and projected into the future. These patterns are obtained through extrapolation from time-series data.

2. **Forecasting Using Causal Models**   A relationship is found between the unknown variable and one or more other known variables. The values of the known variables are then used to predict the value of the variable of interest.

3. **Forecasting Using Judgment**   Quantitative representations are used to express judgments in terms of subjective probabilities. These methods can incorporate the forecaster's actual "batting average" and may provide a way to express collective judgments.

Chapter 7 surveys the forecasting methods commonly used in each of these three categories.

DECISION PROBLEM

Bugoff Chemical Company

Bugoff Chemical Company is a Midwestern firm that sells industrial chemicals and pesticides throughout the United States. At a recent meeting of the Executive Committee, a number of long-range plans were discussed. One of the products, the pesticide Malabug, was of particular concern to Amy Johnson, vice-president of sales. Although sales of the pesticide had more than doubled over the last few years, costs had increased and profit margins had decreased. To get a better handle on future sales and profit margins, after the meeting Johnson met again with Warren Williams, manager of the Planning and Forecasting Department, and Wilson Chou, the comptroller. She asked Williams to prepare a quarterly Malabug sales forecast for 2002 and Chou to make accurate forecasts of Malabug's direct processing costs.

After returning to his office, Williams gathered the following historical 1996–2001 quarterly sales data for Malabug:

	QUARTER				
Year	**Winter**	**Spring**	**Summer**	**Fall**	**Total**
1996	18	80	30	22	150
1997	24	105	54	27	210
1998	33	141	48	38	260
1999	40	150	75	48	310
2000	35	180	55	50	320
2001	48	205	70	57	380

After plotting the data, he saw an annual trend and quarterly seasonal variations, and he deemed the data sufficient for preparing the required forecasts. Chou took a different tactic in forecasting the direct cost. He thinks the following information will suggest a relationship between direct cost, technical base, and raw stock that can be used to forecast future costs.

DIRECT COST PER GALLON	**TECHNICAL BASE (GALLONS)**	**RAW STOCK (GALLONS)**
$9.82	500	1,000
9.14	1,000	500
8.75	700	800
9.24	400	1,100
8.33	350	1,150

The material presented in this chapter will assist Williams and Chou in analyzing their data and making forecasts. We will see:

1. How to isolate seasonal effects. This will help make sales forecasts that will help managers plan their manufacturing.
2. How to make forecasts by various methods that explicitly incorporate seasonal information.
3. How to develop a causal model for estimating production costs.

During this chapter, we will revisit Bugoff Chemical with concrete analyses.

7-1 FORECASTING USING PAST DATA: TIME-SERIES ANALYSIS

A **time series** is a numerical sequence in which individual values are generated at regular intervals of time. The goal of **time-series analysis** is to identify the swings and fluctuations of a time series and then to sort them into various categories by the arithmetic manipulation of the numerical values obtained.

Several models can be used to characterize time series. The classical model used by economists provides the clearest explanation of the four components of time-series variation and how they relate to each other.

1. secular trend (T_t)
2. cyclical movement (C_t)
3. seasonal fluctuation (S_t)
4. irregular variation (I_t)

These components can be related to the forecast variable by mathematical equations. The forecast variable is denoted by the symbol Y_t, where the subscript t refers to a period of time. Examples of Y_t are annual sales, passenger miles flown by domestic airlines, and acre-feet of water supplied to a city.

The Classical Time-Series Model

The classical time-series model originally used by economists combines the four components of time-series variation.

CLASSICAL TIME-SERIES MODEL

$$Y_t = T_t \times C_t \times S_t \times I_t$$

This equation states that factors associated with each of these components can be multiplied to provide the value of the forecast variable.

This model can be explained by means of a hypothetical time series—the sales Y_t of stereo speakers by the Speak E-Z Company. Figure 7-1 shows how the final time

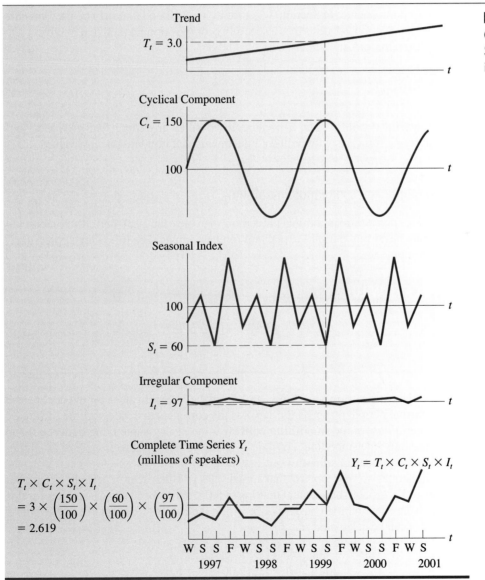

FIGURE 7-1

Complete time series for Speak E-Z sales, using individual components

series (bottom graph) might be obtained by combining the four components. But only a hypothetical time series can be synthesized from the assumed characteristics of the four components. In actual applications, we may not know anything about T_t, C_t, S_t, or I_t. Usually, we begin with the raw time-series data and reverse the procedure, sifting the data to sort out and identify the components.

Forecasting with Time Series

We discuss two major approaches to arrive at forecasts using past data. **Exponential smoothing** averages past time-series values in a systematic fashion. The resulting smoothed values are created using one of several averaging processes that agrees with the underlying nature of the data. Section 7-2 describes three popular procedures, each utilizing a set of parameters. Those parameters may be fine-tuned to the historical time series in order to achieve a best fit. In the following sections, we will encounter the second approach. There, **decomposition methods** are applied in isolating one or more time-series components. In Section 7-3, a trend line is found that may be used in making forecasts. Section 7-5 describes a second decomposition method that uncovers seasonal indexes for making forecasts.

7-2 EXPONENTIAL SMOOTHING

Exponential smoothing is a popular forecasting procedure that produces self-correcting forecasts with built-in adjustments that regulate forecast values.

Single-Parameter Exponential Smoothing

The basic exponential-smoothing procedure provides the next period's forecast directly from the current period's actual and forecast values. The following expression is used to compute the

FORECAST VALUE

(Single-Parameter Smoothing)

$$F_{t+1} = \alpha Y_t + (1 - \alpha)F_t$$

where t is the current time period, F_{t+1} and F_t are the forecast values for the next period and the current period, respectively, and Y_t is the current actual value. α (the lowercase Greek letter *alpha*) is the **smoothing constant**—a chosen value lying between 0 and 1. Because only one smoothing constant is used, we refer to this procedure as **single-parameter exponential smoothing.**

To illustrate, we will suppose that actual sales of Blitz Beer in period 10 (October 2000) were $Y_{10} = 5{,}240$ barrels and that $F_{10} = 5{,}061.6$ had been forecast earlier for this period. Using a smoothing constant of $\alpha = .20$, the forecast for period 11 (November 2000) sales can be calculated as

$$F_{11} = .20Y_{10} + (1 - .20)F_{10}$$
$$= .20(5{,}240) + .80(5{,}061.6) = 5{,}097.3 \text{ barrels}$$

Elementary exponential smoothing is extremely simple, because only one number—last period's forecast—must be saved. But, in essence, the entire time series is embodied in that forecast. If we express F_t in terms of the preceding actual Y_{t-1} and forecast F_{t-1} values, then the equivalent expression for the next period's forecast is

$$F_{t+1} = \alpha Y_t + \alpha(1 - \alpha)Y_{t-1} + (1 - \alpha)^2 F_{t-1}$$

Continuing this for several earlier periods shows us that all preceding Y's are reflected in the current forecast. The name for this procedure is derived from the successive weights $\alpha, \alpha(1 - \alpha), \alpha(1 - \alpha)^2, \alpha(1 - \alpha)^3, \ldots$, which *decrease exponentially*. Thus, the more current is the actual value of the time series, the greater is its weight. Progressively less forecasting weight is assigned to older Y's, and the oldest Y's are eventually wiped out. The forecasting procedure can be modified at any time by changing the value of α.

Table 7-1 provides the actual and forecast Blitz Beer sales for 20 periods when $\alpha = .20$. There, the actual sales figure for period 1 has been used for the initial forecast for period 2. (Eventually, the same F's will be achieved in later time periods, regardless of the initial value.)

The actual and forecast values may be compared in the plot provided in Figure 7-2. Notice that the forecast values deviate considerably from the actual values. This

TABLE 7-1 Forecast of Blitz Beer Sales by Single-Parameter Exponential Smoothing ($\alpha = .20$)

MONTH	PERIOD t	ACTUAL SALES Y_t	FORECAST SALES F_t	ERROR $Y_t - F_t$	ABSOLUTE PROPORTION $\frac{\lvert Y_t - F_t \rvert}{Y_t}$	ERROR^2 $(Y_t - F_t)^2$
January 2000	1	4,890	—	—	—	—
February	2	4,910	4,890.0	20.0	.004	400.00
March	3	4,970	4,894.0	76.0	.015	5,776.00
April	4	5,010	4,909.2	100.8	.020	10,160.64
May	5	5,060	4,929.4	130.6	.026	17,056.36
June	6	5,100	4,955.5	144.5	.028	20,880.25
July	7	5,050	4,984.4	65.6	.013	4,303.36
August	8	5,170	4,997.5	172.5	.033	29,756.25
September	9	5,180	5,032.0	148.0	.029	21,904.00
October	10	5,240	5,061.6	178.4	.034	31,826.56
November	11	5,220	5,097.3	122.7	.024	15,055.29
December	12	5,280	5,121.8	158.2	.030	25,027.24
January 2001	13	5,330	5,153.5	176.5	.033	31,152.25
February	14	5,380	5,188.8	191.2	.036	36,557.44
March	15	5,440	5,227.0	213.0	.039	45,369.00
April	16	5,460	5,269.6	190.4	.035	36,252.16
May	17	5,520	5,307.7	212.3	.038	45,071.29
June	18	5,490	5,350.2	139.8	.025	19,544.04
July	19	5,550	5,378.1	171.9	.031	29,549.61
August	20	5,600	5,412.5	187.5	.033	35,156.25
September	21	—	5,450.0	—	—	—
				2,800.0	.527	460,797.99

$$MSE = 460,797.99/19 = 24,252.53$$
$$MAD = 2,800/19 = 147.37$$
$$MAPE = (.527/19) \times 100 = 2.77\%$$

FIGURE 7-2
Single-parameter
exponential-smoothing
results for Blitz Beer sales
$(\alpha = .20)$

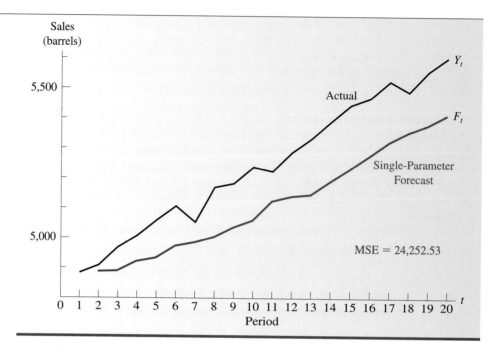

reflects a poorness of fit in using this particular model and level for α. The overall fore-casting quality may be assessed in terms of the forecasting errors.

Forecasting Errors

The errors in a forecasting procedure are determined by subtracting the forecasts from their respective actual values,

$$\epsilon_t = Y_t - F_t$$

α should be set at a level that minimizes these errors. Often several separate sets of fore-casts are required to "tune" the smoothing constant to past data. Large α levels assign more weight to current values, whereas small α levels emphasize past data. By trial and error, an optimal level can be found for α that minimizes *variability* in forecasting errors.

For any set of actual and forecast values, the **mean squared error,** denoted as *MSE,* is used to summarize this variability. The following expression is used to compute the

MEAN SQUARED ERROR

$$MSE = \frac{\Sigma(Y_t - F_t)^2}{n}$$

Here n denotes the number of time periods for which forecast errors are determined. A value of $MSE = 24,252.53$ applies to the Blitz Beer data in Table 7-1.

Although the mean squared error is the primary forecasting accuracy measure, two others are in common use. The **mean absolute deviation,** or *MAD,* is the mean of the absolute value of the errors. It is computed from

$$MAD = \frac{\Sigma |Y_t - F_t|}{n}$$

As can be seen in Table 7-1, $MAD = 147.37$ for the Blitz Beer sales data. Some prefer the *MAD,* finding it easier to relate to the average error.

The **mean absolute percent** error, or *MAPE,* is the average of the absolute value of the errors when they are expressed as a percentage of the actual values. It is computed from

$$MAPE = \frac{\Sigma |Y_t - F_t|/Y_t}{n} \times 100$$

The Blitz Beer sales data in Table 7-1 give a $MAPE = 2.77\%$. It is easy to visualize *MAPE* because it is the average percentage absolute error.

Two-Parameter Exponential Smoothing

The forecast sales found earlier for Blitz Beer are smaller than (lag behind) the actual sales. Whenever there is a pronounced upward trend in actual data (here, increasing sales), forecasts resulting from the single-parameter exponential smoothing will be consistently low.

Two-parameter exponential smoothing eliminates such a lag by explicitly accounting for trend by using a second smoothing constant for the slope of the line. A total of three equations are employed in computing the

FORECAST VALUES

(Two-Parameter Smoothing)

$T_t = \alpha Y_t + (1 - \alpha)(T_{t-1} + b_{t-1})$	(smooth the data to get trend)
$b_t = \gamma(T_t - T_{t-1}) + (1 - \gamma)b_{t-1}$	(smooth the slope in trend)
$F_{t+1} = T_t + b_t$	(forecast)

Here, T_t represents the smoothed value for period t. This quantity conveys the underlying *trend* in the data. The difference between the current and the prior trend values provides the current slope in trend: $T_t - T_{t-1}$. The second equation contains the **slope-smoothing constant** γ (the lowercase Greek letter *gamma*), which is used to obtain smoothed-trend line slopes, represented by b_t. The third equation provides the forecast.

Table 7-2 lists the forecasts of Blitz Beer sales when $\alpha = .20$ and $\gamma = .30$. (The initial trend value of $T_2 = 4,890$ is the actual sales for period 1. The first slope value of $b_2 = 20$ is the difference in actual sales for periods 1 and 2.) The actual and forecast values are plotted in Figure 7-3.

As an illustration, to forecast period 8 sales, first we obtain the smoothed-data value or trend for period 7.

$$T_7 = .20Y_7 + (1 - .20)(T_6 + b_6)$$
$$= .20(5,050) + .80(5,045 + 35.7)$$
$$= 5,075 \text{ barrels}$$

TABLE 7-2 Forecast of Blitz Beer Sales by Two-Parameter Exponential Smoothing ($\alpha=.20$ and $\gamma=.30$)

MONTH	PERIOD t	ACTUAL SALES Y_t	TREND T_t	TREND SLOPE B_t	FORECAST SALES F_t	ERROR $Y_t - F_t$	ERROR² $(Y_t - F_t)^2$
January 2000	1	4,890	—	—	—	—	—
February	2	4,910	4,890	20.0	—	—	—
March	3	4,970	4,922	23.6	4,910.0	60.0	3,600.00
April	4	5,010	4,958	27.3	4,945.6	64.4	4,147.36
May	5	5,060	5,000	31.7	4,985.3	74.7	5,580.09
June	6	5,100	5,045	35.7	5,031.7	68.3	4,664.89
July	7	5,050	5,075	34.0	5,080.7	−30.7	942.49
August	8	5,170	5,121	37.6	5,109.0	61.0	3,721.00
September	9	5,180	5,163	38.9	5,158.6	21.4	457.96
October	10	5,240	5,210	41.3	5,201.9	38.1	1,451.61
November	11	5,220	5,245	39.4	5,251.3	−31.3	979.69
December	12	5,280	5,283	39.0	5,284.4	−4.4	19.36
January 2001	13	5,330	5,324	39.6	5,322.0	8.0	64.00
February	14	5,380	5,367	40.6	5,363.6	16.4	268.96
March	15	5,440	5,414	42.5	5,407.6	32.4	1,049.76
April	16	5,460	5,457	42.7	5,456.5	3.5	12.25
May	17	5,520	5,504	44.0	5,499.7	20.3	412.09
June	18	5,490	5,536	40.4	5,548.0	−58.0	3,364.00
July	19	5,550	5,571	38.8	5,576.4	−26.4	696.96
August	20	5,600	5,608	38.3	5,609.8	−9.8	96.04
September	21	—	—	—	5,646.3	—	—
							31,528.51

MSE = 31,528.51/18 = 1,751.58

Then we compute the smoothed slope in trend for period 7.

$$b_7 = .30(T_7 - T_6) + (1 - .30)b_6$$
$$= .30(5,075 - 5,045) + .70(35.7)$$
$$= 34.0$$

which indicates that sales were increasing at a rate of 34.0 barrels per period at that time. The forecast for period 8 is the sum of the preceding period's trend and slope values.

$$F_8 = T_7 + b_7 = 5,075 + 34.0 = 5,109.0 \text{ barrels}$$

The forecasts that result from this procedure are close to the actual sales values. The current trend itself is readjusted for each period to coincide with the latest growth in the raw data.

Notice, in Figure 7-3, how closely the forecasts from two-parameter smoothing lie to the actual sales figures. When the underlying time series exhibits a pronounced trend, two-parameter exponential smoothing will ordinarily provide better forecasts than those made with a single parameter. The *MSE* will then be smaller, as is the case with the two sets of Blitz Beer forecasts.

$$MSE = 24,252.53 \quad \text{(single parameter)}$$
$$MSE = 1,751.58 \quad \text{(two parameters)}$$

MSE can also be used to gauge how well different levels for α and γ provide forecasts that fit past time-series data.

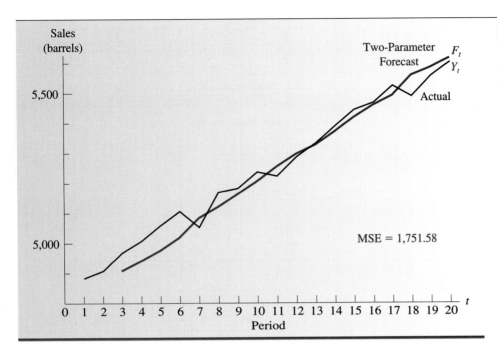

FIGURE 7-3

Two-parameter exponential-smoothing results for Blitz Beer sales ($\alpha = .20$, $\gamma = .30$)

Smoothing with Spreadsheets

Computer assistance is an obvious advantage when performing exponential smoothing. It is helpful for tuning the model (by adjusting the smoothing constants) to the historical data and obtaining a best fit.

Single-Parameter Exponential Smoothing   Figure 7-4 shows an Excel spreadsheet for single-parameter exponential smoothing applied to the same Blitz Beer sales data seen earlier. Those data appear in columns B through D. The forecasts in column E were found by pulling down the Tools menu, then selecting Data Analysis and Exponential Smoothing. That brought to the screen the Exponential Smoothing dialog box in Figure 7-5, in which the cells corresponding to the actual sales data, $D$6:$D$25, were designated as the *Input Range.* Excel requires as an input parameter the *damping factor*, which is 1 minus the smoothing constant α. For Blitz Beer, the damping factor is $1 - .2 = .8$.

The results from Excel exponential smoothing are shown on the spreadsheet itself (Figure 7-4). That is done by first specifying in the dialog box the *Output Range*, which was entered as $E$6:$E$25. Clicking the OK button created the results in column E of Figure 7-4.

Further results are shown in the spreadsheet. The forecast in cell E26 was found after copying cell E25 down to cell E26. The value of *MSE* in cell D28 was obtained by using the Excel functions SUMXMY2 and COUNT. The first function calculates the sum of the squared errors. (SUM represents sum. XMY2 is Excel shorthand for *X* minus *Y* quantity squared.) The second function counts the cells in a range of the spreadsheet. The D28 formula is

$$= \text{SUMXMY2}(D7:D25,E7:E25)/(\text{COUNT}(D6:D25)\text{-}1)$$

FIGURE 7-4

Single-parameter
exponential-smoothing
spreadsheet for Blitz Beer
sales

	A	B	C	D	E	F
1		**Forecast of Blitz Beer Sales by Single-Parameter Smoothing**				
2			$\alpha =$	0.2		
3						
4			Period	Actual	Forecast	
5		Month	t	Sales, Y_t	Sales, F_t	
6		January 2000	1	4,890		
7		February	2	4,910	4890.0	
8		March	3	4,970	4894.0	
9		April	4	5,010	4909.2	
10		May	5	5,060	4929.4	
11		June	6	5,100	4955.5	
12		July	7	5,050	4984.4	
13		August	8	5,170	4997.5	
14		September	9	5,180	5032.0	
15		October	10	5,240	5061.6	
16		November	11	5,220	5097.3	
17		December	12	5,280	5121.8	
18		January 2001	13	5,330	5153.5	
19		February	14	5,380	5188.8	
20		March	15	5,440	5227.0	
21		April	16	5,460	5269.6	
22		May	17	5,520	5307.7	
23		June	18	5,490	5350.2	
24		July	19	5,550	5378.1	
25		August	20	5,600	5412.5	
26		September	21		5450.0	
27						
28			MSE =	24,254		
29						
30				D		
31		28	=SUMXMY2(D7:D25,E7:E25)/COUNT(E7:E25)			

FIGURE 7-5

Exponential-smoothing
Excel dialog box for Blitz
Beer sales

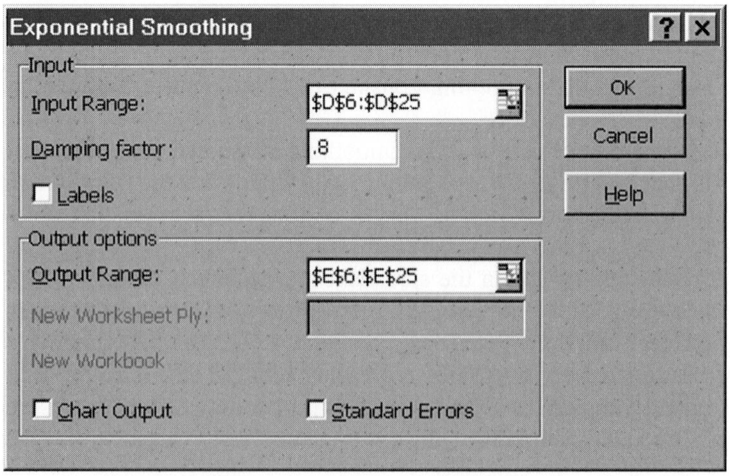

Exponential Smoothing   ? ✕

Input
Input Range: $D$6:$D$25

Damping factor: .8

☐ Labels

OK
Cancel
Help

Output options
Output Range: $E$6:$E$25

New Worksheet Ply:

New Workbook

☐ Chart Output   ☐ Standard Errors

The first argument in the SUMXMY2 function is the range of actual sales Y_t, here D7:D25. The second argument E7:E25, contains the forecasts. The COUNT function counts the number of cells in the range D6:D25. The model requires that 1 be subtracted from the count.

Two Parameter Exponential Smoothing Model   Figure 7-6 presents the Blitz Beer spreadsheet for the two-parameter exponential smoothing mode. It was convenient there to build the model directly into the spreadsheet itself instead of using a dialog box. The necessary formulas appear below the spreadsheet. The first of these is the first trend value T_2, appearing as the value in cell D7 and which is set equal to the value in cell C6. The next trend value T_3 appears in cell D8 and is found using the Excel version of the smoothing formula

$$= \$C\$2*C8+(1-\$C\$2)*(D7+E7) \qquad [\text{trend } T_3 = \alpha Y_3 + (1 - \alpha)(T_2 + b_2)]$$

Only the above was actually entered from the keyboard. Cell D8 was then copied down to cells D9:D25, thereby giving all the trend values shown in the spreadsheet.

	A	B	C	D	E	F
1			Forecast of Blitz Beer Sales by Two-Parameter Smoothing			
2			$\alpha =$ 0.20		$\gamma =$ 0.30	
3						
4		Period	Actual	Trend	Trend	Forecast
5	Month	t	Sales, Y_t	T_t	Slope, b_t	Sales, F_t
6	January 2000	1	4,890			
7	February	2	4,910	4,890	20.0	
8	March	3	4,970	4,922	23.6	4,910.0
9	April	4	5,010	4,958	27.5	4,945.6
10	May	5	5,060	5,001	31.9	4,985.9
11	June	6	5,100	5,046	35.9	5,032.7
12	July	7	5,050	5,076	34.0	5,082.1
13	August	8	5,170	5,122	37.6	5,109.7
14	September	9	5,180	5,164	38.9	5,159.4
15	October	10	5,240	5,210	41.1	5,202.4
16	November	11	5,220	5,245	39.3	5,251.0
17	December	12	5,280	5,283	39.0	5,284.1
18	January 2001	13	5,330	5,324	39.5	5,322.3
19	February	14	5,380	5,367	40.5	5,363.3
20	March	15	5,440	5,414	42.5	5,407.2
21	April	16	5,460	5,457	42.7	5,456.2
22	May	17	5,520	5,504	43.9	5,499.6
23	June	18	5,490	5,536	40.5	5,547.6
24	July	19	5,550	5,571	38.9	5,576.5
25	August	20	5,600	5,608	38.3	5,610.1
26	September	21				5,646.3
27						
28			MSE =	1,734.64		

	D	E	F
7	=C6	=C7-C6	
8	=$C$2*C8+(1-$C$2)*(D7+E7)	=$E$2*(D8-D7)+(1-$E$2)*E7	=D7+E7
9	=$C$2*C9+(1-$C$2)*(D8+E8)	=$E$2*(D9-D8)+(1-$E$2)*E8	=D8+E8

FIGURE 7-6
Spreadsheet for two-parameter exponential smoothing with Blitz Beer sales data

The first slope value b_2 is shown in cell E7. It is the difference between February and January sales, C7-C6. The rest of the slopes b_t are calculated from the Excel version of the slope formula. For cell E8 this is

$$= \text{\$E\$2*(D8-D7)+(1-\$E\$2)*E7} \qquad [\text{slope } b_3 = \gamma(T_3 - T_2) + (1 - \gamma)b_2]$$

which was keyed once and then copied down to cells E9:E25 to obtain the remainder of the smoothed trend-line slopes.

The forecasts are given in column F. The period 3 forecast is in cell F8, having the formula

$$= \text{D7+E7} \qquad [\text{forecast } F_3 = T_2 + b_2]$$

Copying the above formula down to cells F9:F26 gives all the forecasts shown in the spreadsheet.

Using Solver to Find Best Parameters

Excel's Solver can be used to find the best values of α and γ to minimize the *MSE*. That is done from the Solver dialog box shown in Figure 7-7, which we get by selecting Solver from the Tools menu. It is easy to set the Solver parameters.

The Target Cell refers to the location of the value to be minimized—*MSE* in this case. We typed the cell address $D$28 in that box. Then we clicked on the Min button in the *Equal To* line, thereby requesting that the value in the target be minimized. Next, we entered the cell locations of α and γ, $C$2,$E$2, into the *By Changing Cells* field, which tells Solver to find the optimal levels of those parameters.

We want to make sure that α and γ are both ≤ 1. That is accomplished with constraints, which we created by clicking inside the *Subject to the Constraints* box and then selecting the Add button. The Add Constraint dialog box appeared on-screen, as shown in Figure 7-8. We typed C2 ($C$2 would also work) in the *Cell Reference* line, made sure that the inequality box in the middle had the entry $<=$, and typed 1 in the Constraint box. We then clicked the Add button to incorporate that constraint. The second constraint, E2 $<=$ 1, was created in the same manner.

Clicking on OK returned the Solver Parameter dialog box. There, we clicked the Options button, selected the Assume Non-Negative option from another box (not shown) from which clicking OK returned the Solver Parameter dialog box. A final

---

FIGURE 7-7

Excel Solver Parameters dialog box for finding best smoothing constants, α and γ

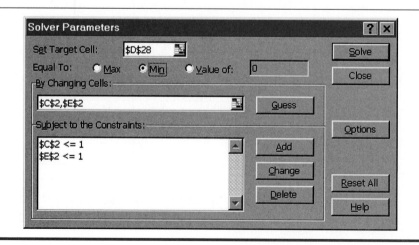

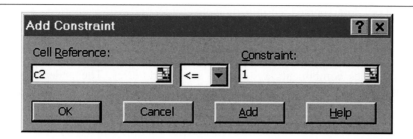

FIGURE 7-8
Excel Add Constraint
dialog box

click on the Solve button activated the optimization and gave the following smoothing constant results that minimize the mean squared error: $\alpha = 0.45$ and $\gamma = 0.23$. (The report screen is not shown.)

Seasonal Exponential Smoothing with Three Parameters

The two exponential-smoothing procedures described thus far ignore any seasonal aspects. Consider the quarterly sales data for Stationer's Supply, plotted in Figure 7-9. A retail outlet, Stationer's Supply has historically experienced two busy periods,

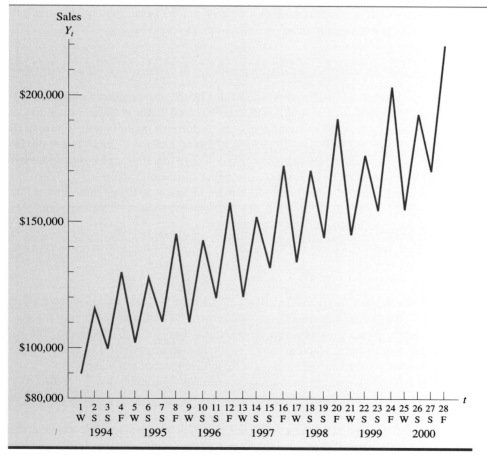

FIGURE 7-9
Actual quarterly sales data for Stationer's Supply

spring and fall, interspersed with the quieter summer and winter quarters. The results show a very pronounced seasonal pattern that gives a saw-toothed effect to the time series.

Seasonal exponential smoothing makes forecasts by isolating the trend and seasonal time-series components as separate smoothed series. The underlying model extends the two-parameter procedure, incorporating the **seasonal-smoothing constant** β (Greek lowercase letter *beta*) as the third parameter. The following four equations apply:

FORECAST VALUES

(Seasonal Smoothing with Three Parameters)

$$T_t = \alpha\left(\frac{Y_t}{S_{t-p}}\right) + (1 - \alpha)(T_{t-1} + b_{t-1}) \qquad \text{(smooth the data to get trend)}$$

$$b_t = \gamma(T_t - T_{t-1}) + (1 - \gamma)b_{t-1} \qquad \text{(smooth the slope in trend)}$$

$$S_t = \beta\left(\frac{Y_t}{T_t}\right) + (1 - \beta)S_{t-p} \qquad \text{(smooth the seasonal factor)}$$

$$F_{t+1} = (T_t + b_t)S_{t-p+1} \qquad \text{(forecast)}$$

The first equation smooths the past data to obtain the trend. In doing this, the current value Y_t is first *deseasonalized*.

$$\frac{Y_t}{S_{t-p}}$$

This is accomplished by dividing the actual value by the latest applicable seasonal factor, S_{t-p}. The $t - p$ subscript signifies that the seasonal factor is taken from p periods earlier. The letter p denotes the number of periods during a major period. There would be $p = 4$ *quarters* in a year, $p = 12$ *months* in a year, and $p = 7$ *days* in a week. For Stationer's Supply, the data are quarterly, and $p = 4$, so that the current spring sales total is divided by the S applicable for the preceding spring, and so on.

The second equation smooths the slope in trend, just as in the previous model. The third equation smooths the seasonal factor. The current portion of the seasonal factor is defined by the following ratio:

$$\frac{Y_t}{T_t}$$

This ratio is weighted (by β) and added to $1 - \beta$ times the prior matching seasonal factor value.

The final equation creates a new deseasonalized projection, adding the prior period's trend and the latest slope in trend. That quantity is multiplied by the latest applicable known seasonal factor S_{t-p+1} (not S_t) to give the forecast value.

Table 7-3 shows the detailed summary obtained from applying the above to the Stationer's Supply sales data, with $\alpha = .4$, $\gamma = .5$, and $\beta = .7$. We will use period 20 to illustrate the calculations with the seasonal model.

Taking, as the current period, $t = 20$ (fall 1998) and all available data from that and the prior periods, we will determine the forecast for period 21 (winter 1999). The first

TABLE 7-3 Seasonal Exponential-Smoothing Results for Stationer's Supply ($\alpha=.4$, $\gamma=.5$, $\beta=.7$)

QUARTER	t	ACTUAL Y_t	TREND T_t	SLOPE b_t	SEASONAL S_t	FORECAST F_t	ERROR $Y_t - F_t$
1994 W	1	90,640	—	—	—	—	—
S	2	115,540	90,640.00	24,900.00	1.27	—	—
S	3	99,190	109,000.00	21,630.00	.91	—	—
F	4	128,800	129,898.00	21,264.00	.99	—	—
1995 W	5	102,350	131,637.20	11,501.60	.78	—	—
S	6	127,440	125,873.46	2,868.93	1.09	182,460.92	−55,020.92
S	7	112,530	126,709.17	1,852.32	.89	117,155.58	−4,625.58
F	8	145,080	135,663.61	5,403.38	1.05	127,474.79	17,605.21
1996 W	9	110,490	141,482.77	5,611.27	.78	109,681.81	808.20
S	10	143,000	140,679.34	2,403.92	1.04	160,498.08	−17,498.08
S	11	119,700	139,367.03	545.81	.87	128,011.98	−8,311.98
F	12	157,760	144,273.64	2,726.21	1.08	146,355.97	11,404.03
1997 W	13	123,710	151,647.84	5,050.21	.81	114,647.37	9,062.63
S	14	153,360	153,066.75	3,234.56	1.01	162,791.25	−9,431.25
S	15	131,950	154,474.06	2,320.93	.86	135,922.52	−3,972.52
F	16	173,160	158,254.92	3,050.90	1.09	169,220.94	3,939.06
1998 W	17	135,900	164,310.22	4,553.10	.82	129,853.54	6,046.46
S	18	164,780	166,383.72	3,313.30	1.00	171,059.64	−6,279.64
S	19	146,010	169,823.34	3,376.46	.86	145,738.78	271.22
F	20	190,400	173,810.45	3,681.79	1.09	188,736.47	1,663.53
1999 W	21	145,070	177,220.66	3,545.99	.82	145,627.08	−557.08
S	22	175,960	179,044.81	2,685.08	.99	180,252.36	−4,292.36
S	23	155,480	181,397.27	2,518.76	.86	156,194.73	−714.73
F	24	202,960	184,576.81	2,849.16	1.10	201,153.27	1,806.73
2000 W	25	157,500	189,364.59	3,818.47	.83	153,529.97	3,970.03
S	26	192,240	193,811.88	4,132.88	.99	190,688.30	1,551.70
S	27	168,330	197,257.61	3,789.30	.85	169,803.64	−1,473.64
F	28	218,960	200,407.03	3,469.36	1.09	220,716.22	−1,756.22
2001 W	29	—	—	—	—	168,800.52	—
S	30	—	—	—	—	205,365.31	—
S	31	—	—	—	—	180,182.80	—
F	32	—	—	—	—	234,460.20	—

step is to compute the smoothed values for trend and slope in trend, averaging current values with those of period 19.

Trend:
$$T_{20} = .40\left(\frac{Y_{20}}{S_{16}}\right) + (1 - .40)(T_{19} + b_{19})$$

$$= .40\left(\frac{\$190,400}{1.09}\right) + .60(\$169,823.34 + \$3,376.46)$$

$$= \$173,810.45$$

Slope:
$$b_{20} = .50(T_{20} - T_{19}) + (1 - .50)b_{19}$$

$$= .50(\$173,810.45 - \$169,823.34) + .50(\$3,376.46)$$

$$= \$3,681.79$$

(Values may differ slightly due to rounding. The table values were computed by hand and vary slightly from those generated by Excel.)

Notice that $S_{16} = 1.09$ (Fall 1997) is used as the divisor to find T_{20}, not S_{20} (which would not be available until T_{20} has been computed). The seasonal factor for period 20 is computed with T_{20}, however.

Seasonal:
$$S_{20} = .70\left(\frac{Y_{20}}{T_{20}}\right) + (1 - .70)S_{16}$$
$$= .70\left(\frac{\$190,400}{\$173,810.45}\right) + .30(1.09)$$
$$= 1.09$$

Finally, the forecast is made for period 21.

Forecast:
$$F_{21} = (T_{20} + b_{20})S_{17}$$
$$= (\$173,810.45 + \$3,681.79)(.82)$$
$$= \$145,627.08$$

(Rounding affects the result. The above was computed using a more precise level for S_{17} instead of .82, as listed in Table 7-3. Also, initial values cannot be computed from the earlier formulas and must be approximated. Thus, trend T_2 equals Y_1, and slope b_2 is $Y_2 - Y_1$. Seasonal factor S_2 is the ratio Y_2/T_2; S_3 through S_5 are computed the same way.)

The complete set of forecast values are plotted alongside the actual sales figures in Figure 7-10. Notice that the F_t's become close to the Y_t values only after the process has settled down, after three full years of data have been incorporated. This slowness in attaining forecasting accuracy is mainly due to poor starting values. Rather than rely on guesswork, the illustrated procedure uses the actual Y_1 as the first T_2 (which appears to be quite low in relation to later T's). That in turn distorts the initial seasonal values. As with any exponential-smoothing process, earlier inaccuracies eventually wash out.

When applying the seasonal model, forecasts may be found for the entire seasonal cycle using the following expression:

$$F_{t+m} = (T_t + b_t m)S_{t-p+m}$$

This equation was used to obtain the last set of four Stationer's Supply forecast values, shown in Figure 7-10 and at the bottom of Table 7-3.

Using Spreadsheets

A spreadsheet for seasonal exponential smoothing with three parameters is given in Figure 7-11. There, the earlier Stationer's Supply data are listed in columns A through C, starting in row 6. As with two-parameter smoothing, we must build the spreadsheet. The Excel formulas created for this purpose are shown at the bottom of the spreadsheet. The initial value of the trend T_1 is given in cell D7. It is the first quarter's sales, the value in cell C6, and the formula =C6 applies there. Likewise, the first slope factor b_2 appears in cell E7. That quantity is the increase in sales between the first and second quarter, $Y_2 - Y_1$, which is the difference between the values in cells C6 and C7; the formula is =C7-C6. The first seasonal factor S_2 appears in cell F7. It is the ratio of the second quarter's sales, Y_2, to the trend value for that quarter, T_2; the formula is =C7/D7.

From these initial values the trend and slope factors for the third, fourth, and fifth quarters ($t = 3, 4,$ and 5) are found using the Excel counterparts to the formulas on page 216, which in cells D8 and E8 are

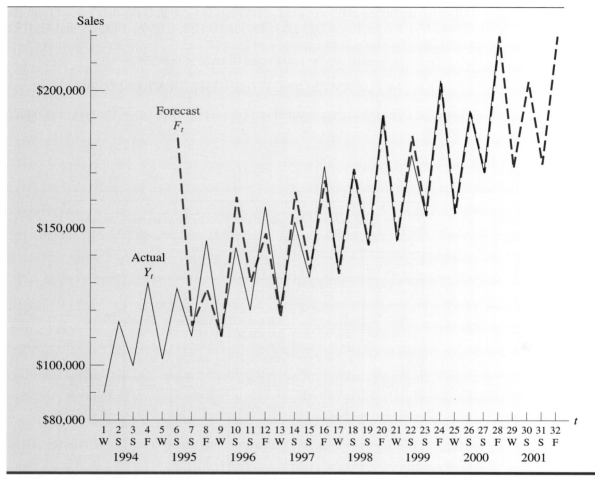

FIGURE 7-10 Actual and forecast quarterly sales data for Stationer's Supply ($\alpha = .4, \gamma = .5, \beta = .7$)

$$= \text{\$C\$2*C8+(1-\$C\$2)(D7+E7)} \qquad \text{(trend)}$$
$$= \text{\$E\$2*(D8-D7)+(1-\$E\$2)*E7} \qquad \text{(slope)}$$

The seasonal factors for the third, fourth, and fifth quarters, S_3, S_4, and S_5, are calculated as the ratio of the actual sales and their respective trend. In cells F8, F9, and F10, the formulas are = C8/D8, = C9/D9, and = C10/D10, respectively.

The trend formula on page 216 for the subsequent quarter is represented in cell D11 by the Excel formula

$$= \text{\$C\$2*(C11/F7)+(1-\$C\$2)(D10+E10)} \qquad \text{(trend)}$$

The seasonal factor and forecast formulas are re-adapted from page 216, giving the Excel counterparts in cells F11 and G11

$$= \text{\$G\$2(C11/D11)+(1-\$G\$2)*F7} \qquad \text{(seasonal factor)}$$
$$= \text{(D10+E10)*F7} \qquad \text{(forecast)}$$

All of the remaining cell formulas for columns D through G are then copied from the above, D11 for the range D12:D33, E8 for E9:E33, F11 for F12:F33 and G11 for G12:G37.

The Excel formula for the mean squared error in cell E39 is

$$= \text{SUMXMY2(C11:C33,G11:G33)/(COUNT(G11:G33))}$$

Figure 7-11 gives the mean squared error for a particular set of the three smoothing constants.

FIGURE 7-11

Spreadsheet for seasonal exponential-smoothing with three parameters using the Stationer's Supply data

	A	B	C	D	E	F	G
1	Seasonal Exponential Smoothing Results for Stationer's Supply						
2		α =	0.4		γ =	0.5	β = 0.7
3							
4			Actual	Trend	Slope	Seasonal	Forecast
5	Quarter	t	Sales, Y_t	T_t	b_t	S_t	F_t
6	1994 W	1	90,640				
7	S	2	115,540	90,640.00	24,900.00	1.27	
8	S	3	99,190	109,000.00	21,630.00	0.91	
9	F	4	128,800	129,898.00	21,264.00	0.99	
10	1995 W	5	102,350	131,637.20	11,501.60	0.78	
11	S	6	127,440	125,873.45	2,868.93	1.09	182,460.91
12	S	7	112,530	126,709.16	1,852.32	0.89	117,155.57
13	F	8	145,080	135,663.60	5,403.38	1.05	127,474.78
14	1996 W	9	110,490	141,482.77	5,611.27	0.78	109,681.80
15	S	10	143,000	140,679.34	2,403.92	1.04	160,498.09
16	S	11	119,700	139,367.04	545.81	0.87	128,011.99
17	F	12	157,760	144,273.63	2,726.20	1.08	146,355.98
18	1997 W	13	123,710	151,647.84	5,050.21	0.81	114,647.37
19	S	14	153,360	153,066.75	3,234.56	1.01	162,791.25
20	S	15	131,950	154,474.07	2,320.94	0.86	135,922.52
21	F	16	173,160	158,254.92	3,050.89	1.09	169,220.96
22	1998 W	17	135,900	164,310.21	4,553.09	0.82	129,853.53
23	S	18	164,780	166,383.71	3,313.29	1.00	171,059.64
24	S	19	146,010	169,823.32	3,376.45	0.86	145,738.78
25	F	20	190,400	173,810.42	3,681.78	1.09	188,736.44
26	1999 W	21	145,070	177,220.62	3,545.99	0.82	145,627.06
27	S	22	175,960	179,044.78	2,685.07	0.99	180,252.32
28	S	23	155,480	181,397.24	2,518.76	0.86	156,194.71
29	F	24	202,960	184,576.76	2,849.15	1.10	201,153.27
30	2000 W	25	157,500	189,364.54	3,818.46	0.83	153,529.94
31	S	26	192,240	193,811.82	4,132.87	0.99	190,688.25
32	S	27	168,330	197,257.56	3,789.30	0.85	169,803.61
33	F	28	218,960	200,406.97	3,469.36	1.09	220,716.23
34	2001 W	29					168,800.51
35	S	30					205,365.30
36	S	31					180,182.79
37	F	32					234,460.18
38							
39				MSE =	182,250,569		

	F	G
11	=$G$2*(C11/D11)+(1-$G$2)*F7	=(D10+E10)*F7
12	=$G$2*(C12/D12)+(1-$G$2)*F8	=(D11+E11)*F8
13	=$G$2*(C13/D13)+(1-$G$2)*F9	=(D12+E12)*F9

	D	E	F
7	=C6	=C7-C6	=C7/D7
8	=$C$2*C8+(1-$C$2)*(D7+E7)	=$E$2*(D8-D7)+(1-$E$2)*E7	=C8/D8
9	=$C$2*C9+(1-$C$2)*(D8+E8)	=$E$2*(D9-D8)+(1-$E$2)*E8	=C9/D9
10	=$C$2*C10+(1-$C$2)*(D9+E9)	=$E$2*(D10-D9)+(1-$E$2)*E9	=C10/D10

	D	E
11	=$C$2*(C11/F7)+(1-$C$2)*(D10+E10)	=SUMXMY2(C11:C33,G11:G33) /COUNT(G11:G33)
12	=$C$2*(C12/F8)+(1-$C$2)*(D11+E11)	39
13	=$C$2*(C13/F9)+(1-$C$2)*(D12+E12)	

Decision Problem Revisited: Bugoff Chemical Company

Warren Williams gives the 1996–2001 Malabug quarterly sales data to his Senior Forecasting Analyst, Sam Morgan, and asks him to use exponential smoothing to make quarterly forecasts for the year 2002. His report follows:

```
MEMORANDUM
TO: Warren Williams
FROM: Sam Morgan
SUBJECT: Results
```

To find the four quarterly forecasts for Malabug in 2002, I used three-parameter exponential smoothing. This method takes into account both the increasing trend in Malabug sales and the seasonal variations in sales during the four quarters of each year. The forecasts are:

Winter	46,660
Spring	242,480
Summer	86,080
Fall	62,200

The smoothing parameters used are alpha = .5, beta = .5, and gamma = .5. The following [see Table 7-4] shows how the trend, slope, and seasonal terms are determined, in addition to the forecasts and errors. The mean squared error obtained in making the forecasts is 5,514.

TABLE 7-4 Malabug Sales Forecasts Using Seasonal Exponential Smoothing

QUARTER	PERIOD t	ACTUAL Y_t	TREND T_t	SLOPE b_t	SEASONAL S_t	FORECAST F_t	ERROR $Y_t - F_t$
1996 W	1	18.00	—	—	—	—	—
S	2	80.00	18.00	62.00	51.34	—	—
S	3	30.00	55.00	49.50	68.76	—	—
F	4	22.00	63.25	28.88	20.92	—	—
1997 W	5	24.00	58.06	11.84	108.68	—	—
S	6	105.00	46.77	0.27	62.91	310.69	−205.69
S	7	54.00	73.02	13.26	0.64	25.66	28.34
F	8	27.00	81.95	11.10	0.34	30.01	−3.01
1998 W	9	33.00	86.44	7.79	0.40	38.46	−5.46
S	10	141.00	68.20	−5.23	2.71	315.22	−174.22
S	11	48.00	68.84	−2.29	0.67	40.46	7.54
F	12	38.00	89.38	9.12	0.38	22.54	15.46
1999 W	13	40.00	99.56	9.65	0.40	39.16	0.84
S	14	150.00	82.32	−3.79	2.26	295.55	−145.55
S	15	75.00	95.24	4.56	0.73	52.60	22.40
F	16	48.00	112.75	11.03	0.40	38.12	9.88
2000 W	17	35.00	105.68	1.98	0.37	49.47	−14.47
S	18	180.00	93.58	−5.06	2.09	243.77	−63.77
S	19	55.00	82.00	−8.32	0.70	64.50	−9.50
F	20	50.00	98.75	4.22	0.46	29.75	20.25
2001 W	21	48.00	117.16	11.31	0.39	37.63	10.37
S	22	205.00	113.19	3.67	1.95	269.00	−64.00
S	23	70.00	108.45	−0.53	0.67	81.77	−11.77
F	24	57.00	116.59	3.80	0.47	49.11	7.89
2002 W	25	—	—	—	—	46.66	—
S	26	—	—	—	—	242.48	—
S	27	—	—	—	—	86.08	—
F	28	—	—	—	—	62.20	—

Fine-Tuning Exponential-Smoothing Parameters

With computer assistance, it is practical to fine-tune the parameters to the historical data, thereby achieving a best fit (minimum *MSE*). Generally, the following applies to any parameter:

Fine-tuning parameters to past data does indeed provide a best historical fit. But, there are no guarantees that the parameters thereby obtained will continue to fit the actual data well. And, should the historical fit result in a parameter that is very close to 0 or to 1, it may be wise to choose a less extreme number that sacrifices past *MSE* for greater future stability or responsiveness.

Figure 7-12 shows the results of using different β levels with the Stationer's Supply data (all with the same α and γ as before). Each *MSE* value was obtained with a separate computer run. Notice that *MSE* declines steadily as β is increased, but the curve flattens out around $\beta = .7$. That number appears to be a good compromise for future forecasts of Stationer's Supply sales, allowing for both stability and responsiveness to a seasonal pattern that will likely prevail with little change. Using that β, the other parameters were fine-tuned.

With a spreadsheet application, we can easily optimize the parameters by finding those levels for α, β, and γ that minimize *MSE*. Using Solver as described in the previous section, we found the following best smoothing constants: $\alpha = .51$, $\beta = 1$, and $\gamma = .49$. These parameters gave *MSE* = 193,571,705, a 7.6% decrease from the *MSE* for the spreadsheet in Figure 7-11 with the original parameter levels.

FIGURE 7-12

Relationship between *MSE* and level for β using Stationer's Supply data ($\alpha = .40$, $\gamma = .50$)

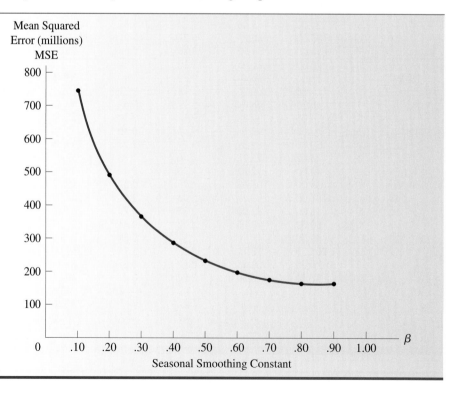

Decision Problem Revisited: Bugoff Chemical Company

Warren Williams studies Sam Morgan's Malabug forecasts and suggests changes.

MEMORANDUM
TO: Sam Morgan
FROM: Warren
Williams
SUBJECT:
  Exponential
  Smoothing
  Forecasts
	Your memo giving three-parameter exponential-smoothing forecasts for 2002 quarterly Malabug sales was interesting. Although your forecasts look very good, I wonder why you chose the three smoothing parameters alpha = .5, beta = .5, and gamma = .5? These seem arbitrary. Can you find smoothing parameters that give better forecasts?
	    By the way, are there any other forecasting procedures that we might use to check the exponential smoothing results you obtained?

MEMORANDUM
TO: Warren
Williams
FROM: Sam Morgan
SUBJECT:
  Smoothing
  Parameters
	I went back to the drawing board and redid the calculations, first finding the best values of the smoothing parameters. The mean squared error is minimized when alpha = .94, beta = .50, and gamma = .54. These smoothing parameters result in the following forecasts:
	
	        Winter 74,580
	        Spring 353,710
	        Summer 82,990
	        Fall 73,351
	The above have an *MSE* of 787.1, much better than before.
	    Regarding your question about other forecasting methods, the decomposition method is another one. I will look into this and get back to you later.

7-3 FORECASTING TREND USING REGRESSION

The secular trend component T_t of a time series may be the most valuable variable in forecasting. Trend analysis focuses on finding the appropriate trend line or curve that provides the best fit to the historical scatter of Y_t over time.

Describing Trend

In the hypothetical time series for stereo speaker demand that was discussed in Section 7-1, secular trend was represented by a straight line. A straight-line trend assumes that Y_t changes at a constant rate.

Most time series do not involve long-term behavior that changes constantly over time. In business or economic situations, a variable will usually increase or decline at a rate that itself changes from period to period. Some basic shapes of nonlinear trend curves frequently encountered are provided in Figure 7-13. For example, consider the movement in GDP levels over a prolonged period. The GDP for the United States has increased by more in the recent past than it did following World War II, so that the trend is represented best by a curve with increasing and positive slope as in Figure 7-13(a). In absolute terms, the U.S. GDP has been increasing in recent times at an increasing rate.

Diagram (b) in Figure 7-13 shows the trend for a time series that decreases at a decreasing rate. The level of activity for a declining industry may sometimes be

FIGURE 7-13
Basic shapes of common trend curves

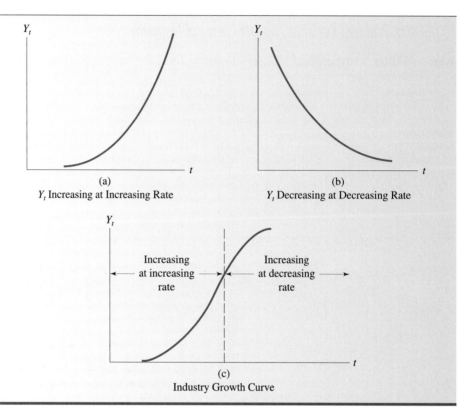

(a)
Y_t Increasing at Increasing Rate

(b)
Y_t Decreasing at Decreasing Rate

Increasing at increasing rate

Increasing at decreasing rate

(c)
Industry Growth Curve

represented by such a curve. The decline is initially dramatic but becomes more gradual with time. An example of such a trend is the number of railroad passengers carried in the United States each year during the past five decades.

The long-range growth of a firm or an industry may sometimes be explained in terms of a trend having the shape shown in Figure 7-13(c). Here, output increases at an increasing rate when innovative products are brought onto the market to satisfy emerging needs. As the industry matures, rapid growth is replaced by a period of gradual increases; product sales still increase, but at a decreasing rate. Ultimately, sales peak and a period of stagnation begins. Such S-shaped curves are therefore called **growth curves.** Two growth curves frequently encountered in statistics are the logistic and the Gompertz.

The particular shape to portray the trend of a specific time series is selected partly by studying the scatter of the data on a graph. The choice should be a basic shape that not only seems to fit the historical data closely but also coincides with good judgment about how it should be related to future data. There are no rules to tell us which shape must be used. Judgment and experience play the dominant role, so that fitting a trend curve to make forecasts is as much an art as a science.

Determining Linear Trend Using Regression

Time series covering a small number of years usually may be fitted by a straight line. This involves finding the following

REGRESSION EQUATION

$$\hat{Y}(X) = a + bX$$

Here, Y represents the **dependent variable** (the variable being forecast) of the time series, and X represents the **independent variable** (the time period). We use X instead of t, because it is simpler to express time relative to a base period. The values a and b in this expression are referred to as **estimated regression coefficients.** It is traditional to place a caret over the letter Y, using $\hat{Y}$ (Y-hat) to denote the predicted or forecast value for Y.

The regression coefficients are calculated from the equations

$$b = \frac{\sum XY - n\bar{X}\bar{Y}}{\sum X^2 - n\bar{X}^2}$$

$$a = \bar{Y} - b\bar{X}$$

where $\bar{Y}$ and $\bar{X}$ are the respective mean values.

Trend in Civilian Employment

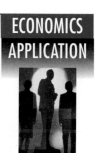

ECONOMICS APPLICATION

The total civilian employment Y in the United States from 1978 through 1987 is given in column (3) of Table 7-5. We want to determine the regression equation for forecasting that variable and use it to make a forecast of 2002 civilian employment.

TABLE 7-5 Computations for Fitting Trend Line to Employment Data

(1) YEAR	(2) YEAR IN TRANSFORMED UNITS X	(3) TOTAL CIVILIAN EMPLOYMENT (MILLIONS) Y	(4) XY	(5) X²
1978	0	96.1	0	0
1979	1	98.8	98.8	1
1980	2	99.3	198.6	4
1981	3	100.4	301.2	9
1982	4	99.5	398.0	16
1983	5	100.8	504.0	25
1984	6	105.0	630.0	36
1985	7	107.2	750.4	49
1986	8	109.6	876.8	64
1987	9	112.4	1,011.6	81
	45 = $\sum X$	1,029.1 = $\sum Y$	4,769.4 = $\sum XY$	285 = $\sum X^2$

Source: Economic Report of the President, 1989.

THE PROBLEM SOLUTION

Columns (1) and (2) of Table 7-5 give the year and the year in transformed units (X) with the base year, $1978 = 0$. Columns (4) and (5) contain the product of columns (2) and (3) and the square of column (2), respectively. Both (4) and (5) provide elements of the regression equation. The totals are then computed for columns (2)–(5). The totals for columns (2) and (3) are then used to compute the means for each variable (using $n = 10$):

$$\bar{X} = \frac{\sum X}{n} = \frac{45}{10} = 4.5$$

$$\bar{Y} = \frac{\sum Y}{n} = \frac{1,029.1}{10} = 102.91$$

The slope of the regression line is computed from the means and the totals from columns (4) and (5).

$$b = \frac{\sum XY - n\bar{X}\bar{Y}}{\sum X^2 - n\bar{X}^2} = \frac{4{,}769.4 - 10(4.5)(102.91)}{285 - 10(4.5)^2} = 1.68$$

Using the b value, the Y-intercept can be computed.

$$a = \bar{Y} - b\bar{X} = 102.91 - 1.68(4.5) = 95.35$$

Putting it all together, the regression equation is solved.

$$\hat{Y}(X) = 95.35 + 1.68X \qquad (X = 0 \text{ at } 1978)$$

This equation indicates that the trend value for 1978 is an employment level of 95.35 million and that Y increases by 1.68 million per year. Because we have transformed the calendar years, it is important to indicate the base year: $X = 0$ at 1978. The trend line and time series obtained are plotted in Figure 7-14.

The trend line may be used to project the level of employment for 2002. We must use $X = 24$ because this year is $X = 2002 - 1978 = 24$ periods beyond the base year. From the trend equation, we project employment for 2002 as

$$\hat{Y}(X) = 95.35 + 1.68(24)$$
$$= 135.67 \text{ million}$$

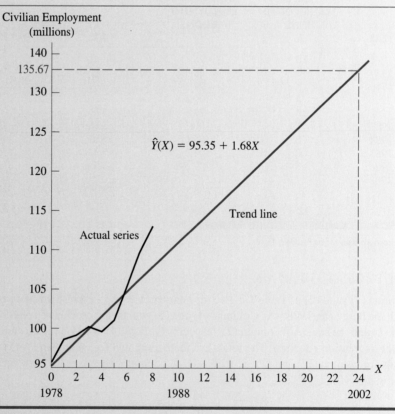

FIGURE 7-14   Actual data and trend line for U.S. civilian employment

The projected trend line for civilian employment is shown in Figure 7-14 as the portion of the line extending beyond the time periods actually observed. It is emphasized that the estimate of 135.67 million is an *extrapolation;* its validity depends on the assumption that the ensuing 15 years has exhibited growth similar to that existing in the past. The assumption of linearity is perhaps a poor one to use here, for the labor force grows in the same manner as the population, which for the United States has been nonlinear. Had more past years been used, a curve with a slope increasing over time would have provided a closer fit to the actual time-series data. Even then, good judgment would be an essential element.

Forecasting Sales Using a Trend Line

In business decision making, sales must often be forecast for planning purposes.

Forecasting Sales of BriDent Toothpaste

MANAGERIAL APPLICATION

Figure 7-15 shows the trend line for sales of BriDent toothpaste, using the 1992 through 2001 data in column (3) of Table 7-6. Using those data, we want to verify the regression equation used to plot that line and to forecast the 2002 BriDent sales.

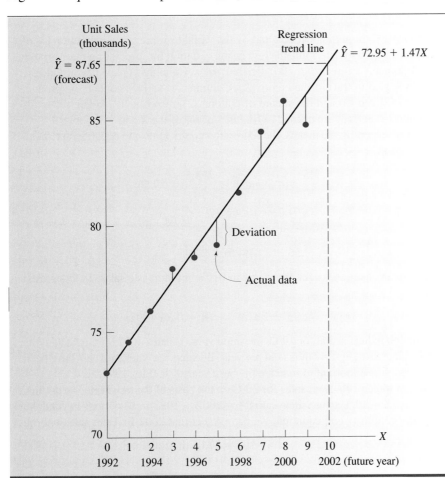

FIGURE 7-15 Regression line for trend in unit sales of BriDent toothpaste

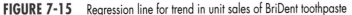

TABLE 7-6   Computations for Fitting Trend Line to BriDent Toothpaste Sales

(1) YEAR	(2) YEAR IN TRANSFORMED UNITS X	(3) UNIT SALES (THOUSANDS) Y	(4) XY	(5) X²
1992	0	72.9	0	0
1993	1	74.4	74.4	1
1994	2	75.9	151.8	4
1995	3	77.9	233.7	9
1996	4	78.6	314.4	16
1997	5	79.1	395.5	25
1998	6	81.7	490.2	36
1999	7	84.4	590.8	49
2000	8	85.9	687.2	64
2001	9	84.8	763.2	81
	45 $=\sum X$	795.6 $=\sum Y$	3,701.2 $=\sum XY$	285 $=\sum X^2$

THE PROBLEM SOLUTION

Sales from 1992 through 2001, denoted by the variable Y, are given in column (3) of Table 7-6. We want to determine the regression equation for forecasting that variable and use it to make a forecast of 2002 BriDent sales. Columns (1) and (2) provide the year and the year in transformed units (X). Columns (4) and (5) contain the product of columns (2) and (3) and the square of column (2), respectively. Again, the totals for columns (2) and (3) are needed to find the means of the X and Y variables.

After determining the means, the regression coefficients and equation are found (using $n = 10$).

$$\bar{X} = \frac{45}{10} = 4.5 \text{ and } \bar{Y} = \frac{795.6}{10} = 79.56$$

$$b = \frac{3,701.2 - 10(4.5)(79.56)}{285 - 10(4.5)^2} = 1.47$$

$$a = 79.56 - 1.47(4.5) = 72.95$$

The regression equation for the trend line in BriDent toothpaste sales (in thousands) is therefore

$$\hat{Y}(X) = 72.95 + 1.47X \qquad (X = 0 \text{ for } 1992)$$

This equation indicates that for 1992, the trend value is sales of 72.95 thousand units and that Y_t increases by 1.47 thousand per year. Because the calendar years have been transformed, it is important to indicate the base year: $X = 0$ for 1992.

We can forecast BriDent sales for 2002 on the basis of the trend line. To do this, we must use $X = 10$, because this year is $X = 2002 - 1992 = 10$ periods beyond the base year. From the trend equation, we can project that 2002 BriDent sales will be

$$\hat{Y}(X) = 72.95 + 1.47(10) = 87.65 \text{ thousand units}$$

	A	B	C	D	E	F	G
1				Fitting Trend Line to BriDent Toothpaste Sales Using Regression			
2				SUMMARY OUTPUT			
3		Year in	Unit				
4		Transformed	Sales	*Regression Statistics*			
5		Units	(thousands)	Multiple R	0.98		
				R Square	0.96		
6	Year	X	Y	Adjusted R Square	0.96		
7	1992	0	72.9	Standard Error	0.90		
8	1993	1	74.4	Observations	10		
9	1994	2	75.9				
10	1995	3	77.9	ANOVA			
					df	*SS*	*MS*	*F*	*Significance F*
11	1996	4	78.6	Regression	1	177.47	177.47	219.86	0.00
12	1997	5	79.1	Residual	8	6.46	0.81		
13	1998	6	81.7	Total	9	183.92			
14	1999	7	84.4					
15	2000	8	85.9		*Coefficients*	*Standard Error*	*t Stat*	
				Intercept	72.96	0.53	138.17	
16	2001	9	84.8	X	1.47	0.10	14.83	

FIGURE 7-16   Excel's Regression tool used on BriDent toothpaste sales

Linear Regression Using Spreadsheets

Excel offers several ways to perform regression analysis. Most convenient for our purposes is the Regression tool under Excel's Data Analysis option. Other methods utilizing special-purpose Excel functions and the Chart Wizard will be illustrated in the problems at the end of the chapter.

Figure 7-16 shows the results of a spreadsheet regression with the original BriDent Toothpaste data appearing in columns A through C, starting in row 7. The Summary Output gives the intercept $a = 72.96$ and the slope $b = 1.47$, so that the regression equation is

$$\hat{Y}(X) = 72.96 + 1.47X$$

Due to rounding, these results differ slightly from the earlier hand computation. To launch the regression, we began by selecting Data Analysis from the Tools menu. That activated the Data Analysis dialog box in Figure 7-17. From that box, we selected Regression, causing the Regression dialog box in Figure 7-18 to appear. In that second box, we entered C7:C16 as the *Input Y Range* and B7:B16 as the *Input X Range*. Then

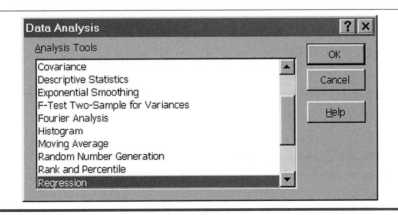

FIGURE 7-17
Excel Data Analysis dialog box

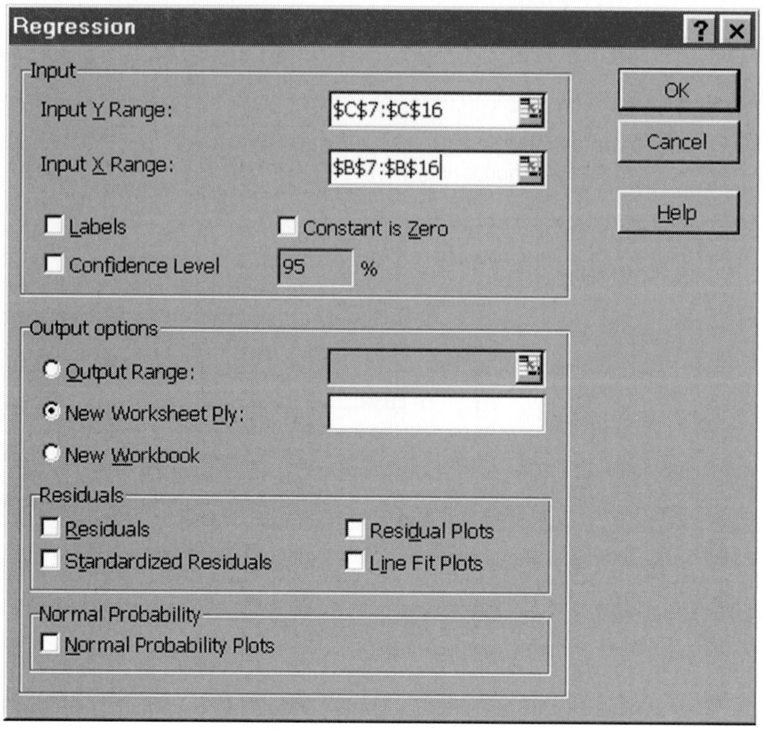

FIGURE 7-18
Excel Regression dialog
box for BriDent toothpaste

after clicking OK, the Summary Output shown on the right-hand side of Figure 7-16 was obtained. That report can appear on the original spreadsheet or on a new one, depending on which option is chosen. (The statistical portions of the output are not meaningful with time-series data.)

A forecast for year 2002 BriDent sales may be found from the regression line determined above by substituting 10 (representing the year 2002) for X.

$$\hat{Y}(10) = 72.96 + 1.47(10) = 87.7$$

However, Excel has a special function that gives the forecast in one step, FORE-CAST. Entering the equation = FORECAST(10,B7:B16,C7:C16) in any cell yields a more precise 87.6 directly, without the need to do a separate regression. The first argument is 10, the year for which the forecast is required. The second argument is the range of the X variable, B7:B16. The third argument is the range of the Y variable, C7:C16.

More information about interpreting the results in Figure 7-16 is given in Section 7-7. The least-squares criterion, sum of squares, coefficient of determination (r square), standard error of estimate, and F- and t-values are all discussed there.

7-4   FORECASTING USING CAUSAL MODELS: REGRESSION ANALYSIS

Thus far, we have discussed forecasting procedures based only on extrapolations from time-series data, and until this point, our conclusions have been somewhat tenuous. Such forecasts—especially long-range ones—can severely err because they are based on historical patterns that will not necessarily continue in the future. Often the cause for such patterns cannot even be identified.

TABLE 7-7	Sample Observations of Rail Distance and Transportation Times for 10 Shipments by a Parts Supplier	

CUSTOMER	RAIL DISTANCE TO DESTINATION X	TRANSPORTATION TIME (DAYS) Y
1. Muller Auto Supply	210	5
2. Taylor Ford	290	7
3. Auto Supply House	350	6
4. Parts 'n' Spares	480	11
5. Jones & Sons	490	8
6. A. Hausman	730	11
7. Des Moines Parts	780	12
8. Pete's Parts	850	8
9. Smith Dodge	920	15
10. Gulf Distributors	1,010	12

Sometimes we can achieve more satisfactory forecasts by using a causal model that explains the dependent forecast variable in terms of the level for one or more predictor variables (rather than simply in terms of a period of time). Ideal predictors *lead* (have values that are determined in advance of) the main variable. Thus, a student's success at college might be predicted from his or her high school grade point average. Predictions of future growth in GDP might be based on today's prices, level of employment, and plant capacities. Or a product's sales forecast might be determined from its current share of the market and planned advertising expenditures.

Table 7-7 shows the observations of distances and transportation times for a sample of 10 rail shipments made by an automobile parts supplier. These data will be used to arrive at predictions of transit times for future shipments.

A linear equation relating the transportation time Y (the forecast or dependent variable) to the rail distance X (the independent variable) can be found using regression. Computer assistance is ordinarily used for this.

Regression Using a Spreadsheet

Figure 7-19 shows the Excel spreadsheet for the transportation times. The following regression equation applies:

$$\hat{Y}(X) = 4.017681 + .008973X$$

The intercept $a = 4.017681$ and slope $b = .008973$ are read from the Summary Output, in the last table at the bottom of Figure 7-19.

We may now use the above regression equation to predict the transportation time $\hat{Y}(X)$ for a shipment of known rail distance X from the parts supplier's plant. For instance, when $X = 490$, we have

$$\hat{Y}(490) = 4.017681 + .008973(490)$$
$$= 8.4 \text{ days}$$

Thus, the prediction for the transportation time to a customer 490 miles away is $\hat{Y}(490)$ = 8.4 days.

Statistical Evaluation

Excel's statistical evaluation is included in the Summary Output at the bottom of Figure 7-19. Here we only briefly describe the results. (You may get further statistical background from the optional Section 7-7 at the end of this chapter.)

The multiple R square value .638995 gauges the overall quality of the regression analysis and is less useful than the standard error of the estimate, 2.020859. We are familiar with the square of this quantity, which is equal to the *MSE*. We have

$$MSE = (2.020859)^2 = 4.083869$$

As we have seen, the *MSE* is a useful quality assessment of a forecasting procedure.

The *MSE* value also appears in the residual row of the ANOVA segment in Figure 7-19. There, the computed level of the *F* statistic is reported. The value achieved indicates that the parts supplier regression results are highly statistically significant.

The statistical information in the last five columns of the final table in the Summary Output allows us to draw inferences regarding *a* and *b*. Notice that the confidence interval for *b* is quite wide. A larger sample size than the one used with these data should provide a better estimate of the true regression line slope.

	A	B	C	D	E	F	G
1		Regression Analysis for the Parts Supplier					
2							
3			Transportation				
4		Rail	Time				
5		Distance	(days)				
6	Customer	X	Y				
7	1	210	5				
8	2	290	7				
9	3	350	6				
10	4	480	11				
11	5	490	8				
12	6	730	11				
13	7	780	12				
14	8	850	8				
15	9	920	15				
16	10	1,010	12				
17							
18	SUMMARY OUTPUT						
19							
20	Regression Statistics						
21	Multiple R	0.799372					
22	R Square	0.638995					
23	Adjusted R Square	0.593869					
24	Standard Error	2.020859					
25	Observations	10					
26							
27	ANOVA						
28		df	SS	MS	F	Significance F	
29	Regression	1	57.829045	57.829045	14.160356	0.005520	
30	Residual	8	32.670955	4.083869			
31	Total	9	90.500000				
32							
33		Coefficients	Standard Error	t Stat	P-value	Lower 95%	Upper 95%
34	Intercept	4.017681	1.590887	2.525435	0.035507	0.349088	7.686274
35	X	0.008973	0.002384	3.763025	0.005520	0.003474	0.014471

FIGURE 7-19   Spreadsheet and results for regression analysis with parts supplier

Multiple Regression Analysis

Predictions made from a regression line relating Y to a single independent variable are categorized as **simple regression analysis.** The procedure may be extended, so that Y is related simultaneously to several independent predictors. The resulting predictions involve **multiple regression analysis.** Multiple regression can dramatically improve forecasting accuracy.

The sample data in Table 7-8 may be used to predict the sales for retail outlets of the Deuce Hardware chain. In doing this, two possible independent predictor variables are available for each store, floorspace X_1, and monthly advertising expenditure, X_2. A simple regression using only X_1 as the predictor provides the following equation:

$$\hat{Y}(X_1) = 3,895 + 6.66X_1$$

We will now consider how an expanded multiple regression using *both* X_1 and X_2 as predictors might provide improved sales predictions.

The essential advantage of considering two or more independent variables is that it permits greater use of available information. For example, a regression line that expresses a new store's sales in terms of the population of the city it serves should yield a poorer sales forecast than an equation that also considers median income, number of nearby competitors, and the local unemployment rate. A plant manager ought to predict more precisely the cost of processing a new order if he considers, in addition to the size of the order, the total volume of orders, his current staffing levels, and the production capacity of available equipment. A marketing manager ought to gauge more finely the sales response to a magazine advertisement if she considers, in addition to the magazine's circulation, the demographical features of its readers, such as median age, median income, and proportion of urban readers.

Linear multiple regression analysis involves two or more independent variables. In the case of two independent variables, denoted by X_1 and X_2, the **estimated multiple regression equation** is

$$\hat{Y} = a + b_1X_1 + b_2X_2$$

TABLE 7-8 Sales, Floorspace, and Advertising Expenditure Data for Deuce Hardware Store

STORE	MONTHLY SALES Y	FLOORSPACE (SQUARE FEET) X_1	MONTHLY ADVERTISING EXPENDITURE X_2
1	$20,100	3,050	$350
2	14,900	1,300	980
3	16,800	1,890	830
4	9,100	1,750	760
5	15,500	1,010	930
6	26,700	2,690	770
7	34,600	4,210	440
8	7,200	1,950	570
9	21,800	2,830	310
10	23,400	2,030	920

FIGURE 7-20
A regression plane for
multiple regression using
three variables

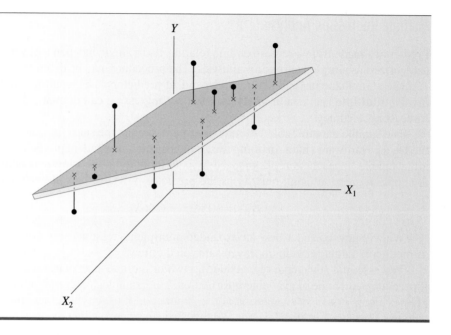

Here, two independent variables and one dependent variable, or a total of three variables, are considered. The sample data will consist of three values for each sample unit observed, so that a scatter diagram of these observations will be three dimensional.

To explain how multiple regression data can be portrayed in three dimensions, we will draw an analogy using the walls and floor of a room. Letting a corner of the room represent the case when all three variables have a value of zero, the data points may be represented by suspending marbles in space at various distances from the floor and the two walls. A marble's height above the floor can be the value of Y for that observation. Its distance along the wall on the right then measures the observed value of X_1, and its distance along the wall on the left expresses the observed value of X_2. Figure 7-20 is a pictorial representation of a three-dimensional scatter for a hypothetical set of data.

The regression equation corresponds to a plane. This plane must be slanted in such a way that it provides the best least-squares fit to the sample data. The three-dimensional surface that results is the **regression plane.** Slanting this plane can be compared to determining how to position a pane of glass through the suspended marbles so that its incline approximates the incline of the pattern of the scatter. As with the regression line, a, b_1, and b_2 are chosen in such a way that the vertical deviations between the actual values and the regression plane are minimized.

To illustrate, we will consider our Deuce Hardware data again. Monthly sales Y can now be predicted using floorspace X_1 and monthly advertising expenditure X_2 as a set of independent variables. A computer solution provides the following values (rounded):

$$a = -22,979$$
$$b_1 = 11.42$$
$$b_2 = 23.41$$

The values of a, b_1, and b_2 provide the estimated multiple regression equation

$$\hat{Y} = -22,979 + 11.42X_1 + 23.41X_2$$

which can be used to forecast the sales of a particular store. Suppose a new store is to be built that will have 2,500 square feet of floorspace and spend $750 a month on advertising. The forecast sales level is then

$$\hat{Y} = -22,979 + 11.42(2,500) + 23.41(750)$$
$$= \$23,128.50$$

These results were obtained using Excel.

Multiple Regression with Spreadsheets

The Excel Regression tool can be used to do multiple regression, as before. We must be sure to list *all* the X variable columns when designating the *Input X Range*. Figure 7-21 illustrates how this is done for the Deuce Hardware Store.

	A	B	C	D	E	F	G
1		**Multiple Regression for the Deuce Hardware Store**					
2							
3				Monthly			
4		Monthly	Floorspace	Advertising			
5		Sales	(square feet)	Expenditure			
6	Store	Y	X_1	X_2			
7	1	20,100	3,050	350			
8	2	14,900	1,300	980			
9	3	16,800	1,890	830			
10	4	9,100	1,750	760			
11	5	15,500	1,010	930			
12	6	26,700	2,690	770			
13	7	34,600	4,210	440			
14	8	7,200	1,950	570			
15	9	21,800	2,830	310			
16	10	23,400	2,030	920			
17							
18	SUMMARY OUTPUT						
19							
20	*Regression Statistics*						
21	Multiple R	0.89332611					
22	R Square	0.798031538					
23	Adjusted R Sqr	0.740326264					
24	Standard Error	4168.371133					
25	Observations	10					
26							
27	ANOVA						
28		*df*	*SS*	*MS*	*F*	*Significance F*	
29	Regression	2	480581774.7	240290887.3	13.8294383	0.003702478	
30	Residual	7	121627225.3	17375317.9			
31	Total	9	602209000				
32							
33		*Coefficients*	*Standard Error*	*t Stat*	*P-value*	*Lower 95%*	*Upper 95%*
34	Intercept	-22979	10546.50	-2.18	0.07	-47917.10	1959.87
35	X_1	11.42	2.29	4.98	0.00	5.99	16.84
36	X_2	23.41	8.64	2.71	0.03	2.99	43.84

FIGURE 7-21 Spreadsheet for multiple regression using the Deuce Hardware Store data

As seen previously, the regression equation may be used to find a forecast. For example, when X_1 = 2,500 square feet of floorspace and the monthly advertising expenditure is X_2 = 750 dollars, the forecast monthly sales is

$$\hat{Y} = -22,979 + 11.42(2,500) + 23.41(750) = \$23,128.50$$

The F statistic is computed to be 13.83 (rounded), shown in the ANOVA portion of the Summary Output. That measures the overall statistical significance of the results. To the right of that quantity is the significance level, .0037. This is the probability that such a regression result could have been obtained when the true regression coefficients are both zero. Further data, shown in the last rows of the Summary Output, provide the computed t values and analogous probabilities for the individual regression coefficients. Also reported are the confidence intervals for these. Notice that the confidence intervals are quite wide, detracting from the quality of any estimates made from the regression equation. (Greater statistical "accuracy" can ordinarily be achieved by using a larger number of observations.)

Comparison of Simple and Multiple Regression

Table 7-9 shows the Deuce Hardware sales forecasts made by applying both simple and multiple regression to the actual data. Note that multiple regression provides greater accuracy because the forecasting errors tend to be smaller when this procedure is used. Including the second predictor variable (advertising expenditure) allows us to "explain" more variation in sales Y.

Multiple regressions can involve higher dimensions, so that as many as 10 or 15 independent X's might be used in making predictions. It is not clear whether including more variables generally reduces forecasting error. In some cases, adding independent variables can even confuse the analysis. Independent variables must be chosen with care and must have some rational basis for affecting Y.

Special Problems in Causal Regression Analysis

In order for probability to be used in qualifying regression results, certain assumptions must apply. In addition to those mentioned earlier, a key theoretical requirement is that the residual values (error terms) be normally distributed with mean zero and constant

TABLE 7-9   Comparison of Forecasting Errors Using Simple and Multiple Regression

ACTUAL DATA			SIMPLE REGRESSION		MULTIPLE REGRESSION	
			Forecast $\hat{Y}$	Error $Y - \hat{Y}$	Forecast $\hat{Y}$	Error $Y - \hat{Y}$
X_1	X_2	Y				
3,050	350	20,100	24,195	−4,095	20,036	64
1,300	980	14,900	12,547	2,353	14,809	91
1,890	830	16,800	16,474	326	18,032	−1,232
1,750	760	9,100	15,542	−6,442	14,795	−5,695
1,010	930	15,500	10,617	4,883	10,327	5,173
2,690	770	26,700	21,799	4,901	25,760	940
4,210	440	34,600	31,915	2,685	35,386	−786
1,950	570	7,200	16,874	−9,673	12,629	−5,429
2,830	310	21,800	22,731	−931	16,588	5,212
2,030	920	23,400	17,406	5,994	21,738	1,662
				MSE = 31,170,000		MSE = 17,380,000

variance (regardless of the level for X). When those ideal conditions do not apply, the price paid is wrongful probabilities.

Time-series data may present special difficulties arising from a **serial correlation** between observations made in successive time periods. A serial correlation or **auto-correlation** exists whenever there is a tendency for similar values to follow the earlier number. For example, the following successive monthly seasonally adjusted unemployment rates show a serial correlation.

7.3   7.4   7.6   7.5   7.3   7.1   7.0   6.9   6.9   7.1   7.2   7.3

Notice that each successive monthly rate lies close to the preceding level, reflecting the inertia in the economy.

Multiple regression presents additional challenges. A potential problem can arise when two independent variables are highly correlated. For example, consider retail sales and foot traffic or magazine advertising revenue and number of pages. In a three-variable situation, such a relationship would provide sample data that are scattered closely about a single line lying inside the least-squares regression plane. Although the estimated regression equation can be found with no special difficulty when X_1 and X_2 are highly correlated, a second set of sample observations may result in drastically different regression coefficients, even when the second line of scatter is nearly identical to the first one. Because many different regression planes can contain the same line, the regression exhibits **multicollinearity.** Including a third independent variable might eliminate the problem created by the multicollinearity.

Further Considerations

We have barely scratched the surface of regression analysis. For example, we have entirely avoided an examination of nonlinear relationships, such as exponential trends, growth functions, or polynomial relationships. (Problems 7-26 and 7-27 discuss using these.)

Forecasts made from the regression line or plane can be qualified in a statistical sense by means of confidence intervals. The procedures involved, however, are based on formidable theoretical assumptions that are too complex to discuss here. Regression analysis is often accompanied by **correlation analysis,** where the major concern is how strongly the variables are related. Advanced techniques, such as **stepwise multiple regression,** help determine not only the regression equation but also the particular predictor variables it is best to include. An area of statistics and economics called **econometrics** considers causal models in great depth and wide breadth.

DECISION PROBLEM

Decision Problem Revisited: Bugoff Chemical Company

Comptroller Wilson Chou asks financial analyst Jason Brown to use regression analysis to develop reliable forecasts of Malabug direct costs, using technical base and raw stock as independent predictors. In particular, he wants an estimate of direct costs for the four cases listed below.

CASE	TECHNICAL BASE (GALLONS)	RAW STOCK (GALLONS)
1	1000	1000
2	500	750
3	750	500
4	400	600

After some study and a number of computer runs, Jason summarizes his results.

```
MEMORANDUM          To find out if there is a relationship between Malabug's
TO: Wilson Chou     direct cost and the technical base or the raw stock, I
FROM: Jason Brown   ran a multiple regression on the data you provided. The
SUBJECT:            equation obtained is
  Direct                     Y = 14.03 − 0.00316X₁ − 0.00342X₂
  Cost            Overall, this is a statistically reliable relationship,
  Forecasts       because the F value is about 14. The coefficient of de-
                  termination is .98, which means that the equation ex-
                  plains 98% of the variation in the data.
                       Using the regression equation given above and the
                  data provided, I obtained the following forecasts.
```

Case	Forecasted Direct Cost (dollars per gallon)
1	7.45
2	9.89
3	9.95
4	10.71

7-5 FORECASTING USING SEASONAL INDEXES

In this section, we will examine a procedure for isolating seasonal fluctuations in time-series data. Identifying seasonal patterns is a necessary first step in short-range planning. The management of a firm whose business drops in May is not alarmed if it is only the beginning of an annual seasonal trough. Likewise, government economists recognize that the consumer price index will rise or fall in certain months solely due to the influence of seasonal factors such as changing varieties of produce on the market. To monitor the performance of a business or an economy, it is useful to "deseasonalize" time-series data to determine whether a current drop or rise is greater than normal.

Ratio-to-Moving-Average Method

The **ratio-to-moving-average method** is widely used to isolate seasonal fluctuations. Beginning with the actual time series, the trend and cyclical elements are isolated together in what is referred to as a "smoothed" time series. The isolation of the long-term elements is accomplished by means of **four-quarter moving averages.**

In the context of the classical time-series model, the ratio-to-moving-average method is summarized by the expression

$$\frac{Y_t}{\text{Moving average}} = \frac{T_t \times C_t \times S_t \times I_t}{T_t \times C_t} = S_t \times I_t$$

The moving average provides both trend and cycle, so that $T_t \times C_t$ is obtained for each time period. Dividing Y_t by the moving average is therefore equivalent to canceling the $T_t \times C_t$ terms from the multiplicative model, so that only the seasonal and irregular components, expressed by $S_t \times I_t$, remain.

The procedure is carried out in a number of steps. First, the first four successive values in the original time series are summed. That total is divided by 4 to get the first four-quarter moving average, which represents one complete year. These computations are repeated, except the initial quarter is dropped and the fifth is added, so that the second four-quarter average also represents a full year. The process is continued until you have run out of new quarters. The final step is to center the data by computing for each period the **centered moving average.** This is accomplished by averaging each successive pair of four-quarter averages.

To illustrate the procedure, Table 7-10 provides data for Haskin-Dobbins ice cream sales (in thousands of gallons). The first four-quarter average is found by adding the actual sales for the quarters of 1995 and dividing by 4.

$$\frac{5,100 + 9,800 + 15,200 + 11,300}{4} = 10,350$$

This value corresponds to that point in time when the spring 1995 quarter ends and the summer 1995 quarter begins—midnight, June 30, 1995.

TABLE 7-10   Time Series for Haskin-Dobbins Data

(1) QUARTER	(2) SALES (IN THOUSANDS OF GALLONS)	(3) FOUR-QUARTER MOVING AVERAGE	(4) CENTERED MOVING AVERAGE	(5) ORIGINAL AS A PERCENTAGE OF MOVING AVERAGE	(6) SEASONAL INDEX
1995					
Winter	5,100				53.58
Spring	9,800				101.04
		10,350			
Summer	15,200		10,475	145.11	144.97
		10,600			
Fall	11,300		10,913	103.55	100.40
		11,225			
1996					
Winter	6,100		11,625	52.47	53.58
		12,025			
Spring	12,300		12,263	100.30	101.04
		12,500			
Summer	18,400		12,638	145.59	144.97
		12,775			
Fall	13,200		13,000	101.54	100.40
		13,225			
1997					
Winter	7,200		13,513	53.28	53.58
		13,800			
Spring	14,100		14,000	100.71	101.04
		14,200			
Summer	20,700		14,375	144.00	144.97
		14,550			
Fall	14,800		14,850	99.66	100.40
		15,150			
1998					
Winter	8,600		15,575	55.22	53.58
		16,000			
Spring	16,500		16,213	101.77	101.04
		16,425			
Summer	24,100		16,575	145.40	144.97
		16,725			
Fall	16,500		17,088	96.56	100.40
		17,450			
1999					
Winter	9,800		18,113	54.10	53.58
		18,775			
Spring	19,400		18,988	102.17	101.04
		19,200			
Summer	29,400				144.97
Fall	18,200				100.40

The second four-quarter average is found by dropping sales for winter 1995 and including the figure for winter 1996:

$$\frac{9,800 + 15,200 + 11,300 + 6,100}{4} = 10,600$$

As before, this value applies to the point in time separating summer 1995 from fall 1995—midnight, September 30. Because the values apply between quarters, the column of four-quarter averages is positioned one-half line off the rest of the table.

Column (4) contains the centered moving averages. The first of these is found by averaging the first two four-quarter averages.

$$\frac{10,350 + 10,600}{2} = 10,475$$

This value applies to the midpoint of summer 1995, coinciding in time with the original data.

The irregular component (I_t) must be removed before a final set of seasonal indexes can be obtained. This is accomplished by first finding for each season the *median* **percentage of moving average** for the applicable quarters. (Although the mean could be used, the median is preferred because it is less affected by unusually large or small values.) Then the median percentages are adjusted so that the final indexes average to 100% for the entire year.

The first percentage of moving average is computed for summer 1995 by dividing the original sales level of 15,200 by that quarter's centered moving average of 10,475. This is then multiplied by 100.

$$\frac{15,200}{10,475} \times 100 = 145.11$$

Sales for summer 1995 were thus 145.11% of the trend and cyclical components.

Table 7-11 shows all the percentages of moving averages. There are four percentages for each quarter, with the median obtained by averaging the middle-sized two. The sum of the medians is 400.79. To obtain indexes that sum to 400% (and that average to

TABLE 7-11   Calculation of Seasonal Indexes for Haskin-Dobbins Sales

Year	QUARTER Winter	Spring	Summer	Fall
1995			145.11	103.55
1996	52.47	100.30	145.59	101.54
1997	53.28	100.71	144.00	99.66
1998	55.22	101.77	145.40	96.56
1999	54.10	102.17		
Median	53.69	101.24	145.26	100.60

Sum of medians = 400.79

$$\text{Seasonal index} = \text{Median} \times \frac{400}{400.79}$$

| | 53.58 | 101.04 | 144.97 | 100.40 |

100% throughout the year), each median is multiplied by 400/400.79. These seasonal indexes provide the S_t values for ice cream sales.

When the original time series is given by months, the general procedures illustrated for quarterly data can also be applied. A year's worth of successive monthly figures is averaged to provide twelve-month moving averages. Each successive pair of these is then averaged to obtain the **twelve-month centered moving average.** These indexes must sum to 1,200%.

Making the Forecast

Seasonal indexes are useful in making short-term forecasts. First, a trend over the annual period is determined, and then seasonal adjustments are made for each period within the year. For example, suppose that the managers of a department store who want to forecast monthly sales for the year 2000 determine the trend equation:

$$\hat{Y} = 1{,}025{,}000 + 50{,}000X$$

where X is in months and $X = 0$ for January 15, 2000. Calculations of the monthly forecasts for department store sales are provided in Table 7-12. The 12 monthly seasonal indexes appear in column (3), and the monthly sales trend levels are calculated in column (4) from the managers' trend equation. For January, the trend value of $1,025,000 is multiplied by 56.7% to obtain the forecast sales of $581,175. The sales forecasts for all 12 months are listed in column (5).

Analysis with Spreadsheets

Spreadsheets are useful in isolating seasonal indexes, which require several calculations. Figure 7-22 shows a spreadsheet using the same Stationer's Supply data evaluated earlier by exponential smoothing. (Rows 28–41 are not printed.) The procedure for obtaining the year 2001 sales forecasts in cells C47:C50 is described below.

TABLE 7-12 Calculations of the Monthly Forecasts for Department Store Sales

(1) MONTH	(2) X	(3) SEASONAL INDEX	(4) MONTHLY SALES TREND LEVEL $\hat{Y}$	(5) MONTHLY SALES FORECAST $[(3) \times (4)] \div 100$
January	0	56.7	$1,025,000	$ 581,175
February	1	64.5	1,075,000	693,375
March	2	62.1	1,125,000	698,625
April	3	99.9	1,175,000	1,173,825
May	4	83.6	1,225,000	1,024,100
June	5	67.4	1,275,000	859,350
July	6	58.2	1,325,000	771,150
August	7	100.1	1,375,000	1,376,375
September	8	110.6	1,425,000	1,576,050
October	9	137.7	1,475,000	2,031,075
November	10	167.3	1,525,000	2,551,325
December	11	191.9	1,575,000	3,022,425
		1,200.0		

CLASSICAL TIME SERIES ANALYSIS

PROBLEM: Stationer's Supply

	C
6	=MEDIAN(F23,F27,F31,F35,F39,F43)
7	=MEDIAN(F24,F28,F32,F36,F40,F44)
8	=MEDIAN(F21,F25,F29,F33,F37,F41)
9	=MEDIAN(F22,F26,F30,F34,F38,F42)

Quarter	Ratio	Index
Winter	88.15%	88.18%
Spring	105.92%	105.95%
Summer	90.43%	90.46%
Fall	115.36%	115.40%

	D
6	=C6*4/SUM($C$6:$C$9)
7	=C7*4/SUM($C$6:$C$9)
8	=C8*4/SUM($C$6:$C$9)
9	=C9*4/SUM($C$6:$C$9)

	H
19	=C19/G19
20	=C20/G20
21	=C21/G21

PROBLEM: Stationer's Supply

PROBLEM DATA

	D	E	F
20	=AVERAGE(C19:C22)		
21	=AVERAGE(C20:C23)	=AVERAGE(D20:D21)	=C21/E21
22	=AVERAGE(C21:C24)	=AVERAGE(D21:D22)	=C22/E22

	Quarter	t	Actual Sales, Y_t	Four-Quarter Moving Average	Centered Moving Average	Original as a Percentage of Moving Average	Seasonal Index	Seasonally Adjusted
19	1994 W	1	90,640				88.18%	102,786.7
20	S	2	115,540	108,543			105.95%	109,046.3
21	S	3	99,190	111,470	110,006	90.17%	90.46%	109,646.5
22	F	4	128,800	114,445	112,958	114.03%	115.40%	111,612.8
23	1995 W	5	102,350	117,780	116,113	88.15%	88.18%	116,066.0
24	S	6	127,440	121,850	119,815	106.36%	105.95%	120,277.5
25	S	7	112,530	123,885	122,868	91.59%	90.46%	124,392.8
26	F	8	145,080	127,775	125,830	115.30%	115.40%	125,720.3
27	1996 W	9	110,490	129,568	128,671	85.87%	88.18%	125,296.9
42	F	24	202,960	177,045	175,010	115.97%	115.40%	175,876.7
43	2000 W	25	157,500	180,258	178,651	88.16%	88.18%	178,606.7
44	S	26	192,240	184,258	182,258	105.48%	105.95%	181,435.6
45	S	27	168,330				90.46%	186,075.1
46	F	28	218,960				115.40%	189,741.7
47	2001 W	29	168,488				88.18%	191,066.8
48	S	30	205,759				105.95%	194,194.5
49	S	31	178,505				90.46%	197,322.3
50	F	32	231,317				115.40%	200,450.1

	C
47	=H47*G47
48	=H48*G48
49	=H49*G49
50	=H50*G50

	H
47	=FORECAST(B47,$H$19:$H$46,$B$19:$B$46)
48	=FORECAST(B48,$H$19:$H$46,$B$19:$B$46)
49	=FORECAST(B49,$H$19:$H$46,$B$19:$B$46)
50	=FORECAST(B50,$H$19:$H$46,$B$19:$B$46)

FIGURE 7-22   The classical time-series analysis spreadsheet for Stationer's Supply

The calculations begin with the four-quarter moving averages in column D, where cell D20 contains the formula

$$= AVERAGE(C19:C22)$$

to calculate the first moving average from the historical sales in column C. The above formula was copied down to the cells in the range D21:D44, where the subsequent moving averages appear. (Cells D45 and D46 have no moving averages because the year 2001 sales are presently unknown.)

Column E centers the four-quarter moving averages from column D. There, cell E21 has the formula

$$= AVERAGE(D20:D21)$$

which has been copied down to cells E22:E44.

Column F determines the original sales as a percentage of the centered moving averages in column E. There, cell F21 has the formula

$$= C21/E21$$

which has been copied down to the range F22:F44.

The seasonal indexes appearing near the top of the spreadsheet were calculated from the column F results. The ratios in cells C6:C9 were found by taking the median of the respective seasons from column F. Thus, the winter ratio in cell C6 is 88.15%, the median of all the winter values from column F, as calculated by the formula

$$= MEDIAN(F23,F27,F31,F35,F39,F43)$$

The other ratio formulas were built in the same way.

The seasonal indexes at the top of column D are the normalized ratios, which sum to 400%. Thus, cell D6 contains the formula

$$= C6*4/SUM(\$C\$6:\$C\$9)$$

which was copied down to cells D7:D9. These seasonal indexes are paste linked (Edit, Paste Special, Paste Link) to the values in column G for the corresponding seasons, cells G19:G50 (for more details, see the *Guide to Excel* on the CD-ROM accompanying this book).

The seasonally adjusted values in column H are found by dividing the actual sales by the seasonal indexes in column G. The formula in cell H19 is

$$= C19/G19$$

which was copied down to cells H20:H46.

The quarterly sales forecasts appear at the bottom of the spreadsheet in cells H47:H50. These were obtained using Excel's FORECAST function. In cell H47 this is used in the formula

$$= FORECAST(B47,\$H\$19:\$H\$46,\$B\$19:\$B\$46)$$

The first argument is B47, the cell containing the period being forecast. The second and third arguments are the applicable cell ranges, H19:H46 (seasonally adjusted values as the *Y*'s) and B19:B46 (periods as the *X*'s). The above formula was copied down to cells H48:H50 at the bottom of the spreadsheet.

Actual sales forecasts for the year 2001 appear at the bottom of the spreadsheet in cells C47:C50. These are the product of seasonally adjusted sales and the seasonal factors in column G. They are based on the cell C47 formula

$$= H47*G47$$

which was copied down to cells C48:C50.

7-6   FURTHER FORECASTING PROCEDURES AND THE ROLE OF JUDGMENT

The third major forecasting technique is based on judgment. In a sense, all forecasting involves some judgment, even when data are extensively analyzed. But we can use judgment to make forecasts even when no data at all are available.

Until now, all of the forecasting methods we have discussed involve *point forecasts;* that is, they provide future predictions in the form of specific numerical values. Such forecasts are almost certain to be in error. The actual data will inevitably differ in some way from the forecasts; at best, the forecasts will be slightly above or below the actual values. It may therefore be more realistic to predict a *range of values*. An even better method might be to include future uncertainty by treating it as a random variable with a *probability distribution*. A detailed discussion of two methods for finding judgmental probability distributions was given in Chapter 4.

In one popular prediction procedure called **Delphi forecasting,** individual judgments regarding future events are combined to express a collective opinion. Delphi forecasting has been successfully employed in predicting technological breakthroughs and scientific advancements. It has also been used to forecast long-range sales and profits.

Another judgmental application, **scenario projection,** is often employed in government and military planning. Here, detailed circumstances are used as stage settings to provide background for a future analysis that simulates reality. **Industrial** and **world dynamics** operate in the same vein. In these procedures, mathematical models are employed to make long-range predictions and to simulate future conditions.

There are many other types of forecasting methods, too numerous to mention here. More detailed discussions of forecasting methods can be found in some of the references in the bibliography.

USING JUDGMENT

Selecting a Procedure for Forecasting

The forecasting methods applied in this chapter all involve judgment. There is no way to know that trends will continue in the same linear fashion as in the past. Seasonal patterns may not repeat themselves. It is a judgment call whenever past data are used to predict the future, and no procedure should be employed without acknowledging that. Judgment is also a necessary component of implementing a chosen procedure—we somewhat arbitrarily choose smoothing constants for exponential smoothing and independent variables for a multiple regression. Forecasting is as much an art as it is a science.

DECISION PROBLEM

Decision Problem Revisited: Bugoff Chemical Company

When Sam Morgan finished his study of using the decomposition method, he wrote the following memorandum to Warren Williams:

```
MEMORANDUM          The decomposition procedure is a good alternative method
TO: Warren          for forecasting with data that appear to have an in-
Williams            creasing trend and seasonal variations, such as for Mal-
FROM: Sam Morgan    abug's quarterly sales. The quarterly forecasts for Mal-
SUBJECT:            abug pesticide in the year 2002 are given in the
  Malabug Sales     following table:
  Forecasts                                       Forecast
  Using                          Quarter         (gallons)
  Decomposition                  Winter           54,700
                                 Spring          229,100
                                 Summer           82,000
                                 Fall             62,000
                    Long-range forecasts can be determined from this method
                    also. For example, Malabug sales are estimated to be
                    424,600 gallons in 2002, 599,500 gallons in 2006, and
                    finally 818,100 gallons by 2011.
```

Tables 7-13, 7-14, and 7-15 summarize the computations used by Mr. Morgan. The long-range Malabug sales forecasts are made from the decomposition trend line

$$\hat{Y} = 162.4 + 43.7X \qquad (X = 0 \text{ in } 1996)$$

In the year 2002, the variable X is 6. Substituting this value in the above equation gives 424.6, or 424,600 gallons.

TABLE 7-13 Finding Seasonal Indexes and Deseasonalized Sales for Malabug

(1) QUARTER	(2) SALES	(3) FOUR-QUARTER MOVING AVERAGE	(4) CENTERED MOVING AVERAGE	(5) PERCENTAGE OF MOVING AVERAGE	(6) SEASONAL INDEX	(7) DESEASONALIZED SALES
1996 W	18					
S	80	37.50	38.250	78	77.2	38.9
S	30	39.00	42.125	52	55.4	39.7
F	22	45.25	48.250	50	51.5	46.6
1997 W	24	51.25	51.875	202	215.8	48.7
S	105	52.50	53.625	101	77.2	69.9
S	54	54.75	59.250	46	55.4	48.7
F	27	63.75	63.000	52	51.5	64.1
1998 W	33	62.25	63.625	222	215.8	65.3
S	141	65.00	65.875	73	77.2	62.2
S	48	66.75	67.875	56	55.4	68.6
F	38	69.00	72.375	55	51.5	77.7
1999 W	40	75.75	76.625	196	215.8	69.5
S	150	77.50	76.875	98	77.2	97.2
S	75	76.25	80.000	56	55.4	81.2
F	45	83.75	81.250	43	51.5	68.0
2000 W	35	78.75	79.375	227	215.8	83.4
S	180	80.00	81.625	67	77.2	71.2
S	55	83.25	86.375	58	55.4	90.3
F	50	89.50	91.375	53	51.5	93.2
2001 W	48	93.25	94.125	218	215.8	95.0
S	205	95.00				
S	70					
F	57					

TABLE 7-14 Seasonal Index Calculations for Malabug Sales

		PERCENTAGES OF MOVING AVERAGE		
YEAR	W	S	S	F
1996			78	52
1997	50	202	101	46
1998	52	222	73	56
1999	55	196	98	56
2000	43	227	67	58
2001	53	218		
Median	52	218	78	56

Sum of medians = 404

Seasonal index = Median $\times \dfrac{400}{404}$

	51.5	215.8	77.2	55.4

TABLE 7-15 Quarterly Malabug Sales Forecasts

(1) QUARTER	(2) SEASONAL INDEX	(3) ANNUAL FORECAST ÷ 4	(4) QUARTERLY FORECAST [(2) × (3) ÷ 100]
2002 W	51.5	106.18	54.7
S	215.8	106.18	229.1
S	77.2	106.18	82.0
F	58.4	106.18	62.0

7-7 (OPTIONAL) STATISTICAL FUNDAMENTALS OF REGRESSION ANALYSIS

The Least-Squares Criterion

The estimated linear regression coefficients a and b in Section 7-3 are chosen so that the following sum is minimized:

$$\Sigma[Y - \hat{Y}(X)]^2 = \Sigma[Y - a - bX]^2$$

The resulting regression line is fit to the data so that the sum of the *squares* of the *vertical deviations* separating the points from the line will be a minimum. Figure 7-23 shows how vertical deviations relate to their regression line in the scatter diagram for the parts supplier's data in Table 7-7. The deviations are the lengths of the vertical lines that connect each point to the regression line.

To explain how this procedure may be interpreted, we investigate the shipment to Jones & Sons at a distance of $X = 490$ miles from the supplier's plant. Our data show that $Y = 8$ days were required for the shipment to arrive. This transportation time is represented on the graph by the vertical distance to the corresponding data point along the dashed line from the X axis at $X = 490$. The predicted or estimated transportation time for the *next* shipment to Jones & Sons equals the vertical distance all the

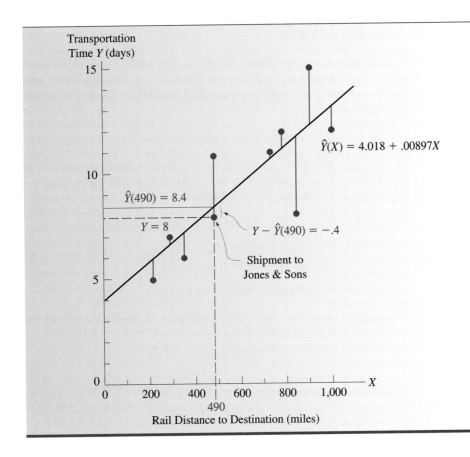

FIGURE 7-23
Fitting the regression line
to the parts supplier's data

way up to the regression line, a total of $\hat{Y}(X) = \hat{Y}(490) = 8.4$ days. The difference between the observed transportation time, $Y = 8$ days, and the predicted value for Y is the deviation $Y - \hat{Y}(X) = Y - \hat{Y}(490) = 8 - 8.4 = -.4$ days. This is represented by the vertical line segment connecting the point to the regression line. The vertical deviation represents the amount of *error associated with using the regression line to predict* a future shipment's transportation time. We want to find the values of a and b that will minimize the sum of the squares of these vertical deviations (or prediction errors).

One reason for minimizing the sum of the *squared* vertical deviations is that some of the deviations are negative and others are positive. For any set of data, a great many lines can be drawn for which the sum of the unsquared deviations is zero, but most of these lines would fit the data poorly.

Regression analysis employs inferential statistics in reaching conclusions from the observed values, which are themselves ordinarily sample data. Thus, a and b are only *estimates* of the true regression parameters, and the computed values may deviate from the true levels. In order to use statistical methodology in qualifying these estimates, certain assumptions must be made regarding the nature of the X-Y relationship. Among these is the assumption that the variability in Y's is constant, unaffected by the level for X. Another assumption is that the levels for X are nonrandom. Further assumptions of statistical regression analysis—and the associated pitfalls—will be discussed shortly.

Regression Variation and Residuals

Figure 7-24 shows the regression line found earlier for the parts supplier's original transportation times. Suppose the parts supplier predicts how long the next order will take to ship without using that line. That sample mean (derived from Table 7-7) would then give a suitable estimate.

$$\bar{Y} = 9.5 \text{ days} \qquad \text{(prediction without regression)}$$

But, this estimate ignores how far the shipment will go. Suppose that this shipment goes to Smith Dodge, for which the distance is known to be $X = 920$ miles. This information allows the supplier to make a better forecast.

$$\hat{Y}(920) = 12.3 \text{ days} \qquad \text{(prediction using regression line)}$$

Although the actual time of the next shipment to Smith Dodge is uncertain, it can be represented by the time originally observed in the sample,

$$Y = 15.0 \text{ days} \qquad \text{(observed time)}$$

The first prediction falls wide of the mark, providing a **total deviation** of $Y - \bar{Y} = 15.0 - 9.5 = 5.5$ days, none of which can be explained. The second prediction is better because it yields a smaller prediction error of $Y - \hat{Y}(X) = 15.0 - 12.3 = 2.7$

FIGURE 7-24
Illustration of total, explained, and unexplained variation in Y

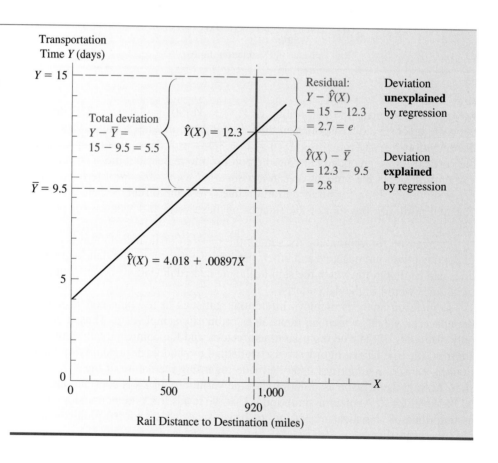

days. By using the regression line, the total error is reduced by the amount $\hat{Y}(X) - \bar{Y} =$ 12.3 − 9.5 = 2.8 days. Thus, part of the total error may be attributed to using the regression line, so that $\hat{Y}(X) - \bar{Y} = 2.8$ days is the **explained deviation.** The remaining portion of the error is due to unidentifiable causes, so that $Y - \hat{Y}(X) = 2.7$ days is an **unexplained deviation.** The total deviation of the observed Y may then be expressed as

$$[Y - \bar{Y}] = [\hat{Y}(X) - \bar{Y}] + [Y - \hat{Y}(X)]$$

Stated in words, we have

Total deviation = Explained deviation + Unexplained deviation

The unexplained deviations are often referred to as the **residuals** and are defined by the differences

$$e_i = Y_i - \hat{Y}(X_i)$$

By squaring both deviations and then summing, we extend the relationship to the entire collection of observations.

Total variation		Explained variation		Unexplained variation
$\sum[Y - \bar{Y}]^2$	=	$\sum[\hat{Y}(X) - \bar{Y}]^2$	+	$\sum[Y - \hat{Y}(X)]^2$
SSTO	=	*SSR*	+	*SSE*

The total variation expresses the amount that the individual Y's deviate from their mean $\bar{Y}$ without regard to the regression relationship. The result is referred to as the **total sum of squares** (*SSTO*).

$$SSTO = \sum[Y - \bar{Y}]^2$$

As shown in Figure 7-24, the distance between Y and the regression line at X explains a portion of the deviation in the observed Y from its mean $\bar{Y}$. The explained variation summarizes the collective squared distances between the regression line $\hat{Y}(X)$ and the sample mean $\bar{Y}$. This is expressed by the **regression sum of squares** (*SSR*).

$$SSR = \sum[\hat{Y}(X) - \bar{Y}]^2$$

The final component of total variation involves the residuals and measures the overall observed error in the sample. This is the **error sum of squares** (*SSE*).

$$SSE = \sum[Y - \hat{Y}(X)]^2$$

The method of least squares selects the regression coefficients a and b, so that the above quantity is minimized. The above term expresses the collective dispersion in Y about the regression line. The regression line leaves those deviations *unexplained.*

The Coefficient of Determination and Correlation Coefficient

Rearranging the terms, the identity

Explained variation	=	Total variation	−	Unexplained variation
SSR	=	*SSTO*	−	*SSE*

is used to construct a useful index. Dividing the unexplained variation by the total variation provides the **sample coefficient of determination.**

$$r^2 = \frac{\text{Explained variation}}{\text{Total variation}} = \frac{SSTO - SSE}{SSTO} = \frac{\Sigma[Y - \bar{Y}]^2 - \Sigma[Y - \hat{Y}(X)]^2}{\Sigma[Y - \bar{Y}]^2}$$

An equivalent expression is

$$r^2 = \frac{\text{Explained variation}}{\text{Total variation}} = 1 - \frac{\Sigma[Y - \hat{Y}(X)]^2}{\Sigma[Y - \bar{Y}]^2}$$

The sample coefficient of determination expresses the proportion of the total variation in Y explained by the regression line.

The coefficient of determination for the parts supplier's data is $r^2 = .64$, indicating that the regression line explains 64% of the variation in transportation time.

A related index is the **sample correlation coefficient r.**

$$\text{Coefficient of determination} = (\text{Correlation coefficient})^2$$

The sign for r may be positive (when the slope of the regression line is positive, and $b > 0$) or negative (when $b < 0$). For the parts supplier illustration, the sample correlation coefficient is

$$r = \sqrt{.64} = +.80$$

This relationship provides another perspective on how the coefficient of determination measures the strength of association between X and Y. In the special case when all the data points fall directly on the regression line, so that there is a perfect correlation and $r = +1$ or $r = -1$, all of the variation in Y is explained and r must then be equal to one. At the other extreme, a horizontal regression line is obtained when X and Y exhibit zero correlation, so that all of the variation in Y is unexplained and r^2 must then be equal to zero.

Forecasting Accuracy in Regression Analysis

We have seen that the mean squared error *MSE* may be used to compare two sets of forecasts in terms of how well they fit the actual data. In regression evaluations the *MSE* is computed from

$$MSE = \frac{\Sigma[Y - \hat{Y}]^2}{n - m} = \frac{\Sigma e^2}{n - m}$$

where n denotes the number of observations (data points) and m represents the number of variables used.

Table 7-16 shows the *MSE* calculations for the parts supplier's illustration. There, a value of $MSE = 4.084$ applies to the data. Because the quantity is in units of squared days, it is common to take the square root, giving the same information in original units.

$$\sqrt{MSE} = \sqrt{4.084} = 2.02 \text{ days}$$

TABLE 7-16   MSE Calculations for the Parts Supplier's Data

CUSTOMER	RAIL DISTANCE TO DESTINATION X	TRANS-PORTATION TIME (DAYS) Y	PREDICTED TIME FROM REGRESSION LINE $\hat{Y}(X)=4.018+.00897X$	ERROR OR RESIDUAL $e=Y-\hat{Y}(X)$	SQUARED ERROR $e^2=[Y-\hat{Y}(X)]^2$
1	210	5	5.9027	−.9027	.8149
2	290	7	6.6203	.3797	.1442
3	350	6	7.1585	−1.1585	1.3421
4	480	11	8.3246	2.6754	7.1578
5	490	8	8.4143	−.4143	.1716
6	730	11	10.5671	.4329	.1874
7	780	12	11.0156	.9844	.9690
8	850	8	11.6435	−3.6435	13.2751
9	920	15	12.2714	2.7286	7.4453
10	1,010	12	13.0787	−1.0787	1.1636
					32.6710

$$MSE = \frac{32.6710}{10-2} = 4.084$$

This calculation gives easier-to-use values that are smaller in size. This quantity is often referred to as the **standard error of the estimate.**

Under the theoretical assumptions of the regression model, *MSE* is a statistical estimator of the variance for the probability distribution in residuals that might be obtained when they are computed using the true regression line.

A second mean square is employed in regression analysis. The **regression mean square** is found from

$$MSR = \frac{SSR}{m-1}$$

This quantity can be used in conjunction with *MSE* to perform a key statistical test. That test is based on the statistic

$$F = \frac{MSR}{MSE}$$

which allows analysts to find the probability that the observed regression line could have been obtained when the true regression coefficient for the independent variable(s) is (are) in fact zero.

Analyzing Regression Results

To assess the quality of a regression equation, four numbers are useful: the standard error of the estimate (square root of the *MSE*), the coefficient of determination, the *F* statistic, and the *t* statistic. The smaller the standard error of the estimate, the better will be the estimates made from the regression equation. Because the coefficient of determination represents the proportion of the total variation explained by the regression

equation, the forecasts generated from it will be sharper the closer it is to 1. The F statistic tests the null hypothesis that the regression equation explains nothing; a bigger F signifies a better overall regression analysis. Likewise, the t statistic tests the null hypothesis that the slope coefficient in the regression equation is 0.

The parts supplier's data in Figure 7-19 yields a standard error of the estimate of 2.02, which is about 20% of the average transportation time. The coefficient of determination is .64, so that the regression equation explains about 64% of the variation in the data. These results indicate a possible relationship exists and are confirmed by the other two measures. $F = 14.16$ confirms a statistically significant relationship. (A value of 5.32 would give 95% confidence.) Likewise, $t = 3.76$ is large enough for us to conclude that the true slope coefficient in the regression equation differs from zero. (A value of 2.31 yields 95% confidence.)

PROBLEMS

7-1 Managers of the Variety Galore Store want to forecast its sales for the next calendar year. These components have been determined by the store accountant.

Quarter t	Trend T_t	Cyclical Component C_t	Seasonal Index S_t
Winter	$100,000	90	80
Spring	110,000	110	70
Summer	121,000	100	100
Fall	133,100	90	150

Use the multiplicative time-series model to determine the forecasts of sales Y_t for each quarter.

7-2 The sales data for Humpty Dumpty Toys have been analyzed, and the trend, cyclical, seasonal, and irregular components have been determined for operations during the preceding four quarters. Supply the missing values in the following table, assuming that the time-series components are multiplicative.

Quarter t	Trend T_t	Cyclical Component (%) C_t	Seasonal Index (%) S_t	Irregular Component (%) I_t	Sales Y_t
Winter	$1,000,000	107	50	101	—
Spring	1,100,000	105	70	—	$820,000
Summer	1,200,000	105	—	98	987,840
Fall	1,300,000	—	200	97	2,622,880

7-3 Tuti-Fruti Yogurt's seasonally adjusted quarterly sales data (thousands of gallons) are given below.

Period	Sales	Period	Sales
1	2	9	12
2	3	10	14
3	5	11	15
4	7	12	17
5	6	13	18
6	8	14	22
7	9	15	24
8	10	16	27

(a) Use single-parameter exponential smoothing with $\alpha = .20$ to forecast sales levels.

(b) Compute the mean squared error.

7-4 Repeat Problem 7-3. Use $\alpha = .50$.

7-5 Refer to the Tuti-Fruti data in Problem 7-3.

(a) Use two-parameter exponential smoothing with $\alpha = .40$ and $\gamma = .10$ to forecast sales levels.

(b) Compute the mean squared error.

7-6 Big Mountain Power serves a region in which the following amounts of annual electricity usage (millions of kilowatt-hours) have been recorded:

Year	Consumption	Year	Consumption
1990	205	1995	241
1991	206	1996	267
1992	223	1997	268
1993	231	1998	277
1994	234	1999	290

(a) Plot the time-series data on graph paper.

(b) Use single-parameter exponential smoothing with $\alpha = .20$ to forecast values for each past

year. Then, compute the *MSE* and find the forecast usage for 2000.

(c) Repeat (b), using two-parameter exponential smoothing with $\alpha = .30$ and $\gamma = .20$.

(d) Which forecast appears better? Explain.

7-7 Garment Suspenders recorded the following quarterly sales data (millions of dollars):

	1995	1996	1997	1998	1999
Winter	3.9	7.8	12.9	13.9	13.5
Spring	6.1	10.6	15.2	14.4	18.2
Summer	4.3	6.9	10.3	10.2	14.2
Fall	10.8	13.5	18.7	17.3	20.7

(a) Plot the time-series data on graph paper.

(b) Use three-parameter seasonal exponential smoothing with $\alpha = .3$, $\gamma = .2$, and $\beta = .4$ to forecast sales levels for the past quarters.

(c) Determine quarterly sales forecasts for 2000.

7-8 In arranging for short-term credit with its bank, the Make-Wave Corporation must project its cash needs on a monthly basis. Management wants to use the following historical data (in hundred thousand dollars) to project monthly cash requirements:

	1995	1996	1997	1998	1999
January	2.7	2.9	3.5	2.5	4.2
February	5.4	6.4	7.3	8.1	9.6
March	9.3	10.1	11.3	7.9	12.4
April	2.4	4.1	3.8	5.2	6.2
May	6.1	7.8	8.1	9.2	8.7
June	7.3	7.4	6.9	8.1	8.3
July	6.5	5.5	6.5	7.6	6.6
August	9.7	9.6	8.9	9.3	9.8
September	13.4	13.5	14.3	15.8	16.3
October	10.6	10.7	11.5	12.6	13.4
November	5.1	4.8	6.5	7.2	6.9
December	3.4	2.8	3.9	4.1	6.1

(a) Plot the time-series data on graph paper.

(b) Use three-parameter seasonal exponential smoothing with $\alpha = .2$, $\gamma = .1$, and $\beta = .3$ to forecast cash requirements for past months.

(c) Determine forecast monthly requirements for 2000.

7-9 Refer to the data provided in Problem 7-6.

(a) Using the method of least squares, determine the equation for the estimated regression line

$\hat{Y}(X) = a + bX$, with X in years and X = 0 in 1990. Plot this line on your graph.

(b) What is the forecast consumption for 2000?

7-10 McFadden's has experienced the following annual sales:

Year	Sales	Year	Sales
1989	$18 million	1995	$ 82 million
1990	28	1996	89
1991	26	1997	108
1992	43	1998	121
1993	55	1999	155
1994	54		

(a) Plot the time-series data on graph paper.

(b) Would a straight line provide a suitable summary of the trend in sales? Explain.

7-11 A statistician wants to determine the equation relating destination distance to freight charge for a standard-sized crate. The following data were obtained for a random sample of 10 freight invoices:

Distance (Hundreds of Miles) X	Charge (to Nearest Dollar) Y
14	68
23	105
9	40
17	79
10	81
22	95
5	31
12	72
6	45
16	93

(a) Plot the scatter diagram for the data.

(b) Using the method of least squares, determine the equation for the estimated regression line. Then, plot the regression line on your scatter diagram.

7-12 The manufacturer of Spinex floppy discs wants to conduct a regression analysis to estimate the average lifetime (hours) at various drive-unit tracking forces X (grams). The regression equation $\hat{Y}(X) = 1{,}300 - 200X$ has been obtained for a sample of $n = 100$ discs that were run at various tracking forces until they were worn out. Find the forecast lifetimes when (a) $X = 1$ gram, (b) $X = 2$ grams, and (c) $X = 3$ grams.

7-13 The Old Ivy College admissions director relies on high school GPA X_1 and IQ scores X_2 to predict college GPA Y. The following regression equation applies:

$$\hat{Y} = .5 + .8X_1 + .003X_2$$

Forecast the college GPA for each of the following students:

Student	High School GPA X_1	IQ Score X_2
(a)	2.9	123
(b)	3.0	118
(c)	2.7	105
(d)	3.5	136

7-14 Megaphonetrics uses special machines to press recording grooves onto blank discs from a die. Each die lasts for about 1,000 pressings. Due to the time constraints inherent in the record business, it is sometimes necessary to use several pressing machines simultaneously. Because each machine requires an expensive die disc and many production runs are completed before the useful lifetime of each die disc is exhausted, this increases production costs. For $n = 100$ production runs, the total manufacturing cost Y (thousands of dollars) has been determined for the number of pressings made X_1 (thousands) and the number of die discs required X_2. The following regression equation applies:

$$\hat{Y} = 1.082 + 1.2X_1 + .553X_2$$

Forecast the cost $\hat{Y}$ of each of the following production runs:

Run	Number of Pressings (Thousands)	Number of Die Discs
(a)	15	5
(b)	20	3
(c)	15	4
(d)	100	10

7-15 The following percentages of moving average values have been obtained for the sales of High Tower Publications:

Year	Winter	Spring	Summer	Fall
1993	—	—	156	111
1994	49	92	137	109
1995	53	93	148	108
1996	52	91	162	104
1997	51	89	153	110
1998	51	90	151	112
1999	48	88		

Determine the seasonal index for each quarter.

7-16 Refer to the data provided in Problem 7-7.
   (a) Determine the four-quarter moving averages.
   (b) Calculate the percentages of moving average values and determine the seasonal indexes.

7-17 Refer to the data provided in Problem 7-8.
   (a) Using 12-month moving averages, determine the seasonal index for each month by means of the ratio-to-moving-average method.
   (b) Make-Wave's cash needs for the coming year are forecast to be $1 million per month on the average. Using the seasonal indexes you calculated in (a), estimate the cash requirements for each month.

Spreadsheet Problems

7-18 Telesat Corporation obtained message volumes (thousands) relayed on successive days by a new communications satellite. (File: Problem07-18.xls)

   Using two-parameter exponential smoothing to forecast message volumes, compute the mean squared error for each of the following cases:
   (a) $\alpha = .10$; $\gamma = .10$
   (b) $\alpha = .10$; $\gamma = .20$
   (c) $\alpha = .10$; $\gamma = .30$
   (d) $\alpha = .20$; $\gamma = .10$
   (e) Which of these parameter levels provides the best fit to the actual data? Find, to the nearest .01, the best-fitting levels for α and γ.

7-19 Refer to the data provided in Problem 7-8. Use three-parameter seasonal exponential smoothing to determine the optimal levels for α and γ (to the nearest .01) and associated *MSE* when (a) $\beta = .2$, (b) $\beta = .5$, (c) $\beta = .7$, and (d) $\beta = .9$.

7-20 Restaurant sales predictions are to be made from a regression equation based on total floorspace and number of employees. The following data have been obtained for a sample of $n = 5$ restaurants:

Sales (Thousands of Dollars) Y	Floorspace (Thousands of Square Feet) X_1	Number of Employees X_2
20	10	15
15	5	8
10	10	12
5	3	7
10	2	10

Construct and calculate the multiple regression equation for those data.

7-21 A systems programmer for Infosoft wants to predict run times Y (minutes) of payroll programs on a particular software-hardware configuration. Data have been obtained for 20 runs. (File: Problem07-21.xls)

(a) Using required memory X_1 (thousands of bytes) and amount of output X_2 (thousands of lines) as the independent variables and run time as the dependent variable, determine the estimated multiple regression equation.

(b) Forecast the run times for the following jobs:

	Memory	Output	Input
(1)	100	10	5
(2)	50	5	5
(3)	20	8	2
(4)	30	5	10

7-22 Refer to the data provided in Problem 7-21. Determine the estimated multiple regression equation. Include the amount of input X_3 (thousands of lines) as a third predictor.

7-23 The Druid's Drayage truck dispatcher wants to predict how many driver hours Y it will take to deliver less-than-truckload shipments over any one of a number of routes. Using four independent variables, he has collected 20 sample observations. (File: Problem07-23.xls)

(a) Determine the estimated multiple regression equation using distance X_1 (miles), load X_2 (tons), deliveries X_3, and speed X_4 (mph) as independent variables.

(b) Forecast driver time for the following trips:

	Distance	Load	Deliveries	Speed
(1)	100	2	5	40
(2)	50	3	8	50
(3)	60	2	2	45
(4)	70	3	5	45

7-24 Redo Problem 7-16 (using the suspender data in Problem 7-7) and then forecast quarterly suspender sales for the year 2000.

7-25 Refer to the data in Problem 7-7. Use a spreadsheet to determine the quarterly forecasts for 2000.

7-26 Refer to the McFadden sales data in Problem 7-10.

(a) Use Excel to find the exponential trend curve $y = ab^x$. The equation may be found using the LOGEST function. That function has four arguments: (1) range of dependent variable, (2) range of independent variable, (3) coefficient setting—use TRUE, and (4) coefficient setting—use FALSE. LOGEST is an array formula, so it must be array-entered (depress the control, shift, and enter keys simultaneously). To obtain the coefficients a and b, highlight two adjacent cells such as E4:F4, type in the LOGEST formula, and then array enter the formula. See the *Guide to Excel* on the CD-ROM for more details about array entering formulas.

(b) Use the Excel GROWTH function to make a forecast for 2004. That function has three arguments: (1) range of dependent variable, (2) range of independent variable, and (3) the independent variable for which the forecast is being made.

7-27 A chemical engineer for GetGo provided the following fuel consumption data for sample test car runs:

Fuel Consumption (mpg) Y	Speed (mph) X	Fuel Consumption (mpg) Y	Speed (mph) X
28.9	56	27.3	22
30.2	34	29.8	47
29.3	32	26.3	57
23.8	59	28.6	21
29.5	25	29.9	28
29.5	40	28.8	52

Use Excel to find an order-2 degree polynomial to fit the above data. The initial step employs the Chart Wizard to graph the data. In the

first Chart Wizard box (Step 1 of 4—*Chart Type*) select *XY Scatter* and pick the first chart sub-type: *Scatter, Compare pairs of values.* When the chart is complete, click on the data series in the chart, depress the right mouse button, and select *Add Trendline* from the drop-down menu. Under *Type,* there are six choices: linear, logarithmic, polynomial, power, exponential, and moving average. Choose polynomial of order 2. Next, select the *Options* tab, click the *Display Equation on Chart* button, and then click OK. The equation will appear on the chart.

CASE 7-1   *Well-Bread Bakeries*

Gerald J. Maxwell
San Jose State University

Bread is the most widely eaten food in the world. In the United States, most bread is made by commercial bakeries and then sold by the approximately 20,000 independent retail bakeries (providing annual gross sales of about $5.9 billion) or by the approximately 24,000 retail bakery departments within supermarkets (doing an annual volume of about $8.6 billion). Sweet products such as cakes, cookies, pies, and brownies are included in these gross sales figures.

Ed and Mildred Ferguson had worked for several years in retail bakeries when in 1986 they acquired sufficient capital to start their own shop, Well-Bread Bakery. Ed and Mildred seemed to have the magic touch for success. In 1987 they bought a second store, commencing operations in the spring. They started a third bakery during the summer of 1989, a fourth in the spring of 1991, and a fifth during the spring of 1993.

Over the years, the total sales increases met the Fergusons' objectives, despite two major setbacks. The first occurred in the spring of 1991, when their original store was heavily damaged by a fire. The second misfortune came in the fall of 1993, when their fourth bakery had to be closed because of fierce competition in the neighborhood.

Baked goods are a highly seasonal business. The greatest activity takes place near major holidays. When annual sales are broken down by quarters, from highest to lowest volume, the following ranking applies:

Fall (Q4)—includes both Thanksgiving and Christmas
Winter (Q1)—Valentine's Day is the key holiday
Summer(Q3)—no holidays, but lots of hot dog buns are sold
Spring (Q2)

File WellBread1.xls contains the quarterly sales data (thousands of dollars) for Well-Bread Bakeries.

The Fergusons' experience from working and managing retail bakeries has shown that bread sales produce low margins, only 2% to 3% of sales volume. They have also experienced a somewhat flat trend in sales of bread. Also, in the years since they opened their first bakery in 1987, sales have declined somewhat for the higher-margin items: cakes, cookies, and other sweet bakery products.

Industry research revealed that similar declines in sales of sweet bakery goods were being experienced by bakeries throughout the nation. Bakery authorities attribute the decline to increasing weight-consciousness among the general population. An objective measurement of this trend was found in sales of diet and fitness books, which, according to booksellers' estimates, were increasing in proportion to total bookstore sales over the past several years. File WellBread2.xls provides sales figures for diet and fitness books for 1986 through 1994.

The Fergusons believe that an additional factor affecting Well-Bread's sales is national personal income. Bread is a daily staple for many families, but demand for sweet bakery products tends to fluctuate as personal income rises and falls. Personal income data are given in file WellBread3.xls.

In spite of the national trend toward weight-consciousness, the Fergusons have been using a three-tiered strategy, beginning in the first quarter of 1995, to increase their bakery sales:

1. Emphasize the staples and continue to sell a variety of breads, recognizing that sales will remain flat for the foreseeable future and that gross margins will be low.

2. Because their discontinuance would adversely affect business and encourage customers to try other stores, continue to sell higher-margin sweet bakery goods, even though sales are declining.

3. Add a line of gourmet coffees. This supplementary line is designed to more than offset declining sales of sweet bakery products and to increase total sales volumes.

QUESTIONS

1. To aid them in forecasting future quarterly sales, the Fergusons have asked you to develop seasonal indexes.
   a. Using the data from Store A, determine the seasonal indexes.
   b. Using the total sales for all bakeries, determine the seasonal indexes.
   c. Do you notice major differences between the two sets of indexes? For planning purposes, which set of indexes would be more suitable? Discuss.

2. The Fergusons are thinking about opening another bakery. They need help in forecasting sales for each of their stores and for their total operation.
   a. Using the chain's total sales, apply two-parameter exponential smoothing—incorporating both trend and slope of trend—to make a chainwide forecast of sales for the first quarter of 1995. In doing this, find levels for the two smoothing constants (α and γ) that minimize *MSE*.
   b. Apply exponential smoothing separately to each store's sales to forecast the sales level for Q1 1995. In each case, use the α and γ values found in part (a).
   c. Would forecasting the sales in one store be helpful to forecasting the sales in a brand new store? Comment.

3. The forecasts in Question 2 ignore the underlying seasonality.
   a. Using the chain's total sales, apply three-parameter exponential smoothing—incorporating seasonal smoothing—to make a chainwide forecast of sales in the *four* quarters of 1995. In doing this, find levels for the two smoothing constants (α and γ) that minimize *MSE*. In all cases, use $\beta = .50$ for the seasonal smoothing constant.
   b. Apply exponential smoothing separately to each store's sales to forecast the sales levels for each quarter of 1995. In each case, use the α and γ values found in part (a), with $\beta = .50$.

4. An alternative procedure for forecasting future sales is to employ regression analysis to find the trend line. This must be done using deseasonalized data and letting time period serve as the independent variable. Once a trend value is known, the forecast value can be obtained by multiplying it by the applicable seasonal index.
   a. Deseasonalize the historical sales for the bakery chain as a whole, using the indexes found in Question 1(b).
   b. Determine an equation for the least squares trend line, using $X = 1$ for Q1 of 1986.
   c. Ignoring the impact of the new store, forecast the chainwide sales trend for each quarter of 1995 by multiplying each trend value by the respective seasonal index found in Question 1(b) to get the forecast sales values.
   d. Compare your solution in part (d) and to your solution for Question 3(a). Which set of values do you prefer? Why?

5. As an alternative to using past values as the basis for forecasting future levels, it is sometimes advantageous to use another independent variable for this purpose. Two possible independent variables are given in files WellBread2.xls and WellBread3.xls.
   a. Determine an estimated regression equation to forecast the quarterly sales of Well-Bread's Store A, using diet book sales as the independent variable. If diet book sales in a future quarter were $70 million, what would be the chainwide total sales forecast?
   b. One measure of how good such forecasts might be is the coefficient of determination. The closer that value is to 1, the greater is the proportion of variation in Y (sales) that can be explained by the regression relationship. But if the coefficient of determination is close to zero, then poor predictions should be expected. Does the regression equation found in part (a) appear to be promising on this basis alone?
   c. One way to improve a regression-based forecast is to use several independent variables in a multiple-regression analysis. Suppose that personal income is also used as an independent variable. Determine the estimated multiple-regression equation, and compute the coefficient of determination. Then forecast sales when the values identified in Table 7-17 apply.

TABLE 7-17	1995 Quarterly Sales of Diet Books and Personal Income Figures

	Diet Literature	
Quarter	Sales (Millions)	Personal Income (Billions)
Q1	$70	$1,400
Q2	75	1,410
Q3	80	1,420
Q4	85	1,430

d. Does it appear that better forecasts may be achieved from the equation used in part (c) than from the equation used in part (a)? Explain.

6. Discuss some of the practical difficulties of using independent variables to predict the level of a dependent variable such as bakery sales.

7. Besides sales forecasts for existing stores, what types of information might Well-Bread consider in making a decision about whether to open a new store?

CASE 7-2 Morgan Stanley Emerging Markets Fund

Surendra K. Mansinghka
San Francisco State University

Sam N. Basu
California State University, Hayward

Morgan Stanley Emerging Markets Fund (MSF) is a closed-end mutual fund designed for investors who wish to allocate part of their investment portfolio to emerging markets' equity securities. An emerging country is any country that the World Bank has classified as having a low- or middle-income economy; thus, countries with high per capita income are excluded. Mutual funds such as MSF provide foreign investment to promote growth and development of emerging countries' capital markets.

The fund commenced operations on November 1, 1991, with an initial public offering of approximately $150 million and slightly more than 10.5 million shares. It is a closed-end fund, meaning that new shares are issued only at the discretion of the fund managers. Like stocks, it trades on the New York Stock Exchange; the ticker symbol is MSF. Since the fund's inception, it has issued 6 million new shares, and on March 31, 1995, the net assets and number of shares of the fund were $270.6 million and 16.63 million, respectively. The shares of the fund have traded both at a premium and at a discount in relation to net asset value. Table 7-18 provides historical information on the market price (high and low), trading volume, net asset value (high and low), and premium (or discount) to net asset value on a quarterly basis from 1991 through May 30, 1995. File Morgan1.xls contains the daily prices of the shares of MSF from March 1, 1995, through June 20, 1995.

On May 30, 1995, the fund announced that current shareholders would be given one *right* for each share they owned. The rights could either be used to purchase additional shares or they could be sold. To purchase additional shares, called *exercising* the right, shareholders would need three rights plus $14 (called the *exercise price*) to buy one additional share. If they did not want to buy the shares by exercising the rights, they could sell them in the market at any time prior to the rights' expiration date, June 20, 1995. The rights began to trade on the New York Stock Exchange under the ticker symbol MSF.RT on May 30, 1995. File Morgan2.xls contains daily prices of the rights from May 30, 1995, through June 20, 1995.

Prior to the announcement of the rights, the shares of MSF closed at $18.50 on May 30, 1995. On May 31, 1995, the rights began trading on the New York Stock Exchange, and the price of MSF declined because of the rights to $17.25.[1]

In a famous paper, Black and Scholes[2] presented a formula that can be used for estimating the value of a right:

$$R = pN(d_1) - Ee^{-it}N(d_2)$$

where R stands for the estimated value of the right, p represents the stock price, E is exercise price of the right, i is the interest rate, t is the length of time until the expiration date of the right, and $N(z)$ represents the value of the normal distribution for a standard normal variable z and gives the probability that a

---

[1]Assume that a shareholder owns three shares on May 30, 1995. His portfolio is worth $55.50 (3 × $18.50). He receives three rights entitling him to buy one additional share by paying $14.00. In other words, he now owns four shares worth $69.50 (3 × 18.50 + 1 × 14.00). The price per share, therefore, should go down to $17.375. This is an example of what is called the *dilution effect* in finance and accounting.

[2]Fischer Black and Myron Scholes, "The Pricing of Options and Corporate Liabilities," *Journal of Political Economy* (May–June 1973) p. 1981. This paper gives a formula for estimating the value of a call option. Rights are similar to call options.

TABLE 7-18 Morgan Stanley Emerging Markets Fund Stock Data*

CALENDAR QUARTERS	MARKET PRICE		QUARTERLY TRADING VOLUME (1,000s)	NET ASSET VALUE		PREMIUM (DISCOUNT)/ TO NET ASSET VALUE
	High	Low		High	Low	
Year ended December 31, 1991						
Fourth quarter†	$16.25	$13.375	2,434.4	$14.67	$13.98	−3.13%
Year ended December 31, 1992						
First quarter	18.125	14.5	2,301.8	16.97	14.80	5.33%
Second quarter	19.0	16.25	1,898.8	18.11	16.69	−2.63%
Third quarter	17.5	16.125	1,158.6	17.74	16.17	−1.73%
Fourth quarter	18.25	15.75	1,277.8	17.07	15.95	8.27%
Year ended December 31, 1993						
First quarter	19.5	16.5	1,067.0	16.79	15.37	11.67%
Second quarter	21.5	18.0	2,943.0	18.98	16.72	9.66%
Third quarter	23.875	19.125	2,942.0	20.77	17.73	14.85%
Fourth quarter	31.625	23.25	3,316.0	28.20	20.72	12.15%
Year ended December 31, 1994						
First quarter	32.5	22.25	5,028.0	29.24	24.73	−5.98%
Second quarter	27.75	22.5	2,607.0	24.63	22.06	9.28%
Third quarter	30.25	25.5	1,789.0	28.78	23.37	3.73%
Fourth quarter	30.375	21.5	2,084.0	28.44	19.86	7.34%
Year ended December 31, 1995						
First quarter	21.5	14.75	3,037.0	19.62	15.05	9.10%
Second quarter (through May 30, 1995)‡	19.875	17.75	1,813.6	18.12	16.59	3.41%

*"Morgan Stanley Emerging Markets Fund Prospectus" (May 30, 1995), p. 11.

†From October 25, 1991, the commencement of trading, through December 31, 1991.

‡The last reported sale price, net asset value per share, and percentage premium to net asset value of the common stock on May 30, 1995, were $18.50, $17.89, and 3.41%, respectively.

value of z or less occurs. The values of d_1 and d_2 are given by

$$d_1 = \frac{\left[ln\left(\frac{p}{E}\right) = \left(i + \frac{\sigma^2}{2}\right)t \right]}{\sqrt{\sigma^2 t}}$$

$$d_2 = d_1 - \sqrt{\sigma^2 t}$$

The Black-Scholes formula implies that the higher the stock price, the higher the value of the right. Higher exercise prices mean lower value of the right. The higher the volatility, as measured by the variance of the stock prices' daily relative returns[3] σ^2, the higher the value of the right because there is a greater

chance that the market price will exceed the exercise price. The longer the length of time until the right expires (i.e., the maturity), the higher the value of the right, because there is more time for the market price to exceed the exercise price. The interest rate usually is measured by the treasury bill rate. The higher the interest rate, the higher the price of the right, because the exercise price need not be paid until the right is exercised. This delayed payment is more valuable when the interest rate is high.

QUESTIONS

The following questions involve substantial computations, so be sure to use a spreadsheet.

1. The Black-Scholes formula indicates that the higher MSF's stock price, the higher the value of the right. Analyze whether this is true by plotting a

---

[3]If p_j represents the price of MSF on day j, then the daily relative return is $\frac{p_j}{p_{j-1}}$.

scatter diagram for these two variables for the time period May 31 through June 16. Calculate the correlation coefficient. Develop a regression model relating the value of rights (as the dependent variable) to MSF's stock price. What are your conclusions?

2. Repeat Question 1, this time examining the relationship between the value of the right and interest rates. Are the results consistent with the implications of the Black-Scholes formula?

3. Develop a regression model relating the value of the rights (as the dependent variable) to MSF's stock price and treasury bill rates (as the independent variables). Use the model, together with the June 19 data for MSF's stock price and the treasury bill rate, to forecast the value of the right on that day. Is the regression model any good?

4. Repeat Question 3, this time using MSF's prices and treasury rates lagged one day as the independent variables.

5. Use the price p_j of MSF on day j from March 1, 1995, through May 30, 1995 (the day the rights were an-

nounced) to calculate the natural logarithm of the daily relative returns, $\ln(p_j/p_{j-1})$.

6. Calculate the mean and the variance of the natural logarithm of the relative returns determined in Question 1. Find the annual variance by multiplying the variance just determined by 365.

7. Determine $N(d_1)$ and $N(d_2)$, using a normal table.

8. Using the Black-Scholes formula, estimate for the price of one right. Make sure that all time units are consistent and are expressed in years. Compare the estimate with the actual price. How well does the Black-Scholes formula estimate? Discuss.

9. The answer to Question 8 depends on the time period selected—March 1 through June 20, in this case. How would the answers to Questions 5, 6, 7, and 8 change if other time periods, such as April 1 through May 30, were used? Compare the new results with those obtained in the prior questions, and focus on how one might select an appropriate time period.

PART III

RESOURCE ALLOCATION

Linear programming is used to allocate resources, plan production, schedule workers, plan investment portfolios, and formulate marketing (and military) strategies. The versatility and economic impact of linear programming in today's industrial world is truly awesome.

Eugene Lawler

W e live in a world of scarce resources in which individuals and groups must make good allocations of limited goods and services. From the beginning of time, people have had to make the best of these limitations. Today, we have new procedures to improve our decision making in these matters. One of those is linear programming. This topic and some of its extensions are covered in Chapters 8–10, followed in Chapter 11 by the advanced concepts of integer and goal programming.

The momentousness of linear programming surprises people. A *Wall Street Journal* article lists the use of linear programming as one of the greatest technological innovations of the past 1,000 years, ranking alongside Gutenberg's Bible, Thomas Edison's electric light bulb, and the creation of the Internet. The 1975 Nobel Prize for economics was shared by T. C. Koopmans and L. V. Kantoprovich for their early contributions to the field. The 1992 prize went to Harry Markowitz for pioneering work involving linear programming extensions.

CHAPTER 8

LINEAR PROGRAMMING

If one would take statistics about which mathematical problem is using most of the computer time in the world (not including data base handling problems like sorting and searching) the answer would probably be linear programming.

Laslo Lavasz

In this chapter, we consider perhaps the most successful quantitative procedure currently used to facilitate the process of making resource allocation decisions. The collection of tools referred to as **linear programming** has a wide variety of applications. It is used by oil companies to determine the best mixture of ingredients for blending gasoline. It has successfully served in the development of optimal schedules for transportation, production, and construction. And, it has been applied in such diverse areas as finance and advertising. Without a doubt, linear programming has had the widest impact of all modern quantitative methods. Billions of dollars in annual cost savings have been attributed to it alone.

What is linear programming? The use of the word *programming* here should not be confused with the written instructions to a computer called "programs." In the present context, we speak of programming as a form of planning that involves the economic allocation of scarce resources to meet all of the basic requirements. Thus, *programming establishes a plan that efficiently allocates limited resources to achievement of a desired objective*. For example, a linear program will tell a refinery manager the precise number of gallons of various petroleum distillates to use in blending a batch of gasoline with a certain octane rating. Moreover, the plan will achieve this in such a way that costs are minimized and the ultimate automobile exhaust meets environmental pollution limits.

By linear programming we mean that the ultimate plan is obtained by employing a mathematical procedure that involves *linear relationships;* that is, the entire problem may be expressed in terms of straight lines, planes, or analogous geometrical figures. There can be no curved surfaces in any graphical representation of the problem. The mathematical model expressing the problem relates all requirements and management's goals by means of algebraic expressions representing straight lines.

MANAGERIAL DECISION

Finding the Best Way to Synthesize Crude Oil

Shale Bituminous Processors (SBP) is a medium-sized oil company. Using its own patented process, it produces low- and high-sulfur crude from coal and shale. These oils are used by refiners who process them into products such as gasoline, jet fuel, industrial lubricating oils, greases, and much more. Marketing director William Stanforth is reviewing an order from a best customer for 10,000 gallons of low-sulfur and

5,000 gallons of high-sulfur crude. Normally such a small order would be sent directly to the Production Department, but something is bothering him. Company president T. J. Bass mentioned recently that this year was going to have record profits, with high product demand and all operations running at nearly full capacity. Checking, Mr. Stanforth learns that only 100 tons of coal and 150 tons of shale remain unallocated. Mr. Stanforth doesn't want to turn down the order, losing its profit and alienating a good customer. But inability to produce the ordered quantities would damage SBP's credibility and reputation.

Mr. Stanforth asks analyst Barry Ginocchio to determine whether or not SBP has sufficient capacity to fulfill the order and, if so, to estimate its corresponding profit. Barry checks with the Purchasing Department and learns that coal costs $20 per ton and shale $25 per ton. The Marketing Department advises him that low-sulfur crude sells for $.50 per gallon and high-sulfur crude for $.30. The Production Department tells him there are two ways to make low-sulfur and high-sulfur crude oil: gasification and pressurization batch processes. A gasification batch requires 1 ton of coal and 2 tons of shale to yield 100 gallons of low-sulfur crude and 200 gallons of high-sulfur crude. Under pressurization, each batch requires 2 tons of coal and 1 ton of shale to yield 150 gallons of low-sulfur crude and 100 gallons of high-sulfur crude.

Barry recently received a bachelor's degree in business from State University. From his quantitative methods course, he knows that his data can be used with linear programming to determine if the customer's order can be fulfilled with the coal and shale available and, if so, to calculate its corresponding profit. This chapter shows how to use linear programming to solve resource allocation problems such as Barry's. His situation will be revisited at the end of the chapter.

8-1   THE REDWOOD FURNITURE PROBLEM

The Redwood Furniture Company manufactures tables and chairs as part of its line of patio furniture. Table 8-1 shows the resources consumed and the unit profits for each product. For simplicity, we will assume that only two resources are consumed in manufacturing the patio furniture: wood (300 board feet in inventory) and labor (110 hours available). The owner wants to determine how many tables and chairs should be made to maximize the total profit for patio furniture.

Linear programming is not essential to establishing such a production plan. After all, it is a recent technique that has been used widely for only the last 40 years, and people have been making furniture for several thousand years. Without any knowledge of linear programming, the owner may decide to make as many chairs as possible,

TABLE 8-1   Data Obtained for the Redwood Furniture Problem

	UNIT REQUIREMENTS		
RESOURCE	Table	Chair	AMOUNT AVAILABLE
Wood (board feet)	30	20	300
Labor (hours)	5	10	110
Unit profit	$6	$8	

because chairs are more profitable than tables. Altogether, there is enough labor to produce exactly 11 chairs, and the owner's profit would be $88. But this plan would leave 80 board feet of wood unused. Would it be more profitable for the owner to make some tables and fewer chairs? If so, how many of each item should be produced? Which brings us back to where we began. Linear programming will tell the owner of Redwood Furniture the exact number of tables and chairs that will *maximize profit*.

8-2   FORMULATING THE LINEAR PROGRAM

Defining the Variables

We begin by treating the number of tables and the number of chairs as unknown quantities, or **variables.** We then express the problem algebraically, using the following symbols:

$$X_T = \text{Number of tables made}$$
$$X_C = \text{Number of chairs made}$$

Our usual convention is to represent a problem's essential variables in terms of X, with subscripts taken directly from the variable's description. Thus, using X_T ("X sub T") to represent the number of tables, where T is the first letter in the word *table*, eases our task of abstracting the problem to a *mathematical model*. Occasionally, letters other than X are employed and numbers are used as subscripts.

Expressing the Constraints

Each resource places limitations on the values of X_T and X_C. In the case of wood, any production plan must meet the following requirement:

Wood for tables + Wood for chairs ≤ Available wood

This **constraint** tells us that the amount of wood used cannot exceed the amount of wood that is available. Note that this constraint does not require that every single foot of wood be used, but only that we do not use more wood than there is. This is why we use the "less than or equal to" symbol, ≤. It would be less flexible, and therefore less desirable, to be unduly restrictive and require the use of all wood, which is what using = in this constraint would indicate.

The wood constraint is referred to as an **inequality.** It is convenient to express this inequality in terms of the quantity variables for tables and chairs.

$$30X_T + 20X_C \le 300 \qquad \text{(wood)}$$

The first term on the left side ($30X_T$) expresses the total amount of wood to be used in the manufacture of tables and is found by multiplying the 30 board feet of wood required for each table by the number of tables X_T. Similarly, because each chair requires 20 board feet, $20X_C$ represents the total amount of wood that will be used in the manufacture of chairs.

An analogous constraint pertains to the labor resource.

$$5X_T + 10X_C \le 110 \qquad \text{(labor)}$$

As before, this simply says that the total quantity of labor expended on either tables or chairs cannot exceed the 110 hours available. Together, these two constraint inequalities establish limits for the values of X_T and X_C.

The Objective Function

The profit objective may also be stated algebraically. Denoting total profit by P, we relate this to the variables by

$$P = 6X_T + 8X_C$$

because total profit consists of the profit derived by selling tables at $6 each plus the profit derived by selling chairs at $8 each. Thus, $6X_T$ is the profit for making and selling tables, and $8X_C$ is the corresponding profit for making chairs. Remember that the owner wants to achieve the greatest possible profit, or to maximize P. We may incorporate this objective directly into the mathematical model by writing the profit equation as

$$\text{Maximize} \quad P = 6X_T + 8X_C \quad \text{(objective)}$$

In this form, the profit expression provides the **objective function.**

Before proceeding, we should note that there are two fundamental types of objective functions, depending on the goal. Instead of maximizing profit, in some problems our goal is to minimize cost. In such situations, the objective function would take the form "minimize C," where C represents the unknown cost variable.

Not all linear programming applications involve cost or profit objectives. A marketing manager may want to maximize *sales*, an advertiser may desire to maximize *exposure* to potential buyers, and an investor may want to maximize *rate of return*. Similarly, a project manager may want to minimize *time* needed to finish, while a freight dispatcher may want to minimize *delays*. For simplicity, we will still use the letter P to express the level of the objective function for all maximization problems and the letter C when minimizing.

The Complete Mathematical Model

We are now ready to incorporate all of these expressions into a single mathematical model, which will prescribe exactly what is to be done within the resource limitations. The model itself, referred to as a **linear program,** is

$$
\begin{aligned}
\text{Letting} \quad & X_T = \text{Number of tables made} \\
& X_C = \text{Number of chairs made} \\
\text{Maximize} \quad & P = 6X_T + 8X_C \quad \text{(objective)} \\
\text{Subject to} \quad & 30X_T + 20X_C \le 300 \quad \text{(wood)} \\
& 5X_T + 10X_C \le 110 \quad \text{(labor)} \\
\text{where} \quad & X_T, X_C \ge 0 \quad \text{(nonnegativity)}
\end{aligned}
$$

This linear program identifies the variables and specifies the problem objective, subject to the constraints that limit what may be done.

The Nonnegativity Conditions

The linear program includes further limitations that we have not previously encountered. The **nonnegativity conditions** state that the variables cannot assume negative values. Although a negative quantity of tables or chairs makes no sense at all, without these prescriptions it would be mathematically possible to obtain a solution such as $X_T = -10$, $X_C = 16$ with a profit of $68. Obviously, this solution is impossible, because

it implies the absurdity of disassembling 10 tables, retrieving all the wood and labor used to manufacture them, and channeling both of the "saved" resources into the production of more chairs than could have been made with the original wood and labor!

8-3   SOLVING LINEAR PROGRAMS GRAPHICALLY

A linear program is only a mathematical *formulation*. It merely sets up the problem. We still do not know how many tables and chairs should be made. This answer is provided by the **solution** to the linear program.

Several different approaches, or **algorithms,** may be used to solve this problem. In Chapter 9, we will discuss the algorithm developed by George B. Dantzig in 1947. To help us understand that procedure, we first describe an easy way for solving simple problems using the **graphical method.** The graphical method is based on the fact that only a small number of alternatives need to be checked.

A graph of all possibilities has a special contiguous shape called the **feasible solution region.** The search for the best alternative is limited to this area. Only some alternatives are candidates for being the best. These are the **corner points,** which are so few in number that little effort is required to find which corresponds to the best solution.

We begin by constructing a graph that represents the linear program in two dimensions—one for the number of tables X_T, and the other for the number of chairs X_C. We use a ruler to make a heavy horizontal line for the X_T axis and a heavy vertical line for the X_C axis on a piece of graph paper, as shown in Figure 8-1. For convenience, we place tick marks every five squares along the respective axes and label these in increments of 5, starting at 0 in each case. Any point in this two-dimensional space corresponds to a production quantity combination or plan for tables and chairs.

FIGURE 8-1

Linear programming axes constructed on graph paper

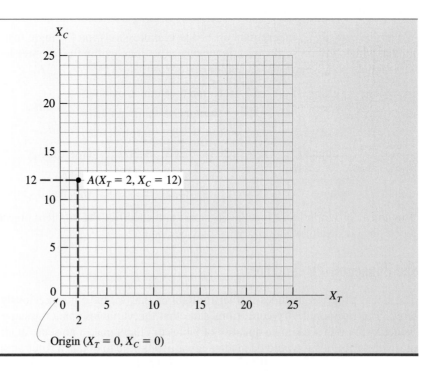

The **origin** is the point where the two axes cross and may be represented in terms of its coordinates along the respective axes ($X_T = 0$, $X_C = 0$). The coordinates for point $A(X_T = 2, X_C = 12)$ represent its distance of 2 units along the X_T axis and its height of 12 units along the X_C axis. This same point represents a production plan for 2 tables and 12 chairs.

Plotting Constraint Lines

Our next step is to plot the constraints on the graph. Begin with the wood constraint, which we expressed as

$$30X_T + 20X_C \leq 300 \qquad \text{(wood)}$$

Temporarily, consider the special case in which the left side of this expression (wood used) is precisely equal to the right side (wood available), which provides the wood *equation*

$$30X_T + 20X_C = 300 \qquad \text{(wood)}$$

When plotted on our graph, this equality is linear. It is therefore referred to as the wood **constraint line.** All points falling on this line represent combinations of table and chair quantities that consume the exact amount of wood that is available.

In constructing the wood constraint line (Figure 8-2), we apply the geometrical principle that any line may be defined by two points. These may then be connected by positioning a straightedge beside both points and drawing the connecting line.

Generally, it is simplest to locate the two points where the line cuts the respective axes. First, consider the X_T axis. The intersection point on the horizontal axis is called the **horizontal intercept.** Since it has no vertical height, one of its coordinates is $X_C = 0$. Plugging this value of X_C into the wood equation gives us

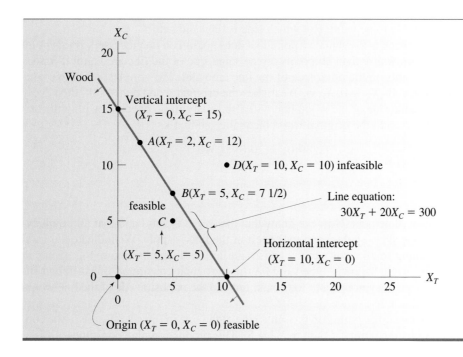

FIGURE 8-2

Plotting the wood constraint line for the Redwood Furniture problem

$$30X_T + 20(0) = 300$$

Because $20 \times 0 = 0$, we may ignore the second term on the left, so that we have

$$30X_T = 300$$

Dividing both sides of this equation by 30, we obtain

$$X_T = 300/30 = 10$$

Thus, the remaining coordinate for the horizontal intercept is $X_T = 10$. In a similar way, we obtain the **vertical intercept** by setting $X_T = 0$ and solving the wood equation for X_C.

$$30(0) + 20X_C = 300$$
$$X_C = 300/20 = 15$$

We then plot these intercepts in Figure 8-2 and draw the wood constraint line to connect them. (For clarity, the grid squares have been omitted in this figure.)

The wood constraint line represents all possible production plans that call for the consumption of the entire 300 board feet of available wood. This is true for the vertical intercept ($X_T = 0$, $X_C = 15$), which corresponds to 0 tables and 15 chairs, and for the horizontal intercept ($X_T = 10$, $X_C = 0$), which corresponds to 10 tables and 0 chairs. For any other point on the wood constraint line, such as point A ($X_T = 2$, $X_C = 12$) or point B ($X_T = 5$, $X_C = 7\frac{1}{2}$), exactly 300 board feet of wood are used. Note that *it is possible to have fractional quantities in linear programming*; coordinates do not have to be whole numbers.

Finding the Valid Side of the Constraint Line

Of course, the original wood constraint does not require us to use all of the available wood. We must reconsider the inequality $\leq$ that we temporarily discarded so that we could work with the wood equation. Actually, an inequality relationship may be incorporated in a linear graph. Any inequality allows all of the points that fall on one side of the constraint line to be valid. But which side is the valid side?

A simple check is to evaluate a point that does not fall on the line itself. If that point satisfies the constraint, then all points on the same side of the line are valid; if it does not, then all points on the other side of the line are valid. The simplest point to evaluate is the origin. If ($X_T = 0$, $X_C = 0$) satisfies the original wood constraint, then every point on the same side of the wood line will also satisfy it. To check this, plug the origin's coordinates into the original wood inequality, so that

$$30(0) + 20(0) \leq 300$$

Thus,

$$0 \leq 300$$

which is a true statement. Now we know that the origin is valid and that all points lying on the same side—below and to the left of the line—apply. We indicate the valid side by attaching small arrows to the constraint line, as shown in Figure 8-2. (Keep in mind that the origin happens to be valid for this particular constraint. In a different situation, the origin may not satisfy the constraint and the opposite side of the line would be the valid side.)

To show that other points on the same side of the line in Figure 8-2 satisfy the constraint, consider the point C ($X_T = 5$, $X_C = 5$). This production plan consumes $30(5) +$

$20(5) = 250$ board feet of wood, which is less than the available 300 board feet. Point C is a valid point. However, point D ($X_T = 10$, $X_C = 10$), which lies above the wood line, is *infeasible*, because it would consume $30(10) + 20(10) = 500$ board feet of wood, which is more than the existing amount of 300 board feet.

The Feasible Solution Region

The entire procedure that we followed to determine the wood constraint must now be duplicated for the labor constraint. The labor equation (again ignoring the $\leq$) is

$$5X_T + 10X_C = 110 \qquad \text{(labor)}$$

The horizontal intercept is $X_T = 110/5 = 22$, and the vertical intercept is $X_C = 110/10 = 11$. The labor line and the wood line are plotted on the same graph in Figure 8-3. The valid side of the labor line includes the origin (doing nothing meets the labor constraint).

Any workable production plan must simultaneously satisfy these wood and labor constraints. Any such plan is called a **feasible solution.** The feasible solutions correspond to the points that lie on the valid sides of both constraint lines, or within the shaded area in Figure 8-3, which is called the **feasible solution region.** Since the non-negativity conditions do not permit negative levels of either X_T or X_C, the feasible solution region is bounded not only by the two constraint lines but also by the vertical and horizontal axes.

Corner Points

A maximum profit solution to the Redwood Furniture Company problem corresponds to a corner point of the feasible solution region. In Figure 8-3, corner points occur where two lines intersect. There are only four that are a part of the feasible solution region:

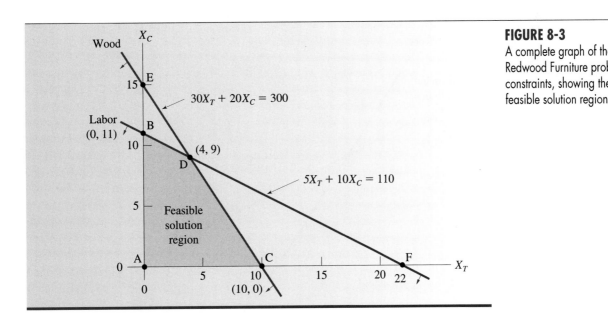

FIGURE 8-3
A complete graph of the Redwood Furniture problem constraints, showing the feasible solution region

$$A \ (X_T = 0, X_C = 0) \quad P = 0 \qquad\qquad C \ (X_T = 10, X_C = 0) \quad P = 60$$
$$B \ (X_T = 0, X_C = 11) \quad P = 88 \qquad\qquad D \ (X_T = 4, X_C = 9) \quad P = 96$$

The values for P were computed by plugging the (X_T, X_C) coordinates into the objective function.

The optimal solution occurs at D. This is called the **most attractive corner.** This corresponds to producing four tables and nine chairs and yields a maximum profit of $96. In this example, it is easy to find the best solution by evaluating the four corner points. The graphical procedure described next is simpler for more complex problems that have many more corners because it avoids the detailed evaluation of every corner.

Finding the Most Attractive Corner Graphically

The Redwood Furniture Company can produce the number of tables and chairs that corresponds to any point in the feasible solution region, because all of these solutions are possible. However, the owner's objective is to maximize total profit, as expressed by the equation

$$P = 6X_T + 8X_C$$

To complete the graphical solution method, we must therefore incorporate profit into our graph.

Because P itself is unknown, various values of profit must be considered. If $P = 48$, for example, the objective function may be written as

$$48 = 6X_T + 8X_C$$

which we recognize as the equation for a straight line. This *profit line* has intercepts of $X_T = 48/6 = 8$ and $X_C = 48/8 = 6$ and is plotted in Figure 8-4 as a dashed line to dis-

FIGURE 8-4
Finding the direction of increasing profit and the most attractive corner for the Redwood Furniture problem

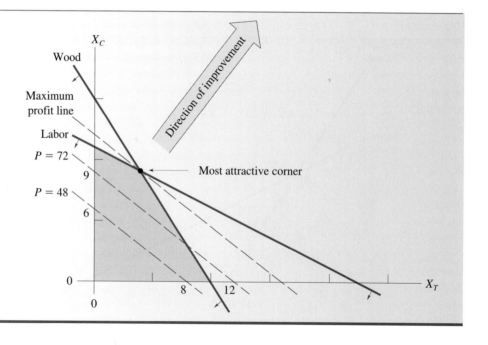

for any other value of P, such as 47, 49, or 53. We chose $P = 48$ because it is evenly divisible by both unit profits, so that the $P = 48$ profit line is easy to construct.

Each point that lies on the $P = 48$ profit line and that also lies inside the feasible solution region corresponds to a production plan yielding a profit of exactly \$48. But we need to know if we can do better and, if so, what the best possible profit is. Let's see what happens if we consider a larger profit, such as $P = 72$ (again a value that is evenly divisible by \$6 and \$8). The corresponding profit line has been plotted as a second dashed line in Figure 8-4. Notice that the $P = 72$ profit line lies above the $P = 48$ profit line. All feasible points on the $P = 72$ profit line will yield the larger profit of \$72.

Note that these two profit lines are *parallel*. This is characteristic of any linear program and any value of P. This property of parallel profit lines is all that we need to know to find the maximum profit. Together, the two profit lines in our graph indicate the **direction of improvement** shown by the large arrow in Figure 8-4.

Now, we may begin to put the solution to our problem together. We still do not know the maximum P, but we do know that as larger possible values of P are considered, the profit lines we plot will be parallel to the first two lines and will lie above them. But there is a limit to how large P can become, because we are only interested in determining the maximum profit that can be achieved by a feasible production plan. By positioning a straightedge parallel to the original two profit lines in Figure 8-4 and sliding it in the direction of increasing profit, we see by a visual inspection of the graph that the highest allowable profit line must just touch the corner of the feasible solution region where the wood and labor constraint lines intersect. Any higher profit line will lie outside the feasible solution region. We refer to the highest allowable point as the **most attractive corner.** A third dashed profit line passes through this corner in Figure 8-4. We must now determine what value of P this *maximum profit line* represents.

Finding the Optimal Solution

The most attractive corner provides us with the production plan that will yield the maximum possible profit. We refer to this plan as the **optimal solution.** Mathematically, the coordinates of the most attractive corner are determined by simultaneously solving the wood and labor equations with two unknowns.

$$30X_T + 20X_C = 300 \quad \text{(wood)}$$
$$5X_T + 10X_C = 110 \quad \text{(labor)}$$

The simplest procedure is to use the method of elimination. We do this by subtracting a multiple of one equation from the other equation in such a way that one of the variables has a coefficient of 0 in the resulting equation difference. The value of the remaining unknown may then be found directly. We can eliminate X_C from the equation difference if we multiply the labor equation by 2 and subtract the result from the wood equation.

$$
\begin{array}{ll}
30X_T + 20X_C = 300 & \text{(wood)} \\
\underline{-2(5X_T + 10X_C = 110)} & \text{(labor)} \\
20X_T + 0X_C = 80 &
\end{array}
$$

Thus,

$$X_T = 80/20 = 4 \text{ tables}$$

Substituting this value into either of the constraint equations, we solve for the value of X_C. Using the wood equation,

FIGURE 8-5

The optimal solution to the Redwood Furniture problem

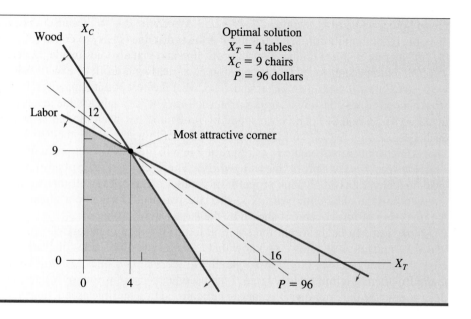

$$30(4) + 20X_C = 300$$
$$20X_C = 300 - 30(4) = 300 - 120 = 180$$

so that

$$X_C = 180/20 = 9 \text{ chairs}$$

The optimal solution to the Redwood Furniture linear program is therefore

$$X_T = 4 \text{ tables}$$
$$X_C = 9 \text{ chairs}$$

and the profit obtained is calculated by substituting these numbers into the objective function.

$$P = 6(4) + 8(9) = 96 \text{ dollars}$$

Figure 8-5 illustrates the profit line that corresponds to $P = 96$. Notice that this line touches the most attractive corner, confirming our earlier conclusion that the profit line that passes through this point will represent the maximum profit.

The graphical method just illustrated shows that the most attractive corner can be found without having to evaluate all the corner points of the feasible solution region. Unfortunately, most linear programming problems have so many variables that they cannot be graphed. Those problems must ordinarily be solved with a computer, using the simplex method to be discussed in Chapter 9.

8-4   SPECIAL PROBLEMS IN CONSTRUCTING LINES

Earlier, we indicated that most constraint lines may be constructed by connecting the horizontal and vertical intercepts. Even though we generally restrict solutions to the positive quadrant, there is no reason why one of these intercepts cannot be negative. Consider the line

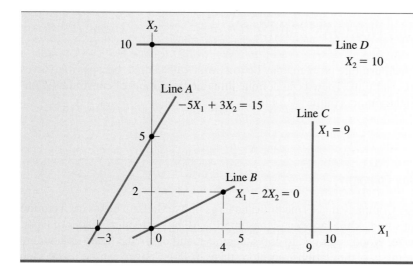

FIGURE 8-6
Examples of special types of lines

$$-5X_1 + 3X_2 = 15$$

which is graphed as line A in Figure 8-6. Notice that the horizontal intercept is *negative*.

$$X_1 = 15/-5 = -3$$

The equation for line B in Figure 8-6 is

$$X_1 - 2X_2 = 0$$

Both the vertical and horizontal intercepts for this equation occur at the *origin*. Because the intercept method yields a single point in this case, a second point must be found. The choice of this second point is arbitrary. We can plug the value of $X_2 = 2$ into the equation to obtain the other coordinate.

$$X_1 - 2(2) = 0$$
$$X_1 = 0 - [-2(2)] = 0 - (-4) = 4$$

Connecting the origin with the point ($X_1 = 4$, $X_2 = 2$) will then give us the required line.

A third type of line has only one intercept. These lines are either horizontal or vertical and have equations of the form

$$X_1 = 9 \quad \text{(line } C\text{)}$$
$$X_2 = 10 \quad \text{(line } D\text{)}$$

where only one variable appears in the equation. For $X_1 = 9$, the value of X_1 is restricted to exactly 9, regardless of the value of X_2, which may be any quantity whatsoever. This relationship is illustrated by line C, a vertical line perpendicular to the X_1 axis and parallel to the X_2 axis. For the equation $X_2 = 10$, line D is plotted as a horizontal line perpendicular to the X_2 axis at a height of 10 units. For that matter, the axes themselves may be represented in terms of the equations $X_2 = 0$ (for the horizontal axis) and $X_1 = 0$ (for the vertical axis).

8-5 PROBLEMS WITH MORE THAN TWO CONSTRAINTS

The Redwood Furniture problem may be somewhat misleading, because it involves only two constraints. There is no definite limit on the number of constraints. Consider a slightly more complex problem.

The Planter Box Company

The Planter Box Company makes medium and large units. Medium boxes each require 9 square feet of wood, while large ones consume 15. All boxes require .5 hour of labor, regardless of size. Wood is limited to 450 square feet, and only 20.3 hours of labor are available. Due to space limitations, no more than 20 large boxes can be made each day. Also, customers can absorb at most 30 medium boxes. Subject to these constraints, any number of boxes can be made. Medium boxes yield a profit of $6; large ones earn only $2.

We will formulate this problem as a linear program and then solve it graphically.

THE PROBLEM SOLUTION

There are two variables. Although any symbol might be used for each, it is traditional to use the letter X to identify them, with a different subscript for each. Using the first letter of the box type we have

$$X_M = \text{number of medium boxes to be made}$$
$$X_L = \text{number of large boxes to be made}$$

The objective is to

Maximize $P = 6X_M + 2X_L$

Subject to:

$$9X_M + 15X_L \leq 450 \qquad \text{(wood)}$$
$$.5X_M + .5X_L \leq 20.3 \qquad \text{(labor)}$$
$$X_L \leq 20 \qquad \text{(space)}$$
$$X_M \leq 30 \qquad \text{(customer)}$$

where $X_M, X_L \geq 0$

In addition to the wood and labor constraints, there are two others: a space limitation and a customer requirement. The space limitation applies only to the large boxes, so that only X_L appears on the left-hand side of that constraint's inequality. Analogously, only X_M appears on the left-hand side of the customer restriction constraint.

Figure 8-7 provides the graph for this problem. The wood and labor lines are constructed similarly to their counterparts in the Redwood Furniture problem. The space constraint, plotted as a *horizontal* line, intersects only the X_L axis. Likewise, the customer constraint, a *vertical* line, intersects only the X_M axis. The origin or "point of doing nothing" satisfies all constraints, so that each constraint line has a valid side facing that point. Putting it all together, the shaded area reveals the feasible solution region.

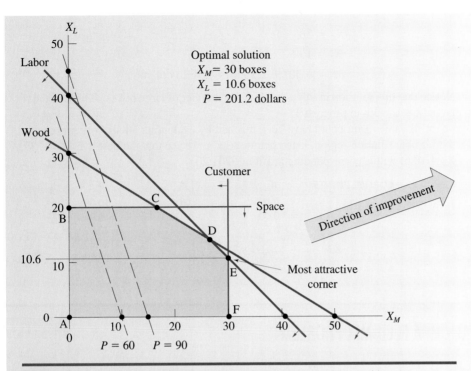

FIGURE 8-7 Graph showing optimal solution to Planter Box Company problem

The most attractive corner for this problem is *not* where the wood and labor lines cross. To identify the most attractive corner, we could evaluate all six corners of the feasible solution region and then find the one with the greatest value for P. That would be a lot of work. Instead we let the graph tell us where that corner lies.

We choose arbitrarily two profit levels, $P = 60$ and $P = 90$, for their convenience and fit on the graph. (Any pair of values might work, but it would be disadvantageous to use profits that would require more arithmetic to find intercepts [61 and 93], require constructing lines that extend far beyond the axes [600 and 900], or involve intercepts too close together to create clearly delineated lines [6 and 9].) All that matters is that these parallel lines present an easy-to-see angle with respect to the corners, and that they make the direction of improvement obvious.

With all lines in place, a *visual* inspection of the graph tells us that the most attractive corner is where the labor line crosses the customer line. To get accurate coordinates for the most attractive corner we simultaneously solve the equations for these lines.

$$.5X_M + .5X_L = 20.3 \qquad \text{(labor)}$$
$$X_M \qquad\quad = 30 \qquad \text{(customer)}$$

That will give us the optimal solution. The second equation directly gives $X_M = 30$ as the solution for medium boxes. Substituting that value into the first equation, we have

$$.5(30) + .5X_L = 20.3$$
$$.5X_L = 20.3 - .5(30) = 5.3$$
$$X_L = 5.3/.5 = 10.6 \text{ boxes}$$

and the complete solution is

$$X_M = 30$$
$$X_L = 10.6$$
$$P = 6(30) + 2(10.6) = 201.20 \text{ dollars}$$

Notice that this solution involves a fractional number of large boxes. (Think of the .6 large box as work in progress.)

This same result could have been reached by evaluating all six corner points of the feasible solution region, listed below. Again, we see that the best is E ($X_M = 30$, $X_L = 10.6$) with a corresponding profit of $201.20.

CORNER POINTS	X_M	X_L	P
A	0.00	0.00	$0.00
B	0.00	20.00	$40.00
C	16.67	20.00	$140.02
D	26.50	14.10	$187.20
E	30.00	10.60	$201.20
F	30.00	0.00	$180.00

8-6   COST MINIMIZATION: A FEED-MIX PROBLEM

We will now consider a simplified problem that may be faced by a seed packager—determining the number of pounds of two types of seeds that should be mixed to formulate the wheat portion of a batch of wild birdseed. Table 8-2 shows the nutritional content of two seed types—buckwheat and sunflower wheat—along with the minimum required pounds of fat and protein. In addition, there is a maximum limit of 1,500 pounds of roughage. Unlimited quantities of either seed type can be purchased at the costs indicated. The packager's goal is to minimize the total cost of satisfying the nutritional requirements of the birdseed mix.

The linear program for this problem may be formulated as follows:

Letting X_B = Pounds of buckwheat in mixture
X_S = Pounds of sunflower wheat in mixture
Minimize $C = .18X_B + .10X_S$ (objective)
Subject to $.04X_B + .06X_S \geq 480$ (fat)
$.12X_B + .10X_S \geq 1,200$ (protein)
$.10X_B + .15X_S \leq 1,500$ (roughage)
where $X_B, X_S \geq 0$

TABLE 8-2   Data Obtained for the Feed-Mix Problem

NUTRITIONAL ITEM	PROPORTIONAL CONTENT Buckwheat	Sunflower Wheat	TOTAL REQUIREMENT
Fat	.04	.06	≥ 480 lb
Protein	.12	.10	$\geq 1,200$
Roughage	.10	.15	$\leq 1,500$
Cost per pound	$.18	$.10	

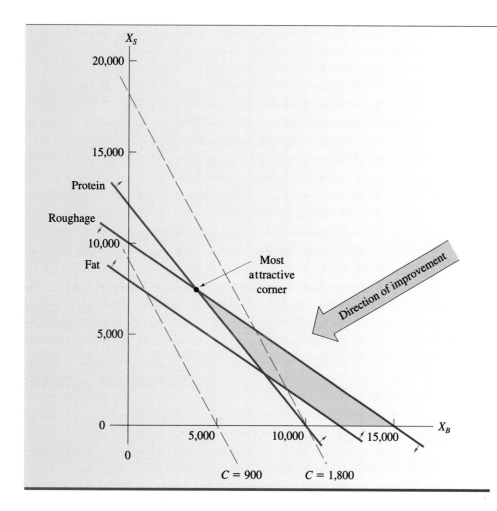

FIGURE 8-8
The graphical solution to
the feed-mix problem

The fat and protein constraints are represented by ≥ (greater than or equal to) inequalities because minimum quantities of each have been established, and the total pounds of fat or protein (provided on the left sides of the respective inequalities) must be at least as large as these quantities. The roughage constraint is a ≤ (less than or equal to) inequality, because total mixture roughage (again represented on the left side) cannot exceed 1,500 pounds.

Figure 8-8 is a graphical representation of the feed-mix problem. Notice that the valid sides of the fat and protein constraints are opposite to the origin side (0 pounds of both seed types will satisfy neither constraint). Cost lines for $C = 1,800$ and $C = 900$ dollars have been plotted. (Even though the $C = 900$ cost line lies outside the feasible solution region, the direction of decreasing cost is readily determined.) The most attractive corner occurs at the intersection of the protein and roughage constraint lines.

Solving the protein and roughage equations simultaneously, we determine the optimal solution.

$$
\begin{array}{ll}
.12X_B + .10X_S = 1,200 & \text{(protein)} \\
-\frac{2}{3}(.10X_B + .15X_S = 1,500) & \text{(roughage)} \\
\hline
.053333X_B + \quad 0X_S = \quad 200 & \\
\end{array}
$$

$$X_B = 200/.053333 = 3,750 \text{ pounds}$$

Plugging the value of X_B into the protein equation, we then find the value of X_S.

$$.12(3,750) + .10X_S = 1,200$$
$$.10X_S = 1,200 - .12(3,750) = 1,200 - 450 = 750$$
$$X_S = 750/.10 = 7,500 \text{ pounds}$$

The optimal solution to the feed-mix problem is therefore

$$X_B = 3,750 \text{ pounds}$$
$$X_S = 7,500 \text{ pounds}$$

and the minimum cost is

$$C = .18(3,750) + .10(7,500) = 1,425 \text{ dollars}$$

8-7 STEPS AND RATIONALE FOR GRAPHICAL SOLUTION

Although the graphical solution procedure just illustrated only works for two-variable problems that may be plotted in two dimensions, this method will be helpful in presenting the concepts common to solving larger linear programs. Before proceeding, let's examine a formal summary of the graphical solution procedure.

Because beginners to linear programming often do not immediately grasp the implications of certain steps, they tend to take shortcuts that often lead to wrong solutions. An appreciation of the rationale for each step in the solution procedure may help prevent those blunders.

SOLUTION PROCEDURE

SUMMARY OF THE GRAPHICAL SOLUTION PROCEDURE

The steps in solving a linear program may now be summarized.

1. **Formulate the linear program.** A proper formulation begins with a definition of the variables that clearly describes how the symbols apply. The rest is algebraic representation. First, the objective function (maximize P or minimize C) is stated in an equation, followed by the expressions for the constraints. No formulation is complete without a final statement of nonnegativity conditions.

2. **Construct a graph and plot the constraint lines.** Ordinarily, this involves locating two points and connecting them. The points are usually the horizontal and vertical intercepts found from each constraint equation. But as we have seen for certain constraints, a different pair of points must be found to draw these lines.

3. **Determine the valid side for each inequality constraint.** The simplest approach is to see whether the origin (the point of "doing nothing") satisfies the constraint by plugging its coordinates (0, 0) into the inequality. If it does, then all points on the origin's side of the line are valid, and the rest are infeasible. If the origin does not satisfy the constraint, then the valid points lie on the side of the line that is opposite the origin. The *two exceptions* to this rule of thumb will be discussed shortly.

4. **Identify the feasible solution region and corner points.** This region will be indicated by the group of points on the graph that are valid for all constraints

collectively. These points correspond to the feasible plans. Ordinarily, the feasible solution region is a contiguous area lying in the positive quadrant, because the nonnegativity conditions preclude negative variable values.

5. **Plot two objective function lines and determine the direction of improvement.** When profit maximization is the goal, two P lines will tell us the direction of increasing P. Two lines are necessary because the direction cannot always be predicted from a single line. The two P lines do not have to intersect the feasible solution region to indicate the direction of increasing P. When the goal is to minimize cost, two C lines are plotted. In this case, the direction of improvement is a decrease in C.

6. **Find the most attractive corner by visual inspection.** This corner will be the last point in the feasible solution region touched by the P or C line that is formed by sliding a straightedge in the direction of improvement while holding it parallel to the two original objective lines.

7. **Determine the optimal solution by algebraically calculating coordinates of the most attractive corner.** The optimal solution is often represented by the intersection of two constraint lines. However, it might also be denoted by the coordinates of a corner point formed by the horizontal or vertical intercept of one constraint equation. When this is the case, the algebraic calculations have already been performed and the optimal solution may be read directly from the coordinates shown on the graph without error.

8. **Determine the value of the objective function for the optimal solution.** This is found by substituting the optimal variable values into the P or C equation. No solution is complete until the maximum value of P or the minimum value of C is stated.

Rationale for Procedure and Practical Suggestions

The following comment is common from students encountering linear programming for the first time:

> "I don't know what the fuss is. I just solved two equations, getting the same answer, and *I didn't even construct a graph*!"

Of course, the Redwood Furniture problem has been kept simple on purpose. And, for that problem, many shortcuts could have been taken in reaching the correct solution. But, there is a reason for every step, and shortcuts may lead to wrong answers.

The Graph Guarantees Feasibility of Solution   Figure 8-9 shows a graph for a similar production problem involving *six* constraints. Including those on the axes, there are 26 possible points of intersection, any of which may contain the solutions. Which pair of equations should we solve simultaneously?

Without the graph, we would fly blindly, perhaps picking one of the 17 *infeasible* intersection points.

Plot Objective Lines to Avoid Picking a Nonoptimal Point   Another comment commonly heard among beginners is

FIGURE 8-9

Possible points of
intersection for a typical
linear program

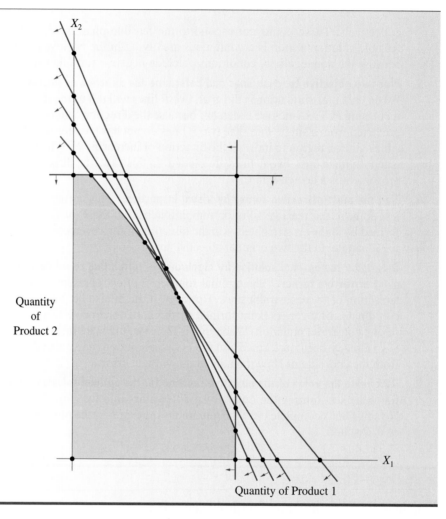

"Yeah, I drew the graph. But why do we need to draw *P* lines? Solving for the intersection point, I got the correct answer. Isn't the maximum profit always where the two constraint lines cross?"

This objection may apply only to problems with two binding constraints. (Why?)

Consider the graph in Figure 8-10. By raising the chair profit, the *P* lines become flatter. The most attractive corner is point *A* when profit is $15 per chair (leaving table unit profit unchanged). Lowering the chair profit results in steeper *P* lines. Point *B* is the most attractive corner when the chair profit is only $3 (and table profit is held fixed). In either case, point *C* is *not* a most attractive corner.

Find the Most Attractive Corner by Rolling Your Pencil in the Direction of Improvement *Two P* lines are helpful in isolating the most attractive corner visually. The two lines must be parallel, and the direction of improvement is toward the line with the better objective (higher *P*, lower *C*). The second line is optional, but safest if the objective function involves a negative coefficient for one of the variables. (In those cases, the direction of improvement may be down, up, right, or left, depending on the form of the objective function.) Once the direction of improvement is determined, place your pencil at any spot on the graph and set it parallel to the plotted line; it lies on top of an imaginary *P* line (*C* line) that is either better or worse. As you roll the pencil in the direction

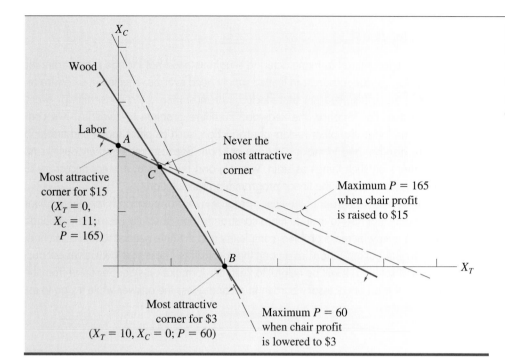

FIGURE 8-10
Illustration of how the most attractive corner and solution may shift as objective coefficients change

of improvement, it describes progressively better lines. The most attractive corner is the *last* feasible point your pencil rolls past.

If it looks like two points may be the most attractive corners, then a separate algebraic evaluation should be made of each. That point with the best P or C is the most attractive one. *There may be a tie.*

Skipping the Algebra May Lead to Inaccuracies

The graph itself minimizes only the more glaring errors. But it is, by itself, not foolproof. To illustrate, suppose that one extra hour of labor becomes available, so that we change the right-hand side of the labor constraint to 111. The graph in Figure 8-5 will change slightly, with a tiny upward shift in the labor line. Visually, it will still look like $X_T = 4$ and $X_C = 9$ is the solution. That is not the case. The solution becomes

$$X_T = 3.90$$
$$X_C = 9.15$$
$$P = 96.60 \quad (111 \text{ labor hours})$$

(Verify this to your satisfaction.)

The graph provides the same essential information as before, showing that the most attractive corner is where the labor and wood lines cross. *The purpose of the most attractive corner is to identify which algebra problem to solve* (here, the simultaneous solution of the wood and labor equations).

Linear Programs Do Not Require Integer Solutions

Notice that the modified problem's optimal solution involves variable values that are not integers. Linear programming does not require that solutions be integer values. (But integers may nevertheless be a legitimate requirement. In those cases, a related procedure, called *integer programming,* would apply. This topic will be discussed in Chapter 11.)

What Constraints to Use

Linear programs encountered in manufacturing situations need not include a constraint for every resource. Only those resources in limited supply need ever be reflected in a constraint. The entire bill of materials need not be reflected, nor must there be a constraint for every stage of production. For instance, the Redwood Furniture problem involves just two constraints: wood and labor. But other factors of production, such as plant space and finishing materials, must also be used in making a table or chair. Because Redwood encounters no practical limitations on such things as stain, varnish, and floorspace, it is not necessary to include constraints for these in the linear programming formulation.

What to include or leave out of the linear programming formulation is largely a matter of judgment. It does not hurt to include more constraints than absolutely essential, although an extra constraint may increase problem complexity and the time needed to find a solution.

Do not worry about redundancies among the constraints. These sort themselves out during the process of solution. It will be helpful to keep the formulation stage separate from the solution process. It is an unnecessary burden to second guess the answer while trying to establish the constraints.

8-8 MIXTURE AND EQUALITY CONSTRAINTS

A line that passes through the origin generally applies to a special type of restriction called a **mixture constraint.** Such a constraint arises in manufacturing applications when some products must be made in a fixed ratio to other products. The Redwood Furniture problem can be modified slightly to incorporate a mixture constraint.

Ordinarily, Redwood's tables and chairs are sold in sets of 4 chairs and 1 table. However, there is an occasional need for extra chairs. Thus, Redwood wants to make at least 4 chairs for every table, which means that the number of chairs must be at least as large as the number of tables multiplied by 4. This adds a further mixture constraint to the problem of the form

$$4 \times \text{Number of tables} \leq \text{Number of chairs}$$

Expressed in terms of the variable symbols used in the previous Redwood problem, this constraint tells us that

$$4X_T \leq X_C \qquad \text{(mixture)}$$

For convenience, all variables are usually collected on the left side of the inequality. Subtracting X_C from both sides, we obtain

$$4X_T - X_C \leq 0 \qquad \text{(mixture)}$$

Temporarily ignoring the inequality gives us the following equation for the mixture constraint line.

$$4X_T - X_C = 0 \qquad \text{(mixture)}$$

This is the expression for a line that passes through the origin.

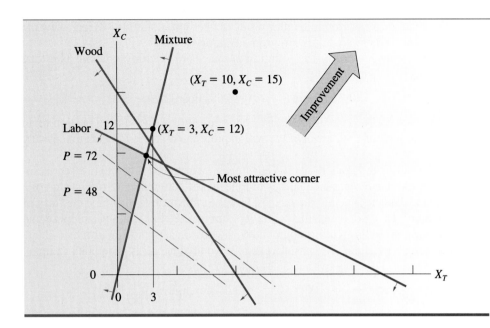

FIGURE 8-11
The graphical solution to
the Redwood Furniture
problem expanded to
include a mixture constraint

The graph for the expanded Redwood Furniture problem is provided in Figure 8-11. (The original wood and labor constraints are replotted here.) The mixture constraint line is found by connecting the origin with the point ($X_T = 3$, $X_C = 12$), because when 3 tables are made, $3 \times 4 = 12$ chairs must be produced.

Finding the valid side of the mixture constraint line is a little complicated. Because the line passes through the origin, we cannot use the origin for this purpose. Instead, we must evaluate some point that does not lie on the line. Any such point will do, so we choose ($X_T = 10$, $X_C = 15$). Substituting these coordinates into the mixture inequality gives us

$$4(10) - 15 \le 0$$
$$25 \le 0$$

which is certainly not true. Thus, the valid side of the mixture constraint line lies opposite this point.

The feasible solution region obtained by including the mixture constraint is smaller than the feasible solution region for the original Redwood Furniture problem in Figure 8-3. (Additional constraints ordinarily reduce the number of possible solutions. Why?) Visual inspection indicates that the most attractive corner for this new linear program lies at the intersection of the mixture and labor constraint lines. The simultaneous solution of these equations

$$4X_T - X_C = 0 \quad \text{(mixture)}$$
$$5X_T + 10X_C = 110 \quad \text{(labor)}$$

provides the optimal solution.

$$X_T = 22/9 = 2\tfrac{4}{9} \text{ tables}$$
$$X_C = 88/9 = 9\tfrac{7}{9} \text{ chairs}$$
$$P = 836/9 = 92\tfrac{8}{9} \text{ dollars}$$

Remember that linear programming may produce fractional solutions. We can view the extra $\frac{4}{9}$ table and $\frac{7}{9}$ chair as work-in-progress inventory items.

One interesting feature of this solution is that there is leftover wood. The total amount of wood consumed is

$$30(22/9) + 20(88/9) = 268\tfrac{8}{9} \text{ board feet}$$

leaving $300 - 268\tfrac{8}{9} = 31\tfrac{1}{9}$ board feet of wood in inventory. The unused portion of an inventoried resource is called *slack*. We will explore the concept of slack extensively in Chapter 9.

Thus far, all of the constraints we have encountered have been expressed as inequalities. As we have seen, inequalities produce valid points that lie to one side of a bisected plane. Under some circumstances, however, constraints may take the form of a strict equality. They are then called **equality constraints.** For example, suppose that Redwood Furniture sells all of its tables and chairs only in sets and that *exactly* 4 chairs are required for each table. The basic constraint would have no $<$ inequality in it and would be expressed directly by the equation for the line

$$4X_T - X_C = 0 \qquad \text{(revised mixture)}$$

Figure 8-12 is a graph of the linear program that reflects this further amendment. Notice that *there is no valid side of the mixture line:* Valid points must lie exactly on the line. The feasible solution region consists of that *line segment* of the mixture constraint that also satisfies the remaining resource constraints. In general, when there is one equality constraint, the feasible points will lie on a line segment, but there are no other basic changes in the linear programming steps.

lously simple. Suppose that Redwood wants to produce 2 tables because exactly this number can be sold. In this case, the **quantity constraint** would be

$$X_T = 2 \qquad \text{(table quantity)}$$

FIGURE 8-12

The graphical solution to the Redwood Furniture problem amended to incorporate an equality mixture constraint

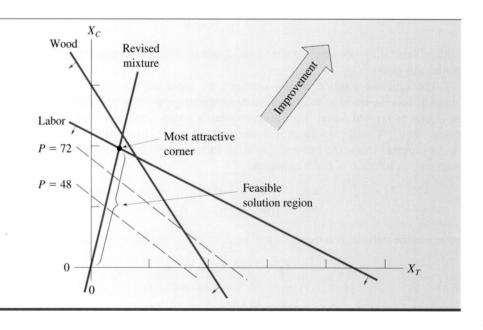

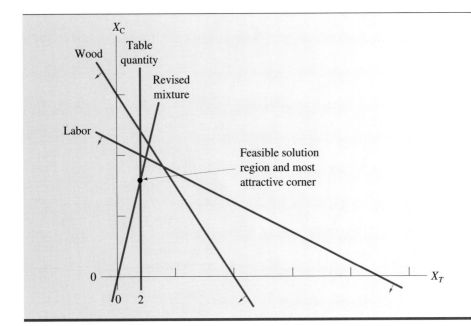

FIGURE 8-13
The graphical solution to the Redwood Furniture problem restricted by two equality constraints

Figure 8-13 is a graph of this more restricted linear program. The constraint is plotted as a vertical line intersecting the X_T axis at 2. Notice that the *feasible solution region consists of the single point* where the two equality constraints intersect. The most attractive corner is the same point! In this case, the optimal solution is $X_T = 2$ tables and $X_C = 8$ chairs, with a profit of $P = 76$ dollars.

8-9   MULTIPLE OPTIMAL SOLUTIONS

Until now, we have examined linear programs with unique optimal solutions corresponding to the most attractive corner. Although the solution to a linear program is generally represented by a corner point of the feasible solution region, more than one corner can be equally most attractive. As an example, consider the following linear program:

$$\begin{array}{llll} \text{Maximize} & P = 10X_1 + 12X_2 & & \text{(objective)} \\ \text{Subject to} & 5X_1 + 6X_2 \leq 60 & & \text{(resource } A) \\ & 8X_1 + 4X_2 \leq 72 & & \text{(resource } B) \\ & 3X_1 + 5X_2 \leq 45 & & \text{(resource } C) \\ \text{where} & X_1, X_2 \geq 0 \end{array}$$

This problem is graphed in Figure 8-14. Visual inspection indicates that there are two candidates for the most attractive corner: the intersection of the A and C lines at point (1) or the intersection of the A and B lines at point (2). To resolve this potential ambiguity, we must determine which point is the last one touched by the highest P line. A visual analysis is not precise enough, because if we slide a straightedge in the direction of increasing P, it is impossible to make a distinction between the two corner points. Alternatively, we can simultaneously solve the respective equation pairs for both points and choose the one with the greatest P. Doing this, we obtain

FIGURE 8-14

The graphical solution
to a problem that has
multiple optimal solutions

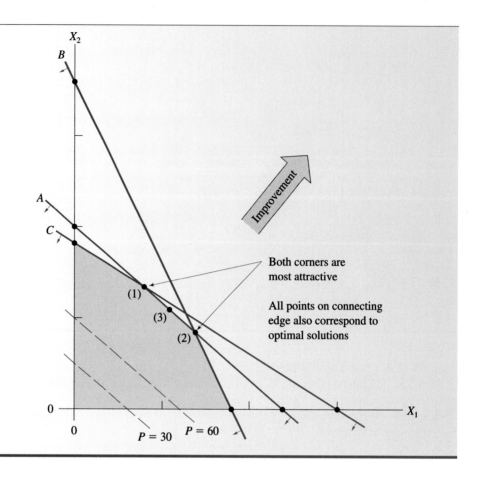

	(1)	(2)
	$X_1 = 4\frac{2}{7}$	$X_1 = 6\frac{6}{7}$
	$X_2 = 6\frac{3}{7}$	$X_2 = 4\frac{2}{7}$
	$P = 120$	$P = 120$

which both yield the same profit. This means that both points are equally attractive, and we have *two most attractive corners*. Thus, both of these solutions are optimal, and the maximum profit is $P = 120$.

Why did we obtain two most attractive corners? The answer is because *the objective function line is parallel to one of the constraint lines*, so that the maximum P line must coincide with that constraint. This can be verified visually in Figure 8-14, where the $P = 30$ and $P = 60$ profit lines are parallel to the resource A constraint line. It is possible to prove mathematically that all lines for P are parallel to that line by comparing their equations.

$$P = 10X_1 + 12X_2 \qquad \text{(objective)}$$
$$5X_1 + 6X_2 = 60 \qquad \text{(resource } A\text{)}$$

Notice that the coefficients of the variables in the resource equation exhibit a constant ratio to the respective coefficients in the P equation. The X_1 terms are 10 and 5, so that the ratio is $10/5 = 2$; this same ratio result $12/6 = 2$ applies to X_2. Thus, the coefficients in the P equation are exactly *twice* the value of the coefficients in the resource A

equation. Whenever all of the coefficients in one equation are the same multiple of their counterparts in another equation, the two lines must be parallel.

Whenever more than one corner provides the optimal solution, all points on the connecting edge will also correspond to optimal solutions. For example, consider point (3), which is midway on the optimal edge in Figure 8-14, with coordinates ($X_1 = 5\frac{4}{7}$, $X_2 = 5\frac{5}{14}$). The maximum profit for this solution is also

$$P = 10(5\tfrac{4}{7}) + 12(5\tfrac{5}{14}) = 120$$

Any other point on the *most attractive edge* will also represent an optimal solution with a profit of $P = 120$, reflecting the fact that the maximum P line must coincide with this edge.

8-10 INFEASIBLE PROBLEMS

Thus far, we have encountered only problems that have solutions. It is possible, however, for constraints to be so restrictive that no solution exists. Such a linear program is called an **infeasible problem.** Consider the following linear program:

$$\begin{aligned} \text{Maximize} \quad & P = 6X_1 + 4X_2 \\ \text{Subject to} \quad & X_1 + X_2 \le 5 \\ & X_2 \ge 8 \\ \text{where} \quad & X_1, X_2 \ge 0 \end{aligned}$$

This problem is graphed in Figure 8-15. Notice that there is no feasible solution region, because the constraints are mutually incompatible.

Ordinarily, an infeasible problem indicates that a mistake has been made in the initial formulation. The remedy is to check the constraint expressions to verify that they properly reflect the problem. One number may have been miscopied or assigned the wrong sign; or perhaps a $\le$ should really be a $\ge$. Once the mistake has been remedied, the corrected linear program can be solved again. It is more perplexing when the formulation properly reflects the problem, indicating that the problem itself represents contradictory requirements. Then unless the impasse is resolved, the decision maker will never be able to solve the problem. (No kind of answer—not even a poor one—is possible for an infeasible problem.)

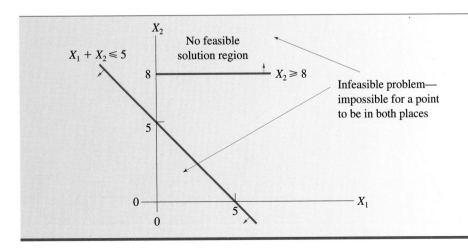

FIGURE 8-15
Graph for the infeasible problem

8-11 UNBOUNDED PROBLEMS

A nother category of linear programs yields ridiculous solutions that place no effective limit on one or more variables. Thus, any level of profit is possible—even a profit level of trillions of dollars, or more. Such a linear program is called an **unbounded problem.** As an example, consider the following linear program:

$$\text{Maximize} \quad P = 3X_1 + 6X_2$$
$$\text{Subject to} \quad 3X_1 + 4X_2 \geq 12$$
$$-2X_1 + X_2 \leq 4$$
$$\text{where} \quad X_1, X_2 \geq 0$$

The graph of this linear program in Figure 8-16 shows that the feasible solution region lies open and becomes wider in the direction of improvement. There is no most attractive corner, and P can be as large as we want it to be. No matter how large a P is chosen, lines for larger and larger P levels can be drawn through the feasible solution region. In essence, P can be infinite.

In the real world, no economic situations are literally unbounded. Thus, when a linear program turns out to be unbounded, some essential restriction (plant capacity, initial inventory level, and so on) has been left out of the formulation. Once the missing constraint is determined, the properly formulated linear program should result in a realistic solution.

FIGURE 8-16
Graph for the unbounded problem

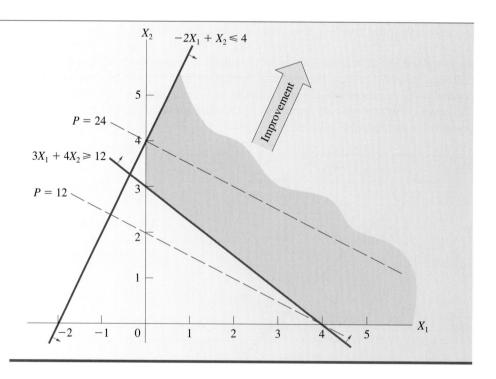

8-12 LINEAR PROGRAMMING APPLICATIONS AND SOLUTION PROCEDURES

L inear programming has been very successful in a variety of business applications. Chapter 9 describes in detail how linear programming can help a portfolio manager select securities. Also described there is a product distribution application, where shipments of skis are scheduled. The range of linear programming applications is a wide one. Chapter 9 also shows how it can be used to select advertising media and to blend liquids. It may even be helpful in making personnel decisions, indicating the optimal assignments of workers to jobs.

In this chapter, we have considered the essential features of linear programming. But we have only scratched the surface of this subject. By nature, the graphical solution method is limited to problems that contain two variables, because our graphs can only represent two dimensions. It would be possible for us to extend this analysis to three variables, using three-dimensional graphs, but to do so would be cumbersome. When four or more variables are involved, entirely different algorithms must be used. In Chapter 9, we will consider the most generally used solution procedure in linear programming—the **simplex method.** In later chapters, more efficient special-purpose algorithms will be described.

Managerial Decision Revisited: Synthesizing Crude Oil

**MANAGERIAL
DECISION**

Barry formulates the following linear program:

Letting X_G = number of gasification batches

X_P = number of pressurization batches

Maximize $P = 40X_G + 40X_P$

Subject to

$$100X_G + 150X_P = 10,000 \quad \text{(low-sulfur)}$$
$$200X_G + 100X_P = 5,000 \quad \text{(high-sulfur)}$$
$$1X_G + 2X_P \leq 100 \quad \text{(coal)}$$
$$2X_G + 1X_P \leq 150 \quad \text{(shale)}$$

where

$$X_G, X_P \geq 0$$

The coefficients for unit profits are computed from the given data.

$.50(100) + .30(200) - 20 - 2(25) = \$40$ per gasification batch

$.50(150) + .30(100) - 2(20) - 25 = \$40$ per pressurization batch

The first two constraints express the demand levels for the two crudes. These are equalities, because the demands must be met exactly. The other two constraints stipulate that no more coal and shale resources may be used beyond the available quantities.

Because the linear program has two variables, Barry knows that the solution can be obtained by the graphical procedure explained in this chapter. The graph is shown in Figure 8-17. The solution must fall at the intersection of the two crude lines, because the respective constraints are equalities. It must also fall inside the shaded region defined by the two resource availability inequalities and nonnegativity conditions. The intersection point falls outside, making the original linear program infeasible. Such problems are common in linear programming and arise whenever there are mutually

FIGURE 8-17
Graph for synthetic crude
oil problem

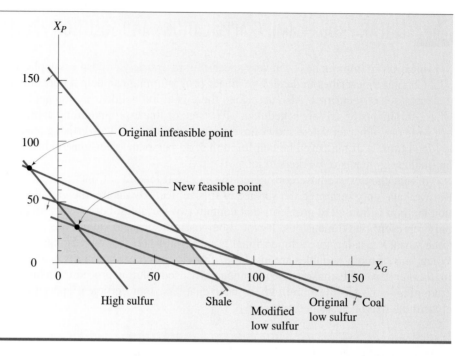

incompatible requirements. Barry concludes from this infeasible solution that the customer's order cannot be fulfilled. Sufficient coal and shale are not available to meet the customer's requirements.

After reading Barry's analysis, Mr. Stanforth thinks of two new possibilities: (1) obtain additional coal and shale from the spot market or (2) persuade the customer to accept only part of the order. Following up on these, he learns that no additional coal and shale are available. Discussion with the customer leads to a revised order involving half of the original low-sulfur crude. Mr. Stanforth gives this revised order to Barry, who re-solves the linear programming model with a new constraint:

$$100X_G + 150X_F = 5,000$$

and gets an optimal solution of

$$X_G = 12.5 \quad X_F = 25 \quad P = \$1,500.$$

Because the revised order can be profitably fulfilled, Mr. Stanforth accepts the order and sends it on to the Production Department. The company will produce 12.5 gasification batches and 25 pressurization batches, and the profit from the order will be $1,500.

8-13 GRAPHING USING A SPREADSHEET

A spreadsheet can be used to graph a linear programming problem. That has several advantages over graphing by hand. The resulting display is more accurate, makes it easier to find the direction of improvement for P or C, and makes it simple to observe how problem changes will alter the graph. We will illustrate this using the Redwood Furniture Company problem on page 265.

The first step is to algebraically express each constraint and the objective function in terms of the variable to appear on the horizontal axis. In this case, solving for X_C give

$$X_C = (300 - 30X_T)/20 \qquad \text{(wood)}$$
$$X_C = (110 - 5X_T)/10 \qquad \text{(labor)}$$
$$X_C = (P - 6X_T)/8 \qquad \text{(profit)}$$

These formulas underlie the Excel spreadsheet shown in Figure 8-18.

The first column is for X_T, whose levels will appear on the horizontal axis. In our example X_T takes on the values 0 through 10, as shown in cells A9 through A19. The above are translated into Excel formulas. For row 9, we have

Cell B9: $X_C = (300 - 30X_T)/20 =$ ($B$4-30*A9)/20 (for wood)

Cell C9: $X_C = (110 - 5X_T)/10 =$ ($B$5-5*A9)/10 (for labor)

Cell D9: $X_C = (P - 6X_T)/8 =$ ($B$3-6*A9)/8 (for profit)

It is only necessary to key the above for the row 9 cells. They are then copied down onto rows 10 through 19. (That may be done by highlighting the above cells and dragging. Alternatively, the same result may be achieved by selecting Edit, Copy, and Paste from the menu bar or from the drop-down menu appearing after right clicking the mouse.)

Chapter 2 shows how to construct a graph using Excel's Chart Wizard. It was used to graph the wood, labor, and profit lines in Figure 8-19.

With the chart on the spreadsheet, it is easy to observe the movement of the objective function. If we change the number in cell B3 to 60 and then to 72 and finally to 96, the dotted objective-function line moves upward toward the right until it passes

	A	B	C	D
1	Redwood Furniture Company			
2				
3	Profit	48		
4	Wood	300		
5	Labor	110		
6				
7		Chairs, X_C		
8	Tables, X_T	Wood	Labor	Profit
9	0	15	11	6
10	1	13.5	10.5	5.25
11	2	12	10	4.5
12	3	10.5	9.5	3.75
13	4	9	9	3
14	5	7.5	8.5	2.25
15	6	6	8	1.5
16	7	4.5	7.5	0.75
17	8	3	7	0
18	9	1.5	6.5	-0.75
19	10	0	6	-1.5

	A	B	C	D
8	Tables, X_T	Wood	Labor	Profit
9	0	=($B$4-30*A9)/20	=($B$5-5*A9)/10	=($B$3-6*A9)/8
10	1	=($B$4-30*A10)/20	=($B$5-5*A10)/10	=($B$3-6*A10)/8
11	2	=($B$4-30*A11)/20	=($B$5-5*A11)/10	=($B$3-6*A11)/8
12	3	=($B$4-30*A12)/20	=($B$5-5*A12)/10	=($B$3-6*A12)/8
13	4	=($B$4-30*A13)/20	=($B$5-5*A13)/10	=($B$3-6*A13)/8
14	5	=($B$4-30*A14)/20	=($B$5-5*A14)/10	=($B$3-6*A14)/8
15	6	=($B$4-30*A15)/20	=($B$5-5*A15)/10	=($B$3-6*A15)/8
16	7	=($B$4-30*A16)/20	=($B$5-5*A16)/10	=($B$3-6*A16)/8
17	8	=($B$4-30*A17)/20	=($B$5-5*A17)/10	=($B$3-6*A17)/8
18	9	=($B$4-30*A18)/20	=($B$5-5*A18)/10	=($B$3-6*A18)/8
19	10	=($B$4-30*A19)/20	=($B$5-5*A19)/10	=($B$3-6*A19)/8

FIGURE 8-18 Excel spreadsheet for graphing the Redwood Furniture Company problem

FIGURE 8-19

Graph of the Redwood
Furniture Company
problem for $P = 48$

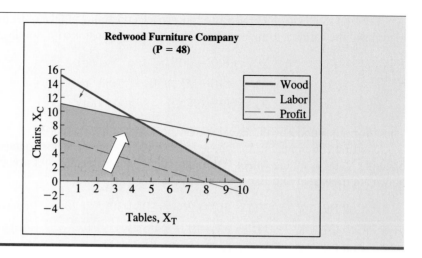

through the intersection of the other two lines. This is the direction of improvement for the objective function. Figure 8-20 shows the case when $P = 96$.

In a similar manner, varying the amount of wood (B4) and labor (B5) automatically changes the graph, permitting us to see the effects of changing resource availabilities. Figure 8-21 shows the effect of putting 80 available labor hours into B5.

Additional Formatting

Three formatting features are not discussed in Chapter 2: the arrows indicating feasible directions, the arrow showing objective function movement, and the shading denoting the feasible area. To draw the first type of arrows, click on the arrow icon on the drawing tool bar (▧). (If the tool bar is not showing, click on View, Toolbars, and then select Drawing.) This changes the cursor to a cross. An arrow is inserted by depressing the left mouse button, dragging the mouse where the arrow is to be inserted, and lifting up on the mouse button.

FIGURE 8-20

Graph of the Redwood
Furniture Company
problem for $P = 96$

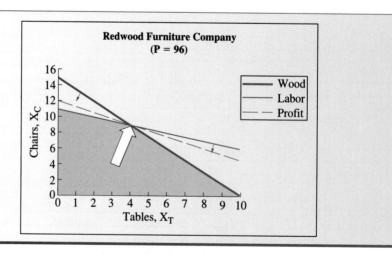

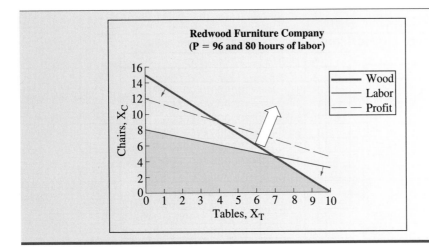

FIGURE 8-21

Graph of the Redwood Furniture Company problem with $P = 96$ and 80 hours of labor

Clicking on the AutoShapes icon (AutoShapes) and selecting Block Arrows draws the objective function arrow. Use the rotate icon (⟳) to change the arrow's direction.

Shading is done by first outlining the shaded area using the freeform polygon option (⬠) from Lines under AutoShapes. After clicking on the freeform polygon icon, click the left mouse button. (Make sure you just click; do not hold the button down.) Move the mouse to a corner point of the area to be shaded, click once, and move to another corner point and click once again. Continue the process until you return to the original starting point, where you double click to finish. To shade the area just outlined, make sure it is highlighted, click on the down arrow on the Fill Color icon (◈), select Fill Effects, and then choose the Pattern tab to find all the different types of shading available. To eliminate the line around the shading, highlight the filled area, right click, select Format AutoShapes on the drop-down menu, and choose the Colors and Lines tab. In the Line section of the resulting dialog box, click on the down arrow in the Color line to display the options, and select No Line.

Drawing Horizontal and Vertical Lines

Drawing horizontal and vertical lines with Excel requires special attention. For example, on a standard X-Y layout, the equation $Y = 3$ would plot as a horizontal line and $X = 7$ would be a vertical line. Figure 8-22 shows an Excel spreadsheet for these two equations. Excel's Chart Wizard can be used with this data to graph the lines.

Column A contains values along the horizontal X axis. Columns B and C give the values of the horizontal line $Y = 3$ and the vertical line $X = 7$ for each of the values on the X axis. The formulas in column C are determined from the general equation for a line

$$Y = a + bX$$

where b represents the slope and a is the Y-intercept. A vertical line can be approximated by an ordinary line with a very large Y-intercept a and a very large negative slope b. In our illustration, $a = 100,000$ and $b = -100,000/c$. These two values give a line appearing vertical on an Excel chart. (Imagine the line as a taut string dangling from

	A	B	C	D	E	F	G	H
1			**Graphing Horizontal and Vertical Lines**					
2					A	B	C	
3	X	Y = 3	X = 7	3	X	Y = 3	X = 7	
4	0	3	100000	4	0	3	=100000-(100000/7)*A4	
5	1	3	85714	5	1	3	=100000-(100000/7)*A5	
6	2	3	71429	6	2	3	=100000-(100000/7)*A6	
7	3	3	57143	7	3	3	=100000-(100000/7)*A7	
8	4	3	42857	8	4	3	=100000-(100000/7)*A8	
9	5	3	28571	9	5	3	=100000-(100000/7)*A9	
10	6	3	14286	10	6	3	=100000-(100000/7)*A10	
11	7	3	0	11	7	3	0	
12	8	3	-14286	12	8	3	=100000-(100000/7)*A12	
13	9	3	-28571	13	9	3	=100000-(100000/7)*A13	
14	10	3	-42857	14	10	3	=100000-(100000/7)*A14	
15								

FIGURE 8-22   Excel spreadsheet for horizontal and vertical lines

high up on a skyscraper and hitting the ground inches from the building's edge. We are graphing only the bottom 10 inches or so.) Using $c = 7$, we have the equation

$$Y = 100,000 - (100,000/7)X$$

The formulas in cells C4:C14 in Figure 8-22 come from this equation. Adapting the steps shown earlier, Excel's Chart Wizard provides the horizontal and vertical lines shown in Figure 8-23.

Make sure the vertical axis scale is adjusted so it appears as in the figure. To do this, select the axis by clicking on it and then right click to get a drop-down menu. Click on the Format Axis option, select the Scale tab, and enter 0 for the minimum, 10 for the maximum, 2 for the major unit, and 1 for the minor unit.

FIGURE 8-23
Plotting horizontal and
vertical lines with Excel

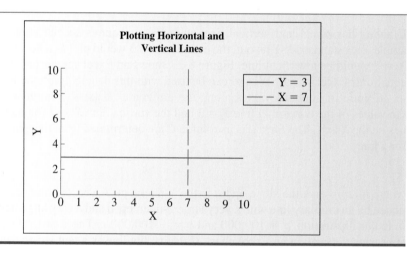

PROBLEMS

8-1 Labeling the horizontal axis X_1 and the vertical axis X_2, plot these lines on a graph.

(a) $X_1 + X_2 = 5$ (d) $X_1 = 12$
(b) $2X_1 + 3X_2 = 18$ (e) $X_2 = 9$
(c) $-3X_1 + 6X_2 = 24$ (f) $X_1 - 2X_2 = 0$

8-2 Solve each equation pair simultaneously.

(a) $X_1 + X_2 = 10$ (c) $8X_1 + 7X_2 = 10$
$X_1 - X_2 = 5$ $4X_1 + 5X_2 = 8$

(b) $2X_1 + 3X_2 = 6$ (d) $4X_1 + 4X_2 = 12$
$X_2 = 1$ $5X_1 + 3X_2 = 6$

8-3 Use the graphical procedure to determine the optimal solution to this linear program.

Maximize $P = 5X_A + 6X_B$
Subject to $3X_A + 2X_B \leq 12$ (labor)
$2X_A + 3X_B \leq 12$ (materials)
where $X_A, X_B \geq 0$

8-4 Use the graphical procedure to determine the optimal solution to this linear program.

Minimize $C = .5X_A + .3X_B$
Subject to $X_A + 2X_B \geq 10$ (protein)
$X_A + X_B \geq 8$ (fiber)
where $X_A, X_B \geq 0$

8-5 Solve this linear program graphically.

Maximize $P = 4X_1 + 7X_2$
Subject to $X_1 + X_2 \leq 5$ (labor)
$2X_1 + 3X_2 \leq 12$ (machine time)
$X_1 \leq 4$ (finishing time)
$X_2 \leq 3$ (assembly time)
where $X_1, X_2 \geq 0$

8-6 Use the graphical procedure to determine the optimal solution to this linear program.

Maximize $P = 2X_1 - 3X_2$
Subject to $4X_1 + 5X_2 \leq 40$ (resource A)
$2X_1 + 6X_2 \leq 24$ (resource B)
$3X_1 - 3X_2 \geq 6$ (mixture)
$X_1 \geq 4$ (demand)
where $X_1, X_2 \geq 0$

8-7 Solve this linear program graphically.

Minimize $C = 3X_1 - 2X_2$
Subject to $5X_1 + 5X_2 \geq 25$ (restriction A)
$2X_1 \leq 20$ (resource B)
$X_2 \leq 3$ (resource C)
$3X_1 + 9X_2 \leq 36$ (resource D)
where $X_1, X_2 \geq 0$

8-8 Consider this linear program.

Maximize $P = 2X_1 + 4X_2$
Subject to $4X_1 + 8X_2 \leq 48$ (resource)
$8X_1 + 4X_2 \geq 48$ (requirement)
$X_2 \leq 5$ (limitation)
where $X_1, X_2 \geq 0$

(a) Plot the constraint lines on a graph. Then, determine the feasible solution region and plot two profit lines. Indicate the direction of increasing profit.
(b) How many attractive corners are there? Find the optimal solution that corresponds to each corner you find.
(c) Plot point ($X_1 = 8$, $X_2 = 2$) on your graph. What profit level corresponds to this point? What can you conclude about this point?

8-9 Consider this problem.

Maximize $P = 2X_1$
Subject to $X_1 + X_2 \leq 5$ (resource)
$X_2 \geq 6$ (demand)
where $X_1, X_2 \geq 0$

Attempt to solve it graphically and briefly state any difficulties you encounter.

8-10 Consider this linear program.

Maximize $P = 10X_1 + 15X_2$
Subject to $5X_1 + 6X_2 \geq 30$ (mixture)
$-7X_1 + 6X_2 \leq 42$ (resource)
$X_2 \leq 10$ (limitation)
where $X_1, X_2 \geq 0$

(a) Attempt to solve this problem using the graphical procedure.

(b) Do you notice anything unusual? Explain.

(c) The following constraint was missing.

$$X_1 \leq 10 \quad \text{(quantity)}$$

Find the optimal solution to the corrected problem.

8-11 Consider this linear program.

Minimize $C = 3X_A + 1X_B$

Subject to
$$X_A + \quad X_B \geq 2 \quad \text{(mixture)}$$
$$X_A + 2X_B \leq 5 \quad \text{(resource)}$$
$$X_B \geq 3 \quad \text{(quantity)}$$

where
$$X_A, X_B \geq 0$$

(a) Attempt to solve this problem using the graphical procedure.

(b) Do you notice anything unusual? Explain.

(c) The right-hand side of the "quantity" constraint should have been 1. Find the optimal solution to the corrected problem.

8-12 Ace Widgets makes two models of its ubiquitous product—regular and deluxe. Both models are assembled from an identical frame. The regular model differs from the deluxe model only in terms of the finish work, which takes 5 hours of labor on the regular version and 8 hours on the deluxe model. In planning the current month's production, Ace's foreman finds that only 12 frames and 80 hours of finishing labor are available. The supply of all other required materials and labor is unlimited. Any number of widgets can be sold at a profit: $10 per regular widget, and $15 per deluxe widget. The foreman wants to produce quantities of the two models that will maximize company profits.

(a) Formulate the foreman's problem as a linear program.

(b) Solve the linear program graphically.

8-13 Refer to the Ace Widgets decision in Problem 8-12 and your answers to that exercise. The circumstances are now modified to reflect an order for three new deluxe widgets, so that production must now include at least three units of that product. Furthermore, a plant remodeling has reduced the work area such that at most nine regular widgets can be made.

(a) Formulate the revised linear program.

(b) Suppose that a special promotion with deluxe widgets reduces the unit profit of production

from $15 to $8. Express the new objective function. Then solve the problem graphically to find the optimal solution.

(c) The promotion in (b) is switched to regular widgets instead, reducing the unit profit for that product from $10 to $5. Express the new objective function. Then, using a new graph, solve the problem to find the optimal solution.

(d) Identify on your graph the most attractive corners from the original problem and those found in (b) and (c). What may you conclude regarding the most attractive corner and the changes in unit profit?

8-14 The marketing manager of Hops Brewery must determine how many television spots and magazine ads to purchase within an advertising budget of $100,000. Each spot is expected to increase sales by 30,000 cans, whereas each magazine ad will account for 100,000 cans in sales. Hops's gross profit on sales is $.10 per can. One television spot costs $2,000; each magazine ad requires an expenditure of $5,000. To have a balanced marketing program, the advertising budget must involve no more than $70,000 in magazine ads and no more than $50,000 in television spots.

(a) Determine the net increase in beer profits for each television spot and magazine ad (that reflects their respective costs).

(b) Assuming that Hops's management wants to maximize the net increase in beer profits, formulate the marketing manager's decision as a linear program.

(c) Solve the linear program graphically.

8-15 Mildred's Tool and Die shop must provide exactly 10 experimental bits to a pneumatic drill company. The bits can be shaped either by forging or by machining. Both procedures involve a final milling stage, but the forged bits require more milling because they are not as smooth initially. In either case, only one bit can be shaped at a time using either process, and the order must be filled within two working days. The table on page 297 summarizes the restrictions.

(a) Assuming that the proprietor, Ms. Mildred Riveter, wants to maximize profits, formulate a linear program specifying the number of bits that should be shaped using each process.

(b) Solve this problem graphically.

	Hours Per Item		Total Hours Available
Process	**Forged**	**Machined**	
Forging	3	—	15
Machining	—	2	16
Milling	2	4/3	16
Unit profit	$12	$9	

8-16 Net Electronics Inc. (NEI) sells 56K voice and 56K voice/fax modems. The profit from the first is $40, and the company estimates that at least 100,000 can be sold during the next year. The voice/fax modem yields a profit of $60, but no more than 90,000 can be sold. Each day, NEI can make either 1,000 voice modems or 500 voice/fax modems, but not both.

(a) Use a linear program to help NEI's management determine the number of days to schedule for production of voice and voice/fax modems during the coming year. Assume 200 working days per year.

(b) The voice modem sales estimate in part (a) should have been *no more than* 100,000 because this is the company's voice modem production capacity. How does this change the answer in part (a)?

8-17 Bill Bates is going to invest $1,000,000. He is considering two sectors in which to invest: hi-tech and conservative. Hi-tech includes high-technology stocks in the Internet, computer, and software areas. Conservative involves more defensive stocks mixed with some bonds. Bill thinks hi-tech investments have the highest return but also the highest risk. Over the next year, he estimates the annual return to be 30% on hi-tech investments and 5% for the conservative sector. Develop a linear program to assist Bill Bates with a decision for each of the following three cases. Assume all $1,000,000 is invested in the two sectors.

(a) To keep risk low, he wishes to invest at least half of his money in the conservative sector. However, he knows that if everything is invested in the conservative sector, his portfolio might not keep up with inflation, so he decides to have at least 25% in the hi-tech sector.

(b) Bill Bates decides that the best mix of hi-tech and conservative sectors is to have two dollars invested in conservative stocks for each dollar in hi-tech, along with a minimum of $100,000 in each sector.

(c) Suppose that the mix in part (b) is to have *at least* two dollars invested in conservative stocks for each dollar in hi-tech. How does part (b)'s answer change? Explain why.

8-18 WebFood.com is a new company that allows customers to do grocery shopping over the Internet. It carries products that need three different types of care. Fresh items, such as fruit, require special handling so they always look fresh and do not spoil. Frozen items need cool or frozen storage so that they do not warm up. All the other items, including canned goods, paper products, and kitchenware, require minimal special attention and are just stocked on shelves. The warehouse for storing these items has 100,000 square feet of storage space. The Marketing Department thinks that no more than 60,000 square feet should be devoted to fresh goods, 45,000 to frozen goods, and 70,000 to all the other items. The accounting department estimates that the storage cost is $5 per square foot for fresh items, $10 per square foot for frozen items, and $1 per square foot for all other items. Company policy limits the storage cost to $1,000,000. Frozen goods have the highest profit margin at $30 per square foot, followed by fresh items at $20 per square foot, and $10 per square foot from the other items. Develop a linear program to determine the floorspace that should be devoted to each of the three item groups so that total profit margin is maximized.

8-19 The computer lab at State College is open from 8 A.M. to midnight every day of the week. To start developing a schedule for the coming quarter, the managers of the lab estimate that four assistants will be needed in the morning from 8 A.M. to noon, eight from noon to 4 P.M., five from 4 P.M. to 8 P.M., and only three from 8 P.M. to midnight. Because lab assistants work 8-hour shifts, they start at 8 A.M., noon, or 4 P.M. Develop a linear program to help the lab managers find the minimum number of assistants that need to be hired and their schedules. Hint: Let X_j, $j = 8, 12, 4$, represent the number of assistants hired at 8:00 A.M., noon, and 4:00 P.M.

8-20 Hard Drives Inc. manufactures computer hard drives. Because demand has seasonal variations it is difficult to schedule production to keep costs to a minimum. Next year, management estimates that the demand for a 10-GB hard drive will be 50,000 units in the first quarter followed by

100,000, 50,000, and 200,000 in the second, third, and fourth quarters. Because the company's production capacity is 125,000 units per quarter, during the slow seasons the company must produce extra hard drives and store them in inventory to help meet demand during the high seasons, particularly during the fourth quarter because Christmas sales makes this the highest sales quarter of the year. The production cost of a hard drive is $25 per unit and company policy is to charge an inventory holding cost of $1 per hard drive per quarter for each unit in inventory at the beginning of a quarter. Assume that the company starts off the first quarter with 10,000 units in inventory and wishes to end the last quarter with 20,000 in inventory. Formulate a linear program to determine how many hard drives should be produced in each quarter in order to minimize total cost. Hint: Let H_j and I_j represent the number of hard drives produced and ending inventory for each quarter, $j = 1, 2, 3, 4$, and note that $I_4 = 20,000$.

8-21 Toby Tucker is on a very strict diet and is allowed a bonus on Saturday night if he remains on his diet throughout the week. The bonus must contain no more than 200 mg sodium (Na) and no more than 60 g carbohydrate (CHO). Toby wants to consume as many calories as he can within these constraints. He has selected apple pie a la mode, for which the following data apply.
(a) Formulate Toby's decision as a linear program and then solve it graphically.
(b) How much pie and ice cream will Toby eat?

Dessert	Calories	Na	CHO
Piece of pie	100	120	15
Scoop of ice cream	140	40	15

Spreadsheet Problems

8-22 Graph the linear program in Problem 8-3 using a spreadsheet. Use $P = 30$ for the value of the objective function.

8-23 Graph the linear program in Problem 8-4 using a spreadsheet. Use $C = 3$ for the value of the objective function.

8-24 Graph the linear program in Problem 8-5 using a spreadsheet. Use $P = 14$ for the value of the objective function.

8-25 Graph the linear program in Problem 8-6 using a spreadsheet. Use $P = 15$ for the value of the objective function.

8-26 Repeat Problem 8-25 using 15, 17, 19, 20, 21, 23, and 25 for the value of P. How does the objective function line move as P changes?

8-27 Repeat Problem 8-25 using 36, 40, 44, 48, and 52 as the right-hand side of the first constraint (resource A). How does the optimal solution vary as the right-hand side changes?

CASE 8-1   Cee's Candy Company

Cee's Candy Company mixes its Rainbow Box from two basic confections — chocolates and pastels. To meet its packaging requirements and to reflect changing ingredient costs, the company runs a linear program periodically to determine the number of pounds of each type of candy to put into the mix. The costs and requirements for a one-pound box are provided on the right.

Item	Proportion of Candy Weight		Minimum Mix Requirement
	Chocolates	Pastels	
Nuts	.15	.05	.10 lb
Soft centers	.50	1.00	.60
Hard centers	.50	0.00	.20
Cost per pound	$4.00	$1.00	

For example, in each pound of chocolate candy, 15% of the contents consist of nuts, 50% of the pieces have soft centers, and 50% have hard centers. These percentages do not add to 100% because nuts are included in some candies of both types (hard and soft centers). The total weight restriction guarantees that boxes contain at least 1 pound of candy.

A batch of chocolate-coated candies is to be made using the same cream base. The chef wants to determine how many pounds to make of the creamy fudge and Burgundy cherry. Each pound of these candies requires the following amounts of ingredients:

Item	Flavor		Amount Available
	Creamy Fudge	Burgundy Cherry	
Pecans	.5 oz	.3 oz	500 oz
Chocolate	2.0 oz	2.0 oz	3,000 oz
Vanilla	3 ml	1 ml	2,400 ml
Cherries	0	24	28,000

All other ingredients are in plentiful supply. Each pound of Burgundy cherry contributes $1.00 to overhead and profit, while the creamy fudge brings $2.00. The total weight of the cherry candy must be at least half that of the fudge.

QUESTIONS

1. Consider the problem of deciding how much of each candy type to put into a Rainbow Box.
    (a) Formulate Cee's linear program and then solve it graphically to determine the optimal weights of chocolates and pastels to put in a Rainbow Box. Assume that each box must contain exactly 1 pound.
    (b) Suppose that the total weight restriction is relaxed, so that *at least* 1 pound of candy must be included in each box. Find the new most attractive corner and the optimal solution.

2. Formulate Cee's second linear program regarding the amount of the two candy types to make. Determine the optimal number of pounds to make of the two types. (Do not bother converting units of measurement.)

CHAPTER 9

LINEAR PROGRAMMING APPLICATIONS AND COMPUTER SOLUTIONS

Before Gauss [in 1820], solving one linear equation in one unknown was a tough problem. . . .
In 1947 the solution of a nine constraint [and 27 variable] . . . problem . . . took 120 person-days
of work with electromechanical desk calculators to solve. . . . In 1950 . . . it was reasonable to
solve problems [on computers] with up to 200 constraints. By 1960 it was reasonable to solve
problems with up to about 1,000 constraints. In 1970 it was reasonable to solve problems with
up to about 10,000 constraints. In 1980 . . . it was ok to go up to about 100,000 constraints.
And in 1990 . . . one can deal reasonably with problems of up to a million constraints.

Alex Orden

Linear programming is perhaps the most successful quantitative method, as evidenced by its widespread use at virtually all levels of business and in every major industry. It is well accepted and is used in most functional areas—particularly finance, management, marketing, and production. Linear programming has an excellent track record for achieving operational efficiencies and cost savings. In this chapter, we will examine a variety of resource allocation situations and show how they can be solved with linear programming. The solution procedures rely on special-purpose software such as *QuickQuant* 2000 and spreadsheet programs such as Excel. Both packages use the same underlying algorithm, which will be briefly explained.

Allocating limited resources to meet specified objectives always has been important to individuals and organizations wanting to do the best. Before linear programming, such problems were solved by evaluating possible allocations and ranking each in terms of benefit or profitability. With just a few simple options, it was easy to pick the one having the best resource allocation. But complex modern problems can have so many alternatives that the fastest computers would require billions of years to evaluate all possible alternatives.

In the late 1940s, George Dantzig discovered a much simpler way to solve many resource allocation problems by taking shortcuts to quickly home in on the best alternative. He gave us the name **linear programming** and called his solution procedure the **simplex method.**

Determining Production Quantities

Swatville Sluggers is a small manufacturer of custom baseball bats. The obscure company is unfamiliar to the general public because it sells exclusively to professional baseball teams, mainly minor league clubs. Swatville sells its entire production at pre-negotiated prices, and the availability of essential resources—especially wood—dictates the final quantities in each monthly production run.

Sluggers are handmade from high-quality 3-by-3-inch blocks of hardwood. They come in six models, depending on length. The owner, George Herman "Sultan" Swat, wants to set the quantities for March production. The following data apply for that month.

| | LENGTH (inches) | | | | | | AVAILABLE |
RESOURCE	30	32	34	36	38	40	QUANTITY
Lathe time	10	10	11	11	12	12	5,000 min
Finishing time	25	27	29	31	33	35	8,000 min
Boxes	1	1	1	1	1	1	500
Stain	2	2	2	3	3	3	1,000 oz
Varnish	5	5	6	6	7	7	2,000 oz

In addition, after allowing for scrap, only 10,000 inches of wood blocks are on hand. Numerous other materials are needed, and further functions must be performed in making the bats, but the quantities are so ample and capacities so high that they place no practical limitations on production.

Further restrictions are (1) the number of 34-inch bats cannot exceed the combined total of 30-inch and 32-inch models; (2) the number of 38-inch bats cannot exceed the combined total of the 32-inch and 34-inch varieties; and (3) the number of 30-inch bats must be less than or equal to the total number of 36-inch and 38-inch lengths.

The following costs apply:

Wood cost per inch	$.08
Lathe cost per minute	.05
Finishing cost per minute	.02
Box cost	.50
Stain cost per ounce	.30
Varnish cost per ounce	.25

The selling prices are $21 for 30-inch and 32-inch bats, $22 for the 34-inch and 36-inch versions, and $25 for the 38-inch and 40-inch lengths. Other direct costs are $2 per bat, regardless of model.

In previous months, production quantities have been established by trial and error. Swat's nephew, Babe, has just completed a course in linear programming. He will use it to help his uncle maximize profit.

At the end of the chapter, Swat's decision will be evaluated using linear programming.

9-1 LINEAR PROGRAMMING IN MANUFACTURING: PRODUCT-MIX SELECTION

Production planning is an extensive area of linear programming application. A detailed schedule of which items to make and what quantities of each item to produce falls into the broad category of **product-mix selection.** Such a detailed listing is one type of production plan that linear programming can generate in such a way that the most profitable mix is found for a given set of constraints. This can be done to ensure that the customer demand for each product is met. All resources used in manufacturing—raw materials, labor, supplies, and facilities—can be explicitly accounted for to ensure that limitations are satisfied by a feasible production plan that employs these resources most efficiently. Special interrelationships between two or more products—for example, the requirement that at least four chairs must be manufactured for each table—may also be reflected as constraints in the linear program.

Microcircuit Production Plan

The plant superintendent for a custom microcircuit manufacturer must decide how many modules to assemble in each of five different sizes. The following variables are defined:

$$X_E = \text{Number of extra-large modules to assemble}$$
$$X_L = \text{Number of large modules to assemble}$$
$$X_R = \text{Number of regular modules to assemble}$$
$$X_S = \text{Number of small modules to assemble}$$
$$X_M = \text{Number of miniature modules to assemble}$$

Each module is mounted on a printed circuit board, which has been cut to size from available stock of large sheets. All modules contain varying quantities of two component chips, type A and type B, supplies of which are limited. There is also a limited number of assembly time hours.

All other needed materials (such as solder and photographic etching chemicals), additional components (such as connectors), and other categories of labor (such as that for etching, coating, and finishing) are in plentiful supply.

The Objective Function

However, everything must be reflected in the *objective* by incorporating *costs* of all labor, freight, and component materials. By subtracting a per-unit total of all direct charges from unit revenue, the unit *profit* of each final product is determined. These unit profits have been determined for each module, and the following objective function applies:

$$\text{Maximize} \quad P = 58X_E + 43X_L + 25X_R + 17X_S + 28X_M$$

Resource Availability Constraints

A 25-square-inch printed circuit board is needed for the extra-large modules. The areas are 15, 10, 5, and 1 square inches for the large, regular, small, and miniature modules, respectively. Altogether, there are 50,000 square inches of available material. The following constraint applies:

$$25X_E + 15X_L + 10X_R + 5X_S + 1X_M \leq 50{,}000 \quad \text{(PC board availability)}$$

The following numbers of component chips are needed in the various module units:

MODULE	TYPE A	TYPE B
Extra-large	28	52
Large	24	48
Regular	18	40
Small	12	60
Miniature	5	75

There are 10,000 type A chips and 25,000 type B chips available. The following availability constraints apply:

$$28X_E + 24X_L + 18X_R + 12X_S + 5X_M \leq 10{,}000 \quad \text{(A availability)}$$
$$52X_E + 48X_L + 40X_R + 60X_S + 75X_M \leq 25{,}000 \quad \text{(B availability)}$$

The assembly times are 1.50, 1.25, 1.00, .75, and 1.50 hours for the extra-large, large, regular, small, and miniature modules, respectively. There are 2,000 hours available in the present production cycle. The following constraint applies:

$$1.50X_E + 1.25X_L + 1.00X_R + .75X_S + 1.50X_M \leq 2{,}000 \quad \text{(assembly time)}$$

Linear program constraints are needed only for those limited resources that might be potential bottlenecks. Not all production factors need to be reflected in the linear program's *constraints.*

Minimum Quantity Constraints

There are orders on hand for 200 regular modules and for 100 small modules. These minimum quantities must be produced. The following two constraints apply:

$$X_R \geq 200 \quad \text{(regular quantity)}$$
$$X_S \geq 100 \quad \text{(small quantity)}$$

$2(x_c + x_f) \leq x_B$

$x_B \geq 2(x_c + x_f)$

Mixture Constraints

The large and extra-large modules are usually ordered in groups, with, on the average, at least 2 large modules ordered for every extra-large one. Wanting to keep enough large units on hand, the superintendent obtains the following constraint:

$$\text{Form (1)} \quad 2X_E \leq X_L \quad \text{(oversized mixture)}$$

The preceding formula says that the number of large modules must be at least two times the number of extra-large. (The coefficient 2 goes with X_E, not with X_L, which must be the greater quantity.)

The preceding statement is mathematically equivalent to the following:

$$\text{Form (2)} \quad X_L \geq 2X_E \quad \text{(oversized mixture)}$$

which reverses the direction of the inequality and lists the variables in reverse sequence. Other mathematically equivalent forms could be used.

$$X_E \le .5X_L \quad \text{and} \quad .5X_L \ge X_E$$

(These are found from (1) and (2) by dividing both sides of each inequality by 2.)

A similar constraint applies to the miniature modules. These cannot exceed half the combined total of all other module types.

$$(1) \qquad X_M \le .50(X_E + X_L + X_R + X_S) \qquad \text{(miniature mixture)}$$

This can be rewritten in the following form:

$$(2) \qquad .50(X_E + X_L + X_R + X_S) \ge X_M \qquad \text{(miniature mixture)}$$

Nonnegativity Conditions

Mathematically, the linear program is incomplete without stating the nonnegativity conditions. These are essential. This statement is achieved by the following,

$$\text{where} \quad X_E, X_L, X_R, X_S, X_M \ge 0$$

When there are many variables in a linear program, a statement to the effect that "all variables are nonnegative" is sufficient.

The Complete Linear Program

The following complete linear program has been formulated.

Letting X_E, X_L, X_R, X_S, and X_M denote the respective number of extra-large, large, regular, small, and miniature modules to assemble, the objective is to

Maximize	$P = 58X_E +\ \ 43X_L +\ \ 25X_R +\ 17X_S +\ \ 28X_M$			
Subject to	$25X_E +\ \ 15X_L +\ \ 10X_R +\ \ 5X_S +\ \ \ 1X_M \le 50,000$		(PC board)	
	$28X_E +\ \ 24X_L +\ \ 18X_R +\ 12X_S +\ \ \ 5X_M \le 10,000$		(A availability)	
	$52X_E +\ \ 48X_L +\ \ 40X_R +\ 60X_S +\ \ 75X_M \le 25,000$		(B availability)	
	$1.50X_E + 1.25X_L + 1.00X_R + .75X_S + 1.50X_M \le\ \ 2,000$		(assembly time)	
	$X_R \ge\ \ \ \ 200$		(regular quantity)	
	$X_S \ge\ \ \ \ 100$		(small quantity)	
	$2X_E \le X_L$		(oversized mixture)	
	$X_M \le .50(X_E + X_L + X_R + X_S)$		(miniature mixture)	
where	$X_E, X_L, X_R, X_S, X_M \ge 0$			

9-2   FORMULATING CONSTRAINTS AND THE STANDARDIZED FORMAT

Any of the constraint forms in the previous problem mathematically expresses the correct requirement. The hardest part is getting the "first draft" for the constraint, which may then be rearranged later.

STEPS IN ARRIVING AT A CORRECT MATHEMATICAL CONSTRAINT

The following optional steps may be used in mathematically expressing a constraint.

1. **Identify the constraint from the problem description.** For example, consider again the first mixture constraint for the oversized modules (page 303). The passage in the description that provides this constraint is

   "...at least 2 large modules ordered for every extra-large one."

2. **Paraphrase the original descriptive wording in a form suitable for introducing symbols.** One such rewording would be

   "The number of large modules must be at least (greater than or equal to) twice (two times) the number of extra-large modules."

   The parenthetical portions more precisely express in mathematical terms the preceding verbal concept.

3. **Position the variables, fitting them into the reworded phrase.** This step provides that

   $$X_L \text{ must be greater than or equal to } 2X_E$$

   This makes it easy to accomplish the fourth step.

4. **Substitute mathematical symbols.** Doing this, we achieve the constraint

   $$X_L \geq 2X_E \quad \text{or} \quad 2X_E \leq X_L$$

Of course, it is not necessary to slavishly go through all of these steps, many of which may be skipped entirely for most constraints. But it is important to realize that formulating linear programs is basically an exercise in translating English into the language of mathematics. Like mastery of any new language, skill in doing this comes with practice.

Although not required by the mathematics of linear programming, it is desirable to identify each constraint by a short parenthetical description, as done in this example. These descriptions will prove helpful when introducing auxiliary variables during the solution. (The procedures for doing this are described in Section 9-3.)

THE STANDARDIZED FORMAT

Eventually it will be necessary to rearrange the constraints in **standardized format**. Such refinements are needed in preparing input data for computer solution or in setting up a linear program for solution using the simplex method (described in Section 9-11). The basic requirements of this arrangement are listed here.

1. **All variables should be listed in a single row on the left-hand side of the expression.** Thus, the first version of the oversized module quantity constraint is expressed as

   $$2X_E - X_L \leq 0$$

   and the second version has the standardized format

$$-2X_E + X_L \geq 0$$

The preceding constraints must still be fixed in accordance with requirements 3 and 4 below.

2. The sequence of the variables should be in the same order as that used in defining the original list of variables. As the preceding statements show, X_E is positioned before X_L, because that was the order in which they were listed originally.

3. Each variable receives its own numerical coefficient. Thus, the first form of the miniature module mixture constraint, originally given as

$$X_M \leq .50(X_E + X_L + X_R + X_S)$$

would end up with all terms collected on the left and the .50 appearing as the coefficient for each individual X that was inside the original parentheses.

$$-.50X_E - .50X_L - .50X_R - .50X_S + 1X_M \leq 0$$

The first four variables are collected on the left-hand side and appear in the original list sequence, each with coefficient $-.50$. A 1 now appears as the coefficient for X_M.

Notice that the right-hand side is now equal to 0. The direction of any inequality constraint with a 0 on the right-hand side may be reversed by changing the signs of all variable coefficients. As we shall see, it is advantageous to express such constraints in the ≤ 0 form rather than as ≥ 0.

4. A zero coefficient appears in front of those variables not represented in the constraint. Thus, the first version of the oversized module mixture constraint would appear as

$$2X_E - 1X_L + 0X_R + 0X_S + 0X_M \leq 0$$

And, the quantity constraint for regular modules would appear as

$$0X_E + 0X_L + 1X_R + 0X_S + 0X_M \geq 200$$

This last step preserves a space for each variable in every constraint. This becomes useful when constraints are algebraically manipulated in the process of solving them.

The following is the complete standardized format formulation of the linear program in Section 9-1.

Letting X_E, X_L, X_R, X_S, and X_M denote the respective number of extra-large, large, regular, small, and miniature modules to assemble, the objective is to

Maximize $P = 58X_E + 43X_L + 25X_R + 17X_S + 28X_M$

Subject to

$$25X_E + 15X_L + 10X_R + 5X_S + 1X_M \leq 50{,}000 \quad \text{(PC board)}$$
$$28X_E + 24X_L + 18X_R + 12X_S + 5X_M \leq 10{,}000 \quad \text{(A availability)}$$
$$52X_E + 48X_L + 40X_R + 60X_S + 75X_M \leq 25{,}000 \quad \text{(B availability)}$$
$$1.50X_E + 1.25X_L + 1.00X_R + .75X_S + 1.50X_M \leq 2{,}000 \quad \text{(assembly time)}$$
$$0X_E + 0X_L + 1X_R + 0X_S + 0X_M \geq 200 \quad \text{(regular quantity)}$$
$$0X_E + 0X_L + 0X_R + 1X_S + 0X_M \geq 100 \quad \text{(small quantity)}$$
$$2X_E - 1X_L + 0X_R + 0X_S + 0X_M \leq 0 \quad \text{(oversized mixture)}$$
$$-.50X_E - .50X_L - .50X_R - .50X_S + 1X_M \leq 0 \quad \text{(miniature mixture)}$$

where

$$X_E, X_L, X_R, X_S, X_M \geq 0$$

9-3 SLACK AND SURPLUS VARIABLES

The preceding example involves constraints with *inequalities,* allowing one side to be greater or smaller than the other. The traditional procedure for solving large linear programs is the *simplex method* (described in optional Section 9-11). Rather than rely on graphs, that procedure solves a series of algebra problems and requires that each constraint be expressed in *equation* form. Constraints are transformed from inequalities to equations through the incorporation of auxiliary variables. There are two types of these variables, which we will illustrate using the foregoing microcircuit example.

The first auxiliary variable type acknowledges the existence of *slack* to represent unused resources. The **slack variable** for the PC board constraint is defined as

$$S_P = \text{quantity of unused PC boards}$$

The letter S is traditionally used for this type of auxiliary variable. (The original problem variables X_E, X_L, X_R, X_S, and X_M are sometimes called *main variables* to distinguish them from the slacks.)

The original constraint says that the quantity of PC boards used must be less than or equal to the total available (50,000). That requirement may be equivalently expressed as

$$\text{PC boards used} + \text{unused PC boards} = \text{available PC boards}$$

By adding the quantities of PC boards on the left side, this constraint tells us "what we use plus what we don't use must equal what we start with." The meaning of the constraint has not changed. Stated algebraically, our revised PC board constraint is

$$25X_E + 15X_L + 10X_R + 5X_S + 1X_M + S_P = 50{,}000 \qquad \text{(PC board)}$$

which is equivalent to the original expression. Adding the slack variable converts an inequality into an equality. The S_P term bridges the gap, taking up the slack between the less than ($<$) and the equal ($=$) signs.

In the same way, the other resource constraints may be converted using

$$S_A = \text{quantity of unused resource } A$$
$$S_B = \text{quantity of unused resource } B$$
$$S_T = \text{quantity of unused assembly time}$$

Each slack variable is unique to a specific constraint. All $\leq$ inequalities are assigned one by computer solution procedures.

The left-hand side of a constraint may be greater than the right-hand side, as in the regular quantity constraint

$$X_R \geq 200$$

It stipulates that the number of regular modules must be at least as great as the minimum of 200. That may be stated another way:

$$\text{regulars made} - \text{surplus regulars} = 200$$

The surplus quantity may be represented by another type of auxiliary variable, called the **surplus variable.** We denote this as

$$S_{RQ} = \text{surplus regular modules beyond the minimum required}$$

The equivalent constraint is

$$X_R - S_{RQ} = 200$$

Another surplus variable for the microcircuit problem is

$$S_{SQ} = \text{surplus small modules beyond the minimum required}$$

All constraints of form $\leq$ (with all main variables collected on the left-hand side) need a slack variable before the linear program (LP) can be solved algebraically. All constraints with a $\geq$ need a surplus variable. (Constraints originally in equation form need neither; some procedures will then employ an artificial variable, which is manipulated mathematically much like a slack variable.)

The microcircuit problem has two nonresource constraints that would be assigned slack variables:

$$S_{OM} = \text{slack variable for oversized mixture constraint}$$
$$S_{MM} = \text{slack variable for miniature mixture constraint}$$

Slack and surplus variables have economic connotations and must always be non-negative.

9-4 SOLVING PROBLEMS USING THE COMPUTER

So far we have seen how to use graphical procedures to solve linear programs. Unfortunately that approach will not work for the preceding problem because we cannot ordinarily graph linear programs that have more than two variables. Instead, we must use an algebraic procedure called the *simplex method*. Such problems are almost always solved with *computer assistance*.

Solving Linear Programs with *QuickQuant*

The *QuickQuant 2000* software package available to users of this book has a segment for solving linear programs. The program is *user friendly,* with screen-prompt questions guiding all necessary choices and inputs. The program allows you to go back and fix your selections before it continues into the next phase.

This approach is especially helpful in translating the linear programming expressions into computer input. *QuickQuant* does this by displaying on the screen the objective function and constraints with blank spaces for you to fill in. *QuickQuant* gives you the chance to make corrections to all or a portion of the completed expressions before proceeding to solve the linear program.

You will have the opportunity to save the problem input data on a disc in case you want to run it again. You may then modify the saved problem with minimal keyboard data entry. *QuickQuant* will let you change any constants and expressions to the current problem or one created earlier and saved on disc. You may also expand existing problems by incorporating additional variables or constraints.

To illustrate how *QuickQuant* works, we continue with the microcircuit production plan linear program introduced earlier in the chapter.

QuickQuant is launched by clicking on its icon (📁) or selecting it from the programs menu. That brings to screen the title box and *QuickQuant* menu bar. Linear programming is selected from Application, as shown below.

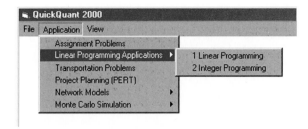

That activates the File menu. Once an application has been selected, problems saved earlier may be retrieved or new problems may be entered. A new linear program is created for *QuickQuant* starting with the following dialog box, into which basic problem information is supplied.

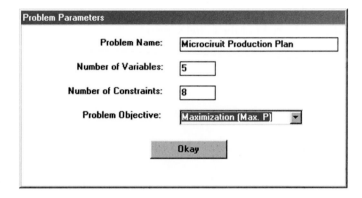

The next *QuickQuant* screen involves supplying problem names. The default names, X1, X2, . . ., may be replaced here.

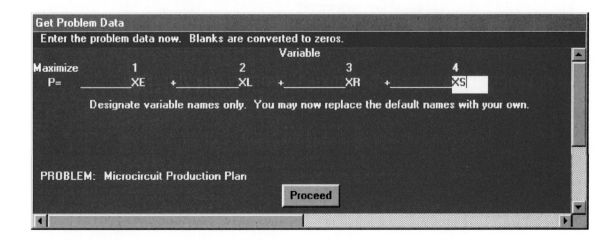

A similar screen appears next, into which the objective coefficients are entered.

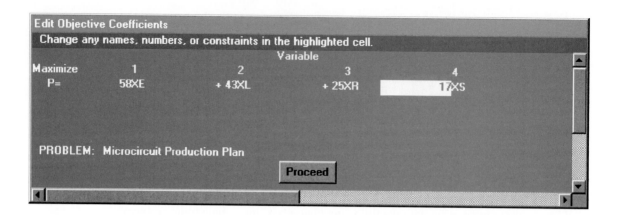

The next screen provides data entry for all the constraint information. The scroll bar at the bottom of the screen accesses portions not shown. (In this example, the fifth variable, XM, lies to the right of the initial screen.)

```
Enter Constraint Data
 Enter the problem data now.  Blanks are converted to zeros.
                                    Variable
Maximize        1               2               3               4
   P=          58XE          + 43XL          + 25XR          + 17XS      Enter <, =, or >
                                                                              ↓
Subject to:
   C1          25XE          + 15XL          + 10XR          + 5XS        <      50000
   C2          28XE          + 24XL            ▢▢XR        +_____XS   _+_____
   C3+_____XE    +_____XL    +_____XR    +_____XS   _+_____
   C4+_____XE    +_____XL    +_____XR    +_____XS   _+_____
   C5+_____XE    +_____XL    +_____XR    +_____XS   _+_____
   C6+_____XE    +_____XL    +_____XR    +_____XS   _+_____
   C7+_____XE    +_____XL    +_____XR    +_____XS   _+_____
   C8+_____XE    +_____XL    +_____XR    +_____XS   _+_____



PROBLEM:  Microcircuit Production Plan
                                    Proceed
```

The solution is next obtained after selecting from the Run menu. *QuickQuant* has two modes for solving linear programs. The Quick Solve choice skips the intermediate steps.

After a great deal of computation (conducted at such high speeds that time seems imperceptible), *QuickQuant* supplies the following report:

SOLUTION TO LINEAR PROGRAM

PROBLEM: Microcircuit Production Plan

Original Variable	Value	Slack/Surplus Variable	Value
XE	67.54032	S1	43771.89000
XL	135.08060	S2	0.00000
XR	200.00000	S3	0.00000
XS	100.00000	S4	1434.75800
XM	13.38710	S5	0.00000
		S6	0.00000
		S7	0.00000
		S8	237.92340

Objective Value: P = 16800.65

[Finished]   [Get Dual]

The optimal main (original) variable values are listed first, along with the corresponding objective value. The second listing gives values for the amount of slack or surplus on the left-hand sides of the respective constraints. The simplex method assigns a *slack variable* to each "≤" constraint and a *surplus variable* to each "≥" constraint. *Quick-Quant* automatically creates these variables. The solution states that there are 43,771.9 units of slack (S1) for the PC board material and 1,434.758 slack (S4) for the assembly time; these amounts represent the unused quantities of the two resources. The 0 solution values for S5 and S6 indicate that there is no surplus for the two "≥" quantity constraints; they are consumed completely by the solution.

Remember that linear programs allow for fractional solutions. If fractional results would not be permitted, the problem must be solved instead as an *integer program.* (Procedures for doing this are described in Chapter 11.)

Solving Linear Programs with a Spreadsheet

The three steps involved in solving linear programming problems with spreadsheets are: (1) write out the formulation table; (2) put the formulation table into a spreadsheet, and (3) use Excel's Solver to obtain a solution.

FIGURE 9-1

Formulation table for the microchip production plan LP

VARIABLES	X_E	X_L	X_R	X_S	X_M	SIGN	RHS
Objective	58	43	25	17	28	5	P(max)
PC Board	25	15	10	5	1	$\leq$	50,000
A availability	28	24	18	12	5	$\leq$	10,000
B availability	52	48	40	60	75	$\leq$	25,000
Assembly time	1.5	1.25	1	0.75	1.50	$\leq$	2,000
Regular quantity			1			$\geq$	200
Small quantity				1		$\geq$	100
Oversized mixture	2	−1				$\leq$	0
Miniature mixture	−0.5	−0.5	−0.5	−0.5	1	$\leq$	0

The Formulation Table   A formulation table arranges the problem in a tabular format, as shown in Figure 9-1 for the microchip production planning decision presented earlier. The first row lists the variables, which become column headings, followed by a sign column and an RHS (right-hand side) column. The second row lists the objective function, beginning with the respective coefficients, an equality sign designation, and an indication in the RHS column whether the problem is to maximize or minimize. Each constraint has its own row listing the variable coefficients, the sign ($\leq$, $\geq$, or $=$), and the RHS value. (The nonnegativity conditions are assumed to apply and do not need to be accounted for in the formulation table.)

The formulation table contains the essential features of the linear programming spreadsheet itself.

The Formulation Spreadsheet   Figure 9-2 shows the Excel formulation spreadsheet for microcircuit production. The left margin numbers (1, 2, 3, . . .) identify the rows and the top margin letters (A, B, C, . . .) identify the columns, allowing spreadsheet cells to be easily referenced. For example, cell H5 gives the number of PC boards available (50,000).

The formulation spreadsheet must be expanded to incorporate the calculations involved in solving linear programming problems. Figure 9-3 shows the expanded spreadsheet for solving the microchip production plan linear program. Two new rows have been added below the formulation portion. For ease of use, the listing of all the variables appears again in row 14. Row 15 lists in each cell the values of the respective variable.

	A	B	C	D	E	F	G	H
1				Microcircuit Production Plan				
2								
3	Variables	X_E	X_L	X_R	X_S	X_M	Sign	RHS
4	Objective	58	43	25	17	28	$=$	P(max)
5	PC Board	25	15	10	5	1	$\leq$	50000
6	A Availability	28	24	18	12	5	$\leq$	10000
7	B Availability	52	48	40	60	75	$\leq$	25000
8	Assembly Time	1.50	1.25	1.00	0.75	1.50	$\leq$	2000
9	Regular Quantity			1			$\geq$	200
10	Small Quantity				1		$\geq$	100
11	Oversized Mixture	2	-1				$\leq$	0
12	Miniature Mixture	-0.50	-0.50	-0.50	-0.50	1.00	$\leq$	0

FIGURE 9-2   Excel formulation spreadsheet for the microchip production plan LP

	A	B	C	D	E	F	G	H	I	J
1				**Microcircuit Production Plan**						
2										
3	Variables	X_E	X_L	X_R	X_S	X_M	Sign	RHS		
4	Objective	58	43	25	17	28	=	P(max)	Profit	8420
5	PC Board	25	15	10	5	1	≤	50000	PC Board	3060
6	A Availability	28	24	18	12	5	≤	10000	A Availability	5610
7	B Availability	52	48	40	60	75	≤	25000	B Availability	16230
8	Assembly Time	1.50	1.25	1.00	0.75	1.50	≤	2000	Assembly Time	330
9	Regular Quantity			1			≥	200	Regular Quantity	200
10	Small Quantity				1		≥	100	Small Quantity	100
11	Oversized Mixture	2	-1				≤	0	Oversized Mixture	0
12	Miniature Mixture	-0.50	-0.50	-0.50	-0.50	1.00	≤	0	Miniature Mixture	-155
13				Solution						
14		X_E	X_L	X_R	X_S	X_M			J	
15		10.00	20.00	200.00	100.00	10.00		4	=SUMPRODUCT(B4:F4,$B$15:$F$15)	
16								5	=SUMPRODUCT(B5:F5,$B$15:$F$15)	
17								6	=SUMPRODUCT(B6:F6,$B$15:$F$15)	
18								7	=SUMPRODUCT(B7:F7,$B$15:$F$15)	
19								8	=SUMPRODUCT(B8:F8,$B$15:$F$15)	
20								9	=SUMPRODUCT(B9:F9,$B$15:$F$15)	
21								10	=SUMPRODUCT(B10:F10,$B$15:$F$15)	
22								11	=SUMPRODUCT(B11:F11,$B$15:$F$15)	
								12	=SUMPRODUCT(B12:F12,$B$15:$F$15)	

FIGURE 9-3   Expanded Excel spreadsheet for solving the microchip production plan LP. A feasible (but not optimal) solution is shown.

Two new columns have been added to the expanded spreadsheet. Column I duplicates the labels from column A. Column J calculates the value of the objective function and the left-hand sides of each of the constraints. For resource constraint rows, the column J cells provide the total amount of resources used.

For any values of variables in cells B15:F15, cell J4 gives the value of the objective function. It is calculated by the formula

$$=SUMPRODUCT(B4:F4, \$B\$15:\$F\$15)$$

The dollar signs ($) make the cell references absolute so that when the cells are copied the solution values in cells B15:F15 are always used. Thus, we need only copy cell J4 into cell J5 to get the left-hand side for the PC board constraint. The formulas in the cells J6:J12 are also obtained by copying J4. (It is not necessary to retype them; see Chapter 2 for information about copying.) All of the formulas used to calculate numbers in Figure 9-3 are shown with corresponding cell references.

Figure 9-3 shows the results when $X_E = 10$, $X_L = 20$, $X_R = 200$, $X_S = 100$, and $X_M = 10$. In that spreadsheet, Column J shows 3,060 PC boards (cell J5), 5,610 A chips (cell J6), 16,230 B chips (cell J7), and 330 hours of assembly time (cell J8) are required. In addition, the regular and small quantity constraints are satisfied because cell J9 is 200 and cell J10 is 100, both the same as their minimum required values in cells H9:H10. In the same manner, cells J11 (0) and J12 (-155) are not greater than their maximum possible values in cells H11:H12 (0) and the oversized mixture and miniature mixture constraints are satisfied. The profit of this solution is $8,420 (cell J4).

By varying the number of modules assembled, any solution can be evaluated quickly. In the case illustrated, a comparison of cells J5:J12 with the RHS column (H5:H12) indicates whether or not a solution is feasible. The solution in Figure 9-3 is feasible, but the one in Figure 9-4 is not feasible. That second solution shows that producing 200 of each module would give a profit of $34,200, but that production plan is impossible, because it would require 17,400 type A chips (cell J6) and only 10,000 are available (cell H6). There are other violations of feasibility. (Can you find them?)

	A	B	C	D	E	F	G	H	I	J
1				**Microcircuit Production Plan**						
2										
3	Variables	X_E	X_L	X_R	X_S	X_M	Sign	RHS		
4	Objective	58	43	25	17	28	=	P(max)	Profit	34200
5	PC Board	25	15	10	5	1	≤	50000	PC Board	11200
6	A Availability	28	24	18	12	5	≤	10000	A Availability	17400
7	B Availability	52	48	40	60	75	≤	25000	B Availability	55000
8	Assembly Time	1.50	1.25	1.00	0.75	1.50	≤	2000	Assembly Time	1200
9	Regular Quantity			1			≥	200	Regular Quantity	200
10	Small Quantity				1		≥	100	Small Quantity	200
11	Oversized Mixture	2	-1				≤	0	Oversized Mixture	200
12	Miniature Mixture	-0.50	-0.50	-0.50	-0.50	1.00	≤	0	Miniature Mixture	-200
13					Solution					
14		X_E	X_L	X_R	X_S	X_M				
15		200.00	200.00	200.00	200.00	200.00				

FIGURE 9-4 Excel spreadsheet (infeasible) for assembling 200 units of each module

Finding Optimal Solutions Using the Excel Solver

Excel has a tool called Solver for finding the *optimal* solutions to LPs like the microcircuit production plan. We will use Solver with the microcircuit production spreadsheet to solve the linear program. We begin by selecting Tools in the menu bar, clicking on the Solver choice. That brings to screen the Solver Parameters dialog box, shown in Figure 9-5. There are three principal features to this dialog box: the Target Cell, the Changing Cells, and the Constraints.

The Target Cell refers to the value to be optimized, which is the value of the objective function, located in cell $J4. That has been typed into the *Set Target Cell* box. (Clicking on the icon with the red arrow [🔺] and then cell J4 it will also automatically enter that cell's address into the box.) The dollar signs ($) are optional. The Max button was clicked on the *Equal To* line, because our objective is to maximize. (Other choices are to minimize or to make the objective equal to a particular value.) The Changing Cells $B$15:$F$15 correspond to the variables of the linear programming problem. This range of cells may be directly typed into the *By Changing Cells* box. (Clicking on the icon with the red arrow and then highlighting the spreadsheet cells will also automatically enter their addresses.)

FIGURE 9-5

The Solver Parameters dialog box for the microchip production plan LP

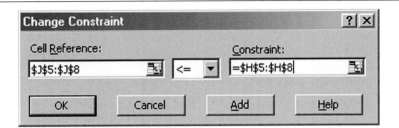

FIGURE 9-6
The Add Constraint dialog box

To enter the constraints, we first click anywhere inside the *Subject to the Constraints* box and then on the Add button to its right. The Add Constraint dialog box in Figure 9-6 appears on-screen. We may enter the constraint information in groups, depending on the signs. The first four constraints (rows 5–8 of the spreadsheet) are entered together. We do that by typing the total resources used for the first four constraints, cells $J$5:$J$8, into the *Cell Reference* line. We then enter the appropriate sign for those constraints, less than or equal to ($\leq$) in this case, from the pull-down list in the box in the middle of the dialog box. (Note that Excel uses the signs $<=$ for the inequality $\leq$.) This brings a drop-down menu with the constraint sign options shown in Figure 9-7. Next we enter the right-hand sides, $=$H$5:$H$8, in the *Constraint* line. (Solver will put the equal sign automatically if it is not entered.)

The next group of constraints are entered analogously, clicking on the Add button again and typing $J$9:$J$10 in the *Cell Reference* line, entering $>=$ (for $\geq$) as the constraint sign, and putting $H$9:$H$10 in the *Constraint* box. That leaves two remaining constraints, which we finish entering, repeating these steps by once more clicking on the Add button, putting $J$11:$J$12 in the *Cell Reference* line, designating $<=$ as the constraint sign, and entering $H$11:$H$12 in the *Constraint* box. Finally, we click the OK button, returning the Solver Parameters dialog box (Figure 9-5).

To enter the nonnegativity conditions, we click on the Options button on the right-hand side of the Solver Parameters dialog box, which brings to screen the Solver Options dialog box shown in Figure 9-8. We make sure that the *Assume Linear Model* and *Assume Non-Negative* boxes are checked, leaving the other settings in this dialog box at their default values. (See the Solver section in the *Guide to Excel* on the CD-ROM that accompanies this book for more details.) Finally, clicking on OK brings back the Solver Parameters dialog box.

Clicking on the Solve button launches Solver. That routine examines many possible solutions until the optimal one is found. When finished, the Solver Results dialog box appears as shown in Figure 9-9. We see that the first two lines in the Solver Results dialog box read, "Solver found a solution. All constraints and optimality conditions are satisfied." No special difficulties (infeasibility, unboundedness) were found. We verify that the Keep Solver Solution option is selected and we click OK. The spreadsheet returns, as shown in Figure 9-10, which shows the optimal solution: $X_E = 67.54$, $X_L = 135.08$, $X_R = 200$, $X_S = 100$, $X_M = 13.39$, and $P(\text{max}) = \$16,800.65$.

FIGURE 9-7
Drop-down menu for constraint signs

FIGURE 9-8
The Solver Options
dialog box

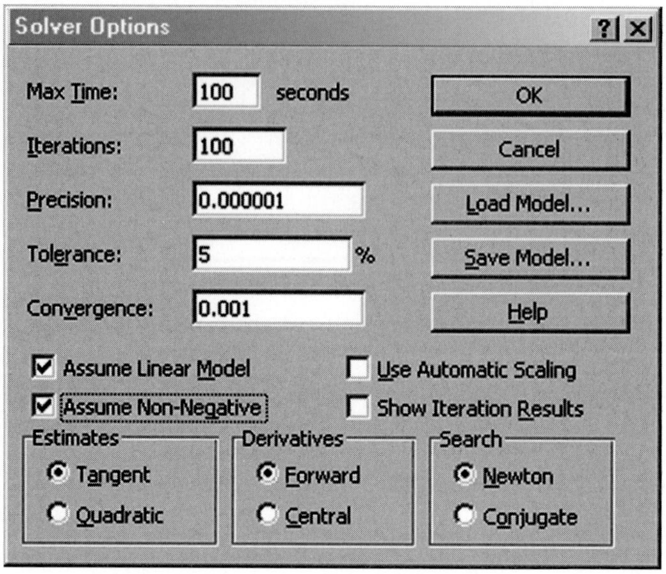

We may use Solver to easily find optimal solutions after changing the problem data. As an illustration, suppose that only 5,000 PC boards are available due to a strike at the supplier. A new solution may be found by changing cell H5 to 5,000 from 50,000 in the latest version of the spreadsheet in Figure 9-10. We rerun Solver by clicking on Tools and Solver. (When the Solver Parameters dialog box appears this time, all the data from the previous run are in the appropriate places because Solver has remembered the information.) Simply clicking on the Solve button gives the new answer: $X_E = 0$, $X_L = 163.88$, $X_R = 200$, $X_S = 100$, $X_M = 41.78$, and $P(\text{max}) = \$14,916.81$.

Solver Reports   The answers seen so far are all found in the Excel spreadsheet itself. Solver also provides answers in various formats. The Solver Results dialog box in Figure 9-9 lists three types of reports in the Reports segment: Answer, Sensitivity, and Limits. Besides more conveniently arranging the results already seen, these reports provide additional useful information. The Answer Report is most commonly used.

To obtain the Answer Report in Figure 9-11 for the original microcircuit LP, we highlight that choice in the *Reports* box and click OK. It appears on a new spreadsheet. (Check the tabs at the bottom of the screen for the one saying Answer Report.) There are three parts to the report: the Target Cell, the Adjustable Cells, and the Constraints. The first, the Target Cell, gives the profit, $P(\text{max}) = \$16,800.65$. Next, the Adjustable

FIGURE 9-9
Solver Results dialog box

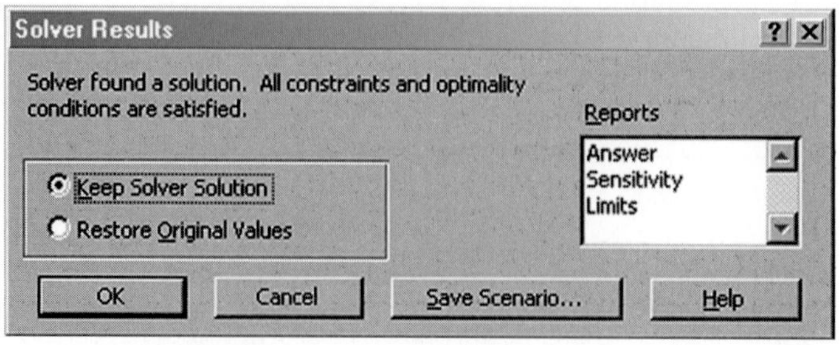

	A	B	C	D	E	F	G	H		I	J
1					**Microcircuit Production Plan**						
2											
3	Variables	X_E	X_L	X_R	X_S	X_M	Sign	RHS			
4	Objective	58	43	25	17	28	=	P(max)		Profit	16800.65
5	PC Board	25	15	10	5	1	≤	50000		PC Board	6228.10
6	A Availability	28	24	18	12	5	≤	10000		A Availability	10000.00
7	B Availability	52	48	40	60	75	≤	25000		B Availability	25000.00
8	Assembly Time	1.50	1.25	1.00	0.75	1.50	≤	2000		Assembly Time	565.24
9	Regular Quantity			1			≥	200		Regular Quantity	200.00
10	Small Quantity				1		≥	100		Small Quantity	100.00
11	Oversized Mixture	2	-1				≤	0		Oversized Mixture	0.00
12	Miniature Mixture	-0.50	-0.50	-0.50	-0.50	1.00	≤	0		Miniature Mixture	-237.92
13					Solution						
14			X_E	X_L	X_R	X_S	X_M				
15			67.54	135.08	200.00	100.00	13.39				

FIGURE 9-10   Spreadsheet and corresponding solution for original microchip production plan LP

Cells give the values of the variables: $X_E = 67.54$, $X_L = 135.08$, $X_R = 200$, $X_S = 100$, and $X_M = 13.39$.

The Constraints section of the Answer Report shows the left-hand side of each constraint and whether or not the constraints are *binding*. A constraint that is binding has no slack (for the ≤ case) or surplus (for the ≥ case), and the corresponding auxiliary variable has a value of zero. Nonbinding constraints have nonzero slack or surplus variables. We see that the PC board constraint is not binding, which means that the available stock of PC boards will not be used up, and positive slack exists for this constraint in the amount of 43,771.90 boards. On the other hand, the chip A availability constraint is binding, so that all of the A chips will be utilized, and the slack is zero for this constraint.

Target Cell (Max)

Cell	Name	Original Value	Final Value
$J$4	Profit	0.00	16800.65

Adjustable Cells

Cell	Name	Original Value	Final Value
$B$15	XE	0.00	67.54
$C$15	XL	0.00	135.08
$D$15	XR	0.00	200.00
$E$15	XS	0.00	100.00
$F$15	XM	0.00	13.39

Constraints

Cell	Name	Cell Value	Formula	Status	Slack
$J$5	PC Board	6228.10	$J$5<=$H$5	Not Binding	43771.90
$J$6	A Availability	10000.00	$J$6<=$H$6	Binding	0.00
$J$7	B Availability	25000.00	$J$7<=$H$7	Binding	0.00
$J$8	Assembly Time	565.24	$J$8<=$H$8	Not Binding	1434.76
$J$9	Regular Quantity	200.00	$J$9>=$H$9	Binding	0.00
$J$10	Small Quantity	100.00	$J$10>=$H$10	Binding	0.00
$J$11	Oversized Mixture	0.00	$J$11<=$H$11	Binding	0.00
$J$12	Miniature Mixture	-237.92	$J$12<=$H$12	Not Binding	237.92

FIGURE 9-11

Solver's Answer Report for the original microchip production plan LP

9-5   LINEAR PROGRAMMING IN FINANCE: PORTFOLIO SELECTION

Portfolio managers use linear programming and its extensions to determine what investments to make.

U.S.A. Funds is starting a new income mutual fund. To initiate the registration process with the Securities and Exchange Commission, it will begin with assets of $100,000. The fund's principal objective is to provide high income, and its secondary objective is to limit risk by having a diversified portfolio. The portfolio manager has narrowed the initial portfolio to the bonds in the following table:

BOND	CURRENT YIELD (%)	SCHEDULED REDEMPTION	QUALITY RATING
A	8.5	2006	Excellent
B	9.0	2015	Very good
C	10.0	2002	Fair
D	9.5	2003	Fair
E	8.5	2007	Excellent
F	9.0	2010	Very good

To quantify the diversified portfolio objective, the fund's management has decided to invest no more than 25% in any one bond, to have at least one-half of the investments in longer maturing issues (post-2005), and to have no more than 30% of all funds placed in bonds rated in categories lower than "very good."

The first step in developing a linear programming model is to define the variables. In this case, there are six variables, which represent the amount invested in each bond.

$$X_i = \text{the dollar investment in company } i \text{ bonds}$$

Here, i represents any one of the six companies: A, B, C, D, E, or F.

The second step is to determine the objective function. In this case, the objective is to choose the values of the X's that will maximize total interest income. The current yields from the second column of the table above give

Maximize $P = 0.085X_A + 0.090X_B + 0.100X_C + 0.095X_D + 0.085X_E + 0.090X_F$

The last step is to find the constraints. There are nine in total, one for the $100,000 total amount to be invested, six for the 25% limit in any bond, one for the maturities, and one for the quality.

The initial portfolio investment will be $100,000, so the individual bond purchases must sum to this amount.

$$X_A + X_B + X_C + X_D + X_E + X_F = 100,000 \qquad \text{(funds)}$$

Public investment funds are often diversified by placing limitations on the proportion of the portfolio applied to any particular issue. In this case, the 25% limit on investments in bond A yields

$$X_A \leq 25,000$$

Identical constraints are applicable to X_B, X_C, X_D, X_E, and X_F.

Investment policy is that at least one-half of the funds be placed in longer maturity (post-2005) issues. This requirement provides the maturity constraint

$$X_A + X_B + X_E + X_F \geq 50,000 \qquad \text{(maturity)}$$

It is also investment policy that no more than 30% of all funds be placed in bonds rated in categories lower than "very good." This requirement is represented by the quality constraint

$$X_C + X_D \leq 30{,}000 \qquad \text{(quality)}$$

Nonnegativity conditions ordinarily apply to the variables in portfolio selection,

$$\text{where} \quad X_A, X_B, X_C, X_D, X_E, X_F \geq 0$$

The preceding linear program involves six variables. The graphical methods of Chapter 8 *will not work*. The following solution has been obtained using *QuickQuant*:

SOLUTION TO LINEAR PROGRAM

Original Variable	Value
XA	20000.00000
XB	25000.00000
XC	25000.00000
XD	5000.00000
XE	0.00000
XF	25000.00000

Objective Value: P = 9175.0002

Excel's Solver provides the identical solution.

	A	B	C	D	E	F	G	H	I	J	K
1	Bond Portfolio Selection										
2											
3	Variables	X_A	X_B	X_C	X_D	X_E	X_F	Sign	RHS		
4	Objective	0.085	0.09	0.1	0.095	0.085	0.09	=	P(max)	Profit	9,175
5	Funds	1	1	1	1	1	1	=	100,000	Funds	100,000
6	Diversification - A	1						≤	25,000	Diversification - A	20,000
7	B		1					≤	25,000	B	25,000
8	C			1				≤	25,000	C	25,000
9	D				1			≤	25,000	D	5,000
10	E					1		≤	25,000	E	0
11	F						1	≤	25,000	F	25,000
12	Maturity	1	1			1	1	≥	50,000	Maturity	70,000
13	Quality			1	1			≤	30,000	Quality	30,000
14		Solution									
15		X_A	X_B	X_C	X_D	X_E	X_F				
16		20,000	25,000	25,000	5,000	0	25,000				

Notice that none of bond E is purchased—a plausible result considering its low yield of 8.5%. But more money must be invested in bond F at 9% than in bond D at 9.5%. This is largely due to maturity and quality differences. Collectively, several linear programming constraints may provide surprising—even perplexing—results. Linear programming has been used extensively by many mutual funds and other large financial institutions to facilitate portfolio selections.

9-6   LINEAR PROGRAMMING IN TRANSPORTATION: SHIPMENT SCHEDULING

A large category of linear programs arises from the need to control distribution costs. A typical problem is faced by a multiplant manufacturer who must schedule shipments to several regional warehouses. When the number of sources and

destinations is great, linear programming solutions may involve a great number of un-obvious shipping assignments. Cost savings in transportation may be huge. Many companies of moderate size have saved millions of dollars in freight charges by using linear programming to schedule shipments.

Consider the operations of a sporting goods company that makes skis in three plants throughout the world. The plants supply four company-owned warehouses that distribute the skis directly to ski shops. Depending on which mode is cheaper, the product is air-freighted or trucked from the plants to the warehouses. The monthly capacities of the plants in terms of the number of pairs of skis that can be made are

PLANT	CAPACITY
Juarez	100
Seoul	300
Tel Aviv	200
Total	600

and warehouse demand requirements for the next month are

WAREHOUSE	DEMAND
Frankfurt	150
New York	100
Phoenix	200
Yokohama	150
Total	600

Table 9-1 provides the various point-to-point costs of shipping a pair of skis. To determine how many pairs of skis should be shipped from each plant to the various warehouses, the shipping schedule shown in Table 9-2 is constructed. The numbers of pairs of skis sent via each route are unknown and are represented as variables by the letter X with the appropriate subscripts. In general, we will adopt the convention

$$X_{ij} = \text{Quantity of skis shipped from plant } i \text{ to warehouse } j$$

where each possible i or j may be represented by a number $(1, 2, 3, 4, \ldots)$ or a letter $(A, B, C, D, \ldots)$ corresponding to the identity of the respective plant or warehouse.

The X's are chosen to minimize total shipping costs. The total cost over each route is the shipping cost per pair of skis multiplied by the quantity shipped. From Juarez to Frankfurt, this cost would be $19X_{JF}$. Summing the values from all routes, our problem objective is to

TABLE 9-1   The Shipping Costs per Pair of Skis

FROM PLANT	TO WAREHOUSE			
	Frankfurt	New York	Phoenix	Yokohama
Juarez	$19	$ 7	$ 3	$21
Seoul	15	21	18	6
Tel Aviv	11	14	15	22

TABLE 9-2 The Shipment Schedule for Skis

FROM PLANT	TO WAREHOUSE				Plant Capacity
	F	N	P	Y	
J	X_{JF}	X_{JN}	X_{JP}	X_{JY}	100
S	X_{SF}	X_{SN}	X_{SP}	X_{SY}	300
T	X_{TF}	X_{TN}	X_{TP}	X_{TY}	200
Warehouse Demand	150	100	200	150	600

$$\text{Minimize} \quad C = \quad 19X_{JF} + 7X_{JN} + 3X_{JP} + 21X_{JY}$$
$$+ 15X_{SF} + 21X_{SN} + 18X_{SP} + 6X_{SY}$$
$$+ 11X_{TF} + 14X_{TN} + 15X_{TP} + 22X_{TY}$$

The problem involves two kinds of constraints. One set applies to the plants and specifies that *the total number of units shipped from each plant must equal that plant's capacity.* The three plant capacity constraints for this problem are

$$X_{JF} + X_{JN} + X_{JP} + X_{JY} = 100 \qquad \text{(Juarez capacity)}$$
$$X_{SF} + X_{SN} + X_{SP} + X_{SY} = 300 \qquad \text{(Seoul capacity)}$$
$$X_{TF} + X_{TN} + X_{TP} + X_{TY} = 200 \qquad \text{(Tel Aviv capacity)}$$

Analogously, every warehouse must meet a second set of constraints, so that *the total number of units shipped to each warehouse must equal that warehouse's demand.* The four warehouse demand constraints for our problem are expressed explicitly as

$$X_{JF} + X_{SF} + X_{TF} = 150 \qquad \text{(Frankfurt demand)}$$
$$X_{JN} + X_{SN} + X_{TN} = 100 \qquad \text{(New York demand)}$$
$$X_{JP} + X_{SP} + X_{TP} = 200 \qquad \text{(Phoenix demand)}$$
$$X_{JY} + X_{SY} + X_{TY} = 150 \qquad \text{(Yokohama demand)}$$

Finally, we include the nonnegativity conditions,

$$\text{where} \quad \text{all } X_{ij}\text{'s} \geq 0$$

Our example illustrates a class of linear programming situations that are referred to as **transportation problems.** In Chapter 12, we will learn how such problems are solved using the **transportation method.** The optimal solution to this problem (which will be discussed in detail in Chapter 12) is

$X_{JF} = 0$	$X_{JN} = 0$	$X_{JP} = 100$	$X_{JY} = 0$
$X_{SF} = 50$	$X_{SN} = 0$	$X_{SP} = 100$	$X_{SY} = 150$
$X_{TF} = 100$	$X_{TN} = 100$	$X_{TP} = 0$	$X_{TY} = 0$

$$C = 6,250$$

This solution provides the most economical plan. Some of the results are obvious—for example, that Seoul (Korea) supplies Yokohama (Japan) but not New York. It seems a little odd that Seoul supplies Phoenix, but its demand outstrips Juarez's capacity and the Korean supplier must take up the slack.

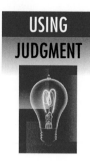

USING JUDGMENT

The Pros and Cons of Double Subscripting

The use of double subscripting when choosing symbols for linear programming variables can have significant advantages. It enables us to construct constraints in a blending problem or transportation problem; symbols representing disparate constraints fall into place naturally with a minimum of thought and little need for double checking. Think how difficult it would be in the ski transportation problem if instead of X_{TF} for the quantity shipped from Tel Aviv to Frankfurt we used X_9. We would continually have to refer to the master list of variable definitions to build demand and capacity constraints.

Beginners tend to overuse double subscripting, especially in manufacturing situations. Let good judgment be your guide when deciding whether or not to use double subscripts. Use them when they are helpful. If they only clutter or confuse the situation, don't use double subscripts for that problem.

9-7 LINEAR PROGRAMMING IN MARKETING: BUDGETING ADVERTISING EXPENDITURES

Linear programming may be employed in establishing advertising budgets to designate a firm's level of expenditures for each medium such as television, radio, billboards, or magazines. Linear programming may even be used to determine how much space or time should be allocated to each medium, as the following example illustrates.

Real Reels is a medium-sized company that manufactures high-quality fishing equipment. Company policy is to sell the products for a little more than competitors' products, because Real Reels considers its quality and reputation to be higher. A recent sales slowdown has prompted the owner to consider advertising for the first time. He has allocated $100,000 for the advertising and has narrowed down his decisions to placing quarter-page ads in *Playboy, True,* and *Esquire.* His goal with the advertising is to maximize total product exposure to significant buyers of expensive fishing gear. Exposure in any particular magazine is the number of ads placed multiplied by the number of significant buyers. The following data apply for a single ad placement:

	PLAYBOY	**TRUE**	**ESQUIRE**
Readers	10 million	6 million	4 million
Significant buyers	10%	15%	7%
Cost per ad	$10,000	$5,000	$6,000
Exposures per ad	1,000,000	900,000	280,000

The exposure for a *Playboy* ad is $.10 \times 10,000,000 = 1,000,000$. It will be convenient to express everything in millions. The owner has already determined that no more than five ads should be placed in *True* and that at least two ads apiece should be placed in *Playboy* and *Esquire.*

The first step in formulating the linear programming model is to define the variables. In this case, they are the numbers of ads to place in each of the three magazines.

$$X_P = \text{the number of quarter-page ads in } Playboy$$
$$X_T = \text{the number of quarter-page ads in } True$$
$$X_E = \text{the number of quarter-page ads in } Esquire$$

The second step is to determine the objective function. In this case, Real Reels wishes to maximize the total advertising exposure. Using the numbers in the last row of the above table yields

$$\text{Maximize}\quad P = 1X_P + .9X_T + .28X_E$$

Finally, the constraints are determined. Four exist for Real Reels, one for the $100,000 budget and three for the maximum and minimum ad placement conditions specified by the owner. Those are listed below, along with the nonnegativity conditions.

$$
\begin{aligned}
10{,}000X_P + 5{,}000X_T + 6{,}000X_E &\leq 100{,}000 &&\text{(budget)}\\
1X_T &\leq 5 &&\text{(maximum } True \text{ ads)}\\
1X_P &\geq 2 &&\text{(minimum } Playboy \text{ ads)}\\
1X_E &\geq 2 &&\text{(minimum } Esquire \text{ ads)}
\end{aligned}
$$

where $\qquad X_P, X_T, X_E \geq 0$

Using *QuickQuant*, the optimal solution in the following abbreviated printout is obtained.

SOLUTION TO LINEAR PROGRAM

Original Variable	Value
XP	6.30000
XT	5.00000
XE	2.00000

Objective Value: P = 11.3600

The following Excel Solver answer is identical:

	A	B	C	D	E	F	G	H
1				Real Reels				
2								
3	Variables	X_P	X_T	X_E	Sign	RHS		
4	Objective	1	0.9	0.28	=	P(max)	Profit	11.36
5	Budget	10000	5000	6000	≤	100,000	Budget	100000.00
6	Maximum *True* ads		1		≤		5 Maximum *True* ads	5.00
7	Minimum *Playboy* ads	1			≥		2 Minimum *Playboy* ads	6.30
8	Minimum *Esquire* ads			1	≥		2 Minimum *Esquire* ads	2.00
9			Solution					
10		X_A	X_B	X_C				
11		6.30	5.00	2.00				

Notice that this solution involves a fractional amount for the *Playboy* ads. Remember that linear programming permits this. Fractional solutions may not be troublesome when quantities are large. In Chapter 11, we will examine **integer programming,** where variables are restricted to whole numbers.

The preceding example only partially illustrates the power of linear programming in advertising decision making. Many more magazines and media types may be considered simultaneously and several time periods may even be incorporated in a linear programming problem. Various demographic characteristics in the target audiences, such as reader ages and earnings, may also be included. Constraints may result in more or less emphasis on certain groups of people. Advertising problems involving thousands of variables with hundreds of constraints have been solved by using the linear programming approach.

9-8 LINEAR PROGRAMMING AND HUMAN RESOURCES: ASSIGNING PERSONNEL

Linear programming is widely used to assign workers to specific jobs. Such linear programs fall into the broad class of **assignment problems.** These are discussed in detail in Chapter 12.

Mildred Riveter runs a small machine shop, where each worker operates different pieces of equipment at varying skill levels. The following average times apply to each item processed by the shop:

INDIVIDUAL	TIME REQUIRED TO COMPLETE ONE JOB		
	Drilling	Grinding	Lathe
Ann	5 min	10 min	10 min
Bud	10	5	15
Chuck	15	15	10

Management wants to make assignments of operators to jobs that will minimize the total time required to process one item.

As in shipment scheduling, it is convenient to designate the variables with double subscripts. In this case,

$$X_{ij} = \text{Fraction of time individual } i \text{ is assigned to job } j$$

Notice that we have $3 \times 3 = 9$ variables (the number of individuals multiplied by the number of jobs). The objective function is to

$$\text{Minimize} \quad C = \quad 5X_{AD} + 10X_{AG} + 10X_{AL}$$
$$+ 10X_{BD} + 5X_{BG} + 15X_{BL}$$
$$+ 15X_{CD} + 15X_{CG} + 10X_{CL}$$

One set of constraints applies to the availability of the operators, thereby ensuring that every individual is fully occupied.

$$X_{AD} + X_{AG} + X_{AL} = 1 \quad \text{(Ann's availability)}$$
$$X_{BD} + X_{BG} + X_{BL} = 1 \quad \text{(Bud's availability)}$$
$$X_{CD} + X_{CG} + X_{CL} = 1 \quad \text{(Chuck's availability)}$$

Another set of constraints applies to the jobs, each of which requires a complete assignment.

$$X_{AD} + X_{BD} + X_{CD} = 1 \qquad \text{(drill-press requirement)}$$
$$X_{AG} + X_{BG} + X_{CG} = 1 \qquad \text{(grinder requirement)}$$
$$X_{AL} + X_{BL} + X_{CL} = 1 \qquad \text{(lathe requirement)}$$

Of course, nonnegativity is a condition for all variables.

The optimal solution to this problem is

$$X_{AD} = 1 \qquad\qquad X_{CL} = 1$$
$$X_{BG} = 1 \qquad \text{all other } X\text{'s} = 0$$
$$C = 20$$

9-9 LINEAR PROGRAMMING IN REFINING: LIQUID BLENDING

Many products, from toothpaste to gasoline, are blended from a variety of raw ingredients. The processes involved are often highly flexible because these products must meet various restrictions, such as limited ingredient availability and minimum product demand. Managers may apply linear programming to determine the particular blend of ingredients that will meet all constraints and still maximize total profit.

Linear programming is used extensively by oil and chemical companies to solve **liquid blending problems.** Managers at many large oil refineries routinely employ linear programs in operational planning. One refinery makes a daily computer run to solve a linear program that indicates the day's gasoline blending plan. Shifts in ingredient availabilities and costs and slight variations in ingredient composition require frequent planning, and linear programming has proved to be a very valuable tool in accomplishing this task.

Chanel 2000 Inc. makes and sells perfumes for men and women that are a blend of natural and synthetic scents. Valerie St. Johns is project manager in charge of handling an order for 1,500 liters of aftershave and 500 liters of cologne, as shown below.

PRODUCT	AGENTS (%)		SELLING PRICE ($)	QUANTITY ORDERED
	Emulsion	Evaporatives		
Aftershave	—	20	10	1,500
Cologne	30	—	20	500

The secret to obtaining the high-quality aftershave and cologne products sold by Chanel 2000 is the amounts of emulsion and evaporative agents. The preceding table shows the secret minimum percentages: at least 30% of the cologne must be emulsion and at least 20% of the aftershave must be evaporative agents. Also given in the table are the sales prices of the aftershave and cologne and the quantities ordered.

Both the aftershave and cologne are made of essentially the same three active ingredients: oil, rinse, and stabilizer. The following table gives the amounts of the two agents in those raw materials, their costs, and the quantities available:

INGREDIENT	AGENTS (%) Emulsion	AGENTS (%) Evaporatives	COST ($)	AVAILABILITY
Oil	50	0	2	2,000
Rinse	100	25	30	500
Stabilizer	10	50	4	1,000

Valerie is wondering if those quantities will be sufficient to fill the order. She would also like to determine whether the order is profitable and, if so, what the profit will be.

She begins her linear programming formulation by defining the variables. It is convenient to use double-subscript notation, so that

$$X_{ij} = \text{Volume (liters) of ingredient } i \text{ used in blending product } j$$

The letters O, R, and S will be used to denote the respective ingredients; A and C denote the products.

Of course, all X's must be nonnegative. The objective is to maximize total profit. We begin to express this by considering total sales. The value per liter of active ingredients is $10 for aftershave and $20 for cologne. This gives us total sales of

$$10(X_{OA} + X_{RA} + X_{SA}) + 20(X_{OC} + X_{RC} + X_{SC})$$

Ingredient costs are $2 per liter of oil, $30 per liter of rinse, and $4 per liter of stabilizer. Total cost is therefore expressed as

$$2(X_{OA} + X_{OC}) + 30(X_{RA} + X_{RC}) + 4(X_{SA} + X_{SC})$$

By subtracting total cost from total revenue and collecting and rearranging terms, we obtain the objective function

$$\text{Maximize} \quad P = 8X_{OA} - 20X_{RA} + 6X_{SA} + 18X_{OC} - 10X_{RC} + 16X_{SC}$$

There are seven constraints: three for the ingredient availabilities, two for the order quantities, and two for the secret ingredient minimum percentages. We begin with constraints pertaining to liquid availabilities (in liters).

$$X_{OA} + X_{OC} \leq 2,000 \quad \text{(available oil)}$$
$$X_{RA} + X_{RC} \leq 500 \quad \text{(available rinse)}$$
$$X_{SA} + X_{SC} \leq 1,000 \quad \text{(available stabilizer)}$$

The left-hand sides of these inequalities represent the total quantities of the respective ingredients actually used; the right-hand sides indicate the current inventory levels.

A second set of constraints pertains to volume (quantity) requirements for the final products.

$$X_{OA} + X_{RA} + X_{SA} \geq 1,500 \quad \text{(aftershave volume)}$$
$$X_{OC} + X_{RC} + X_{SC} \geq 500 \quad \text{(cologne volume)}$$

Here, the left-hand sides represent the total volumes of active liquid ingredients in the present production run of the respective products, and the right-hand sides indicate the minimum volumes required to meet the product demands.

A final set of constraints pertains to the proportional content of the ingredients in each product. For example, at least 30% of the volume of cologne must be emulsions. The oil is 50% emulsions, the rinse is 100%, and the stabilizer is only 10%. The emulsion requirement may therefore be summarized as

$$\frac{.50X_{OC} + 1.00X_{RC} + .10X_{SC}}{X_{OC} + X_{RC} + X_{SC}} \geq .30 \qquad \text{(emulsions in cologne)}$$

where the numerator expresses the total emulsion volume of the cologne ingredients and the denominator indicates the total volume of the cologne. This ratio must be at least .30.

A similar restriction applies to the aftershave, which must contain at least 20% evaporative agents. The rinse is 25% evaporatives, the stabilizer is 50%, and the oil contains none. The evaporative requirement is summarized as

$$\frac{.25X_{RA} + .50X_{SA}}{X_{OA} + X_{RA} + X_{SA}} \geq .20 \qquad \text{(evaporatives in aftershave)}$$

These two proportional content constraints are ordinarily rearranged by multiplying both sides of the inequality by the denominator, canceling, and then collecting X terms on the left-hand side.

$$.20X_{OC} + .70X_{RC} - .20X_{SC} \geq 0 \qquad \text{(emulsions in cologne)}$$
$$- .20X_{OA} + .05X_{RA} + .30X_{SA} \geq 0 \qquad \text{(evaporatives in aftershave)}$$

In standardized format, the constraints for this problem are provided below.

$$
\begin{array}{llllllll}
1X_{OA} + & 0X_{RA} + & 0X_{SA} + & 1X_{OC} + & 0X_{RC} + & 0X_{SC} \leq 2{,}000 & \text{(available oil)} \\
0X_{OA} + & 1X_{RA} + & 0X_{SA} + & 0X_{OC} + & 1X_{RC} + & 0X_{SC} \leq 500 & \text{(available rinse)} \\
0X_{OA} + & 0X_{RA} + & 1X_{SA} + & 0X_{OC} + & 0X_{RC} + & 1X_{SC} \leq 1{,}000 & \text{(available stabilizer)} \\
1X_{OA} + & 1X_{RA} + & 1X_{SA} + & 0X_{OC} + & 0X_{RC} + & 0X_{SC} \geq 1{,}500 & \text{(aftershave volume)} \\
0X_{OA} + & 0X_{RA} + & 0X_{SA} + & 1X_{OC} + & 1X_{RC} + & 1X_{SC} \geq 500 & \text{(cologne volume)} \\
0X_{OA} + & 0X_{RA} + & 0X_{SA} + & .20X_{OC} + & .70X_{RC} - & .20X_{SC} \geq 0 & \text{(emulsions in cologne)} \\
-.20X_{OA} + & .05X_{RA} + & .30X_{SA} + & 0X_{OC} + & 0X_{RC} + & 0X_{SC} \geq 0 & \text{(evaporatives in aftershave)}
\end{array}
$$

Using *QuickQuant*, the optimal solution in the following abbreviated printout is obtained:

SOLUTION TO LINEAR PROGRAM
PROBLEM: Scent Mixing

Original Variable	Value
XOA	500.00000
XRA	0.00000
XSA	1000.00000
XOC	1500.00000
XRC	0.00000
XSC	0.00000

Objective Value: P = 37000.00000
This problem has multiple optimal solutions.

The Excel Solver provides the identical solution:

	A	B	C	D	E	F	G	H	I	J	K
1						Scent Mixing					
2											
3	Variables	X_{OA}	X_{RA}	X_{SA}	X_{OC}	X_{RC}	X_{SC}	Sign	RHS		
4	Objective	8	-20	6	18	-10	16	=	P(max)	Profit	37000
5	Available oil	1			1			≤		2000	Available oil	2000
6	Available rinse		1			1		≤		500	Available rinse	0
7	Available stabilizer			1			1	≤		1000	Available stabilizer	1000
8	Aftershave volume	1	1	1				≥		1500	Aftershave volume	1500
9	Cologne volume				1	1	1	≥		500	Cologne volume	1500
10	Emulsions in cologne				0.2	0.7	-0.2	≥		0	Emulsions in cologne	300
11	Evaporatives in aftershave	-0.2	0.05	0.3				≥		0	Evaporatives in aftershave	200
12					Solution						
13		X_{OA}	X_{RA}	X_{SA}	X_{OC}	X_{RC}	X_{SC}				
14		500	0	1000	1500	0	0				

The product manager would find the preceding solution a bit disconcerting, because it indicates that the cologne must consist of nothing but oil. Of course, the overall problem has been simplified, and only a few essential requirements are shown. However, an important step in any linear programming application is to examine the results to see if they make sense. An unreasonable solution could result from a missing requirement or an improperly formulated constraint.

Special Considerations in Defining Variables

Perhaps the most challenging part of the linear program formulation is properly defining the variables and separating variables from their constraints. Liquid blending problems are particularly troublesome to beginners. Keep in mind that the X's are what the decision maker wants to find. In the present illustration, the question is, How much of each available ingredient (oil, rinse, and stabilizer) is to go into each final product (cologne and aftershave)? There is a separate variable for each ingredient-product combination, and it is convenient to have a double subscript for the *OA, RA, SA, OC, RC,* and *SC* variable designations.

In determining what is a variable (and to be decided) and what is a secondary quantity, keep in mind that the latter will ordinarily occur in *fixed proportion* to another unknown quantity to be decided. For example, the amount of *wood* used by Redwood Furniture (page 263) in making tables is *not* what is to be decided (even though the amount is not known). Exactly 30 board feet will be used in making each table (the variable). Once the number of tables and chairs has been determined, of course, the amount of wood and labor to go into each product can be readily determined. Wood and labor are not variables, and there are not separate *WT* and *WC* or *LT* and *LC* variables. Wood and labor are not blended, with finished furniture emerging from a melting pot.

Although also unknown, the level of emulsions in cologne or aftershave is *not* a variable, but rather a secondary quantity that is automatically fixed once values have been determined for the X's defined earlier.

Keep your list of variables as short as possible. In the scent-mixing problem, the total amounts to be used of oil, rinse, and stabilizer are unknowns and are equal to the following:

$$\text{Total volume of oil} = X_{OA} + X_{OC}$$
$$\text{Total volume of rinse} = X_{RA} + X_{RC}$$
$$\text{Total volume of stabilizer} = X_{SA} + X_{SC}$$

Still, it only "muddies the water" to have additional separate O, R, and S variables for the totals. If a constraint involves a specification on the total amount of oil, the variable *sum* $X_{OA} + X_{OC}$ should be used whenever the total oil is needed.

A similar conclusion may be made regarding the amount of final product.

$$\text{Total volume of aftershave} = X_{OA} + X_{RA} + X_{SA}$$
$$\text{Total volume of cologne} = X_{OC} + X_{RC} + X_{SC}$$

There should be no separate A and C variables. Use the *sum* of the double-subscripted X's whenever expressing the total amount of a final product.

9-10 LINEAR PROGRAMMING IN FOOD PROCESSING: THE DIET PROBLEM

An important linear programming application is the **diet problem.** In this problem, quantities are selected for various ingredients used in mixing a final product so that minimum nutritional requirements are met while at the same time minimizing costs.

Yosemite Ann's supplies hikers with a variety of provisions. One of these is Trail-Mix Delight, a 1-kilogram package made up of natural ingredients. Each package provides the hiker with the complete nutritional requirements for one day, in accordance with the requirements given in Table 9-3.

All ingredients are readily available from local suppliers, so that there are no quantity limitations. Yosemite Ann wants to determine the weight of the various ingredients that will be mixed together to give exactly 1 kilogram of the product. She defines the following variables:

TABLE 9-3   Trail-Mix Delight Dietetic Requirements

	NUTRITIONAL VALUE OF INGREDIENTS PER KILOGRAM					
NUTRIENTS	**Dried Currants**	**Roasted Peanuts**	**Roasted Walnuts**	**Pumpkin Kernels**	**Dried Milk**	**MINIMUM REQUIREMENT**
Calories	540	5,720	6,540	5,530	4,990	3,000 cal
Protein	20	270	150	290	260	56 g
Iron	10	30	20	110	10	10 mg
Vitamin A	230	0	300	700	9,200	1,000 µg
Thiamin	.5	2.5	4.8	2.4	2.9	1.4 mg
Riboflavin	.5	2.6	1.3	1.9	12.1	1.6 mg
Niacin	3	170	12	24	7	18 mg
Calcium	600	720	830	510	9,120	800 mg
Ascorbic Acid	2,000	10	30	0	90	60 µg RE
Cost per kilogram	$1.50	$2.50	$4.00	$1.00	$1.50	

Source: Louise Bullock

X_C = Weight of dried currants in a 1-kilogram package

X_P = Weight of roasted peanuts in a 1-kilogram package

X_W = Weight of roasted walnuts in a 1-kilogram package

X_K = Weight of pumpkin kernels in a 1-kilogram package

X_M = Weight of dried milk in a 1-kilogram package

These quantities are to be selected in such a way that total ingredient cost is minimized. Yosemite's objective function is to

$$\text{Minimize } C = 1.50X_C + 2.50X_P + 4.00X_W + 1.00X_K + 1.50X_M$$

Diet problems usually involve a constraint for the total weight of the final product, which is the sum of the ingredient weights.

$$X_C + X_P + X_W + X_K + X_M = 1 \quad \text{(total weight)}$$

This constraint is essential because there is no other way to guarantee that a kilogram of ingredients will be put into the 1-kilogram package.

Each nutritional requirement provides a separate constraint.

$$
\begin{aligned}
540X_C + 5{,}720X_P + 6{,}540X_W + 5{,}530X_K + 4{,}990X_M &\geq 3{,}000 \quad &\text{(calories)} \\
20X_C + 270X_P + 150X_W + 290X_K + 260X_M &\geq 56 \quad &\text{(protein)} \\
10X_C + 30X_P + 20X_W + 110X_K + 10X_M &\geq 10 \quad &\text{(iron)} \\
230X_C + 0X_P + 300X_W + 700X_K + 9{,}200X_M &\geq 1{,}000 \quad &\text{(vitamin A)} \\
.5X_C + 2.5X_P + 4.8X_W + 2.4X_K + 2.9X_M &\geq 1.4 \quad &\text{(thiamin)} \\
.5X_C + 2.6X_P + 1.3X_W + 1.9X_K + 12.1X_M &\geq 1.6 \quad &\text{(riboflavin)} \\
3X_C + 170X_P + 12X_W + 24X_K + 7X_M &\geq 18 \quad &\text{(niacin)} \\
600X_C + 720X_P + 830X_W + 510X_K + 9{,}120X_M &\geq 800 \quad &\text{(calcium)} \\
2{,}000X_C + 10X_P + 30X_W + 0X_K + 90X_M &\geq 60 \quad &\text{(ascorbic acid)}
\end{aligned}
$$

Of course, the nonnegativity conditions are assumed to apply.

It does not matter that the units vary from constraint to constraint. (Indeed, as we have seen, one constraint might be in board feet, another in hours of labor, and so on.) In linear programming, it is only essential that the same units are used on the left and the right side of each constraint.

Using *QuickQuant*, the optimal solution in the following abbreviated printout is obtained:

SOLUTION TO LINEAR PROGRAM
PROBLEM: Yosemite Ann

Original Variable	Value
XC	0.02834
XP	0.00000
XW	0.00000
XK	0.93483
XM	0.03686

Objective Value: C = 1.03263

The Excel Solver provides the following identical results:

	A	B	C	D	E	F	G	H	I	J
1					Yosemite Ann					
2										
3	Variables	X_C	X_P	X_W	X_K	X_M	Sign	RHS		
4	Objective	1.50	2.50	4.00	1.00	1.50	=	C(min)	Cost	1.0326
5	Total weight	1.00	1.00	1.00	1.00	1.00	=	1	Total weight	1
6	Calories	540	5720	6540	5530	4990	≥	3000	Calories	5369
7	Protein	20	270	150	290	260	≥	56	Protein	281
8	Iron	10	30	20	110	10	≥	10	Iron	103
9	Vitamin A	230	0	300	700	9200	≥	1000	Vitamin A	1,000
10	Thiamin	0.5	2.5	4.8	2.4	2.9	≥	1.4	Thiamin	2
11	Riboflavin	0.5	2.6	1.3	1.9	12.1	≥	1.6	Riboflavin	2
12	Niacin	3	170	12	24	7	≥	18	Niacin	23
13	Calcium	600	720	830	510	9120	≥	800	Calcium	830
14	Ascorbic acid	2000	10	30	0	90	≥	60	Ascorbic acid	60
15				Solution						
16		X_C	X_P	X_W	X_K	X_M				
17		0.0283	0.0000	0.0000	0.9348	0.0369				

Yosemite Ann finds the results extremely unsatisfactory because no peanuts or walnuts are included in the solution.

Fearing that nobody will buy the insipid, but nutritional, mix, she decides to add two constraints guaranteeing that at least 10% of the total weight are peanuts and 10% are walnuts. The following two constraints are added to the earlier problem:

$$0X_C + 1X_P + 0X_W + 0X_K + 0X_M \geq .10 \qquad \text{(peanuts)}$$
$$0X_C + 0X_P + 1X_W + 0X_K + 0X_M \geq .10 \qquad \text{(walnuts)}$$

QuickQuant allows us to add those two constraints to the original problem without having to reenter all the data. A computer run with the modified problem provides the new optimal solution.

SOLUTION TO LINEAR PROGRAM

Original Variable	Value
XC	0.02577
XP	0.10000
XW	0.10000
XK	0.72457
XM	0.04966

Objective Value: C = 1.4877

Managerial Decision Revisited: Determining Production Quantities

MANAGERIAL DECISION

The following linear program applies:

Letting X_{30}, X_{32}, X_{34}, X_{36}, X_{38}, and X_{40} denote the number of bats to be made in the respective sizes, Swat's problem is to

Maximize $P = 13.25X_{30} + 13.05X_{32} + 13.55X_{34} + 13.05X_{36} + 15.55X_{38} + 15.35X_{40}$

Subject to

$$30X_{30} + 32X_{32} + 34X_{34} + 36X_{36} + 38X_{38} + 40X_{40} \leq 10{,}000 \quad \text{(wood)}$$
$$10X_{30} + 10X_{32} + 11X_{34} + 11X_{36} + 12X_{38} + 12X_{40} \leq 5{,}000 \quad \text{(lathe)}$$
$$25X_{30} + 27X_{32} + 29X_{34} + 31X_{36} + 33X_{38} + 35X_{40} \leq 8{,}000 \quad \text{(finishing)}$$
$$1X_{30} + 1X_{32} + 1X_{34} + 1X_{36} + 1X_{38} + 1X_{40} \leq 500 \quad \text{(boxes)}$$
$$2X_{30} + 2X_{32} + 2X_{34} + 3X_{36} + 3X_{38} + 3X_{40} \leq 1{,}000 \quad \text{(stain)}$$
$$5X_{30} + 5X_{32} + 6X_{34} + 6X_{36} + 7X_{38} + 7X_{40} \leq 2{,}000 \quad \text{(varnish)}$$
$$-1X_{30} - 1X_{32} + 1X_{34} + 0X_{36} + 0X_{38} + 0X_{40} \leq 0 \quad \text{(restriction 1)}$$
$$0X_{30} - 1X_{32} - 1X_{34} + 0X_{36} + 1X_{38} + 0X_{40} \leq 0 \quad \text{(restriction 2)}$$
$$1X_{30} + 0X_{32} + 0X_{34} - 1X_{36} - 1X_{38} + 0X_{40} \leq 0 \quad \text{(restriction 3)}$$

where   all X's $\geq$ 0

The solution is

$$X_{30} = 94.12 \qquad X_{36} = 0$$
$$X_{32} = 94.12 \qquad X_{38} = 94.12$$
$$X_{34} = 0 \qquad\quad X_{40} = 0$$
$$P = \$3{,}938.82$$

9-11 (OPTIONAL) THE SIMPLEX METHOD

Computers are used to solve linear programs containing too many variables to plot on a two-dimensional graph. Both *QuickQuant* and Excel use an algorithm based on the **simplex method.**

The word *simplex* was *not* formed by adding the ubiquitous suffix *-ex* to the word *simple* (as in Kleenex and Memorex). *Simplex* is a legitimate term in the language of mathematics that represents the simplest object in an *n*-dimensional space connecting $n + 1$ points. In one dimension, a simplex is a line segment connecting two points. In two dimensions, a simplex is a triangle formed by joining three points. A three-dimensional simplex is a four-sided pyramid having just four corners. Such geometrical objects, extended to higher dimensions, are used to explain how and why the simplex method works. Although the procedure itself is quite simple to master, the mathematical arguments justifying this procedure are fairly complex.

Even though its underlying concepts are geometrical, the simplex algorithm itself is fundamentally an algebraic procedure. George B. Dantzig developed the algorithm after World War II and, with other mathematicians, has since extended and expanded it in a variety of ways. Like the graphical method discussed in Chapter 8, the simplex algorithm finds the most attractive corner of the feasible solution region, thereby solving the linear program. Ordinarily, the region itself exists in a higher dimensional space that may be imagined but not pictured. An underlying theoretical concept of the simplex method is that *any problem having a solution at all must have an optimal solution that corresponds to a corner point.*

This means that we need to evaluate only the corner points. Although finding and evaluating corners would seem to be child's play, remember that they are not pictured,

so we cannot see them. Furthermore, the number of corners associated with even a moderately large linear program may be huge. For example, solving a 10-product planning problem with 10 resource constraints would involve nearly 200,000 corners. In our lifetimes, the biggest, fastest computer could not evaluate the trillions and trillions of corners in a problem just 10 times that size.[1] A second feature of the simplex method incorporates a reliable search through the formidable thicket of corners to rapidly find the most attractive one. Based on *economic analysis,* this searching procedure is so efficient that only about 20 corners are evaluated in the 10-product case just mentioned.

The simplex method embodies geometry, but it combines algebra with economic principles to solve linear programs. Simplex is really an odyssey in n-dimensional space where you visit a few corner points on a multifaceted "gem stone" you cannot see. Each time you stop, a small analysis finds out where you should stop next; your journey ends at the most attractive corner.

Because the simplex method cannot "see" corner point solutions the way you can see them in a graph, it uses a table of numbers, called a **simplex tableau,** to represent a corner point. The corner point solution can be read from the table, with the simplex tableau playing a role similar to the accountant's balance sheet. Rules are used in constructing a balance sheet, and company information can be found from it. Likewise for a simplex tableau. We will next present the rules for constructing a simplex tableau, how to read a solution from it, and how to calculate a new tableau if another would give a better solution. The geometrical interpretation of the simplex method is that it is a journey from one corner point to another; that is equivalent to going from one simplex tableau to another.

Basic Simplex Concepts

To introduce the simplex method, we will continue our Redwood Furniture problem. As before, X_T and X_C represent the number of tables and chairs. The following linear program applies:

$$\begin{aligned}
\text{Maximize} \quad & P = 6X_T + 8X_C & \text{(objective)} \\
\text{Subject to} \quad & 30X_T + 20X_C \leq 300 & \text{(wood)} \\
& 5X_T + 10X_C \leq 110 & \text{(labor)} \\
\text{where} \quad & X_T, X_C \geq 0 &
\end{aligned}$$

The first step to solving a linear program with the simplex method is to express the problem as a series of equations. This is accomplished by adding a new variable to each constraint and incorporating them into the objective function.

$$\begin{aligned}
\text{Maximize} \quad & P = 6X_T + 8X_C + 0S_W + 0S_L & \text{(objective)} \\
\text{Subject to} \quad & 30X_T + 20X_C + 1S_W + 0S_L = 300 & \text{(wood)} \\
& 5X_T + 10X_C + 0S_W + 1S_L = 110 & \text{(labor)} \\
\text{where} \quad & X_T, X_C, S_W, S_L \geq 0 &
\end{aligned}$$

The new variables are the slack variables and represent the amount of unused resources. Here, S_W is the amount of unused wood and S_L the amount of unused labor. Note that the slack variables S_W and S_L appear in the objective equation with coeffi-

---

[1]George Dantzig calculated that evaluating all corner point solutions could take longer than 15 billion years, which some estimate to be the approximate age of the universe.

cients of 0, reflecting the fact that unused resources contribute nothing to profit (or to cost) but remain assets in inventory. The nonnegativity conditions apply to S_W and S_L as well as to X_T and X_C. Slack variables cannot be negative. (If they were, it would mean that more of the resource than was originally available could be consumed, which would remove the limitation of the original constraint.)

The feasible solution region to the new problem cannot be completely graphed, because we now have four variables and our problem is four dimensional. Our algebraic system contains two constraint equations with four unknowns.

$$30X_T + 20X_C + 1S_W + 0S_L = 300$$
$$5X_T + 10X_C + 0S_W + 1S_L = 110$$

We learned how to solve two equations with two unknowns in Chapter 8 when we found the coordinates for the most attractive corner. But here *we have more unknowns than equations*. How do we find the solution?

In our Redwood Furniture problem, there are two more variables than equations. The values of these extra variables must be fixed before the equations can be solved algebraically. Part of our problem is deciding which variables are assigned arbitrary values and which variables are "free" to be solved algebraically. We must also determine what arbitrary values to use.

We will refer to the variables that must be solved algebraically as the **basic variable mix.** As we have seen, their values can be found only after the other variables have been fixed at some arbitrary level. The fixed-value variables are identified as not being in the basic mix. Table 9-4 shows all of the possible combinations of basic and nonbasic variables for the Redwood Furniture problem. In each of the six cases, two complementary pairs of variables are involved.

We have noted that an essential feature of simplex is to evaluate corner points only. *Such a corner point is the algebraic solution to the constraint equations when the nonbasic variables have been arbitrarily set at 0.* This fact considerably simplifies finding solutions and allows us to greatly streamline the overall simplex method.

Each of the six basic mix pairs in Table 9-4 for the Redwood Furniture problem provides a different **corner point solution.** All of these corner points are graphed in Figure 9-12. (You may verify any solution in Table 9-4 by zeroing out the nonbasic variables in the preceding four-variable equations and then solving algebraically to get the levels of the basic variables.) Only corner points A, B, C, and D are feasible. Point E is infeasible because it violates the labor constraint (the algebraic solution leads

TABLE 9-4	Possible Basic Variable-Mix Combinations and Their Algebraic Solutions for the Redwood Furniture Problem

CORNER POINT	BASIC VARIABLE MIX (free variables)	NONBASIC VARIABLES (arbitrarily set at 0)	ALGEBRAIC SOLUTION				
			X_T	X_C	S_W	S_L	P
A	$S_W \, S_L$	$X_T \, X_C$	0	0	300	110	$ 0
B	$S_W \, X_C$	$X_T \, S_L$	0	11	80	0	88
C	$S_L \, X_T$	$X_C \, S_W$	10	0	0	60	60
D	$X_T \, X_C$	$S_W \, S_L$	4	9	0	0	96
E	$S_L \, X_C$	$S_W \, X_T$	0	15	0	−40	Infeasible
F	$S_W \, X_T$	$S_L \, X_C$	22	0	−360	0	Infeasible

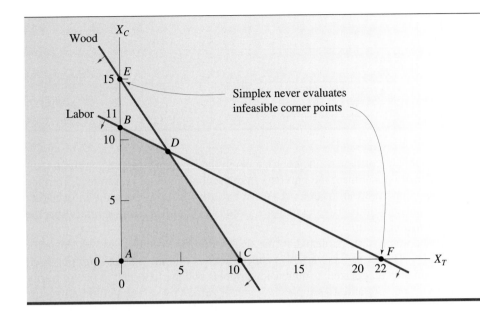

FIGURE 9-12

Possible corner point projections for the Redwood Furniture problem

to a negative quantity for S_L), and point F is infeasible because it violates the wood constraint.

Although the Redwood Furniture problem has been graphed in Figure 9-12, the augmented problem incorporating slacks S_W and S_L is *four-dimensional*. The feasible solution region is a polyhedron in that space. Thus, simplex evaluates the corners of a geometrical surface that cannot be pictured on an ordinary graph. Figure 9-12 only shows *projections* of that higher dimensional region onto the two-dimensional X_T-X_C plane.

Simplex ordinarily begins at the corner that represents "doing nothing," where the basic variable mix is composed only of slack variables. It then moves to the neighboring corner point that improves the solution at the greatest rate. It continues to move progressively from neighboring corner to neighboring corner, making the greatest possible improvement in the solution on each successive move. When no more improvements can be made in the solution, the most attractive corner has been found.

The process for doing this is not graphical. Problems solved through simplex ordinarily have too many dimensions to be pictured. Rather, each corner is represented by a set of equations manipulated in tabular form. Simplex makes those evaluations one at a time, through a series of iterations, skipping many corners that may be infeasible or unattractive. Each new corner is reached by pivoting from the previous one. That is achieved by replacing one basic-mix variable (the **exiting variable**) with a nonbasic variable (the **entering variable**).

Illustration of the Simplex Method

Simplex begins with the equations in standard format, with slack and surplus variables included. Ordinarily, all computations are done on a computer. To streamline things, symbols are removed from the underlying equations, each represented by a row in the simplex tableau. Figure 9-13 shows the initial simplex tableau for the Redwood Furniture problem. Along the top of the central portion we list the problem variables in their original order of appearance in the formulated constraint equations. In the top margin, we list the corresponding per-unit profits for the objective equation. The first row in the

FIGURE 9-13
Initial simplex tableau for
the Redwood Furniture
problem

UNIT PROFIT		6	8	0	0	
	Basic Mix	X_T	X_C	S_W	S_L	Sol.
0	S_W	30	20	1	0	300
0	S_L	5	10	0	1	110

body of the tableau consists of the coefficients in the first constraint equation in their original order of appearance; the numbers in the second row are reproduced from the second constraint equation. In essence, these two rows supply the same information that the original equations provide; *they are streamlined and equivalent versions of the original constraint equations.*

The first column of the tableau lists the slack variables S_W and S_L; we will solve for these variables. The basic-mix variables appear in this column. All variables not listed in this column are categorized as nonbasic variables and are assumed to be arbitrarily fixed at zero. Thus, X_T and X_C are presently set at zero. The solution column lists the values of the basic variables: $S_W = 300$ and $S_L = 110$. This tells us that all of the available wood and labor are unused. Figure 9-14 shows the corners that will be evaluated. This first simplex iteration corresponds with the corner point for "doing nothing," for which there is a zero profit.

The values in the body of the tableau represent the original constraint coefficients and are sometimes referred to as **exchange coefficients,** because they indicate how many units of the variable listed on the left must be given up to accommodate a unit increase in the variable listed at the top of the tableau. Thus, the value 30 in the S_W row and the X_T column indicates that 30 board feet of unused wood may be exchanged for one table. We can also see that exactly 20 board feet of wood must be provided to produce one chair. Similarly, 5 hours of unused labor must be given up to produce one

FIGURE 9-14
Graphical illustration
of successive corners
evaluated in simplex

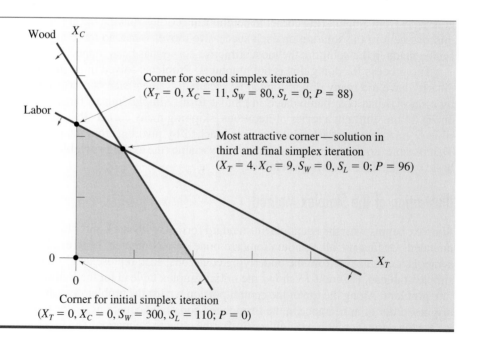

Wood X_C

Corner for second simplex iteration
$(X_T = 0, X_C = 11, S_W = 80, S_L = 0; P = 88)$

Labor

Most attractive corner—solution in
third and final simplex iteration
$(X_T = 4, X_C = 9, S_W = 0, S_L = 0; P = 96)$

0 X_T

0

Corner for initial simplex iteration
$(X_T = 0, X_C = 0, S_W = 300, S_L = 110; P = 0)$

table, and 10 hours must be given up to produce one chair. The exchange coefficients are 0 or 1 for the basic-mix variables and are not very meaningful. They indicate, for example, that 1 board foot of unused wood may be traded for 1 more board foot and that no unused wood is required to accommodate more unused labor.

The simplex tableau for the Redwood Furniture problem is expanded in Figure 9-15. In the left margin, we list the per-unit profits for the basic variables. For the slack variables S_W and S_L, per-unit profits are 0. Below the dark line are two special rows where economic data are compiled that tell us which corner point to evaluate next. Values in the **sacrifice row** tell us what we will lose in per-unit profits by making a change. The **improvement row** indicates the per-unit change in profits that will result from making that same change.

The sacrifice entry for each column is determined by making the following computation:

$$\text{Unit sacrifice} = \text{Unit profit column} \times \text{Exchange coefficient column}$$

For example, in the X_T column, we have

UNIT PROFIT COLUMN	$\times$	X_T COLUMN	
0	$\times$	30	= 0
0	$\times$	5	= 0
		Sacrifice for X_T = 0	

The first product (0×30) is the unit profit of unused wood multiplied by the amount needed to make one table; this is the reduction in unused wood profit required to produce one table. The second product (0×5) is the unused labor profit that must be given up to make that table. Together, these products constitute the profit that must be sacrificed by the basic mix variables to accommodate a unit increase in tables.

This computation can also be made for the solution column. The entry obtained, which is $P = 0$ in Figure 9-15, is the current value of the objective function.

Because the unit profit column for the current basic mix (the slack variables) consists of zeros, all of the sacrifice terms result in product sums of zero. This concept seems obvious now—we give up no profit to make tables or chairs if the unused resource has no profit to begin with—but it will prove crucial later.

The entries in the improvement row are found by subtracting each sacrifice term from the corresponding unit profit listed at the top of the tableau.

$$\text{Unit improvement} = \text{Unit profit} - \text{Unit sacrifice}$$

UNIT PROFIT		6	8	0	0		
	Basic Mix	X_T	X_C	S_W	S_L	**Sol.**	
0	S_W	30	20	1	0	300	Exchange
0	S_L	5	10	0	1	110	coefficients
	Sac.	0	0	0	0	0	Current P
	Imp.	6	8	0	0	—	

FIGURE 9-15
An expanded simplex tableau for the Redwood Furniture problem

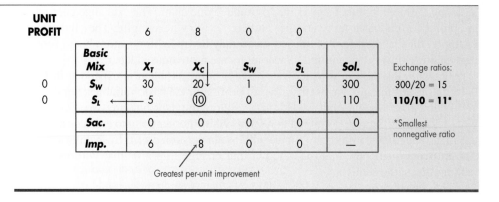

FIGURE 9-16
Simplex tableau showing the entering and exiting variables and the pivot element

UNIT PROFIT		6	8	0	0		
	Basic Mix	X_T	$X_C \downarrow$	S_W	S_L	Sol.	Exchange ratios:
0	S_W	30	20	1	0	300	300/20 = 15
0	S_L ←	5	⑩	0	1	110	**110/10 = 11***
	Sac.	0	0	0	0	0	*Smallest nonnegative ratio
	Imp.	6	8	0	0	—	

Greatest per-unit improvement

In the tableau in Figure 9-15, all of the improvement terms are identical to the unit profits, since all the sacrifices are zero.

We must now determine the **entering variable** through economic analysis. In our profit maximization problem we accomplish this by finding the largest positive value in the improvement row.

Referring to Figure 9-16, we can see that 8 in the X_C column is the largest per-unit improvement. This means that we can improve the current solution by $8 per unit for each chair made. Increasing the value of the X_C variable from 0 (remember, X_C is a nonbasic variable and all such variables equal 0) to some positive quantity is the best change to make. (Another change—increasing tables—has a smaller per-unit improvement of only $6.) Thus, X_C is the entering variable. We indicate this on the simplex tableau by placing a small arrow pointing downward just to the right of the X_C column. Next, we find the **exiting variable.** As the name implies, one variable will enter the basic mix and replace another, which *exits* from the basic mix and assumes a nonbasic status. Such an exchange of variables is referred to as a **pivot operation.** Simplex involves a sequence of such pivots. In each case, the pivot identifies the next corner point to be evaluated. The current basic mix differs by only one variable from the subsequent basic mix created by the pivot. The two corresponding corners are often called *neighbors.*

At this point, we want to increase our entering variable X_C as much as possible from 0. Dividing the solution value by the corresponding exchange coefficient in the X_C column, we obtain

$$300/20 = 15 \quad \text{for the } S_W \text{ row}$$
$$110/10 = 11 \quad \text{for the } S_L \text{ row}$$

These **exchange ratios** tell us how many chairs Redwood can make by trading away all of the current level of the respective basic variable. By trading 300 board feet of unused wood, Redwood can produce 15 chairs, because one chair can be exchanged at the rate of 20 board feet. Likewise, by trading all 110 hours of unused labor at an exchange rate of 10 hours per chair, Redwood can produce 11 chairs.

The **exit criterion** requires that we find the smallest ratio; here, it is 11. This value limits the number of chairs that can result from the exchange. It is impossible to make more than 11 chairs because all of the available labor will be used to produce that quantity. An easy way to remember this rule is the rhyme, "the row that's low has to go." The importance of this rule is that it determines the critical resource at this stage in the

solution, that is, the resource in shortest supply. The exiting variable is therefore S_L, so that X_C will replace S_L in the basic mix. S_W will remain in the basic mix, because labor will be depleted before wood and some unused wood will still remain once the exchange is made. We indicate that unused labor exits the basic mix by placing a small arrow pointing toward the S_L in Figure 9-16.

The circled value in the X_C column and the S_L row is called the **pivot element.** This value is used to evaluate the new corner point represented by exchanging X_C and S_L. The evaluation is achieved by means of a *new* simplex tableau.

We must next construct a new simplex tableau that provides the solution values for the new corner point. Each basic-mix variable row must also represent an equation, and, together, these equations must preserve the underlying constraint relationships. We begin with the following constraint equations:

$$30X_T + 20X_C + 1S_W + 0S_L = 300 \quad \text{(old } S_W \text{ row)}$$
$$5X_T + 10X_C + 0S_W + 1S_L = 110 \quad \text{(old } S_L \text{ row)}$$

Set at 0

Since X_C is to replace S_L, we want to transform the second equation so that X_C will have a coefficient of 1. Dividing both sides of the second equation by 10 gives us

$$\left(\frac{5}{10}\right)X_T + \left(\frac{10}{10}\right)X_C + \left(\frac{0}{10}\right)S_W + \left(\frac{1}{10}\right)S_L = \frac{110}{10}$$

and provides us with the equivalent expression

$$\tfrac{1}{2}X_T + 1X_C + 0S_W + \tfrac{1}{10}S_L = 11 \quad \text{(new } X_C \text{ row)}$$

which we will refer to as the new X_C row. If the latest nonbasic variables, X_T and S_L, are set at 0, this equation directly provides the solution $X_C = 11$.

Now consider the following two equations:

$$30X_T + 20X_C + 1S_W + 0S_L = 300 \quad \text{(old } S_W \text{ row)}$$
$$\tfrac{1}{2}X_T + 1X_C + 0S_W + \tfrac{1}{10}S_L = 11 \quad \text{(new } X_C \text{ row)}$$

The variable X_C can be eliminated from the first equation so that X_C will appear in only one equation. Then $X_C = 11$ is a solution value that satisfies both equations. Subtracting 20 times the second equation from the first, we obtain

$$30X_T + 20X_C + 1S_W + 0S_L = 300$$
$$-20\left(\tfrac{1}{2}X_T + 1X_C + 0S_W + \tfrac{1}{10}S_L = 11\right)$$
$$\overline{20X_T + 0X_C + 1S_W - 2S_L = 80} \quad \text{(new } S_W \text{ row)}$$

We will refer to the equation for this difference as the new S_W row, because it provides the solution $S_W = 80$ when the nonbasic variables are set at 0 ($X_T = 0$, $S_L = 0$). This reflects the fact that when 11 chairs—each requiring 20 board feet of wood—are made, exactly $300 - 11(20) = 80$ board feet will remain unused.

Our two new constraint equations are then

$$20X_T + 0X_C + 1S_W - 2S_L = 80 \quad \text{(new } S_W \text{ row)}$$
$$\tfrac{1}{2}X_T + 1X_C + 0S_W + \tfrac{1}{10}S_L = 11 \quad \text{(new } X_C \text{ row)}$$

Set at 0

Because we obtained each equation by dividing both sides of an original constraint equation by a constant or by subtracting equal amounts from both sides of an original constraint equation, the two new equations preserve the problem constraints.

The beauty of the simplex method is that we do not have to perform all of these steps to obtain these new equations. We can work directly from the previous tableau to determine the values for the new tableau. The following procedure summarizes the steps for obtaining new rows.

SOLUTION PROCEDURE

STEPS FOR CALCULATING NEW SIMPLEX TABLEAU ROWS

a. **Modify pivot row.** Divide all values in the row of the exiting variable by the pivot element. (Such calculations can be easily made in your head.) Place the answers in the *same position* in the new tableau. Label this row with the symbol of the newly entered variable.

b. **Get zero coefficients for exiting variable.** To obtain each of the remaining rows, find the value in that row in the old tableau that is also in the pivot element column. Then, multiply the first number in the new row found in step (a) by this quantity and *subtract* that product from the old value in the first position. The result is the first term in the new row. Repeat this process for all positions in the new row, including the solution position. Then, repeat this process for all the remaining rows until the tableau is complete. The basic variables for these rows will be the same as they were in the old tableau.

c. **Update unit profit margin values.** Place the appropriate unit profits (costs) for the basic variables in the left margin.

Applying this procedure to the simplex tableau in Figure 9-16 results in the bottom tableau provided in Figure 9-17 for the Redwood Furniture problem. Every term in the new X_C row is found by dividing the respective old S_L row value by 10 (the pivot element). The new S_W row values are found by successively subtracting from the old S_W row the product of 20 (the old S_W row value in the pivot element column) multiplied by the new X_C row value for that column position. Notice that the new tableau is exactly what we would obtain if we transferred the coefficients from the equations at the bottom of the previous page. Also notice that this procedure yields *column* values for each basic-mix variable with a 1 where the basic variable's row and column intersect and a 0 elsewhere in the column. This feature ensures that the underlying equations will provide solution values when the nonbasic variables are zeroed out.

We must also find the per-unit sacrifice and improvement values for the new simplex tableau, which is given in Figure 9-18. But before we perform the calculations to obtain these values, let's assess the exchange coefficients in the X_T column. The value in the S_W row is 20, which indicates that Redwood must give up a net amount of 20 board feet of unused wood to make one table—not the 30 board feet specified in the original problem statement. Where are the missing 10 board feet? The second number in that column, 1/2, tells us that Redwood must also relinquish one-half of a chair to produce one table. This happens because some labor currently being spent on chairs must be diverted to that table. That one-half chair returns 5 hours of labor as well as the missing 10 board feet of wood to Redwood.

The exchange coefficients in the S_L column tell a similar story. To increase S_L by one unit—that is, to increase unused labor by 1 hour—we must trade $-2S_W$. In other words, if 1 hour of labor is *taken away* (which is what increasing unused resources

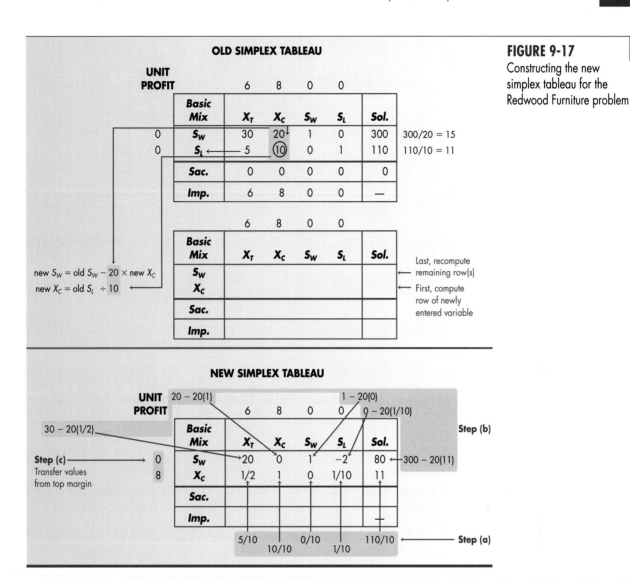

FIGURE 9-17
Constructing the new simplex tableau for the Redwood Furniture problem

means), Redwood must give up -2 board feet of unused wood; that is, Redwood gets back $+2$ board feet of unused wood (so that it uses 2 feet less than before). The net changes in unused resources correspond to the requirements for a fraction of a chair ($1/10$, to be exact) that must be relinquished if S_L is increased by 1 hour (remember, it takes 10 hours to make a whole chair). This is why the second exchange coefficient in the X_C row is $1/10$.

The per-unit profits for S_W and X_C are \$0 and \$8. The per-unit sacrifice for X_T is therefore

UNIT PROFIT	×	EXCHANGE COEFFICIENT	
0	×	20	= 0
8	×	1/2	= 4
		Sacrifice for X_T	= 4

FIGURE 9-18
Completed second
simplex tableau

UNIT PROFIT		6	8	0	0	
	Basic Mix	X_T	X_C	S_W	S_L	**Sol.**
0	S_W	20	0	1	−2	80
8	X_C	1/2	1	0	1/10	11
	Sac.	4	8	0	8/10	88 ← Current P
	Imp.	2	0	0	−8/10	—

This represents the $4 profit forgone by giving up the 1/2 chair to accommodate one table. For S_L, we obtain

UNIT PROFIT	×	EXCHANGE COEFFICIENT	
0	×	−2	= 0
8	×	1/10	= 8/10
		Sacrifice for S_L	= 8/10

which is the $8/10 profit (one-tenth of $8) lost by giving up the 1/10 of a chair that cannot be made if unused labor is increased by 1 hour. The value computed in the solution column is

$$0 \times 80 = 0$$
$$8 \times 11 = \underline{88}$$
$$88$$

which is the $88 profit represented by the current basic variable-mix solution.

The solution for the new basic variable mix may be read directly from Figure 9-18 as

$$X_T = 0 \qquad S_W = 80$$
$$X_C = 11 \qquad S_L = 0$$
$$P = 88$$

X_T and S_L are not in the basic variable mix and must therefore be 0. Figure 9-14 shows that we have now reached a second corner of the feasible solution region that must be evaluated further. For this purpose, we must determine the possible per-unit profit improvements from increasing each of the nonbasic variables.

The values in the per-unit improvement row of the latest simplex tableau, shown again as the top tableau in Figure 9-19, are found by subtracting the sacrifice values from the profits listed in the top margin. We can see that only one value is positive (the 2 in the X_T column). This indicates that increasing X_T will result in a net increase in profits of $2 per unit. Redwood does not receive the full profit of $6 on each table because for every table made we must "steal" back resources that could be used to make one-half a chair, thereby losing $4 of chair profit. Thus, Redwood receives a profit of only $6 − $4 = $2 per table.

We have now finished a complete iteration of the simplex method for the Redwood Furniture problem. At this point, according to the procedure, we return to step 2 and begin a new iteration with a new tableau and basic variable mix. Each iteration repeats the earlier ones, using new values.

UNIT PROFIT		6	8	0	0		
	Basic Mix	X_T	X_C	S_W	S_L	**Sol.**	Exchange ratios:
0	S_W ←	⑳	0	1	−2	80	**80/20 = 4***
8	X_C	1/2	1	0	1/10	11	11/(1/2) = 22
	Sac.	4	8	0	8/10	88	*Smallest
	Imp.	2	0	0	−8/10	—	nonnegative ratio

[old S_W ÷ 20]	6	X_T	1	0	1/20	−1/10	4
[old X_C − 1/2 × new X_T]	8	X_C	0	1	−1/40	3/20	9
		Sac.	6	8	1/10	6/10	96
		Imp.	0	0	−1/10	−6/10	—

No per-unit improvement is positive;
no further improvement is possible

FIGURE 9-19
Constructing the third simplex tableau from the second tableau for the Redwood Furniture problem

Our entering variable is X_T. According to the exit criterion, we see that the smallest exchange ratio applies to S_W, which limits table production more (Redwood would run out of unused wood before giving back all chairs). This exchange will result in 4 tables and no unused wood, so that the exiting variable is S_W. The present pivot element occurs where the S_W row and X_T column intersect and has a value of 20.

The new (third) simplex tableau, constructed by transforming the second tableau, appears as the bottom tableau in Figure 9-19. This tableau provides the solution

$$X_T = 4 \qquad\qquad S_W = 0$$
$$X_C = 9 \qquad\qquad S_L = 0$$
$$P = 96$$

which we know from Figure 9-14 is the optimal solution. Simplex tells us that this must be the stopping point, because none of the per-unit improvement row values is positive. No further improvement is possible.

It will be helpful to summarize the required steps in the simplex method.

STEPS OF THE SIMPLEX METHOD

SOLUTION PROCEDURE

1. **Formulate the linear program in standardized format.** Add slack variables to the problem, eliminating any inequality constraints. Construct the initial simplex tableau, using slack variables in the starting basic variable mix.

2. **Find the sacrifice and improvement rows.**

3. **Apply the entry criterion.** Find the current nonbasic variable that increasing its value from zero will improve the objective at the greatest rate, breaking any ties arbitrarily. This variable is the **entering variable.** If no improvement can be found, the optimal solution is represented by the present tableau.

4. **Apply the exit criterion.** Use the current tableau's exchange coefficient values from the column of the entering variable to calculate the following **exchange ratio** for each row:

$$\frac{\text{Solution value}}{\text{Exchange coefficient}}$$

Ignoring ratios with zero or negative denominators, find the smallest *nonnegative* exchange ratio,* again breaking ties arbitrarily. The basic variable for the row of this ratio is the **exiting variable.** Mark this variable's row with an arrow pointing left.

5. **Construct a new simplex tableau using steps a–c (page 340).**   Replace the basic mix label of the exiting variable with that of the entering variable. All other basic variable-mix labels remain the same. Also, change the unit profit (unit cost) column value to correspond to the newly entered basic variable. Then, recompute the row values to obtain a new set of exchange coefficients applicable to each basic variable.

6. **Go back to step 2.**

---

*A divisor of zero results in an infinitely large ratio (and is treated as such, even when the numerator is zero, too). If all divisors are zero or negative, the problem is unbounded.

HISTORICAL NOTE

George B. Dantzig is known as the "Father of Linear Programming." Born in 1914, he was a graduate student at the University of California, Berkeley, in the 1940s when he displayed a "unique brand of genius that would eventually elevate him to almost mythical status."[1] In Dantzig's own words:

"I was a grad student at Berkeley working on my Ph.D. I wasn't very good at getting to his class on time. [The professor] had a habit of putting homework assignments up on the blackboard at the start of the class. When I came in late I'd copy the problem, take it home and work on it.

On this particular day there were two problems. They seemed more difficult than usual. When I handed in the assignment, I apologized for taking so long [and I] left, never expecting to hear about it again.

One Sunday morning a couple of weeks later he came running over to my house and banged on the door. He rushed in and said he had written an introduction to the problems and was going to submit the paper for publication. It turns out that those two problems were two very well-known, unsolved statistical problems. I had solved them both."[2]

Subsequently, Dantzig's achievement was retold in the media as an inspirational story. Believing he was working on a homework assignment, he had solved two famous "unsolvable" problems that had stumped generations of statisticians. A legend was born.

---

[1] Peter Horner, "Interview with a Living Legend," *OR/MS Today* (October 1999), p. 26.
[2] Horner, ibid, p. 27.

Simplex with the Computer

Before modern computing, all of the simplex steps were done by hand. Now, linear programs are almost always solved on computers. Most software employ the simplex method, although many programs only provide users with the final answer. Even though we won't do the calculations by hand, it can be helpful to see the details. *Quick-Quant* allows us the option of doing that. Figure 9-20 shows the screens created in solving the Redwood Furniture problem.

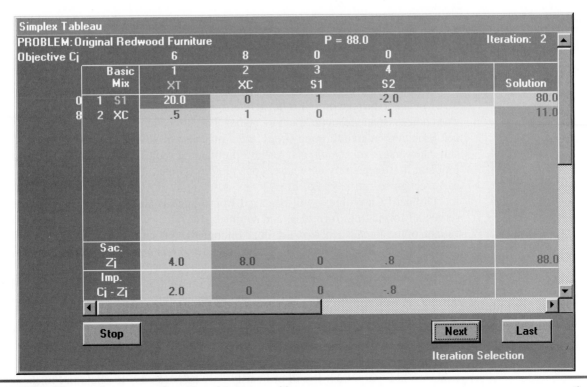

FIGURE 9-20 Simplex iterations for Redwood Furniture problem

continued

Simplex Tableau

PROBLEM: Original Redwood Furniture				P = 96.0			Iteration: 3
Objective Cj		6	8	0	0		
	Basic Mix	1 XT	2 XC	3 S1	4 S2		Solution
6 1	XT	1	0	.05	-.1		4.0
8 2	XC	0	1	-.025	.15		9.0
Sac. Zj		6.0	8.0	.1	.6		96.0
Imp. Cj - Zj		0	0	-.1	-.6		

Done   Next   Last

Optimal Solution   Iteration Selection

FIGURE 9-20 *(continued)*

9-12 (OPTIONAL) SAVING PROBLEM DATA AND EXCHANGING FILES

Regardless of which program is used in running a problem, it is always a good idea to save the problem data. *QuickQuant* can save a problem either as a .prb file (meant to be read only by *QuickQuant*) or a .txt file (readable by other programs). The choice is made from the main menu bar. The latter file type can be accessed by Excel. Problems entered through *QuickQuant* may also be solved using Microsoft Excel, and vice versa. *QuickQuant* can retrieve problems saved as .txt files by Excel and any problem files created by earlier versions of *QuickQuant*. The program will automatically recognize either type of file.

Ordinarily, a problem will be saved from Excel as an .xls file because that preserves all formatting, formulas, and settings. But Excel will also save a streamlined version of the spreadsheet as a .txt file. Although the formatting, formulas, and settings cannot be included in the .txt file, that storage format is portable, and the .txt file can be directly accessed by *QuickQuant*.

Excel can open a .txt file orginally created by itself or by *QuickQuant*. In the latter case, all Excel formatting, settings, and formulas must then be supplied for the imported spreadsheet. The Excel procedure for accessing any text file is a bit elaborate. Figure 9-21 shows the dialog box for doing this. There, "Text Files" or "All Files" must be designated to get a listing of possibilities.

After the .txt file has been selected, Excel brings to screen its Text Import Wizard, as shown in Figure 9-22. It will ordinarily only be necessary to click on Finish. That

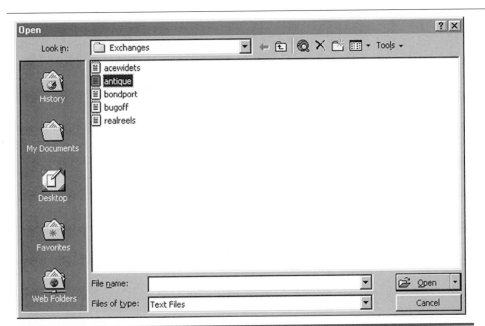

FIGURE 9-21
Excel's Open File
dialog box

will bring to screen a complete spreadsheet containing the imported problem. The spreadsheet may then be formatted, with formulas incorporated as needed, and evaluated like any other Excel problem.

When Excel saves a spreadsheet as an .xls file, all formatting, formulas, and settings are preserved. It is recommended that spreadsheet problems be saved that way. But only a streamlined .txt file can be accessed by *QuickQuant*, so the same problem

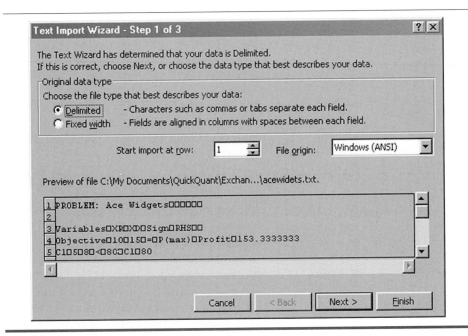

FIGURE 9-22
Excel Text Import Wizard
dialog box

FIGURE 9-23
Excel screen dialog box for saving spreadsheet as a text file

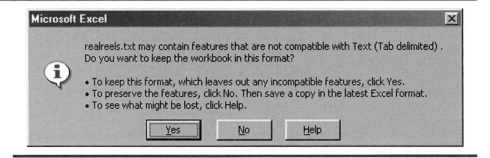

can be saved a second time in the .txt mode. It is important that the problem formats follow those shown in the book. (For details, see the guides to *QuickQuant* and Excel on the CD-ROM accompanying this book.) While creating the .txt file, Excel will present the dialog box in Figure 9-23. Clicking on Yes completes the process.

Warning: *QuickQuant* cannot accommodate numerical input with commas. The Excel spreadsheet must be edited to eliminate them before creating the .txt file.

PROBLEMS

The following problems all involve too many variables to be solved graphically and are to be *formulated only*. Standardized formats are optional.

9-1 Rott Irony manufactures four types of light fixtures. A fancy lamp yields a profit of $100, takes 10 hours of labor and 2 hours of machine time, and requires 10 square feet of sheet metal. An ornate lamp yields a profit of $150, takes 8 hours of labor and 3 hours of machine time, and requires 20 square feet of metal. The plain and rococo lamps each yield a $200 profit and involve 1 hour of machine time. However, the rococo lamp requires 20 hours of labor and 30 square feet of metal, and the plain lamp requires 10 hours of labor and 15 square feet of metal. Rott must produce at least twice as many plain as rococo lamps. Only 1,000 hours of labor and 200 hours of machine time are available, and 5,000 square feet of sheet metal are in inventory. Rott wants to determine how many of each type of lamp to make to maximize total profits. Formulate this problem as a linear program.

9-2 You have been given the assignment of scheduling the production of Hoopla Hoops. There are four basic models, with the following resource usages:

	Model				
Resource	A	B	C	D	Available
Plastic	5	6	6	7	100 ft
Beads	10	12	15	15	500 oz
Nylon	4	5	5	0	600 ft
Teflon	0	2	3	4	200 gal
Labor	.5	.4	.5	.8	300 hr

The number of model A's cannot exceed the combined total of the other models. Hoopla must make at least 50 model B and 20 model D hoops.

Hoopla wants to determine the number of models of each type that should be made in order to maximize total profit. The unit profits are $2 for models A and C, $1.50 for model B, and $2.50 for model D. Formulate Hoopla's problem as a linear program.

9-3 The Myrtlewood Box Company manufactures small, medium, and large boxes. Wood usages are 4, 8, and 16 board feet for the respective products. Assembly time requirements are 1, 2, and 3 hours, respectively. Only 500 board feet of wood and 200 hours of assembly time are presently available. All boxes produced will be sold for the following unit profits: small, $10; medium, $15; and large, $30. How many boxes of each type should Myrtlewood produce? Formulate this problem as a linear program.

9-4 Quicker Oats must determine how much of its $200,000 advertising and promotional budget should be spent in the following media: television, radio, magazines, and prize promotion. Each dollar spent on television advertising increases sales $10; both radio and magazine ads result in half that return, and prize promotion returns $20 in sales for each dollar invested. Television advertising cannot exceed half of the total budget, and total radio advertising must be at least 20% of total TV advertising. At least $20,000 must be spent on magazine ads, and no more than $25,000 may be spent on the prize promotion. Management's objective is to maximize the total increase in Quicker's sales volume. Formulate the decision as a linear program.

9-5 CompuQuick must determine which of its computer facilities should process client company payrolls. Based on the complexity and size of the payroll and on processing speed, data-transmission requirements, and volumes of input and output, the following costs apply:

	Company Payroll		
Facility	**Blitz Beer**	**WaySafe Markets**	**Quicker Oats**
Arizona	$500	$750	$400
California	600	500	300
Illinois	700	600	300

Each facility has the capacity to process only one payroll. CompuQuick wants to minimize its total data-processing costs. Formulate this problem as a linear program, using double subscripts in defining your variables.

9-6 A trust officer for the Million Bank wants to invest in the following bonds:

Bond	**Yield**	**Maturity**	**Risk**	**Tax-Free**
A	8%	Long	High	Yes
B	9	Short	Low	No
C	9	Long	High	No
D	10	Short	Low	No
E	9	Short	High	Yes

She will use a linear program to find the dollar investment in each bond that will maximize total interest income.

(a) Define the variables that apply and then express her linear programming objective in terms of these.

(b) Express each of the following linear programming constraints using the variables defined in (a).
(1) Exactly $100,000 will be invested altogether.
(2) At least $50,000 must be placed in short maturity bonds.
(3) No more than $30,000 may be invested in high-risk issues.
(4) At least $25,000 must be placed in tax-free issues.
(5) Total funds invested in low-risk bonds must be less than or equal to total funds placed in long-maturity issues.
(6) The interest income derived from tax-free bonds must be at least one-fourth of the total income.

9-7 Ima Hogg wants to determine the quantity of ingredients to use in making each pound of sausage at a minimum cost. The available ingredients and their costs are provided in the following table:

Pound of Ingredient	**Cost**	**Protein**	**Fat**	**Water**
Hog bellies	$.30	3 oz	5 oz	6 oz
Tripe	.20	5	3	4
Beef	.70	4	2	5
Pork	.60	3	4	9
Chicken	.45	3	3	4

Ima must meet the specified weight exactly, and there are further restrictions. Not more than 10% of the sausage weight can be composed of hog bellies and tripe, chicken cannot exceed 25% of the total content, and at least 30% of the sausage must consist of beef. In addition, a minimum of 3 ounces of protein must be present in each pound of sausage. Furthermore, each pound of sausage may contain a maximum of 4 ounces of fat and a maximum of 8 ounces of water. Formulate the decision as a linear program.

9-8 The BugOff Chemical Company manufactures three pesticides—Ant-Can't, Boll-Toll, and Caterpillar-Chiller—at respective profits of $5, $6, and $7 per gallon. BugOff must decide what quantities of each pesticide to produce. Regardless of brand, each gallon requires 100 milligrams (.1 gram) of catalyst. Every gallon of Ant-Can't and Caterpillar-Chiller requires 1/10 gallon of malathion, and each gallon of Boll-Toll and Caterpillar-Chiller must contain 2/10 gallon of

parathion. Seasonal requirements dictate that the quantity of Ant-Can't may exceed the quantity of Boll-Toll by no more than 500 gallons. The available ingredients are 1,000 grams of catalyst, 1,000 gallons of malathion, and 2,000 gallons of parathion. BugOff wants to produce the most profitable quantities of each pesticide. Formulate this problem as a linear program.

9-9 Willy B. Rich wants to invest $100,000 of current receipts to maximize total annual interest income. He has narrowed his choices to a municipal bond yielding 6%, an industrial bond yielding 8%, Treasury bills at 10%, and certificates of deposit (CDs) at 9%. For safety, at least one-half of the funds must be placed in bonds. For liquidity, at least 25% of the funds must be invested in CDs. Due to volatile Fed policies, no more than 20% of the portfolio can be in Treasury bills. Tax-sheltering considerations dictate that at least 30% of the investment must be in municipal bonds. Formulate this problem as a linear program.

9-10 Refer to the scent-mixing problem described in Section 9-9. Formulate each of the following constraints in a form suitable for incorporation into the original linear program.
(a) The proportion of alcohol in cologne cannot exceed 50% of the total volume. The oil contains no alcohol, but the rinse is 50% alcohol and the stabilizer is 20% alcohol.
(b) The volume of skin-bracing agents in the aftershave cannot exceed 30% of the total volume. These agents comprise 10% of the oil, 20% of the rinse, and 20% of the stabilizer.

9-11 Druid's Drayage hauls rock from two quarries to three tombstone masons. The manager, H. Priest, wants to minimize total shipping costs in such a way that every quarry operates precisely at full capacity and each mason receives exactly the number of stones demanded. The unit shipping costs and quantity requirements for tombstones are provided in the following table:

From Quarry	To Mason			Quarry Capacity
	Cedrick	Dunstan	Eldred	
Abinger	£10	£ 15	£ 8	100
Barnesly	12	9	10	200
Mason Demand	50	150	100	300

A linear program may be used to establish a shipping schedule that indicates how many tombstones should be supplied from each quarry to the various masons. A quarry can service any number of masons, and any mason can receive shipments from one or more quarries. Formulate this problem as a linear program, using variables defined with double subscripts.

9-12 All-American Meat Processors is mixing the ingredients for a batch of German and Italian sausages. The following cuts are to be used:

Meat	Cost per Pound	Available Quantity (lbs)
Beef rib	$1.00	200
Beef shank	1.50	500
Beef tongue	1.00	700
Pork	.90	1,000
Lamb	1.20	800

All-American wants to determine the minimum cost mixture that will provide at least 500 pounds of German sausage and 300 pounds of Italian. This must be done so that at least 60% of the German sausage is beef and at least 80% of the Italian sausage is beef. Furthermore, the German sausage can contain no more than 10% lamb, while the Italian sausage cannot have more than 20% pork. Using double-subscripted variables throughout, formulate All-American's problem as a linear program.

9-13 ChipMont manufactures silicon wafer circuits for use in microprocessors. Computer makers presently buy ChipMont's entire production of the following types of silicon chips: central processing unit (CPU), integrated circuit, and core memory.

Item	Chip Types			Available Maximums
	CPU	Integrated	Memory	
Silicon	.005	.02	.01	10,000 sheets
Sorting labor	.2	.5	.1	200,000 minutes
Chemical wash	.10	.40	.15	400,000 hours
Profit per wafer	$.25	$.40	$.15	

ChipMont must decide how many of each chip to manufacture. The number of integrated circuits must be at least as large as the combined total for the other two types of wafers.

(a) Formulate ChipMont's decision as a linear program.

(b) One possible production plan is to make 50,000 CPU's, 300,000 integrated circuits, and 200,000 core memories. Place these quantities in each of your linear programming constraints to verify that this plan is feasible. Then, find the corresponding profit.

9-14 Channel Zee blends two fragrance bases, Mystery and Anomaly, which are used by perfume makers worldwide. The ingredients include gland extract, spice oil, and brandy. Channel wants to use linear programming in determining what volume of each ingredient to mix in one batch each of the final products. This will be done to maximize total profit. Costs per liter are: gland, $5,000; spice, $100; and brandy, $10. Mystery sells for $200 per liter and Anomaly for $300.

(a) Define the variables that apply and then express the linear programming objective.

(b) The following proportions of ingredient volumes contain agents for fixing perfumes:

Ingredient	Preserving	Accentuating	Stabilizing
Gland extract	.01	.20	.01
Spice oil	.10	.02	.05
Brandy	.20	.01	.01

Express each of the following constraints using the variables defined in (a):

(1) Preserving agents in the Mystery batch must be at least 10% of the total volume for that product.

(2) Accentuating agents cannot exceed 15% of the total Anomaly volume.

(3) Stabilizing agents must be at least 2% of the total Mystery volume.

(4) Stabilizing agents cannot exceed 3% of the total Anomaly volume.

(5) The preserving agents in Mystery must occupy at least twice the volume of the accentuating agents.

(6) The stabilizing agents in Anomaly cannot exceed one-tenth the volume of the preserving agents.

9-15 Conformity Systems has three employees: a clerk, a typist, and a stenographer. Each employee will be assigned exactly one of the following tasks: filing, bookkeeping, or report preparation. The man-

ager wants to assign workers to jobs so that total cost is minimized. The costs for each possible employee–job assignment are provided in the following table:

Employee	Job		
	Filing	Bookkeeping	Reports
Clerk	$20	$25	$35
Typist	25	20	30
Stenographer	30	25	25

Treating each possible employee–job assignment as a separate variable, formulate this problem as a linear program.

9-16 Blitz Beer has allotted $10,000 for radio advertising in Gotham City and must determine the placement of spot ads that will maximize increased sales. Top-40 stations attract a heavier beer-drinking audience than do golden-oldie stations, but top-40 stations also charge more for each spot. The following data apply:

Station	Cost per Spot	Sales Increase per Spot	Spots Available	Format
KBAT	$100	$300	30	Top-40
WJOK	50	120	Unlimited	Golden-oldie
WROB	75	150	Unlimited	Golden-oldie
KPOW	150	400	40	Top-40

At least 25% of the spots must be placed with golden-oldie stations. Formulate Blitz's problem as a linear program.

9-17 Geo-Pet is the managing partner in a variety of oil-exploration ventures. It must decide its level of dollar investment in the five ventures described in the following table:

Joint Venture	Expected Return	Minimum Investment	Primary Product
Athabasca Tar Sands (Canada)	100%	$100,000	Crude
Kern County (USA)	30	None	Crude
Louisiana Miocene Trend (USA)	50	50,000	Gas
Persian Gulf (Arabia)	150	None	Crude
West Texas (USA)	75	100,000	Gas

Geo-Pet wants to maximize its expected rate of return on a maximum total investment of $700,000 and still meet the dollar minimums given here. At

least \$300,000 must be placed in gas-producing investments, and no more than one-half of the total amount can be invested outside the United States. Formulate this problem as a linear program.

9-18 Ace Widgets manufactures products in plant *A* at a cost of \$10 each and products in plant *B* at a cost of \$11 each. The products are shipped to warehouses at a cost of \$.01 per mile. The following distances apply:

From	Distance to C	D	E
A	100	200	300
B	200	100	200

Plant *A* can manufacture 1,000 units; plant *B* has the capacity to manufacture only 500 units. Warehouse demands are 500 units for each. Ace Widgets must determine the manufacturing and shipping schedule that will meet these exact limitations at the least total cost. Formulate Ace's problem as a linear program.

9-19 Backpacker's Budget Shoppe is concocting a package to sell under the label "Hiker's Daily Dried Gruel." Designed only with nutritional value and ease of preparation in mind, each kilogram of the mix must meet the nutritional requirements provided in the following table:

Nutrient	Nutritional Value of Ingredient per kilogram: Corn Meal	Beans	Spinach	Peanuts	Milk	Minimum Requirement
Calories	4,000	3,000	250	2,000	2,000	2,500
Protein	100	200	25	100	100	75 g
Iron	12	100	30	8	2	12 g
Vitamin A	4,000	1,000	50,000	5,000	13,000	5,000 units
Thiamin	2	6	1.5	1.5	1	2 mg
Riboflavin	1	5	3	1	6	3 μg
Niacin	12	25	8	80	3	20 mg
Ascorbic Acid	0	0	500	0	15	100 mg
Cost per kilogram	\$.50	\$.75	\$1.25	\$.75	\$1.50	

Formulate a linear program that determines the minimum-cost ingredient weights that satisfy these nutritional requirements.

Linear Programs to Be Solved

Solve the following linear programs either by hand using the simplex procedure, with *QuickQuant* 2000, or by using Excel's Solver:

9-20 Maximize $P = 3X_1 + 2X_2$

Subject to
$$10X_1 + 2X_2 \leq 20$$
$$X_1 + X_2 \leq 6$$
where $X_1, X_2 \geq 0$

9-21 Maximize $P = 8X_1 + 10X_2$

Subject to
$$15X_1 + 5X_2 \leq 45$$
$$10X_2 \leq 30$$
where $X_1, X_2 \geq 0$

9-22 Maximize $P = 7X_1 + 5X_2$

Subject to
$$X_1 + X_2 \leq 3$$
$$2X_1 + X_2 \leq 4$$
where $X_1, X_2 \geq 0$

9-23 Maximize $P = 2X_1 + X_2$

Subject to
$$5X_1 + 4X_2 \leq 40$$
$$12X_1 + 2X_2 \leq 24$$
$$X_1 + X_2 \leq 4$$
where $X_1, X_2 \geq 0$

9-24 Maximize $P = 50X_1 + 40X_2$

Subject to
$$25X_1 + 20X_2 \leq 100$$
$$40X_1 + 100X_2 \leq 200$$
$$2X_1 - X_2 \leq 4$$
where $X_1, X_2 \geq 0$

9-25 Maximize $P = X_1 + 2X_2$

Subject to
$$2X_1 + 2X_2 \leq 8$$
$$4X_1 + 2X_2 \leq 12$$
$$-3X_1 + 5X_2 \leq 15$$
$$X_1 \leq 4$$
where $X_1, X_2 \geq 0$

9-26 Maximize $P = 200X_1 + 150X_2$

Subject to
$$100X_1 + 150X_2 \leq 300$$
$$-200X_1 + 50X_2 \leq 100$$
$$25X_1 + 25X_2 \leq 50$$
$$40X_1 + 20X_2 \leq 60$$

where $X_1, X_2 \geq 0$

9-27 Maximize $P = 10X_1 + X_2 + 4X_3$

Subject to
$$15X_1 + 3X_2 + 8X_3 \leq 75$$
$$15X_1 + X_2 + 2X_3 \leq 30$$

where $X_1, X_2, X_3 \geq 0$

9-28 Maximize $P = 2X_1 + 3X_2 + 4X_3$

Subject to
$$5X_1 + 4X_2 + 3X_3 \leq 12$$
$$X_1 - 4X_2 + 7X_3 \leq 18$$

where $X_1, X_2, X_3 \geq 0$

9-29 Maximize $P = 5X_1 + X_2 + 4X_3$

Subject to
$$5X_1 - X_2 + 2X_3 \leq 10$$
$$-X_1 + X_2 + 2X_3 \leq 2$$
$$3X_1 + 6X_2 + 4X_3 \leq 14$$

where $X_1, X_2, X_3 \geq 0$

9-30 Maximize $P = 16X_1 + 20X_2 + 10X_3$

Subject to
$$10X_1 + 20X_2 + 15X_3 \leq 45$$
$$10X_1 + 10X_2 - 10X_3 \leq 10$$
$$40X_1 + 10X_2 + 30X_3 \leq 80$$

where $X_1, X_2, X_3 \geq 0$

9-31 Maximize $P = 16X_1 + 20X_2 + 40X_3 + 45X_4$

Subject to
$$8X_1 + 3X_2 + 2X_3 + 10X_4 \leq 22$$
$$-2X_1 + 4X_2 + 6X_3 + 8X_4 \leq 30$$
$$14X_1 - X_2 + X_4 \leq 20$$

where $X_1, X_2, X_3, X_4 \geq 0$

9-32 Maximize $P = 7X_1 + 5X_2 + 3X_3 + 6X_4$

Subject to
$$2X_1 + 2X_2 + 2X_3 + 2X_4 \leq 15$$
$$X_1 \leq 5$$
$$X_4 \leq 10$$

where $X_1, X_2, X_3, X_4 \geq 0$

Computer Problems

The following may be solved using *QuickQuant* or some other suitable program, including an electronic spreadsheet.

9-33 Refer to Problem 9-1 and your answer to that exercise. How many lamps of each type should Rott Irony make and what will be his maximum profit?

9-34 Refer to Problem 9-2 and your answer to that exercise. How many models of each type should Hoopla Hoops make and what will be the maximum profit?

9-35 Refer to Problem 9-3 and your answer to that exercise. How many boxes of each size should Myrtlewood make and what will be the maximum profit?

9-36 Refer to Problem 9-4 and your answer to that exercise. How much should Quicker Oats spend on each medium and what will be the maximum increase in sales volume?

9-37 Refer to Problem 9-6 and your answer to that exercise. How much should Million Bank invest in each bond and what will be the maximum annual interest income?

9-38 Refer to Problem 9-7 and your answer to that exercise. What ingredient volumes should Ima Hogg select for making one pound of sausage and what will be the corresponding cost per pound of sausage?

9-39 Refer to Problem 9-8 and your answer to that exercise. How many gallons of each product should BugOff Chemical formulate and what will be the maximum profit?

9-40 Refer to Problem 9-9 and your answer to that exercise. How much should Willy B. Rich invest in

each financial instrument and what will be his annual interest income?

9-41 Sammy Love sells three types of candied apples on the street corner — butterscotch, cinnamon, and peppermint. In making today's batch, Sammy is limited only by the amounts of sugar and gelatin, because all other ingredients are in good supply. Each butterscotch apple requires 1 cup of sugar. Each cinnamon or peppermint apple requires $\frac{1}{2}$ cup of sugar. Cinnamon apples require 2 ounces of gelatin; peppermint apples, 1 ounce; and butterscotch apples, none. Only 200 cups of sugar and 100 ounces of gelatin are available.

Sammy makes a profit of $.10 on each butterscotch apple, $.15 on each cinnamon apple, and $.20 on each peppermint apple. He always sells his entire stock.

(a) Formulate Sammy's linear program.
(b) Identify any slack variables required to solve this problem using the simplex method.
(c) Determine how many candied apples of each type Sammy should make.

9-42 Grubby Stakes Mining Company is establishing a production plan for the current week at its Bonstock Lode, which has three main veins of varying characteristics. The net yields per ton for each of the veins is provided below.

| Ore | Mining Veins | | |
	Eastern	Northern	Tom's Lucky
Gold	.2 oz	.3 oz	.4 oz
Silver	30 oz	20 oz	30 oz
Copper	50 lb	20 lb	25 lb

Gold presently sells for $150 per ounce, silver sells for $5 per ounce, and copper sells for $2 per pound. Eastern is the most accessible vein, requiring 1 worker-hour per ton of ore; Northern and Tom's Lucky veins are more remote and require 2 worker-hours per ton. Only 300 worker-hours are available, and all labor costs are fixed. At least 100 tons must be mined from the Northern vein this week, so that it can be reshored next week; there are no tonnage limitations for the other tunnels. The company must also yield at least 5,000 pounds of copper to meet contractual commitments.

(a) Formulate Grubby's linear program to determine how many tons must be mined from each vein to maximize total revenue.
(b) Find the optimal solution.

9-43 The Flying Chef supplies in-flight dinners to airlines. On a particular run, the passengers are given their choice of beef, chicken, or fish entrees. The owner must decide how many meals of each type to prepare in order to minimize total cost. Historically, 55% of all passengers prefer beef, 30% prefer chicken, and 15% prefer fish. However, to compensate for varying tastes from flight to flight, the number of meals provided must be as great as the above percentages of total passengers. On the current flight, there are 200 passengers and 300 meals must be provided. Airline policy states that at least one-half the extra meals on any given flight must be beef. Costs are $2 for each beef entree, $1.50 for chicken, and $1 for fish.

(a) Formulate the linear program for this problem.
(b) Solve this problem.
(c) How many meals of each type should be provided?

9-44 Morrie's Thrift Shoppe sells three kinds of suits: used, seconds (rejects from large clothing manufacturers), and Hong Kong specials. Morrie is buying his stock for the coming season. The used suits yield an average profit of $30 per suit, each second nets $20, and the Hong Kong suits are the most profitable at $50 each. Because Morrie has a 100% markup policy, the preceding figures also represent his wholesale costs. Morrie can spend no more than $10,000 this year. To maintain his "quality" image, no more than one-fourth of his suits can be used suits. Morrie does not wish to be too exotic, so the Hong Kong suits must not outnumber the used and second suits combined. To maintain his factory contacts, Morrie must buy at least 100 seconds each year.

Morrie always sells his entire inventory every year, and he wants to maximize his total suit profits.

(a) Formulate this problem as a linear program.
(b) Identify any necessary slack and surplus variables separately and solve the problem.

9-45 Hoopla Hoops must decide how to allocate magazine advertising funds for water wheelies. This is to be done so that total exposure, based on circulation, is maximized. No more than $100,000 will be spent. The data on the right apply for one-page ads in various publications.

The total number of teen market ads must be no greater than the number of youth placements. Also, the number of general ads must be less than or equal to half the combined total of youth and teen placements. Finally, no more than $40,000 may be placed in teen-oriented media.

Determine the optimal number of ads to be placed in each of the magazines.

Magazine	Cost Per Ad (thousands)	Circulation (millions)	Maximum Placements	Type of Readership
1. Tiger Club	2.0	1.5	10	Teen
2. Rocky	2.5	1.4	2	Teen
3. Spider Glider	1.5	.7	10	Youth
4. Toy Fans	1.0	.8	3	Youth
5. Mr T's	2.0	1.1	2	Teen
6. Hideaway	2.0	1.5	5	General
7. Mickey Club	.8	.3	4	Youth
8. Sport Rods	1.2	.9	6	General
9. Go Cars	3.0	2.1	7	Youth
10. Two-4-8	1.8	1.9	5	Youth
11. Up We Go	1.5	1.4	5	Teen
12. Fan Times	1.5	1.6	4	Teen
13. Fan Fare	3.0	2.0	2	Teen
14. UpBeat	2.0	1.6	2	General
15. Comic Craze	.8	.9	3	Youth

9-46 Le Petite Fromagerie makes 10 varieties of cheese. Letting X_i denote the number of pounds to be made of variety i, the following linear program applies:

Maximize
$$P = 2.00X_1 + 2.50X_2 + 1.75X_3 + 1.50X_4 + 2.05X_5 + 2.85X_6 + 2.90X_7 + 3.15X_8 + 2.70X_9 + 1.95X_{10}$$

Subject to
$$.5X_1 + .6X_2 + .4X_3 + .9X_4 + .8X_5 + .7X_6 + .6X_7 + .5X_8 + .5X_9 + .7X_{10} \leq 1,000 \quad \text{(gallons of milk)}$$

$$2X_1 + 3X_2 + 1X_3 + 4X_4 + 3X_5 + 2X_6 + 9X_7 + 4X_8 + 3X_9 + 1X_{10} \leq 10,000 \quad \text{(storage cake-weeks)}$$

$$1X_1 + 1X_2 + 1X_3 + 1X_4 + 1X_5 + 1X_6 + 1X_7 + 1X_8 + 1X_9 + 1X_{10} \leq 2,000 \quad \text{(molds)}$$

$$2X_1 + 3X_2 + 1X_3 + 2X_4 + 3X_5 + 2X_6 + 1X_7 + 1X_8 + 2X_9 + 2X_{10} \leq 3,000 \quad \text{(culture packs)}$$

$$.5X_1 + .6X_2 + .7X_3 + .5X_4 + .6X_5 + .5X_6 + .4X_7 + .3X_8 + .3X_9 + .2X_{10} \leq 1,500 \quad \text{(salt ounces)}$$

$$2X_1 + 1X_2 + 2X_3 + 1X_4 + 2X_5 + 1X_6 + 1X_7 + 2X_8 + 2X_9 + 1X_{10} \leq 3,000 \quad \text{(gauze sheets)}$$

$$0X_1 + 0X_2 - 1X_3 + 0X_4 + 0X_5 + 0X_6 + 0X_7 + 1X_8 + 0X_9 + 0X_{10} \leq 0 \quad \text{(product mix 1)}$$

$$-1X_1 + 0X_2 + 1X_3 + 0X_4 + 0X_5 + 0X_6 + 0X_7 + 0X_8 + 0X_9 + 0X_{10} \leq 0 \quad \text{(product mix 2)}$$

$$0X_1 + 0X_2 + 0X_3 + 0X_4 + 0X_5 + 1X_6 + 1X_7 + 1X_8 + 1X_9 + 1X_{10} \leq 1,000 \quad \text{(group limitation)}$$

where
$$\text{all } X\text{'s} \geq 0$$

(a) How many pounds should be made of each type of cheese? What is the corresponding maximum profit?

(b) Indicate the unused amount of each resource.

9-47 Refer to Problem 9-12 and your answer to that exercise. What ingredient volumes should All-American Meat Processors use in blending the batches of the two sausages? What will be the cost?

9-48 Refer to Problem 9-13 and your answer to that exercise. How many chips of each type should Chip-Mont manufacture and what will be the maximum profit?

9-49 Refer to Problem 9-14 and your answer to that exercise. Assume that constraints (1)–(6) apply. Three further constraints are (7) only 100 liters of spice oil are available, (8) up to 10 liters of gland

extract can be used, and (9) at most 40 liters of brandy can be used. What ingredient volumes should Channel Zee use in blending the batches of the two perfumes? What will be the cost?

9-50 Refer to Problem 9-16 and your answer to that exercise. How many spots should Blitz Beer reserve on each station? What will be the increased sales?

9-51 Refer to Problem 9-17 and your answer to that exercise. What should Geo-Pet's dollar investment be in each of the proposed ventures? What will be the expected rate of return?

9-52 Refer to Problem 9-19 and your answer to that exercise. What ingredient volumes should Back-packer's Budget Shoppe use in blending each kilogram of "Hiker's Daily Dried Gruel"? What will be the blended product's cost per kilogram?

Spreadsheet Problems

9-53 Use Solver to find the optimal solution to the following linear program:

	A	B	C	D	E	F	G	H
3	Variables	X_1	X_2	X_3	X_4	X_5	Sign	RHS
4	Objective	18	13	25	17	28	=	P(max)
5	Constraint 1	5	12	7	9	3	≤	100,000
6	Constraint 2	20	14	17	13	4	≤	25,000
7	Constraint 3	1		1			≤	200
8	Constraint 4		1		1		≤	100
9	Constraint 5			1	-1		≤	0
10	Constraint 6					1	≤	0

9-54 Use Solver to find the optimal solution to the following linear program:

	A	B	C	D	E	F	G	H
3	Variables	X_1	X_2	X_3	X_4	X_5	Sign	RHS
4	Objective	100	110	90	98	103	=	P(max)
5	Constraint 1	1	1	1	1	1	≤	75
6	Constraint 2	5	-3	-7	8	9	≤	400
7	Constraint 3	6	7	5	6	4	≤	250
8	Constraint 4				1	1	≤	50
9	Constraint 5			1	1		≤	50
10	Constraint 6	1	1				≤	50

9-55 Use Solver to find the optimal solution to the following linear program:

	A	B	C	D	E	F	G	H
3	Variables	X_1	X_2	X_3	X_4	X_5	Sign	RHS
4	Objective	5	4	7	6	8	=	P(max)
5	Constraint 1	10	7	15	13	12	≤	75,000
6	Constraint 2	5	5	5	5	5	≤	50,000
7	Constraint 3	1					≤	200
8	Constraint 4		1				≤	100
9	Constraint 5			1			≤	100
10	Constraint 6				1		≤	250
11	Constraint 7					1	≤	150

9-56 Use Solver to find the optimal solution to the linear program on Problem09-56.xls.

9-57 Use Solver to find the optimal solution to the linear program on Problem09-57.xls.

9-58 Use Solver to find the optimal solution to the linear program on Problem09-58.xls.

CASE 9-1   Horrible Harry's

Horrible Harry's is a chain of 47 self-service gas stations served by a small refinery and mixing plant. Each day's product requirements are met by blending feedstocks on hand at midnight. The volumes vary daily, depending on the previous day's refinery output and on bulk receipts.

The entire operation is run by the owner, Harry Oldaker. Although dozens of chemicals and byproducts are generated by the refinery, Harry's major concern is the retail distribution of gasoline products.

On a particular Tuesday there are sufficient volumes of leaded and unleaded regular gasolines at the stations. Only the two hybrid petroleum products — gasohol and petrolmeth — will be shipped that day. Both products are blended from 90-octane unleaded gasoline. Ethyl alcohol, the only additive to gasohol, cannot exceed 10% of the final product's volume. Petrolmeth may contain both ethyl and methyl alcohols, but these combined ingredients must not exceed 30% of the final product's volume. The octane ratings are 120 for ethyl alcohol and 110 for methyl alcohol. Final product octane ratings must equal the average octane ratings for the ingredients by volume. Gasohol must have an octane rating of at least 91, and petrolmeth must have a rating of at least 93.

There are 20,000 gallons of gasoline presently available for blending, at a cost of $1.00 per gallon. Up to 5,000 gallons of methyl alcohol can be ac-

quired for $.50 per gallon, and 3,000 gallons of ethyl alcohol are available at $1.50 per gallon. The demands are at least 10,000 gallons for gasohol and 5,000 gallons for petrolmeth.

Until now Harry has determined product blends by trial and error. A new staff analyst says that she can save a considerable amount of money by using linear programming to establish a minimum-cost blending formulation. Harry is a bit skeptical, but he offers her the challenge to do better than the following:

9,000 gallons of unleaded gas to gasohol

1,000 gallons of ethyl alcohol to gasohol

3,500 gallons of unleaded gas to petrolmeth

1,500 gallons of methyl alcohol to petrolmeth

Cost=$14,750

If the analyst can save a significant amount, she will use linear programming for all future blending decisions.

QUESTIONS

1. Formulate Horrible Harry's decision problem as a linear program.

2. Run your linear program on a computer to determine the optimal volumes to be blended. How much lower is the cost of the optimal solution than that of Harry's original plan?

CASE 9-2   Shale—Bituminous Processors I

Reconsider the Shale–Bituminous Processors example (page 262) with the following additions and changes. The objective is to determine the number of gasification and pressurization batches and the number of gallons of low-sulfur and high-sulfur crude to be produced during each of the next two quarters of the coming year that will minimize costs. The quarterly orders for each crude are given in the table. The initial inventory of both high-sulfur and low-sulfur crude is zero. Management wants to end the second quarter with 1,000 gallons of each type of crude. Assume now that 100 tons of coal and 100 tons

of shale are available each quarter for producing the crudes. The variable labor costs for a gasification batch are $10, and $8 for a pressurization batch. Crude not used in a quarter can be used in future periods. The annual inventory holding cost is 8% of the value of the crude.

| Quarter | Crude Orders (Gallons) | |
	Low-Sulfur	High-Sulfur
1	5,000	6,000
2	6,000	11,000

QUESTIONS

1. Formulate a linear program that will help the refinery manager to make a decision about the number of gasification and pressurization batches to schedule and the quantities of low-sulfur and high-sulfur crude to produce each quarter.

2. Solve the linear program in Question 1. Determine the annual cost.

3. The economy is starting to pick up so that now it looks like the orders to be filled next year might be 10% greater than the values shown in the table. How would this affect the original solution?

4. Because of a disagreement between management and the union, there will be a work slowdown affecting the availability of coal and shale. If this slowdown decreases the availability to 95% of the original estimates, how would it affect management's original plans? Supposing the decrease is 20%, what happens in this case?

5. An accident has occurred in the pressurization batch equipment and 20% of the production capacity will be lost during the coming year. Is this a problem? That is, how would such an accident affect the company's production schedule and projected profit? Suppose a *big* accident occurs; yields from pressurization batches are only going to be 50% of that originally anticipated. What happens in this situation?

6. The cost of coal has unexpectedly increased to $26 per ton so that now it costs more than shale ($25). Will it mess up the company's plans? Explain.

7. (a) The refinery manager changes his mind and requires that 2,000 gallons of each crude be in inventory at the end of the second quarter. How does this affect the solution originally obtained?

   (b) After determining the original solution, it is learned that 1,000 gallons of both low-sulfur and high-sulfur crude are available from a supplier at a 20% discount from their normal prices. The refinery manager might buy those crudes as initial inventory at the beginning of the year. Fewer gallons would have to be produced during the year by Shale–Bituminous Processors; she thinks this would decrease costs. Should she make the purchase? Why?

   (c) After reviewing the original linear program, a company engineer advises the refinery manager that the limited storage capacity for the crudes is not included. Tanks can store only 1,990 gallons of each of the crudes at the end of the first quarter. Does this affect the original solution? If so, how?

   (d) An auditor questions Shale–Bituminous Processors about their 8% holding cost figure. It might be higher or maybe even lower. Examine how the original solution changes if the holding cost is half that value; twice the value.

8. Suppose that coal and shale not used in a quarter *are* available for future production. How will this alter the original solution?

CASE 9-3   *Martin Santa Barbara Wines*[1] /

After finishing her business degree at State University, Laura Martin went to work for her father in the family furniture business. However, she always nurtured the idea of branching out on her own. As an amateur viniculturist, her dream was running her own winery. Recently, she bought 5 acres of

land in the hills of Santa Barbara with the option to purchase an additional 50 acres. Initial analysis has shown that the land would be ideal for growing a variety of premium grapes.

Because wine making is capital intensive, and because growing commercial-quality grapes with a full yield of 5 tons per acre takes at least eight years, Laura is planning to start out on a small scale. She plans to plant vines on 4 of the initial 5 acres and tend to the crop on weekends. To help maintain a positive

---

[1] Kurt Martsolf, California State University, Hayward, co-authored this case.

cash flow during the first few years, she plans to buy grapes from other nearby growers so she can make her own label wine. She proposes to market it through a small tasting room that she will build on the land and keep open on weekends.

Laura will begin with $10,000 in savings to finance the initial purchase of grapes from which she will make her first batch of wine. She also intends to apply to a local bank for a loan, so she needs to make a business plan calculating the profitability and cash flows associated with her idea. Her preliminary planning horizon is two years. She must decide how much of the $10,000 should be allocated to purchasing grapes for the first and second years. In addition, she must decide how much to spend purchasing Petite Sirah and Sauvignon Blanc grapes.

Laura estimates that in the first year, grapes for Petite Sirah will cost $.80 for each bottle, and those for Sauvignon Blanc will cost $.70 per bottle. In the second year, the costs will change to $.75 and $.85, respectively. Laura has arranged with a local firm to provide, label, and fill the necessary bottles at $.50 each. However, the bottler has limited capacity and can only fill 35,000 bottles each year. She anticipates that the Petite Sirah will sell for $8 per bottle in the first year and $8.25 in the second year, while Sauvignon Blanc will sell for $7 per bottle for each year.

In addition to the decisions about the grape purchase, Laura must estimate the wine sales during the two years. Because Laura lacks the capital for market research, she is wondering about how much money to spend on promoting each wine each year. The winemaking association says that for each dollar spent in the first year promoting Petite Sirah, a demand of five bottles will be created, and that each dollar spent in the second year will result in a demand for six bottles. Similarly, the respective results for Sauvignon Blanc are 8 bottles in the first year and 10 bottles in the second year.

The first-year funds for grape purchases, bottling, and advertising will come from the initial $10,000. Assume that the cash earned from wine sales the first year is available in the second year. Finally, Laura needs a proper balance of wine products, so the number of bottles of Petite Sirah sold each year must be between 40% and 70% of all bottles of wine sold.

QUESTIONS

1. Laura needs help to decide how many grapes to buy, how much money to spend on advertising, how many bottles of wine to sell, and how much profit she can expect to earn over the 2-year period. Formulate a linear programming model to aid her in this situation.

2. Solve the linear programming model formulated in Question 1.

3. Recently, Chile and Australia have flooded the market with inexpensive, high-quality white wines. The loan officer at the bank has commented that Laura may only be able to command half the price she expects for each bottle of Sauvignon Blanc in the second year. If this is true, what effect will this have on profits?

4. The loan officer also commented that Laura has made no provision for the cost of carrying over inventory from the first to the second year. If the estimated carrying cost is $.10 for each bottle, how would that change Laura's plan?

5. There are rumors that organizers for the local grape worker's union may strike in the next few weeks, even though the workers are not currently unionized. If there is a work stoppage, it may last for years and the price of grapes may rise 50% or 100%. What effect would such an occurrence have on Laura's plan?

6. Laura finds a local wine operation that can bottle as many units of wine as she might require during the second year for $.55 per bottle. Is it possible that she may increase her profits while paying more for bottling? If so, when should she begin using this new bottler? (Once she contracts a bottler, she must use their services exclusively for an entire year. She cannot use the services of both bottlers at the same time.)

7. Suppose that the bank is impressed by the prospects of Laura's wine business and agrees to give her a $10,000 1-year loan at the beginning of the first year at the bank's best small-business rate, 22.8% interest with a 10% compensating balance.[2] Both the principal and interest must be repaid at the

---

[2]This requirement means that only $9,000 of the original $10,000 loan is available. The other $1,000 must remain on deposit in the bank.

beginning of the second year. Should she accept the bank's offer? Why or why not?

8. Suppose that the number of bottles of Petite Sirah and Sauvignon Blanc sold each year are only four and five for each advertising dollar, respectively. What effect does this have on Laura's plan?

9. How would the profit change if Laura's concern for production mixture (the number of bottles of Petite Sirah sold each year is between 40% and 70% of all bottles of wine sold) is ignored? What would be the effect of demanding an equal mix of each wine each year?

CASE   9-4   *The California Arabian Oil Company, Inc.*

Saudi Arabia is a kingdom with an area of 865,000 square miles. It has a population of about 16 million. In 1937, the California Arabian Oil Company (CAARCO) was formed as a joint venture between Standard Oil Company of California (SOCAL) and the government of Saudi Arabia to explore, produce, and market any petroleum found. A discovery was made of what was to be the largest oil field in the world. Called the Ghawar field, it is located about 50 miles inland from the western shores of the Persian Gulf. The productive area covers approximately 900 square miles, and the vertical oil column is about 1,300 feet. It has recoverable reserves of about 75 billion barrels of oil. Total proven reserves in Saudi Arabia are estimated at more than 500 billion barrels, enough for more than a hundred years of production.

During the 1960s, CAARCO hired Dr. George Dantzig as a consultant. He supervised the development of linear programming models to optimize the production of different types of crude oils, their refining, and the marketing of some of their principle products. As a result profits increased substantially.

Now an analyst, Mostafa El Agizy, an Arab-American who recently graduated with a B.S. in Quantitative Methods, has been focusing on production of three types of aviation gasoline from Saudi Arabian crude oil. Aviation petroleum products had become a substantial portion of CAARCO's business. As can be seen from Figure 1, the three aviation gasolines A, B, and C are made by blending four feed stocks: Alkylate, Catalytic Cracked Gasoline, Straight Run Gasoline, and Isopentane.

In Table 1, TEL stands for tetraethyl lead, measured in milliliters per gallon (ml/gal). Thus, a TEL of .5 means that there are .5 ml/gal of tetraethyl lead. It can be seen from Table 1 that TEL influences octane number but not the Reid Vapor Pressure.

Each type of aviation gasoline has a maximum permissible Reid Vapor Pressure of 7. Aviation gasoline A has a TEL level of .5 ml/gal and has a mini-

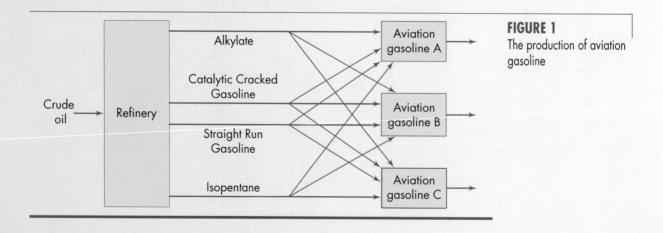

FIGURE 1
The production of aviation gasoline

TABLE 1 Feedstock Availabilities*

Characteristic	Feedstock			
	Alkylate	**Catalytic Cracked Gasoline**	**Straight Run Gasoline**	**Isopentane**
Reid Vapor Pressure	5	8	4	20
Octane Number				
—If TEL is .5	94	83	74	95
—If TEL of 4.0	107.5	93	87	108
Available, barrels/day	3,800	2,700	4,100	1,300
Value, $/barrel	17.00	14.50	13.50	14.00

*Some of the data in this case have been adapted from *Introduction to Linear Programming* by Walter W. Garvin (Ch. 5), McGraw-Hill, 1960.

TABLE 2 Aviation Gasoline Data

Characteristic	Aviation Gasoline		
	A	**B**	**C**
Minimum requirements, barrels/day	1,000	2,000	1,500
Price, $/barrel	15.00	16.00	16.50

mum octane number of 80. The TEL level of aviation gasolines B and C are 4 ml/gal, but the former has a minimum octane number of 91, whereas the latter has a minimum of 100.

All feedstocks used to blend aviation gasoline A are leaded at a TEL level of .5 ml/gal and all those going into aviation gasolines B and C have TEL levels of 4 ml/gal.

QUESTIONS

1. Formulate a linear program to determine how to blend the three grades of gasoline from available input streams so that specifications are met and income is maximized. The demands are the minimum amounts that will be sold and the stock availabilities are the maximums.

2. Solve the linear program formulated in Question 1.

3. Mr. El Agizy sees the potential of a supply shortage due to damage from Iraqi attacks. This could cause the prices of the three gasolines to double (but the stocks will remain the same). How would this affect the refinery's operations? If after current stocks are

exhausted, additional quantities must be obtained at values double those in Table 1, how might CAARCO's plans be affected?

4. Suppose that because of the Iraqi crisis the supply of alkylate is decreased by 800 bbl/day, catalytic cracked gas is decreased by 200 bbl/day, and straight run gasoline is decreased by 100 bbl/day. How does this affect CAARCO's operations?

5. CAARCO is considering trying to fill the aviation gasoline shortage created by the Iraqi crisis by increasing its own production. Mr. El Agizy has learned that additional quantities of alkylate, catalytic cracked gasoline, straight run gasoline, and isopentane are available, and he is wondering if they should be processed, if so how much, and how their values affect the situation.

6. Due to the uncertainty about the Iraqi crisis, CAARCO's economists are considering market research to reestimate the minimum requirement forecasts. It is felt that demand will be decreasing in the future. Management is wondering if changes in the minimum requirements would significantly

affect CAARCO's operations. What is the change in profit from an increase or a decrease in the minimum requirements? Over what ranges of demands do these profit changes apply?

7. Suppose that the Middle East crisis ends and there is a flood of oil in the marketplace so that the prices of aviation gasoline drop to $10, $11, and $11.50, for A, B, and C, respectively. How would this affect the company's plans?

8. Suppose the government is considering mandating the elimination of lead in aviation gasoline to decrease air pollution. This law would be based on new technology that allows jet engines to burn unleaded gasoline efficiently at any octane level. Thus, there would no longer be any need for constraints on octane level. How would such a new law affect CAARCO?

9. There is uncertainty about whether the CAARCO refinery can produce aviation fuel within the specified limit on Reid Vapor Pressure of 7. It is sure that any variation will be within a range of ± 1. Management is concerned about how such errors might affect their profitability.

10. The marketing department has told Mr. El Agizy that CAARCO can increase its share of the market with a new contract. This will require at least as much gasoline A to be produced as B. Because A is the least profitable of the three, Mr. El Agizy feels that the decrease in profit will be too much for the company. The "large" increase in market share, with the concomitant long-run profit increases, may not offset the "temporary small decrease" in profits created by the additional restriction. What do you recommend? Why?

CHAPTER 10

SENSITIVITY ANALYSIS AND DUALITY IN LINEAR PROGRAMMING

The primal linear program solution answers the tactical question when it tells us how much to produce. But the dual linear program can have far greater impact because it addresses strategical issues regarding the structure of the business itself.

W e have seen how linear programming may be used to solve a variety of resource allocation problems. The variables in these applications are generally unknown quantities such as the number of tables, pounds of beef, or dollars spent on television advertising. In production-planning applications, the problem is to determine how much of each product type should be made. An entirely different way to represent the production decision as a linear program will be presented in this chapter.

We know that a linear program actually tells us how to allocate scarce resources to maximize profits. Now suppose that our primary concern is to determine the most efficient application of the production resources themselves. The focus is on *resources,* rather than on products. Only indirectly related to their accounting costs, each of these has a **shadow price** that reflects the true impact of scarcity. To find these amounts, we may look at a wholly different expression of the underlying problem. In effect, we must "cross through the looking glass" into a special mathematical environment that essentially mirrors our ordinary one. In this new linear programming environment, problems are formulated differently but have equivalent solutions. Every ordinary problem has its doppelgänger, which we refer to as the **dual linear program** or, for short, the **dual.**

The dual linear program plays an essential role in the analysis of an operation. It helps identify economic bottlenecks, allowing us to quantify those constraints whose adjustments might bring *incremental* cost or profit improvements. Unfortunately, dual values cannot by themselves tell us the possible *magnitude* of those changes. This chapter shows us how far to carry through a particular change, right up to the point of zero or diminishing returns. An investigation regarding the possible magnitude of a change and its effect on the optimal solution is called a **sensitivity analysis.**

MANAGERIAL DECISION

Determining Production Quantities

Swatville Sluggers is a small manufacturer of baseball bats handmade from high-quality 3-by-3-inch blocks of wood. The owner, George Herman "Sultan" Swat, and his nephew, Babe, want to know where to expand supplies, inventories, and functional capacities. They would also like to know whether it would be profitable to add to the product mix. To answer these questions, Babe gathers the information presented below

about the production of the various types of bats, the limited resources available, and the relevant bat sales prices and costs. The subscripts refer to the bat length in inches. The times are in minutes, and the volumes of stain and varnish are in ounces.

| | SIZE OF BAT | | | | | | AVAILABLE QUANTITY |
CONSTRAINT	X_{30}	X_{32}	X_{34}	X_{36}	X_{38}	X_{40}	
Wood	30	32	34	36	38	40	≤ 12,000
Lathe time	10	10	11	11	12	12	≤ 6,000
Finishing time	25	27	29	31	33	35	≤ 7,000
Boxes	1	1	1	1	1	1	≤ 1,000
Stain	2	2	2	3	3	3	≤ 1,500
Varnish	5	5	6	6	10	10	≤ 3,000
Restriction 1	−1	−1	1	0	0	0	≤ 0
Restriction 2	0	−1	−1	0	1	0	≤ 0
Restriction 3	1	0	0	−1	−1	0	≤ 0

The following cost data apply to the resources used in making bats:

Wood cost per inch	$.12
Lathe cost per minute	.06
Finishing cost per minute	.03
Box cost	.50
Stain cost per ounce	.25
Varnish cost per ounce	.20

These costs differ from the March figures (in Chapter 9, page 301). The larger bats now get an extra coat of varnish, and the available quantities of the resources have changed. Also, the selling prices have been revised for April. These are $22 for 30-inch and 32-inch bats, $24 for 34-inch and 36-inch versions, and $28 for the 38-inch and 40-inch lengths. Other direct costs are now higher, $3 per bat, regardless of model. Further restrictions are (1) the number of 34-inch bats cannot exceed the combined total of 30-inch and 32-inch models, (2) the number of 38-inch bats cannot exceed the combined total of the 32-inch and 34-inch varieties, and (3) the number of 30-inch bats must be less than or equal to the total number of 36-inch and 38-inch bats.

Babe has a concern about a potential customer who would like a 39-inch bat and will pay $23 for each one. Although Swatville Sluggers does not currently produce this size bat, Babe was wondering if the company should expand its production line by accepting the order. He decides to call this new 39-inch bat the Corner Pounder and starts his analysis by gathering the following information: a Corner Pounder would require 10 minutes of lathe time, 30 minutes of finishing time, no box, 4 ounces of stain, and 8 ounces of varnish.

The material presented in this chapter will illustrate how to do a sensitivity analysis of Swatville Sluggers. If extra funds are available, the analysis will help determine if funds should be spent on obtaining more wood or expanding the limited amount of lathe and finishing time available and if more boxes, stain, or varnish should be bought. A related analysis will tell Swat whether or not to accept the Corner Pounder bat order.

10-1 SHADOW PRICES AND OPPORTUNITY COSTS

L et's explore the resource orientation by again evaluating the original Redwood Furniture problem used in Chapters 8 and 9. Table 10-1 shows the essential information regarding that problem in greater detail. Management must decide the number of tables and chairs to be made that will maximize total profit while not exceeding the available quantities of labor and wood. The unit profits for each item of furniture are determined by subtracting the costs of all resources used.

Letting X_T and X_C denote the number of tables and chairs to be made, the following linear program applies:

$$\text{Maximize} \quad P = 6X_T + 8X_C$$
$$\text{Subject to} \quad 30X_T + 20X_C \leq 300 \quad \text{(wood)}$$
$$5X_T + 10X_C \leq 110 \quad \text{(labor)}$$
$$\text{where} \quad X_T, X_C \geq 0$$

(Notice that not all the resources appear in the original linear program, just the ones in scarce supply.)

This linear program was solved graphically in Chapter 8, where we obtained

$$X_T = 4 \quad X_C = 9 \quad P = \$96$$

If we plug the above solution values into the constraint left-hand sides, we find that the optimal plan will use all the available wood

$$30(4) + 20(9) = 120 + 180 = 300 \text{ board feet}$$

and all the available labor

$$5(4) + 10(9) = 20 + 90 = 110 \text{ hours}$$

Because the optimal plan would use all the available resources, it stands to reason that more wood or more labor would bring about improved profits. The graphical solution can tell us the net impact of additional resources.

The Effect of Increasing Available Resource Quantities

Refer to the graphical solution to the Redwood Furniture problem, shown in Figure 10-1. There we can see that increasing the available amount of wood to 301 board feet

TABLE 10-1   Data Obtained for the Original Redwood Furniture Problem

RESOURCE	Unit Cost	EACH TABLE Amount Required	EACH TABLE Product Cost	EACH CHAIR Amount Required	EACH CHAIR Product Cost	AVAILABLE QUANTITY
Wood	$1/ft	30 ft	$ 30	20 ft	$ 20	300 ft
Labor	$10/hr	5 hrs	50	10 hrs	100	110 hrs
Others	Various	Lots	120	Lots	100	Plentiful
	Total cost		$200		$220	
	Selling price		$206		$228	
	Profit		$6		$8	

FIGURE 10-1
The graphical interpretation of the dual variable for the cost of wood

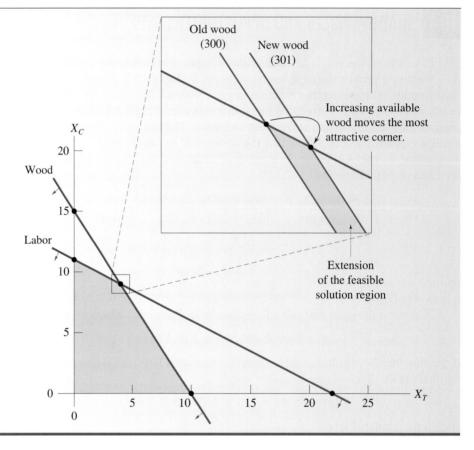

results in a rightward shift of the wood line, making the feasible solution region wider than before. The intersection of the new wood line with the labor line provides the new most attractive corner, which shifts to the right and downward. This indicates that more tables and fewer chairs should be made than before. To determine the optimal solution exactly, we can simultaneously solve the new wood and original labor constraint equations

$$30X_T + 20X_C = 301 \quad \text{(new wood)}$$
$$5X_T + 10X_C = 110 \quad \text{(original labor)}$$

which yields

$$X_T = 4.05$$
$$X_C = 8.975$$

The resulting profit is

$$P = 6(4.05) + 8(8.975)$$
$$= 96.10 \text{ dollars}$$

which is exactly $.10 larger than the maximum profit when only 300 board feet of wood is available.

A similar finding applies to a 1-hour increase in available labor. The optimal solution to that linear program may be determined by simultaneously solving the original wood equation and the new labor equation

$$30X_T + 20X_C = 300 \qquad \text{(original wood)}$$
$$5X_T + 10X_C = 111 \qquad \text{(new labor)}$$

which yields

$$X_T = 3.90$$
$$X_C = 9.15$$

The resulting profit is

$$P = 6(3.90) + 8(9.15)$$
$$= 96.60 \text{ dollars}$$

which is exactly $.60 larger than the maximum profit when only 110 hours of labor is available.

Marginal Values and Shadow Prices

We may refer to the $.10 increase in P resulting from an additional board foot of wood as its **marginal value.** Marginal values are sometimes referred to as **opportunity costs,** because a limitation on available resources may result in the loss of opportunity to earn greater profit. Do not confuse the $.10 marginal value for wood with its accounting cost (given as $1 in Table 10-1). The marginal value reflects the net effect of an additional board foot, and the usual $1 supply cost still applies for the material, which of course could not be obtained for free. Likewise, an additional hour of labor has a marginal value of $.60. This is the added profit that would result, even after paying the worker $10 in wages and benefits.

The marginal values of $.10 for wood and $.60 for labor are sometimes referred to as the **shadow prices** for the resources. In effect, the decision maker would improve total profit by paying a premium for wood and labor not exceeding the shadow price. For example, if more wood could be obtained by making a special trip to the mill, at an added cost under $.10 per board foot, then Redwood should do so. Likewise, Redwood would be better off coaxing workers to give more hours as long as the company does not have to pay more than $.60 per hour (beyond the standard $10) as the incentive.

The shadow prices apply to each resource individually, and any change in the available quantity of one resource can bring about changes in the shadow prices of the others. Also, each shadow price is only valid over a limited range of resource levels. Later, we will see how such limits are established.

10-2 THE DUAL LINEAR PROGRAM

The Redwood Furniture Company linear program in Section 10-1 is referred to as the **primal linear program.** As we have seen, that original model establishes the *product quantities* that will maximize profit. We now consider the **dual linear program,** which focuses on the *resources* used in production.

To formulate the dual, several rules must be observed. First, there is one dual variable for each primal constraint. The letter U always denotes that variable. In this case, there are two nonnegative dual variables, U_W for the wood constraint and U_L for the labor constraint. Second, each row (constraint) of the dual problem corresponds to a column (X variable) of the primal.

$$30U_W + 5U_L \geq 6 \qquad \text{(table)}$$
$$20U_W + 10U_L \geq 8 \qquad \text{(chair)}$$
$$U_W, U_L \geq 0$$

All of the signs in the dual constraints ($\geq$) are the opposite of those in the primal constraints ($\leq$).

Notice from the above that the *column* numbers of the primal provide the *row* numbers of the dual. Thus, the third column of the primal, containing the numbers on the right-hand side of each original resource constraint, become the third row of the dual, which is written below.

$$\text{Minimize} \quad C = 300U_W + 110U_L$$

The above is the dual objective function. It is to minimize C, the opposite of the primal objective (to maximize P).

Notice that the two programs are arranged similarly. The constraint coefficients of the two problems arranged as matrices are

$$\begin{array}{cc} \text{PRIMAL} & \text{DUAL} \end{array}$$

$$\begin{pmatrix} 30 & 20 \\ 5 & 10 \end{pmatrix} \qquad \begin{pmatrix} 30 & 5 \\ 20 & 10 \end{pmatrix}$$

Note that the rows of the dual coefficients are the columns of the primal coefficients and that the columns of the dual are the rows of the primal. We refer to one matrix as the *transpose* of the other. The coefficients of the objective of the primal linear program appear as the right-hand sides of the dual constraints, and the right-hand sides of the primal constraints provide the objective coefficients for the dual. In effect, the position of every constraint in the dual is exactly what we would obtain by rotating the primal $90°$ counterclockwise when the P equation is written last and then by resequencing the inequalities.

The objective of the primal problem is to maximize P. The objective of the dual is the opposite—to minimize C. The primal constraints are $\leq$ inequalities; the dual constraints are $\geq$ inequalities. One linear program is the transpose of the other with totally opposite objective and constraint orientations. (In effect, the primal is the "dual" of the dual.)

Interpreting the Dual

The primal linear program typically represents the perspective of the production manager who optimizes resource allocation by establishing quantities for each product that will maximize profit. The dual linear program approaches the same problem from an *economist's* point of view. The economist wants to achieve a production plan that optimizes resource allocation by ensuring that each product is produced at that quantity such that *its marginal opportunity cost equals its marginal return.*

The economist's problem is to deploy all resources optimally so that the aggregate value of increasing any resource by one more unit is minimized. Thus, the dual linear program has an objective function of the form

$$\text{Minimize} \quad C = \sum_{\text{all resources}} (\text{available quantity}) \times U_{\text{resource}}$$

The available quantity of each resource serves as the objective coefficient for the respective U. Each resource is thus given weight in proportion to its overall impact on the problem.

The economist cannot arbitrarily set the U's at any level. The dual linear program has a separate constraint for *each product* of the form

$$\sum_{\text{all resources}} (\text{requirement per unit}) \times U_{\text{resource}} \geq \text{unit profit} \qquad \text{(for each product)}$$

To make any amount of a product requires the removal of resources, each having unit value equal to its own U, from the available pool. These diversions leave fewer resources available to be deployed in making other products, and doing this is therefore a cost from the economist's point of view. These special costs are *opportunity* costs, only indirectly related to the accounting costs used in computing the unit profit of the product.

The left-hand side of the constraint represents the total drop in resource value, over all resources, needed to accommodate one unit of the product, so that the combined quantity represents the product's *economic marginal opportunity cost;* the right-hand side is the product's *marginal return.* Each constraint therefore states the condition that

product marginal opportunity cost $\geq$ product marginal return

When the left-hand side exactly equals the right-hand side, the product will be made at a volume where its marginal opportunity cost equals its marginal return—the economist's condition of product optimality.

It is of course possible for marginal opportunity cost to exceed marginal return; that is allowed by the constraint. In such a case, the optimal volume for the product would be zero, and thus, it should not be produced at all. The case of $<$ is disallowed by the constraint. This is because no product should ever be produced at a level where its marginal return exceeds its marginal opportunity cost.

Using these guidelines, we can interpret the dual linear program for the Redwood Furniture Company problem. The dual variables are

$$U_W = \text{marginal value of wood (per board foot)}$$
$$U_L = \text{marginal value of labor (per hour)}$$

They are also called the shadow prices of wood and labor.

The objective function is

$$\text{Minimize} \quad C = 300U_W + 110U_L \qquad \text{(objective)}$$

It minimizes the total value of the resources, where the total is calculated using the marginal values (shadow prices).

The table constraint

$$30U_W + 5U_L \geq 6 \quad \text{(table)}$$

stipulates that the marginal opportunity cost of a table (on the left-hand side) must be equal to (or greater than) the marginal return of a table (on the right-hand side).

A second constraint applies to the chair and ensures that the marginal opportunity cost of a chair must be equal to (or greater than) its marginal return:

$$20U_W + 10U_L \geq 8 \quad \text{(chair)}$$

A fundamental fact of linear programming is that for any feasible respective solutions to the dual and primal

$$C \geq P$$

Further, the objective value in both problems is identical for the respective optimal solutions. Thus,

$$\text{Minimum } C = \text{Maximum } P$$

so that the smallest possible cost is equal to the maximum possible profit. We will learn the importance of this feature later.

Solving the Dual Graphically

The dual linear program for the Redwood Furniture problem is solved graphically in Figure 10-2. Because the most attractive corner lies at the intersection of the table and chair constraint lines, the simultaneous solution of these equations provides

$$U_W = \$.10 \text{ per board foot}$$
$$U_L = \$.60 \text{ per hour}$$

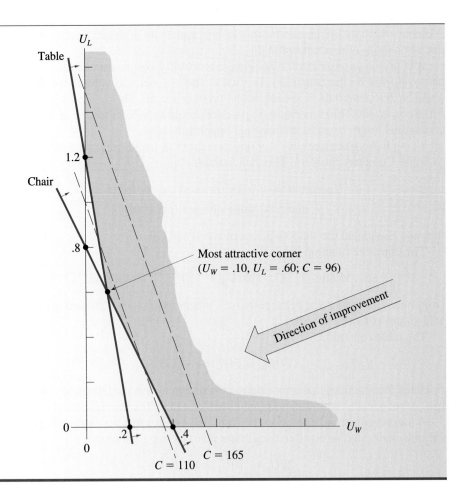

FIGURE 10-2
The graphical solution to the dual for the Redwood Furniture problem

and the minimum value of the objective function is

$$C = 300(.10) + 110(.60)$$
$$= 96 \text{ dollars}$$

This is the figure that we originally obtained in Chapter 9 for the maximum profit of the primal linear program.

Notice that $U_W = \$.10$ and $U_L = \$.60$ are the same increases in profit found in the preceding section after separately raising the available wood and labor, respectively, by one unit and solving each modified linear program. We see that the optimal dual variable levels are the opportunity costs (or shadow prices) for each resource.

Formulating the Dual from the Primal

Although the dual linear program may be formulated by building on the same information as that used to establish the primal linear program, it is easiest to first formulate the primal. The dual may then be found directly from the primal.

Managerial Decision Revisited: Determining Production Quantities

Babe knows that a linear program will help him determine the best April production schedule. His first step is to define the variables. There are six, one for each size bat produced. Each must be nonnegative.

$$X_{30} = \text{the number of 30-inch bats produced in April}$$
$$X_{32} = \text{the number of 32-inch bats produced in April}$$
$$X_{34} = \text{the number of 34-inch bats produced in April}$$
$$X_{36} = \text{the number of 36-inch bats produced in April}$$
$$X_{38} = \text{the number of 38-inch bats produced in April}$$
$$X_{40} = \text{the number of 40-inch bats produced in April}$$

Next he focuses on calculating the objective function, maximizing the total profit from all the bats produced. First, he calculates the unit profits for each bat size and obtains the results in the table below.

COMPONENT	COST ($/UNIT)	30-inch	32-inch	34-inch	36-inch	38-inch	40-inch
Price ($)	NA	22.00	22.00	24.00	24.00	28.00	28.00
Wood (oz)	.12	30	32	34	36	38	40
Lathe (min)	.06	10	10	11	11	12	12
Finishing time (min)	.03	25	27	29	31	33	35
Boxes	.50	1	1	1	1	1	1
Stain (oz)	.25	2	2	2	3	3	3
Varnish (oz)	.20	5	5	6	6	10	10
Fixed cost ($)	3.00	3.00	3.00	3.00	3.00	3.00	3.00
Unit profit	NA	12.05	11.75	13.19	12.64	15.48	15.18

We will use the 30-inch bat as an illustration. The costs are subtracted from its $22 selling price. This includes the fixed cost of $3 per bat and the variable costs, which must be calculated from the given data by summing the products of required resource amounts and their unit costs. The unit profit for the 30-inch bat is

$$\$22 - [3.00 + .12(30) + .06(10) + .03(25) + .50(1) + .25(2) + .20(5)] = \$12.05$$

Incorporating all the bat unit profits, the following objective function is obtained:

$$\text{Maximize}\quad P = 12.05X_{30} + 11.75X_{32} + 13.19X_{34} + 12.64X_{36} + 15.48X_{38} + 15.18X_{40}$$

There are six constraints, one for each resource limitation. These are

$$
\begin{array}{lll}
30X_{30} + 32X_{32} + 34X_{34} + 36X_{36} + 38X_{38} + 40X_{40} \le 12,000 & \text{(wood)} \\
10X_{30} + 10X_{32} + 11X_{34} + 11X_{36} + 12X_{38} + 12X_{40} \le 6,000 & \text{(lathe time)} \\
25X_{30} + 27X_{32} + 29X_{34} + 31X_{36} + 33X_{38} + 35X_{40} \le 7,000 & \text{(finishing time)} \\
1X_{30} + 1X_{32} + 1X_{34} + 1X_{36} + 1X_{38} + 1X_{40} \le 1,000 & \text{(boxes)} \\
2X_{30} + 2X_{32} + 2X_{34} + 3X_{36} + 3X_{38} + 3X_{40} \le 1,500 & \text{(stain)} \\
5X_{30} + 5X_{32} + 6X_{34} + 6X_{36} + 10X_{38} + 10X_{40} \le 3,000 & \text{(varnish)}
\end{array}
$$

In addition to the above, there are three restrictions, each requiring a separate constraint. The first requirement is that the number of 34-inch bats cannot exceed the combined total of the 30-inch and 32-inch models, so that $X_{34} \le X_{30} + X_{32}$. Rearranging terms, Babe gets

$$-1X_{30} - 1X_{32} + 1X_{34} + 0X_{36} + 0X_{38} + 0X_{40} \le 0 \qquad \text{(restriction 1)}$$

In a similar manner, the number of 38-inch bats cannot exceed the combined total of the 32-inch and 34-inch varieties, and the number of 30-inch bats must be less than or equal to the total number of 36-inch and 38-inch bats. These bring the final two constraints:

$$
\begin{array}{ll}
0X_{30} - 1X_{32} - 1X_{34} + 0X_{36} + 1X_{38} + 0X_{40} \le 0 & \text{(restriction 2)} \\
1X_{30} + 0X_{32} + 0X_{34} - 1X_{36} - 1X_{38} + 0X_{40} \le 0 & \text{(restriction 3)}
\end{array}
$$

Solving this linear program with *QuickQuant* gives the following solution. Only 30-inch, 34-inch, and 38-inch bats are produced and the profit is $3,276.32.

Variable	Value
X30	80.45977
X32	0.00000
X34	80.45977
X36	0.00000
X38	80.45977
X40	0.00000

Objective Value: P = 3276.32200

Babe formulates the dual linear program, defining U_W, U_L, U_F, U_B, U_S, and U_V as the respective marginal values of wood, lathe time, finishing time, boxes, stain, and var-

nish. Also, he defines U_1, U_2, and U_3 as the marginal values for restrictions 1, 2, and 3. The dual objective is to minimize C:

$$C = 12{,}000U_W + 6{,}000U_L + 7{,}000U_F + 1{,}000U_B + 1{,}500U_S + 3{,}000U_V + 0U_1$$
$$+ 0U_2 + 0U_3$$

Subject to

$$30U_W + 10U_L + 25U_F + 1U_B + 2U_S + 5U_V - 1U_1 + 0U_2 + 1U_3 \geq 12.05$$
$$32U_W + 10U_L + 27U_F + 1U_B + 2U_S + 5U_V - 1U_1 - 1U_2 + 0U_3 \geq 11.75$$
$$34U_W + 11U_L + 29U_F + 1U_B + 2U_S + 6U_V + 1U_1 - 1U_2 + 0U_3 \geq 13.19$$
$$36U_W + 11U_L + 31U_F + 1U_B + 3U_S + 6U_V + 0U_1 + 0U_2 - 1U_3 \geq 12.64$$
$$38U_W + 12U_L + 33U_F + 1U_B + 3U_S + 10U_V + 0U_1 + 1U_2 - 1U_3 \geq 15.48$$
$$40U_W + 12U_L + 35U_F + 1U_B + 3U_S + 10U_V + 0U_1 + 0U_2 + 0U_3 \geq 15.18$$

where all U's ≥ 0.

With *QuickQuant* it is neither necessary to separately formulate the dual linear program nor to make an additional computer run to solve it. The software provides optimal levels for the dual variables as an automatic option whenever the primal problem is solved. The solution of the Swatville dual is shown in the following *QuickQuant* printout, which lists the dual variable values in the same order as the primal constraints. The symbol annotations are not supplied by the software and were added later.

CONSTR. No. Type		Auxiliary Variable		Value of DUAL Variable	
1	<	S1 =	3793.10	0.000	$= U_W$
2	<	S2 =	3344.83	0.000	$= U_L$
3	<	S3 =	0.00	0.468	$= U_F$
4	<	S4 =	758.62	0.000	$= U_B$
5	<	S5 =	936.78	0.000	$= U_S$
6	<	S6 =	1310.34	0.000	$= U_V$
7	<	S7 =	0.00	0.000	$= U_1$
8	<	S8 =	0.00	0.383	$= U_2$
9	<	S9 =	0.00	0.349	$= U_3$

Notice that only one of the first six dual variables is nonzero, $U_F = 0.47$. This means that Swatville can increase profits by $\$.47$ for each minute of additional finishing time available. Increasing available levels of any of the other five resources will not increase profits. Based on this, Babe will look for ways to increase finishing time.

So far, all the primal linear programs in this chapter involve $\leq$ constraints. Optional Section 10-6 at the end of the chapter describes more complex cases involving $\geq$ and $=$ constraint types. The dual U's associated with one of these constraint types might assume *negative* values. For example, if there is a demand constraint in the Redwood Furniture problem stipulating that

$$X_C \geq 10$$

Adjustable Cells

Cell	Name	Final Value	Reduced Cost	Objective Coefficient	Allowable Increase	Allowable Decrease
$D$17	X30	80.46	0.000	12.05	3.68	0.857
$E$17	X32	0	0.000	11.75	0.50	2.537
$F$17	X34	80.46	0.000	13.19	3.57	0.516
$G$17	X36	0	-1.269	12.64	1.27	1E+30
$H$17	X38	80.46	0.000	15.48	2.01	1.94
$I$17	X40	0	-1.202	15.18	1.20	1E+30

Constraints

Cell	Name	Final Value	Shadow Price	Constraint R.H. Side	Allowable Increase	Allowable Decrease
$N$6	Wood	8206.90	0.000	12000	1E+30	3793.10
$N$7	Lathe	2655.17	0.000	6000	1E+30	3344.83
$N$8	Finishing	7000.00	0.468	7000	3235.29	7000.00
$N$9	Boxes	241.38	0.000	1000	1E+30	758.62
$N$10	Stain	563.22	0.000	1500	1E+30	936.78
$N$11	Varnish	1689.66	0.000	3000	1E+30	1310.34
$N$12	Production	0.00	0.252	0	0	164.71
$N$13	<	0.00	0.635	0	0	250.00
$N$14	Restrictions	0.00	0.601	0	0	114.75

FIGURE 10-3   Excel's Sensitivity Report giving the optimal dual values for Swatville Sluggers
*Note: The values $U_1 = .252$, $U_2 = .635$, and U_3 differ from those reported by *QuickQuant* on page 373 because this dual *LP* has multiple optimal solutions and Excel found a different but equally good solution.

then increasing the minimum quantity from 10 to 11 can have a negative effect on profit, and the dual variable for that constraint will have a nonpositive optimal level.

Dual Values from Excel's Sensitivity Report

Figure 10-3 shows the Excel Sensitivity Report for the Swatville Sluggers problem with the same information presented in a different format. The optimal levels of the dual variables are in the Shadow Price column in the lower part of the report. Dual surplus (or slack) variables are in the Reduced Cost column in the upper part of the output.

10-3   EVALUATING NEW PRODUCTS USING THE DUAL

Suppose that Redwood Furniture is considering the manufacture of two additional products—benches and planter boxes. We will assume that the benches yield a per-unit profit of $7 and the planter boxes yield a per-unit profit of only $2. We will further assume that a bench requires 25 board feet of wood and 7 hours of labor and a planter box only consumes 10 board feet of wood and 2 hours of labor.

Should the new products be made? One way to answer this question would be to start from scratch, formulating a new Redwood Furniture linear program having new variables for the number of benches and planter boxes. That new problem could then be run on the computer. We discuss next a shortcut evaluation involving the dual.

We may use the information from the dual to cost out the benches to determine whether they should be included in the product mix. As shadow prices, the marginal values (U's) for labor and wood establish for each bench the unit opportunity cost of diverting resources from tables and chairs to that product. Applying the required resource quantities for one bench, we determine

$$\text{Opportunity cost of one bench} = 25U_W + 7U_L$$
$$= 25(\$.10) + 7(\$.60) = \$6.70$$

(This differs from the accounting cost of making a bench; that information has already been reflected in the $7 unit profit for that item.) This means that resources currently earning $6.70 in profits with tables and chairs must be diverted from those products in order to make one bench. Because that amount is less than the profit of $7 per bench, benches should be made.

We may also cost out planter boxes:

$$\text{Opportunity cost of one planter box} = 10U_W + 2U_L$$
$$= 10(\$.10) + 2(\$.60) = \$2.20$$

Because this exceeds the unit profit of $2 per box, none should be made. The wood and labor necessary to make a planter box are more profitably employed making tables and chairs.

Managerial Decision Revisited: Determining Production Quantities

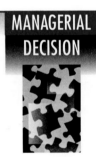

MANAGERIAL DECISION

Returning to the Swatville Sluggers problem, Babe can now determine whether or not to expand the product line by accepting a contract to produce a new 39-inch Corner Pounder bat. The total direct cost is $11.78 for each Corner Pounder. The unit profit is

$$\$23 - 11.78 = \$11.22$$

The increased opportunity cost for making one Corner Pounder is

$$39(0) + 10(0) + 30(\$.47) + 0(0) + 4(0) + 8(0) + 0(0) + 0(\$.38) + 0(\$.35) = \$14.10$$

Because the above amount exceeds the per-unit profit, *no* Corner Pounders should be made. Thus Babe would not accept the contract. However, he did decide to make a counter offer to supply the bats at a price of $26. Should the customer accept, Swatville would earn an extra $.12 per 39-inch bat ($11.22 + 3.00 − 14.10).

Putting Dual Values into Practice

USING JUDGMENT

The dual provides very useful information. It can be used in many different ways, and the information thereby obtained can have immediate use or longer-term value. Consider the following possibilities that might apply to a particular manufacturing situation:

ITEM	DUAL VALUE	SUGGESTED PROFIT IMPROVEMENT	POSSIBLE ACTION		
			Immediate	Short Term	Long Term
Wood	$ 2.30	Increasing available wood	Buy more wood from local retailer for $1 premium	Get supplementary special delivery at a $.50 premium	Make permanent arrangements to get more wood at a favorable negotiated price
Assembly Labor	$ 5.10	Increasing available hours	Put assembly workers on mandatory overtime at $1 premium	Move worker from different department	Hire new permanent staff for assembly
Machine Time	$ 4.17	Increasing available hours	Rent time as available for $2 more than current standard cost	Lease new equipment at premium of $1 per hour	Buy new and faster machine with reduced hourly operating cost
Product X	$10	Raise profit of product	Don't make the product	Increase selling price and try to sell all current production	Reduce production costs by finding greater efficiencies, then reduce price and raise market share

It is essentially a judgment call to determine just how extensively to use the dual in a post-optimality analysis and how far to go in implementing the results.

10-4 SENSITIVITY ANALYSIS IN LINEAR PROGRAMMING

A **sensitivity analysis** of a linear programming solution examines how changes or errors in data affect the optimal solution. Sometimes this is called "what if . . ." analysis because it is useful in answering many types of questions. For example, what if prices change? What if fewer resources are available? What if an accident occurs and the capacity of one of the critical components is decreased? What if a mistake was made in calculating the costs?

To see how sensitivity analysis applies in linear programming, we reconsider the wood and labor constraints of the Redwood Furniture problem. What will happen to the optimal solution if a strike at the lumber mills makes less wood available? How will the new production plan be amended if one of the cabinetmakers goes on sick leave? We will answer these questions for our original linear program.

$$X_T = \text{Number of tables}$$
$$X_C = \text{Number of chairs}$$

$$\text{Maximize} \quad P = 6X_T + 8X_C$$
$$\text{Subject to} \quad 30X_T + 20X_C \leq 300 \quad (\text{wood})$$
$$5X_T + 10X_C \leq 110 \quad (\text{labor})$$
$$\text{where} \quad X_T, X_C \geq 0$$

Sensitivity Limits

A sensitivity analysis utilizes sensitivity limits. These are ordinarily computed for the constraint right-hand sides and the coefficients of the objective function, with the required calculations performed by computer at the same time that the linear program is solved.

The following annotated report was consolidated from the output of a *QuickQuant* run with the Redwood Furniture problem. Solution values for the auxiliary variables are given in the first two columns. The last three columns show each constraint's right-hand side sensitivity limits and current level.

SOLUTION TO LINEAR PROGRAM

PROBLEM: Redwood Furniture

Objective Value: P = 96.0000

SOLUTION TO DUAL AND SENSITIVITY ANALYSIS

				RIGHTHAND SIDE Sensitivity Anal.			
CONSTR.			Value				
No. Type		Auxiliary Variable	of DUAL Variable	Lower Limit	Original Level	Upper Limit	
1	<	S1 =	0.00	0.100	220.00	300.00	660.00	wood
2	<	S2 =	0.00	0.600	50.00	110.00	150.00	labor

Those limits indicate what available levels of the respective resources (i.e., the primal constraint right-hand sides) would still yield an LP solution having identical optimal values for the dual. Thus, the levels $U_W = .10$ and $U_L = .60$ will be the same as long as available wood lies between the **lower sensitivity limit** of 220 board feet and the **upper sensitivity limit** of 660 board feet. This is verified graphically in Figure 10-4. Notice in (a) that although the feasible solution region becomes narrower as the level of available wood is reduced, it maintains the same basic four-sided shape and that, until 220 board feet is reached, the most attractive corner is where the wood and labor constraint lines intersect. At 220 board feet and below, the feasible solution region is triangular and no tables are made and there is slack labor. In Figure 10-4(b), as the level of available wood is raised, the feasible region's shape remains the same and the intersection of the labor and wood constraint lines provides the most attractive corner until 660 board feet is reached. Thereafter, the region is triangular, formed only by the labor constraint line and axes, no chairs are made, and there is slack wood. The values for U_W and U_L will also change for any shift in available wood below 220 or above 660 board feet.

Similar limits apply to changes in unit profits. The underlying rationale is basically the same as it is for right-hand side analysis (which can be applied to the dual problem, in which the right sides are the primal unit profits).

Continuing with our original Redwood Furniture problem, let's see what happens if the profit per table is changed. As Figure 10-5(a) shows, an increase in the table profit results in a new maximum P line. Increasing the profit per table from $6 to $10 yields a steeper profit line, but the most attractive corner remains the same. At a profit

FIGURE 10-4

Graphical illustration of how the feasible solution region changes for various levels of available wood

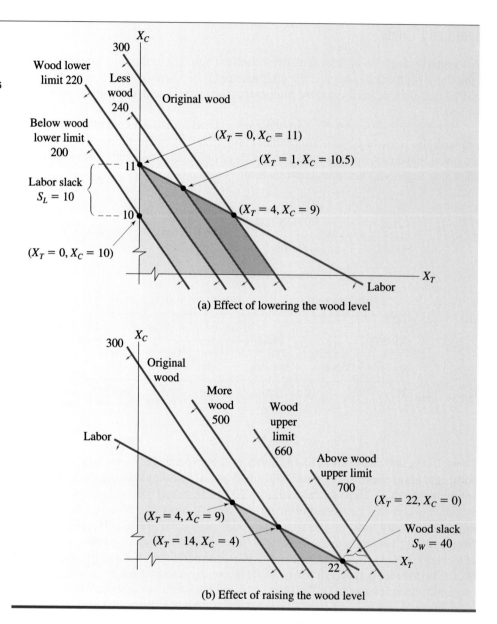

(a) Effect of lowering the wood level

(b) Effect of raising the wood level

of $15 per table, it is no longer attractive to make chairs, and the most attractive corner occurs where the wood line intersects the X_T axis; in effect, the resulting maximum P line is steeper than the wood constraint line. Figure 10-5(b) illustrates the reverse situation—when the unit table profit decreases. At a $5 profit, the maximum P line is flatter than before, and the original corner remains most attractive. At a $3 profit for each table, making tables is no longer attractive, and the most attractive corner occurs where the labor line intersects the X_C axis; the resulting maximum P line is flatter than the labor constraint line.

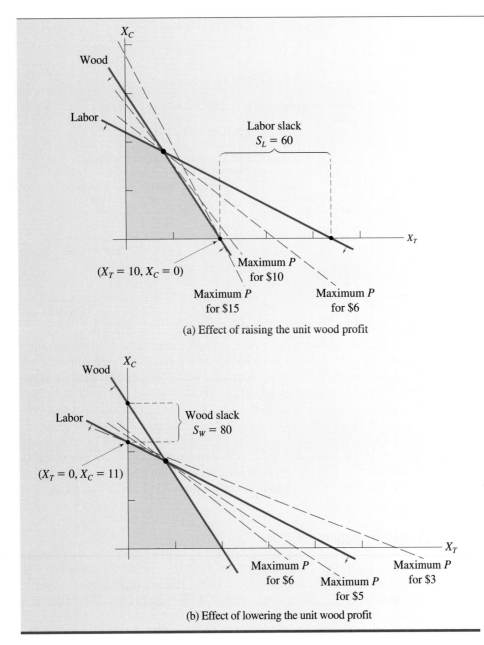

FIGURE 10-5
Graphical illustrations of how the most attractive corner (the optimal solution) changes with different unit profit levels for tables

(a) Effect of raising the unit wood profit

(b) Effect of lowering the unit wood profit

Figure 10-5 tells us that the same primal solution ($X_T = 4$, $X_C = 9$) applies over a wide range of unit profits. Only the level of P is affected.

The following report was output from a *QuickQuant* run with the Redwood Furniture problem. Solution values for the main problem variables are listed in the second column, followed by dual slack or surplus values. Objective coefficient information is provided in the last three columns, where each variable's profit sensitivity limits are listed along with the original unit profit.

SOLUTION TO LINEAR PROGRAM

PROBLEM: Redwood Furniture

ORIGINAL PROBLEM DATA

Objective Value: P = 96.00000

SOLUTION TO DUAL AND SENSITIVITY ANALYSIS

			OBJECTIVE COEFFICIENT Sensitivity		
Main Variable	Optimal Value	DUAL Slack/Surplus	Lower Limit	Original Level	Upper Limit
XT	4.00	0.00	4.00	6.00	12.00
XC	9.00	0.00	4.00	8.00	12.00

We see that the current optimal solution ($X_T = 4$, $X_C = 9$) will remain unchanged for any unit table profit between \$4 and \$12. Coincidentally, the same range \$4 to \$12, applies to the unit chair profit. (Ordinarily each variable will have different limits.)

As an illustration of the use of these limits, suppose that the table profit contribution increases from \$6 to \$12. Common sense might suggest that the new optimal solution should produce more tables, because the table profit contribution doubles. However, the above report shows that the new optimal solution would still produce 4 tables and 9 chairs because the new profit contribution of \$12 falls within the original sensitivity limits. In addition, the 4 tables and 9 chairs still give the highest profit for Redwood. Profits will actually be worse if more tables are produced to take advantage of their increased profit contribution. Even though the optimal number of tables and chairs remain the same in this new optimal solution, the total profit will change; it will increase by \$24, that is 4 (number of tables) multiplied by \$6 (increased unit profit).

The Excel Sensitivity Report

Solver provides a sensitivity report that can be used in a sensitivity analysis. Figure 10-6 is an example of the sensitivity report for the Redwood Furniture Company. There are two parts to this report. The first deals with the adjustable cells and the second provides information about the constraints.

In the adjustable cells section of the report, the Final Value column contains the optimal levels for the tables and chairs, $X_T = 4$ and $X_C = 9$. This solution remains the same as long as the table and chair profit contributions are within the allowable increases and decreases shown in the last two columns. The Objective Coefficient column lists the current table profit contribution as \$6. Subtracting the allowable decrease of 2 provides the same lower limit of \$4 found in the *QuickQuant* run. Adding the allowable increase of 6 provides the upper limit of \$12. As long as the table profit is between \$4 and \$12, the original solution remains unchanged. The same reasoning gives the lower and upper limits for the chair's profit contribution to be \$4 (8 minus 4) and \$12 (8 plus 4), respectively.

The numbers in the Reduced Cost column are the dual surplus values for the corresponding variables. They represent the decrease in profits that occur if the corre-

Adjustable Cells						
Cell	Name	Final Value	Reduced Cost	Objective Coefficient	Allowable Increase	Allowable Decrease
$B$9	XT	4	0	6	6	2
$C$9	XC	9	0	8	4	4

Constraints						
Cell	Name	Final Value	Shadow Price	Constraint R.H. Side	Allowable Increase	Allowable Decrease
$G$5	Wood used	300	0.1	300	360	80
$G$6	Labor used	110	0.6	110	40	60

FIGURE 10-6
Solver's Sensitivity report for the original Redwood Furniture problem

sponding variables are increased to a positive level. In Figure 10-6, the reduced cost for tables is 0 because X_T is already positive (4 in this case).

The Constraints section of the sensitivity report contains similar information. We are familiar with the entries in the Shadow Price column. The 0.1 for wood tells us that P will increase by $.10 to $96.10 when one more unit of wood is made available. Similarly, if two fewer units of wood are available, the profit decreases by $.20 to $95.80. The allowable changes in resource availabilities appear in the last two columns, from which it is easy to calculate sensitivity limits of resource availabilities within which the shadow prices are valid. For wood, the shadow price of .1 is valid as long as the available amount is between 220 (300 minus 80) and 660 (300 plus 360). If the available wood were to fall outside that range, both new shadow prices and new values of X_T and X_C would need to be found with another Solver run.

10-5 POST-OPTIMALITY ANALYSIS

The primal LP solves the immediate problem, allowing management to optimize current production quantities for the present product line. This type of decision making is *tactical* in nature. When solving the tactical primal LP, the companion dual solution can also be employed to address *strategical* issues, such as whether or not to introduce a new product.

The dual's usefulness extends well beyond costing out new products. Its focus on resources pinpoints those limitations that have significant opportunity costs, quantifying each in terms of potential profit improvements. In essence, it identifies *economic bottlenecks*.

In a production situation, the simplest economic bottleneck might be the available quantity of raw material, the expanded supply of which can permit greater production. Such improvements are easy to make. But of even greater significance may be bottlenecks attributable to limitations of other factors of production, such as the time availability with special equipment or the floorspace area of the plant. A **post-optimality analysis** uses the information provided by the dual to pursue such issues.

A complete post-optimality analysis identifies attractive areas in which improvements can be made to the problem itself. The process is iterative, with successive reformulated problems giving solutions that may uncover further revisions, leading to even more improvements.

TABLE 10-2   Data Obtained for Expanded Redwood Furniture Problem

	VARIABLE							
CONSTRAINT	(1) X_{TS}	(2) X_{TR}	(3) X_{TL}	(4) X_{CS}	(5) X_{CA}	(6) X_{BS}	(7) X_{BT}	AVAILABLE QUANTITY
(1) Wood	20	30	40	15	25	20	30	≤3,000
(2) Labor	4	5	6	8	12	6	8	≤1,100
(3) Machine time	2	2	2	3	3	2	2	≤ 250
(4) Quantity, tables	1	1	1					≥ 30
(5) Quantity, chairs				1	1			≥ 20
(6) Quantity, bookcases						1	1	≥ 20
(7) Mix, tables	1	−1	−1					= 0
(8) Mix, chairs				1	−4			= 0
(9) Mix, bookcases						1	−1	= 0
Unit profit	$5	$6	$7	$6	$10	$8	$6	

Dual values pinpoint economic bottlenecks that might be ameliorated through a facility expansion or by relaxing some requirement. But the dual variables are only applicable over specific ranges, the limits of which we now know how to find. Combined with the dual, sensitivity limits will enable us to determine actual problem changes, giving improved optimal profit or cost levels exceeding those of the original problem.

A comprehensive illustration of post-optimality analysis will be provided by the expanded Redwood Furniture problem presented in Table 10-2. This problem involves determining how many pieces of furniture to make: tables in three sizes—small (X_{TS}), regular (X_{TR}), and large (X_{TL}); chairs of two types—standard (X_{CS}) and armed (X_{CA}); and bookcases of two heights—short (X_{BS}) and tall (X_{BT}). That is to be done subject to three resource limitations—on wood, labor, and machine time—three minimum quantities for each furniture group, and three mix requirements for the quantities of various types within groups. The overall objective is to maximize profit.

The problem was solved using *QuickQuant,* with output in Figure 10-7. (See Section 10-6 for a detailed explanation of the dual for this expanded problem.) Perusal of the dual variables uncovers two standouts: $U_M = 3.5$ and $U_{QC} = -3.7$. The first value indicates that a profit improvement of $3.50 might be achieved for each additional hour of machine time obtained at the standard hourly cost. The second value indicates that profit would *drop* by $3.70 for each unit *increase* in minimum chairs.

Redwood can obtain additional machine time (at present cost) beyond the 250 hours currently available. Unfortunately, the impact of additional machine time would be short lived, because the dual only applies for levels of the right-hand side between sensitivity limits 160 and 260.8 hours. Similar profit increases can be achieved by reducing the chair quantity minimum below the current 20 units down to any level greater than 13.41. Management does not want to disturb customer relations by changing the minimum chair quantity.

Additional machine time can be rented in increments of 50 hours. Although getting more machine time would increase the level to 300, beyond the upper sensitivity limit for that resource, management is willing to consider it.

A new simplex run was made with *QuickQuant* incorporating that one change. The new output in Figure 10-8 was obtained. Notice that profit increases only by $98.63—not the $3.50 × 50 expected. The original dual value of 3.5 only applies for the first

SOLUTION TO LINEAR PROGRAM

PROBLEM: Redwood Furniture (Expanded)

Objective Value: P = 771.00000

SOLUTION TO DUAL AND SENSITIVITY ANALYSIS

RIGHTHAND SIDE Sensitivity Anal.

CONSTR. No.	Type	Auxiliary Variable		Value of DUAL Variable	Lower Limit	Original Level	Upper Limit			
1	<	S1 =	135.00	0.000	2865.00	3000.00	None	wood	U_W	= 0
2	<	S2 =	319.00	0.000	781.00	1100.00	None	labor	U_L	= 0
3	<	S3 =	0.00	3.500	160.00	250.00	260.80	mach. t.	U_M	= 3.5
4	>	S4 =	0.00	−1.000	0.00	30.00	57.00	qty., tab.	U_{QT}	= −1
5	>	S5 =	0.00	−3.700	13.41	20.00	50.00	qty., ch.	U_{QC}	= −3.7
6	>	S6 =	45.00	0.000	None	20.00	65.00	qty., bk.	U_{QB}	= 0
7	=	a7 =	0.00	−1.000	−13.50	0.00	30.00	mix, tab.	U_{MT}	= −1
8	=	a8 =	0.00	−.800	−67.50	0.00	20.00	mix, ch.	U_{MC}	= −.8
9	=	a9 =	0.00	1.000	−27.00	0.00	65.00	mix, bk.	U_{MB}	= 1

OBJECTIVE COEFFICIENT Sensitivity

Main Variable	Optimal Value	DUAL Slack/Surplus	Lower Limit	Original Level	Upper Limit		
XTS	15.00	0.00	None	5.00	7.00	U_{TS}	= 0
XTR	0.00	1.00	None	6.00	7.00	U_{TR}	= 1
XTL	15.00	0.00	6.00	7.00	9.00	U_{TL}	= 0
XCS	16.00	0.00	None	6.00	10.62	U_{CS}	= 0
XCA	4.00	0.00	None	10.00	28.50	U_{CA}	= 0
XBS	32.50	0.00	6.00	8.00	None	U_{BS}	= 0
XBT	32.50	0.00	4.00	6.00	None	U_{BT}	= 0

FIGURE 10-7   Portions of the *QuickQuant* report giving primal and dual solutions to the expanded Redwood Furniture problem, with annotations

----

$260.80 - 250 = 10.80$ hours of additional machine time. Notice that the solution values change. There is no more unused wood, and there is now surplus for the chairs quantity. The dual values shift too, and the ranges differ substantially from before.

Perusal of the second *QuickQuant* printout indicates that further profit improvements may be achieved by further increasing machine time, for which the dual value is now $U_M = 1.244$ (smaller than before). There is also an advantage from reducing the table quantity, because $U_{QT} = -1.5$. Doing this has the same customer disadvantages as with the earlier chair quantity reduction (which would now provide *no* improvement, because $U_{QC} = 0$). Another attractive possibility is suggested by $U_{MB} = 1.902$, which indicates that raising the number of short bookcases beyond the number of tall ones, by as much as 68 units, would raise profit by $1.90 for each extra short bookcase made. Management decides that the number of excess short bookcases can be 50 instead of the present 0. (This will not change the basic mix, but all quantities will shift to new levels.)

FIGURE 10-8

Portions of the annotated second *Quick-Quant* report giving solution to the expanded Redwood Furniture problem, modified by increasing machine time availability to 300 hours

```
                       SOLUTION TO LINEAR PROGRAM
         ----------------------------------------------------------------
         PROBLEM: Redwood Furniture (Expanded)

                         Objective Value: P = 869.63420

               SOLUTION TO DUAL AND SENSITIVITY ANALYSIS
         ----------------------------------------------------------------
```

RIGHTHAND SIDE Sensitivity Anal.

CONSTR. No.	Type	Auxiliary Variable	Value of DUAL Variable	Lower Limit	Original Level	Upper Limit		
1	<	S1 =	0.00	0.180	2383.33	3000.00	3340.00	wood U_W = .18
2	<	S2 =	187.20	0.000	912.80	1100.00	None	labor U_L = 0
3	<	S3 =	0.00	1.240	272.80	300.00	375.99	mach. t. U_M = 1.244
4	>	S4 =	0.00	−1.500	0.00	30.00	75.12	qty., tab. U_{QT} = −1.5
5	>	S5 =	16.59	0.000	None	20.00	36.59	qty., ch. U_{QC} = 0
6	>	S6 =	45.12	0.000	None	20.00	65.12	qty., bk. U_{QB} = 0
7	=	a7 =	0.00	0.400	−30.00	0.00	30.00	mix, tab. U_{MT} = .402
8	=	a8 =	0.00	−0.440	−240.00	0.00	33.33	mix, ch. U_{MC} = −.439
9	=	a9 =	0.00	1.900	−47.68	0.00	68.00	mix, bk. U_{MB} = 1.902

OBJECTIVE COEFFICIENT Sensitivity

Main Variable	Optimal Value	DUAL Slack/Surplus	Lower Limit	Original Level	Upper Limit	
XTS	15.00	0.00	None	5.00	8.00	U_{TS} = 0
XTR	15.00	0.00	5.20	6.00	9.00	U_{TR} = 0
XTL	0.00	.80	None	7.00	7.80	U_{TL} = .8
XCS	29.27	0.00	3.45	6.00	8.06	U_{CS} = 0
XCA	7.32	0.00	−0.20	10.00	18.25	U_{CA} = 0
XBS	32.56	0.00	5.80	8.00	14.00	U_{BS} = 0
XBT	32.56	0.00	3.80	6.00	12.00	U_{BT} = 0

Two further changes to the linear program are made next. Available machine time is increased from 300 to 400 (a figure slightly higher than the limit given for that constraint in Figure 10-8), and the right-hand side of the bookcase mixture constraint is changed to 50.

Figure 10-9 shows the *QuickQuant* output from a new run with these changes. As before, many quantities change, and new dual values apply. The profit rises substantially to P = $1,065, a nearly $300 increase. Examination of the dual shows that further increases in machine time will not raise profit. The dual value U_W = .40 indicates that it would be attractive to increase available wood, but the current level is so close to the wood upper sensitivity limit that it appears not worth the bother.

Large dual surplus values of U_{TL} = 3.0 and U_{BT} = 6.0 are obtained. They suggest that raising unit profits for large tables and tall bookcases would increase profit. Because they cannot control the cost of supplies and other production factors, management can increase unit profit only by raising prices. Due to market forces, the only product for which prices can be raised is the large table.

A final run was made with the large table profit increased to $11, accomplished by raising the price by $4. The results are shown in Figure 10-10. Notice that total profit has increased to P = $1,080. Although the new dual values indicate that further im-

FIGURE 10-9
Portions of the annotated third *QuickQuant* report giving solution to the expanded Redwood Furniture problem, modified by increasing machine time availability to 400 hours and allowing a 50-unit difference for the bookcase mixture

SOLUTION TO LINEAR PROGRAM

PROBLEM: Redwood Furniture (Expanded)

Objective Value: P = 1065.0000

SOLUTION TO DUAL AND SENSITIVITY ANALYSIS

RIGHTHAND SIDE Sensitivity Anal.

CONSTR. No.	Type	Auxiliary Variable		Value of DUAL Variable	Lower Limit	Original Value	Upper Limit			
1	<	S1	=	0.00 0.400	2090.00	3000.00	3034.66	wood	U_W	= .4
2	<	S2	=	17.94 0.000	1082.06	1100.00	None	labor	U_L	= 0
3	<	S3	=	19.41 0.000	380.59	400.00	None	mach. t.	U_M	= 0
4	>	S4	=	0.00 -4.500	27.87	30.00	66.40	qty., tab.	U_{QT}	= -4.5
5	>	S5	=	53.53 0.000	None	20.00	73.53	qty., ch.	U_{QC}	= 0
6	>	S6	=	30.00 0.000	None	20.00	50.00	qty., bk.	U_{QB}	= 0
7	=	a7	=	0.00 1.500	-30.00	0.00	8.59	mix, tab.	U_{MT}	= 1.5
8	=	a8	=	0.00 0.000	-200.00	0.00	55.00	mix, ch.	U_{MC}	= 0
9	=	a9	=	0.00 0.000	45.88	50.00	95.50	mix, bk.	U_{MB}	= 0

OBJECTIVE COEFFICIENT Sensitivity

Main Variable	Optimal Value	DUAL Slack/Surplus	Lower Limit	Original Value	Upper Limit	
XTS	15.00	0.00	None	5.00	14.00	$U_{TS} = 0$
XTR	15.00	0.00	3.00	6.00	15.00	$U_{TR} = 0$
XTL	0.00	3.00	None	7.00	10.00	$U_{TL} = 3$
XCS	58.82	0.00	3.45	6.00	None	$U_{CS} = 0$
XCA	14.71	0.00	-0.20	10.00	None	$U_{CA} = 0$
XBS	50.00	0.00	None	8.00	14.00	$U_{BS} = 0$
XBT	0.00	6.00	None	6.00	12.00	$U_{BT} = 6$

provements might be made, the changes are either not significant enough or management is unwilling to make them.

The post-optimality analysis is complete. Substantial profit improvement may be achieved by increasing machine time to 400 hours, allowing for 50 extra short bookcases, and increasing the price of large tables by $4. The optimal production quantities are given in the first two columns of the bottom section of Figure 10-10.

The post-optimality considerations encountered so far all involve changes to one or more constraint right-hand sides or to objective coefficients for one or more variables. These changes are *internal* in nature, each suggested by the linear program solutions alone. Post-optimality analysis also extends to *externally* generated changes, originating outside of the current linear program. One common change is to add new variables or delete current ones. Such a modification would arise in manufacturing applications when modifications to the product mix itself are contemplated. Another externally generated change is to add or delete a constraint. Such a change might be required to reflect changes in the marketplace or a new manufacturing process. In the lat-

FIGURE 10-10

Portions of the annotated final *QuickQuant* report giving solution to the expanded Redwood Furniture problem, modified by raising the large-table price by $4

SOLUTION TO LINEAR PROGRAM

PROBLEM: Redwood Furniture (Expanded)

Objective Value: P =1080.0000

SOLUTION TO DUAL AND SENSITIVITY ANALYSIS

RIGHTHAND SIDE Sensitivity Anal.

CONSTR.			Value					
No.	Type	Auxiliary Variable	of DUAL Variable	Lower Limit	Original Value	Upper Limit		
1	<	S1 =	0.00	0.400	2240.00	3000.00	3155.68	wood $U_W = .4$
2	<	S2 =	80.59	0.000	1019.41	1100.00	None	labor $U_L = 0$
3	<	S3 =	45.88	0.000	354.12	400.00	None	mach. t. $U_M = 0$
4	>	S4 =	0.00	−4.000	22.35	30.00	55.33	qty., tab. $U_{QT} = -4$
5	>	S5 =	44.71	0.000	None	20.00	64.71	qty., ch. $U_{QC} = 0$
6	>	S6 =	30.00	0.000	None	20.00	50.00	qty., bk. $U_{QB} = 0$
7	=	a7 =	0.00	1.000	−30.00	0.00	19.30	mix, tab. $U_{MT} = 1$
8	=	a8 =	0.00	0.000	−176.00	0.00	73.33	mix, ch. $U_{MC} = 0$
9	=	a9 =	0.00	0.000	31.49	50.00	88.00	mix, bk. $U_{MB} = 0$

OBJECTIVE COEFFICIENT Sensitivity

Main Variable	Optimal Value	DUAL Slack/Surplus	Lower Limit	Original Value	Upper Limit	
XTS	15.00	0.00	None	5.00	13.00	$U_{TS} = 0$
XTR	0.00	1.00	None	6.00	7.00	$U_{TR} = 1$
XTL	15.00	0.00	10.00	11.00	19.00	$U_{TL} = 0$
XCS	51.76	0.00	3.45	6.00	8.12	$U_{CS} = 0$
XCA	12.94	0.00	−0.20	10.00	18.50	$U_{CA} = 0$
XBS	50.00	0.00	None	8.00	14.00	$U_{BS} = 0$
XBT	0.00	6.00	None	6.00	12.00	$U_{BT} = 6$

ter case, the nature of a constraint might change by requiring revisions to existing constraint exchange coefficients to reflect equipment upgrades.

Adding a New Variable (Product)

Adding a new variable to the problem can require a realignment of the current solution similar to increasing a unit profit or reducing a cost to a level outside of the sensitivity limits. We have seen how to assess, on a per-unit basis, the effect of a new variable by costing it out and applying dual values as shadow prices. Recall that the resulting opportunity cost arises from the diversion of resources away from other currently profitable products. A new product should be added to the product line only when its unit profit exceeds its opportunity cost.

A shadow price investigation using dual values can also help management establish a viable selling price for a new product. To illustrate, we will continue with the expanded Redwood Furniture problem, incorporating all of the post-optimality changes made so far. Table 10-3 summarizes the current linear program.

TABLE 10-3	Expanded Redwood Furniture after Modifications from First Post-Optimality Analysis

CONSTRAINT	VARIABLE							AVAILABLE QUANTITY
	X_{TS}	X_{TR}	X_{TL}	X_{CS}	X_{CA}	X_{BS}	X_{BT}	
(1) Wood	20	30	40	15	25	20	30	≤3,000
(2) Labor	4	5	6	8	12	6	8	≤1,100
(3) Machine time	2	2	2	3	3	2	2	≤ 400
(4) Quantity, tables	1	1	1					≥ 30
(5) Quantity, chairs				1	1			≥ 20
(6) Quantity, bookcases						1	1	≥ 20
(7) Mix, tables	1	−1	−1					= 0
(8) Mix, chairs				1	−4			= 0
(9) Mix, bookcases						1	−1	= 50
Unit profit	$5	$6	$11	$6	$10	$8	$6	

Suppose that a new product, desks, might be added to the furniture line. Each desk uses 100 board feet of wood, requires 10 hours of labor, and needs 5 hours of machine time. The desks will be priced at $195 and cost $180 to make, yielding a per unit profit of $15. Should desks be added to Redwood's product line?

Using the dual values from Figure 10-10, we cost out one desk.

RESOURCE	DUAL VALUE (COST)	REQUIRED AMOUNT	COST × AMOUNT
Wood	$.40	100 bd ft	$40
Labor	0	10 hr	0
Machine time	0	5 hr	0
			$40

The resources needed to make one desk would have to be diverted from other products, but the calculation shows that doing so would reduce profits by $40 for each desk made. At a standard cost of $180 each, with a $195 selling price, Redwood would net only $15 per desk. The company would lose $40 − 15 = $25 on each desk made. Only by raising the desk price by more than $25 a unit would desks be profitable.

Management decides that they can make a selling price of $230 stick, so that the unit profit is $230 − 180 = $50. That will provide a net increase in current profit of $10 for each desk made, up to some limit yet to be determined.

The final production plan and overall profit can only be determined by solving the problem from scratch. We add a new variable (X_D), using as coefficients the respective required amounts listed in the expanded wood, labor, and machine time constraints. Before doing that, an additional problem modification is required.

Adding a New Constraint

Adding a new constraint presents similar challenges to adding a new variable. Depending on the type of constraint, the expanded problem will require a new row and a new slack variable. Adding the new desk to Redwood's line creates the need for a new constraint. This is because management does not think that they can sell 10 desks at the

FIGURE 10-11

Portions of the annotated *QuickQuant* report giving solution to the expanded Redwood Furniture problem, further modified by adding a new variable, desks, and a new constraint

SOLUTION TO LINEAR PROGRAM

PROBLEM: Redwood Furniture (Expanded)

Objective Value: P = 1130.0000

SOLUTION TO DUAL AND SENSITIVITY ANALYSIS

RIGHTHAND SIDE Sensitivity Anal.

CONSTR.			Value of DUAL Variable	Lower Limit	Original Value	Upper Limit			
No.	Type	Auxiliary Variable							
1	<	S1 =	0.00 .400	2740.00	3000.00	3421.64	wood	U_W	= .4
2	<	S2 =	257.94 0.000	842.06	1100.00	None	labor	U_L	= 0
3	<	S3 =	134.12 0.000	265.88	400.00	None	mach. t.	U_M	= 0
4	>	S4 =	0.00 −4.000	10.68	30.00	38.67	qty., tab.	U_{QT}	= −4
5	>	S5 =	15.29 0.000	None	20.00	35.29	qty., ch.	U_{QC}	= 0
6	>	S6 =	30.00 0.000	None	20.00	50.00	qty., bk.	U_{QB}	= 0
7	=	a7 =	0.00 1.000	−26.00	0.00	30.00	mix, tab.	U_{MT}	= 1
8	=	a8 =	0.00 0.000	−96.00	0.00	40.00	mix, ch.	U_{MC}	= 0
9	=	a9 =	0.00 0.000	20.00	50.00	63.00	mix, bk.	U_{MB}	= 0
10	<	S10 =	0.00 10.000	0.41	5.00	7.60	qty., dk.	U_{QD}	= 10

OBJECTIVE COEFFICIENT Sensitivity

Main Variable	Optimal Value	DUAL Slack/Surplus	Lower Limit	Original Value	Upper Limit		
XTS	15.00	0.00	None	5.00	13.00	U_{TS}	= 0
XTR	0.00	1.00	None	6.00	7.00	U_{TR}	= 1
XTL	15.00	0.00	10.00	11.00	19.00	U_{TL}	= 0
XCS	28.24	0.00	3.45	6.00	8.12	U_{CS}	= 0
XCA	7.06	0.00	−0.20	10.00	18.50	U_{CA}	= 0
XBS	50.00	0.00	None	8.00	14.00	U_{BS}	= 0
XBT	0.00	6.00	None	6.00	12.00	U_{BT}	= 6
XD	5.00	0.00	40.00	50.00	None	U_D	= 0

high price necessary to justify making them. Management adds the restriction that the number of desks cannot exceed 5.

$$X_D \leq 5 \quad \text{(quantity, desks)}$$

The new variable and new constraint are added to the problem. Figure 10-11 shows the *QuickQuant* printout giving the solution to the expanded problem. Profit increases by $50 by adding the new product.

Modifying Constraint Coefficients

The effect of modifying constraint coefficients is hard to assess, and it is recommended that a new solution be obtained from scratch. To illustrate, suppose that after adding desks to the product mix, Redwood wants to determine whether to adopt a special labor-saving process that reduces labor hours 20% per unit while increasing machine time by

TABLE 10-4   Expanded Redwood Furniture Including New Exchange Coefficients and Objective for Special Processes

CONSTRAINT	X_{TS}	X_{TR}	X_{TL}	X_{CS}	X_{CA}	X_{BS}	X_{BT}	X_D	QUANTITY
				VARIABLE					
(1) Wood	20	30	40	15	25	20	30	100	≤3,000
(2) Original labor	4	5	6	8	12	6	8	10	
Less 20%	.8	1	1.2	1.6	2.4	1.2	1.6	2	
New labor	3.2	4	4.8	6.4	9.6	4.8	6.4	8	≤1,100
(3) Original machine time	2	2	2	3	3	2	2	5	
Plus 10%	.2	.2	.2	.3	.3	.2	.2	.5	
New machine time	2.2	2.2	2.2	3.3	3.3	2.2	2.2	5.5	≤ 400
(4) Quantity, tables	1	1	1						≥ 30
(5) Quantity, chairs				1	1				≥ 20
(6) Quantity, bookcases						1	1		≥ 20
(7) Mix, tables	1	−1	−1						= 0
(8) Mix, chairs				1	−4				= 0
(9) Mix, bookcases						1	−1		= 50
(10) Quantity, desks								1	≤ 5
Original unit profit	5	6	11	6	10	8	6	50	
Labor savings	+8	+10	+12	+16	+24	+12	+16	+20	
Added machine cost	−1	−1	−1	−1.5	−1.5	−1	−1	−2.5	
New processing cost	−1	−1	−1	−1	−1	−1	−1	−1	
New unit profit	11	14	21	19.5	31.5	18	20	66.5	

10%. All exchange coefficients must be recomputed, and because the resource costs will change, new unit profits must be computed as well. Labor costs are $10 per hour, while machine time only costs $5 per hour. The new procedure will also add an additional $1 to the final cost of each furniture item. Table 10-4 summarizes the new problem.

This modified problem was run on *QuickQuant,* which provides the output in Figure 10-12. Notice how dramatically the new process increases total profit, from $P =$ $1,130 to $P =$ $2,828.79. Of course, an entire round of fresh internal post-optimality analysis could be performed on this solution to achieve further profitable problem improvements to this radically different solution.

When to Conduct and When to Stop a Post-Optimality Analysis

Deciding whether to do a post-optimality analysis is strictly a judgment call; there is no rule telling us when to stop. Whenever dual values are readily available, a quick perusal can be very enlightening.

There is no *theoretical* stopping point in post-optimality analysis. There will always be some constraint right-hand side or some variable whose dual suggests a favorable outcome from adjustment. But, there is ordinarily some external force, such as scarcity of resource or market intolerance to increased prices, that provides a *natural* stopping point on possible changes. Also, a point of diminishing returns can be reached after which further problem improvements become no longer worth the bother.

USING JUDGMENT

FIGURE 10-12

Portions of the annotated *QuickQuant* report giving solution to the expanded Redwood Furniture problem, further modified by incorporating a new process

SOLUTION TO LINEAR PROGRAM

PROBLEM: Redwood Furniture (Expanded)

Objective Value: P = 2728.78800

SOLUTION TO DUAL AND SENSITIVITY ANALYSIS

| | | | | RIGHTHAND SIDE Sensitivity Anal. | | |
| CONSTR. | | | Value | | | |
No.	Type	Auxiliary Variable	of DUAL Variable	Lower Limit	Original Value	Upper Limit
1	<	S1 =	0.00 .700	2903.94	3000.00	3053.94	wood U_W = .7
2	<	S2 =	306.45 0.000	793.55	1100.00	None	labor U_L = 0
3	<	S3 =	0.00 3.030	389.53	400.00	418.65	mach. t. U_M = 3.03
4	>	S4 =	0.00 −11.667	27.11	30.00	37.03	qty., tab. U_{QT} = −11.67
5	>	S5 =	47.88 0.000	None	20.00	67.88	qty., ch. U_{QC} = 0
6	>	S6 =	30.00 0.000	None	20.00	50.00	qty., bk. U_{QB} = 0
7	=	a7 =	0.00 2.000	−19.21	0.00	5.39	mix, tab. U_{MT} = 2
8	=	a8 =	0.00 −1.000	−48.03	0.00	26.97	mix, ch. U_{MC} = −1
9	=	a9 =	0.00 −4.667	43.78	50.00	61.08	mix, bk. U_{MB} = −4.67
10	<	S10 =	5.00 0.000	0.00	5.00	None	qty., dk. U_{QD} = 0

OBJECTIVE COEFFICIENT Sensitivity

Main Variable	Optimal Value	DUAL Slack/Surplus	Lower Limit	Original Value	Upper Limit	
XTS	15.00	0.00	None	11.00	34.33	U_{TS} = 0
XTR	5.39	0.00	8.12	14.00	16.81	U_{TR} = 0
XTL	9.61	0.00	18.19	21.00	26.88	U_{TL} = 0
XCS	54.30	0.00	7.94	19.50	None	U_{CS} = 0
XCA	13.58	0.00	−14.75	31.50	None	U_{CA} = 0
XBS	50.00	0.00	None	16.00	28.33	U_{BS} = 0
XBT	0.00	10.33	None	20.00	32.33	U_{BT} = 10.33
XD	0.00	20.17	None	66.50	86.67	U_D = 20.17

10-6 (OPTIONAL) DUAL FOR A GENERALIZED LINEAR PROGRAM

The examples of the dual presented thus far involve production-type problems where all constraints pertain to resource availabilities. In a more general context, each constraint in the primal corresponds to a dual variable, even if the constraint involves a nonresource restriction, such as quantity or mixture requirements. In general, for the kth primal constraint in a profit-maximization problem, the dual variable is defined as

U_k = marginal value from increasing the right-hand side of constraint k

The examples of the dual encountered thus far involve a linear program with a *regular form,* in which, for a maximization primal, all the constraints are of the $\leq$ type. But linear programs may also have a more general form, with constraints of the $\geq$ and

= types. The dual linear program corresponding to such a problem will have nonstandard features.

There are various methods of formulating dual linear programs. All are equivalent, although they may look different. The simplest method is to start with the primal in the regular form seen so far in this chapter and then formulate the dual as has been illustrated. The regular form for a primal having a maximize P objective always has constraints with the $\leq$ orientation; its dual will be minimize C, and all the dual constraints will have the $\geq$ orientation. (Should the primal objective be minimize C, regular form primal constraints will have the $\geq$ orientation; the dual will be maximize P with $\leq$ constraints. That case is illustrated in Optional Section 10-7.)

The only two situations not covered by the above rules are when the primal inequality orientations are mixed or when constraints are strict equalities. In those cases, the primal must be reformatted in the regular form before getting the dual.

Consider the following two primal constraints with mixed inequality signs:

$$3X_1 + 2X_2 \leq 5 \qquad \text{(resource } A\text{)}$$
$$4X_1 + X_2 \geq 10 \qquad \text{(limitation } B\text{)}$$

Multiplying both sides of the second constraint by -1

$$(-1) \times (4X_1 + X_2) \quad \text{and} \quad (-1) \times 10$$

we *reverse the direction* of the inequality, so that the two primal constraints have matching inequality orientations and are both in regular form.

$$U_A: \quad 3X_1 + 2X_2 \leq 5 \qquad \text{(resource } A\text{)}$$
$$U_B: \quad -4X_1 - X_2 \leq -10 \qquad \text{(limitation } B\text{)}$$

Theoretically, the dual variables U_A and U_B corresponding to the above formulation would be nonnegative. However, U_B has a -10 coefficient in the dual minimize C objective function. That signifies that increasing the right-hand side of the limitation B constraint by one unit will *reduce* primal LP profit by an amount equal to U_B. In order to provide a consistent interpretation, the software described in this book reverses the sign for the value of a dual variable (like U_B) that was derived from a reversed primal constraint. The output will list a negative quantity, such as $-U_B = -0.50$ or $-U_B = -2.25$, when the value is nonzero.

For a primal constraint that is an equality, such as

$$2X_1 + 3X_2 = 10 \qquad \text{(mixture)}$$

we first rewrite it in an equivalent form as two inequalities of opposite orientations,

$$2X_1 + 3X_2 \leq 10$$
$$2X_1 + 3X_2 \geq 10$$

and then multiply both sides of the last inequality by -1 to reverse the orientation to the regular form:

$$U_1: \quad 2X_1 + 3X_2 \leq 10 \qquad \text{(mixture 1)}$$
$$U_2: \quad -2X_1 - 3X_2 \leq -10 \qquad \text{(mixture 2)}$$

The dual linear program formulated from a primal modified in this manner would have *two* variables, although at most one of them can be nonzero in value. (The

software described in this book gives just one dual listing, either the value of U_1 or $-U_2$, depending on which happens to be nonzero.)

10-7   (OPTIONAL) THE DUAL FOR A COST-MINIMIZATION PRIMAL LINEAR PROGRAM

The dual linear program for cost minimization is the reversal of the primal—the objective is to maximize P and the constraint inequalities point in the opposite direction.

Again, we may explain the dual in terms of the underlying economics. Cost-minimization primals are epitomized by blending or mixing problems in which a processor seeks levels of various ingredients that will minimize total cost subject to a host of restriction constraints. The economist focuses on the restrictions rather than the ingredients.

$$U_{\text{restriction}} = \text{marginal value from decreasing the restriction limit}$$

The marginal value applies to *decreases* in the limit (right-hand side), the opposite focus of dual variables for primal *maximization* problems. The dual U from a cost-minimization primal expresses the *cost savings* a blender would experience when there is a one-unit *decrease* in the *restriction limit*. (The dual U from a profit-maximization primal expresses the *profit increase* from a one-unit *increase* in the *available resource*.)

The economist achieves overall optimization by maximizing the collective marginal values from all restrictions. When the primal is cost minimization, the dual objective takes the form

$$\text{Maximize } P = \sum_{\text{all restrictions}} (\text{restriction limit}) \times U_{\text{restriction}}$$

The limits (primal right-hand sides) serve as the coefficients, giving each restriction weight in accordance with the absolute size of its limit.

As with the primal maximization problem, there is a dual constraint corresponding to each primal variable or ingredient. Ingredient quantities are sought that will equate the marginal cost with the marginal return, the economist's condition for optimality. *Each ingredient* has a constraint of the following form:

$$\sum_{\text{all restrictionss}} (\text{exchange coefficient}) \times U_{\text{restriction}} \leq \text{unit cost} \qquad (\text{for each ingredient})$$

The right-hand side is the ingredient's marginal cost and the left-hand side is its marginal return, so the

$$\text{ingredient marginal return} \leq \text{ingredient marginal cost}$$

Notice that cost and return are on opposite sides from the maximize-P problem typical of production decisions.

As with the dual for a primal maximization problem, an ingredient will be used at some positive level only when there is equality. The case of $<$ occurs only when an ingredient is not used and has zero level. And, the case of $>$ is specifically disallowed; no ingredient should ever be used at a level at which its marginal return exceeds its marginal cost.

Determining Wild Birdseed Mixture

In Chapter 8, a wild birdseed-mixture problem was originally formulated. The following problem data apply for a batch to be blended from buckwheat and sunflower wheat:

NUTRITIONAL ITEM	INGREDIENT PROPORTIONAL CONTENT		LIMIT REQUIREMENT (LB)
	Buckwheat	Sunflower Wheat	
Fat	.04	.06	$\geq$ 480
Protein	.12	.10	$\geq$ 1,200
Roughage	.10	.15	$\leq$ 1,500
Cost per pound	$.18	$.10	

The primal will be formulated, and then from it the dual will be expressed. The primal problem is solved on the computer, which also provides the dual.

THE PROBLEM SOLUTION

Although these are not part of the primal LP, it will be helpful to list to the left of each constraint the symbols representing the dual variable for the respective restrictions.

Primal Let X_B and X_S = weight of buckwheat and sunflower wheat for the birdseed batch, respectively.

$$\text{Minimize} \quad C = .18X_B + .10X_S$$

Subject to

$$U_F: \quad .04X_B + .06X_S \geq 480 \quad \text{(fat)}$$
$$U_P: \quad .12X_B + .10X_S \geq 1,200 \quad \text{(protein)}$$
$$U_R: \quad -.10X_B - .15X_S \geq -1,500 \quad \text{(roughage)}$$

where

$$X_B, X_S \geq 0$$

The roughage constraint

$$.10X_B + .15X_S \leq 1,500$$

had to be adjusted by reversing all signs, giving it the regular format for the minimize C primal.

Dual The formulation of the dual begins with a definition of the dual variables. We use U_F, U_P, and U_R to represent the marginal values for the respective restrictions.

The objective of the dual will have an opposite orientation to that of the primal, and this dual will maximize P. The objective function is formed by multiplying each dual variable by the corresponding primal right-hand side value, and summing terms. We obtain

$$\text{Maximize} \quad P = 480U_F + 1,200U_P - 1,500U_R$$

The constraints are formed analogously, multiplying the exchange coefficients from each product column times the U column, and then summing terms. This provides the left-hand side of the ingredient constraint; the primal objective (cost) coefficient for that ingredient column is used as the right-hand side. For buckwheat, in the first primal column, we get

$$.04U_F + .12U_P - .10U_R \leq .18 \quad \text{(buckwheat)}$$

The sunflower wheat constraint is formed analogously. The complete formulated dual linear program follows.

Let U_F, U_P, and U_R = marginal value from decreasing the limit of fat, protein, and roughage, respectively.

$$\text{Maximize} \quad P = 480U_F + 1{,}200U_P - 1{,}500U_R$$

Subject to

$$.04U_F + .12U_P - .10U_R \leq .18 \quad \text{(buckwheat)}$$
$$.06U_F + .10U_P - .15U_R \leq .10 \quad \text{(sunflower)}$$

where $\quad U_F,\ U_P \text{ and } U_R \geq 0$

The dual variables represent the cost savings per unit relaxation of the respective primal restrictions. Figure 10-13 shows a portion of the computer printout obtained by solving the primal using *QuickQuant*.

The solution indicates that there would be no cost advantage to reducing the minimum fat requirement, but that lowering the minimum protein requirement by one pound would save $2.125 in the overall batch cost, and reducing the roughage minimum by one pound (say, from 1,500 to 1,499) would have negative cost savings of $.75. Reducing the roughage minimum would not be beneficial, but increasing it by a pound would yield $.75 cost savings.

SOLUTION TO LINEAR PROGRAM
```
------------------------------------------------------------
```
PROBLEM: Birdseed Mixture

Objective Value: C = 1425.00000

SOLUTION TO DUAL AND SENSITIVITY ANALYSIS
```
------------------------------------------------------------
```

CONSTR.			Value	RIGHTHAND SIDE Sensitivity Limits				
No.	Type	Auxiliary Variable	of DUAL Variable	Lower Limit	Original Value	Upper Limit		
1	>	S1 =	120.00	0.00	None	480.00	600.00	fat $\quad U_F = 0$
2	>	S2 =	0.00	2.125	1000.00	1200.00	1800.00	protein $\quad U_P = 2.125$
3	<	S3 =	0.00	−.75	1200.00	1500.00	1800.00	roughage $\quad U_R = -.75$

OBJECTIVE COEFFICIENT Sensitivity
```
------------------------------------------------------------
```

Main Variable	Optimal Value	DUAL Slack/Surplus	Lower Limit	Original Value	Upper Limit	
XB	3750.00	0.00	0.12	0.18	None	$U_B = 0$
XS	7500.00	0.00	None	0.10	.15	$U_S = 0$

FIGURE 10-13 Portions of the *QuickQuant* report giving primal and dual solutions to the wild birdseed-mixture problem, with annotations

PROBLEMS

10-1 Formulate the dual for the following primal linear program and then solve it graphically:

Maximize $P = 12X_1 + 16X_2$

Subject to

(resource A)	$4X_1 + 4X_2 \leq 16$
(resource B)	$6X_1 + 4X_2 \leq 24$
where	$X_1, X_2 \geq 0$

10-2 Formulate the dual for the following linear program and then solve it graphically:

Maximize $P = 9X_1 + 6X_2$

Subject to

(wood)	$50X_1 + 20X_2 \leq 200$
(labor)	$10X_1 + 30X_2 \leq 240$
where	$X_1, X_2 \geq 0$

10-3 Formulate the dual for the following linear program and then solve it graphically:

Maximize $P = 5X_1 + 1X_2$

Subject to

(demand)	$X_1 + 3X_2 \geq 10$
(material)	$5X_1 + 2X_2 \leq 20$
where	$X_1, X_2 \geq 0$

10-4 Formulate the dual for the following linear program and then solve it graphically:

Maximize $P = 2X_1 + 3X_2$

Subject to

(mixture)	$12X_1 + 10X_2 = 90$
(labor)	$3X_1 + 6X_2 \leq 43$
where	$X_1, X_2 \geq 0$

10-5 Formulate the dual for the following linear program and then solve it graphically:

Minimize $C = 4X_1 + 3X_2$

Subject to

(ingredient)	$X_1 + 2X_2 \geq 1$
(limitation)	$3X_1 + 1X_2 \leq 2$
where	$X_1, X_2 \geq 0$

10-6 Formulate the dual for the following linear program. Do *not* attempt to solve it.

Maximize $P = 5X_1 + 8X_2$

Subject to

(mixture)	$X_1 - 2X_2 \geq 0$
(labor)	$8X_1 + 7X_2 \leq 20$
(balance)	$X_1 + X_2 = 20$
where	$X_1, X_2 \geq 0$

10-7 Formulate the dual for the following linear program and then solve it graphically:

Minimize $C = 12X_1 + 4X_2$

Subject to

(mixture)	$7X_1 + 2X_2 = 20$
(demand)	$7X_1 + 6X_2 \geq 25$
where	$X_1, X_2 \geq 0$

10-8 Formulate the dual for the following linear program. Do *not* attempt to solve it.

Minimize $C = 5X_1 + 4X_2$

Subject to

(limitation)	$X_1 - 2X_2 \leq 0$
(demand)	$8X_1 + 7X_2 \leq 20$
(balance)	$2X_1 + 2X_2 = 4$
(mixture)	$X_1 - X_2 \geq 0$
where	$X_1, X_2 \geq 0$

10-9 Formulate the dual for the following linear program. Do *not* attempt to solve it.

Maximize P
$$= 100X_1 + 250X_2 + 150X_3$$

Subject to

(limitation)	$10X_1 + 20X_2 + 15X_3 \leq 1{,}000$
(mixture)	$50X_1 + 30X_2 + 14X_3 = 875$
(restriction)	$X_1 + X_2 + X_3 \geq 1$
where	$X_1, X_2, X_3 \geq 0$

10-10 Formulate the dual for the following linear program. Do *not* attempt to solve it.

Minimize $C = .55X_1 + .75X_2 + .45X_3$

Subject to

(quantity)	$X_1 + X_2 + X_3 \leq 100$
(mixture)	$4X_1 + 2X_2 + X_3 = 10$
(restriction)	$-X_1 + X_2 - X_3 \geq 20$
where	$X_1, X_2, X_3 \geq 0$

10-11 The Redwood Furniture problem in the chapter is expanded for August to include the number of bookcases (X_B) and desks (X_D) to be made. Available wood and labor have increased, and new prices result in changed profits. Now there must be exactly 4 chairs for each table, and there must be at least 5 bookcases made. The following linear program applies:

Maximize

$$P = 8X_T + 8X_C + 8X_B + 12X_D$$

Subject to

(wood)	$30X_T + 20X_C + 25X_B + 40X_D \leq 800$
(labor)	$5X_T + 10X_C + 7X_B + 15X_D \leq 250$
(mix.)	$4X_T - X_C = 0$
(quan.)	$X_B \geq 5$
where	$X_T, X_C, X_B, X_D \geq 0$

Formulate the dual.

10-12 The Redwood Furniture problem is expanded for September to include the number of bookcases (X_B) and desks (X_D) to be made. Available wood and labor have increased, and new prices result in changed profits. Now there may be any number of chairs, subject to resource availability, but there must be at least four bookcases and the number of desks must be equal to that of bookcases. The following linear program applies:

Maximize

$$P = 9X_T + 7X_C + 9X_B + 11X_D$$

Subject to

(wood)	$30X_T + 20X_C + 25X_B + 40X_D \leq 900$
(labor)	$5X_T + 10X_C + 7X_B + 15X_D \leq 300$
(quan.)	$X_B \geq 4$
(mix.)	$X_B - X_D = 0$
where	$X_T, X_C, X_B, X_D \geq 0$

Formulate the dual.

10-13 The birdseed mix problem originally described in Chapter 8 (page 276) is modified for January to include two new seed quantities (pounds): rye (X_R) and cracked corn (X_C). In addition to the original constraints, there is now a requirement that at least 10% of the total batch weight be sunflower seeds and that no more than 20% of the final mixture weight can be cracked corn:

Minimize

$$C = .18X_B + .10X_S + .12X_R + .09X_C$$

Subject to

(fat)	$.04X_B + .06X_S + .05X_R + .10X_C \geq 480$
(protein)	$.12X_B + .10X_S + .12X_R + .10X_C \geq 1{,}200$
(roughage)	$.10X_B + .15X_S + .10X_R + .12X_C \leq 1{,}500$
(wt. sunflower)	$.10X_B + .90X_S - .10X_R - .10X_C \geq 0$
(wt. corn)	$.20X_B - .20X_S - .20X_R + .80X_C \leq 0$
where	$X_B, X_S, X_R, X_C \geq 0$

Formulate the dual.

10-14 The birdseed mix problem is modified for February to include one new seed quantity (pounds): poppy (X_P). In addition to the original constraints, there is now a requirement that the final mix contain at least 500 pounds of poppy seeds and that the weight of the buckwheat not exceed that of the sunflower. The following linear program applies:

Minimize

$$C = .18X_B + .10X_S + .11X_P$$

Subject to

(fat)	$.04X_B + .06X_S + .05X_P \geq 480$
(protein)	$.12X_B + .10X_S + .10X_P \geq 1{,}200$
(roughage)	$.10X_B + .15X_S + .07X_P \leq 1{,}500$
(quan. poppy)	$X_P \geq 500$
(mixture)	$X_B - X_S \leq 0$
where	$X_B, X_S, X_P \geq 0$

Formulate the dual.

10-15 Reconsider Ace Widgets' problem of deciding how many regular and deluxe models to produce. The regular model requires 5 hours of finishing labor and 1 frame. The deluxe version requires 8 hours and 1 frame. Only 12 frames and 80 hours of labor are available. The per-unit profits are $10 for the regular model and $15 for the deluxe version.
  (a) Formulate the primal linear program and solve it graphically.
  (b) Formulate the dual linear program. State in words the meaning of your dual variables.
  (c) Solve the dual graphically.

10-16 Now suppose that Ace Widgets in Problem 10-15 makes a third product—the super widget—at a per-unit profit of $25. Each super widget requires 10 hours of labor and 1 frame.

(a) Formulate Ace's new primal linear program.
(b) Formulate the dual linear program and solve it graphically.
(c) Suppose that Ace can sell a fourth model—the cheap widget—at a per-unit profit of $6. This model requires 2 hours of labor and 1 frame. Should any cheap models be made?

10-17 The Piney Woods Furniture Company makes tables (T), chairs (C), and bookcases (B). The following linear program applies:

Maximize
$$P = 20X_T + 15X_C + 15X_B$$
Subject to
(wood) $\quad 10X_T + 3X_C + 10X_B \le 100$
(labor) $\quad 5X_T + 5X_C + 5X_B \le 60$
where $\quad X_T, X_C, X_B \ge 0$

The dual linear program is

Minimize
$$C = 100U_W + 60U_L$$
Subject to
(table) $\quad 10U_W + 5U_L \ge 20$
(chair) $\quad 3U_W + 5U_L \ge 15$
(bookcase) $\quad 10U_W + 5U_L \ge 15$
where $\quad U_W, U_L \ge 0$

and the solution to the dual is

$$U_W = \frac{5}{7} \quad U_L = \frac{18}{7} \quad C = \frac{1580}{7} \text{ dollars}$$

(a) What is the maximum premium that Piney Woods would pay for an additional unit of wood? For an additional unit of labor?
(b) Letting U_T, U_C, and U_B represent the dual surplus variables for the respective constraints, determine the optimal values of these variables.
(c) Suppose that Piney Woods can sell desks at a per-unit profit of $50 each and that each desk requires 30 board feet of wood and 10 hours of labor. Should any desks be made?

10-18 Pumpkin-Goblins must decide how many gallons of pumpkin (X_P) and licorice (X_L) ice cream to make for sale during Halloween week. All ingredients are in plentiful supply, except for artificial carbon black, vanilla extract, and orange food coloring. The following linear program applies:

Maximize
$$P = 2.00X_P + 1.50X_L$$
Subject to
(carbon) $\quad .50X_L \le 1,000$
(vanilla) $\quad .02X_P + .01X_L \le 25$
(orange) $\quad .10X_P \le 50$
where $\quad X_P, X_L \ge 0$

Formulate the dual linear program.

10-19 A brewery president wants to develop a monthly production schedule that will maximize gross profits. He sells three products: light beer, dark beer, and malt liquor. The respective production quantities (in gallons) are denoted by X_L, X_D, and X_M. The president is faced with three constraints pertaining to the respective usages and availabilities of hops-handling capacity (bushels), fermentation space (cubic feet), and bottling time (hours). A computer run provides the solution.

$$X_L = 100,000 \quad X_D = 20,000 \quad X_M = 10,000$$
$$P = 155,000$$

and the optimal levels for the dual variables

$$U_H = \$.10 \quad U_F = \$3 \quad U_B = \$.50$$

for the respective resources.
The president is contemplating a capital expansion. The following incremental monthly costs of three alternatives are to be added to capacities.

1 bushel of hops-handling capacity, $.20
1 cubic foot of fermentation space, $1.00
1 hour of bottling time, $.10

Assuming that you can use the information in the final simplex tableau, what alternative investment would be most profitable if the capital expansion is very limited? Explain.

10-20 Refer to the bond portfolio selection problem in Section 9-5. Formulate the dual linear program and define all variables.

10-21 Refer to the Real Reels advertising decision problem in Section 9-7. Formulate the dual linear program and define all variables.

10-22 Refer to Yosemite Ann's final cost-minimization linear program for producing trail mix, described in Section 9-10. Formulate the dual linear program and define all variables.

10-23 Refer to Sammy Love's candied apple decision in Problem 9-41 (page 354).

(a) Formulate Sammy's linear program and separately identify any slack variables required to solve this problem using the simplex method.

(b) Formulate the dual linear program and separately identify any surplus variables required to solve this problem using the simplex method.

(c) Solve the dual *graphically*. What are the optimal values of the dual main variables? Of the dual surplus variables?

(d) What is the maximum premium that Sammy would pay for extra cups of sugar? For extra ounces of gelatin?

(e) Suppose that Sammy is considering selling a caramel apple with chopped nuts because he will make a profit of $.30 on each one. Should Sammy sell this new candied apple if two ounces of sugar and one ounce of gelatin are required for each one?

10-24 The Redwood Furniture Company opened a new plant in Australia to manufacture the same items identified in Table 10-2 (page 382). Changes were made to the costs and revenues, as well as changes in the labor and machine constraints. The machine time constraint was divided between machine A and machine B and the labor coefficients have changed. Complete items (a) through (f) with the changes using the linear program given below. The *QuickQuant* report (right) was obtained after solving the primal:

SOLUTION TO LINEAR PROGRAM

PROBLEM: Australian Redwood

ORIGINAL PROBLEM DATA

Objective Value: P = 1105.0000

SOLUTION TO DUAL AND SENSITIVITY ANALYSIS

RIGHTHAND SIDE Sensitivity Anal.

CONSTR. No.	Type	Auxiliary Variable		Value of DUAL Variable	Lower Limit	Original Value	Upper Limit	
1	<	S1	=	0.00	.60	2510.00	2700.00	3020.00	wood
2	<	S2	=	202.65	0.00	797.35	1000.00	None	labor
3	<	S3	=	37.65	0.00	162.35	200.00	None	mach. t. A
4	>	S4	=	178.82	0.00	121.18	300.00	None	mach. t. B
5	>	S5	=	0.00	-7.00	30.61	50.00	57.60	qty., tab.
6	>	S6	=	11.18	0.00	None	30.00	41.18	qty., ch.
7	=	a7	=	0.00	-5.50	10.61	30.00	37.60	qty., bk.
8	=	a8	=	0.00	3.00	-38.00	0.00	50.00	mix, tab.
9	=	a9	=	0.00	-0.00	-95.00	0.00	46.67	mix, ch.
10	<	S10	=	0.00	3.50	-30.00	0.00	30.00	mix, bk.

OBJECTIVE COEFFICIENT Sensitivity

Main Variable	Optimal Value	DUAL Slack/Surplus	Lower Limit	Original Value	Upper Limit
XTS	25.00	0.00	None	8.00	22.00
XTR	25.00	0.00	4.00	8.00	22.00
XTL	0.00	4.00	None	10.00	14.00
XCS	32.94	0.00	4.33	9.00	None
XCA	8.24	0.00	-3.70	15.00	None
XBS	15.00	0.00	None	10.00	21.00
XBT	15.00	0.00	None	9.00	20.00

(a) Formulate the dual.

(b) Identify the optimal levels for each dual variable defined in (a).

(c) What is the effect on profit from increasing by one unit available (1) wood, (2) labor, (3) machine A time, (4) machine B time?

$$\text{Maximize} \quad P = 8X_{TS} + 8X_{TR} + 10X_{TL} + 9X_{CS} + 15X_{CA} + 10X_{BS} + 9X_{BT}$$

Subject to

$20X_{TS} +$	$30X_{TR} +$	$40X_{TL} +$	$15X_{CS} +$	$25X_{CA} +$	$20X_{BS} +$	$30X_{BT} \leq 2{,}700$	(wood)
$4X_{TS} +$	$5X_{TR} +$	$6X_{TL} +$	$5X_{CS} +$	$12X_{CA} +$	$6X_{BS} +$	$5X_{BT} \leq 1{,}000$	(labor)
$1X_{TS} +$	$1X_{TR} +$	$1X_{TL} +$	$2X_{CS} +$	$2X_{CA} +$	$1X_{BS} +$	$1X_{BT} \leq 200$	(machine A time)
$1X_{TS} +$	$1X_{TR} +$	$1X_{TL} +$	$1X_{CS} +$	$1X_{CA} +$	$1X_{BS} +$	$1X_{BT} \leq 300$	(machine B time)
$1X_{TS} +$	$1X_{TR} +$	$1X_{TL} +$	$0X_{CS} +$	$0X_{CA} +$	$0X_{BS} +$	$0X_{BT} \geq 50$	(quantity tables)
$0X_{TS} +$	$0X_{TR} +$	$0X_{TL} +$	$1X_{CS} +$	$1X_{CA} +$	$0X_{BS} +$	$0X_{BT} \geq 30$	(quantity chairs)
$0X_{TS} +$	$0X_{TR} +$	$0X_{TL} +$	$0X_{CS} +$	$0X_{CA} +$	$1X_{BS} +$	$1X_{BT} \geq 30$	(quantity bookcases)
$1X_{TS} -$	$1X_{TR} -$	$1X_{TL} +$	$0X_{CS} +$	$0X_{CA} +$	$0X_{BS} +$	$0X_{BT} = 0$	(mix tables)
$0X_{TS} +$	$0X_{TR} +$	$0X_{TL} +$	$1X_{CS} -$	$4X_{CA} +$	$0X_{BS} +$	$0X_{BT} = 0$	(mix chairs)
$0X_{TS} +$	$0X_{TR} +$	$0X_{TL} +$	$0X_{CS} +$	$0X_{CA} +$	$1X_{BS} -$	$1X_{BT} = 0$	(mix bookcases)

where   all variables $\geq$ 0

(d) What is the effect on profit from increasing by one unit the group minimum quantities for (1) tables, (2) chairs, (3) bookcases? The group minimum quantities are referred to in the *QuickQuant* printout. There, qty., tab., qty., ch., and qty., bk. denote quantity tables, quantity chairs, and quantity bookcases.

(e) What is the effect on profit from increasing by one unit the allowable mixture difference for (1) tables, (2) chairs, (3) bookcases? (See the *QuickQuant* printout annotations.)

(f) Consider the following new products, listed with their profits and unit resource requirements:

Product	Unit Profit	Required Wood (board feet)	Required Labor (hours)	Required Machine Time A (hours)	Required Machine Time B (hours)
Desk	$10	30	5	2	3
Bench	15	20	3	1	0
Swing	25	70	10	3	4

Indicate for each whether Redwood would find it profitable to add it to the current period production.

10-25 Re-solve Problem 10-24 (b)–(f) using the Excel Sensitivity Report shown below.

Adjustable Cells

Cell	Name	Final Value	Reduced Cost	Objective Coefficient	Allowable Increase	Allowable Decrease
$B$20	XTS	25.00	0.00	8.00	14.00	1E+30
$C$20	XTS	25.00	0.00	8.00	14.00	4.00
$D$20	XTL	0.00	-4.00	10.00	4.00	1E+30
$E$20	XCS	32.94	0.00	9.00	1E+30	4.68
$F$20	XCA	8.24	0.00	15.00	1E+30	18.70
$G$20	XBS	15.00	0.00	10.00	11.00	1E+30
$H$20	XBT	15.00	0.00	9.00	11.00	1E+30

Constraints

Cell	Name	Final Value	Shadow Price	Constraint R.H. Side	Allowable Increase	Allowable Decrease
$L$7	1	2700.00	0.60	2700.00	320.00	190.00
$L$8	2	653.53	0.00	1000.00	1E+30	346.47
$L$9	3	162.35	0.00	200.00	1E+30	37.65
$L$10	4	121.18	0.00	300.00	1E+30	178.82
$L$11	5	50.00	-7.00	50.00	7.60	19.39
$L$12	6	41.18	0.00	30.00	11.18	1E+30
$L$13	7	30.00	-5.50	30.00	7.60	19.39
$L$14	8	0.00	3.00	0.00	50.00	38.00
$L$15	9	0.00	0.00	0.00	46.67	95.00
$L$16	10	0.00	3.50	0.00	30.00	30.00

Computer Problems

10-26 Rott Irony makes three fancy door hinges: Baltic, chic, and Gothic. All of the materials used in making these hinges are plentiful, except that only 100 square feet of brass plate are on hand and a maximum of 200 hours of hand-crafting labor can be spared. A set of heavy Baltic hinges requires 2 square feet of brass plate; a set of chic or Gothic hinges requires 1 square foot. Handcrafting takes 1 hour for a set of Baltic hinges, 3 hours for a set of chics, and $1\frac{1}{4}$ hours for a set of Gothics. Rott can sell the entire production run at a profit of $10 for a set of Baltic or Gothics and $15 for a set of chics.

(a) Formulate Rott's linear program and separately identify any slack variables required to solve this problem using the simplex method.

(b) Formulate the dual linear program and separately identify any surplus variables required to solve this problem using the simplex method.

(c) Solve the dual graphically. What are the optimal values of the dual main variables? Of the dual surplus variables?

(d) What is the maximum premium that Rott would pay for each extra square foot of brass plate? For each extra hour of handcrafting?

(e) Solve the primal linear program. How many sets of each type of hinge should Rott make? What will Rott's maximum profit be?

(f) Suppose that Rott Irony is considering a new model door hinge called Antique. It yields a profit of $20 per hinge and requires 1 hour of labor and 2 square feet of plate. Should the new Antique model be produced? If so, how many?

10-27 Consider Willy B. Rich's investment decision originally described in Problem 9-9 (page 350).

(a) Formulate Willy's decision problem as a linear program.

(b) Formulate the dual linear program.
(c) Using a computer, solve the primal problem and determine the solution to the dual from the same computer run.

10-28 Consider the Blitz Beer advertising decision originally described in Problem 9-16 (page 351).
(a) Formulate the decision problem as a linear program.
(b) Formulate the dual linear program.
(c) Using a computer, solve the primal problem and determine the solution to the dual from the same computer run.

10-29 Consider the All-American Meat Processors' decision for mixing sausage batches, originally described in Problem 9-12 (page 350).
(a) Formulate the decision problem as a cost-minimization linear program.
(b) Formulate the dual linear program.
(c) Using a computer, solve the primal problem and determine the solution to the dual from the same computer run.

10-30 Consider Le Petite Fromagerie's decision in Problem 9-46 (page 355).
(a) Formulate the dual linear program.
(b) Determine the solution to the dual.
(c) For which resources would it be profitable to expand the available quantities?

10-31 Consider the Hoopla Hoops advertising decision in Problem 9-45 (page 355).
(a) Formulate the dual linear program.
(b) Determine the solution to the dual.
(c) How much will profit increase for each additional dollar added to the total funds available for advertising?
(d) How much will profit increase for each additional dollar allowed beyond $40,000 for ads in teen media?

10-32 Consider the Blitz Beer advertising decision in Problem 10-28 and your answers to that exercise.
(a) Determine the sensitivity limits within which the present basic mix remains optimal for the following limitations:
(1) available funds
(2) available spots on KBAT
(3) available spots on KPOW

(b) Determine the sensitivity limits within which the present solution remains optimal for the sales increase per spot on
(1) KBAT   (3) WROB
(2) WJOK   (4) KPOW
(c) Find the dual values for the quantities represented by each constraint and the dual surplus values for every station spot.
(d) What one change to the problem will bring about the greatest increase in total sales without disturbing the basic variable mix?

10-33 Refer to Problem 10-32 and your answers to that exercise. Perform a post-optimality analysis to determine how the decision maker might improve the maximum sales increase. In doing this, you may not increase expenditures beyond the original budget. Discuss all assumptions that must be made to accomplish any problem changes.

10-34 Consider the sausage ingredient decision in Problem 9-7 (page 349).
(a) Formulate the linear program and find the optimal solution.
(b) Determine the sensitivity limits within which the present basic mix remains optimal for the following limitations:
(1) allowable chicken
(2) minimum beef
(3) minimum protein
(4) maximum fat
(c) Determine the sensitivity limits within which the present solution remains optimal for the cost of the following:
(1) hog bellies   (3) beef
(2) tripe   (4) chicken
(d) Find the dual values for the quantities represented by each constraint and the dual slack values for every ingredient.
(e) What one change to the problem will bring about the greatest decrease in total cost without disturbing the basic variable mix?

10-35 Refer to Problem 10-34 and your answers to that exercise. Perform a post-optimality analysis to determine how the decision maker might improve the minimum cost. In doing this you may not reduce the content weight of the sausage below one pound. Discuss all assumptions that must be made to accomplish any problem changes.

10-36 Consider Le Petite Fromagerie's decision in Problem 9-46 (page 355).
  (a) Find the optimal solution.
  (b) Determine the sensitivity limits within which the present basic mix remains optimal for the following resources:
    (1) milk   (3) molds
    (2) storage   (4) salt
  (c) Determine the sensitivity limits within which the present solution remains optimal for the unit profit of each type of cheese.
  (d) Find the dual values for the quantities represented by each constraint and the dual surplus values for each cheese type.
  (e) What one change to the problem will bring about the greatest increase in total profit without disturbing the basic variable mix?

10-37 Refer to Problem 10-36 and your answers to that exercise. Perform a post-optimality analysis to determine how the decision maker might improve the maximum profit. Discuss all assumptions that must be made to accomplish any problem changes.

10-38 Consider the Hoopla Hoops advertising decision in Problem 9-45 (page 355).

  (a) Find the optimal solution.
  (b) Determine the sensitivity limits within which the present basic mix remains optimal for the following limitations:
    (1) available funds
    (2) maximum teen placement expenditures
  (c) Determine the sensitivity limits within which the present solution remains optimal for the circulation of the following:
    (1) Tiger Club   (3) Spider Glider
    (2) Rocky   (4) Toy Fans
  (d) Find the dual values for the quantities represented by each constraint and the dual surplus values for every magazine.
  (e) What one change to the problem will bring about the greatest increase in total exposure without violating the sensitivity limits?

10-39 Refer to Problem 10-38 and your answers to that exercise. Perform a post-optimality analysis to determine how the decision maker might improve the maximum exposure. In doing this you may not spend more than the original budgeted amount. Discuss all assumptions that must be made to accomplish any problem changes.

CASE   10-1   *La República Oriental de Amazonia*

The Inter-American Development Bank (IDB) is an international financial institution established in 1959 to help accelerate economic and social development in Latin America and the Caribbean. In its 28 years of operations, the bank has helped to provide, secure, and organize financing for projects which represent a total investment of more than $115 billion.[1]

According to Dr. Miguel Urrutia, manager of IDB's Economic and Social Development Department, the underlying structural problem of many Latin American economies is the debt crisis, which is in many ways a fiscal crisis due to government spending and taxation being out of sync with the capacities and needs of the economy.[2]

As a part of IDB's long-term plan to help Latin American countries restructure their spending, Dr. Urrutia has sent one of his senior advisors, Professor Rafael Betancourt, to assist the Minister of Finance and Planning, Dr. José Luis Cagigal Garcia, of La República Oriental de Amazonia, a small country of 10 million inhabitants located on the eastern bank of the Amazon River. Amazonia, as the country is usually called, has recently returned to a democratic system of government after 20 years of military dictatorships.

Professor Betancourt's assignment is to help the Ministry of Finance and Planning develop a strategic plan to maximize the output of Amazonia (as measured by the Producto Interno Bruto [PIB] which, roughly, is equivalent to the GDP in the United States) while at the same time efficiently utilizing the country's resources.

For rough planning purposes, the economy of Amazonia has been broken down into four principal sectors: energy, manufacturing, agriculture, and services. Each of these has been further subdivided into

[1] The Inter-American Development Bank, 1300 New York Avenue, N.W., Washington, DC 20577.

[2] *The Inter-American Development Bank Bulletin,* February 1989, p. 8.

two subsectors: energy into "petroleum" and "other energy" (for example, mining and power generation); manufacturing into "automobiles" and "other manufacturing"; agriculture into "coffee" and "other agricultural products" (mainly cacao and bananas); and services into "tourism" and "other services" (such as finance and real estate).

Dr. Cagigal indicates that the two critical limiting factors in the growth of the economy are labor and money. The active work force is only 40% of the population (and 20% of these individuals are unemployed). Current social policy is to grant a universal 5-week vacation (25 working days) to all workers regardless of length of service, and the government also has legally specified 15 holidays during the year. The normal workweek is 5 days, 8 hours per day. With respect to financial resources, Dr. Cagigal estimates that 11 trillion Nuevos Pesos (NP for short) will be available to the country from all sources, including foreign borrowing. The current exchange is NP 1,000 to U.S. $1.

Economists in the Ministry of Finance and Planning have developed economic data that show the relationship between the sectors of the economy. This information is shown in Table 1. It shows the quantity of inputs required to produce one unit of output for each of the economic sectors, and hence is called an input–output table. For example, the first row (petroleum sector) shows that .04 unit of petroleum is needed to produce 1 unit of output in the petroleum

TABLE 1   Input–Output Coefficients for the República Oriental de Amazonia

	Energy		Manufacturing	
Economic Sector	**Petroleum**	**Other Energy**	**Automobiles**	**Other Manufacturing**
Energy				
Petroleum	.04	.16	.26	.18
Other energy	.10	.01	.32	.02
Manufacturing				
Automobiles	.40	.23	.15	.21
Other manufacturing	.10	.17	.10	.11
Agriculture				
Coffee	.01	.08	.03	.01
Other agriculture	.15	.04	.01	.15
Services				
Tourism	—	.05	—	.15
Other services	.06	—	.09	.21

	Agriculture		Services	
Economic Sector	**Coffee**	**Other Agriculture**	**Tourism**	**Services**
Energy				
Petroleum	.21	.15	.13	.39
Other energy	.18	.18	.09	.16
Manufacturing				
Automobiles	.17	.21	.32	.05
Other manufacturing	.20	.11	.05	.01
Agriculture				
Coffee	.01	.17	.21	—
Other agriculture	.05	.05	—	—
Services				
Tourism	.05	.10	.05	.30
Other services	.10	—	.10	—

sector, .26 unit of petroleum is needed to produce one unit of output in the automobile sector, and .21 unit of petroleum is needed to produce one unit in the coffee sector. Viewed in another way, in order to produce NP 1 worth of petroleum, the first column indicates that NP .04 of petroleum input is needed, NP .10 of other energy products is needed, NP .40 worth of output from the automobile sector is needed, and NP .10 worth of output from other manufacturing sectors is needed. Because of the current capacity in place in each sector of the economy and due to pressures from the Ministry of Labor to keep unemployment to a minimum, the final demand from each sector must be no less than 1,000 units.

Engineers in the Ministry of Industry have done technical studies of all the sectors and provided the information in Table 2. It shows the quantity of labor (in worker-hours) and financial resources (in Nuevos Pesos) required to produce one unit of output in each sector of the economy.

Finally, Dr. Cagigal requests that the Ministry of Commerce provide the final demand of each economic sector, taking into account competition. This results in it being known that each unit of final demand in the petroleum sector is worth NP 16,000,000 and that from the other energy sector, NP 10,000,000. Likewise, it is known that the values of each unit of demand from the other sectors are NP 20,524,000, automobile; NP 5,000,000, other manufacturing; NP 17,000,000, coffee; NP 10,000,000, other agricultural products; NP 18,150,000, tourism; and NP 4,000,000, other services.

TABLE 2 Labor and Funds Required to Produce One Unit of Output

Economic Sector	Labor (Worker-Hours)	Funds (Nuevos Pesos)
Energy		
Petroleum	3,000	1,000,000
Other energy	1,500	3,000,000
Manufacturing		
Automobiles	20,000	49,000,000
Other manufacturing	3,750	10,000,000
Agriculture		
Coffee	15,000	1,500,000
Other agriculture	4,500	2,500,000
Service		
Tourism	2,250	12,000,000
Other services	6,000	11,000,000

QUESTIONS

1. Formulate a linear program of this situation that will help the República Oriental de Amazonia decide how to most efficiently allocate its resources to maximize its PIB for the next year.

2. Solve the linear program formulated in Question 1.

3. Suppose that Professor Betancourt learns that FUTA (Frente Unido de Trabajadores de Amazonia — Amazonian Worker's United Front), is planning a 1-day nationwide work stoppage. How would this affect the plan developed in Question 1? Suppose the 1-day work stoppage degenerates into a protracted 2-week strike because of alleged police brutality. Would this have a significant effect on the country's economic plan?

4. Suppose Dr. Urrutia is seeking an extra billion dollar loan to Amazonia. What kind of effect would this have on the country? Would the effect critically depend on the interest rate and terms of the loan? Why or why not?

5. Suppose that Dr. Cagigal, the Minister of Industry, has just returned from a visit to Japan and brings with him an offer to modernize the petroleum industry with special credits to Amazonia. It is estimated that this would increase its efficiency by 100% (that is, all of the input coefficients to the petroleum industry in Table 1, column 1, and also the numbers in Table 2, row 1, would be cut in half) by providing both the latest technology and special training for all the workers in the industry. Would you accept the Japanese offer? Why or why not?

6. Suppose an earthquake destroys one of the principal pipelines that carries oil from refineries in the interior of the Amazonian jungle to the populated areas of the country so that oil production is cut in half. How does this affect the economy of Amazonia?

7. If the price of oil decreases by 30% because of the discovery of a giant oil field in Africa, how would this affect Amazonia's plan? Suppose coffee prices drop by 10% because of a worldwide surplus. How would this affect the country's plan?

8. Increased tourism is causing a difference of opinion among some of the ministers. The Minister of Tourism explains that this is a happy event because of tourist dollars contributing to development of the country. Dr. Cagigal believes the negative impact of

tourism will absorb investments more beneficial elsewhere. Analyze these two situations under the supposition that tourist demand triples.

9. Suppose that the National Congress is considering implementing a free-market economic system in Amazonia. This would eliminate the requirements that the central government mandate a minimum final demand of 1,000 units for each sector of the economy so that each firm, and hence each sector, would be free to produce whatever the market could support. What are the ramifications of this elimination of the minimum production quantities?

CASE 10-2 *Operation Desert Shield* [1] /

Many countries throughout the world have treaties and agreements with other nations. Particularly since World War II, as one of the world's two superpowers, the United States has made many mutual defense pacts and other arrangements that would commit U.S. military forces in certain situations.

One mission of the Department of Defense (DOD) is to ensure that such treaties, pacts, and other agreements can be met by existing U.S. military forces, anywhere on the globe. That might require calling up and deploying additional forces from the reserves or National Guard. In both cases, means must be provided to move the forces quickly, utilizing fleets of transport aircraft and/or fleets of fast-deployment logistic ships. A second way to meet U.S. commitments is with overseas bases, including prepositioning forces or stockpiling material.

In the early 1960s, DOD's Office of the Assistant Secretary of Defense (Systems Analysis) studied this problem of strategic mobility by performing cost-effectiveness evaluations. Such planning for rapid deployment of large military forces successfully met a major test when Iraq invaded Kuwait in 1991. Within two months, the Military Airlift Command (MAC) moved 155 kilotons of equipment and 164,000 personnel 7,500 miles to the Middle East. Three times these amounts were sent afterward.

For simplicity, we now suppose that Brigadier General W. D. Walker, Chief of the Crisis Action Team (CAT) of the U.S. Central Command (CENT-

COM) has broken down the world into three theaters of operation: the Middle East, the Far East, and Africa. Various obligations with countries in these areas might require the United States to send military assistance. The current plan is to maintain a limited quantity of quick-response forces in the continental United States (CONUS) that would be able to go to any theater very rapidly by air, using transport aircraft such as the C-141 and/or C-5A.

Suppose that 200 aircraft are available to MAC at annual operating costs of $15 million each. Protracted problems in the theaters would require the continual deployment and resupply of larger quantities of troops than could be handled by air. Thus, another alternative is to stock forward bases prepositioned closer to the various theaters of operations with large tonnages of equipment. If a contingency arose, fast-deployment logistic ships at these forward bases would be able to deploy the supplies much more quickly than ships from CONUS and in larger quantities than using just air transports. The United States has maintained such forward bases in Guam, Hawaii, Italy, Okinawa, the Philippines, and Turkey, in addition to various Western European countries.

For simplicity, we suppose that there is one forward base in the Indian Ocean (Diego Garcia) and the second is a collection of several locations in Western Europe. In addition, we assume that the U.S. Navy is trying to decide how many ships will be needed to meet U.S. commitments.

CAT has estimated the requirements needed to meet the contingencies in the various theaters, depending on different scenarios. Although thousands of items must be supplied for any emergency, for planning purposes all of them are summarized by the term "force unit," which consists of everything needed (the troops, armor, artillery, aircraft, supplies).

The estimated force unit requirements for the first three weeks of deployment are given in Table 1.

[1] Based on "Crisis Analysis: Operation Desert Shield" by Col. Robert Roehrkasse and Lt. Col. George C. Hughes, *OR Today*, December 1990, and "Programming the Procurement of Airlift and Sealift Forces: A Linear Programming Model for the Analysis of the Least-Cost Mix of Strategic Deployment Systems" by George R. Fitzpatrick, Jerome Bracken, Mary J. O'Brien, Lee G. Wentling, and Justin C. Whilton, *Naval Research Logistics Quarterly,* vol. 14, no. 2 (June 1967).

| TABLE 1 | Cumulative Force Unit Deployments Required (Kilotons) | | |

Week	Theater of Operations		
	Middle East	**Far East**	**Africa**
1	20	40	60
2	60	100	140
3	100	200	300

The limiting factor in delivering a force unit to the theaters is its weight, one kiloton. Thus from Table 1, a contingency in the Middle East would require 20 force units during the first week, 60 by the second week, and 100 by the third week. That is, sufficient transportation capacity, utilizing both aircraft and ships, must be available to transport 20 kilotons to the Middle East during the first week, an additional 40 during the second week (for a cumulative total of 60), and an additional 40 during the third week (for a cumulative total of 100).

The only means of reaching the three theaters during the first week is by aircraft from CONUS. Fast-deployment ships from the forward bases would arrive a week later. Consequently, the earliest force units via ship transportation would begin to arrive in the second week. The average annual cost, including initial investment and annual operation and maintenance, is $10 million per force unit for ships at Diego Garcia and $11 million per force unit for ships in Europe. Each ship has the capacity to carry 1 kiloton.

The number of air transports needed to deliver one force unit per week varies. Table 2 gives the estimated productivity factors for aircraft flying to the three theaters from CONUS.

Although the number of available aircraft is 200, this analysis can determine if more or less will be needed. In addition, the size of the prepositioned forces and the number of ships needed to carry force

units must be determined. U.S. political considerations dictate that the forward base in the Indian Ocean region can be no larger than the one in Europe.

The purpose of the present study is to permit the United States to meet all treaty commitments that might involve military forces, while minimizing the cost to U.S. taxpayers. It is assumed that only one of the theaters of operation will be active at any one time; that is, there will not be demands on U.S. forces from two or more theaters at the same time.

QUESTIONS

1. Formulate a linear program of this situation that will assist General Walker in determining the quantities of transport aircraft and fast-logistic ships that will be needed to satisfy the treaty commitments of the United States at minimum cost.

2. Solve the linear program formulated in Question 1.

3. New estimates made by MAC indicate that there is a good possibility that enemy fighters would be able to shoot down 10% of the air transports during the second week and an additional 10% during the third week. How might this affect the strategic mobility deployment plan, if at all?

4. A routine safety investigation discovers cracks in the tail sections of 20% of the transport aircraft so they have to be grounded for a 6-month period while they are being repaired. Evaluate the effect of this finding.

5. The Central Intelligence Agency (CIA) indicates that current military plans seriously underestimate the magnitude of the possible contingencies. Its study indicates that the number of troops and associated equipment—the number of force units actually required—would be about 10% higher than previously predicted. How would this affect the current strategic mobility deployment plan? What about a 25% increase?

6. Suppose anti-American demonstrations in Europe about the American bases have become widespread. To decrease the visibility of the U.S. presence, the State Department recommends that bases be reduced to a maximum capacity of 50 force units. How would this change the current plans? What about a maximum capacity of only 40 force units?

| TABLE 2 | Air Transport Productivity |

Theater	Productivity (Aircraft/Kiloton)
Middle East	2.5
Far East	1.5
Africa	3.0

7. Lockheed Corporation informs DOD that it would consider cutting the prices of its C-5A and C-141s by 20% if DOD will purchase more. Should they purchase more? If so, why and how many? If not, why not and what price cuts would be needed before DOD would reconsider and purchase more?

8. Although political considerations originally dictated that the forward bases in the Indian Ocean be no larger than those in Europe, economic factors are playing a more significant part in decisions. Costs are so much lower in the Indian Ocean area that it might make sense to eliminate this political constraint to allow the forward base there to be expanded. What is your analysis of this situation?

9. The Navy has many old Victory ships mothballed at various bases on both the East and West Coasts. They are old and slow, but are relatively cheap to operate, about $6 million per force unit annually. Troops and supplies sent in these ships would not arrive at the various theaters of operation until the third week. Analyze whether they should be used. If so, how many? If not, why not? Assume that the capacity of Victory ships is 1 kiloton.

CHAPTER **11**

INTEGER AND GOAL PROGRAMMING

A number of important scheduling problems . . . require the study of an astronomical number of arrangements to determine which one is best. . . . Mathematicians have been working on improved techniques.

George Dantzig

This chapter discusses two extensions of linear programming procedures for solving resource allocation problems, beginning with the more common integer programming. An **integer program** is structurally like the linear programming models encountered so far, but it has one distinguishing feature: the solution must be whole numbers, or **integers.** That simple requirement makes these problems especially challenging to solve.

The second linear programming extension is the **goal program,** used to evaluate multicriteria decisions. As the name implies, such a model allows for simultaneous consideration of multiple goals. These models are linear programs formulated especially to incorporate those separate and possibly competing goals into a single omnibus objective function.

MANAGERIAL DECISION

Determining Production Quantities

Swatville Sluggers is a small manufacturer of baseball bats. In evaluating earlier analysis of March and April production using linear programming, owner George Herman "Sultan" Swat is dissatisfied with the fractional values obtained. He suggested to his nephew, Babe, that those answers be rounded to the nearest whole numbers. Babe objects, stating that doing so would not necessarily be optimal and might even give an infeasible production plan. (The respective linear programming formulations appear on pages 332 and 372.)

11-1 INTEGER PROGRAMMING

We have seen that linear programs permit fractional solutions, which is satisfactory for most applications. In manufacturing, the completion of one-half or one-third of a unit might merely signify that the production period is ending with unfinished goods or some work-in-progress inventory. Even at the end of a production run, when no unfinished goods are held over, one-third of an item may be inconsequential when quantities are in the hundreds or thousands.

But there is a significant class of situations for which the solution values must be whole numbers or integers. For example, an airline might use a linear program to determine what aircraft to buy. A linear programming solution involving $5\frac{2}{3}$ Boeing 747's and $9\frac{3}{8}$ DC-10's would not be very meaningful. Furthermore, a rounded solution—with respective values of 6 and 9, in this case—may not even be feasible or may cost millions of dollars more than the truly optimal solution. Problems that may otherwise be solved by employing linear programming, except that there are integer restrictions on the variables involved, fall into the category of integer programs.

Graphical Solutions

As an example, consider the following integer program:

$$\text{Maximize} \quad P = 14X_1 + 16X_2$$
$$\text{Subject to} \quad 4X_1 + 3X_2 \leq 12 \quad (A)$$
$$6X_1 + 8X_2 \leq 24 \quad (B)$$

where X_1 and X_2 are nonnegative integers

In place of the requirement that all X's ≥ 0, we specify that X_1 and X_2 must be non-negative integers.

It is convenient to begin by treating the problem as a linear program, which is solved graphically in Figure 11-1. If this solution involves only integer values, then it will be the solution to the integer program as well. But, we obtain

$$X_1 = 1\frac{5}{7} \qquad X_2 = 1\frac{5}{7}$$
$$P = 51\frac{3}{7}$$

which does not meet the integer specifications. It is tempting to round this solution off to ($X_1 = 2$, $X_2 = 2$), but our graph indicates that this is infeasible. The dots in Figure 11-1, which are sometimes referred to as **lattice points,** represent all of the integer solutions that lie within the feasible solution region of the linear program. The optimal integer solution is

$$X_1 = 0 \qquad X_2 = 3$$
$$P = 48$$

Notice that its lattice point is not even adjacent to the most attractive linear programming corner.

The Branch-and-Bound Method

The branch-and-bound method is an effective search procedure that involves solving a succession of carefully formulated linear programs. Each linear program shares the original program constraints, with new ones added in accordance with findings from previous solutions. The process begins with the original integer program solved as a *linear* program (LP), so some of the solution values will ordinarily involve fractional parts.

This **parent linear program** provides essential information about the more restrictive integer program. In a profit-maximization problem, its optimal P establishes an **upper bound** on the level of P for the integer program. It is easy to understand why this must be so. Although the integer program shares all the restrictions of the LP, it

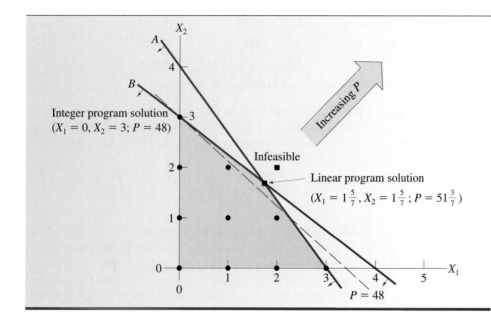

FIGURE 11-1

Graphical solutions to a problem formulated as a linear program and as an integer program

must meet further limitations, so that its best P cannot be better than the maximum profit of the less restrictive LP.

The solution to the first parent linear program allows investigators to identify two potential **descendant linear programs** that share all of the parent problem's constraints. Each descendant has just one additional constraint. The new problems are selected by picking from the parent's solution one of the noninteger-valued variables, which becomes the **branching variable.** One descendant LP has the new restriction that this variable must lie at or below the largest integer not exceeding its solution value for the parent problem; the second limits that X to be greater than or equal to the next larger integer from its sibling's restriction. The two descendant LPs partition the feasible solution region of the parent. The respective optimal P's can at best be less than or equal to the maximum profit for the parent.

A tree portrayal may be used to keep track of the whole process. Each problem is represented by a node, followed by branches leading to the descendant LPs. As the tree gets bigger, more information becomes known about the solution to the original integer program.

The process of subdividing LPs continues until one solution is so restrictive that it *happens* (but is not forced) to end up with all integer values. This is a feasible solution to the original *integer* program, although it may not be optimal. The P for this first integer solution, called the **best-solution-so-far** establishes a **lower bound** on profit, which can be no worse. The tree may then be pruned, with LPs having P's worse than this lower bound eliminated from further consideration. Eventually, the tree becomes fully pruned, and the optimal solution is found.

Illustration: A Profit-Maximization Problem

To illustrate the procedure, we will use a modified version of the original Redwood Furniture problem. The objective is to

$$\text{Maximize} \quad P = 6X_T + 8X_C$$

$$\text{Subject to} \quad 30X_T + 20X_C \leq 310 \quad \text{(wood)}$$

$$5X_T + 10X_C \leq 113 \quad \text{(labor)}$$

where X_T and X_C are nonnegative integers

(The right-hand sides differ slightly from those in Chapter 8.)

Relaxing the integer requirements, the Redwood objective gives rise to Problem 1, the first linear program. This problem is solved graphically in Figure 11-2. We obtain the following results:

Problem 1 $X_T = 4.2$ $X_C = 9.2$

$$P = 98.8$$

Because both X_T and X_C are nonintegers, either quantity may serve as the branching variable. We will arbitrarily choose X_T. The value $X_T = 4.2$ serves to determine a partition for the Problem 1 feasible solution region. Because no lattice points lie on the strip where X_T is >4 and also <5, all of those points may be eliminated from further consideration. The feasible solution region is partitioned to exclude that strip, with one part having the restriction that

$$X_T \leq 4$$

and the other that

$$X_T \geq 5$$

Two descendant linear programs are thereby defined. Each incorporates the constraints of the parent problem, plus one of the branching variable restrictions.

FIGURE 11-2
Graphical solution to
Problem 1

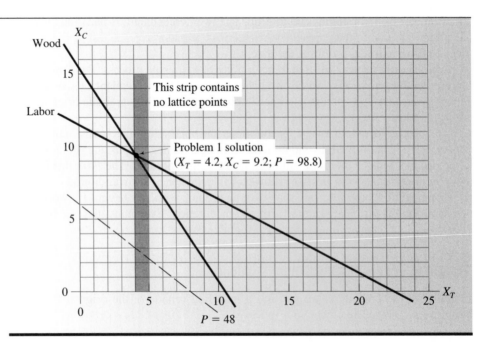

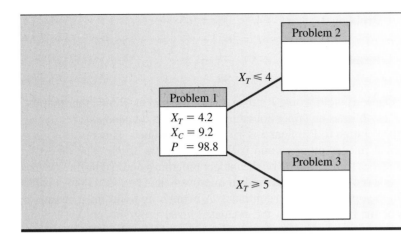

FIGURE 11-3
Initial tree for the branch-and-bound method applied to the modified Redwood Furniture problem

Problem 2

Maximize $P = 6X_T + 8X_C$

Subject to $30X_T + 20X_C \leq 310$

$5X_T + 10X_C \leq 113$

$X_T \leq 4$

where $X_T, X_C \geq 0$

Problem 3

Maximize $P = 6X_T + 8X_C$

Subject to $30X_T + 20X_C \leq 310$

$5X_T + 10X_C \leq 113$

$X_T \geq 5$

where $X_T, X_C \geq 0$

Figure 11-3 summarizes, on a tree diagram, the current situation. The further growth of the tree will depend on what solution values are obtained for these LPs.

Problems 2 and 3 are solved graphically in Figure 11-4. We obtain the following results.

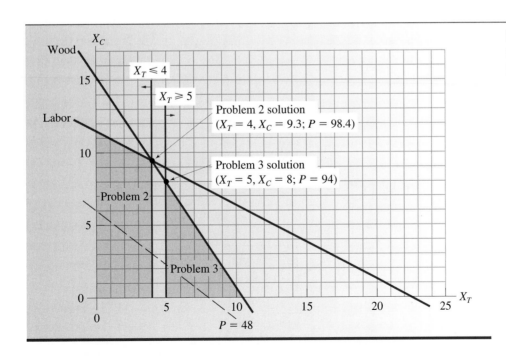

FIGURE 11-4
Graphical solutions to Problems 2 and 3

Problem 2 $X_T = 4$ $X_C = 9.3$
$$P = 98.4$$

Problem 3 $X_T = 5$ $X_C = 8$
$$P = 94$$

Notice that both solutions yield worse P's than that of the parent. Remember that the parent's optimal P establishes an upper bound on the P's of its descendants.

We see that the solution to Problem 3 is 100% integer valued. This result is a solution to the original integer program and is the *best-solution-so-far*. The objective value $P = 94$ establishes a *lower bound* on the integer program's optimal profit. We can do no worse than this profit, but we may find an improvement.

The search for the optimal solution continues. A **branching point** must be found. This will always be the box for one of the evaluated linear programs not yet having descendants and which involves at least one noninteger solution value. Only Problem 2 falls into this category, and the next branching takes place from there. Should there be a choice, *that candidate having the greatest P would be selected as the next branching point.*

The branching variable is X_C (the only non-integer-valued variable in the Problem 2 solution). The descendant LPs involve the following constraints:

$$X_C \leq 9 \text{ (for Problem 4)} \quad \text{and} \quad X_C \geq 10 \text{ (for Problem 5)}$$

Figure 11-5 shows the current tree. The new linear programs are

Problem 4	**Problem 5**
Maximize $P = 6X_T + 8X_C$	Maximize $P = 6X_T + 8X_C$
Subject to $\quad 30X_T + 20X_C \leq 310$	Subject to $\quad 30X_T + 20X_C \leq 310$
$\quad\quad\quad\quad 5X_T + 10X_C \leq 113$	$\quad\quad\quad\quad 5X_T + 10X_C \leq 113$
$\quad\quad\quad\quad X_T \quad\quad\quad \leq \quad 4$	$\quad\quad\quad\quad X_T \quad\quad\quad \leq \quad 4$
$\quad\quad\quad\quad\quad X_C \leq \quad 9$	$\quad\quad\quad\quad\quad X_C \geq \quad 10$
where $\quad\quad\quad\quad X_T, X_C \geq \quad 0$	where $\quad\quad\quad\quad X_T, X_C \geq \quad 0$

FIGURE 11-5

Continuation of the tree for the branch-and-bound method applied to the modified Redwood Furniture problem

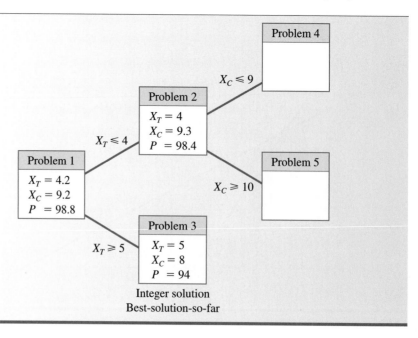

Problem 4

$X_C \leq 9$

Problem 2
$X_T = 4$
$X_C = 9.3$
$P = 98.4$

$X_T \leq 4$

Problem 1
$X_T = 4.2$
$X_C = 9.2$
$P = 98.8$

Problem 5

$X_C \geq 10$

Problem 3
$X_T \geq 5$
$X_T = 5$
$X_C = 8$
$P = 94$

Integer solution
Best-solution-so-far

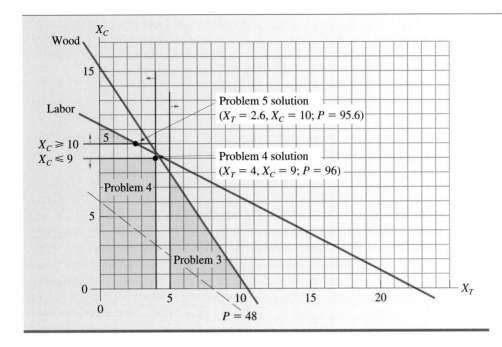

FIGURE 11-6
Graphical solutions to
Problems 4 and 5

These problems are solved graphically in Figure 11-6. We obtain the following results:

Problem 4 $X_T = 4$ $X_C = 9$
$$P = 96$$

Problem 5 $X_T = 2.6$ $X_C = 10$
$$P = 95.6$$

The solution to Problem 4 involves all integers. Because its P exceeds that of the best-solution-so-far, it replaces Problem 3, which may be pruned from the tree, as shown in Figure 11-7. The new lower bound on profit is now 96. Because this amount exceeds

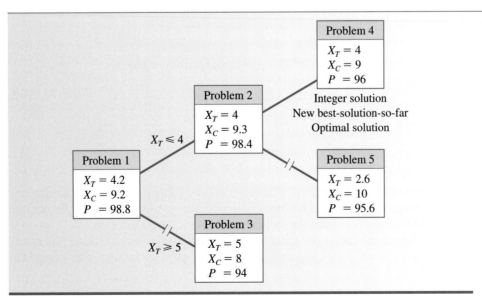

FIGURE 11-7
Pruned final tree for the
branch-and-bound method
applied to the modified
Redwood Furniture problem

$P = 95.6$ for Problem 5, that problem is also pruned from the tree. (None of the descendants of Problem 5 need to be investigated, because none will have a better P than 95.6.) Figure 11-7 indicates that there are no further branching points. The best-solution-so-far is optimal, and the solution to the original integer program is

$$X_T = 4 \qquad X_C = 9$$
$$P = 96$$

Solving Larger Problems

If a problem can be graphed, the branch-and-bound method is not needed at all. The solution can be obtained, as in Figure 11-1, by locating the feasible lattice point that has the best objective value. But by working a two-dimensional problem we can see why that method must still work for problems that cannot be graphed. In a three-variable problem, the linear programs must all be solved on a computer, and the only picture available is the tree. This tree can grow to be quite large before any pruning takes place.

Once tree-pruning begins, the bounds get progressively tighter, providing a bidirectional pincer action that converges on the optimum. Unfortunately, that process can be agonizingly slow, and hundreds of LPs may have to be solved before uncovering the answer to a problem having a half-dozen variables.

Cost-Minimization Problems

The branch-and-bound method works analogously for cost-minimization problems. The parent LP is obtained from the original problem by ignoring integer restrictions. The optimal C to any parent problem establishes a *lower bound* on the C's of its descendants. The C for the first integer solution establishes an *upper bound* on all remaining solutions, and any problem having a worse-cost solution may be pruned from the tree. The most promising branching point will be the nonparent linear program with the best C, which has some noninteger solution values.

As an illustration, consider the following integer program:

$$\text{Minimize} \quad C = 4X_1 + 3X_2 + 5X_3$$
$$\text{Subject to} \qquad 2X_1 - 2X_2 + 4X_3 \geq 7$$
$$2X_1 + 4X_2 - 2X_3 \geq 5$$
$$\text{where } X_1, X_2, \text{ and } X_3 \text{ are nonnegative integers}$$

We will temporarily ignore the integer restriction and refer to the resulting linear program as Problem 1. The simplex method provides the following linear programming solution.

$$\textbf{Problem 1} \quad X_1 = 2\tfrac{5}{6} \qquad X_2 = 0 \qquad X_3 = \tfrac{1}{3}$$
$$C = 13$$

Because two of the variables have noninteger values, further steps are required to uncover the integer solution. As our branching variable, we may use X_1 or X_3, both of which have noninteger values. We arbitrarily choose X_1.

The solution provides $X_1 = 2\tfrac{5}{6}$, so 2 is the highest integer not exceeding this value. Thus, the descendant linear programs include the original constraints, plus one of the following:

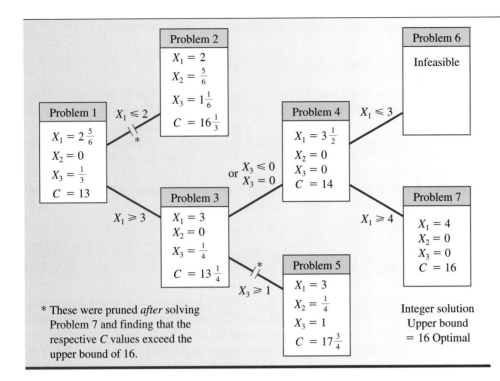

FIGURE 11-8
The branch-and-bound method applied to an integer program involving cost minimization

Problem 2
$X_1 = 2$
$X_2 = \frac{5}{6}$
$X_3 = 1\frac{1}{6}$
$C = 16\frac{1}{3}$

Problem 6
Infeasible

Problem 1
$X_1 = 2\frac{5}{6}$
$X_2 = 0$
$X_3 = \frac{1}{3}$
$C = 13$

$X_1 \leqslant 2$
$X_1 \geqslant 3$

Problem 4
$X_1 = 3\frac{1}{2}$
$X_2 = 0$
$X_3 = 0$
$C = 14$

$X_1 \leqslant 3$

or $\begin{array}{c} X_3 \leqslant 0 \\ X_3 = 0 \end{array}$

Problem 3
$X_1 = 3$
$X_2 = 0$
$X_3 = \frac{1}{4}$
$C = 13\frac{1}{4}$

$X_3 \geqslant 1$

$X_1 \geqslant 4$

Problem 7
$X_1 = 4$
$X_2 = 0$
$X_3 = 0$
$C = 16$

Problem 5
$X_1 = 3$
$X_2 = \frac{1}{4}$
$X_3 = 1$
$C = 17\frac{3}{4}$

Integer solution
Upper bound
= 16 Optimal

* These were pruned *after* solving Problem 7 and finding that the respective C values exceed the upper bound of 16.

Problem 2 $X_1 \leq 2$
Problem 3 $X_1 \geq 3$

The respective solutions to these linear programs obtained using simplex are shown in Figure 11-8, which provides a tree summary of the entire procedure. Neither linear program has an integer solution, so further branching will be the next step.

Problem 3 has the smallest minimum cost of $C = 13\frac{1}{4}$, so it becomes the new parent linear program and the subset problems are partitioned from it. The only noninteger solution value is $X_3 = \frac{1}{4}$, which makes X_3 the branching variable. The following descendant linear programs are obtained by adding the respective constraint to the parent problem. Thus,

Problem 4 $X_3 \leq 0$ or $X_3 = 0$
Problem 5 $X_3 \geq 1$

Both of these linear programs involve the original constraints and the restriction in Problem 3 that $X_1 \geq 3$.

The solutions are provided in Figure 11-8. Of all the nonparent LPs, Problem 4 has the smallest objective of $C = 14$. This linear program is then partitioned, again using X_1 as the branching variable. This time $X_1 \leq 3$, which is the largest integer $< 3\frac{1}{2}$ (the solution value). The descendants include the earlier constraints for Problem 4 plus one of the following:

Problem 6 $X_1 \leq 3$
Problem 7 $X_1 \geq 4$

In Problem 6, we include $X_1 \geq 3$ (the earlier constraint for Problem 3). This constraint together with the new constraint yields the restriction that $X_1 = 3$ exactly.

Problem 6 is infeasible. Problem 7 yields the following solution.

$$\textbf{Problem 7} \qquad X_1 = 4 \qquad X_2 = 0 \qquad X_3 = 0$$
$$C = 16$$

Because all of the variables have integer values, this is a solution to the original integer program. This is the best-solution-so-far. The objective establishes an upper bound of 16 on the C values of any further integer solutions to be evaluated.

Referring to Figure 11-8, we can see that Problems 2 and 5 remain childless. Because the respective C values (lower bounds) of these subsets exceed the upper bound of 16, these linear programs can be eliminated and the branches leading to them can be pruned. This leaves no nonparent LPs having noninteger solutions and our solution to Problem 7 is redesignated as the optimal integer solution.

11-2 COMPUTER APPLICATIONS WITH INTEGER PROGRAMMING

A small integer program evaluation may involve hundreds of separate linear programs. This is a job best done with computer assistance. *QuickQuant* 2000 will automatically solve integer programs using the branch-and-bound procedure. All you have to do is enter the data in the same fashion as a simple linear program. You must then wait a while as the program builds and prunes the solution tree (maintained internally, but not displayed). This could take dozens of iterations. *QuickQuant* will terminate the run after 300 iterations, providing the best-solution-so-far, if at that point any integer solution has been found.

To illustrate, consider the expanded Redwood Furniture problem. There are three table sizes—small (X_{TS}), regular (X_{TR}), and large (X_{TL}); two chair styles—standard (X_{CS}) and armed (X_{CA}); and two bookcase sizes—short (X_{BS}) and tall (X_{BT}). Greater resource quantities are available, and machine shop time is now in short supply. There are minimum quantities for each product group, and there are mixture constraints that must be met exactly.

Table 11-1 summarizes the production requirements. The following report was obtained. (The printer types $<$ for $\leq$ and $>$ for $\geq$.)

TABLE 11-1 Data Obtained for the Expanded Redwood Furniture Problem

| CONSTRAINT | VARIABLE | | | | | | | AVAILABLE |
	(1) X_{TS}	(2) X_{TR}	(3) X_{TL}	(4) X_{CS}	(5) X_{CA}	(6) X_{BS}	(7) X_{BT}	QUANTITY
(1) Wood	20	30	40	15	25	20	30	$\leq 3,000$
(2) Labor	4	5	6	8	12	6	8	$\leq 1,100$
(3) Machine time	2	2	2	3	3	2	2	≤ 250
(4) Quantity, tables	1	1	1					≥ 30
(5) Quantity, chairs				1	1			≥ 20
(6) Quantity, bookcases						1	1	≥ 20
(7) Mix, tables	1	−1	−1					$= 0$
(8) Mix, chairs				1	−4			$= 0$
(9) Mix, bookcases						1	−1	$= 0$
Unit profit	$5	$6	$7	$6	$10	$8	$6	

SOLUTION TO INTEGER PROGRAM

PROBLEM: Redwood Furniture (Expanded)

DETAILED RECORD OF LINEAR PROGRAMS EVALUATED IN SOLVING INTEGER PROGRAM

Problem Number	Profit Upper Bound	Parent Problem	Branching Variable	Problem Status
1	771.000			
2	770.000	1	XBS (< 32)	
3	Infeasible	1	XBS (> 33)	
4	768.533	2	XTS (< 15)	
5	769.000	2	XTS (> 16)	
6	768.000	5	XBS (< 31)	
7	Infeasible	5	XBS (> 32)	
8	764.000	4	XCS (< 16)	Integer
9	766.375	4	XCS (> 17)	
10	766.533	6	XTS (< 16)	
11	767.000	6	XTS (> 17)	
12	766.000	11	XBS (< 30)	
13	Infeasible	11	XBS (> 31)	
14	762.000	10	XCS (< 16)	Integer
15	764.375	10	XCS (> 17)	
16	Infeasible	9	XCA (< 4)	
17	752.500	9	XCA (> 5)	
18	764.533	12	XTS (< 17)	
19	765.000	12	XTS (> 18)	
20	764.000	19	XBS (< 29)	
21	Infeasible	19	XBS (> 30)	
22	760.000	18	XCS (< 16)	Integer
23	762.375	18	XCS (> 17)	
24	Infeasible	15	XCA (< 4)	
25	750.500	15	XCA (> 5)	

This problem illustrates *profit maximization.* Notice that the P for each parent linear program establishes an *upper bound* on the P values of all descendant problems. The P for the best-solution-so-far establishes a *lower bound* on profit. Any problem having a P smaller than that lower bound is pruned from the evolving tree. The first such solution was not obtained until Problem 8, the first linear program to have all integer values. It took 17 more problems to establish that Problem 8 is indeed optimal.

QuickQuant provides the following report for the large Redwood Furniture problem:

SOLUTION TO INTEGER PROGRAM

PROBLEM: Redwood Furniture (Expanded)

Original Variable	Value	Status
XTS	15.00000	Integer
XTR	0.00000	Integer
XTL	15.00000	Integer
XCS	16.00000	Integer
XCA	4.00000	Integer
XBS	32.00000	Integer
XBT	32.00000	Integer

Objective Value: P =764.00000

Solving Integer Programs with a Spreadsheet

Spreadsheets can be used to solve integer programming problems very much like ordinary LPs. All we need to do is add the integer condition to the problem formulation. To illustrate, we use the original Redwood Furniture Company problem in Figure 11-9, where the available quantities of wood and labor have been changed.

FIGURE 11-9

Formulation table for the original Redwood Furniture Company problem with increased resource availabilities

Variables	X_T	X_C	Sign	RHS
Objective	6	8	=	P(max)
Wood	30	20	≤	310
Labor	5	10	≤	113

Figure 11-10 shows the Excel spreadsheet for this problem when the variables are not constrained to be integers; the solution obtained is $X_T = 4.2$, $X_C = 9.2$, and $P = 98.8$.

FIGURE 11-10

Optimal solution to the increased-resource Redwood Furniture Company problem without the integer restriction

	A	B	C	D	E	F	G
1		**Redwood Furniture Company**					
2							
3	Variables	X_T	X_C	Sign	RHS		
4	Objective	6	8	=	P(max)	Profit	98.8
5	Wood	30	20	≤	310	Wood used	310
6	Labor	5	10	≤	113	Labor used	113
7		Solution					
8		X_T	X_C		G		
9		4.2	9.2	4	=SUMPRODUCT(B4:C4,$B$9:$C$9)		
10				5	=SUMPRODUCT(B5:C5,$B$9:$C$9)		
11				6	=SUMPRODUCT(B6:C6,$B$9:$C$9)		

The integer programming version of the problem uses the same spreadsheet with one small change in the Solver Parameters dialog box, as shown in Figure 11-11. There the condition of integer values is introduced into Solver by adding a new constraint in the *Subject to the Constraints* box: $B$9:$C$9 = integer. That was done by clicking on the Add button, which brought to screen the Add Constraint dialog box shown in

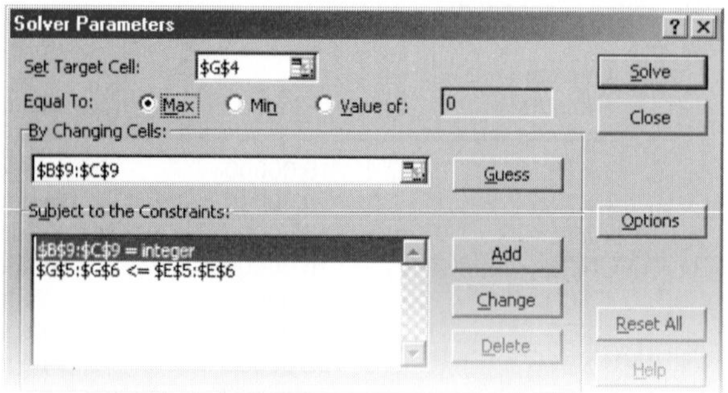

FIGURE 11-11

Solver Parameters dialog box for increased-resource Redwood Furniture Company problem with the integer restriction

Figure 11-12. The integer constraint is obtained by typing in the cell reference $B$9:$C$9 and then pulling down the menu to select *int* for integer.

Change Constraint	? X
Cell Reference: $B$9:$C$9	Constraint: int ▼ =integer
OK	Cancel	Add	Help

FIGURE 11-12
The Change Constraint dialog box for setting up the Redwood Furniture Company problem

Clicking Solve in the Solver Parameters dialog box launches the program, which revises the earlier spreadsheet, shown in Figure 11-13. The optimal solution is $X_T = 4$, $X_C = 9$, and $P = 96$.

	A	B	C	D	E	F	G
1		Redwood Furniture Company					
2							
3	Variables	X_T	X_C	Sign	RHS		
4	Objective	6	8	=	P(max)	Profit	96
5	Wood	30	20	≤	310	Wood used	300
6	Labor	5	10	≤	113	Labor used	110
7			Solution				
8		X_T	X_C			G	
9		4	9		4	=SUMPRODUCT(B4:C4,$B$9:$C$9)	
10					5	=SUMPRODUCT(B5:C5,$B$9:$C$9)	
11					6	=SUMPRODUCT(B6:C6,$B$9:$C$9)	

FIGURE 11-13
Spreadsheet and solution for integer increased-resource Redwood Furniture Company problem with the integer restriction

Managerial Decision Revisited: Determining Production Quantities

MANAGERIAL DECISION

Babe solved the March and April production problems using *QuickQuant* 2000. He found it helpful to first solve each problem as *linear* programs and then round those values by hand and calculate separately the total profit. Then he made a second computer run for each problem solved as an *integer* program. The following results were obtained:

	MARCH			APRIL		
Variable	Linear Program Solution	Rounded Solution	Integer Program Solution	Linear Program Solution	Rounded Solution	Integer Program Solution
X_{30}	94.12	94	94	80.46	80	80
X_{32}	94.12	94	89	0.00	0	0
X_{34}	0.00	0	5	80.46	80	80
X_{36}	0.00	0	0	0.00	0	0
X_{38}	94.12	94	94	80.46	80	80
X_{40}	0.00	0	0	0.00	0	1
Maximum P	$3,938.82	$3,933.30	$3,936.40	$3,276.32	$3,257.60	$3,272.78
Subproblems Evaluated			147			255

Notice that the linear programs have greater P's than the integer program solutions. (That must be the case, because the LPs are the beginning parent problems for the branch-and-bound procedure.) Notice also that the rounded LP solutions are feasible but have worse P's than the integer programs. (A feasible rounded LP solution can never have an objective value better than that of the corresponding integer programming solution.)

11-3   INTEGER PROGRAMMING APPLICATIONS

Integer programming has been applied to a wide variety of decision-making situations. Although it is not used as extensively as linear programming, integer programming is suited to almost as wide a range of applications. As we noted earlier, solving an integer programming problem requires a lot of computer time. Integer programming procedures are often used to solve problems involving a large number of variables, although computations are usually terminated before the optimal solution can be firmly established. The best-solution-so-far is then used in place of the optimal solution.

One popular application of integer programming is *facility location.* For instance, the problem of locating warehouses can be a significant decision for a manufacturer of bulky items, such as a chemical company. Hundreds of candidate cities could accommodate warehouses, but only a few cities will be chosen. These sites may be selected to minimize total distribution costs. If the warehouse locations are already fixed, the problem can be solved as a linear program, using the transportation method to determine the quantities to be shipped from source to destination. But when the warehouse locations are variables, an entire set of integer-valued, zero–one variables must be considered—one for each possible site. The fixed cost of operating a warehouse site applies only when a facility is built there. (Its variable is equal to *one,* and the fixed cost is charged in the objective function.) Otherwise, there is no fixed cost and the site variable has a value of *zero.*

The use of zero–one variables can be extended to other applications. Production runs usually involve fixed set-up costs, regardless of what quantities are eventually made. In any planning period, each product is assigned a zero–one variable indicating whether or not it will be produced in that period. The concepts encountered in warehouse location also apply to a variety of capital-budgeting decisions that involve not only physical facilities but also the introduction of new products and research and development projects, among others.

A fractional item may make no practical sense in a product-mix decision. A production run may be practical only in batches of a particular size—say, 1,000 items at a time. Integer requirements must be met in these cases.

MANAGERIAL APPLICATION

Maui Miser Car Rentals

Maui Miser Car Rentals specializes in economy cars for tourists on a low budget. Owner Tony Yamato wants to determine the optimal mix of cars to order in his next fleet purchase of up to $500,000. Tony has narrowed the possibilities to three vehicles: economy vans, compact cars, and large cars. The respective fleet-purchase costs per vehicle are $25,000, $15,000, and $21,000. Past experience establishes the following expected annual rental incomes: $15,000 for vans, $7,600 for compacts, and $10,600 for

large cars. Subject to further limitations, Tony wants to maximize expected annual revenue from the fleet additions. The purchase must include at least 5 vans, at least 5 large cars, and at least 12 passenger cars altogether. Altogether, the purchase must involve at least 25 vehicles. The number of large cars cannot exceed the number of compacts. The average daily rental rates are $50 for vans, $30 for compacts, and $40 for large cars. To maintain the miser's image, Tony wants to keep the average rental rate for the new fleet at or below $39.

    Tony's daughter Tanya has just completed a course in quantitative methods. She volunteers to formulate his problem as an integer program, which she will then solve with her personal computer.

THE PROBLEM SOLUTION

The following integer program applies:

$$X_V = \text{number of economy vans to purchase}$$
$$X_C = \text{number of compact cars to purchase}$$
$$X_L = \text{number of large cars to purchase}$$

Maximize

$$P = 15{,}000X_V + 7{,}600X_C + 10{,}600X_L$$

Subject to					
$25{,}000X_V +$	$15{,}000X_C +$	$21{,}000X_L \leq$	$500{,}000$	(budget)
$11X_V -$	$9X_C +$	$1X_L \leq$	0	(average rental)
$X_V +$	$X_C +$	$X_L \geq$	25	(vehicle minimum)
X_V		$\geq$	5	(van minimum)
		$X_L \geq$	5	(large car minimum)
	$X_C +$	$X_L \geq$	12	(car minimum)
	$-X_C +$	$X_L \leq$	0	(car mix)

where X_V, X_C, X_L are nonnegative integers

    Tanya used *QuickQuant* to solve this problem. After entering the data, to check for feasibility Tanya first solved the integer program as a *linear* program, getting the following solution:

SOLUTION TO LINEAR PROGRAM

PROBLEM: Maui Miser Rental Cars

Original Variable	Value
XV	8.92308
XC	11.46154
XL	5.00000

Objective Value: P = 273953.8100

She then rounded the number of vans to 9 and the number of compacts to 11. Evaluating this as a possible solution, Tanya found the rounded LP solution to be *infeasible*. A second *QuickQuant* run provided the following results:

SOLUTION TO INTEGER PROGRAM

PROBLEM: Maui Miser Rental Cars

DETAILED RECORD OF LINEAR PROGRAMS EVALUATED IN SOLVING INTEGER PROGRAM

Problem Number	Profit Upper Bound	Parent Problem	Branching Variable	Problem Status
1	273953.810			
2	271800.000	1	XV (< 8)	Integer
3	Infeasible	1	XV (> 9)	

SOLUTION TO INTEGER PROGRAM

Original Variable	Value	Status
XV	8.00000	Integer
XC	13.00000	Integer
XL	5.00000	Integer

Objective Value: P = 271800.0000

Tanya recommends that Tony purchase 8 economy vans, 13 compact cars, and 5 large cars. This will maximize expected annual rental revenue.

When Is Rounding the LP Good Enough?

For problems having a small number of variables, the integer program may usually be solved with no difficulty. Bigger problems may require so many iterations that computer programs terminate before an optimum has been found, although a best-solution-so-far might be satisfactory. If no integer solution has been found, a rounded LP solution might be used, provided that the result is feasible. Which solution to use becomes a judgment call.

11-4 MULTI-OBJECTIVE EVALUATIONS USING GOAL PROGRAMMING

The linear programming applications encountered so far in this book all involve a *single objective*. For those problems, maximizing profit or minimizing cost seems like a proper thing to do. But that approach can be a serious oversimplification when the decision maker has *multiple goals*. For example, a manufacturer may want not only to maximize profit, but also to increase share of market, to keep within a capital-spending budget, to maintain a minimum cash reserve, and to achieve steady workforce growth. All of these goals are important and should be incorporated into the process of selecting a solution.

Of course, it may not be possible to achieve all the goals absolutely. Consider the traditional investor dilemma, illustrated by Willy B. Rich, who makes his choice of stock with the two following objectives in mind:

Maximize return   and   Minimize risk

The market structures for securities make it impossible for an investor to achieve both goals. Although Willy expects High-Volatility Engineering to give a high dividend pay-out and to have substantial opportunity for appreciation, he feels so uncomfortable with the stock's potential for losing its market value that he buys Stability Power—a stock having lower expected returns but a lot less risk of losing its market value. This purchase decision achieves for Willy his *optimal balance* in attaining the conflicting goals.

The concepts of linear programming may be extended to achieve such an optimal balance in meeting multiple objectives. The procedure is aptly called **goal programming.** Like the investor, however, it may be impossible for decision makers to meet all of their goals. More realistically, the focus aims at achieving certain *targets* for each goal. The overall objective is to find the solution that collectively minimizes deviations from these targets.

Linear Programming and Multiple Objectives

To lay the foundation for a new method for accommodating multiple goals, we consider once more the familiar Redwood Furniture problem. There are now three main objectives that must be met to establish a production plan. These objectives are to

> Maximize *profit*
>
> Maximize *revenue* to maintain market share growth
>
> Maximize *training time* to increase work-force productivity

Suppose that Redwood wants to achieve all of these while still meeting the original constraints in establishing quantities of tables X_T and chairs X_C to produce. The following data apply:

	TABLE	CHAIR
Profit per unit	$ 6	$ 8
Revenue per unit	$50	$25
Training time per unit	1 hour	3 hours

These data indicate that chairs actually generate higher profits with less revenue. Chairs are also richer in the amount of training time they provide.

The constraints are

$$30X_T + 20X_C \le 300 \qquad \text{(wood)}$$
$$5X_T + 10X_C \le 110 \qquad \text{(labor)}$$
$$\text{where } X_T, X_C \ge \quad 0$$

Standard linear programs have a single objective. The linear programming approach would treat this problem as three separate LPs, all sharing the same constraints, but each having just one of the following objectives:

FIGURE 11-14

Graphical solutions to separate linear programs with different goals for the Redwood Furniture problem

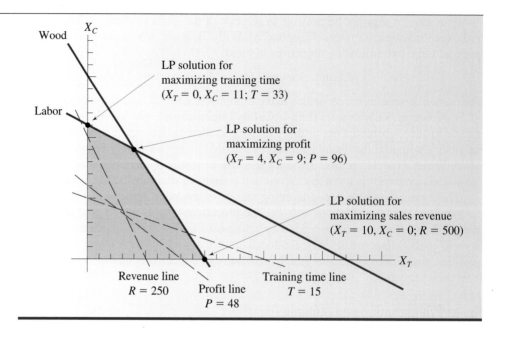

Objective 1	Maximize	$P = 6X_T + 8X_C$	(profit)
Objective 2	Maximize	$R = 50X_T + 25X_C$	(revenue)
Objective 3	Maximize	$T = 1X_T + 3X_C$	(training)

The separate problems are solved graphically using Figure 11-14. We see that each LP has different optimal levels for the X's with the respective solutions corresponding to different most-attractive corners of the common feasible solution region.

As with Willy B. Rich's investment decisions, this problem illustrates in more detail that it is usually impractical to meet several objectives in an absolute sense through direct maximization or minimization. A more realistic set of multiple goals, however, can be accommodated by extending the linear programming approach.

Linear Programming with Goal Targets

Redwood management establishes the following realistic **goal targets:**

Profit	$ 90
Sales revenue	$450
Achieved training time	30 hours

Using these targets, individual goals may be expressed as inequalities (or equations).

Goal 1	$6X_T + 8X_C \geq 90$	(profit)
Goal 2	$50X_T + 25X_C \geq 450$	(revenue)
Goal 3	$1X_T + 3X_C \geq 30$	(training)

Treating each separately, the goals are plotted in Figure 11-15. Each goal has its own line and valid side. The figure also shows the original resource constraints and feasible solution region bordered by the wood and labor lines. Notice that Goal 2 has no feasi-

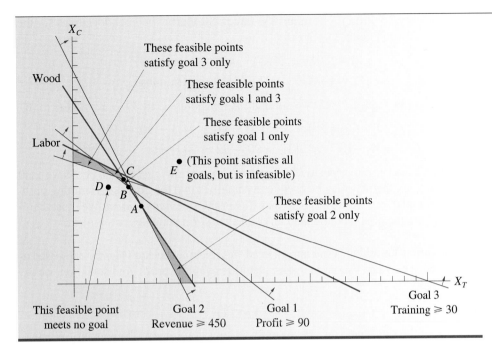

FIGURE 11-15
Graphical representation of the goal program for the Redwood Furniture problem

ble points in common with the other goals, while there is a small overlapping region where both Goal 1 and Goal 3 are met. (Should a goal target be too high, there may be no feasible point satisfying that goal.)

The graph in Figure 11-15 illustrates a further inadequacy in the straight linear programming approach. No matter what objective function is used, *there may be no feasible solution satisfying all goals.*

Goal Programming

Unlike standard linear programming, goal programming is flexible in accommodating multiple goals, allowing a trade-off to be made between them. This is accomplished by allowing some of the goals to be only partially met. An optimal balance between goals may be achieved in several ways.

Goal Deviations   What distinguishes the goal program from a simple linear program is that the goals are treated as *constraints* of a less rigid type than those encountered so far in this book. These special constraints permit goal attainment to be measured in terms of how the achieved levels deviate from their targets.

The amount of deviation from a target is itself treated as a *variable*. Thus, each goal will have its own **goal deviation.** These may be illustrated using the profit goal for the Redwood Furniture problem. We let

$$Y_P = \text{the amount by which profit deviates from the target level}$$

This may be expressed in terms of the other elements in the problem as

$$Y_P = (6X_T + 8X_C) - 90 \qquad \text{(profit)}$$

so that Y_P is the solution profit minus the target. Similarly, the goal deviations for the two other Redwood goals are

$$Y_R = (50X_T + 25X_C) - 450 \qquad \text{(revenue)}$$
$$Y_T = (\ 1X_T + \ 3X_C) - \ 30 \qquad \text{(training)}$$

Referring to Figure 11-15, we compute Y_P for points C (4.29, 8.57) and D (3, 8).

C: $Y_P = (6[4.29] + 8[8.57]) - 90 = 94.3 - 90 = +4.3$
D: $Y_P = (6[3] + 8[8]) - 90 = 82 - 90 = -8$

Notice that Y_P can be either positive or negative. It is *unrestricted as to sign*. As we shall see, the simplex method may be used to eventually solve the goal programming problem. The simplex procedure requires that all variables be *nonnegative*. We must therefore reexpress the goal deviations in an equivalent form suitable for simplex.

Goal Deviation Variables   Any unrestricted variable may be equivalently expressed as the difference between two nonnegative quantities. For the profit goal deviation, we express this as

$$Y_P = Y_P^+ - Y_P^-$$

Only one of the right-hand side terms in this expression can ever be nonzero. When Y_P is positive, Y_P^+ is equal to that goal deviation and is a positive quantity. And, when Y_P is negative, it will be equal to $-Y_P^-$, so that Y_P^- is itself also a positive quantity. The two component variables are referred to as **goal deviation variables.** All goal deviation variables must be *nonnegative*.

Consider once more points C and D from Figure 11-15. The goal deviation variable values are as follows:

C: $Y_P = +4.3 = 4.3 - 0 = Y_P^+ - Y_P^-$, so that $Y_P^+ = 4.3$ and $Y_P^- = 0$
D: $Y_P = -8 = 0 - 8 = Y_P^+ - Y_P^-$, so that $Y_P^+ = 0$ and $Y_P^- = 8$

For the two remaining Redwood goals, the goal deviation variables are defined analogously.

$$Y_R = Y_R^+ - Y_R^-$$
$$Y_T = Y_T^+ - Y_T^-$$

The Goal Program   We are now ready to express the goal program for the Redwood Furniture problem. A goal program is a special linear program that ties all of the goals together through a set of **goal deviation constraints,** with one constraint for each goal. For the Redwood Furniture problem the profit goal is represented by the following constraints:

Goal 1 $6X_T + \ 8X_C - (Y_P^+ - Y_P^-) = 90$ (profit)

The remaining goal constraints are expressed analogously.

Goal 2 $50X_T + 25X_C - (Y_R^+ - Y_R^-) = 450$ (revenue)
Goal 3 $1X_T + \ 3X_C - (Y_T^+ - Y_T^-) = \ 30$ (training)

The goal program is a linear program having a single **omnibus objective function** involving nonzero coefficients for the goal deviation variables only. The objective is to minimize the collective cost of the goal deviations.

It only costs Redwood $1 to fall a dollar below the profit target, so that the coefficient for Y_P^- is 1; because exceeding the profit target is desirable, the other goal deviation variable Y_P^+ will have a coefficient of 0. Redwood has found that falling below its revenue target diminishes future market share. The present value of lost earnings potential is judged to be $2 for each current dollar under the revenue target. (Revenues beyond target are assumed to have a negligible impact on future profitability.) Thus, the coefficient of Y_R^- is $2 per dollar of revenue, while the coefficient of Y_R^+ is 0. Finally, training time up to 30 hours will enhance future efficiencies. This is assumed to be worth $.50 per hour obtained. Beyond 30 hours the training effect would be unnoticeable. Thus, for Y_T^- the coefficient is .50 per hour, while for Y_T^+ it is 0.

Including the original resource constraints, we may finally express the complete goal program in terms of the following linear program:

$$\text{Minimize} \quad C = 0X_T + 0X_C + 0Y_P^+ + 1Y_P^- + 0Y_R^+ + 2Y_R^- + 0Y_T^+ + .5Y_T^-$$

Subject to

Regular Constraints

(wood):	$30X_T + 20X_C$	≤ 300
(labor):	$5X_T + 10X_C$	≤ 110

Goal Deviation Constraints

G1	(profit):	$6X_T + 8X_C - (Y_P^+ - Y_P^-)$		$= 90$
G2	(revenue):	$50X_T + 25X_C$	$- (Y_R^+ - Y_R^-)$	$= 450$
G3	(training):	$1X_T + 3X_C$	$- (Y_T^+ - Y_T^-) =$	30

where   all variables $\geq$ 0

This linear program has 8 main variables and 5 constraints. Denoting by S_W the unused wood and S_L the unused labor, the following solution

$$
\begin{array}{ccc}
X_T = 6 & Y_P^+ = 0 & Y_P^- = 6 \\
X_C = 6 & Y_R^+ = 0 & Y_R^- = 0 \\
S_W = 0 & Y_T^+ = 0 & Y_T^- = 6 \\
S_L = 20 & &
\end{array}
$$

$$C = 9$$

corresponds to point A in Figure 11-15, where the revenue goal is exactly on target, and $Y_R^+ = Y_R^- = 0$. The profit lies $Y_P^- = 6$ dollars below target and the training time falls $Y_T^- = 6$ hours under target. Not all of the labor gets used, so production falls below resource capacity, with only 6 tables and 6 chairs to be made. The cost of this solution is 9 dollars, the minimum possible, which establishes an optimal compromise among the three goals.

The goal program solution depends on the objective coefficients used. Should the relative costs of the goal deviations change, a different solution may be obtained. For example, by increasing the coefficients for Y_P^- to 5 dollars and for Y_T^- to 1 dollar, the optimal solution becomes point B (5, 7.5) in Figure 11-15. Point B then provides the best

balance among goal deviations. Should the cost for Y_T^- be bumped up to 10 dollars per hour, point C (4.29, 8.57) becomes optimal.

Other Goal Forms

The Redwood Furniture problem involves only goals of the $\geq$ form, for which the targets are *minimums*. Goals may also take the $\leq$ form, so that the target is a *maximum*. For example, suppose that Redwood Furniture desires a working capital budget of $325. Tables involve direct costs of $44 each, while chairs involve an expenditure of $17. This goal may be expressed as

$$44X_T + 17X_C \leq 325 \qquad \text{(budget)}$$

The goal program involves two goal deviation variables, denoted here as Y_B^+ and Y_B^-, so the budget goal gives rise to the following goal deviation constraint:

$$44X_T + 17X_C - (Y_B^+ - Y_B^-) = 325 \qquad \text{(budget)}$$

Although the constraint has the same form as the original three, the objective must be to keep Y_B^+ small to avoid exceeding the budgetary limit; Y_B^- may be any amount without violating the goal. Thus, the omnibus objective function would have coefficients such as 1 for Y_B^+ and 0 for Y_B^-.

A third form involves goals that aim at targets that ought to be met *exactly*. For Redwood Furniture, such a goal may be to produce exactly 4 chairs for each table. This may be expressed as

$$4X_T - 1X_C = 0 \qquad \text{(mixture)}$$

This goal involves two goal deviation variables Y_M^+ and Y_M^-, so the following goal deviation constraint applies:

$$4X_T - 1X_C - (Y_M^+ - Y_M^-) = 0 \qquad \text{(mixture)}$$

Both of the variables Y_M^+ and Y_M^- may have nonzero coefficients in the omnibus objective function.

Other Goal Programming Approaches

Some goal programming applications have no natural costs for use as objective coefficients. These problems can still be solved using *penalty points* arbitrarily chosen to coincide with the relative importance of the goals.

11-5 SOLVING GOAL PROGRAMS ON THE COMPUTER

As with any larger linear program, computer assistance is needed to solve goal programs. The computer treats goal programs as linear programs with extra variables and constraints.

Solving Goal Programs with QuickQuant

To run a goal program with *QuickQuant* 2000, the data are entered exactly as with any linear program. The program requires the user to create the goal deviation variables (Y_1^+, Y_1^-, Y_2^+, etc.) and to supply coefficients for the goal-deviation constraints.

Maui Miser Car Rentals Combining Goal and Integer Programming

Maui Miser Car Rentals specializes in economy cars for tourists on a low budget. Owner Tony Yamato wants to determine the optimal mix of cars to order in his next fleet purchase of three vehicles: economy vans, compact cars, and large cars. In Section 11-3, this problem was formulated as an integer program. Tony's daughter Tanya suggests that, although important, annual revenue might best be considered as one of a family of goals, with a targeted amount, such as $300,000. She also recommends that the budget should not be a hard $500,000, and that some leeway be permitted. Likewise, the average daily rental of $39 per vehicle can instead be treated as a "soft" constraint, best handled by means of a goal deviation constraint.

Tanya recommends three goals:

1. Achieve annual rental income of at least $300,000 from the fleet addition.

2. Spend as close to $500,000 as is practicable.

3. Do not exceed the annual average daily rental of $39 for the vehicles in the fleet addition.

Tanya assigns an omnibus objective value of $1 for each dollar violation of Goals 1 and 2. Tanya and Tony agree that violating the "miser" image should involve a penalty of $10,000 for each dollar above the $39 average rental target.

Tanya wants to express her father's problem as a goal program to be solved with *QuickQuant* as a *linear* program with an appropriate omnibus objective and goal deviation constraints. Because fractional vehicle amounts do not make sense, she will then solve the goal problem as a *mixed integer* program (allowing goal deviation variables to be nonintegers).

THE PROBLEM SOLUTION

Using the original problem data, the problem goals are expressed as follows:

$$\text{Goal 1} \quad 15{,}000X_V + 7{,}600X_C + 10{,}600X_L \geq 300{,}000$$
$$\text{Goal 2} \quad 25{,}000X_V + 15{,}000X_C + 21{,}000X_L = 500{,}000$$
$$\text{Goal 3} \quad 11X_V - 9X_C + 1X_L \leq 0$$

Tanya ran the completed goal program and received the following results:

```
                        SOLUTION TO LINEAR PROGRAM
-----------------------------------------------------------------------------------------
PROBLEM: Maui Miser Rental Cars

                        ORIGINAL PROBLEM DATA
Minimize C =
            + 0  XV        + 0  XC        + 0  XL        + 0  Y1+
            + 1  Y1-       + 1  Y2+       + 1  Y2-       + 10000  Y3+
            + 0  Y3-
Subject to:

    C1:     + 1  XV        + 1  XC        + 1  XL        + 0  Y1+
            + 0  Y1-       + 0  Y2+       + 0  Y2-       + 0  Y3+
            + 0  Y3-                                          >      25
```

C2:	+ 1 XV	+ 0 XC	+ 0 XL	+ 0 Y1+	
	+ 0 Y1-	+ 0 Y2+	+ 0 Y2-	+ 0 Y3+	
	+ 0 Y3-				> 5
C3:	+ 0 XV	+ 0 XC	+ 1 XL	+ 0 Y1+	
	+ 0 Y1-	+ 0 Y2+	+ 0 Y2-	+ 0 Y3+	
	+ 0 Y3-				> 5
C4:	+ 0 XV	+ 1 XC	+ 1 XL	+ 0 Y1+	
	+ 0 Y1-	+ 0 Y2+	+ 0 Y2-	+ 0 Y3+	
	+ 0 Y3-				> 12
C5:	+ 0 XV	- 1 XC	+ 1 XL	+ 0 Y1+	
	+ 0 Y1-	+ 0 Y2+	+ 0 Y2-	+ 0 Y3+	
	+ 0 Y3-				< 0
C6:	+ 15000 XV	+ 7600 XC	+ 10600 XL	- 1 Y1+	
	+ 1 Y1-	+ 0 Y2+	+ 0 Y2-	+ 0 Y3+	
	+ 0 Y3-				= 300000
C7:	+ 25000 XV	+ 15000 XC	+ 21000 XL	+ 0 Y1+	
	+ 0 Y1-	- 1 Y2+	+ 1 Y2-	+ 0 Y3+	
	+ 0 Y3-				= 500000
C8:	+ 11 XV	- 9 XC	+ 1 XL	+ 0 Y1+	
	+ 0 Y1-	+ 0 Y2+	+ 0 Y2-	- 1 Y3+	
	+ 1 Y3-				= 0

```
Original
Variable          Value
-----------------------------------
   XV            8.92308
   XC           11.46154
   XL            5.00000
   Y1+           0.00000
   Y1-       26046.15000
   Y2+           0.00000
   Y2-           0.00000
   Y3+           0.00000
   Y3-           0.00000

Objective Value: C = 26046.1538
```

Solving Goal Programs with Spreadsheets

From a computational point of view, goal programming problems are just linear programs with extra variables and constraints, and they can be solved in the same manner. Figure 11-16 is the formulation table for the Maui Miser Car Rentals problem. Figure 11-17 shows the Excel spreadsheet with the optimal solution. Figure 11-18 shows the Solver Parameters dialog box for this problem, where in addition to the constraints listed, the *Assume Linear Model* and *Assume Non-Negative* boxes have been checked. (An integer solution could be

Variables	X_V	X_C	X_L	Y_1^+	Y_1^-	Y_2^+	Y_2^-	Y_3^+	Y_3^-	Sign	RHS
Objective	0	0	0	0	1	1	1	10,000	0	=	C (min)
Vehicle minimum	1	1	1							≥	25
Van minimum	1									≥	5
Large car minimum			1							≥	5
Car minimum		1	1							≥	12
Car mix		-1	1							≤	0
Goal 1	15,000	7,600	10,600	-1	1					=	300,000
Goal 2	25,000	15,000	21,000			-1	1			=	500,000
Goal 3	11	-9	1					-1	1	=	0

FIGURE 11-16   Formulation table for the Maui Miser Car Rentals problem

	A	B	C	D	E	F	G	H	I	J	K	L	M	N
1						Maui Miser Car Rentals Managerial								
2														
3	Variables	X_V	X_C	X_L	Y_1^+	Y_1^-	Y_2^+	Y_2^-	Y_3^+	Y_3^-	Sign	RHS		
4	Objective				1		1	1	10,000		=	C(min)	Profit	26046.154
5	Vehicle minimum	1	1	1							≥	25	Vehicle minimum	25.38
6	Van minimum	1									>	5	Van minimum	8.92
7	Large car minimum			1							>	5	Large car minimum	5.00
8	Car minimum		1	1							≥	12	Car minimum	16.46
9	Car mix		-1	1							≤	0	Car mix	-6.46
10	Goal 1	15000	7600	10600	-1	1					=	300000	Goal 1	300000.00
11	Goal 2	25000	15000	21000			-1	1			=	500000	Goal 2	500000.00
12	Goal 3	11	-9	1					-1	1	=	0	Goal 3	0.00
13						Solution							N	
14		X_V	X_C	X_L	Y_1^+	Y_1^-	Y_2^+	Y_2^-	Y_3^+	Y_3^-	4	=SUMPRODUCT(B4:J4,$B$15:$J$15)		
15		8.923	11.462	5	0	26046.154	0	0	0	0	5	=SUMPRODUCT(B5:J5,$B$15:$J$15)		
16											6	=SUMPRODUCT(B6:J6,$B$15:$J$15)		
17											7	=SUMPRODUCT(B7:J7,$B$15:$J$15)		
18											8	=SUMPRODUCT(B8:J8,$B$15:$J$15)		
19											9	=SUMPRODUCT(B9:J9,$B$15:$J$15)		
20											10	=SUMPRODUCT(B10:J10,$B$15:$J$15)		
21											11	=SUMPRODUCT(B11:J11,$B$15:$J$15)		
22											12	=SUMPRODUCT(B12:J12,$B$15:$J$15)		

FIGURE 11-17   Optimal solution for the Maui Miser Car Rentals goal programming problem

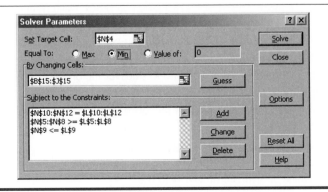

FIGURE 11-18
Solver Parameters dialog box for the Maui Miser Car Rentals problem

obtained by adding a new constraint in which X_V, X_C, and X_L are integers using $B$15:$D$15 as the designated field.) This solution involves fractional numbers of vehicles. Tanya next directed *QuickQuant* to solve the same problem as an integer program, obtaining the following results:

SOLUTION TO INTEGER PROGRAM

PROBLEM: Maui Miser Rental Cars

DETAILED RECORD OF LINEAR PROGRAMS
EVALUATED IN SOLVING INTEGER PROGRAM

Problem Number	Cost Lower Bound	Parent Problem	Branching Variable	Problem Status
1	26046.150			
2	28200.000	1	XV (< 8)	Integer
3	27511.110	1	XV (> 9)	
4	78257.140	3	XC (< 11)	
5	30800.000	3	XC (> 12)	Integer

SOLUTION TO INTEGER PROGRAM

Original Variable	Value	Status
XV	8.00000	Integer
XC	13.00000	Integer
XL	5.00000	Integer
Y1+	0.00000	Unrestricted
Y1-	28200.00000	Unrestricted
Y2+	0.00000	Unrestricted
Y2-	0.00000	Unrestricted
Y3+	0.00000	Unrestricted
Y3-	24.00000	Unrestricted

Objective Value: C = 28200.0000

USING JUDGMENT

Should a Requirement be a Goal or a Constraint?

In the Maui Miser example, two requirements expressed as constraints in the original linear (integer) program of Section 11-3 are now treated as goals. Each goal is in effect a "soft" constraint, the "violation" of which extracts some penalty instead of creating an infeasible problem. As the example shows, budget limitations need not be absolutes whenever actual amounts needed might be obtained by reducing expenditures elsewhere or by utilizing an existing line of credit. In those cases, right-hand sides for the original constraint can instead serve as the target for a goal, and the constraint itself can be eliminated.

Some absolutes are just that. Consider the labeling requirements for a food product. A meat packer cannot let the water content of the sausage exceed the minimum because it provides a good trade-off among competing goals to do so.

When a substitution of a "soft" goal for a "hard" constraint makes sense, it is still a matter of judgment which analytical framework to use.

Managerial Decision Revisited: Determining Production Quantities

Having learned of his uncle's multiple goals, Babe now wants to reconsider the problem of determining March production quantities.

The following goals are applicable to Swatville Sluggers:

Goal 1   Achieve a profit of at least $3,000.

Goal 2   Use no more than 4,000 minutes of lathe time in order to allow for preventive maintenance scheduling.

Goal 3   Use exactly 7,500 minutes of finishing time in order to level-out workforce scheduling.

Goal 4   Use no more than 7,000 inches of wood to stabilize long-run inventories.

Babe chooses to evaluate the problem using goal programming. On his own, Babe decides to assign weights to the various goals. He assigns zero weight (no penalty) to bettering the targets for Goals 1, 2, and 4.

He uses weights of .40 for Goal 1, .20 each for Goals 2 and 4, and .10 each for falling under or over the target for Goal 3.

Using standard notation, Babe's omnibus objective function is to

$$
\begin{aligned}
\text{Minimize} \quad C = \; & + 0X_{30} + 0X_{32} + 0X_{34} + 0X_{36} \\
& + 0X_{38} + 0X_{40} + 0Y_1^+ + .4Y_1^- \\
& + .2Y_2^+ + 0Y_2^- + .1Y_3^+ + .1Y_3^- \\
& + .2Y_4^+ + 0Y_4^-
\end{aligned}
$$

Subject to the goal deviation constraints:

Goal 1
$$
\begin{aligned}
& + 13.25X_{30} + 13.05X_{32} + 13.55X_{34} + 13.05X_{36} \\
& + 15.55X_{38} + 15.35X_{40} - 1Y_1^+ + 1Y_1^- \\
& + 0Y_2^+ + 0Y_2^- + 0Y_3^+ + 0Y_3^- \\
& + 0Y_4^+ + 0Y_4^- = 3000
\end{aligned}
$$

Goal 2
$$
\begin{aligned}
& + 10X_{30} + 10X_{32} + 11X_{34} + 11X_{36} \\
& + 12X_{38} + 12X_{40} + 0Y_1^+ + 0Y_1^- \\
& - 1Y_2^+ + 1Y_2^- + 0Y_3^+ + 0Y_3^- \\
& + 0Y_4^+ + 0Y_4^- = 4000
\end{aligned}
$$

Goal 3
$$
\begin{aligned}
& + 25X_{30} + 27X_{32} + 29X_{34} + 31X_{36} \\
& + 33X_{38} + 35X_{40} + 0Y_1^+ + 0Y_1^- \\
& + 0Y_2^+ + 0Y_2^- - 1Y_3^+ + 1Y_3^- \\
& + 0Y_4^+ + 0Y_4^- = 7500
\end{aligned}
$$

Goal 4
$$
\begin{aligned}
& + 30X_{30} + 32X_{32} + 34X_{34} + 36X_{36} \\
& + 38X_{38} + 40X_{40} + 0Y_1^+ + 0Y_1^- \\
& + 0Y_2^+ + 0Y_2^- + 0Y_3^+ + 0Y_3^- \\
& - 1Y_4^+ + 1Y_4^- = 7000
\end{aligned}
$$

and subject to the original constraints (see page 332). The non-negativity conditions apply.

The solution to this goal program is

VARIABLE	VALUE	VARIABLE	VALUE
X_{30}	71.68	Y_1^+	0.00
X_{32}	71.68	Y_1^-	0.00
X_{34}	0.00	Y_2^+	0.00
X_{36}	0.00	Y_2^-	1706.09
X_{38}	71.68	Y_3^+	0.00
X_{40}	0.00	Y_3^-	1406.81
		Y_4^+	168.46
		Y_4^-	0.00

Objective Value: $C = 174.3728$

The solution shows that it is possible to attain Goals 1 and 2 but not 3 and 4. Goal 1 (a profit of at least \$3,000) is achieved because $Y_1^+ = Y_1^- = 0$. Goal 2 (using no more than 4,000 minutes of lathe time) also is satisfied because $Y_2^- = 1,706.09$ indicates that only 2,293.91 minutes are used. Goal 3 (exactly 7,500 minutes of finishing time) is impossible because $Y_3^- = 1,406.81$. This means that only 6,093.19 minutes are used. Goal 4 (use no more than 7,000 inches of wood) is not met because $Y_4^+ = 168.46$ indicates that 7,168.46 board feet are used.

PROBLEMS

11-1 Consider the following integer program:

Maximize $P = 3X_1 + 4X_2$
Subject to $X_1 + 2X_2 \le 8$
                      $3X_1 + X_2 \le 10$

where X_1 and X_2 are nonnegative integers

(a) Ignoring the integer constraints, solve this problem graphically as a linear program.
(b) Identify all of the lattice points in your graph that lie inside the feasible solution region of the linear program.
(c) Find the most profitable lattice point and the optimal solution to the original integer program.

11-2 Solve the following integer program graphically:

Minimize $C = 6X_1 + 8X_2$
Subject to $6X_1 + 7X_2 \ge 84$
                      $2X_1 \qquad \ge 11$
                            $3X_2 \ge 14$

where X_1 and X_2 are nonnegative integers

11-3 Solve the following integer program graphically:

Maximize $P = 5X_1 + 7X_2$
Subject to $12X_1 + 7X_2 \le 84$
                      $5X_1 + 7X_2 \ge 35$
                            $2X_2 \le 7$

where X_1 and X_2 are nonnegative integers

11-4 Refer to Problem 8-12 (page 296). Assume that Ace Widgets must produce only whole items. Formulate the problem as an integer program and solve it graphically.

11-5 Apply the branch-and-bound method to solve the integer program in Problem 11-1. Do this by solving graphically a succession of linear programs. Summarize the procedure using a tree diagram.

11-6 Repeat Problem 11-5 using instead the integer program in Problem 11-2.

11-7 The solutions to several linear programs appearing in the table below have been obtained in the process of solving the following integer program:

Minimize $C = 5X_1 + 2X_2 + 3X_3$
Subject to $3X_1 - 2X_2 + 4X_3 \ge 8$
                      $3X_1 + 4X_2 - 2X_3 \ge 6$

where X_1, X_2, and X_3 are nonnegative integers

Problem	Latest Branching Variable	X_1	X_2	X_3	C	
1	none	$2\frac{2}{9}$	0	$\frac{1}{3}$	$12\frac{1}{9}$	
2	X_1	2	$\frac{1}{3}$	$\frac{2}{3}$	$12\frac{2}{3}$	
3	X_1	3	0	0	15	
4	X_2	—	—	—	—	(infeasible)
5	X_2	$1\frac{5}{9}$	1	$1\frac{1}{3}$	$13\frac{7}{9}$	
6	X_1	1	$1\frac{5}{6}$	$2\frac{1}{6}$	$15\frac{1}{6}$	
7	X_1	2	1	1	15	

Construct a tree diagram summarizing the problem solution. Indicate the optimal solution(s).

11-8 The solutions to several linear programs appearing in the table below have been obtained in the process of solving the following integer program:

$$\text{Maximize } P = 3X_A + 5X_B + 4X_C$$

$$\text{Subject to} \quad 2X_A + 3X_B + 3X_C \le 13$$

$$5X_A + 4X_B + 5X_C \le 17$$

where X_A, X_B, X_C are nonnegative integers

Construct a tree diagram summarizing the problem's solutions. Indicate the optimal solution(s).

Problem	Latest Branching Variable	X_A	X_B	X_C	P	
1	none	0	4.25	0	21.25	
2	X_B	0	4	.2	20.8	
3	X_B	—	—	—	—	(infeasible)
4	X_C	.2	4	0	20.61	
5	X_C	0	3	1	19	
6	X_A	0	4	0	20	
7	X_A	1	3	0	18	

11-9 Ace Widgets must determine how many regular and deluxe widgets to produce. Each regular widget requires 5 hours of labor, while 8 hours are needed to complete a deluxe widget; only 80 hours are available. Each unit requires exactly 1 frame, and there are just 12 frames available. The following information applies:

	Regular	Deluxe
Selling price	$30	$60
Unit cost	20	45
Unit profit	10	15

Find the optimal solution assuming that the objective is (a) to maximize profit and (b) to maximize sales revenue. (You may use graphical methods.)

11-10 Refer to the information given in Problem 11-9. The following goals must be met:

Goal 1	Sales revenue $\ge$ \$500
Goal 2	Production cost $\le$ \$400 budget
Goal 3	Profit $\ge$ \$140
Goal 4	At least as many regular widgets as deluxes must be made.

The cost of violating Goals 1–3 is \$1 per dollar, while there is a \$2 cost per unit violation of Goal 4.

(a) Formulate the decision as a goal program.
(b) Determine the value of each goal deviation variable under a production plan to make 4 regular and 7 deluxe widgets. What is the omnibus objective value under that plan?

Computer Problems

11-11 Solve the following integer program:

$$\text{Minimize} \quad C = 2X_1 + 3X_2 + 4X_3$$

$$\text{Subject to} \quad 2X_1 - 3X_2 + 3X_3 \ge 7$$

$$-3X_1 + 2X_2 + 4X_3 \ge 5$$

where X_1, X_2, and X_3 are nonnegative integers

11-12 Refer to Problem 10-17 (page 396). Determine the integer programming solution to the Piney Woods Furniture problem originally stated as a linear program.

11-13 Refer to the Real Reels advertising decision in Chapter 9 (page 322). Find the integer programming solution to this problem.

11-14 Refer to the microcircuit production decision of Chapter 9 (page 304). Find the integer programming solution to this problem.

11-15 Computer printouts from running integer programs do not list the variable solution values for intermediate problems. These may be found in

a separate computer run by solving the corresponding linear program.

Consider the expanded Redwood Furniture problem whose tree is summarized on page 417.

(a) Formulate and solve the linear program for Problem 23 of the tree.

(b) List the optimal values for the variables in Problem 23 of the tree.

11-16 Consider the decision in Problems 11-9 and 11-10. Solve the goal program.

11-17 Refer to Problem 9-16 (page •••). The following demographics apply to Blitz Beer's radio advertising linear program:

Station	Female Listeners	Male Listeners	High-Income Listeners	Low-Income Listeners
KBAT	50,000	75,000	40,000	85,000
WJOK	15,000	10,000	20,000	5,000
WROB	23,000	19,000	5,000	37,000
KPOW	175,000	200,000	250,000	125,000

These are averages. Each category has an exposure goal. Exposure is the sum of the products obtained by multiplying the number of listeners times the number of spots. The following goals apply:

Goal 1　Female exposure $\geq 1,000,000$

Goal 2　Male exposure $\leq 500,000$

Goal 3　High-income exposure $\geq 1,500,000$

Goal 4　Low-income exposure $\leq 500,000$

In achieving the goals, all of the original constraints in Problem 9-16 must be satisfied. Violations of the goals are equally serious, so that coefficients of 1 may be used on the applicable goal deviation variables in the omnibus objective function.

(a) Formulate this problem as a goal program.

(b) Find the optimal solution.

11-18 Consider the Real Reels advertising decision described in Chapter 9 (page 323). The following three goals must be met, in addition to the original constraints:

Goal 1　A minimum total exposure of 12 million buyers (penalty 5)

Goal 2　Total number of ads to be at least 15 (penalty 3)

Goal 3　Dollar expenditure in *Playboy* not to exceed $50,000 (penalty 2)

(a) Formulate Real Reels' goal program.

(b) Solve the goal program.

11-19 A mutual fund manager wants to determine the level of future purchases to be made in the categories that follow:

	Growth	Income	New Issues	Warrants
Expected appreciation	15%	10%	20%	15%
Loss exposure	20%	5%	30%	40%
Avg. holding time (yrs.)	2	1	.3	.1
Brokerage cost	1%	.5%	2%	5%

There is $1,000,000 to invest, and no more than half of the funds may be invested in any single category. The following goals must be met:

Goal 1　At least $140,000 in annualized price appreciation

Goal 2　Total potential loss exposure no greater than $200,000

Goal 3　Average portfolio holding time no greater than 1.5 years

Goal 4　Total brokerage cost not to exceed $15,000

These goals are listed in decreasing priority. The manager uses penalty points of 5, 3, 2, and 1 for violating the respective goals.

(a) Formulate this problem as a goal program.

(b) Find the optimal solution.

11-20 Consider the portfolio selection problem in Chapter 9 (pages 318–319). The following goals must be met, in addition to the original constraints.

Goal 1　A minimum return of $9,500 is desired (penalty 5)

Goal 2　The dollar investment in any particular bond should not be more than 20% of the total committed funds (six goals, each of penalty 1)

(a) Formulate the manager's goal program.

(b) Solve the goal program.

11-21 Consider the birdfeed-mix problem described in Chapter 8 (page 276). The following four goals must be met, in addition to the original constraints:

Goal 1   A maximum total cost of $1,500 is desired (penalty 5)

Goal 2   Sunflower seeds must be at least 8,000 pounds of the mixture bulk (penalty 3)

Goal 3   The protein level must be at least 1,300 (penalty 2)

Goal 4   The fat level must be at least 500 (penalty 1)

(a) Formulate the birdfeed-mix decision as a goal program.

(b) Solve the goal program.

11-22 Consider the final version of Yosemite Ann's Trail-Mix Delight formulation problem described in Chapter 9 (page 329). Suppose that Yosemite has appearance goals that dried currants and roasted walnuts each be at least 15% of the total ingredient weight (Goals 1 and 2). She furthermore wants dried milk and pumpkin kernels combined not to exceed 50% of the total weight (Goal 3). All of this is to be done so that total cost does not exceed $2 per kilogram (Goal 4). These goals are not absolute, although the original constraints still apply and must all be satisfied. Yosemite assigns equal penalty weights to falling on the wrong side of each goal target.

(a) Formulate Yosemite Ann's goal program.

(b) Solve the goal program.

CASE 11-1   *National Bank of Hayward I*

Hayward's first bank, the National Bank of Hayward, opened for business in 1883. Suppose that you are the manager of Operations Analysis and Control for the bank. Recently, you had lunch with Dr. W. D. Hayward, vice-president of Human Resources and a great-great grandson of founder William Hayward, who complained about the difficulties in hiring employees for one particular back office operation of the bank because of its variable workload. As the day goes on, the workload picks up rapidly, peaking during midday, and then decreasing until closing time. This contrasts with the resources available to do the work, which, normally, are relatively constant. Fridays and Saturdays are different from other days, and the first few days of the month are always more busy. Seeing this as a perfect situation in which linear programming could be used, you appeared politely interested and asked Dr. Hayward for more details.

Dr. Hayward is currently using part-time employees to smooth out the workload. This option is particularly attractive because they do not need any special training to perform the required work. In addition, they are not entitled to benefits. Dr. Hayward is constrained by a bank policy that only allows the use of 40% or fewer part-time workers.[1] The agency requires that they be guaranteed at least 4 hours of work per day. Furthermore, the bank also dictates that part-time workers cannot work more than 7 hours per day. As part-time workers, they are expected to eat a sandwich while on their regularly scheduled two 15-minute breaks because they are not allowed a lunch break.

Full-time employees work 8 hours, 1 hour of which is a lunch break so that productive time is only 7 hours (they also get two breaks). However, a complicating factor here is that the bank's policy requires that one half of the full-time workers take a lunch break from 11:00 A.M. to noon and the others between noon and 1:00 P.M. so that 50% of the full-time employees are on duty at all times during the middle of the day.

Another especially troublesome problem for Dr. Hayward is that the department in question works until 7:00 P.M. This means that some full-time employees must work overtime. However, the company policy is that such employees are not allowed to work more than 5 hours of overtime per week. The ostensible reason for this is that full-time employees work 35 hours a week (not counting the lunch hours, for which they are not paid) so that 5 hours of overtime gives a total of 40 hours per week. Thus, the pay for up to 5 hours of overtime is the normal rate and *not* time and a half (which would be applicable to hours in excess of 40 hours per week).

---

[1] Adapted from "An LP Model for Work Force Scheduling for Banks," by Shyam L. Moondra, *Journal of Bank Research*, Winter 1976.

TABLE 1 Work-Force Requirements

Time Period	Number of Personnel Required
9–10 A.M.	10
10–11	20
11–12 P.M.	25
12–1	35
1–2	50
2–3	55
3–4	55
4–5	32
5–6	15
6–7	11

TABLE 2 Friday Work-Force Requirements

Time Period	Number of Personnel Required
3–4 P.M.	60
4–5	40
5–6	40
6–7	20

The next day after the lunch, Dr. Hayward sent you the information he had gathered about how the workload varies during a typical weekday. It is presented in Table 1.

Through further discussions with Dr. Hayward, you find out that his goal is to meet the workload requirements in Table 1 at a minimum possible personnel cost, subject to all the bank's and agency's policies and requirements. From the bank's accounting department you learn that the average cost per full-time employee is $14 per hour including fringe benefits and $10 per hour excluding fringe benefits. This later figure, you are informed, is applicable to the first 5 hours of overtime for any employee. The bank pays $8 per hour to the agency for the part-time employees.

QUESTIONS

1. Formulate a linear program that will assist Dr. Hayward in resolving his employee scheduling and part-time hiring problems.

2. Solve the linear program formulated in Question 1. In addition, solve it using integer programming.

3. Suppose that the bank is considering eliminating the 5-hour-per-week limit on overtime because of the heavy workload. Would this have any effect on the solution? In addition, what if the union demands that all overtime be compensated at time and a half ($15 per hour)? How would this change your recommendations?

4. Suppose it is pointed out to you that the demand on Fridays does not taper off as indicated in Table 1, but usually increases to that shown in Table 2. How would this affect your answer?

5. Suppose that the bank is considering raising the 40% part-time limit up to 50% to permit more part-time workers. How would this change the solution? Suppose that part-time workers are not as efficient as full-time workers so the bank is considering decreasing the limit to 30%. How would this affect the solution?

6. Suppose that the temporary agency from which you hire the part-time workers has raised its rate to $9 per hour. How would this affect your recommendations to Dr. Hayward? Now, suppose the full-time employees are willing to forgo a wage increase for an increase in benefits so that the bank still covers all their medical care. This means that the cost of benefits goes from $4 to $5. How does this affect the solution? Is it more or less significant than the increase in wages that might be paid to the part-time employees?

7. As a result of a recent merger with another small bank, your branch is going to handle all the clients of the other branch, which is going to be closed, in addition to your own customers. How will you be able to meet the new increased demand, given by Table 3?

TABLE 3 Work-Force Requirements after the Merger

Time Period	Number of Personnel Required
9–10 A.M.	16
10–11	30
11–12 P.M.	36
12–1	44
1–2	70
2–3	82
3–4	80
4–5	46
5–6	22
6–7	22

8. Suppose the temporary agency indicates that the maximum number of part-time employees that they can furnish on any given day is 25. Describe how this might affect the original solution obtained.

9. What happens if more people want to have lunch at noon? To be more specific, what would be the effect of changing the bank's policy so that only 25% of the employees must have lunch at 11:00 A.M.? What about everyone having lunch at noon? Is that possible? Why? How would it change the solution? On the other hand, suppose the bank proposes to have one-third of the employees take their lunch between 11:00 A.M. and noon, with another one-third between noon and 1 P.M., with the rest between 1:00 P.M. and 2:00 P.M. How would this change the situation?

10. Finally, suppose that part-timers have been complaining that they need a lunch break if they work 6 hours or more; eating sandwiches during their breaks is not satisfactory. Consequently, the bank is thinking about limiting part-time workers to 5 hours or less so that the scheduling problem does not become more complicated by having to schedule lunch breaks for the part-time workers. What is the effect of this proposed management change?

CASE 11-2   *National Bank of Hayward II*

Dr. Hayward's immediate questions were answered from solving National Bank of Hayward I. However, he is troubled with conflicts that crop up whenever he attempts to meet several goals. He therefore thinks that the earlier analyses do an unsatisfactory job of balancing conflicting goals. You have been retained for a second consultation. You may use the data from the original case in answering the questions below.

Dr. Hayward has four goals being discussed by the bank.

1. Keep total labor cost at or below $4,000.

2. Keep part-time work below 50 hours per week.

3. Keep overtime premium at or below $100 per week.

4. Have an equal number of full- and part-time employees during peak hours.

He wishes to find out how the goals might affect a problem solution that just minimizes costs.

Dr. Hayward assigns a penalty of 1 point for every dollar exceeding the cost target, 2 points for each part-timer hour above the weekly target, 3 points for each overtime dollar exceeding the cost target, and 1 point for every hour that the part-timers and full-timers are out of balance.

QUESTIONS

Do the following for Questions 1–5 below.

(a) Formulate and solve the employee-scheduling and part-time hiring decision problem as a goal program, ignoring the integer conditions. Indicate whether or not the solution meets any goal exactly, and if not, give the amount of deviation. Determine total labor cost of the solution.

(b) Round the solution in (a) to a whole number of employees, and check to see if it is feasible.

(c) Solve the goal program in (a) with integer conditions for numbers of employees.

1. Evaluate with zero penalty points for all goals but Goal 1.

2. Evaluate with zero penalty points for all goals but Goal 2.

3. Evaluate with zero penalty points for all goals but Goal 3.

4. Evaluate with zero penalty points for all goals but Goal 4.

5. Evaluate with the original penalty points for all goals.

6. Based on the answers to Questions 1–5, what can you say about using rounded solutions?

7. Based on the answers to Questions 1–5, what are your conclusions about using integer programming as compared with linear programming and rounded linear programming solutions?

8. Compare the solutions to Questions 1–5 with the solution to National Bank of Hayward I. What are your conclusions about using goal programming instead of linear or integer programming for National Bank of Hayward?

CASE 11-3 Shale—Bituminous Processors II

Reconsider Case 9-2 (Shale—Bituminous Processors I) and find the solutions using integer programming. Compare the results with the solutions obtained using linear programming, and comment on what you find.

CASE 11-4 Martin Santa Barbara II

Reconsider Case 9-3 (Martin Santa Barbara I) and find the solutions using integer programming. Compare the results with the solutions obtained using linear programming, and comment on what you find.

CASE 11-5 Operation Desert Shield II

Reconsider Case 10-2 (Operation Desert Shield I) and find the solutions using integer programming. Compare the results with the solutions obtained using linear programming, and comment on what you find.

PART IV

DISTRIBUTION, ROUTING, AND SCHEDULING

Perhaps the greatest impact of quantitative methods has been in distribution, where they result in billions of dollars saved every year.

This segment presents models and algorithms for solving problems from a wide class encompassing scheduling, routing, and distribution. Although most of these problems could be solved using linear programming methodology, they also can be evaluated by efficient special-purpose algorithms exploiting their structural idiosyncrasies.

Chapter 12 describes one of these procedures, the transportation method, used for scheduling shipments through a distribution system. That same algorithm provides optimal assignments of persons to jobs. Another set of procedures solves problems expressed as network models. Chapter 13 describes four applications structurally represented by graphs constructed using nodes and arcs. These include finding the shortest routes, identifying a critical set of arcs called a tree, and determining arc values that maximize the flow in and out of key nodes. Each problem type is solved by its own set of rules. Chapter 14 deals with project scheduling. It discusses the PERT procedure for managing projects efficiently within time and budget constraints.

CHAPTER 12

TRANSPORTATION AND ASSIGNMENT PROBLEMS

By trial and error, it is easy to find the best assignment of 3 people to 3 jobs, because there are only 6 ways to get the work done. But the number of cases grows to 120 for 5 persons, 720 for 6 persons, and 3,628,800 for 10 persons. With 20 people and jobs, a superfast computer making a billion evaluations per second would need over 700 years to singly enumerate all possibilities. But that same computer could use linear programming software to solve the 20-person problem in a fraction of a second.

One of the most important and successful applications of quantitative analysis in solving business problems has been in the area of the physical distribution of products. Great cost savings have been achieved by the more efficient routing of freight from supply points to required destinations. In this chapter, we will consider the **transportation problem,** which serves as the framework for analyzing such decisions. The purpose of the transportation problem is to minimize the total cost of shipping goods from plants to warehouse distribution centers in such a way that the needs of each warehouse are met and every factory operates within its capacity.

Ordinarily, it is convenient to express such a problem mathematically in terms of a linear program. The transportation problem can be solved like any linear program, but the special structure of the transportation problem permits us to solve it by using a faster, more streamlined algorithm. In studying the transportation problem, we will therefore gain a new insight into quantitative analysis: *The judicious choice of the solution procedure itself can result in savings of both time and money.* This chapter illustrates another way to "skin a cat" that is better for certain kinds of cats.

Another important managerial decision is personnel assignment. People vary so widely in their skill and competence levels that it is challenging to determine which workers are best suited to perform specific jobs. A classical application of the **assignment problem** is provided by a small machine shop, where individual machinists are assigned to particular machines or jobs. This must be done so that every worker is assigned to exactly one job and every job is assigned to a worker. The assignments must minimize the combined time or cost for completing all of the required jobs.

As we saw in Chapter 9, the linear programming approach is well suited to machine shop personnel assignments because each task is well defined and the respective productivities (time required per item) of each worker can be accurately measured. Moreover, machine shop jobs require similar skills, so that workers can easily be shifted to new assignments.

Scheduling Shipments

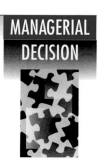

Thread-Bare, Ltd., is a Hong Kong–based firm that distributes textiles worldwide. The company is owned by the Lao family. Present plans are to remain in Hong Kong because the People's Republic of China has continued its economic renaissance. The company hopes to use its current base to expand operations to the mainland. Thread-Bare has mills in the Bahamas, Hong Kong, Korea, Nigeria, and Venezuela, each weaving fabrics out of two or more raw fibers: cotton, polyester, and/or silk. The mills service eight company distribution centers located near the customers' geographical centers of activity.

Because transportation costs historically have been less than 10% of total expenses, management has paid little attention to extracting savings through judicious routing of shipments. Ching Lao is returning from the United States, where he has just completed his bachelor's degree in marketing. He believes that each year he can save Thread-Bare hundreds of thousands of dollars—perhaps millions—just by better routing of fabrics from mills to distribution centers. One glaring example of poor routing is the current assignment of fabric output to the Mexico City distribution center from Nigeria instead of from Venezuela, less than a third the distance. Similarly, the Manila center now gets most of its textiles from Nigeria and Venezuela, although the mills in Hong Kong itself are much closer.

Of course, the cost of shipping a bolt of cloth does not depend on distance alone. The table below provides the actual costs supplied to Mr. Lao from company head-

	DISTRIBUTION CENTERS							
MILLS	**Los Angeles**	**Chicago**	**London**	**Mexico City**	**Manila**	**Rome**	**Tokyo**	**New York**
Bahamas	2.00	2.00	3.00	3.00	7.00	4.00	7.00	1.00
Hong Kong	6.00	7.00	8.00	10.00	2.00	9.00	4.00	8.00
Korea	5.00	6.00	8.00	11.00	4.00	9.00	1.00	7.00
Nigeria	14.00	12.00	6.00	9.00	11.00	7.00	5.00	10.00
Venezuela	4.00	3.00	5.00	1.00	9.00	6.00	11.00	4.00

quarters. Distribution center demands are seasonal, so a new shipment plan must be made each month. The next table below provides the fabric requirements for the month

	FABRIC DEMAND (BOLTS)							
TYPE	**Los Angeles**	**Chicago**	**London**	**Mexico City**	**Manila**	**Rome**	**Tokyo**	**New York**
Cotton	500	800	900	900	800	100	200	700
Polyester	1,000	2,000	3,000	1,500	400	700	900	2,500
Silk	100	100	200	50	400	200	700	200

of March. Thread-Bare's mills have varying capacities for producing the various types of cloth. The last table provides the quantities that apply during March.

MILLS	PRODUCTION CAPACITY (BOLTS)		
	Cotton	Polyester	Silk
Bahamas	1,000	3,000	0
Hong Kong	2,000	2,500	1,000
Korea	1,000	3,500	500
Nigeria	2,000	0	0
Venezuela	1,000	2,000	0

Mr. Lao wants to schedule production and shipments in such a way that the most costly customers are shorted when there is insufficient capacity and the least efficient plants operate at less than full capacity when demand falls below maximum production capacity.

12-1 A SKI SHIPMENT SCHEDULING ILLUSTRATION

In this section, we will return to the shipment-scheduling application concerning the operation of the sporting goods company first discussed in Chapter 9. To review, the company makes skis in three plants throughout the world. The plants supply four company-owned warehouses that distribute the skis directly to ski shops. Depending on which mode is cheaper, the product is air-freighted or trucked from plants to the warehouses. Table 12-1 provides the various point-to-point costs of shipping a pair of skis. The problem is to find how many pairs of skis should be shipped from each plant to the various warehouses to minimize total cost. This is accomplished by determining the quantities for the shipment schedule shown in Figure 12-1, where X_{ij} represents the quantity shipped from plant i to warehouse j.

In Chapter 9, we formulated this problem as

$$\text{Minimize} \quad C = 19X_{JF} + 7X_{JN} + 3X_{JP} + 21X_{JY}$$
$$+ 15X_{SF} + 21X_{SN} + 18X_{SP} + 6X_{SY}$$
$$+ 11X_{TF} + 14X_{TN} + 15X_{TP} + 22X_{TY}$$

Subject to
$$X_{JF} + X_{JN} + X_{JP} + X_{JY} = 100 \quad \text{(Juarez capacity)}$$
$$X_{SF} + X_{SN} + X_{SP} + X_{SY} = 300 \quad \text{(Seoul capacity)}$$
$$X_{TF} + X_{TN} + X_{TP} + X_{TY} = 200 \quad \text{(Tel Aviv capacity)}$$
$$X_{JF} + X_{SF} + X_{TF} = 150 \quad \text{(Frankfurt demand)}$$
$$X_{JN} + X_{SN} + X_{TN} = 100 \quad \text{(New York demand)}$$
$$X_{JP} + X_{SP} + X_{TP} = 200 \quad \text{(Phoenix demand)}$$
$$X_{JY} + X_{SY} + X_{TY} = 150 \quad \text{(Yokohama demand)}$$

where
$$\text{all } X\text{'s} \geq 0$$

TABLE 12-1 The Shipping Costs per Pair of Skis

FROM PLANT	TO WAREHOUSE			
	Frankfurt	New York	Phoenix	Yokohama
Juarez	$19	$ 7	$ 3	$21
Seoul	15	21	18	6
Tel Aviv	11	14	15	22

FROM PLANT	TO WAREHOUSE				Plant Capacity
	F	N	P	Y	
J	X_{JF}	X_{JN}	X_{JP}	X_{JY}	100
S	X_{SF}	X_{SN}	X_{SP}	X_{SY}	300
T	X_{TF}	X_{TN}	X_{TP}	X_{TY}	200
Warehouse Demand	150	100	200	150	600

FIGURE 12-1
The shipment schedule for skis

Special Requirements of Transportation Problems

The number of constraints is dictated by the number of plants (or rows in the shipment schedule) and the number of warehouses (or columns in the shipment schedule). Every transportation problem must have exactly the following number of equality constraints:

Number of constraints = Number of rows + Number of columns

As we can see in Figure 12-1, each X is represented exactly once in the capacity constraints and exactly once in the demand constraints. This can happen if and only if the total quantity shipped is exactly equal to the total quantity received: *Total plant capacity must equal total warehouse demand.* In our example, the capacities sum to 600, which is also the sum of the demands.

$$600 = 100 + 300 + 200 = 150 + 100 + 200 + 150$$

Later, we will see that this fact plays an important role in solving a transportation problem.

You may wonder why each plant must produce exactly at its capacity and each warehouse must receive precisely its demand. Isn't that unrealistic? These requirements are needed to solve the problem by the most efficient means. Of course they are unrealistic, but we will see that it will always be possible to formulate any transportation problem in this manner, even when true demands and capacities are not in balance.

Solving Transportation Problems

Optimal shipping schedules for transportation problems may be obtained in a variety of ways. One of the more efficient procedures involves the **transportation method,** described next. Although a transportation problem may be optimized using the same simplex procedures for solving any general linear program, the special-purpose transportation method is more streamlined.

Although large transportation problems will be solved with computer assistance, it is very instructive to solve a few smaller problems by hand. That is helpful not only for understanding how to set up transportation problems but also in removing some of the mystery regarding exactly what the computer is doing as it so quickly finds the answer. The transportation method is a great algorithm for "getting your hands dirty," be-

cause its calculations involve only simple addition and subtraction that can be done in your head without a calculator.

12-2 GETTING STARTED: THE NORTHWEST CORNER METHOD

We solve the transportation problem in iterations proceeding from solution to solution much like we do in simplex. We begin with an initial solution that satisfies all constraints. A convenient starting point is to apply the **northwest corner method.** We begin with a blank shipment schedule, shown in Figure 12-2. Each plant-warehouse route is represented by a cell. For convenience, the unit shipping costs are placed in the upper-right-hand corner of each cell. The central portion of the cell is reserved for the quantity to be shipped.

The northwest corner method begins in the cell in the upper-left-hand corner of the schedule. (On a map, this would be called the "northwest corner.") In this cell, we place the largest possible quantity that satisfies the capacity and demand constraints. This means that we look in the row and column margins of Figure 12-2 for the smallest demand or capacity applicable and write this number in the northwest corner cell. Further cell allocations are made by moving down or to the right in the direction of leftover demand or capacity and inserting the maximum feasible quantity at each step. We stop when the southeast corner has been allocated. The cell-to-cell movement in this procedure is analogous to the movement of chess pieces. Only horizontal and vertical movements, like those of the "rook," are allowed; no diagonal "bishop" moves are permitted.

The northwest corner solution for the ski distribution problem is provided in Figure 12-3. Our beginning corner receives an allocation of 100 pairs to be shipped from Juarez to Frankfurt. This is the largest possible number of pairs of skis that can be shipped over that route, because Juarez's capacity is 100 pairs; Frankfurt must receive 150 pairs, but we cannot ship more skis from Juarez than it can make. This leaves an unfilled demand of $150 - 100 = 50$ pairs for Frankfurt, so our next cell for skis

---

FIGURE 12-2
A blank shipment schedule

To From	F	N	P	Y	Capacity
J	19	7	3	21	100
S	15	21	18	6	300
T	11	14	15	22	200
Demand	150	100	200	150	600

From \ To	F	N	P	Y	Capacity
J	[19] (100)	[7]	[3]	[21]	100
S	[15] (50)	[21] (100)	[18] (150)	[6]	300
T	[11]	[14]	[15] (50)	[22] (150)	200
Demand	150	100	200	150	600

FIGURE 12-3
The shipment schedule for the ski-distribution problem found by the northwest corner method

shipped from Seoul to Frankfurt lies directly below. The largest possible allocation to that cell is 50 pairs, because the gap in Frankfurt's demand is exhausted before this warehouse takes up Seoul's capacity. This leaves us with an unused capacity for Seoul in the amount of 300 − 50 = 250 pairs. We therefore move to the cell at the right, where we must allocate a shipment from Seoul to New York. There, we fill New York's total demand of 100, leaving 300 − 50 − 100 = 150 pairs under capacity at Seoul. We move to the right again, where we allocate 150 pairs from Seoul to Phoenix. This does not exhaust that warehouse's demand, leaving 200 − 150 = 50 pairs short at Phoenix. Moving down, we pick up 50 pairs from Tel Aviv to take care of Phoenix, and then move to the right, where we allocate the rest of Tel Aviv's capacity as a 150-pair shipment to Yokohama. At this point, all constraints are satisfied.

The solution in Figure 12-3 serves as the starting feasible solution. The cell entries are the values of the corresponding problem variables; empty cells correspond to zero quantities. The total cost of this shipment schedule is computed to be $C = 11{,}500$ dollars.

QUANTITY	UNIT COST	ROUTE COST
$X_{JF} = 100$	$C_{JF} = 19$	$19 \times 100 = 1{,}900$
$X_{SF} = 50$	$C_{SF} = 15$	$15 \times 50 = 750$
$X_{SN} = 100$	$C_{SN} = 21$	$21 \times 100 = 2{,}100$
$X_{SP} = 150$	$C_{SP} = 18$	$18 \times 150 = 2{,}700$
$X_{TP} = 50$	$C_{TP} = 15$	$15 \times 50 = 750$
$X_{TY} = 150$	$C_{TY} = 22$	$22 \times 150 = 3{,}300$
		$C = 11{,}500$

In applying the northwest corner method, there sometimes will be no remaining capacity or unfilled demand before the process is complete. In those cases, a circled ⓪ must be placed in the cell directly to the right (or below) the newest quantity before proceeding. That cell is treated as nonempty and guarantees a start having the proper

number of nonempty cells. (More will be said later about the required number of nonempty cells.)

SOLVING THE PROBLEM: THE TRANSPORTATION METHOD

We have just begun to solve this transportation problem. Our next task is to search for improvements. We could try the trial-and-error approach, reallocating cell values until it becomes hard to find improvements. Not only would this procedure be inefficient, but there is no guarantee that the optimal solution would be found. We would probably give up in frustration, not knowing if more improvements were possible. Instead, we will take a systematic approach to the problem.

The northwest corner method only provides us with a *starting* solution. We will try to improve that solution by means of a pivot procedure in which the *status* of the cells is exchanged: A currently nonempty cell becomes empty, and a presently empty cell receives a quantity allocation. The new nonempty cell is referred to as the **entering cell,** and the cell it replaces is called the **exiting cell.** Such an exchange will result in a cheaper shipment schedule. We continue this procedure until we reach a set of quantities that cannot be improved. This is the optimal solution.

Finding the Entering Cell: Row and Column Numbers

The entering cell is found through economic analysis. In the transportation problem, we evaluate every empty cell by determining the per-unit cost improvement associated with allocating one unit to that cell. Our procedure for doing this may seem roundabout at first, but it is really quite efficient.

We begin by assigning special values to each row and column of the current shipment schedule. The unit shipping cost for a cell is denoted by c_{ij}. The **row numbers** are represented by r_i, and the **column numbers** are represented by k_j. These values are calculated so that the following relationship holds:

> **For nonempty cells:** $c_{ij} = r_i + k_j$
> (Cost = row number + column number)

We begin by assigning zero as the row number for the first row. The pattern of the non-empty cells and their unit costs can then dictate the values of the remaining row and column numbers. These are found algebraically by solving a sequence of equations, each with one unknown.

Returning to our ski-distribution example, consider the present solution shown in Figure 12-4. The row and column numbers appear outside the shipment schedule in the respective margins. The circled letters indicate the *sequence* in which these values were obtained. The proper sequence is extremely important when computing the r and k values. A general rule in finding the row and column numbers is to work from the last number found, proceeding through a nonempty cell in its row or column and solving for the missing opposite value. Then move to the row or column of that new value and repeat the procedure. Always use the newest r value to obtain the next k value, and vice versa. Continue this zigzagging process until there are no new nonempty cells needing a number. Occasionally, there will be more than one nonempty cell to choose from in making the next assignment. Break the tie by picking just one of them arbitrarily. Mark

FIGURE 12-4
Row and column numbers for the initial solution to the ski-distribution problem

From \ To	F	N	P	Y	Capacity	
J	[19] (100)	[7]	[3]	[21]	100	$r_J = 0$ (a)
S	[15] (50)	[21] (100) *	[18] (150)	[6]	300	$r_S = -4$ (c)
T	[11]	[14]	[15] (50)	[22] (150)	200	$r_T = -7$ (e)
Demand	150	100	200	150	600	
	$k_F = 19$ (b)	$k_N = 25$ (g)	$k_P = 22$ (d)	$k_Y = 29$ (f)	* skipped cell	

the skipped cells and return to them (in any order) after exhausting the chain of r and k assignments made by working from that cell where you broke the original tie.

The following detailed explanation tells how the row and column numbers were obtained for the ski-distribution example:

ⓐ We begin with the first row. It always receives a zero row number. Thus, $r_J = 0$.

ⓑ Looking at row J, we see that there is one nonempty cell, JF, that does not yet have a column number. For this cell

$$c_{JF} = r_J + k_F$$

must hold. We know that $c_{JF} = 19$, and we have just found $r_J = 0$. Plugging these numbers into this equation, we obtain

$$19 = 0 + k_F$$

and we find that $k_F = 19$.

ⓒ There are no other nonempty cells in row J. We now look in column F for any nonempty cell that does not have a row number. SF does not. We know that

$$c_{SF} = r_S + k_F$$

Plugging $c_{SF} = 15$ and $k_F = 19$ into this equation gives us

$$15 = r_S + 19$$

which yields

$$r_S = 15 - 19 = -4$$

ⓓ There are no other nonempty cells in column F. We then search row S, where we see that both cell SN and cell SP do not yet have a column number. Cell SN is skipped and marked (*) for a later return. Working through cell SP, we plug $c_{SP} = 18$ and $r_S = -4$ into

$$c_{SP} = r_S + k_P$$

which yields

$$18 = -4 + k_P$$

so that $k_P = 18 - (-4) = 22$.

(e) We can see that column P contains nonempty cell TP, which has no row number. Plugging $c_{TP} = 15$ and $k_P = 22$ into

$$c_{TP} = r_T + k_P$$

we obtain

$$15 = r_T + 22$$

so that $r_T = 15 - 22 = -7$.

(f) One more nonempty cell, TY, remains in row T without a column number. Substituting $c_{TY} = 22$ and $r_T = -7$ into

$$c_{TY} = r_T + k_Y$$

gives us

$$22 = -7 + k_Y$$

and $k_Y = 22 - (-7) = 29$.

(g) Now only column N needs a number. Returning to cell SN, skipped earlier, we substitute $r_S = -4$ and $c_{SN} = 21$ into

$$c_{SN} = r_S + k_N$$

getting

$$21 = -4 + k_N$$

so that $k_N = 21 - (-4) = 25$.

All rows and columns now have their numbers.

With practice, you can make these computations very rapidly in your head without having to use scratch paper.

The r and k values obtained in this way are now used in conjunction with the present shipment schedule to find the entering cell. To do this, we calculate *for the empty cells only* the

Improvement difference: $c_{ij} - r_i - k_j$

This difference indicates the per-unit cost improvement that can be achieved by raising the shipment allocation in the corresponding cell from its present level of zero. *The empty cell with the greatest absolute negative improvement difference is the entering cell.*

Figure 12-5 shows how the entering cell is found for our example. There, the differences have been entered in the lower-left-hand corners of each empty cell. For example, the improvement difference in cell JN is

$$c_{JN} - r_J - k_N = 7 - 0 - 25 = -18$$

This tells us that raising the quantity allocated to that cell will reduce costs by $18 per pair of skis. The other differences are calculated in the same way.

We can see that cells JP and SY in Figure 12-5 are tied for the greatest cost improvement at $19 per pair. We will break this tie arbitrarily and choose JP as the entering cell. Our next step is to determine just how much we can allocate to the cell.

FIGURE 12-5
Improvement values and the closed-loop path for the initial solution to the transportation problem

To From	F	N	P	Y	Capacity	
J	19 (100) (−)	7 −18	3 −19	21 (+) −8	100	$r_J = 0$
S	15 (50) (+)	21 (100)	18 (150) (−)	6 −19	300	$r_S = -4$
T	11	14	15 (50)	22 (150)	200	$r_T = -7$
	−1	−4				
Demand	150	100	200	150	600	
	$k_F = 19$	$k_N = 25$	$k_P = 22$	$k_Y = 29$		

Finding the New Solution: The Closed-Loop Path

We begin by placing a (+) in cell *JP* to indicate that its allocation (the shipment from Juarez to Phoenix) will be increased from zero quantity. Whatever change we make must be *balanced,* so that the new quantities in row *J* and column *P* sum to the respective capacity of 100 for Juarez and demand of 200 for Phoenix. Thus, we must reduce cell *JF* by the amount of the change. We place a (−) there to reflect this reduction. But if we reduce cell *JF,* we must make a compensating change in column *F.* Our rule is that *there can be only one increasing and one decreasing cell in any row or column. Except for the entering cell, all changes must involve nonempty cells.* Thus, we place a (+) in cell *SF,* because it is the only nonempty cell in column *F.* This leaves us in row *S,* where a compensating (−) change must be made. We can readily see that cell *SN* must be skipped because it is the only nonempty cell in its column, so we place the (−) in cell *SP.* All of our changes now balance.

Connecting the (+) and (−) signs with line segments, we can see that they provide a **closed-loop path.** This path highlights the changes involved in reallocating the shipments. *For any entering cell, the closed-loop path is unique.* Its corners are alternating (+) and (−) cells, and only the entering cell is empty. *Only the corner cells on the path will be changed.* (Those cells that a line segment passes through are not involved.) We can find the closed-loop path by proceeding either clockwise or counterclockwise and starting up, down, right, or left (but never moving diagonally). We proceed, turning at each new (+) or (−), until our path closes. If we reach an impasse, ending up in a cell where we cannot turn (because all other cells in its column or row are empty), then we backtrack to the last turning point and go the other way or move forward to another nonempty cell in the same row or column.

The closed-loop path verifies that we will indeed save $19 by increasing the quantity allocated to cell *JP.* Tracing its trajectory counterclockwise, we have

Change:	(+)	(−)	(+)	(−)
Cell:	*JP*	*JF*	*SF*	*SP*

Each unit shifted along this path will produce a cost increase in the $(+)$ cells and a cost reduction in the $(-)$ cells, so that the net unit cost change is

$$3 - 19 + 15 - 18 = -19$$

The fact that we obtain -19 by using the r and k values is not coincidental. (The $c_{ij} - r_i - k_j$ differences are analogous to the entries in the per-unit improvement row of a simplex tableau.)

We must now make our change in the shipment schedule. The shift in quantities will occur only in the cells at the corners of the closed-loop path. *The amount shifted each time is equal to the smallest quantity in the losing cells.* The smallest $(-)$ quantity is selected because all affected cells will change by plus or minus the same amount, and the resulting quantities cannot be negative. The smallest losing-cell shipment quantity occurs in cell *JF*, where 100 pairs can be taken away. The following changes are made:

CELL ON CLOSED-LOOP PATH	PRESENT QUANTITY	CHANGE	NEW QUANTITY
JP	(empty)	+100	100
JF	100	-100	(empty)
SF	50	+100	150
SP	150	-100	50

Because cell *JF* becomes empty, it is the *exiting cell.*

Figure 12-6 shows the new shipment schedule that results from the new allocations. The total cost savings is

$$100 \times 19 = 1,900 \text{ dollars}$$

so that the total route cost is now $C = 11,500 - 1,900 = 9,600$ dollars.

Our example involves rectangular closed-loop paths. But *closed-loop paths may assume unusual shapes,* such as *L*'s, figure-8's, and even loops inside loops.

FIGURE 12-6
The second solution to the transportation problem

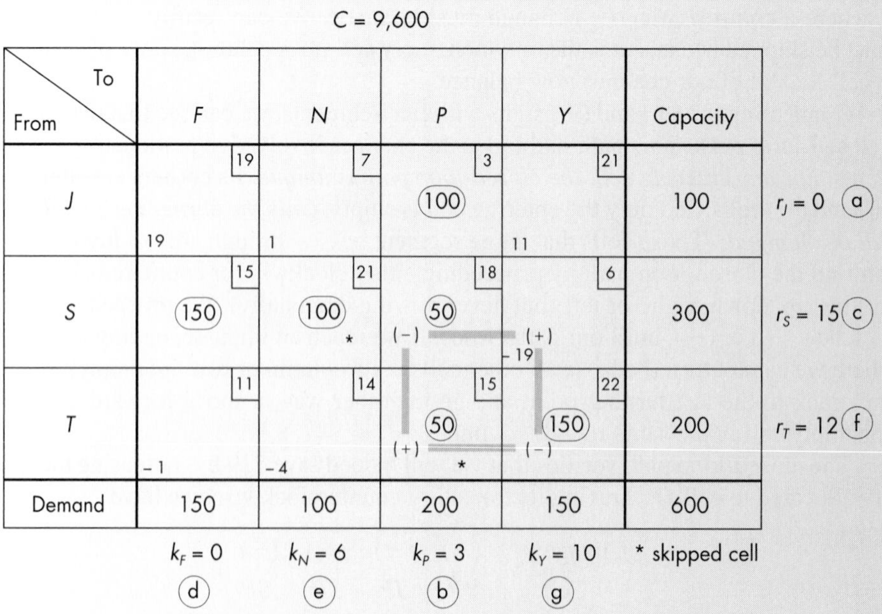

Further Iterations to Find the Optimal Solution

Now we begin again, using the new row and column numbers. Notice that except for $r_J = 0$, all of the r and k values in Figure 12-6 are different from before. This is because the set of nonempty cells has changed. The sequence in which these numbers are obtained is different as well. There are no shortcuts; the r and k values must be recomputed from scratch for each new shipment schedule. Next, we find the differences for the empty cells. We can see that cell SY is the entering cell, where costs are reduced by $19 per unit (coincidentally, the same amount as before). The closed-loop path is indicated in Figure 12-6, and the smallest quantity in the losing cells is 50 pairs.

Figure 12-7 provides the next shipment schedule, where total cost has been reduced by $19 \times 50 = 950$ dollars to $C = 9,600 - 950 = 8,650$ dollars. Recomputing the row and column numbers and the empty-cell differences, we find that cell TN is the entering cell. Increasing its allocation will save $23 per unit.

The smallest quantity in the losing cells is 100 pairs, which happens to be the same for cells SN and TY. Whenever there is a tie for the exiting cell, more than one cell will be reduced to zero. This presents a problem we have not encountered previously. Before we proceed, a few more observations must be made.

The Required Number of Nonempty Cells

In our illustration, there have always been exactly six nonempty cells. All of the successive changes made in the shipment schedules guarantee this. This number is one less than the number of rows and columns. In general,

Number of nonempty cells = Number of rows + Number of columns − 1

Every transportation problem has as many constraints as there are rows and columns in the shipment schedule. But together these constraints are redundant, because when the constraints are combined with the underlying condition that total capacity must be equal to total demand, any one constraint can be eliminated without affecting

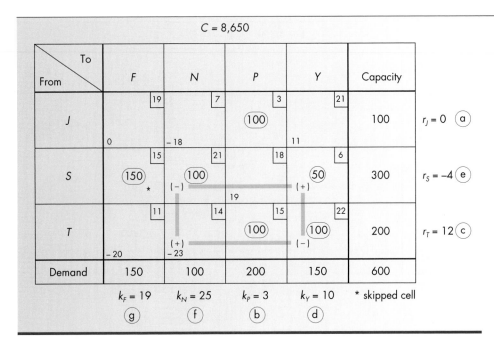

FIGURE 12-7
The third solution to the transportation problem

the problem solution. Our illustration involves three plant-capacity requirements (rows) and four warehouse-demand limitations (columns), or seven constraints in all. But both total capacity and demand must equal 600. If we left out the Yokohama demand constraint, for example, the other six constraints combined with this condition would still ensure that the Yokohama warehouse received its required 150 pairs of skis. Only six constraints are nonredundant. This is why the number of nonempty cells is one less than the number of rows and columns in the shipment schedule.

If there were fewer than the necessary number of nonempty cells, it would be impossible to obtain a unique set of row and column numbers and, in some cases, to form closed-loop paths. (Too many nonempty cells cause similar problems.) This does not mean that our example cannot have a solution with only five non-zero cells, but it does mean that a total of six cells must be treated as nonempty.

Ties for the Exiting Cell

Whenever there is a tie for the exiting cell, both cells will lose all of their allocation and be reduced to 0. To meet the required number of nonempty cells, exactly one of these tying cells must thereafter be treated as nonempty. Referring to Figure 12-7, we can see that both cell SN and cell TY will be reduced to 0 by reallocating 100 units along the closed-loop path. Either cell SN or cell TY must, however, continue to be treated as if it were nonempty. It does not matter which cell we choose, because ties can almost always be broken arbitrarily in linear programming.

Figure 12-8 provides the new shipment schedule. The cost savings are $23 \times 100 = 2,300$ dollars, and the new total cost is $C = 8,650 - 2,300 = 6,350$ dollars. We place a circled zero in cell TY and treat it as nonempty, even though the shipping quantity is 0.

We can see that increasing the allocation into cell TF will save \$20 per unit. However, one of the losing cells is TY, which involves a zero quantity. Shifting 0 around the closed-loop path gives us the new schedule in Figure 12-9. The total cost for this schedule is exactly the same as before, but the zero shipping quantity now appears in cell TF. No quantities changed, but the new pattern for the nonempty cells is an improvement.

FIGURE 12-8
The fourth solution to the transportation problem

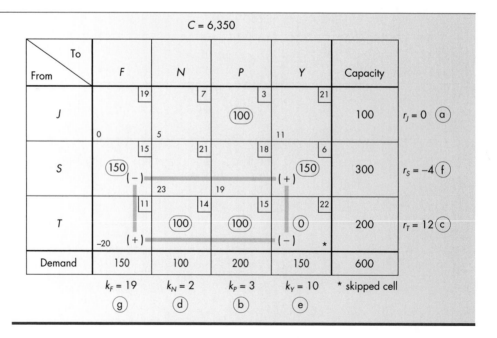

C = 6,350

From \ To	F	N	P	Y	Capacity	
J	19	7	3 (100)	21	100	$r_J = 0$ (a)
	20	5		31		
S	15 (150) (−)	21	18 (+)	6 (150)	300	$r_S = 16$ (e)
		3	−1			
T	11 (0) (+)	14 (100)	15 (100) (−)	22	200	$r_T = 12$ (c)
			*	20		
Demand	150	100	200	150	600	

$k_F = -1$ (d) $k_N = 2$ (g) $k_P = 3$ (b) $k_Y = -10$ (f) * skipped cell

FIGURE 12-9
The fifth solution to the transportation problem

Determining the Optimal Solution

Cell *SP* in Figure 12-9 provides a $1 cost improvement. The smallest quantity in the losing cells is 100 pairs in cell *TP*. Reallocating this amount along the closed-loop path, we obtain the new shipment schedule in Figure 12-10, where the cost saving is $1 \times 100 = 100$ and $C = 6{,}350 - 100 = 6{,}250$ dollars.

The schedule in Figure 12-10 is optimal. No empty cells yield potential cost reductions, so that *further improvements are impossible.*

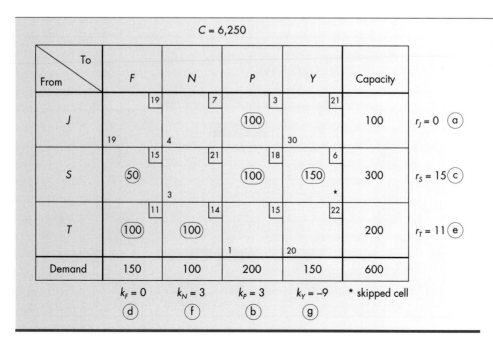

C = 6,250

From \ To	F	N	P	Y	Capacity	
J	19	7	3 (100)	21	100	$r_J = 0$ (a)
	19	4		30		
S	15 (50)	21	18 (100)	6 (150)	300	$r_S = 15$ (c)
		3		*		
T	11 (100)	14 (100)	15	22	200	$r_T = 11$ (e)
			1	20		
Demand	150	100	200	150	600	

$k_F = 0$ (d) $k_N = 3$ (f) $k_P = 3$ (b) $k_Y = -9$ (g) * skipped cell

FIGURE 12-10
The optimal solution to the transportation problem

12-4 COMPUTER SOLUTION TO TRANSPORTATION PROBLEMS

The transportation method is a procedure well suited to computer solution. It is not uncommon for a distribution problem to involve hundreds, even thousands, of sources and destinations. Such problems obviously cannot be solved by hand; even problems as small as 10-by-10 would be difficult to solve by hand.

Solving Transportation Problems with *QuickQuant*

The *QuickQuant* 2000 software package available to users of this book has a segment for solving transportation problems. The program is user friendly, with screen-prompt questions guiding all necessary choices and inputs. The program allows you to go back and fix your selections before it continues into the next phase.

We illustrate using *QuickQuant* 2000 to solve the ski-distribution problem. The data are entered into two windows. First is the parameters window in Figure 12-11.

FIGURE 12-11

QuickQuant Problem Parameters dialog box for the ski-distribution transportation problem

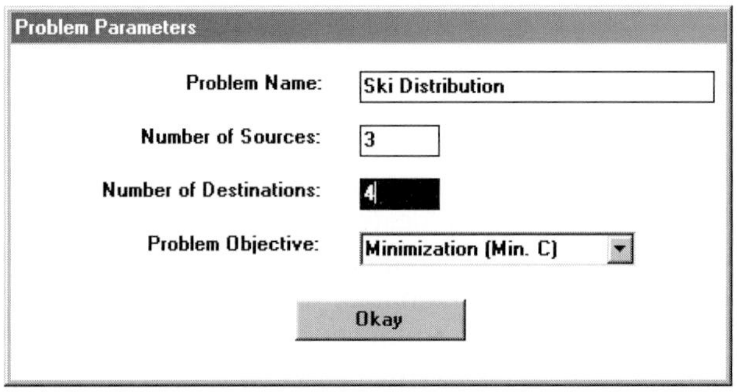

FIGURE 12-12

QuickQuant transportation problem data entry screen for ski distribution

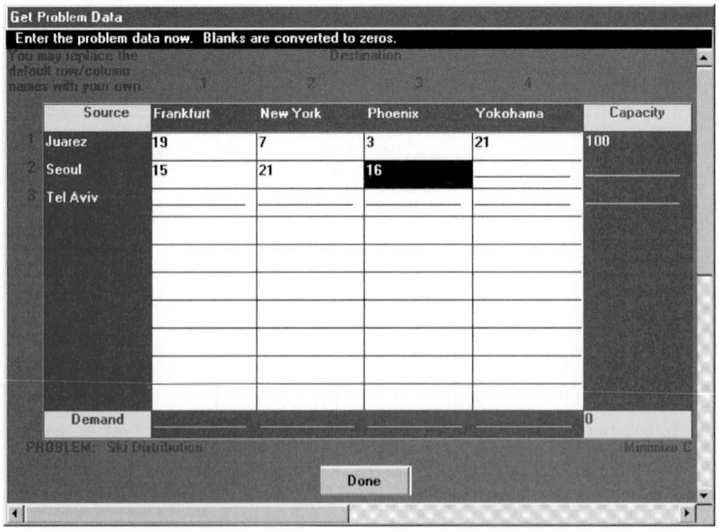

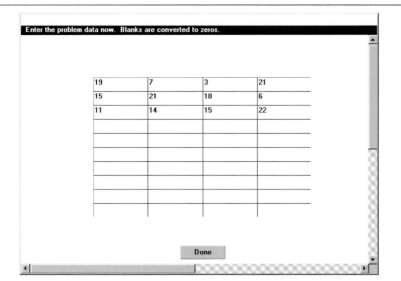

FIGURE 12-13
Completed *QuickQuant* transportation data entry screen for ski distribution

The complete problem data are then entered into the window shown in Figure 12-12. When all the data are entered, the complete screen in Figure 12-13 applies.

We click on the Done button, activating the menu bar. The solution is next obtained after selecting from the Run menu.

QuickQuant has two modes for solving linear programs. The Quick Solve choice skips the intermediate steps. The screen in Figure 12-14 resulted from selecting Detailed Solve. It provides the first iteration and matches Figure 12-5.

FIGURE 12-14
QuickQuant screen for first iteration of the ski-shipment problem

				Destination					
Source	1 Frankfurt		2 New York		3 Phoenix		4 Yokohama		Capacity
1 Juarez	(-)	19 100		7	(+)	3		21	100
			-18		-19		-8		
2 Seoul	(+)	15 50		21 100	(-)	18 150		6	300
							-19		
3 Tel Aviv		11		14		15 50		22 150	200
	-1		-4						
Demand	150		100		200		150		600

FIGURE 12-15

QuickQuant solution
screen for ski-distribution
problem

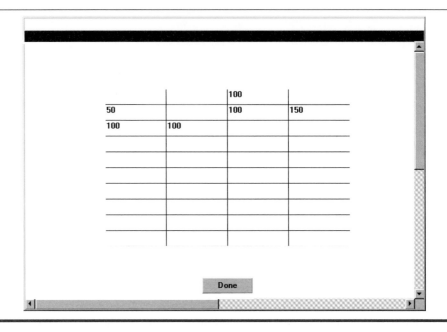

FIGURE 12-15

QuickQuant solution
screen for ski-distribution
problem

The northwest corner method was used as the starting procedure. *QuickQuant* has a
menu choice for a second type of start, Vogel's approximation, discussed in Optional
Section 12-8.

The same shipping schedules shown earlier for this problem are obtained by clicking on the Next button in the Iteration Selection. After examining the last schedule,
clicking on the Done button provides the report in Figure 12-15.

Solving Transportation Problems with a Spreadsheet

There are three steps involved in solving a transportation problem with an Excel
spreadsheet. First, a transportation formulation table is set up. Second, that table is entered into a matching blank spreadsheet. Third, Solver is used to get the solution.

A transportation *formulation* table expresses the problem in a tabular format, as
shown in Figure 12-16 for the ski-distribution problem. The body of the table contains

FIGURE 12-16

Transportation for-
mulation table for ski-
distribution problem

FROM PLANT	TO WAREHOUSE				Capacity
	Frankfurt	New York	Phoenix	Yokohama	
Juarez	19	7	3	21	100
Seoul	15	21	18	6	300
Tel Aviv	11	14	15	22	200
Demand	150	100	200	150	C(min)

	A	B	C	D	E	F	G	H
1			**Ski Shipment-Scheduling Illustration**					
2								
3	From		To Warehouse					
4	Plant	Frankfurt	New York	Phoenix	Yokohama	Capacity		
5	Juarez	19	7	3	21	100		
6	Seoul	15	21	18	6	300		
7	Tel Aviv	11	14	15	22	200		F
8	Demand	150	100	200	150	Cost		=SUMPRODUCT
9			Solution			$0	9	(B5:E7,B12:E14)
10	From		To Warehouse					
11	Plant	Frankfurt	New York	Phoenix	Yokohama	Total		F
12	Juarez	0	0	0	0	0	12	=SUM(B12:E12)
13	Seoul	0	0	0	0	0	13	=SUM(B13:E13)
14	Tel Aviv	0	0	0	0	0	14	=SUM(B14:E14)
15	Total	0	0	0	0			
16								
17		B		C		D	E	
18	15	=SUM(B12:B14)		=SUM(C12:C14)		=SUM(D12:D14)	=SUM(E12:E14)	

FIGURE 12-17   Excel spreadsheet for solving the ski-distribution problem

the unit point-to-point shipping costs, with the right-hand and bottom margins containing the source capacities and destination demands. The lower-right-hand corner indicates whether the objective is cost minimization or profit maximization.

Figure 12-17 shows the same data after they have been entered into a blank Excel spreadsheet. The top portion gives the original problem data, and the lower segment provides the solution by showing all the shipment quantities. All shipments are initially set equal to zero.

Key Excel formulas used in the spreadsheet are displayed in the right portion of Figure 12-17. There we list for cell F9 the formula

$$= \text{SUMPRODUCT(B5:E7;B12:E14)}$$

which causes F9 to display the value of the objective function. This formula calculates the total shipping cost by summing the products of unit costs with quantities shipped. Because the shipping quantities are all zero, the F9 cell value is $0.

The second set of formulas for cells F12:F14 sum the shipments out of each source (plant) or row of the formulation table. Cell F12 has =SUM(B12:E12), determining the total number of pairs of skis shipped from Juarez to the warehouses (in Frankfurt, New York, Phoenix, and Yokohama). This formula was copied down to cells F13 and F14 to get the counterparts for those cells.

The last group of similar formulas for cells B15:E15 sum the shipments received at each destination (warehouse), or column. Cell B15, =SUM(B12:B14), determines the total number of pairs of skis shipped to the warehouse in Frankfurt (from Juarez, Seoul, and Tel Aviv). This formula was copied horizontally to get the counterpart formulas for cells C15 through E15.

FIGURE 12-18
Solver Parameters dialog
box for the ski-distribution
problem

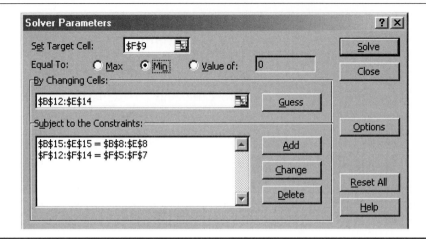

Finding Optimal Solutions Using Solver

The Solver Parameters dialog box for solving the ski-distribution problem is shown in Figure 12-18. The *Target Cell* is the value of the objective function located in $F$9. Because the problem is minimization, we clicked on *Min* in the *Equal To* line. The *Changing Cells* are the shipments from each source to the various destinations. There, we entered $B$12:$E$14.

There are two types of constraints in the *Subject to the Constraints* box. The first requires that the sum of the shipments from each source equals the respective capacity, accomplished by the formula $F$12:$F$14=$F$5:$F$7. The second constraint type requires that the shipments received at each destination sum to the respective capacity, achieved with the formula $B$15:$E$15=$B$8:$E$8.

Clicking on the Options button allowed us to make sure that the *Assume Linear Model* and *Assume Non-Negative* boxes were selected. The Solve button was then selected. Excel's Solver finds the optimal solution and the resulting spreadsheet is shown in Figure 12-19. The solution is identical to those given earlier.

	A	B	C	D	E	F	G	H	I	J	K
1	**Ski Shipment-Scheduling Illustration**										
2											
3	From		To Warehouse								
4	Plant	Frankfurt	New York	Phoenix	Yokohama	Capacity	Cell	Name	Original Value		Final Value
5	Juarez	19	7	3	21	100	B12	Juarez Frankfurt	0		0
6	Seoul	15	21	18	6	300	C12	Juarez New York	0		0
7	Tel Aviv	11	14	15	22	200	D12	Juarez Phoenix	0		100
8	Demand	150	100	200	150	C(min)	E12	Juarez Yokohama	0		0
9			Solution			$6,250	B13	Seoul Frankfurt	0		50
10	From		To Warehouse				C13	Seoul New York	0		0
11	Plant	Frankfurt	New York	Phoenix	Yokohama	Total	D13	Seoul Phoenix	0		100
12	Juarez	0	0	100	0	100	E13	Seoul Yokohama	0		150
13	Seoul	50	0	100	150	300	B14	Tel Aviv Frankfurt	0		100
14	Tel Aviv	100	100	0	0	200	C14	Tel Aviv New York	0		100
15	Total	150	100	200	150		D14	Tel Aviv Phoenix	0		0
							E14	Tel Aviv Yokohama	0		0

FIGURE 12-19   Optimal solution for the ski-shipment-scheduling illustration

12-5 IMBALANCED CAPACITY AND DEMAND: DUMMY ROWS AND COLUMNS

So far we have encountered only transportation problems for which the total demand exactly matches total capacity. There is no reason why a real-world distribution system must have this feature, which is only a requirement of the solution algorithm and not the linear program. In this section we will see how a problem for a distribution system having *imbalanced capacity and demand* may still be solved. This is accomplished by reexpressing the problem in a standard form through the creation of dummy rows or columns, resulting in an equivalent problem where total demand equals total capacity.

We began our ski-distribution example with total demand and total capacity in balance. Ordinarily, distribution systems are not so perfectly balanced. There is usually excess capacity or more demand than can possibly be filled. In such cases, the shipment schedule must include an additional plant or warehouse to take up the slack. We refer to these fictional distribution points as **dummy sources** or **dummy destinations.**

Consider the following example, involving two plants and three warehouses.

PLANT	CAPACITY	WAREHOUSE	DEMAND
A	500	W	250
B	300	X	400
	800	Y	300
			950

Total demand is for 950 units, which exceeds the total capacity of 800 units by 150 units. The shortage in total capacity is made up by including a dummy plant with a 150-unit capacity. Figure 12-20 provides the optimal shipment schedule for this expanded problem. All shipments from the dummy plant have zero cost because they represent product items that are not being made and not being sent. Notice that 150 units from the dummy plant are allocated to warehouse X. This means that warehouse X is shorted

From \ To	W		X		Y		Capacity
		2		4		6	
A	(250)		(250)				500
		3		3		1	
B					(300)		300
		0		0		0	
Dummy			(150)		(0)		150
Demand	250		400		300		950

C = 1,800

FIGURE 12-20
The optimal shipment schedule for the problem requiring a dummy plant

FIGURE 12-21

The optimal schedule for the problem requiring a dummy warehouse

From \ To	W	X	Y	Dummy	Capacity
A	13	14	10 (250)	0 (50)	300
B	12	8 (350)	11	0 (50)	400
C	6 (200)	10	13	0 (0)	200
Demand	200	350	250	100	900

C = 6,500

150 units. In effect, X is the most costly warehouse to service, so it receives fewer units than its demand.

Now, consider the following example:

PLANT	CAPACITY	WAREHOUSE	DEMAND
A	300	W	200
B	400	X	350
C	200	Y	250
	900		800

Here, the total plant capacity of 900 units exceeds the total demand for 800 units by 100 units. The surplus capacity is handled by including a dummy warehouse with a demand equal to the difference of 100. Figure 12-21 provides the optimal solution to this problem. We use zero unit shipping costs to the dummy warehouse, reflecting the fact that allocations to those cells represent product items that are not being made and not being sent. We can see that 50 units apiece are allocated to the dummy warehouse from plants A and B. These amounts represent the unused surplus capacities of these plants. In terms of distribution costs, plants A and B are less efficient than plant C, operating at full capacity.

QuickQuant creates dummy rows or columns as needed. These must be created in advance in spreadsheet evaluations.

12-6   THE TRANSSHIPMENT PROBLEM

The distribution systems encountered so far have just two sets of locations, one to ship and the other to receive. A more general problem is faced by manufacturers with three sets of locations: plants, warehouses, and customers. Warehouses in such systems both receive and transship a product. A distribution optimization for such a system falls into a special class of linear programs called the **transshipment problem.** Such a problem may be solved using the transportation method by including for

From \ To	C1	C2	C3	C4	Warehouse	Capacity
Plant	12	7 ⟨300⟩	8 ⟨300⟩	9 ⟨200⟩	2 ⟨200⟩	1,000
Warehouse	5 ⟨200⟩	6	7	8	0 ⟨300⟩	500
Demand	200	300	300	200	500	1,500

$C = 7,700$

FIGURE 12-22

The optimal shipping schedule for the transshipment problem

each **transshipment point** (warehouse) a row and a column, with identical capacity and demand. Shipments may be allowed between transshipment points, although the respective cells may be made impossible when this is not allowed. Each transshipment point will have a zero-cost **dummy cell** representing the quantity it "ships" to itself; any entry into such a cell represents the amount by which that location operates below its capacity.

To illustrate, consider a single-plant manufacturer with four customers. The 1,000-unit capacity plant makes shipments directly to customers, C1, C2, C3, and C4, as shown in Figure 12-22. But by first making shipments at reduced bulk rates to a company warehouse, overall savings in freight costs are achieved. The warehouse has capacity to handle 500 units and is represented by both a column and a row. The warehouse receives only 200 units from the plant, which are transshipped to C1. It operates 300 units below its capacity, as reflected by the entry in the dummy cell of the warehouse row and column.

Solving a transshipment problem proceeds exactly like a transportation problem.

ABC Evaluates Warehouse Sites

MANAGERIAL APPLICATION

ABC Container Corp. services four major customers from two plants. The average monthly distribution has been optimized using the transportation method, with the problem data and solution shown in Figure 12-23. The capacities and demands are in tons, with the unit costs in dollars per ton. The optimal solution gives a monthly cost of $C = 20,600$ dollars. ABC wants to determine if there are any savings from using warehouses.

Two warehouse sites have been temporarily added to ABC's distribution network, shown in Figure 12-24. The following shipping costs (dollars per ton) apply:

PLANT TO WAREHOUSE		WAREHOUSE TO CUSTOMER			
P1-W1	2	W1-C1	3	W2-C1	6
P1-W2	13	W1-C2	4	W2-C2	1
P2-W1	7	W1-C3	5	W2-C3	11
P2-W2	9	W1-C4	12	W2-C4	10

FIGURE 12-23
Original ABC Container
transportation problem

C = 20,600

To / From	C1	C2	C3	C4	Dummy	Capacity
P1	14 (300)	15 (200)	20	17	0	500
P2	18	19 (50)	16 (450)	21 (250)	0 (250)	1,000
Demand	300	250	450	250	250	1,500

Warehouse $W1$ has a capacity (and hence demand) of 400 tons; the capacity for warehouse $W2$ is 500. Warehouses can ship to each other at a cost of $8 per ton.

The shipment schedule is modified in Figure 12-24 into a transshipment problem. For each warehouse, there is a column and row intersection over a dummy (zero cost) cell. The original dummy column is unaffected by the addition of the warehouses. The optimal solution is shown.

ABC management is pleased with the results. They can save $20,600 − $14,850 = $5,750 each month under the new plan. Of course, the cost of opening and then operating the two warehouses must be considered before a final decision can be made.

FIGURE 12-24
Optimal Solution of ABC
Container transshipment
problem

C = 14,850

To / From	C1	C2	C3	C4	W1	W2	Dummy	Capacity	r
P1	14 / 2	15 / 7	20 / 6	17 (100)	2 (400)	13 / 6	0 / 2	500	0
P2	18 / 4	19 / 9	16 (350)	21 / 2	7 / 3	9 (400)	0 (250)	1,000	2
W1	3 (300)	4 / 5	5 (100)	12 / 4	0 / 7	8 / 10	0 / 11	400	−9
W2	6 / 1	1 (250)	11 / 4	10 (150)	8 / 13	0 (100)	0 / 9	500	−7
Demand	300	250	450	250	400	500	250	2,400	
k	12	8	14	17	2	7	−2		

Managerial Decision Revisited: Determining Shipment Quantities

The following optimal shipping schedules for Thread-Bare Fabrics were provided by *QuickQuant*:

Cotton C=15400

Mill :	L.A.	Chi.	Lon.	Mex.	Man.	Rome	Tok.	N.Y.	Dum* :	Capacity
Baha :	0	300	0	0	0	0	0	700	0 :	1000
Hong :	0	100	0	0	800	0	0	0	1100 :	2000
Kor :	500	300	0	0	0	0	200	0	0 :	1000
Nig :	0	0	900	0	0	100	0	0	1000 :	2000
Ven :	0	100	0	900	0	0	0	0	0 :	1000
Demand :	500	800	900	900	800	100	200	700	2100 :	7000

Polyester C=40300

Mill :	L.A.	Chi.	Lon.	Mex.	Man.	Rome	Tok.	N.Y. :	Capacity
Baha :	0	0	500	0	0	0	0	2500 :	3000
Hong :	0	0	2100	0	400	0	0	0 :	2500
Kor :	1000	1500	100	0	0	0	900	0 :	3500
Nig :	0	0	Zero	0	0	0	0	0 :	0
Ven :	0	500	0	1500	0	0	0	0 :	2000
Dum* :	0	0	300	0	0	700	0	0 :	1000
Demand :	1000	2000	3000	1500	400	700	900	2500 :	12000

Silk C=5000

Mill :	L.A.	Chi.	Lon.	Mex.	Man.	Rome	Tok.	N.Y. :	Capacity
Baha :	0	0	0	0	0	0	0	Zero :	0
Hong :	100	100	200	0	400	0	200	0 :	1000
Kor :	0	0	0	0	0	0	500	0 :	500
Nig :	0	0	Zero	0	0	0	0	0 :	0
Venz :	0	0	0	Zero	0	0	0	0 :	0
Dum* :	0	0	Zero	50	0	200	0	200 :	450
Demand :	100	100	200	50	400	200	700	200 :	1950

12-7   THE ASSIGNMENT PROBLEM

We will expand the machine shop example described in Chapter 9 to include six individual machinists who are to be assigned to six jobs, each to be performed on a different type of machine. Each of the six tasks is to be completed suc-

TABLE 12-2	Average Times (in Minutes) for Machine Shop Assignments					
INDIVIDUAL i / **JOB** i	**Drilling**	**Grinding**	**Lathe**	**Milling**	**Polishing**	**Routing**
Ann	13	22	19	21	16	20
Bud	18	17	24	18	22	27
Chuck	20	22	23	24	17	31
Eduardo	14	19	13	30	23	22
Sam	21	14	17	25	15	23
Tom	17	23	18	20	16	24

cessively on aluminum castings that will be shaped into a final product. Past records provide individual performance data for all six workers. Table 12-2 summarizes the average times (in minutes) that each worker takes to complete each job for one item.

Our objective is to assign the individuals to jobs in such a way that the total average labor time per item is minimized. The assignments are summarized in the assignment schedule in Figure 12-25. The unknown cell quantities are represented by the variables

$$X_{ij} = \text{Fraction of time individual } i \text{ is assigned to job } j$$

The marginal row and column totals are 1. Thus, every person must be fully occupied (so that the row X's sum to 1) and every job must be completely assigned (so that the

FIGURE 12-25
The machine shop
assignment schedule

Individual i / Job i	D	G	L	M	P	R	Availability
A	13 X_{AD}	22 X_{AG}	19 X_{AL}	21 X_{AM}	16 X_{AP}	20 X_{AR}	1
B	18 X_{BD}	17 X_{BG}	24 X_{BL}	18 X_{BM}	22 X_{BP}	27 X_{BR}	1
C	20 X_{CD}	22 X_{CG}	23 X_{CL}	24 X_{CM}	17 X_{CP}	31 X_{CR}	1
E	14 X_{ED}	19 X_{EG}	13 X_{EL}	30 X_{EM}	23 X_{EP}	22 X_{ER}	1
S	21 X_{SD}	14 X_{SG}	17 X_{SL}	25 X_{SM}	15 X_{SP}	23 X_{SR}	1
T	17 X_{TD}	23 X_{TG}	18 X_{TL}	20 X_{TM}	16 X_{TP}	24 X_{TR}	1
Requirement	1	1	1	1	1	1	6

column X's sum to 1). The average completion times for individual and job combinations serve the same function as the unit shipping costs in a transportation problem.

Solving the Assignment Problem

Assignment problems have all the structural elements of the transportation problem. Thus, the transportation method can be used to solve that class of problems as well. Figure 12-26 shows the initial assignment. (This was obtained using the cheapest cell method described in Optional Section 12-8.)

Figure 12-27 shows the second iteration for solving the machine shop assignment problem using the transportation method. Cell *CD,* which has an improvement value of -10, is the entering cell. The closed-loop path turns out to be a double figure-8. Notice that the losing cells all contain circled zeros. The maximum quantity to be reallocated along the closed-loop path is 0, and exactly one of the losing cells will go blank in the next solution. We break the tie by choosing the most expensive losing cell, and the circled zero from cell *CR* moves to cell *CD.* The total time savings is $10 \times 0 = 0$.

After several more iterations that involve only the movement of circled zeros, we can establish that the present assignment of workers to jobs is in fact optimal. Actually, there is a tie for the optimal solution. Either of the following assignments will minimize total average time. And any solution in which Ann and Tom split the drilling and routing jobs—say, spending one-half of their time on each job—would also be optimal.

Individual i \ Job j	D	G	L	M	P	R	Availability	
A	13 (1)	22	19	21	16	20	1	$r_A = 0$
B	18	17 (0)	24	18 (1)	22	27	1	$r_B = 8$
C	20	22	23	24	17 (0)	31 (1)	1	$r_C = 11$
E	14 (0)	19	13 (1)	30	23	22	1	$r_E = 1$
S	21	14 (1)	17 (0)	25	15	23	1	$r_S = 5$
T	17	23	18	20 (0)	16 (1)	24	1	$r_T = 10$
Requirement	1	1	1	1	1	1	6	
	$k_D = 13$	$k_G = 9$	$k_L = 12$	$k_M = 10$	$k_P = 6$	$k_R = 20$		

FIGURE 12-26
Starting solution for the machine shop assignment problem using the transportation method

FIGURE 12-27

The second iteration for solving the machine shop assignment problem using the transportation method

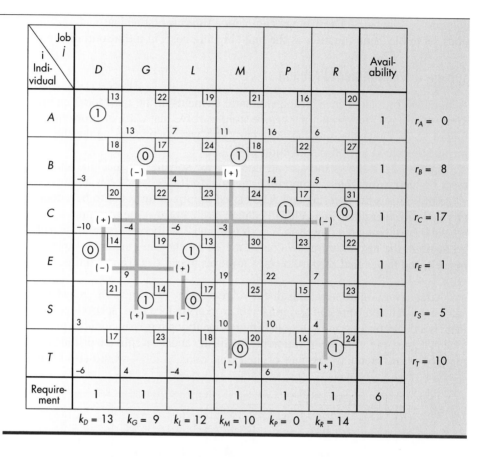

Worker	OPTIMUM Job	OPTIMUM Time	ALTERNATIVE OPTIMUM Job	ALTERNATIVE OPTIMUM Time
Ann	Drilling	13 min	Routing	20 min
Bud	Milling	18	Milling	18
Chuck	Polishing	17	Polishing	17
Eduardo	Lathe	13	Lathe	13
Sam	Grinding	14	Grinding	14
Tom	Routing	24	Drilling	17
		99 min		99 min

Because it requires many circled zeros, and thus many vacuous iterations that do not reposition any ones, the general transportation method may involve more work than faster algorithms designed specifically for solving assignment problems. But because large assignment problems are solved on the computer using the same software as transportation problems, the potential computational disadvantages are insignificant.

Profit-Maximization Problems

The transportation and assignment problems encountered so far have had the objective to minimize C. Although a maximization objective may not be too meaningful in a distribution context, where controlling shipping costs is the major concern, the trans-

portation format can be used for more general problem types. In these cases, maximizing P can sometimes be a more realistic objective. A maximization objective is natural in assignment problems, where instead of trying to keep small the total cost of an assignment schedule a manager might instead want to maximize efficiency or value added.

The following illustration discusses an assignment problem with a maximization objective that is solved using the computer:

Assigning Programmers for a Personal Computer Flight Simulator

MANAGERIAL APPLICATION

AeroSoft specializes in software products for general aviation. Management is putting together a team of programmers to develop version 3.0 of its popular personal computer flight simulator program, PCFly. The job has been divided into 10 tasks, with a different programmer to be assigned to each.

The possibilities follow. Each programmer has been subjectively evaluated in terms of an efficiency index for each task.

	TASK									
	1	**2**	**3**	**4**	**5**	**6**	**7**	**8**	**9**	**10**
PROGRAMMER	**Joy Stick**	**Avionics**	**Flight Physics**	**Fore-ground Art**	**Back-ground Art**	**Key-board Templates**	**Gauge Controls**	**Condi-tion Generator**	**Chart Graphics**	**Main Logic**
1 Smith	120	150	110	75	65	100	110	130	140	100
2 Johnson	100	90	70	50	40	100	80	100	110	120
3 Brown	150	140	120	100	110	80	120	100	100	130
4 Lichtberg	70	60	40	120	130	100	60	70	110	60
5 Pagani	100	90	90	100	100	95	90	95	100	90
6 Wong	50	130	170	50	50	50	80	115	80	80
7 Keesoo	70	70	150	40	30	120	120	110	90	100
8 Kikuchi	100	90	80	150	140	100	90	80	90	100
9 Gorski	130	100	70	90	80	100	130	100	110	70
10 Nugent	90	100	150	50	60	100	110	130	130	100

AeroSoft wants to find an assignment schedule maximizing the aggregate project efficiency index. This will be done using computer assistance.

THE PROBLEM SOLUTION

This problem is solved using *QuickQuant*. Data are input in the same way as before, except that the program automatically gives every programmer a capacity (availability) of 1 and every task a demand (requirement) of 1.

COMPUTER SOLUTION

Flight Simulator Assignment Problem

The following report was obtained from a *QuickQuant* run with the problem data:

FIGURE 12-28
QuickQuant solution
for PC Fly Assignment
problem

ASSIGNMENT PROBLEM SOLUTION

PROBLEM: PC Fly

===

| : | | | Task | | | : | |
Person :	T1	T2	T3	T4	T5	:	Capacity
P1 :	0	1	0	0	0	:	1
P2 :	0	0	0	0	0	:	1
P3 :	1	0	0	0	0	:	1
P4 :	0	0	0	0	1	:	1
P5 :	0	0	0	0	Zero	:	1
P6 :	0	Zero	1	0	0	:	1
P7 :	0	0	0	0	0	:	1
P8 :	0	0	0	1	Zero	:	1
P9 :	Zero	0	0	0	0	:	1
P10 :	0	0	0	0	0	:	1
Demand :	1	1	1	1	1	:	10

===

| : | | | Task | | | : | |
Person :	T6	T7	T8	T9	T10	:	Capacity
P1 :	0	0	0	Zero	0	:	1
P2 :	0	0	0	0	1	:	1
P3 :	0	0	0	0	Zero	:	1
P4 :	0	0	0	0	0	:	1
P5 :	0	0	0	1	Zero	:	1
P6 :	0	0	0	0	0	:	1
P7 :	1	Zero	0	0	0	:	1
P8 :	0	0	0	0	0	:	1
P9 :	0	1	0	0	0	:	1
P10 :	0	0	1	Zero	0	:	1
Demand :	1	1	1	1	1	:	10

===

Maximum profit is P = 1350

From the data and solution, the following optimal assignments are determined:

PROGRAMMER	TASK	EFFICIENCY
1 Smith	2 Avionics	150
2 Johnson	10 Main Logic	120
3 Brown	1 Joy Stick	150
4 Lichtberg	5 Background Art	130
5 Pagani	9 Chart Graphics	100
6 Wong	3 Flight Physics	170
7 Keesoo	6 Keyboard Templates	120
8 Kikuchi	4 Foreground Art	150
9 Gorski	7 Gauge Controls	130
10 Nugent	8 Condition Generator	130
		1,350

Total efficiency index (profit) is $P = 1,350$.

12-8 (OPTIONAL) STARTING PROCEDURES BASED ON COST

Two starting solutions are popular in solving transportation problems. First to be described is the **cheapest cell method.** This is followed by a brief summary of the more elaborate **Vogel's approximation.**

The cheapest cell method is very simple. The following steps apply:

SOLUTION PROCEDURE

STEPS FOR CHEAPEST CELL STARTING METHOD

1. Starting with a blank shipping schedule, find the cheapest (lowest cost) cell. Allocate the maximum possible quantity into that cell.

2. Cross out the column or row into which further quantity allocations are impossible. (In some cases, both a column and a row must be crossed out.)

3. Find the cheapest cell in the portions of the shipping schedule not yet crossed out. Place the maximum possible quantity into that cell.

4. Repeat steps 2 and 3 until only one or two cells remain which do not lie in a row or column already crossed out. Allocate into the remaining cell(s) whatever quantities will make a feasible schedule. The cell quantities obtained provide the *starting solution.*

In performing these steps, ties may be broken arbitrarily.

We will illustrate this method on a new transportation problem in Figure 12-29, where the results of step 1 are shown. The cheapest cell is *CK,* with a unit shipping cost of $6. The maximum quantity allocation for that cell is 300 units, which equals both the capacity of *C* and the demand of *K*. Both row *C* and column *K* are crossed out, since neither can receive further quantity allocations. Step 3 indicates that the next allocation

To From	H	I	J	K	Capacity
A	13	10	8	7	100
B	10	14	13	12	100
C	7	10	8	6 (300)	300
D	9	9	15	8	200
Demand	100	50	250	300	700

FIGURE 12-29
Transportation schedule showing steps 1 and 2 of the cheapest cell method

From \ To	H	I	J	K	Capacity
A	13	10	8 (100)	7	100
B	10	14	13	12	100
C	7	10	8	6 (300)	300
D	9	9	15	8	200
Demand	100	50	250	300	700

must go into cell *AJ,* with 100 units being the maximum allocation there. Going back to step 2, no further quantities can be placed into row *A,* which must be crossed out.

Figure 12-30 shows the resulting status of the shipping schedule. We see that a tie exists for cheapest remaining cell, either *DH* or *DI,* both at a cost of $9. The tie is broken arbitrarily with the selection of *DH,* which receives a maximum allocation of 100 units. This necessitates the removal of column *H* from further allocations.

Figure 12-31 shows the new quantities. There we see that cell *DI* is the cheapest remaining cell of those not yet crossed out. Cell *DI* can receive at most 50 units. Figure 12-32 shows the result of this allocation, with column *I* now crossed out.

From \ To	H	I	J	K	Capacity
A	13	10	8 (100)	7	100
B	10	14	13	12	100
C	7	10	8	6 (300)	300
D	9 (100)	9	15	8	200
Demand	100	50	250	300	700

From \ To	H	I	J	K	Capacity
A	13	10	8 (100)	7	100
B	10	14	13	12	100
C	7	10	8	6 (300)	300
D	9 (100)	9 (50)	15	8	200
Demand	100	50	250	300	700

FIGURE 12-32

Transportation schedule showing the fourth iteration of the cheapest cell method

Only two cells, *BJ* and *DJ*, remain uncrossed out. Both receive maximum quantities. Figure 12-33 shows the completed starting solution, with all the cross lines erased. The total cost is $C = 6,000$.

Positioning Circled Zeros

The cheapest cell method does *not guarantee* that exactly the required number of nonempty cells will be obtained. The present 4×4 problem requires exactly $4 + 4 - 1 = 7$ nonempty cells. Figure 12-33 shows that only six nonempty cells were obtained. One circled zero must therefore be included in the shipping schedule.

It is easiest to position the circled zeros as we determine the row and column numbers. Figure 12-34 illustrates the procedure. We start with $r_A = 0$. From this and nonempty cell *AJ*, we obtain $k_J = 8$. We then work through cell *BJ* to get $r_B = 5$ and cell *DJ* to get $r_D = 7$. Proceeding in row *D* from that number, working through cell *DI*, $k_I = 2$ is obtained. Also in row *D*, working through cell *DH*, $k_H = 2$ is obtained.

An impasse is reached at this point, because column *H* has no other nonempty cells through which further row numbers could be found. This obstacle is surmounted by identifying in column *H* those empty cells lying in rows that need numbers, and placing in one of these a circled zero. There is only one such cell, *CH*. By placing a ⓪ into cell *CH*, it is then possible to get the value $r_C = 5$. From there, working through cell *CK*, the value $k_K = 1$ is found.

All row and column numbers are obtained, and there is precisely the correct number of nonempty cells. The basic steps of the original transportation method may now be continued until the optimal solution is found.

It is common for a starting solution to need more than one ⓪. Just add a ⓪ to the problem as each impasse is reached while assigning row and column numbers. If there is more than one empty cell where the ⓪ might be placed, pick the cheapest and break any ties arbitrarily.

Once a complete quantity assignment has been achieved (so that the number of nonempty cells is exactly equal to the number of rows plus the number of columns

FIGURE 12-33

Transportation schedule showing the completed starting solution with the cheapest cell method

To From	H	I	J	K	Capacity
A	13	10	8 (100)	7	100
B	10	14	13 (100)	12	100
C	7	10	8	6 (300)	300
D	9 (100)	9 (50)	15 (50)	8	200
Demand	100	50	250	300	700

minus one) and a set of row and column numbers is found, the transportation method proceeds as before. The starting solution, with $C = 6,000$ dollars, is shown in Figure 12-34. There the entering cell is found to be *CJ*, and the corresponding closed-loop path is identified. The minimum quantity in the losing cells is 0, so that in the next iteration the Ⓞ will be in a new spot. It takes two intermediate iterations of the main

FIGURE 12-34

Row and column numbers and positioning circled zero for the starting solution

$C = 6,000$

To From	H	I	J	K	Capacity	
A	13 [11]	10 [8]	8 (100)	7 [6]	100	$r_A = 0$ ⓐ
B	10 [3]	14 [7]	13 (100)	12 [6]	100	$r_B = 5$ ⓒ
C	7 (−) (0) [3]	10 (+) [−5]	8	6 (300)	300	$r_C = 5$ ⓖ
D	9 (100) (+)	9 (50)	15 (50) (−)	8 [0]	200	$r_D = 7$ ⓓ
Demand	100	50	250	300	700	

$k_H = 2$ ⓕ $k_I = 2$ ⓔ $k_J = 8$ ⓑ $k_K = 1$ ⓗ

transportation method algorithm to find the optimal solution. (As an exercise, you might finish the problem.)

Vogel's Approximation

The more elaborate Vogel's approximation may sometimes provide better starting solutions than the cheapest cell method. This also involves crossing out rows and columns.

STEPS FOR VOGEL'S APPROXIMATION STARTING METHOD

SOLUTION PROCEDURE

1. Find for each uncovered (not yet crossed-out) row and column the difference between the cheapest and next cheapest uncovered cell.

2. Identify that row or column having the greatest difference and place the maximum possible quantity in the cheapest uncrossed cell in that row or column.

3. Cross out any row or column that can receive no further quantities.

4. Repeat steps 1 through 3 until only one or two uncovered cells remain. Place into the cells the quantities needed to make a feasible schedule.

The Vogel's approximation starting method is applied in Figure 12-35 to the preceding problem. To begin, the row and column differences are obtained. The following steps are taken:

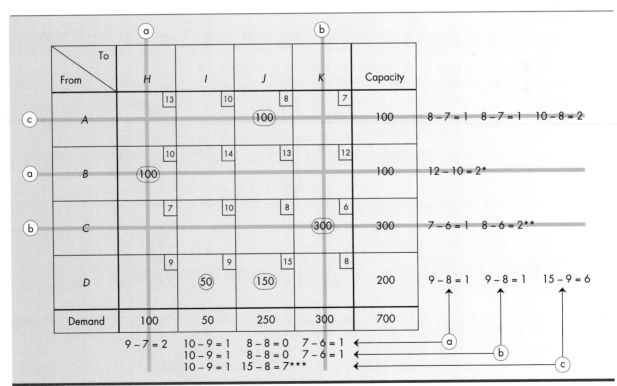

FIGURE 12-35 Getting transportation problem started with Vogel's approximation

(a) There is a tie for greatest difference between column *H* and row *B* (2). Row *B* is chosen arbitrarily. Place 100 units into its cheapest cell, *BH,* then cross out row *B* and column *H.*

(b) Recompute the row and column differences, ignoring covered (crossed-out) cells. The greatest difference occurs for row *C.* Place 300 units into its cheapest uncovered cell, *CK,* then cross out row *C* and column *K.*

(c) Recompute the row and column differences, ignoring the covered cells. The greatest difference occurs for column *J.* Place 100 units into its cheapest uncovered cell, *AJ,* then cross out row *A.* (Column *J* is *not* crossed out because it can receive more units.)

(d) This leaves only two uncovered cells. Place 50 units into *DI* and 150 units into *DJ.*

The optimization proceeds similarly to the preceding one. Vogel's approximation gives a start requiring the same number of iterations for this problem as the cheapest cell method. But, for larger problems, Vogel's method will usually get to the answer faster.

Modified Cheapest Cell Method

In applying the cheapest cell method to problems involving dummies, a more efficient start requiring fewer subsequent iterations can usually be achieved by avoiding the dummy cells until the end. Under that *modified* cheapest cell method, no quantity is placed into a dummy (zero shipping cost) cell as long as an uncovered regular cell remains.

USING JUDGMENT

Selecting a Starting Procedure

Because it focuses on position only, ignoring cell costs, the northwest corner method gives inefficient starts. It is, however, easy to understand and is fail-safe. More-efficient starts, requiring fewer optimization iterations to complete the solution, may be obtained with the cheapest cell method. But that procedure loses some of its advantages when there are several cells having the same costs, because ties must then be broken arbitrarily. Vogel's approximation is the most elaborate, but it is generally more efficient than the cheapest cell method. One big disadvantage, shared with the cheapest cell method, is that there often are insufficient nonzero cells, so that circled zeros must be inserted later during the first optimization iteration.

Which start to use is essentially a matter of judgment. The optimal solution will eventually be reached regardless of which method is used.

12-9 (OPTIONAL) OTHER APPLICATIONS OF THE TRANSPORTATION PROBLEM

The scope of the transportation problem can be expanded to consider production costs as well as freight charges. For example, suppose that the three plants in the ski-distribution illustration all operated at different unit costs—$60 for Juarez, $50 for Seoul, and $65 for Tel Aviv. Cost differentials are just as important in choosing which plants will service which warehouses as the physical distances separating the

production and consumption centers. By adding 60 to row *J* costs, 50 to row *S* costs, and 65 to row *T* costs, the ski distribution transportation problem can be solved so that all distribution costs—instead of just the freight costs—can be optimized. Indeed, any formulation that does not reflect all cost differentials between plants is undesirable and generally leads to an inferior solution. (This revised problem will be left as an exercise.)

The transportation problem is so named because it was originally used to determine shipment schedules in distribution systems. However, its basic source–destination structure makes it suitable for solving many other types of problems that do not involve the physical distribution of items. For example, this format can be used to establish a plant's production schedule for several time periods.

Transportation Method Used in Production Scheduling

As an illustration, we will suppose that the Juarez ski plant can actually operate at as much as 150% of its stated capacity during the August–November period by placing its workforce on overtime. We will also assume that the company policy is to use this plant exclusively to service the Phoenix warehouse. Moreover, we will assume that Juarez can make up to 100 pairs of skis monthly at a cost of $60 per pair using regular labor; for an additional $20 per pair, Juarez can make 50 additional pairs of skis per month using overtime labor. Finally, we will assume that the factory can store extra skis for later distribution at a cost of $1 per pair per month.

Now, suppose that the following demands occur at the Phoenix warehouse:

August	100 pairs
September	150
October	200
November	100
	550 pairs

Figure 12-36 provides the optimal ski production schedule. There are eight "plants," each representing the month and type of production (*R* = regular, *O* = overtime). There are four "warehouses"—one for each monthly demand, plus one dummy warehouse (because total capacity exceeds total demand).

In constructing Figure 12-36, we have omitted the unit freight charge, because it is the same for all cells. Notice that it is impossible to satisfy an earlier demand from later production. For the sake of completeness, however, the cells representing these situations appear in the table. Such allocations receive a very large unit cost of *M* dollars. Any starting solution that involved such a cell would exit early. Also notice that each cell in the dummy column has a unit cost of 0.

The transportation problem format may be used for certain production-scheduling problems where the nature of the physical items themselves, not just the timing, is to be decided. This approach might be used in an assembly operation, where various components are joined together into final products. Supply constraints exist for the components, and these must be allocated to final products to meet demand constraints. All other production factors must be assumed in plentiful supply, so that there are no labor or machine time constraints, for example. (The coefficients of the *X*'s must always be 1, and all constraints must involve simple addition with the *X*'s.)

FIGURE 12-36
The optimal ski production schedule

From Month \ To Month	A	S	O	N	Dummy	Capacity
AR	60 (100)	61 (0)	62	63	0	100
AO	80	81 (50)	82	83	0 (0)	50
SR	M	60 (100)	61 (0)	62	0	100
SO	M	80	81 (50)	82	0	50
OR	M	M	60 (100)	61	0	100
OO	M	M	80 (50)	81	0	50
NR	M	M	M	60 (100)	0	100
NO	M	M	M	80 (0)	0 (50)	50
Demand	100	150	200	100	50	600

Profit-Maximization Problems

Assembly production problems have an overall objective of maximizing profit rather than minimizing cost. The transportation method is easily adapted for that objective. The simplest approach would be to reverse the entry criterion, selecting as the entering cell the one having the greatest *positive* difference $c_{ij} - r_i - k_j$. The northwest corner start would be identical. A faster start could be achieved by using a most-profitable-cell method, analogous to the cheapest cell method, in which the most profitable cell in the uncovered portion is given a maximum allocation at each step.

PROBLEMS

12-1 Use the northwest corner method to find the starting solution to the problem shown in Figure 12-37.

12-2 Use the cheapest cell method to find the starting solution to Problem 12-1.

12-3 The starting solution has been obtained for a transportation problem (see Figure 12-38). It is not optimal.
(a) Find a complete set of row and column numbers.

FIGURE 12-37
Blank shipment schedule for Problem 12-1

$C =$

From \ To	H	I	J	K	Capacity
A	15	9	8	7	200
B	11	14	13	12	150
C	6	16	5	4	200
D	17	18	20	3	200
Demand	150	200	250	150	750

FIGURE 12-38
Starting shipment schedule for Problem 12-3

From \ To	A	B	C	D	Capacity	
P1	11	12	6 (150)	9	150	$r_1 =$
P2	14 (50)	10	10	13	50	$r_2 =$
P3	17 (150)	8 (0)	15	11 (50)	200	$r_3 =$
P4	15	12	13	10 (200)	200	$r_4 =$
P5	17	8 (150)	9 (100)	11	250	$r_5 =$
Demand	200	150	250	250	850	
	$k_A =$	$k_B =$	$k_C =$	$k_D =$		

(b) Determine the improvement value for each empty cell.

(c) Identify the entering cell and indicate the closed-loop path.

(d) Construct the new shipment schedule and compute the new total cost.

12-4 Consider the following distribution problem for Ace Widgets:

Plants	Shipping Costs to Warehouses				Capacity
	W1	W2	W3	W4	
P1	2	6	4	12	100
P2	7	3	10	11	250
P3	5	8	9	13	300
Demand	50	150	200	250	

(a) Set up a blank shipping schedule and apply the northwest corner method to determine a starting solution. Compute the total cost of that solution.

(b) Determine the row and column numbers. Then determine for each cell the improvement values. Indicate on your shipping schedule the closed-loop path. Which cell is the entering cell?

(c) Set up another blank shipping schedule. Determine the new quantities according to the closed-loop path from the schedule set up in (a). Then compute the total shipping cost. Recompute the row and column numbers, find the improvement values for the empty cells, and indicate the closed-loop path. Find the entering and exiting cells.

(d) Repeat (c) starting with the latest solution until the optimal schedule is determined.

12-5 Consider the following distribution problem for the Ace Widgets warehouses and customers in the Western region:

Warehouse	Shipping Costs to Customers			Capacity
	C1	C2	C3	
W1	7	2	8	30
W2	5	3	1	50
W3	4	6	7	40
Demand	60	40	20	

(a) Set up a blank shipping schedule and apply the northwest corner method to determine a starting solution. Compute the total cost of that solution.

(b) Set up another blank shipping schedule and apply the cheapest cell method to determine a starting solution. Compute the total cost of that solution.

(c) Subtract the total cost found in (a) from that found in (b). What would be the total cost savings by using the shipping schedule from (b) instead of the one in (a)?

(d) Establish the optimality of your shipping schedule from (b) by attempting to calculate the row and column numbers. Do you notice anything unusual?

12-6 Use the cheapest cell method to find the starting solution to the ski manufacturer's transportation problem in Figure 12-2.

12-7 Use Vogel's approximation to find the starting solution to the ski manufacturer's transportation problem in Figure 12-2.

12-8 Consider the following distribution problem for the BugOff Chemicals plants and warehouses:

Plants	Shipping Costs to Warehouses				Capacity
	C1	C2	C3	C4	
P1	2	6	9	4	200
P2	7	1	10	12	300
P3	5	11	3	8	400
Demand	100	200	300	400	

(a) Compute total demand and total capacity. In applying the transportation method, is a dummy source or a dummy destination required? If so, incorporate the new row or column into the problem.

(b) Set up a blank shipping schedule and apply the northwest corner method to determine a starting solution. Compute the total cost of that solution.

(c) Determine the row and column numbers. Then determine for each cell the improvement value. Indicate on your shipping schedule the closed-loop path. Which cell is the entering cell?

(d) Set up another blank shipping schedule. Determine the new quantities in accordance

with the closed-loop path from the schedule set up in (c). Then compute the total shipping cost. Recompute the row and column numbers, find the improvement values for the empty cells, and indicate the closed-loop path. Is there an entering cell?

(e) Repeat (d) starting with the latest solution until the optimal schedule is determined.

12-9 Refer to Problem 12-8. A new plant with a capacity of 200 is added to BugOff's distribution system. Its unit shipping cost to each customer is $5. Repeat (a)–(e) as in Problem 12-8.

12-10 Penny-Saver Markets sends supplies from two regional centers to its seven stores. The requirements and costs per ton follow:

Centers	Shipping Costs to Stores							Capacity
	10th St.	Country Center	Hale St.	East Side	South Side	City Center	Brook-side	
1st St.	2	3	8	6	11	13	11	500
River Rd.	5	4	9	7	10	7	14	1,000
Required Cartons	50	60	110	220	310	170	230	

Set up the initial blank shipping schedule.

12-11 Refer to Problem 12-10 and your answer to that problem. The current plan for stocking stores follows:

Centers	Stores						
	10th St.	Country Center	Hale St.	East Side	South Side	City Center	Brook-side
1st St.	25	40	—	70	200	50	50
River Rd.	25	20	110	150	110	120	180

(a) What is the total cost of this plan?

(b) Using the schedule found in Problem 12-10, apply the cheapest cell method (modified version if applicable) to find a starting solution. Break any ties arbitrarily.

(c) What is the total cost of your solution from (b)? How much will Penny-Saver save using your solution from (b) instead of the one in (a)?

(d) Can you find a cheaper solution than the one in (b)? If so, determine the cheapest possible solution and its cost. How much would Penny-Saver save over the current plan in (a) by using your optimal solution?

12-12 Solve the following transportation problem to find the minimum-cost solution:

	W1	W2	W3	W4	Capacity
A	5	4	7	5	1,000
B	3	2	7	5	2,000
C	5	5	6	6	5,000
Demand	2,000	2,000	2,000	2,000	

12-13 Solve the following transportation problem to find the minimum-cost solution:

	SF	NY	NO	LA	Capacity
Hong Kong	33.20	25.00	30.50	42.25	150,000
Tokyo	27.00	28.50	30.00	31.50	300,000
Taipei	30.00	26.00	31.00	30.00	250,000
Demand	240,000	260,000	50,000	150,000	

12-14 A distribution system must meet the following requirements:

Plant	Capacity	Warehouse	Demand
A	100	U	150
B	150	V	200
C	300	W	200

Unit shipping costs are

Source	Shipping Cost to Destination		
	U	V	W
A	10	7	8
B	15	12	9
C	7	8	12

(a) Formulate this transportation problem as a linear program.

(b) Determine the optimal solution using the transportation method.

12-15 Refer to Problem 12-14. Suppose that a new plant D is opened that has a capacity of 200 units. It costs $8 per unit for this plant to service each warehouse. Use the transportation method to determine the shipment schedule that minimizes total transportation cost.

FIGURE 12-39

Intermediate shipment schedule for Problem 12-19

To\From	J	K	L	M	N	O	P	Capacity
A	[2]	[10]	[8]	[8]	[5] (100)	[6] (100)	[7]	200
B	[21]	[15]	[14]	[24]	[7]	[14] (100)	[9]	100
C	[10]	[8] (200)	[8]	[14] (100)	[10]	[9]	[9]	300
D	[10]	[11]	[11] (200)	[10]	[14]	[16]	[10]	200
E	[3]	[3] (200)	[2]	[8]	[1]	[4] (100)	[5]	300
F	[9] (200)	[11]	[12]	[8] (200)	[9]	[8]	[7]	400
G	[12]	[11] (200)	[10]	[11]	[13]	[10]	[11] (100)	300
H	[10]	[8]	[12]	[17]	[10] (200)	[12]	[10] (100)	300
Demand	200	400	400	300	300	300	200	2,100

12-16 Refer to Problem 12-14. Suppose that a new warehouse X is opened that has a demand of 100 units. It costs $15 to ship each unit to this warehouse, regardless of the origin. Use the transportation method to determine the shipment schedule that minimizes total transportation cost.

12-17 Solve the following transportation problem to find the minimum-cost solution:

	W1	W2	W3	Capacity
Plant 1	1.00	2.00	3.00	150
Plant 2	2.00	1.00	2.00	100
Plant 3	2.00	2.00	2.00	350
Demand	200	100	150	

12-18 Solve the following transportation problem to find the minimum-cost solution:

	W1	W2	W3	W4	Capacity
Plant 1	16.00	15.00	17.00	14.00	800
Plant 2	18.00	12.00	15.00	13.00	200
Demand	500	500	500	500	

12-19 Consider the intermediate shipment schedule shown in Figure 12-39 for a transportation problem. Determine the row and column numbers. Then, find the closed-loop path. (Remember, the closed-loop path is defined only by the turning points.) *Do not solve the problem further.* Indicate the new solution by crossing out the numbers that have changed and by adding the new shipment quantities to the revised cells.

12-20 Refer to Problem 12-14. Suppose that a hub center is added with a capacity of 300 units. The hub will receive large shipments from plants and transship units to warehouses. The following transportation costs apply:

Plant to Hub		Hub to Warehouse	
A	2	U	5
B	3	V	6
C	2	W	7

Find the minimum-cost solution.

12-21 Use the transportation method to determine the optimal tombstone shipment schedule for Druids' Drayage in Problem 9-11 (page 350).

12-22 Refer to Problem 12-21. An alternative (tying) optimal solution exists for a transportation problem whenever an empty cell in the final schedule has an improvement value of zero. Beginning with your final table in Problem 12-21, find the alternative optimal solution for shipping tombstones.

12-23 Use the transportation method to determine the optimal production and shipment schedule for Ace Widgets in Problem 9-18 (page 352).

12-24 An assignment schedule in Figure 12-40 has been obtained using a cost-based starting procedure. Use the transportation method to determine the optimal solution or to verify that the current solution is optimal.

12-25 The following possible person–job assignments and costs apply.

Person	Cost for Job			
	W	X	Y	Z
A	5	10	12	7
B	6	13	8	16
C	9	8	14	15
D	19	11	18	17

Use each of the following methods to find the minimum-cost solution. Time yourself to see how long it takes under each method. In each case, provide (1) a table showing the person–job assignments, (2) total cost, and (3) minutes required to reach the solution.
(a) Solve the problem using trial and error.
(b) Solve the problem using the transportation method. Start using the northwest corner.

12-26 These costs apply to an assignment problem:

Individual	J	K	L	M	N
A	3	17	5	21	13
B	10	4	14	24	7
C	10	15	26	8	20
D	23	6	9	19	25
E	11	18	27	12	22

Determine the optimal assignment.

FIGURE 12-40
Blank shipment schedule for Problem 12-24

C = 27

Person \ Task	V	W	X	Y	Z	Availability
A	6	17	7	13	5 ①	1
B	15	2 ①	8	19	25	1
C	9	14	18	1 ①	12	1
D	3 ①	16	4	24	23	1
E	21	10 ①	20	11	22	1
Demand	1	1	1	1	1	5

12-27 Hans and Fritz, and their cousins Gert and Zelda, want to divide their chores to minimize total combined working time and to maximize their playing time. Each is faster at certain daily chores. The following times apply:

	Chase Hippos	Pen Ostriches	Retrieve the Captain's Pipe	Scare Cannibals
Fritz	15 min	30 min	10 min	15 min
Hans	10	20	15	10
Gert	20	15	15	20
Zelda	10	20	10	15

Each brat must do one chore, and all chores must be done. Solve this assignment problem using the transportation method.

12-28 Consider the following assignment problem for a project manager in charge of redesigning one of the Ace Widgets plants:

	Total Employee Cost for Job ($1,000)					
Employee	J	K	L	M	N	O
A	1	3	8	3	3	4
B	2	5	6	7	4	5
C	3	4	9	2	5	3
D	4	5	10	1	6	8
E	5	6	9	5	5	7
F	6	7	7	2	4	9

Using the transportation method, find an optimal assignment schedule and determine its cost.

12-29 A six-person team is entered in the World Greased-Pig Wrestling Championship. The following wrestler–task assignments, along with the average penalty points assessed in preliminary contests, are possible:

Wrestler	Grab-bing	Hold-ing	Identi-fying	Jerk-ing	Kick-ing	Load-ing
Anastasia	0	18	7	2	21	14
Basil	9	1	15	24	31	6
Carlos	19	28	10	20	34	12
Daphne	4	16	16	3	13	32
Elsie	17	23	8	26	15	29
Fred	5	25	22	11	35	27

An assignment is to be made that will minimize the total average penalty points for the entire team. Determine the optimal assignment.

12-30 Use the transportation method to solve Compu-Quick's assignment decision in Problem 9-5 (page 349).

12-31 Use the transportation method to solve Conformity Systems' assignment decision in Problem 9-15 (page 351).

12-32 Solve the flight simulator assignment problem described in the chapter. (*Hint:* Use negative efficiency indexes as the costs.)

12-33 AeroSoft must assign programmers to a new computer globetrotting game, Hop-Skip-and-Jump. Altogether, there are 8 tasks, but only 7 programmers are available. The following table provides the total expected cost (hundreds of dollars) for the various assignment possibilities. The next new programmer hired will be assigned to whichever task remains.

	Task							
	1	2	3	4	5	6	7	8
Programmer	Game Con-trols	Event Gener-ator	Logic Tables	Carto-graphic Art	Special Art	Video Driver	Sound Effects	Main Pro-gram
1 Latrec	71	88	52	75	65	100	110	98
2 Parker	45	93	66	59	73	105	119	101
3 Raster	91	58	70	93	88	83	120	106
4 Bitberg	72	49	55	58	92	99	112	107
5 Paganini	93	67	84	74	76	102	103	111
6 Magellan	69	56	69	54	68	104	109	115
7 Russell	52	70	36	62	77	105	122	113

Find the optimal solution. (Hint: A dummy person is needed.)

12-34 Suppose that the following demands apply instead for providing skis from the Juarez plant to the Phoenix warehouse in the problem discussed in Section 12-9.

August	25 pairs
September	175
October	150
November	150

Also, suppose that now the regular production cost is $50 per pair, the overtime premium is $25 per pair, and the storage cost is $5 per pair. Solve this problem using the transportation method to determine the optimal plan for ski production at the Juarez plant.

12-35 Love and Peace Leather Works creates products from exotic skins obtained by the owner on hunting trips. After each hunt, the skins are cut into strips to make purse straps, belts, plant hangers, and hatbands. These items are sold to The Skin Boutique at an agreed price. On the latest trip, our hunter has obtained the following number of

strips: 30 rattlesnakes, 100 crocodiles, 50 armadillos, and 20 Gila monsters. Each strip is of equal size, and any one type of skin can be used for each final product. The Skin Boutique will buy up to 50 purse straps, 100 belts, 50 plant hangers, and 100 hatbands—regardless of the material used to make them. The prices yield the following profits to Love and Peace:

Skin	Product			
	Purse Strap	Belt	Plant Hanger	Hatband
Rattlesnake	$ 5	$12	$ 5	$10
Crocodile	10	15	5	10
Armadillo	8	10	10	5
Gila monster	10	20	20	15

Solve this problem using the transportation method to determine how Love and Peace can maximize its profits.

12-36 Hoopla Hoops produces Wendy Bendies at a unit cost of $3. A total of 500 units per month can be fabricated. The product may be produced in December, January, February, and March. Demands are: 300 for December, 400 for January, 300 for February, and 400 for March. There is a unit carrying cost of $.10 per month. Determine Hoopla's optimal production schedule.

Computer Problems

12-37 WaySafe Markets services eleven district warehouses from three regional centers. The following traffic volumes apply. The average cost of moving goods from a center to a warehouse is $.50 per ton per mile. Find the optimal shipment schedule and its cost.

Center	Distance (Miles)											Center Capacity (kilotons)
	W1	W2	W3	W4	W5	W6	W7	W8	W9	W10	W11	
C1	10	22	29	45	11	31	42	61	36	21	45	500
C2	25	35	17	38	9	17	65	45	42	5	41	750
C3	18	19	22	29	24	54	39	78	51	14	38	400
Warehouse Demand (kilotons)	112	85	138	146	77	89	101	215	53	49	153	

12-38 Refer to Problem 12-37 and your answers to that problem. Several modifications have been suggested. Consider each independently, modifying the original problem in each case. Solve the modified problem and answer the questions.

(a) A modernization program at center C1 will increase its capacity by 100 kilotons and reduce by 10% the cost of all shipments originating there.
  (1) By how much does total cost decrease?
  (2) By how much does the volume shipped out of C1 increase?

(b) Warehouse W8 is closed. Operations are consolidated at W7, so the demands are combined and the costs of W7 apply for all traffic originally slated for W8.
  (1) Does total cost increase or decrease?
  (2) Which centers now ship to W7?

(c) Center C1 is closed, and the capacity of C3 is raised from 400 to 500.
  (1) Does total cost increase or decrease?
  (2) What level of net fixed operating cost savings would justify the changes?

12-39 DanDee Assemblers ships parts from 4 manufacturing plants to 10 assembly plants. The following data apply:

Manufacturing Plant	Cost of Shipping for One Pound of Items										Manufacturing Capacity (thousand lbs.)
	A1	A2	A3	A4	A5	A6	A7	A8	A9	A10	
M1	$ 7	$11	$15	$ 8	$19	$12	$12	$6	$ 9	$10	155
M2	13	14	9	10	13	11	15	9	12	14	245
M3	8	9	12	20	10	5	4	8	15	12	325
M4	17	11	8	15	7	6	9	7	11	16	175
Assembly Demand (thousand lbs.)	75	155	120	130	75	95	115	55	145	195	

Find the optimal shipment schedule and its cost.

12-40 DanDee Assemblers in Problem 12-39 adds two new distribution centers, each with a capacity of 200. The following shipping cost from distribution centers to assembly plants data apply:

Centers	A1	A2	A3	A4	A5	A6	A7	A8	A9	A10
D1	2	1	1	2	2	3	2	3	3	3
D2	1	3	2	1	1	1	2	2	2	2

The following shipping cost from plants to distribution centers data apply:

Plant	D1	D2
M1	2	3
M2	3	2
M3	4	1
M4	1	3

Distribution centers may send items to each other at a one-way cost of $5 per thousand pounds. Find the optimal shipment schedule and its total cost.

12-41   Consider the assignment problem in file Problem12-41.xls. Determine the minimum-cost assignment schedule.

CASE 12-1   *Fast-Gro Fertilizer Company I*

Fast-Gro Fertilizer Company currently operates in California with two plants, located in Red Bluff (annual capacity 1,500,000 tons) and Bakersfield (1,000,000 tons). Fast-Gro has two warehouses, each with a capacity of 500,000 tons, situated in Sacramento and Visalia. Each facility lies near the center of gravity of a local sales territory. The California market is divided into five more territories, each containing hundreds of individual customers.

Fast-Gro plants serve the warehouse function for the territory in which they are situated. Any warehouse may deliver to customers in neighboring territories, within geographical constraints. Table 12-3 provides the territory demands and the applicable distances. Blank entries indicate that no shipments are allowed over that route.

The numbers along the main diagonal represent average delivery distances from the central point to customers within the territory. For example, 10 miles is the average distance from the center to customers within the Imperial territory. That distance will be used as the miles to the Imperial customer group aggregation. A shipment from the Bakersfield plant to the Imperial customer group will go by truck over a distance of 240 + 10 = 250 miles. A shipment to the Turlock customer group may be made directly from the Bakersfield plant, a truck distance of 150 + 25 = 175 miles. The same Turlock customer group might instead receive shipments through the Visalia warehouse; those items would travel 50 miles by rail from Bakersfield to Visalia, then another 95 + 25 = 120 miles by truck. (Because rail and truck routes differ, the total distances are not the same.)

TABLE 12-3   Mileage Data and Allowed Routes for the Fast-Gro Fertilizer Company

Territory	Distance									Demand (Thousand Tons)
	1	2	3	4	5	6	7	8	9	
1. Bakersfield (plant)	35	240	240	—	210	150	140	150	50	250
2. Imperial	—	10	—	—	—	—	130	—	—	300
3. Napa/North Coast	—	—	20	—	50	100	—	100	—	150
4. Red Bluff (plant)	—	—	120	30	110	240	—	200	280	200
5. Sacramento (whse.)	—	—	50	—	25	140	—	70	—	400
6. Salinas	—	—	100	—	—	15	—	80	160	400
7. San Bernardino	—	130	—	—	—	—	15	—	—	200
8. Turlock	—	—	100	—	—	80	—	25	—	150
9. Visalia (whse.)	—	—	—	—	—	160	—	95	20	300

Freight costs per ton-mile are $.02 by truck and $.01 by rail. Rail shipments are made only from a plant to a warehouse.

QUESTIONS

1. Construct a transportation problem matrix for Fast-Gro's distribution. Be sure to set up the schedule as a *transshipment* problem, so that each warehouse has both a row and a column. Warehouses may not ship to another warehouse, and the corresponding variables should be represented in the shipment schedule as *impossible cells,* as would forbidden routings. These cells should each have an arbitrarily high cost. As a final step, add a dummy row or column to make total demand equal total capacity.

2. Solve the transportation problem in (1) and find the minimum transportation cost, using a computer if possible. If you solve it by hand, use the cheapest cell method or Vogel's approximation to start. Make no allocations to impossible cells, and proceed to determine the optimal solution.

3. Suppose that the warehouse capacities are increased to 750,000 tons each. Determine the new optimal shipment schedule and its total cost.

CASE 12-2 *Panamint Springs Resort*

Natalia Detroit operates the Panamint Springs Resort, a small casino complex in rural Nevada. She wants to use linear programming concepts to determine where to locate slot machines; they come in five different types. Natalia has determined that machines of various types should be grouped together, reasoning that overall activity of the machines as a group will draw customers to them. The basic configuration of the slot area is established, beginning with assignments of leading slots to the corners and heavy foot traffic areas.

Figure 12-41 shows a floor plan of the Panamint casino area. Every slot location is represented by a small rectangle. Numbers are shown for the leading locations.

Natalia wants to position machines of similar type throughout the casino in roughly the same proportion as the first 23 to be assigned to the leading locations. The following baseline mix of machines might be assigned in the first group:

Machine Type	Number of Machines	Identity Numbers
$1.00 Poker	3	100P1, 100P2, 100P3
.25 Poker	6	25P1, 25P2, 25P3, 25P4, 25P5, 25P6
.25 Fruit	5	25F1, 25F2, 25F3, 25F4, 25F5
.10 Fruit	3	10F1, 10F2, 10F3
.05 Fruit	6	5F1, 5F2, 5F3, 5F4, 5F5, 5F6

Natalia is considering various criteria for deciding slot placement. She hired several college students to count the number of persons passing nine strategic points (A–I in Figure 12-41). From their data, the following 24-hour average foot traffic counts were estimated:

Strategic Point	24-Hour Foot Traffic
A	1,950
B	1,780
C	3,200
D	1,850
E	3,500
F	4,800
G	1,600
H	950
I	1,840

Prior testing has established that 5% of casino customers passing near any slot group will stop to play at the first empty machine.

Net receipts from a particular slot machine vary with machine type. Past experience provides the following data:

Machine Type	Average Duration of Play	Number of Plays per Minute
$1.00 Poker	5 minutes	3
.25 Poker	10	3
.25 Fruit	20	4
.10 Fruit	30	4
.05 Fruit	30	4

Regardless of denomination, Panamint machines provide average net receipts equal to 10% of the amount bet at each pull.

The length of play is also affected by general casino area as well as by slot type. Special studies provide the data in Table 12-4.

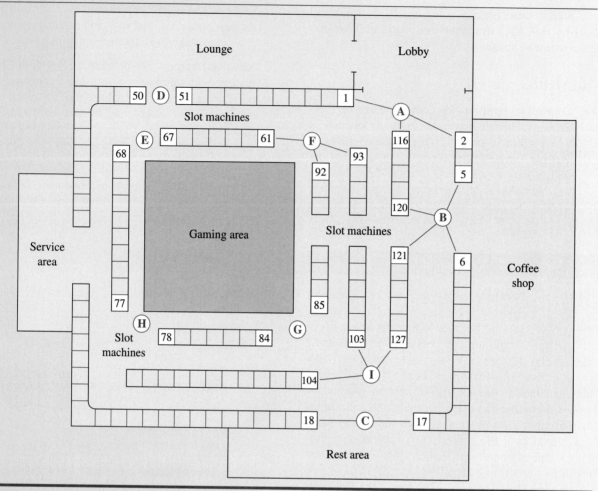

FIGURE 12-41   Casino area of Panamint Springs Resort

TABLE 12-4	Important Data for Panamint Springs Resort				
	Average Play Time (Minutes)				
Machine Type	**Near Coffee Shop**	**Near Lobby**	**Near Lounge**	**Gaming Area**	**Rest Area**
$1.00 Poker	2	10	10	10	3
.25 Poker	5	5	10	5	10
.25 Fruit	15	10	20	25	10
.10 Fruit	15	10	30	30	45
.05 Fruit	25	10	30	30	45
Slot Locations	5, 6, 120, 121	1, 2, 116	50, 51	61, 67, 68, 77, 78, 84, 85, 92, 93	17, 18, 103, 104, 127

The exact machine mix is flexible. Besides the baseline mix, the following four variations are being considered:

Machine Type	(a) Smoothed Out	(b) High-End Skew	(c) Low-End Skew	(d) Poker Skew
$1.00 Poker	4	8	2	8
.25 Poker	4	4	2	6
.25 Fruit	5	5	5	2
.10 Fruit	5	3	7	3
.05 Fruit	5	3	7	4

Identity numbers for these possibilities follow the pattern of the baseline mix.

Natalia wants to maximize 24-hour slot machine net receipts from the 23 strategic locations and their extended groups.

QUESTIONS

1. Using foot traffic counts for the nearest strategic spot and casinowide average durations of play, determine Panamint's average 24-hour net receipts for each slot type and possible leading location for a group of identical machines. (For simplicity, assume there is always at least one free machine in any group.)

2. Using the baseline machine mix, find that assignment for the 23 locations that will maximize Panamint's average 24-hour net receipts.

3. Natalia does not feel that the results in Question 1 reflect differences in major casino area types. Using the average play time for the five areas instead of the casinowide average, determine Panamint's average 24-hour net receipts for each slot type and possible leading location for a group of identical machines.

4. Using the baseline machine mix, find the assignment for the 23 locations that will maximize Panamint's average 24-hour net receipts based on your answers to Question 3.

5. Natalia wants to determine if there is a better machine mix than the baseline. Using the payoffs from Question 3, determine for each type mix (a)–(d) the optimal assignment for the 23 locations.

6. From your answers to Questions 4 and 5, which machine mix provides the maximum net receipts?

7. Provide Natalia with suggestions that might help her reach a final choice of slot machine locations.

CHAPTER 13

NETWORK MODELS

Mathematical models of networks give us algorithms so computationally efficient that we can employ them to evaluate problems too big to be solved any other way.

As we have seen, resource allocations are made in a tremendous variety of decisions. This chapter focuses on special applications that may all be represented in terms of a network. The models described are especially useful in distribution applications, allowing us to evaluate different kinds of problems from those encountered in Chapter 12 as well as similar problems that are far too complex to be efficiently solved with the transportation methods described there.

Network models have applicability ranging from project scheduling to production planning and facilities layout decisions. All problem situations described in this chapter may be represented in terms of a physical network, which makes them easy to formulate. Network problems have a structure making them easier to solve than most linear programs, because the underlying algorithms are graphical and less abstract. Their simplicity has been advantageously used with computers to very efficiently solve linear programming problems of very large size. Many such problems would be extremely unwieldy to tackle with the general simplex method.

DECISION PROBLEM

WaySafe Markets Determines Retail Districts

Lela Sanchez is the operations manager of WaySafe Markets. One of her responsibilities is to establish boundaries for districts. A district is defined as a retail store grouping in the neighborhood of one company warehouse that is assigned responsibility for servicing those outlets. The current groupings of stores and warehouses are 12 years old, and Lela believes that a complete reorganization is necessary.

To start her evaluation, Lela focused on a retail store group in which one warehouse supplies two stores. Looking at a map, she saw that it is possible to go directly from the warehouse located at B to one of the stores, at D, in 2 hours (120 minutes). The store, at G, can be reached only by passing through another city. Because there are alternative routes from the warehouse to each store, which pass through other cities, Lela determined all the distances and calculated the times shown in Table 13-1. Looking at this table, Lela wonders if routes exist through other cities that are shorter than the direct route she initially calculated. For example, she sees that going from warehouse B directly to store site D takes 120 minutes, but going to C first and then to D

TABLE 13-1   Mean WaySafe Point-to-Point Travel Times (Minutes)

FROM \ TO	A (Warehouse)	B (Warehouse)	C	D (Store Site)	E	F	G (Store Site)	H	I
A	—	25	NA	NA	25	40	150	30	NA
B (Warehouse)		—	40	120	NA	NA	NA	45	30
C			—	55	35	25	NA	25	NA
D (Store Site)				—	20	35	30	NA	25
E					—	20	30	40	NA
F						—	35	NA	35
G (Store Site)							—	35	20
H								—	35
I									—

requires only 95 minutes. Lela wonders if even quicker routes exist. What is the quickest route from warehouse B to store site D?

Once she knows the quickest routes for all of WaySafe's warehouses and stores, Lela would like to determine the optimal shipping quantities from each warehouse to each store. The determination of those shipments is complicated because demands are different at each store and because the delivery trucks have limited capacities. The material presented in this chapter will assist Lela in finding the answers to these and other similar questions.

13-1 THE STRUCTURE OF NETWORK PROBLEMS

Network problem situations are represented graphically by a chart as in Figure 13-1. Such a network is like a road map — lines connect points to represent roads joining cities. The linkages in a network are generally referred to as **arcs,** each connecting two **nodes,** just like a road segment that begins in one city and ends at another.

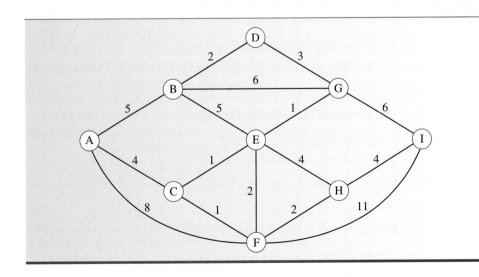

FIGURE 13-1
Network structure

TABLE 13-2	Examples of Situations for Which Network Models Have Been Used			
NETWORK TYPE	**NODES**	**ARCS**	**ARC VALUE**	**FLOW**
Computer network	Work stations	Cable links	Connection, yes or no	Messages
Distribution system	Loading facilities	Roads	Capacity	Cargo
Airline	Airports	Airplanes	Flights	Traffic
Project	Milestones	Activities	Cost	Time
Road map	Cities	Highways	Distance	Route

We may think of a road map as an *iconic* or graphical model representing a transportation network. Although the arc "lines" can curve, the network is ordinarily an abstract rendering, so that the actual road's bends and curves are left out. Like a map showing cities that take up space, the nodes are "points" represented as circles. Each arc has some distance between nodes, which on a map is implicit by the physical length of the road. Some maps even mark the distance with a number; such a quantity is an **arc value.** Other arc values, usually not appearing on a physical map, might include driving time between nodes or the cost of traversing a particular arc. Usually one or more **node values** apply to a network as well. In this chapter, we represent networks with both a graphical model and a mathematical model to symbolically represent the various elements and values.

The network linkages in Figure 13-1 are **undirected arcs.** Some network problems involve instead **directed arcs;** movement along these arcs would always begin at a particular node and terminate at another. Such arcs would appear on a chart as *arrows.*

We will look at network situations that involve decision making, such as what route to take or how to send shipments to minimize time or cost. All such problems involve determining **flow.** These problems can be expressed as linear programs involving a **flow variable** for each arc. The network model is a very general one, and the road map is just one of the most familiar situations imaginable. Table 13-2 shows some of the variety of situations that might be so represented.

Although network problems may be solved like any linear program, some can be best solved using a special-purpose algorithm that combines the graph or chart with a set of rules. These algorithms involve a series of iterations, some requiring a new chart at each step.

We will begin with the **shortest route** problem, which tells us that route which minimizes traveling distance from the start to any city in the network. Then we will investigate the **minimal spanning tree** problem, which seeks to find that set of linkages connecting all nodes with the minimum possible combined distance. This is followed by the **maximum flow** problem, which could be used to determine how a military convoy could send the maximum amount of traffic from one source to a single destination. The last model is the **maximum flow minimum cost** problem, which could be used — very much like the transportation problem — to optimize shipments for a multiechelon distribution system with arcs having both lower and upper bounds.

13-2   THE SHORTEST ROUTE PROBLEM

The **shortest route** problem is conceptually the simplest network model. To illustrate, we will consider the plight of a long-haul dispatcher for Yellow Jacket Freightways who is responsible for routing trucks over the network in Figure 13-2.

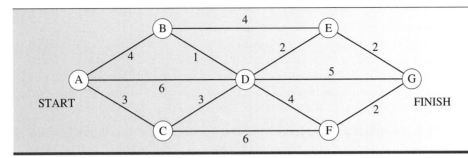

FIGURE 13-2
Network for the Yellow
Jacket Freightways
distribution

You may think of that chart as exactly like a road map with all nonessential information missing; it is not drawn to scale. The *arcs* are shown as lines and represent the highway linkages connecting distribution centers. Because two-way movement is possible between all distribution centers, the network arcs are *undirected.* These centers, A through G, are the network *nodes.* Along each arc is a number indicating the distance (in hundreds of miles) between the two centers when that route is taken. Node A is designated as the START and node G as the FINISH.

The dispatcher wants to find the shortest **route** or **path**— represented on the network by a sequence of arcs — from the START at node A to the FINISH at node G. (As we shall see, in solving this problem the dispatcher will also get the shortest route from START to *each* node, not just the FINISH.)

The Algorithm

We want to find the shortest path from center A to center G. Various approaches might be taken. One possibility would be to trace through all paths, adding the arc distances along the way, to get the total distance from taking each path. That would be very inefficient because there are so many possibilities.

It has proven much more efficient to find the minimum distance from START to each node, beginning with the closest ones. Always working away from those nodes whose minimum distances are known, a series of evaluations can be made using all the information obtained to determine the next closest nodes. Eventually the minimum distance between START and FINISH, and the path that corresponds, will become known.

All of the work can be done on the original network chart, with a few simple calculations (easily done in your head) and with annotations penciled in at each iteration. Once the shortest route to a node becomes known, it becomes *evaluated,* which is indicated by placing a node value above it equal to the minimum distance from START and shading in the node.

SOLUTION PROCEDURE

ALGORITHM FOR THE SHORTEST ROUTE

The following steps apply:

1. **Assign START a node value of 0 and shade in its node.** This becomes the first evaluated node.

2. **Mark all arcs connecting an evaluated node to an unevaluated one.** Calculate for each arc the sum of its evaluated node's value and the arc length. This establishes the minimum cumulative distance from START to the node at the unevaluated end of the arc.

3. **Select the arc having the minimum sum.** Locate the unevaluated node for this *key arc* and place the minimum sum near it as the node value. That node value equals the minimum distance to it from START. Shade in that node, which is now evaluated. Place a pointer near this newest evaluated node, alongside the key arc, aiming at the key arc's opposite node. (Repeat for all arcs that tie for minimum sum.) If the FINISH is not yet evaluated, return to step 2.

4. **Find the shortest route from START to FINISH.** The shortest route is identified by that path found by tracing backward from the FINISH to the START, following the pointers. (There may be ties for shortest route.) The minimum distance from START to FINISH is the node value for the FINISH node.

Illustration

We will illustrate the algorithm by solving the Yellow Jacket Freightways problem. The process begins with iteration 1 in Figure 13-3. There the START, node A, has been shaded in and assigned a node value of 0. We mark the following arcs

$$(A, B) \ (A, D) \ (A, C)$$

which are the only ones connecting evaluated node (A) to unevaluated nodes (B, C, and D). The minimum distance from A to each of these unevaluated nodes can be determined now. The cumulative distance to a selected unevaluated node equals the sum of the node number 0 for its connecting arc's evaluated node (A in all cases) and the respective arc length. These sums are shown in color beside the respective nodes. We have

$$0 + 4 = 4 \text{ to node B}$$
$$0 + 3 = 3^* \text{ to node C}$$
$$0 + 5 = 5 \text{ to node D}$$

(You do not actually have to enter the colored information on your chart. It is simple enough to keep track of in your head. It might help for a while to lightly pencil it in, erasing what is no longer needed as you go along.)

The minimum sum (marked with the asterisk) occurs for node C. Arc (A, C) is on the shortest route from A to C. We lightly pencil in "yes" beside arc (A, C), as shown in color, to denote that fact. Although the other two arcs, (A, B) and (A, D), might also be on a shortest route to their respective nodes, we will not worry about that for now. We cross out the sums in Figure 13-3 and lightly pencil in a "no" beside those arcs.

FIGURE 13-3

Iteration 1 of the Yellow Jacket Freightways shortest route problem

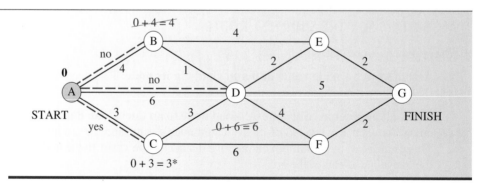

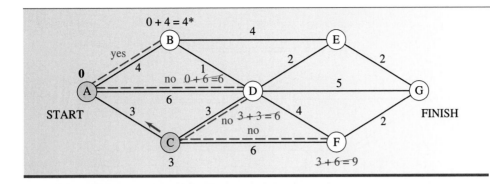

FIGURE 13-4
Iteration 2 of the Yellow Jacket Freightways shortest route problem

Although we would ordinarily do everything on a single chart, marking, crossing out, and erasing as we go along, it will be helpful to show a separate partial diagram at each iteration. Figure 13-4 shows how a permanent record has been made of our findings so far. A permanent node value of 3 is entered below node C, now shaded in. A pointer (little arrow) is placed beside arc (A, C) aiming back to node A to indicate the direction of the shortest route from START to C. All the other temporary information shown in color in Figure 13-3 has been erased. A brand new iteration 2 begins in Figure 13-4.

We identify all arcs connecting evaluated (shaded) nodes (A and C) directly to unevaluated nodes (B, D, and F). The dashed colored lines highlight these, arcs (A, B), (A, D), (C, D), and (C, F). A cumulative distance is computed as before from START to each of these arcs' unevaluated node.

$$0 + 4 = 4* \text{ to node B (from A)}$$
$$0 + 6 = 6 \text{ to node D (from A)}$$
$$3 + 3 = 6 \text{ to node D (from C)}$$
$$3 + 6 = 9 \text{ to node F (from C)}$$

For all arcs connecting node C, the minimum distance of 3 found in the previous iteration is added to each link distance to get the total distance over that route from the start. The minimum cumulative distance is 4, ending at node B via arc (A, B). The sums for the other nodes are crossed out, and node B will now be included in the evaluated nodes, at a minimum distance of 4.

Figure 13-5 shows the network for iteration 3. Node B is now shaded and temporary marks from before are erased. A pointer is placed along arc (A, B) aiming back to node A. Those arcs directly connecting evaluated nodes to unevaluated ones —(A, D),

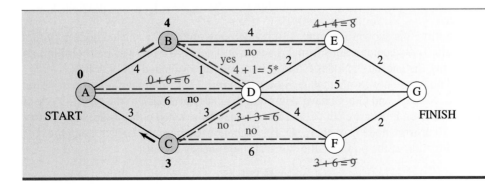

FIGURE 13-5
Iteration 3 of the Yellow Jacket Freightways shortest route problem

FIGURE 13-6
Iteration 4 of the Yellow Jacket Freightways shortest route problem

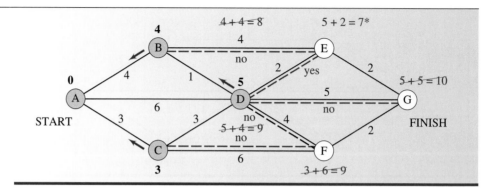

(B, D), (B, E), (C, D), and (C, F)— are again highlighted. The following cumulative distances to the ending nodes of those arcs are found:

$$0 + 6 = 6 \text{ to node D (from A)}$$
$$4 + 1 = 5^* \text{ to node D (from B)}$$
$$4 + 4 = 8 \text{ to node E (from B)}$$
$$3 + 3 = 6 \text{ to node D (from C)}$$
$$3 + 6 = 9 \text{ to node F (from C)}$$

The minimum distance is 5 to D along (B, D). Node D now joins the evaluated set, with a node value of 5 that is equal to the minimum distance from START to that node.

Iteration 4 starts on the new chart shown in Figure 13-6. The temporary marks from before have been erased, node D is shaded and given a node value of 5, and a new pointer aims in the direction of the minimum distance back to START. The highlighted arcs directly connecting evaluated nodes to unevaluated ones are (B, E), (C, F), (D, E), (D, F), and (D, G). The following cumulative distances to the ending nodes of these arcs are found:

$$4 + 4 = 8 \text{ to node E (from B)}$$
$$5 + 2 = 7^* \text{ to node E (from D)}$$
$$3 + 6 = 9 \text{ to node F (from C)}$$
$$5 + 4 = 9 \text{ to node F (from D)}$$
$$5 + 5 = 10 \text{ to node G (from D)}$$

The minimum, 7, establishes the minimum distance to node E, which joins the evaluated set.

Iteration 5 is shown in Figure 13-7, which now includes a shaded node E with a node value of 7; a pointer aims from E back to D. There is a three-way tie for minimum cumulative distance at 9. Nodes F and G both join the evaluated set of nodes.

All nodes are now evaluated, as shown in Figure 13-8, where the solution has been reached. Nodes F and G both have minimum distances of 9 back to the START. Node G is reached from E over arc (E, G) and node F may be reached either from node C over arc (C, F) or from node D over arc (D, F). Tracing back from the FINISH along the arcs in the direction of the pointers, the shortest route (heavy arcs) is

A-B-D-E-G

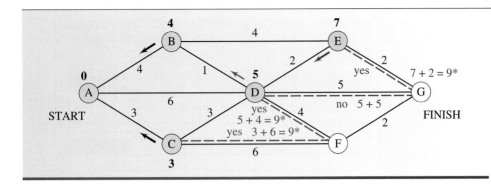

FIGURE 13-7
Iteration 5 of the Yellow Jacket Freightways shortest route problem

The minimum distance from START to FINISH equals the sum of the arc lengths on this path

$$C = 4 + 1 + 2 + 2 = 9$$

Solving Problems with Computer Assistance

Although it is easy to solve small shortest route problems by hand, larger problems will generally be solved with computer assistance. *QuickQuant* 2000 has a module for solving all network problems presented in this chapter, including the Yellow Jacket Freightways problem.

After *QuickQuant* is instructed that there are 7 nodes for the Yellow Jacket Freightways problem, a series of screens appear into which the arc data are entered by filling in the blanks. Figure 13-9 shows the data input screen. The screen window moves as needed until all data are entered correctly. Those cells corresponding to nonexistent arcs must be left *blank*. Clicking on "Done" activates the menu bar.

The problem data may then be stored on file for future use. After selecting the "Run" choice from the *QuickQuant* menu, the program creates its own network, in accordance with the underlying logic, and then solves the problem. The report in Figure 13-10 is provided on the screen. The same report may also be stored on file or printed as hard copy.

The positioning of nodes may differ from a hand-drawn sketch, because there are many equivalent charts possible for the same network. The arc distance is shown within the respective line, with the shortest route indicated by the heavy lines. The arrow pointers from each node are placed above the line for that arc on the shortest path back to START, with the corresponding cumulative distance shown below the nodes.

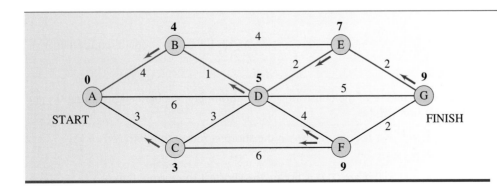

FIGURE 13-8
Solution of the Yellow Jacket Freightways shortest route problem

FIGURE 13-9
Main *QuickQuant* data input screen for the Yellow Jacket Freightways shortest route problem

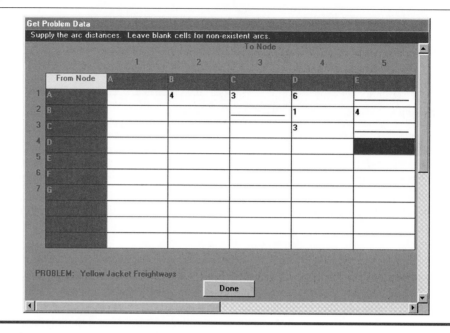

The Linear Programming Model and Excel Solution

The shortest route problems may be expressed as linear programs. When so formulated, the same problems can be solved a second way using Excel's Solver.

The network contains nodes identified by code numbers $0, 1, 2, \ldots, N$. Node 0 is the START and node N is the FINISH. The flow variables X_{ij} represent the amount of flow along undirected arc (i, j) from node i to node j. (There is no variable for those node pairs not connected by an arc.) Each arc (i, j) has a length or distance c_{ij} between nodes i and j. The mathematical model for this dispatcher problem is stated in general terms by the following linear program. The objective is to

$$\text{Minimize} \quad C = \sum_{i=0}^{N} \sum_{j=0}^{N} c_{ij} X_{ij}$$

Subject to

$$\sum_{i=0}^{N} X_{ik} = \sum_{j=0}^{N} X_{kj} \quad \text{for intermediate nodes } k = 1, 2, \ldots, N-1 \quad \text{(conservation of flow)}$$

$$\sum_{j=0}^{N} X_{0j} = 1 \qquad\qquad\qquad\qquad\qquad\qquad\qquad\qquad \text{(path requirement)}$$

$$\sum_{i=0}^{N} X_{iN} = 1 \qquad\qquad\qquad\qquad\qquad\qquad\qquad\qquad \text{(path requirement)}$$

where all $X_{ij} \geq 0$

Due to the nature of the constraints, a solution may be obtained involving 0's and 1's. The solution will be

$$X_{ij} = \begin{cases} 1 \text{ if arc } (i, j) \text{ lies on the shortest route from 0 to } N \\ \qquad\qquad\qquad\qquad \text{or} \\ 0 \text{ if arc } (i, j) \text{ is not on the shortest route from 0 to } N \end{cases}$$

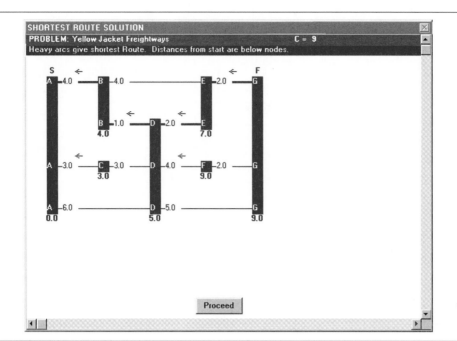

FIGURE 13-10

QuickQuant solution screen for the Yellow Jacket Freightways shortest route problem

Because those X's having a value of 1 will lie on the shortest route connecting 0 to N, the minimum distance will be the sum of the c's for arcs on that path. The first group of constraints expresses *conservation of flow* for the intermediate nodes, so that combined flow *into* a node must be equal to the combined flow *out*. These conditions prohibit nonsensical solutions that loop, end early, or start from the wrong place. The path requirement constraint forces the solution to have exactly one route from the START. Flow conservation guarantees that the selected path will end at node N.

To illustrate, the Excel solution to the Yellow Jacket Freightways linear program is given in Figure 13-11. The spreadsheet is organized with a from-to distance matrix at the top and a to-from solution report below that. Impossible routes have a cell distance of 1,000. To start, any values (or blanks) may be entered into the solution portion (B21:H27). The total outflows are given in column I and the total inflows in row 28; their cells may contain any value (or be blank) to start.

The total outflow in cell I21 has the formula =SUM(B21:H21) (copied down to B29), with the values in I21:I27 transferred into B29:H29. The total inflow in cell B28 has the formula =SUM(B21:B27) (copied over to H28). The net flow in row 30 is the total outflow minus the total inflow, so that cell B30 has the formula =B29-B28 (copied over to H30). The required flows in cells B31:H31 reflect the conservation of flow requirements for the intermediate nodes (all of which are given a value of zero) and the path requirements for the start and end nodes. Thus, the starting node A receives a 1 (cell B31) indicating that the path leaves from that node and the ending node G gets −1 (cell H31) signifying that the path arrives at that node.

The solution C in cell E17 has the formula

$$=SUMPRODUCT(B9:H15,B21:H27)$$

FIGURE 13-11

Excel spreadsheet for finding the Yellow Jacket Freightways shortest route using linear programming

	A	B	C	D	E	F	G	H	I	J	K
1				SHORTEST ROUTE SOLUTION							
2											
3	PROBLEM:		Yellow Jacket Freightways								
4											
5					Distances						
6											
7					To Node						
8	From Node	A	B	C	D	E	F	G			
9	A	1000	4	3	6	1000	1000	1000			
10	B	4	1000	1000	1	4	1000	1000			
11	C	3	1000	1000	3	1000	6	1000			
12	D	6	1	3	1000	2	4	5			
13	E	1000	4	1000	2	1000	1000	2			
14	F	1000	1000	6	4	1000	1000	2			
15	G	1000	1000	1000	5	2	2	1000			
16											
17				Solution C =	9				E17 =SUMPRODUCT(B9:H15,B21:H27)		
18											
19					To Node				Total		
20	From Node	A	B	C	D	E	F	G	Outflow		
21	A	0	1	0	0	0	0	0	1	21 =SUM(B21:H21)	
22	B	0	0	0	1	0	0	0	1	22 =SUM(B22:H22)	
23	C	0	0	0	0	0	0	0	0	23 =SUM(B23:H23)	
24	D	0	0	0	0	1	0	0	1	24 =SUM(B24:H24)	
25	E	0	0	0	0	0	0	1	1	25 =SUM(B25:H25)	
26	F	0	0	0	0	0	0	0	0	26 =SUM(B26:H26)	
27	G	0	0	0	0	0	0	0	0	27 =SUM(B27:H27)	
28	Total Inflow	0	1	0	1	1	0	1			
29	Total Outflow	1	1	0	1	1	0	0			
30	Net Flow	1	0	0	0	0	0	-1			
31	Required Flow	1	0	0	0	0	0	-1			

	B	C	D	E
28	=SUM(B21:B27)	=SUM(C21:C27)	=SUM(D21:D27)	=SUM(E21:E27)
29	=I21	=I22	=I23	=I24
30	=B29-B28	=C29-C28	=D29-D28	=E29-E28
31	1	0	0	0

	F	G	H
28	=SUM(F21:F27)	=SUM(G21:G27)	=SUM(H21:H27)
29	=I25	=I26	=I27
30	=F29-F28	=G29-G28	=H29-H28
31	0	0	-1

and is minimized using Solver, with B21:H27 as the changing cells. Because the net flows must equal the required flows, the only Solver constraint (except for the non-negativity conditions) is that B30:H30=B31:H31. Figure 13-12 shows the Solver Parameters dialog box.

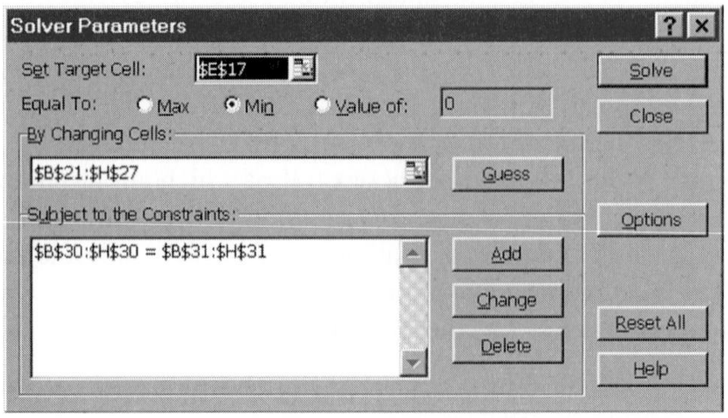

FIGURE 13-12

The Solver Parameters dialog box for Yellow Jacket Freightways

Solver Parameters

Set Target Cell: $E$17

Equal To: ○ Max   ● Min   ○ Value of: 0

By Changing Cells:
$B$21:$H$27   Guess

Subject to the Constraints:
$B$30:$H$30 = $B$31:$H$31   Add   Change   Delete

Solve   Close   Options   Reset All   Help

The 1's in the solution table at the bottom of Figure 13-11 indicate the same shortest route found earlier, A-B-D-E-G, with a minimum total distance of 9 (cell E17).

WaySafe Managerial Decision Revisited: Determining Routings

Before she can solve the final problem of determining the best quantities to send from each warehouse to particular stores. Lela Sanchez must determine the warehouse-to-store routings. There are many possibilities. For example, from Table 13-1, two possible routings between the warehouse in city B and the store at city G are

B-C-E-G at 40 + 35 + 30 = 105 minutes and B-D-G at 120 + 30 = 150 minutes

Although with the relatively small set of cities in Table 13-1 an exhaustive listing of all possibilities could determine the optimal routing between B and G and between B and D, it would be quite time consuming. A complete enumeration would be impractical for larger networks of cities. Instead, Lela solved the shortest route problems to the two store sites from city B, finding

B-I-D at 30 + 25 = 55 minutes
B-I-G at 30 + 20 = 50 minutes

13-3 MINIMAL SPANNING TREE PROBLEM

An interesting class of problems is concerned with selecting certain arcs in a network to receive a special treatment. An important group of such problems involves finding a set of arcs that connect all nodes. Once the arcs have been selected, they can provide a plan for setting up a system in which every node can communicate with every other node along some path connecting them. An efficient plan would not use all arcs in the original network, thereby conserving scarce resources needed in making the physical connections over the chosen linkages.

To illustrate the concept of selecting connecting arcs, consider the problem faced by Security Alarm Company in installing a motion detection system in a building. Altogether, the plan requires 10 sensor sites, shown as nodes in the network in Figure 13-13. The arcs connecting these sites are feasible linkages that might be included in

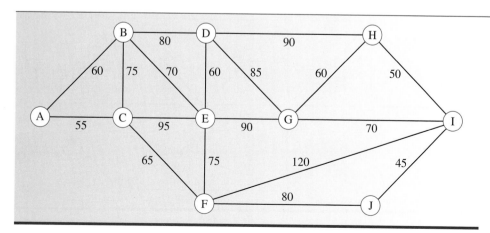

FIGURE 13-13
Network for the Security Alarm Company motion detection system

FIGURE 13-14
Possible solution (nontree) for the Security Alarm Company motion detection system

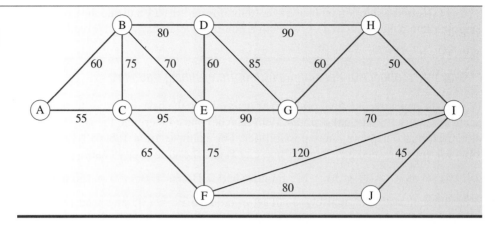

the final design, with the arc lengths representing the distance (feet) between the respective pair of nodes. The sensor sites will be joined by a series of optical fiber cable connections over which intruder alarms can be relayed, via any open route through connected sensors, to a central processor (CPU) located at one of the sites. The company wants to find that plan which minimizes the total cable distance.

One possible solution is shown in Figure 13-14. The colored arcs form a **connected set** in which each node has at least one path connecting it to every other node in the set. Although workable, the illustrated plan forms a **loop** through all the arcs, resulting in redundant linkages. The illustrated plan will not minimize the total connecting distance.

A connected set having no loops is called a **tree.** Figure 13-15 provides a possible Security Alarm plan involving two trees. The nodes A, B, C, D, and E are connected by arcs forming one tree, while nodes F, G, H, I, and J are connected with a second tree. The plan would be infeasible, however, because not all nodes are connected to the rest through some path; thus only five sites can communicate with the CPU if it is located at A.

A feasible solution is shown in Figure 13-16, which provides a **spanning tree** that connects all nodes with a single tree. A spanning tree will have a total number of branches equal to the number of nodes minus one. As we shall see, another spanning tree provides a solution requiring even less cable. We want to find the solution with the

FIGURE 13-15
Infeasible solution for the Security Alarm Company problem showing two separate trees

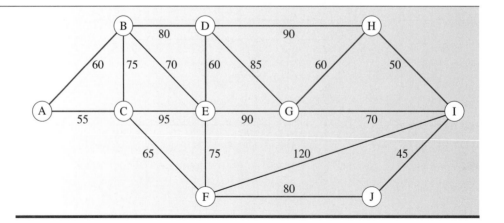

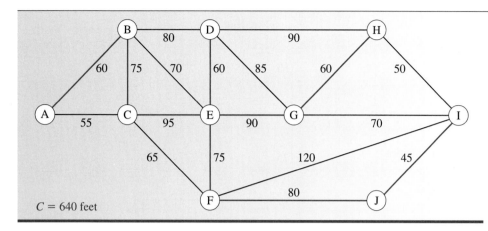

FIGURE 13-16
A spanning tree for the
Security Alarm Company
problem that is not minimal

minimum cable requirement. A solution that minimizes the combined arc length is called a **minimal spanning tree.**

The Algorithm

For small problems, the minimal spanning tree can be found by trial and error. It will be far more efficient to construct the tree in stages, adding at each iteration the single most attractive branch, until the solution has been found. This can be done simply, with the results of each iteration marked directly on the network graph.

SOLUTION PROCEDURE

ALGORITHM FOR MINIMAL SPANNING TREE

The following steps apply.

1. **Pick any node as the initial *connected* node.** Shade in that node.

2. **Identify all arcs joining a connected node (shaded) with an unconnected node.**

3. **Select the arc from step 2 having the minimum length.** Join that arc to the tree, reinforcing its arc line, and include its unconnected node in the connected set, shading it.

4. **Stop when all arcs are shaded.** The reinforced arcs are on the minimal spanning tree. Otherwise, go back to step 2.

Illustration

The Security Alarm Company problem illustrates the algorithm. It does not matter which node is the start; we designate node A as the initial connected node. Although only one network chart is needed to establish the minimal spanning tree, we will use several to help explain the process. Figure 13-17 shows the first iteration, where node A might be connected to node B (connections are marked by dashed lines) at a distance of 60 feet over arc (A, B), or to node C at a distance of 55 feet over (A, C). Because arc (A, C) is the shortest, it will be added to the tree and node C will join the connected set of nodes.

FIGURE 13-17
Iteration 1 of the Security
Alarm minimal spanning
tree problem

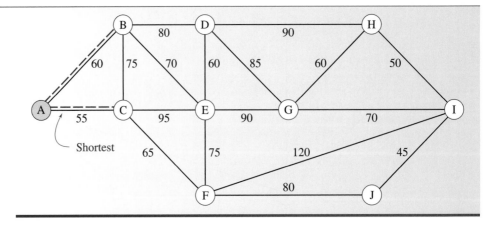

The second iteration is shown in Figure 13-18. There the temporary information is erased, node C is shaded, and arc (A, C) is now reinforced (appearing as a solid colored line). We use *both* connected nodes, A and C, in defining the candidate arcs to be added to the tree. The possible additions are (A, B) at 60 feet, (B, C) at 75 feet, (C, E) at 95 feet, and (C, F) at 65 feet. The shortest arc (A, B) will be added to the tree. Node B will join the connected nodes.

Iteration 3 is shown in Figure 13-19, where node B is shaded and the reinforced arc (A, B) is shown in solid color. Only arcs (B, D) at 80 feet, (B, E) at 70 feet, (C, E) at 95 feet, and (C, F) at 65 feet are candidates to join the tree. [Arc (B, C) will never be considered again because it joins two already connected nodes.] Arc (C, F), the shortest, will be added to the tree, with node F joining the connected nodes.

The process continues, but for brevity, we leave out several charts. In iteration 4, arc (B, E) is added to the tree and node E is connected (Figure 13-20). In iteration 5, arc (D, E) joins the tree and node D is connected. Iteration 6 joins arc (F, J) to the tree and connects node J. Iteration 7 joins arc (I, J) to the tree and connects node I. Iteration 8 joins arc (H, I) and connects node H.

Figure 13-20 shows iteration 9. The candidate arcs are (D, G) at 85 feet and (G, H) at 60 feet. The shortest arc is (G, H), which becomes the last branch to be added to the tree. The final solution is shown in Figure 13-21, where the minimal spanning tree is portrayed by the colored arcs. This tree has a combined length of 545 feet.

FIGURE 13-18
Iteration 2 of the Security
Alarm minimal spanning
tree problem

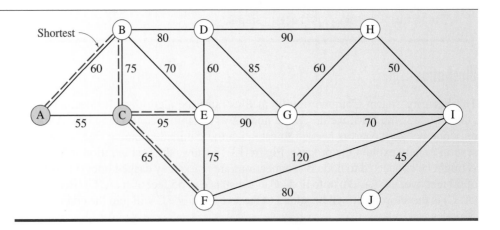

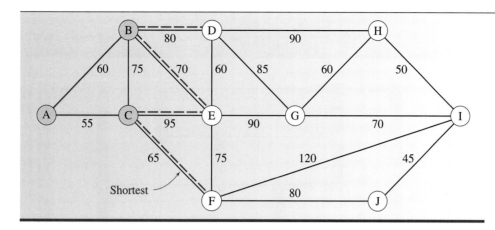

FIGURE 13-19
Iteration 3 of the Security Alarm minimal spanning tree problem

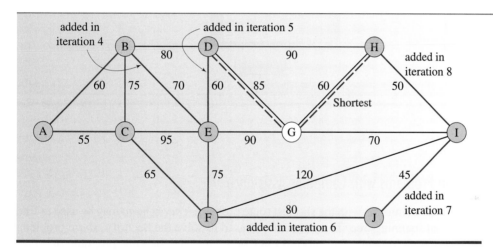

FIGURE 13-20
Iteration 9 of the Security Alarm minimal spanning tree problem

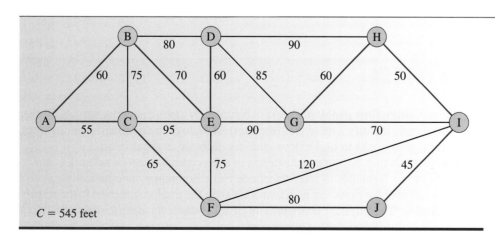

FIGURE 13-21
Solution to the Security Alarm minimal spanning tree problem

FIGURE 13-22

QuickQuant composite screen showing solution of Security Alarm minimal spanning tree problem

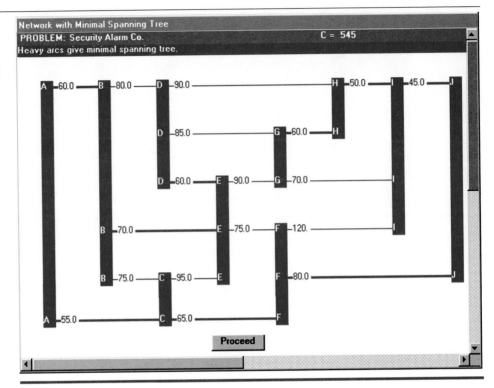

Solving Problems with Computer Assistance

In a similar manner as with the shortest route problem, *QuickQuant* may be used to find a minimal spanning tree. The program was used to solve the Security Alarm problem. The data input is identical to shortest route problems, and the same program logic creates the network. The *QuickQuant* report is provided in Figure 13-22. As with the shortest route problem, the arc distance is shown within each arc line. The arcs on the minimal spanning tree are shown as heavy lines, and the combined length is indicated at the top of the report.

13-4   THE MAXIMUM FLOW PROBLEM

The **maximum flow problem** is next in complexity among network models. Rather than merely identify a set of arcs (the shortest route or the minimal spanning tree), this problem seeks to find a flow value for each arc in the network.

This problem may be illustrated in terms of a telecommunications network connecting various trunk terminals to relay telephone calls. Equipment automatically routes a particular call over the first clear path found between the trunks connected to the respective telephones. The physical configuration of the system for determining how many

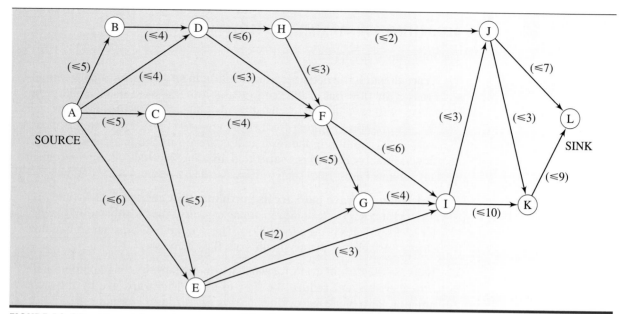

FIGURE 13-23 Network for trunk connections of the Lilliput Telephone Company

calls can be made between any two connected trunks must be set in advance. How well a particular telephone system works can be quantified in terms of the maximum number of calls it can accommodate. That quantity may be found for a particular network configuration by treating each call routed between two trunks as a unit of *flow*. Total flow through the network will be maximized.

Figure 13-23 shows the trunk network for the Lilliput Telephone Company. Each node is a switching trunk. The arcs represent linkage between trunks. The arcs are *directed*, proceeding from a **beginning node** (originating trunk) to an **ending node** (destination trunk), as indicated with the arrowheads. Each arc value indicates the **arc capacity,** or maximum number of calls that may be connected from the originating trunk to the destination.

Lilliput will measure performance in terms of how many calls might be routed from trunk A through the network to trunk L. Lilliput arbitrarily designates trunk A as the **source node** and trunk L, the **sink node.** Lilliput wants to determine a routing scheme that will maximize the number of calls originating at the source and terminating at the sink.

The Algorithm

The procedure is based on finding a series of paths from the SOURCE to the SINK. Once a path is selected, the maximum flow amount is added to all the arcs on that path. That quantity is determined by the lowest remaining capacity for all arcs on the path. Eventually, no path can be found that may receive further flow, at which point the optimal solution has been found. As with the preceding two network algorithms, all the work may be done directly on the network chart, and the computations are extremely simple.

SOLUTION PROCEDURE

ALGORITHM FOR MAXIMIZING FLOW

The following steps apply.

1. **Trace through the network from SOURCE to SINK, finding a path that increases the flow out of the SOURCE and into the SINK.** Each arc in the sequence will have its flow changed by the same absolute amount, increasing for *forward* arcs (pointing from SOURCE to SINK) and decreasing for *backward* arcs (pointing in the reverse direction). Any arc that cannot have its flow favorably changed is a **saturated arc.** The selected path cannot contain any saturated arcs. If no such path exists, the current flows are optimal.

2. **Determine for each path arc its maximum flow change.** That quantity for forward arcs (i, j) will be the remaining capacity. The maximum flow change for backward arcs is the current flow. The minimum of these maximum flow changes establishes the maximum path flow increase.

3. **Increase the flow of every forward arc on the path by the maximum path flow increase and reduce the flow of every backward arc by the same amount.** Put a block mark on any arrows where the arc is saturated.

Illustration

The Lilliput Telephone Company problem illustrates the algorithm. We begin the first iteration with all arcs at zero flow. It does not matter which of the many paths from SOURCE to SINK is chosen in step 1. We choose path A-B-D-H-J-K-L, whose arcs are shown in color in Figure 13-24. The maximum possible flow change for each of these

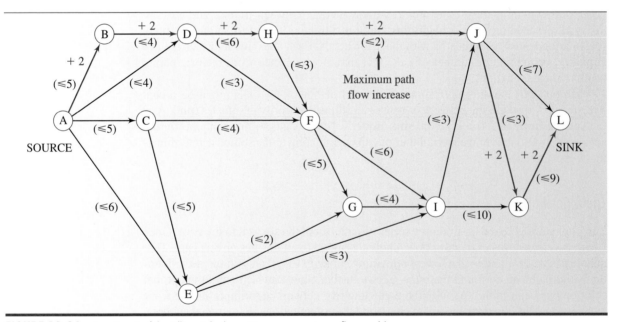

FIGURE 13-24   Iteration 1 of the Lilliput Telephone Company maximum flow problem

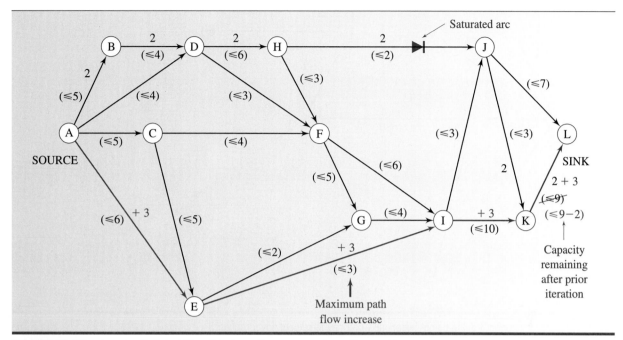

FIGURE 13-25 Iteration 2 of the Lilliput Telephone Company maximum flow problem

arcs is the original arc capacity. The smallest of these is 2, indicated by the short heavy colored arrow, for arc (H, J). This quantity is the maximum path flow increase. Because all arcs on this path are forward arcs, each path arc will have its flow increased by 2 (as indicated by the colored numbers).

Iteration 2 is shown in Figure 13-25. Because its forward flow cannot be increased further, a colored arrowhead and bar marks arc (H, J) as saturated. (In a later iteration, that arc's flow can only be reduced.) The current flows appear beside the arcs. Numerous paths exist for further flow increases. The bottommost path, A-E-I-K-L, is chosen arbitrarily. Notice that the remaining capacity of arc (K, L), $9 - 2 = 7$ (shown in color), serves as the maximum possible flow change for that arc. Because the remaining arcs have a flow of 0 (they were not altered by iteration 1), their maximum possible flow changes are their respective capacities. The smallest of these is 3, for arc (E, I). Again, all arcs on the selected path are forward arcs, so the flow of each will be increased by 3.

Iteration 3 is shown in Figure 13-26. Arc (E, I) joins (H, J) as now saturated and receives a colored bar. The current flows have been updated in accordance with the prior iteration. The choice narrows for possible paths to receive further flow increases. We arbitrarily choose path A-C-F-G-I-K-L. Two arcs on this path already have flow, and their remaining capacities, $9 - 5 = 4$ for (K, L) and $10 - 3 = 7$ for (I, K) are noted in color. There is a three-way tie for the minimum of the maximum possible arc flow changes, 4, marked by the thick colored arrows at (C, F), (G, I), and (K, L). Again, all arcs on the selected path are forward arcs, so the flow of each will be increased by 4.

Iteration 4 is shown in Figure 13-27. Arcs (C, F), (G, I), and (K, L) join the set of saturated arcs. The current flows have been updated. The next path choice is A-D-F-I-J-L, for which the maximum path flow increase is 3. Again, all arcs are forward and have their flow increased by this amount.

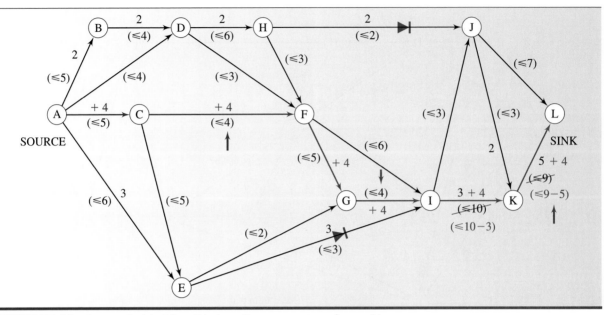

FIGURE 13-26   Iteration 3 of the Lilliput Telephone Company maximum flow problem

Figure 13-28 for iteration 5 reflects all changes made so far. The choice of path is now severely limited. The least complicated possibility is A-B-D-H-F-I-K-J-L. This path contains a *backward* arc (J, K), which has the reverse direction of the other arcs. In effect, the flow from J to K must be reduced, so that the quantity will be shifted to flow over arc (J, L). To emphasize that the flow is going to be reversed out of arc

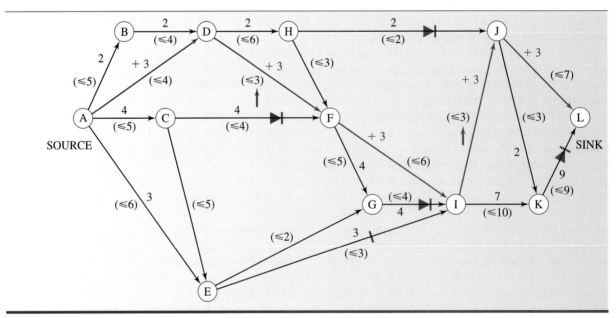

FIGURE 13-27   Iteration 4 of the Lilliput Telephone Company maximum flow problem

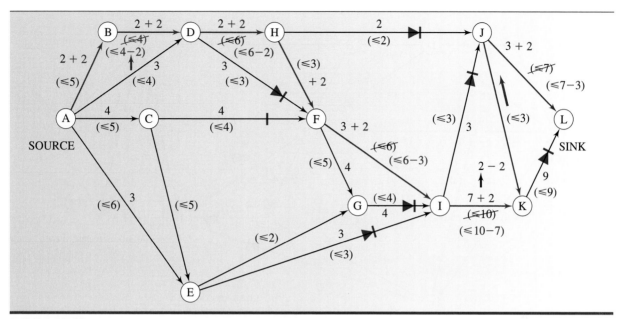

FIGURE 13-28   Iteration 5 of the Lilliput Telephone Company maximum flow problem

(J, K), a second colored arrow points in the same direction as the overall path flow from K to J. The maximum path flow, 2, is determined by a two-way tie for the minimum arc flow change equal to the remaining capacity of arc (B, D) and the current flow of backward arc (J, K).

Whether an arc is forward or backward depends on its direction with respect to the other arcs in its path. Figure 13-24 for iteration 1 shows arc (J, K) as forward because for the selected path at that iteration the arc had the same direction as the flow from SOURCE to SINK. However, in the selected path in Figure 13-28 arc (J, K) is backward, pointing opposite the path's flow from SOURCE to SINK.

Figure 13-29 shows the final optimal solution. No further paths from the SOURCE to the SINK can be formed. The SINK cannot be reached by further flow-augmenting paths, because no increased flow is possible through either J or K. All arcs ending at J are saturated, so there can be no increased flow through it. Likewise, all arcs beginning at K are saturated, so again there can be no increased flow through it. The maximum network flow is 14, determined by the combined flow of all arcs originating at the SOURCE.

$$(A, B) = 4$$
$$(A, C) = 4$$
$$(A, D) = 3$$
$$(A, E) = \underline{3}$$
$$14$$

This is also the combined flow for all arcs terminating at the SINK.

$$(J, L) = 5$$
$$(K, L) = \underline{9}$$
$$14$$

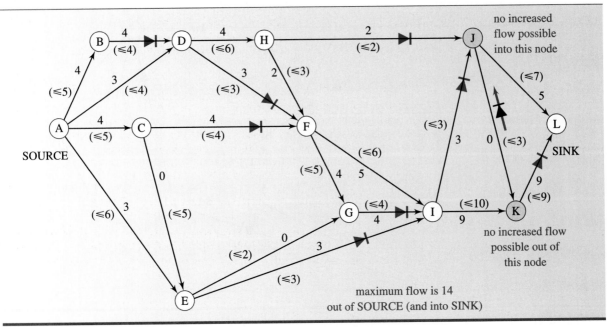

FIGURE 13-29   Optimal solution for the Lilliput Telephone Company maximum flow problem

Ties for Optimal Solution

Numerous ties exist for the optimal solution to the Lilliput Telephone Company problem. For example, it is possible to divert some of the flow over leg C-F-G through leg C-E-G. Also, some of the flow over A-C-F-G could instead go over leg A-E-G. Another possibility would be to take some of the flow over A-B-D-H-F and redirect it over A-D-F. Any combination of these changes, in various amounts, would also lead to a tying optimal solution. Any one of the many tying solutions might have been obtained as the final optimum had a different set and sequence of paths been selected.

Solving Problems with Computer Assistance

QuickQuant may be used to find network maximum flow quantities, as in the Lilliput Telephone Company problem. The data input is identical to shortest route problems, except that arc upper bounds are entered in place of distances. The same program logic creates the network. *QuickQuant* provides the report for Lilliput Telephone in Figure 13-30. The arc capacity is preceded by "<=" (which signifies ≤) and is shown below each arc line. The optimal flow is shown above the respective arc line, with the maximum network flow provided at the top of the report.

The Linear Programming Model and Excel Solution

The shortest route problems may be expressed as linear programs. When so formulated, the same problems can be solved a second way using Excel's Solver.

The network contains nodes identified by code numbers 0, 1, 2,..., N. Node 0 is the SOURCE and node N is the SINK. The flow variables X_{ij} represent the amount of flow along directed arc (i, j) from beginning node i to ending node j. (There is no variable

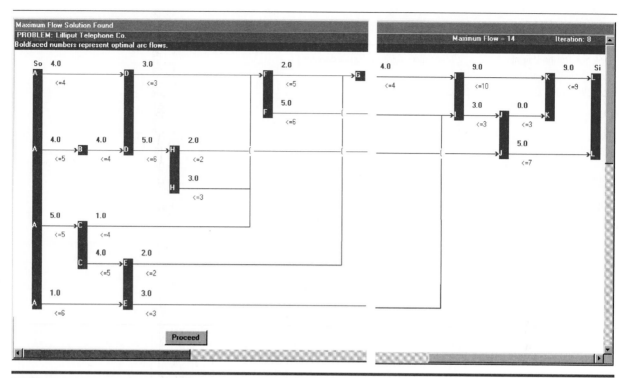

FIGURE 13-30   *QuickQuant* composite screen for solution of the Lilliput Telephone Company maximum flow problem

for those node pairs not connected by an arc.) Each arc (i, j) has a capacity K_{ij}. The mathematical model for this problem is stated in general terms by the following linear program. The objective is to

$$\text{Maximize} \quad P = \sum_{j=1}^{N-1} X_{0j} \equiv \sum_{i=1}^{N-1} X_{iN}$$

Subject to

$$\sum_{i=0}^{N} X_{ik} = \sum_{j=0}^{N} X_{kj} \text{ for intermediate nodes } k = 1, 2, \ldots, N - 1 \quad \text{(conservation of flow)}$$

$$X_{ij} \leq K_{ij} \text{ for all arcs} \quad \text{(capacity)}$$

where all $X_{ij} \geq 0$

The objective function indicates that the problem may be approached either by maximizing the flow out of the SOURCE or by maximizing the flow into the SINK. Those quantities must be the same, as guaranteed by conservation of flow, throughout the remainder of the network.

The identical Excel solution to the linear program for the Lilliput Telephone Company problem is shown in Figure 13-31 and is based on Figure 13-11. The only structural differences are that the required flows in cells B41:M41 are all zero (from the linear programming formulation), a large number is entered for the upper limit of the flow from the ending to the beginning node (20 in this case in cell B20), the objective in E22 has the formula = B37 (the total flow out of A), and the maximum capacity constraints B25:M37<=B9:M20 are added. (See the Solver Parameters dialog box in Figure 13-32.)

FIGURE 13-31
Linear programming solution for the Lilliput Telephone Company problem using Excel

Note: The solution has different flows than those found earlier, but the total is the same. This problem has multiple possible solutions.

MAXIMUM FLOW SOLUTION

PROBLEM: Lilliput Telephone Company

Capacities

To Node

From Node	A	B	C	D	E	F	G	H	I	J	K	L
A		5	5	4	6							
B				4								
C					5	4						
D						3		6				
E							2		3			
F							5		6			
G									4			
H						3				2		
I										3	10	
J										3	7	
K											9	
L		20										

Solution C =   14

	E
22	=B37

To Node

From Node	A	B	C	D	E	F	G	H	I	J	K	L	Total Outflow
A	0	1	4	4	5	0	0	0	0	0	0	0	14
B	0	0	0	1	0	0	0	0	0	0	0	0	1
C	0	0	0	0	0	4	0	0	0	0	0	0	4
D	0	0	0	0	0	3	0	2	0	0	0	0	5
E	0	0	0	0	0	0	2	0	3	0	0	0	5
F	0	0	0	0	0	0	1	0	6	0	0	0	7
G	0	0	0	0	0	0	0	0	3	0	0	0	3
H	0	0	0	0	0	0	0	0	0	2	0	0	2
I	0	0	0	0	0	0	0	0	0	3	9	0	12
J	0	0	0	0	0	0	0	0	0	0	0	5	5
K	0	0	0	0	0	0	0	0	0	0	0	9	9
L	14	0	0	0	0	0	0	0	0	0	0	0	14
Total Inflow	14	1	4	5	5	7	3	2	12	5	9	14	
Total Outflow	14	1	4	5	5	7	3	2	12	5	9	14	
Net Flow	0	0	0	0	0	0	0	0	0	0	0	0	
Required Flow	0	0	0	0	0	0	0	0	0	0	0	0	

	N
26	=SUM(B26:M26)
27	=SUM(B27:M27)
28	=SUM(B28:M28)
29	=SUM(B29:M29)
30	=SUM(B30:M30)
31	=SUM(B31:M31)
32	=SUM(B32:M32)
33	=SUM(B33:M33)
34	=SUM(B34:M34)
35	=SUM(B35:M35)
36	=SUM(B36:M36)
37	=SUM(B37:M37)

	B	C	D	E	F	G	H
38	=SUM(B26:B37)	=SUM(C26:C37)	=SUM(D26:D37)	=SUM(E26:E37)	=SUM(F26:F37)	=SUM(G26:G37)	=SUM(H26:H37)
39	=N26	=N27	=N28	=N29	=N30	=N31	=N32
40	=B38-B39	=C38-C39	=D38-D39	=E38-E39	=F38-F39	=G38-G39	=H38-H39
41	0	0	0	0	0	0	0

	I	J	K	L	M
38	=SUM(I26:I37)	=SUM(J26:J37)	=SUM(K26:K37)	=SUM(L26:L37)	=SUM(M26:M37)
39	=N33	=N34	=N35	=N36	=N37
40	=I38-I39	=J38-J39	=K38-K39	=L38-L39	=M38-M39
41	0	0	0	0	0

FIGURE 13-32
The Solver Parameters dialog box for the Lilliput Telephone Company

Solver Parameters   ? ×

Set Target Cell: $E$22

Equal To: ● Max   ○ Min   ○ Value of: 0

By Changing Cells:

$B$26:$M$37

Subject to the Constraints:

$B$26:$M$37 <= $B$9:$M$20
$B$40:$M$40 = $B$41:$M$41

Solve
Close
Guess
Options
Add
Change
Delete
Reset All
Help

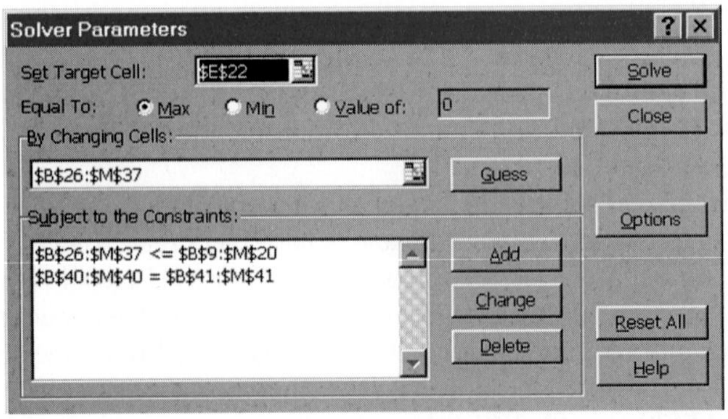

13-5 THE MINIMUM COST MAXIMUM FLOW PROBLEM

The most general network model described in this book is the **minimum cost maximum flow problem.** It accommodates a variety of distribution problems, including the transportation problems described in Chapter 12. The network model more realistically portrays actual situations by including lower and upper bounds on shipment quantities over a particular *route*. (The transportation problems in Chapter 12 represent a route as a shipping schedule cell, for which a separate constraint is not recognized.)

To illustrate the minimum cost maximum flow problem, we consider a decision faced by the regional manager of the BigCo discount retail chain. She is in charge of five stores supplied from two distribution centers. Weekly store demand tonnages and center capacities are provided in Table 13-3.

TABLE 13-3   BigCo Distribution Requirements and Shipping Costs

FROM CENTER	COST PER TON TO STORE					Capacity (Tons)
	(3) Jay Street	(4) 7th Avenue	(5) River Cross	(6) Downtown	(7) Exurbia	
(1) Centralia	$10	$12	$11	$13	$13	500
(2) Gotham	15	12	9	14	9	600
Demand (tons)	200	250	350	150	150	1,100

Trucks have a capacity of 20 tons. Due to distance, driver availability, and loading and unloading times, each route has a different upper limit on weekly tonnage. Because certain items can only be shipped from a particular center, some routes have a minimum weekly quantity as well. Table 13-4 summarizes these.

As with the maximum flow problem discussed in Section 13-4, network arcs must be *directed* and have SOURCE and SINK nodes. These nodes are not physical distribution points and serve only to connect the various components in a **circuit network,** which has flow backward from the SINK to the SOURCE. Figure 13-33 shows the network for the BigCo problem. There is one arc for each possible shipment route (center–store combination). Additionally, special arcs connect the SOURCE to each distribution center; the arc upper bounds are the *capacities* of the respective distribution centers. Another five special arcs connect the stores to the SINK; the lower bounds are equal to the *demands* of the respective stores. For all special arcs, the lower bound must equal the

TABLE 13-4   Route Quantity Limits for BigCo Distribution

FROM CENTER	TO STORE				
	(3) Jay Street	(4) 7th Avenue	(5) River Cross	(6) Downtown	(7) Exurbia
	Weekly Minimum Route Quantities				
(1) Centralia	40	60	40	0	60
(2) Gotham	0	40	80	40	0
	Weekly Maximum Route Quantities				
(1) Centralia	300	200	200	200	100
(2) Gotham	200	200	200	200	200

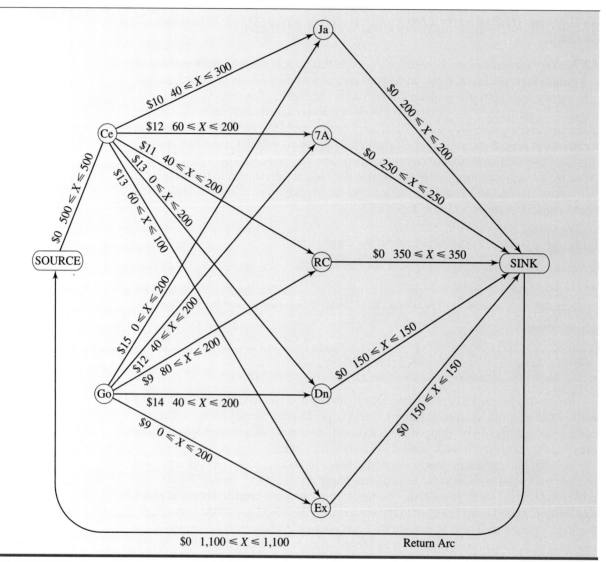

FIGURE 13-33 Network for BigCo regional distribution

upper bound. A final special **return arc** ties the SINK to the SOURCE; both of the return arc's bounds equal total demand (1,100; which must be the same as total capacity). All special arcs have a unit cost of $0.

Figure 13-34 shows the optimal solution to the BigCo distribution problem. Notice that the sum of the flows into each node matches the total flow out of it. The solution was obtained using the special-purpose **out-of-kilter algorithm.**

Solving the Problem

The algorithm begins with a starting solution. Unlike other linear programming procedures described in this book, the starting solution might not even be feasible.

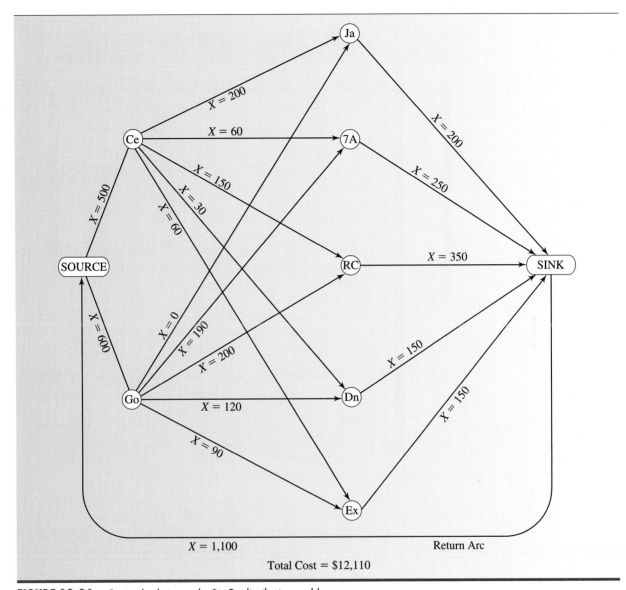

FIGURE 13-34 Optimal solution to the BigCo distribution problem

The procedure is governed by a complex set of rules that test each arc to see whether or not it conforms to its own bounds. Such problems are invariably solved on the computer, so it is not necessary to give the details here. (You may elect to read more about the out-of-kilter algorithm in Optional Section 13-7.) You can get a flavor of the process by following some of the iterations obtained from a computer run using *Quick-Quant*.

The first iteration of the BigCo distribution problem is shown in Figure 13-35. Like most iterations, this one finds a flow-augmenting path, just like those in maximum flow problems. The heavy arcs show the selected path, which includes the gray return arc to complete the circuit. All of those arcs will have their flows increased by 200 units

FIGURE 13-35

QuickQuant composite screens for iteration 1 of the BigCo distribution problem

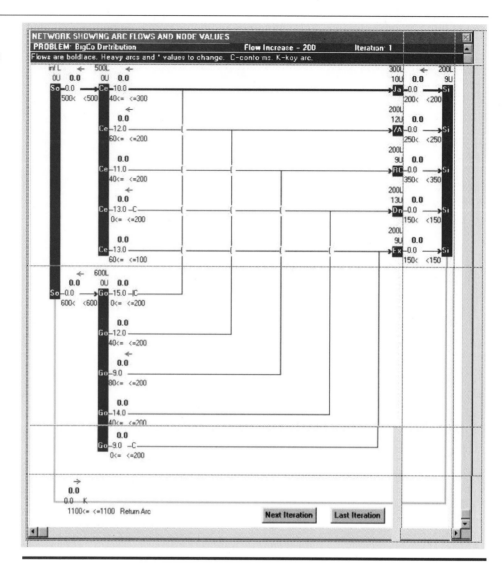

from their starting levels of zero. Even before those changes are made, the following three arcs

Ce-Dn   Go-Ja   Go-Ex

are found to conform (their arrows are marked by a capital C) because their current flows (all zero) lie between the lower and upper bounds. Arc Go-Ja is blocked (its arrow is marked by a bar), a special condition having to do with the relation between quantity limits and arc costs. A blocked arc cannot have its flow increased.

The node value, or U, appears above each node (for example, the $U = 9$ for Si) and expresses the total cost of the path leading to that particular node. The node values are used to identify blocked arcs. The node labels, or L's, also appear above the nodes. (Node Si has $L = 200$.) These convey the maximum flow that may be brought from the start to that node. The node labels are used to select the flow-augmenting path that can shift the maximum quantity. In doing that, ties are broken arbitrarily. (Optional Section 13-7 describes how the U's and L's are found.)

When expressed as a linear program, maximizing flow at minimum cost has a primal and dual problem. The out-of-kilter algorithm massages the current solution, making changes that bring either the primal or dual solution a step closer to feasible. When both problems have feasible solutions, the optimums have been reached, and no further steps are required.

In iterations 2 through 7, a succession of flow-augmenting paths are identified and flows increased on their arcs. All of those paths start at the source, go through the sink, and return to the source. At that stage a total of 940 units are moved out of the source and into the sink. That amount is sent back along the return arc, which in those iterations serves as the key arc. (Once the return arc conforms, the key arc designation moves to a different place. Depending on conditions, the start of a flow-augmenting path will be at the beginning or at the end of the key arc.)

Figure 13-36 shows the path (heavy arcs) found in iteration 8. A net flow increase of 40 units will be made along this path. Its trajectory is

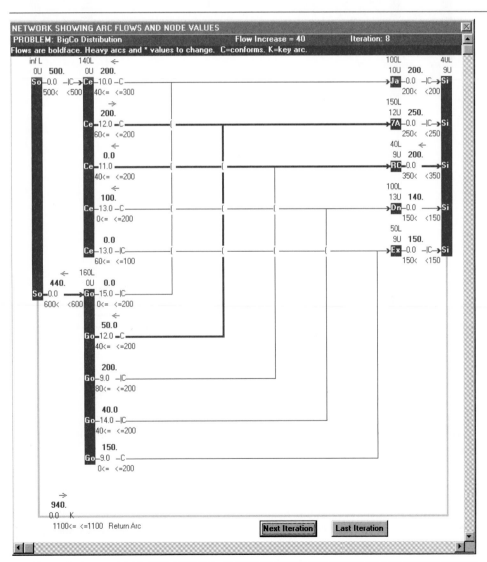

FIGURE 13-36

QuickQuant composite screens for iteration 8 of the BigCo distribution problem

FIGURE 13-37

QuickQuant composite screens for iteration 10 of the BigCo distribution problem

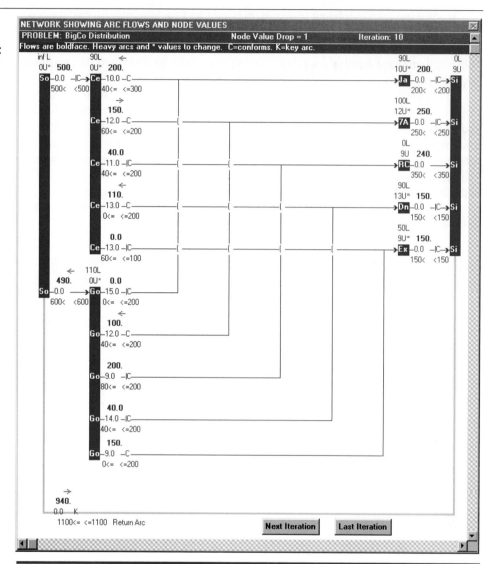

$$\text{SOURCE} \to \text{Go} \to \text{7A} \to \text{Ce} \to \text{RC} \to \text{SINK} \to \text{SOURCE}$$

The arc leading from Seventh Avenue (7A) to Centralia (Ce) is sequenced in reverse of its direction of flow, so that arc 7A-Ce will have its flow *reduced* by 40 units. Iteration 9 is similar. A very different type of change is made with iteration 10.

Figure 13-37 shows the findings for iteration 10. Here, no path can be found along the key arc. The U's (dual variable levels) must be changed before further flow modifications can be made. Iteration 11 also involves changes to the U's.

Figure 13-38 shows iteration 12, in which a further 90 units can be shifted along the same path used in iteration 8. A total of 15 iterations are taken to reach the optimal solution in Figure 13-39.

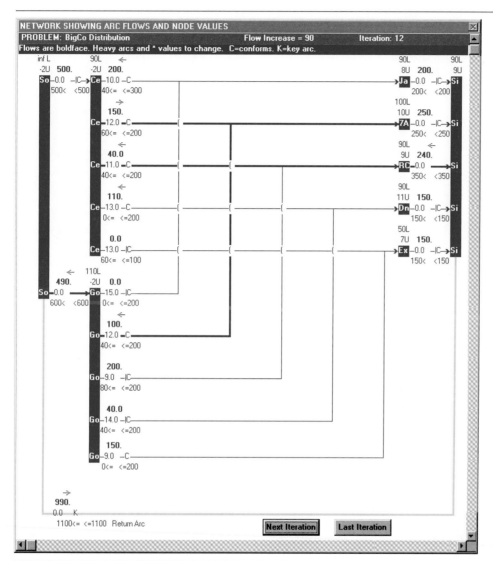

FIGURE 13-38
QuickQuant composite screens for iteration 12 of the BigCo distribution problem

The Linear Programming Model and Excel Solution

As with finding a shortest route or a maximum flow, the minimum cost network flow problems may be solved as linear programs. They may be solved using *QuickQuant* or Excel.

The network contains nodes identified by code numbers 0, 1, 2,..., N. Node 0 is the SOURCE and node N is the SINK. The flow variables X_{ij} represent the amount of flow along directed arc (i, j) from its beginning node i to its ending node j. (There is no variable for those node pairs not connected by an arc.) Each arc (i, j) has a lower limit L_{ij} and an upper limit K_{ij}. Each arc also has a unit cost c_{ij}. The mathematical model

FIGURE 13-39

QuickQuant composite screens for the optimal solution of the BigCo distribution problem

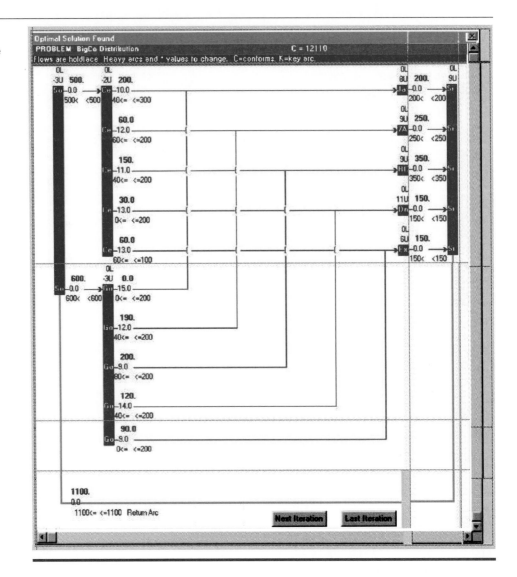

for this problem is stated in general terms by the following linear program. The objective is to

$$\text{Minimize}\quad C = \sum_{i=0}^{N}\sum_{j=0}^{N} c_{ij} X_{ik}$$

Subject to

$$\sum_{i=0}^{N} X_{ik} = \sum_{j=0}^{N} X_{kj} \quad \text{for all nodes } k = 0, 1, 2, \dots, N \qquad \text{(conservation of flow)}$$

$$X_{ij} \geq L_{ij} \quad \text{for all arcs} \qquad \text{(arc lower bound)}$$

$$X_{ij} \leq K_{ij} \quad \text{for all arcs} \qquad \text{(arc upper bound)}$$

where all $L_{ij} \geq 0$

	A	B	C	D	E	F	G	H
1	\multicolumn{8}{c}{MINIMUM COST MAXIMUM FLOW SOLUTION}							
2								
3	PROBLEM:	BigCo Discount Retail Chain						
4								
5			Costs, Capacities, and Demands					
6			To Node					
7	From Node	Jaystreet	7th Avenue	River Cross	Downtown	Exurbia	Capaciy	
8	Centralia	10	12	11	13	13	500	
9	Gotham	15	12	9	14	9	600	
10	Demand	200	250	350	150	150		
11								
12			Minimum Quantities (Lower Bounds)					
13			To Node					
14	From Node	Jaystreet	7th Avenue	River Cross	Downtown	Exurbia		
15	Centralia	40	60	40	0	60		
16	Gotham	0	40	80	40	0		
17								
18			Maximum Quantities (Upper Bounds)					
19			To Node					
20	From Node	Jaystreet	7th Avenue	River Cross	Downtown	Exurbia		
21	Centralia	300	200	200	200	100		
22	Gotham	200	200	200	200	200		
23							E	
24			Solution Quantities, C =		$ 12,110		24 =SUMPRODUCT(B8:F9,B27:F28)	
25			To Node					
26	From Node	Jaystreet	7th Avenue	River Cross	Downtown	Exurbia	Total Quantity	
27	Centralia	200	60	150	30	60	500	G
28	Gotham	0	190	200	120	90	600	27 =SUM(B27:F27)
29	Total Quantity	200	250	350	150	150		28 =SUM(B28:F28)
30		B	C	D	E	F		
31	29 =SUM(B27:B28)	=SUM(C27:C28)	=SUM(D27:D28)	=SUM(E27:E28)	=SUM(F27:F28)			

FIGURE 13-40   Excel spreadsheet for the BigCo distribution problem

Nonnegativity conditions are superseded by the arc lower bounds, each of which must be ≥ 0. The conservation of flow applies to all nodes, so that the total flow into any node exactly matches the total flow out of that node.

The Excel solution for the BigCo discount retail chain is shown in Figure 13-40. The minimum cost, $12,110, is in cell E24, and the shipping schedule is in cells B27:F28, identical with that determined with the out-of-kilter algorithm. Figure 13-40 is an extension of the spreadsheet in Figure 12-17 for a transportation problem. Only the minimum and maximum quantities tables (cells B15:F16 and B21:F22) have been added and those necessitate two additional Solver constraints

$$=B27:F28<=B21:F22$$
$$=B27:F28>=B15:F16$$

The Solver Parameters dialog box is shown in Figure 13-41.

FIGURE 13-41
The Solver Parameters dialog box for the BigCo distribution problem

DECISION PROBLEM

WaySafe Managerial Decision Revisited: Determining Optimal Shipment Quantities and Assigning Groups

For the peninsular region of the WaySafe marketing area, Lela Sanchez reduced the overall transportation problem to two warehouses and eight stores. After Lela Sanchez had determined the best routes from each warehouse to all the stores, she wanted to find the amounts to ship that would minimize shipping costs. Her first step was to compute the shipping costs from both of the warehouses to the eight stores. They are shown in the first table below. Two factors complicate the decision about shipping amounts. Some stores require minimum amounts, and different limited truck capacities exist on a few routes. These minimum and maximum restrictions are shown in the second table below.

To From	Sa	Sc	Sd	Se	Sg	St	Su	Sw	Weekly Capacity (Tons)
W5	$13	$15	$ 8	$ 9	$12	$11	$10	$13	2,500
W8	7	10	11	13	15	9	12	15	2,000
Weekly Demand (tons)	500	750	400	510	370	535	440	605	

The following limitations apply to particular routes:

	W5-Sd	W5-Su	W8-Sg	W8-Sw
Maximum Route Tonnage	300	300	—	—
Minimum Route Tonnage	—	—	100	200

The following shipments were determined for maximizing quantity flow at minimum cost:

To From	Sa	Sc	Sd	Se	Sg	St	Su	Sw	Weekly Capacity (Tons)
W5			300	510	270	325	300	405	2,500
W8	500	750	100		100	210	140	200	2,000
Weekly Demand (tons)	500	750	400	510	370	535	440	605	

From the above, Lela made the following district assignments:

W5: Sd Se Sg St Su Sw

W8: Sa Sc

13-6 FURTHER NETWORK CONSIDERATIONS

The network models presented in this chapter extend linear programming concepts into a broad range of applications. The first three solution algorithms presented are far simpler to apply than the other linear programming procedures in this book. Although the out-of-kilter algorithm for minimum cost maximum flow problems is quite a bit more elaborate than the others, this procedure is computationally very efficient and is well suited for solving large distribution problems on the computer.

Chapter 14 introduces one of the most successful applications involving networks: PERT (Program Evaluation and Review Technique). This project management tool employs a network tying various activities. A primary objective of PERT is to provide information that managers can use in taking action to ensure that project activities are completed in a timely fashion.

13-7 (OPTIONAL) THE OUT-OF-KILTER ALGORITHM

The out-of-kilter algorithm involves a series of steps to reach the optimum. The steps are based on both the primal (original) linear program and its dual. (These concepts are described in Chapter 10.) The dual linear program involves one variable for each constraint in the original linear program. The out-of-kilter algorithm uses some of the dual variable values as node values and employs a set of rules involving those values and the arc flows. (The node variables are represented symbolically as U's.) At each iteration, changes are made that result in either modified flows or reduced node values. These are guided partly by the principle of complementary slackness between the primal and the dual. The solutions themselves need not be feasible. With successive iterations, the deviations from feasibility diminish. Eventually, either an optimum is reached or it is established that the problem has no feasible solution.

Figure 13-42 shows the initial network for the BigCo distribution problem, shown in a worksheet format with a set of boxes and marginal entries for each arc. The legend at the bottom indicates the worksheet elements, which include a two-sided oval for each node. The worksheet is updated at each iteration.

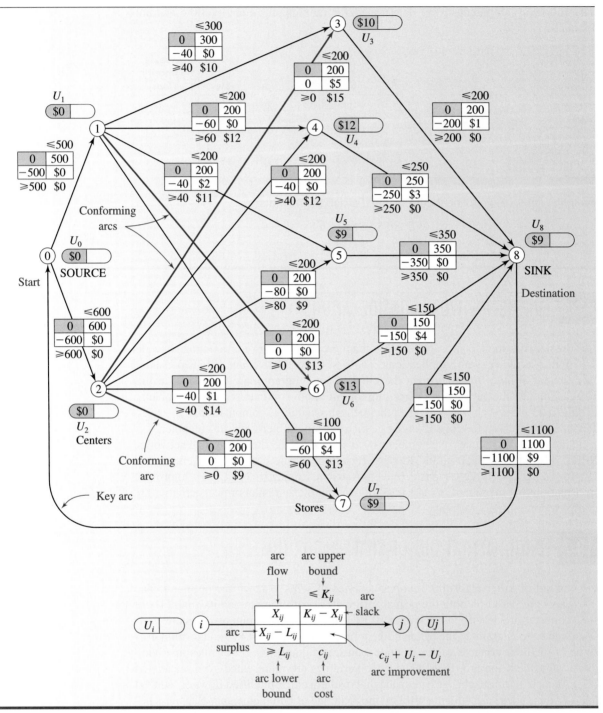

FIGURE 13-42   BigCo network with arc slack, surplus, and improvement values added

STEPS FOR OUT-OF-KILTER ALGORITHM

0.   Initial quantities. Assign starting flows meeting the conservation constraints, but which do not need to satisfy the arc limitations. [Beginning flows for each arc (i, j) equal to 0 will work.] For each node i determine a node value U_i equal to the cost for the cheapest path leading to it from the SOURCE. (Those node values can be found by treating cost as "distance" and applying the shortest route algorithm.)

1.   Determine for each network arc whether or not it conforms. Arc (i, j) *conforms* if one of the following conditions applies:

$$c_{ij} + U_i - U_j > 0 \quad \text{and} \quad X_{ij} = L_{ij}$$
$$c_{ij} + U_i - U_j = 0 \quad \text{and} \quad L_{ij} \le X_{ij} \le K_{ij}$$
$$c_{ij} + U_i - U_j < 0 \quad \text{and} \quad X_{ij} = K_{ij}$$

If all arcs conform, the current solution is optimal.

2.   Set Start and Destination. As long as the return arc (SINK, SOURCE) is non-conforming, it is the **key arc.** If the return arc conforms, choose *any* non-conforming arc as the key arc. Then apply the rules in Figure 13-43 to determine the Start and Destination nodes.

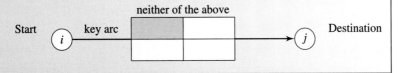

FIGURE 13-43   Rules for designating the Start and the Destination when the return arc is not the key arc during step 2

3.   Evaluate arcs and get node quantity labels. Begin with all nodes unlabeled, except for the Start, which receives a label quantity of $N_{\text{Start}} = \infty$. Substep (a) determines which arcs are next evaluated.

a. *Evaluate arcs.* If all arcs (except the key arc) that connect with labeled nodes have been evaluated, or if the Destination has been labeled, go to substep (c). Otherwise, evaluate each unevaluated arc (i, j) beginning or ending at a labeled node. The evaluation consists of finding a **shift quantity** or marking the arc as **blocked,** according to one of the rules in Figure 13-44.

b. *Get node quantity labels and place pointers.* Skip any unlabeled node connected only to an unevaluated or a blocked arc; such a node cannot be labeled yet. For all remaining unlabeled nodes, determine its quantity label

$$N_i = \text{maximum shift quantity from all unblocked evaluated arcs}$$

Enter this quantity in the right half of the node's oval. Then place a pointer near the newly labeled node alongside the arc yielding this maxi-

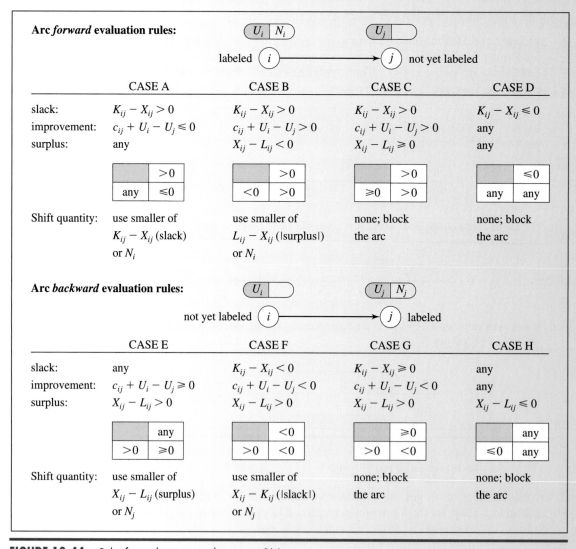

FIGURE 13-44   Rules for evaluating arcs during step 3(a)

mum quantity, with the pointer aimed at the opposite end of the arc. After checking all nodes, return to substep (a).

c.   If the Destination node is unlabeled, go to step 5. Otherwise, find the shift quantity for the key arc according to whichever rule in Figure 13-44 applies when treating the Destination as the labeled node. Place a pointer beside the Start node alongside the key arc, aiming at the Destination.

4. **Get new flows, slacks, and surpluses.** Trace backward from the Destination, according to the pointers, to identify a circuit of arcs looping through the Start and back to the Destination. The **circuit shift quantity** is the shift quantity found for the key arc in step 3(c). Proceed from the Start along the circuit. Add the circuit shift quantity to the flow on the forward arcs (those having the same direction as Start-to-Destination) and subtract it from the flow on the backward arcs. Revise the arc box slack and surplus quantities accordingly. Erase all node quantity labels and return to step 1.

5. **Revise node values and recompute arc improvement values.** Use the procedure in Figure 13-45 to find the **node value reduction** θ. If $\theta = \infty$, stop; the problem is *infeasible*. Otherwise, subtract θ from each node value U_i for *labeled* nodes only. Erase the old node labels in the *left* portion of the respective ovals, replacing them with the new U_i's. Then recompute the improvement value of each affected arc, placing the new values in the respective arc boxes. Erase the node quantity labels (*right* side of the oval) and return to step 1.

---

a. Consider all arcs beginning at labeled nodes and ending at unlabeled nodes having nonnegative slack ($K_{ij} - X_{ij} \geqslant 0$) and *strictly* positive improvement ($c_{ij} + U_i - U_j > 0$):

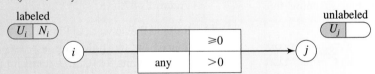

Determine the minimum *positive* improvement, θ_1. Set $\theta_1 = \infty$ if there are no such values.

b. Consider all arcs beginning at unlabeled nodes and ending at labeled nodes having nonnegative surplus ($X_{ij} - L_{ij} \geqslant 0$) and *strictly* negative improvement ($c_{ij} + U_i - U_j < 0$):

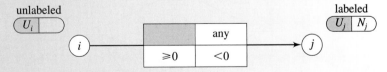

Determine the minimum of the absolute values of the *negative* improvements, θ_2. Set $\theta_2 = \infty$ if there are no such values.

c. Determine the node value reduction

$$\theta = \text{minimum } (\theta_1, \theta_2)$$

FIGURE 13-45   Procedure for finding node value reduction during step 5

PROBLEMS

13-1 Refer to the network in Figure 13-1. Using node A as the START and I as the FINISH, determine the shortest route and its total length.

13-2 Refer to the network in Figure 13-1. Determine a minimal spanning tree and its total length.

13-3 Consider the network in Figure 13-46. Find the maximum flow.

13-4 Refer to the Ace Widgets transportation decision in Problem 12-4 (page 480). The following limits apply:

Plants	Lower Bounds				Upper Bounds			
	W1	W2	W3	W4	W1	W2	W3	W4
P1	0	0	30	0	50	50	50	100
P2	10	0	30	20	20	100	100	50
P3	0	20	40	0	30	100	100	150

Determine the quantities that minimize total cost.

13-5 Refer to the Security Alarm Company network in Figure 13-13. Find the shortest route from site A to site I.

13-6 Refer to the Yellow Jacket Freightways network in Figure 13-2. Find a minimal spanning tree connecting all centers.

13-7 Refer to the Yellow Jacket Freightways network in Figure 13-2. Redesignate center C as the START and center G as the FINISH. Then find the shortest route.

13-8 Suppose the Lilliput Telephone Company raises the capacities on three trunk lines in Figure 13-23 as follows: (E, I)— 4, (H, J)— 4, and (K, L)— 11. Find the new maximum flow solution.

13-9 A company is developing a 5-year plan indicating when to purchase and replace its trucks. In any year that a truck is sold, a replacement must be bought. The following table gives the net cost for each combination. Construct a network for this problem with an arc for each feasible year-of-buy, year-of-sale combination. Then solve the shortest route problem to determine the optimal purchase schedule.

Year of Buy	Year of Sale				
	1	2	3	4	5
0	3	10	17	23	28
1		3	10	17	23
2			3	10	17
3				3	10
4					3

13-10 Find a minimum cost solution for the maximum flow problem summarized by the network in Figure 13-47.

13-11 Refer to the network in Figure 13-46. The lower bounds for the following arcs are 3 units for (B, D), 3 units for (C, E), 4 units for (E, G), and 5 units for (G, I). The remaining arcs have 0 as the lower bound. The following unit costs apply.

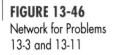

FIGURE 13-46
Network for Problems
13-3 and 13-11

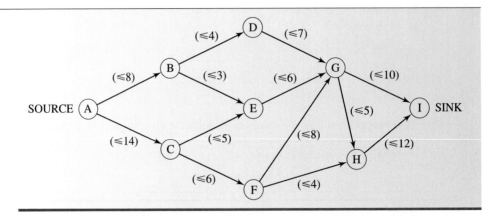

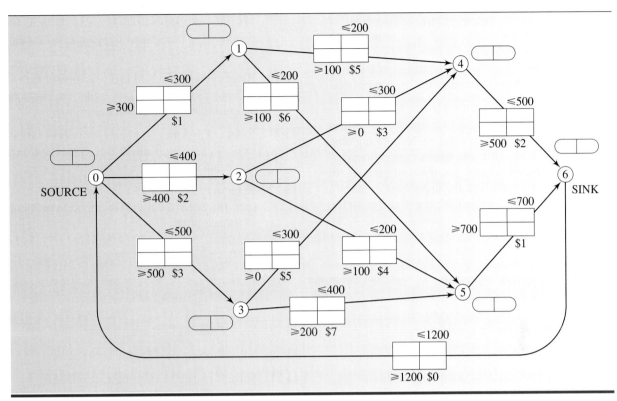

FIGURE 13-47   Network for Problem 13-10

To From	A	B	C	D	E	F	G	H	I
A	—	5	7	—	—	—	—	—	—
B	—	—	—	2	3	—	—	—	—
C	—	—	—	—	2	8	—	—	—
D	—	—	—	—	—	—	6	—	—
E	—	—	—	—	—	—	7	—	—
F	—	—	—	—	—	—	5	4	—
G	—	—	—	—	—	—	—	3	7
H	—	—	—	—	—	—	—	—	6
I	—	—	—	—	—	—	—	—	—

Find the minimum cost maximum flow solution.

13-12 The BigCo manager described in the chapter experiences increased weekly demands; the new quantities are 200 tons for Downtown and 250 for Exurbia. To meet these needs, center capacities have been increased; the new quantities are 700 tons for Gotham and 550 tons for Centralia. All other data remain the same.

Find the optimal solution for the revised problem.

13-13 Consider the Yellow Jacket Freightways shortest route problem discussed in the chapter. Using the network data in Figure 13-2, formulate the linear program. In doing this, you may use the letter codes of the distribution centers as subscripts.

13-14 Consider the Lilliput Telephone Company maximum flow problem. Using the network data in Figure 13-23, formulate the linear program. In doing this, you may use the letter code of the trunks as subscripts.

13-15 Consider the BigCo distribution problem. Using the network data in Figure 13-33, formulate the linear program.

13-16 Consider the arc distances for a telecommunications network in file Problem 13-16.txt.
(a) Find the shortest route from A to L.
(b) Find the shortest route from G to J.

13-17 Refer to the network data in Problem 13-16. Use *QuickQuant* to find the minimal spanning tree.

13-18   The daily carrying capacities (in hundreds of acre feet) for water distribution channels are given in file Problem 13-18.txt.

Using A as the SOURCE and M as the SINK, find the channel volumes that maximize total flow.

13-19   Refer to Problem 12-39 on page 485. Add a dummy plant having capacity 160 and shipping costs of $0. All routes have an upper bound of 100 pounds, except for those originating in plant $M1$, for which the upper bounds are 50. All routes have lower bounds of 0 except for the following: $M1$-$A1$ — 20 pounds, $M2$-$A2$ — 30,

$M3$-$A3$ — 20, $M4$-$A10$ — 25, and $M3$-$A4$ — 10 pounds. Find the optimal shipping schedule and its cost.

13-20   Refer to Problem 13-13 and your answer to that exercise. Solve the Yellow Jacket Freightways shortest route problem as a linear program.

13-21   Refer to Problem 13-14 and your answer to that exercise. Solve the Lilliput Telephone Company maximum flow problem as a linear program.

13-22   Refer to Problem 13-15 and your answer to that exercise. Solve the BigCo distribution problem as a linear program.

Spreadsheet Problems

13-23   Solve Problem 13-1 using a spreadsheet.

13-24   Solve Problem 13-3 using a spreadsheet.

13-25   Solve Problem 13-4 using a spreadsheet.

13-26   Solve Problem 13-5 using a spreadsheet.

13-27   Solve Problem 13-7 using a spreadsheet.

13-28   Solve Problem 13-8 using a spreadsheet.

13-29   Solve Problem 13-9 using a spreadsheet.

13-30   Solve Problem 13-12 using a spreadsheet.

13-31   Solve Problem 13-16 using a spreadsheet.

13-32   Solve Problem 13-18 using a spreadsheet.

13-33   Solve Problem 13-19 using a spreadsheet.

CASE   13-1 *Papua New Guinea Mining Company*

The Papua New Guinea Mining Company (PNGM Co.) mines gold, silver, and copper from three sites on the Island of New Guinea. The mining activities take place in the highlands and have no major sources of water. Water is an essential ingredient in the bacterial leaching, done at three sites at lower elevations. Currently only pilot operations are being conducted while the ore sites are surveyed and final planning is done.

The overall scheme is to extract the ore and transport it to one of the leaching sites. There, the metals will be separated from the nonmetallic compounds using several strains of *Thiobacillus*. The concentrated metallic "soup" will then be transported to the port facility, loaded onto tankers, and shipped to Australia to be refined and smelted.

New Guinea is an extremely underdeveloped place with few roads. Except for the port facility, the PNGM Co. sites are in remote jungle or mountain locations not connected by roads or navigable waterways. Three major transportation projects are being considered. One is to construct a railway connecting the various sites. The railway may just connect the mines to the leaching sites, or it may also connect the latter to the port. If the shorter rail option is used, the enriched slurry will be routed to port through pipelines. A series of aqueducts must also be constructed connecting the leaching sites to water sources.

The final railroad bed and pipeline choices will be based on the distances separating the various sites. These are shown in Table 13-5 in which the distances (in kilometers) between neighboring sites are listed as candidate routes.

TABLE 13-5

Site	Site							
	A	B	C	D	E	F	G	H
A (mine)	—	55	50	60	—	—	—	—
B (leaching)	—	—	—	25	40	—	—	—
C (mine)	—	—	—	30	—	35	—	—
D (leaching)	—	—	—	—	45	—	—	—
E (mine)	—	—	—	—	—	—	15	80
F (mine)	—	—	—	—	—	—	65	70
G (leaching)	—	—	—	—	—	—	—	75
H (port)	—	—	—	—	—	—	—	—

The water sources include two lakes (L1 and L2), two rivers (R1 and R2), and one well (W). The maximum possible flows (millions of cubic liters per hour) are shown in Table 13-6, along with the maximums required or available.

TABLE 13-6

Water Source	Leaching Source			Available
	B	D	G	
L1	2	0	0	5
L2	3	0	4	5
R1	0	5	3	6
R2	4	8	0	6
W	1	1	1	2
Maximum	10	10	10	

Chief engineer Roy Youngblatt has selected a special gondola car for hauling ore to the leaching sites. When empty, these cars can accommodate a large removable rubber bladder which will contain the metal-enriched liquid drawn from the leaching sites, so that the same cars can be used to move the liquid to port. Empty rail cars can be returned to the leaching sites with empty bladders, which will then be removed before returning the empty cars to the mines.

In volumes measured in the number of filled gondola cars, the following daily ore quantity limitations apply to the shipments from the mines:

Site	Lower Bound	Upper Bound
A	0	50
C	0	60
E	0	80
F	0	70

For the routes from mine to leaching sites there is no lower bound on the number of gondola carloads. Generally at most 40 carloads can be shipped. There are several exceptions. The maximum number of carloads is 30 over (A, D), 20 over (C, D), and 10 over (E, G). The minimum number of carloads is 20 each over (A, G) and (C, G).

When each ore car is emptied it will be reconfigured as a gondola-bladder car. Thus, every car entering a leaching site full of ore will leave it loaded with a full bladder of metallic soup pumped from the holding ponds. The following carload limitations apply for shipments to and from leaching sites to the port:

Site	Lower Bound	Upper Bound
B	20	80
D	30	80
G	40	100

QUESTIONS

1. Each site will be connected to at least one other site by the railroad. The rail links will traverse some subset of the linkages in Table 13-5.
   (a) Determine the minimum track length and the corresponding routes and spurs that will be needed if the port and leaching sites are included.
   (b) Repeat (a), leaving out the linkages to the port.

2. Determine the minimum pipeline length for connecting the port to the leaching sites, leaving out the linkages to mine sites A, C, and F. Prune any legs ending at a mine site.

3. Find the aqueduct volumes that will maximize the flow from the water sources to the leaching sites.

4. Suppose that the metallic liquid pipelines are not built, and the leaching sites are connected to the port by rail. Due to land ownership disputes, the track routing found in Question 1(a) cannot be used. The rail links are

   A-D   B-D   C-D   C-F   D-E   E-G   G-H

   It is possible to route shipments from one site to another, going through a third site without loading or unloading there.
   (a) Prepare a new railroad mileage table showing how far cars will have to travel between mines

and leaching sites and between leaching sites and the port, allowing for all possibilities, no matter how unattractive.

(b) In solving the shipment problem as a minimum cost maximum flow problem, can all necessary constraints be met? Explain.

(c) Sketch a network that portrays all arcs and nodes needed to solve the problem. Then indicate for each arc the lower bound and upper bound. Assuming that each car-mile costs PNGM Co. $1, use your distances from (a) to determine the unit cost for each arc.

5. Find the transportation schedule that minimizes daily shipping cost.

6. Consider the problem of getting gondola cars back to the mines and the bladders back to the leaching sites. Suggest how you would solve this problem.

PROJECT PLANNING
WITH PERT AND CPM

A construction superintendent explained to his client the massive cost overruns. He told of concrete trucks arriving too soon and having to dump their loads, of having to repour the foundation because the gravel underlay had not been set, of having to cut many holes through the concrete floor pad because the pipes had been covered before being inspected. Everything happened as scheduled, the poor man lamented. "You should have used PERT," the client admonished.

I mportant applications of quantitative methods can be made in the area of project management, where a great deal of effort is aimed at a specific accomplishment. Such a program might be the construction of a dam, the development of a new aircraft, the implementation of a new computer system, or the introduction of a new product. All of these examples require management that is oriented toward directing and coordinating the activities of disparate organizations and people. Each project is fraught with uncertainties and takes a great deal of time to complete.

14-1 THE IMPORTANCE OF TIME IN PLANNING

T ime is often a paramount factor in selecting alternative ways of completing such projects. This is especially true of construction projects, which must generally be completed by the builder by the date the user plans to begin operating the facilities. A new headquarters building for a corporation illustrates the importance of timely completion.

Suppose that a company's present lease expires in June and that it is planning to move from New York to San Francisco in July. The builder may receive a bonus of thousands of dollars per day for early completion, with a substantial penalty imposed on each day's delay.

The builder will want to finish the job as quickly as possible and will have every expectation of achieving an acceptable profit. This requires a lot of planning. The efforts of dozens of subcontractors, who will be separately responsible for such components as air-conditioning, excavation, glasswork, and carpeting, will have to be coordinated. Because the sequence of work is not very flexible (for instance, the framework must be completed before the plumbing or wiring can begin), this coordination must be achieved through the judicious *scheduling of activities*. All subcontractors must adhere to this overall schedule, because a delay on the part of any one of them could make the entire project late.

535

One procedure generally used to establish schedules for large projects is the **Program Evaluation and Review Technique,** usually referred to by the acronym **PERT.** This procedure may also be referred to as the **Critical Path Method,** or **CPM.** In addition to helping establish schedules, PERT can serve as a management tool for controlling the progress of any large project when timely completion is important.

PERT was developed in the late 1950s, when it came into extensive use in military research and development. Its first important application was in the Polaris program for the first submarine-launched ballistic missiles. PERT has been credited with saving several months in completion time compared with the expected results if more traditional procedures had been used. Since then, PERT and other project management tools have been adopted by the Defense Department for most large research and development efforts. PERT has also been adopted by the construction industry, and to a lesser extent it has been successfully employed in other types of industrial applications.

DECISION PROBLEM

MaxiSoft Schedules Development of Manufacturing Management System

Penny Saver is a project director for MaxiSoft, a software company. Her current project is developing a manufacturing management system, which she has broken down into 16 activities. These were the result of many hours spent with employees identifying the work to be done and arranging the tasks into meaningful groupings. Additional time was spent ironing out the underlying order of the tasks and arriving at expected completion times. The following table is the result of that effort. For example, beta testing (code TB) is expected to take 5 months, and it cannot be started until alpha testing (TA), getting platform versions (PV), and writing manuals (WM) are all completed.

ACTIVITY CODE	DESCRIPTION	EXPECTED TIME (MONTHS)	IMMEDIATELY PRECEDING ACTIVITIES
PP	Do project plan	2	—
IO1	Set screen formats	2	—
IO2	Set report formats	2	—
CI	Code interface modules	4	CG
CG	Code graphics	6	IO1
CO	Code optimizations	5	PP
DB	Code database manager	3	IO1
WM	Write manuals	4	CI, DB
TA	Alpha testing	4	CO, CG, TD
TB	Beta testing	5	TA, PV, WM
TD	Develop test data	2	IO2
PV	Get platform versions	4	IP
IP	Write interfacing protocols	3	CG
MP	Do marketing plan	2	TA
PO	Get product on-line	2	MS, TB
MS	Train marketing staff	1	MP

As project director, Penny would like to do a good job of planning, scheduling, and controlling this project. A first step will be using PERT as a project scheduling tool. This will help provide her supervisor with a preliminary estimate of the project's completion time and its total cost. Penny plans to use PERT to determine a master schedule and finalize overall project planning.

14-2 THE BASIC CONCEPTS OF PERT

PERT builds on a foundation of basic work groupings called **activities.** In construction, an activity is usually a function, such as excavating or installing plumbing, that is the responsibility of a single subcontractor. In the development of an aircraft, designing the landing gear may be one activity; that same component may involve several more activities in successive stages: testing materials, establishing final specifications, fabricating test gears, ground testing, and flight testing. Regardless of how the activities are identified, they have one feature in common: *Activities take time.* Usually, activities also consume resources in the form of labor, material, or money.

The number of activities to be identified will vary with the scope of the project. There may be only a handful of activities involved in building a house, but the construction of a nuclear power plant or an oil refinery may involve several thousand activities. One ballistic missile development program involved more than 2,000 activities at the top-management level, where the U.S. Air Force established schedules and directly monitored the progress of contractors. Several major contractors were responsible for separate systems of the missile, such as propulsion or guidance. Each organization had its own activities to control, so that each contractor monitored several thousand activities for internal PERT purposes. Altogether, tens of thousands of activities were involved in the development of this particular missile.

PERT involves structuring the various project activities in such a way that schedules are developed, alternative plans are investigated, and the project's status is continuously monitored. This is accomplished by employing a graphical procedure.

The PERT Network

The central focus of any PERT procedure is a logical representation of the project activities. This is accomplished by means of a **PERT network,** which graphically indicates the interrelationships between the activities in chronological order. Figure 14-1 provides the PERT network for constructing a small home. Each activity is represented by a single *arrow,* and each arrow is connected with another in such a way that the required sequence of activities is followed. Before a network can be constructed, all activities must be identified and the immediately preceding activities must be determined. The information is provided in Table 14-1 for the home construction illustration.

We see that the project starts with excavating, which is activity (*a*). The foundation (*b*) and the outside plumbing (*c*) follow immediately. Both the framing (*d*) and the brickwork (*h*) are preceded by the foundation (*b*), which must be completed before these activities can begin. The basic principle underlying a PERT network is that certain activities must be completed before others can begin, whereas some activities can be conducted simultaneously. The network must follow the basic chronological logic dictated by the characteristics of the project. In constructing a home, grading and excavation must be completed before the foundation can be poured. And the foundation must be present before the framework can be installed.

Notice that the arrows for framing (*d*) and brickwork (*h*) activities begin at *circle 3.* This circle constitutes that *point in time* when the foundation (activity *b*) is completed. The PERT network for this project has 11 circles, which are called **events.** An event signals the completion or the starting point of one or more activities. The events themselves consume neither time nor resources. They serve mainly as **project milestones** and provide the logical "glue" that connects the various activities.

FIGURE 14-1
A PERT network for constructing a home

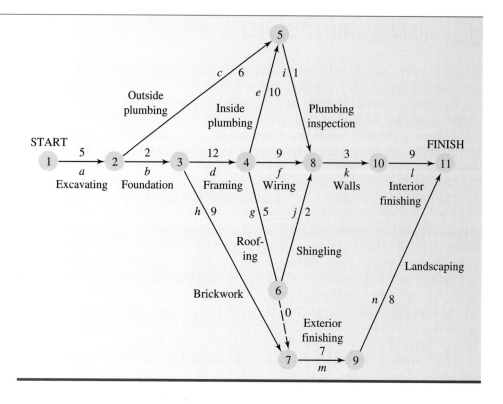

The activities in any neighboring collection exhibit one of two basic relationships to each other. When activities must be completed in a strict sequence, they appear in a *series,* as shown in Figure 14-2. For example, excavating (*a*), pouring the foundation (*b*), and framing (*d*) must be performed in that order. The activity sequence *a-b-d* must be represented by a succession of arrows, each following the other, indicating that an activity cannot begin until the preceding activity has been completed. Such a sequence

TABLE 14-1 | Basic Data Used to Construct a PERT Network for Building a Home

ACTIVITY	IMMEDIATELY PRECEDING ACTIVITY	EXPECTED COMPLETION TIME
(a) Excavating	—	5 days
(b) Pour foundation	a	2
(c) Outside plumbing	a	6
(d) Framing	b	12
(e) Inside plumbing	d	10
(f) Wiring	d	9
(g) Roofing	d	5
(h) Brickwork	b	9
(i) Plumbing inspection	c, e	1
(j) Shingling	g	2
(k) Cover walls	f, i, j	3
(l) Interior finishing	k	9
(m) Exterior finishing	h, g	7
(n) Landscaping	m	8

FIGURE 14-2
Activities in series

of activities forms a portion of a particular *path* through the network from START to FIN-ISH. The sequence *a-b-d-f-k-l* in Figure 14-1 is one of several such paths.

Activities that may occur simultaneously can be stacked, as shown in Figure 14-3. Any such arrangement involves *parallel* activities. Conceivably, plumbers, electricians, and roofers could all work on the house on the same day. Because parallel activities may be of varying durations, it is not necessary that they actually occur simultaneously, but we allow for that possibility in our PERT network. If, for some reason, electricians and plumbers cannot work together (perhaps because quarters are cramped), then the present portrayal becomes unrealistic and the project network should be restructured to reflect a series arrangement between inside plumbing and wiring. *But activities should not be placed in series unless it is absolutely necessary.* Whenever two or more jobs may be done at the same time, this possibility should be reflected in the network—even if it has never been done that way before. This approach allows greater flexibility in planning and may actually shorten the project's duration.

Once the required activity sequence has been specified, the construction of the PERT network can begin. It is best to use a very large sheet of paper for this and to begin with a rough draft. The network can then be copied and some events can be repositioned to keep the number of crossing arrows small. In some applications, the PERT network is drawn in successive revised versions as new activities or interrelationships come to mind.

Computer routines have been written as an aid in arriving at a final graphical display. It may be impractical to have any pictorial representation at all of very large projects. (If drawn, a PERT network with several thousand activities could completely cover the walls of a big room.) Such projects are usually processed entirely on a computer.

Dummy Activities

The broken arrow leading from event 6 to event 7 in Figure 14-1 is an example of a **dummy activity.** Such a portrayal is required to meet the underlying chronology of the work groupings without introducing spurious constraining relationships. The requirements in Table 14-1 indicate that shingling (*j*) is preceded by roofing (*g*) and that exterior finishing (*m*) is preceded by both brickwork (*h*) and roofing (*g*). All of these constraints are met by the network arrangement shown in Figure 14-4.

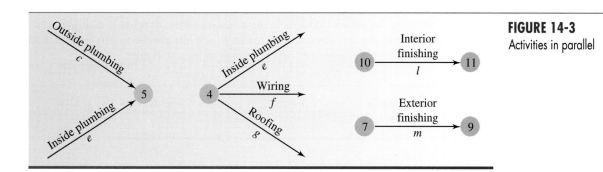

FIGURE 14-3
Activities in parallel

FIGURE 14-4

An incorrect network representation

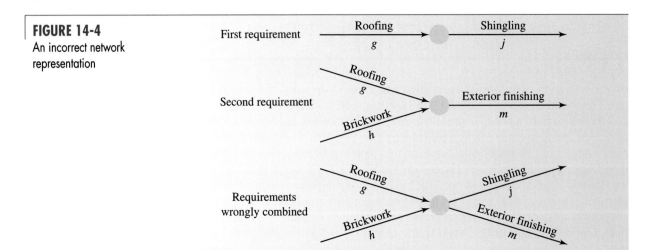

FIGURE 14-4

An incorrect network representation

However, the final portion of Figure 14-4 is incorrect, because it improperly indicates that shingling (j) cannot start until brickwork (h) is completed (see Figure 14-5). No such requirement exists, and there is no apparent reason why shingling cannot commence while the bricklayers are still working (this particular house does not have a fireplace protruding through the roof). This means that the X formed by the activities in the bottom portion of Figure 14-4 does not apply; only the first three portions shown in Figure 14-6 are correct.

The graphical dilemma is solved by using two events in place of one and letting the precedence of activity g before activity m be represented by a broken arrow pointing downward. The resulting dummy activity explicitly disallows the spurious constraint indicated earlier. A dummy activity is necessary only to preserve the interactivity logic; it consumes neither time nor resources.

A quick way to see where a dummy activity is needed is to scan the list of immediately preceding activities to see if the same activity code appears on two or more lines and not all the codes are the same. For example, the Immediately Preceding Activity Column of Table 14-1 shows that code g appears in the shingling line and again in the exterior finishing line. But the listed predecessors are not the same for both of those activities. This signals that a dummy activity is required to properly represent these activities. Although code a appears on both the pour foundation and outside plumbing lines, the listed predecessors are identical and no dummy is required.

Activity Completion Times

The duration of an activity is usually uncertain. It is impossible to predict the exact number of working days it will take to frame a house, although reliable estimates, accurate to plus or minus a few days, can be made. Much less precision can be expected in estimating how long a research effort or a series of tests will take.

FIGURE 14-5

Spurious requirement induced by not employing a dummy activity

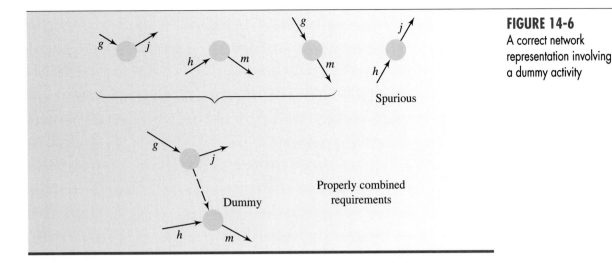

FIGURE 14-6
A correct network representation involving a dummy activity

In its most general form, PERT treats activity completion times as random variables, each having a distinct probability distribution. To further simplify the analysis, each variable is usually represented by a mean value called the *expected activity completion time*. The numbers appearing above the arrows in the PERT network in Figure 14-1 are the expected completion times for the various activities. For instance, framing (activity *d*) has a mean completion time of 12 days. After the job is done, the builder's records may show that it actually took 11.50 or 13.25 days to erect the frame. But before building begins, the actual time is an unknown future value, and the expected time of 12 days is a convenient number to use in planning.

14-3 AN ANALYSIS OF THE PERT NETWORK

Thus far, we have seen what a PERT network represents and how such a network may be constructed. We will soon see how PERT may be used in project planning and control. A major advantage of PERT is that *the network provides a basis for establishing a compatible activity schedule that permits project completion in a minimum amount of time.* Additional PERT concepts will be discussed when the steps leading to a final schedule are described.

Keep in mind that much of the following discussion is essentially *deterministic*, because expected activity times are treated as actual durations. Later in the chapter, we will investigate some of the implications of this approach.

The Earliest Possible Event Times

PERT analysis begins by focusing on events. Recall that an event is simply a point in time that represents either the completion of one activity or group of parallel activities or the start of one or more activities. An event is therefore a milestone that must be reached by all activities that directly precede it before future activities can begin. For example, event 4 in the network for constructing a home, redrawn for convenience in Figure 14-7, must occur just after framing is finished and before inside plumbing, wiring, or roofing can begin.

FIGURE 14-7

A PERT network for constructing a home, showing the earliest possible event times (*TE*'s)

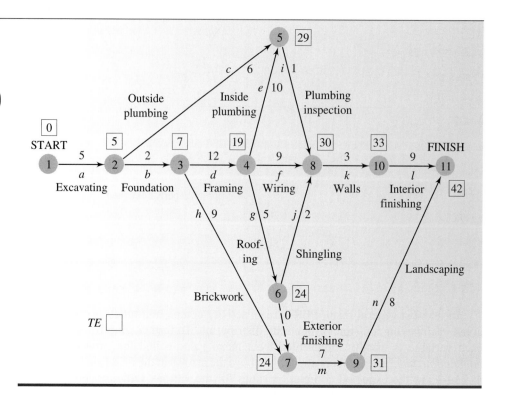

Our first step is to find the *event times* when the respective events occur. If we want to schedule each activity so that it begins as soon as possible, the permissible starting time for a particular activity can be no later than the **earliest possible event time** for the event preceding that activity.

For convenience, we use the letters *TE* to represent the earliest possible event times that can be expected. We begin at the start of the project, designated as time zero (so that it can represent any calendar time desired, such as 8 A.M. on Friday, November 18, 2002). A *TE* value of 0 applies to event 1 in Figure 14-7. For ease of identification, each *TE* is placed in the *square* alongside its corresponding event. The *TE* for any event is based on the sum of the preceding event's *TE* plus the expected completion time for the connecting activity.

Figure 14-8 shows how to apply this principle. There, event 2 is connected to event 1 by excavating (activity *a*), which takes a mean of 5 days to complete. Thus, the *TE* for event 2 is 0 + 5 = 5 days, and the earliest that event 2 can be expected to occur is at the *end* of the fifth working day of the project. Likewise, the *TE* for event 3 is obtained by adding the *TE* for event 2 to the 2-day expected completion time for the foundation (activity *b*, which connects events 2 and 3) to obtain 5 + 2 = 7 days. At event 4, we add this time to the mean framing (activity *d*) time of 12 days to obtain a *TE* of 7 + 12 = 19 days.

When two or more activities terminate at a single event, that event cannot occur until all those activities are completed. Thus, its *TE* is equal to the earliest point in time when the last activity is expected to be completed. Consider event 5, where both outside and inside plumbing (*c* and *e*) terminate. We find the respective expected numbers of working days for the earliest completion of these activities to be

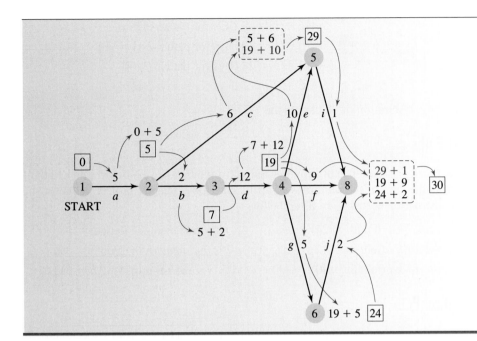

FIGURE 14-8
An illustration of how to
find event *TE* values

$$5 + 6 = 11 \text{ days for outside plumbing } (c)$$
$$19 + 10 = 29 \text{ days for inside plumbing } (e)$$

The largest sum of 29 days is required for inside plumbing (*e*), which is expected to be the last of the two activities to be completed. Thus, a *TE* of 29 is the earliest possible time for event 5. In general, the *TE* for an event must be the largest sum applicable to those activities that terminate there.

Now, consider event 8, where three activities terminate. The earliest possible completion times for these activities are

$$29 + 1 = 30 \text{ days for plumbing inspection } (i)$$
$$19 + 9 = 28 \text{ days for wiring } (f)$$
$$24 + 2 = 26 \text{ days for shingling } (j)$$

As before, the *TE* for event 8 must be the largest of these values, or 30.

TE values are found by making a *forward pass* through the network to establish the earliest possible times expected for the respective events. By adding successive activity completion times, we can see that an *event's earliest possible time* (TE) *is equal to the longest duration of all activity paths leading to it from the start.* For instance, paths *a-c* and *a-b-d-e* lead to event 5: the durations of these paths are

$$5 + 6 = 11 \text{ days for path } a\text{-}c$$
$$5 + 2 + 12 + 10 = 29 \text{ days for path } a\text{-}b\text{-}d\text{-}e$$

The longer duration path to event 5 takes 29 days—the same figure found for its *TE*. Likewise, there are four paths leading to event 8. The durations of these paths are

$$5 + 6 + 1 = 12 \text{ days for path } a\text{-}c\text{-}i$$
$$5 + 2 + 12 + 10 + 1 = 30 \text{ days for path } a\text{-}b\text{-}d\text{-}e\text{-}i$$
$$5 + 2 + 12 + 9 = 28 \text{ days for path } a\text{-}b\text{-}d\text{-}f$$
$$5 + 2 + 12 + 5 + 2 = 26 \text{ days for path } a\text{-}b\text{-}d\text{-}g\text{-}j$$

and the longest duration of 30 days is the TE for event 8.

Project Paths

A project path is a sequence of activities going from the START to FINISH. The length of the path is the sum of the durations of all its activities. The six project paths for the home construction network are listed below.

$a\text{-}c\text{-}i\text{-}k\text{-}l$ (length = 24)	$a\text{-}b\text{-}d\text{-}g\text{-}j\text{-}k\text{-}l$ (length = 38)
$a\text{-}b\text{-}d\text{-}e\text{-}i\text{-}k\text{-}l$ (length = 42)	$a\text{-}b\text{-}d\text{-}g\text{-}dummy\text{-}m\text{-}n$ (length = 39)
$a\text{-}b\text{-}d\text{-}f\text{-}k\text{-}l$ (length = 40)	$a\text{-}b\text{-}h\text{-}m\text{-}n$ (length = 31)

The Critical Path

The path with the longest total time through the PERT network from START to FINISH is called the **critical path.** The shaded arrows in Figure 14-9 indicate this particular activity sequence for the home construction project, giving us

$$\text{Critical path} = a\text{-}b\text{-}d\text{-}e\text{-}i\text{-}k\text{-}l$$

Notice that this is the longest of the six project paths. The following table represents the succession of activities on the critical path:

ACTIVITY SEQUENCE		EXPECTED COMPLETION TIME
	START	
(a)	Excavating	5 days
(b)	Pour foundation	2
(d)	Framing	12
(e)	Inside plumbing	10
(i)	Plumbing inspection	1
(k)	Cover walls	3
(l)	Interior finishing	9
	FINISH	Total 42 days

Because they compose the critical path, the tasks in this table are called **critical activities.** They are critical because a delay in completing any one of them will cause a delay in completing the entire project.

    The duration (or length) of the critical path is equal to the TE for the last event in the project, which is event 11 in our example. That final milestone can occur no sooner than 42 working days from the START. This is also the earliest time that all activities—and therefore the project itself—can be finished. Thus, *the duration of the critical path is here used to estimate the expected completion time for the entire project.* (As we shall see, for technical reasons this will often underestimate the true expected project completion time.)

Several activity sequences may tie for the longest amount of time in a PERT network. In such cases, each sequence will be a critical path. There is no reason why a project cannot have several critical paths.

The critical path has many ramifications. Before investigating these further, however, we will describe two additional preliminary PERT procedures.

Latest Allowable Event Times

By themselves, the earliest possible event times are insufficient to establish schedules because not all activities must start at the earliest opportunity. Many "harmless" or noncritical activities can actually be started later without delaying the entire project. A second set of numbers for the network events, called the **latest allowable event times,** serves to establish limits on the degree of scheduling flexibility.

The latest allowable event times, abbreviated TL, appear inside the *circles* beside the respective events in Figure 14-9. The TL value establishes the point in time by which an event must occur before an automatic delay can be expected in everything that follows, including the project itself.

For example, consider event 9, which follows exterior finishing (m). If this milestone does not occur before its latest allowable time of $TL = 34$ days, the project cannot be expected to be completed in the shortest possible duration of 42 working days. To see why this is so, suppose that event 9 does not occur until the end of the 36th working day. Because 8 more days are expected for landscaping, the project could then be expected to take 44 days to complete.

The TL and the TE values are determined similarly, but the TL values are computed in a *backward pass* through the network, and expected activity completion times are

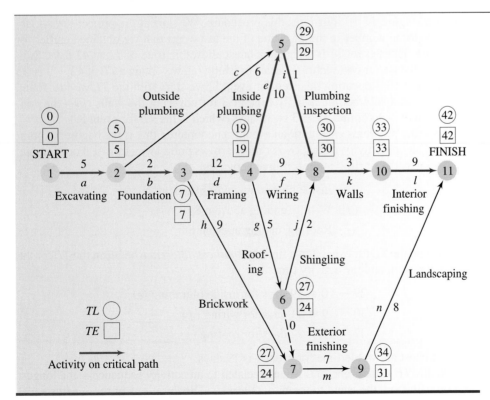

FIGURE 14-9

A PERT network for constructing a home, showing the critical path, the earliest possible event times (TE's), and the latest allowable event times (TL's)

FIGURE 14-10

An illustration of how to find event *TL* values

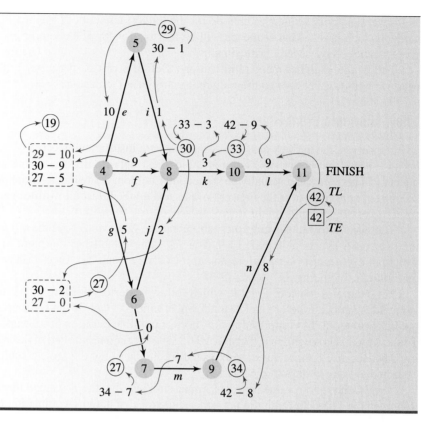

subtracted. Figure 14-10 illustrates this procedure. We start at the project FINISH, assigning the same number to the *TL* value of the last event that we obtained earlier for its *TE* value. Thus, event 11 is assigned a latest allowable time of $TL = 42$ days. Subtracting the 9 days for completing interior finishing (*l*), we obtain a *TL* of $42 - 9 = 33$ days for event 10. Repeating this step for event 8, we start with the *TL* we just found for event 10 and subtract the activity time of 3 for covering the walls (*k*)—the connecting activity—to obtain $33 - 3 = 30$ days, which is the *TL* for event 8.

No special problems exist until an event is encountered that is the beginning point for more than one activity, so that two or more arrows point away from it. For example, event 4 signals the starting point for three activities.

> (*e*) Inside plumbing, ending at event 5
>
> (*f*) Wiring, ending at event 8
>
> (*g*) Roofing, ending at event 6

To determine the *TL* for event 4, we find the *smallest difference* between the *TL* for the terminating event and the activity time.

$$29 - 10 = 19 \text{ days for inside plumbing } (e)$$
$$30 - 9 = 21 \text{ days for wiring } (f)$$
$$27 - 5 = 22 \text{ days for roofing } (g)$$

Thus, the latest allowable time for event 4 is 19 days.

Like the *TE* values, each *TL* value is related to an activity sequence—the longest duration path from the event to the project FINISH. The durations of these paths equal

the sum of the applicable activity times as well as the earliest *project* completion time minus the *TL* value. (In our example, the longest path leading from event 4 to the FINISH is expected to take $42 - 19 = 23$ days.)

The significance of the *TL* values in project scheduling will be discussed later. We will now examine the importance of the information that can be gleaned when the *TE* and *TL* values are considered together.

Event Slack Times: Finding the Critical Path

The *TE* value of an event establishes the earliest possible time within which it can be expected to occur; the *TL* value of that event is the latest allowable time that it can occur without causing expected delays in the entire project. The difference between these quantities tells the project manager how much leeway exists in achieving such an event. This duration, called the **event slack time,** is computed

$$\text{Event slack time} = TL - TE$$

As an example, consider event 9, which has a *TL* of 34 days and a *TE* of 31 days; its event slack time is therefore $34 - 31 = 3$ days. The slack times for other home construction events are computed similarly. These slack times appear in the triangles beside the respective events in Figure 14-11.

The main advantage of event slack times in PERT analysis is that they provide another way to identify the critical path. Although the *TE* for the terminal event tells us the length of the critical path, it can be hard to identify exactly which acts compose that

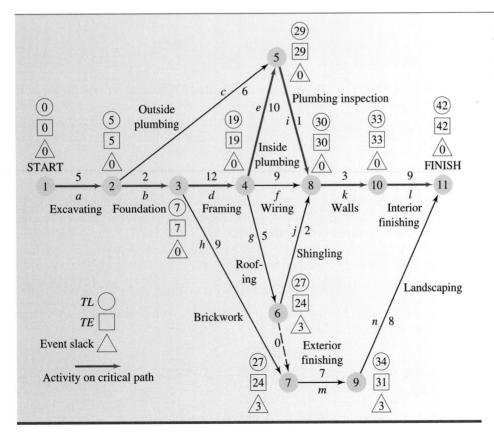

FIGURE 14-11
The complete PERT network for the home construction illustration

path without some guideline. In a network of several hundred activities, there can be millions of distinct paths from START to FINISH, but there may be only one critical path. It would be an incredible waste of time, money, and human resources to attempt to locate it by trial and error or by listing all project path possibilities to see which is longest.

Because the critical path is the longest activity sequence from START to FINISH, it should be readily apparent that *all connecting events in the critical path must have zero slack times.* This limits our search to those paths connecting zero-slack events. In Figure 14-11, there are three such sequences.

$$a\text{-}c\text{-}i\text{-}k\text{-}l$$
$$a\text{-}b\text{-}d\text{-}e\text{-}i\text{-}k\text{-}l$$
$$a\text{-}b\text{-}d\text{-}f\text{-}k\text{-}l$$

Two of these paths are not critical because their activity times do not sum to the project duration of 42 days that we found earlier. The activity times in the first path sum to 24 days; in the last path, they total only 40 days. The middle sequence describes the critical path identified in the network in Figure 14-11.

14-4 PLANNING AND CONTROL USING THE PERT NETWORK

The PERT network information in Figure 14-11 can be used to establish project schedules and to aid in controlling activities so that delays can be avoided.

Activity Scheduling

Recall that the earliest possible event time, *TE,* sets a lower limit on when successive activities can be expected to start and that the latest allowable event time, *TL,* sets an upper limit on when preceding activities can end without causing expected delays in the project. Thus, considered together, the *TE* and *TL* values provide the basis for scheduling activities.

A schedule for an activity consists of a starting date and a completion date. The PERT network establishes limits for these dates. An activity can be expected to begin on any date between its **early starting time, *ES,*** and its **late starting time, *LS.*** By adding the estimated activity completion time, these dates determine the **early finishing time, *EF,*** and the **late finishing time, *LF.***

An activity's early starting time is equal to the earliest possible time *TE* in which the immediately preceding event can be attained, or

$$ES = TE \text{ for preceding event}$$

By adding the expected activity completion time, represented by the letter *t,* we can then compute the early finishing time for each activity, or

$$EF = ES + t$$

The late finishing time for an activity is equal to the *TL* for the event at the point when the activity ends, or

$$LF = TL \text{ for succeeding event}$$

TABLE 14-2 Limits for Scheduling Home Construction Activities

		STARTING TIMES		FINISHING TIMES	
		ES	LS	EF	LF
ACTIVITY	t	Preceding TE	LF − t	ES + t	Succeeding TL
(a) Excavating	5	0	0	5	5
(b) Pour foundation	2	5	5	7	7
(c) Outside plumbing	6	5	23	11	29
(d) Framing	12	7	7	19	19
(e) Inside plumbing	10	19	19	29	29
(f) Wiring	9	19	21	28	30
(g) Roofing	5	19	22	24	27
(h) Brickwork	9	7	18	16	27
(i) Plumbing inspection	1	29	29	30	30
(j) Shingling	2	24	28	26	30
(k) Cover walls	3	30	30	33	33
(l) Interior finishing	9	33	33	42	42
(m) Exterior finishing	7	24	27	31	34
(n) Landscaping	8	31	34	39	42

Subtracting the expected activity completion time, we calculate the late starting time as

$$LS = LF - t$$

Table 14-2 shows these quantities for the home construction illustration. Consider, for example, wiring (activity f). From Figure 14-11, we see that this activity is preceded by event 4 (with an earliest possible time of $TE = 19$) and succeeded by event 8 (with a latest allowable time of $TL = 30$). Thus, the early starting time for wiring is $ES = 19$ days from the project START. Adding the expected completion time of $t = 9$ days for this activity, the early finishing time for wiring is $EF = 19 + 9 = 28$ days from time zero. The late finishing time for wiring is $LF = 30$ days, and the late starting time is $LS = 30 - 9 = 21$ days.

In scheduling the project, the builder can start wiring anytime between the early starting time of $ES = 19$ days and the late starting time of $LS = 21$ days. Thus, if the project is to start at 8 A.M. on Wednesday, August 3, 2002, wiring may be scheduled to begin sometime just after 19 working days, or at 8 A.M. on August 30 (the beginning of the 20th day) but not later than after 21 working days (8 A.M. on September 2). If the early starting time is chosen, wiring can be scheduled for completion at any time between the two corresponding finishing dates. But, if a late starting time is chosen, wiring must be scheduled for completion exactly at the late finishing time (the end of the 30th working day, or 5 P.M. on September 14—assuming that Labor Day is a working day).

Activity Slack Times

We have now identified the points in time that are associated with the activities themselves. These points provide another set of measures, called **activity slack times,** that are useful in project planning. Like their event counterparts discussed earlier, these values indicate how much leeway exists in completing an activity before project delays

TABLE 14-3	Activity Slack Times for the Home Construction Illustration		
	FINISHING TIME		
ACTIVITY	**LF**	**EF**	**ACTIVITY SLACK TIME**
(a) Excavating	5	5	0
(b) Pour foundation	7	7	0
(c) Outside plumbing	29	11	18
(d) Framing	19	19	0
(e) Inside plumbing	29	29	0
(f) Wiring	30	28	2
(g) Roofing	27	24	3
(h) Brickwork	27	16	11
(i) Plumbing inspection	30	30	0
(j) Shingling	30	26	4
(k) Cover walls	33	33	0
(l) Interior finishing	42	42	0
(m) Exterior finishing	34	31	3
(n) Landscaping	42	39	3

can be expected. For any particular activity, the activity slack time is computed from the difference between the late and early finishing times, or

$$\text{Activity slack time} = LF - EF$$

(The same results can be obtained from the difference $LS - ES$.)

The activity slack times for our home construction example are computed in Table 14-3. Notice that some activities have zero slack. A *critical path connects only zero-slack activities, and all such activities lie on at least one critical path.* Our example has only one critical path, *a-b-d-e-i-k-l.*

Although they are very similar, activity slack measures something different than event slack does, and one set of values cannot generally be computed directly from the other set.

Managing with PERT/CPM

PERT can provide a structure for controlling the multitude of activities in a complex project. When separate organizations are responsible for work that must be done in small pieces over a long period of time at widely separated locations, good coordination of these efforts is a prerequisite for success. Strict adherence to mutually compatible schedules almost assures this. Although it is by no means a panacea, PERT accomplishes this function well.

Management through PERT does not stop with the publication of schedules. Remember, the PERT analysis we have examined so far is based on a single set of numbers—the *expected* activity completion times. The amount of time actually required for a particular activity is uncertain. Consider the framing of a house. Inclement weather, an accident on the job, poor workmanship, illness, or a variety of other circumstances might delay its completion. As we have seen in our home construction example, this particular activity is critical. A delay in framing will delay the project unless the lost time can be made up by speeding up the completion of one or more later activities on the critical path.

If the timely completion of the entire project is extremely important, the critical activities deserve special attention. This is an excellent application of the *management-by-exception principle.* Less attention should be paid to activities that are not on the critical path simply because small delays in completing them will not delay the entire project.

Again, it should be emphasized that the expected activity completion times themselves are only estimated values. If some activity that was not on the critical path were unduly delayed, the critical path from that point in time onward may actually shift and a new set of activities may become critical. Special managerial attention should therefore be given to the critical and near-critical (low-slack time) activities.

14-5 COMPUTER APPLICATIONS WITH PERT/CPM

Since their inception, network planning methods have been successfully employed with computer assistance. PERT has been employed on projects involving thousands of activities, each of which is represented on a common network. It would be impracticable to evaluate such networks by hand. Indeed, the network can be too big to physically diagram without papering the walls of a large room.

Large-scale implementation of PERT must incorporate the computer, with all details stored in a database. These stored details include the estimated completion times for the activities and how the activities are logically connected. Also maintained in the database are data for the various event times and scheduling information for events. The database may be updated constantly as activities are completed, delayed, or accelerated. Additional activities may be added as they are identified.

PERT Network Evaluations with *QuickQuant*

The *QuickQuant* software package has a segment for evaluating PERT networks. The program is user friendly, with screen-prompt questions guiding all necessary choices and inputs. (Operating instructions for this program are provided in the *Guide to QuickQuant* on the CD-ROM accompanying this textbook.)

Data are entered in tabular form, and only the basic logical structure needs to be known in advance. *QuickQuant* internally constructs the network and allows you to not only correct problem inputs, but to modify the problem for a slightly different case. *QuickQuant* allows you to save problem data for later use.

Shown in Figures 14-12 and 14-13 are two output reports from a *QuickQuant* run for the home construction illustration described earlier. The first of these is an activity report that summarizes essential information for scheduling and monitoring the activities.

Using the Computer to Organize the PERT Data

The biggest challenge in implementing PERT is identifying the project activities and then finding the logical relationships among them. It is sufficient in constructing the PERT network to identify for each activity which activities immediately precede it. That firmly establishes the logical foundation for drawing the complete network. When done by hand, that can involve a lot of trial and error. It may be helpful to first run the problem on the computer because the information thereby generated can unscramble and organize the many interconnections.

FIGURE 14-12

QuickQuant PERT activity report for the home construction illustration

```
PROBLEM: Home Construction

                        PERT ACTIVITY REPORT

      Activity          Events               Planning Times
  ------------------   --------   ------------------------------------------
  No  Code    Name     Beg. End.  Exp. t  ES     LS     EF     LF    Slack
  ---------------------------------------------------------------------------
   1   a    Excavating    1    2    5.0   0.0    0.0    5.0    5.0    0.0
   2   b    Pour founda   2    3    2.0   5.0    5.0    7.0    7.0    0.0
   3   c    Outside plu   2    5    6.0   5.0   23.0   11.0   29.0   18.0
   4   d    Framing       3    4   12.0   7.0    7.0   19.0   19.0    0.0
   5   e    Inside plum   4    5   10.0  19.0   19.0   29.0   29.0    0.0
   6   f    Wiring        4    7    9.0  19.0   21.0   28.0   30.0    2.0
   7   g    Roofing       4    6    5.0  19.0   22.0   24.0   27.0    3.0
   8   h    Brickwork     3    8    9.0   7.0   18.0   16.0   27.0   11.0
   9   i    Plumbing in   5    7    1.0  29.0   29.0   30.0   30.0    0.0
  10   j    Shingling     6    7    2.0  24.0   28.0   26.0   30.0    4.0
  11   k    Cover walls   7    9    3.0  30.0   30.0   33.0   33.0    0.0
  12   l    Interior fi   9   11    9.0  33.0   33.0   42.0   42.0    0.0
  13   m    Exterior fi   8   10    7.0  24.0   27.0   31.0   34.0    3.0
  14   n    landscaping  10   11    8.0  31.0   34.0   39.0   42.0    3.0
  15   D*1  Dummy--1      6    8    0.0  24.0   27.0   24.0   27.0    3.0


  Expected Project Duration: 42

  The following critical path(s) apply.

        a     b     d     e     i     k     l
```

FIGURE 14-13

QuickQuant PERT event milestone report for the home construction illustration

```
PROBLEM: Home Construction

                        PERT EVENT MILESTONE REPORT

          Event Connections          Times          Activity Connections
        ----------------------   ---------------    ----------------------
  Event Predecessors Successors   TE    TL   Slack   Ending      Starting
  ---------------------------------------------------------------------------
    1   : none       : 2  -- --  : 0.0   0.0  0.0 : none      : a    ----
    2   : 1  -- --   : 3  5  --  : 5.0   5.0  0.0 : a    ---- : b    c
    3   : 2  -- --   : 4  8  --  : 7.0   7.0  0.0 : b    ---- : d    h
    4   : 3  -- --   : 5  7  6   :19.0  19.0  0.0 : d    ---- : e    f
        :            :           :                :          : g    ----
    5   : 2  4  --   : 7  -- --  :29.0  29.0  0.0 : c    e    : i    ----
    6   : 4  -- --   : 7  8  --  :24.0  27.0  3.0 : g    ---- : j    D*1
    7   : 4  5  6    : 9  -- --  :30.0  30.0  0.0 : f    i    : k    ----
        :            :           :                : j    ---- :
    8   : 3  6  --   :10  -- --  :24.0  27.0  3.0 : h    D*1  : m    ----
    9   : 7  -- --   :11  -- --  :33.0  33.0  0.0 : k    ---- : l    ----
   10   : 8  -- --   :11  -- --  :31.0  34.0  3.0 : m    ---- : n    ----
   11   : 9  10  --  : none      :42.0  42.0  0.0 : l    n    : none

  Expected Project Duration: 42

  The following critical path(s) apply.

      1  2  3  4  5  7  9  11
```

Decision Problem Revisited: MaxiSoft Constructs PERT Network and Finds the Critical Path

Penny Saver used *QuickQuant* to construct the PERT network for the manufacturing management system. After supplying the program with the project name and number of activities, Penny filled in the detailed project data as shown on the screen in Figure 14-14.

She then ran the problem, getting on-screen the network in Figure 14-15. The program automatically created two *dummy activities,* shown with gray arrow lines, needed to preserve the underlying predecessor-successor requirements. From the network, we see that the critical path for the project is

$$I01\text{-}CG\text{-}CI\text{-}WM\text{-}TB\text{-}PO$$

which is expected to take 23 months.

Penny was generally satisfied with the results and planned to use an activity report (not shown) similar to the one in Figure 14-12 to schedule starting and finishing times for the individual activities. She planned to fit the *ES* times onto an actual calendar, with 0 being the first week in July, and convert them into preliminary activity starting dates.

PERT Network

Change any labels or numbers in the highlighted cells.

Activity Data for: MaxiSoft Manufacturing Management

No.	Letter Code	Name	Specified Expected Completion Time	Upper/Lower Case Must Match Letter Code for Immediately Preceding Activities						
				1	2	3	4	5	6	7
1	PP	do project plan	2.00							
2	I01	set screen fmts	2.00							
3	I02	set report fmts	2.00							
4	CI	cd intfce models	4.00	CG						
5	CG	code graphics	6.00	I01						
6	CO	code optimizers	5.00	PP						
7	DB	cd dBase mgmt	3.00	I01						
8	WM	write manuals	4.00	CI	DB					
9	TA	alpha testing	4.00	CO	CG	TD				
10	TB	beta testing	5.00	TA	PV	WM				
11	TD	develop test dat	2.00	I02						
12	PV	get platform ver	4.00	IP						
13	IP	wrt intfc prots	3.00	CG						
14	MP	do marketing pln	2.00	TA						
15	PO	get prod on-line	2.00							

Proceed

FIGURE 14-14   *QuickQuant* data entry screen for the MaxiSoft PERT evaluation

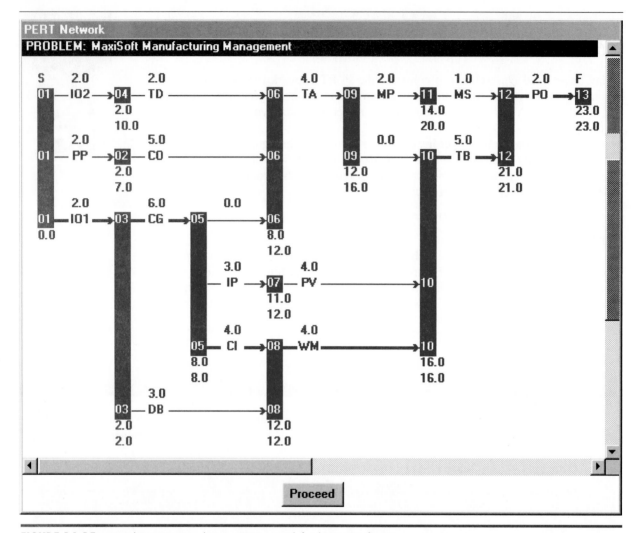

FIGURE 14-15 *QuickQuant* screen showing PERT network for the MaxiSoft project

She would use the *LF* times analogously to get initial scheduled finishing times. These would be shuffled to account for vacations and other as yet unforeseen circumstances.

But first Penny wanted to fine-tune the overall project design itself in an attempt to shave time from the project. Penny decided to refine the activities, splitting the manual writing into preliminary and final drafts. Only the preliminary draft is needed before beta testing, and the final draft can be finished while testing takes place. The lengthy beta testing can also be split into two rounds, the last one following the first and running concurrently with getting the product on-line. Those bugs found in the second beta-testing round should have miniscule effect on the manual and will signal late improvements in the program itself. Those fixes can all be accommodated just before program discs are produced, the very last step.

The following changes are made to the project:

	ACTIVITY CODE	DESCRIPTION	EXPECTED TIME (MONTHS)	IMMEDIATELY PRECEDING ACTIVITIES
Replace	WM	Write manuals	4	CI, DB
New	PMD	Preliminary manual draft	2	CI, DB
New	FMD	Final manual draft	2	PMD
Replace	TB	Beta testing	5	TA, PV, WM
New	TB1	Beta testing round 1	2	TA, PV, PMD
New	TB2	Beta testing round 2	3	TB1
Modify	PO	Get product on-line	2	MS, FMD

Again, *QuickQuant* is used. The original problem is easily modified through the Edit menu. First, WM is renamed and recoded as PMD, with a new expected time of 2. A new activity, coded FMD, is added to the problem as in the updated table. Then TB is renamed and recoded as TB1, with an expected time of 2. A new activity, coded TB2, is, similarly, added to the problem. Finally, the predecessor activity list for PO is modified as in the table to accommodate the changes.

The *QuickQuant* run provides a new critical path,

$$IO1\text{-}CG\text{-}IP\text{-}PV\text{-}TB1\text{-}TB2$$

expected to take only 20 months.

Further activity modifications might yield even more time savings. For example, PV (get platform versions) can be broken into two equal-duration phases in a manner similar to beta testing, with only the first phase needed before round 1 of beta testing, with the second phase preceding round 2. (This assessment is left as a problem for the reader.)

14-6 TIME—COST TRADE-OFF EVALUATIONS WITH PERT

As we have seen, PERT involves much more than setting schedules. If situations that cause unusual delays are encountered, PERT must somehow accommodate them. Also, our discussions until now have focused on time to the exclusion of resources that might be consumed in completing a project. This is natural, because PERT is essentially a time-minimizing procedure. But a project manager should also be concerned with minimizing the *cost* of the resources being used.

The Time—Cost Trade-off

The expected activity completion times used in the basic PERT analysis are predicated on some assumed level of resource commitment. Labor is the dominant resource in most projects that lend themselves to PERT analysis, and management has the greatest flexibility and control over this resource. For instance, it is possible to shorten the time it takes to complete an activity by concentrating more labor on it. This can be accomplished in framing a house simply by using a larger crew of carpenters than originally planned.

FIGURE 14-16

Time–cost trade-off curve for a project

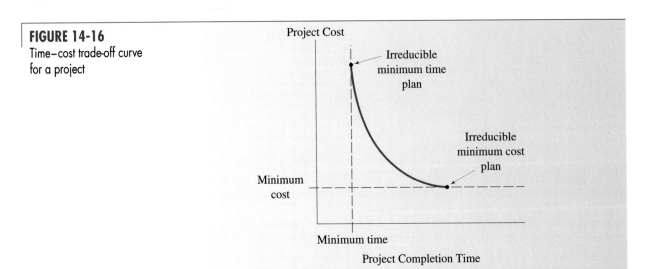

Ordinarily, an activity can be shortened only by increasing its cost. For example, adding a third carpenter will shorten the work completion time but will not necessarily increase overall crew output by 50%, which can happen only if the work of the original two carpenters is less than optimal (from a productivity point of view). Beyond the optimal crew size, the marginal productivity of each extra worker decreases so that the total framing cost will be higher if three carpenters are employed. Another way to get the job done faster is to permit overtime work, but any overtime wage premium would also raise the total cost of completing the job.

Figure 14-16 shows how project completion time and cost are related by a curve. Each point on this **time–cost trade-off curve** corresponds to a possible project plan. Note the dilemma faced by a project manager: It is possible to reduce the duration of a project only by increasing its cost and possible to reduce its cost only by increasing the duration of the project. Moreover, there are irreducible minimum plans with respect to time and cost. Only these plans and the ones lying in between, represented by the solid portion of the time–cost trade-off curve will ever be considered.

Unless time savings can be expressed in terms of a dollar return, quantitative analysis cannot identify the optimal point on the curve, because minimizing time and minimizing cost are competing objectives.

Regular and Crash Activity Plans

A good activity manager should be aware not only of how long a particular task may take under varying working conditions, but also of how much these various working arrangements should cost. When quantified, such information provides a graph such as the one shown in Figure 14-17, where two planning extremes determine a time–cost trade-off for an activity. The **crash activity plan** brings the expected activity completion time to its irreducible minimum, regardless of cost. At the other extreme, the **regular activity plan** involves the most efficient working arrangement in terms of resource use; it is the minimum-cost plan. Either of these plans, or one between them, may be chosen.

Table 14-4 provides some potential data for regular and crash activity plans for our home construction project. We can see that excavating (activity *a*) is expected to take

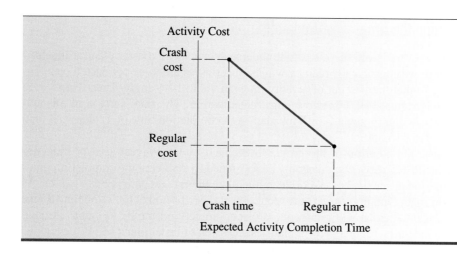

FIGURE 14-17
Time—cost trade-off line for
an activity

5 days and to cost $1,000 in labor under the regular plan. On a crash basis, larger equipment can be rented to reduce the completion time of excavating by 1 day to a crash time of 4 days for a total direct crash cost of $1,300; the additional cost of shortening this activity's completion time is $300 per day reduced. Pouring the foundation (activity *b*) cannot be shortened. The expected regular time for outside plumbing (activity *c*) is 6 days and the regular cost is $900. But if the plumbers work overtime, an expected crash time of 4 days and a crash cost of $1,300 can be achieved; the added cost reflects the overtime pay, so that the crash program for outside plumbing costs $400 more and saves 2 days, and the daily cost of reducing that activity's completion time is $200. Altogether, the direct costs (nonmaterial) total $16,350 under the regular plans and $20,150 if all possible activities are crashed.

TABLE 14-4   Regular and Crash Programs for Constructing a Home

	EXPECTED ACTIVITY TIMES		DIRECT COST		ADDITIONAL COST PER DAY SAVED
ACTIVITY	**Regular**	**Crash**	**Regular**	**Crash**	
(a) Excavating	5 days	4 days	$1,000	$1,300	$300
(b) Pour foundation	2	2	500	500	—
(c) Outside plumbing	6	4	900	1,300	200
(d) Framing	12	8	2,400	2,800	100
(e) Inside plumbing	10	7	1,500	2,100	200
(f) Wiring	9	6	1,800	2,250	150
(g) Roofing	5	3	1,000	1,400	200
(h) Brickwork	9	7	1,800	2,150	175
(i) Plumbing inspection	1	1	50	50	—
(j) Shingling	2	2	400	400	—
(k) Cover walls	3	2	300	425	125
(l) Interior finishing	9	8	1,500	1,725	225
(m) Exterior finishing	7	5	1,200	1,650	225
(n) Landscaping	8	4	2,000	2,100	25
			$16,350	$20,150	

Constructing the Time–Cost Trade-off Curve

The time–cost trade-off curve can help the manager select a master plan for the project. To start, we consider the plan by which all activities are to be conducted on a regular basis, so that the first set of activity times in Table 14-4 apply. These times were used in the original PERT network constructed earlier. The final version of this network is repeated in Figure 14-18. This plan has a completion time of 42 days and total direct costs of $16,350.

Because the duration of the project is dictated by the longest activity sequence through the PERT network, it can only be shortened by reducing the completion times of activities on the critical path. For the initial plan, the critical path is *a-b-d-e-i-k-l*. As long as this path remains critical, any reduction in the expected completion time of one of the critical activities will reduce the project completion time by the same amount.

From the initial regular project plan, a succession of faster plans will be developed by crashing various activities in such a way that each new plan is the cheapest possible one for the indicated project completion time. Table 14-5 shows the plans that result.

The procedure is started by crashing the cheapest critical activity, which happens to be framing (activity *d*), because this increases the direct costs by the smallest amount (only $100 per day saved). A maximum reduction of 4 days is possible. This faster plan yields a project completion time of 38 days and a larger total direct cost of $16,750.

The third plan is to crash activity *k* (walls), the next cheapest critical activity at $125, for a reduction of 1 day in completion time. This plan takes 37 days and costs $16,875.

FIGURE 14-18

A PERT network for the home construction illustration when all activities have regular expected completion times (plan 1)

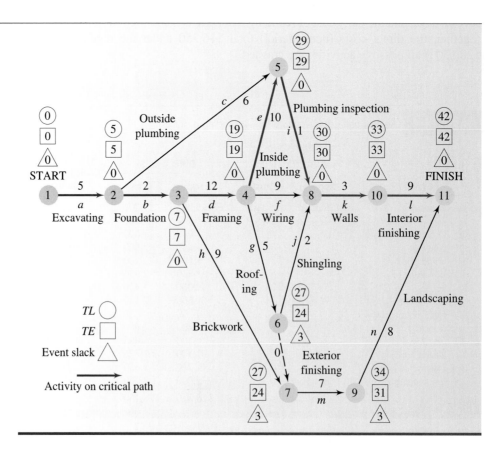

PROJECT PLAN	PROJECT COMPLETION TIME	TOTAL DIRECT COST	LAST ACTIVITY CRASHED	ADDITIONAL COST PER DAY SAVED	CRITICAL PATH

TABLE 14-5 Potential Home Construction Project Plans, Listed in Increasing Order of Additional Cost per Day Saved

PROJECT PLAN	PROJECT COMPLETION TIME	TOTAL DIRECT COST	LAST ACTIVITY CRASHED	ADDITIONAL COST PER DAY SAVED	CRITICAL PATH
1	42 days	$16,350	None	—	a-b-d-e-i-k-l
2	38	16,750	d by 4 days	$100	a-b-d-e-i-k-l
3	37	16,875	k by 1 day	125	a-b-d-e-i-k-l
4	35	17,275	e by 2 days	200	a-b-d-e-i-k-l
					a-b-d-f-k-l
					a-b-d-g-m-n
5	34	17,525	l by 1 day	225	a-b-d-e-i-k-l
			n by 1 day	25	a-b-d-f-k-l
				$\overline{250}$	a-b-d-g-m-n
6	33	17,825	a by 1 day	300	a-b-d-e-i-k-l
					a-b-d-f-k-l
					a-b-d-g-m-n
7	32	18,200	e by 1 day	200	a-b-d-e-i-k-l
			f by 1 day	150	a-b-d-f-k-l
			n by 1 day	25	a-b-d-g-m-n
				$\overline{375}$	

The cheapest critical activity remaining to be crashed is inside plumbing (*e*), which costs $200 extra for each day's reduction. Although activity *e* can be crashed from 10 to 7 days to save 3 days, just 2 days of this reduced completion time will be felt by the project as a whole. This is because two other paths (*a-b-d-f-k-l* and *a-b-d-g-m-n*) also become critical when the time for activity *e* is reduced by 2 days. Thus, the fourth plan incorporates a 2-day reduction (a partial crash) in the expected completion time for activity *e* to 8 days. This lowers the project time to 35 days and increases the cost to $17,275. This plan, reflecting all of the time changes made so far, has the PERT network shown in Figure 14-19. Each of the *three* critical paths takes 35 days. (If activity *e* were completely crashed all the way to 7 days, the project would still take 35 days, because that activity does not lie on the two new critical paths.)

The next time reduction is complicated by the fact that there are several critical paths. *The durations of all three paths must be reduced to shorten the project further.* This could be accomplished in a variety of ways. By trial and error, we can find the cheapest method. This is to crash interior finishing (*l*) and to partially crash landscaping (*n*), saving 1 day on each activity at a combined cost of $250. This fifth plan allows the project to be completed in 34 days at a cost of $17,525.

All three critical paths involve excavating (*a*). Crashing this activity is the next cheapest change, costing $300 for a 1-day reduction in completion time. This results in plan 6, which reduces the project completion time to 33 days and increases total direct costs to $17,825.

The seventh plan must involve a 1-day reduction in activity *e*, because this is the only activity remaining in the original critical path that has not been completely crashed. In the other two critical paths, a 1-day partial crash reduction combination for activities *f* and *n* provides the least costly change. Altogether, these time reductions raise to-

FIGURE 14-19
The PERT network for plan 4

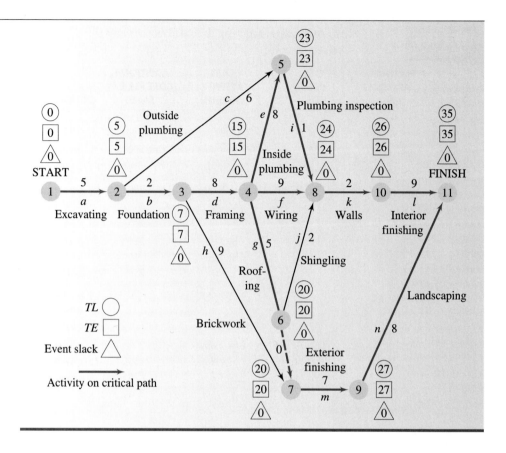

tal direct cost by $375 to $18,200 and reduce project completion time to 32 days. The PERT network for plan 7 is provided in Figure 14-20. No further time reductions are possible, because every activity in the critical path *a-b-d-e-i-k-l* is completely crashed. Because that critical path cannot be shortened, any further crashing of critical activities will only increase total direct cost without providing a compensatory time savings for the project as a whole.

The procedure just outlined for finding each new plan is strictly a matter of trial and error. It will be helpful to begin with several blank copies of the basic PERT network. The project time for new plans should be reduced in *1-day increments* to avoid making large time reductions that might not be valid for the project as a whole due to the unnoticed emergence of new critical paths. (Two or more successive plans involving identical activity changes can be combined later.) For each new plan, start with a fresh network, change the activity times on the arrows, and recompute the *TE, TL,* and slack values. Then clearly mark the critical paths. As you go along, put an × on the arrows of those activities on your latest diagram that cannot be crashed further and cross the respective activities off your original list (like the one in Table 14-4). Ignoring earlier networks, study your latest diagram to find further time-reduction alternatives. Changes will become more complex as the number of critical paths grows. Fortunately, fewer possibilities are left to be considered after each new plan.

The time–cost trade-off curve for the home construction project appears in Figure 14-21. This curve provides the builder with a comprehensive summary of possible

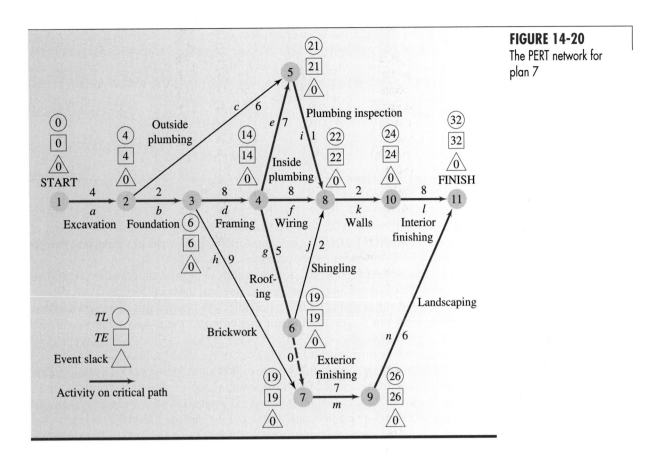

FIGURE 14-20
The PERT network for plan 7

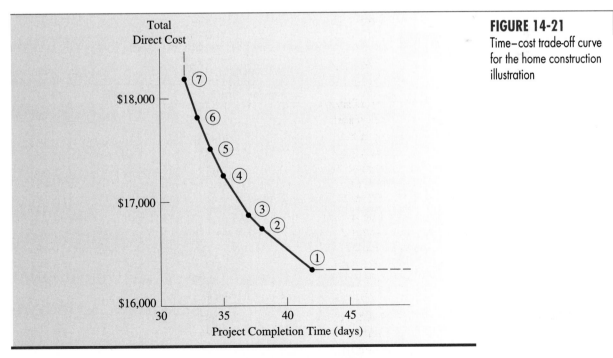

FIGURE 14-21
Time—cost trade-off curve for the home construction illustration

master plans and indicates the most efficient plan for successive reductions in project completion time. For example, if there is some advantage in shaving 5 days off the original completion time, then plan 3 should be adopted if the gain outweighs the added cost. (In-between plans are also possible, such as a 2-day reduction in expected project completion time by only partially crashing activity *d* by 2 days instead of the full 4 days possible.)

DECISION PROBLEM

Decision Problem Revisited: The Time–Cost Trade-Off

Besides breaking the project activities into smaller modules to increase the amount of parallel effort, MaxiSoft can revise planning for the manufacturing management software by accelerating the pace of some activities. Because the initial planning was based on the most efficient resource utilization, speedups will cause staff productivity drops because of inefficiencies arising from job splitting and the need for additional coordination. This will result in disproportionate increases in an activity's cost. Nevertheless, Penny Saver feels that project completion time savings might more than justify the added cost.

She evaluated the time–cost trade-off, using the problem data in Table 14-6. After picking a plan, further analysis would be performed to get more detailed planning data. Using *QuickQuant,* she retrieved the file containing the modified problem data from the last run (page 555). *QuickQuant* requested more data. Then after selecting the menu choice for the time–cost trade-off analysis, a run yielded the following report, listing eight possible plans, each reducing project completion time, but at progressively steeper increases in total cost.

TABLE 14-6   Time–Cost Trade-off Data for Modified MaxiSoft PERT Problem

		TIME (MONTHS)		COST	
	Activity	Regular	Crash	Regular	Crash
PP	Do project plan	2	1	$ 5,000	$ 6,000
IO1	Set screen formats	2	1	4,000	4,500
IO2	Set report formats	2	1	2,500	2,800
CI	Code interface modules	4	2	10,000	11,500
CG	Code graphics	6	3	15,000	19,000
CO	Code optimization	5	3	12,500	15,500
DB	Code database manager	3	2	6,000	6,700
PMD	Preliminary manual draft	2	1.5	5,000	5,400
TA	Alpha testing	4	3	6,000	8,000
TB1	Beta testing round 1	2	1.5	7,500	8,500
TD	Develop test data	2	1.5	2,000	2,500
PV	Get platform versions	4	3	3,500	3,700
IP	Write interfacing protocols	3	2	1,000	1,500
MP	Do marketing plan	2	1.5	3,000	4,000
PO	Get product on-line	2	2	35,000	35,000
MS	Train marketing staff	1	1	5,000	5,000
FMD	Final manual draft	2	1.5	6,000	7,000
TB2	Beta testing round 2	3	2	7,000	10,000

```
                   PERT TIME-COST TRADEOFF ANALYSIS

          Project     Project    Time
   Plan    Cost        Time     Savings    Last Activities Crashed
   ------------------------------------------------------------------
    1     136000.00    20.00     ----       ----
    2     136200.00    19.00     1.00       PV
    3     136700.00    18.00     1.00       IO1
    4     137950.00    17.00     1.00       CI    IP
    5     139283.32    16.00     1.00       CG
    6     141616.70    15.00     1.00       PP    CG
    7     144450.00    14.00     1.00       CG    CO
    8     146450.00    13.50     0.50       TB1   MP
```

Penny was very intrigued by the results, which show that it may be possible to complete the project in 13.5 months, 6.5 months sooner than suggested by the original PERT analysis. But, the total project cost would rise from $136,000 to $146,450. The time savings might be worth the extra cost because it could give MaxiSoft a big jump on the competition in the race for market share.

Penny needed more details regarding plan 8. She retrieved the problem from the saved data file, editing it to reduce the expected completion times: 1 month each for PV, IO1, IP, CI, PP, and CO; 3 months for CG; and .5 month for TB1 and MP. A new *QuickQuant* run shows that all the fat gets squeezed out of the project, with all activities critical except IO2, DB, TD, and FMD. Four critical paths were obtained, each expected to take 13.5 months:

PP-CO-TA-MP-MS-PO

IO1-CG-CI-PMD-D*3-TB1-TB2

PP-CO-TA-D*2-TB1-TB2

IO1-CG-IP-PV-TB1-TB2

14-7 PROBABILISTIC PERT ANALYSIS WITH THREE TIME ESTIMATES

Our introduction would not be complete without acknowledging the *uncertainty* that permeates project planning. There is no way to know how long most activities will take. Due to weather, the actual time needed to frame a house might vary considerably. The time value used for that activity in the home construction example is just the *expected* completion time. It and analogous values are actually *means* for underlying probability distributions for completion times.

All of the PERT procedures presented so far are essentially *deterministic* in nature. Except for the adjective *expected,* those procedures do not explicitly incorporate underlying project uncertainties. (Although good managers should always be cognizant of uncertainties.)

Uncertainty in PERT is handled in two primary ways. In this section we discuss a single-path evaluation that gives probabilities for how long the critical path will take. Chapter 18 describes in detail how simulation procedures can provide similar information regarding the project as a whole.

Probability Distribution for Activity Completion Time

So far we have not considered how we arrive at expected activity completion times. Although the techniques presented in Chapter 4 can be used for this purpose, in traditional PERT analysis, expected activity completion times are obtained from a special procedure that involves three time estimates.

$$a = \text{Optimistic time}$$
$$m = \text{Most likely time}$$
$$b = \text{Pessimistic time}$$

These estimates are fairly easy for activity line managers to provide.

The activity duration will almost certainly exceed the optimistic time a, and the actual completion time will almost certainly be below the pessimistic time b. The most likely time m is analogous to the *mode* in statistics. These three time estimates specify a particular continuous probability distribution that is a member of the **modified beta distribution** family. Such a distribution can be symmetrical or skewed (positively or negatively), depending on the relative positions of a, m, and b. The frequency curves for each case appear in Figure 14-22. The expected activity completion time may be computed from these three estimates.

$$t = \frac{a + 4m + b}{6}$$

The values calculated from this equation can then be used in the main PERT analysis.

It may also be useful to know the variance in completion time, which is computed

$$\text{Variance} = \left(\frac{b - a}{6}\right)^2$$

FIGURE 14-22
Three basic shapes of frequency curves for the PERT modified beta distribution

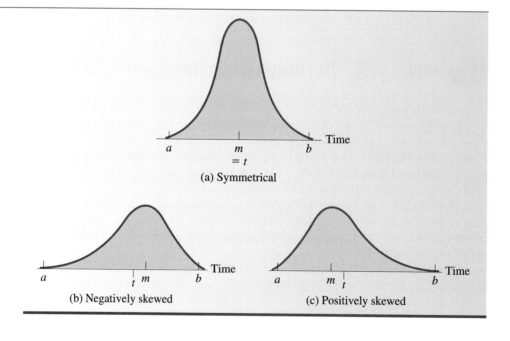

(a) Symmetrical

(b) Negatively skewed

(c) Positively skewed

TABLE 14-7	Three Time Estimates Used to Compute the Expected Values and Variances of Activity Completion Times for the Home Construction Illustration				
ACTIVITY	**OPTIMISTIC TIME** a	**MOST LIKELY TIME** m	**PESSIMISTIC TIME** b	**EXPECTED TIME** $t = \dfrac{a + 4m + b}{6}$	**VARIANCE** $\left(\dfrac{b - a}{6}\right)^2$
a	3	5	7	5	.444
b	1	1.5	5	2	.444
c	4	5	12	6	1.778
d	8	10	24	12	7.111
e	7	10	13	10	1.000
f	5	9.5	11	9	1.000
g	3.5	5	6.5	5	.250
h	6	8	16	9	2.778
i	1	1	1	1	0
j	1	2	3	2	.111
k	1.5	3	4.5	3	.250
l	7	9	11	9	.444
m	6	6.5	10	7	.444
n	5	7.5	13	8	1.778

Table 14-7 shows the three time estimates applicable to the activities for the home construction illustration. In each case, the three estimates yield the same expected time used in the earlier illustrations. Also listed are the variances in the completion time for each activity.

Although we could use the modified beta distribution to determine probabilities for the completion time of any single activity, managers are ordinarily interested in the probability for the duration of the project. It is easier to instead use the knowledge about individual activities to find probabilities for how long the *critical path*, or any other designated path, will take.

Finding Single-Path Probabilities

Notice in Table 14-7 that there is considerable variability in the completion time for most activities listed. Thus, any of the various events in the PERT network could occur at a wide variety of points in time, and the project completion time could be considerably shorter or longer than the 42 days originally anticipated.

As a result, the duration T of the original critical path *a-b-d-e-i-k-l* cannot be predicted precisely. We do know that its expected value, represented by μ, is the sum of the expected completion times for the component activities, or

$$\mu = 5 + 2 + 12 + 10 + 1 + 3 + 9 = 42 \text{ days}$$

If we assume that the activity times are *independent,* then we can closely approximate the complete probability distribution of the length of T of this particular path. Its variance σ^2 is then the sum of the variances of the individual completion times for the critical activities, or

$$\sigma^2 = .444 + .444 + 7.111 + 1.000 + 0 + .250 + .444 = 9.693$$

And the standard deviation for T is

$$\sigma = \sqrt{9.693} = 3.11 \text{ days}$$

A general form of the central limit theorem indicates that T is approximately normally distributed with a mean of μ and a variance of σ^2. Thus, we can establish the probability that 50 days or less will be required to complete path a-b-d-e-i-k-l as

$$z = \frac{50 - 42}{3.11} = 2.57$$

$$\Pr[T \le 50] = .5 + .4949 = .9949$$

and the probability that it will take more than 40 days as

$$z = \frac{40 - 42}{3.11} = -.64$$

$$\Pr[T > 40] = .5 + .2389 = .7389$$

Computer Solution

QuickQuant takes much of the pain out of the single-path probabilistic analysis. By selecting the menu choice for that procedure, the original problem data can be augmented by incorporating the three time estimates as supplemental input. This involves filling in the blanks in two screens.

Along with the standard PERT reports seen earlier, *QuickQuant* provides the results of the single-path probability analysis in Figure 14-23. Based on the underlying normal distribution, fractile values are given for the completion time of the critical path a-b-d-e-i-k-l. Notice that there is a .99 probability that this path will take less than 49.25 days.

There is one major fallacy in this analysis. *T is the duration for a particular path—not for the project itself.* This point has been widely misunderstood. There is a considerable chance that some path other than the one we identify as the critical path will actually take longer. Thus, $\mu = 42$ days is not really a measure of how long the *project*

FIGURE 14-23
QuickQuant PERT single-path probability analysis report for the home construction problem

```
PROBLEM: Home Construction

    Critical Path:
             a    b    d    e    i    k    l

         Mean Duration: 42
    Standard Deviation: 3.11

         Fractile .01: 34.75
         Fractile .05: 36.89
         Fractile .10: 38.01
         Fractile .25: 39.91
         Fractile .50: 42
         Fractile .75: 44.09
         Fractile .90: 45.99
         Fractile .95: 47.11
         Fractile .99: 49.25
```

may be expected to take, and it can considerably understate the true value of the project's expected length.

Simulation Correctly Assesses the Project Duration

Getting exact probabilities for the *project* duration of any but the simplest of PERT networks is mathematically too complex. The difficulties arise because of statistical dependency among the numerous path durations that occur in most projects. Unlike individual activity durations on the same path, for which the assumption of independence is generally plausible, independence cannot be assumed for path durations because they share the same activities.

The mathematical difficulties can be avoided by *simulating* the project. This might involve building the home, on paper only, hundreds of times. Useful patterns emerge from such simulations that can provide management with the same type of information that could otherwise be obtained only from a complex mathematical analysis.

Although you must read Chapter 18 to learn about the details of such a simulation, Figure 14-24 shows the results for the home construction illustration from building the home 200 times. Notice that the mean project completion time is 42.59 days, exceeding the expected completion time found earlier for path *a-b-d-e-i-k-l* by .59 day. Aside from the statistical sampling error inherent in any simulation, the discrepancy may be explained by the fact that the simulation sometimes found *different* paths to be critical, so that the project was found to on the average take longer than the expected duration of the original single critical path. With different data or for more complex projects, the discrepancies between the single-path analysis and the simulation might be far more dramatic.

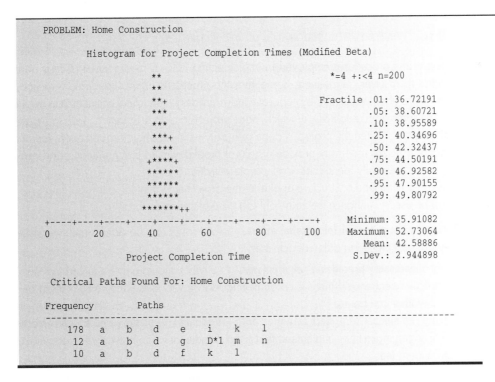

FIGURE 14-24
QuickQuant PERT simulation report for the home construction problem

14-8   IMPLEMENTING PERT AND FURTHER CONSIDERATIONS

Once a plan has been established, the appropriate schedules can be determined and the project can be started. PERT can still be used as the project progresses. The actual completion times of the early activities can deviate, perhaps considerably, from the expected values identified at the outset due to such factors as strikes, poor weather, illness, or chance. Or the expected completion times for some future activities may have to be revised in the light of new information. Or a subcontractor may simply not be able to start work on the scheduled date. Such discrepancies may necessitate revising the PERT network, because much of the earlier analysis is no longer applicable. For example, a delay of several days in the completion of the brickwork could effectively shift the critical path in our home construction example to a portion of the network never considered critical before.

When the project is well underway, PERT procedures are the same as before, except that completed activities will have actual rather than expected completion times. New time–cost trade-offs can be made (completed activities, of course, cannot be changed), and a new master plan can be developed that involves revised schedules.

The ability to update PERT networks is especially important in long projects with considerable uncertainties, such as those encountered in weapon system development. Such projects can take more than five years to complete and often involve major technological breakthroughs. In such cases, all of the activities cannot even be identified in detail before the project starts. Initial PERT planning often begins with educated guesses about the specific tasks that will be required three or four years into the project. As planning becomes more precise, the PERT network can grow and be based on more sophisticated time estimates. As the PERT network is modified, revised schedules reflecting current planning can be periodically published.

How Should Work Be Arranged into Separate Activities?

Regardless of the procedures employed in implementing PERT, a fundamental issue is how the activities themselves get defined. Sometimes the process is natural, as in construction, where tasks are often performed by separate subcontractors, so distinct activities can apply to each. The same applies to R&D, in which many projects are done under contract with government agencies. When the project is done primarily within a single organization, the organizational structure itself may provide a natural breakdown, so that marketing and production efforts are easily identifiable as separate activities.

No matter what kind of structure applies to the project environment, a few guiding principles can be used to enhance the value of PERT as a planning and control tool.

1. **Maximize the potential for parallel effort.**   If two tasks can be done simultaneously, they are best placed in different activities.

2. **Avoid unnecessary precedence requirements.**   Activities should only be forced to follow a particular sequence if there is a compelling reason why one must be completed before the other can begin.

3. **Balance the number of project activities with the complexity of the project.**   Too many activities can make PERT implementation a formidable task. Too few activities can make PERT superfluous.

14-9 (OPTIONAL) ALTERNATIVE NETWORK GRAPH: THE CPM NETWORK

An alternative portrayal of the PERT network is for *each activity to be represented by a circle.* The circles are connected with arrows in accordance with the required logical sequence, forming a network like the one in Figure 14-25 for the home construction example. The expected activity completion times appear inside the respective circles. (For convenience, circles are also used to represent the project's start and finish.)

The critical path is located by a similar procedure. First, a forward pass is made to obtain the *ES* and *EF* values. A value of zero is used for the START; the *ES* is the largest *EF* of immediately preceding activities. An activity's *ES* value represents the longest path of activities that must be completed before it can start. The *LF* and *LS* values are found in a backward pass. The *LS* used to begin this process is equal to the *ES* for FINISH; the *LF* is always the smallest *LS* of immediately preceding activities. An activity's *LF* is the longest duration from its completion to FINISH. In this procedure, the following relationships are used:

$$EF = ES + t$$
$$LS = LF - t$$
$$\text{Activity slack} = LF - EF = LS - ES$$

The critical path is one connecting zero-slack activities.

One distinct disadvantage of the alternative network is that it is clumsy for identifying events, which makes it less desirable for milestone scheduling. Each divergence or convergence of arrows corresponds to the standard PERT network event. Earliest possible and latest allowable event times may be obtained from the following:

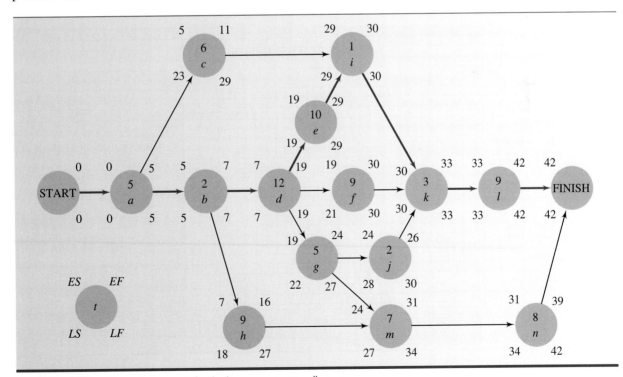

FIGURE 14-25   Alternative network for the home construction illustration

$$TE = \text{Largest } EF \text{ for preceding activity}$$
$$TL = \text{Smallest } LS \text{ for succeeding activity}$$

Another disadvantage of the alternative network is that it is harder to identify activities for computer processing; in standard PERT, each activity can be defined in terms of predecessor and successor events. The main advantage of the CPM network is that it is easier to graph than the PERT network, because dummy activities are not required.

14-10 (OPTIONAL) PERT NETWORK EVALUATIONS USING SPREADSHEETS

PERT networks may be evaluated as linear programs. Excel can be employed to do that. Figure 14-26 shows the Excel spreadsheet for evaluating the home construction example described earlier. The same results were obtained. The spreadsheet can serve as a template for other PERT applications in this text.

The earliest possible overall project completion time of 42 weeks is given in cell N26; the earliest possible event times appear in cells C26:M26.

In using Excel to evaluate PERT networks as linear programs, it is first necessary to have a drawing of the network to identify the events. The LP formulation begins with an *activity-event table,* appearing in cells A6:N22 for the home construction example. There, column A lists the activity codes, including any dummies, and column B lists the activity names. The activity durations (expected completion times) are given in column N. For example, the first activity's code is *a* (in cell A8), its name is "Excavating" (in cell B8), and its duration is 5 (in cell N8). The events are numbered and are listed in the top row in cells C7:M7. Each activity gets a -1 in the column of its beginning event and a $+1$ in the column of its ending event. For instance, activity *e* (in row 12)

PERT/CPM EVALUATION RESULTS

PROBLEM: Home Construction Example

Activity - Event Table

Activities	Name	1	2	3	4	5	6	7	8	9	10	11	Duration	Activities	Name	TE_end − TE_beg	On Critical Path?
a	Excavating	-1	1										5	a	Excavating	5	Yes
b	Pour Foundation		-1	1									2	b	Pour Foundation	2	Yes
c	Outside plumbing		-1			1							6	c	Outside plumbing	24	No
d	Framing			-1	1								12	d	Framing	12	Yes
e	Inside plumbing				-1	1							10	e	Inside plumbing	10	Yes
f	Wiring				-1				1				9	f	Wiring	11	No
g	Roofing				-1		1						5	g	Roofing	5	No
h	Brickwork			-1			1						9	h	Brickwork	17	No
i	Plumbing inspection					-1			1				1	i	Plumbing inspection	1	Yes
j	Shingling						-1		1				2	j	Shingling	6	No
k	Cover walls								-1		1		3	k	Cover walls	3	Yes
l	Interior finish										-1	1	9	l	Interior finish	9	Yes
m	Exterior finish							-1		1			7	m	Exterior finish	7	No
n	Landscaping									-1		1	8	n	Landscaping	11	No
D1	Dummy 1						-1	1					0	D1	Dummy 1	0	No

Solution (Earliest Event Times, TE_i)

	1	2	3	4	5	6	7	8	9	10	11	Project Time	N 26 =M26
	0	5	7	19	29	24	24	30	31	33	42	42	Sum of Earliest Event Times = 244

	O	P	Q	R	R
8	=A8	=IF(ISBLANK(B8),"",B8)	=SUMPRODUCT($C$26:$M$26,C8:M8)	=IF(R38=1,"Yes","No")	26 =SUM(C26:M26)
9	=A9	=IF(ISBLANK(B9),"",B9)	=SUMPRODUCT($C$26:$M$26,C9:M9)	=IF(R39=1,"Yes","No")	
10	=A10	=IF(ISBLANK(B10),"",B10)	=SUMPRODUCT($C$26:$M$26,C10:M10)	=IF(R40=1,"Yes","No")	

FIGURE 14-26   Excel spreadsheet PERT evaluation results for home construction example

starts at event 4 (in column F) and ends at event 5 (in column G); the activity-event table thus has a -1 in cell F12 and a $+1$ in cell G12. All other entries in row 12 are blank.

The main portion of the PERT solution is shown below the activity-event table, in rows 25 and 26. There the earliest possible event times (*TE* values) are listed. Originally unknown with cells blank, the *TE* values were computed during the problem solution process. For convenience, the event numbers are repeated in row 25, and *TE* values appear directly below in row 26. For instance, the *TE* of 29 days for event 5 appears in cell G26. The values in row 26 are provided by Solver.

The formulas used in the spreadsheet are shown in Figure 14-26. For ease in reading the table, columns O and P repeat the activity codes and names. Column Q contains the differences between the earliest possible times for the respective activity's ending and beginning events; the column header is $TE_{end} - TE_{beg}$. The Excel SUMPRODUCT function is used to compute these. For instance, in cell Q8 the formula is

$$=SUMPRODUCT(\$C\$26:\$M\$26,C8:M8)$$

The above formula was copied down to cell Q22.

Only the activity-event table and durations were entered onto the spreadsheet. The solution process began by clicking on Tools and then Solver. That brought the Solver Parameters dialog box shown in Figure 14-27. Using $ prefixes to make references absolute, the changing cells were designated as $C$26:$M$26 (the earliest possible event times or *TE* values). The project time is to be minimized, so that the objective equation formula is =N26, which serves as the Target Cell. The constraints require that the differences between the ending and beginning early times for each activity be at least as great as the corresponding activity durations, and

$$\$Q\$8:\$Q\$22>=\$N\$8:\$N\$22$$

was added in the *Subject to the Constraints* field. On the *Equal To* line the *Min* button was clicked as the objective. Clicking the Options button brought to screen the *Assume Linear* and *Assume Non-Negative* boxes to be checked.

Each activity having a Yes in column R lies on the critical path. The Yes answers were generated after the problem was solved using Excel's Sensitivity Report in Figure 14-28, which is stowed in the lower-right portion of the spreadsheet. Any activity hav-

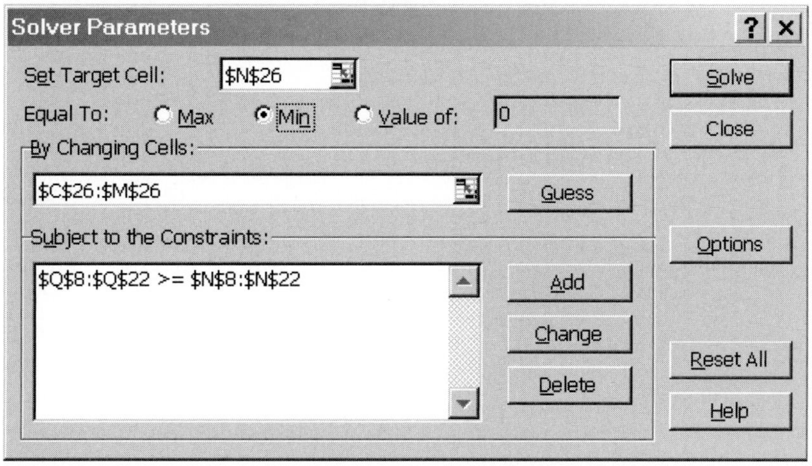

FIGURE 14-27
The Solver Parameters dialog box for the home construction example

	N	O	P	Q	R	S	T	U
35	Constraints							
36				Final	Shadow	Constraint	Allowable	Allowable
37		Cell	Name	Value	Price	R.H. Side	Increase	Decrease
38		$Q$8	Excavating TEend - TEbeg	5	1	5	1E+30	5
39		$Q$9	Pour Foundation TEend - TEbeg	2	1	2	1E+30	7
40		$Q$10	Outside plumbing TEend - TEbeg	24	0	6	18	1E+30
41		$Q$11	Framing TEend - TEbeg	12	1	12	1E+30	11
42		$Q$12	Inside plumbing TEend - TEbeg	10	1	10	1E+30	2
43		$Q$13	Wiring TEend - TEbeg	11	0	9	2	1E+30
44		$Q$14	Roofing TEend - TEbeg	8	0	5	3	1E+30
45		$Q$15	Brickwork TEend - TEbeg	20	0	9	11	1E+30
46		$Q$16	Plumbing inspection TEend - TEbeg	1	1	1	1E+30	2
47		$Q$17	Shingling TEend - TEbeg	3	0	2	1	1E+30
48		$Q$18	Cover walls TEend - TEbeg	3	1	3	1	3
49		$Q$19	Interior finish TEend - TEbeg	9	1	9	1	3
50		$Q$20	Exterior finish TEend - TEbeg	7	0	7	3	1
51		$Q$21	Landscaping TEend - TEbeg	8	0	8	3	1
52		$Q$22	Dummy 1 TEend - TEbeg	0	0	0	3	1

FIGURE 14-28   Portion of Excel's Sensitivity Report showing the critical path

ing a shadow price 1 is a critical activity. The entries in column R were created by the formula for cell R8 (of the spreadsheet in Figure 14-26)

$$=IF(R38=1,\text{``Yes''},\text{``No''})$$

which was copied down to cells R9:R22.

A last step is required to ensure that the solution in cells C26:M26 contains all of the earliest event times: Run Solver once more, using cell R26, the sum of the earliest event times, as the Target Cell. In other words, click on Tools, Solver; in the Target Cell line enter R26 and click on the solve button.

It is a simple matter to modify the spreadsheet in Figure 14-26 to incorporate crashing activities.

PROBLEMS

14-1   Find the critical path for the PERT network in Figure 14-29.

FIGURE 14-29
The PERT network for
Problem 14-1

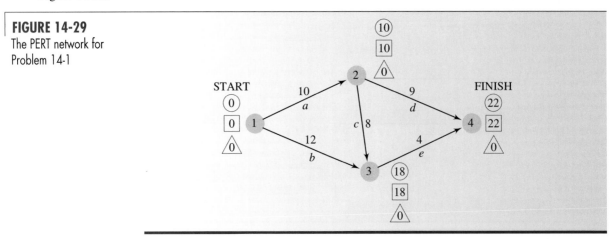

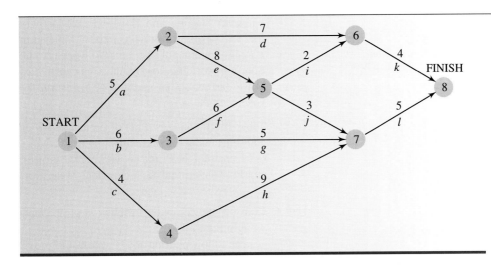

FIGURE 14-30
The PERT network for
Problem 14-2

14-2 Copy the PERT network in Figure 14-30 on a piece of paper.
   (a) Determine the *TE, TL,* and slack values for each event.
   (b) Find the critical path(s). What project duration is indicated?
   (c) Determine the *ES, EF, LS, LF,* and slack values for each activity.

14-3 For the PERT network in Figure 14-31, determine (1) the earliest event completion times, (2) the latest allowable event completion times, (3) the event slack times, and (4) the critical path(s).

14-4 Table 14-8 contains a list of project activities and the sequencing requirements.
   (a) Construct a PERT network for the project.
   (b) Determine the *TE, TL,* and slack values for each event. Indicate these values on your diagram, using a square, circle, and triangle, respectively, for each event.
   (c) Find the critical path(s).

14-5 Table 14-9 contains a list of project activities and sequencing requirements.

TABLE 14-8   Data for Problem 14-4

Activity	Immediately Preceding Activity	Expected Completion Time
a	—	8 days
b	—	7
c	—	6
d	a	6
e	b	7
f	c	6
g	c	3
h	a	5
i	d, e, f	3
j	c	3
k	h, i, j	4

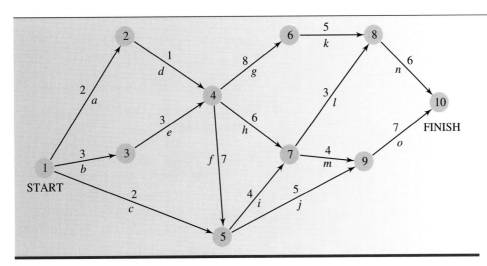

FIGURE 14-31
The PERT network for
Problem 14-3

TABLE 14-9 Data for Problem 14-5

Activity	Immediately Preceding Activity	Expected Completion Time
a	—	2 days
b	—	3
c	—	2
d	b	4
e	a, b	3
f	b	2
g	f, c	5
h	g	4
i	f	3
j	i, d	2
k	j	1
l	e	6

(a) Construct a PERT network for the project.
(b) Find the critical path(s).

14-6 Refer to Problem 14-5 and your answers. Suppose that activity g is split into two activities, g_1 (expected to take 2 days) and g_2 (expected to take 3 days). Activity g_1 has the same predecessors as the original g. Activity g_2 is only preceded by activity g_1. Activity h is now preceded only by activity g_2. In addition to j, activity k is now immediately preceded by g_1.
(a) Construct the PERT network for the project.
(b) Find the critical path(s).
(c) Do the changes result in a shorter critical path(s) than found in Problem 14-5?

14-7 Consider the PERT network in Figure 14-29, where the expected completion times are in 8-hour working days. Assuming that the project will start at 8 A.M. on Monday, September 1, determine a set of mutually compatible schedule

TABLE 14-10 Data for Problem 14-8

Activity	Immediately Preceding Activity	Expected Completion Time
a	—	5 days
b	—	4
c	—	3
d	a	4
e	a, b	5
f	a, b	6
g	c	8
h	d, e	3
i	h	1
j	f, g	1
k	i	2
l	h, j	4

dates for starting and finishing each activity that will permit the projects to be completed in a minimum amount of time. (No work is to be done on weekends or holidays, and activities must start at 8 A.M. and end at 5 P.M. on the scheduled dates.)

14-8 Table 14-10 contains a list of project activities and sequencing requirements.
(a) Construct the PERT network for the project.
(b) Find the critical path. How long is the project expected to take?

14-9 Consider the computer installation project network in Figure 14-32.
The following time and cost data apply:

Activity	Time (Weeks) Regular	Crash	Cost Regular	Crash	Additional Cost/Week Saved
a	2	1	$1,000	$2,000	$1,000
b	6	6	1,000	1,000	—
c	2	1	500	700	200
d	2	1	600	700	100
e	6	4	400	1,000	300
f	4	1	500	1,700	400
g	3	3	1,000	1,000	—
h	3	1	1,000	2,000	500
i	2	1	1,000	1,600	600

The following is a partially completed listing of the succession of plans for the time–cost trade-off. Complete the list, identifying each successive plan that will save one week in project completion time at the smallest increase in cost.

Project Plan	Project Completion Time (Weeks)	Total Direct Cost	Last Activities Crashed	Additional Cost per Week Saved	Critical Paths
1	13	$7,000	none	—	a-e-h-i
2	12	7,300	e by 1 week	$300	a-e-h-i
3	11	7,600	e by 1 week	300	a-e-h-i c-f-h-i a-f-h-i

14-10 The following table provides information on a research project:

Activity	Expected Time Regular	Crash	Direct Cost Regular	Crash
a	9 days	9 days	$500	$500
b	18	17	400	600
c	10	9	300	500
d	22	20	700	900
e	21	20	600	900

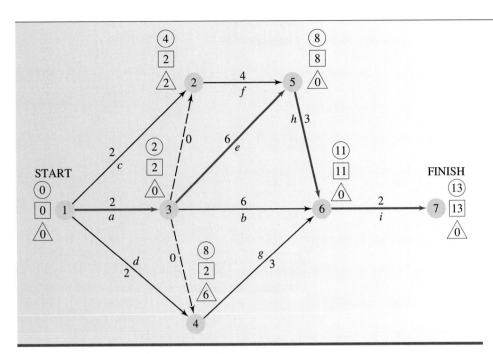

FIGURE 14-32
The PERT network for
Problem 14-9

The PERT network is provided in Figure 14-33.
(a) Using regular times, find the critical path. How long is the project expected to take? How much will it cost?
(b) Determine the plans that the project manager should want to consider in making a time–cost trade-off. List these, beginning with the most lengthy duration plan and ending with the most costly plan. (Do not list plans that should not be considered at all.)
(c) Suppose that the project manager saves $150 in late penalties for each day that the project is completed ahead of regular time.
   (1) Which of the plans in (b) would be used?
   (2) If he saves, instead, $300 per day, which of the plans would be used?

14-11 The activities in the table (right) apply to the computerization of a company's accounting system, presently operated manually.

Activity		Expected Completion Time
(a)	Select computer	2 months
(b)	Assemble and install computer	6
(c)	Design data input forms	2
(d)	Design output report forms	2
(e)	Write main processing programs	6
(f)	Write input routines	4
(g)	Write output routines	3
(h)	Generate accounting data bank	3
(i)	Test and revise system	2

All of the program routines can be written independently before the computer is installed and can be debugged using computer time rented from another company. No programs or routines can be written until the particular computer model has been selected, although forms and reports can be designed while alternative computers are being evaluated. No input or output routines can be written until the corresponding forms have been designed. The main processing programs and input routines are

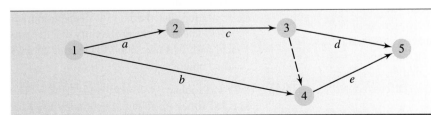

FIGURE 14-33
The PERT network for
Problem 14-10

required to establish the accounting data bank, which can be created on rental equipment. The final activity before implementation is complete is to test and revise the system.

(a) Construct a PERT network for converting the accounting system.

(b) What is the earliest time that the conversion can be finished assuming that the completion times are certain?

(c) Establish the early and late starting and finishing times for each activity. Which activities are critical?

14-12 Consider the PERT network in Figure 14-30. Suppose that the following regular and crash data apply:

	Expected Time		Direct Cost	
Activity	Regular	Crash	Regular	Crash
a	5 days	4 days	$100	$ 120
b	6	4	200	260
c	4	4	300	300
d	7	5	500	580
e	8	6	700	800
f	6	5	500	560
g	5	5	400	400
h	9	8	950	1020
i	2	2	200	200
j	3	2	250	325
k	4	3	350	440
l	5	3	500	700

(a) Construct the time–cost trade-off curve for this project. (*Hint:* Before starting, make several copies of the PERT network, omitting the activity times; use a new network for each plan.)

(b) Suppose that the project manager values each day of the project completion time saved at $85. Which point on your curve is optimal? What direct cost and project completion time apply?

14-13 In publishing a textbook, the following simplified sequence of activities applies, as shown in Table 14-11.

(a) Construct the PERT network and find the critical path for this activity sequence. How long should the project take from start to finish?

(b) If the project is well managed, it is possible to produce a book in 18 months or less without crashing any activities. This contradicts your findings in (a). Discuss each of the following:

TABLE 14-11 Data for Problem 14-13

Activity		Preceding Activity	Expected Completion Time
(a)	Write book	—	12 months
(b)	Design book	a	1
(c)	Edit manuscript	a	6
(d)	Check editing	c	2
(e)	Accept design	b	1
(f)	Copy edit	d, e	2
(g)	Prepare artwork	d, e	4
(h)	Accept and correct artwork	g	.5
(i)	Set galleys	f	4
(j)	Check and correct galleys	i	1
(k)	Pull page proofs	h, j	2
(l)	Check and correct pages	k	1
(m)	Prepare index	k	1
(n)	Set and correct index	m	.5
(o)	Check camera-ready copy	l, n	.5
(p)	Print and bind book	o	1

(1) How do you think publishers get the job done so quickly?

(2) Does this mean that PERT is not applicable to book publishing?

(3) Publishers usually require an author's complete manuscript before they begin to work on the book. In light of your answer to (2), suggest how PERT may be used to shorten the publication time of a book even further.

14-14 Consider a small project that involves the following activities:

Activity	Preceding Activity	Completion Times (Days)		
		Optimistic	Most Likely	Pessimistic
a	—	5	6	7
b	—	4	5	18
c	a	4	15	20
d	b, c	3	4	5
e	a	16	17	18

(a) Determine the expected value and the variance of the completion time for each activity.

(b) Use the expected times from (a) to find the critical path.

(c) Assuming that the normal distribution applies, determine the probability that the critical path will take between 18 and 26 days to complete.

14-15 Refer to Problem 14-13 and your answers. The expected times (in months) originally used for

TABLE 14-12 Three Time Estimate Data for Problem 14-15

Activity	Optimistic Time	Most Likely Time	Pessimistic Time
(a) Write book	10	12	14
(b) Design book	1	1	1
(c) Edit manuscript	3	6	9
(d) Check editing	2	2	2
(e) Accept design	1	1	1
(f) Copy edit	1	2	3
(g) Prepare artwork	3	4	5
(h) Accept and correct artwork	.5	.5	.5
(i) Set galleys	2	4	6
(j) Check and correct galleys	1	1	1
(k) Pull page proofs	2	2	2
(l) Check and correct pages	1	1	1
(m) Prepare index	1	1	1
(n) Set and correct index	.5	.5	.5
(o) Check camera-ready copy	.5	.5	.5
(p) Print and bind book	1	1	1

the activities were obtained using three time estimates and the modified beta distribution with the data in Table 14-12.

(a) Compute the expected values and variances in activity completion times.

(b) Calculate the expected value and variance for the duration of the critical path found in Problem 14-13.

(c) Find the probability that the path in (b) takes (1) less than 30 months, (2) more than 31 months, and (3) more than 33 months.

(d) Repeat (b) using the path a-c-d-g-h-k-l-o-p.

(e) Repeat (c) using the path from (d).

14-16 Suppose that the variance for some of the home construction activities in Table 14-7 is increased, leaving the expected times unchanged. This is accomplished by subtracting 1 day from the optimistic time and adding 1 day to the pessimistic time for activities a, e, g, and l.

(a) Compute the new variances.

(b) Determine the probability that the original critical path a-b-d-e-i-k-l falls (1) below 50 days and (2) above 40 days.

(c) Comparing the results from (b) with those on page 566, what may you conclude regarding activity-time variability and single-path duration probabilities?

Computer Problems

14-17 The activities in Table 14-13 apply to the research and development of a new pharmaceutical product.

(a) Obtain the activity report. From this, find (1) the critical path(s) and (2) the expected duration of that path.

(b) Obtain the event milestone report. From this, determine the event sequence taken by the critical path.

14-18 (Continuation of Problem 14-17): Suppose that a new activity, pp, expected to take 12 weeks, is added to the project. The new activity is immediately preceded by activity y only, and it is an immediate predecessor only to activity aa. All other activity data remain exactly the same.

(a) Obtain the activity report. From this, find (1) the critical path(s) and (2) the expected duration of that path.

(b) Obtain the event milestone report. From this, determine the event sequence taken by the critical path.

TABLE 14-13 Activities for Pharmaceutical Product

Activity	Preceding Activity	Expected Completion Time (Weeks)	Activity	Preceding Activity	Expected Completion Time (Weeks)
a	—	6.3	v	l, mm	8.3
b	—	6.0	w	l, mm	13.1
c	—	2.9	x	t, u, v	8.1
d	—	8.5	y	t, u, v	4.2
e	—	3.8	z	t, u, v	5.9
f	a	5.9	aa	s, x	25.9
g	a	4.7	bb	y	13.3
h	b	6.3	cc	k, w, z	12.6
i	c	6.8	dd	y, aa	4.9
j	d	11.6	ee	y, aa	11.4
k	e	13.7	ff	y, aa	9.7
l	e, j	16.2	gg	bb, ff	9.1
m	e, j	7.9	hh	bb, ff	6.8
n	g, h, i	11.8	ii	ee, hh	5.7
p	f	11.6	jj	r, dd	14.3
q	f	4.1	kk	ii, jj	9.8
r	q	5.4	ll	cc, gg	2.5
s	q	4.1	mm	m, n, p	11.4
t	q	4.5	nn	ee, hh	9.2
u	mm	9.5			

FIGURE 14-34
The PERT network for
Problem 14-22

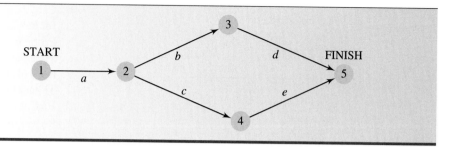

14-19 *(Continuation of Problem 14-17):* Additional information has been obtained regarding expected completion times for the original activities in the project. The following now apply:

Activity	Time
h	11.5
x	7.5
ee	18.0
ii	7.5

All other original activity data remain exactly the same (with activity *pp* not included).

(a) Obtain the activity report. From this, find (1) the critical path(s) and (2) the expected duration of that path.

(b) Obtain the event milestone report. From this, determine the event sequence taken by the critical path.

14-20 Enter the data for the MaxiSoft problem from page 536, incorporating the modifications on page 555. Save those data for further use. Then, split activity PV into two activities: PT (test candidate platforms) and TC (translate program code). Each new activity is expected to take 2 months to complete. Activity PT has the same predecessor activities as the old PV, TC has only PT as its predecessor, PT replaces PV as one of the predecessors for activity TB1, and TC becomes an additional predecessor to TB2.

(a) Using computer assistance, construct the PERT network for the modified project. Determine the critical path and its expected duration.

(b) Would you recommend the new project structure to MaxiSoft? Explain.

14-21 Refer to Problem 14-20 and your answers.

(a) Suggest an alternative change to the original project structure.

(b) Retrieve the original data (first saved in Problem 14-20) and make a computer run with your new problem to determine the PERT network, critical path(s), and expected duration.

(c) Would you recommend the new project structure to MaxiSoft? Explain.

14-22 *Probability analysis.* Consider the PERT network in Figure 14-34. Suppose that the following probabilities (in parentheses) apply to the completion times for the various activities:

a	b	c	d	e
$8(1)$	$5(\frac{1}{2})$	$2(\frac{1}{2})$	$5(\frac{1}{4})$	$8(\frac{3}{4})$
	$6(\frac{1}{2})$	$3(\frac{1}{2})$	$6(\frac{3}{4})$	$9(\frac{1}{4})$

(a) Use these data to compute the expected activity completion times. Then, determine the critical path and its duration based on the expected values.

(b) What actual durations are possible for the critical path you found in (a)? Assuming that activity times are independent events, determine the probability for each duration.

(c) Repeat (b) for the other (noncritical) path.

(d) Use your answers to (b) and (c) and the multiplication law to construct the joint probability table for the durations of the two paths.

(e) From your joint probability table, identify the situations in which the "critical" path is actually of shorter duration than the "noncritical" path. What is the probability that any one of these situations will occur?

(f) Use your joint probability table to determine the probability distribution for the length of the longest path(s) from START to FINISH. This distribution represents the *project* completion time. What is its expected value? Is this the same as the duration you found in (a)? Explain.

14-23 (This problem uses concepts from Chapter 13.) Refer to Problem 14-3 and your answers. Consider again the PERT network in Figure 14-31.

(a) Make a fresh copy of Figure 14-31. Then using event 1 as the START node, modify the shortest route procedure to find the *longest* route (in time) from there to each event node. In doing this, move forward along the arrows. Place the respective cumulative times into a box near the respective event node. Those values should correspond to the *TE* values found for Problem 14-3.

(b) Using event 10 as the START, work backward along the arc arrows to establish the longest route (using time as distance) to each event node. Write the respective cumulative times near the respective event node.

(c) The *TL* for event 10 is 28. Subtract each node value found in (b) from 28, placing the difference in a circle near the respective event node. These should correspond to the *TL* values found for Problem 14-3.

Spreadsheet Problems

14-24 Solve Problem 14-1 using a spreadsheet.

14-25 Use a spreadsheet to find the critical path for the project in Figure 14-30. How long will the project take?

14-26 Repeat Problem 14-25 using Figure 14-31.

14-27 Construct the PERT network for the data in Table 14-8. Then find the critical path and project completion time using a spreadsheet.

14-28 Repeat Problem 14-27 using the data in Table 14-9.

14-29 Solve Problem 14-27 using the changes given in Problem 14-6.

14-30 Solve Problem 14-8 using a spreadsheet.

14-31 Solve Problem 14-11 (a) and (b) using a spreadsheet.

14-32 Solve Problem 14-13(a) using a spreadsheet

CASE 14-1   *A House with Seven Gables*

Salem Daughters Construction Company has contracted with a Mr. Hawthorne to build a classic house having seven gables. The customer wants to complete the house as soon as possible, at a minimum cost. The preliminary data in Table 14-14 apply for the various activities.

Samantha Salem believes that the data in Table 14-14 reflect optimal expenditures of labor and resources. The following cost estimates correspond:

Activity	Cost	Activity	Cost
a	$1,000	k	$ 200
b	2,500	l	1,500
c	4,400	m	2,300
d	5,500	n	1,000
e	2,000	o	3,200
f	500	p	8,000
g	3,000	q	3,000
h	500	r	3,000
i	4,000	s	5,000
j	2,300	t	0

TABLE 14-14   Data for the Construction Activities

Activity	Immediately Preceding Activity	Expected Completion Time
(a) Grade	—	3 days
(b) Excavate	—	4
(c) Basement	b	1
(d) Foundation	a, c	2
(e) Floor joists	d	3
(f) Exterior plumbing	a, c	3
(g) Floor	e, f	2
(h) Power on	d	1
(i) Walls	g	10
(j) Wire	h, i	2
(k) Com lines	i	1
(l) Inside plumbing	i	5
(m) Windows	l	2
(n) Doors	l	2
(o) Sheetrock	k, l	3
(p) Interior trim	n, o	5
(q) Exterior trim	n	4
(r) Paint	m, p, q	3
(s) Carpet	r	1
(t) Buyer inspection	s	1

The preceding includes the cost of materials supplied by subcontractors. Additional Salem materials costs are $51,000.

A few activities can be speeded up. By working extended hours, carpenters can complete the walls in 8 days at a total cost of $4,500. Working at night, workers can complete the sheetrock in 2 days at a total cost of $3,500. For a premium of $700, the plumbing contractor can complete inside plumbing in 3 days. Using night lighting, crews can finish the excavation in 2 days at a total cost of $3,500 and complete the grading in 2 days for $1,600.

QUESTIONS

1. Construct a PERT network for the project, entering the expected activity completion times alongside the applicable arrows.

2. For each event, find the earliest possible, latest allowable, and slack times. Then, establish the critical path. How long is the project expected to take?

3. Determine a sequence of plans for Salem Daughters Construction Company, each plan representing a 1-day savings in project completion time at a minimal increase in cost.

4. Salem has accepted an incentive clause which provides for a payment of $400 for each day saved from an anticipated 40-day duration until project completion. Which plan identified in Question 3 should be implemented? Specify which activities should be speeded up and by how many days. What is Salem's net project cost using the optimal plan?

5. Analysis in Questions 1–4 has been based on expected activity completion times. Samantha is concerned that the uncertainties in the project have been downplayed. The expected activity completion times given earlier were computed from the three time estimate data (in days) given in Table 14-15. Compute the variance in completion time for each activity.

6. The modified beta distribution for each activity time (1) is *positively skewed* if m is closer to a than

TABLE 14-15 Three Time Estimate Data for the Construction Activities

Activity	Optimistic Time	Most Likely Time	Pessimistic Time
(a) Grade	2	3	4
(b) Excavate	2	3	10
(c) Basement	1	1	1
(d) Foundation	2	2	2
(e) Floor joists	1	3	5
(f) Exterior plumbing	3	3	3
(g) Floor	2	2	2
(h) Power on	1	1	1
(i) Walls	7	9	17
(j) Wire	1.5	2	2.5
(k) Com lines	.5	1	1.5
(l) Inside plumbing	3	5.25	6
(m) Windows	1	2	3
(n) Doors	2	2	2
(o) Sheetrock	2.5	3	3.5
(p) Interior trim	4	4.75	7
(q) Exterior trim	3	4	5
(r) Paint	3	3	3
(s) Carpet	1	1	1
(t) Buyer inspection	1	1	1

to b, (2) is *symmetrical* if m falls midway between a and b, (3) is *negatively skewed* if m is closer to b than to a, and (4) has *zero variance* if a, m, and b are all equal.
   (a) Determine for each activity which case applies.
   (b) For the zero-variance activity times, what may you conclude regarding the completion time probabilities?

7. Consider the critical path found in Question 2.
   (a) Find the variance for the duration of that path.
   (b) Determine the probability that the path will take more than 42 days.

8. Consider the "nearly" critical path b-c-d-e-g-i-j-k-o-p-r-s-t.
   (a) Find the expected duration and variance of that path.
   (b) Determine the probability that the path will take more than 42 days.
   (c) Compare your answers in Question 7(b). What may you conclude regarding using any single-path probability to estimate a probability for project completion time?

PART V

INVENTORY MANAGEMENT

Good inventory management is a trait common to all successful businesses, large or small.

I nventory management begins with establishing ordering policies for items to be used for resale, as supplies, as parts in manufacturing, or as raw materials. In all cases, a policy specifies what quantities to order and how often to order them. Quantitative methods provide mathematical optimization models for determining the policy that minimizes cost.

The inventory models described in this book comprise two main groups. The models in Chapter 15 all involve certainty. Although a key element for inventory decisions is demand, which is almost always uncertain, the simplicity achieved by assuming demand to be fixed and known gives us a convenient point of departure. A pleasant surprise is that those simple models can give good results even when more complex realities are taken into account.

Chapter 16 tackles the issues raised by the uncertainty of demand. There, several problem types are encountered that may be evaluated using probability and expected value.

CHAPTER 15

INVENTORY DECISIONS WITH CERTAIN FACTORS

If I order too little, I make no profit. If I order too much, I may go broke. Every product is different. Help me!

A Retailer's Plea

One area of business decision making in which quantitative methods have played a highly successful role in achieving cost savings is the area of inventory control. A primary reason for this success story is that inventory represents such a vast segment of total economic activity. In the United States alone, hundreds of billions of dollars are invested in inventory. Due to the sheer size of inventory investments, even minor improvements in controlling inventory can create large savings.

Two phenomena have contributed to improvements in controlling inventory. One has been the application of mathematical models and optimization techniques to achieve efficiencies. In this chapter, we will focus on these quantitative methods. A second source of savings has been the development of the digital computer with improved information processing and retrieval capabilities. Managers in complex organizations now have immediate access to all kinds of information relevant to inventory that was once impossible to obtain quickly. The closing of this information gap has dramatically reduced the need to maintain inventory. Many inventory systems are automated to the extent that even orders to replenish stock are issued by computer.

The central problem we face in making any decision involving physical storage is finding an efficient **inventory policy.** A key element in establishing such a policy is to determine how many items should be stocked periodically and when replenishment should occur. It is convenient to refer to the number of items to be stocked as the **order quantity** and to the level of inventory when the requisition is made as the **order point.** For example, a family might always purchase two gallons of milk (the order quantity) and repurchase milk only when all of it has been drunk (so that the order point is zero).

Our objective is to determine optimal inventory policies. In this chapter, we will consider the basic structure of inventory decisions and present some of the models that are applicable when all factors are certain. These models will serve to explain the essential concepts that are common to more advanced models. In Chapter 16, we will consider inventory decisions made under uncertainty.

The House of Fine Wines and Liquors

DECISION PROBLEM

Shortly after arriving in the United States, Rigoberto Zúñiga started in San Francisco's Mission District a small liquor store specializing in brands favored by the Latin Americans in the neighborhood. Over the years, as his business grew and prospered, he expanded his line of products and opened upscale stores throughout California under the name The House of Fine Wines and Liquors. At a recent conference of the American Association of Liquor Dealers, Mr. Zúñiga attended a session on modern inventory control in the liquor industry and learned how inventory models could improve inventory management and cut costs. He has asked one of his assistants, Alex Mullen, to look into using them. To get started, Mr. Zúñiga suggested using the Tres Equis brand of beer as a test case. If results are good, then the use of inventory models will be expanded to other products.

Because this will be his first mathematical analysis of inventory models, Alex starts with the simplest economic order quantity model. Checking sales data for the last few years, he learns that The House of Fine Wines and Liquors sells 5,200 cases of Tres Equis at a constant rate each year. The company obtains the beer from a wholesaler in Tijuana, Mexico, who charges $1.50 per case plus $.50 per case for shipping to the company's central warehouse in San Francisco. Delivery occurs the day after the order is placed. Under the present policy, the Purchasing Department telephones the wholesaler at the beginning of each week to place an order for 100 cases of Tres Equis. Those calls cost $10 per order, regardless of the quantity ordered. The Accounting Department informs Alex that the company's only working capital is tied up in inventory and these funds have been borrowed from Bank of America at a simple annual interest rate of 10%. In addition, the company must pay a state franchise tax of 5% of the annual inventory value and another 5% for theft insurance. Alex concludes that all other operating costs are either fixed in nature or do not depend on the amount of beer ordered.

Before returning to talk with Mr. Zúñiga about the results of using the economic order quantity model, Alex needs answers to the following questions:

1. What is the total annual relevant cost of the company's current inventory policy?

2. What is the optimal order quantity and its cost? Will ordering that amount provide significant savings?

3. How would the same type of analysis work on another product, one of the fine Chilean wines?

4. Mr. Zúñiga habitually warns his staff, "Garbage in, garbage out," and Alex is nervous about the accuracy of the data supplied by the Purchasing and Accounting Departments. When Alex presents his results to Mr. Zúñiga, how can he guarantee the results?

5. The simple inventory quantity model is that there will be no shortages. How can Alex incorporate the inevitability of shortages?

6. A long-standing company policy requires that customers should be able to find their desired products on the store shelves at least 90% of the time. Mr. Zúñiga especially wishes to know if inventory models can reflect this policy.

This chapter will show how inventory models can be used to answer these and other similar questions.

15-1 FACTORS INFLUENCING INVENTORY POLICY

The usual long-run objective of an inventory policy is to maximize profits or to minimize costs. In the simpler situations we will encounter in this chapter, those two goals coincide. The desired end result is ordinarily achieved by minimizing the average inventory cost over a short period of time, such as one year. Our initial models will all be based on minimizing *annual* cost.

Inventory Cost Components

In typical business situations, the various costs considered in evaluating inventory systems are as follows:

1. ordering and procurement costs for items to be stocked
2. holding or carrying costs
3. shortage costs

Inventory ordering and procurement costs represent all expenses incurred in ordering or manufacturing items, including not only the acquisition costs but also the costs of transporting, collecting and sorting, and placing the items in storage. Also included in this category are any managerial and clerical costs associated with placing an order. These costs often vary with the size of the order; for example, this occurs when products are priced with quantity discounts. Ordering and procurement costs are of two kinds: (1) a fixed portion for each order that is independent of the number of items stocked, and (2) a variable portion for each order that is dependent on the number of items stocked. We will refer to the *fixed* portion as the *ordering costs* and to the *variable* portion as the *procurement costs*.

Inventory holding or carrying costs are the expenses incurred during the storage of items. This includes physical costs — the most common being the operation of warehouse facilities — as well as the costs of insurance and property taxes. Other cost components might be expenses arising from pilferage, spoilage, and obsolescence. A very important portion of inventory holding costs is the **opportunity cost** of those funds invested in inventory that might have been used profitably elsewhere. All such costs depend on *how many* items are stored and for *how long*. Such costs can be 20 – 25% of the value of the items held in inventory.

Inventory shortage costs occur whenever there is a demand for items that are not currently in stock. For items that are usually backordered, such as a new car of a particular color with special options, shortage costs may have only a fixed component — the extra paperwork and managerial expenses incurred in processing the order. For shortages of more mundane items such as a particular brand of paint, an additional variable cost component that depends on the duration of the shortage must be considered. This cost is due largely to the potential loss of customer goodwill that may be expected to increase in proportion to the length of the delay; such a decline in goodwill might be reflected in the loss of future business. In extreme cases of convenience products such as cigarettes, or necessities such as gasoline, there is no backordering at all. Under those circumstances, a shortage results in the loss of a sale. The minimum cost of a lost sale is the marginal profit that the item would have earned, but it may be larger due to the loss of goodwill.

In evaluating an inventory policy, some or all of these types of costs might be considered. But it is very important that only **relevant costs** be used. These involve only those expenses that are in some way affected by the inventory policies themselves. Certain legitimate accounting costs may therefore be ignored. For instance, the rent on a warehouse would not be included as a carrying cost if the same facility were to be used regardless of the number of items stocked. Instead, the rent would be considered properly as an overhead item, like the company president's salary. No proration of overhead items should be reflected in the inventory costs, unless these items somehow differ from policy to policy. But certain nonaccounting costs, such as the opportunity cost of invested capital and the loss of customer goodwill, are definitely relevant and should be incorporated into the evaluation.

The Nature of Demand and Supply

In a typical business situation, demand occurs erratically. The demand for most items also occurs discretely; that is, a few items are demanded at a time. In this chapter, demand is assumed to occur *continuously* (as if each item is a cubic foot of natural gas fed into a heater that is always lit—either from a pilot light or by the main flame) and *at the same rate over time* (as if the gas heater were always on full flame). As long as demand is predictable, such a simplifying assumption makes little difference in the inventory costs or in the particular policy that minimizes cost.

But one element does matter. Demand typically occurs *randomly* over time, so that the overall level is generally uncertain. In this chapter, however, we will consider only cases in which the demand is *certain* and known in advance. These cases will prepare us for the discussion in Chapter 16, where uncertainty in demand will be explicitly considered.

How items are supplied is another important element in establishing inventory policies. Generally, this is handled in one of two ways. From the retailer's or the wholesaler's point of view, the only question is how long it will take to fill an order. This is the *lead time* that it will take to receive the units ordered. Like demand, lead time is often uncertain. Here, we will only consider *constant* lead times. This greatly simplifies the analysis and allows us to analyze most problems without explicitly considering the lead time at all, as if inventories were instantaneously replenished. In Chapter 16, we will consider how the choice of policy is affected by uncertain lead times.

The method of supply differs for the manufacturer who must produce items for later sale. Here, replenishment cannot be instantaneous. Instead, items must be added to the inventory at a rate equal to the speed at which they are produced.

15-2   THE ECONOMIC ORDER QUANTITY (EOQ) MODEL

The simplest inventory model involves one type of item that has a known and constant demand and that is resupplied instantaneously. No backordering of items is allowed. The problem objective is to select an inventory policy—that is, to choose the order quantity (which in turn establishes the time when an order must be placed)—in such a way that the annual inventory cost is minimized.

The Mathematical Model

The following parameters are used to establish a mathematical model for this problem:

$$k = \text{Fixed cost per order}$$
$$A = \text{Annual number of items demanded}$$
$$c = \text{Unit cost of procuring an item}$$
$$h = \text{Annual cost per dollar value of holding items in inventory}$$
$$T = \text{Time between orders}$$

The objective is to choose the number of items to order

$$Q = \text{Order quantity}$$

such that

$$\text{Total annual cost} = \text{Ordering cost} + \text{Holding cost} + \text{Procurement cost}$$

is minimized.

The features of this inventory system are illustrated in Figure 15-1, where the inventory level is plotted against calendar time. This graph will help to explain the development of the mathematical model. Figure 15-1 tells us that Q items are replenished periodically, at which time a new **inventory cycle** begins and an old one ends. Each cycle has a duration of T years (some fraction of one year), which is determined by the order quantity Q. The length of time is equal to the proportion of the annual demand consumed in one inventory cycle, or

$$T = \frac{Q}{A}$$

The items are depleted at the rate of A units per year, so that the slanted line segments, each with a slope of $-A$, indicate the level of inventory at any given point in time. The sawtooth effect of the graph represents the sequence of inventory depletions and replenishments of successive inventory cycles. Because it costs something to hold items in inventory, there is no advantage to restocking until the inventory is zero. Thus, each inventory cycle can be pictured as a triangle of height Q and base T, with a new cycle

FIGURE 15-1

Inventory system for the simple economic order quantity model

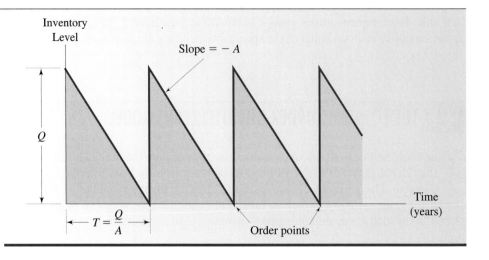

or triangle beginning at the order point, where the leg of the preceding triangle touches the time axis.

To find a mathematical expression for the problem objective, we begin with the first cost component, the **annual ordering cost,** which is based on how many orders are placed each year. The number of annual orders depends on two factors: (1) the annual number of items demanded A, and (2) the order quantity Q. It follows that

$$\text{Number of annual orders} = \frac{A}{Q}$$

Multiplying this equation by the cost per order k, we obtain

$$\text{Annual ordering cost} = \left(\frac{A}{Q}\right)k$$

The second cost component, the **annual holding cost,** is based on the number of items placed in inventory and the duration they are held in inventory. Individually, some items will be sold immediately; others will be held until the inventory is restocked. However, we need to concern ourselves only with an average value. Because the inventory level in any cycle ranges from Q downward to zero and there is a constant rate of depletion, we have, for any cycle,

$$\text{Average inventory} = \frac{Q}{2}$$

This same quantity applies from cycle to cycle and therefore represents the *average inventory level* throughout the entire operating life of the inventory system.

It is realistic to base the holding cost on the value of the items held. This is certainly true of the opportunity cost of the invested capital and applies to other costs, such as insurance and property taxes, as well. (Physical storage costs are usually highly correlated with an item's value, too.) Here, we base the value of an item on its procurement cost. The cost of holding an item in inventory for one year is therefore the product of the annual holding cost per dollar h and the unit procurement cost c, or

$$\text{Annual holding cost of one item} = hc$$

We can now determine the annual holding cost of all the items involved by multiplying the above cost by the average inventory, or

$$\text{Annual holding cost} = hc\left(\frac{Q}{2}\right)$$

[handwritten annotation: cost of holding of one unit for one year.]

For the entire year, A items will be demanded, so that

$$\text{Annual procurement cost} = Ac$$

Adding the three cost components (ordering + holding + procurement), we find that

$$\text{Total annual cost} = \left(\frac{A}{Q}\right)k + hc\left(\frac{Q}{2}\right) + Ac$$

The problem objective is to select the value Q that minimizes this total annual cost.

However, we need to consider only relevant costs (which differ, depending on the inventory policy). We can therefore ignore the procurement cost Ac, because that expense will arise regardless of the value of Q. Equivalently, the objective for our simple inventory model is to minimize

TOTAL ANNUAL RELEVANT COST

$$TC(Q) = \left(\frac{A}{Q}\right)k + hc\left(\frac{Q}{2}\right)$$

where $TC(Q)$ is a function of Q.

USING JUDGMENT

The Worth of a Mathematical Model

The economic order quantity (EOQ) mathematical model is only an approximation to reality. For instance, it would be rare for demand to be known in advance, let alone be uniform and constant over time. But, making these assumptions allows for simplicity in the mathematical model, permitting us to more easily find solutions. A simple mathematical model's value is that it brings insight to an evaluation, even if it does not perfectly reflect reality. If its results are good, that is a bonus. The inventory model fits that bill because the solutions it provides agree closely with those of more elaborate models that more closely reflect reality.

Finding the Optimal Solution

The TC equation is a mathematical expression that we refer to as the **objective function.** The value of TC depends on the order quantity Q. $TC(Q)$ is plotted in Figure 15-2, where the vertical axis indicates the annual cost and the horizontal axis represents the order quantity Q. The total annual relevant cost has two components: (1) annual ordering cost and (2) annual holding cost. Each of these components is also plotted in Figure 15-2. Because $TC(Q)$ is the sum of ordering and holding costs, the height of the TC curve at any level of Q is the sum of the respective heights of the ordering-cost curve and the holding-cost line.

The annual ordering-cost curve has the geometric shape of a hyperbola. Recall that the cost of each order is an amount k, regardless of how many items are requested each

FIGURE 15-2

Graphical representation of inventory cost components

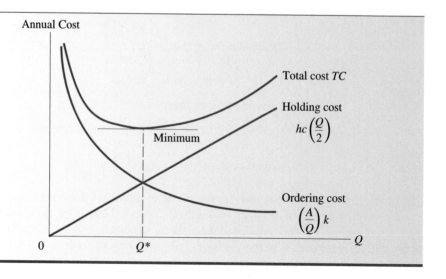

time. Thus, very low levels of Q will involve a great number of orders throughout the year, and ordering costs will be huge. As Q becomes larger, fewer orders are required and the annual ordering cost declines as we move to the right on the ordering-cost curve. The annual holding cost is plotted as a straight line because this component is a constant multiple of the average inventory level. This line begins at the origin with zero holding cost at $Q = 0$, where no inventory is held. Each item is sold as demanded, so that the holding-cost line rises with constant slope as Q increases. This is because progressively larger order quantities raise the average inventory level, causing holding costs to rise proportionately.

The **optimal solution** to the objective function occurs at the point where total annual relevant cost is minimized. We denote the optimal order quantity by Q^*. This level corresponds to the *minimum cost point* on the TC curve, where its slope is zero. The slope equation for a curve may be determined by using mathematical procedures. Once the equation for the slope has been found, it can be set equal to zero and algebraically solved to determine the corresponding order quantity.[†]

The following equation is used to compute the

OPTIMAL ORDER QUANTITY

$$Q^* = \sqrt{\frac{2Ak}{hc}}$$

which is sometimes called the **economic order quantity,** or **EOQ.** This equation is often referred to as the *Wilson formula,* in honor of R. H. Wilson, who first proposed it. Once Q^* has been obtained, the corresponding reorder time is automatically determined to be

$$T^* = \frac{Q^*}{A}$$

and a complete optimal inventory policy is thereby obtained, which tells how much should be ordered and when each order should be placed. The total annual relevant cost of this policy can be determined by substituting the value of Q^* for Q in the TC equation.

Referring again to Figure 15-2, we can see that Q^* happens to be the order quantity at which holding cost is equal to ordering cost. The Wilson formula can be verified by setting the respective component cost equations equal to each other and algebraically solving for Q. Study of the Q^* formula allows us to draw some interesting conclusions. The economic (optimal) order quantity increases with the square root of the annual demand A instead of becoming proportional to it. Also, it is inversely pro-

---

[†]To do this, we employ calculus. The first derivative of the objective function $TC(Q)$ is obtained and set equal to zero.

$$\frac{dTC(Q)}{dQ} = -\frac{A}{Q^2}k + \frac{hc}{2} = 0$$

Because $TC(Q)$ is convex from below, if we solve for Q, the minimum cost occurs when

$$Q = \sqrt{\frac{2Ak}{hc}}$$

portional to the square root of the unit procurement cost c, indicating that all else being equal, fewer expensive items should be ordered than would be the case for cheaper items. Thus, the various **parameters** k, A, c and h really serve to determine the optimal inventory policy, and widely different results may be obtained for different levels of these constants.

MANAGERIAL APPLICATION

Establishing an Optimal Inventory Policy: The House of Fine Wines and Liquors

Alex Mullen decides that the first task in utilizing inventory models is to determine the values of all of the model parameters. He calculates that they are

$$k = \$10 \text{ per order}$$
$$A = 5,200 \text{ cases per year}$$
$$c = \$2 \text{ per case}$$
$$h = \$.20 \text{ annual cost per dollar value of beer held in inventory}$$

where the $10 ordering cost is from telephone charges, the $2 procurement cost is the sum of the $1.50 per case of beer and the $.50 per case shipping cost, and the $.20 holding cost is the dollar equivalent from summing the 10% bank interest, the 5% state franchise tax, and the 5% theft insurance rate.

The present policy of ordering every week involves an order quantity of

$$Q = \frac{5,200}{52} = 100 \text{ cases}$$

The total annual relevant cost of this policy is

$$TC(Q) = \left(\frac{A}{Q}\right)k + hc\left(\frac{Q}{2}\right)$$

$$= \left(\frac{5,200}{100}\right)10 + .20(2)\left(\frac{100}{2}\right)$$

$$= 520 + 20$$

$$= 540 \text{ dollars per year}$$

Alex notes that the annual ordering cost of $520 is much larger than the annual $20 holding cost. These two cost components should be the same to achieve an optimal inventory policy.

To establish the optimal inventory policy, he uses the Wilson formula to determine the economic order quantity.

$$Q^* = \sqrt{\frac{2Ak}{hc}}$$

$$= \sqrt{\frac{2(5,200)10}{.20(2)}}$$

$$= \sqrt{260,000}$$

$$= 509.9, \text{ or } 510 \text{ cases of beer}$$

The optimal time between orders is

$$T^* = \frac{510}{5,200}$$
$$= .098 \text{ year}$$

which can be converted to once every $365(.098) = 35.8$ or 36 days. The optimal inventory policy is therefore to order 510 cases of beer every 36 days. The resulting total annual relevant cost is

$$TC(510) = \left(\frac{5,200}{510}\right)10 + .20(2)\left(\frac{510}{2}\right)$$
$$= 101.96 + 102.00$$
$$= 203.96 \text{ dollars per year}$$

(The two cost components differ by \$.04 because we rounded the value of Q^* to the nearest whole number.) Thus, Alex concludes that more than \$300 in annual beer costs alone can be saved by switching to the optimal inventory policy.

Using a Spreadsheet with the Basic EOQ Model

The spreadsheet used for the model is shown in Figure 15-3, using The House of Fine Wines and Liquors Tres Equis beer example. The first formula in the spreadsheet is in cell F15

$$=(F7/F12)*F6+F9*F8*(F12/2)$$

This is equivalent to the formula for the total annual relevant cost, $TC(Q)$, given earlier. The second formula in cell F16 is $=F12/F7$, which gives the time between orders, $T = Q/A$. Consequently, the spreadsheet in Figure 15-3 calculates the total annual relevant cost and time between orders for any set of parameter values and order quantity.

	A	B	C	D	E	F	G	H	I
1	INVENTORY ANALYSIS - ECONOMIC ORDER QUANTITY MODEL								
2									
3	PROBLEM:	House of Fine Wines and Liquors - Tres Equis Beer							
4									
5	Parameter Values:								
6		Fixed Cost per Order: k =				\$ 10.00			
7		Annual Number of Items Demanded: A =				5,200			
8		Unit Cost of Procuring an Item: c =				\$ 2.00			
9		Annual Holding Cost per Dollar Value: h =				\$ 0.20			
10									
11		Decision Variables:							
12			Order Quantity: Q =			100			
13									
14		Results:						F	
15			Total Annual Relevant Cost: TC =			\$ 540.00	15 =(F7/F12)*F6+F9*F8*(F12/2)		
16			Time Between Orders (years): T =			0.0192	16 =F12/F7		

FIGURE 15-3   Excel spreadsheet for the basic model with supplied Q values applied to ordering Tres Equis beer

	A	B	C	D	E	F	G	H	I
1	INVENTORY ANALYSIS - ECONOMIC ORDER QUANTITY MODEL								
2									
3	PROBLEM:	House of Fine Wines and Liquors - Tres Equis Beer							
4									
5	Parameter Values:								
6			Fixed Cost per Order: k =			$ 10.00			
7			Annual Number of Items Demanded: A =			5,200			
8			Unit Cost of Procuring an Item: c =			$ 2.00			
9			Annual Holding Cost per Dollar Value: h =			$ 0.20			
10									
11		Decision Variables:					F		
12			Order Quantity: Q =			509.9	12 =SQRT((2*F7*F6)/(F9*F8))		
13									
14		Results:					F		
15			Total Annual Relevant Cost: TC =			$ 203.96	15 =(F7/F12)*F6+F9*F8*(F12/2		
16			Time Between Orders (years): T =			0.098	16 =F12/F7		

FIGURE 15-4   Modified Excel spreadsheet for finding optimal solutions with the EOQ model applied to ordering Tres Equis beer

For an order quantity of $Q = 100$ (cell F12), the total annual relevant cost is $540 and the time between orders is .0192 years (once a week). The same values were calculated previously by hand.

The spreadsheet in Figure 15-3 is on the CD-ROM that accompanies the text and can be used as a template to calculate the results of any order quantity. For example, the optimal order quantity for this example was calculated previously to be $Q = 509.9$. Putting this value in cell F12 results in a total annual cost of $203.96, as obtained in the example.

Note that the value of Q was supplied to Excel, and it was not the optimal level. One way of finding the optimal order quantity is by trial and error, accomplished by varying the order quantity Q in cell F12 until the minimum cost is obtained. That would be time consuming and would involve substantial calculations, even with a spreadsheet. It is preferable to incorporate the EOQ formula directly into the spreadsheet. To do that, we need only modify the spreadsheet in Figure 15-3, replacing the order quantity data value of 100 in cell F12 by the formula for $Q*$, which takes the following form in Excel

$$=SQRT((2*F7*F6)/(F9*F8))$$

The resulting spreadsheet provides the optimal solution for any set of parameter values entered into F6:F9.

Figure 15-4 shows the modified spreadsheet for the beer example with the formula entered in cell F12. Notice how the results in cells F12, F15, and F16 changed. This spreadsheet is on the accompanying CD-ROM and can be used to solve other economic order quantity problems in this text.

The Effect of Parameter Values on the Solution

The optimal solution will depend greatly on the parameter values used. Any change in A, k, c, or h will be reflected in a different value for $Q*$. These parameters interact in complex ways. The following application shows how great the effects of different parameters may be.

Establishing an Optimal Inventory Policy for Wine—The House of Fine Wines and Liquors

Alex Mullen wishes to apply the EOQ model to a product with lower sales, a particular variety of Chilean wine that sells 1,000 cases annually. The cost is $20 per case. A telephone call to Chile to place an order costs $100, independent of the number of cases ordered. The holding costs are the same as for Tres Equis beer.

To find the EOQ and the total annual relevant cost, the first step is to calculate the values of the model parameters.

$k = \$100$ per order

$A = 1,000$ cases per year

$c = \$20$ per case

$h = \$.20$ annual cost per dollar value of wine held in inventory

The optimal inventory policy (again, assuming a known, constant demand rate and a predictable lead time for inventory replenishment) is

$$Q^* = \sqrt{\frac{2(1,000)100}{.20(20)}} = \sqrt{50,000}$$

$$= 223.6, \text{ or } 224 \text{ cases of wine}$$

$$T^* = \frac{224}{1,000} = .224 \text{ year, or approximately 82 days}$$

The total annual relevant cost is

$$TC(224) = \left(\frac{1,000}{224}\right)100 + .20(20)\left(\frac{224}{2}\right)$$

$$= 894.43 \text{ dollars per year}$$

Notice the difference between the results for wine and beer.

Spreadsheet Solution   The Excel spreadsheet gives the same results, as shown in Figure 15-5. The optimal order quantity is $Q^* = 223.6$ cases of wine, the optimal time between orders is $T^* = .224$ years (or approximately 82 days), and the total annual relevant cost is $TC(Q^*) = \$894.43$.

FIGURE 15-5
Excel spreadsheet showing optimal solution for Chilean wine ordering decision

	A	B	C	D	E	F	G	H	I
1		INVENTORY ANALYSIS - ECONOMIC ORDER QUANTITY MODEL							
2									
3	PROBLEM:	House of Fine Wines and Liquors - Chilean Wine							
4									
5	Parameter Values:								
6		Fixed Cost per Order: k =				$ 100.00			
7		Annual Number of Items Demanded: A =				1,000			
8		Unit Cost of Procuring an Item: c =				$ 20.00			
9		Annual Holding Cost per Dollar Value: h =				$ 0.20			
10									
11		Decision Variables:						F	
12			Order Quantity: Q =			223.6	12	=SQRT((2*F7*F6)/(F9*F8))	
13									
14		Results:						F	
15			Total Annual Relevant Cost: TC =			$ 894.43	15	=(F7/F12)*F6+F9*F8*(F12/2)	
16			Time Between Orders (years): T =			0.224	16	=F12/F7	

Sensitivity Analysis Even when the level for one or more parameters has been based on guesswork, the solution obtained might still be close to the true optimum— it could also widely miss the mark. Evaluating how the optimal solution will change with different assumed levels of the parameters is sometimes referred to as a **sensitivity analysis.**

DECISION PROBLEM

Sensitivity Analysis for Wine Parameters: The House of Fine Wines and Liquors

Spreadsheets make it easy to perform a sensitivity analysis. Figure 15-6 shows how the wine-ordering solution changes when the ordering cost varies. To accomplish that sensitivity analysis, cells F6:F16 were copied to cells G6:I16. That was done by highlighting cells F6:F16, putting the cursor on the fill handle in the lower right-hand corner of the highlighted area, and dragging it to cell I16. The copied parameter-value cells may then be changed to the desired levels. In this illustration, we changed the ordering cost (k) in cells F6, H6, and I6 to $50, $150, and $200. The resulting solution values then appeared in the respective positions in cells F12:I16.

	A	B	C	D	E	F	G	H	I
1	INVENTORY ANALYSIS - ECONOMIC ORDER QUANTITY MODEL								
2									
3	Parameter Values:								
4			Fixed Cost per Order: k =			$ 50.00	$ 100.00	$ 150.00	$ 200.00
5			Annual Number of Items Demanded: A =			1,000	1,000	1,000	1,000
6			Unit Cost of Procuring an Item: c =			$ 20.00	$ 20.00	$ 20.00	$ 20.00
7			Annual Holding Cost per Dollar Value: h =			$ 0.20	$ 0.20	$ 0.20	$ 0.20
8									
9		Decision Variables:							
10			Order Quantity: Q =			158.1	223.6	273.9	316.2
11									
12		Results:							
13			Total Annual Relevant Cost: TC =			$ 632.46	$ 894.43	$ 1,095.45	$ 1,264.91
14			Time Between Orders (years): T =			0.16	0.22	0.27	0.32

FIGURE 15-6 Sensitivity analysis for ordering Chilean wine, varying ordering cost

Simplicity of graphing is another nice feature of spreadsheet sensitivity analysis, making it easier to visualize the results. Figure 15-7 plots the wine ordering sensitivity analysis, in which we can see how Q^* and the total annual relevant cost vary with k. Notice that changes in the fixed cost per order have diminishing effects on the results, so that a 100% increase from $k = \$100$ to $k = \$200$ causes both Q^* and $TC(Q^*)$ to increase by smaller percentages, about 41%.

Section 5 in Chapter 2 shows how to construct such a graph using the Chart Wizard. Excel's Data Table option also can be used to do sensitivity analysis. This option is discussed in Chapter 17 and in the *Guide to Excel* on the CD-ROM accompanying the text.

Alex noted that a similar evaluation may be made for different levels of annual holding cost h. He did that, each time setting the ordering cost at the original level of $k = \$100$. He obtained the following results:

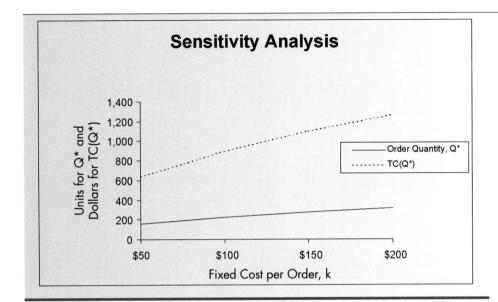

FIGURE 15-7
Graph resulting from
the sensitivity analysis
spreadsheet in
Figure 15-6

	h = $.19	h = $.20	h = $.21
Q*	229	224	218
TC(Q*)	$871.78	$894.43	$916.52

Here, small fluctuations in the level for h affect Q^* (drops as h increases) and $TC(Q^*)$ (rises with h).

Some Limitations of the Model

Applying economic order quantity analysis to two different items is only valid under special conditions. Here, we must assume that beer and wine have independent demands and that the storage capacity is sufficient to handle any contemplated quantities of each product. If beer and wine must compete for limited space, or if there is a constraint on the amount of working capital that can be tied up in inventories, then the products must be analyzed jointly and the mathematics can become quite complicated.

15-3   OPTIMAL INVENTORY POLICY WITH BACKORDERING

The simple inventory model we have just described assumes that backordering is not possible. We will now consider how items can be sold even after the inventory has been exhausted. Such a situation could apply when buying automobile tires, for example; a retailer might not have the exact size in current stock but might be willing to place a special order to satisfy a customer. An inventory system that permits backordering is summarized in Figure 15-8. As before, Q represents the order quantity. Because sales may be made even after the on-hand inventory reaches the zero level, it may be desirable to use part of each successive order to fill backordered items. The **order level** is represented by S; this quantity is the on-hand inventory position at the beginning of each inventory cycle. The optimal inventory policy must specify the values of both Q and S that minimize total annual cost.

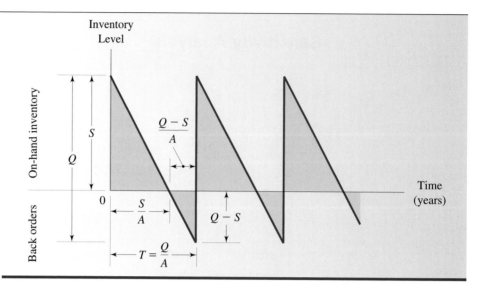

FIGURE 15-8

Inventory system for the EOQ model when backordering is allowed

The New Model

We will now assume that a shortage cost applies and that, like a holding cost, this cost depends on how many items are short and on the amount of time that each shortage lasts. Such a **shortage penalty,** represented by p, arises largely from loss of goodwill. The inventory models of this chapter are all expressed on an *annual* basis, and p is the cost of being short one item for an *entire year.* (An additional fixed shortage penalty that is based only on the number of items short is sometimes applied, but for simplicity, that second penalty is not included here.)

Thus, we may now express total annual relevant cost as

$$TC = \text{Ordering cost} + \text{Holding cost} + \text{Shortage cost}$$

The total annual relevant cost may be expressed as a function of both Q and S.

$$TC(Q, S) = \left(\frac{A}{Q}\right)k + \frac{hcS^2}{2Q} + \frac{p(Q - S)^2}{2Q}$$

The problem objective is to find the values of Q and S that minimize TC. The following expressions may be used to calculate the optimal values.[†]

ORDER QUANTITY AND ORDER LEVEL

(Backordering)

$$Q^* = \sqrt{\frac{2Ak}{hc}}\sqrt{\frac{p + hc}{p}}$$

$$S^* = \sqrt{\frac{2Ak}{hc}}\sqrt{\frac{p}{p + hc}}$$

[†]It can be established that the function $TC(Q, S)$ is convex over the ranges being considered. These equations are derived by setting the partial derivatives with respect to Q and S equal to zero and solving them algebraically.

The time between orders is

$$T^* = \frac{Q^*}{A}$$

and the maximum number of backorders is $Q^* - S^*$.

The Backordering Model Applied to Chilean Wine—The House of Fine Wines and Liquors

The Marketing Department tells Alex that beer is a convenience product that cannot be backordered. (Customers will always buy it elsewhere rather than wait.) However, some wine customers are connoisseurs who are willing to order out-of-stock items. Nevertheless, the store owner will incur some penalty if there is a shortage of wine.

Suppose that each day that a customer must wait for a favorite wine costs the store a penny per case; this means that the annual penalty is $p = \$3.65$ per case. What is the optimal inventory policy?

Using the same constants for wine ($k = \$100$, $A = 1,000$, $c = \$20$, and $h = \$.20$), Alex calculates the optimal inventory policy.

$$Q^* = \sqrt{\frac{2(1,000)100}{.20(20)}} \sqrt{\frac{3.65 + .20(20)}{3.65}} = 324$$

$$S^* = \sqrt{\frac{2(1,000)100}{.20(20)}} \sqrt{\frac{3.65}{3.65 + .20(20)}} = 154$$

and

$$T^* = \frac{324}{1,000} = .324 \text{ year, or approximately 118 days}$$

The optimal inventory policy is to order 324 cases of wine every 118 days. Only 154 of these cases will be stored in inventory; the remaining $Q^* - S^* = 170$ cases will be used to satisfy outstanding backorders. The total relevant cost of this policy is

$$TC(324, 154) = \left(\frac{1,000}{324}\right)100 + \frac{.20(20)(154)^2}{2(324)} + \frac{3.65(170)^2}{2(324)}$$

$$= 617.82 \text{ dollars per year}$$

Alex notes that this is smaller than the optimal cost of $894.43 when no backordering was allowed. He sees that this is because fewer orders are placed when backordering is permitted, so the average on-hand inventory level is lower. Although shortage costs now exist, these costs are lower than the combined cost reduction for ordering and holding items.

Solving with a Spreadsheet   The basic spreadsheet in Figure 15-4 can be easily modified for the backordering models. We need to shift the contents to incorporate two new rows and then alter the formulas for $TC(Q)$ and T, the new locations of which are cells F17:F18, and for Q, now in cell F13. We illustrate this using the revised wine example, for which the spreadsheet in Figure 15-9 (and on the CD-ROM accompanying the text) applies. There we see that the economic order quantity is $Q^* = 324$ cases, the economic order level is $S^* = 154$ cases, the total annual relevant cost is $TC(Q^*, S^*) = \$617.82$, and the time between orders is $T^* = .32$ years (about 118 days).

	A	B	C	D	E	F	G	H	I	J
1	INVENTORY ANALYSIS - ECONOMIC ORDER QUANTITY MODEL WITH BACKORDERING									
2										
3	PROBLEM:	House of Fine Wines and Liquors - Chilean Wine								
4										
5	Parameter Values:									
6			Fixed Cost per Order: k =			$ 100.00				
7			Annual Number of Items Demanded: A =			1,000				
8			Unit Cost of Procuring an Item: c =			$ 20.00		F		
9			Annual Holding Cost per Dollar Value: h =			$ 0.20	=SQRT((2*$F$7*$F$6)/($F$9*$F$8))			
10			Annual Cost of Being Short One Item: p =			$ 3.65	13	*SQRT(($F$10+$F$9*$F$8)/$F$10)		
11										
12		Decision Variables:					=SQRT((2*$F$7*$F$6)/($F$9*$F$8))			
13			Economic Order Quantity: Q =			324	14	*SQRT($F$10/($F$10+$F$9*$F$8))		
14			Economic Order Level: S =			154		F		
15							=($F$7/$F$13)*$F$6+$F$9*$F$8*			
16		Results:					((($F$14^2)/(2*F13))+((F10*(F13-			
17			Total Annual Relevant Cost: TC =			$ 617.82	17	F14)^2/(2*F13)))		
18			Time Between Orders (years): T =			0.32	18	=F13/F7		

FIGURE 15-9   Spreadsheet for the backordering model with Chilean wine

The underlying spreadsheet formulas are shown in Figure 15-9. Cell F13 has the following equivalent backordering formula for the economic order quantity Q^*

$$= SQRT((2*F7*F6)/(F9*F8))*SQRT((F10+F9*F8)/F10)$$

Likewise, cell F14 has the following companion formula for the economic order level, S^*

$$= SQRT((2*F7*F6)/(F9*F8))*SQRT(F10/(F10+F9*F8))$$

Cell F17 has the backordering version of the formula for total annual relevant cost $TC(Q^*, S^*)$

$$= (F7/F13)*F6+F9*F8*((F14^2)/(2*F13))+((F10*(F13-F14)^2/(2*F13)))$$

Finally, cell F18 contains = F13/F7, the formula for T^*.

Shortage Penalty Considerations

Implementation of the preceding model may be hampered because of difficulties in establishing a value for the shortage penalty p. It must be emphasized that the model assumes that shortage costs vary only with time, as shown in Figure 15-10(a). Furthermore, an item's shortage penalty is an *annualized* amount, so that, when the actual shortage lasts just a month, week, or day, the experienced shortage cost must be converted.

$$p = \ 12 \times \text{one month's shortage cost}$$
$$p = \ 52 \times \text{one week's shortage cost}$$
$$p = 365 \times \text{one day's shortage cost}$$

Such a cost may arise from the loss of goodwill (reduced future business) with the shorted customer, who may become increasingly disenchanted as the waiting times become longer.

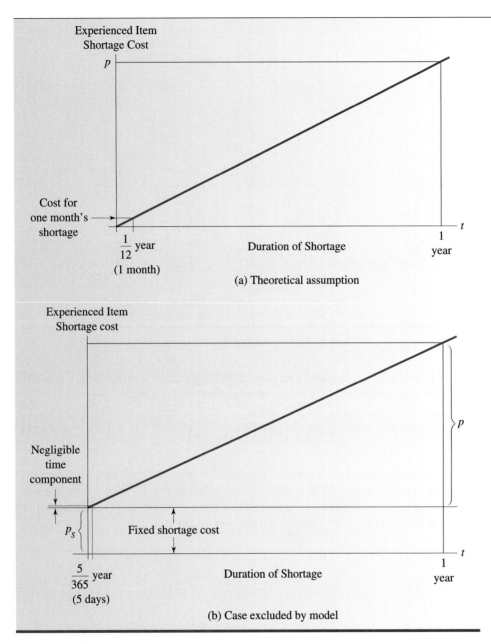

FIGURE 15-10
Shortage penalty
considerations showing
(a) how penalty relates to
length of shortage and (b)
the presence of a fixed
penalty p_s

The given model allows no *fixed* shortage-cost component. A retailer may experience such a one-shot cost, p_S, as shown in Figure 15-10(b). That cost element may reflect the added labor of logging in backorders, removing items on arrival, storing them, and notifying customers. Included in p_S would be any immediate goodwill impact that does not depend on the duration of shortage. And, if the stockout period is very short, the fixed component may be dominant. In Chapter 16, we will consider models that explicitly incorporate p_S. (For those models, it will be the negligible time-based component p that is left out.)

Loss of goodwill is hard to quantify accurately. Often only a ballpark figure can be established for p. That amount may be used to find Q^* and could result in acceptable inventory evaluations, because Q may be *insensitive* over a wide range of levels for p.

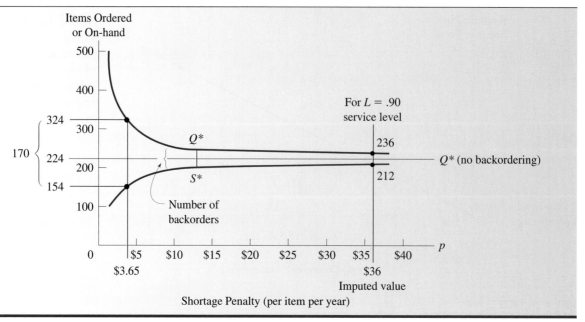

FIGURE 15-11   Effect of *p* on order quantity and order levels for the wine ordering illustration.

In Figure 15-11, the optimal item quantities are plotted for various levels of *p*. Notice that beyond $5 the level for *p* has a minor effect on Q^* and S^*.

15-4 ESTABLISHING INVENTORY POLICIES BASED ON SERVICE LEVEL

An alternative approach for establishing an inventory policy is based on achieving a desired **service level.** A common measure of service level in inventory evaluations is the *proportion of demand met on time.* Using the **service level proportion** *L,* the order quantity and order level are chosen, so that

$$\frac{Q^* - S^*}{Q^*} = 1 - L \quad \text{or} \quad Q^* - S^* = (1 - L)Q^*$$

It follows that

$$LQ^* = S^*$$

Using the individual expressions for Q^* and S^*, this can be reexpressed as

$$L\sqrt{\frac{2Ak}{hc}}\sqrt{\frac{p + hc}{p}} = \sqrt{\frac{2Ak}{hc}}\sqrt{\frac{p}{p + hc}}$$

from which an expression for the *imputed* shortage penalty is found:

IMPUTED SHORTAGE PENALTY

$$p = \frac{hcL}{1 - L}$$

DECISION
PROBLEM

Using Service Level to Get Inventory Policy for Wine—The House of Fine Wines and Liquors

We illustrate this procedure by returning to the wine retailer's decision. Suppose that the retailer wants to provide a service level in which 90% of the customer demand is filled on time (so that shortages occur just 10% of the time). Using the same parameters as before, except for p, the optimal inventory policy with backordering is found.

The service level is $L = .90$.  Using $A = 1,000$, $k = \$100$, $c = \$20$, and $h = \$.20$, Alex calculates

$$p = \frac{.20(20)(.90)}{1 - .90} = 36$$

The corresponding optimal quantities are

$$Q^* = \sqrt{\frac{2(1,000)100}{.20(20)}}\sqrt{\frac{36 + 4}{36}} = 223.6\sqrt{1.11}$$
$$= 235.7, \quad \text{or} \quad 236$$

and

$$S^* = \sqrt{\frac{2(1,000)100}{.20(20)}}\sqrt{\frac{36}{36 + 4}} = 223.6\sqrt{.90}$$
$$= 212.1, \quad \text{or} \quad 212$$

These quantities are much closer together than those obtained from the backordering model using $p = 3.65$. Alex can see that a higher level of service corresponds to using a greater p.

15-5 INVENTORY POLICY FOR LOST SALES

A s we have already noted, items like convenience products cannot be backordered. When a demand for such an item cannot be met from on-hand inventory, a sale is lost. It is possible to extend the model we have developed with backordering to accommodate this special case. However, a complete analysis of the case of lost sales is merely a mathematical exercise. If an inventory system is to be in operation at all, it can be shown that the basic economic order quantity model should be used, so that no shortages leading to lost sales should be allowed as long as demand is predictable.

Remember that in this chapter we have been dealing with certain, constant demand and predictable lead time for replenishment. We know that many successful retail establishments occasionally run out of convenience items like cigarettes and lose some sales. But these businesses are faced with *uncertain* demand. Stores would never run out of convenience items if demand could be predicted precisely and lead time never varied.

In Chapter 16, we will consider inventory policy when uncertainty leads to unplanned shortages, and how to make evaluations when those shortages result either in backorders or in lost sales.

15-6   ECONOMIC PRODUCTION-QUANTITY MODEL

In the models presented thus far, orders have been filled instantaneously. Identical results are obtained when the lead time is constant, so that all items arrive at some future date that is fixed when the order is placed. We will now consider the special case encountered when a manufacturer can supply demanded items either from inventory or from current production. Because production itself requires some time, the replenishment of inventory items is not instantaneous. We assume that production, like demand, occurs at some known and constant rate. The **annual production rate,** in items per year, is denoted by B. We further assume that no backorders are allowed and that the production rate exceeds the demand rate, or $B > A$.

Figure 15-12 illustrates such an inventory system. Each inventory cycle consists of two phases, depending on whether or not production is occurring. The **production phase** is represented by the upward-sloping triangle on the left. Although the total amount produced is Q, a portion of the items produced is siphoned off to customers before it can be stored, so that the maximum inventory buildup is

$$\text{Maximum inventory} = Q\left(\frac{B - A}{B}\right)$$

at which point production stops. The net accumulation of on-hand inventory occurs at the rate of $B - A$ units; the duration of the production phase is T_1. The **demand-only phase,** represented by the downward-sloping triangle, then begins. During this stage, all demands are filled from inventory until the stock is totally depleted; the duration of the demand-only phase is T_2. The respective phase durations are

$$T_1 = \frac{Q}{B}$$

$$T_2 = T - T_1 = \frac{Q}{A} - \frac{Q}{B}$$

$$= Q\left(\frac{B - A}{AB}\right)$$

FIGURE 15-12

The production and inventory system when items are produced at a uniform rate

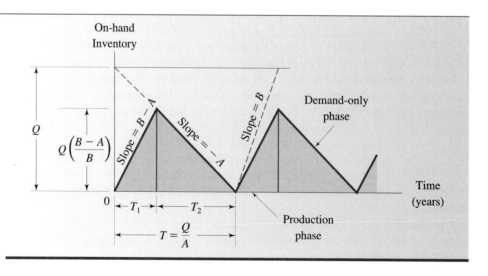

In place of the usual ordering cost k, we now substitute the *fixed* cost of making a production run. This quantity is referred to as a **set-up cost** or a **start-up cost.** The **variable production cost** per item is denoted as c. The total annual relevant cost is

$$TC(Q) = \left(\frac{A}{Q}\right)k + hc\left(\frac{Q}{2}\right)\left(\frac{B-A}{B}\right)$$

which differs only slightly from this cost in the simple EOQ model. The minimum cost production (order) quantity is often referred to as the

ECONOMIC PRODUCTION QUANTITY

$$Q^* = \sqrt{\frac{2Ak}{hc}}\sqrt{\frac{B}{B-A}}$$

MANAGERIAL
APPLICATION

An Instrument Manufacturer

Finding the Economic Production Quantity

Lambda Optics makes microscope lens housings. Annual demand is $A = 100{,}000$ units per year. Assume that the product can be produced at the rate of $B = 200{,}000$ units per year. Each production run costs $k = \$5{,}000$ to set up, and the variable production cost of each item is $c = \$10$. The annual cost per dollar value of holding items in inventory is $h = \$.20$. We find the economic production quantity and total relevant inventory cost.

THE PROBLEM SOLUTION

The optimal production run size is

$$Q^* = \sqrt{\frac{2(100{,}000)5{,}000}{.20(10)}}\sqrt{\frac{200{,}000}{200{,}000 - 100{,}000}}$$

$$= 31{,}623 \text{ items}$$

and each production run lasts

$$T_1^* = \frac{Q^*}{B} = \frac{31{,}623}{200{,}000} = .158 \text{ year, or approximately 58 days}$$

A new production run occurs every

$$T^* = \frac{Q^*}{A} = \frac{31{,}623}{100{,}000} = .316 \text{ year, or approximately 115 days}$$

The total annual relevant cost of this production plan is

$$TC = \left(\frac{100{,}000}{31{,}623}\right)5{,}000 + .20(10)\left(\frac{31{,}623}{2}\right)\left(\frac{200{,}000 - 100{,}000}{200{,}000}\right)$$

$$= 15{,}811 + 15{,}812$$

$$= 31{,}623 \text{ dollars per year}$$

	A	B	C	D	E	F	G	H	I
1	INVENTORY ANALYSIS - ECONOMIC PRODUCTION-QUANTITY MODEL								
2									
3	PROBLEM:	Lambda Optics							
4									
5	Parameter Values:								
6		Fixed Set-Up Cost per Run: k =				$ 5,000.00			
7		Annual Number of Items Demanded: A =				100,000			
8		Annual Production Rate: B =				200,000			
9		Variable Production Cost per Unit: c =				$ 10.00			
10		Annual Holding Cost per Dollar Value: h =				$ 0.20		F		
11							=SQRT((2*F7*F6)/(F10*F9))*S		
12		Decision Variables:					13 QRT((F8)/(F8-F7))		
13		Economic Production Quantity: Q =				31,623	F		
14							16 =F13/F7		
15		Results:					17 =F13/F8		
16		Time Between Production Runs (year): T =				0.32	=(F7/F13)*F6+F10*F9*(F13/2)*		
17		Duration of Production Run (year): T1 =				0.16	18 ((F8-F7)/F8)		
18		Total Annual Relevant Cost: TC =				$ 31,623			

FIGURE 15-13   Spreadsheet for the economic production-quantity model as applied to Lambda Optics

Solving with a Spreadsheet   Figure 15-13 gives the spreadsheet for this problem. (It is also on the CD-ROM accompanying the text.) The optimal production run size is $Q^* = 31{,}623$ items, each production run lasts $T_1 = .16$ years (approximately 56 days), a new production run occurs every $T = .32$ years (approximately 115 days), and the total annual relevant cost of this production plan is $TC(Q^*) = \$31{,}623$ per year. The formulas used in the spreadsheet are shown in the spreadsheet. Cell F13 contains the equivalent formula for the optimal production run size Q^*

$$=\text{SQRT}((2\text{*}F7\text{*}F6)/(F10\text{*}F9))\text{*}\text{SQRT}((F8)/(F8\text{-}F7))$$

The two cells F16 and F17 have the formulas for the time between production runs T and the duration of the production run T_1: =F13/F7 and =F13/F8, respectively. The equivalent formula for the total relevant cost, $TC(Q)$, in cell F18 is

$$=(F7/F13)\text{*}F6\text{+}F10\text{*}F9\text{*}(F13/2)\text{*}((F8\text{-}F7)/F8)$$

15-7   ADDITIONAL REMARKS

The EOQ models discussed in this chapter have been purposely simplified. More complex models are available. For instance, a second shortage penalty that does not depend on the duration of a backorder is sometimes included in more general representations. The models described here can be expanded to include several different types of items. These more advanced models consider constraints that might reflect limitations on storage space or on the dollar investment in inventory. Slight extensions of the basic EOQ models also permit the treatment of quantity discounts.

Perhaps the greatest deficiency of the simple EOQ models is that they do not reflect that uncertainties exist. Few real-life inventory systems are based on predictable, constant demands. Yet the models presented in this chapter set the stage for our examination of inventory policy formulation under uncertainty in Chapter 16. There, we will see that the basic Wilson formula can often provide a solution that is very close to optimal, even though many of the assumptions on which it is based are not strictly true.

PROBLEMS

15-1 Compu-Fast is a retailer that sells 1,000 personal computer disc drives per year. The units cost $400 each, and it costs $2,000 to place an order with the supplier. The annual cost per dollar value of holding items in inventory is $.25.

    (a) Determine the economic disc-drive order quantity.

    (b) How often should orders be placed?

15-2 Albers, Crumbly, and Itch (AC&I) sells mosquito repellents all over the world. Demand for the Malabug brand is 10,000 bottles per year. The African supplier charges AC&I $2 per bottle, and the fixed cost of placing an order for Malabug is $100. AC&I targets a 15% annual rate of return on working-capital funds. The physical storage cost of Malabug is fixed.

    (a) Determine the optimal order quantity and inventory cycle duration for Malabug.

    (b) How many orders should be placed each year?

    (c) Compute the total annual relevant inventory cost of Malabug.

    (d) Suppose, for managerial convenience, that AC&I orders 2,500 bottles of Malabug each quarter.

        (1) Compute the total annual relevant inventory cost.

        (2) Is this sum larger or smaller than the amount in (c)? Explain.

15-3 Mini Stock is a car parts wholesaler that supplies 20 batteries to various service stations on each weekday. Batteries are purchased from the manufacturer in lots of 100 for $1,000 per lot. Multiple and fractional lots can be ordered at any time, and all orders are filled the next day. Each order placed with the manufacturer incurs a $50 handling charge and a $200 per-lot freight charge. The incremental cost is $.50 per year to store a battery in inventory. Mini Stock finances inventory investments by paying its holding company $1\frac{1}{2}$% monthly for borrowed funds.

    (a) Determine the values of k, A, c, and h.

    (b) How many batteries should be ordered, and how often should orders be placed to minimize total annual inventory cost?

15-4 Emergency Supply Distributor Inc. (ESD) supplies to public and private elementary schools kits that contain items that might be needed after an emergency such as an earthquake or other disaster. Each kit costs ESD $5, and ESD sells them for $10 each. Ordering the emergency kits from the manufacturer costs ESD $50 per order. A cost study recently done found that holding items in inventory has an opportunity cost of 12% per year. ESD estimates the demand for the emergency supply kits to be 10,000 per year.

    (a) Using the economic order quantity model, determine (1) the optimal order quantity, (2) the number of orders placed per year, and (3) the total annual relevant cost.

    (b) Repeat (a) for a demand of 20,000 per year.

    (c) Repeat (a) for a demand of 5,000 per year.

15-5 ZIP Electric Bike Company buys special batteries to power its most popular model, called the Zippy. Since ZIP's successful IPO last year and because of high-profile endorsements by several well-known sports figures, demand has taken off, and the company is selling about 100,000 Zippies per year. The batteries cost $50 each. ZIP figures that the impact of holding inventory is 15% per year and placing an order costs the company $200.

    (a) Using the economic order quantity model, determine (1) the optimal order quantity, (2) the number of orders placed per year, and (3) the total annual relevant cost.

    (b) Repeat (a) for a demand of 200,000 Zippies.

    (c) Repeat (a) for a demand of 50,000 Zippies.

15-6 Suppose that the store in Problem 15-2 can backorder Malabug when it is out of stock. Because most customers are simply itching to go backpacking and may have to delay their departure if they must wait to purchase the repellent, there is a penalty of $10 per year in lost goodwill for every bottle short.

    (a) Determine the optimal order quantity, order level, and time between orders. What proportion of the time is Malabug out of stock?

    (b) Compute the total annual relevant inventory cost of the policy you found in (a). Is this cost larger or smaller than your answer to Problem 15-2(c)? Do you think the same conclusion would be reached if the annual shortage penalty were $1,000 per bottle?

15-7 Paul Bunyan's Lumber Company periodically buys tenpenny size nails. The supplier will deliver any quantity of a particular order size for a charge of $1 plus $.20 per pound. It costs the store $.15 per dollar value of inventory items stored for one year. A total of 600 pounds of tenpenny nails are sold each year.

   (a) How many pounds of nails should be ordered, and how often should orders be placed to minimize total annual inventory cost?

   (b) Suppose that Paul Bunyan's has patient customers who will backorder tenpenny nails when they are out of stock. The annual cost of each pound of nails short is $.01.

      (1) Determine the optimal order quantity.

      (2) How many pounds of nails will have been backordered when each new shipment arrives?

15-8 Deuce Hardware satisfies a yearly demand of 10,000 36-inch fluorescent lamp tubes. These are obtained from the supplier for $.75 each. Orders cost Deuce an average of $20 to process, and the company earns 15% annually on idle funds.

   (a) Determine the economic order quantity and total annual relevant inventory cost, assuming that no shortages are allowed. Should that cost be bigger or smaller than the counterpart for the optimal policy when backordering occurs?

   (b) Suppose that Deuce fills all tube demands that occur when out of stock by taking backorders. Each tube short reduces Deuce's expected future profit by a present value of $.01 per day, including weekends and holidays. Find the annual cost of being short one tube.

   (c) Using your answer to (b), determine Deuce's optimal order level and quantity and compute the corresponding total annual relevant inventory cost. How many items are backordered per inventory cycle?

15-9 Suppose that Emergency Supply Distributor Inc. in Problem 15-4 runs out of the emergency kits. That causes some unhappiness among its customers, because of the delays in getting the kits. Sometimes parents or the PTA must make the kits themselves. The cost of the delays is estimated to be $5 per kit per year.

   (a) Answer the following:

      (1) What are the optimal order quantity and the maximum inventory level?

      (2) How many times per year should ESD reorder the emergency kits?

      (3) What is the total annual relevant cost?

      (4) Calculate the maximum number of backorders.

   (b) Re-solve (a) for a penalty cost of $1 per year.

   (c) Re-solve (a) for a penalty cost of $10 per year.

   (d) Re-solve (a) for a penalty cost of $100 per year.

   (e) Using Excel's Chart Wizard, draw a graph of Q^*, S^*, and TC on the Y-axis versus the shortage cost, p, on the X-axis. Comment on how the solution changes as the penalty cost varies.

15-10 In Problem 15-5, suppose that when ZIP is out of batteries, the company cannot sell its Zippy electric bike. The company determines that this costs it $20 per bike per year because of the unhappy customers.

   (a) Answer the following:

      (1) What are the optimal order quantity and the maximum inventory level?

      (2) How many times per year should ZIP Electric Bike Company place orders for the batteries?

      (3) What is the total annual relevant cost?

      (4) Compute the maximum number of backorders.

   (b) Re-solve (a) for a penalty cost of $5 per year.

   (c) Re-solve (a) for a penalty cost of $50 per year.

   (d) Re-solve (a) for a penalty cost of $100 per year.

   (e) Using Excel's Chart Wizard, draw a graph of Q^*, S^*, and TC on the Y-axis versus the shortage cost, p, on the X-axis. Comment on how the solution changes as the penalty cost varies.

15-11 Wheeling Wire Works, the manufacturer of the nails in Problem 15-7, makes the nails at an annual rate of 400 tons, even though only 300 tons are demanded per year. The unit cost of manufacturing is $100 per ton, and it costs an additional $30 to set up a production run. The annual holding cost of the nails is $.20 per dollar value.

   (a) Determine the optimal number of tons that should be manufactured in a single produc-

tion run. How often should the nails be produced? How long will a production run last?

(b) Compute Wheeling's total annual relevant inventory and production cost using the optimal policy you found in (a).

15-12 DanDee Assemblers buys SX-3 printed circuit boards for $10 each. Annual demand is 1,000 boards. No shortages are permitted. It costs DanDee $500 to process an order. The annual holding cost per dollar value is unknown.

(a) Suppose that $Q = 100$ boards are ordered. What imputed value is necessary for h in order for that policy to be optimal?

(b) Suppose that h is $.25. Determine the optimal order quantity and relevant inventory cost.

15-13 The Getco headquarters office buys 1,000 boxes of computer paper every two months at a cost of $5 per box. Paper usage is uniform and constant over time. The cost of placing an order with the supplier is $50. Assume that the present inventory policy is optimal, so that it minimizes annual paper inventory cost.

(a) How many boxes will be demanded in one year?

(b) What annual cost per dollar value of holding items in inventory is implicit under the present policy?

15-14 Referring to Problem 15-4, Emergency Supply Distributor Inc. is considering making the emergency kits instead of buying them. The company estimates that it can make as many as 20,000 kits per year for only $3 per kit. However, it will cost ESD $50 to prepare to make each batch of the kits.

(a) Find the optimal production quantity.

(b) What is the maximum inventory of kits ESD will have during the year?

(c) How many times per year should ESD make the emergency kits?

(d) What is the duration of the optimal production run?

(e) What is the total annual relevant cost?

(f) Should ESD continue to buy the kits as in Problem 15-4 or start making them?

(g) What happens to the solution when the demand is 20,000 per year? Why?

15-15 The manufacturing vice-president of ZIP Electric Bike Company (refer to Problem 15-5) is thinking about manufacturing the special batteries used in the company's electric bikes, because of recent shortages by its supplier. He estimates that the company could do it cheaper, for about $40 per battery, and that it could make about 150,000 batteries per year with the current idle capacity in the manufacturing plant. The setup cost to manufacture the batteries would be $1,000.

(a) Find the optimal production quantity.

(b) What is the maximum inventory of batteries that ZIP will have during the year?

(c) How many times per year should ZIP make the batteries?

(d) What is the duration of the optimal production run?

(e) What is the total annual relevant cost?

(f) Should ZIP continue to buy the batteries as in Problem 15-5 or start making them?

(g) What happens to the solution when the demand is 150,000 per year? Why?

15-16 Suppose that it costs the office in Problem 15-13 $2 to hold a box of paper in inventory for one year.

(a) Determine the annual cost per dollar value of holding items in inventory.

(b) Suppose that the policy of ordering 1,000 boxes every two months must be reevaluated because shortages are now allowed. Assume an annual penalty of $10 per box short.

(1) Determine the optimal order quantity and order level.

(2) How often should orders be placed?

(c) Suppose, instead, that shortages are allowed only 5% of the time.

(1) Determine the optimal order quantity, order level, and imputed shortage penalty.

(2) Compute the corresponding total annual relevant inventory cost.

15-17 Mini Stock is reevaluating the company policy for meeting an annual demand for 5,000 standard car headlamps. These are imported from Brazil at a variable cost of $2 each, including freight. Regardless of order quantity, its agent charges a $100 fee for processing a shipment through customs, and Mini Stock also estimates that a further $50 must be spent on clerical and management time with each shipment. All working capital, including inventory, is financed

through the holding company at a monthly fee of 1.5%.

(a) Management wants to maintain sufficient inventory to satisfy demand 95% of the time. Find (1) the imputed annual unit shortage penalty, (2) the optimal order quantity and level, and (3) the corresponding total annual relevant inventory cost.

(b) Repeat (a) using instead a requirement that current demand be met 99% of the time.

15-18 WysiWyg Systems lives up to its name. They provide word processing software for which *what you see* on the screen *is what you get* when printed. Company programs are distributed on floppy diskettes. Usage averages 500 diskettes per day, and the production schedule runs 300 days per year. WysiWyg currently earns 40% .4₀ on invested capital. Each diskette order costs $100 to initiate and track, and the vendor supplies diskettes for $.35 each. Freight charges amount to $.05 per disc.

(a) Assuming that no shortages are permitted, determine the optimal order quantity and total annual relevant inventory cost.

(b) Actual WysiWyg company policy is to allow shortages no more than 1% of the time. Suppose that this policy is extended to diskettes.
    (1) Determine the optimal order quantity, order level, and imputed shortage penalty.
    (2) Compute the corresponding total annual relevant inventory cost.

15-19 The manufacturer of Snail Hail, a garden mollusk pesticide, distributes its product from a plant warehouse. The plant has the capacity to produce 1,000 tons per year at a variable cost of $100 per ton. However, only 200 tons of Snail Hail are sold annually. The cost of setting up a production run is $2,000. The net cost of holding the highly volatile Snail Hail in inventory is $.40 per dollar value per year.

(a) Determine the economic production quantity.

(b) How long is each inventory cycle?

(c) How long will a production run last?

15-20 Water Wheelies manufactures high-pressure sprinkler heads. These are produced periodically at a rate of 100,000 per month. Demand is steady at 20,000 per month. Each production

run has a setup cost of $2,000. Variable direct production costs are $1.55 for labor, $2.15 for parts, and $6.55 for raw materials. Water Wheelies can earn 25% annually on idle funds.

(a) Determine the economic production quantity and the total annual relevant inventory cost.

(b) Water Wheelies can double its production rate by using a new technology, but the setup cost per production run will also double. Determine the economic production quantity and the total annual relevant inventory cost.

(c) In terms of total annual relevant inventory cost only, is the faster production method better? Should Water Wheelies adopt the new technology? Explain.

15-21 AlphaComp buys memory chips from overseas for $5 each. It costs $200 to place an order with the supplier. Annual demand is 100,000 units, and the company earns 30% on invested capital.

(a) Assuming that no shortages are allowed, determine the optimal order quantity.

(b) Suppose that some shortages do occur, so that 100 chips are backordered per inventory cycle. For Q^*, AlphaComp uses the answer found in (a) plus half of the number backordered.
    (1) Determine the order level for this policy.
    (2) Determine the implied service level percentage.
    (3) Compute the imputed shortage penalty.

15-22 *Quantity discounts.* Refer to Problem 15-7. Suppose that Paul Bunyan's Lumber Company buys tenpenny nails according to the following price schedule:

	Quantity (pounds)	Price Per Pound
(1)	0–200	$.20
(2)	201–500	.19
(3)	more than 500	.18

Assume that no shortages are allowed.

(a) Determine the economic order quantity and the corresponding total annual inventory cost (including total procurement cost) for each price.

(b) Indicate, for each price level, whether the optimal order quantity you found in (a) is feasible, so that the quantity agrees with the

price schedule. If it is not feasible, replace Q^* for that price by the minimum price break quantity and recompute total annual cost.

(c) The overall optimal order quantity will be feasible and have the minimum total annual cost. Which of the three order quantities is optimal?

15-23 Ace Widgets Supply distributes two products — Regular and Deluxe widgets — throughout the Midwest. The demands for the two items are independent; a total of 2,000 Regular and 4,000 Deluxe items are sold every year. The Regular items cost Ace $10 each; the Deluxe models cost twice as much. Ace's annual holding cost is $.25 for each dollar invested in inventory. The ordering cost is $100 per batch for each item. The Regular item may be ordered only when a Deluxe order is placed, but Regular widgets may be ordered less frequently than Deluxe widgets.

(a) Determine the optimal order quantity and the total annual relevant inventory cost for each item.

(b) Assume that a maximum of $10,000 may be invested in inventory at any given time. Are the quantities you found in (a) still possible?

(c) Ace's warehouse can store a maximum of only 1,000 items. Are the quantities you found in (a) still possible?

(d) Suppose that the Regular and the Deluxe models must be ordered at the same time and that each order costs $200. Treat combinations of 1 Regular and 2 Deluxe units as a single item.

(1) Determine the economic order quantity and the corresponding total annual relevant cost.

(2) Is this procedure less costly than the one in (a)? Explain.

15-24 The Coin-Op is a vending machine operator that must establish a policy for periodically restocking its candy machines and collecting the coins deposited by customers. The total labor cost of restocking a machine is $7, most of which is due to travel time. Each machine can hold quite a lot of candy, so the machines do not need to be filled to capacity. All machines are identical, and each satisfies a demand of 5,000 candy bars per year. Candy bars cost $.10 each and are sold for $.25. The firm's annual opportunity cost of working capital is 20%. A significant aspect in establishing a policy is that all those quarters are uselessly locked up in coin boxes, so that the quicker retrieval of these funds translates directly into smaller working-capital requirements.

(a) Determine the values of c and h. (Assume that the same cost of working capital applies to the value of the candy and to the value of the coins. Also assume that the average inventory of candy bars is the same as the average inventory of quarters.)

(b) Determine the restocking quantity that minimizes total annual cost. How often should the machines be restocked?

Spreadsheet Problems

15-25 Refer to Paul Bunyan's nail-buying decision in Problem 15-7. The actual holding cost is unknown.

(a) Determine Paul Bunyan's economic order quantity and total annual relevant inventory cost for the following assumed annual holding costs: (1) $.08, (2) $.12, (3) $.16, (4) $.20, and (5) $.24.

(b) Graph the optimal order quantity and the total annual relevant cost versus the various assumed holding costs. What can you conclude regarding the influence of h on Q^* and $TC(Q^*)$?

15-26 Refer to Getco's paper-buying decision in Problem 15-13. The actual ordering cost may only be guessed.

(a) Determine Getco's economic order quantity and total annual relevant inventory cost for the following assumed ordering costs (1) $10, (2) $25, (3) $50, (4) $75, and (5) $100. An annual holding cost of $.15 is assumed.

(b) Graph the optimal order quantity and the total annual relevant cost versus the various assumed ordering costs. What can you conclude regarding the influence of k on Q^* and $TC(Q^*)$?

15-27 Mrs. Moo's is a self-sufficient dairy; all feed grasses are grown on the premises. To rejuvenate the grass and trigger growth, periodic fertilizing is necessary. The dairy herd eats full-grown grass at the rate of 5,000 acres per year. Each fertilizing costs $100 to set up and requires $50 worth of chemicals per acre to create full growth. It takes a fertilized acre one-tenth of a year to reach maturity. There are 1,000 acres of grassland at Mrs. Moo's. The dairy finances its chemical purchases through the local bank at a 10% annual interest rate.

(a) Determine the number of acres that should be fertilized in each application. How often should fertilization take place? How many applications should be made each year?

(b) Do you think that it is totally satisfactory to apply the EOQ model to this problem? Explain.

15-28 Refer to Problem 15-1.

(a) Find the economic disc-drive order quantity by using a spreadsheet that follows the format in Figure 15-3 and varying the order quantity Q by trial and error until the lowest total annual relevant cost is obtained.

(b) Following the format in Figure 15-4, solve using a spreadsheet that utilizes the economic order quantity formula to compute the economic disc-drive quantity.

15-29 Solve Problem 15-2 using a spreadsheet as in Problem 15-28.

15-30 Solve Problem 15-7 with a spreadsheet that follows the formats in Figures 15-4 and 15-9.

15-31 Solve Problem 15-8 with a spreadsheet that follows the formats in Figures 15-4 and 15-9.

15-32 Solve Problem 15-11 with a spreadsheet that follows the format in Figure 15-13.

15-33 Solve Problem 15-19 with a spreadsheet that follows the format in Figure 15-13.

CASE   15-1   *Ingrid's Hallmark Shop I*

Ingrid's Hallmark Shop is a card and gift store specializing in Hallmark cards and related items. A substantial portion of the business is with allied gift items for non-Hallmark suppliers and with toys. Altogether there are several hundred different products in this group that are ordered throughout the year.

One item demanded with some regularity is balloons, usually sold inflated with helium at the time of purchase. The balloons come in a variety of shapes and styles. It generally takes Ingrid two hours to place a balloon order, track it, and eventually pay the supplier. Her average cost per balloon is $.50, plus about $.25 for the helium, string, and clamps.

Before taxes, Ingrid's Hallmark Shop has been netting about 20% on invested capital. The physical costs of storing merchandise are fixed. The store volume is too small to take advantage of any significant supplier quantity discounts.

Ingrid has no evidence regarding what shortage penalty applies when the store runs out of a particular balloon. She wishes to achieve a 95% service level, so that no particular balloon is out of stock more than 5% of the time.

Ingrid estimates that her shop will sell between 1,500 and 2,000 balloons in the coming year.

QUESTIONS

1. Comment on the suitability of using an EOQ model to determine how many balloons to order, and how often.

2. Remember, costs for inventory decisions may be assigned differently than those of traditional accounting. Discuss why it would not be appropriate to include the costs of the supplies—string, clamps, and helium—as part of the procurement cost for balloons.

3. Ingrid values her time at $10 per hour.
   (a) Establish values for (1) the unit procurement cost, (2) the ordering cost, and (3) the annual cost of holding a dollar's value in inventory.
   (b) State any assumptions you must make.

4. Refer to the parameters found in Question 3. Determine the optimal order quantity, assuming that no shortages are permitted and that annual demand

is for (a) 1,500, (b) 1,600, (c) 1,700, (d) 1,800, (e) 1,900, and (f) 2,000 units.

5. Assuming that backorders are taken, with an annual shortage penalty of $10 per balloon, determine the EOQ and order level when annual demand is 2,000 balloons.

6. Assume, instead, a 95% service level and an annual demand of 2,000 balloons.

(a) Compute the value of p that would be imputed from this policy.
(b) Determine the EOQ and order level.

7. The EOQ models described in this chapter are based on a single product.
(a) Comment on the suitability of lumping together different balloon topics and designs, treating all as a single item.
(b) What do you suggest for Ingrid?

CASE 15-2   *Fantasia Greeting Cards*

Freddy Phail is a marketing analyst for Fantasia Greeting Cards. The company supplies cards to more than 10,000 retailers of various types and sizes. Freddy is evaluating the current company policy of bundling multiples of the same card into wholesale units. That is now done using price category as the guide, with the objective of assembling packets with a retail value of approximately $12. The following data apply:

Retail Price	Number of Cards in Wholesale Packet
(1) $1.00	12
(2) 1.50	8
(3) 2.00	6
(4) 2.50	5
(5) 3.00	4
(6) 4.00	3
(7) 5.00	3

Retailers pay Fantasia half of the retail price for their cards. Freddy wants to use EOQ models to determine a better way of picking packet sizes.

Cards are distinguished by design, which is a combination of graphical layout and overall message sentiment and topic. The following data apply to a typical Fantasia dealer:

Retail Price	Average Annual Demand per Design	Number of Different Designs
(1) $1.00	150	150
(2) 1.50	200	245
(3) 2.00	75	330
(4) 2.50	50	178
(5) 3.00	25	56
(6) 4.00	10	85
(7) 5.00	10	36
		1,080

Freddy assumes a 15% return on working capital for a typical store. The cost of placing an order is small, amounting to only $.25 per design.

Fantasia policy is that, at any time, a retailer should have at least 95% of its display pockets filled with the design assigned to it, with obsolete filler cards inserted into the other 5% until they can be restocked. Customers do not backorder any card that is out of stock, taking the filler instead. Because the customers are not ordinarily fully satisfied with the filler, Freddy feels that the actual shortage penalty experienced grows with the duration of a shortage. He believes that the amount and effect would be similar to what might be experienced if backordering made sense and were to be literally followed.

QUESTIONS

1. The EOQ models in the chapter can only be used to approximately optimize the retailer's ordering decisions. Discuss some of the assumptions that may not strictly apply here. Comment on the suitability of using the models in spite of their limitations.

2. Determine how many cards of a single design in each retail category a typical store should order to minimize total annual relevant inventory cost. Freddy will recommend that these amounts be adopted as the packet quantities.

3. Compute the total annual relevant inventory cost for ordering a design in each price category with the order quantities you found in Question 2.

4. Compute the same costs assuming that Fantasia only lets retailers order exactly one, two, or three old-type packets for a particular design, and that the retailer orders the number of packets containing that total number of cards that best meets the EOQ found in Question 2. Then determine the net annual

inventory cost savings per design in each price category by using instead the true EOQ.

5. The above analysis was based on the assumption that each design has the same annual demand as the average for that price category. Actual experience shows that each card in a particular price category has its own demand, independent of the rest. Comment on the validity of the EOQs computed in Question 2.

6. Fritzi's Gift Boutique experiences the following annual demands for selected $2 cards.

(1) Humorous Birthday	(2) Elegant Anniversary	(3) Fancy Sympathy	(4) Retirement
632	157	54	62

(a) Determine Fritzi's EOQ for each of these.

(b) If Fantasia accepts Freddy's recommendations, the company will only accept orders for any number of new-type wholesale packets of the size found in Question 2. Determine for each design which number of the new-type packets comes closest to achieving the optimal order sizes found in (a).

C A S E   15-3   *All Star Driving School*

by Manuel Bernardo
California State University, Hayward

All Star Driving School has two lines of customers: the general public and corporations. It is located in Fremont, California, and its instructors are officially licensed by the state of California.

General public customers are those wanting to obtain Class C licenses (to drive a car), Class B licenses (to drive fire engines, ambulances, and so forth), or Class A licenses (to drive trucks). School districts also need to train bus drivers, and many public agency employees need defensive driving courses to operate official vehicles.

With corporate and government agency customers, All Star operates under contract to train a specified number of drivers. Each contract differs and its profitability must be evaluated carefully. Currently, All Star is evaluating a proposal by National Carrier, Inc. (NCI), a trucking company with headquarters in Fresno. NCI is interested in having All Star provide a truck-driving program for its new drivers. NCI's reason for the contract is that it wants to have a steady supply of newly trained drivers because of a combination of high turnover and growth in demand for shipping via trucks.

All Star estimates that a 4-week trucker-training course costs $2,000 for the instructor, $350 for the fa-

cilities and equipment, and $50 for office and support fees. In addition, for each trucker waiting to be trained, NCI incurs an additional opportunity cost of $1,400 per month, because the truckers are being paid but cannot be used productively.

QUESTIONS

1. If NCI needs five trained truck drivers per month for the foreseeable future, how big should the training classes be in order to minimize total annual relevant cost? Assume that All Star guarantees that the trained drivers will be available and that the EOQ model with no shortages applies. How many classes would be offered each year? What is the total annual relevant cost associated with the training classes?

2. Notice that the class size found in Question 1 is not an integer. Round it off and see how this would affect the total annual relevant cost.

3. It looks like the economy will improve next year. That would mean an increased demand for truck shipments in general and for NCI in particular. It is estimated that this could mean that as many as eight newly trained drivers per month would be needed. How would this affect the answers obtained in Question 1? What about a decrease in demand to four drivers per month?

4. Salary negotiations with the Teamsters are going to increase trucker wages next year. That would increase the opportunity cost associated with drivers waiting to start driving to $1,600 per month. How would this affect the answers obtained in Question 1?

5. Suppose that NCI is considering a proposal to streamline its operations because of the difficult economy. This would decrease the opportunity cost to $1,200 per month. How would this affect the answers obtained in Question 1?

6. (a) The instructor is threatening to quit unless his fee is increased from $2,000 to $2,500. Does this materially affect the answers obtained in Question 1?

(b) Unfortunately, the company can offer the instructor only $2,410, instead of the $2,500. How does this affect the answers obtained in Question 1?

7. In all of the previous questions, the fact that the class size must be a whole number was not explicitly considered. In Question 2, for instance, it was assumed that rounding would give the better answer. Is this always the case? To investigate this more precisely, re-solve Questions 1 through 6 with class sizes obtained by rounding both down and up. Calculate the cost of both cases and summarize your results. That is, if Q^* is 10.3, then recalculate the cost for an order quantity of 10 and 11.

8. In Question 1 All Star guaranteed that the drivers would be available. Now All Star is not so sure that this is for the best. It is thinking about renegotiating the contract to allow for the possibility of delays in the training of new drivers. NCI is amenable to delays, but they indicate that this would cost the company an additional $1,400 per month. A 1-week delay would incur an additional cost of $350, a 2-week delay $700; and so on. How would permitting delays affect the answers obtained in Question 1? What about delay costs of $2,000 per month?

9. Reanalyzing the situation in which delays are possible, suppose that NCI finds it difficult to put a cost on the delays. Instead it wants to have a policy that allows no more than 10% of the drivers to wait for the training classes to begin. How would this policy change the answers in Question 8? What about service levels of 99% and 50%?

CASE 15-4 *Mike's Imprints*

by Manuel Bernardo
California State University, Hayward

Mike's Imprints is an all-custom garment-printing business. Its main line of business is designing and printing custom designs or symbols on T-shirts, baseball caps, and nylon jackets. The firm also provides other products such as bumper stickers and posters. The company has been profitable with customers such as school and college clubs, little league baseball teams, church groups, and various businesses such as car dealers, hotels, nightclubs, bands, and music groups.

Mike's Imprints started as a hobby for Mike and then became a second source of income. Mike has one assistant, who helps him with production and runs the shop when he is not present.

The balance sheet for December 31, 1999, is given in Table 15-1. The marketable securities consist of a 2-year investment Certificate of Deposit (CD)

TABLE 15-1 Balance Sheet, December 31, 1999

Assets	
Cash	$2,000
Marketable Securities	20,000
Accounts Receivable	2,000
Supplies	
Office	460
Imprint Materials	1,900
Gross Plant and Equipment	
(Net of Depreciation)	23,000
TOTAL ASSETS	**$49,360**

Liabilities	
Accounts Payable	$2,000
Notes Payable	4,000
Accrued Taxes	1,140
Mortgage Payable	14,000
TOTAL LIABILITIES	**$21,140**
Capital (Mike)	28,220
TOTAL LIABILITIES AND CAPITAL	**$49,360**

that pays an annual rate of 7%. Money can be added once a month to this investment CD. However, there is a $40 penalty for early withdrawal (prior to maturity). The minimum required balance for the investment CD is $2,500, and no more than $3,500 can be withdrawn at any one time. Imprint material supplies include T-shirts, ink, screens, squeezes, and all other materials that will be used to produce a finished T-shirt product. The $4,000 notes payable is due January 1, 2002 and carries an annual interest rate of 7.5%. The $2,000 accounts payable is due on March 31, 2001. It has an interest rate of 6%.

Mike's concern is his cash flow during 2000. Although Mike's Imprints is profitable, it is subject to chronic cash shortages. This occurs because at times expenditures precede receipts. When there is excess cash generated, it is accumulated in the cash account, and when sufficient, it is put into the investment CD. When Mike brought up the issue of the cash shortages with his CPA, the CPA suggested that Mike set targets for his cash balance through the use of an EOQ model. The CPA's reasoning was that Mike could have no investments in the CDs and have cash available all the time, but there would be an opportunity cost involved with doing this: the interest lost from not putting the money in the investment CD. If additional cash is needed, it is withdrawn from the investment CD if funds are available.

Because Mike is in an evening M.B.A. program at a nearby university, he knows that if it is applied, the EOQ model will have Mike's Imprints' cash balance drop to zero at times. Because Mike's Imprints is a small business and only a source of part-time income for him, Mike realizes that he will have difficulty obtaining a loan to cover such zero balances on short notice. Consequently, he decides subjectively to maintain a minimum cash balance of $2,000 so that the total cash level will be that given by the EOQ model plus $2,000.

Although cash expenditures vary a little during the year, based on past experience Mike thinks that he can approximate them with a constant monthly rate. Table 15-2 shows the monthly cash expenditures.

Although cash expenditures and cash receipts do not match each other exactly (with cash flows positive in some months and negative in others), experience has shown that cash receipts are always at least 70% of cash expenditures. Consequently, it is the

TABLE 15-2 Monthly Cash Expenditures

Utilities	$300
Misc. Office Expenses	60
Monthly Mortgage Payment	323
Telephone	70
Purchase of Imprint Materials	2,000
Shop Assistant ($7/hour)	700

30% of cash expenditures that Mike is concerned about covering with the EOQ model.

Assuming that Mike uses the EOQ model to solve his cash balance problem, answer the following questions.

QUESTIONS

1. (a) How much cash should be withdrawn periodically from the investment CD during 2000? What will be the average cash balance? How often will Mike make withdrawals from the investment CD?

   (b) What will be the firm's total annual cost associated with following the EOQ model? Include the interest cost for the $2,000 minimum cash balance. What proportion of this is associated with the $2,000 minimum cash balance?

2. The monthly expenditures in Table 15-2 are just estimates. The actual expenditures might vary within a range of ±20%. Analyze whether such variations would change the answers in Question 1 significantly.

3. Reanswer Question 1 if the bank eliminates the $3,500 limit on withdrawals.

4. When Mike's CD matures, it might be renewed for 9% instead of the current 7%. How would this affect the answers to Question 1? If the renewal rate is only 5%, what happens?

5. Suppose that the penalty for withdrawing money from the investment CD account is increased to $60. How would that change the answers to Question 1?

6. Assume that the cost of making a withdrawal from the investment CD account is $40 plus 2% of the amount withdrawn. How would that change the answers to Questions 1 and 2?

CHAPTER 16

INVENTORY DECISIONS WITH UNCERTAIN FACTORS

When demands are unknown, expected values are the keys for deciding how much to order and how often.

Most inventory decisions must be made under uncertain conditions, requiring that one or more quantities be represented by random variables with probability distributions. Real-world demands are usually not constant and uniform, and probabilities should be used to represent them. Mathematical models involving probability are often referred to as **stochastic models.** In situations that do not involve uncertainty, such as those discussed in Chapter 15, the analytical procedures employ **deterministic models.**

Deterministic models are limited in scope and may be applied only approximately to most real-world decision-making problems. They do, however, provide points of departure for developing more realistic methods of analysis. It is easier to cope with uncertainty when an analytical framework has already been established by means of deterministic models. But making the leap from certainty into the world of uncertainty presents new difficulties.

Inventory models involving probability are generally based on expected values. The optimal inventory policy is found by considering *expected* profits or costs, so that the best we can do is to maximize or minimize long-run "average" profits or costs. Thus, even an optimal policy may lead to a range of outcomes from poor to excellent. The actual result is determined largely by luck. Such a lack of determinism on the part of the decision maker is an unavoidable burden we face whenever we attempt to cope with uncertainty.

DECISION PROBLEM

Betty's Stationery Stores

When John and Anita Johnson started a stationery store during the 1960s, they named it after their new daughter, Betty. Times were difficult at the beginning, but the store began to prosper after a few years, and Betty worked part time in the store during high school and college. As a business administration major, she was required to take a course in quantitative methods in which she learned about using inventory models to improve inventory management. In 2000, Betty inherited the store, which by that time had expanded to five locations around the San Francisco Bay Area.

Betty was now in a position to implement her business education by trying inventory models on a particular brand of printer cartridge. She wanted to see what inventory policy the models would recommend and what would be the cost savings.

Betty began by gathering data about the printer cartridge demand. Historical experience indicated a mean annual demand of 1,500 cartridges per year, although the actual demand and lead time for receiving an order were uncertain. A tabulation of the printer cartridge demand during the lead time yielded the following:

DEMAND	NUMBER OF OCCURRENCES	DEMAND	NUMBER OF OCCURRENCES
0	1	6	10
1	7	7	6
2	16	8	3
3	20	9	1
4	19	10	1
5	16		

Betty checked further and learned that each separate order took about half an hour to do the paper work and to enter the data into the company's computer system. Betty determined that at a labor rate of $10 per hour, the cost for placing an order was $5. The store paid $1.50 for each cartridge purchased from the supplier and financed its working capital through bank loans at an interest rate of 12%. From talking with store employees, Betty learned that when the cartridges are out of stock, customers usually are willing to wait the short time until the next shipment arrives. Betty is sure that the store suffers a loss in goodwill while the customers wait. She estimates the penalty from lost future profits to be $.50 for each cartridge short and backordered.

Current store policy is to order 100 cartridges whenever the inventory drops to 25 or less. Betty hopes her analysis will answer the following questions:

1. What type of inventory model should she select?

2. What inventory policy should Betty adopt for printer cartridges? How many items should be ordered? How often should orders be placed?

3. What are the costs associated with the inventory model? Are they less than the cost of the current inventory policy?

This chapter will show how inventory models can be used to answer these and other similar questions. For example, Betty is concerned about the assumption that customers will wait around for printer cartridges to arrive. Although this may be true for the cartridges, she knows it is not true for all products. Sometimes customers will go elsewhere, rather than backorder missing items, and sometimes they will fail to pick up their backorder requests. She wonders how those cases can be handled.

16-1 MAKING AN INVENTORY DECISION: MAXIMIZING EXPECTED PAYOFF

To set the stage for analyzing inventory decisions from explicit mathematical models, we identify the alternative inventory policies and use them, together with uncertain demand events, to construct a payoff table. Applying probability values for

each possible demand level, we then choose the inventory policy that provides the best expected payoff. At this point, the optimal decision is indicated.

The Nature of Uncertain Demand

As an illustration, consider the problem a small drugstore faces in trying to determine how many copies of various magazines to order. In particular, the drugstore owner wants to estimate how many copies of the October issue of *Fortune* to stock. Assume that past demand has provided a history of customer interest in this product and that the owner knows the frequencies of the various demand levels, which serve to establish probabilities for demand in future months.

Demand is a totally distinct notion from *sales.* A retailer can only sell a product if it is in stock or if a customer is willing to order and wait for it. *Fortune* is not an item that customers will order (except by subscription); if they do not see it on the shelf, no sale can be made. Yet, the desire to buy a copy of *Fortune* is a demand. Thus, we may define the **demand** for an item as the *intent to buy* it. Such a demand results in either a sale or the loss of a potential sale (when the item is not in stock).

Suppose that the drugstore owner has determined the following probability distribution for the demand for the October issue of *Fortune:*

COPIES DEMANDED	PROBABILITY
D = 20	.2
D = 21	.4
D = 22	.3
D = 23	.1

Alternative order quantities must be considered. Obviously, *Fortune* is a profitable item to include on the magazine rack, so the owner will not want to stock less than the minimum demand (if any issues are stocked at all, which is another question entirely). Also, there is no advantage to stocking more than the maximum demand.

Maximizing Expected Profit

Fortune is purchased directly from the local distributor at an assumed price of $2.10 and sells for $3.00 per copy. Unsold copies are returned at the end of the month for a $.70 credit. We assume that the drugstore owner's goal is to maximize profit, so the **payoff table** in Table 16-1 applies. In calculating the profits for each act and event

TABLE 16-1 Payoff Table for the *Fortune* Problem

DEMAND EVENT	ORDER QUANTITY ACT			
	Q = 20	Q = 21	Q = 22	Q = 23
D = 20	$18.00	$16.60	$15.20	$13.80
D = 21	18.00	18.90	17.50	16.10
D = 22	18.00	18.90	19.80	18.40
D = 23	18.00	18.90	19.80	20.70

TABLE 16-2   Expected Payoffs for the *Fortune* Problem

DEMAND EVENT	PROBABILITY	PROFIT × PROBABILITY			
		Q = 20	**Q = 21**	**Q = 22**	**Q = 23**
D = 20	.2	$3.60	$3.32	$3.04	$2.76
D = 21	.4	7.20	7.56	7.00	6.44
D = 22	.3	5.40	5.67	5.94	5.52
D = 23	.1	1.80	1.89	1.98	1.07
	Expected profits	$18.00	$18.44	$17.96	$16.79
			Maximum		

combination, we assume that whenever Q is greater than D, that $Q - D$ unsold *Fortune* magazines will be returned for the $.70 credit. Also, when Q is smaller than D, we assume that the excess demand is not filled and the disappointed customer must buy the October *Fortune* elsewhere. No penalty is considered for being short.

We assume that the owner will choose the value of Q that maximizes expected profit. Table 16-2 shows the calculations involved. The optimal order quantity is $Q = 21$ *Fortune* magazines.

Using Spreadsheets to Maximize Expected Profits

Figure 16-1 presents the payoff table spreadsheet for the *Fortune* illustration. It shows that the optimal order quantity is $Q = 21$ magazines and that this yields an expected profit of $18.44. (See Chapter 5 for a detailed description of the spreadsheet methodology.)

FIGURE 16-1

Payoff table spreadsheet for the *Fortune* magazine example

	A	B	C	D	E	F
1			PAYOFF TABLE EVALUATION			
2						
3	PROBLEM:	Fortune Magazine				
4						
5			Problem Data			
6						
7			Act 1	Act 2	Act 3	Act 4
8	Events	Probability	Q = 20	Q = 21	Q = 22	Q = 23
9	1 D = 20	0.2	$18.00	$16.60	$15.20	$13.80
10	2 D = 21	0.4	$18.00	$18.90	$17.50	$16.10
11	3 D = 22	0.3	$18.00	$18.90	$19.80	$18.40
12	4 D = 23	0.1	$18.00	$18.90	$19.80	$20.70
13						
14			Act Summary			
15						
16			Act 1	Act 2	Act 3	Act 4
17			Q = 20	Q = 21	Q = 22	Q = 23
18	Expected Payoff		$18.00	$18.44	$17.96	$16.79

16-2 SINGLE-PERIOD INVENTORY DECISION: THE NEWSVENDOR PROBLEM

The *Fortune* problem typifies inventory policy decisions when the demand for a product is uncertain and its lifetime is limited, so a single time period applies. Such a perishable product is epitomized by the daily newspaper, which has an effective demand lasting only one day. A newsvendor has one opportunity to decide how many copies of today's *Wall Street Journal* to stock. An entire class of inventory decisions of identical structure is here referred to as the **newsvendor problem.**

It is convenient to develop a mathematical model to solve this type of problem. Although analysis using a payoff table or a decision tree is effective for small-scale problems like our *Fortune* example, a large number of alternatives or possible events makes these procedures impractical.

The Mathematical Model

In its simplest form, the objective of the newsvendor problem is to decide how many items Q should be stocked at the beginning of the inventory cycle. The uncertain demand D expresses the number of items that customers will require during this period. Two types of outcomes may occur. If demand is less than or equal to the order quantity, sales will equal the quantity demanded; if demand is greater than the initial stock, sales will equal the order quantity.

$$\text{Sales} = \begin{cases} D & \text{if } D \le Q \\ Q & \text{if } D > Q \end{cases}$$

Four cost elements are considered.

$c =$ Unit procurement cost

$h_E =$ Additional cost of each item held at the *end* of the inventory cycle

$p_S =$ Penalty for each item short (loss of goodwill)

$p_R =$ Selling price

Single-period inventory decisions usually involve a short cycle, and none of the above parameters is time based. Here, we use subscripts to expand the notation from Chapter 15. In this model, the holding cost applies only at the *end* of the inventory cycle, and h_E has the subscript E to distinguish this usage of holding cost from that in previous inventory models. Likewise, instead of one shortage penalty p, there are now two, p_S and p_R. We will assume that there is no fixed ordering cost. The unit holding cost ordinarily represents the disposal cost of the unsold items in the ending inventory. If these items have any further limited economic use, h_E represents the unit disposal cost minus the salvage value (so that h_E may be negative).

These parameters are used to form two familiar cost components encountered with the deterministic inventory models of Chapter 15.

$$\text{Cost of each leftover item} = (h_E + c)$$
$$\text{Cost of each item short} = (p_S + p_R - c)$$

The cost of each leftover item $(h_E + c)$ adds the item's procurement cost c to its disposal cost h_E. The cost of each item short $(p_S + p_R - c)$ equals the goodwill cost p_S plus the profit $p_R - c$ lost because of not making the sale. The combined shortage cost acknowledges two sources of lost profit: p_S, which is primarily the present value of

future profits from that business expected to be lost from present customers disappointed by a shortage, and the *current* transaction profit $p_R - c$.

When demand is some level d, the total inventory cost may be computed beginning with the total procurement cost for those items, $c \times d$. That quantity must then be adjusted upward by the holding cost or the shortage cost. The holding cost is found by multiplying the cost of leftovers ($h_E + c$) by the number of items leftover ($Q - d$) when demand falls below supply ($d < Q$). The shortage cost is found by multiplying the unit shortage cost ($p_S + p_R - c$) by the number of items short ($d - Q$) when demand exceeds supply ($d > Q$). Thus, treating Q as a variable, the total cost is

$$TC(Q) = cd + \begin{cases} (h_E + c)(Q - d) & \text{if } d \le Q \quad \text{(holding cost)} \\ (p_S + p_R - c)(d - Q) & \text{if } d > Q \quad \text{(shortage cost)} \end{cases}$$

Of course we cannot know the level of d in advance, so this expression is used only to explain the underlying cost relationship.

The proper inventory cost calculation reflects the uncertainty regarding demand. The demand is assumed to have a probability distribution, so that for each possible demand d there is a given probability $\Pr[D = d]$. Because demand is uncertain, the optimal order quantity Q is one that minimizes total *expected* cost.

To find that quantity, we begin by applying the probability weights, in effect averaging the demand levels, getting the

EXPECTED DEMAND

$$\mu = \sum_d d\Pr[D = d]$$

This is used to compute **total expected cost,** which has three components:

$$TEC(Q) = \frac{\text{Procurement Cost}}{\text{for Expected Demand}} + \frac{\text{Expected}}{\text{Holding Cost}} + \frac{\text{Expected}}{\text{Shortage Cost}}$$

For the procurement cost we replace the unspecified demand level d with μ, so that all possible levels of demand are reflected. As with individual demands, we multiply the holding and shortage cost terms by their respective probabilities, summing these to obtain a final expected value. The following expression provides the

TOTAL EXPECTED COST

$$TEC(Q) = c\mu + \sum_{d=0}^{Q} (h_E + c)(Q - d)\Pr[D = d] + \sum_{d>Q} (p_S + p_R - c)(d - Q)\Pr[D = d]$$

MANAGERIAL APPLICATION

Ordering Wall Street Journals

Part A: Computing Expected Demand and Total Expected Cost

A newsvendor places daily orders for the *Wall Street Journal*. For simplicity, we assume that the vendor pays $c = \$.20$ for each paper and sells it for $p_R = \$.23$. Unsold papers must be hauled to the recycling center for a cost each of $h_E = \$.01$. There is a goodwill cost of $p_S = \$.02$, representing the loss of *future* profits that may arise from a shortage and a *current* loss of profit, $p_R - c = \$.23 - .20 = \$.03$. Altogether, the per-unit shortage cost is the sum of these two components, $\$.02 + .23 - .20 = \$.05$.

| **TABLE 16-3** | Probability Distribution for Daily *Wall Street Journal* Demand, Showing Expected Value Calculations When Q = 50 |

(1)	(2)	(3)	(4) HOLDING COST		(5) SHORTAGE COST	
POSSIBLE DEMAND *d*	PROBABILITY Pr[D = d]	DEMAND × PROBABILITY *d* Pr[D = d]	COST (.20 + .01) × (50 − d)	COST × PROBABILITY	COST (.02 + .23 − .20) × (d − 50)	COST × PROBABILITY
45	.05	2.25	$1.05	$.0525	—	—
46	.06	2.76	.84	.0504	—	—
47	.09	4.23	.63	.0567	—	—
48	.12	5.76	.42	.0504	—	—
49	.17	8.33	.21	.0357	—	—
50 (=Q)	.20	10.00	.00	.0000	—	—
51	.12	6.12	—	—	.05	.0060
52	.08	4.16	—	—	.10	.0080
53	.06	3.18	—	—	.15	.0090
54	.04	2.16	—	—	.20	.0080
55	.01	.55	—	—	.25	.0025
		$\mu = 49.50$		$.2457		$.0335

$$TEC(50) = \$.20(49.50) + .2457 + .0335 = \$10.1792$$

Table 16-3 provides the newsvendor's probability distribution for daily *Wall Street Journal* demand. These data will be used to evaluate her current inventory policy of ordering $Q = 50$ newspapers each day.

THE PROBLEM SOLUTION

The expected demand is computed using the given probability data in columns (1) and (2) of Table 16-3. The calculations are made in column (3), where each possible demand is multiplied by its corresponding probability. The sum of these products provides the expected daily *Wall Street Journal* demand of $\mu = 49.50$.

The expected holding cost is computed in column (4). The first subcolumn provides the holding cost computed for each demand level for which there would be an excess of newspapers. A cost of $.00 applies when demand exactly equals order quantity. The second subcolumn is the product of the holding cost and the respective demand probability. The total of these products is the expected holding cost, $.2457. Because the disposal cost is so small, this amount is dominated by the sunk procurement cost for leftover papers.

The expected shortage cost is determined in column (5), where the first subcolumn lists the shortage cost for the applicable demand. The second subcolumn multiplies those costs by the respective probabilities. The sum of those products provides the expected shortage cost, only $.0335 for this problem. This amount is small because the number of possible shortages is not great, their likelihood is small, and the goodwill cost and unit profit for lost sales is small.

Total expected cost is

$$TEC(50) = \$.20(49.50) + .2457 + .0335 = \$10.1792$$

found by adding the holding and shortage costs to the procurement cost for the expected demand.

As with previous inventory models, an optimal order quantity Q must be found that minimizes total expected inventory cost. This quantity Q^* will achieve an optimal balance between the expected holding cost and the expected shortage cost.

Finding the Optimal Solution Through Marginal Analysis

Although the optimal solution might be obtained by computing a separate *TEC* for each possible Q and finding the one with the smallest expected cost, that would be very computationally inefficient. (There are 11 demand levels possible in the preceding example.) It is far simpler to follow another approach called **marginal analysis.**

Marginal analysis is based on *convexity*— a mathematical property of expressions of the form *TEC(Q)*. In principle, any mathematical expression is convex when its value decreases steadily at a progressively slower rate for increasing levels of the independent variable until a minimum is achieved, after which values of the expression increase steadily at an increasing rate. This means that *TEC(Q)* achieves its minimum value at the lowest level of Q that is followed by an increase in total expected cost. This feature is illustrated in Figure 16-2.

We can find the smallest order quantity that is followed by an increase in total expected cost by considering all of the differences between successive *TEC* values.

$$\text{Difference} = TEC(Q + 1) - TEC(Q)$$

The smallest Q with a nonnegative difference is optimal.

A mathematical analysis shows that the successive total cost difference[†] is

$$\text{Difference} = (h_E + c)\,\Pr[D \le Q] - (p_S + p_R - c)(1 - \Pr[D \le Q])$$

which must be greater than or equal to zero. Notice that this expression involves only the unit cost constants and the cumulative probability that demand falls at or below the order quantity. The condition for the optimal order quantity is established by setting the total expected cost difference greater than or equal to zero and rearranging terms.

We get the following result for the

OPTIMAL ORDER QUANTITY

Q^* is the smallest possible demand such that

$$\Pr[D \le Q^*] \ge \frac{p_S + p_R - c}{(p_S + p_R - c) + (h_E + c)}$$

[†]The difference in *holding costs only* is

$$\sum_{d=0}^{Q+1} (h_E + c)[(Q + 1) - d]\Pr[D = d] - \sum_{d=0}^{Q} (h_E + c)(Q - d)\Pr[D = d]$$
$$= (h_E + c)\Pr[D \le Q]$$

Likewise, the difference in *shortage costs only* is

$$\sum_{d>Q+1} (p_S + p_R - c)[d - (Q + 1)]\Pr[D = d] - \sum_{d>Q} (p_S + p_R - c)(d - Q)\Pr[D = d]$$
$$= -(p_S + p_R - c)(1 - \Pr[D \le Q])$$

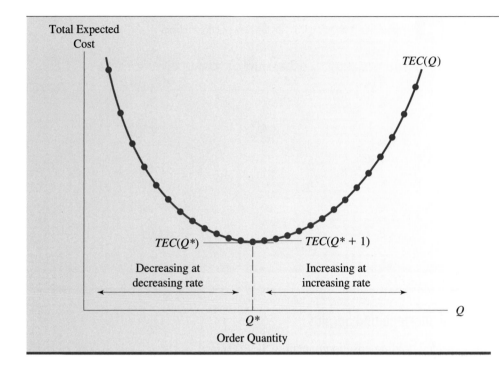

FIGURE 16-2
The convexity principle in marginal analysis

This tells us that we need to calculate only the above ratio, using the constants given for the problem, and establish the cumulative probability for demand. The smallest demand with a cumulative probability greater than or equal to this ratio is equal to the order quantity that minimizes total expected cost.

Ordering Wall Street Journals

MANAGERIAL
APPLICATION

Part B: Finding Optimal Order Quantity

Marginal analysis can find the optimal number of *Wall Street Journals* for the newsvendor to order.

THE PROBLEM SOLUTION

The cumulative demand probabilities are computed in Table 16-4. Using the constants provided earlier, we calculate the ratio

$$\frac{p_S + p_R - c}{(p_S + p_R - c) + (h_E + c)} = \frac{.02 + .23 + \ -.20}{(.02 + .23 + \ -.20) + (.01 + .20)} = .192$$

From column (3) of Table 16-4, we see that the smallest cumulative demand probability that exceeds this value is .20, which applies when the demand is for 47 papers. Thus, $Q^* = 47$, and the newsvendor will minimize expected cost by stocking exactly 47 papers. Notice that this optimal order quantity is less than the expected demand of 49.50 (Table 16-3). Depending on the values for c, h_E, p_S, and p_R, Q^* may lie above or below the expected demand.

TABLE 16-4	Probability Distribution Data for the Newsvendor Problem	
(1) POSSIBLE DEMAND d	(2) PROBABILITY $\Pr[D = d]$	(3) CUMULATIVE PROBABILITY $\Pr[D \leq d]$
45	.05	.05
46	.06	.11
47	.09	.20
48	.12	.32
49	.17	.49
50	.20	.69
51	.12	.81
52	.08	.89
53	.06	.95
54	.04	.99
55	.01	1.00
	1.00	

Expected Shortage and Surplus

The expected holding cost component of $TEC(Q)$ is

$$\sum_{d=0}^{Q} (h_E + c)(Q - d)\Pr[D = d]$$

Pulling the $(h_E + c)$ terms outside of the summation, this is equivalently expressed as

$$(h_E + c) \sum_{d=0}^{Q} (Q - d)\Pr[D = d] = (h_E + c) \times \text{Expected surplus}$$

The portion involving the summation is the **expected surplus.** That quantity is the weighted average of $(Q - d)$ terms, each representing the possible number of items left over because the demand falls at or below the order quantity $(d \leq Q)$.

Similarly, the expected shortage cost component of $TEC(Q)$ is

$$\sum_{d>Q} (p_S + p_R - c)(d - Q)\Pr[D = d]$$

This may be equivalently expressed as

$$(p_S + p_R - c) \sum_{d>Q} (d - Q)\Pr[D = d] = (p_S + p_R - c) \times \text{Expected shortage}$$

The portion involving the summation is the **expected shortage.** That quantity is the weighted average of $(d - Q)$ terms, each representing the possible number of items short because the demand exceeds the order quantity $(d > Q)$. Because it is so frequently used, the expected shortage is represented by the symbol $B(Q)$. We use the following expression to compute the

EXPECTED SHORTAGE

$$B(Q) = \sum_{d>Q} (d - Q)\Pr[D = d]$$

The **expected surplus** may be expressed in terms of the expected shortage:

EXPECTED SURPLUS

$$Q - \mu + B(Q) = \sum_{d=0}^{Q} (Q - d)\Pr[D = d]$$

An Alternative Expression for Total Expected Cost

An alternative expression for $TEC(Q)$ will prove helpful in later inventory models. Expressing total expected cost in terms of its components, we have

$$TEC(Q) = c\mu + (h_E + c) \times \text{Expected surplus} + (p_S + p_R - c) \times \text{Expected shortage}$$

This is expressed in final form by

TOTAL EXPECTED COST

$$TEC(Q) = c\mu + (h_E + c)[Q - \mu + B(Q)] + (p_S + p_R - c)B(Q)$$

Ordering Wall Street Journals

MANAGERIAL APPLICATION

Part C: Using Expected Shortage in Computing Total Expected Cost

The expected shortage applicable when the optimal order quantity is $Q^* = 47$ is next computed for the newsvendor's *Wall Street Journal* problem. The resulting $B(Q)$ value is used in the revised $TEC(Q)$ expression to compute the corresponding minimum total expected cost.

THE PROBLEM SOLUTION

Table 16-5 shows the preliminary computations. The expected surplus is computed in column (3) by first subtracting from the order quantity those demands for which there would be a surplus. The probability weights are applied, and when totaled, the expected surplus of .16 items is computed. This same quantity can be found another way, after the expected shortage is computed.

The expected shortage $B(47)$ for the optimal order quantity is computed in column (4). There, the order quantity is first subtracted from each demand for which a shortage would arise. Applying the respective probability weights, as before, and summing those products yields the expected shortage $B(47) = 2.66$.

The expected surplus can also be computed indirectly, employing this quantity. We have

$$\text{Expected surplus} = Q - \mu + B(Q) = 47 - 49.50 + 2.66 = .16$$

The total expected cost is easily determined.

$$TEC(47)$$
$$= \$.20(49.50) + (.01 + .20)(47 - 49.50 + 2.66) + (.02 + .23 - .20)(2.66)$$
$$= \$10.0666$$

TABLE 16-5	Calculations for Expected Surplus and Shortage for Newsvendor's *Wall Street Journal* Problem When $Q^* = 47$					
(1)	(2)	(3) SURPLUS		(4) SHORTAGE		
Possible Demand d	Probability $\Pr[D = d]$	Items $(Q - d)$	Items × Probability	Items $(d - Q)$	Items × Probability	
45	.05	2	.10	—	—	
46	.06	1	.06	—	—	
47 ($= Q^*$)	.09	0	.00	—	—	
48	.12	—	—	1	.12	
49	.17	—	—	2	.34	
50	.20	—	—	3	.60	
51	.12	—	—	4	.48	
52	.08	—	—	5	.40	
53	.06	—	—	6	.36	
54	.04	—	—	7	.28	
55	.01	—	—	8	.08	
			.16		$B(47) = 2.66$	

Solving the Newsvendor Problem with a Spreadsheet

Figure 16-3 gives the spreadsheet solution for the *Wall Street Journal* example. The optimal order quantity appears in cell G13, and the total expected cost is in cell G15. This spreadsheet is on the CD-ROM that accompanies the text and can be used as a template to solve other newsvendor problems. The development of the spreadsheet is shown in Appendix 16-1 at the end of this chapter.

The Effect of Cost Elements on Total Expected Cost

The shortage penalty p_S is perhaps the most elusive cost element in inventory decisions because it is difficult to quantify the loss of goodwill. For this reason, it may be desirable to analyze the inventory decision for a range of levels of p_S. Such optional additional work is referred to as **sensitivity analysis,** because it tells us just how sensitive the optimal solution is to variations in the value assumed for the parameter constant. Table 16-6 shows the total expected costs for the newsvendor problem when p_S is .02, .07, .12, .17, or .22, with $p_R = .23$, $c = .20$, and $h_E = .01$. Notice that within each row, at each level of Q, the *TEC* values increase as p_S increases (except in the last row, where Q is equal to the maximum possible demand and shortages are impossible).

It is interesting to see how Q^* changes as p_S is increased. When p_S is raised from .02 to .07, the optimal order quantity jumps from $Q^* = 47$ to $Q^* = 49$ and remains at that level through $p_S = .17$. At $p_S = .22$, the optimal order quantity jumps again to $Q^* = 50$. Thus, we can see that when shortage penalties are more severe, larger order quantities (larger levels of Q^*) are required to minimize total expected costs.

Similar conclusions may be drawn about the other cost parameters. In general, *TEC* will increase as either c or h_E increases, but the relationship to Q^* will differ. Because the optimal order quantity is determined by the ratio $(p_S + p_R - c)/[(p_S + p_R - c) + (h_E + c)]$ and the cumulative probability for demand, Q^* increases as the ratio increases. Thus, holding p_S, p_R, and h_E fixed, a reduction in c will make the numerator

	A	B	C	D	E	F	G
1	SINGLE PERIOD INVENTORY MODEL -- NEWSVENDOR PROBLEM						
2							
3	PROBLEM:		Wall Street Journal				
4							
5			Parameter Values:				
6			Cost per Item Procured: c =				0.20
7			Additional Cost for Each Leftover Item Held: h_E =				0.01
8			Penalty for Each Item Short: p_S =				0.02
9			Selling Price per Unit: p_R =				0.23
10			Number of demands for probability distribution =				11
11							
12			Optimal Values:				
13			Optimal Order Quantity: Q^* =				47
14			Expected Demand: mu =				49.5
15			Total Expected Cost: $TEC(Q^*)$ =				$10.07
16			Expected Shortages: $B(Q^*)$ =				2.66
17			Probability of Shortage: $P[D>Q^*]$ =				0.80
18							
19					Cumulative	Number of	
20			Demand	Probability	Probability	shortages	
21			45	0.05	0.05	0.0	
22			46	0.06	0.11	0.0	
23			47	0.09	0.20	0.0	
24			48	0.12	0.32	1.0	
25			49	0.17	0.49	2.0	
26			50	0.20	0.69	3.0	
27			51	0.12	0.81	4.0	
28			52	0.08	0.89	5.0	
29			53	0.06	0.95	6.0	
30			54	0.04	0.99	7.0	
31			55	0.01	1.00	8.0	

FIGURE 16-3
Spreadsheet for newsvendor problems applied to the *Wall Street Journal* example

TABLE 16-6 Total Expected Costs for the Newsvendor Problem at Several Levels for the Shortage Penalty

ORDER QUANTITY Q	TOTAL EXPECTED COST $TEC(Q)$				
	$p_S = .02$	$p_S = .07$	$p_S = .12$	$p_S = .17$	$p_S = .22$
45	$10.1250	$10.3500	$10.5750	$10.8000	$11.0250
46	10.0880	10.2655	10.4430	10.6205	10.7980
47	10.0666*	10.1996	10.3326	10.4656	10.5986
48	10.0686	10.1616	10.2546	10.3476	10.4406
49	10.1018	10.1608*	10.2198*	10.2788*	10.3378
50	10.1792	10.2127	10.2462	10.2797	10.3132*
51	10.3086	10.3266	10.3446	10.3626	10.3806
52	10.4692	10.4777	10.4862	10.4947	10.5032
53	10.6506	10.6536	10.6566	10.6596	10.6626
54	10.8476	10.8481	10.8486	10.8491	10.8496
55	11.0550	11.0550	11.0550	11.0550	11.0550
$\dfrac{p_S + p_R - c}{(p_S + p_R - c) + h_E + c}$	.192	.323	.417	.488	.543
Q^*	47	49	49	49	50

larger and increase Q^*, whereas the reverse is true for an increase in c. This reflects the fact that a smaller procurement cost makes it less painful to hold unsold items. Increasing the level of h_E will increase the denominator, thereby reducing the ratio, and lowering the level of Q^*, whereas a reduction in h_E will increase Q^*. Thus, everything else being equal, the more expensive it is to dispose of unsold items, the lower the order quantity should be.

16-3 CONTINUOUS PROBABILITY DISTRIBUTION FOR DEMAND: THE CHRISTMAS TREE PROBLEM

When the number of possible demands is large — as it would be when hundreds of thousands of units are sold daily — it is usually convenient to use a continuous approximation for the demand probability distribution. The single-period models discussed thus far may be adapted to continuous probability distributions. As was true for the discrete probabilities applicable in these earlier models, the order level depends only on the cumulative probability for demand. However, there is one change: Q^* is chosen, so that the ratio is exactly equal to the cumulative probability that demand lies at or below that level. When demand is a continuous random variable, we use the following expression to find the

OPTIMAL ORDER QUANTITY

Q^* is that level of possible demand where

$$\Pr[D \le Q^*] = \frac{p_S + p_R - c}{(p_S + p_R - c) + (h_E + c)}$$

MANAGERIAL APPLICATION

Christmas Tree Seller's Decision

Part A: Inventory Policy for Noble Firs ($Q^* \ge \mu$)

Suppose that the demand for noble fir Christmas trees experienced by a particular Gotham City seller is approximately normally distributed with a mean of $\mu = 2,000$ trees and a standard deviation of $\sigma = 500$ trees. The trees sell for an average of $9 and cost $3 each. The loss of goodwill arising from shortages is judged to be $1 per tree short. The city license requires that all unsold trees be converted into mulch pulp, which is donated to the Gotham City Parks Department; the cost of pulverization averages $.50 per tree. The seller has already committed funds to any fixed costs involved. How many trees should be ordered from Canadian suppliers to minimize inventory costs (and thereby maximize profits)?

THE PROBLEM SOLUTION

The applicable cost constants (in dollars) are

$$c = 3 \qquad h_E = .50 \qquad p_S = 1 \qquad p_R = 9$$

The following ratio applies:

$$\frac{p_S + p_R - c}{(p_S + p_R - c) + (h_E + c)} = \frac{1 + 9 - 3}{(1 + 9 - 3) + (.50 + 3)} = .6667$$

This ratio establishes the cumulative demand probability that determines Q^*:

$$\Pr[D \le Q^*] = .6667$$

Figure 16-4(a) helps to explain how the value of Q^* is obtained. The shaded area under the normal curve for noble fir demand is equal to the cumulative probability of .6667. The portion of this area that is above the mean is equal to .1667, which corresponds to a normal deviate value of $z = .43$ (see Appendix Table B). This expresses the number of standard deviations that Q^* lies beyond the mean, so that

$$Q^* = \mu + z\sigma$$

Substituting $\mu = 2{,}000$ and $\sigma = 500$ trees into this equation, we obtain

$$Q^* = 2{,}000 + .43(500) = 2{,}215 \text{ noble firs}$$

The Gotham City seller should order 2,215 noble firs.

The optimal order quantity can lie *below* μ, so that the corresponding cumulative demand probability may be less than .5. Figure 16-4(b) for the next application represents such a probability as a shaded area under the left tail of the normal curve. The normal deviate will be *negative*.

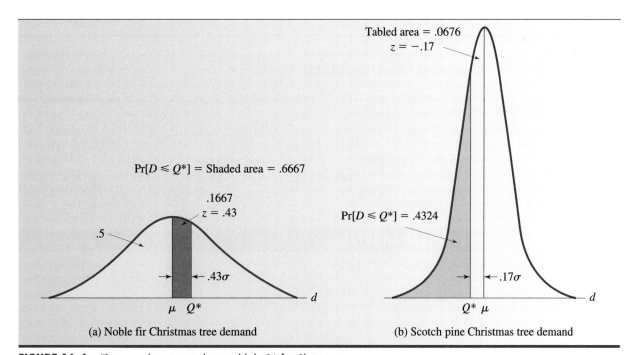

(a) Noble fir Christmas tree demand   (b) Scotch pine Christmas tree demand

FIGURE 16-4   The normal curves used to establish Q^* for Christmas trees

Christmas Tree Seller's Decision

Part B: Inventory Policy for Scotch Pines ($Q^* < \mu$)

The tree seller carries a variety of trees. Another popular tree is the Scotch pine, for which

$$c = 10 \qquad h_E = .50 \qquad p_S = 1 \qquad p_R = 17 \qquad \mu = 1,000 \qquad \sigma = 200$$

THE PROBLEM SOLUTION

The optimal order quantity is that demand level with a cumulative probability equal to the ratio

$$\frac{p_S + p_R - c}{(p_S + p_R - c) + (h_E + c)} = \frac{1 + 17 - 10}{(1 + 17 - 10) + (.50 + 10)} = .4324$$

That area lies totally below μ and is not directly represented in Appendix Table B, which only gives areas (and z's) for quantities lying between the *mean* and levels for d larger than the mean. To find the tabled area corresponding to a tail, we must subtract the tail area from .5, which represents an entire half of the normal curve. For the Scotch pine normal curve in Figure 16-4(b), the applicable tabled area in Appendix Table B is

$$.5 - .4324 = .0676$$

for which $z = -.17$ is the nearest normal deviate.

Because Q^* will fall below μ, the corresponding normal deviate must be negative, and we use $z = -.17$ to compute the optimal order quantity.

$$Q^* = \mu + z\sigma = 1,000 + (-.17)(200) = 966 \text{ Scotch pines}$$

Computing Total Expected Cost

When demand is normally distributed, the total expected cost will be computed from the alternative expression,

$$TEC(Q) = c\mu + (h_E + c)[Q - \mu + B(Q)] + (p_S + p_R - c)B(Q)$$

where the expected shortage $B(Q)$ must be found first.

Because of the difficulties in computing $B(Q)$ directly when demand is normally distributed, we employ the following expression and a special tabled function to find the values for

EXPECTED SHORTAGE

(Normally Distributed Demand)

$$B(Q) = \begin{cases} \sigma L\left(\dfrac{Q - \mu}{\sigma}\right) & Q \geq \mu \\[2ex] \mu - Q + \sigma L\left(\dfrac{\mu - Q}{\sigma}\right) & Q < \mu \end{cases}$$

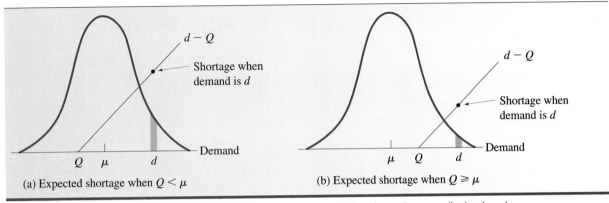

(a) Expected shortage when $Q < \mu$

(b) Expected shortage when $Q \geqslant \mu$

FIGURE 16-5   Suggested approximation for finding expected shortage when demand is normally distributed

$L(x)$ is the **normal loss function,** the values for which apply to the distance x that separates μ and Q (measured in standard deviation units). These values are listed in Appendix Table C. The values of $L(x)$ were constructed by approximating the normal curve (Figure 16-5), formed by a large number of narrow intervals. The area of each interval serves as the probability value for a demand falling there. Using the interval midpoints as the respective d's, a lengthy calculation similar to the one in column (4) of Table 16-5 establishes the expected shortage. We don't have to do that here because the result is already given by the respective entry in Appendix Table C. Those quantities were computed for $\sigma = 1$, so that we can customize the scale to any particular application by multiplying the L value by the applicable σ.

Christmas Tree Seller's Decision

Part C: Computing the Expected Shortage and *TEC(Q)*
The expected shortage and $TEC(Q)$ may be computed for any designated order quantity Q. We illustrate those computations for the Christmas tree seller using the respective Q^* values found earlier for the noble fir and Scotch pine orders.

THE PROBLEM SOLUTION
Noble fir: For $Q^* = 2{,}215$ trees, which exceeds the mean of $\mu = 2{,}000$, using the standard deviation of $\sigma = 500$ we compute the expected shortage.

$$B(2{,}215) = 500L\left(\frac{2{,}215 - 2{,}000}{500}\right) = 500L(.43)$$

From Appendix Table C, $L(.43) = .2203$, so that we have

$$B(2{,}215) = 500(.2203) = 110.15 \text{ trees}$$

Using $c = \$3$, $h_E = \$.50$, $p_S = \$1$, and $p_R = \$9$, the total expected cost is

$$TEC(2{,}215) = \$3(2{,}000) + (.50 + 3)[2{,}215 - 2{,}000 + B(2{,}215)] + (1 + 9 - 3)B(2{,}215)$$

$$= \$6{,}000 + 3.50(2{,}215 - 2{,}000 + 110.15) + 7(110.15)$$

$$= \$6{,}000 + 1{,}138.03 + 771.05 = \$7{,}909.08$$

Scotch pine: For $Q^* = 966$ trees, which falls below the mean of $\mu = 1{,}000$, using the standard deviation of $\sigma = 200$ we compute the expected shortage.

$$B(966) = 1000 - 966 + 200L\left(\frac{1{,}000 - 966}{200}\right) = 34 + 200L(.17)$$

From Appendix Table C, $L(.17) = .3197$, so that we have

$$B(966) = 34 + 200(.3197) = 97.94 \text{ trees}$$

Using $c = \$10$, $h_E = \$.50$, $p_S = \$1$, and $p_R = \$17$, the total expected cost is

$$TEC(966) = \$10(1{,}000) + (.50 + 10)[966 - 1{,}000 + B(966)] + (1 + 17 - 10)B(966)$$

$$= \$10{,}000 + 10.50(966 - 1{,}000 + 97.94) + 8(97.94)$$

$$= \$10{,}000 + 671.37 + 783.52 = \$11{,}454.89$$

Using Spreadsheets for Christmas Tree Problems

Figure 16-6 gives the spreadsheet solution for the noble fir problem. The optimal order quantity appears in cell F14 and the total expected cost is in cell F16 (answers differ slightly due to rounding). This spreadsheet is on the CD-ROM that accompanies the text and can be used as a template to solve other Christmas tree problems. The development of the spreadsheet is shown in Appendix 16-1 at the end of this chapter.

FIGURE 16-6

Spreadsheet for Christmas tree problems as applied to the noble fir example

	A	B	C	D	E	F	G
1	SINGLE PERIOD INVENTORY MODEL - CHRISTMAS TREE PROBLEM						
2							
3	PROBLEM:		Noble Fir				
4							
5			Parameter Values:				
6				Mean of Demand Distribution: mu =			2000
7				Stand. Deviation of Demand Distribution: sigma =			500
8				Cost per Item Procured: c =			3.00
9				Additional Cost for Each Leftover Item Held: h_E =			0.50
10				Penalty for Each Item Short: p_S =			1.00
11				Selling Price per Unit: p_R =			9.00
12							
13			Optimal Values:				
14				Optimal Order Quantity: Q* =		2215	
15				Expected Demand: mu =		2000	
16				Total Expected Cost: TEC(Q*) =		$7,910.35	
17				Expected Shortages: B(Q*) =		110.15	
18				Probability of Shortage: P[D>Q*] =		0.33	

16-4 MULTIPERIOD INVENTORY POLICIES

Until this point, we have discussed only single-period inventory problems. These models generally apply to perishable items that may be ordered only once and that may not be held in inventory to satisfy demands occurring in another period. It is far more common, however, to encounter the problem of establishing an inventory policy for items that may be stored over several time periods and that may be reordered with considerable flexibility.

We began our initial discussion of inventory decisions in Chapter 15 with what we may now refer to as **multiperiod inventory policies.** At this point, we must begin to cope with uncertainties. The two major uncertain variables encountered in inventory decisions are **demand** and **lead time** required to fill orders.

The mathematical procedures for analyzing multiperiod inventory decisions in this book involve *continuous review models.* They assume that a continuous monitorship of inventory positions takes place, so that decision rules regarding replenishment are based on the current inventory position. These models give rise to (r, Q) policies, and orders are triggered whenever the current inventory position falls below the **reorder point r,** at which point Q items are ordered.

Figure 16-7 illustrates the behavior of an inventory system when demand and lead time are uncertain. Notice that inventory depletion occurs erratically due to the varying intensities of demand. Orders are placed whenever the inventory position falls below r. But continued variations in demand and unpredictable lead times cause shortages to occur in some periods and not in others. This erratic behavior results in varying cycle durations and beginning inventory positions.

The EOQ Model for Uncertain Demand

Several time periods are involved, so we will return to the problem objective in Chapter 15 of minimizing total annual relevant cost. Because demand and lead time are now uncertain, we minimize *expected cost,* which is the following sum of expected values:

Annual ordering cost + Annual holding cost + Annual shortage cost

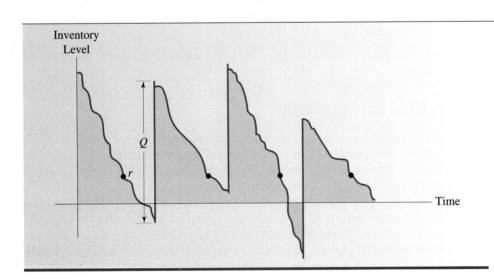

FIGURE 16-7

Inventory system using (r, Q) policy with uncertain demand and lead time

Although demand is no longer presumed to be certain, we will assume that the mean annual demand rate applies uniformly over time. We use the symbol

$$A = \text{Mean annual demand rate}$$

(The *mean* demand rate is constant, but demand may vary from period to period.) If Q items are ordered each time at a cost of k per order, it follows that

$$\text{Expected annual ordering cost} = \left(\frac{A}{Q}\right)k$$

which was true for the earlier models described in Chapter 15.

The actual demand D over any interval of time is uncertain and must be specified in terms of a probability distribution. Instead of focusing on some fixed calendar period like a day, week, or month, our model will consider the level of demand during the *lead time* for filling an order. For this purpose, we will employ the probability distribution for **lead-time demand,** which we will distinguish from the earlier single-period distributions by a subscript L.

$$\text{Probability for } d \text{ units demanded in lead time} = \Pr_L[D = d]$$

This distribution reflects two uncertainties: one regarding the demand itself and one surrounding the duration of the lead time. Our model will focus on the expected value of D.

$$\mu = \text{Mean lead-time demand}$$

There are two major cases considered in inventory evaluations. These are based on how shortages are handled.

1. **Backordering** occurs when items are out of stock. Any demand occurring during this time will be filled when the outstanding order arrives. A shortage penalty applies that includes the added cost of processing plus any cost assigned to the loss of customer goodwill.

2. **Lost sales** arise from any demand occurring while items are out of stock. The shortage penalty reflects the seller's gross profit (margin) for the missing items that would otherwise have been sold, plus the cost of the diminished goodwill that results from the shortage.

The two cases have very similar models. We begin with a detailed discussion of the backordering case.

Inventory Model with Backordering

This model is appropriate whenever items are ordinarily backordered. For example, it applies to printed computer forms or similar items that have no substitutes. There may be a special cost for processing a backorder, and there may be some loss of goodwill that could impact future business with the shorted customer.

Each inventory cycle begins when an order arrives. Stock is then depleted until it falls below the reorder point r, which is assumed to exceed μ, at which time a new order is placed. Continued depletion occurs until the order arrives. Any items short are then provided from the incoming shipment. The expected level of inventory just before the order arrives is $r - \mu$, so that the subsequent cycle begins with an expected inven-

tory of $Q + r - \mu$ items. Because the mean rate of depletion is uniform, the average inventory level during a cycle must be the average of these quantities. Thus,

$$\text{Expected average cycle inventory} = \frac{1}{2}[(Q + r - \mu) + r - \mu]$$

$$= \frac{Q}{2} + r - \mu$$

As we did in the EOQ models described in Chapter 15, we let h represent the *annual* cost per *dollar value* of holding items in inventory. From this, it follows that

$$\text{Expected annual holding cost} = hc\left[\frac{Q}{2} + r - \mu\right] \quad \text{(with backordering)}$$

The most complicated part of the EOQ models for uncertain demand involves the shortage cost component. That cost depends on the number of shortages in each cycle, which is a random variable due to the uncertain lead-time demand. Because items are only backordered when lead-time demand exceeds the reorder point r, we may use the following expression to determine the

EXPECTED SHORTAGE PER INVENTORY CYCLE

$$B(r) = \sum_{d > r} (d - r)\text{Pr}_L[D = d]$$

In the backordering case, all shortages will eventually be filled, and $B(r)$ may then be viewed as the expected number of backorders. Multiplying $B(r)$ by the expected number of cycles per year A/Q and the penalty p_S for each item short, we obtain

$$\text{Expected annual shortage cost} = p_S\left(\frac{A}{Q}\right)B(r) \quad \text{(with backordering)}$$

In keeping with the single-cycle models employed in this chapter, we let p_S represent the cost of each item short, regardless of how long it is backordered. (This parameter therefore differs from its counterpart in the backordering model we examined in Chapter 15, where the penalty instead applied to the duration of the shortage.) Because backordering occurs, no lost sales revenue from *current* transactions is included in p_S. But p_S will largely reflect *future* lost profits arising from business lost because some disappointed present customers may begin to shop elsewhere.

The following expression provides the

TOTAL ANNUAL EXPECTED COST

(With Backordering)

$$TEC(r, Q) = \left(\frac{A}{Q}\right)k + hc\left[\frac{Q}{2} + r - \mu\right] + p_S\left(\frac{A}{Q}\right)B(r)$$

Our objective is to find the values of Q and r that minimize this expression.

The following procedure permits us to determine the optimal levels of these variables:

1. For a given order quantity Q, the **optimal reorder point r^*** is the *smallest* quantity having a cumulative lead-time demand probability meeting the

---

CONDITION FOR REORDER POINT

$$\Pr[D \leq r^*] \geq 1 - \frac{hcQ}{p_S A} \quad \text{(with backordering)}$$

---

2. For a given reorder point r, the **optimal order quantity Q^*** is found.

OPTIMAL ORDER QUANTITY

$$Q^* = \sqrt{\frac{2A[k + p_S B(r)]}{hc}} \quad \text{(with backordering)}$$

To solve for either r or Q, the value of the other variable must be known. Before we may begin, a seed value must be obtained for one of these variables. This value is then used to determine the level of the second variable, which in turn is used to refine the value of the first variable. This procedure continues — using the last Q to obtain the next r and that r to obtain the next Q — until no values change.

A good starting or seed value may be obtained by using the Wilson formula from Chapter 15 for the economic order quantity when no backordering is allowed.

STARTING ORDER QUANTITY

$$Q_1 = \sqrt{\frac{2Ak}{hc}}$$

The subscript 1 simply indicates that this is the first attempt to determine the value of the order quantity.

DECISION PROBLEM

Decision Problem Revisited: Betty's Stationery Stores (Printer Cartridges)

Based on the information she obtained, Betty decides to use the multiperiod inventory model under conditions of uncertainty, assuming backorders, with the discrete lead-time demand distribution in Table 16-7. The following parameters apply:

$$A = 1,500 \text{ items per year}$$
$$k = \$5 \text{ per order}$$
$$c = \$1.50 \text{ per item}$$
$$h = \$.12 \text{ per dollar value per year}$$
$$p_S = \$.50 \text{ per unit short (no matter how long)}$$

TABLE 16-7 Lead-Time Demand Probability Distribution for Printer Cartridges

POSSIBLE DEMAND d	PROBABILITY $Pr_L[D = d]$	DEMAND × PROBABILITY	CUMULATIVE PROBABILITY $Pr_L[D \leq d]$
0	.01	0	.01
1	.07	.07	.08
2	.16	.32	.24
3	.20	.60	.44
4	.19	.76	.63
5	.16	.80	.79
6	.10	.60	.89
7	.06	.42	.95
8	.03	.24	.98
9	.01	.09	.99
10	.01	.10	1.00
	1.00	$\mu = 4.00$	

THE PROBLEM SOLUTION

The mean lead-time demand is computed in Table 16-7, where $\mu = 4$.

First Iteration   The starting value for the order quantity is

$$Q_1 = \sqrt{\frac{2(1,500)5}{.12(1.5)}} = 289$$

The following steps permit Betty to determine the optimal levels of Q and r.

1. Using the value $Q = 289$, she computes

$$1 - \frac{hcQ}{p_S A} = 1 - \frac{.12(1.5)289}{.5(1,500)} = .93$$

The smallest cumulative lead-time demand probability greater than or equal to this value in Table 16-7 is

$$Pr_L[D \leq 7] = .95$$

so that the optimal reorder point is $r^* = 7$ cartridges.

2. Using $r = 7$, Betty first evaluates the corresponding expected number of back-orders per cycle, $B(r) = B(7)$. This quantity is computed as follows:

Demand d	Probability $Pr_L[D = d]$	Difference $d - r = d - 7$	Difference × Probability
8	.03	1	.03
9	.01	2	.02
10	.01	3	.03
			$B(7) = .08$

Substituting $B(7) = .08$ into the expression for Q^* gives

$$Q^* = \sqrt{\frac{2(1,500)[5 + .5(.08)]}{.12(1.5)}} = 290$$

Because this result differs from the initial value of $Q = 289$, Betty must continue the procedure with a second iteration.

Second Iteration   Betty uses $Q = 290$ to recompute the reorder point. First, she finds

$$1 - \frac{hcQ}{p_s A} = 1 - \frac{.12(1.5)290}{.5(1,500)} = .93$$

which is identical to the cumulative probability for $r^* = 7$ found before. The reorder point does not change, so that no step 2 calculations are required.

Thus, the values in the optimal (r, Q) policy are

$$r^* = 7 \quad \text{and} \quad Q^* = 290$$

so that $Q^* = 290$ cartridges should be ordered whenever the current inventory falls below $r^* = 7$. The total annual expected cost of this policy is

$$TEC(7,290) = \left(\frac{1,500}{290}\right)5 + .12(1.5)\left[\frac{290}{2} + 7 - 4\right] + .50\left(\frac{1,500}{290}\right)(.08)$$

$$= 25.86 + 26.64 + .21$$

$$= 52.71 \text{ dollars}$$

Comparison to Original Policy   Redoing the total annual cost calculation for the current policy, $Q = 100$ and $r = 25$ gives

$$TEC(25,100) = \left(\frac{1,500}{100}\right)(5) + .12(1.5)\left(\frac{100}{2} + 25 - 4\right) + (.5)\left(\frac{1,500}{100}\right)(0)$$

$$= 87.78 \text{ dollars}$$

Based on those calculations, Betty was pleasantly surprised that the inventory model decreases total annual expected costs by $87.78 - $52.71 = 35.07, or 40%.

Notice that in the preceding example the Wilson formula for the simple inventory model provides an order quantity of $Q_1 = 289$, which is very close to the final optimal solution of $Q^* = 290$. Although the starting and final values will not always be so close (this depends on the various parameter values and on the lead-time demand distribution), this illustration shows that sometimes the simple inventory model works quite well — even though it assumes that demand is certain and constant.

The expected inventory on-hand when an order arrives is called the **safety stock.** This is the difference between the reorder point and mean lead-time demand, or

$$\text{Safety stock} = r - \mu$$

In the preceding application, the safety stock is $7 - 4 = 3$ cartridges. On the average, when the optimal $(7, 290)$ policy is employed, 3 cartridges will be on hand when any order arrives.

Safety stock as computed above may be *negative,* so that there may be, on the average, some backorders outstanding whenever a shipment arrives. Certain combinations of levels for the problem parameters may bring about such a solution.

Solving with Spreadsheets

The spreadsheet for multiperiod models with backorders and discrete lead-time demand is similar to the newsvendor spreadsheet in Figure 16-3. The principal difference is that some calculations in that figure must be repeated because of the iterative nature of the multiperiod solution process. Figure 16-8 gives the spreadsheet solution for the printer cartridge problem. The optimal order quantity appears in cell G14, the optimal reorder point in cell G15, and the total expected cost in cell G17. This spreadsheet is on the CD-ROM that accompanies the text and can be used as a template to solve other multiperiod problems with backordering. The development of the spreadsheet is shown in Appendix 16-1.

Inventory Model with Lost Sales

A different model is appropriate whenever it is impossible to backorder items or when customers will simply find another source of supply. Many convenience items, such as

	A	B	C	D	E	F	G
1	\multicolumn{7}{l}{**MULTI-PERIOD EOQ MODEL (Backordering) -- DISCRETE LEAD-TIME DEMAND**}						
2							
3	PROBLEM:	Printer Cartridges					
4							
5		Parameter Values					
6			Fixed Cost per Order: k =				5
7			Annual Demand Rate: A =				1500
8			Unit cost of Procuring an Item: c =				1.5
9			Annual Holding Cost per Dollar Value: h =				0.12
10			Shortage Cost per Unit: ps =				0.5
11							
12		Optimal Values:					
13			Optimal Order Quantity: Q* =				290
14			Optimal Reorder Poind: r* =				7
15			Expected Lead-Time Demand: mu =				4
16			Total Expected Cost: TEC(Q*) =				$52.71
17			Expected Shortage: B(Q*) =				0.08
18			Probability of Shortage: P[D>r*] =				0.05
19							
20					Cumulative		
21			Demand	Probability	Probability		
22			0	0.01	0.01		
23			1	0.07	0.08		
24			2	0.16	0.24		
25			3	0.20	0.44		
26			4	0.19	0.63		
27			5	0.16	0.79		
28			6	0.10	0.89		
29			7	0.06	0.95		
30			8	0.03	0.98		
31			9	0.01	0.99		
32			10	0.01	1.00		

FIGURE 16-8

Spreadsheet for the printer cartridge problem

cigarettes, should be evaluated in terms of *lost sales.* Immediate necessities fall into this category.

This lost sales case is easiest to describe in terms of how it differs from back-ordering. The expected average inventory level will be the same as in backordering, except that the expected shortage $B(r)$ must be added back (because any short items will not be sold). Thus, the expected annual holding cost becomes

$$\text{Expected annual holding cost} = hc\left[\frac{Q}{2} + r - \mu + B(r)\right] \quad \text{(with lost sales)}$$

The shortage penalty is more elaborate than before. In addition to the penalty p_S (reflected here primarily as the value of lost goodwill arising from a shortage), we must account for the gross profit on the lost sale. We denote the lost revenue per short item by p_R (selling price), so that the lost gross profit is computed by subtracting the item procurement cost c.

$$\text{Expected shortage penalty per item} = \text{Loss of goodwill} + \text{Lost profit}$$

$$= p_S + (p_R - c)$$

(You may think of p_S as the net present value of *future* losses in expected profit arising from the disappointment caused by each unit of current shortage and $p_R - c$ as the lost profit from each unit short from *current* transactions.)

Multiplying the expected shortage penalty by the expected size of shortage $B(r)$, we obtain the expected shortage cost per inventory cycle. When the resulting quantity is multiplied by the number of orders, the expected annual shortage cost is obtained. Using A/Q to *approximate* that quantity, we have

$$\text{Expected annual shortage cost} = (p_S + p_R - c)\left(\frac{A}{Q}\right)B(r) \quad \text{(with lost sales)}$$

The expected relevant inventory cost is determined in a way similar to the back-ordering case, except the holding and shortage cost components reflect the above adjustments. A further modification must be made in the number of orders, reduced in this model by the annual level of lost sales. That reduction is accomplished by replacing annual *demand A* by the annual *sales A',* from which all lost sales have been removed. Thus, we have a new expression for

TOTAL EXPECTED COST

(With Lost Sales)

$$TEC(r, Q) = \left(\frac{A'}{Q}\right)k + hc\left[\frac{Q}{2} + r - \mu + B(r)\right] + (p_S + p_R - c)\left(\frac{A'}{Q}\right)B(r)$$

$$\text{where} \quad A' = A(1 - B(r)/Q)$$

The same iterative approach is used here as with backordering. Different expressions are used for finding r and Q. The following steps apply, using Q_1 (as before) as the seed value.

1. For a given order quantity Q, the **optimal reorder point r^*** is the smallest quantity with a cumulative lead-time demand probability meeting the

CONDITION FOR REORDER POINT

$$\Pr_L[D \le r^*] \ge \frac{(p_S + p_R - c)A}{hcQ + (p_S + p_R - c)A} \quad \text{(with lost sales)}$$

2. For a given reorder point r, the **optimal order quantity Q^*** is found.

OPTIMAL ORDER QUANTITY

$$Q^* = \sqrt{\frac{2A[k + (p_S + p_R - c)B(r)]}{hc}} \quad \text{(with lost sales)}$$

Decision Problem Revisited: Betty's Stationery Stores (Compact Discs)

Betty was concerned about the backorder assumption made for the printer cartridge inventory model. Although customers are willing to suffer a slight delay in getting those items when out of stock, users of compact discs are not so patient. Those customers will go elsewhere to purchase their discs during shortages. Not only is the markup on the sale lost, but some amount of future business (not just for discs) may be lost after these customers locate a new source of supply for the missing items. Each disc short is estimated to cost an average of $.10 in future profits.

Betty decided to use a multiperiod model under conditions of uncertainty with lost sales and discrete lead-time demand for the compact discs. She assumed that the following parameters apply:

$$A = 5,000 \text{ items per year}$$
$$k = \$20 \text{ per order}$$
$$c = \$.45 \text{ per item}$$
$$h = \$.12 \text{ per dollar value per year}$$
$$p_S = \$.10 \text{ per item short}$$
$$p_R = \$.90 \text{ per item}$$

The lead-time demand probability distribution for compact discs is given in Table 16-8.

THE PROBLEM SOLUTION

The mean lead-time demand is computed in Table 16-8 to be $\mu = 123.4$.

First Iteration   The starting value for the order quantity is

$$Q_1 = \sqrt{\frac{2(5,000)20}{.12(.45)}} = 1,925$$

The following steps permit Betty to determine the optimal levels of Q and r.

TABLE 16-8 Lead-time Demand Probability Distribution for Compact Discs

POSSIBLE DEMAND d	PROBABILITY $\text{Pr}_L[D = d]$	DEMAND × PROBABILITY	CUMULATIVE PROBABILITY $\text{Pr}_L[D \leq d]$
90	.05	4.5	.05
100	.12	12.0	.17
110	.17	18.7	.34
120	.22	26.4	.56
130	.19	24.7	.75
140	.14	19.6	.89
150	.05	7.5	.94
160	.03	4.8	.97
170	.02	3.4	.99
180	.01	1.8	1.00
	1.00	$\mu = 123.4$	

1. Using the value $Q = 1,925$, Betty computes the ratio

$$\frac{(p_S + p_R - c)A}{hcQ + (p_S + p_R - c)A} = \frac{(.10 + .90 - .45)5,000}{.12(.45)(1,925) + (.10 + .90 - .45)5,000}$$

$$= .964$$

The smallest cumulative lead-time demand probability greater than or equal to this value in Table 16-8 is

$$\text{Pr}_L[D \leq 160] = .97$$

so the optimal reorder point is $r^* = 160$ compact discs.

2. Using $r = 160$, Betty first evaluates the corresponding expected number of items short per inventory cycle $B(r) = B(160)$. This quantity is computed as follows:

DEMAND d	PROBABILITY $\text{Pr}_L[D = d]$	DIFFERENCE $d - 160$	DIFFERENCE × PROBABILITY
170	.02	10	.2
180	.01	20	.2
			$B(160) = .4$

Substituting $B(160) = .4$ into the expression for Q^* gives

$$Q^* = \sqrt{\frac{2A[k + (p_S + p_R - c)B(r)]}{hc}} = \sqrt{\frac{2(5,000)[20 + (.10 + .90 - .45)(.4)]}{.12(.45)}}$$

$$= 1,935$$

Because this result differs from the initial value of $Q = 1,925$, Betty must continue the procedure with a second iteration.

Second Iteration Betty uses $Q = 1,935$ to recompute the reorder point. First, she finds the ratio

$$\frac{(.10 + .90 - .45)5,000}{.12(.45)(1,935) + (.10 + .90 - .45)5,000} = .963$$

which yields the identical tabled cumulative demand probability found before, and $r^* = 160$. The reorder point does not change. Thus, no step 2 is required, and the values in the optimal (r, Q) policy are

$$r^* = 160 \quad \text{and} \quad Q^* = 1,935$$

so that $Q^* = 1,935$ discs should be ordered whenever the current inventory falls below $r^* = 160$. The expected annual disc sales total is

$$A' = (1 - B(r)/Q)A = (1 - .4/1,935)(5,000) = 4,999$$

(with only 1 disc shortage expected per year). The total annual expected cost of this policy is

$$TEC = \left(\frac{4,999}{1,935}\right)20 + .12(.45)\left[\frac{1,935}{2} + 160 - 123.4 + .4\right]$$
$$+ (.10 + .90 - .45)\left(\frac{4,999}{1,935}\right)(.4)$$
$$= 51.67 + 54.24 + .57 = 106.48 \text{ dollars}$$

Solving with a Spreadsheet

The spreadsheet for the lost sales case involves minor variations from the backordering case. Figure 16-9 gives the main segment of the spreadsheet for the compact disc problem. The optimal order quantity appears in cell G15, the optimal reorder point in

FIGURE 16-9
Spreadsheet for the compact disc example with lost sales

	A	B	C	D	E	F	G
1	MULTI-PERIOD EOQ MODEL (Lost Sales) - DISCRETE LEAD-TIME DEMAND						
2							
3	PROBLEM:		Compact Disks				
4							
5			Parameter Values				
6			Fixed Cost per Order: k =				20
7			Annual Demand Rate: A =				5000
8			Unit cost of Procuring an Item: c =				0.45
9			Annual Holding Cost per Dollar Value: h =				0.12
10			Shortage Cost per Unit: p_S =				0.1
11			Shortage Cost per Unit: p_R =				0.9
12			Number of demands for probability distribution =				10
13							
14			Optimal Values:				
15			Optimal Order Quantity: Q* =				1935
16			Optimal Reorder Point: r* =				160
17			Expected Lead-Time Demand: mu =				123
18			Total Expected Cost: TEC(Q*) =				$ 106.48
19			Expected Shortage: B(r*) =				0.40
20			Probability of Shortage: P[D>r*] =				0.03
21							
22					Cumulative	Number of	
23			Demand	Probability	Probability	Shortages	
24			90	0.05	0.05	0	
25			100	0.12	0.17	0	
26			110	0.17	0.34	0	
27			120	0.22	0.56	0	
28			130	0.19	0.75	0	
29			140	0.14	0.89	0	
30			150	0.05	0.94	0	
31			160	0.03	0.97	0	
32			170	0.02	0.99	10	
33			180	0.01	1.00	20	

cell G16, and the total expected cost is in cell G18. This spreadsheet is on the CD-ROM that accompanies the text and can be used as a template to solve other multiperiod problems with lost sales. The development of the spreadsheet is shown in the Appendix 16-1 at the end of this chapter.

16-5   THE EOQ MODELS FOR NORMALLY DISTRIBUTED DEMAND

When large inventory systems comprise many units or when a product such as gasoline is sold in divisible quantities, it is convenient to represent lead-time demand with a continuous probability distribution. Only slight modifications are required to use the preceding model to find the optimal (r, Q) policy when lead-time demand is normally distributed.

The primary change is the way in which the expected number of shortages $B(r)$ is computed. As with the previous model involving normal curves (page 630), this may be accomplished by a simple computation using a tabled value.

EXPECTED SHORTAGE

(Normally Distributed Lead-Time Demand)

$$B(r) = \begin{cases} \sigma L\!\left(\dfrac{r - \mu}{\sigma}\right) & \text{if } r \geq \mu \\[3mm] \mu - r + \sigma L\!\left(\dfrac{\mu - r}{\sigma}\right) & \text{if } r < \mu \end{cases}$$

---

where

$$\mu = \text{Mean lead-time demand}$$
$$\sigma = \text{Standard deviation in lead-time demand}$$

L is the normal loss function, and its values are listed in Appendix Table C.

The Backordering Case

The following example shows how the EOQ model with backordering is applied when lead-time demand is normally distributed.

MANAGERIAL APPLICATION

Unleaded Gasoline at Oil Refinery

Optimal Inventory Policy with Backordering

The normal demand model may be illustrated with an example of how to find the optimal inventory policy for unleaded gasoline at an oil refinery. Due to the varying availability of crude oil and other petroleum processing requirements, the starting time for processing a batch of unleaded gasoline is unpredictable. The lead time is the period from the point that an order is issued until the unleaded gasoline product begins to flow into the holding tanks. We will assume that the demand while this is happening is normally distributed with a mean of $\mu = 200{,}000$ liters and a standard deviation of $\sigma = 20{,}000$ liters. When the unleaded tanks are empty, trucks scheduled to deliver that fuel

are dispatched with other gasolines, and the unleaded customers receive their back-orders later via a special delivery.

The mean annual demand rate for unleaded fuel from this refinery is $A = 40$ million liters per year. The fixed cost of a production run is $k = \$1,000$, and the wholesale value of this gasoline is $c = \$.40$ per liter. The annual opportunity cost per dollar value of funds tied up in inventory is $h = \$.20$. From the refinery's point of view, the only shortage cost for backordering fuel is the expense of the special delivery, which exceeds regular costs by $p_S = \$.05$ per liter. (For simplicity, we will assume that the production rate is so much greater than the inventory depletion rate that the savings in holding costs while simultaneously filling and emptying the holding tanks are too small to be significant.)

THE PROBLEM SOLUTION

First Iteration   The starting value for the order quantity is

$$Q_1 = \sqrt{\frac{2(40,000,000)(1,000)}{.20(.40)}} = 1,000,000 \text{ liters}$$

The following steps permit us to determine the optimal levels of Q and r.

1. Using the value of $Q = 1,000,000$, we compute

$$1 - \frac{hcQ}{p_S A} = 1 - \frac{.20(.40)(1,000,000)}{.05(40,000,000)} = .96$$

The optimal reorder point r^* is the lead-time demand with a cumulative probability *equal* to this result (because the distribution is continuous). This corresponds to a normal deviate z for the area under the standard normal curve. We choose the normal deviate with the area between the mean and z that is closest to $.96 - .5 = .46$. Reading Appendix Table B in reverse, we obtain $z = 1.75$. This means that the reorder point r^* lies $z = 1.75$ standard deviations above the mean lead-time demand. Thus,

$$r^* = \mu + z\sigma$$
$$= 200,000 + 1.75(20,000)$$
$$= 235,000 \text{ liters}$$

2. This figure is then used to calculate Q^*. This requires computing the expected number of backorders in an inventory cycle $B(r)$. For $r = 235,000$ liters,

$$B(235,000) = (20,000)L\left(\frac{235,000 - 200,000}{20,000}\right)$$
$$= (20,000)L(1.75)$$

From Appendix Table C, we find that $L(1.75) = .01617$, so that

$$B(235,000) = (20,000)(.01617) = 323.4$$

Substituting this value and the other parameter values into the equation for Q^* gives us the improved order quantity value

$$Q^* = \sqrt{\frac{2(40,000,000)[1,000 + .05(323.4)]}{.20(.40)}} = 1,008,050 \text{ liters}$$

Because this result differs from the initial value of $Q = 1,000,000$, a second iteration is required.

Second Iteration   Returning to step 1, we use the improved order quantity to recompute the reorder point. First, we find

$$1 - \frac{hcQ}{p_sA} = 1 - \frac{.20(.40)(1,008,050)}{.05(40,000,000)} = .9597$$

The closest normal deviate corresponding to .9597 is $z = 1.75$, which is identical to the normal deviate in the first iteration. *No further steps are required*, because the values of r^* and, therefore, Q^*, do not change.

The optimal policy is

$$Q^* = 1,008,050 \text{ liters}$$
$$r^* = 235,000 \text{ liters}$$

The total annual expected cost of this policy is

$$TEC = \left(\frac{40,000,000}{1,008,050}\right)1,000 + .20(.40)\left[\frac{1,008,050}{2} + 235,000 - 200,000\right]$$
$$+ .05\left(\frac{40,000,000}{1,008,050}\right)323.4$$
$$= 39,680.57 + 43,122 + 641.63$$
$$= 83,444.20 \text{ dollars}$$

Solving with a Spreadsheet

The spreadsheet for this model is a variation of that described in Section 16-3 for the Christmas tree problem, with the normal lead-time demand distribution replacing the discrete one. Figure 16-10 shows the spreadsheet for the unleaded gasoline at an oil refinery example. The optimal order quantity appears in cell F15, the optimal reorder

FIGURE 16-10

Spreadsheet for unleaded gasoline at an oil refinery

	A	B	C	D	E	F	G
1		MULTI-PERIOD EOQ MODEL (Backordering) - NORMAL LEAD-TIME DEMAND					
2							
3	PROBLEM:	Unleaded Gas at Oil Refinery					
4							
5		Parameter Values:					
6			Mean of Demand Distribution: mu =				200,000
7			Stand. Deviation of Demand Distribution: sigma =				20,000
8			Fixed Cost per Order: k =				1,000
9			Annual Demand Rate: A =				40,000,000
10			Unit Cost of Procuring an Item: c =				0.40
11			Annual Holding Cost per Dollar Value: h =				0.20
12			Shortage Cost per Unit: ps =				0.05
13							
14		Optimal Values:					
15			Optimal Order Quantity: Q* =			1,008,256	
16			Optimal Reorder Point: r* =			234,937	
17			Expected Demand: mu =			200,000	
18			Total Expected Cost: TEC(Q*) =			83,455.46	
19			Expected Shortages: B(r*) =			331.60	
20			Probability of Shortage: P[D>r*] =			0.04	

point in cell F16, and the total expected cost in cell F18. (These answers differ slightly from earlier due to rounding.) This spreadsheet is on the CD-ROM that accompanies the text and can be used as a template to solve other multiperiod problems with a normal lead-time demand distribution and backordering. The development of the spreadsheet is shown in Appendix 16-1.

Negative Safety-Stock Policies

In the preceding illustration, r was always greater than μ. That is not always the case.

Pesticide Production

MANAGERIAL APPLICATION

Optimal Inventory Policy with Backordering (Negative Safety Stock)
Suppose that the BugOff Chemical Company experiences the following parameters for its Bug-a-Cider technical pesticide base:

$$A = 1,000 \text{ gallons per year}$$
$$k = \$600 \text{ per cycle}$$
$$c = \$50 \text{ per gallon}$$
$$h = \$.50 \text{ per dollar held one year}$$
$$p_S = \$10 \text{ per gallon short}$$
$$\mu = 50 \text{ gallon lead-time demand}$$
$$\sigma = 9 \text{ gallons}$$

THE PROBLEM SOLUTION

First Iteration   The starting value for the order quantity is

$$Q_1 = \sqrt{\frac{2(1,000)600}{.50(50)}} = 219$$

The following steps permit us to determine the optimal levels of Q and r.

1. Using the value of $Q = 219$, we compute

$$1 - \frac{hcQ}{p_S A} = 1 - \frac{.50(50)219}{10(1,000)} = .4525$$

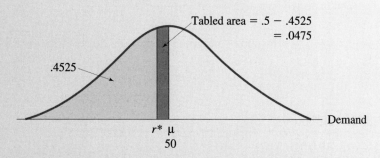

This value corresponds to a cumulative probability lying in the *lower tail* of the lead-time demand normal curve. To find the tabled area, the cumulative

probability must be *subtracted* from .5, giving us $.5 - .4525 = .0475$. This corresponds to the closest normal deviate value $z = -.12$. (The negative sign applies because the indicated cumulative probability is a lower-tailed area.)

The optimal reorder point when $Q = 219$ is

$$r^* = \mu + z\sigma$$
$$= 50 + (-.12)9$$
$$= 48.9, \text{ or } 49$$

2. Using the expression applicable when $r < \mu$, the above result will give us the expected number of backorders in an inventory cycle $B(r)$.

$$B(49) = 50 - 49 + 9L\left(\frac{50 - 49}{9}\right) = 1 + 9L(.11) = 1 + 9(.3464) = 4.1176$$

Using $B(49) = 4.1176$, the optimal order quantity is

$$Q^* = \sqrt{\frac{2(1,000)[600 + 10(4.1176)]}{.50(50)}} = 226.48, \text{ or } 226$$

Second Iteration   Returning to step 1, we use $Q = 226$ to recompute the reorder point. First, we find

$$1 - \frac{.50(50)226}{10(1,000)} = .4350$$

As before, the area under the lead-time demand normal curve lies in the lower tail. For a table area of $.5 - .4350 = .0650$, the nearest normal deviate is $z = -.16$, and the optimal reorder point is

$$r^* = 50 + (-.16)9 = 48.56, \text{ or } 49$$

No further steps are required, since the values of r^* and therefore Q^* do not change. The optimal policy is

$$r^* = 49 \text{ gallons}$$
$$Q^* = 226 \text{ gallons}$$

The total expected annual inventory cost is

$$TEC(49, 226) = \left(\frac{1,000}{226}\right)600 + .50(50)\left[\frac{226}{2} + 49 - 50\right] + 10\left(\frac{1,000}{226}\right)4.1176$$

$$= 5,637.06 \text{ dollars}$$

Computer Solution

PESTICIDE PRODUCTION

The following Excel spreadsheet is for the pesticide production evaluation:

	A	B	C	D	E	F	G
1	MULTI-PERIOD EOQ MODEL (Backordering) - NORMAL LEAD-TIME DEMAND						
2							
3	PROBLEM:	Bug-a-Cider					
4							
5			Parameter Values:				
6				Mean of Demand Distribution: mu =			50
7				Stand. Deviation of Demand Distribution: sigma =			9
8				Fixed Cost per Order: k =			600
9				Annual Demand Rate: A =			1,000
10				Unit Cost of Procuring an Item: c =			50.00
11				Annual Holding Cost per Dollar Value: h =			0.50
12				Shortage Cost per Unit: ps =			10.00
13							
14			Optimal Values:				
15				Optimal Order Quantity: Q* =		227	
16				Optimal Reorder Point: r* =		48	
17				Expected Demand: mu =		50	
18				Total Expected Cost: TEC(Q*) =	$	5,638.28	
19				Expected Shortages: B(r*) =		4.45	
20				Probability of Shortage: P[D>r*] =		0.57	

(Again, rounding leads to slightly different answers than those found before.)

The Lost Sales Case

The following example shows how the EOQ model with lost sales is applied.

Unleaded Gasoline at Service Station

MANAGERIAL APPLICATION

Optimal Inventory Policy with Lost Sales

Although the refinery in our earlier illustration may backorder those demands arising during a shortage, the service stations may not do the same. The drivers that need unleaded gasoline will simply drive away, searching until they find a gas station that has the needed fuel. Demands arising during shortages become *lost sales*.

We assume that Roger's Sentinel Station experiences an annual demand of $A = 500,000$ gallons for unleaded gasoline. The lead-time demand is assumed to be normally distributed with a mean $\mu = 1,000$ gallons and standard deviation $\sigma = 50$ gallons. Deliveries to Roger's involve a tanking charge averaging $k = \$100$, and fuel costs of $c = \$1.48$ per gallon. Roger's net proceeds average to $p_R = \$1.75$ per gallon. Some of the customers who leave with unfilled tanks are lost permanently. Roger estimates that he loses $p_S = \$.25$ in future profits for every gallon short. Roger presently earns 19% on his invested capital, so that $h = \$.19$ applies to each dollar's worth of inventory tied up for one year.

THE PROBLEM SOLUTION

First Iteration   The starting value for the order quantity is

$$Q_1 = \sqrt{\frac{2(500,000)100}{.19(1.48)}} = 18,858 \text{ gallons}$$

The following steps permit us to determine the optimal levels of Q and r.

1. Using the value $Q = 18,858$, we compute

$$\frac{(p_S + p_R - c)A}{hcQ + (p_S + p_R - c)A} = \frac{(.25 + 1.75 - 1.48)500,000}{.19(1.48)18,858 + (.25 + 1.75 - 1.48)500,000}$$

$$= .9800$$

This value corresponds to a nearest tabled normal deviate of $z = 2.05$. Thus, the optimal reorder point is

$$r^* = \mu + z\sigma$$
$$= 1,000 + 2.05(50)$$
$$= 1,103 \text{ gallons}$$

2. This figure is then used to calculate Q^*. This requires computing the expected number of gallons short per inventory cycle $B(r)$. For $r = 1,103$ gallons,

$$B(1,103) = 50L\left(\frac{1,103 - 1,000}{50}\right)$$

$$= 50L(2.05) = 50(.007418)$$

$$= .371 \text{ gallons}$$

Substituting this value and the other parameter values into the equation for Q^* on page 641 we obtain the improved EOQ value

$$Q^* = \sqrt{\frac{2(500,000)[100 + (.25 + 1.75 - 1.48)(.371)]}{.19(1.48)}} = 18,876$$

Because this result differs from the starting value of $Q = 18,858$, a second iteration is required.

Second Iteration   Returning to step 1, use $Q = 18,876$ to recompute the reorder point. First, we find

$$\frac{(p_S + p_R - c)A}{hcQ + (p_S + p_R - c)A} = \frac{(.25 + 1.75 - 1.48)500,000}{.19(1.48)18,876 + (.25 + 1.75 - 1.48)500,000}$$

$$= .9800$$

Because this ratio is unchanged, z remains the same. The subsequent r^* and Q^* will also not change.

The optimal policy is

$$r^* = 1,103 \text{ gallons}$$
$$Q^* = 18,876 \text{ gallons}$$

The adjusted annual demand is

$$A' = (1 - .371/18,876)500,000 = 499,990$$

and the total annual expected cost is

$$TEC = \left(\frac{499,990}{18,876}\right)100 + .19(1.48)\left[\frac{18,876}{2} + 1,103 - 1,000 + .371\right]$$

$$+ (.25 + 1.75 - 1.48)\left(\frac{499,990}{18,876}\right)(.371)$$

$$= 2,648.81 + 2,683.03 + 5.11$$

$$= 5,336.95 \text{ dollars}$$

Using a Spreadsheet

Figure 16-11 shows the spreadsheet for the unleaded gasoline example. It is derived from that for the backordering case by making slight modifications to incorporate lost sales. The optimal order quantity appears in cell F16, the optimal reorder point in cell F17, and the total expected cost in cell F19. (These differ slightly from before due to rounding.) This spreadsheet is on the CD-ROM that accompanies the text and can be used as a template to solve other multiperiod problems with a normal lead-time demand distribution and backordering. The development of the spreadsheet is shown in Appendix 16-1.

	A	B	C	D	E	F	G
1			MULTI-PERIOD EOQ MODEL (Lost Sales) - NORMAL LEAD-TIME DEMAND				
2							
3	PROBLEM:	Roger's Sentinel Station					
4							
5			Parameter Values:				
6				Mean of Demand Distribution: mu =			1,000
7				Stand. Deviation of Demand Distribution: sigma =			50
8				Fixed Cost per Order: k =			100
9				Annual Demand Rate: A =			500,000
10				Unit Cost of Procuring an Item: c =			1.48
11				Annual Holding Cost per Dollar Value: h =			0.19
12				Shortage Cost per Unit: pS =			0.25
13				Selling Price per Unit: pR =			1.75
14							
15			Optimal Values:				
16				Optimal Order Quantity: Q* =		18,876	
17				Optimal Reorder Point: r* =		1,103	
18				Expected Demand: mu =		1,000	
19				Total Expected Cost: TEC(Q*) =		5,336.87	
20				Expected Shortages: B(r*) =		0.37	
21				Probability of Shortage: P[D>r*] =		0.02	

FIGURE 16-11
Spreadsheet for Roger's Sentinel station example

16-6 ANALYTIC AND NUMERICAL SOLUTION METHODS

Methods for analyzing multiperiod inventory decisions can be quite complex. These methods may be divided into two categories. **Analytic methods** solve the model mathematically, giving precise answers that lead to truly optimal inventory policies. All of the procedures we have described thus far are analytic methods. Unfortunately, we have found that the problem situations to which a particular mathe-

matical model may be applied are severely limited. Often, the representation of the inventory system itself must be simplified or slightly changed to make an existing model fit the situation. This may lead to decidedly inferior solutions despite the mathematical perfection of the analytic method.

To avoid this pitfall, complex inventory systems are often evaluated by **numerical methods.** Strict optimization is not the goal of a numerical method; instead, a reasonably good inventory policy is sought. A numerical solution may be obtained essentially by a "trial-and-error" process or by making suitable approximations. Two types of numerical methods are primarily employed. One of these methods embodies **heuristic procedures** and might be called an "optimal-seeking" approach. Under such a policy, a starting solution is obtained and successively improved through minor modifications until further improvements are hard to make.

When uncertainty is present, **Monte Carlo simulation** is a very satisfactory numerical solution procedure. (Chapter 18 is devoted entirely to this topic.) Usually performed with the assistance of a digital computer, Monte Carlo simulation evaluates alternatives "on paper" through exhaustive trial-and-error operations. Various combinations of (r, Q) policies may be evaluated by applying each one to an inventory decision over a very long time frame of, say, 100 years. The (r, Q) policy that yields the minimum average cost is then chosen for actual use. Simulation may be used to tackle highly complex problems that are too intractable to solve realistically any other way.

APPENDIX 16-1 DEVELOPMENT OF THE INVENTORY MODEL SPREADSHEETS

Newsvendor Model

The optimal order quantity in Figure 16-3 appears in cell G13 and is computed from

$$=\text{INDEX(C21:C40,MATCH(LOOKUP((G8+G9-G6)} $$
$$/\text{(G8+G9+G7),E21:E40,C21:C40),C21:C40)+1)}$$

The LOOKUP function calculates the ratio of probabilities on the right-hand side of the formula for the optimal order quantity in Section 16-2, finds the row in which the cumulative probability is just larger than this ratio in column E21:E40, and then goes to column in C21:C40 and returns the number in the cell in the same row. The order quantity is the number in the cell just below the row. It is found using Excel's MATCH and INDEX functions. MATCH yields the position in column C21:C40 of the row found by LOOKUP, that is, 1, 2, 3, etc. Then the INDEX function determines the optimal order quantity as the value in the following position, that is, the number in C21:C40 one row below the row determined by LOOKUP.

The formula for the expected demand in cell G14 is the sum of the products of the demands and their respective probabilities

$$=\text{SUMPRODUCT(C21:C40,D21:D40)}$$

The total expected cost in cell G15 is computed from

$$=\text{G6*G14+(G7+G6)*(G13-G14+G16)+(G8+G9-G6)*G16}$$

The expected number of shortages $B(Q)$ is computed from the following in cell G16

$$=\text{SUMPRODUCT(D21:D40,F21:F40)}$$

This Excel function multiplies the probabilities in cells D21:D40 by the number of shortages in cells F21:F40.

The probability of a shortage in cell G17, $\Pr[D > Q^*]$, is found from

$$=1\text{-VLOOKUP(G13,C21:F40,3)}$$

which is the Excel formula for $1 - \Pr[D \le Q^*]$.

The cumulative probabilities in column E21:E40 are found by adding the probabilities in column D21:D40. Stopping at row 40 permits newsvendor problems with as many as 20 probability distribution demands to be solved. This is adequate for all problems in the text. It is a simple matter to solve larger problems by increasing the stopping point to a larger row number and adjusting the appropriate formulas in cells G13, G14, G16, and G17 to account for this.

The formula in cell E21 is

$$=\text{IF(ROW(C21)-20}\text{<=}\text{\$G\$10,D21,""))}$$

which transfers the probability from cell D21 to this cell. In cell E22 the formula is

$$=\text{IF(ROW(C22)-20}\text{<=}\text{\$G\$10,D22+E21,""))}$$

and this is copied down to the remaining cells E23:E40. The sum D22+E21 yields the cumulative probability. Consequently, this formula yields cumulative probabilities for the probability distribution of the problem (if ROW(C22)-20<=$G$10) and blanks for cells that exceed the number of demands for the probability distribution (""). The Excel ROW function used above gives the row number of a cell. For example, ROW(C22) = 22.

Column F21:F40 gives the number of shortages, zero if $Q \ge D$, or $D - Q$ if $Q < D$. In cell F21, the Excel formula for this is

$$=\text{IF(ROW(C21)-20}\text{<=}\text{\$G\$10,IF(\$G\$13}\text{>}\text{C21,0,C21-\$G\$13),""))}$$

and it is copied down to cells F22:F40.

Christmas Tree Model

Figure 16-6 is the first of two worksheets for the Christmas tree model. The other contains the normal loss function from Table C in the Appendix. The values in the table are in cells A2:B501 of the L(D) worksheet, indicated by the L(D) tab, and are not shown here, to save space. In Figure 16-6, the formula for the optimal order quantity, Q^*, in cell F14 comes from finding the value of Q that satisfies the conditions in Section 16-3. The Excel formula is

$$=\text{NORMINV((G10+G11-G8)/(G10+G11+G9),G6,G7)}$$

where the ratio (G10+G11-G8)/(G10+G11+G9) is the ratio on the right-hand side of the formula for the optimal order quantity at the beginning of Section 16-3, and the second and third arguments, G6 and G7, are the mean and standard deviations of the normal demand distribution.

The total expected cost is computed from the expression from Section 16-2 using the expected number of shortages $B(Q)$. The latter is calculated in cell F17

$$=\text{IF(F14}\text{<}\text{G6,G6-F14+G7*VLOOKUP((G6-F14)/G7,'L(D)'!A2:B501,2),}$$
$$\text{G7*VLOOKUP((F14-G6)/G7,'L(D)'!A2:B501,2))}$$

There are two cases: $Q \ge \mu$ and $Q < \mu$. The VLOOKUP functions find the appropriate values of the normal loss function table in cells A2:B501 on the worksheet indicated by the tab L(D) ('L(D)'!).

The total expected cost, *TEC(Q)* is determined in cell F16

$$=G8*F15+(G9+G8)*(F14-F15+F17)+(G10+G11-G8)*F17$$

The last calculation is for the probability of a shortage, P[*D* > *Q**]. The formula in cell F18 uses the Excel function for the normal distribution, NORMDIST

$$=1-NORMDIST(F14,G6,G7,TRUE)$$

where F14 is the value for which the probability is desired, G6 is the mean, G7 is the standard deviation, and the last argument, TRUE, indicates that the cumulative normal distribution is used.

Multiperiod Models with Backordering and Discrete Lead-Time Demand

The workbook for multiperiod models with backorders and discrete lead-time demand is based on the newsvendor spreadsheet in Figure 16-3. It varies in two respects. Some formulas are a little different, and it contains many worksheets because of the iterative nature of the multiperiod solution process. Figure 16-8 is one worksheet from this workbook.

The first worksheet (tab 1) is for the first iteration. Cell G14 contains the EOQ formula

$$=SQRT((2*G7*G6)/(G9*G8))$$

The reorder point *r* in cell G15 is found from the newsvendor optimal order quantity at the beginning of this appendix

$$=INDEX(C23:C42,MATCH(LOOKUP(1-((G9*G8*G14)/(G10*G7)),E23:E42,C23:C42),C23:C42,0)+1)$$

All of the remaining formulas except for one, the total expected cost, are identical with the newsvendor formulas except that all cell references are shifted down two cells. For example, C21:C40 in the newsvendor problem becomes C23:C42 for the multiperiod backordering model with discrete lead-time demand. This is true for the expected lead-time demand (cell G16), the expected shortage (cell G18), the probability of a shortage (cell G19), the cumulative probabilities (cells E23:E42), and the number of shortages (cells F23:F42). One exception occurs for cell G10 in the newsvendor problem, the number of demands for probability distribution. It is shifted down one cell for the multiperiod model, to cell G11.

Cell G17 calculates the total expected cost using the formula

$$=(G7/G14)*G6+G9*G8*(G14/2+G15-G16)+G10*(G7/G14)*G18$$

The worksheet for the second iteration (tab 2) is obtained by making a copy of the above worksheet. Click on Edit, select Move or Copy Sheet, click the Create a Copy box, click on (Move to End) in the Before sheet box, and click on the OK button. Name the tab 2 (for iteration 2) by double clicking on it. Only one formula changes in this worksheet; all the others remain the same as for the first iteration. In cell G14, the new formula for the order quantity is

$$=SQRT((2*G7*(G6+'1'!G18*G10))/(G9*G8))$$

where '1'!G18 is the value of the expected number of shortages from the first iteration (cell G18 from the worksheet indicated by tab 1 ('1'!).

Each following iteration is done in a similar manner. For example, the third iteration is copied from the second with '2'! replacing '1'! in the above formula so that the

third iteration is linked to the expected number of shortages found in the second iteration. Usually only a few iterations are needed to find the optimal solution. The workbook on the CD-ROM that accompanies this text does 10 iterations. It can be used as a template for solving other multiperiod problems with backordering and discrete lead-time demand and is sufficient for all problems in this book. Figure 16-8 results when the results do not change from one iteration to another.

As for the newsvendor problem, as many as 20 probability distribution demands are allowed. This is adequate for all problems in the text. It is a simple matter to solve larger problems by increasing the stopping point to a larger row number and adjusting the appropriate formulas in cells G15, G16, G18, and G19 to account for this.

In the workbook on the CD-ROM, data entered on the first worksheet (tab 1, or iteration 1) is linked to all the other worksheets (tabs or iterations), so all numbers need be entered only once. The linking causes blank cells from the first worksheet to carry over to subsequent iterations as zeros. To ensure that blank cells result in columns C and D on subsequent tabs whenever no data is entered in a corresponding cell (that is, a cell is blank), on the first worksheet a formula like

$$=IF('1'!C34="","",'1'!C34)$$

can be used. This ensures that a number or a blank entered in cell C34 on the first iteration carries over as the same number or a blank in cell C34 in subsequent worksheets or iterations.

Multiperiod Model with Lost Sales and Discrete Lead-Time Demand

The workbook for the lost sales case in Figure 16-9 is based on the backordering case in Figure 16-8. The formulas for the reorder point (cell G16) and total expected cost (cell G18) in Figure 16-9 are modified to take into account the lost sales, and the formulas in cells G17, G19, G20 and in the table in cells C24:F43 are shifted down one cell as described in the above section.

The formula for the reorder point in cell G16 is

$$=INDEX(C24:C43,MATCH(LOOKUP((G10+G11-G8)*G7/(G9*G8*G15+(G10+G11-G8)*G7),E24:E43,C24:C43),C24:C43,0)+1)$$

and the formula for the total expected cost in cell G18 is

$$((G7*(1-G19/G15))/G15)*G6+G9*G8*(G15/2+G16-G17+G19)+(G10+G11-G8)*(G7*(1-G19/G15)/G15)*G19$$

The final modification comes in the worksheet for the second iteration (tab 2) where the formula for the order quantity in cell G15 uses the expected number of shortages from the first iteration '1'!G19.

$$=SQRT((2*G7*(G6+'1'!G19*(G10+G11-G8))/(G9*G8)))$$

Multiperiod Model with Backordering and Normal Lead-Time Demand

The spreadsheet in Figure 16-10 is a variation of the Christmas tree model described in Section 16-3. In addition, it incorporates features from the multiperiod model with backordering and discrete lead-time demand in Figure 16-8, utilizing a normal rather than a discrete lead-time distribution. This causes the Excel formulas to change in the iterations that are necessary to find the solution. The formulas for the first iteration, with tab 1, are shown in Figure 16-12.

FIGURE 16-12

The Excel formulas for the multiperiod EOQ model with backordering and a normal lead-time demand

	F
15	=SQRT((2*G9*G8)/(G11*G10))
16	=NORMINV(1-((G11*G10*F15)/(G12*G9)),G6,G7)
17	=G6
18	=(G9/F15)*G8+G11*G10*(F15/2+F16-G6)+G12*(G9/F15)*F19
19	=IF(F16<F17,F17-F16+G7*VLOOKUP((F17-F16)/G7,'L(D)'!A2:B501,2),G7*VLOOKUP((F16-F17)/G7,'L(D)'!A2:B501,2))
20	=1-NORMDIST(F16,G6,G7,TRUE)

In the second and subsequent iterations, identified by tabs 2, 3, . . . , 10, only the formula for the order quantity in cell F15 must be modified to take into account the expected number of shortages from the prior iteration. For example, cell F15 on the second spreadsheet is

$$=\text{SQRT}((2*\text{G9}*(\text{G8}+\text{G12}*'1'!\text{F19}))/(\text{G11}*\text{G10}))$$

where '1'!F19 is the expected number of shortages from the first iteration.

Multiperiod Model with Lost Sales and Normal Lead-Time Demand

Figure 16-13 gives the formulas for the first iteration of the multiperiod model with lost sales and normal lead-time demand in Figure 16-11. They are analogous to those for the backordering case just above.

In the second and subsequent iterations, identified by tabs 2 and higher, only the formulas for the order quantity in cell F16 must be modified to take into account the expected number of shortages from the prior iteration. For example, cell F16 on the second spreadsheet is

$$=\text{SQRT}((2*\text{G9}*(\text{G8}+'1'!\text{F20}*(\text{G12}+\text{G13-G10}))/(\text{G11}*\text{G10})))$$

where '1'!F20 is the expected number of shortages from the first iteration.

FIGURE 16-13

The Excel formulas for the multiperiod EOQ model with lost sales and normal lead-time demand

	F
16	=SQRT((2*G9*G8)/(G11*G10))
17	=NORMINV((G12+G13-G10)*G9/(G11*G10*F16+(G12+G13-G10)*G9),G6,G7)
18	=G6
19	=(G9*(1-F20/F16))/F16*G8+G11*G10*(F16/2+F17-F18+F20)+(G12+G13-G10)*(G9*(1-F20/F16)/F16)*F20
20	=IF(F17<F18,F18-F17+G7*VLOOKUP((F18-F17)/G7,'L(D)'!A2:B501,2),G7*VLOOKUP((F17-F18)/G7,'L(D)'!A2:B501,2))
21	=1-NORMDIST(F17,G6,G7,TRUE)

PROBLEMS

16-1 Clark Kent's aunt sells *Daily Planets* from a stand for $.10 each. The following probability distribution for demand applies:

Copies	Probability
31	.05
32	.11
33	.18
34	.21
35	.17
36	.13
37	.10
38	.05

She pays $.05 for each paper. Unsold papers are thrown away at no further cost to Ms. Kent. How many copies should she stock in order to maximize her expected profit? Use marginal analysis.

16-2 The Green Thumb roadside fruit and vegetable stand must order its cherries from a nearby orchard before they are picked. The following probability distribution for seasonal cherry demand applies:

Possible Demand	Probability
$D = 100$ boxes	.15
$D = 150$	.20
$D = 200$	.30
$D = 250$	.20
$D = 300$	.15

Green Thumb buys its cherries for $2 a box and sells them for $3 a box. Unsold, overripe cherries are picked up for disposal by a hog farmer, who charges $.10 for each box. Green Thumb must determine how many boxes to order so that expected profit is maximized.
(a) Construct the payoff table.
(b) Determine which quantity of cherries should be ordered.

16-3 Refer to Problem 16-2.
(a) Construct the cumulative probability distribution for Green Thumb's cherry demand.
(b) Use the newsvendor problem approach to determine the optimal number of cherries to order to minimize total expected cost.

16-4 Personalized Printing Company must decide how many Christmas gift calendars should be made this season. All unsold calendars will be purchased by schools for $.10 each. Each calendar costs $.50 and ordinarily sells for $1. Loss of goodwill for shortages is $.05 per calendar. The following probability distribution for demand applies:

Demand	Probability
2,000	.05
3,000	.20
4,000	.25
5,000	.30
6,000	.20

(a) Compute the expected demand and determine the cumulative probabilities.
(b) How many calendars should be ordered?
(c) For the quantity in (b), determine (1) the expected shortage, (2) the expected surplus, and (3) total expected cost.
(d) For the quantity in (b), determine the probability that there will be a shortage.

16-5 The demand for Halloween pumpkins at the Black Cat's Patch is normally distributed with a mean of 1,000 and a standard deviation of 200. Each pumpkin costs $.50 and sells for $.90. Unsold pumpkins are disposed of at a cost of $.10 each.
(a) How many pumpkins should be ordered?
(b) For the quantity in (a), determine (1) the expected shortage, (2) the expected surplus, and (3) total expected cost.
(c) For the quantity in (a), determine the probability that there will be a shortage.

16-6 A newsvendor must decide how many copies of the *Berkeley Barb* he should leave in a sidewalk stand. Each paper sells for $.50 and costs him a quarter. Unsold papers are then converted into fireplace logs, giving them a nickel in value. The newsvendor believes that any quantity between 51 and 70 papers, inclusively, is equally likely to be demanded. There is no goodwill lost due to unfilled demands.
(a) How many *Berkeley Barbs* should be placed to minimize total expected daily cost?

(b) What is the total expected daily cost of the optimal inventory policy?

(c) What is the newsvendor's maximum expected daily profit from selling *Berkeley Barbs?*

16-7 A baker must decide how many dozen donuts to bake. Leftovers are ordinarily sold the next day, but she is closing her shop today to take a vacation. The following probability distribution for daily demand applies:

Dozen Donuts	Probability
5	.10
10	.15
15	.30
20	.20
25	.15
30	.10

Donuts cost $.50 per dozen to make, and they sell for $1 per dozen. Before closing the shop, the baker plans to throw away any unsold donuts.

(a) Compute the expected demand and determine the cumulative probabilities.

(b) How many donuts should be baked?

(c) For the quantity in (b), determine (1) the expected shortage, (2) the expected surplus, and (3) total expected cost.

(d) For the quantity in (b), determine the probability that there will be a shortage.

16-8 The captain of a tramp steamer picks up a load of cocoa beans whenever he travels to West Africa. He always sells them to a candymaker in Rotterdam for twice what he paid for them. The candymaker buys only what she needs, and the captain must dispose of any excess beans at less than cost to a cocoa dealer who also resides in Rotterdam. The present African price is 2 guilders per kilogram, and the Dutch cocoa dealer buys the beans for 1.50 guilders per kilogram. The following probability distribution for the candymaker's demand applies:

Demand	Probability
100 kg	.05
200	.12
300	.18
400	.25
500	.22
600	.09
700	.09

(a) How many kilograms of cocoa beans should the captain take on?

(b) For the quantity in (a), determine (1) the expected shortage, (2) the expected surplus, and (3) total expected cost.

16-9 Horatio Dull is a college professor who supplements his paltry salary each year by selling Christmas trees — a venture that has been immensely successful in the past. He must order his trees in October for delivery in early December. His net cost for each tree is $5, and the trees sell for an average of $15. On those occasions when there have been unsold trees, Horatio has managed to dispose of every excess tree on Christmas Eve for a price of $0.50. Having built up a loyal clientele, Dull values any goodwill lost for each tree short at $20. Demand for his trees has been established as approximately normally distributed, with a mean of $\mu = 5,000$ trees and a standard deviation of $\sigma = 1,000$.

(a) How many trees should Professor Dull order to minimize the total expected cost?

(b) For the quantity in (a), determine (1) the expected shortage, (2) the expected surplus, and (3) total expected cost.

16-10 The annual demand for Water Wheelies is 5,000. Due to uncertain deliveries and customer requirements, the following distribution for lead-time demand applies:

Items	Probability
20	.05
25	.10
30	.30
35	.25
40	.25
45	.05

(a) Determine the mean value and the cumulative probability distribution for lead-time demand.

(b) Each Water Wheelie costs $100 and the ordering charge is $500, regardless of the quantity ordered. Assuming an annual holding cost of $.20 and a goodwill loss of $5 per item short, determine the optimal reorder point and order quantity when backordering occurs.

16-11 The normal distribution is often used in inventory analysis as an *approximation* to the true de-

mand probability distribution. This may be done for the tramp steamer captain in Problem 16-8.

(a) Use the data from Problem 16-8 to compute the (1) expected demand and (2) standard deviation for demand.

(b) Using your results as μ and σ, assume that a normal distribution now applies for demand. Find the optimal order quantity and determine the total expected cost.

(c) Compare your answers from (b) to those found for Problem 16-8. Comment on the worthiness of using a normal distribution in similar problems and the amount of lost accuracy from making that approximation.

16-12 Miller's Mothballs are stocked by a pesticide supply house. The annual demand is 1,000 boxes. Due to uncertain deliveries and customer requirements, the following distribution for lead-time demand applies:

Boxes	Probability
11	.10
12	.25
13	.30
14	.20
15	.15

(a) Determine the mean value and the cumulative probability distribution for lead-time demand.

(b) Each box of mothballs costs $10, and the ordering charge is $10, regardless of the quantity ordered. Assume an annual holding cost of $.20 per dollar value and a goodwill loss of $1 per box short.

    (1) Determine the optimal reorder point and order quantity when backordering occurs.

    (2) What is the total expected cost?

16-13 Refer to Problem 16-10. Assume that no backordering is possible. Using the same parameters, and a $120 selling price, determine the optimal reorder point and order quantity.

16-14 Refer to Problem 16-12. Assume that no backordering is possible. Use the same parameters and a $13 selling price.

(a) Determine the optimal reorder point and order quantity.

(b) Compute the total annual expected cost.

16-15 Sylvester's Bootery caters to customers who cannot obtain the more specialized shoe sizes anywhere else. An optimal policy is sought for stocking size $8\frac{1}{2}$ EEE men's wingtip shoes, which cost Sylvester $20 a pair. The manufacturer charges a flat $10 for each size and style that is special ordered, regardless of quantity. When it is out of stock, all customers will back-order this shoe. But they will usually reheel and resole their present shoes while waiting, so Sylvester loses some amount of future profits, which he estimates to be $5 for each pair short. He finances his inventory with a bank loan at a 10% annual interest rate. The following distribution for lead-time demand applies.

Demand	Probability
5	.1
6	.2
7	.3
8	.2
9	.1
10	.1

Sylvester sells an average of 100 size $8\frac{1}{2}$ EEE pairs of wingtip shoes each year.

(a) Determine the mean lead-time demand.

(b) Determine the optimal reorder point and order quantity, assuming backordering.

(c) What is the safety stock level?

(d) Determine the expected annual inventory cost for this particular shoe.

16-16 The cost data given in Problem 16-15 apply for Sylvester's size 10 AA shoes, which are rarer. An average of only 50 pairs of these shoes are sold per year. The following distribution for lead-time demand applies:

Demand	Probability
8	.05
9	.13
10	.21
11	.36
12	.11
13	.07
14	.04
15	.03

Answer (a)–(d) in Problem 16-15 for this shoe.

16-17 Refer to the oil refinery illustration on pages 644–646. Suppose that the refinery experi-

ences identical costs for its leaded or regular gasoline, which has a mean annual demand of 100 million liters and a normally distributed lead-time demand of 500,000 liters with a standard deviation of 100,000 liters. Determine the optimal reorder point and order quantity.

16-18 Buster Black is contemplating a mail-order shoe business for super sizes. He will contract with a manufacturer in Italy to make shoes. For each size, the supplier charges Buster $500 per order as a set-up charge, plus $25 per pair (including shipping, taxes, and handling). Buster will receive $35 per pair after selling expenses. No backordering is possible and no goodwill is lost from shortages. Expected annual demand is 100 pairs of size 18D shoes per year. A 20% annual rate of return is assumed on Buster's invested capital. The following distribution for lead-time demand applies:

Demand	Probability
4	.08
5	.12
6	.21
7	.29
8	.19
9	.11
	1.00

(a) Determine the applicable inventory parameters and expected demand.
(b) Determine the optimal reorder point and order quantity.
(c) What is the safety stock level?

16-19 Refer to the BugOff Chemical illustration on pages 647–648. A related product is Caterpillar-Chiller, having an expected annual demand of 2,000 gallons and a direct manufacturing cost of $30 per gallon. The product is sold for $35, and lost goodwill costs $3 per gallon short. The same setup and holding costs apply. No backordering is allowed, and the lead-time demand is normally distributed with a mean of 60 gallons and a standard deviation of 12. Determine the optimal reorder point and order quantity.

16-20 Refer to Roger's Sentinel Station illustration on pages 649–651. Suppose that Roger has a mean annual demand of 100,000 gallons of leaded

regular gasoline. A separate tanking charge of $50 applies to this fuel, which costs Roger $.85 per gallon and yields him revenue of $1.07 per gallon. The lead-time demand is normally distributed with a mean of 500 gallons and a standard deviation of 100. Assume no appreciable loss of goodwill arising from shortages and that the same $.19 holding cost applies.
(a) Determine the optimal reorder point and order quantity.
(b) Compute the total annual expected cost.

16-21 A chemical manufacturer periodically formulates batches of SX-100. There is a setup cost of $500 for each production run, and the variable cost is $5 per gallon. Each dollar invested in inventory costs $.20 per year, and each backordered gallon represents a loss of $.25. Annual demand is for 100,000 gallons. Assume that the lead-time demand is normally distributed, with a mean of $\mu = 5,000$ gallons and a standard deviation of $\sigma = 1,000$ gallons. Determine the optimal reorder point and order (production) quantity.

16-22 The BugOff Chemical Company periodically formulates batches of Ant-Can't pesticide. There is a set-up cost of $1,000 for each production run, and the variable cost is $10 per pound. Each dollar invested in inventory costs $.25 per year, and each backordered pound of Ant-Can't represents a loss of $2.00. Annual demand is 500,000 pounds. Assume that the lead-time demand is normally distributed, with a mean of $\mu = 10,000$ pounds and standard deviation of $\sigma = 1,000$ pounds. Determine the optimal reorder point and order (production) quantity.

16-23 Refer to the Bug-a-Cider pesticide application on pages 647–648. The normal distribution may not strictly apply for lead-time demand. Suppose instead that a *uniform* distribution applies over the range $a = \mu - 3\sigma = 23$ to $b = \mu + 3\sigma = 77$. The expected demand μ is still 50, as in the original illustration. The reorder point (fractile for demand) corresponding to a particular ratio can be computed from

$$r = a + \text{ratio} \times (b - a)$$

The corresponding expected shortage can be computed from

$$B(r) = \frac{(b - r)^2}{2(b - a)}$$

(a) Find the optimal inventory policy and compute the total expected cost.

(b) Compare your answers to those given in the text when the normal distribution is assumed.
(c) Does the assumption of normality appear to be very critical to the original problem?

Spreadsheet Problems

16-24 (a) Refer to the *Daily Planets* decision in Problem 16-1. Using a payoff table evaluation, determine which quantity Clark Kent's aunt should stock.
(b) Solve for the optimal order quantity using the formula in Section 16-2.

16-25 (a) Refer to Green Thumb's cherry decision in Problem 16-2. Perform a decision tree analysis to determine which number of boxes will maximize expected payoff.
(b) Solve for the optimal order quantity using the formula in Section 16-2.

16-26 Solve Problem 16-8 using a spreadsheet following the format in Figure 16-3.

16-27 Solve Problem 16-5 for the optimal order quantity using a spreadsheet following the format in Figure 16-6.

16-28 Refer to Problem 16-6. Solve using a spreadsheet following the format in Figure 16-3.

16-29 Solve Problem 16-12 using a spreadsheet following the format in Figure 16-8.

16-30 Solve Problem 16-13 using a spreadsheet following the format in Figure 16-9.

16-31 Solve Problem 16-14 using a spreadsheet following the format in Figure 16-9.

16-32 Solve Problem 16-15 using a spreadsheet following the format in Figure 16-8.

16-33 Solve Problem 16-17 using a spreadsheet following the format in Figure 16-10.

16-34 Solve Problem 16-18 using a spreadsheet following the format in Figure 16-9.

16-35 Solve Problem 16-20 using a spreadsheet following the format in Figure 16-11.

16-36 Solve Problem 16-21 using a spreadsheet following the format in Figure 16-11.

16-37 Refer to the Personalized Printing decision in Problem 16-4. There is some loss in future business associated with current shortage, but an amount for that penalty is not known.

(a) Perform a sensitivity analysis to determine the economic order quantity and total expected cost, assuming that the shortage penalty is (1) \$.03, (2) \$.04, (3) \$.05, (4) \$.06, and (5) \$.07.
(b) Do you think that the optimal inventory policy is sensitive to the chosen level for the shortage penalty? Explain.

16-38 (a) and (b) Repeat Problem 16-10 using a spreadsheet program.
(c) Repeat (a) and (b) using a uniform demand distribution over the range 20 to 45.
(d) Find the expected value and standard deviation for demand using the original data. Then use those as parameters for a normally distributed demand. Repeat (a) and (b) using the new distribution.

16-39 Refer to the Black Cat's Patch decision in Problem 16-5. There is some loss in future business associated with current shortage, but an amount for that penalty is not known.
(a) Perform a sensitivity analysis to determine the economic order quantity and total expected cost, assuming that the shortage penalty is (1) \$.05, (2) \$.10, (3) \$.15, (4) \$.20, and (5) \$.25.
(b) Graph Q^* and $TEC(Q^*)$ versus p_S. Do you think that the optimal inventory policy is sensitive to the chosen level for the shortage penalty? Explain.

16-40 Refer to the SX-100 decision in Problem 16-21. There is some loss in future business associated with current shortage, but an amount for that penalty is not known.
(a) Perform a sensitivity analysis to determine the optimal inventory policy and total expected cost, assuming that the shortage penalty is (1) \$.15, (2) \$.20, (3) \$.25, (4) \$.30, and (5) \$.35. Graph Q^*, r^*, and $TEC(r^*, Q^*)$ versus p_S. Do you think that

the optimal inventory policy is sensitive to the chosen level for the shortage penalty? Explain.

(b) The holding cost is another assumed value. Keeping the shortage penalty at the original level, perform a sensitivity analysis to determine the optimal inventory policy and total expected cost, assuming that the annual holding cost is (1) $.18, (2) $.19, (3) $.20, (4) $.21, and (5) $.22. Graph Q^*, r^*, and $TEC(r^*, Q^*)$ versus h. Do you think that the optimal inventory policy is sensitive to the chosen level for the holding cost? Explain.

16-41 Refer to the Roger's Sentinel Station illustration on pages 649–651. Apply the backordering model with $p_S = .25 + 1.75 - 1.48 = .52$.

(a) Determine the optimal reorder point and order quantity.

(b) Compare your answers to the solution on page 650. What may you conclude regarding the use of the backordering model to approximate the lost-sales case?

16-42 Refer to the printer cartridge illustration on pages 636–638. Suppose that the shortage penalty p_S for the cartridges is unknown.

(a) Determine the optimal inventory policy when (1) $p_S = \$1.00$, (2) $p_S = \$2.00$, and (3) $p_S = \$3.00$.

(b) What may you conclude regarding the relationship between safety stock and p_S for this problem?

CASE 16-1 *Ingrid's Hallmark Shop II*

Ingrid's Hallmark Shop is a retail store specializing in "social expression" products, such as greeting cards, stationery, albums, and party goods. The social expression industry is noted for its seasonal volatility—an average December day outselling an average August day by 10 to 1.

Christmas merchandise must be ordered many months in advance. It is impossible to reorder most items once the selling season begins. Consider Ingrid's decision regarding how many angel ornaments to order. She believes that there is equally likely demand for any quantity between 16 and 25 items, inclusive. Her cost (including freight) is $5.50, and the ornaments retail for $10. Unsold angels will be disposed of during the half-off sale after Christmas.

Everyday merchandise never goes on sale, so there is less concern about over-ordering. Hallmark Cards has a systematic program, where certain items are reordered automatically. This is achieved when a store employee pulls a "ticket" that is sent to Hallmark. It then takes about two weeks for the requested merchandise to arrive. Tickets are to be pulled only when store stock for that item falls below the reorder point. The order quantities and reorder points have been established for retailers in various size categories. For example, a "Happy Birthday—Wife" counter card is assumed to have a lead-time demand in small stores of one card every two days—on the average—and total lead-time demand is equally likely to fall between 6 and 10 cards, inclusively.

Ingrid's son, Daniel, wants to establish order quantities and reorder points for both seasonal and everyday items.

QUESTIONS

1. Determine the optimal number of angels for Ingrid to order.

2. Why isn't Ingrid concerned with the reorder point for angels?

3. An average of 3 minutes of clerk time is spent in activities associated with pulling a ticket. Each clerk costs $5 per hour. Determine the optimal order quantity for the "Happy Birthday—Wife" counter card costing $.50 and selling for $1.00. You may assume the shortage penalty to be a minuscule $.05 per card, reflecting a high degree of product substitutability. Assume also that the annual holding cost is $.20 per dollar and that all lead-time demands from 5 to 10 are equally likely. Determine, also, the optimal reorder point, assuming lost sales for out-of-stock cards.

4. A typical Hallmark store has several hundred different counter cards. Lower-priced cards are shipped presealed in packets of 10 or 12. Dealers may arrange for shipments of 1, 2, or 3 packets per design. Suppose you were the store manager. Discuss how you might implement the policy determined in Question 3. Do you think any compromises would be necessary?

CASE 16-2 *Fantasia Greeting Cards II*

Fantasia Greeting Cards offers its dealers a line of figurines. These are either regular items or limited editions. Regular figurines are shipped as ordered. Limited editions are offered on an allocated basis to any dealer requesting them until the supply is exhausted. Fantasia orders both types of figurines from an Asian supplier. Although turnaround is 20 days for a Fantasia order of regular figurines, the limited editions are made just once and are long lead-time items for which Fantasia must establish lot quantities a year in advance, before dealer demand can be known. Limited edition molds are destroyed after production, so that Fantasia can never reorder those figurines.

All figurines retail for $20. The supplier charges a flat $5 per item, regardless of quantity. Fantasia sells them to dealers for $10, FOB (Free on Board) the distribution center. Unsold limited edition figurines will be rendered through a collectibles dealer who pays $2 each. Regular figurines are always backordered, with the shortage penalty not precisely known. The goodwill cost of running short of limited editions is also not known. For each dollar invested in inventory, Fantasia loses the opportunity to earn $.25 on an annual basis. It costs Fantasia $5,000 to set up production for each limited edition. The relevant cost for ordering regular items is only $200 for each figurine design.

Freddy Phail is in charge of placing Fantasia figurine orders and wants to establish inventory policies that will always minimize total expected cost.

Freddy uses as his mean lead-time demand that fraction of annual demand that occurs during the time for an order to turn around. His experience shows that during about 95% of those times total dealer demand fell within ±20% of the mean lead-time demand. This means a standard deviation in lead-time demand that equals 10% of the mean level. A normal distribution is assumed.

QUESTIONS

1. Demand for a limited edition bisque clown is judged to be normally distributed with mean 10,000 and standard deviation 2,000. The cost of lost goodwill for each clown short is judged to be $25. How many clowns should Fantasia order?

2. Fantasia sells about 100,000 porcelain cocker spaniels every year. The shortage penalty is judged to be $2 per item. What is the optimal inventory policy and total annual expected inventory cost for these items?

3. The GreenWall Drugstore chain has a special bunny sold only to stores in that chain in unlimited quantities, just like other regular Fantasia items. The bunny demand is 200,000 per year. Unlike other Fantasia items, GreenWall stores do not backorder those bunnies, for which there is not a special shortage penalty; sales are instead lost for GreenWall bunny orders that occur during a stockout. Find Fantasia's optimal inventory policy for GreenWall bunnies.

4. GreenWall wants Fantasia to supply a limited edition 50th anniversary piece to its stores exclusively. GreenWall does not know how many units its stores will order altogether. Freddy judges the following demands to be equally likely: 5,000, 6,000, 7,000, and 8,000. The goodwill cost for each piece short is judged to be $10. How many pieces should Fantasia order?

5. Fantasia is experimenting with the limited edition peace dove. A second production run for that item will be made if unfilled customer orders from the first run exceed 2,000. The first run demand is assumed to be normally distributed with mean 15,000 and standard deviation 2,500, shortages of which will bring a penalty of only $5 per item.
   (a) Determine the optimal number of first run peace doves Fantasia should order.
   (b) Using your answer to (a), what is the probability that there will be a second run?
   (c) Comment on the long-run effect of having second runs for limited editions.

PART VI

SIMULATION AND WAITING LINES

If mathematical analysis is too difficult, we can try out each possibility on paper. That way we can find which alternative appears to work best over a series of hypothetical futures.

W aiting line (queuing) evaluations are key quantitative methods. They employ mathematical models that allow us to quickly determine how many servers are needed to achieve an optimal balance between the costs of providing service and the costs arising from customers having to wait. But Chapter 17 tells us why the assumptions built into those common queuing models, deceptively simple to apply, can lead to results that are drastically wrong. Improperly applied textbook formulas can lead to ludicrous results, such as gross overstaffing or, worse, overbuilt service facilities. It is the promise of huge benefits and the threat of terrible blunders that make the study of queuing models so important.

Chapter 18 differs from the preceding portions of the book. It describes a problem-solving approach that does not utilize a general model that may or may not closely fit the current problem circumstances. Rather, the simulation approach is presented as an alternative. In place of mathematics, simulation substitutes number crunching designed specifically to duplicate reality in ways essential for making comparisons and reaching a final decision.

CHAPTER 17

WAITING LINES (QUEUES)

Standing in line—at the bank, the market, the movies—is the time-waster everyone loves to hate. Stand in just one 15-minute line a day, every day, and kiss goodbye to almost four days of idle time by year's end.

Kathleen Doheny

Quantitative methods have been successfully applied to waiting-line situations. Although it may seem that no one cares how long you have to wait in line to cash a check or to buy groceries, most businesses pay a great deal of attention to customer waiting times. Many large retail establishments have actually been designed to achieve an optimal balance between customer inconvenience and operational efficiency. This explains why a supermarket may have ten checkout counters, even though only two or three are in operation most of the time; during the Saturday afternoon rush hours, all of these counters may be open. Retailers do not dare to make their customers wait in line for long, because people value their time highly and would rather switch to a competing store than wait for service.

In management science or operations research, a waiting line is called a **queue.** As a field of study, **queuing theory** is one of the richest areas of operations research methodology. The number of models representing specific situations has grown steadily over the years, and new ones are being reported even now. Queuing theory is one of the earliest quantitative methods. Its origins were published in a 1909 paper by a Danish telephone engineer, A. K. Erlang, whose name is associated with a large class of probability distributions used in conjunction with mathematical queuing models. Since then, thousands of articles and numerous books have been written on the subject.

The usual objective of a queuing model is to determine how to provide service to customers in such a way that an efficient operation is achieved. Unlike the inventory or linear programming models encountered earlier in this book, a minimum-cost or a maximum-profit solution is not always sought. Rather, the aim of these models is to determine various characteristics of the queuing system, such as the mean waiting time and the mean length of the waiting line. These mean values may then be used in a later cost analysis. Or a targeted level of satisfactory customer service is established, and facilities and operations are planned to meet this goal.

To the uninitiated, it may seem that any waiting line is a sign of inefficiency and that good management should eliminate the nuisance of waiting entirely. This viewpoint probably results from the fact that we are all somebody's customers, but relatively few of us operate public establishments. If we reflect on this problem, we see that elimi-

nating waiting lines entirely would be prohibitively costly for banks, stores, or gas stations. The main reason we have to wait in line at the bank is that customers arrive unpredictably (sometimes creating congestion) and seek a variety of services, each requiring a varying amount of a teller's time. Several times the usual number of tellers may be required to completely eliminate waiting lines, and many tellers would then be idle almost all the time. No bank has fewer tellers than are needed to service its customers within a reasonable time span, and these employees still spend many idle minutes. We rarely remember the days when we did not have to wait in a line at all!

Million Bank

DECISION PROBLEM

Neena Pangal manages the Commercial Branch of Million Bank. She is concerned about the long lines on Friday afternoons between 4 and 6 P.M. More tellers would solve the problem. Neena asks Sylvia Smith to look into this situation and to recommend the best number to have on duty during the Friday rush.

After Sylvia watches the lines that Friday afternoon to get an idea about the severity of the problem, she decides to gather data for use with a multiple-server queuing model. She finds that an average of 500 customers seek service during the 2-hour Friday rush. Although individual service times will vary, she finds that they may be crudely approximated by an exponential distribution with a mean service time of 2 minutes per customer. The accounting department advises Sylvia that the hourly cost of tellers is $12.

Of course, customers hate to wait. Every once in a while a frustrated customer closes his accounts and moves to another bank, complaining about the lines at Million. Such a breaking point is believed to be reached after a cumulative amount of waiting has been reached, and only an average effect can be accommodated in a queuing analysis. Neena judges that each minute a customer spends in line (waiting time only) costs Million an average of $.10 in the present value of future profits in eventual loss of business.

How many tellers should Million have on station so that average hourly cost is minimized?

Sylvia goes over the data with her manager and presents a plan to use a multiple-server queuing model. Although Neena likes the plan, there is concern about the numbers gathered. The $12 hourly teller cost is affected by three factors: (1) the possible use of part-time employees costing only $10 per hour; (2) a potential general salary increase, which would raise teller cost by 10 or 20%; and (3) the possibility of using more-expensive managerial employees, costing $24 or $36 per hour, as fill-in tellers during rush periods. Neena is also bothered by the average customer arrival rate and the mean teller service time data, which can vary from week to week. She would like to know how such variations would affect Sylvia's results.

The material presented in this chapter will illustrate how to apply a queuing model to find the best number of tellers for the bank to use. In addition, the chapter will show how to analyze uncertainty in data and determine its significance and its effect on results.

17-1 | BASIC QUEUING SITUATIONS

All queuing situations involve customer arrivals at a **service facility,** where some time may be spent waiting for and then receiving the desired service. We usually think of customers as people, but customers may also be objects, such as cars being repaired in a garage, unfinished items proceeding to the next stage of production, aircraft waiting to land, or jobs being processed on a computer. A service facility may be a single person, such as a barber or a hairdresser, or several persons, such as a surgical team. A server may also be a machine that dispenses candy bars, stamps parts, or processes data, or a complex entity such as an airport runway or an oil refinery port facility.

Structures of Queuing Systems

The simplest queuing system involves a single-service facility that handles one customer at a time, so that any customer arriving while an earlier customer is being serviced must wait in line. Such a system is represented schematically in Figure 17-1. In this **single-server single-stage queue,** all the required services are performed before each customer leaves. The waiting line itself is not necessarily a physical string of customers, like the line that forms at a theater ticket window. The waiting line may simply be some identifiable grouping of customers whose sequence of service may or may not be designated (perhaps by a number, as is often the case in a retail store where physical lines are inconvenient). The customers do not even have to comingle physically. For example, several inquiries (customers) may stack up in a central computer system, even though they have been processed by remote terminals scattered across a huge geographical expanse, or planes attempting to land at New York's Kennedy Airport may be spread over tens of thousands of square miles of air space.

Somewhat more complicated is the queuing system depicted in Figure 17-2, which is a **multiple-server single-stage queue** with several service facilities. In the simplest case, each facility provides identical service, a single waiting line forms, and the leading customer proceeds to the first free server. Many banks employ such a system, where a single line feeds customers to the teller windows. Slightly different characteristics apply when arriving customers must select one server and wait in separate server lines, as is still the case when checking out of a large self-service market.

Queue Disciplines

An important aspect of any queuing situation is the *order* in which customers receive service. We refer to the manner of customer sequencing as the **queue discipline.** The mathematical models developed for essentially the same queuing structure may differ, depending on the discipline that applies.

The most common queue discipline is a physical **FIFO** (*first in, first out*) discipline, where customers receive service in the order of their arrival. Retail establishments

---

FIGURE 17-1
Schematic of a single-server single-stage queue

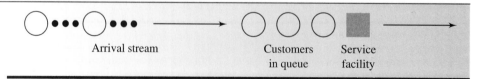

Arrival stream　　　　　Customers in queue　　Service facility

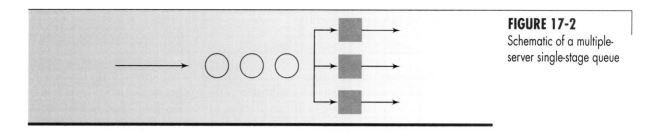

FIGURE 17-2
Schematic of a multiple-server single-stage queue

and public service agencies usually employ this system. Indeed, FIFO has become almost a basic human right—like freedom of speech. In our generally calm modern society, few actions evoke as strong emotions as line cutting.* Many successful establishments rigidly enforce FIFO by issuing numbers to arriving customers. FIFO applies to all of the queuing models discussed in this chapter.

Arrival and Service Patterns

Arrival and service patterns are very important aspects of waiting-line situations. Customers typically arrive at the queuing system randomly. Various probability distributions may be used to represent the time between arrivals; the most common of these is the **exponential distribution,** described in Chapter 4. Service time also usually varies (although it may be *constant*), and a variety of probability distributions may be used to characterize service patterns as well. Queuing models may differ considerably for various combinations of arrival and service patterns.

17-2 | THE SINGLE-SERVER QUEUING MODEL WITH EXPONENTIAL SERVICE TIMES

Basic queuing models are concerned with the state of the system. Under various assumptions regarding the queue discipline and service, a probability distribution may be obtained for the number of customers in the system (either waiting or receiving service) at any future point in time. This probability information may then be used to derive certain useful results mathematically, such as the amount of time that a customer may expect to wait in line.

Our initial model represents the single-server single-stage queuing system. We assume "first come, first served," so that the FIFO discipline applies. Arrivals are assumed to be a Poisson process, so that the arrivals are events that occur randomly over time and meet the other necessary conditions of that process. Thus, the interarrival times have an exponential distribution, and the number of customers arriving in any specified time interval has a Poisson distribution. Arrivals are assumed to occur at a **mean arrival rate** λ. Due to the resulting mathematical convenience, our basic model further assumes that *the service times are exponentially distributed.* The **mean service rate** (customers per minute, second, or hour) is represented by μ (lowercase Greek mu). It follows that the mean service time is $1/\mu$. Moreover, we assume that *the mean service rate must exceed the mean arrival rate,* or $\mu > \lambda$, so that the queuing system must have more than enough capacity to service all customers. (Without this last restriction, a queuing system would be unstable and the waiting line would grow indefinitely.)

---

*Prior to Christmas 1973, a man was killed in an altercation that resulted when a family crowded into a line of people waiting to see Santa Claus.

Some Important Queuing Results

The queuing model provides the following important results:

1. **The probability distribution for the number of customers in the system P_n**
   This distribution is the basis for establishing all the other results listed here. It may also be useful in designing facilities that can physically hold waiting customers.

2. **The mean number of customers in the system L**   This quantity accounts for the number of customers either waiting in line or receiving service. It is useful primarily as an intermediate device for finding the mean customer time spent in the system.

3. **The mean customer time spent in the system W**   This is an average amount representing the total time spent by a customer in the system. When a cost may be associated with each unit of a customer's time, it may be used to make economic comparisons of alternative queuing systems.

4. **Mean number of customers waiting (length of line) L_q**   This quantity is similar to the mean number of customers in the system, but only involves the customers who are actually waiting in line and not being serviced. Knowing the average number of customers waiting in line can help to establish the size of holding facilities such as hospital waiting rooms and is used in an intermediate step to establish the mean customer waiting time.

5. **The mean customer waiting time W_q**   This is an average value that may be used to evaluate the quality of service. Like the mean customer time spent in the system, this quantity may sometimes be used in economic analysis, but it is unsatisfactory for this purpose if alternative queuing systems involve different service-time distributions.

6. **The server utilization factor ρ (Greek rho)**   This is the proportion of time that the server actually spends with customers—the time during which the server is busy. It provides an estimate of the expected amount of server idle time that may be devoted to secondary tasks not directly involved with service.

Although a discussion of them is beyond the scope of this book, other important results, such as complete probability distributions for a customer's waiting time and the duration of the server's busy period, may be obtained from queuing models.

Basic Queuing Formulas

Although many of the mathematical details are beyond the scope of this book, algebraic expressions have been derived for all of the results provided by the present queuing model. We express all results in terms of two parameters.

$$\lambda = \text{Mean customer arrival rate}$$
$$\mu = \text{Mean service rate}$$

We will begin with the probability distribution for the number of customers in the system. This distribution may be found by considering each possible number of customers either waiting or receiving service as a distinct *state* that may be entered by the arrival of a new customer or left by the completion of the leading customer's service. The schematic representation in Figure 17-3 will help to explain this process. Consider

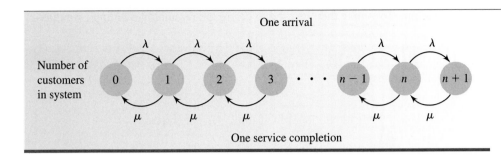

FIGURE 17-3

Schematic of single-server queuing system states

a barbershop with a single barber. There are two ways in which there may be exactly one customer in the shop. There may be no customers in the shop and then one arrives; or there may be two customers in the shop and the first customer's service is completed. These two cases are represented by the two arrows pointing to 1 in Figure 17-3—one at the top leaving 0 and one at the bottom leaving 2. Likewise, the barbershop can leave the one-customer state either by the arrival of a new customer or by finishing with the present one. Again, these possibilities are shown as two arrows leaving 1—the top one pointing to 2 and the bottom one to 0. This same feature is exhibited for any number of customers n in the system. Beside each arrow, the mean rate is indicated for the possible change in state—λ for an arrival and μ for a departure.

$$P_n = \Pr[n \text{ customers in system}]$$

Under the assumption of exponentially distributed arrival and service times, the probability for leaving a state must be equal to the probability of entering that state, and, in short time intervals, movement is possible only between neighboring states (two to three customers, five to four, six to seven, and so on). There are two ways to enter and two ways to leave any state except zero, depending on the preceding number of customers and on whether a departure or an arrival occurs first. The probability for one movement (arrival or service completion) is approximately the product of the corresponding rate (λ or μ) with the duration of time considered between changes. These facts lead to the following *balance equations:*

$$\lambda P_0 = \mu P_1$$
$$\lambda P_1 + \mu P_1 = \lambda P_0 + \mu P_2$$
$$\lambda P_2 + \mu P_2 = \lambda P_1 + \mu P_3$$

A solution of the balance equations provides the

QUEUING SYSTEM STATE PROBABILITIES

(Basic Model)

$$P_0 = 1 - \frac{\lambda}{\mu}$$

$$P_n = \left(\frac{\lambda}{\mu}\right)^n P_0$$

$$n = 1, 2, 3, \dots$$

These expressions may then be used to derive the remaining queuing formulas.

QUEUING FORMULAS

(Basic Model)

Mean Number of Customers in the System

$$L = \frac{\lambda}{\mu - \lambda}$$

Mean Customer Time Spent in the System

$$W = \frac{L}{\lambda} = \frac{1}{\mu - \lambda}$$

Mean Number of Customers Waiting (length of line)

$$L_q = \frac{\lambda^2}{\mu(\mu - \lambda)}$$

Mean Customer Waiting Time

$$W_q = \frac{L_q}{\lambda} = \frac{\lambda}{\mu(\mu - \lambda)}$$

Server Utilization Factor

$$\rho = \frac{\lambda}{\mu}$$

Shorthand symbols sometimes are used to designate queuing models. The designation *M/M/*1 represents a single-server queuing model (the number 1) with exponential distributions for interarrival time (the first M) and service time (the second M).

A Supply Room Example

Consider the queuing system involved in the operation of a central supply room for a large office. Employees pick up needed supplies there, just like customers who make purchases at a stationery store. An average of 25 employee customers withdraw supplies during each hour of normal operation. A full-time clerk is required to check persons out of central supply, primarily to ensure proper accounting control of requisitioned items. Each requisition takes an average of 2 minutes, so the clerk may check out 30 customers per hour. We will assume that the pattern of arrivals at the checkout counter is a close approximation to a Poisson process and that the checkout times are exponentially distributed. Thus,

$$\lambda = 25 \text{ customers per hour}$$
$$\mu = 30 \text{ customers per hour}$$

The mean number of customers either waiting in line or being checked out is

$$L = \frac{\lambda}{\mu - \lambda} = \frac{25}{30 - 25} = 5 \text{ customers}$$

and the mean time spent by customers in the system is

$$W = \frac{1}{\mu - \lambda} = \frac{1}{30 - 25} = \frac{1}{5} \text{ hour}$$

or 12 minutes, which could also have been calculated $W = L/\lambda = 5/25 = 1/5$.
   The mean number of customers in the waiting line (or its length) is

$$L_q = \frac{\lambda^2}{\mu(\mu - \lambda)} = \frac{(25)^2}{30(30 - 25)} = \frac{25}{6} = 4\frac{1}{6} \text{ customers}$$

and the mean customer waiting time is

$$W_q = \frac{\lambda}{\mu(\mu - \lambda)} = \frac{25}{30(30 - 25)} = \frac{1}{6} \text{ hour}$$

or 10 minutes, which could also have been calculated $W_q = L_q/\lambda = (25/6) \div 25 = 1/6$.
   The server utilization factor is

$$\rho = \frac{\lambda}{\mu} = \frac{25}{30} = \frac{5}{6}$$

so that the supply room clerk is busy five-sixths of the time.

Finding the System State Probabilities

The system state probabilities are computed for the supply room using the expressions given earlier.

$$P_0 = 1 - \frac{\lambda}{\mu} = 1 - \frac{25}{30} \qquad\qquad = .1667$$

$$P_1 = \left(\frac{\lambda}{\mu}\right)^1 P_0 = \left(\frac{25}{30}\right)(.1667) = .1389$$

$$P_2 = \left(\frac{\lambda}{\mu}\right)^2 P_0 = \left(\frac{25}{30}\right)^2 (.1667) = .1158$$

The basic queuing model has no theoretical limit to the number of customers that might be in the supply room, so that these calculations might be made for any level of n, such as 10, 50, or 100.
   Although these calculations are easy to make by hand, they can be done faster and with greater accuracy with computer assistance.

Using Spreadsheets for Single-Server Models

A spreadsheet for the supply room example is shown in Figure 17-4. The shown formulas indicate that this spreadsheet can be used as a template for solving other single-server queuing models. (It is stored on the CD-ROM accompanying the book.)

FIGURE 17-4

Spreadsheet (M/M/1) for
the supply room example

FIGURE 17-4

Spreadsheet (M/M/1) for the supply room example

	A	B	C	D	E	F	G	H	I	J
1				BASIC QUEUING SYSTEM EVALUATION -- SINGLE SERVER						
2										
3	PROBLEM: Supply Room									
4										
5			Parameter Values:							
6			Mean Customer Arrival Rate: lambda =				25			
7			Mean Customer Service Rate: mu =				30			
8										
9			Queuing Results:							
10			Mean Number of Customers in System: L =				5			
11			Mean Customer Time Spent in System: W =				0.2			
12			Mean Number of Customers Waiting							
13					(Length of Line): L_q =		4.166667			
14			Mean Customer Waiting Time: W_q =				0.166667			
15			Server Utilization Factor: rho =				0.833333			
16										
17			Number in	Probability	Cumulative					
18			System n	P_n	Probability					
19			0	0.1667	0.1667					
20			1	0.1389	0.3056					
21			2	0.1157	0.4213					
22			3	0.0965	0.5177					
23			4	0.0804	0.5981					
24			5	0.0670	0.6651					
25			6	0.0558	0.7209					
44			25	0.0017	0.9913					
45			26	0.0015	0.9927					
46			27	0.0012	0.9939					
47			28	0.0010	0.9949					
48			29	0.0008	0.9958					
71			52	0.0000	0.9999					
72			53	0.0000	0.9999					
73			54	0.0000	1.0000					

Inset (column G formulas):

	G
10	=G6/(G7-G6)
11	=1/(G7-G6)
12	
13	=G6^2/(G7*(G7-G6))
14	=G6/(G7*(G7-G6))
15	=G6/G7

Inset (columns D and E formulas):

	D	E
19	=1-G15	=D19
20	=$D$19*$G$15^C20	=E19+D20
21	=$D$19*$G$15^C21	=E20+D21
22	=$D$19*$G$15^C22	=E21+D22
23	=$D$19*$G$15^C23	=E22+D23
24	=$D$19*$G$15^C24	=E23+D24
25	=$D$19*$G$15^C25	=E24+D25
44	=$D$19*$G$15^C44	=E43+D44
45	=$D$19*$G$15^C45	=E44+D45
46	=$D$19*$G$15^C46	=E45+D46
47	=$D$19*$G$15^C47	=E46+D47
48	=$D$19*$G$15^C48	=E47+D48
71	=$D$19*$G$15^C71	=E70+D71
72	=$D$19*$G$15^C72	=E71+D72
73	=$D$19*$G$15^C73	=E72+D73

The Excel formula for cell G10 is

$$=G6/(G7-G6)$$

representing the number of customers in the system, L. The Excel formula in cell G11 is

$$=1/(G7-G6)$$

for the mean customer time spent in the system, W. The formulas in cells G13 and G14 are

$$=G6^2/(G7*(G7-G6)) \quad \text{and} \quad =G6/(G7*(G7-G6))$$

representing the mean number of customers waiting (the length of the line), L_q, and the mean customer waiting time, W_q, respectively. The formula in cell G15 is =G6/G7 for the server utilization factor.

Cell D19 contains the Excel formula =1-G15 to represent $P_0 = 1 - \lambda/\mu$. Cell D20 gives the probability P_1 using the Excel formula

$$=\$D\$19*\$G\$15^C20$$

Copying this cell down to cells D21:D73 gives all the probabilities, P_n, for $n = 1$, $2, \ldots, 54$. (Dollar signs [$] appear in the first two terms of this formula to make the cell references absolute.)

Note that the number in the system jumps from $n = 6$ to 25 (cells C25 and C44) and from $n = 29$ to 52 (cells C48 and C71). (Rows for $n = 7$ to 24 and 30 to 51 have

been suppressed for printing purposes. That is done by highlighting the rows to be suppressed, clicking on Format, selecting Row [or Column] and then selecting Hide. Unhide makes the rows [or columns] appear again. More details on suppressing rows or columns are given in the *Guide to Excel* found on the CD-ROM accompanying the text.)

A Queuing System Cost Analysis

These results may be used to determine the average daily cost of the waiting-line situation. Suppose that the cost of the supply room clerk's labor is $5 per hour, whereas the unproductive time of employee customers is valued at an average hourly payroll figure of $7. Each customer spends an average of $W = 1/5$ hour getting supplies and then checking out of the supply room, so that the average queuing cost per customer is

$$\$7 \times 1/5 = \$1.40$$

During any hour, an average of 25 customers request supplies, so the average hourly queuing cost is

$$\$1.40 \times 25 = \$35$$

The average total hourly cost of checking out of the supply room is therefore

$$\$35 \text{ (queuing cost)} + \$5 \text{ (clerk's cost)} = \$40$$

This amount does not include the time that each employee spends selecting supplies off the shelves—time that is independent of the queuing system itself, which encompasses only the checkout process.

Management should consider this hourly cost figure highly excessive, especially because the average cost of the labor lost checking out of the supply room is seven times as great as the cost of the clerk. Two remedies are possible. The checkout process itself could be speeded up by hiring a faster clerk, by making the customers do some of the bookkeeping, or by partially automating the system. Or one or more extra clerks could be hired to assist the first clerk. The latter alternative would involve a *multiple-server queue,* which will be described later in the chapter.

Now, we will consider a partially automated system that enables the clerk to double his service rate, so that $\mu = 60$ customers per hour. The mean customer time spent in the system then becomes

$$W = \frac{1}{\mu - \lambda} = \frac{1}{60 - 25} = \frac{1}{35} \text{ hour, or 1.7 minutes}$$

The faster service considerably reduces the average hourly cost of the labor lost in checking out to

$$25 \times \$7 \times 1/35 = \$5$$

Suppose that the special equipment and handling required for automation costs $6.25 per hour in addition to the clerk's wages. The average total hourly cost would then be

$$\$5 \text{ (queuing cost)} + \$6.25 \text{ (equipment cost)} + \$5 \text{ (clerk's cost)} = \$16.25$$

Partial automation would yield an average savings of $40 - \$16.25 = \$23.75$ per hour over manual operation with one clerk.

17-3 INTERPRETING QUEUING FORMULAS AND ALTERNATIVE EXPRESSIONS

An interpretation of the basic queuing formulas may prove helpful at this point. We might view λ as a measurement of the "demand" for service and μ as an expression of the "capacity" of the service facility. The difference $\mu - \lambda$ then represents the "excess capacity" of the system to fill demand. Thus, the mean number of customers in the system is the ratio of demand to excess capacity, or

$$L = \frac{\text{Demand}}{\text{Excess capacity}} = \frac{\lambda}{\mu - \lambda}$$

When excess capacity is small in relation to demand, congestion is heavy and a large number of customers can be expected in the system. In the supply room operated manually by one clerk, demand is $\lambda = 25$ customers per hour, which is five times the excess capacity of $\mu - \lambda = 5$ customers per hour, so that $L = 5$ customers.

The mean customer time spent in the system may be determined by multiplying the mean time between customer arrivals $1/\lambda$ and the mean number of customers L, or

$$W = \left(\frac{1}{\lambda}\right) L = \frac{L}{\lambda}$$

When the supply room is operated manually with one clerk, we find an average of 5 customers in the system, who arrive once every $1/\lambda = 1/25$ hour. Each customer may therefore expect to spend $1/25 \times 5 = 1/5$ hour checking out of the supply room. (It may seem perplexing that to obtain W from L, we multiply by the mean time between arrivals $1/\lambda$ instead of the mean service time $1/\mu$. But remember that $L = 5$ is only a mean figure—not the actual number in the system, which at any given time may be more or less than 5. If it is known in advance that exactly 5 customers are in the system, then the fifth customer would indeed expect to spend $(1/\mu)(5) = (1/30)(5) = 1/6$ hour being checked out. But that result is not W, which applies only when the number of customers is unspecified.)

A customer's mean waiting time is simply the difference between the mean time that customer spends in the system and the mean service time for that customer, or

$$W_q = W - \frac{1}{\mu}$$

This is algebraically equivalent to $\lambda/[\mu(\mu - \lambda)]$. The mean customer waiting time is also equal to the product of the mean time between arrivals and the mean number of customers in the waiting line, or

$$W_q = \left(\frac{1}{\lambda}\right) L_q = \frac{L_q}{\lambda}$$

Multiplying both sides of this equation by λ, we obtain the expression for the mean number of customers in the waiting line.

$$L_q = \lambda W_q$$

We see that all of the queuing results may be obtained by beginning with L, which we may view as the ratio of "demand" (λ) to "excess capacity" ($\mu - \lambda$). We could start

with W, L_q, or W_q instead and obtain the other results without memorizing all four basic formulas. And, some of the relationships described here apply to other queuing situations, where one result may be easier to obtain directly than the others. Alternative expressions for the queuing results using the server utilization factor are described below.

It is easy to see that when the checkout clerk operates the supply room manually, he will only be busy an average of 5 minutes out of every 6. In an eight-hour day, the clerk will check out $8 \times 25 = 200$ customers. This will take an average of 2 minutes (1/30 hour), so that a total of 400 minutes will be spent checking out customers. Each working day comprises $60 \times 8 = 480$ minutes. The proportion of busy minutes is therefore 400/480 = 5/6.

The expression for W_q may be obtained from the expression for W by multiplying by the server utilization factor ($\rho = \lambda/\mu$), so that

$$W_q = \left(\frac{\lambda}{\mu}\right)W$$

This same fact applies to L_q and to L, so that

$$L_q = \left(\frac{\lambda}{\mu}\right)L$$

Thus, we see why the values of L_q and W_q, which do not consider that customer receiving service, are both smaller than L and W, which do. Because the clerk is only busy $\lambda/\mu = 5/6$ of the time under manual operation, L_q and W_q are only five-sixths as large as L and W. The expression for L_q may also be arrived at by subtracting the server utilization factor from the mean number of customers in the system.

$$L_q = L - \frac{\lambda}{\mu}$$

This is algebraically equivalent to $\lambda^2/[\mu(\mu - \lambda)]$. One rationale for this result is that L_q does not include the one customer who may be receiving service. Because the server is only busy λ/μ of the time, then on the average, we expect that fraction of a customer to be receiving service at any time. Thus, the fraction λ/μ of a customer must be subtracted to provide the expected number of customers who are waiting only.

17-4 THE MULTIPLE-SERVER QUEUING MODEL

We now extend the basic queuing model for a one-service facility to the case of several facilities. We will assume that each facility is identical in all respects and that each is capable of performing service at the rate of μ customers per unit of time. As before, the pattern of arrivals is assumed to be a Poisson process and the service times are presumed to be exponentially distributed. The queuing formulas given here are based on the FIFO discipline, and we will assume that the customer at the head of the line proceeds to the first free server.

The shorthand symbol for the multiple-server queuing model is *M/M/S*. The two letters *M* stand for the exponential interarrival and service times, and the letter *S* represents the number of servers.

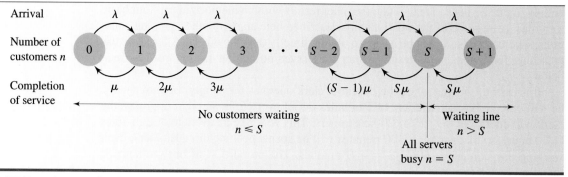

FIGURE 17-5   Schematic of multiple-server queuing system states

Queuing Formulas

The queuing formulas for a multiple-channel system are based on principles similar to those used for a single server, but a new parameter is needed to represent the number of channels.

$$S = \text{Number of service channels}$$

Figure 17-5 shows how movement occurs between customer states. As in the single-server model, the arrows represent changes and the quantity beside an arrow corresponds to the applicable rate for that particular change.

Notice that when all servers are not busy—that is, when the number of customers n is less than S—no customers are waiting in line and the combined rate of service is $n\mu$. For example, consider a bank that has 5 tellers, so that $S = 5$. When $n = 3$ customers are present, each is being served and the combined rate at which service is being performed is 3μ. For any increment of time, it is therefore three times as likely that service will be completed for any one of these three customers as a group as it is that service will be completed individually for any specific customer. When the number of customers is at least as large as the number of servers, so that $n \geq S$, all servers are busy and the combined rate of service is $S\mu$. If the bank has $n = 7$ customers, then two customers are waiting in line and the combined service rate is 5μ. As in our earlier model, we assume that total service capacity must exceed customer requirements, so that $S\mu > \lambda$.

The queuing formulas that result with S service channels are a little more complex than those that apply to the single-channel case. When there are S service channels, queuing formulas are based on the following probabilities:

QUEUING SYSTEM STATE PROBABILITIES

(Multiple Servers)

$$P_0 = 1 \left/ \left[\sum_{n=0}^{S-1} \frac{(\lambda/\mu)^n}{n!} + \frac{(\lambda/\mu)^S}{S!} \left(\frac{1}{1 - \lambda/S\mu} \right) \right] \right.$$

$$P_n = \begin{cases} \dfrac{(\lambda/\mu)^n}{n!} P_0 & \text{if } 0 \leq n \leq S \\[2ex] \dfrac{(\lambda/\mu)^n}{S! \, S^{n-s}} P_0 & \text{if } n \geq S \end{cases}$$

The remaining queuing expressions are all based on first calculating L_q.

QUEUING FORMULAS

(Multiple Servers)

Mean Number of Customers Waiting (length of line)

$$L_q = \frac{(\lambda/\mu)^S(\lambda/S\mu)}{S!(1 - \lambda/S\mu)^2}P_0$$

Mean Customer Waiting Time

$$W_q = \frac{L_q}{\lambda}$$

Mean Customer Time Spent in the System

$$W = W_q + \frac{1}{\mu}$$

Mean Number of Customers in the System

$$L = L_q + \frac{\lambda}{\mu}$$

Server Utilization Factor

$$\rho = \frac{\lambda}{S\mu}$$

Notice that the server utilization factor differs from that of a single-server system. In a multiple-server system, it is not possible to express the mean customer waiting time as the product of λ/μ and the mean customer time in the system. Thus,

$$W_q \neq \left(\frac{\lambda}{\mu}\right)W \quad \text{and} \quad L_q \neq \left(\frac{\lambda}{\mu}\right)L$$

One reason for this is that λ/μ does not represent the same thing in a multiple-server queuing system.

Two Copying Machines Example

A company is considering renting office copying machines. One alternative is to lease two model *A* machines that can make 100 copies per minute. However, because items must be manually placed on the machine to be copied, the effective copying rate is quite a bit slower. The actual machine time will also vary from user to user, depending on the number of copies required and the originals used. Based on the manufacturer's historical experience for offices with similar workloads, the total time per user is

approximately exponentially distributed with a mean of 2 minutes per job. The effective service rate is therefore .5 job per minute. The demand for copying by company employees occurs at the rate of three jobs every 5 minutes, or an average of .6 job per minute. Historical experience shows that the need for copying occurs randomly over time and that a Poisson process applies to jobs arriving at the copying center. The parameters of this problem are

$$S = 2 \text{ service channels}$$
$$\mu = .5 \text{ job per minute}$$
$$\lambda = .6 \text{ job per minute}$$

The probability that no jobs are in the copying system is

$$P_0 = 1 \Big/ \left[\frac{(\lambda/\mu)^0}{0!} + \frac{(\lambda/\mu)^1}{1!} + \frac{(\lambda/\mu)^2}{2!} \left(\frac{1}{1 - \lambda/2\mu} \right) \right]$$

$$= 1 \Big/ \left[\frac{(.6/.5)^0}{0!} + \frac{(.6/.5)^1}{1!} + \frac{(.6/.5)^2}{2!} \left(\frac{1}{1 - .6/2(.5)} \right) \right]$$

$$= 1 \Big/ \left[1 + 1.2 + \frac{(1.2)^2}{2} \left(\frac{1}{1 - .6} \right) \right]$$

$$= 1/[1 + 1.2 + 1.8] = 1/4 = .25$$

The mean number of jobs waiting to be copied is therefore

$$L_q = \frac{(.6/.5)^2[.6/2(.5)]}{2![1 - .6/2(.5)]^2} (.25) = .68 \text{ job}$$

and the mean waiting time per job is

$$W_q = \frac{L_q}{\lambda} = \frac{.68}{.6} = 1.13 \text{ minutes}$$

The mean time each job spends in the copying center is

$$W = W_q + \frac{1}{\mu} = 1.13 + \frac{1}{.5} = 3.13 \text{ minutes}$$

and the mean number of jobs at the copying center at any given time is

$$L = L_q + \frac{\lambda}{\mu} = .68 + \frac{.6}{.5} = 1.88 \text{ jobs}$$

Solving with Spreadsheets

Figure 17-6 shows a spreadsheet for the multiple-server model applied to the copy machine example. It is included on the accompanying CD-ROM and can be used as a template for solving other multiple-server queuing problems in the book. The development of this spreadsheet is shown in Appendix 17-1.

	A	B	C	D	E	F	G
1	**BASIC QUEUING EVALUATION -- MULTIPLE SERVERS**						
2							
3	PROBLEM: Supply Room						
4							
5			Parameter Values:				
6				Mean Customer Arrival Rate: lambda =			0.6
7				Mean Customer Service Rate: mu =			0.5
8				Number of Servers: S =			2
9							
10			Queuing Results:				
11				Mean Number of Customers in System: L =			1.8750
12				Mean Customer Time Spent in System: W =			3.1250
13				Mean Number of Customers Waiting			
14					(Length of Line): L_q =		0.6750
15				Mean Customer Waiting Time: W_q =			1.1250
16				Server Utilization Factor: rho =			0.6000
17							
18			Number in	Probability	Cumulative		
19			System, n	P_n	Probability		
20			0	0.2500	0.2500		
21			1	0.3000	0.5500		
22			2	0.1800	0.7300		
23			3	0.1080	0.8380		
24			4	0.0648	0.9028		
38			18	0.0001	0.9999		
39			19	0.0000	1.0000		

FIGURE 17-6

Spreadsheet (*M/M/S*) for a multiple-server model applied to the two copying machine example

Establishing the Queuing System Cost

Management is concerned about the average hourly cost of operating two model *A* machines. Each job is personally processed by the user, whose average hourly payroll cost is $10. Machine rental is a straight $.05 per copy, and an average job involves 12 copies. The average number of jobs per hour is

$$.6 \times 60 = 36 \text{ jobs}$$

and each employee using the machine spends an average of $W = 3.13$ minutes, or

$$\frac{3.13}{60} = .0522 \text{ hour}$$

in the copying center. The average hourly cost of the labor lost in making copies is therefore

$$\$10 \times 36 \times .0522 = \$18.79$$

The hourly rental cost for the two machines is

$$\$.05 \times 12 \times 36 = \$21.60$$

The total hourly average cost of operating two model *A* machines is therefore

$$\$18.79 \text{ (labor lost)} + \$21.60 \text{ (equipment rental)} = \$40.39$$

Optimizing the Number of Servers

Deciding on the number of servers is one of the most useful queuing applications. This is done by finding the total queuing system cost for the various alternatives. The following example illustrates how this may be done with computer assistance.

Decision Problem Revisited: Million Bank

Because Sylvia has selected a multiple-server queuing model, her first step is to develop a spreadsheet to make her evaluation. The spreadsheet is shown in Figure 17-7 and may be used as a template (included on the accompanying CD-ROM) for doing a cost analysis of other single- or multiple-server queuing problems. The development of this spreadsheet is shown in Appendix 17-1.

Sylvia begins by calculating the arrival and service rates and the server and customer hourly costs. The mean arrival rate is $\lambda=500/2=250$ customers per hour, which is entered in cell G6. Because tellers take an average of 2 minutes per customer, the mean service rate is $\mu=60/2=30$ customers per hour, entered in cell G7. The customer cost per hour waiting in line, $\$.10 \times 60 = \$6$, and server cost of \$12 per hour are entered in cells G8 and G9. The results list the possible number of servers, beginning with $S = 9$. (The minimum number of servers is 9, such that total service capacity $S\mu$ exceeds total demand for service λ.) The listing stops at $S = 18$, after which there is a negligible customer cost because of the miniscule customer waiting times. The optimal number of servers, providing minimum total cost of \$134.63 per hour (cell I23), is $S = 10$ (cell A23). (This evaluation assumes that there is a penalty only for *waiting* time, not time in the system. Otherwise, column K would have been used to select the minimum cost.)

	A	B	C	D	E	F	G	H	I	J	K
1	BASIC QUEUING SYSTEM EVALUATION -- MULTIPLE SERVERS										
2											
3	PROBLEM: Million Bank Tellers										
4											
5		Parameter Values:									
6			Mean Customer Arrival Rate: lambda				250				
7			Mean Customer Service Rate: mu =				30				
8			Customer Cost per Unit of Time =				6				
9			Server Cost per Unit of Time =				12				
10											
11											
12							Server	Customer	Total	Customer	Total
13	Servers	P₀	Lq	L	Wq	W	Cost	Cost(Wq)	Cost(Wq)	Cost(W)	Cost(W)
22	9	0.0001	9.5049	17.8382	0.0380	0.0714	$108.00	$57.03	$165.03	$107.03	$215.03
23	10	0.0002	2.4381	10.7714	0.0098	0.0431	$120.00	$14.63	$134.63	$64.63	$184.63
24	11	0.0002	0.9363	9.2696	0.0037	0.0371	$132.00	$5.62	$137.62	$55.62	$187.62
25	12	0.0002	0.3999	8.7333	0.0016	0.0349	$144.00	$2.40	$146.40	$52.40	$196.40
26	13	0.0002	0.1761	8.5094	0.0007	0.0340	$156.00	$1.06	$157.06	$51.06	$207.06
27	14	0.0002	0.0774	8.4107	0.0003	0.0336	$168.00	$0.46	$168.46	$50.46	$218.46
28	15	0.0002	0.0334	8.3668	0.0001	0.0335	$180.00	$0.20	$180.20	$50.20	$230.20
29	16	0.0002	0.0141	8.3474	0.0001	0.0334	$192.00	$0.08	$192.08	$50.08	$242.08
30	17	0.0002	0.0057	8.3391	0.0000	0.0334	$204.00	$0.03	$204.03	$50.03	$254.03
31	18	0.0002	0.0023	8.3356	0.0000	0.0333	$216.00	$0.01	$216.01	$50.01	$266.01

FIGURE 17-7 Cost analysis spreadsheet for the Million Bank

Two Servers Compared with One Server Who Is Twice as Fast

An interesting result arises from queuing theory. To the uninitiated, it may seem that one server who is twice as fast will produce results identical to two separate facilities, each servicing customers at the regular rate. *This is not true.* (If it were, we would not

need a separate model for multiple-channel queues; the single-channel system with twice as large a value of μ could be used instead.)

Suppose that the effective service rate of the model T copying machine is twice as fast as that of the model A. If $\mu = 1$ job per minute, the single-server model provides a mean number of jobs waiting of

$$L_q = \frac{\lambda^2}{\mu(\mu - \lambda)} = \frac{(.6)^2}{1(1 - .6)} = .9 \text{ job} \quad \text{(one model } T\text{)}$$

which is larger than the comparable number when two model A machines are used. The mean waiting time per job using one model T would be

$$W_q = \frac{L_q}{\lambda} = \frac{.9}{.6} = 1.5 \text{ minutes} \quad \text{(one model } T\text{)}$$

which is longer than before. Of course, the service rate of the model T is twice as fast, so the average time a job spends in the system is smaller than it would be if two model A machines were used, or

$$W = \frac{1}{\mu - \lambda} = \frac{1}{1 - .6} = 2.5 \text{ minutes} \quad \text{(one model } T\text{)}$$

This results in a smaller hourly lost labor cost of

$$\$10 \times 36 \times \frac{2.5}{60} = \$15.00$$

Even if the faster model T rents for a little more per copy than the slower model A does, it would still be cheaper for management to rent one model T instead of two model A machines.

Finding the Cost of Waiting

The cost-per-minute or -hour for customer waiting is a key element used to establish the optimal number of servers. The actual cost of waiting will be the result of a future loss of business and associated profits from some percentage of those customers who refuse to come back because they had to wait. That amount may never be known, and a good guess must ordinarily be used. A sensitivity analysis may be applied to assess how the optimal S varies with different levels for the cost of waiting.

USING
JUDGMENT

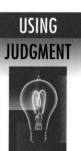

17-5 SENSITIVITY ANALYSIS WITH SPREADSHEETS

Spreadsheets are useful in simplifying **sensitivity analysis,** in which the impact is assessed of changes in assumed parameter levels. They help answer "what if. . ." questions such as, What is the effect on total costs and the best number of servers if the service rate differs or if labor rates change by various amounts?

DECISION PROBLEM

Decision Problem Revisited: Million Bank

Million Bank manager Neena Pangal has questions about Sylvia's solution indicating that $S = 10$ tellers are optimal for the Friday rush, at a cost of $134.63: (1) What happens to this solution if the server cost goes up or down? (2) What happens if the mean customer arrival rate is greater than expected or if the mean customer service rate is less than expected?

To answer the first question, Sylvia changes the server cost value in her spreadsheet to get the new solutions summarized in Table 17-1. Notice that as the hourly server cost increases, the original $S = 10$ remains optimal until it reaches $42.41, above which it is best to cut back to only $S = 9$ servers. Everything else being equal, normal teller salary increases have little effect on the optimal staffing level. Using $10-per-hour part-time workers will not change the optimal number of tellers either. Only the minimum total cost will change.

TABLE 17-1   Variations in Minimum Total Cost and the Optimal Number of Million Bank Tellers

SERVER COST	MINIMUM TOTAL COST	NUMBER OF SERVERS, S
$10.00	$114.63	10
$12.00	$134.63	10
$20.00	$214.63	10
$40.00	$414.63	10
$42.00	$434.63	10
$42.40	$438.63	10
$42.41	$438.72	9
$42.42	$438.81	9

To answer her manager's second question, Sylvia changes the spreadsheet arrival rate, λ, to various values from 230 to 270 customers per hour and the service rate μ to values from 20 to 40. Tables 17-2 and 17-3 summarize the results. We see that the optimal number of servers varies between $S = 7$ and $S = 16$ and that the minimum total cost ranges between $98.68 and $205.46. Staffing requirements are highly sensitive to assumed levels for λ and μ.

You may verify some of the values in these tables. (Although such tables might be constructed by trial and error, the process can be automated using Excel's Data Table option. A detailed discussion is found in the *Guide to Excel* on the CD-ROM accompanying this book.)

TABLE 17-2   Optimal Number of Million Bank Tellers for Various Arrival and Service Rate Combinations

ARRIVAL RATE, λ	SERVICE RATE, μ				
	20	25	30	35	40
230	14	11	10	8	7
240	14	12	10	9	8
250	15	12	10	9	8
260	15	13	11	9	8
270	16	13	11	10	9

| TABLE 17-3 | Minimum Million Bank Total Cost for Variations in Arrival and Service Rates | | | | |

ARRIVAL RATE, λ	SERVICE RATE, μ				
	20	25	30	35	40
230	$178.65	$146.58	$126.68	$109.94	$ 98.68
240	$185.34	$152.85	$129.82	$114.78	$102.43
250	$192.04	$157.48	$134.63	$117.66	$104.96
260	$199.33	$164.42	$140.05	$121.90	$108.61
270	$205.46	$168.54	$143.62	$127.05	$113.95

17-6 A MODEL FOR NONEXPONENTIAL SERVICE TIMES

Some distribution other than the exponential—such as the normal distribution—could more appropriately represent the service pattern of a queuing system. Recall from Chapter 4 that a normal distribution is specified by two parameters—the mean and the standard deviation σ. A different queuing model applies when only the arrivals form a Poisson process, while the service times follow some other distribution. That model depends only on the standard deviation σ for service time and assumes no particular form for the distribution itself. The following equations apply:

$$P_0 = 1 - \lambda/\mu$$

$$L_q = \frac{\lambda^2\sigma^2 + (\lambda/\mu)^2}{2(1 - \lambda/\mu)} \qquad L = L_q + \frac{\lambda}{\mu}$$

$$W_q = \frac{L_q}{\lambda} \qquad\qquad W = W_q + \frac{1}{\mu}$$

The state probabilities are the same as in the earlier single-server model. Notice that L_q—and therefore all the other queuing results—depends on the standard deviation σ of the service-time distribution. L_q, L, W_q, and W all become larger as σ increases. Thus, greater variability in service time will result in longer lines and longer waiting times. This indicates that consistency in service times is very important to the overall quality of the service provided.

Recall from Chapter 4 that the exponential distribution has a mean and standard deviation that are both equal to $1/\mu$. The preceding equations provide identical results to the earlier ones when $\sigma = 1/\mu$. Should σ be larger or smaller, however, results will vary. Consider the following three cases applicable to the supply room example given earlier:

ORIGINAL VARIABILITY ($\sigma = 1/\mu = 1/30$)	LESS VARIABILITY ($\sigma = 1/60$)	GREATER VARIABILITY ($\sigma = 1/15$)
$L_q = 4.167$ customers	$L_q = \dfrac{(25)^2(1/60)^2 + (25/30)^2}{2(1 - 25/30)}$	$L_q = \dfrac{(25)^2(1/15)^2 + (25/30)^2}{2(1 - 25/30)}$
	$= 2.61$ customers	$= 10.42$ customers
$W_q = .167$ hr	$W_q = 2.61/25 = .10$ hr	$W_q = 10.42/25 = .42$ hr
$W = .20$ hr	$W = .10 + 1/30 = .133$ hr	$W = .42 + 1/30 = .453$ hr
Cost $= $320	Cost $= 7(.133)200 + 40$	Cost $= 7(.453)200 + 40$
	$= $226	$= $674

The shorthand representation of this model is *M/G/*1. As with the earlier models, the *M* denotes exponential interarrival times, the *G* denotes a general service time distribution, and the 1 signifies one server.

Sammy Lee Evaluates His Barbershop

Sammy Lee operates a one-man barbershop. Past experience shows that customers arrive at a mean rate of $\lambda = 4$ per hour, and an exponential distribution is assumed. Experience has established that service occurs at a mean rate of $\mu = 5$ customers per hour. This means that Sammy spends an average of $1/\mu = .2$ hour (12 minutes) per customer. He believes that service times have some unspecified positively skewed unimodal *two-tailed* distribution with a standard deviation $\sigma = .05$ hour (3 minutes).

Sammy wants to determine the queuing characteristics of his shop. He would also like to see just how much the assumption of exponential service times would distort these values.

Using the equations on page 685, he obtains the following results, assuming the service times are

*nonexponential (M/G/*1): $L = 12.5$ $W = .625$ $L_q = 1.7$ $W_q = .425$

Distorted results would be obtained by the basic queuing model due to its faulty (here) exponential service-time requirement. Applying the equations on page 672, the following would apply with service times that are

*exponential (M/M/*1): $L = 4$ $W = 1$ $L_q = 3.2$ $W_q = .8$

Notice that both the customer times and the number of customers are greater than the correct ones, regardless of whether customers are waiting or are just in the system.

The above barbershop example illustrates just how critical the assumption of exponential service times can be and how important it is to ascertain the correct probability distribution before embarking on a queuing evaluation.

Solving with a Spreadsheet

A spreadsheet for Sammy's barbershop with nonexponential service times is shown in Figure 17-8. This spreadsheet (on the CD-ROM accompanying the book) can be used as a template for single-server nonexponential queuing evaluations.

The Excel formula for the server utilization factor λ/μ in cell G16 is =G6/G7. The Excel formula in cell G14 is for the mean number of customers waiting (the length of line) L_q:

=(G6^2*G8^2+G16^2)/(2*(1-G16))

Once this is known, L, the mean number of customers in the system, can be calculated in cell G11 from the Excel formula =G14+G16. The next calculations are the mean customer waiting time W_q, having Excel formula =G14/G6 in cell G15, and the mean customer time spent in the system W, represented by =G15+1/G7 in cell G12.

	A	B	C	D	E	F	G	H	I	J
1	QUEUING EVALUATION FOR SINGLE SERVER WITH NON-EXPONENTIAL TIMES									
2										
3	PROBLEM: Sammy's Barbershop									
4										
5		Parameter Values:								
6			Mean Customer Arrival Rate: lambda =				4			
7			Mean Customer Service Rate: mu =				5			
8			Standard Deviation of Service Time: sigma =				0.05			
9										
10		Queuing Results:								
11			Mean Number of Customers in System: L =				2.5		G	
12			Mean Customer Time Spent in System: W =				0.625	11 =G14+G16		
13			Mean Number of Customers Waiting					12 =G15+1/G7		
								13		
14					(Length of Line): L_q =		1.7	14 =(G6^2*G8^2+G16^2)/(2*(1-G16))		
15			Mean Customer Waiting Time: W_q =				0.425	15 =G14/G6		
16			Server Utilization Factor: rho =				0.8	16 =G6/G7		

FIGURE 17-8 Spreadsheet for Sammy's Barbershop

17-7 FURTHER QUEUING PROBABILITY TOPICS

The queuing models seen so far are based on the assumption that the exponential distribution applies for times between successive customer arrivals. That distribution is a natural consequence for events occurring randomly over time and meeting the assumptions of a Poisson process, as described in Chapter 4. Although those assumptions are plausible for many queuing applications, in this section we introduce a statistical testing procedure that may be helpful in establishing whether empirical data fit a particular distribution. Such a test can be especially important with service times, for which the justification of the exponential distribution is much less compelling than for arrival times.

Finding Probabilities for Interarrival and Service Times

Recall that the exponential is a continuous probability distribution from which specific probability values may only be established for *intervals,* similar to those found with the normal curve. Although specific details may be found in Chapter 4, we can easily determine such values using a spreadsheet.

Figure 17-9 shows a spreadsheet for finding probabilities of interarrival times as applied to the supply room example. It can be used for service time probabilities also. This spreadsheet (on the CD-ROM) can be used as a template for other exponential distributions.

The Excel formulas for determining the exponential probabilities in cells C18:D23 are shown in Figure 17-9 and come from Figure 4-16. To calculate $\Pr[X \leq a]$ in cell F9 (where $a = .05$ in cell D6), the Excel formula is

$$=\text{EXPONDIST(D6,D5,TRUE)}$$

where the first argument D6 is the cell location of the nonnegative lower point a, the second argument D5 is the cell location of the mean process rate λ, and the last argument

FIGURE 17-9

Spreadsheet for
calculating inter-arrival-
time probabilities for the
supply room example

	A	B	C	D	E	F	G	H	I
1		**EXPONENTIAL DISTRIBUTION**							
2									
3	PROBLEM: Supply Room Arrival								
4						F			
5	Mean process rate lambda =			25		9 =EXPONDIST(D6,D5,TRUE)			
6	Lower point a =			0.05		10 =1-F11-F9			
7	Upper point b =			0.2		11 =1-EXPONDIST(D7,D5,TRUE)			
8									
9	Area to the left of a: Pr[X ≤ a] =					0.713495			
10	Area between a and b: Pr[a < X < b] =				E	0.27977			
11	Area to the right of b: Pr[X ≥ b] =				13 =B13	0.00674			
12			B				C		
13	Mean =	0.04	13 =1/D5	Stand. Dev. =	0.04	18 =EXPONDIST(B18,$D$5,FALSE)			
14						19 =EXPONDIST(B19,$D$5,FALSE)			
15		Interarrival	Frequency	Cumulative		20 =EXPONDIST(B20,$D$5,FALSE)			
16		Time	Curve	Distribution		21 =EXPONDIST(B21,$D$5,FALSE)			
17		t	f(t)	F(t)		22 =EXPONDIST(B22,$D$5,FALSE)			
18		0	25	0		23 =EXPONDIST(B23,$D$5,FALSE)			
19		0.05	7.16262	0.71350		D			
20		0.1	2.05212	0.91792		18 =EXPONDIST(B18,$D$5,TRUE)			
21		0.2	0.16845	0.99326		19 =EXPONDIST(B19,$D$5,TRUE)			
22		0.3	0.01383	0.99945		20 =EXPONDIST(B20,$D$5,TRUE)			
23		0.4	0.00113	0.99995		21 =EXPONDIST(B21,$D$5,TRUE)			
						22 =EXPONDIST(B22,$D$5,TRUE)			
						23 =EXPONDIST(B23,$D$5,TRUE)			

TRUE indicates that a *cumulative* distribution applies. The Excel formula in cell F11 is

$$=1\text{-EXPONDIST(D7,D5,TRUE)}$$

which calculates $Pr[X \geq b]$. The arguments have the same meaning as before, with D7 denoting the cell location of the upper point b. The Excel formula $Pr[a < X < b]$ in cell F10 is

$$=1\text{-F11-F9}$$

To find service time probabilities, the mean service rate μ is used as the value in cell D5 instead of λ. When $\mu = 30$, the modified spreadsheet in Figure 17-10 indicates that

FIGURE 17-10

Spreadsheet for
calculating service
time probabilities

	A	B	C	D	E	F
1		**EXPONENTIAL DISTRIBUTION**				
2						
3	PROBLEM:	Supply Room Service				
4						
5	Mean process rate lambda =			30		
6	Lower point a =			0.05		
7	Upper point b =			0.2		
8						
9	Area to the left of a: Pr[X ≤ a] =					0.77687
10	Area between a and b: Pr[a < X < b] =					0.22065
11	Area to the right of b: Pr[X ≥ b] =					0.00248
12						
13	Mean =	0.033333		Stand. Dev. =	0.033333	
14						
15		Interarrival	Frequency	Cumulative		
16		Time	Curve	Distribution		
17		t	f(t)	F(t)		
18		0	30	0		
19		0.05	6.69390	0.77687		
20		0.1	1.49361	0.95021		
21		0.2	0.07436	0.99752		
22		0.3	0.00370	0.99988		
23		0.4	0.00018	0.99999		

the mean and standard deviation of the service times are .03333 (cells B13 and E13), $\Pr[X \le a] = 0.77687$ (cell F9), $\Pr[a < X < b] = .22065$ (cell F10), and $\Pr[X \ge b] = .00248$ (cell F11), where $a = .05$ in cell D6 and $b = .2$ in D7.

Finding Probabilities for the Number of Arrivals within a Fixed Time Span

In Chapter 4 we saw that the exponential distribution gives one representation of the underlying Poisson process. That distribution is concerned with times *between* successive events. A second representation is provided by the Poisson distribution, which provides probabilities for the number of events occurring in a fixed time span. Although you should refer to Chapter 4 for the details of the Poisson distribution, a spreadsheet may be readily used to establish probabilities.

Figure 17-11 gives a spreadsheet for finding the probability of a certain number of arrivals for the supply room example. It can be used to calculate the probabilities of various numbers of service completions during a specified time. The Excel formulas shown in Figure 17-11 for calculating individual Poisson probabilities in cells B20:C33 are discussed in Chapter 4 (and appear in Figure 4-17).

FIGURE 17-11
Spreadsheet for calculating the probabilities for numbers of arrivals for the supply room example

	A	B	C	D	E	F	G
1	**POISSON DISTRIBUTION**						
2							
3	PROBLEM: Number of Arrivals at Supply Room						
4							
5	Mean process rate lambda =				25		
6	Duration t =				0.1		
7	Lower limit for the number of events, a =				0		
8	Upper limit for the number of events, b =				8		
9							
10	Pr[X ≤ a] =		0.08208	Pr[X < a] =	0		
11	Pr[a ≤ X ≤ b] =		0.99886		E		
12	Pr[a ≤ X < b] =		0.99575	10	=IF(E7>0,POISSON(E7-1,E5*E6,TRUE),0)		
13	Pr[a < X ≤ b] =		0.91677		E		
14	Pr[a < X < b] =		0.91367	15	=1-POISSON(E8,E5*E6,TRUE)		
15	Pr[X ≥ b] =		0.00425	Pr[X > b] =	0.00114		
16							
17	Number of		Cumulative		C		
18	Arrivals	Probability	Probability	10	=POISSON(E7,E5*E6,TRUE)		
19	x	Pr[X = x]	Pr{X ≤ x]	11	=POISSON(E8,E5*E6,TRUE)-E10		
20	0	0.08208	0.08208	12	=POISSON(E8-1,E5*E6,TRUE)-E10		
21	1	0.20521	0.28730	13	=POISSON(E8,E5*E6,TRUE)-C10		
22	2	0.25652	0.54381	14	=POISSON(E8-1,E5*E6,TRUE)-C10		
23	3	0.21376	0.75758	15	=1-POISSON(E8-1,E5*E6,TRUE)		
24	4	0.13360	0.89118				
25	5	0.06680	0.95798		B		
26	6	0.02783	0.98581	20	=POISSON(A20,$E$5*$E$6,FALSE)		
27	7	0.00994	0.99575	21	=POISSON(A21,$E$5*$E$6,FALSE)		
28	8	0.00311	0.99886	22	=POISSON(A22,$E$5*$E$6,FALSE)		
29	9	0.00086	0.99972				
30	10	0.00022	0.99994		C		
31	11	0.00005	0.99999	20	=POISSON(A20,$E$5*$E$6,TRUE)		
32	12	0.00001	1.00000	21	=POISSON(A21,$E$5*$E$6,TRUE)		
33	13	0.00000	1.00000	22	=POISSON(A22,$E$5*$E$6,TRUE)		

In calculating the probabilities in cells C10:C15, E10, and E15, the process mean λt is needed by all the Poisson Excel functions. In Excel, the process mean is the product of λ and t, expressed in terms of their cell locations by the expression E5*E6. Cell E10 gives the probability that the number of arrivals is less than the nonnegative lower limit in cell E7. Normally, this is found from the Excel formula

$$=IF(E7>0,POISSON(E7-1,E5*E6,TRUE),0)$$

which returns 0 if E7 = 0; otherwise, it yields the Poisson probability corresponding to the value in cell E7. In the first argument, 1 is subtracted from E7 because the probability we seek is for the number of arrivals *less than* the value located in cell E7. The second argument is the process mean, described earlier. The last argument, TRUE, signifies that a *cumulative* probability is required.

To find the probability for a certain number of service completions during a specified time, the spreadsheet can be modified, substituting the mean customer service rate μ for λ in cell E5. In the supply room example, the probability that one customer is handled during a 6-minute period (.1 hour) may be read from the spreadsheet so constructed in Figure 17-12. That probability is .14936 (cell C13).

Finding Probabilities for a Customer's Waiting Time

Besides its good empirical fit, the exponential distribution is assumed in queuing models because it has nice mathematical properties. Whenever a single-server queue has exponential arrival and service times at rates λ and μ, respectively, the exponential distribution applies to an individual customer's *waiting time* as well. The mean rate parameter for the waiting time distribution is the difference, $\mu - \lambda$.

Customers may spend a lot of time waiting, so it is useful to find probabilities of waiting various lengths of time. Two important formulas give the cumulative probability distribution functions for waiting time $W_q(t)$ and time in the system $W(t)$.

FIGURE 17-12
Spreadsheet for calculating probabilities for the number of customers being served during a specified time span for the supply room example

	A	B	C	D	E
1			**POISSON DISTRIBUTION**		
2					
3	PROBLEM: Number of Arrivals at Supply Room				
4					
5	Mean process rate lambda =				30
6	Duration t =				0.1
7	Lower limit for the number of events, a =				0
8	Upper limit for the number of events, b =				1
9					
10	Pr[X ≤ a] =		0.04979	Pr[X < a] =	0
11	Pr[a ≤ X ≤ b] =		0.19915		
12	Pr[a ≤ X < b] =		0.04979		
13	Pr[a < X ≤ b] =		0.14936		
14	Pr[a < X < b] =		0.00000		
15	Pr[X ≥ b] =		0.95021	Pr[X > b] =	0.800852
16					
17	Number of		Cumulative		
18	Arrivals	Probability	Probability		
19	x	Pr[X = x]	Pr{X ≤ x]		
20	0	0.04979	0.04979		
21	1	0.14936	0.19915		

	A	B	C	D	E	F	G	H	I	J
1				**WAITING TIME PROBABILITIES**						
2										
3	PROBLEM: Supply Room Waiting Times									
4										
5			Parameter Values:							
6			Mean Customer Arrival Rate: lambda =				25			
7			Mean Customer Service Rate: mu =				30			
9										
10			Time, t	$W_q(t)$	W(t)					
11			0.05	0.3510	0.2212					
12			0.10	0.4946	0.3935					
13			0.15	0.6064	0.5276					
14			0.20	0.6934	0.6321					
15			0.25	0.7612	0.7135					
16			0.30	0.8141	0.7769					
17			0.35	0.8552	0.8262					
18			0.40	0.8872	0.8647					
19			0.45	0.9122	0.8946					
20			0.50	0.9316	0.9179					

Inset (column D):

	D
11	=1-($G$6/$G$7)*EXP(-1*($G$7-$G$6)*C11)
12	=1-($G$6/$G$7)*EXP(-1*($G$7-$G$6)*C12)
13	=1-($G$6/$G$7)*EXP(-1*($G$7-$G$6)*C13)

Inset (column E):

	E
11	=1-EXP(-1*($G$7-$G$6)*C11)
12	=1-EXP(-1*($G$7-$G$6)*C12)
13	=1-EXP(-1*($G$7-$G$6)*C13)

FIGURE 17-13 Spreadsheet to calculate waiting time probabilities for the supply room example

$$W_q(t) = 1 - \frac{\lambda}{\mu}e^{-(\mu-\lambda)t}$$
$$W(t) = 1 - e^{-(\mu-\lambda)t}$$

Figure 17-13 shows the spreadsheet for calculating these probabilities. In the supply room illustration, the probability of waiting no more than 15 minutes (.25 hour) is .7612 (cell D15). The probability for spending no more than 15 minutes in the system is .7135 (cell E15). The Excel formula for $W_q(t)$ uses the Excel EXP function. Cell D11 has the formula

=1-($G$6/$G$7)*EXP(-1*($G$7-$G$6)*C11)

where $t = .05$ is the value for cell C11. Cell E11 has the Excel formula for $W(t)$

=1-EXP(-1*($G$7-$G$6)*C11)

These are copied down to cells D12:E20 for the remaining probabilities. (To ensure that this copying operation gives the correct results, the Excel formulas in cells D11:E11 must have the dollar signs [$] so that, when copied, the results always refer back to cells G6 and G7.)

17-8 ADDITIONAL REMARKS

In this chapter, we have described only three queuing models in detail. These models presume exponential distributions for interarrival and service times. Many other queuing situations exist and have been studied in detail. Several additional queuing models are described in the following optional section.

Arrivals that occur *singly* over time often historically fit the Poisson distribution. It is inappropriate to use this distribution when customers arrive in groups—for example, when customers pick up their luggage after a flight. Generally, a Poisson process is of limited duration, so that the basic queuing formulas are really only applicable for

short periods of time. As we have seen, a bank or a toll station will exhibit different characteristics at different times of the day or on different days of the week. Thus, a different value of λ may be appropriate for any particular period, and different mean waiting times and queuing results would apply to each.

As with certain other applications of quantitative methods, various mathematical queuing models have limited scope and often only approximate reality because of the many simplifying assumptions that must ordinarily be made to accommodate the mathematical analysis. To avoid erroneous results, numerical solution procedures are often used instead of standard queuing formulas to evaluate complex queuing situations. One useful procedure—*Monte Carlo simulation*—is in Chapter 18.

17-9   (OPTIONAL) SOME FURTHER QUEUING MODELS

A tremendous variety of queuing models exists. Each model applies to a particular situation in which any one or a combination of differences occurs in the underlying structure, queue discipline, or arrival or service pattern. This section provides three additional queuing models that are widely applicable. All of these models assume a Poisson process for arrivals. The first two models also assume that service times are exponentially distributed.

A Single-Server Model for a Finite Queue

Often the number of customers that a queuing system can handle at any given time is limited. For example, a hospital emergency room only has enough beds to accommodate a specific number of patients waiting to see the attending doctors, and any additional patients must be diverted to other hospitals. A waiting line of limited length is called a *finite queue*. A finite queue may arise due to a physical constraint, such as the emergency room. Or customers may simply give up when the waiting line becomes too long. In either case, a customer who is turned away does not return to the system. Systems involving finite queues differ from the queuing systems discussed in this chapter, where no limits were placed on the number of customers waiting for service. The underlying queuing formulas must be modified to reflect this structural difference. The resulting model may be expressed in terms of the constant

$$M = \text{Maximum number of customers in the system}$$

The probabilities for the number of customers in the system are

$$P_0 = \frac{1 - \lambda/\mu}{1 - (\lambda/\mu)^{M+1}}$$

$$P_n = (\lambda/\mu)^n P_0 \quad \text{for } 1 \leq n \leq M$$

The mean number of customers in the system is

$$L = \frac{\lambda/\mu}{1 - \lambda/\mu} - \frac{(M+1)(\lambda/\mu)^{M+1}}{1 - (\lambda/\mu)^{M+1}}$$

The remaining queuing results may be found from this expression. The mean length of the waiting line is found by subtracting the proportion of time the server is busy, which is $1 - P_0$ here.

$$L_q = L - (1 - P_0)$$

	A	B	C	D	E	F	G	H	I	J
1	QUEUING EVALUATION -- SINGLE SERVER WITH A FINITE QUEUE									
2										
3	PROBLEM: Supply Room									
4										
5		Parameter Values:						G		
6			Mean Customer Arrival Rate: lambda =				25	=(G16/(1-G16))-		
7			Mean Customer Service Rate: mu =				30	(((G8+1)*(G16)^(G8+1))/		
8			Maximum Number of Customers in System: M =				5	11	(1-G16^(G8+1)))	
9								12	=G11/(G6*(1-D25))	
10		Queuing Results:						13		
11			Mean Number of Customers in System: L =				1.9788	14	=G11-(1-D20)	
12			Mean Customer Time Spent in System: W =				0.0880	15	=G14/(G6*(1-D25))	
13			Mean Number of Customers Waiting					16	=G6/G7	
14				(Length of Line): L_q =			1.2294			
15			Mean Customer Waiting Time: W_q =				0.0547			
16			Traffic Intensity: rho =				0.8333			
17										
18			Number in	Probability	Cumulative					
19			System n	P_n	Probability			D	E	
20			0	0.2506	0.2506			=(1-G16)/(1-G16^(G8+1))	=D20	
21			1	0.2088	0.4594			=$D$20*$G$16^C21	=E20+D21	
22			2	0.1740	0.6334			=$D$20*$G$16^C22	=E21+D22	
23			3	0.1450	0.7784			=$D$20*$G$16^C23	=E22+D23	
24			4	0.1208	0.8993			=$D$20*$G$16^C24	=E23+D24	
25			5	0.1007	1.0000			=$D$20*$G$16^C25	=E24+D25	

FIGURE 17-14 Spreadsheet for a single-server model with a finite queue for the supply room example

The respective mean customer waiting times are

$$W_q = \frac{L_q}{\lambda(1 - P_M)} \qquad W = \frac{L}{\lambda(1 - P_M)}$$

Figure 17-14 represents the spreadsheet for a single-server queuing model with a finite queue. All the required Excel formulas are shown.

A Single-Server Model for a Limited Population

A related queuing model arises when the customers arriving at the system represent a small population. Although this case resembles the model for a finite queue, here the potential customers (rather than the line itself) are limited. Such a situation may arise in a plant that contains several machines that need to be serviced when they break down. Each malfunctioning machine is treated as an arriving customer, and the breakdowns can be assumed to be a Poisson process. The model involves the constant

M = Maximum number of customers that may need service

The probabilities for the number of customers either waiting or receiving service are

$$P_0 = 1 \left/ \sum_{n=0}^{M} \left[\frac{M!}{(M - n)!} \left(\frac{\lambda}{\mu} \right)^n \right] \right.$$

$$P_n = \frac{M!}{(M - n)!} \left(\frac{\lambda}{\mu} \right)^n P_0 \quad \text{for } 1 \le n \le M$$

The parameter λ represents the arrival rate of a *single* customer, and unlike λ in other queuing models it does not represent the customer group as a whole.

FIGURE 17-15
Spreadsheet for a single-server model with a limited population

	A	B	C	D	E	F	G	H
1	**QUEUING EVALUATION WITH A LIMITED POPULATION**							
2								
3	PROBLEM:		Supply Room					
4								
5			Parameter Values:					
6			Mean Customer Arrival Rate: lambda =				2	
7			Mean Customer Service Rate: mu =				10	
8			Size of Customer Population: M =				10	
9								
10			Queuing Results:					
11			Mean Number of Customers in System: L =				5.0919	
12			Mean Customer Time Spent in System: W =				0.5187	
13			Mean Number of Customers Waiting					
14				(Length of Line): L_q =			4.1103	
15			Mean Customer Waiting Time: W_q =				0.4187	
16			Traffic Intensity: rho =				0.2000	
17								
18			Number in	Probability	Cumulative			
19			System, n	P_n	Probability			
20			0	0.0184	0.0184			
21			1	0.0368	0.0552			
22			2	0.0662	0.1213			
23			3	0.1059	0.2272			
24			4	0.1483	0.3755			
25			5	0.1779	0.5534			
26			6	0.1779	0.7313			
27			7	0.1423	0.8736			
28			8	0.0854	0.9590			
29			9	0.0342	0.9932			
30			10	0.0068	1.0000			

The remaining results are

$$L_q = M - \frac{\lambda + \mu}{\lambda}(1 - P_0) \qquad L = L_q + (1 - P_0)$$

$$W_q = \frac{L_q}{\lambda(M - L)} \qquad\qquad W = \frac{L}{\lambda(M - L)}$$

As an illustration, the spreadsheet is shown in Figure 17-15. (It is on the CD-ROM accompanying the text and can be used as a template for solving other single-server applications with a limited population.) The development of this spreadsheet is shown in Appendix 17-1.

A Single-Server Model with Constant Service Times

As a special case, suppose that service times are constant, so that it takes time $1/\mu$ to serve each customer. Because successive customers will all require the same amount of time, the variance is zero. Substituting $\sigma^2 = 0$ into the model in Section 17-6, we find

$$L_q = \frac{(\lambda/\mu)^2}{2(1 - \lambda/\mu)}$$

The results for L, W_q, and W may then be calculated as before, using this level for L_q. As an illustration, the spreadsheet is shown Figure 17-16.

FIGURE 17-16
Spreadsheet for the
single-server model with
constant service times
for the supply room
illustration

17-10 (OPTIONAL) TESTING FOR GOODNESS OF FIT

Because the form of the probability distribution assumed for arrival and service times is so crucial, it may be desirable to do a statistical verification. The usual statistical procedure for doing this is the **goodness-of-fit test.** We describe one such procedure, the Kolmogorov–Smirnov test. This test indicates whether we should accept or reject the null hypothesis that a particular distribution applies.

For instance, we use the goodness-of-fit procedure to test whether the checkout times at a WaySafe market are exponential with mean rate $\mu = 12$ customers per hour, or .20 per minute (so that the mean checkout time is $1/12 = .0833$ hour, or 5 minutes). The test compares the expected frequencies for various times with actual sample data, assessing the magnitude of the deviation between the two sets of values. If that deviation is significant (in a statistical sense), the null hypothesis must be rejected, and we would have to conclude that the checkout times are represented by some distribution other than the exponential. A small deviation requires the opposite, and we would then accept the null hypothesis and conclude that the exponential distribution applies.

The Kolmogorov–Smirnov test requires that we establish for each actual level t of the random variable T two cumulative relative frequencies. These are the actual frequencies, denoted as $F_a(t)$, which correspond to the sample data, and the expected frequencies $F_e(t)$, computed under the assumed distribution. The test statistic involves computing the greatest absolute difference between these frequencies.

KOLMOGOROV–SMIRNOV TEST STATISTIC

$$D = \max \left| F_a(t) - F_e(t) \right|$$

For various sample sizes n and significance levels α, a critical value D_α for D may be determined from Appendix Table G.

| TABLE 17-4 | Random Sample of Actual Checkout Times at a WaySafe Market |

CHECKOUT TIME (MINUTES)				
2.5	1.5	.5	11.0	.5
1.5	2.0	19.5	11.5	17.5
.5	3.0	1.0	2.0	3.5
10.0	4.5	6.0	1.5	5.0
1.5	8.5	14.5	1.0	.5
		Total = 131.0		

Consider the data in Table 17-4, which lists $n = 25$ checkout times observed at a WaySafe market. We will test the null hypothesis that an exponential distribution applies with a mean rate of $\mu = .20$ customer per minute.

The test statistic D is computed in Table 17-5. The sample data have been first sorted in increasing sequence, providing the observed checkout times as the t values, shown in column (1) of Table 17-5. Each sample value has a relative frequency of $1/n = 1/25 = .04$. This is the increment used to compute the cumulative relative frequencies $F_a(t)$ shown in column (2). The expected cumulative relative frequencies are equal to the respective cumulative exponential probabilities applicable under the null hy-

| TABLE 17-5 | Computation of the Test Statistic D for Checkout Times at a WaySafe Market |

(1) POSSIBLE TIME t	(2) ACTUAL FREQUENCY $F_a(t)$	(3) EXPECTED FREQUENCY $F_e(t) = 1 - e^{-.20t}$	(4) DEVIATION $F_a(t) - F_e(t)$
.5	.04	.095163	-.055163
.5	.08	.095163	-.015163
.5	.12	.095163	.024837
.5	.16	.095163	.064837
1.0	.20	.181269	.018731
1.0	.24	.181269	.058731
1.5	.28	.259182	.020818
1.5	.32	.259182	.060818
1.5	.36	.259182	.100818
1.5	.40	.259182	.140818
2.0	.44	.329680	.110320
2.0	.48	.329680	**.150320**
2.5	.52	.393469	.126531
3.0	.56	.451188	.108812
3.5	.60	.503414	.096586
4.5	.64	.593430	.046570
5.0	.68	.632121	.047879
6.0	.72	.698806	.021194
8.5	.76	.817316	-.057316
10.0	.80	.864665	-.064665
11.0	.84	.889197	-.049197
11.5	.88	.899741	-.019741
14.5	.92	.944977	-.024977
17.5	.96	.969803	-.009803
19.5	1.00	.979758	.020242

pothesis. In Chapter 4 we saw that for any possible time t the cumulative probability may be obtained from the expression.

$$\Pr[T \le t] = 1 - e^{-\mu t}$$

Here, the symbol μ represents the process rate (which is sometimes denoted as λ). The cumulative relative frequencies $F_e(t)$ for the present illustration, computed using $\mu = .20$ are listed in column (3). Column (4) lists the differences between the actual and expected frequencies. The maximum of these, shown in boldface, establishes the value of the test statistic

$$D = .150320$$

With $n = 25$, the smallest tabled value for D_α is .20790 for $\alpha = .10$. Because the computed test statistic value is smaller, the null hypothesis of exponential distribution can only be rejected at a higher significance level than .10, such as .15 or .20. This means that the test results are not statistically significant. The null hypothesis must be *accepted,* and we must conclude that the exponential distribution applies with a mean rate of $\mu = .20$ customer per minute (12 customers per hour).

Accepting the null hypothesis does not mean that the exponential distribution must apply. The same conclusion might also have been reached with some other probability distribution assumed for the null hypothesis. Only after repeated observation can we ever be certain that the exponential distribution with the stated parameter applies. Only then can we be totally confident that the basic queuing models most accurately convey the underlying relationships.

Using *BestFit* Software

The chi-square test discussed in statistics texts is another procedure useful in finding a best-fit distribution. Its weakness is that there are no clear guidelines for selecting intervals. The Kolmogorov–Smirnov test discussed above is more powerful than the chi-square test in the sense that it does not depend on the number of intervals used. A weakness of the Kolmogorov–Smirnov test is that it does not detect tail discrepancies very well. The Anderson–Darling test can be used to do that. The *BestFit* 4.0 software program on the CD-ROM accompanying this book compares data with more than 30 different distributions and does all of these statistical tests automatically. It fits data to the following distributions: beta, binomial, chi-square, error, Erlang, exponential, gamma, geometric, hypergeometric, inverse Gaussian, logistic, log normal, negative binomial, normal, Pareto, Poisson, Rayleigh, Student t, triangular, uniform, and Weibull, among others.

To illustrate how to use *BestFit* 4.0 on the WaySafe data, we enter the 25 numbers in the Sample column of the *BestFit* opening screen, click on Fitting on the menu bar, and select Run Fit. This initiates the process of fitting all the distributions selected by *BestFit* to the data. Figure 17-17 shows part of the Fit Results dialog box that appears. On the left-hand side is a list of all the distributions fitted, from the best (inverse Gaussian) to the worst (uniform). In the line *Rank by,* K-S means that the Kolomogorov–Smirnov test statistic, D, was used as the criterion for ranking the distributions. Clicking on the down arrow to the right of K-S gives other ranking options, such as chi-square, Anderson–Darling, or root-mean-square error. The middle of the figure shows a graph of the best distribution and the data. Figure 17-17 also shows that $D = 0.1195$ for the best distribution. This is found under the GOF (goodness of fit) tab on the right-hand side of the Fit Results dialog box in the K-S column.

FIGURE 17-17

Fit Results dialog box showing all the fitted distributions and a graph of the best one (inverse Gaussian) compared with the WaySafe data

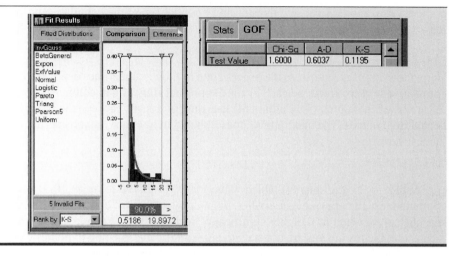

An exponential distribution (with mean time of 5.05) is the third-best fit. Figure 17-18 shows a graph of how it compares with the WaySafe data. *BestFit* calculates $D = 0.1802$ (a little larger than the .1503 calculated above).

Plausibility of the Exponential Distribution

The exponential distribution, like the normal distribution, is a theoretical model that only approximates reality. Such probability models may be quite useful even if some literal interpretations are absurd. Some obvious inadequacies of theoretical distributions may be outweighed by the overall closeness of their approximations to reality. Although the normal curve provides a nonzero probability that a randomly selected man will be over 20 feet tall, it reflects the immense rarity of such an event. Even though theoretically such a giant might be expected to be born only once in every billion tril-

FIGURE 17-18

Comparison of Exponential to WaySafe data

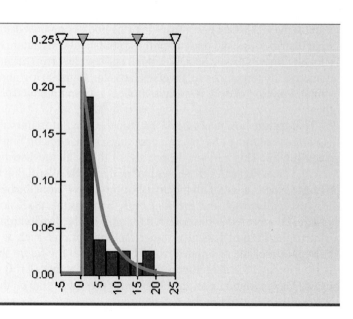

lion lifetimes of the universe, or even longer, the value of the normal distribution is that it provides accurate probabilities for more ordinary heights.

Consider one implication of the exponential distribution which can be seen in the probability density function curve in Figure 4-15(b) on page 100. Notice that when $t = 0$, the density function is highest, which implies that the most likely values are in the neighborhood of 0. That may be a good representation for arriving cars, but it would poorly match reality for supermarket checkouts, for which a zero checkout time is an *impossibility!* Nevertheless, actual checkout data may have other properties (a near-zero mode, a very pronounced positive skew) so that the exponential distribution can actually provide a good empirical approximation overall.

PROBLEMS

17-1 For each of the following single-server queuing systems, determine the values of L, W, L_q, W_q, and ρ:

(a)	(b)	(c)	(d)
$\lambda = 20$	$\lambda = 8$	$\lambda = 2$	$\lambda = .4$
$\mu = 25$	$\mu = 12$	$\mu = 5$	$\mu = .7$

17-2 Patrons arrive at the Dogpatch post office at the rate of 30 per hour. There is one clerk on duty, who takes an average of 1 minute to serve each customer. Service times are approximately exponential.
  (a) Calculate the mean customer time (1) spent waiting in line and (2) spent receiving or waiting for service. Also, find the mean number of customers (3) in line and (4) receiving or waiting for service.
  (b) Construct the probability distribution for the number of customers inside the post office (stopping at that n where the probability rounds to zero to two decimal places).

17-3 For each of the following waiting-line situations, give at least one reason why the models provided in this chapter may be inappropriate for determining the mean customer waiting time:
  (a) Telephone calls being placed through a manually operated switchboard
  (b) Customers arriving at a restaurant for dinner
  (c) Patients visiting a dermatologist, who sees patients only by appointment
  (d) A bottling machine filling empties with ingredients
  (e) Plant workers showing their badges to a security guard while passing through the corridor into the main building

17-4 Refer to Problem 17-2 regarding the Dogpatch post office and your answers. Determine the probabilities for the following events:
  (a) The next customer arrives at least 1 minute after his predecessor.
  (b) It will take at least 1 minute to complete service for the 13th customer.
  (c) The 46th customer waits no more than 30 seconds.
  (d) Exactly 5 customers arrive between 10:00 and 10:10 A.M.

17-5 Sammy Lee is the sole operator of a barbershop. Between noon and 6 P.M. on Saturday afternoons, 1 customer arrives every 15 minutes on the average. Sammy takes an average of 10 minutes to trim each customer. His little shop has chairs for only 2 waiting customers in addition to the customer getting a haircut.
  (a) What is the probability that any particular customer will have to spend part of his waiting time standing up?
  (b) What percentage of an average Saturday afternoon is Sammy busy? How many hours is he idle on an average Saturday afternoon?
  (c) What is the probability that any particular customer will have to wait more than 20 minutes before getting a haircut?
  (d) What is the probability that any particular haircut takes more than 15 minutes?

17-6 Refer to the supply room example in the chapter when no automation is used. Suppose that the service rate can be raised to 35 customers per hour by sending the clerk to special training. This results in a salary increase for the clerk, bringing the cost to $6 per hour. Suppose further that each un-

productive employee now costs $8 per hour. Determine the average hourly queuing system cost.

17-7 Refer to the copying machine example in the chapter. Suppose that three machines are installed. This will require a bigger room, raising rent by $1 per hour. All the other costs are the same.

(a) Determine the average hourly cost with three machines.

(b) Are three machines cheaper overall than two machines? Explain.

17-8 Ace Airlines has one reservations clerk on duty at a time to handle information about flight times and make reservations. All calls to Ace Airlines are answered by an operator. If a caller requests information or reservations, the operator transfers the call to the reservations clerk. If the clerk is busy, the operator asks the caller to wait. When the clerk becomes free, the operator transfers the call of the person who has been waiting the longest. Assume that arrivals and services can be approximated by a Poisson process. Calls arrive at a rate of 10 per hour, and the reservations clerk can service a call in an average of 4 minutes.

(a) What is the average number of calls waiting to be connected to the reservations clerk?

(b) What is the average time that a caller must wait before reaching the reservations clerk?

(c) What is the average time it takes for a caller to complete a call?

(d) What is the probability that a caller takes more than 10 minutes to complete a reservation?

(e) What is the probability that there will be no callers in a 15-minute period?

(f) What is the probability that there will be 3 callers in a 15-minute period?

17-9 Suppose that the management of Ace Airlines in Problem 17-8 is considering installing some visual display equipment and a new reservations system. One of the benefits of this system is that it will reduce the average time required to service a call from 4 to 3 minutes.

(a) Under the new system, what would be the average number of calls waiting to be connected?

(b) Under the new system, what would be the average waiting time for a caller?

(c) Suppose that instead of installing the new system, a second reservations clerk is added.

Calls could then be referred to whichever clerk was free.

(1) What would be the average number of calls waiting?

(2) What would then be the average waiting time for a caller?

17-10 Mildred's Tool and Die Shop has a central tool cage manned by a single clerk, who takes an average of 5 minutes to check and carry parts to each machinist who requests them. The machinists arrive once every 8 minutes on the average. Times between arrivals and for service are assumed to both have exponential distributions. A machinist's time is valued at $15 per hour; a clerk's time is valued at $9 per hour. What are the average hourly queuing system costs associated with the tool cage operation?

17-11 Mildred wants to improve the costs for the tool cage operation in Problem 17-10. Two alternatives are (1) use two clerks who are equally fast and (2) have a machinist instead of a clerk operate the tool cage. (Special knowledge enables the machinist to provide service twice as fast as the clerk.)

(a) Determine the mean machinist time spent checking out tools for both alternatives.

(b) Find the average hourly queuing system costs for both alternatives. Which one would be cheaper?

(c) Discuss any advantages of each alternative that cannot be measured by applying queuing models.

17-12 The multiple-server model described in the chapter assumes that customers will form a single queue and that FIFO will be used. In one BetaAlpha market there is insufficient holding space for such an operation. Customers instead select a checkout lane and stay there until checking out. There are two lanes, and each can serve customers at a mean rate of 20 per hour. Customers arrive at the checkout area at a mean rate of 30 per hour.

(a) Determine the mean waiting time that would apply if there were room for a single line to form, feeding to the first free checkout lane.

(b) Determine the mean waiting time applicable to a customer who randomly chooses one of the two checkout lines. The customer

stays put, and each lane experiences a mean arrival rate of 15 per hour.

(c) Are your answers to (a) and (b) different? Give a nonmathematical explanation.

(d) Would either the solution in (a) or (b) be the correct one if a customer always joined the shortest line? Give a nonmathematical explanation.

17-13 Samantha Lee is the owner and sole operator of a hair salon. She can service customers at a mean rate of 2 per hour. Customers arrive at the salon at a mean rate of 1.5 per hour.

(a) Samantha's customers currently arrive randomly. Determine (1) the mean number of customers in the salon, (2) the mean number of customers waiting, (3) the mean customer waiting time, (4) the mean customer time in the system, and (5) Samantha's utilization factor.

(b) Each customer-hour spent waiting results in lost business having a net present value of $2.

    (1) Ignoring Samantha's salary, determine Samantha's average hourly queuing system cost.

    (2) Compute Samantha's average hourly gross profit when each customer spends $20.

(c) Samantha implements a reservation system that boosts her mean arrival rate to 1.9 customers per hour. There is no waiting.

    (1) What will be Samantha's average profit per hour?

    (2) If the reservation system involves purchasing a computer and software for $1,000, how many hours will it take Samantha to break even?

17-14 C. A. Gopher & Sons is to excavate a site from which 100,000 cubic yards of dirt must be removed. Gopher has the choice of using a scoop loader or a shovel crane. He has leased 10 trucks at $20 per hour. A scoop loader costs $40 per hour, and a shovel crane costs $60 per hour. Once work has been started, the trucks will arrive according to a Poisson process at a mean rate of $\lambda = 7$ trucks per hour. Truck-filling times are approximately exponentially distributed. A scoop loader can fill an average of 10 trucks per hour. The shovel crane is faster and is capable of filling 15 trucks per hour on the average. (For simplicity, we will assume that the truck arrival rate is the same, regardless of the equipment used.)

Because the number of truck arrivals required to excavate the site is fixed by the amount of dirt to be removed, the optimal choice of filling equipment will be the one that minimizes the combined average hourly costs of unproductive truck time plus the cost of the filling equipment. Determine the optimal choice.

17-15 The manager of a WaySafe market with 10 checkout counters wants to determine how many counters to operate on Saturday morning. His decision will be determined in part by the costs assigned to each additional minute that a customer spends checking out of the store. In a special experiment in obsolete stores about to be closed, customers were forced to wait in line for an abnormally long time. The study concluded that an average of $.05 in future profits is lost for every minute that a customer spends waiting.

Assume that WaySafe customer arrivals at the checkout area are approximated by a Poisson process with a mean rate of $\lambda = 2$ per minute, that each attendant can check out customers at a mean rate of .5 per minute, and that the service time is exponentially distributed. Assume that a single waiting line feeds customers to the first available checker.

(a) What is the minimum number of checkers required for the service capacity to *exceed* the demand for service? Determine the mean customer waiting time when that many checkers are providing service.

(b) What is the mean customer waiting time if one more checker is added?

(c) The salary expense for each checker is $10 per hour. What number of checkers will minimize the total hourly queuing system cost—the number in (a) or in (b)? (Ignore service time, because no penalty applies for actual checkout time spent.)

17-16 The following service times (in minutes) were observed for teller transactions at Million Bank:

.4	.6	.8	1.2	1.4
1.8	2.0	4.0	5.6	7.2

Apply a goodness-of-fit test with the null hypothesis that the service times have an exponential distribution with a mean rate of .5 per minute.

17-17 Consider the WaySafe checkout time data in Table 17-4. Apply the Kolmogorov–Smirnov test with the null hypothesis that the checkout times are normally distributed with mean $1/\mu = 5$ minutes per customer and standard deviation of $\sigma = 3$ minutes.
  (a) Should the null hypothesis be accepted or rejected?
  (b) Does your finding contradict the test applied in the chapter with the same data? Explain.

17-18 Refer to Problem 17-2(a). Solve the problem when the service time is normally distributed with a mean of $1/\mu = 1$ minute and a standard deviation of $\sigma = .30$ minutes.

17-19 Refer to Problem 17-8. Solve the problem assuming that the standard deviation in service time is (1) $\sigma = 2$ minutes (1/30 hour) and (2) $\sigma = 5$ minutes (1/12 hour).

17-20 A hospital emergency room can accommodate a maximum of $M = 5$ patients. The patients arrive at a rate of 4 per hour. The single staff physician can only treat 5 patients per hour. Any patient overflow is directed to another hospital.
  (a) Determine the probability distribution for the number of patients either waiting for or receiving treatment at any given time.
  (b) Determine the mean values of the number of patients in the emergency room, the number of patients waiting to see the doctor, the patient waiting time, and the patient time spent in the emergency room.
  (c) Repeat the calculations in (b) assuming that there is no restriction on the number of patients to receive treatment.

17-21 A machinist services $M = 5$ machines as they break down. Individual machines fail at a rate of 1 per day, and the machinist fixes them at a rate of 2 per day.
  (a) Determine the probability distribution for the number of machines that will break down at any given time.
  (b) Calculate L_q, L, W_q, and W.
  (c) Repeat the calculations in part (b) for (1) $M = 6$, (2) $M = 7$, and (3) $M = 8$.
  (d) Repeat the calculations in (b) for a machinist who services a population of thousands of machines. Assume that machine failures and service times occur at the given rates.

17-22 Customers arrive at a coffee vending machine randomly at a mean rate of 50 per hour. Although service times may vary slightly, a constant service model is a good approximation. The mean service rate is 100 per hour. Determine the values of L, W, L_q, W_q, and ρ.

Spreadsheet Problems

17-23 For Problem 4-23, determine tables and charts for the frequency curve and cumulative distribution for $t = 0, .5, 1, 1.5, 2, \ldots, 5$. Show the formulas on the same page.

17-24 For Problem 4-24 determine tables and charts for the probability distribution and the cumulative distribution for $x = 0, 1, 2, 3, \ldots, 14$. Show the formulas on the same page.

17-25 For Problem 17-8(d), determine tables and charts for the cumulative distribution of the waiting time in the system and in line for $t = 0, 5, 10, 15, \ldots, 45$ minutes. Show the formulas on the same page.

17-26 Solve Problem 17-4 using a spreadsheet.

17-27 Solve Problem 17-1 using a spreadsheet.

17-28 Solve Problem 17-2 using a spreadsheet.

17-29 Solve Problem 17-7 using a spreadsheet.

17-30 Another WaySafe supermarket manager is analyzing her operations on Saturday mornings, when six full-service checkout stands are currently in operation. The arrival rate (Poisson process) to the stands is 1 customer per minute. The mean checkout time is 5 minutes per customer (assuming an exponential distribution) and is the same for all checkers. By analyzing the records used to obtain these data, the manager has determined that one-half of the customers

buy five items or fewer. This group can be serviced in an average of 1 minute each (again, assuming an exponential distribution); it takes a mean of 9 minutes to serve the longer customers. The manager wants to know if she should convert one full-service checkout stand to serve customers who buy only five items or fewer.

(a) What is the expected waiting time per customer for the present operational setup?

(b) For the proposed operational setup, what is the expected waiting time for customers buying (1) six or more items and (2) five or fewer items, assuming that the latter customers can only go through the small-item checkout stand?

(c) If you were buying more than five items, which system would you prefer? Why?

(d) Which system would be more efficient if the cost of a (1) customer's waiting time is $.05 per minute and the cost of a (2) customer's waiting time is $.20 per minute?

(e) Re-solve under the assumption that six independent single-channel queues are changed into five independent queues for six or more items and one single-channel express queue for customers with five or fewer items.

17-31 Refer to the Million Bank example in the chapter. Suppose that each weekday between 10 A.M. and noon, customers arrive at a mean rate of 150 per hour. All the other data are the same. Find the number of tellers that will minimize average hourly cost during these periods.

17-32 (a) Solve Problem 17-8 using a spreadsheet.
(b) Solve Problem 17-9 using a spreadsheet.

17-33 (a) Solve Problem 17-10 using a spreadsheet.
(b) Solve Problem 17-11 using a spreadsheet.

17-34 Solve Problem 17-15 using a spreadsheet.

17-35 Solve Problem 17-13 using a spreadsheet.

17-36 Refer to Problem 17-13. Analyze the sensitivity of the answer in (a) to variations in the mean customer arrival rate from 100 to 500 per hour.

17-37 Solve Problem 17-20 using a spreadsheet.

17-38 Solve Problem 17-21 using a spreadsheet.

17-39 Solve Problem 17-22 using a spreadsheet.

17-40 How many technical support representatives are needed to answer customer questions in a Bell Computer Corporation's Customer Service Department? The department's policy is that calls should be answered within 20 seconds. Although it is impossible to guarantee it, the department would like that to happen 95% of the time on the average. Data indicate that the average service rate is 30 calls per hour and the arrival rate is 20 calls per hour. Assume an $M/M/S$ model and use the formula

$$W_q(t) = \Pr[W_q \le t] = \frac{\left(\frac{\lambda}{\mu}\right)^S [1 - e^{-(\mu S - \lambda)t}]}{(S-1)!\left(S - \frac{\lambda}{\mu}\right)} P_0 + 1 - \frac{S\left(\frac{\lambda}{\mu}\right)^S}{S!\left(S - \frac{\lambda}{\mu}\right)} P_0$$

where P_0 is the same as in the text.

17-41 Refer to Problem 17-40. Use Excel's Data Table option to analyze the sensitivity of your answer to variations in customer arrival rates, technical support representative service times, the .95 probability, and the 20-second time. That is, find the number of technical support representatives for the following two tables:

λ	25	26	27	28	29	μ 30	31	32	33	34
15										
16										
17										
18										
19										
20										
21										
22										
23										
24										
25										

t(sec)	0.50	0.60	0.70	Probability 0.80	0.85	0.90	0.925	0.975	0.99
1									
5									
10									
15									
20									
25									
30									
35									
40									
50									
60									

BestFit *Problems*

17-42 The following table gives the results of a count of the number of customers arriving during 60 1-minute intervals during a Friday morning:

Number of Customers	Frequency
0	31
1	16
2	5
3	4
4	3
5	0
6	1

   (a) Use *BestFit* to find the discrete distribution that best fits the data.

   (b) Is the Poisson distribution a reasonable fit to the data? Explain why or why not.

17-43 The following table gives the results of a count of the number of customers arriving during 60 1-minute intervals during a Friday afternoon:

Number of Customers	Frequency
0	6
1	30
2	15
3	5
4	3
5	0
6	1

   (a) Use *BestFit* to find the discrete distribution that best fits the data.

   (b) Is the Poisson distribution a reasonable fit to the data? Explain why or why not.

17-44 A study of 25 transactions at a bank teller window during a Friday morning yields the following table. It gives the length of time, in minutes, for each of 25 transactions.

Time for a Teller to Serve a Customer (Minutes)				
.86	.44	.80	.40	.37
.86	.39	.91	.56	.86
.57	.77	.98	1.25	.57
.60	.41	.46	.36	1.74
1.20	.67	.40	.65	1.39

   (a) Use *BestFit* to find the continuous distribution that best fits the data (1) using chi-square as the goodness-of-fit statistic and (2) using the Kolmogorov–Smirnov D as the goodness-of-fit statistic.

   (b) Is the exponential distribution a reasonable fit to the data based on the chi-square and Kolmogorov–Smirnov D statistics? Explain why or why not.

17-45 A study of 25 transactions at a bank teller window during a Friday afternoon yields the following table. It gives the length of time, in minutes, for each of 25 transactions.

Time for a Teller to Serve a Customer (Minutes)				
1.1	1.0	0	.8	2.6
.6	2.8	.8	1.3	.8
2.0	.2	.9	.4	.2
1.8	2.5	.7	.1	1.9
5.4	1.4	1.4	1.9	.2

   (a) Use *BestFit* to find the continuous distribution that best fits the data (1) using chi-square as the goodness-of-fit statistic and (2) using the Kolmogorov–Smirnov D as the goodness-of-fit statistic.

   (b) Is the exponential distribution a reasonable fit to the data based on the chi-square and Kolmogorov–Smirnov D statistics? Explain why or why not.

17-46 A study of the weekly sales of boxes of ZIP discs at a particular branch of USA Computers results in the data in the following table.

Week	Sales	Week	Sales	Week	Sales	Week	Sales
1	61	14	66	27	55	40	67
2	43	15	43	28	40	41	62
3	42	16	43	29	40	42	35
4	59	17	51	30	53	43	51
5	67	18	55	31	49	44	50
6	54	19	53	32	52	45	52
7	40	20	52	33	30	46	54
8	55	21	64	34	41	47	61
9	65	22	32	35	55	48	52
10	52	23	40	36	50	49	66
11	49	24	62	37	48	50	57
12	68	25	34	38	48	51	57
13	72	26	41	39	65	52	66

(a) Use *BestFit* to find the distribution that best fits the data (1) using continuous distributions and both the chi-square and Kolmogorov–Smirnov *D* statistics and (2) using discrete distributions.

(b) Is the normal distribution a reasonable fit to the data based on the chi-square and Kolmogorov–Smirnov *D* statistics?

(c) Is the Poisson distribution a reasonable fit to the data? Explain why or why not.

CASE   17-1 *Caledonia Bank*

Peter McGregor is the operations manager for Caledonia Bank. He is establishing teller schedules for the Seventh Street Branch. The following data apply to the arrivals of customers at various times of the week.

Period	Daily Average Number of Arrivals
(1) Monday–Friday 10 A.M.–12 P.M.	155
(2) Monday–Friday 12–1 P.M.	242
(3) Monday–Friday 1–3 P.M.	290
(4) Friday 3–6 P.M.	554

The bank opens at 10 A.M. and closes at 3 P.M., except for Friday, when it closes at 6 P.M. Past study shows that arrivals over each period constitute a Poisson process. The mean time to complete customer transactions is 2 minutes, and individual service times are approximated by an exponential distribution.

Tellers all work part-time and cost $10 per bank hour. Past experience shows that a significant drop-off in clientele soon follows when customers are forced to experience lengthy waits.

McGregor also needs to decide whether or not to install an automated teller machine (ATM). The equipment supplier claims that other banks experience a 30% diversion of regular business away from human tellers, plus a further 10% expansion in the previous level of overall client transactions (with all of the increase going to the ATM).

ATM business takes place on a 24-hour basis, although traffic is negligible between 11 P.M. and 6 A.M. During the busier hours, times between customer arrivals are assumed to be represented by a single exponential distribution.

The mean service time at an ATM is .5 minute, and again the exponential distribution serves as an adequate approximation. McGregor believes that once an ATM is installed, the human tellers would be left with a greater proportion of the more involved and lengthy transactions, raising the mean service time to 2.5 minutes.

QUESTIONS

1. Assume that Caledonia Bank uses human tellers only.
   (a) For each time period, determine the minimum number of tellers needed on station to service the customer stream.
   (b) Assume that the numbers of tellers in (a) are used. For each time period, determine the mean customer waiting time.
   (c) For each time period, determine the mean customer waiting time when the number of tellers is one more than found in (a).

2. Past experience shows that the drop-off in clientele due to waiting translates into an expected net present value in lost future profits of $.10 per minute. For each time period, determine the average hourly queuing system costs, assuming that the bank uses (a) the minimum number of human tellers necessary to service the arriving customers and (b) one teller more than is found in (a) of Question 1.

3. Suppose that the ATM is installed and that customers themselves decide whether to use human tellers or to use the ATM, and that two queues form independently for each. Finally, assume that there is a 10% traffic increase generated by the ATM within each open time period, and that all of it is for the ATM. Determine, in each case, the mean customer arrival rate (a) at the human teller windows and (b) at the ATM. Then, find (c) the minimum number of human tellers required to be on station during each time period.

4. Determine for Peter McGregor the mean customer waiting time during each open time period for those customers who seek (a) human tellers and (b) access to the ATM. Assume that the number of human

tellers used is one more than that found in (c) of Question 3.

5. The hourly cost of maintaining and operating the ATM is $5. Increased customer traffic results in additional bank profit estimated to be $.20 per transaction. Determine, for Peter McGregor, the net hourly queuing system cost, reflecting any profit increase, for operating with the ATM for periods (1)–(4). Use the mean waiting times from Question 4.

CASE   17-2   *Banco Espírito Santo e Comercial de Lisboa*

by Manuel Bernardo
California State University, Hayward

Banco Espírito Santo e Comercial de Lisboa (BESCL) is one of the largest and oldest banks in Portugal. All of Espírito Santo businesses, including BESCL, were nationalized in the 1970s.

In the 1980s, Portugal was moving away from centralized government ownership and toward a more free-market economy. The new government of Prime Minister Cavaco Silva began setting the trend of selling government-owned businesses. In 1986, the Espírito Santo Group regained the Banco Espírito Santo e Comercial de Lisboa. Currently, BESCL controls approximately 9% of Portuguese retail banking. The Espírito Santo family wants the bank to improve its operations and be more efficient.

In the past, Banco Espírito Santo e Comercial's motto was, "If it works, don't change it." However, under the new Espírito Santo ownership, times have changed, operational efficiency is being monitored and evaluated, and many improvements are being made. One improvement being considered in particular has to do with a branch located in Almada. If successful, it could be implemented in other branches. The Almada Branch is the only banking institution

TABLE 17-6	Customer Arrival Log Sheet Monday, Wednesday, and Friday 9:00–11:00 A.M. (Customers per half hour)

Customers	Frequency	Customers	Frequency
33	1	51	6
34	2	52	5
35	1	53	4
36	1	54	13
37	3	55	3
38	8	56	2
39	2	57	1
40	2	58	3
41	2	59	2
42	3	60	2
43	2	61	2
44	4	62	2
45	4	63	0
46	0	64	1
47	4	65	1
48	1	66	1
49	0	67	6
50	6	68	0

TABLE 17-7	Customer Arrival Log Sheet Monday, Wednesday, and Friday 11:00 A.M.–1:00 P.M. (Customers per half hour)

Customers	Frequency	Customers	Frequency
86	1	110	4
87	0	111	5
88	0	112	4
89	0	113	1
90	1	114	4
91	1	115	3
92	0	116	3
93	1	117	0
94	1	118	4
95	2	119	3
96	3	120	2
97	2	121	2
98	1	122	1
99	2	123	3
100	4	124	2
101	3	125	1
102	3	126	2
103	3	127	2
104	4	128	0
105	3	129	1
106	2	130	1
107	3	131	0
108	4	132	1
109	6	133	1

with no ATMs. If service and efficiency continue to be inadequate, BESCL risks losing dissatisfied customers to its main competitors. David Rodrigues, district operations manager of BESCL headquarters in Lisbon, wants to consider certain areas in which BESCL could become more efficient. He contacted the branch manager in Almada, Carlos Periera, and both agreed to work together on the problem.

Customer surveys showed that customers were satisfied with the physical appearance and maintenance of the branch; it was clean and organized. Tellers were also found to be polite, helpful, and accurate. However, there were complaints about waiting times in lines, even though recently the branch had switched to using a single line for all the windows, instead of having a line for each one, in an effort to improve service. Rodrigues also surveyed former customers who had moved to other banks. Two problem areas pointed out by these customers were waiting times and lack of ATMs. Another concern was about the number of teller windows. Currently, there are 10 in the branch, and Periera is considering rearranging the lobby so that there will be room for 2 more.

Rodrigues has decided to tackle the waiting-line problem first. It seems to be an indirect result of what appears to be the inadequacy of BESCL's teller-staffing policy. BESCL's policy is to use the minimum number of tellers needed, no matter what the occasion. Rodrigues is considering revising this policy and asks Periera to help gather data. First, Rodrigues needs information about customer arrivals at the bank. He asks Periera to count customers as they enter the lobby during each half-hour period during the day, making sure that only customers who join a line or go to a window are counted. He emphasizes that this information is not the same as that provided by teller log sheets, which record the number of customers served based on those customers waiting in line. The information Periera obtains is shown on the log sheets in Tables 17-6–17-11. Furthermore, Rodrigues asks Periera to monitor tellers and record the time required to service a customer. This includes the processing time for all of a customer's transactions. If a customer makes a savings deposit and cashes a personal check, then the customer service time includes the time to process both of those transactions. The information gathered about customer service times is shown in Table 17-12.

Like its competitors, BESCL operates its branch Monday through Friday, 9:00 A.M. to 3:00 P.M. Periera reminds Rodrigues that in a typical 5-day week, Monday and Friday are the busiest days and accordingly asks that data be arranged in that way.

TABLE 17-8	Customer Arrival Log Sheet Monday, Wednesday, and Friday 1:00–3:00 P.M. (Customers per half hour)

Customers	Frequency	Customers	Frequency
48	1	66	5
49	2	67	4
50	1	68	5
51	1	69	4
52	1	70	3
53	2	71	4
54	1	72	4
55	3	73	3
56	2	74	3
57	3	75	2
58	3	76	2
59	2	77	2
60	4	78	1
61	5	79	1
62	5	80	0
63	7	81	1
64	6	82	1
65	5	83	1

TABLE 17-9	Customer Arrival Log Sheet Tuesday and Thursday 9:00–11:00 A.M. (Customers per half hour)

Customers	Frequency	Customers	Frequency
20	0	35	7
21	1	36	7
22	0	37	6
23	1	38	5
24	0	39	5
25	2	40	4
26	1	41	5
27	3	42	3
28	4	43	3
29	5	44	2
30	5	45	2
31	6	46	1
32	5	47	1
33	7	48	1
34	8	49	0

TABLE 17-10	Customer Arrival Log Sheet Tuesday and Thursday 11:00 A.M.–1:00 P.M. (Customers per half hour)		
Customers	**Frequency**	**Customers**	**Frequency**
34	0	52	7
35	1	53	5
36	0	54	4
37	1	55	3
38	2	56	3
39	1	57	3
40	3	58	3
41	4	59	1
42	3	60	2
43	3	61	3
44	5	62	1
45	4	63	1
46	7	64	1
47	4	65	1
48	5	66	1
49	6	67	0
50	5	68	0
51	6	69	1

TABLE 17-11	Customer Arrival Log Sheet Tuesday and Thursday 1:00–3:00 P.M. (Customers per half hour)		
Customers	**Frequency**	**Customers**	**Frequency**
25	1	40	5
26	1	41	5
27	0	42	6
28	1	43	5
29	1	44	4
30	2	45	6
31	3	46	4
32	3	47	4
33	4	48	3
34	2	49	2
35	5	50	2
36	6	51	3
37	6	52	1
38	7	53	0
39	7	54	1

Tellers are hired on a part-time basis and are paid $12 per hour.[*] Additional useful information is an estimate of $.15 per minute of lost profits attributed to customers who get tired of waiting in lines and leave.

When Periera gave Rodrigues his data on the arrivals and service times, Rodrigues told him that he already had all the information he needed. The next step, he said, is to determine the optimal number of tellers for each two-hour period. In thinking more deeply about the problem, Rodrigues knows that at some point he will have to make some sort of trade-off between achieving minimum operating cost and a satisfactory level of service. Rodrigues also decides that the method for applying customer cost will be the waiting time in line only, because the environment is more of a retail type.

Another area of concern for Rodrigues is the introduction of ATMs at the branch. ATMs are in use at the main branch in Lisbon. This makes matters simpler because cost data are available. The hourly cost of maintaining and operating an ATM is $6.50 per hour. The mean service time at an ATM is 1 minute. A total of three ATMs are installed at the main branch. For each ATM installed the bank experiences an average diversion from regular customer service of 10% during the 9:00–11:00 A.M. and 1:00–3:00 P.M. time

periods. During the 11:00 A.M.–1:00 P.M. time period, the average diversion rate for each ATM is 12%.

QUESTIONS

1. (a) Determine the average customer arrival rates for the six time periods given in Tables 17-6–17-11. Is the Poisson distribution a good approximation to the data? Use the Kolmogorov–Smirnov test to answer this question.
   (b) Determine the average service time from Table 17-12. Is the exponential distribution a good approximation to the data? Use BestFit to answer this question.

In answering the following questions, assume that customers arrive according to a Poisson distribution and that the teller service time is exponential, both with mean rates as determined in Question 1.

2. Rodrigues claims that he has enough information to determine the minimum number of tellers needed. Verify his claim for each of the six time periods during the day and determine:
   (a) the minimum number of tellers needed
   (b) the mean customer waiting time
   (c) the total cost (teller and waiting cost) per week

3. Rodrigues is wondering how increasing the number of tellers would affect the waiting time in the lines and total cost. Suppose the number of tellers available for each time period increases by one, two, or three. (Note: Use the minimum number of tellers found in Question 2(a) as the starting point.) Ro-

---

[*]The currency used in Portugal is the Escudo (Esc). For simplicity, the U.S. dollar notation is used.

TABLE 17-12   Service Time Log Sheet (all times in minutes)

Customers	Frequency	Customers	Frequency
1	.23	51	5.26
2	1.43	52	3.44
3	2.98	53	.25
4	.98	54	2.61
5	.53	55	.50
6	2.22	56	.93
7	6.66	57	.88
8	3.54	58	7.78
9	.45	59	.42
10	5.43	60	.21
11	2.34	61	.78
12	3.34	62	2.35
13	1.26	63	1.53
14	.18	64	1.68
15	2.75	65	.35
16	4.87	66	1.58
17	.34	67	3.65
18	7.03	68	1.05
19	1.14	69	1.47
20	1.05	70	2.78
21	1.37	71	4.12
22	.64	72	.34
23	3.23	73	1.89
24	.80	74	3.57
25	3.39	75	1.01
26	.77	76	1.50
27	5.67	77	.39
28	4.23	78	2.42
29	4.31	79	4.60
30	5.69	80	1.94
31	.51	81	.78
32	6.09	82	1.22
33	8.44	83	5.70
34	.17	84	.86
35	.12	85	1.66
36	1.11	86	1.78
37	2.48	87	2.16
38	3.72	88	.09
39	.79	89	3.12
40	2.51	90	2.10
41	2.01	91	.51
42	.42	92	2.62
43	10.37	93	1.00
44	.69	94	1.83
45	1.76	95	.33
46	9.58	96	6.82
47	.56	97	1.56
48	.83	98	2.59
49	11.15	99	.99
50	4.90	100	3.94

drigues is interested in keeping track of (1) the mean waiting time in line for each period, and (2) total costs (teller and waiting costs).

4. Using the information from Questions 2 and 3 determine:
    (a) the number of tellers for each time period as-
    suming that the objective is the minimum waiting time
    (b) the number of tellers for each time period assuming that the objective is minimum total cost

5. On reflection, Rodrigues thinks that the solution to Question 4(a) can be improved. The incremental increases in tellers for all time periods together seem arbitrary, because a change in one time period may not be optimal for another. Consider instead determining independently the number of tellers for each time period. Analyze this situation to see if Rodrigues's hunch is correct.

6. (a) Suppose a 10% salary increase is being considered for the part-time workers. Does this affect the above answers?
    (b) Rodrigues reasons that the higher the tellers' salaries, the fewer tellers should be used. Help him by determining the range of salary increases for which the solution to Question 4(b) would remain the same. Then find the range for which a smaller number of tellers should be used.

7. Suppose the union is demanding that all part-time employees be given full-time jobs. This would mean that the number of tellers working during the day would be equal to the number needed during the peak period. How would this affect the answers in Question 4(b)?

8. Carlos Periera is thinking about the meeting he will be having with Rodrigues to explain his recommendations. He realizes that there will be concern expressed about the $.15 lost profit estimate, because this includes qualitative terms such as goodwill costs and lost future profits. Neither of these factors can be determined with much precision. Does this matter? That is, suppose the lost profit estimate is $.28. How would this affect the solution determined in Question 4(b)? What if the lost profit is $.29?

9. One of the major bottlenecks appears to be during 11:00 A.M.–1:00 P.M. on Mondays and Fridays. The reason for this is the large number of customers that come into the bank. Although the bank has more teller windows open during this time than during any other, there are only 10 available, and this appears to be too few. Rodrigues thinks that remodeling the lobby and adding 2 more windows would help alleviate this bottleneck. He has received an estimate of $25,000 from a company to do all of the remodeling and expansion work. Calculate the in-

ternal rate of return for this investment to determine if it is worthwhile. Assume a 5-year time period when calculating the rate of return, and suppose that the bank has a minimum required return on all investments of 10%. Assume the bank is open for business 50 weeks per year.

10. (a) Rodrigues wants to see the effect of using an ATM. There will be two lines, one for the tellers and the other for the ATM. Assuming the number of tellers determined in 4(b), calculate the mean waiting time for the teller line, the mean waiting time for the ATM line, and the total weekly cost consisting of the costs of the tellers, the cost of operating the ATM, and the

costs of waiting for both tellers and the ATM.

(b) What about adding a second or even a third ATM? Assume 1 line in front of each ATM.

(c) As mentioned in Question 5, the number of tellers determined in Question 4(b) might not be the best, because the assumption is made that increases in tellers must occur simultaneously for all time periods. Analyzing each time period independently of the others, determine the best number of tellers in conjunction with the ATM machine. Do the results change the answers obtained in part (a) or part (b)? Explain.

CASE 17-3 *West to East Food Market*

by Manuel Bernardo
California State University, Hayward

West to East Food Markets (WEFM) are located in seven cities in California: San Francisco, Sacramento, Oakland, Fresno, San Jose, Los Angeles, and San Diego.

The Oakland store differs from all the others. It is more of a wholesale outlet modeled after chains such as Costco. The Oakland store has a deli and a small "take-out" stand. Manager Juan Perez has followed the guidelines for setting the number of checkers needed but still receives many complaints from customers regarding long checkout lines. Typically, the manager uses the minimum number of checkers needed given the customer arrival rate and service rates. The Oakland store has 10 checkout stands. Arrival information is listed in Table 17-13 and was obtained by having someone count the prospective customers as they got in line to buy the products they had selected.

As can be seen in Table 17-13, the time period 12–2 P.M. on Mondays through Fridays is the busiest. Of particular interest is that many of the customers purchase "food to go" for lunch. During this time period, it takes a checker approximately 3 minutes to check out a customer. For the other periods, the average service time is 4 minutes. This is due to the fact that many customers purchase fewer items during that time period. Therefore, the average service time is lower. The service times for all of the time periods are approximated by an exponential distribution.

Of concern to Perez is the mean number of customers waiting in line and the mean customer waiting time when a minimum number of checkers is used. These are summarized in Table 17-14 and are estimated for the average number of customer arrivals (from Table 17-13) and the average service times.

The minimum number of servers, mean number of customers waiting, and mean customer waiting

TABLE 17-13 Daily Customer Arrivals

Period	Day	Time	Average Number of Arrivals
1	Monday–Friday	9:00 A.M.–12:00 P.M.	162
2	Monday–Friday	12:00–2:00 P.M.	220
3	Monday–Friday	2:00–5:00 P.M.	114
4	Monday–Friday	5:00–7:00 P.M.	98
5	Saturday	12:00–6:00 P.M.	414

TABLE 17-14 Waiting Times

Period	Minimum Number of Servers	Mean Number of Customers Waiting (L_q)	Mean Customer Waiting Time (W_q) in Minutes
1	4	8	36
2	6	10	33
3	3	5	22
4	4	4	18
5	5	11	46

time are estimated for all those that join the lines. For example, period 1 has 4 checkout stands in operation. This number was estimated by taking the mean arrival rate during that period (54) and the mean service rate (15) and then finding the minimum number of servers needed—four in this case. The number of servers can be anything above the minimum, but the company policy is to use only the minimum number of checkout stands required by the situation. Perez thinks that the policy of using the minimum number of checkers will need to be evaluated and possibly revised. Some of the lines and waiting times are obviously too excessive, leading to lost profits because many customers with only a few items are discouraged and leave the store. Even the smallest estimated average waiting times in line, in period 2 and period 3, have customers taking about twenty minutes to check out. If more checkers were used, the waiting times would be lower.

To aid him in his analysis, Perez estimates the lost profit per minute accountable to dissatisfied customers, the ones who enter the store and are so discouraged by the lines that they do not even bother getting in line. Perez knows that estimating the lost profits due to these discouraged customers is difficult. One measure he uses is the estimated cost of the goods left in abandoned carts, in other words, the customers who started to accumulate goods in the store but left without getting in line. Another way is surveying those customers who leave the store without making purchases to get an estimate of how much they might have spent; the membership card numbers are recorded, and past purchases are used as a measure of lost profits. There are variations for some periods because of differences in purchasing habits. For example, during period 2 customers spend less on lunch than those during period 5, who purchase groceries for the following week. By combining information from all of the procedures just described, Perez arrives at the data in Table 17-15.

In general, the longer the lines, the higher the number of customers who are "lost"; in other words, the periods with longer waiting times have a higher percentage of lost customers. The checkout clerks are paid $12 per hour. An average of $.10 in future profits is lost for every minute that a customer spends waiting. With this information Perez is sure that the cost of the current policy can be estimated. In addition, he feels that this cost can be lowered by using additional checkers.

Two other options are (1) have quick checkout stands and (2) have "courtesy clerks" bag the groceries, thus reducing the service time. The "courtesy clerks" would be paid $9 an hour, and there would be one for each checker used. If the number of checkers used is 6, then the number of "courtesy clerks" used will be 6. For analysis of the quick checkout option, Perez estimated the number of shoppers who buy 10 or fewer items and estimated new service rates. Table 17-16 provides this information.

On a 2-week trial basis, one quick checkout lane was used. The mean service time for a regular lane was 5 minutes per customer (4 minutes for period 2) and for a quick lane, 1.5 minutes.

In answering the following questions, use waiting cost, not idle cost, when determining customer cost.

QUESTIONS

1. Calculate the total cost for the minimum number of checkers used in Table 17-14. The cost should include the checker cost, the cost of waiting in line, and the opportunity cost (associated with the lost profits from Table 17-15).

2. Assume that adding a checkout clerk for each time period will reduce the percentage of customers lost due to the long line (Table 17-15) by two percentage points. For example, for period 1 the percentage of lost customers would decrease from 4% to 2%, for period 2 from 8% to 6%, and so on. In other

TABLE 17-15	Lost Sales Costs	
Period	Lost Profit per Customer Lost	Percentage of Customers Lost Due to Long Lines
1	$15	4%
2	5	8%
3	15	4%
4	25	4%
5	30	8%

TABLE 17-16	Percentage of Customers Purchasing 10 or Fewer Items
Period	Percentage of Shoppers Purchasing 10 or Fewer Items
1	15%
2	33%
3	15%
4	15%
5	15%

words, by having shorter lines, not as many cus-tomers will be "lost." Assume that this will be the case every time a checkout clerk is added. An addi-tional requirement is that a minimum of 2% of the customers will always be lost for whatever the rea-sons may be; in other words, the percentages in Table 17-15 can go only as low as 2%.

(a) Add one more checkout clerk (besides those in Table 17-14) for each time period and calculate the total cost. Note that the maximum number of checkout clerks is 10.

(b) Re-solve for 2, 3, and 4 more checkout clerks.

3. Assume that the objective is to minimize total costs. Which policy (1, 2a, or 2b) will provide lowest cost?

4. What will be the number of checkout clerks, length of waiting line, and waiting time for the minimum cost policy in Question 3? Are there other factors

that should be taken into account when choosing the best solution?

5. Is it better to have one lane of the optimal solution just determined as a quick check lane? Explain.

6. Repeat Question 5 making two of the lanes quick check lanes.

7. Carrying Question 6 one step further, now add "courtesy clerks" (in addition to the two quick lanes) and see if this improves the situation. As-sume that by using a "courtesy clerk," the service time is reduced by 30 seconds for the quick check lanes, by 1.5 minutes for the regular lanes during periods 1, 3, 4, and 5, and by 1 minute for period 2.

8. What if "courtesy clerks" are used with the number of checkers determined in Question 4 (and no quick check lanes)? Would this be an improvement?

APPENDIX 17-1   SPREADSHEET DEVELOPMENT

Multiple-Server Model

The workbook for the multiple-server model has two worksheets. The first is the spreadsheet in Figure 17-6 (MMS tab). The second (Sum tab) contains a table that per-forms a summation in the denominator of the P_0 formula.

All of the calculations in Figure 17-6 are based on P_0, the probability that there are no customers in the system. In several places, the Excel formulas use the value in G8, the cell location for the number of servers, S. Cell D20 has the formula

$$=1/(VLOOKUP(G8-1,Sum!A2:C102,3)$$
$$+VLOOKUP(G8,Sum!A2:C102,2)*(1/(1-G6/(G7*G8))))$$

which utilizes the Excel VLOOKUP function. The initial VLOOKUP has first argu-ment G8-1 (i.e., S-1), which gives the stopping point (here, $2-1=1$) of the summation in the denominator of the P_0 calculation; it indicates the value to be looked up in the table in the second worksheet (Sum tab), shown in Figure 17-19. The second argument, Sum!A2:C102, defines the lookup range of that table. The last argument is 3, which identifies the column (here, the third one) of the sum table from which the looked up value is obtained. Consequently, this VLOOKUP uses the table in Figure 17-19, goes to cell A3 (in row 3) because it has the value 1 (G8-1), and returns the value 2.2 (cell C3), which is the value in the third column. See the *Guide to Excel* on the CD-ROM accompanying the text for more details about the VLOOKUP function.

Column B in Figure 17-19 finds the values of formula

$$\frac{(\lambda/\mu)^n}{n!}$$

	A	B	C
1	n	$(\lambda/\mu)^n/n!$	Sum from 0 to n
2	0	1.000E+00	1.000E+00
3	1	1.200E+00	2.200E+00
4	2	7.200E-01	2.920E+00
5	3	2.880E-01	3.208E+00
6	4	8.640E-02	3.294E+00
101	99	7.395E-149	3.320E+00
102	100	8.874E-151	3.320E+00

FIGURE 17-19
Excel worksheet table for the summations in the denominator of P_0 (Sum tab)

for the values of n in column A, $n = 0, 1, \ldots, S$. They are used in the denominator of the P_0 calculations. Column C adds these terms from $n = 0$ to $n = S$ and yields the summation in the denominator of the P_0 formula. The formula for cell B2 is

$$=((\text{MMS!}\$G\$6/\text{MMS!}\$G\$7)^{\wedge}(\text{A2}))/\text{FACT(A2)}$$

The above uses the Excel FACT function to compute the factorial values. The formula is copied down to B102. (We assume that the number of servers is 100 or less.) Column C then sums the values in column B. The first number, in cell C2, is 1 because cell B2 is 1. Cell C3 is the sum of cells B2 and B3, which is the same as the formula =C2+B3. Cell C4 is the sum of cells B2:B4. That is equivalent to using the Excel formula =C3+B4 for cell C4, which is copied down the column.

Once P_0 is known, the rest of the results in Figure 17-6 can be determined. The formula in cell G14 gives the mean number of customers waiting L_q:

$$=((\text{G6/G7})^{\wedge}\text{G8})*(\text{G6}/(\text{G8}*\text{G7}))*\text{D20}/(\text{FACT(G8)}*(1-\text{G6}/(\text{G7}*\text{G8}))^{\wedge}2)$$

The next three formulas derive from the above. Cell G15 has the mean customer waiting time W_q, which in Excel is =G14/G6. The mean customer time spent in the system W is in cell G12 with formula =G15+(1/G7), and the mean number of customers in the system L is in cell G11 with formula =G14+(G6/G7). Cell G16 contains the server utilization factor ρ, determined by the formula =G6/(G7*G8).

The formulas in cells D21:D39 determine the probabilities of n customers (jobs in the copying system). Cell D21 contains the Excel formula for P_1.

$$=\text{IF(C21}>\$G\$8,(\$D\$20*((\$G\$6/\$G\$7)^{\wedge}(\text{C21/2}))$$
$$*((\$G\$6/\$G\$7)^{\wedge}(\text{C21/2})))/(\text{FACT}(\$G\$8)*(\$G\$8^{\wedge}((\text{C21}-\$G\$8)/2))$$
$$*(\$G\$8^{\wedge}((\text{C21}-\$G\$8)/2))),$$
$$(\$G\$6/\$G\$7)^{\wedge}\text{C21}*(\$D\$20/\text{FACT(C21)}))$$

The Excel IF function is used because there are two ways to compute P_n, depending on whether $n \leq S$ or $n > S$. Once this formula is entered in cell D21, it is copied down to cells D22:D39.

The cumulative probabilities are in cells E20:E39. Cell E20 has the formula =D20 and cell E21 has =E20+D21. The latter cell is copied down to cells E22:E39 for this example. For other problems, we may not know how many rows are needed, and more can be added until P_n for the last one rounds to zero. (It cannot hurt to have too many rows.)

Cost Analysis

The workbook for a cost analysis has two worksheets like those of the multiple-server model. Figure 17-20 summarizes the Excel formulas for P_0, L_q, L, W_q, and W applicable to cells B22:F22 in the first worksheet (Cost Analysis tab), shown as the spreadsheet

FIGURE 17-20
Excel formulas for
Figure 17-7

	B	C
22	=1/(VLOOKUP(A22-1,Sum!A2:C102,3)+VLOOKUP(A22,Sum!A2:C102,2)*(1/(1-$G$6/($G$7*A22))))	=(($G$6/$G$7)^A22)*($G$6/(A2 2*$G$7))*B22/(FACT(A22)*(1-$G$6/($G$7*A22))^2)

	D	E	F	G
22	=C22+($G$6/$G$7)	=C22/$G$6	=E22+(1/$G$7)	=$G$9*A22

	H	I	J	K
22	=$G$6*E22*$G$8	=G22+H22	=$G$6*F22*$G$8	=G22+J22

in Figure 17-7. They are based on the Excel formulas for the multiple-server model. Assuming no more than 100 servers, we copy row 22 down to row 113. The second worksheet (Sum tab) contains a table that performs a summation in the denominator of the P_0 formula. It is identical to the one in Figure 17-19 for the multiple-server model.

The only new formulas are for the server cost, customer cost (based on W_q or W), and total cost (based on W_q or W) in cells G22:K22. The cost in cell G22 is the server cost per unit time (cell G9) multiplied by the number of servers from column A and has the formula =$G$9*A22. The customer cost based on W_q is in cell H22 and has the formula

$$=\$G\$6*E22*\$G\$8$$

The alternative customer cost based on W is in cell J22 and has the formula

$$=\$G\$6*F22*\$G\$8$$

The total cost based on W_q is in column I and is the sum of the server cost in column G plus the customer cost in column H. Cell I22 thus contains the formula =G22+H22. In the same manner, the total cost based on W is in cell K22 and has the formula =G22+J22.

Rows 14 through 21 contain analogous formulas but are missing from Figure 17-7 because they have been suppressed by using Excel's Group and Outline option (click on Data on the menu bar and select Group and Outline) to shorten the *printed* spreadsheet. For more information about this option, see the CD-ROM accompanying the text.

Single-Server Model with a Limited Population

The workbook for the limited population model has two worksheets like the preceding models. The first is Figure 17-15 (Limited Pop tab). The second worksheet (Sum tab), not shown in Figure 17-15, contains a table that performs a summation in the denominator of the P_0 formula, here computed differently than with earlier models.

All of the calculations in Figure 17-15 are based on P_0, which is found in cell D20 by the formula

$$=1/(VLOOKUP(G8,Sum!A2:C12,3))$$

where the second argument refers to cells A2:C12 on the Sum tab. The cell reference C12 in the range A2:C12 depends on the limited population size. In this example, $M = 10$, so C12 is used, but if $M = 5$ then the range is A2:C7 or if $M = 27$ then the range is A2:C27, and so forth, for other limited population sizes up to an assumed maximum of $M = 100$.

FIGURE 17-21
Excel worksheet (Sum tab) for the summation in the denominator of P_0

	A	B	C
1	n	$[M!/(M-n)!](\lambda/\mu)^n$	Sum from 0 to n
2	0	1	1
3	1	2	3
4	2	3.6	6.6
5	3	5.76	12.360000
6	4	8.064	20.424000
7	5	9.6768	30.100800
8	6	9.6768	39.777600
9	7	7.74144	47.519040
10	8	4.644864	52.163904
11	9	1.8579456	54.021850
12	10	0.37158912	54.393439

The worksheet corresponding to the Sum tab is used to find the required summations. Column B in this worksheet, shown in Figure 17-21, finds the values of

$$\frac{M!}{(M-n)!}\left(\frac{\lambda}{\mu}\right)^n$$

for the values of n in column A, $n = 1, 2, \ldots, S$, for $S \leq M$. They are used in the denominator of the P_0 calculations. Column C adds terms from $n = 0$ to $n = S$ and yields the summation in the denominator of the P_0 formula. In this example, $M = 10$. Cell B2 has the Excel formula

=(FACT('Limited Pop'!$G$8)/FACT('Limited Pop'!$G$8-A2))
*('Limited Pop'!$G$6/'Limited Pop'!$G$7)^A2

which uses the Excel FACT function to compute the various factorials. It is copied down to cell B102 (the population is assumed to be no more than 100). Column C sums the terms in column B so that cell C2 contains 1 and cell C3 has =C2+B3. This last cell, C3, is copied down to the rest of the cells in column C.

With P_0 known, the rest of the results in Figure 17-15 can be calculated using the formulas in Figure 17-22.

The formulas in column D of Figure 17-15 determine the probabilities for n customers in the system. Cell D21 contains the Excel formula for P_1

=(FACT($G$8)/FACT($G$8-C21))*$D$20*($G$6/$G$7)^C21

It is copied down the rest of the column. Column E contains the cumulative probabilities, having the formula =D20 in cell E20 and =E20+D21 in cell E21. The latter is copied down to the rest of the cells in the column.

FIGURE 17-22
Excel formulas for Figure 17-17

	G
11	=G14+1-D20
12	=G15+(1/G7)
13	
14	=$G$8-(($G$6+$G$7)/$G$6)*(1-$D$20)
15	=G14/(G6*(G8-G11))
16	=G6/G7

CHAPTER 18

SIMULATION

Want to improve the odds of saving enough to put the kids through college or have a nest egg to last through retirement? Try Monte Carlo simulation.

Karen Hube

I n the **analytic solution procedures** we have examined thus far, an algorithm provides a problem solution that can be mathematically proved to be optimal. In decision making under uncertainty, a solution obtained in this manner generally provides a maximum expected payoff or a minimum expected cost. All of these problems therefore involve variables whose values are determined by chance, so that probability distributions must be specified in advance.

We will now consider a **numerical solution procedure** that seeks optimal alternatives essentially through a trial-and-error process. This simulation technique may be applied to practically any decision problem that involves uncertainty. It is a problem-solving approach that offers several advantages over traditional analytic methods. The most significant advantage of simulation is that it can provide answers for problems that are difficult, or even impossible, to solve in a purely mathematical way.

Simulation thoroughly evaluates each alternative by generating a series of values for each random variable at the frequencies indicated by their probability distributions. This is done by sampling from populations of possible values of the variables. The resulting quantities are combined in accordance with an underlying mathematical model to provide a particular value for the payoff measure. After a number of repetitions, a statistical pattern in the results can be discerned. Simulation is therefore a procedure that tries out each alternative "on paper" over and over again; in effect, it represents a sample from the future. As in most random sampling procedures, random numbers are used to generate the events and quantities involved, as if they were determined by spins of a roulette wheel. For this reason, the procedure has become known as **Monte Carlo simulation.**

A variety of problems have been analyzed using Monte Carlo simulations. The oil-tanker port facility study described in Chapter 1 was analyzed using this procedure. Each design alternative was evaluated by more than 1,000 years of simulated operation to arrive at a statistically reliable estimate of its expected rate of return. Monte Carlo simulation has been used to establish baseball batting orders, select rocket combinations to use in launching satellites, and evaluate starting-time policies at golf courses. It has served in planning restaurant menus, in choosing cars, and in estimating how many tellers a bank should hire. It has determined optimal inventory policies for small retailers and large conglomerates. It has proved useful in production control in the

manufacture of automobiles, bicycles, and submarines. Monte Carlo simulation has been used to evaluate queuing systems of all kinds—even those without first-come, first-served policies or exponentially distributed service times.

18-1 CONCEPTS AND PROCEDURES: A WAITING-LINE SIMULATION

As an aid in our discussion of the concepts and procedures of Monte Carlo simulation, we will apply the technique to a simple waiting-line situation.

Illustration: A One-Man Barbershop

Sammy Lee, owner of a one-man barbershop, is contemplating adding a part-time assistant on Saturdays—the busiest day of the week. His daughter Samantha, who is studying quantitative methods at a distant university, has offered to perform a study to help her father make his decision. As a first step, Samantha wants to evaluate the characteristics of the present operation.

Samantha knows that customers arrive at Sammy's more or less randomly over time and that the time Sammy spends with a particular customer may vary substantially. To help in performing her final analysis, she wants to establish applicable Saturday values for the following:

1. Mean arrival rate (λ)
2. Mean time between arrivals ($1/\lambda$)
3. Mean service rate (μ)
4. Mean service time ($1/\mu$)
5. Mean customer waiting time (W_q)
6. Mean customer time in the system (shop) (W)
7. Mean number of customers in the waiting line (L_q)
8. Mean number of customers in the system (shop) (L)
9. Server utilization factor (proportion of time the barber is busy with customers) (ρ)

Samantha knows the textbook formulas for computing these values, but she also knows that they depend on a series of crucial assumptions that may not apply in her father's case. Because she is too far away to observe what goes on at Sammy's shop directly, she will have to simulate the Saturday operations to estimate the preceding parameters.

Duplicating Reality

Any Monte Carlo simulation seeks to duplicate reality as closely as possible within practical limitations. Thus, Samantha wants to conduct a simulation that resembles in all important respects what she would find if she actually observed her father's shop in operation.

If Samantha were watching the true operation, what information would she need to find the desired parameter values and how should she arrange the data to obtain the target results?

The simplest solution is to maintain a log, as illustrated in Figure 18-1, identifying each customer and recording when he arrives, when he receives his haircut, and when

FIGURE 18-1

Simple customer log for actual observations at a barbershop

Customer	Clock Time at Arrival	Clock Time at Beginning of Service	Clock Time at End of Service
Mr. Jones	9:15	9:15	9:30
Mr. Smith	9:25	9:30	9:45
Mr. Green	9:30	9:45	10:00

he is finished. As we will see, such a log contains the minimum amount of information necessary to answer the questions.

However, by giving a little additional thought to the design of such a log, Samantha can save some work later on. Items 2 and 4 on Samantha's list of parameters are the mean times between arrivals and for service, respectively. The data needed to compute these means exist in the original log, but, by adding two more columns, the bored log keeper can list the times between successive customer arrivals and the service time for each customer. Another new column can record how long each customer must wait before receiving service. Because a new customer's service cannot begin until the barber is finished with those customers ahead of him, waiting time is the elapsed clock time between his arrival and the end of service for the preceding customer (and thus the beginning of service for him). Figure 18-2 shows what this more detailed log may look like.

Of course, Samantha cannot be there, so she must use fictional customers. Her simulated log, discussed later, will be similar to the one in Figure 18-2. Because she is only interested in the queuing aspects of the barbershop, it is important that the arrival and service patterns of her fictional customers match those of the real ones. In this way, the interactions between the timing of various events in her simulation will be representative of those occurring in real life.

Probability Distributions

The essential inputs for Samantha's simulation are probability data regarding the patterns of customer arrivals and service. Because much of her analysis involves time, two probability distributions are sought: one for the time between successive customer arrivals and another for the service times of individual customers. Although the basic data for generating these distributions may best be determined by clocking customers during the actual operation of the shop, Sammy cannot afford to hire someone to do

Customer	Time Between Arrivals	Clock Time at Arrival	Clock Time at Beginning of Service	Service Time	Clock Time at End of Service	Waiting Time
Mr. Jones		9:15	9:15	15	9:30	0
Mr. Smith	10	9:25	9:30	15	9:45	5
Mr. Green	5	9:30	9:45	15	10:00	15

FIGURE 18-2   Detailed customer log for actual observations at a barbershop

TABLE 18-1 Probability Distributions for Times between Customer Arrivals and Customer Service Times

TIMES BETWEEN ARRIVALS		CUSTOMER SERVICE TIMES	
Time	Probability	Time	Probability
5 min	.10	5 min	.05
10	.15	10	.20
15	.25	15	.40
20	.25	20	.20
25	.15	25	.10
30	.10	30	.05
	1.00		1.00

this. Samantha therefore must apply the techniques presented in Chapter 4 to help her father establish subjective probabilities for these random variables.

Although both variables are continuous, Samantha determines the discrete approximations in Table 18-1 for the underlying probability distributions. Her hypothetical customers must therefore arrive randomly, and the frequency of interarrival times must be consistent with the probabilities given in Table 18-1. The amount of time taken to cut any customer's hair should also be unpredictable and vary according to the respective probabilities.

Generating Events Using Random Numbers

A Monte Carlo simulation generates events so that they occur with long-run frequencies that are identical to their probabilities. This process is similar to a statistical study in which **random numbers** are used to select a sample from a population of values.

You may recall from an earlier study of statistics that random numbers have no particular pattern and could record the outcomes from successive spins of a wheel of fortune, when any digit between 0 and 9 is equally likely to occur. Appendix Table F contains a list of random numbers created by the RAND Corporation. For convenience, we will use the following partial listings taken from the first two columns of that table:

*12*651 *61*646
*81*769 *74*436
*36*737 *98*863
*82*861 *54*371
*21*325 *15*732
*74*146 *47*887
*90*759 *64*410
*55*683 *98*078
*79*686 *17*969
*70*333 *00*201

Notice that the random numbers listed here contain five digits. Because the probability values for the barbershop simulation are accurate only to two places, we may therefore ignore all but the first two digits and use only the italicized portion of each number.

It really does not matter how random numbers are picked from the table, as long as the values of earlier numbers do not influence the choice of future ones.

In simulating the operations of Sammy Lee's barbershop, each hypothetical customer may be considered to be a sample observation taken from the population of all future clients seeking a Saturday haircut. In traditional statistics, sample customers are randomly selected from a master list. But in a simulation, the customers are imaginary ones with all the essential characteristics of real customers, so that they must be created in such a way that they could have come from a list like the log in Figure 18-2 that has not been and may never be constructed under actual operation. Although they are used differently in simulation than in an ordinary sampling study, random numbers serve this purpose.

In the actual operation of a barbershop, the chance events—each customer's arrival and service times—occur randomly. These events are simulated by translating successive entries on the list of random numbers. Thus, a random number of 67 for the tenth customer could mean that he arrives 20 minutes after the ninth. *A separate random number is used for each variable.* Thus, the next random number on the list might be 19, which could represent a service time of 10 minutes for this customer.

Before the actual simulation begins, exactly which random numbers are to correspond to each event or uncertain quantity must be determined. The barbershop study requires two random number assignments—one for each of the time random variables. Consider the time between arrivals first.

Table 18-1 indicates that an interarrival time of 5 minutes occurs with a probability of .10. This outcome should result 10% of the time in a simulation. Of course, there is no reason why more or less than 10% of these 5-minute outcomes cannot occur, just as a sequence of coin tosses may result in more or less than 50% heads. But when a large number of cases are considered, the frequency of occurrence for any event should be very close to its probability. We let random numbers determine when a 5-minute outcome will occur. Because any possible number is equally likely to appear in any position on a list of random numbers, we want to assign exactly 10% of these so that they correspond to an interarrival time of 5 minutes.

Any 10% of the random numbers will suffice, but these numbers must be identified in advance. It's easiest if we assign the smallest 10% of them to represent 5 minutes. Thus, we will set any two-digit random number between 01 and 10, inclusively, to correspond to a 5-minute interarrival time.

The next possible interarrival time is 10 minutes, which occurs with a probability of .15. Thus, the second 15% of the random numbers—those between 11 and 25—will be assigned to that event. To speed the process of assigning random numbers, it is helpful to construct a cumulative probability distribution like the one shown in Table 18-2. Each successive set of random numbers begins where the last set left off, ending with

TABLE 18-2   Random Number Assignment for Times between Arrivals Using Cumulative Probabilities

TIME BETWEEN ARRIVALS	PROBABILITY	CUMULATIVE PROBABILITY	RANDOM NUMBERS
5 min	.10	.10	01–10
10	.15	.25	11–25
15	.25	.50	26–50
20	.25	.75	51–75
25	.15	.90	76–90
30	.10	1.00	91–00

TABLE 18-3   Random Number Assignment for Service Times

SERVICE TIME	PROBABILITY	CUMULATIVE PROBABILITY	RANDOM NUMBERS
5 min	.05	.05	01–05
10	.20	.25	06–25
15	.40	.65	26–65
20	.20	.85	66–85
25	.10	.95	86–95
30	.05	1.00	96–00

the value that is identical (except for the decimal point) to the respective cumulative probability. This approach guarantees that the proportion of random numbers assigned will always be identical to the probability for the outcome. In doing this, 00 is treated as 100.

The same procedure is used to assign random numbers to service times in Table 18-3.

Setting Up the Simulation

Before starting her simulation, Samantha Lee must set it up so that she can create a hypothetical log. She begins by making up the *worksheet* in Figure 18-3. For convenience, each customer is given an identity number corresponding to the order of arrival. Notice that two additional columns ([1] and [5]) are required for the random numbers that determine the times between arrivals and the service times. The numbers in these columns may be entered in advance or one at a time as they are needed.

In general, a simulation is a series of **trials,** each of which is a repetition of the basic steps. In our example, the entries made in each customer row constitute a trial. The steps taken compose a portion of the **simulation model.** In the barbershop simulation, the worksheet itself spells out that part of the overall model in which the trials are generated. Later, we will discuss the remaining parts of the particular model.

The simulation model is basically mathematical and may be defined in terms of algebraic expressions. It is often more convenient, however, to indicate the procedures of the model in a worksheet that clearly delineates each step. In large-scale simulations that must be run on a digital computer, the model is generally embedded in the programming instructions.

Trial or Cust. No.	(1) Rand. No.	(2) Time Betw. Arriv.	(3) Clock Time at Arriv. [last (3) + (2)]	(4) Clock Time at Beg. of Serv. [(3) or last (7)]	(5) Rand. No.	(6) Serv. Time	(7) Clock Time at End of Serv. [(4) + (6)]	(8) Waiting Time [(4) − (3)]
1								
2								
3								

FIGURE 18-3   Worksheet for the one-man barbershop simulation

Conducting the Simulation

We are now ready to conduct the simulation. The worksheet entries for one customer at a time appear in Table 18-4.

Samantha begins with the first customer, obtaining the random number 12 from the first list provided earlier. This appears in column (1) and corresponds to a time between arrivals of 10 minutes, which is entered in column (2). Because there is no prior customer, these minutes are simply added to the shop's 9:00 opening time, providing 9:10 as the clock time at arrival for customer number 1. This time is entered in column (3) and also in column (4) for the clock time at the beginning of service, because Sammy is free to serve that customer immediately on his arrival. The next random number, 61, is read from the second list and entered in column (5). This corresponds to the service time of 15 minutes, which is placed in column (6). Adding the values in columns (4) and (6) yields a clock time of 9:25 when service ends, which is entered in column (7). Because this customer is served immediately, there is no waiting time.

The second customer is assigned the random number 81 and arrives at 9:35, 25 minutes after the first. Sammy Lee has finished with the preceding customer at 9:25, so service begins immediately at 9:35 with no waiting. The next random number, 74, corresponds to a 20-minute service time, so customer 2 is finished at 9:55.

TABLE 18-4   Worksheet Entries for the Barbershop Simulation

TRIAL OR CUST. NO.	(1) RAND. NO.	(2) TIME BETW. ARRIV.	(3) CLOCK TIME AT ARRIV. [LAST (3) + (2)]	(4) CLOCK TIME AT BEG. OF SERV. [(3) OR LAST (7)]	(5) RAND. NO.	(6) SERV. TIME	(7) CLOCK TIME AT END OF SERV. [(4) + (6)]	(8) WAITING TIME [(4) − (3)]
Open			9:00					
1	(12)	10	9:10	9:10	(61)	15	9:25	0
2	(81)	25	9:35	9:35	(74)	20	9:55	0
3	(36)	15	9:50	9:55	(98)	30	10:25	5
4	(82)	25	10:15	10:25	(54)	15	10:40	10
5	(21)	10	10:25	10:40	(15)	10	10:50	15
6	(74)	20	10:45	10:50	(47)	15	11:05	5
7	(90)	25	11:10	11:10	(64)	15	11:25	0
8	(55)	20	11:30	11:30	(98)	30	12:00	0
9	(79)	25	11:55	12:00	(17)	10	12:10	5
10	(70)	20	12:15	12:15	(00)	30	12:45	0
11	(14)	10	12:25	12:45	(53)	15	1:00	20
12	(59)	20	12:45	1:00	(08)	10	1:10	15
13	(62)	20	1:05	1:10	(62)	15	1:25	5
14	(57)	20	1:25	1:25	(97)	30	1:55	0
15	(15)	10	1:35	1:55	(90)	25	2:20	20
16	(18)	10	1:45	2:20	(23)	10	2:30	35
17	(74)	20	2:05	2:30	(68)	20	2:50	25
18	(11)	10	2:15	2:50	(16)	10	3:00	35
19	(41)	15	2:30	3:00	(17)	10	3:10	30
20	(32)	15	2:45	3:10	(91)	25	3:35	25
		345				360		250

Elapsed time = 3:35 − 9:00
              = 6 hours and 35 minutes
              = 395 minutes

Meanwhile, the third customer arrives 15 minutes after the second, at 9:50. Sammy is busy with customer 2 until 9:55, so customer 3's service cannot begin until then and he must wait 5 minutes. In general, the clock time at beginning of service is the *greater* of the entries in columns (3) and (7).

The simulation continues until 20 customers have been monitored. It is now possible for Samantha to estimate the various parameters. This procedure constitutes the remaining portion of the simulation model.

Summing the values in column (2) and dividing by the number of customers, we calculate the first result as follows:

Estimated Mean Time Between Arrivals

$$\frac{\text{Total time between arrivals}}{\text{Number of customers}} = \frac{345}{20} = 17.25 \text{ minutes per customer}$$

The reciprocal of this result, in units of customers per minute, provides the following:

Estimated Mean Arrival Rate

$$\frac{1}{\text{Mean time between arrivals}} = \frac{1}{17.25} = .058 \text{ customer per minute}$$
$$(3.48 \text{ customers per hour})$$

Summing the entries in column (6) and dividing by 20 customers, we calculate the following result:

Estimated Mean Service Time

$$\frac{\text{Total service time}}{\text{Number of customers}} = \frac{360}{20} = 18.00 \text{ minutes per customer}$$

And the reciprocal of this result provides the following:

Estimated Mean Service Rate

$$\frac{1}{\text{Mean service time}} = \frac{1}{18} = .056 \text{ customer per minute}$$
$$(3.36 \text{ customers per hour})$$

The true values of these parameters may be computed from the initial probability distributions, so that it is unnecessary to use these estimates. But some interesting points may be made by comparing the estimates with their true values (the expected values calculated in Table 18-5 using the initial probability distributions).

Notice that the true mean time between arrivals is 17.50 minutes per customer, which is quite close to the simulation result of 17.25. However, the true mean service time of 16.25 minutes per customer is considerably smaller than the simulated value of 18.00. We must keep in mind that a simulation is a sample result, and like any statistical estimate, it may be expected to contain sampling errors. In this particular simulation, the service times were longer than usual, reflecting the fact that abnormally large random numbers were used. This should not detract from the value of the simulation, however, because the service times actually observed on any particular Saturday may also tend to be longer than usual.

As in any sampling situation, the only protection against sampling error is to increase the precision or the reliability of the simulation estimates by conducting a suf-

TABLE 18-5 Expected Value Calculations to Determine True Parameter Values

POSSIBLE TIMES	PROBABILITY	TIME × PROBABILITY
Between arrivals:		
5 min	.10	.50 min
10	.15	1.50
15	.25	3.75
20	.25	5.00
25	.15	3.75
30	.10	3.00
	$1/\lambda$ = Mean time between arrivals = 17.50 min	
For service:		
5 min	.05	.25 min
10	.20	2.00
15	.40	6.00
20	.20	4.00
25	.10	2.50
30	.05	1.50
	$1/\mu$ = Mean service time = 16.25 min	

ficiently large number of trials. If 200 rather than 20 customers were evaluated, we would expect the estimated mean service time to be much closer to the true parameter value. Later we will consider the question of just how many trials ought to be used.

Samantha's other parameters must be estimated because they cannot be computed as easily as the simple expected values we just determined. Returning to Table 18-4, we divide the total of the column (8) values by the number of customers to determine the following:

Estimated Mean Customer Waiting Time

$$\frac{\text{Total waiting time}}{\text{Number of customers}} = \frac{250}{20} = 12.50 \text{ minutes}$$

Including the total of the column (6) service times in the numerator, we obtain the following expression:

Estimated Mean Customer Time Spent in the System

$$\frac{\text{Total waiting time + Total service time}}{\text{Number of customers}} = \frac{250 + 360}{20}$$
$$= 30.50 \text{ minutes}$$

This calculation reflects that a customer's time in the barbershop must be spent waiting for and then receiving service. This result is therefore equivalent to the sum of the mean waiting and service times.

$$12.50 + 18.00 = 30.50$$

The remaining parameter estimates require some thought. Consider the problem of finding the average number of customers waiting at any given time. This could be accomplished by taking every 5-minute time interval in the simulation and determining how many customers are waiting in each one. A relative frequency distribution indicating the proportion of times 0, 1, 2, 3, or 4 persons were waiting could then be found,

and their weighted average would provide the desired result. Fortunately, all of this extra work is unnecessary. Instead, we divide the total waiting time in column (8) by the simulation's **elapsed time,** or its duration from start to finish (calculated in Table 18-4 to be 395 minutes) to obtain the following result:

Estimated Mean Number of Customers Waiting

$$\frac{\text{Total waiting time}}{\text{Elapsed time}} = \frac{250}{395} = .63 \text{ customer}$$

It may seem a bit odd that customers result when we divide minutes by minutes, but this computation is the mathematical equivalent of the weighted average approach. We may view total waiting time as the product of the times when customers wait and the number of customers waiting, so that the numerator is in units of customer-minutes.

Similarly, the totals for columns (6) and (8) can be added and divided by elapsed time to provide the following:

Estimated Mean Number of Customers in the System

$$\frac{\text{Total service time} + \text{Total waiting time}}{\text{Elapsed time}} = \frac{360 + 250}{395}$$
$$= 1.54 \text{ customers}$$

This represents the average number of customers either waiting or receiving service at any point in time.

To find the proportion of time the barber is busy with a customer, we divide the total from column (6) by the elapsed time to obtain a value for the following:

Estimated Server Utilization Factor

$$\frac{\text{Total service time}}{\text{Elapsed time}} = \frac{360}{395} = .91$$

We see that Sammy Lee spends about 91% of the time that the shop is in operation on Saturday actually cutting hair. Another interpretation of .91 is that it represents the fraction of a customer who may be receiving service at any point in time. By subtracting this value from the estimated mean number of customers in the barbershop, we obtain the estimated mean number of customers who are waiting, or

$$1.54 - .91 = .63$$

Transient Simulation States

You may have wondered why Samantha Lee stopped her simulation abruptly with the twentieth customer at 3:35, in the middle of a busy period that started at about 2 P.M. Shouldn't she have continued her simulation until closing time?

All simulations must begin and end some time, and the number of trials is generally established in advance. In the barbershop example, this can lead to distortions near the beginning and the end of the simulation. Sammy Lee opened his shop at 9 A.M., and customers started trickling in at 9:10. No opening-time congestion, which may occur in reality, was possible. Also, no successful barber quits for the day when customers are still waiting. The middle of the simulation is the closest approximation of reality. Distortions encountered at the beginning and the end arise because the simulation is then in *transient states.* An analogy with the performance test on an automobile engine

may be helpful. An engine exhibits different characteristics while warming up than it does when it has been running for a while. To realistically assess performance, only the results obtained after the engine has warmed up should be considered. Also, a slight sputtering or coughing the instant after the ignition switch is shut off should not be reflected in the performance rating.

The impact of transitional distortions can be minimized by conducting the simulation over a longer period of time. If Samantha uses 1,000 customers (so that 50 Saturdays are considered back-to-back), distortions at the beginning and the end may be safely ignored.

It is another matter entirely if the barbershop actually goes through transient states when it is in actual operation. This may happen if customers are usually lined up at the door when Sammy arrives or if he varies his closing time to accommodate stragglers. Also, arrivals may be more concentrated at 2 or 3 P.M. than at other times. And Sammy may slow down in the afternoon, thereby increasing the service times. The simulation model itself must be sufficiently complex to realistically reflect the varying characteristics of a system.

Decision Making with Simulation

Samantha Lee's simulation provides a variety of estimates for the key parameters that may be helpful in any further analysis. Remember that Sammy Lee's basic problem is deciding whether or not to hire a second barber to work on Saturdays. To evaluate this alternative, a second simulation must be performed that involves a somewhat more complex procedure (which is left as an exercise for the reader to determine). A similar set of estimated parameter values will be obtained in this later simulation and may then be compared with the initial ones.

The comparison of two or more simulations may be a demanding task, especially when several kinds of information are provided by each one. To a certain extent, such a comparison presents the same problems we encountered when we evaluated samples taken from several populations. The statistical aspects of simulation will be discussed in Section 18-9.

18-2 SIMULATION AND THE COMPUTER

Monte Carlo simulation involves many repetitions of the same computational steps, which makes computers ideal for applying simulations. Once the computer program has been written, each alternative may be simulated and thousands of trials may be conducted at a relatively modest cost. Indeed, perhaps no other management science technique has been nurtured so dramatically by the advent of faster and more powerful computers.

Simulation Programs and Languages

The evolution of computer simulation programs has paralleled the dramatic changes in computers themselves. Early simulations were conducted on the initial generations of "mainframe" computers. Early users had to write their own programs from scratch. Special computer languages were written to streamline that process.

With the advent of personal computers, simulation software blossomed at a rapid pace. Some of these packages require a host program for inputting data and making displays. Section 18-7 discusses *@RISK*, a spreadsheet add-in program with which users

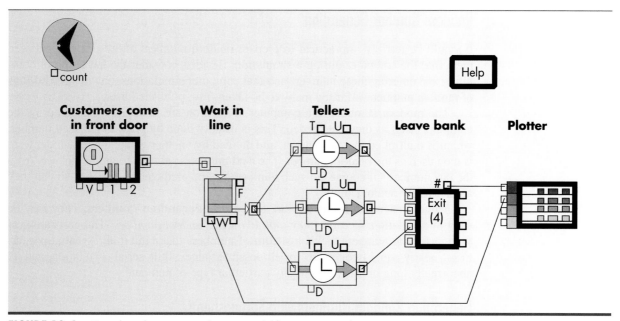

FIGURE 18-4   *Extend* simulation screen showing model for queuing simulation

may create a simulation model of considerable complexity. Even more elaborate "stand-alone" programs have recently appeared. One of these is *Extend,* which allows users to create models using blocks of various types, represented on a flow diagram by icons.

Figure 18-4 shows an *Extend* model for a 3-server queuing system. A variety of parameter settings may be made using pull-down menus. The simulation may be run in an animation mode showing customers arriving and receiving service. The output is generated in real time on-screen in graphical form, as in Figure 18-5.

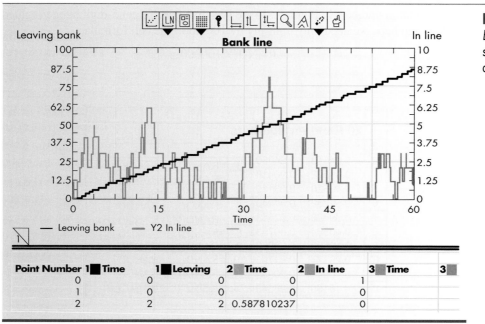

FIGURE 18-5
Extend simulation screen showing output from queuing simulation

Point Number	1	Time	1	Leaving	2	Time	2	In line	3	Time	3	
0		0		0		0		0		1		
1		0		0		0		0		0		
2		2		2		2	0.587810237		0				

Random Number Generation

It would be terribly impractical to prepare random numbers ahead of time and feed them into the computer during a simulation. Besides, consider the awful job of compiling and entering these numbers and that computer simulations may involve billions of random numbers—far too many to be taken from published lists.

The random numbers in a computer simulation are invariably generated by the computer itself as they are needed. This is usually done by providing a seed number, which is multiplied by one constant and divided by another value; the remainder term is then used as the random number. The next number is always found in this way from the last number. Of course, all such numbers can be predicted in advance, so that they are not really random at all.

Values generated in this way are called **pseudorandom numbers.** They may be used in simulations because *they look like true random numbers*. The generation of pseudorandom numbers yields a stream of numbers that exhibit all essential properties—nearly equal frequencies for all possible values, little serial correlation, and no abnormally long or short runs of any particular type of number.

Generating Random Numbers with Spreadsheets

Excel has a handy function for generating random numbers. Entering =RAND() in a spreadsheet cell returns a random number between zero and one. Figure 18-6 shows a spreadsheet with this formula entered 20 times in cells B3:C12. The formula was typed into cell B3 and then copied to the other cells.

No two spreadsheets will be alike. Each time the initial RAND formula is copied into another cell, the random numbers will change. This will occur normally whenever something is entered into another cell and the Enter key is depressed, causing Excel to recalculate all formulas in a spreadsheet. (To prevent the numbers from changing, the spreadsheet may be set in the manual recalculation mode: Tools, Options, Calculation tab, Manual button.)

There are many ways of using the RAND function to generate random numbers. All the random numbers in Figure 18-6 are less than one. To get 5-digit integer-valued random numbers, we need only multiply by 100,000. The cell formula

$$=RAND()*100000$$

FIGURE 18-6

Twenty random numbers generated by Excel RAND function

	A	B	C	D	E
1	**20 Random Numbers**				
2					
				A	B
3	0.04513	0.54380	3	=RAND()	=RAND()
4	0.81522	0.90410	4	=RAND()	=RAND()
5	0.49520	0.33119	5	=RAND()	=RAND()
6	0.59232	0.84140	6	=RAND()	=RAND()
7	0.39428	0.57553	7	=RAND()	=RAND()
8	0.40504	0.50753	8	=RAND()	=RAND()
9	0.10550	0.68953	9	=RAND()	=RAND()
10	0.29177	0.04796	10	=RAND()	=RAND()
11	0.70949	0.20935	11	=RAND()	=RAND()
12	0.10150	0.26348	12	=RAND()	=RAND()

generates random numbers from 00000 to 99999. Make sure to change the cell formats so decimals are not displayed (Format, Cells, Number tab, Number, Decimal places). Two-digit random numbers from 00 to 99 are generated if we instead multiply by 100.

Simulation Using Spreadsheets

Figure 18-7 gives the spreadsheet for the Sammy Lee barbershop simulation. It is on the CD-ROM accompanying the text and can be used to assist in other queuing evaluations. The format of the spreadsheet is a streamlined version of the manual one in Figure 18-4, with no need for random number columns. Column B calculates the time between arrivals using a generated random number and the interarrival time distribution stored at the bottom of the spreadsheet in cells A29:B34 (shown in Figure 18-8). Cell B6 has the formula

$$=VLOOKUP(RAND(),\$A\$29:\$B\$34,2)$$

	A	B	C	D	E	F	G
1		**Sammy Lee's Barbershop Simulation Example**					
2							
3		Time	Clock	Clock time		Clock time	
4		Between	time at	at begin.	Service	at end of	Waiting
5	Trial	Arrivals	arrival	of service	time	service	time
6	1	0:10	9:10 AM	9:10 AM	0:25	9:35 AM	0:00
7	2	0:10	9:20 AM	9:35 AM	0:15	9:50 AM	0:15
8	3	0:25	9:45 AM	9:50 AM	0:10	10:00 AM	0:05
9	4	0:20	10:05 AM	10:05 AM	0:15	10:20 AM	0:00
10	5	0:20	10:25 AM	10:25 AM	0:20	10:45 AM	0:00
11	6	0:05	10:30 AM	10:45 AM	0:15	11:00 AM	0:15
12	7	0:10	10:40 AM	11:00 AM	0:10	11:10 AM	0:20
13	8	0:15	10:55 AM	11:10 AM	0:05	11:15 AM	0:15
14	9	0:15	11:10 AM	11:15 AM	0:20	11:35 AM	0:05
15	10	0:05	11:15 AM	11:35 AM	0:20	11:55 AM	0:20
16	11	0:20	11:35 AM	11:55 AM	0:10	12:05 PM	0:20
17	12	0:15	11:50 AM	12:05 PM	0:15	12:20 PM	0:15
18	13	0:15	12:05 PM	12:20 PM	0:30	12:50 PM	0:15
19	14	0:20	12:25 PM	12:50 PM	0:15	1:05 PM	0:25
20	15	0:25	12:50 PM	1:05 PM	0:30	1:35 PM	0:15
21	16	0:15	1:05 PM	1:35 PM	0:10	1:45 PM	0:30
22	17	0:25	1:30 PM	1:45 PM	0:15	2:00 PM	0:15
23	18	0:15	1:45 PM	2:00 PM	0:15	2:15 PM	0:15
24	19	0:10	1:55 PM	2:15 PM	0:15	2:30 PM	0:20
25	20	0:30	2:25 PM	2:30 PM	0:15	2:45 PM	0:05
26	Average	0:16:15			0:16:15		0:13:30

	B	C	D	E	F	G
27						
35	26	=AVERAGE(B6:B25)		=AVERAGE(E6:E25)		=AVERAGE(G6:G25)

	B	C	D
36			
37	6	=VLOOKUP(RAND(),\$A\$29:\$B\$34,2)	=+B6+9/(24)	=+C6
38	7	=VLOOKUP(RAND(),\$A\$29:\$B\$34,2)	=+C6+B7	=IF(C7<F6,F6,C7)
39	8	=VLOOKUP(RAND(),\$A\$29:\$B\$34,2)	=+C7+B8	=IF(C8<F7,F7,C8)
	9	=VLOOKUP(RAND(),A\$29:B\$34,2)	=+C8+B9	=IF(C9<F8,F8,C9)

	E	F	G
40			
41	6	=VLOOKUP(RAND(),\$D\$29:\$E\$34,2)	=D6+E6	=D6-C6
42	7	=VLOOKUP(RAND(),\$D\$29:\$E\$34,2)	=D7+E7	=D7-C7
43	8	=VLOOKUP(RAND(),\$D\$29:\$E\$34,2)	=D8+E8	=D8-C8

FIGURE 18-7

Spreadsheet simulation output for the Sammy Lee barbershop example

FIGURE 18-8

The arrival and service distributions for Sammy Lee's barbershop

	A	B	C		D	E	F	
28	Arrival Distribution			B	Service Distribution			E
29	0	0:05	29	=5/(24*60)	0	0:05	29	=5/(24*60)
30	0.1	0:10	30	=10/(24*60)	0.05	0:10	30	=10/(24*60)
31	0.25	0:15	31	=15/(24*60)	0.25	0:15	31	=15/(24*60)
32	0.5	0:20	32	=20/(24*60)	0.65	0:20	32	=20/(24*60)
33	0.75	0:25	33	=25/(24*60)	0.85	0:25	33	=25/(24*60)
34	0.9	0:30	34	=30/(24*60)	0.95	0:30	34	=30/(24*60)
35								

The first argument of the Excel VLOOKUP function is the random number created by the program. The second argument locates the interarrival time distribution table. The last argument is a 2, indicating that the value sought will be the one in the second column of that lookup table (interarrival times) having the closest cumulative probability equal to or less than ($\leq$) the random number. For example, if the random number is .1647, Excel looks in cell A29 and then in A30, selecting A30 because it is the closest cumulative probability value $\leq$ the random number. VLOOKUP selects 10 minutes from B30 as the interarrival time (0:10). The time between arrivals in cell B6 is displayed as 0:10 (in time format).

Figure 18-8 displays times in columns B and E, where each time is divided by 24*60, the number of minutes in a day, because Excel denotes time of day in fractions of 24 hours. Thus, Excel uses .5 for 12:00 noon, .75 for 6:00 P.M., and 1.0 for 12:00 midnight. To get the units of the time cells in columns B and C in minutes, they must be converted to a fraction of 24 hours. (The Excel value for 5 minutes is 5/(24*60)= .00347222, and that is used in all computations. But .00347222 is displayed on screen as 0:05 in a time format.)

After the interarrival time is found in cell B6, cell C6 gives the clock time of the arrival based on the assumption that the barbershop opens at 9:00 A.M. The Excel formula in this cell is =B6+9/24. (Because there are 24 hours in a day, 9:00 A.M. is 9/24 under the Excel time measure.) This is added to the arrival time in B6 and becomes the clock time of the first arrival. (Cell C6 must have a time format for the clock time to display properly.)

Cell D6 contains the clock time at the beginning of service. This is just the time of the first arrival, =C6. Cell E6 contains the service time, found the same way as time between arrivals. Cell F6 contains the clock time at the end of the service, equaling clock time at the beginning of the service (in cell D6) plus the service time (in cell E6). Finally, the waiting time in cell G6 is the difference between the customer's time when service begins and his arrival time, so that the formula is =D6-C6.

The formulas in row 7 are obtained by copying B6, E6, F6, and G6. Slight changes are made to cells C7 and D7.

Cell C7 contains the clock time at the arrival of the second customer, which is found by adding the clock time of the first arrival and the second randomly generated time between arrivals. The formula is =C6+B7.

Clock time at the beginning of the second service shown in cell D7 has the formula

$$=IF(C7<F6,F6,C7)$$

	G	H	I	J	K
27					
28	W_q =	00:13:30			
29	W =	00:29:45			
30	L_q =	0.78			
31	L =	1.72			

	H
28	=G26
29	=SUM(E6:E25,G6:G25)/20
30	=SUM(G6:G25)/(F25-(C6-B6))
31	=SUM(G6:G25,E6:E25)/(F25-(C6-B6))

FIGURE 18-9
Summary measures from Sammy Lee's barbershop simulation: W_q, W, L_q, and L

which utilizes the Excel IF function. The formula indicates that if the second customer's arrival time (the value in cell C7) is less than (earlier than) the time when the first customer is finished (the value in cell F6), then the customer must wait until the time in cell F6 (when the earlier customer is done) before his service begins. But if the opposite is true, then the second customer's service begins immediately on arrival (the value in cell C7).

Cells B7 through G7 are copied down through row 25, giving a simulation with 20 trials. At the foot of the main spreadsheet are the average time between arrivals, the average service time, and the average waiting time, appearing in cells B26, E26, and G26, respectively. The formulas shown in Figure 18-7 all use the Excel AVERAGE function.

Additional summary simulation measures help analyze the results. These are shown in Figure 18-9, another portion of the original spreadsheet. Four usual queuing results are determined. The estimated queuing characteristics in column G are calculated just like they would be in a hand simulation, using the Excel formulas in column H.

The computer simulation results differ from the hand simulation, which can be seen by comparing the original simulation's mean waiting time of 12.5 minutes with the analogous computer result, 13.5 minutes. Whether done by hand or on the computer, simulation results will vary. Each set of waiting times represents just a *sample* from a theoretically infinite population of waiting times that Sammy's customers would experience in continuous operation. Like any random sample, simulation results are subject to sampling error, so that none can ever precisely portray the true population with complete reliability. Later in the chapter we will pursue some of these statistical issues.

18-3 SIMULATION AND PERT

In our discussion of PERT (Program Evaluation and Review Technique) in Chapter 14, we saw that much of the analysis ignores the uncertainties about activity times. Using only expected times, we can provide the project manager with a time–cost trade-off curve for deciding which activities, if any, should be crashed. Unfortunately, the project completion times obtained in this manner can seriously understate the true expected project completion times.

Consider the PERT network in Figure 18-10, which illustrates a project with five activities. Each activity is represented by an arrow, and the regular activity completion times appear on the respective arrows. The times in boldface for activities *b* and *d* are *certain* and cannot vary; the times for activities *a, c,* and *e* are *expected* times. Traditional PERT analysis is based on the **critical path,** which is the longest duration activity sequence from START to FINISH. Given the times in this network, all paths (*a-d, a-c-e,* and *b-e*) are critical, and each path is expected to take 20 days.

FIGURE 18-10
A PERT network illustrating a project with five activities

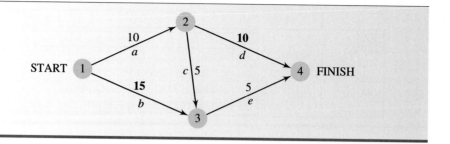

The continuous probability distributions for the three activity completion times are represented in Figure 18-11 by cumulative probability graphs. The project will be simulated using random numbers to determine the times that will be obtained in each trial.

FIGURE 18-11
Cumulative probability distributions for PERT expected activity completion times

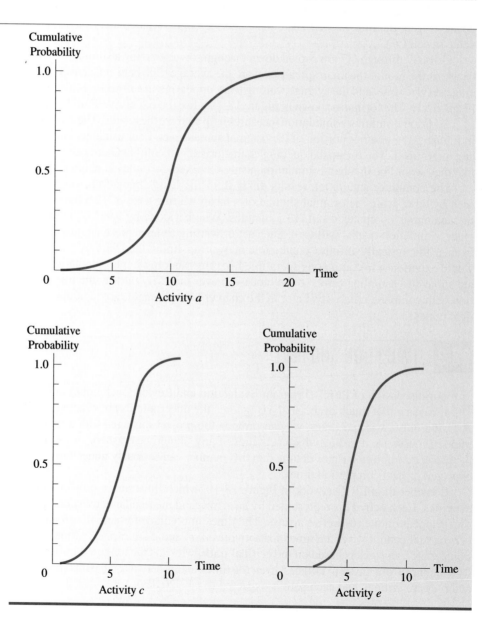

Using Random Numbers with Continuous Distributions

When a cumulative probability graph has been constructed for a continuous random variable (see Chapter 4 to find out how this is done), the graph may be used to determine which quantities correspond to the random numbers. As we saw in the barbershop simulation, random numbers can be assigned to trial variable values by establishing the *range* for the random numbers. The upper limit of that range is identical to the cumulative probability for the value, except for the decimal point. When the variable is continuous, cumulative probability serves the same purpose, except that only single quantities—not ranges—are involved. Because fractional activity times are possible, it is convenient to use all of the digits in each random number.

Figure 18-12 illustrates the procedure for generating completion times for activity *a*. Consider 12651 as the first random number; this corresponds to a cumulative probability of .12651, representing a height on the graph slightly below .13. From the curve, we can see that the time corresponding to this cumulative probability is roughly 6.8 days. Similarly, we may locate the cumulative probability corresponding to a second random number, 81769. The curve at that height represents a time of approximately 12.3 days. Because any random number between 00000 and 99999 is equally likely, each possible height on the curve is just as likely on each trial. Notice that the steepest portion of the curve occurs around 10 days, indicating that more possible random numbers will yield times falling near 10 than any other time. The curve is flatter near 5 days, so that fewer random numbers will lead to times near that level. The graphical procedure therefore generates times more frequently for the more typical levels and less frequently for the rarer levels. For a large number of trials, the frequencies can be expected to match the underlying probabilities exactly, which is just what a simulation is supposed to do.

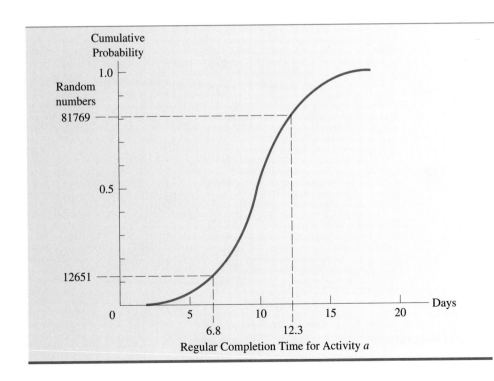

FIGURE 18-12

Using a cumulative probability curve to assign random numbers to quantities

The Simulation

The results of $n = 20$ trials for the PERT simulation are provided in the worksheet shown in Table 18-6. Each trial involved reading three random numbers onto the respective cumulative probability graphs for activities *a, c,* and *e* to determine the corresponding activity completion times. The path with the longest total time through the network was then determined, and the duration of that critical path established the project completion time for the particular trial.

The simulation provides some interesting results. Notice that the simulated mean project completion time of 21.96 days is almost 2 days *longer* than the 20-day completion time indicated using expected values alone. Because only 20 trials were used, we must rely on statistical analysis to tell us whether this difference is significant or the natural result of sampling error. However, studies have established that similar results are generally the case in PERT simulations with a larger number of trials. Also notice that if the mean simulation times for the various activities are considered, all three paths based on these averages are shorter than 21.96 days. This illustrates the tendency of traditional PERT procedures, which are based on average times and individual paths, to understate the mean completion time for the project as a whole. One explanation for this is that no particular path can really be considered singly, for there is some probability that any one of several paths will actually be the longest. Notice that all three paths turned out to be critical in at least one trial and that in no trial was there more than one critical path.

TABLE 18-6   Worksheet and Results for the PERT Simulation

	ACTIVITY TIMES (DAYS)									LONGEST	
	a		**b**	**c**		**d**	**e**			**(CRITICAL)**	**PROJECT**
TRIAL	**Random Number**	**Time**	**Time**	**Random Number**	**Time**	**Time**	**Random Number**	**Time**		**PATH**	**DURATION**
1	(12651)	6.8	15	(61646)	6.3	10	(11769)	4.2		b-e	19.2
2	(81769)	12.3	15	(74436)	6.8	10	(02630)	2.7		a-d	22.3
3	(36737)	9.4	15	(98863)	8.5	10	(77240)	6.2		a-c-e	24.1
4	(82861)	12.6	15	(54371)	6.2	10	(76610)	6.2		a-c-e	25.0
5	(21325)	7.8	15	(15732)	4.0	10	(24127)	4.6		b-e	19.6
6	(74146)	11.3	15	(47887)	6.0	10	(62463)	5.4		a-c-e	22.7
7	(90759)	13.9	15	(64410)	6.5	10	(54179)	5.1		a-c-e	25.5
8	(55683)	10.2	15	(98078)	8.3	10	(02238)	2.7		a-c-e	21.2
9	(79686)	12.0	15	(17969)	4.2	10	(76061)	6.2		a-c-e	22.4
10	(70333)	11.0	15	(00201)	.5	10	(86201)	6.9		b-e	21.9
11	(14042)	7.0	15	(53536)	6.1	10	(07779)	3.8		b-e	18.8
12	(59911)	10.3	15	(08256)	3.1	10	(06596)	3.6		a-d	20.3
13	(62368)	10.4	15	(62623)	6.4	10	(62742)	6.0		a-c-e	22.8
14	(57529)	10.2	15	(97751)	8.2	10	(54976)	5.4		a-c-e	23.8
15	(15469)	7.1	15	(90574)	7.5	10	(78033)	6.3		b-e	21.3
16	(18625)	7.6	15	(23674)	4.6	10	(53850)	5.1		b-e	20.1
17	(74626)	11.3	15	(68394)	6.7	10	(88562)	7.2		a-c-e	25.2
18	(11119)	6.4	15	(16519)	4.1	10	(27384)	4.7		b-e	19.7
19	(41101)	9.6	15	(17336)	4.2	10	(48951)	4.9		b-e	19.9
20	(32123)	9.0	15	(91576)	7.6	10	(84221)	6.7		a-c-e	23.3
Totals		196.2	300		115.8	200		103.9			439.1
Averages		9.81	15		5.79	10		5.20			21.96

Using Three Time Estimates to Find Distribution for Project Duration

The preceding illustration uses for each activity a general cumulative probability distribution represented by a graph. In standard PERT applications the subjective probability distributions for activity completion times may instead be more directly specified through parameters. In Chapter 14 we saw how a probabilistic PERT evaluation may be based on three time estimates for each activity. These are the optimistic time a, the most likely time m, and the pessimistic time b. The three parameters together specify a particular member of a modified beta distribution family. That distribution may be used directly in simulating a project with a PERT network. Because of complications in tabulating the modified beta distribution, such a simulation requires computer assistance.

Computer Applications

The simulation module of *QuickQuant* 2000 will conduct a PERT network simulation using the modified beta distribution. (A detailed discussion of the *QuickQuant* structure is contained on the CD-ROM accompanying this book.)

To illustrate, we consider again the original home construction example with a PERT network solution in Figure 14-11 (page 547). The three time estimates for the home construction example are provided in Table 14-7 (page 565).

After entering the problem data, a *QuickQuant* simulation was performed involving 200 trials. Each trial represents a separate hypothetical construction of the home. Figure 18-13 shows the results. The simulation provides a mean project completion time of 42.59 days, which exceeds by .59 day the expected completion time found in

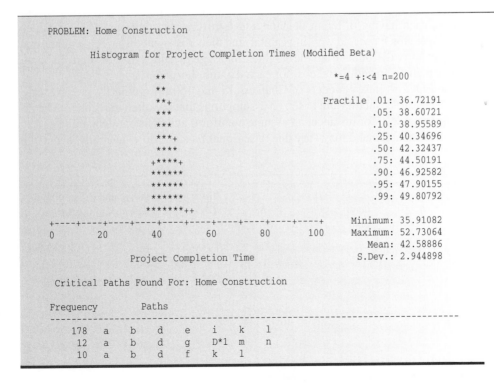

FIGURE 18-13
Portion of *QuickQuant* PERT simulation report for the home construction problem

Figure 14-11 for the original critical path *a-b-d-e-i-k-l*. Notice that the simulation found three *different* paths to be critical, so that the project was found to on the average take longer than the expected duration of the original single critical path. The histogram shows that a considerable amount of variety exists in the project duration; 1% of the trials resulted in times of 36.72 days or less, while 99% of the trials gave times falling at or below 49.81 days (so that 1% of the times exceeded that duration).

18-4 SIMULATING INVENTORY POLICIES

Simulation can also be used to evaluate alternative inventory policies. Figure 18-14 shows the log a retailer may use to record the actual operations of an inventory system for a single product. From this log format, a more detailed simulation worksheet may be developed to simulate various inventory policies, such as "order 500 items whenever any day starts with fewer than 60 units."

Daily demand is one random variable for which a probability distribution must be obtained. Some probability distribution would apply to the number of days until an order arrives, and another uncertainty may be reflected in the lead time it takes to receive the order. The values of both variables would apply to the number of days until an order arrives and would be generated with random numbers.

The log pictured in Figure 18-14 indicates that all items demanded will be sold unless the inventory is depleted, in which case short items will be backordered and supplied when the next shipment arrives. Inventory holding costs are presumed to be $.01 per item held at the start of each day, which represents a daily proration of annual holding costs (usually expressed as a monetary amount per dollar value). A straight penalty of $.10 is assumed to apply for each item short, and the ordering cost is $5.00, regardless of how many items are ordered.

The same approach may be taken for more elaborate problems that involve several products, each having different demand and lead-time distributions. These products may compete for space and working capital, and their costs will differ. Some items may receive quantity discounts from the supplier. Shortage penalties may be more elaborate and may include an additional cost for each day the shortage lasts.

The EOQ inventory models of Chapters 15 and 16 will ordinarily give basically accurate answers. But they are based on assumptions that are often unrealistic. The deterministic models, for instance, all assume a uniform and constant demand rate. As a practical matter, demand may vary due to seasonal factors. More generally, demand is

Day	Starting Inventory	Items Received	Items Demanded	Items Sold	Items Back-ordered	Items Ordered	Days for Order to Arrive	Holding and Shortage Costs	Ordering Cost
6/7	150	0	100	100	0	0	—	$1.50	—
6/8	50	0	75	50	25	500	2	3.00	$5.00
6/9	0	0	85	0	85	0	—	8.50	—
6/10	0	500	55	55	0	0	—	0.00	—
6/11	335	0	60	60	0	0	—	3.35	—

FIGURE 18-14   Hypothetical log for the actual daily operation of an inventory system

treated as an uncertain quantity, so it is represented by a probability distribution. Costs may vary. In particular, the procurement cost need not be a uniform constant, as the basic models require, but may instead vary with the quantity ordered according to a quantity discount schedule.

Many of the inadequacies of the EOQ models may be overcome by instead basing evaluations on simulation. Simulations may be formulated to adhere to any conditions, matching reality to a high degree.

Computer Simulation of Inventory Systems

Excel may be used for simulating inventory systems. Quantity discounts are allowed, and varied demands may be entered according to a fixed schedule, so that a deterministic simulation can be performed. Alternatively, demand may be treated as a random variable, with a variety of distribution forms possible in a Monte Carlo simulation.

Each period represents a trial. As with the EOQ models, the holding cost parameter h is the annual cost per dollar value held, and the period holding cost is based on average inventory. A period's initial inventory equals the beginning inventory plus the arriving shipment quantity; its ending inventory is then found by subtracting the demand from the initial level. Should the ending inventory be negative, the initial physical units are prorated over the earliest times and then an average is computed. The period holding cost is the product of average inventory and h, divided by the number of periods per year.

A one-shot shortage penalty p_S applies to each item short, independent of the shortage duration. The unit selling price p_R is also used. In the backordering case, the latter is ignored, and backordered items are removed from the incoming shipment before the initial inventory is determined. The unit shortage cost is p_S for the backordering case and $p_R + p_S$ for the lost sales case. A period's shortage cost equals the product of the number of items short and the unit shortage cost.

Shipments can only arrive at the beginning of a subsequent period, according to the amount of lead time specified. The program assigns a shipment's ordering and procurement costs to the period when it arrives. Period total inventory cost is the sum of the procurement, ordering, holding, and shortage cost components. The simulation total cost is computed by summing the total costs for all periods in the simulation. Simulation totals are found for the individual cost components as well.

To compare simulations, net total cost is used. That amount is determined by subtracting from simulation total cost the average procurement cost of the items in the last period's ending inventory. (When the ending inventory is negative, the procurement cost computed for that quantity is instead added to total simulation cost.) A simpler basis for comparison is the average net cost, found by dividing net total cost by the number of simulation periods.

MANAGERIAL APPLICATION

Evaluating an Inventory Policy for Copy Paper

Part A: A Deterministic Simulation with No Quantity Discounts

A regional office of XYZ Corporation orders $8\frac{1}{2}$-by-11-inch white copy paper several times a year. Currently XYZ pays $c = \$2.00$ per ream, regardless of quantity ordered. XYZ experiences an annual holding cost of $h = \$.25$ for each dollar's value held in inventory. It costs $k = \$20.00$ to place an order, regardless of quantity. When out of stock, XYZ borrows paper at a nearby retail stationery store. The operational cost of such borrowing is negligible, but the full retail markup of $2.00 must be paid for each ream

borrowed. (That is, each borrowed ream is purchased for $4.00 and later returned for a $2.00 credit.) Thus, there is a shortage penalty of $p_S = \$2.00$ per ream short. When the next shipment arrives, the borrowed reams are paid back to the stationery store, so that in effect a backordering case applies.

Based on previous usage patterns, the following forecast usage applies for the next 8 months. The mean monthly demand is $1,600/8 = 200$ reams.

PERIOD (MONTH)	PROJECTED USAGE (DEMAND)
1	150
2	100
3	200
4	250
5	200
6	150
7	300
8	250
	1,600

XYZ places orders for office supplies at the beginning of each month. The basic EOQ model of Chapter 15 provides a first approximation for the optimal order quantity Q. The annual demand rate is obtained by multiplying the average monthly usage of 200 reams by 12 months in a year, so that $A = 12(200) = 2,400$. We have

$$Q^* = \sqrt{\frac{2Ak}{hc}} = \sqrt{\frac{2(2,400)20}{.25(2)}} = 438$$

The XYZ supplier requires 1 month's lead time to complete delivery of an order. Because the average monthly usage is 200 reams, that will be the reorder point. A new order will be placed at the beginning of any month having an initial inventory of $r = 200$ reams or less.

The average net per-period cost of this policy (including procurement costs) is determined. Then other combinations of r and Q are evaluated in an attempt to find a policy with a lower total cost.

Figure 18-15 presents the Excel spreadsheet for performing the XYZ copy paper inventory simulation. (This spreadsheet is on the CD-ROM accompanying the text and can be used for making similar evaluations.) The problem parameters are listed toward the top of column G.

Cell B43 contains the initial inventory from the problem information (cell G12). Column C gives the quantity received, with either the amount of the previous order or zero if the time period in column A is less than the lead time. The Excel OFFSET function is used to determine that amount. It is imbedded with an IF statement in the formula of cell C43:

$$=IF(A43<=\$G\$15,0,OFFSET(C43,-\$G\$15,1)$$

The OFFSET function has three arguments. The first is the cell where offsetting starts (here, C43). The second argument is the number of rows to move up (negative value) or down (positive value). In this illustration, the lead time given is cell G15, and the argument is -$G$15, which means to go up as many rows as the amount in cell G15. The third argument is the number of columns to move to the right (here that is 1, which lists the order quantities in column D).

INVENTORY SIMULATION (Backordering, Discrete Demand)

	A	B	C	D	E	F	G	H	I	J	K	L
1						INVENTORY SIMULATION (Backordering, Discrete Demand)						
2												
3	PROBLEM:		XYZ Copying Paper Policy									
4												
5		Problem Information										
6				Fixed Cost per Order:		k =	20					
7				Unit Cost of Procuring an Item:		c =	2					
8				Annual Holding Cost per Dollar Value:		h =	0.25					
9				Penalty for Each Item Short:		p_s =	2					
10				Selling Price per Unit:		p_R =	4					
11				Number of Periods per Year:			12					
12				BeginningInventory:			200					
13				Order Quantity:		Q =	438					
14				Reorder Point:		r =	200					
15				Lead Time:			1					
16												
17				Period	Demand							
18				1	150							
19				2	100							
20				3	200							
21				4	250							
22				5	200							
23				6	150							
24				7	300							
25				8	250							
26												
27				Simulation Results (Backordering)								
28				Number of periods			8					
29				Procurement cost		$2628.00						
30				Ordering cost		$60.00						
31				Holding cost		$45.50						
32				Shortage cost		$296.00						
33				Total cost		$3029.50						
34				Ending inventory		-86						
35				Value of ending inventory		-$172.00						
36				Net cost		$3201.50						
37				Average net cost per period		$400.19						
38				Number of trial periods simulated		8						
39												
40												
41					Log of Inventory Simulation (Backordering)							

Log of Inventory Simulation (Backordering)

	Period	Beginning Inventory	Quantity Received	Order Quantity	Due In	Demand	Ending Inventory	Procurement Cost	Order Cost	Holding Cost	Shortage Cost	Total Cost
43	1	200	0	438	2	150	50	$0.00	$0.00	$5.21	$0.00	$5.21
44	2	50	438	0	-	100	388	$876.00	$20.00	$9.13	$0.00	$905.13
45	3	388	0	0	-	200	188	$0.00	$0.00	$12.00	$0.00	$12.00
46	4	188	0	438	5	250	-62	$0.00	$0.00	$3.92	$124.00	$127.92
47	5	-62	438	0	-	200	176	$876.00	$20.00	$3.67	$0.00	$899.67
48	6	176	0	438	7	150	26	$0.00	$0.00	$4.21	$0.00	$4.21
49	7	26	438	0	-	300	164	$876.00	$20.00	$3.96	$0.00	$899.96
50	8	164	0	438	9	250	-86	$0.00	$0.00	$3.42	$172.00	$175.42
51	Ave.	141	164	219		200	106	$328.50	$7.50	$5.69	$37.00	$378.69

Formula insets

Column C:

	B	C
43	=G12	=IF(A43<=$G$15,0,OFFSET(C43,-$G$15,1))
44	=G43	=IF(A44<=$G$15,0,OFFSET(C44,-$G$15,1))
45	=G44	=IF(A45<=$G$15,0,OFFSET(C45,-$G$15,1))

Column D:

	D
43	=IF(B43+C43<=$G$14,$G$13,0)
44	=IF(B44+C44<=$G$14,$G$13,0)
45	=IF(B45+C45<=$G$14,$G$13,0)

Column E:

	E
43	=IF(D43>0,A43+$G$15,"-")
44	=IF(D44>0,A44+$G$15,"-")
45	=IF(D45>0,A45+$G$15,"-")

Columns F, G, H, I:

	F	G	H	I
43	=E18	=B43+C43-F43	=C43*$G$7	=IF(C43>0,$G$6,0)
44	=E19	=B44+C44-F44	=C44*$G$7	=IF(C44=$G$13,$G$6,0)
45	=E20	=B45+C45-F45	=C45*$G$7	=IF(H39=$G$13,$G$6,0)

Column J:

	J
43	=((IF(B43>0,B43,0)+IF(G43>0,G43,0))/2)*($G$8/$G$11)*$G$7
44	=((IF(B44>0,B44,0)+IF(G44>0,G44,0))/2)*($G$8/$G$11)*$G$7
45	=((IF(B45>0,B45,0)+IF(G45>0,G45,0))/2)*($G$8/$G$11)*$G$7

Columns K, L:

	K	L
43	=IF(G43<0,-G43*$G$9,0)	=H43+I43+J43+K43
44	=IF(G44<0,-G44*$G$9,0)	=H44+I44+J44+K44
45	=IF(G45<0,-G45*$G$9,0)	=H45+I45+J45+K45

Column F (results):

	F
28	=MAX(D18:D25)
29	=SUM(H43:H50)
30	=SUM(I43:I50)
31	=SUM(J43:J50)
32	=SUM(K43:K50)
33	=SUM(L43:L50)
34	=G50
35	=G50*G7
36	=ABS(F35-F33)
37	=F36/F28
38	=MAX(D18:D25)

Column B (average):

	B
51	=AVERAGE(B43:B50)

FIGURE 18-15   Excel spreadsheet for the XYZ copy paper inventory example

The order quantity in cell D43 has the Excel formula

$$=IF(B43+C43<=\$G\$14,\$G\$13,0)$$

The above states that the order quantity is the value in cell G13 if the beginning inventory (cell B43) plus the quantity received (cell C43) is less than or equal to the reorder point (cell G14); otherwise, the order quantity is zero. If the above formula results in an order, its due date is calculated in cell E43 by adding the lead time to the time period in column A, using the Excel formula

$$=IF(D43>0,A43+\$G\$15,"-")$$

The demand (cell F43) is taken from the problem information. The ending inventory (cell G43) is the beginning inventory (cell B43) plus the quantity received (cell C43) minus the demand (cell F43): =B43+C43-F43.

The procurement cost (cell H43) is the quantity received (cell C43) multiplied by the unit cost of procuring an item (cell G7): =C43*$G$7. The order cost (cell I43) is the fixed cost per order when an order is placed and zero otherwise. The formula is

$$=IF(C43>0,\$G\$6,0)$$

Cell J43 contains the holding cost. It is the average inventory multiplied by the holding cost per period (the annual holding cost per dollar value divided by the number of periods per year) multiplied by the cost of each item. If both the beginning and ending inventories are nonnegative, the average inventory is half of their sum. If either one is negative, its value is replaced by zero in the average computation. The Excel formula in cell J43 is thus

$$((IF(B43>0,B43,0)+IF(G43>0,G43,0))/2)*(\$G\$8/\$G\$11)*\$G\$7$$

where the two IF functions replace negative inventory levels at the beginning or ending of a period with zero for the average calculation, $G$8/$G$11, is the per-period holding cost, and $G$7 is the unit cost.

The shortage cost in cell K43 is obtained by multiplying the number of shortages and the unit shortage penalty. The formula is

$$=IF(G43<0,-G43*\$G\$9,0)$$

The total cost for the period in cell L43 is the sum of the procurement cost (cell H43), order cost (cell I43), holding cost (cell J43), and shortage cost (cell K43):

$$=H43+I43+J43+K43$$

All the formulas in row 43 are copied down to row 44, except for those in column B (beginning inventory). Cell B44 contains the previous ending inventory (cell G43). Row 44 is copied down as many rows as periods in the simulation. (In this illustration, there are 8 periods, so row 44 is copied down to row 50.)

The last row of the simulation gives the averages. For example, cell B51 is

$$=AVERAGE(B43:B50)$$

This formula is copied over to cells C51:L51. The second argument is B50, because the formulas were copied down to row 50. For other numbers of simulation periods, this argument is adjusted so that the average includes all periods. For example, for 10 periods, the argument would be B43:B52.

The simulation results formulas are given in cells F28:F38. Cells F28 and F38 contain the number of periods, =MAX(D18:D25). Cells F29:F32 have the total procurement, ordering, holding, and shortage costs, and cell F33 contains the sum of the total costs. A typical Excel formula is the one in cell F29

$$=SUM(H43:H50)$$

The others just change the range. For example, the range is I43:I50 to find the total ordering cost in cell F30.

The ending inventory in cell F34 comes from cell G50. Multiplying the ending inventory in cell G50 by the unit cost gives the value of the ending inventory in cell F35.

Cell F36 gives the net cost, the difference between the total cost and the value of the ending inventory, =ABS(F35-F33). The average net cost in cell F37 is the net cost divided by the number of periods, =F36/F28.

To modify Figure 18-15 for simulating with the lost sales case, three minor alterations are needed: (1) change the ending inventory formulas in column G so that the values are not negative, (2) add a new column for computing each period's lost sales, and (3) replace the shortage cost component formula in column L with the Excel counterpart for $p_S + p_R - c$. (The CD-ROM accompanying the book contains the lost sales spreadsheet template.)

Evaluating an Inventory Policy for Laser Printer Paper

MANAGERIAL APPLICATION

Part B: A Simulation with Uncertain Demands and Quantity Discounts

The preceding analysis involves a scheduled demand. Such a schedule would be appropriate when (1) there is a seasonal pattern to demand and (2) uncertainties are ignored. That does not apply to XYZ Corporation's laser printer paper. This high-grade paper is obtained from another supplier, who provides quantity discounts according to the following schedule:

QUANTITY	PRICE PER REAM
0 – 99	$3.00
100 – 199	2.90
200 – 499	2.75
500 – 999	2.50
≥ 1,000	2.15

The lead time in filling orders is one month.

Monthly usage is approximately normally distributed with mean $\mu = 150$ and standard deviation $\sigma = 25$ reams. As before, shortages are made up by buying retail as needed at $p_R = \$5.00$ per ream. There is no cooperative arrangement with the retail supplier, so this situation is a lost sales case. Aside from the price penalty of buying paper at retail, no shortage penalty applies, and $p_S = \$0$. The ordering cost is $k = \$20.00$, and the annual cost of holding a dollar's value is $h = \$.25$.

An initial order quantity is found using the basic EOQ formula, with an annual demand equal to 12 times the expected monthly demand: $A = 12(150) = 1,800$.

$$Q^* = \sqrt{\frac{2Ak}{hc}} = \sqrt{\frac{2(1,800)(20)}{.25(3)}} = 310$$

This quantity was computed using the highest possible unit cost from the price schedule, so that $c = \$3.00$. Using 310 units as the order quantity, the price schedule gives a cost of $2.75. Recomputing the order quantity with $c = \$2.75$, we obtain the final order quantity:

$$Q^* = \sqrt{\frac{2Ak}{hc}} = \sqrt{\frac{2(1,800)(20)}{.25(2.75)}} = 324$$

A reorder point of $r = 150$ reams will be used to start.

Using an initial inventory of 200 reams, this inventory policy is simulated. Based on the results obtained, further inventory policies are determined and simulated to arrive at an (r, Q) combination that appears attractive.

The lost sales version of the Excel spreadsheet in Figure 18-15 discussed earlier can be used to solve this problem. Only two minor modifications are required: (1) the demands in column E must be generated randomly according to a normal distribution using

$$=\text{NORMINV}(\text{RAND}(),\mu,\sigma)$$

where μ and σ are the mean and the standard deviation of demand (100 and 25 respectively, in this example) and (2) the number of periods is 20, so the formulas in the inventory simulation log must be copied down 20 rows and the average row must be shifted accordingly with 20 as the divisor.

Once the simulation spreadsheet is completed, it is easy to do additional simulations by depressing the F9 key. For instance, pressing the F9 key 20 times gives 20 different simulations.

The results from four 20-trial Excel simulations give total costs of $415.34 and $348.98 for two runs with $Q = 324$ and $r = 150$, $393.91 for $Q = 500$ and $r = 300$, and $345.76 for $Q = 1,000$ and $r = 300$.

18-5 SIMULATION AND FORECASTING

In Chapter 7, various forecasting models are presented. The procedures involving exponential smoothing are essentially deterministic in nature. Levels for the smoothing parameters are chosen to provide the best fit for *past* data. Unfortunately, history does not repeat, and a model tuned to one set of data may not work well with another.

Simulation allows us to take a different perspective in "tuning" exponential smoothing models. Rather than selecting simulation parameters to fit a few past periods very well, we consider tuning the forecasting model to the *process* that generates individual times-series values.

The Forecasting Simulation

The procedure employs the two-parameter exponential smoothing model:

$$T_t = \alpha Y_t + (1 - \alpha)(T_{t-1} + b_{t-1}) \qquad \text{(smooth to get trend)}$$
$$b_t = \gamma(T_t - T_{t-1}) + (1 - \gamma)b_{t-1} \qquad \text{(smooth trend)}$$
$$F_{t+1} = T_t + b_t \qquad \text{(forecast)}$$

The model assumes that each Y_t is generated by a process that is *linear*. This suggests that we may generate values of Y_t using the equation for a line. Rather than given values, the Y_t's are obtained from

$$Y_t = a + bt + \epsilon_t$$

where a and b are given parameters for the underlying line. The random deviation term ϵ_t is assumed to be normally distributed with mean 0 and some stipulated standard deviation.

Each trial of the Monte Carlo simulation first generates a set of Y_t's. From these, a set of F_t's is next generated using the stipulated α and γ in the exponential-smoothing

equations. The mean squared error (*MSE*) is then computed to summarize how well the actual and forecast values agree. The whole procedure is repeated with a new set of Y_t's, generated randomly each time, until the desired number of trials is reached. The simulation gives a final statistical summary of *MSE*s achieved that may be compared to similar results for another simulation with a different (α, γ) parameter pair.

   The preceding outlined process would be too complex to perform by hand. A simulation template can make all the calculations.

Forecasting Diesel Fuel Sales

MANAGERIAL APPLICATION

Sentinel Oil Company used a two-parameter exponential-smoothing model to forecast sales. This did not employ the previously described process. Rather, the forecasts were tuned to the past data, with the choice of (α, γ) as the pair that minimizes *MSE*, re-computed many times with exactly the same data. The values of α and γ were revised periodically as new data points became available. Unfortunately, Sentinel experienced an oscillation in the levels for α between .10 and .20 and for γ between .20 and .30. They could not settle on a long-term (α, γ) pair even though the actual diesel fuel data presented a fairly steady, nearly linear trend lacking the pronounced seasonality for other Sentinel products. Past experience shows that sales are growing from their current level of 100,000 gallons at a rate of approximately 2,000 gallons per day. Daily oscillations appear to have a standard deviation of about 500 gallons per day.

   Figure 18-16 shows the Excel spreadsheet for the Sentinel diesel fuel forecasting example, adapted from the template for the two-parameter exponential smoothing

FIGURE 18-16
Excel spreadsheet for the Sentinel diesel fuel forecasting example (adapted from Figure 7-6)

	A	B	C	D	E
1		**FORECASTING SIMULATION RESULTS**			
2					
3	PROBLEM:		Sentinel Diesel Fuel Forecasting		
4					
5			Problem Parameters		
6					
7	Slope of Actual Trend Line =				20
8	Standard Deviation for Actual Trend Line =				5
9	Smoothing Constant α =				0.10
10	Trend Smoothing Constant γ =				0.20
11	Number of Trials =				100

	B
16	1000
17	=1000+$E$7*A16+ NORMINV(RAND(),0,$E$8)

	Period	Actual	Trend	Trend	Forecast
14	t	Sales, Y_t	T_t	Slope, b_t	Sales, F_t
16	1	1,000			
17	2	1,026	1,000	25.8	
18	3	1,045	1,028	26.2	1,025.8
19	4	1,062	1,055	26.38	1,054.0
20	5	1,079	1,081	26.3	1,081.2
21	6	1,096	1,106	26.1	1,107.3
22	7	1,120	1,131	25.9	1,132.3
23	8	1,140	1,155	25.5	1,157.0
24	9	1,155	1,178	25.0	1,180.7
25	10	1,184	1,201	24.6	1,203.2
26	11	1,200	1,223	24.1	1,225.9
112	97	2,919	2,918	19.6	2,917.8
113	98	2,941	2,938	19.7	2,937.6
114	99	2,963	2,958	19.8	2,957.6
115	100	2,976	2,978	19.8	2,978.0
116					
117		MSE =	138.59		

model in Figure 7-6. Minor formatting modifications have been made, moving some of the problem parameters to different cell locations and deleting the month column. The only other alteration is that the actual sales Y_t are calculated according to the linear process equation, which in Excel is

$$=1000+\$E\$7*A16+NORMINV(RAND(),0,\$E\$8)$$

applicable to cell B17. This formula is copied down to the cell corresponding to the last period, which is B115 in this case. (Rows 27–111 have been suppressed in Figure 18-16 to shorten the presentation.) The *MSE* is 138.59. As discussed in Chapter 7, Excel's Solver can be used to find the values of the two smoothing parameters that minimize *MSE* for a series of simulations.

18-6   FURTHER SPREADSHEET APPLICATIONS

It is easy to perform additional spreadsheet simulations. Consider again Sammy Lee's barbershop simulation. (Refer to the spreadsheets in Figures 18-7 through 18-9). Depressing the F9 key to recalculate the spreadsheet yields another simulation with a completely different set of random numbers. Pressing the F9 key 10 times gives 10 simulations of 20 trials each in a matter of seconds.

One problem with performing many separate simulations is that the results of one simulation are lost when the next one is performed. That difficulty may be resolved using Excel's Data Table option. Figure 18-17 is a portion of the spreadsheet results of 100 repetitions of Sammy Lee's barbershop simulation. (Rows 49–138 have been suppressed. The CD-ROM accompanying the text contains the spreadsheet with this data table for use in additional simulations.) Cell references for W_q, W, L_q, and L were entered in cells B43:E43. The trial numbers, 1, 2, ..., 100 were entered in cells A44:A143. We then highlighted cells A43:E143, clicked on Data on the menu bar, and selected Table, and the Data Table dialog box appeared. After clicking the column input cell line and then on an empty cell on the spreadsheet and clicking the OK button, the spread-

FIGURE 18-17

100 repetitions of Sammy Lee's barbershop simulation example using Excel's Data Tables

	B	C	D	E
43	=$H$28	=$H$29	=$H$30	=$H$31

	A	B	C	D	E
42		Wq	W	Lq	L
43	Trial	12.50	29.25	0.6757	1.5811
44	1	17.75	37.50	0.8256	1.7442
45	2	3.75	19.25	0.1807	0.9277
46	3	1.75	17.75	0.0729	0.7396
47	4	6.75	22.75	0.3418	1.1519
48	5	24.75	43.75	1.1786	2.0833
139	96	17.75	34.00	0.9221	1.7662
140	97	4.75	20.00	0.2500	1.0526
141	98	2.75	17.50	0.1358	0.8642
142	99	12.50	29.75	0.6757	1.6081
143	100	6.75	24.50	0.3553	1.2895

sheet in Figure 18-17 appeared on the screen. (The numbers you obtain will be different because of the random nature of the simulation process.)

If the F9 key is depressed with a data table on the spreadsheet, everything will be recalculated. This is an easy way to do the 100 repetitions in Figure 18-17 a second or third time. However, be careful, because Excel is doing many calculations and each repetition can take from a few seconds to a few minutes, *or even longer,* depending on the speed of the computer being used. Consequently, Excel's recalculation option has been set to the manual mode. (Otherwise, each time something is typed in a cell and the Enter key is depressed, the worksheet will recalculate, possibly delaying for several minutes to finish all of the calculations.)

Although Excel makes it possible to do some simulations simply, as just demonstrated, that simplicity yields results that encompass many numbers. Analyzing and understanding a large mass of numbers has its own difficulties. That can be alleviated by computing summary statistics (means and standard deviations) or by preparing frequency tables or graphs.

Excel makes it easy to construct frequency tables, graphs, and histograms. These props help analysts see patterns and results hidden by the sheer mass of data. Figure 18-18 shows a graph of L found from 100 repetitions of the barbershop simulation.

The mean L from all 100 20-trial simulations was computed to be 1.45 customers, with a standard deviation of .54. Compare these results with those in Figure 18-9 that came from the original single 20-trial simulation with mean 1.72 customers.

Generating Events with Other Distributions

Excel functions can be used to generate numbers that follow other probability distributions such as the exponential or uniform. Excel also can generate random numbers from other useful probability distributions, including the Bernoulli, binomial, discrete, patterned, and Poisson.

To compute a series of exponentially distributed numbers, Excel uses the formula

$$=-m*LN(RAND())$$

where m is the mean of the distribution and LN is Excel's function for natural logarithm. The symbol m is used for the mean of the distribution to avoid confusion with

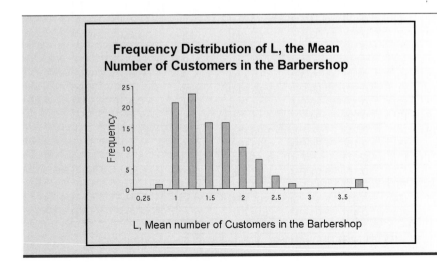

FIGURE 18-18
Frequency distribution of the mean number of customers in the system, L, for 100 repetitions of the 20-trial Sammy Lee barbershop simulation

the symbol μ (the queuing-model service rate, equivalent to the *reciprocal, 1/m*). It is easy to overlook the *minus sign* in front of the *m*.

Numbers uniformly distributed between a lower limit a and an upper limit b can be generated with the following formula

$$=a+(b-a)*RAND()$$

As an illustration of these formulas, reconsider the Sammy Lee barbershop example in Figure 18-7. Now assume that customers arrive according to a Poisson distribution and that service times are exponentially distributed with the same mean interarrival and service times as for the discrete distributions in Figure 18-8. To calculate these means, enter the formulas

$$=SUMPRODUCT(A29:A34,B29:B34)$$

$$=SUMPRODUCT(D29:D34,E29:E34)$$

in cells B36 and E36. The results are a mean interarrival time of 17.5 and a mean service time of 16.25.

A second change from the original spreadsheet is in the times between arrivals, column B, and the service times, column E. In Figure 18-19 we entered

$$=-B\$36*LN(RAND())/(24*60)$$

in cell B6 and copied it down to cells B7:B25. (Note the minus sign before the first term.) Because the units of cell B6 are in minutes, the arrival time randomly generated

FIGURE 18-19

Revised Sammy Lee's barbershop simulation using exponential arrivals and service times

	A	B	C	D	E	F	G
1		Sammy Lee's Barbershop Simulation Example					
2			Exponential Arrivals and Service Times				
3			Time	Clock	Clock time		Clock time	
4			Between	time at	at begin.	Service	at end of	Waiting
5	Trial	Arrivals	arrival	of service	time	service	time
6	1	0:05	9:05 AM	9:05 AM	0:12	9:18 AM	0:00
7	2	0:17	9:23 AM	9:23 AM	0:23	9:46 AM	0:00
8	3	0:44	10:08 AM	10:08 AM	0:12	10:20 AM	0:00
9	4	0:17	10:25 AM	10:25 AM	0:14	10:39 AM	0:00
10	5	0:06	10:31 AM	10:39 AM	0:01	10:40 AM	0:07
11	6	0:02	10:34 AM	10:40 AM	0:02	10:43 AM	0:06
12	7	0:29	11:03 AM	11:03 AM	0:05	11:09 AM	0:00
13	8	0:15	11:19 AM	11:19 AM	0:17	11:37 AM	0:00
14	9	0:00	11:20 AM	11:37 AM	0:22	11:59 AM	0:17
15	10	0:09	11:29 AM	11:59 AM	0:05	12:05 PM	0:29
16	11	0:39	12:09 PM	12:09 PM	1:02	1:11 PM	0:00
17	12	0:31	12:40 PM	1:11 PM	0:00	1:11 PM	0:30
18	13	0:23	1:04 PM	1:11 PM	0:06	1:17 PM	0:06
19	14	0:24	1:28 PM	1:28 PM	0:06	1:34 PM	0:00
20	15	0:10	1:38 PM	1:38 PM	0:00	1:39 PM	0:00
21	16	0:07	1:45 PM	1:45 PM	0:31	2:17 PM	0:00
22	17	0:15	2:01 PM	2:17 PM	0:20	2:38 PM	0:16
23	18	0:12	2:14 PM	2:38 PM	0:24	3:02 PM	0:24
24	19	0:01	2:15 PM	3:02 PM	0:13	3:16 PM	0:46
25	20	0:45	3:01 PM	3:16 PM	0:37	3:54 PM	0:14

	B		E
6	=-B\$36*LN(RAND())/(24*60)	6	=-E\$36*LN(RAND())/(24*60)

FIGURE 18-20
Summary measures of
Sammy Lee's barbershop
simulation

	G	H
30	Wq =	00:10
31	W =	00:26
32	Lq =	0.48
33	L =	1.26

FIGURE 18-20
Summary measures of
Sammy Lee's barbershop
simulation

by Excel's LN formula is also in minutes. That must be converted to a fraction of 24 hours, dividing by the number of minutes in a day. Likewise, in cell E6 we typed

$$=-E\$36*LN(RAND())/(24*60)$$

and copied it down to cells E7:E25. (Each time the F9 key is depressed, a new 20-trial simulation with Poisson arrivals and exponential service times will be performed.)

The summary measures are shown in Figure 18-20. Comparing them with those from Figure 18-9 for the original simulation, we see that all the summary values are similar.

18-7   SIMULATION IN FINANCE: RISK ANALYSIS

Risk analysis is a method for evaluating investment decisions involving uncertainty that will be assessed through simulation. To illustrate, we consider Four Seasons Villages, a proposed Los Angeles–area entertainment complex having hotels, motels, restaurants, theaters, bowling, billiards, archery, ice skating, retail stores, and snack shops. Figure 18-21 shows the computations that developers performed to calculate the 20% rate of return anticipated from a $125 million investment.

FIGURE 18-21
Original spreadsheet for
computing the return on
invested capital for Four
Seasons Villages

	A	B	C	D	E	F
1		**Four Seasons Villages**				
2						
3	Revenue					
4		Hotel		$ 20,400,000		
5		Motel		$ 5,740,000		
6		Restaurants		$ 12,770,000		
7		Theaters		$ 14,640,000		
8		Bowling		$ 1,960,000		
9		Billiards		$ 850,000		
10		Archery		$ 345,000		
11		Ice Skating		$ 1,544,000		
12		Retail Stores		$ 18,345,000		
13		Snack Shops		$ 950,000		
14		Total Revenues		$ 77,544,000	D	
15	Expenses				14 =SUM(D4:D13)	
16		Common Area		$ 13,100,000		
17		Advertising		$ 5,400,000		
18		Insurance		$ 1,100,000		
19		Security Guards		$ 5,100,000		
20		Parking Attendants		$ 2,870,000		
21		Real Estate Taxes		$ 8,530,000	D	
22		Land Lease		$ 16,000,000	23 =SUM(D16:D22)	
23		Total Expenses		$ 52,100,000		
24	Net Operating Profit				D	
25		Depreciation		$ 4,186,400	26 =D23-D25	
26	Profit Before Taxes			$ 47,913,600	27 =D26*0.48	
27		Taxes		$ 22,998,528	28 =D26-D27	
28	Net Profit After Taxes			$ 24,915,072	29 =D28/125000000	
29	Return on Investment			19.93%		

The original analysis was seriously flawed, because no provision was made for the uncertainties involved. Actual revenues and expenses might deviate from the values shown in Figure 18-21. For instance, suppose that the economy slows down and revenues fall or that expenses are higher than anticipated. How would the return on investment be affected? What are the chances of any of the various possibilities happening? Although the return on investment had been originally estimated to be 20%, what is the chance that Four Seasons Villages might actually lose money? Risk analysis is designed to answer those and similar questions.

To illustrate the simulation approach, Figure 18-22 shows the rate of return calculations when the revenue and most of the costs are normally distributed with the means and standard deviations given in various cells. Cell D4 contains the Excel formula

$$=\text{NORMINV(RAND(),E4,F4)}$$

which computes the hotel revenue when the mean and the standard deviation have the values in E4 and F4. All other row variables have their own normal distributions. By copying this formula down to the other cells in column F, a simulated value will be generated for the respective variable. Each time the F9 key is depressed, a simulation occurs and the return on investment is calculated in cell D29 (20.81% in the illustrated case).

Excel's Data Table option was used to perform 100 simulations (like those done for Sammy Lee's barbershop), yielding the histogram in Figure 18-23. It shows that the return on investment varies from 18% to 23% and the majority is from 20% to 21%. This histogram suggests that, although the developer's original estimate was 20%, the odds appear high that the actual return on investment will be somewhat larger. It also indicates that the chance of a negative return on investment is zero.

An Excel add-in helpful in performing risk analysis is @RISK 4.0. (It is available on the CD-ROM accompanying this book.) The program is easy to use, with input

FIGURE 18-22

Spreadsheet showing the risk analysis simulation of Four Seasons Villages

	A	B	C	D	E	F
1				Four Seasons Villages		
2						Standard
3	Revenue			Normal	Mean	Deviation
4		Hotel		$ 25,344,365	$ 20,400,000	$ 5,340,000
5		Motel		$ 5,686,791	$ 5,740,000	$ 1,000,000
6		Restaurants		$ 10,941,615	$ 12,770,000	$ 4,350,000
7		Theaters		$ 10,964,598	$ 14,640,000	$ 3,300,000
8		Bowling		$ 1,801,710	$ 1,960,000	$ 505,000
9		Billiards		$ 820,415	$ 850,000	$ 200,000
10		Archery		$ 275,917	$ 345,000	$ 100,000
11		Ice Skating		$ 1,673,893	$ 1,544,000	$ 200,000
12		Retail Stores		$ 14,321,316	$ 18,345,000	$ 5,000,000
13		Snack Shops		$ 868,605	$ 950,000	$ 300,000
14		Total		$ 72,699,225	$ 77,544,000	
15	Expenses					
16		Common Area		$ 14,781,892	$ 13,100,000	$ 1,500,000
17		Advertising		$ 6,221,008	$ 5,400,000	$ 1,000,000
18		Insurance		$ 1,301,882	$ 1,100,000	$ 200,000
19		Security Guards		$ 4,617,922	$ 5,100,000	$ 1,000,000
20		Parking Attendants		$ 2,998,575	$ 2,870,000	$ 500,000
21		Real Estate		$ 8,457,940	$ 8,530,000	$ 100,000
22		Land Lease		$ 16,000,000	$ 16,000,000	$ -
23		Total		$ 54,379,219	$ 52,100,000	
24	Net Operating Profit					
25		Depreciation		$ 4,354,205	$ 4,186,400	$ 200,000
26	Profit Before Taxes			$ 50,025,014	$ 47,913,600	
27		Taxes		$ 24,012,007	$ 22,998,528	
28	Net Profit After Taxes			$ 26,013,007	$ 24,915,072	
29	Return on			20.81%	19.93%	

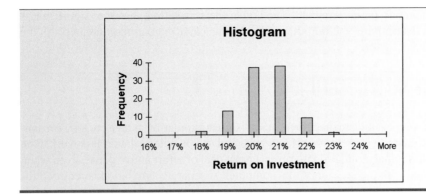

lifted from a spreadsheet like Figure 18-22. Its outputs are similar to those obtained with Excel's Data Table option and in Figure 18-23, however @*RISK* has several distinct advantages. Among these are more probability distributions and many more methods for analyzing results. The program has the capability to incorporate correlation between input variables, reflecting their tendency to move together. For example, Four Seasons Villages hotel and motel revenues might be positively correlated, both tending to go up or down as general business conditions change.

Some of the more than 30 probability distributions in @*RISK* include beta, binomial, chi-square, error, Erlang, exponential, gamma, geometric, hypergeometric, logistic, log normal, negative binomial, normal, Pareto, PERT, Poisson, Rayleigh, Student *t*, triangular, uniform, and Weibull.

In addition to the usual simulation output illustrated in Figure 18-23, @*RISK* provides several analytical tools, including information on the sensitivity of each output variable to the input distributions. Among the results, it creates tornado graphs that assist in identifying the most critical inputs in a model. Figure 18-24 shows a tornado graph for Four Seasons Villages. The horizontal bars give the correlation between each

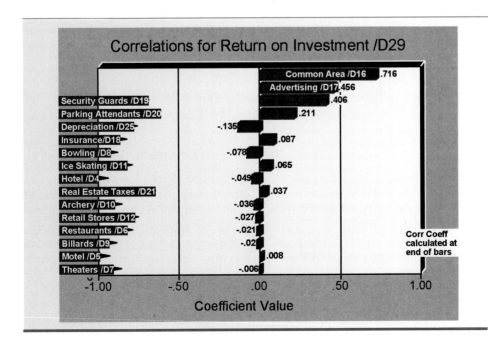

FIGURE 18-24
Tornado graph for Four Seasons Villages

input and the return on investment.* The higher the correlation, the more significant is the input in determining the output's value. In this case, the common area cost is the most significant factor.

18-8 SIMULATION VERSUS THE ANALYTIC SOLUTION

Whenever possible, management scientists use simulation as a last resort. An analytic solution is preferable if it is valid and can be obtained with less work. One reason is that simulation involves a great deal of effort and expense, even when it is performed with the assistance of a computer. A separate simulation is required for each alternative, and hundreds or thousands of these may have to be performed. After the simulations are finished, only statistical estimates—not true values—are available. It is not surprising that an algebraic expression providing the exact answer would be more desirable.

Simulation should be viewed in its proper perspective and used sparingly. But no one has categorized the situations in which it should and should not be used. We must never force a problem to fit a particular analytic solution simply to avoid the tedium of simulation, unless the assumptions underlying the model closely fit the problem. We illustrate the pitfalls of doing this by considering the barbershop illustration once again.

In Chapter 17, we saw that various formulas can be used to obtain the parameters of a single-channel queue. These formulas depend only on the mean arrival rate λ and the mean service rate μ. In the case of Sammy Lee's barbershop, the reciprocals of these values were computed earlier from the probability data.

$$1/\lambda = 17.50 \text{ minutes per customer}$$
$$1/\mu = 16.25 \text{ minutes per customer}$$

Thus,

$$\lambda = 1/17.50 = .057 \text{ customer per minute}$$
$$\mu = 1/16.25 = .062 \text{ customer per minute}$$

Plugging these values into the formula for the mean customer waiting time gives us

$$W_q = \frac{\lambda}{\mu(\mu - \lambda)} = \frac{.057}{.062(.062 - .057)} = 184 \text{ minutes}$$

which is more than 10 times the value obtained in the simulation. Another queuing formula tells us that the mean arrival rate multiplied by W_q equals the mean number of customers waiting. Thus,

$$L_q = \lambda W_q = .057(184) = 10.5 \text{ customers}$$

which disagrees with the simulation results by the same factor.

Why are these discrepancies so great? The explanation is that the operation of Sammy Lee's barbershop does not agree with an underlying assumption of the queuing model—the often overlooked assumption that the arrival and service times must be *exponentially distributed*. The probability distributions used in the simulation do not even resemble the exponential distribution, which indicates that a time of zero is the most likely to occur.

---

*The Spearman rank correlation coefficient.

The barbershop illustration was purposely picked to dramatize what may happen if an appropriate analytic solution procedure is blindly followed. Not all procedures work so poorly—even when their assumptions are not met exactly. The EOQ (economic order quantity) formulas used to design inventory policies are generally very successful in finding answers that are close to optimal in such cases. They are said to be *robust* with regard to a variety of violations in the underlying assumptions. It may not be worth the extra work to simulate inventory policies when a very good answer can be found much more simply by working a 30-second calculation.

What Alternatives Should Be Simulated?

An entire inventory simulation provides the same type of result that would be obtained by plugging an order quantity Q into the total cost equation (TC, as in Chapter 15). It does not automatically optimize—there is no formula for Q^* and no way to know for sure whether a particular Q is better than another level. Worse yet, we do not even know which levels of Q (or r) to try. In this respect, each simulation run is like trying on a pair of shoes; we may never discover the best pair (solution) unless we try all possibilities—an impracticability. To complicate matters, because of sampling error we cannot even be sure that a particular Monte Carlo simulation run is typical of future results that might be achieved once we have made a final choice. Although simulation is generally more workable than pursuing analytic solutions—especially under complex circumstances—we may never be totally confident that simulation even partially uncovers the most attractive choices. And, our evaluations must of necessity be limited to a handful of alternatives. Selecting which cases to simulate is a judgment call, not a mathematical one.

USING JUDGMENT

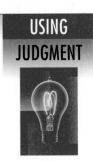

18-9 THE STATISTICAL ASPECTS OF SIMULATION

A simulation is completely analogous to a sampling study. Consider the similarities between estimating the mean customer waiting time and estimating a city's mean disposable family income. Each simulation trial provides one randomly chosen waiting time, whereas a randomly selected family yields a sample observation of income. In either case, planning is involved in setting up the study and in deciding how many observations to make. Although the data are collected differently, the results are qualitatively equivalent. Whether we are reporting results or deciding what to do, we must acknowledge and contend with potential sampling error. Thus, conclusions in either situation are in the nature of *statistical inferences*.

Required Number of Trials

As indicated earlier, the number of simulation trials determines the precision and reliability of the resulting estimate. This number plays the same role as the sample size does in traditional statistics. In the planning stage of the simulation, the number of trials must be treated as a variable, which we denote by n. Samantha Lee used $n = 20$ in her barbershop queuing simulation, but how large should n be in estimating mean waiting time? In determining the answer, we will assume that no simulation data are available.

To simplify our discussion and ease the transition to traditional statistics, we will adopt conventional notation. Each individual waiting time may be represented by an X with the appropriate subscript, so that X_1 represents customer 1's waiting time, X_2 represents customer 2's waiting time, and so on. The arithmetic mean of these X values is denoted by $\bar{X}$. The standard deviation for the population of all future Saturday waiting times is σ. The mean waiting time for the population is denoted by W_q (instead of μ, which represents the true mean service rate in standard queuing formulas). W_q is the quantity to be estimated. The expected value of $\bar{X}$ is W_q, and from the central limit theorem we know that $\bar{X}$ is approximately normally distributed with

$$\text{Mean} = W_q \qquad \text{Standard deviation} = \frac{\sigma}{\sqrt{n}}$$

where σ is known in advance.

Of course, we do not know the value of σ. We must guess its value, and we use the subscript g to distinguish the guessed value of the standard deviation from its true value, so that

$$\sigma_g = \text{Guessed value for standard deviation}$$

A rule of thumb for finding σ_g is that it should equal one-sixth the difference between the largest and smallest conceivable values.*

GUESSED STANDARD DEVIATION

$$\sigma_g = \frac{\text{Largest value} - \text{Smallest value}}{6}$$

Suppose that Sammy Lee occasionally keeps a Saturday customer waiting as long as 60 minutes, but never any longer. The smallest waiting time is obviously 0, so that

$$\sigma_g = \frac{60 - 0}{6} = 10 \text{ minutes}$$

Before finding n, it is necessary to establish target levels for precision and reliability. These are

d = Target precision level (maximum deviation from the true value)

z = Normal deviate for the target reliability level

Statistical theory tells us that $\bar{X}$ is a normally distributed variable. A reliability probability $1 - \alpha$ is desired for getting an $\bar{X}$ that falls within $\pm d$ of the true mean. The normal deviate $z_{\alpha/2}$ corresponds to the area in the normal curve's upper tail that lies above the targeted range. Some of the more common levels for $z_{\alpha/2}$ are listed in Table 18-7.

It should be emphasized that establishing levels for both d and $z_{\alpha/2}$ is essential, because precision and reliability are competing ends. An overly precise estimate such as

---

*If the individual waiting times are normally distributed, then they would fall within $\pm 3\sigma$, or a range of 6σ, of the true mean about 99.7% of the time. Of course, some other distribution may apply, so the rule of thumb is not completely accurate.

TABLE 18-7	Common Normal Deviates Used in Statistical Estimation and Hypothesis Testing

RELIABILITY $1 - \alpha$	CONFIDENCE LEVEL $100(1 - \alpha)\%$	SIGNIFICANCE LEVEL α	NORMAL DEVIATE $z_{\alpha/2}$
.80	80%	.20	$z_{.10} = 1.28$
.90	90	.10	$z_{.05} = 1.64$
.95	95	.05	$z_{.025} = 1.96$
.98	98	.02	$z_{.01} = 2.33$
.99	99	.01	$z_{.005} = 2.57$
.998	99.8	.002	$z_{.001} = 3.08$
.999	99.9	.001	$z_{.0005} = 3.27$

$W_q = 2.343$ minutes $\pm.0005$ is almost totally unreliable. On the other hand, a very imprecise result, such as "W_q lies between 0 and 100 minutes," may be perfectly reliable—even if no simulation is conducted.

The target precision level d expresses the maximum deviation that may be tolerated between the estimate and its true value—either above or below it—in terms of the units involved (minutes, in the present example). The reliability expresses the probability that the target precision level will be met. Because such a probability is obtained from a normal curve centered at the true mean with standard deviation of $\sigma/\sqrt{n}$ (represented by $\sigma_g/\sqrt{n}$), for a specific d, $z_{\alpha/2}$, and σ_g there is a unique n^* yielding the

REQUIRED SAMPLE SIZE

$$n = \frac{z_{\alpha/2}^2 \sigma_g^2}{d^2}$$

Suppose that Samantha wants to be precise to the nearest whole minute, so that $d = 1$, with a reliability of .95, so that the required normal deviate is $z = 1.96$. Plugging these values and $\sigma_g = 10$ into the preceding equation, we find that her required sample size is

$$n = \frac{(1.96)^2(10)^2}{(1)^2} = 384.16, \text{ or } 385$$

(Because n is always expressed in whole numbers, 384.16 is raised to 385.) By using only 20 customers, Samantha has *undersampled* and will not meet her target levels. Often, n values calculated in this manner are huge, so hand simulations by necessity involve undersampling. (In computer simulations, the proper n can usually be applied at minimal cost.) Undersampling produces fuzzy results, which makes it difficult to compare the alternatives simulated.

---

*A complete explanation of the equation is too lengthy to include here. See Lawrence L. Lapin, Statistics for Modern Business Decisions, 6th ed. (Ft. Worth: Dryden Press, 1993), pp. 326–332, for a complete discussion.

The Confidence Interval Estimate

An **interval estimate** is often used to report data from a simulation, just as it is used to report ordinary sample data. When estimating a mean, two values are used to construct such an interval—the sample mean $\bar{X}$ and the

SAMPLE STANDARD DEVIATION

$$s = \sqrt{\frac{\Sigma(X - \bar{X})^2}{n - 1}}$$

The latter statistic may be calculated from simulation data and serves as the estimator of the unknown value of σ. The n used here—and in any other statistical calculation involving data—must be the *actual* number of trials. In the barbershop simulation, $n = 20$ (not the desired level of 385 found earlier).

Ordinarily, some **confidence level,** such as 95% or 99%, is used to report the results. A normal deviate value such as $z_{.025} = 1.96$ or $z_{.005} = 2.57$, corresponds to the level chosen. For the large samples generally used in simulations, the following expression* determines the

100(1 − α)% CONFIDENCE INTERVAL ESTIMATE

$$\text{True mean} = \bar{X} \pm z_{\alpha/2}\frac{s}{\sqrt{n}}$$

Before computing the confidence interval for the mean customer waiting time, the sample standard deviation must be found. This is calculated in Table 18-8 to be $s = 12.4$ minutes. Samantha desires a 95% confidence level, so that $z_{.025} = 1.96$. Plugging these values, along with $\bar{X} = 12.50$ and $n = 20$, into this equation, we determine the confidence interval for the mean customer waiting time.

$$W_q = 12.50 \pm (1.96)\frac{12.4}{\sqrt{20}} = 12.50 \pm 5.43 \text{ minutes}$$

or,

$$7.07 \leq W_q \leq 17.93 \text{ minutes}$$

The proper interpretation of this result is, *if the 20-customer simulation were repeated over and over again, using different random numbers each time, then an interval constructed in this manner would contain the true mean waiting time in about 95 out of every 100 cases, but about 5 of such intervals would lie totally above or below the true value.*

Notice that this confidence interval is quite wide, reflecting the lack of precision due to undersampling.

---

*Although these confidence intervals are traditionally computed using the Student t distribution, the normal approximation is used here. This is satisfactory given the large n's usually encountered in simulation.

TABLE 18-8 Calculations for the Sample Standard Deviation of Customer Waiting Times

CUSTOMER i	WAITING TIME X_i	DEVIATION $(X_i - \bar{X})$	$(X_i - \bar{X})^2$
1	0	-12.50	156.25
2	0	-12.50	156.25
3	5	-7.50	56.25
4	10	-2.50	6.25
5	15	2.50	6.25
6	5	-7.50	56.25
7	0	-12.50	156.25
8	0	-12.50	156.25
9	5	-7.50	56.25
10	0	-12.50	156.25
11	20	7.50	56.25
12	15	2.50	6.25
13	5	-7.50	56.25
14	0	-12.50	156.25
15	20	7.50	56.25
16	35	22.50	506.25
17	25	12.50	156.25
18	35	22.50	506.25
19	30	17.50	306.25
20	25	12.50	156.25
	250	0.00	2,925.00

$$\bar{X} = \Sigma X/n = 250/20 = 12.50 \text{ min}$$

$$s = \sqrt{2,925.00/(20 - 1)} = \sqrt{153.95} = 12.4 \text{ min}$$

Hypothesis Testing and Simulation

Statistical estimation is the weaker form of statistical inference. In keeping with the decision-making theme of this book, we can apply statistical methodology to make comparisons of alternative procedures. For instance, we can compare different activity structures for conducting a project evaluated with PERT. This may be accomplished by performing two separate simulations of the project under each alternative and then choosing the one yielding the smaller mean project completion time. Or, we might compare two inventory policies in terms of average net cost per period using the results from two separate simulations.

Such comparisons are a form of **hypothesis testing** in which two samples (simulations) are used to compare alternative A with alternative B. There is a population for each alternative representing all possible levels of the comparison variable (project completion times with PERT or net cost per period with inventories). The means are denoted as μ_A and μ_B. Ordinarily, the **null hypothesis** is that the means do not differ:

$$\text{Null hypothesis: } \mu_A = \mu_B$$

Based on the simulation results, one of three conclusions is reached:

1. $\mu_A = \mu_B$ (null hypothesis is *true*)
2. $\mu_A > \mu_B$ (null hypothesis is *false*)
3. $\mu_A < \mu_B$ (null hypothesis is *false*)

The final choice will depend on the levels of the two computed means $\bar{X}_A$ and $\bar{X}_B$ and the standard deviations s_A and s_B. The decision rule incorporates the

TEST STATISTIC FOR COMPARING TWO MEANS

$$z = \frac{\bar{X}_A - \bar{X}_B}{\sqrt{\dfrac{s_A^2}{n_A} + \dfrac{s_B^2}{n_B}}}$$

where n_A and n_B are the respective number of simulation trials. The simulations are assumed to be independent (each involving a different set of random numbers).

The null hypothesis is rejected (conclusions 2 or 3 reached) only when the sample means are *significantly* different, in accordance with a prescribed **significance level** α (such as .05 or .01). The significance level is arbitrarily chosen to provide protection against erroneously rejecting the null hypothesis when it is actually true by keeping the probability of such an error at or below α.

To test the null hypothesis, we set in advance a desired significance level. Then we compute z and apply the following rule:

Reject null hypothesis conclude: $\mu_A < \mu_B$	*Accept* null hypothesis conclude: $\mu_A = \mu_B$	*Reject* null hypothesis conclude: $\mu_A > \mu_B$
$-z_{\alpha/2}$	0	$z_{\alpha/2}$

The choice depends on which range the computed z falls into.

MANAGERIAL APPLICATION

PERT Simulations to Compare Alternative Methods for Anchoring Bridge Foundation

A civil engineer can use two different technologies for anchoring a bridge foundation. Method *A* involves driving already formed pilings deep into the ground. Method *B* would instead drill holes and pour raw concrete over a subterranean steel frame. The anchor activity completion time (days) differs under the two methods:

	OPTIMISTIC TIME	MOST LIKELY TIME	PESSIMISTIC TIME
Method A:	2	5	10
Method B:	3.5	5.5	7

Although the most likely time for anchoring under method *B* is greater, the method *A* activity has greater variability. A conclusion regarding which is faster cannot be reached without assessing the overall interactions with the other project activities. This is provided through a PERT evaluation.

The engineer performed two separate PERT simulations, obtaining the project completion times for each. The following results were obtained:

$$\bar{X}_A = 117.6 \qquad \bar{X}_B = 113.5$$
$$s_A = 9.3 \qquad s_B = 7.9$$
$$n_A = 200 \qquad n_B = 100$$

At the $\alpha = .01$ significance level, which method is expected to be faster?

THE PROBLEM SOLUTION

Table 18-7 provides a critical value of $z_{.005} = 2.57$. The computed value of the test statistic is

$$z = \frac{117.6 - 113.5}{\sqrt{\dfrac{(9.3)^2}{200} + \dfrac{(7.9)^2}{100}}} = \frac{4.1}{1.028} = 3.99$$

Because this computed value exceeds the $z_{.005}$ value, the engineer must conclude that $\mu_A > \mu_B$. The mean project completion time is greater under method A than method B; method B is faster. (There is, of course, some chance $< 1\%$ that the null hypothesis, $\mu_A = \mu_B$, is true, so that the two methods would be equally fast. Such residual uncertainty is unavoidable in any simulation.)

Further Statistical Considerations

We have barely scratched the statistical surface of simulation. Many other kinds of inferences may be made involving various hypothesis-testing procedures. If several alternatives are to be simulated, an analysis of variance may be conducted. A detailed discussion of such procedures is beyond the scope of this book, but many good statistical references are provided in the bibliography at the back of the book.

In some simulations, a probability or a proportion is estimated instead of a mean. For example, the optimal number of telephone information operators may be the smallest crew that provides a .95 probability of rendering service within 10 seconds. In simulating various alternatives, the true probability for a particular crew size could be estimated by the proportion of calls (trials) receiving service within 10 seconds. Although there is not enough space to describe them in this book, equivalent expressions can be used to find n and to compute confidence intervals for such quantities.

Hypothesis Testing Using Spreadsheets

Excel can assist hypothesis testing by organizing results to facilitate several statistical tests. These include the z-test for two sample means, the t-test assuming variances that are either equal or unequal, and the paired two-sample t-test.

The t-test is illustrated here for comparing two alternative methods, A and B, for organizing a queuing system. A 10-trial simulation was conducted under each alternative and the customer waiting time was computed. The results are shown in Figure 18-25.

FIGURE 18-25

Customer waiting times for 10-trial simulations of two alternative queuing organizations

	A	B
4	26.3	28.5
5	28.6	30.0
6	25.4	28.8
7	29.2	25.3
8	27.6	28.4
9	25.6	26.5
10	26.4	27.2
11	27.7	29.3
12	28.2	26.2
13	29.0	27.5

Hypothesis testing helps determine if one alternative is better than another. The null hypothesis is that the mean waiting times are identical under the two alternative procedures, under the assumption that the variances are unequal. A 5% significance level is used for the test.

After clicking on Tools on the menu bar and then selecting Data Analysis, we select from the menu t-Test: Two-Sample Assuming Unequal Variances. That brings to screen the dialog box in Figure 18-26, in which we click in the *Variable 1 Range* box and highlight the spreadsheet data for Alternative A, cells A4:A13. That is repeated for the *Variable 2 Range* box, for which the highlighted range is B4:B13. To complete the requested test information, we place a 0 in the *Hypothesized Mean Difference* box and set the significance level in the *Alpha* box to be 0.05. After selecting the *Output Range* button under the *Output options,* highlight a range for the output and then click the OK button.

FIGURE 18-26

The *t*-Test Two-Sample Assuming Unequal Variances dialog box

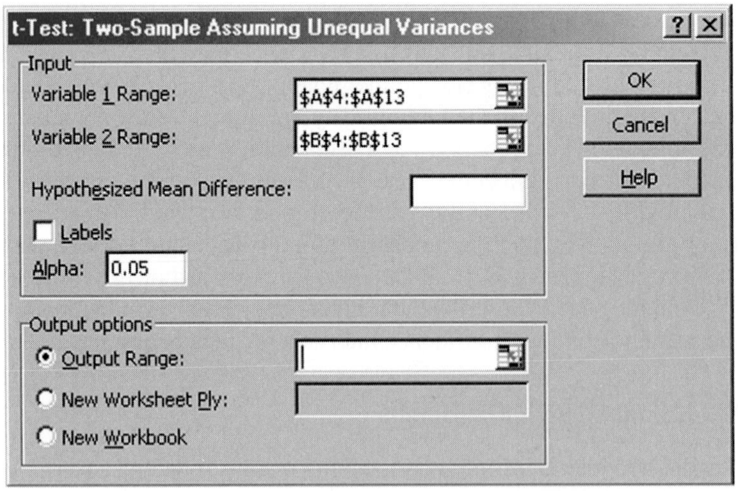

The results in Figure 18-27 report a t value of $-.5744$, which is much smaller than the two-tailed critical value of 2.1009. The null hypothesis that the means do not differ must be accepted. There appears to be no significant difference between the two alternatives. Excel's other statistical tests are performed in a similar manner.

	Variable 1	Variable 2
Mean	27.4	27.77
Variance	1.94	2.209
Observations	10	10
Hypothesized Mean Difference	0	
df	18	
t Stat	-0.5744	
P(T<=t) one-tail	0.2864	
t Critical one-tail	1.7341	
P(T<=t) two-tail	0.5728	
t Critical two-tail	2.1009	

FIGURE 18-27
Excel statistical test results applied to the queuing data in Figure 18-25

PROBLEMS

18-1 Consider the following probability distribution for the times between arrivals of cars stopping at a New Guernsey toll booth:

Time	Probability
5 sec	.35
10	.23
15	.15
20	.11
25	.08
30	.05
35	.03

(a) Construct the cumulative probability distribution and determine a random number assignment suitable for simulation. (Use the first two digits of the random numbers.)
(b) Simulate the arrival of 20 cars and calculate the estimated mean time between arrivals.

18-2 For the probability distribution in Problem 18-1, perform the expected value calculation to find the true mean time between arrivals.

18-3 As part of a simulation to determine advertising response, you must create trial persons who fall into one of the following categories:

Category	Probability
Urban	.36
Suburban	.47
Rural	.17

Prepare a two-digit random number assignment to generate these events.

18-4 Consider the cumulative probability for demand provided in Figure 4-23 on page 116. Use the following random numbers to generate 20 demands:

99582	53390	46357	13244
18080	02321	05809	04898
30143	52687	19420	60061
46683	33761	47452	23551
48672	28736	84994	13071

What is the estimated mean demand?

18-5 A staff analyst for Big-E Corporation has developed a simulation model to estimate the mean annual rate of return for new projects. Separate simulations, each consisting of several investment lifetime trials, will be conducted for the various alternatives. The analyst wants to determine how many trials to create for a particular case if the lifetime annual rate of return may fall between -20% and 40%. How many trials are required to estimate the mean rate of return to the nearest 1% when a reliability of 95% is desired?

18-6 The mean time required by automobile assemblers to hang a car door is to be estimated. Assuming that the guessed value of the standard deviation is 10 seconds, determine the required n under the following conditions:
(a) The desired reliability probability for being in error by no more than 1 second (in either direction) is .99.
(b) The desired reliability probability for being in error by no more than 1 second is .95.
(c) A reliability of .99 is desired, with a target precision of 2 seconds. How does the n you obtain here compare with your answer to (a)?

18-7 Construct a 95% confidence interval for the true mean, given the following simulation results:
(a) $n = 100$; $\bar{X} = 100.53$ minutes; $s = 25.3$ minutes

(b) $n = 200$; $\bar{X} = 69.2$ inches; $s = 1.08$ inches

(c) $n = 350$; $\bar{X} = \$12$; $s = \$7$

18-8 Construct a 95% confidence interval estimate for the mean project completion time using the simulation results given in Table 18-6 for the PERT illustration in the chapter.

18-9 The following results were obtained for the weekly net inventory cost for policy A ($r = 200$, $Q = 500$) and policy B ($r = 300$, $Q = 700$):

$$\bar{X}_A = \$153.48 \qquad X_B = \$172.56$$
$$s_A = \$14.95 \qquad s_B = \$20.17$$
$$n_A = 100 \qquad n_B = 100$$

At the $\alpha = .05$ significance level, what may you conclude regarding the mean weekly net inventory cost of the two policies?

18-10 Two operational methods for settling insurance claims were simulated. Method A involves five human adjusters. Method B replaces them with a single analyst using expert systems software. In terms of time a claim spends waiting to be processed, the following results were obtained:

$$\bar{X}_A = 7.3 \text{ days} \qquad \bar{X}_B = 6.7 \text{ days}$$
$$s_A = 5.4 \qquad s_B = 3.8$$
$$n_A = 100 \qquad n_B = 200$$

(a) At the $\alpha = .01$ significance level, what may you conclude regarding the mean claim waiting time under the two methods?

(b) What is the lowest significance level at which you can conclude that expert systems move claims faster?

18-11 Consider the alternative of adding a second barber to Sammy Lee's shop on Saturdays. This will attract more clients, so customers will arrive closer together. Suppose that the following probabilities apply:

Time Between Arrivals	Probability
5 min	.35
10	.25
15	.20
20	.10
25	.10

Also, suppose that the second barber has the same service time distribution as Sammy.

(a) Set up a worksheet for simulating the 2-man barbershop. (*Hint:* Only one random number is needed for each customer's service time.)

(b) Assume that a customer will pick Sammy if both barbers are free and the first free barber otherwise. Conduct a 20-customer simulation with the random numbers used in Table 18-4 (page 722).

(c) Find the estimated mean customer waiting time.

18-12 Consider Sammy's barbershop again. Suppose that enough simulations were conducted to determine the following true mean waiting times:

$$W_q = 15 \text{ minutes for one barber}$$
$$W_q = 5 \text{ minutes for two barbers}$$

Also, suppose that Sammy suffers a loss of goodwill of $\$.05$ for each minute that *each* customer spends waiting. The shop is open for 8 hours on Saturdays. Each customer brings in an average revenue of $\$4.00$, and the second barber costs Sammy $\$5.00$ per hour.

Using the probability data in the chapter and in Problem 18-11, compute Sammy's average Saturday earnings for one barber and for two barbers. What should Sammy do?

18-13 Suppose that the initial decision maker in Section 18-4 is a retailer who experiences a daily demand for items according to the following probability distribution:

Demand	Probability
40	.04
50	.08
60	.15
70	.23
80	.20
90	.15
100	.10
110	.05

The following lead-time distribution for filling an order applies:

Lead Time	Probability
1 day	.20
2	.25
3	.20
4	.15
5	.10
6	.10

(a) Simulate 25 days of operation to estimate the mean daily inventory cost, given an order quantity of 500, if an order is placed whenever a day's starting inventory falls be-

low 60 items and the starting inventory is 150 items.

(b) Repeat your simulation given an order quantity of 1,000 and an order point of 100. Use the same random numbers you did in (a).

(c) Which of the two inventory policies appears to be less costly?

18-14 Although it is not an accepted practice, you can generate your own random numbers in a pinch by tossing a coin. For instance, a list of two-digit numbers can be obtained by generating a list of seven-digit binary numbers from seven tosses of a coin. This is done by assigning a 0 to a tail and a 1 to a head and then converting the results of every seven tosses to a decimal number. For example, the sequence HTHHTTH yields the binary number 1011001. In decimals, this number may be expressed as the following sum:

$$1 \times 2^6 = 64$$
$$0 \times 2^5 = 0$$
$$1 \times 2^4 = 16$$
$$1 \times 2^3 = 8$$
$$0 \times 2^2 = 0$$
$$0 \times 2^1 = 0$$
$$1 \times 2^0 = \underline{1}$$
$$89$$

Any decimal values greater than 99 can be thrown away. Generate a list of 10 two-digit random numbers this way.

18-15 The dice game of "Craps" provides an interesting example of when not to simulate. The outcome is based on the values achieved from tossing 2 six-sided dice. One way to place a bet is to "play the field." Here, the bettor indicates that he or she wants to make a bet with a complicated payoff, depending on which faces of the dice show. If a "field" number (defined by a sum value of 2 through 4 or 9 through 12) occurs, the player wins. If the roll of the dice yields any other total, the player loses. A field gamble is further complicated by varying payoffs: 1 to 1 for all field numbers except 2 or 12, 2 to 1 on a 2, and 3 to 1 on a 12. Winning bettors keep their original bet and are also paid their winnings. Losing players forfeit their wagers.

(a) For a bet of $1, use this information and the basic concepts of probability to determine the probability distribution for a gambler's net winnings.

(b) Suppose that a system player has an initial bankroll of $7. Beginning with a $1 bet, this player's strategy is to place successive field bets until winning once or losing the original $7. Either of these outcomes terminates the play. As long as money remains, the gambler will double the last wager lost.

Simulate 10 runs of this system to estimate the gambler's mean winnings per play. (To simplify things, you may roll dice rather than use random numbers.)

(c) Solve the problem in (b) analytically by determining the appropriate probability values and finding the gambler's expected winnings. Then, compare this with the simulated value you found in (b). (*Hint:* A tree diagram may be helpful.)

18-16 Big-E Corporation's computer microwave transmission network, which connects five cities, is provided in Figure 18-28. Each line represents a

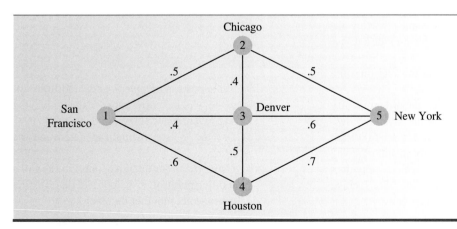

FIGURE 18-28
Network for
Problem 18-16

channel, and transmissions between two cities may be routed over any sequence of clear channels. The number above each line represents the probability for interference on that channel at any given moment. Management is contemplating adding more channels and wants to estimate the probability that San Francisco and New York communications will be completely blocked by interference at any given time.

Estimate this probability by simulating this system for 20 trials. (*Hint:* You may want to make 20 copies of the network before starting so that the blocked channels for each trial can be clearly identified.)

18-17 Million Bank experiences Friday afternoon arrivals at a mean rate of 1.5 per minute; an exponential distribution applies. Service times are normally distributed with mean 2 minutes and

standard deviation .5 minute. There are four tellers on duty. Mean waiting time is to be estimated through simulation.

(a) Suppose that the longest conceivable wait is 20 minutes, with 0 as the shortest. Find a good guess for the standard deviation in waiting time.

(b) Suppose that mean waiting time will be estimated to a precision of $\pm.10$ minute with a reliability of .99. How many simulation trials are required?

(c) Simulate 200 customers. (1) What is the simulation's mean waiting time? (2) What is the simulation's standard deviation in waiting time?

(d) Using your answers to (c), construct a 95% confidence interval estimate of the true mean customer waiting time.

Computer Problems

18-18 Refer to Part B of the Managerial Application for XYZ Corporation's purchases of laser printer paper. Oversized sheets of 11-by-17-inch laser paper have a monthly demand approximately normally distributed with mean $\mu = 50$ and a standard deviation $\sigma = 10$ reams. The following supplier cost schedule applies:

Quantity	Price per Ream
0– 49	$4.50
50– 99	4.25
100–199	4.00
200–499	3.75
≥ 500	3.50

Except for the retail price of $10, all other inventory parameters are the same. Starting inventory is 50 reams, and all other conditions are the same.

(a) Use the Wilson formula to determine the EOQ.

(b) Using $n = 100$ trials, use the order quantity found in (a) to simulate the inventory system when the reorder point is $r = 50$. What is the average net monthly inventory cost?

(c) Using $n = 100$ trials in each case, conduct a simulation and determine the average monthly net inventory cost for:

(1) $Q = 100$ $r = 100$
(2) $Q = 200$ $r = 100$
(3) $Q = 500$ $r = 100$

Which case yielded the minimum cost?

18-19 Refer to Part A of the Managerial Application for XYZ Corporation's purchases of copier paper. The company now must determine an inventory policy for copy paper in assorted colors. The following scheduled usage applies:

Month	Usage
January	100
February	150
March	200
April	300
May	200
June	100

The same costs, parameters, and conditions apply as to w3hite copy paper, except that the starting inventory is 100 reams.

(a) Use the Wilson formula to determine the EOQ.

(b) Using the order quantity found in (a) and a reorder point of $r = 200$, simulate to find average net monthly inventory cost.

(c) Using instead an order quantity of $Q = 400$ and a reorder point of $r = 200$, simulate to find average net monthly inventory cost.

18-20 Refer to the textbook publishing project in Problem 14-13 and the three time-estimate data given in Table 14-11.
(a) Using *QuickQuant*, simulate 200 trials.
(b) List the longest duration paths found and their frequency.
(c) Indicate the following fractiles for the duration of the project: (1) .01, (2) .25, (3) .50, (4) .75, (5) .99.

18-21 Refer to Problem 18-20 and your answers. Construct a 95% confidence interval for project completion time.

18-22 Refer to the home construction project in Figure 14-11 (page 547) with activity data given in Table 14-7 (page 565). Keeping the expected activity completion times unchanged, increase the variability in activities *a, e, g,* and *l* by reducing each optimistic time by 1 day and increasing each pessimistic time by 1 day.
Answer (a)–(c) as in Problem 18-20.

18-23 Sentinel Oil Company wants to find which two-parameter exponential-smoothing constants (α, γ) to use in forecasting sales of quart cans of oil. The following cases will be considered:

$$A: \alpha = .10 \qquad \gamma = .20$$
$$B: \alpha = .30 \qquad \gamma = .20$$

The current daily sales are 1,000 cases. Daily linear trend is assumed to be 2 cases. The standard deviation in daily sales is 1 case.
(a) Simulate 100 sets of forecasts using parameters *A* and another set with those of *B*.
(b) Using a .05 significance level, test the null hypothesis that the mean *MSE* is identical under the two forecasts. Does set *A* or set *B* have a significantly lower *MSE*, or must you conclude that they yield the same forecasting accuracy?

18-24 A special type of hypothesis test allows comparisons to be made with *matched pairs*. Such a test is analogous to comparing identical twins raised apart to assess the impact of some environmental factor without having to account for hereditary differences. In simulation, "twins" can be created by generating trials under

method *A* that involve exactly the same random numbers, each used analogously to those in the simulation for method *B*. The primary advantage of using matched pairs is that the statistical test is more powerful in extracting information from the samples (simulations), allowing for smaller sample sizes (fewer trials). This is done by computing the difference for each trial pair, followed by computation of the mean and standard deviation of the differences:

$$d_i = X_{A_i} - X_{B_i} \qquad \bar{d} = \frac{\Sigma d_i}{n}$$

$$s_d = \sqrt{\frac{\Sigma(d_i - \bar{d})^2}{n - 1}}$$

The test statistic is

$$z = \frac{\bar{d}}{s_d(\sqrt{n})}$$

which is used exactly like the z in the chapter to test the null hypothesis that the two methods have the same means.

Consider an inventory decision having the following parameters (no quantity discounts):

$$c = \$1.00 \qquad p_R = \$2.00$$
$$k = \$50 \qquad p_S = \$.50$$
$$h = \$.30$$

Weekly demand is normally distributed with mean $\mu = 500$ and standard deviation $\sigma = 100$ units. There are currently 800 units on hand, and there is a fixed lead time of 2 weeks. Two inventory policies are:

Policy *A:* $r = 1,000$ and $Q = 3,000$
Policy *B:* $r = 2,000$ and $Q = 5,000$

Using $n = 20$ trials and the same random numbers each time, simulate the two policies. From the respective simulation logs, construct a table listing the weekly net costs from the two simulations. Using those as matched pairs, test at the $\alpha = .05$ significance level the null hypothesis that the mean weekly net cost is the same under the two policies. What do you conclude?

18-25 (a) Use Excel's RAND() function to generate 100 single-digit random numbers. If the random numbers change each time a key is depressed, then change the calculation mode to manual. With the manual calcula-

tion mode in effect, the random numbers change only when the key F9 is depressed (or Shift F9).

(b) Use Excel's Histogram tool to do a frequency table for the 100 single-digit random numbers in (a) using the bin numbers given below. Graph the results with the Chart Wizard.

Bin Numbers	Frequency
0	
1	
2	
3	
4	
5	
6	
7	
8	
9	

(c) Repeat (b) using Excel's FREQUENCY function.

18-26 With a spreadsheet, simulate tossing a coin 10,000 times by using the Excel formula

=IF(RAND()<0.5,"Heads","Tails")

Count the number of heads and tails using Excel's COUNTIF function. Put your results in a table like the following:

Result	Number of Times
Heads	
Tails	

18-27 (a) Using Excel's Data Table option, repeat Problem 18-26 100 times so that you have simulated tossing a coin 1,000,000 times. Put the results in a table like the following, which shows the average number of heads and tails for the 100 repetitions. Also, find the maximum and minimum number of heads and tails during the 100 repetitions.

	Heads	Tails
Average		
Maximum		
Minimum		

(b) Use the Histogram tool or the FREQUENCY function to graph the frequency of heads for the 100 repetitions. Use bin numbers of 4,750, 4,800, 4,850, ..., 5,250.

(c) Do 10 heads (or tails) in a row or column ever occur? What is the greatest number of consecutive heads or tails you can find?

18-28 (a) Using a spreadsheet, do 20 trials of the Sammy Lee barbershop example following the format in Figure 18-7.

(b) Are the average values of the arrival rate, service rate, W_q, W, L_q, and L the same as the results in Chapter 17? Should they be the same? Explain.

18-29 Repeat the Sammy Lee barbershop simulation example in Figure 18-7 100 times using Excel's Data Table option. Each one of the 100 repetitions should record the values of W_q, W, L_q, and L (see the table below). Calculate the average and the standard deviation of each of the four variables.

Trial	W_q	W	L_q	L
1				
2				
...				
99				
100				
Avg.				
S.D.				

18-30 Repeat Problem 18-28 using exponential distributions with the same means as the distributions in the text. These means need to be computed from the text data.

18-31 Repeat Problem 18-28 using normal distributions with the same means and standard deviations as the text distributions. The means and the standard deviations need to be determined from the text data.

18-32 (a) Re-solve Problem 17-15 replacing the values of λ and μ with values generated from exponential distributions with the same means. For example, in the cell where λ is located, put in the formula =-1*λ*LN(RAND()). Do the same for μ.

(b) Re-solve Problem 17-15 replacing the values of λ and μ with values generated from normal distributions with the same means

and with standard deviations equal to 20% of the means.

(c) Repeat (a) 100 times using data tables. Each of the 100 repetitions should record the results for λ, μ, the minimum cost, the optimal S, L_q, and W_q as shown below. Create charts that show the frequency of the results like those shown below. Compare the charts with the results from Problem 17-15.

Trial	λ	μ	Min Cost	Opt S	L_q	W_q
1						
2						
...						
99						
100						
Avg.						
S.D.						

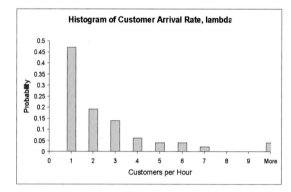

Histogram of Customer Arrival Rate, lambda

18-33 Repeat the Four Seasons Villages 100-trial simulation to determine the mean return on investment. Use the same means and standard deviations as in Figure 18-22.

18-34 Repeat the Four Seasons Villages 100-trial simulation to determine the mean return on investment. Use the same means and standard deviations as in Figure 18-22, but increase the standard deviation for hotel revenue to $7,000,000 and reduce the common area standard deviation to $1,000,000.

18-35 Bill and Sue Eckman would like to retire in about 25 years. They wonder what their current $100,000 stock market portfolio will be worth at that time.

(a) Assume that the portfolio earns 10% each year. What will it be worth at retirement?

(b) Assume that the return each year is normally distributed with a mean of 10% and a standard deviation of 10%. Using Excel's

Data Table option, do 100 simulations of Bill and Sue's portfolio value at retirement.

(c) Construct a frequency distribution of the 100 portfolio values in part (b). What is the probability that the portfolio value at retirement will be at least that found in part (a)?

(d) Find the compound annual return for each of the 100 simulations in part (b).

(e) Construct a frequency distribution for the values determined in part (d).

(f) Using Excel's Chart Wizard, construct a histogram of Bill and Sue's compound annual returns found in part (d).

(1) What is the probability the compound annual return is 10% or more?

(2) What is the probability the compound annual return is 15% or more?

(3) What is the probability the compound annual return is 6% or less?

(4) What is the probability the compound annual return is 4% or less?

18-36 Bill and Sue Eckman are planning to save money to pay for college for their 6-month-old daughter, Amanda, who is their only child. They have decided that they would like to have $200,000 saved by the time Amanda is ready for college in 17 years.

(a) How much money do Bill and Sue need to save each year to reach the $200,000 goal? Assume that they save the same amount each year, that it is available for investment at the beginning of the year, and that it earns 10% each year.

(b) Assume that Bill and Sue invest the money in the stock market and obtain annual returns that are normally distributed with a mean of 10% and a standard deviation of 10%. Use Excel's Data Option and do 100 simulations of the value of Amanda's college fund when she is ready to enter college.

(c) What is the probability that Bill and Sue will meet their $200,000 goal?

18-37 Re-solve the Four Seasons Villages evaluation in Section 18-7 using *@RISK*.

18-38 (a) Re-solve the Four Seasons Villages evaluation in Section 18-7 using *@RISK* and assuming that the revenue sources follow a uniform distribution with the following minimum and maximum values:

Revenue Source	Revenue in Millions	
	Minimum	Maximum
Hotel	$15	$26
Motel	$ 4	$ 7
Restaurants	$10	$16
Theaters	$11	$18
Bowling	$ 1	$ 2
Billiards	$ 1	$ 1
Archery	$ 0	$ 0
Ice Skating	$ 1	$ 2
Retail Stores	$14	$23
Snack Shops	$ 1	$ 1

Revenue Source	Revenue			
	Minimum	Most Likely	Mean	Maximum
Hotel	$15,300,000	$18,360,000	$20,400,000	$26,520,000
Motel	$4,305,000	$5,166,000	$5,740,000	$7,462,000
Restaurants	$9,577,500	$11,493,000	$12,770,000	$16,601,000
Theaters	$10,980,000	$13,176,000	$14,640,000	$19,032,000
Bowling	$1,470,000	$1,764,000	$1,960,000	$2,548,000
Billiards	$637,500	$765,000	$850,000	$1,105,000
Archery	$258,750	$310,500	$345,000	$448,500
Ice Skating	$1,158,000	$1,389,600	$1,544,000	$2,007,200
Retail Stores	$13,758,750	$16,510,500	$18,345,000	$23,848,500
Snack Shops	$712,500	$855,000	$950,000	$1,235,000

(b) Determine the frequency histogram of the return on investment.

18-39 (a) Re-solve the Four Seasons Villages evaluation in Section 18-7 using *@RISK* and assuming that the revenue sources follow a subjective beta distribution with the following parameters:

(b) Determine the frequency histogram of the return on investment.

18-40 (a) Re-solve Problem 18-35 (b), (c), (d), and (e) using *@RISK* and do 1,000 simulations.

(b) How do the results compare with those in 18-35?

18-41 (a) Re-solve Problem 18-36 (b) and (c) using *@RISK* and do 1,000 simulations.

(b) How do the results compare with those in 18-36?

CASE 18-1   *The Balloon Saloon*

The Balloon Saloon is a boutique providing balloons for special occasions. Most of the business is with balloon bouquets for birthdays, anniversaries, promotions, and similar occasions. The proprietor, Mrs. H. E. Lium, wants to establish the best combination of reorder point and order quantity for the more expensive and popular Mylar balloons. The following probability distributions are assumed to apply on any given day for Mylars:

Lium pays $.50 per Mylar balloon, each selling for $1.25 when inflated with helium (which along with other supplies costs $.25 per Mylar). Each dollar tied up in inventory costs Lium $.001 per day. She incurs a cost of approximately $10 to place, track, and process each balloon order—regardless of size. The following probability distributions are assumed to apply for each order. The supplier is rarely able to fill the entire order:

Number of Customers	Probability	Demand per Customer	Probability
15	.05	1	.20
16	.10	2	.15
17	.15	3	.10
18	.15	4	.07
19	.10	5	.07
20	.10	6	.06
21	.10	7	.06
22	.08	8	.05
23	.07	9	.05
24	.06	10	.04
25	.04	11	.04
		12	.04
		13	.03
		14	.02
		15	.02

Lead Time Days	Probability	Proportion of Order Filled	Probability
2	.10	.75	.10
3	.15	.80	.20
4	.20	.85	.25
5	.20	.90	.30
6	.15	.95	.10
7	.10	1.00	.05
8	.10		

When the Balloon Saloon is out of Mylars, 70% of the customers will settle for rubber balloons, which each bring a markup of $.20. The remaining customers will leave without making a purchase. Additionally, Lium believes that the expected present value of future profits lost due to being out of Mylars is $.30 per balloon.

QUESTIONS

1. Set up a schedule of random number assignments for number of customers, demand per customer, lead time, proportion of order filled, and whether or not a customer leaves when out of stock.

2. Set up necessary simulation worksheets for determining the Mylar balloon profit for several days of operation.

3. Conduct a 20-day simulation, using a reorder point of 200 Mylar balloons and an order quantity of 500 Mylar balloons. Then, compute the total Mylar profit for the period. Assume that orders are placed at the beginning of the day, depending on the opening inventory, and that shipments arrive just before the store opens on the date indicated by the lead time. Assume also that the Mylar customer arriving just before stockout will accept any available quantity and fill his or her remaining demand with rubber balloons.

CASE 18-2   *A House with Seven Gables II*

The Salem Daughters Construction Company has contracted with Mr. Hawthorne to build a classic house with seven gables. The activity logic for this project is given in Table 14-14. The activity completion times are uncertain. The three time-estimate activity data are given in Table 14-15. Modified beta distributions apply.

Samantha Salem has enlisted your help in answering several questions.

QUESTIONS (COMPUTER REQUIRED)

1. If you have not already done so, use the PERT module of *QuickQuant* to enter the problem data. Store it under a file for future use or modification.

2. Employing traditional PERT, use *QuickQuant* to perform a single-path probabilistic analysis for the duration of the critical path identified from expected times only. Then identify the 90% probability interval for the duration of that path; the lower limit will be the .05 fractile, the upper limit will be the .95 fractile.

3. Samantha Salem wants the summary statistics from 200 simulated constructions of the house.
   (a) Provide her a complete report using *Quick-Quant.* Highlight your results by specifically pinpointing (1) the mean project completion time; (2) the standard deviation for project completion time; and (3) the 90% frequency interval with the .05 fractile as the lower limit and the .95 fractile as the upper limit.
   (b) Comparing the interval from Question 3, part (a)(3) with the counterpart from Question 2, explain why they differ.

   (c) Compute the 90% confidence interval for the mean project completion time. Explain the meaning of this and discuss why it differs from your answer to part (a)(3).

4. Samantha wants to consider several alternative project activity structures in cases (a)–(c) that follow. For each, perform the following steps:
   (1) Modify the original problem data from Question 1 to reflect the new logic. Use the *Quick-Quant* PERT program module.
   (2) Use *QuickQuant* to simulate 200 trial constructions.
   (3) Record the mean and standard deviation for project completion time.
      (a) Suppose that the exterior trim (activity q) cannot begin until *after* the windows are installed (activity m) in addition to the doors (activity n).
      (b) Suppose instead that laying carpets (activity s) and buyer inspection (activity t) may be done concurrently instead of sequentially, so that both may directly follow painting (activity r).
      (c) Suppose instead that wiring (activity j) and installing communication lines (activity k) may be done concurrently instead of sequentially. Thus, activity k has the same predecessors as activity j, and sheetrocking (activity o) cannot begin until *both* j and k, as well as l, have been completed.

5. The changes in Question 4 (b) and (c) should reduce the true mean project completion time. Compare the two simulation results; test the null hypothesis that the two alternatives have the same mean project completion time at the $\alpha = .05$ significance level. If one alternative is significantly faster, which one?

C A S E   18-3   *Banco Espírito Santo e Comercial de Lisboa II*

Referring to the case of Banco Espírito Santo Comercial de Lisboa I (BESCL I) in Chapter 17, David Rodrigues, District Operations Manager in Lisbon of BESCL, has just returned a little depressed from a meeting with Sr. Periera, Manager of the Almada branch. Rodrigues had presented his recommendations about how to handle the waiting-line problems and his answers to all the questions discussed in that case. Sr. Periera was excited about the findings and ready to implement them on a trial basis in the coming months. However, one of his assistants, Sr. Miguel Silva, was not so enthusiastic. Several years ago, the bank had sent him to the United States for an M.B.A., so he was familiar with queuing models and he had several technical questions that finally caused Sr. Periera to delay a decision. At the end of the meeting, Sr. Periera asked Rodrigues and Silva to schedule further meetings during the week to resolve all potential doubts and difficulties in time for the bank's management board meeting the following week. Because BESCL recently was returned to the control of the Espírito family, it is becoming more aggressive and many improvements are being considered. The purpose of the management board meeting is to bring together, on a bankwide basis, all the steps being taken to become more efficient and to increase market share. Consequently, Sr. Periera wants to present the plans about what is going to be done at the Almada branch.

QUESTIONS

1. One of Sr. Silva's concerns is that the calculations in Question 1 of BESCL I suggest that the assumption of Poisson arrivals may not be very good for the Monday and Friday 9:00 –11:00 A.M. time period. Thus, he feels that Rodrigues's results and conclusions are in doubt because they are based on the assumption that the arrivals are Poisson. Rodrigues argues that even though the arrivals are not exactly Poisson, they are close enough that his answers and conclusions still are valid. To analyze Sr. Silva's concern a little further, simulate this situation using the actual distribution of arrivals from Table 17-6 of BESCL I and compare the results with those obtained by using the queuing model. That is, simulate the 9:00 –11:00 A.M. period for four weeks us-

ing the minimum number of tellers as found in Question 2 of BESCL I. Repeat for the minimum number of tellers plus one, plus two, and plus three. Let the number of simulation trials for each day be equal to the expected number of arrivals.

2. From Question 1 results, calculate the mean of the 20 waiting times in line, the mean of the 20 teller utilization factors, and 95% confidence limits for both of these estimates. Compare the results with those obtained from Question 3 of BESCL I. What can be concluded about whether the Poisson is a good approximation?

3. After looking at the results of Questions 1 and 2, Sr. Silva worries that the 20 simulations are not long enough because 20 was picked arbitrarily. He says, "Why not run the simulation for a year? Wouldn't this give much more accurate results?" To address this concern, Rodrigues decides to use the mean and the standard deviation of the waiting times found in Question 2 to calculate the number of simulations runs necessary to obtain a target precision level of ±10% of the mean value for confidence levels of 90%, 95%, and 99%. "Who knows," he says, "maybe doing more simulation will increase the accuracy of the results only marginally, and it might not be worth the extra effort and cost to do all of the additional calculations."

4. To examine the issue whether the difference between the Poisson and the actual arrival distribution is significant, use the mean waiting times from Question 2, and recalculate the best number of tellers from among the four alternatives presented above—in other words, the minimum number of tellers or the minimum number plus one, two, or three. Compare the results with those of Question 3 of BESCL I.

5. One of Sr. Periera's concerns at the meeting was that it is difficult to relate to an average waiting time of, say, .02. To be more precise, he wanted to know how many customers would have to wait in line during each time period and how long each of these customers would have to wait. As an example, he said, "If I know that five customers will have to wait during an hour on the average, with one waiting five minutes and the other four waiting one minute, I can relate to this better than to an average wait, includ-

ing those who do not wait, of .02." Determine the average waiting time distribution for the simulations in Question 1, and present the results in a table, chart, or histogram. Do these results support the customers' complaints that they encounter long lines?

6. Another concern of Sr. Silva is that he knows that the queuing models used in BESCL I make an assumption that the waiting-line situation is in "steady state"— that is, it has been operating for a long time. He wonders if two hours really satisfies this assumption. If so, then the use of the queuing

models is appropriate. However, if not, then he worries that the results—that is, the average waiting times—are meaningless. Rodrigues decides that to investigate this worry, Questions 1–5 should be resolved using the Poisson assumption for arrivals. What can be concluded about the appropriateness of the steady-state queuing models?

7. Are the means of the 20 average waiting times from Question 6 different from the mean determined in Question 2? Use a *t*-test to see if the difference in means is statistically significant at a 95% confidence level.

CASE 18-4 *Brown-Henderson Industries**

by Manuel Bernardo
California State University, Hayward

Brown-Henderson Industries (BHI) of Sunnyvale, California, is a company that focuses on electronics and communications.

BHI's operation center and main plant are located on Central Expressway in Sunnyvale. Central Expressway and El Camino Real are used by many commuters in traveling through Sunnyvale to and from San Jose. In addition, Central Expressway runs almost parallel to Highway 101. When traffic is moving slowly on 101, many commuters try to use Central Expressway. These factors lead to major congestion problems for those trying to get to the BHI center from Central Expressway. Steve Courier, director of plant operations, is to conduct a feasibility study on how to improve access to and from the facility and still maintain the same level of security and safety. Everyone entering and leaving the facility must check in or out. The main access to BHI's facility is through the South Gate on Central Expressway as illustrated in Figure 18-29. Outside the operations center there are two lanes for cars or other private vehicles such as pickups, small vans, and motorcycles. These two lanes, called

Lane 1 and Lane 2, merge into one lane at the gate. A third lane is used by buses entering the facility.

During the morning, an average of 170 vehicles per hour and 5 buses per hour enter the facility through the South Gate. This heavy traffic frequently causes long lines to form. The arriving vehicles form a line in Lane 1 that, because it has space for only 30 vehicles, often extends onto the adjacent expressway. The cars waiting in this line on the Central Expressway are a hazard to both their drivers and to drivers of other cars on the expressway. Lane 2 can be used to shorten the line, but drivers frequently prefer not to use it because they find it difficult to merge back into Lane 1 to pass through the gate. Buses pass through the gate in their own lane, Lane 3. They experience little delay, because normally about 5 buses enter the facility during the hour under consideration. This means that only rarely are there 2 buses at the gate at the same time. Once a bus is checked by a security guard, it drops off its passengers at a designated bus stop and then exits the facility by the Northeast Gate. This gate has one lane and is used mainly for bus exits and emergencies. A security guard at the Northeast Gate checks the exiting buses and makes sure that only those individuals who were supposed to get off the bus actually got off. Although the Northeast Gate is closed to private vehicles entering the facility, it is used in the afternoon to permit vehicles to leave in order to ease the traffic congestion at the South Gate. There is one other gate, the North Gate. It is

*Adapted from "Reducing Waiting Time at Security Checkpoints," by Edwin G. Landauer and Linda C. Becker, *Interfaces,* 19:5 September–October 1989.

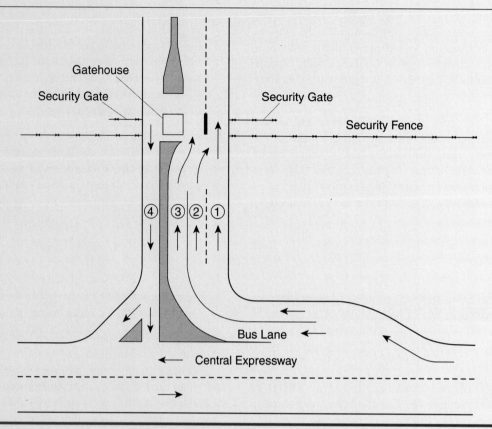

FIGURE 18-29   South Gate at Brown-Henderson Industries

used only by the facility's suppliers or distributors and leads to the Shipping and Receiving Department. This gate cannot be used by private vehicles.

The problem that concerns Steve is the congestion at the South Gate in the morning and the ensuing safety hazards caused by the line of cars extending onto the Central Expressway. He is wondering if a better scheduling of the number of security guards will eliminate the line. The number can vary from one to three on any day. If one guard is on duty, he/she normally is checking cars. When a bus arrives, he/she stops checking the car lane to check the bus, because buses are given priority over other vehicles. With two guards working, one checks the left side of a car while the other checks the passengers on the right side. When a bus arrives, one guard continues to check the cars while the other checks the bus. Finally, when three guards are at the gate, two check cars and one is assigned to the bus lane, because it is not practical to have three guards checking one lane of cars.

This third guard directs and controls traffic when there are no buses.

Steve plans to create a simulation model to evaluate the morning traffic pattern. The first step is to collect data. He has two assistants keep track of the average number of arrivals and the service rates for a 5-day period. Their findings are summarized in Table 18-9 and Table 18-10.

TABLE 18-9   Average Number of Vehicles and Buses Served and Average Service Rates

Average number of cars (private vehicles)	170
Average number of buses	5
Average arrival rate (vehicles/minute)	2.83
Vehicle service rates (vehicles/minute)	
With one security guard	3.67
With two security guards	5.33
With three security guards	6.33
Bus service rate (bus/minute)	0.50

TABLE 18-10	Interval Starting Time and Average Number of Arrivals	

INTERVAL STARTING TIME	AVERAGE NUMBER OF ARRIVALS
7:00	5.00
7:04	6.67
7:08	7.33
7:12	5.00
7:16	12.33
7:20	16.33
7:24	17.67
7:28	22.00
7:32	19.33
7:36	17.33
7:40	18.67
7:44	12.67
7:48	6.67
7:52	1.67
7:56	1.33

Note: Two buses arrive at 7:12, one each at 7:24, 7:40, and 7:48.

QUESTIONS

1. a. Using the average arrival and service data in Table 18-9, ignoring the buses, and assuming that the arrival and service times follow Poisson and exponential distributions, use the appropriate queuing formulas to determine the expected number of cars waiting during each of the 4-minute periods for one, two, and three security guards.
   b. Redo part (a) for each interval in Table 18-10 using the average number of arrivals for the interval.

2. a. Repeat Question 1 using deterministic simulation.
   b. Repeat Question 1, using probabilistic simulation.
   c. Discuss the advantages and disadvantages of using simulation rather than queuing. What is the optimal number of security guards if the objective is to minimize overall queue length?

3. Taking into account the buses, and using the arrival and service rates given in Tables 18-9 and 18-10, do a simulation of the entire hour for one, two, and three security guards. Estimate the expected number of cars waiting in line. Again assuming the objective is to minimize overall queue length, what number of guards is best?

4. Brown-Henderson is thinking about giving the guards special training to help them be more efficient in checking the cars. They would be able to process the cars a little more rapidly; their service rates would be 4, 6, and 7 vehicles per minute after the training. How would this change the results obtained in Question 3?

5. During the summer, the arrival rates decrease by about 20% due to vacations. Should the number of guards be reduced because of this?

6. It is anticipated that the operations center will be hiring additional employees because of a new contract Brown-Henderson has obtained. This means that the arrival rates could increase by 25%. Analyze how such an expansion would affect the assignment of security guards.

BIBLIOGRAPHY

Basic Concepts, Survey of Topics, and Applications

Ackoff, R. L., and P. Rivett. *A Manager's Guide to Operations Research.* New York: John Wiley & Sons, 1963.

Gass, S. I., and C. M. Harris (Eds.). *Encyclopedia of Operations Research and Management Science.* 2nd ed. Boston: Kluwer Academic Press, 2000.

Hillier, F. S., and G. J. Lieberman. *Introduction to Operations Research.* 7th ed. New York: McGraw-Hill, 2000.

Lapin, L. L., and W. D. Whisler. *Cases in Management Science.* Belmont, CA: Duxbury Press, 1996.

Miller, D. W., and M. K. Starr. *Executive Decisions and Operations Research.* 2nd ed. Englewood Cliffs, NJ: Prentice-Hall, 1969.

————. *The Structure of Human Decisions.* Englewood Cliffs, NJ: Prentice-Hall, 1967.

Rivett, P. *Model Building for Decision Analysis.* New York: John Wiley & Sons, 1980.

Wagner, H. M. *Principles of Operations Research with Applications to Managerial Decisions.* 2nd ed. Englewood Cliffs, NJ: Prentice-Hall, 1975.

Winston, W. L. *Operations Research: Applications and Algorithms.* 3rd ed. Belmont, CA: Duxbury Press, 1997.

Excel and Spreadsheet Modeling

Blattner, P. (Ed.), L. Ulrich, K. Cook, and T. Dyck. *Using Microsoft Excel 2000.* Special ed. Indianapolis, IN: Que/Macmillan, 1999.

Grauer, R. T., and M. Barber. *Exploring Microsoft Excel 2000.* Upper Saddle River, NJ: Prentice-Hall, 1999.

Hallberg, B. A., S. Kinkoph, and B. Ray. *Using Microsoft Excel 97.* Special ed. Indianapolis, IN: Que/Macmillan, 1997.

Ragsdale, C. *Spreadsheet Modeling and Decision Analysis.* 3rd ed. Cincinnati, OH: South-Western College Publishing, 2000.

Winston, W. L., and S. C. Albright. *Practical Management Science: Spreadsheet Modeling and Applications.* 2nd ed. Belmont, CA: Duxbury Press, 2000.

Probability Concepts (Chapters 3–4)

Feller, W. *An Introduction to Probability Theory and Its Applications,* Vol. 1. 3rd ed. New York: John Wiley & Sons, 1968.

Feller, W. *An Introduction to Probability Theory and Its Applications,* Vol. 2. 2nd ed. New York: John Wiley & Sons, 1971.

Lapin, L. L. *Statistics for Modern Business Decisions.* 6th ed. Fort Worth, TX: Dryden Press, 1993.

Laplace, Pierre Simon, Marquis de. *A Philosophical Essay on Probabilities.* New York: Dover Publications, 1996. (Previously published by Dover Publications, 1951.)

Parzen, E. *Modern Probability Theory and Its Applications.* Reprint ed. New York: John Wiley & Sons, 1992. (Originally published by John Wiley & Sons. 1960.)

Decision Making (Chapters 5–6)

Aitchison, J. *Choice Against Chance: An Introduction to Statistical Decision Theory.* Reading, MA: Addison-Wesley, 1970.

Chernoff, H., and L. E. Moses. *Elementary Decision Theory.* New York: Dover Publications, 1986. (Originally published by Dover, 1959.)

Lapin, L. L. *Statistics for Modern Business Decisions.* 6th ed. Fort Worth, TX: Dryden Press, 1993.

Luce, R. D., and H. Raiffa. *Games and Decisions: Introduction and Critical Survey.* Reprint ed. New York: Dover Publications, 1989. (Originally published by John Wiley & Sons, 1957.)

Miller, D. W., and M. K. Starr. *Executive Decisions and Operations Research.* 2nd ed. Englewood Cliffs, NJ: Prentice-Hall, 1969.

Pratt, J. W., H. Raiffa, and R. Schlaifer. *Introduction to Statistical Decision Theory.* Cambridge: MIT Press, 1995.

Raiffa, H. *Decision Analysis: Introductory Lectures on Choices Under Uncertainty.* Reading, MA: Addison-Wesley, 1968.

Schlaifer, R. *Analysis of Decisions Under Uncertainty.* Reprint ed. Huntington, NY: R. E. Krieger Publishing, 1978. (Originally published by R. E. Krieger, 1969.)

———. *Introduction to Statistics for Business Decisions.* Melbourne, FL: R. E. Krieger Publishing, 1982. (Originally published by McGraw-Hill, 1961.)

Forecasting (Chapter 7)

Box, G. E. P., G. M. Jenkins, and G. C. Reinsel, *Time Series Analysis: Forecasting and Control.* 3rd ed. Englewood Cliffs, NJ: Prentice-Hall, 1994.

Brown, R. G. *Smoothing, Forecasting, and Prediction of Discrete Time Series.* Englewood Cliffs, NJ: Prentice-Hall, 1963.

Gross, C. W., and R. T. Peterson. *Business Forecasting.* 2nd ed. Boston: Houghton Mifflin, 1983.

Hanke, J. E., A. G. Reitsch, and D. W. Wichern, *Business Forecasting.* 7th ed. Upper Saddle River, NJ: Prentice-Hall, 2001.

Holt, C. C., F. Modigliani, J. F. Muth, and H. A. Simon. *Planning Production, Inventories, and Work Force.* Englewood Cliffs, NJ: Prentice-Hall, 1960.

Makridakis, S. G., and S. C. Wheelwright. *Interactive Forecasting: Univariate and Multivariate Methods.* 2nd ed. San Francisco: Holden-Day, 1978.

———. *Forecasting Methods for Management.* 5th ed. New York: John Wiley & Sons, 1989.

Makridakis, S. G., S. C. Wheelwright, and R. J. Hyndman. *Forecasting: Methods and Applications.* 3rd ed. New York: John Wiley & Sons, 1997.

Pindyck, R. S., and D. L. Rubinfeld, *Econometric Models and Economic Forecasts.* 4th ed. Boston: Irwin/McGraw-Hill, 1998.

Linear, Integer, Goal Programming, and Networks (Chapters 8–13)

Dantzig, G. B. *Linear Programming and Extensions.* Princeton, NJ: Princeton University Press, 1998. (Originally published by Princeton University Press, 1963.)

Daskin, M. S. *Network and Discrete Location Models, Algorithms, and Applications.* New York: Wiley-Interscience, 1995.

Garvin, W. W. *Introduction to Linear Programming.* New York: McGraw-Hill, 1960.

Gass, S. I. *Linear Programming.* 4th ed. New York: McGraw-Hill, 1975.

Goicoechea, A., D. R. Hansen, and L. Duckstein. *Multiobjective Decision Analysis with Engineering and Business Applications.* New York: John Wiley & Sons, 1982.

Hillier, F. S., and G. J. Lieberman. *Introduction to Operations Research.* 7th ed. New York: McGraw-Hill, 2000.

Kolman, B., and R. E. Beck. *Elementary Linear Programming with Applications.* 2nd ed. New York: Academic Press, 1995.

Salkin, H. M., K. Mathur, and R. Haas, *Foundations of Integer Programming.* New York: North-Holland, 1989.

Simonnard, M. *Linear Programming.* Englewood Cliffs, NJ: Prentice-Hall, 1966.

Schneiderjans, M. J. *Linear Goal Programming.* Princeton, NJ: Petrocelli Books, 1984.

Wagner, H. M. *Principles of Operations Research with Applications to Managerial Decisions.* 2nd ed. Englewood Cliffs, NJ: Prentice-Hall, 1975.

Williams, H. P. *Model Building in Mathematical Programming.* 4th ed. New York: John Wiley & Sons, 1999.

PERT/CPM (Chapter 14)

Baker, B. N., and R. L. Ellis. *An Introduction to PERT/CPM.* Homewood, IL: R. D. Irwin, 1964.

Evarts, H. F. *Introduction to PERT.* Boston: Allyn & Bacon, 1964.

Levin, R. I., and C. A. Kirkpatrick. *Planning and Control with PERT/CPM.* New York: Mc-Graw-Hill, 1966.

Lockyer, K. G. *An Introduction to Critical Path Analysis.* 4th ed. London: Pitman, 1984. (Originally published by Pitman, 1969.)

MacCrimmon, K. R., and C. A. Ryavec, "Analytical Study of the PERT Assumptions," *Operations Research,* January 1964, pp. 16–37.

Moder, J. J., C. R. Philips, and E. W. Davis. *Project Management with CPM, PERT, and Precedence Diagramming.* 3rd ed. New York: Van Nostrand Reinhold, 1983.

Weist, J. D., and F. K. Levy. *A Management Guide to PERT/CPM: With GERT/PDM/DCPM and Other Networks.* 2nd ed. Englewood Cliffs, NJ: Prentice-Hall, 1977.

Inventory Decisions (Chapters 15–16)

Arrow, K. J., S. Karlin, and H. Scarf. *Studies in the Mathematical Theory of Inventory and Production.* Stanford, CA: Stanford University Press, 1958.

Greene, J. H. (Ed.), *Production and Inventory Control Handbook.* 3rd ed. New York: McGraw Hill, 1997. (Earlier edition published by McGraw-Hill in 1970.)

Hadley, G., and T. M. Whitin. *Analysis of Inventory Systems.* Englewood Cliffs, NJ: Prentice-Hall, 1963.

Hillier, F. S., and G. J. Lieberman. *Introduction to Operations Research.* 7th ed. New York: Mc-Graw-Hill, 2000.

Holt, C. C., F. Modigliani, J. F. Muth, and H. A. Simon. *Planning Production, Inventories, and Work Force.* Englewood Cliffs, NJ: Prentice-Hall, 1960.

Magee, J. F., and D. M. Boodman. *Production Planning and Inventory Control.* 2nd ed. New York: McGraw Hill, 1967.

Wagner, H. M. *Principles of Operations Research with Applications to Managerial Decisions.* 2nd ed. Englewood Cliffs, NJ: Prentice-Hall, 1975.

———. *Statistical Management of Inventory Systems.* New York: John Wiley & Sons, 1962.

Whitin, T. M. *The Theory of Inventory Management.* Reprint of 1957 ed. Westport, CT: Greenwood Press, 1970.

Zipkin, P. H. *Foundations of Inventory Management.* New York: McGraw-Hill, 2000.

Queues (Chapter 17)

Cooper, R. B. *Introduction to Queueing Theory.* 2nd ed. New York: North Holland, 1981.

Cox, D. R., and W. L. Smith. *Queues.* London: Methuen/New York: Wiley, 1961.

Gross, D., and C. M. Harris. *Fundamentals of Queueing Theory.* 3rd ed. New York: John Wiley & Sons, 1997.

Hillier, F. S., and G. J. Lieberman. *Introduction to Operations Research.* 7th ed. New York: Mc-Graw-Hill, 2000.

Lee, A. M. *Applied Queueing Theory.* New York: St. Martin's Press, 1966.

Morse, P. M. *Queues, Inventories, and Maintenance: The Analysis of Operational Systems with Variable Demand and Supply.* New York: John Wiley & Sons, 1958.

Newell, G. F. *Applications of Queueing Theory.* 2nd ed. New York: Chapman & Hall, 1982.

Saaty, T. L. *Elements of Queueing Theory with Applications.* New York: Dover Publications, 1983.

Wagner, H. M. *Principles of Operations Research with Applications to Managerial Decisions.* 2nd ed. Englewood Cliffs, NJ: Prentice-Hall, 1975.

Simulation (Chapter 18)

Banks, J. (Ed.). *Handbook of Simulation: Principles, Methodology, Advances, Applications, and Practice.* New York: John Wiley & Sons, 1998.

Emshoff, J. R., and R. L. Sisson. *Design and Use of Computer Simulation Models.* New York: Macmillan, 1970.

Fishman, G. S., *Concepts and Methods in Discrete Event Digital Simulation.* New York: John Wiley & Sons, 1973.

Graybeal, W. T., and U. W. Pooch. *Simulation: Principles and Methods.* Boston: Little, Brown, 1982. (Originally published by Winthrop Publishers, 1980.)

Kleijnen, J. P. C. *Statistical Techniques in Simulation.* Parts 1 and 2. New York: Marcel Dekker, 1974, 1975.

Khoshnevis, B. *Discrete Systems Simulation.* New York: McGraw-Hill, 1994.

Pugh, A. L. *DYNAMO User's Manual.* 6th ed. Cambridge, MA: MIT Press, 1983.

Ross, S. M. *Simulation.* 2nd ed. New York: Academic Press, 1996.

Schmidt, J. W., and R. E. Taylor. *Simulation and Analysis of Industrial Systems.* Homewood, IL: R. D. Irwin, 1970.

Shannon, R. E. *Systems Simulation: The Art and Science.* Englewood Cliffs, NJ: Prentice-Hall, 1975.

Watson, H. J. *Computer Simulation in Business.* 2nd ed. New York: Prentice-Hall, 1995.

APPENDIX TABLES

TABLE A   Cumulative Values for the Binomial Probability Distribution

$Pr[R \leq r]$

$n = 1$

P	.01	.05	.10	.20	.30	.40	.50
r							
0	0.9900	0.9500	0.9000	0.8000	0.7000	0.6000	0.5000
1	1.0000	1.0000	1.0000	1.0000	1.0000	1.0000	1.0000

$n = 2$

P	.01	.05	.10	.20	.30	.40	.50
r							
0	0.9801	0.9025	0.8100	0.6400	0.4900	0.3600	0.2500
1	0.9999	0.9975	0.9900	0.9600	0.9100	0.8400	0.7500
2	1.0000	1.0000	1.0000	1.0000	1.0000	1.0000	1.0000

$n = 3$

P	.01	.05	.10	.20	.30	.40	.50
r							
0	0.9703	0.8574	0.7290	0.5120	0.3430	0.2160	0.1250
1	0.9997	0.9927	0.9720	0.8960	0.7840	0.6480	0.5000
2	1.0000	0.9999	0.9990	0.9920	0.9730	0.9360	0.8750
3	1.0000	1.0000	1.0000	1.0000	1.0000	1.0000	1.0000

$n = 4$

P	.01	.05	.10	.20	.30	.40	.50
r							
0	0.9606	0.8145	0.6561	0.4096	0.2401	0.1296	0.0625
1	0.9994	0.9860	0.9477	0.8192	0.6517	0.4752	0.3125
2	1.0000	0.9995	0.9963	0.9728	0.9163	0.8208	0.6875
3	1.0000	1.0000	0.9999	0.9984	0.9919	0.9744	0.9375
4	1.0000	1.0000	1.0000	1.0000	1.0000	1.0000	1.0000

$n = 5$

P	.01	.05	.10	.20	.30	.40	.50
r							
0	0.9510	0.7738	0.5905	0.3277	0.1681	0.0778	0.0313
1	0.9990	0.9774	0.9185	0.7373	0.5282	0.3370	0.1875
2	1.0000	0.9988	0.9914	0.9421	0.8369	0.6826	0.5000
3	1.0000	1.0000	0.9995	0.9933	0.9692	0.9130	0.8125
4	1.0000	1.0000	1.0000	0.9997	0.9976	0.9898	0.9688
5				1.0000	1.0000	1.0000	1.0000

SOURCE: From *Management Science for Business Decisions* by Lawrence L. Lapin, copyright ©1980 by Harcourt Brace Jovanovich, Inc. Reproduced by permission of the publisher.

TABLE A (continued)

n = 10

P	.01	.05	.10	.20	.30	.40	.50
r							
0	0.9044	0.5987	0.3487	0.1074	0.0282	0.0060	0.0010
1	0.9957	0.9139	0.7361	0.3758	0.1493	0.0464	0.0107
2	0.9999	0.9885	0.9298	0.6778	0.3828	0.1673	0.0547
3	1.0000	0.9990	0.9872	0.8791	0.6496	0.3823	0.1719
4	1.0000	0.9999	0.9984	0.9672	0.8497	0.6331	0.3770
5	1.0000	1.0000	0.9999	0.9936	0.9526	0.8338	0.6230
6	1.0000	1.0000	1.0000	0.9991	0.9894	0.9452	0.8281
7				0.9999	0.9999	0.9877	0.9453
8				1.0000	1.0000	0.9983	0.9893
9						0.9999	0.9990
10						1.0000	1.0000

n = 20

P	.01	.05	.10	.20	.30	.40	.50
r							
0	0.8179	0.3585	0.1216	0.0115	0.0008	0.0000	0.0000
1	0.9831	0.7358	0.3917	0.0692	0.0076	0.0005	0.0000
2	0.9990	0.9245	0.6769	0.2061	0.0355	0.0036	0.0002
3	1.0000	0.9841	0.8670	0.4114	0.1071	0.0160	0.0013
4	1.0000	0.9974	0.9568	0.6296	0.2375	0.0510	0.0059
5	1.0000	0.9997	0.9887	0.8042	0.4164	0.1256	0.0207
6	1.0000	1.0000	0.9976	0.9133	0.6080	0.2500	0.0577
7	1.0000	1.0000	0.9996	0.9679	0.7723	0.4159	0.1316
8	1.0000	1.0000	0.9999	0.9900	0.8867	0.5956	0.2517
9	1.0000	1.0000	1.0000	0.9974	0.9520	0.7553	0.4119
10				0.9994	0.9829	0.8725	0.5881
11				0.9999	0.9949	0.9435	0.7483
12				1.0000	0.9987	0.9790	0.8684
13					0.9997	0.9935	0.9423
14					1.0000	0.9984	0.9793
15						0.9997	0.9941
16						1.0000	0.9987
17							0.9998
18							1.0000

TABLE A   (continued)

n = 50

P	.01	.05	.10	.20	.30	.40	.50
r							
0	0.6050	0.0769	0.0052	0.0000	0.0000	0.0000	0.0000
1	0.9106	0.2794	0.0338	0.0002	0.0000	0.0000	0.0000
2	0.9862	0.5405	0.1117	0.0013	0.0000	0.0000	0.0000
3	0.9984	0.7604	0.2503	0.0057	0.0000	0.0000	0.0000
4	0.9999	0.8964	0.4312	0.0185	0.0002	0.0000	0.0000
5	1.0000	0.9622	0.6161	0.0480	0.0007	0.0000	0.0000
6	1.0000	0.9882	0.7702	0.1034	0.0025	0.0000	0.0000
7	1.0000	0.9968	0.8779	0.1904	0.0073	0.0001	0.0000
8	1.0000	0.9992	0.9421	0.3073	0.0183	0.0002	0.0000
9	1.0000	0.9998	0.9755	0.4437	0.0402	0.0008	0.0000
10	1.0000	1.0000	0.9906	0.5836	0.0789	0.0022	0.0000
11	1.0000	1.0000	0.9968	0.7107	0.1390	0.0057	0.0000
12	1.0000	1.0000	0.9990	0.8139	0.2229	0.0133	0.0002
13	1.0000	1.0000	0.9997	0.8894	0.3279	0.0280	0.0005
14	1.0000	1.0000	0.9999	0.9393	0.4468	0.0540	0.0013
15	1.0000	1.0000	1.0000	0.9692	0.5692	0.0955	0.0033
16				0.9856	0.6839	0.1561	0.0077
17				0.9937	0.7822	0.2369	0.0164
18				0.9975	0.8594	0.3356	0.0325
19				0.9991	0.9152	0.4465	0.0595
20				0.9997	0.9522	0.5610	0.1013
21				0.9999	0.9749	0.6701	0.1611
22				1.0000	0.9877	0.7660	0.2399
23					0.9944	0.8438	0.3359
24					0.9976	0.9022	0.4439
25					0.9991	0.9427	0.5561
26					0.9997	0.9686	0.6641
27					0.9999	0.9840	0.7601
28					1.0000	0.9924	0.8389
29						0.9966	0.8987
30						0.9986	0.9405
31						0.9995	0.9675
32						0.9998	0.9836
33						0.9999	0.9923
34						1.0000	0.9967
35							0.9987
36							0.9995
37							0.9998
38							1.0000

TABLE A (continued)

				$n = 100$			
P	.01	.05	.10	.20	.30	.40	.50
r							
0	0.3660	0.0059	0.0000	0.0000	0.0000	0.0000	0.0000
1	0.7358	0.0371	0.0003	0.0000	0.0000	0.0000	0.0000
2	0.9206	0.1183	0.0019	0.0000	0.0000	0.0000	0.0000
3	0.9816	0.2578	0.0078	0.0000	0.0000	0.0000	0.0000
4	0.9966	0.4360	0.0237	0.0000	0.0000	0.0000	0.0000
5	0.9995	0.6160	0.0576	0.0000	0.0000	0.0000	0.0000
6	0.9999	0.7660	0.1172	0.0001	0.0000	0.0000	0.0000
7	1.0000	0.8720	0.2061	0.0003	0.0000	0.0000	0.0000
8	1.0000	0.9369	0.3209	0.0009	0.0000	0.0000	0.0000
9	1.0000	0.9718	0.4513	0.0023	0.0000	0.0000	0.0000
10	1.0000	0.9885	0.5832	0.0057	0.0000	0.0000	0.0000
11	1.0000	0.9957	0.7030	0.0126	0.0000	0.0000	0.0000
12	1.0000	0.9985	0.8018	0.0253	0.0000	0.0000	0.0000
13	1.0000	0.9995	0.8761	0.0469	0.0001	0.0000	0.0000
14	1.0000	0.9999	0.9274	0.0804	0.0002	0.0000	0.0000
15	1.0000	1.0000	0.9601	0.1285	0.0004	0.0000	0.0000
16	1.0000	1.0000	0.9794	0.1923	0.0010	0.0000	0.0000
17	1.0000	1.0000	0.9900	0.2712	0.0022	0.0000	0.0000
18	1.0000	1.0000	0.9954	0.3621	0.0045	0.0000	0.0000
19	1.0000	1.0000	0.9980	0.4602	0.0089	0.0000	0.0000
20	1.0000	1.0000	0.9992	0.5595	0.0165	0.0000	0.0000
21	1.0000	1.0000	0.9997	0.6540	0.0288	0.0000	0.0000
22	1.0000	1.0000	0.9999	0.7389	0.0479	0.0001	0.0000
23	1.0000	1.0000	1.0000	0.8109	0.0755	0.0003	0.0000
24				0.8686	0.1136	0.0006	0.0000
25				0.9125	0.1631	0.0012	0.0000
26				0.9442	0.2244	0.0024	0.0000
27				0.9658	0.2964	0.0046	0.0000
28				0.9800	0.3768	0.0084	0.0000
29				0.9888	0.4623	0.0148	0.0000
30				0.9939	0.5491	0.0248	0.0000
31				0.9969	0.6331	0.0398	0.0001
32				0.9984	0.7107	0.0615	0.0002
33				0.9993	0.7793	0.0913	0.0004
34				0.9997	0.8371	0.1303	0.0009
35				0.9999	0.8839	0.1795	0.0018

TABLE A   (continued)

				$n = 100$			
P	**.01**	**.05**	**.10**	**.20**	**.30**	**.40**	**.50**
r							
36				0.9999	0.9201	0.2386	0.0033
37				1.0000	0.9470	0.3068	0.0060
38					0.9660	0.3822	0.0105
39					0.9790	0.4621	0.0176
40					0.9875	0.5433	0.0284
41					0.9928	0.6225	0.0443
42					0.9960	0.6967	0.0666
43					0.9979	0.7635	0.0967
44					0.9989	0.8211	0.1356
45					0.9995	0.8689	0.1841
46					0.9997	0.9070	0.2421
47					0.9999	0.9362	0.3086
48					0.9999	0.9577	0.3822
49					1.0000	0.9729	0.4602
50						0.9832	0.5398
51						0.9900	0.6178
52						0.9942	0.6914
53						0.9968	0.7579
54						0.9983	0.8159
55						0.9991	0.8644
56						0.9996	0.9033
57						0.9998	0.9334
58						0.9999	0.9557
59						1.0000	0.9716
60							0.9824
61							0.9895
62							0.9940
63							0.9967
64							0.9982
65							0.9991
66							0.9996
67							0.9998
68							0.9999
69							1.0000

TABLE B Areas Under the Standard Normal Curve

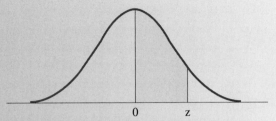

The following table provides the area between the mean and normal deviate value z.

Normal Deviate z	.00	.01	.02	.03	.04	.05	.06	.07	.08	.09
0.0	.0000	.0040	.0080	.0120	.0160	.0199	.0239	.0279	.0319	.0359
0.1	.0398	.0438	.0478	.0517	.0557	.0596	.0636	.0675	.0714	.0753
0.2	.0793	.0832	.0871	.0910	.0948	.0987	.1026	.1064	.1103	.1141
0.3	.1179	.1217	.1255	.1293	.1331	.1368	.1406	.1443	.1480	.1517
0.4	.1554	.1591	.1628	.1664	.1700	.1736	.1772	.1808	.1844	.1879
0.5	.1915	.1950	.1985	.2019	.2054	.2088	.2123	.2157	.2190	.2224
0.6	.2257	.2291	.2324	.2357	.2389	.2422	.2454	.2486	.2518	.2549
0.7	.2580	.2612	.2642	.2673	.2704	.2734	.2764	.2794	.2823	.2852
0.8	.2881	.2910	.2939	.2967	.2995	.3023	.3051	.3078	.3106	.3133
0.9	.3159	.3186	.3212	.3238	.3264	.3289	.3315	.3340	.3365	.3389
1.0	.3413	.3438	.3461	.3485	.3508	.3531	.3554	.3577	.3599	.3621
1.1	.3643	.3665	.3686	.3708	.3729	.3749	.3770	.3790	.3810	.3830
1.2	.3849	.3869	.3888	.3907	.3925	.3944	.3962	.3980	.3997	.4015
1.3	.4032	.4049	.4066	.4082	.4099	.4115	.4131	.4147	.4162	.4177
1.4	.4192	.4207	.4222	.4236	.4251	.4265	.4279	.4292	.4306	.4319
1.5	.4332	.4345	.4357	.4370	.4382	.4394	.4406	.4418	.4429	.4441
1.6	.4452	.4463	.4474	.4484	.4495	.4505	.4515	.4525	.4535	.4545
1.7	.4554	.4564	.4573	.4582	.4591	.4599	.4608	.4616	.4625	.4633
1.8	.4641	.4649	.4656	.4664	.4671	.4678	.4686	.4693	.4699	.4706
1.9	.4713	.4719	.4726	.4732	.4738	.4744	.4750	.4756	.4761	.4767
2.0	.4772	.4778	.4783	.4788	.4793	.4798	.4803	.4808	.4812	.4817
2.1	.4821	.4826	.4830	.4834	.4838	.4842	.4846	.4850	.4854	.4857
2.2	.4861	.4864	.4868	.4871	.4875	.4878	.4881	.4884	.4887	.4890
2.3	.4893	.4896	.4898	.4901	.4904	.4906	.4909	.4911	.4913	.4916
2.4	.4918	.4920	.4922	.4925	.4927	.4929	.4931	.4932	.4934	.4936
2.5	.4938	.4940	.4941	.4943	.4945	.4946	.4948	.4949	.4951	.4952
2.6	.4953	.4955	.4956	.4957	.4959	.4960	.4961	.4962	.4963	.4964
2.7	.4965	.4966	.4967	.4968	.4969	.4970	.4971	.4972	.4973	.4974
2.8	.4974	.4975	.4976	.4977	.4977	.4978	.4979	.4979	.4980	.4981
2.9	.4981	.4982	.4982	.4983	.4984	.4984	.4985	.4985	.4986	.4986
3.0	.49865	.4987	.4987	.4988	.4988	.4989	.4989	.4989	.4990	.4990
4.0	.49997									

SOURCE: From *Statistical Analysis for Decision Making* by Morris Hamburg, copyright ©1970 by Harcourt Brace Jovanovich, Inc. Reproduced by permission of the publisher.

TABLE C   Loss Function for Decision Making with the Normal Curve

D	.00	.01	.02	.03	.04	.05	.06	.07	.08	.09
.0	.3989	.3940	.3890	.3841	.3793	.3744	.3697	.3649	.3602	.3556
.1	.3509	.3464	.3418	.3373	.3328	.3284	.3240	.3197	.3154	.3111
.2	.3069	.3027	.2986	.2944	.2904	.2863	.2824	.2784	.2745	.2706
.3	.2668	.2630	.2592	.2555	.2518	.2481	.2445	.2409	.2374	.2339
.4	.2304	.2270	.2236	.2203	.2169	.2137	.2104	.2072	.2040	.2009
.5	.1978	.1947	.1917	.1887	.1857	.1828	.1799	.1771	.1742	.1714
.6	.1687	.1659	.1633	.1606	.1580	.1554	.1528	.1503	.1478	.1453
.7	.1429	.1405	.1381	.1358	.1334	.1312	.1289	.1267	.1245	.1223
.8	.1202	.1181	.1160	.1140	.1120	.1100	.1080	.1061	.1042	.1023
.9	.1004	.09860	.09680	.09503	.09328	.09156	.08986	.08819	.08654	.08491
1.0	.08332	.08174	.08019	.07866	.07716	.07568	.07422	.07279	.07138	.06999
1.1	.06862	.06727	.06595	.06465	.06336	.06210	.06086	.05964	.05844	.05726
1.2	.05610	.05496	.05384	.05274	.05165	.05059	.04954	.04851	.04750	.04650
1.3	.04553	.04457	.04363	.04270	.04179	.04090	.04002	.03916	.03831	.03748
1.4	.03667	.03587	.03508	.03431	.03356	.03281	.03208	.03137	.03067	.02998
1.5	.02931	.02865	.02800	.02736	.02674	.02612	.02552	.02494	.02436	.02380
1.6	.02324	.02270	.02217	.02165	.02114	.02064	.02015	.01967	.01920	.01874
1.7	.01829	.01785	.01742	.01699	.01658	.01617	.01578	.01539	.01501	.01464
1.8	.01428	.01392	.01357	.01323	.01290	.01257	.01226	.01195	.01164	.01134
1.9	.01105	.01077	.01049	.01022	$.0^29957$	$.0^29698$	$.0^29445$	$.0^29198$	$.0^28957$	$.0^28721$
2.0	$.0^28491$	$.0^28266$	$.0^28046$	$.0^27832$	$.0^27623$	$.0^27418$	$.0^27219$	$.0^27024$	$.0^26835$	$.0^26649$
2.1	$.0^26468$	$.0^26292$	$.0^26120$	$.0^25952$	$.0^25788$	$.0^25628$	$.0^25472$	$.0^25320$	$.0^25172$	$.0^25028$
2.2	$.0^24887$	$.0^24750$	$.0^24616$	$.0^24486$	$.0^24358$	$.0^24235$	$.0^24114$	$.0^23996$	$.0^23882$	$.0^23770$
2.3	$.0^23662$	$.0^23556$	$.0^23453$	$.0^23352$	$.0^23255$	$.0^23159$	$.0^23067$	$.0^22977$	$.0^22889$	$.0^22804$
2.4	$.0^22720$	$.0^22640$	$.0^22561$	$.0^22484$	$.0^22410$	$.0^22337$	$.0^22267$	$.0^22199$	$.0^22132$	$.0^22067$
2.5	$.0^22004$	$.0^21943$	$.0^21883$	$.0^21826$	$.0^21769$	$.0^21715$	$.0^21662$	$.0^21610$	$.0^21560$	$.0^21511$
2.6	$.0^21464$	$.0^21418$	$.0^21373$	$.0^21330$	$.0^21288$	$.0^21247$	$.0^21207$	$.0^21169$	$.0^21132$	$.0^21095$
2.7	$.0^21060$	$.0^21026$	$.0^39928$	$.0^39607$	$.0^39295$	$.0^38992$	$.0^38699$	$.0^38414$	$.0^38138$	$.0^37870$
2.8	$.0^37611$	$.0^37359$	$.0^37115$	$.0^36879$	$.0^36650$	$.0^36428$	$.0^36213$	$.0^36004$	$.0^35802$	$.0^35606$
2.9	$.0^35417$	$.0^35233$	$.0^35055$	$.0^34883$	$.0^34716$	$.0^34555$	$.0^34398$	$.0^34247$	$.0^34101$	$.0^33959$
3.0	$.0^33822$	$.0^33689$	$.0^33560$	$.0^33436$	$.0^33316$	$.0^33199$	$.0^33087$	$.0^32978$	$.0^32873$	$.0^32771$
3.1	$.0^32673$	$.0^32577$	$.0^32485$	$.0^32396$	$.0^32311$	$.0^32227$	$.0^32147$	$.0^32070$	$.0^31995$	$.0^31922$
3.2	$.0^31852$	$.0^31785$	$.0^31720$	$.0^31657$	$.0^31596$	$.0^31537$	$.0^31480$	$.0^31426$	$.0^31373$	$.0^31322$
3.3	$.0^31273$	$.0^31225$	$.0^31179$	$.0^31135$	$.0^31093$	$.0^31051$	$.0^31012$	$.0^49734$	$.0^49365$	$.0^49009$
3.4	$.0^48666$	$.0^48335$	$.0^48016$	$.0^47709$	$.0^47413$	$.0^47127$	$.0^46852$	$.0^46587$	$.0^46331$	$.0^46085$
3.5	$.0^45848$	$.0^45620$	$.0^45400$	$.0^45188$	$.0^44984$	$.0^44788$	$.0^44599$	$.0^44417$	$.0^44242$	$.0^44073$
3.6	$.0^43911$	$.0^43755$	$.0^43605$	$.0^43460$	$.0^43321$	$.0^43188$	$.0^43059$	$.0^42935$	$.0^42816$	$.0^42702$
3.7	$.0^42592$	$.0^42486$	$.0^42385$	$.0^42287$	$.0^42193$	$.0^42103$	$.0^42016$	$.0^41933$	$.0^41853$	$.0^41776$
3.8	$.0^41702$	$.0^41632$	$.0^41563$	$.0^41498$	$.0^41435$	$.0^41375$	$.0^41317$	$.0^41262$	$.0^41208$	$.0^41157$
3.9	$.0^41108$	$.0^41061$	$.0^41016$	$.0^59723$	$.0^59307$	$.0^58908$	$.0^58525$	$.0^58158$	$.0^57806$	$.0^57469$
4.0	$.0^57145$	$.0^56835$	$.0^56538$	$.0^56253$	$.0^55980$	$.0^55718$	$.0^55468$	$.0^55227$	$.0^54997$	$.0^54777$
4.1	$.0^54566$	$.0^54364$	$.0^54170$	$.0^53985$	$.0^53807$	$.0^53637$	$.0^53475$	$.0^53319$	$.0^53170$	$.0^53027$
4.2	$.0^52891$	$.0^52760$	$.0^52635$	$.0^52516$	$.0^52402$	$.0^52292$	$.0^52188$	$.0^52088$	$.0^51992$	$.0^51901$
4.3	$.0^51814$	$.0^51730$	$.0^51650$	$.0^51574$	$.0^51501$	$.0^51431$	$.0^51365$	$.0^51301$	$.0^51241$	$.0^51183$
4.4	$.0^51127$	$.0^51074$	$.0^51024$	$.0^69756$	$.0^69296$	$.0^68857$	$.0^68437$	$.0^68037$	$.0^67655$	$.0^67290$
4.5	$.0^66942$	$.0^66610$	$.0^66294$	$.0^65992$	$.0^65704$	$.0^65429$	$.0^65167$	$.0^64917$	$.0^64679$	$.0^64452$
4.6	$.0^64236$	$.0^64029$	$.0^63833$	$.0^63645$	$.0^63467$	$.0^63297$	$.0^63135$	$.0^62981$	$.0^62834$	$.0^62694$
4.7	$.0^62560$	$.0^62433$	$.0^62313$	$.0^62197$	$.0^62088$	$.0^61984$	$.0^61884$	$.0^61790$	$.0^61700$	$.0^61615$
4.8	$.0^61533$	$.0^61456$	$.0^61382$	$.0^61312$	$.0^61246$	$.0^61182$	$.0^61122$	$.0^61065$	$.0^61011$	$.0^79588$
4.9	$.0^79096$	$.0^78629$	$.0^78185$	$.0^77763$	$.0^77362$	$.0^76982$	$.0^76620$	$.0^76276$	$.0^75950$	$.0^75640$

SOURCE: From Robert O. Schlaifer, *Introduction to Statistics for Business Decisions.* New York: McGraw-Hill Book Co., 1961. Reproduced by permission of the copyright holder, the President and Fellows of Harvard College.

TABLE D Exponential Functions

y	e^y	e^{-y}	y	e^y	e^{-y}
0.00	1.0000	1.000000	3.00	20.086	.049787
0.10	1.1052	.904837	3.10	22.198	.045049
0.20	1.2214	.818731	3.20	24.533	.040762
0.30	1.3499	.740818	3.30	27.113	.036883
0.40	1.4918	.670320	3.40	29.964	.033373
0.50	1.6487	.606531	3.50	33.115	.030197
0.60	1.8221	.548812	3.60	36.598	.027324
0.70	2.0138	.496585	3.70	40.447	.024724
0.80	2.2255	.449329	3.80	44.701	.022371
0.90	2.4596	.406570	3.90	49.402	.020242
1.00	2.7183	.367879	4.00	54.598	.018316
1.10	3.0042	.332871	4.10	60.340	.016573
1.20	3.3201	.301194	4.20	66.686	.014996
1.30	3.6693	.272532	4.30	73.700	.013569
1.40	4.0552	.246597	4.40	81.451	.012277
1.50	4.4817	.223130	4.50	90.017	.011109
1.60	4.9530	.201897	4.60	99.484	.010052
1.70	5.4739	.182684	4.70	109.95	.009095
1.80	6.0496	.165299	4.80	121.51	.008230
1.90	6.6859	.149569	4.90	134.29	.007447
2.00	7.3891	.135335	5.00	148.41	.006738
2.10	8.1662	.122456	5.10	164.02	.006097
2.20	9.0250	.110803	5.20	181.27	.005517
2.30	9.9742	.100259	5.30	200.34	.004992
2.40	11.023	.090718	5.40	221.41	.004517
2.50	12.182	.082085	5.50	244.69	.004087
2.60	13.464	.074274	5.60	270.43	.003698
2.70	14.880	.067206	5.70	298.87	.003346
2.80	16.445	.060810	5.80	330.30	.003028
2.90	18.174	.055023	5.90	365.04	.002739
3.00	20.086	.049787	6.00	403.43	.002479

TABLE E — Cumulative Probability Values for the Poisson Distribution

$$\Pr[X \leq x]$$

λt $\to$ / x $\downarrow$	1.0	2.0	3.0	4.0	5.0	6.0	7.0	8.0	9.0	10.0
0	0.3679	0.1353	0.0498	0.0183	0.0067	0.0025	0.0009	0.0003	0.0001	0.0000
1	0.7358	0.4060	0.1991	0.0916	0.0404	0.0174	0.0073	0.0030	0.0012	0.0005
2	0.9197	0.6767	0.4232	0.2381	0.1247	0.0620	0.0296	0.0138	0.0062	0.0028
3	0.9810	0.8571	0.6472	0.4335	0.2650	0.1512	0.0818	0.0424	0.0212	0.0103
4	0.9963	0.9473	0.8153	0.6288	0.4405	0.2851	0.1730	0.0996	0.0550	0.0293
5	0.9994	0.9834	0.9161	0.7851	0.6160	0.4457	0.3007	0.1912	0.1157	0.0671
6	0.9999	0.9955	0.9665	0.8893	0.7622	0.6063	0.4497	0.3134	0.2068	0.1301
7	1.0000	0.9989	0.9881	0.9489	0.8666	0.7440	0.5987	0.4530	0.3239	0.2202
8		0.9998	0.9962	0.9786	0.9319	0.8472	0.7291	0.5926	0.4557	0.3328
9		1.0000	0.9989	0.9919	0.9682	0.9161	0.8305	0.7166	0.5874	0.4579
10			0.9997	0.9972	0.9863	0.9574	0.9015	0.8159	0.7060	0.5830
11			0.9999	0.9991	0.9945	0.9799	0.9466	0.8881	0.8030	0.6968
12			1.0000	0.9997	0.9980	0.9912	0.9730	0.9362	0.8758	0.7916
13				0.9999	0.9993	0.9964	0.9872	0.9658	0.9262	0.8645
14				1.0000	0.9998	0.9986	0.9943	0.9827	0.9585	0.9165
15					0.9999	0.9995	0.9976	0.9918	0.9780	0.9513
16					1.0000	0.9998	0.9990	0.9963	0.9889	0.9730
17						0.9999	0.9996	0.9984	0.9947	0.9857
18						1.0000	0.9999	0.9993	0.9976	0.9928
19							0.9999	0.9997	0.9989	0.9965
20							1.0000	0.9999	0.9996	0.9984
21								1.0000	0.9998	0.9993
22									0.9999	0.9997
23									1.0000	0.9999
24										0.9999
25										1.0000

SOURCE: From *Management Science for Business Decisions* by Lawrence L. Lapin, copyright ©1980 by Harcourt Brace Jovanovich, Inc. Reproduced by permission of the publisher.

TABLE E   (continued)

λt	11.0	12.0	13.0	14.0	15.0	16.0	17.0	18.0	19.0	20.0
x
0	0.0000	0.0000	0.0000	0.0000	0.0000	0.0000	0.0	0.0	0.0	0.0
1	0.0002	0.0001	0.0000	0.0000	0.0000	0.0000	0.0000	0.0000	0.0000	0.0
2	0.0012	0.0005	0.0002	0.0001	0.0000	0.0000	0.0000	0.0000	0.0000	0.0000
3	0.0049	0.0023	0.0011	0.0005	0.0002	0.0001	0.0000	0.0000	0.0000	0.0000
4	0.0151	0.0076	0.0037	0.0018	0.0009	0.0004	0.0002	0.0001	0.0000	0.0000
5	0.0375	0.0203	0.0107	0.0055	0.0028	0.0014	0.0007	0.0003	0.0002	0.0001
6	0.0786	0.0458	0.0259	0.0142	0.0076	0.0040	0.0021	0.0010	0.0005	0.0003
7	0.1432	0.0895	0.0540	0.0316	0.0180	0.0100	0.0054	0.0029	0.0015	0.0008
8	0.2320	0.1550	0.0998	0.0621	0.0374	0.0220	0.0126	0.0071	0.0039	0.0021
9	0.3405	0.2424	0.1658	0.1094	0.0699	0.0433	0.0261	0.0154	0.0089	0.0050
10	0.4599	0.3472	0.2517	0.1757	0.1185	0.0774	0.0491	0.0304	0.0183	0.0108
11	0.5793	0.4616	0.3532	0.2600	0.1847	0.1270	0.0847	0.0549	0.0347	0.0214
12	0.6887	0.5760	0.4631	0.3585	0.2676	0.1931	0.1350	0.0917	0.0606	0.0390
13	0.7813	0.6815	0.5730	0.4644	0.3632	0.2745	0.2009	0.1426	0.0984	0.0661
14	0.8540	0.7720	0.6751	0.5704	0.4656	0.3675	0.2808	0.2081	0.1497	0.1049
15	0.9074	0.8444	0.7636	0.6694	0.5681	0.4667	0.3714	0.2866	0.2148	0.1565
16	0.9441	0.8987	0.8355	0.7559	0.6641	0.5660	0.4677	0.3750	0.2920	0.2211
17	0.9678	0.9370	0.8905	0.8272	0.7489	0.6593	0.5640	0.4686	0.3784	0.2970
18	0.9823	0.9626	0.9302	0.8826	0.8195	0.7423	0.6549	0.5622	0.4695	0.3814
19	0.9907	0.9787	0.9573	0.9235	0.8752	0.8122	0.7363	0.6509	0.5606	0.4703
20	0.9953	0.9884	0.9750	0.9521	0.9170	0.8682	0.8055	0.7307	0.6472	0.5591
21	0.9977	0.9939	0.9859	0.9711	0.9469	0.9108	0.8615	0.7991	0.7255	0.6437
22	0.9989	0.9969	0.9924	0.9833	0.9672	0.9418	0.9047	0.8551	0.7931	0.7206
23	0.9995	0.9985	0.9960	0.9907	0.9805	0.9633	0.9367	0.8989	0.8490	0.7875
24	0.9998	0.9993	0.9980	0.9950	0.9888	0.9777	0.9593	0.9317	0.8933	0.8432
25	0.9999	0.9997	0.9990	0.9974	0.9938	0.9869	0.9747	0.9554	0.9269	0.8878
26	1.0000	0.9999	0.9995	0.9987	0.9967	0.9925	0.9848	0.9718	0.9514	0.9221
27		0.9999	0.9998	0.9994	0.9983	0.9959	0.9912	0.9827	0.9687	0.9475
28		1.0000	0.9999	0.9997	0.9991	0.9978	0.9950	0.9897	0.9805	0.9657
29			1.0000	0.9999	0.9996	0.9989	0.9973	0.9940	0.9881	0.9782
30				0.9999	0.9998	0.9994	0.9985	0.9967	0.9930	0.9865
31				1.0000	0.9999	0.9997	0.9992	0.9982	0.9960	0.9919
32					0.9999	0.9999	0.9996	0.9990	0.9978	0.9953
33					1.0000	0.9999	0.9998	0.9995	0.9988	0.9973
34						1.0000	0.9999	0.9997	0.9994	0.9985
35							0.9999	0.9999	0.9997	0.9992
36							1.0000	0.9999	0.9998	0.9996
37								1.0000	0.9999	0.9998
38									1.0000	0.9999
39										0.9999
40										1.0000

TABLE F Random Numbers

12651	61646	11769	75109	86996	97669	25757	32535	07122	76763
81769	74436	02630	72310	45049	18029	07469	42341	98173	79260
36737	98863	77240	76251	00654	64688	09343	70278	67331	98729
82861	54371	76610	94934	72748	44124	05610	53750	95938	01485
21325	15732	24127	37431	09723	63529	73977	95218	96074	42138
74146	47887	62463	23045	41490	07954	22597	60012	98866	90959
90759	64410	54179	66075	61051	75385	51378	08360	95946	95547
55683	98078	02238	91540	21219	17720	87817	41705	95785	12563
79686	17969	76061	83748	55920	83612	41540	86492	06447	60568
70333	00201	86201	69716	78185	62154	77930	67663	29529	75116
14042	53536	07779	04157	41172	36473	42123	43929	50533	33437
59911	08256	06596	48416	69770	68797	56080	14223	59199	30162
62368	62623	62742	14891	39247	52242	98832	69533	91174	57979
57529	97751	54976	48957	74599	08759	78494	52785	68526	64618
15469	90574	78033	66885	13936	42117	71831	22961	94225	31816
18625	23674	53850	32827	81647	80820	00420	63555	74489	80141
74626	68394	88562	70745	23701	45630	65891	58220	35442	60414
11119	16519	27384	90199	79210	76965	99546	30323	31664	22845
41101	17336	48951	53674	17880	45260	08575	49321	36191	17095
32123	91576	84221	78902	82010	30847	62329	63898	23268	74283
26091	68409	69704	82267	14751	13151	93115	01437	56945	89661
67680	79790	48462	59278	44185	29616	76531	19589	83139	28454
15184	19260	14073	07026	25264	08388	27182	22557	61501	67481
58010	45039	57181	10238	36874	28546	37444	80824	63981	39942
56425	53996	86245	32623	78858	08143	60377	42925	42815	11159
82630	84066	13592	60642	17904	99718	63432	88642	37858	25431
14927	40909	23900	48761	44860	92467	31742	87142	03607	32059
23740	22505	07489	85986	74420	21744	97711	36648	35620	97949
32990	97446	03711	63824	07953	85965	87089	11687	92414	67257
05310	24058	91946	78437	34365	82469	12430	84754	19354	72745
21839	39937	27534	88913	49055	19218	47712	67677	51889	70926
08833	42549	93981	94051	28382	83725	72643	64233	97252	17133
58336	11139	47479	00931	91560	95372	97642	33856	54825	55680
62032	91144	75478	47431	52726	30289	42411	91886	51818	78292
45171	30557	53116	04118	58301	24375	65609	85810	18620	49198
91611	62656	60128	35609	63698	78356	50682	22505	01692	36291
55472	63819	86314	49174	93582	73604	78614	78849	23096	72825
18573	09729	74091	53994	10970	86557	65661	41854	26037	53296
60866	02955	90288	82136	83644	94455	06560	78029	98768	71296
45043	55608	82767	60890	74646	79485	13619	98868	40857	19415
17831	09737	79473	75945	28394	79334	70577	38048	03607	06932
40137	03981	07585	18128	11178	32601	27994	05641	22600	86064
77776	31343	14576	97706	16039	47517	43300	59080	80392	63189
69605	44104	40103	95635	05635	81673	68657	09559	23510	95875
19916	52934	26499	09821	87331	80993	61299	36979	73599	35055
02606	58552	07678	56619	65325	30705	99582	53390	46357	13244
65183	73160	87131	35530	47946	09854	18080	02321	05809	04898
10740	98914	44916	11322	89717	88189	30143	52687	19420	60061
98642	89822	71691	51573	83666	61642	46683	33761	47542	23551
60139	25601	93663	25547	02654	94829	48672	28736	84994	13071

SOURCE: The Rand Corporation. *A Million Random Digits with 100,000 Normal Deviates* (New York: Free Press, 1955), excerpt from page 387. Copyright 1955 by The Rand Corporation. Used by permission.

TABLE G — Critical Values of D for Kilmogorov-Smirnov Goodness-of-Fit Test

The following table provides the critical values D_α corresponding to an upper tail probability α of the test statistic D. The following relationship holds

$$\alpha = Pr[D \geq D_\alpha]$$

n	α = .10	α = .05	α = .025	α = .01	α = .005
1	.90000	.95000	.97500	.99000	.99500
2	.68377	.77639	.84189	.90000	.92929
3	.56481	.63604	.70760	.78456	.82900
4	.49265	.56522	.62394	.68887	.73424
5	.44698	.50945	.56328	.62718	.66853
6	.41037	.46799	.51926	.57741	.61661
7	.38148	.43607	.48342	.53844	.57581
8	.35831	.40962	.45427	.50654	.54179
9	.33910	.38746	.43001	.47960	.51332
10	.32260	.36866	.40925	.45662	.48893
11	.30829	.35242	.39122	.43670	.46770
12	.29577	.33815	.37543	.41918	.44905
13	.28470	.32549	.36143	.40362	.43247
14	.27481	.31417	.34890	.38970	.41762
15	.26588	.30397	.33760	.37713	.40420
16	.25778	.29472	.32733	.36571	.39201
17	.25039	.28627	.31796	.35528	.38086
18	.24360	.27851	.30936	.34569	.37062
19	.23735	.27136	.30143	.33685	.36117
20	.23156	.26473	.29408	.32866	.35241
21	.22617	.25858	.28724	.32104	.34427
22	.22115	.25283	.28087	.31394	.33666
23	.21645	.24746	.27490	.30728	.32954
24	.21205	.24242	.26931	.30104	.32286
25	.20790	.23768	.26404	.29516	.31657
26	.20399	.23320	.25907	.28962	.31064
27	.20030	.22898	.25438	.28438	.30502
28	.19680	.22497	.24993	.27942	.29971
29	.19348	.22117	.24571	.27471	.29466
30	.19032	.21756	.24170	.27023	.28987
31	.18732	.21412	.23788	.26596	.28530
32	.18445	.21085	.23424	.26189	.28094
33	.18171	.20771	.23076	.25801	.27677
34	.17909	.20472	.22743	.25429	.27279
35	.17659	.20185	.22425	.25073	.26897
36	.17418	.19910	.22119	.24732	.26532
37	.17188	.19646	.21826	.24404	.26180
38	.16966	.19392	.21544	.24089	.25843
39	.16753	.19148	.21273	.23786	.25518
40	.16547	.18913	.21012	.23494	.25205
41	.16349	.18687	.20760	.23213	.24904
42	.16158	.18468	.20517	.22941	.24613
43	.15974	.18257	.20283	.22679	.24332
44	.15796	.18053	.20056	.22426	.24060
45	.15623	.17856	.19837	.22181	.23798
46	.15457	.17665	.19625	.21944	.23544
47	.15295	.17481	.19420	.21715	.23298
48	.15139	.17302	.19221	.21493	.23059
49	.14987	.17128	.19028	.21277	.22828
50	.14840	.16959	.18841	.21068	.22604

TABLE G *(continued)*

n	α= .10	α= .05	α= .025	α= .01	α= .005
51	.14697	.16796	.18659	.20864	.22386
52	.14558	.16637	.18482	.20667	.22174
53	.14423	.16483	.18311	.20475	.21968
54	.14292	.16332	.18144	.20289	.21768
55	.14164	.16186	.17981	.20107	.21574
56	.14040	.16044	.17823	.19930	.21384
57	.13919	.15906	.17669	.19758	.21199
58	.13801	.15771	.17519	.19590	.21019
59	.13686	.15639	.17373	.19427	.20844
60	.13573	.15511	.17231	.19267	.20673
61	.13464	.15385	.17091	.19112	.20506
62	.13357	.15263	.16956	.18960	.20343
63	.13253	.15144	.16823	.18812	.20184
64	.13151	.15027	.16693	.18667	.20029
65	.13052	.14913	.16567	.18525	.19877
66	.12954	.14802	.16443	.18387	.19729
67	.12859	.14693	.16322	.18252	.19584
68	.12766	.14587	.16204	.18119	.19442
69	.12675	.14483	.16088	.17990	.19303
70	.12586	.14381	.15975	.17863	.19167
71	.12499	.14281	.15864	.17739	.19034
72	.12413	.14183	.15755	.17618	.18903
73	.12329	.14087	.15649	.17498	.18776
74	.12247	.13993	.15544	.17382	.18650
75	.12167	.13901	.15442	.17268	.18528
76	.12088	.13811	.15342	.17155	.18408
77	.12011	.13723	.15244	.17045	.18290
78	.11935	.13636	.15147	.16938	.18174
79	.11860	.13551	.15052	.16832	.18060
80	.11787	.13467	.14960	.16728	.17949
81	.11716	.13385	.14868	.16626	.17840
82	.11645	.13305	.14779	.16526	.17732
83	.11576	.13226	.14691	.16428	.17627
84	.11508	.13148	.14605	.16331	.17523
85	.11442	.13072	.14520	.16236	.17421
86	.11376	.12997	.14437	.16143	.17321
87	.11311	.12923	.14355	.16051	.17223
88	.11248	.12850	.14274	.15961	.17126
89	.11186	.12779	.14195	.15873	.17031
90	.11125	.12709	.14117	.15786	.16938
91	.11064	.12640	.14040	.15700	.16846
92	.11005	.12572	.13965	.15616	.16755
93	.10947	.12506	.13891	.15533	.16666
94	.10889	.12440	.13818	.15451	.16579
95	.10833	.12375	.13746	.15371	.16493
96	.10777	.12312	.13675	.15291	.16408
97	.10722	.12249	.13606	.15214	.16324
98	.10668	.12187	.13537	.15137	.16242
99	.10615	.12126	.13469	.15061	.16161
100	.10563	.12067	.13403	.14987	.16081

SOURCE: Reprinted by permission from L. H. Miller, "Table of Percentage Points of Kolmogorov Statistics," *Journal of the American Statistical Association*, 51 (1956), pages 111–121.

ANSWERS TO SELECTED PROBLEMS

1-12 Q = 75, TC(Q) = $503,000

2-1 (d) 425

2-4 (b) Q = 75, TC(Q) = $503,000

2-6 Total estimated sales = $5,935,000

2-8 (b) Total interest earned = $64,000

2-10 (b) 0.3 (c) 26
(d) The average waiting time in line is undefined because when the arrival rate equals the service rate a division by zero occurs.
(e) For an arrival rate of 40 customers per hour the average waiting time is 2 minutes. This is when a second ATM is to be installed.

2-12 (a) 138 (b) 144 (c) 275

3-1 (a) 1/5 (b) 1/10,000 (c) 1/4 (d) 2/3

3-2 1/38

3-4 (a) 1/20 (b) 1/10

3-7 (a) .72 (b) .48 (c) .16 (d) .35

3-9 (a) .7 (b) .5 (c) .7 (d) .3 (c) .6

3-11 (a) 3/10 (b) Yes, not independent
(c) 3/20 No

3-14 (a) (1) .6 (2) .35 (3) .40 (4) .15
(5) .50 (6) .25 (7) .50 (8) .25
(b) (1) .65 (2) .75 (3) .75 (4) .85

3-18 (a)

Sex	Marital Status: Married	Marital Status: Unmarried	Marginal Probability
Male	3/35	17/35	20/35
Female	5/35	10/35	15/35
Marginal Probability	8/35	27/35	1

(b) (1) 3/35 (2) 5/35 (3) 10/35
(4) 17/35

3-23 (a) .12 (b) .48 (c) .08 (d) .32

3-25 (a) .288 (b) .200 (c) .0625 (d) .0714

3-30 (a) .729 (b) .2916 (c) .40951

3-38 (a) (1) .6 (2) .4 (3) .4 (4) .7
(5) .6 (6) .3
(b) (1) .24 (2) .36 (3) .28 (4) .12

3-44 (a) Pr[P] = 1/5 Pr[S] = 4/5
(b) Pr[K | S] = 1/13 Pr[K | P] = 1
Pr[P | K] = .765

3-46 (a) .467 (b) .086

3-51 (a) .82 (b) .11

3-52 (a) No (b) Yes (c) Maybe

3-56 (a)

Result	Unconditional Probability	Posterior Probability: Fair	Posterior Probability: Crooked
7	7/12	1/7	6/7
Not 7	5/12	1	0

4-2 (−$1)(20/38) + $1(18/38) = −$0.053
After many wagers the gambler will lose an average 5.3 cents per play.

4-12 (a) .25 (b) .50 (c) 5

4-15 (a) .0490 (b) .2262 (c) .6723 (d) .9687

4-17 (a) .0565 (b) .0710 (c) .8744 (d) .5956
(e) .2500 (f) .8534

4-20 (a) .4332 (b) .1915 (c) .2420 (d) .0062
(e) .0968 (f) .9861 (g) .97585 (h) .0606

4-26 (a) .0774 (b) .9797 (c) .0286 (d) .6315

4-28 (a) 60 sec; 22.4 sec
(b) (1) .3472 (2) .0594 (3) .5000 (4).8732

4-32 (a) .105 (b) .15 (c) .38 (d) .73

4-38 302

4-39 170

4-41 (a) 3 (b) 45 (c) 190 (d) 4,950

4-43 (b) expected value = 1.5, variance = 0.75, standard deviation = 0.87

4-45 (b) expected value = 12, variance = 4.8, standard deviation = 2.19

4-50 (a) .3935 (b) 1 − .7769 = .2231
(c) 1 − .3935 − .2231 = 0.3834

4-52 (a) 0   (b) .5830   (c) .4170

4-54 (a) .4332   (b) .1915   (c) .2420   (d) .0062
(e) .0968   (f) .9861   (g) .9759   (h) .0606

4-56 (b) Pr[no customers] = .0067
(c) Pr[number of customers ≤ 8] = 0.9319
(d) Pr[number of customers ≥ 8] = 1 − .8666
= .1334

5-5 A_3 and A_5

5-13

Event	Probability	Act				
		A_1	A_2	A_3	A_4	A_5
E_1	.2	10	0	10	5	0
E_2	.2	15	0	15	0	15
E_3	.6	0	10	5	5	5
Expected opportunity loss:		5	6	8	4	6

Act A_4 has the lowest expected opportunity loss.

5-14 (a) 27 for A,   (b) 39   (c) 12   (d) 12
(e) They are the same values.

5-16 (a)

Sales Event	Proba-bility	Tire Act			Row Maximum
		A	B	C	
4,000	.30	$120,000	$130,000	$120,000	$130,000
7,000	.50	255,000	295,000	300,000	300,000
10,000	.20	390,000	460,000	480,000	480,000
Expected payoff:		$241,500	$278,500	$282,000	$285,000

(b) See above. Tire C is best.
(c) EVPI = $285,000 − $282,000 = $3,000
(d)

Sales Event	Probability	Tire Act		
		A	B	C
4,000	.30	$10,000	$ 0	$10,000
7,000	.50	45,000	5,000	0
10,000	.20	45,000	5,000	0
Expected opportunity loss:		$43,500	$ 6,500	$ 3,000

5-18 Spring-action movement

5-20 Test market. If that is successful, market nation-ally; if it is unsuccessful, abort.

5-21 Use no test and hire each candidate.

5-27 (b) Choose method A with an expected payoff of $ 920,000

6-2

	(a)	(b)	(c)	(d)
(1) Expected payoff	$35,000	$19,300	$2,500	$ 0
(2) Risk premium	4,000	1,000	200	20,000
(3) Certainty equivalent	31,000	18,300	2,300	−20,000

6-5 (a) −$10   (b) $5

6-11 (a)

Event	Act	
	Policy	No Policy
Tornado	−$500	−$40,000
No tornado	−500	0

(b) −$500 for a policy; −$4 for no policy
(c) No

6-13 (a) 50   (b) 170   (c) 2,000

6-16 (a) Willing   (b,c) Might be willing
(d) Unwilling   (e) Willing

6-18 No

6-21 (a)

Event	Act	
	Buy	Rent
Win contract	$120,000	$50,000
Lose contract	−40,000	0

(b) $40,000 for buying; $25,000 for renting
(c)

Event	Act	
	Buy	Rent
Win contract	400	300
Lose contract	0	200

(d) 200 for buying; 250 for renting.   (e) Rent

6-26 (a) 1/2   (b) 3/4; 1/4   (c) 1/2 Inconsistent

6-30 Same as Problem 6-21

6-31 (a) Do not test market, do not market nationally.
(b) Test market. If favorable, market, and if un-favorable do not market.

7-1 Winter $ 72,000   Spring $ 84.700
Summer   121,000   Fall   179,685

7-9 (a) $\hat{Y} = 200.67 + 9.673X$ ($X = 0$ at 1984)
(b) 297.40

7-11 (b) $\hat{Y} = 22.405 + 3.619X$

7-12 (a) 1,100   (b) 900   (c) 700

7-15 Winter   50.6   Spring   89.8
Summer   150.9   Fall   108.7

7-16

(a) (b)

Quarter	Percentage of Moving Average	Average	Seasonal Index
1995 W			93.4
S			112.0
S	6.8	63.2	69.2
F	7.8	138.5	125.4
1996 W	8.7	89.7	93.4
S	9.4	112.8	112.0
S	10.3	67.0	69.2
F	11.6	116.4	125.4
1997 W	12.6	102.4	93.4
S	13.6	111.8	112.0
S	14.4	71.5	69.2
F	14.4	129.9	125.4
1998 W	14.3	97.2	93.4
S	14.1	102.1	112.0
S	13.9	73.4	69.2
F	14.3	121.0	125.4
1999 W	15.3	88.2	93.4
S	16.2	112.3	112.0
S			69.2
F			125.4

7-18 (e) $\alpha = 0.9$, $\gamma = 0.38$

7-20 $\hat{Y} = -.5595 + .817X_1 + 1.1605X_2$

7-23 (a) $\hat{Y} = .305 + .104X_1 + .317X_2 + .965X_3$
(b) (1) 18.70 (2) 11.91 (3) 6.85
(4) 14.66

7-25 Q1 forecast = 15.93, Q2 forecast = 21.73, Q3 forecast = 14.58, Q4 forecast = 23.75

7-27 $\hat{Y} = -.0098X^2 + .726X + 16.925$

8-2 (a) $X_1 = 7.5$, $X_2 = 2.5$
(b) $X_1 = 1.5$, $X_2 = 1$
(c) $X_1 = -.5$, $X_2 = 2$
(d) $X_1 = -1.5$, $X_2 = 4.5$

8-3 $X_A = 2.4$, $X_B = 2.4$, $P = 26.4$

8-8 (b) There are two most attractive corners:
(1) $X_1 = 4$, $X_2 = 4$, $P = 24$
(2) $X_1 = 12$, $X_2 = 0$, $P = 24$
(c) $P = 24$ The point represents an optimal solution.

8-12 (a) Letting X_R = Quantity of regular models, X_D = Quantity of deluxe models

Maximize $P = 10X_R + 15X_D$
Subject to $5X_R + 8X_D \le 80$ (labor)
$X_R + X_D \le 12$ (frame)
where $X_R, X_D \ge 0$

(b) $X_R = 5\ 1/3$, $X_D = 6\ 2/3$, $P = 1533$ dollars

8-14 4 forged bits, 6 machined bits, $P = 102$ dollars

8-16 (a) Letting X_V = number of days devoted to producing voice modems
X_F = number of days devoted to producing voice/fax modems

Maximize $P = 40(1,000)X_V + 60(500)X_F$
$= 40,000X_V + 30,000X_F$
Subject to $X_V + X_F = 200$
$1,000X_V \ge 100,000$
$500X_F \le 90,000$
where $X_V, X_F \ge 0$

(b) The first constraint changes to
$$1,000X_V \le 100,000$$

8-20 Letting H_1, H_2, H_3, and H_4 denote the number of hard drives produced in the respective quarters and I_1, I_2, I_3, and I_4 denote the inventory of hard drives at the end of the respective quarters

Minimize
$C = 25(H_1 + H_2 + H_3 + H_4) + 1(I_1 + I_2 + I_3 + I_4)$
Subject to
$H_1 + H_2 + H_3 + H_4 + 1(I_1 + I_2 + I_3 + I_4)$
$H_1 + I_1 = 40,000$
$H_2 + I_1 - I_2 = 100,000$
$H_3 + I_2 - I_3 = 50,000$
$H_4 + I_3 = 220,000$
$H_1 \le 125,000$
$H_2 \le 125,000$
$H_3 \le 125,000$
$H_4 \le 125,000$
where $H_1, H_2, H_3, H_4, I_1, I_2, I_3 \ge 0$

9-1 Letting X_F = quantity of fancy lamps
X_O = quantity of ornate lamps
X_P = quantity of plain lamps
X_R = quantity of rococo lamps

Maximize
$$P = 100X_F + 150X_O + 200X_P + 200X_R$$
Subject to
(labor) $10X_F + 8X_O + 10X_P + 20X_R \le 1,000$
(machine) $2X_F + 3X_O + 1X_P + 1X_R \le 200$
(sheet metal) $10X_F + 20X_O + 15X_P + 30X_R \le 5,000$
(quantity) $-1X_R + 2X_R \le 0$
where $X_F, X_R, X_R, X_R \ge 0$

9-7 Letting X_H = pounds of hog bellies
X_P = pounds of pork
X_T = pounds of tripe
X_C = pounds of chicken
X_B = pounds of beef

Minimize
$$C = .30X_H + .20X_T + .70X_B + .60X_P + .45X_C$$
Subject to

$$
\begin{array}{ll}
X_H + X_T & \le .10 \\
& \text{(restriction)} \\
X_C \le .25 \\
& \text{(chicken)} \\
X_B & \ge .30 \\
& \text{(beef)} \\
3X_H + 5X_T + 4X_B + 3X_P + 3X_C \ge 3 \\
& \text{(protein)} \\
5X_H + 3X_T + 2X_B + 4X_P + 3X_C \le 4 \\
& \text{(fat)} \\
6X_H + 4X_T + 5X_B + 9X_P + 4X_C \le 8 \\
& \text{(water)} \\
X_H + X_T + X_B + X_P + X_C = 1 \\
& \text{(total weight)}
\end{array}
$$

where   all $Xs \ge 0$

9-8   Letting X_A = number of gallons of Ant Can't
X_B = number of gallons of Boll-Toll
X_C = number of gallons of Caterpillar-Chiller

Maximize P
$$= 5X_A + 6X_B + 7X_C$$
Subject to

$$
\begin{array}{ll}
.1X_A + .1X_B + .1X_C \le 1,000 & \text{(catalyst)} \\
.1X_A + \quad .1X_C \le 1,000 & \text{(malathion)} \\
.2X_B + .2X_C \le 2,000 & \text{(parathion)} \\
X_A + X_B \quad \le 500 & \text{(quantity mix)}
\end{array}
$$

where $X_A, X_B, X_C \ge 0$

9-11   Letting X_{ij} = number of tombstones shipped from quarry
i to mason j
i = A or B
j = C, D, or E

Minimize C
$$= 10X_{AC} + 15X_{AD} + 8X_{AE} + 12X_{BC} + 9X_{BD} + 10X_{BE}$$
Subject to

$$
\begin{array}{ll}
X_{AC} + X_{AD} + X_{AE} & = 100 \\
& \text{(Abinger capacity)} \\
X_{BC} + X_{BD} + X_{BE} = 200 \\
& \text{(Barnesly capacity)} \\
X_{AC} + \quad X_{BC} \quad = 50 \\
& \text{(Cedrick's demand)} \\
X_{AD} + \quad X_{BD} \quad = 150 \\
& \text{(Dunstan's demand)} \\
X_{AE} + \quad X_{BE} = 100 \\
& \text{(Eldred's demand)}
\end{array}
$$

where   all $Xs = 0$

9-16   Letting X_B = number of spots on KBAT
X_J = number of spots on WJOK
X_R = number of spots on WROB
X_P = number of spots on KPOW

Maximize P
$$= 300X_B + 120X_J + 150X_R + 400X_P$$
Subject to

$$
\begin{array}{ll}
100X_B + 50X_J + 75X_R + 150X_P \le 10,000 \\
& \text{(funds)} \\
X_B \quad \le 30 \\
& \text{(avail. on KBAT)} \\
X_P \le 40 \\
& \text{(avail. on KPOW)} \\
.25X_B - .75X_J - .75X_R + .25X_P \le 0 \\
& \text{(golden-oldie)}
\end{array}
$$

where   all variables ≥ 0

9-53 $X_1 = 0, X_2 = 0, X_3 = 10, X_4 = 0, X_5 = 50$;
$P = 6,050$

9-55 $X_1 = 200, X_2 = 100, X_3 = 100, X_4 = 250,$
$X_5 = 150; P = 4,800$

9-57 $X_1 = 0, X_2 = 100, X_3 = 0$
$Y_1 = .33, Y_2 = 99.7, Y_3 = 0, Y_4 = 100,$
$Y_5 = 0, Y_6 = 0, Y_7 = 0$
$Z_1 = 0, Z_2 = 0, Z_3 = 0, Z_4 = 0, Z_5 = 0,$
$Z_6 = 96, Z_7 = 3.96$
$P = 34,523$

10-2   Letting U_W = marginal value of resource
wood
U_L = marginal value of resource
labor

Minimize C = $200U_W + 240U_L$
Subject to $50U_W + 10U_L \ge 9$
$20U_W + 30U_L \ge 6$
where $U_W, U_L \ge 0$

10-3   Letting U_D = marginal value for demand
constraint
U_M = marginal value for material
constraint

Minimize C = $-10U_D + 20U_M$
Subject to $-U_D + 5U_M \ge 5$
$-3U_D + 2U_M \ge 1$
where $U_D < U_M \ge 0$

10-6   Letting U_M = marginal value for the mixture constraint

U_L = marginal value for the labor constraint

U_{B1} = marginal value for the first balance constraint

U_{B2} = marginal value for the second balance constraint

Minimize $C = 0U_M + 20U_L + 20U_{B1} - 20U_{B2}$

Subject to $-1U_M + 8U_L + 1U_{B1} - 1U_{B2} \geq 5$

$2U_M + 7U_L + 1U_{B1} - 1U_{B2} \geq 8$

where $U_M, U_L, U_{B1}, U_{B2} \geq 0$

10-9   Letting U_L = marginal value for the limitation constraint

U_{M1} = marginal value for the rst mixture constraint

U_{M2} = marginal value for the second mixture constraint

U_R = marginal value for the restriction constraint

Minimize C

$= 1,000U_L + 875U_{M1} - 875U_{M2} - 1U_R$

Subject to

$10U_L + 50U_{M1} - 50U_{M2} - 1U_R \geq 100$

$20U_L + 30U_{M1} - 3U_{M2} - 1U_R \geq 250$

$15U_L + 14U_{M1} - 14U_{M2} - 1U_R \geq 150$

where $U_L, U_{M1}, U_{M2}, U_R \geq 0$

10-15   (b) Letting U_L = marginal value of labor

U_F = marginal value of a frame

The above reect the increase in prot that results from an additional hour of labor and an extra frame, respectively.

Minimize $C = 80U_L + 12U_F$

Subject to $5U_L + 10U_F \geq 10$ (regular)

$8U_L + 1U_F \geq 15$ (deluxe)

where $U_L, U_F \geq 0$

(c) $U_L = 5/3$, $U_F = 5/3$, C = 460/3 dollars

10-17   (a) \$5/7; \$18/7   (b) $U_T = 0$, $U_C = 0$, $U_B = 5$

(c) $X_T = 64/7$, $X_C = 20/7$, $X_B = 0$,

$P = 1580/7$ dollars   (d) Yes

10-26   (e) Rott should make no Baltics, 400/7 Gothics, and 300/7 chics, at a profit of \$8,500/7

11-1   (c) $X_1 = 2$, $X_2 = 3$; $P = 18$

11-4 $X_R = 6$, $X_D = 6$; $P = 150$

$X_R = 0$, $X_D = 10$; $P = 150$

$X_R = 3$, $X_D = 8$; $P = 150$

11-9   (a) 51⅓ regulars, 6⅔ deluxes, $P = 153⅓$

(b) 0 regulars, 10 deluxes, $R = 600$

11-12 $X_T = 9$, $X_C = 3$, $X_B = 0$; $P = 225$

12-4   C = 5,050

From \ To	W1	W2	W3	W4	Capacity
P1	2	6	4 / 100	12	100
	2	6		4	
P2	7	3 / 150	10	11 / 100	250
	2		3		
P3	5 / 50	8	9 / 100	13 / 150	300
		3			
Demand	50	150	200	250	650

12-12   C = 37,000

From Plant	To Warehouse 1	2	3	4
A	0	0	0	1000
B	0	2000	0	
C	2000	0	2000	1000

12-14   (b) C = 4,350

From \ To	U	V	W	Capacity
A	10	7 / 50	8 / 50	100
	4			
B	15	12	9 / 150	150
	8	4		
C	7 / 150	8 / 150	2	300
			3	
Demand	150	200	200	550

12-17   C = 650

From Plant	To Warehouse W1	W2	W3	Dummy
Plant 1	150	0	0	0
Plant 2	0	100	0	0
Plant 3	50	0	150	150

12-22   Ship 100 tombstones to Eldred from Abinger, and ship 50 tombstones to Cedriclk and 150 tombstones to Dunstan from Barneslv.

12-27

Brat	Chore
Fritz	Retrieve the Captain's pipe
Hans	Scare cannibals
Gert	Pen ostriches
Zelda	Chase hippos

12-34

Production	Used for Demand
August regular-25	August-25
August overtime-75 September regular-100	September-175
October regular-100 October overtime-50	October-150
November regular-100, November overtime-50	November-150

12-37   C = 16,678.50

From Plant	To Warehouse											
	W1	W2	W3	W4	W5	W6	W7	W8	W9	W10	W11	DUMMY
C1	112	0	0	0	0	0	0	0	53	0	0	335
C2	0	0	138	0	77	89	0	215	0	49	85	97
C2	0	85	0	146	0	0	101	0	0	0	68	0

12-39   C = 6,900

From Plant	To Warehouse									
	A1	A2	A3	A4	A5	A6	A7	A8	A9	A10
M1	75	0	0	0	0	0	0	0	80	0
M2	0	0	115	130	0	0	0	0	0	0
M3	0	155	0	0	0	55	115	0	0	0
M4	0	0	5	0	75	40	0	55	0	0
Dummy	0	0	0	0	0	0	0	0	65	95

12-41

P1-T5	P2-T1	P3-T9	P4-T6
P5-T4	P6-T11	P7-T8	P8-T7
P9-T14	P10-T3	P11-T2	P12-T12
P13-T10	P14-T13	C = 344	

13-1   A-C-F-H-I   11

13-2   A-C   B-D   F-H   18
C-E   D-G   H-I
C-F   E-G

13-3

A-B = 7	B-E = 3	E-G = 6	G-H = 5
A-C = 9	C-E = 3	F-G = 5	H-I = E
B-D = 4	C-F = 6	F-H = 1	
B-E = 3	D-G = 4	G-I =10	

maximum flow16

13-4
P1-W1 = 0	P2-W2 = 20	P3-W1 = 30
P1-W2 = 0	P2-W2 = 100	P3-W2 = 100
P1-W3 = 50	P2-W3 = 80	P3-W3 = 100
P1-W4 = 50	P2-W4 = 50	P3-W4 = 150

C = 5,720

13-23   A-C-F-H-I   11

13-24   Same as Problem 13-3

13-25   Same as Problem 13-4

13-28   C = 17

From Node	To Node											
	A	B	C	D	E	F	G	H	I	J	K	L
A	0	3	4	4	6	0	0	0	0	0	0	0
B	0	0	0	3	0	0	0	0	0	0	0	0
C	0	0	0	0	0	4	0	0	0	0	0	0
D	0	0	0	0	0	3	0	4	0	0	0	0
E	0	0	0	0	0	0	2	0	4	0	0	0
F	0	0	0	0	0	0	1	0	6	0	0	0
G	0	0	0	0	0	0	0	0	3	0	0	0
H	0	0	0	0	0	0	0	0	0	4	0	0
I	0	0	0	0	0	0	0	0	0	0	10	0
J	0	0	0	0	0	0	0	0	0	0	0	7
K	0	0	0	0	0	0	0	0	0	0	0	10
L	17	0	0	0	0	0	0	0	0	0	0	0

13-29   C = 15

To Node	From Node								
	B0	S1	B1	S2	B2	S3	B3	S4	S5
B0	0	0	0	0	0	0	0	0	0
S1	1	0	0	0	0	0	0	0	0
B1	0	1	0	0	0	0	0	0	0
S1	0	0	1	0	0	0	0	0	0
B2	0	0	0	1	0	0	0	0	0
S3	0	0	0	0	1	0	0	0	0
B3	0	0	0	0	0	1	0	0	0
S4	0	0	0	0	0	0	1	0	0
B4	0	0	0	0	0	0	0	1	0
S5	0	0	0	0	0	0	0	0	1

13-33   C = $7,475

From Warehouse	To Store									
	A1	A2	A3	A4	A5	A6	A7	A8	A9	A10
M1	50	0	0	20	0	0	0	35	50	0
M2	0	30	100	100	0	0	0	0	15	0
M3	25	100	20	10	0	70	100	0	0	0
M4	0	0	0	0	75	25	15	20	15	25
Dummy	0	25	0	0	0	0	0	0	65	70

14-1   *a-c-e*

14-5   (b) *b-f-g-h*

14-13   (a) *a-c-d-f-i-j-k-m-n-o-p*   32 months

14-14   (a)

Activity	Expected Time	Variance
a	6	.11
b	7	5.44
c	14	7.11
d	4	.11
e	17	.11

(b) *a-c-d*   (c) .7568

14-24   *a-c-e*

14-28   (b) *b-f-g-h*

14-30 The critical path is a-D1-e-h-D2-l. Its expected duration is 17.

14-32 The critical path is a-c-d-f-i-j-D1-k-m-n-o-p. Its expected duration is 32.

15-1 $Q^* = 200$; order once every .2 year.

15-4
(a) $Q^* = 1,291$, order once every 7.75 years, $TC(Q^*) = \$774.60$
(b) $Q^* = 1,825.7$, order once every 11 years, $TC(Q^*) = \$1,095.45$
(c) $Q^* = 912.9$, order once every 5.48 years, $TC(Q^*) = \$547.72$

15-6
(a) $Q^* = 2,620$, $S^* = 2,544$, $T^* = .262$ year Out of stock .029 of the time.
(b) $\$763.23$; smaller

15-7
(a) $Q^* = 1,886$ $TC(Q^*) = \$212.13$, always smaller
(b) $\$3.65$
(c) $Q^* = 1,914$ $S^* = 1,857$ $TC(Q^*, S^*) = \$208.93$ backorders $= 57$

15-9
(a) $Q^* = 1,366$, $S^* = 1,220$, once every 7.32 years, $TC(Q^*) = \$731.92$, maximum backorders 146
(b) $Q^* = 1,633$, $S^* = 1,021$, once every 7.34 years, $TC(Q^*) = \$612.37$, maximum backorders 612
(c) $Q^* = 1,329$, $S^* = 1,254$, once every 7.52 years, $TC(Q^*) = \$752.35$, maximum backorders 75
(d) $Q^* = 1,295$, $S^* = 1,287$, once every 7.72 years, $TC(Q^*) = \$772.31$, maximum backorders 8

15-13
(a) 6,000   (b) $.12

15-14
(a) $Q^* = 2,357$ (b) 2,357
(c) once every 4.24 years
(d) .118 years   (e) $TC(Q^*) = \$424.66$
(f) make, don't buy
(g) There is no answer, because when the production rate equals demand rate, a division by zero occurs.

15-19 (a) 158.1 tons   (b) .79 year   (c) .1581 year

15-27 (a) 632.5 acres   Fertilize every .127 year. or 7.9 times yearly.

15-28 $Q^* = 200$; order once every .2 year.

16-2 Stock 150 boxes.

16-6 (a) 62   (b) $16.235   (c) $14.015

16-9 (a) 6,120 trees   (b) (1) 66   (2) 1,186 (3) $32,315.28

16-15
(a) $\mu = 7.3$ pairs   (b) $r^* = 9$, $Q^* = 32$
(c) 1.7 pairs   (d) $68.21

16-19 $r^* = 67$ $Q^* = 406$

16-21 $r^* = 5,180$ gallons $Q^* = 10,760$ gallons

16-25 (a,b) $Q^* = 250$

16-28 (a) $Q^* = 62$ (b) $16.24

16-32
(a) $\mu = 7$ (b) $Q^* = 32$ $r = 9$
(c) $r - \mu = 2$ (d) $TEC = \$68.21$

16-35 $Q^* = 405$ $r = 67$

16-37 (a)

Case	p_S	Q^*	$TEC(Q^*)$
1	0.03	5,000	$2,626.00
2	0.04	5,000	$2,628.00
3	0.05	5,000	$2,630.00
4	0.06	5,000	$2,632.00
5	0.07	5,000	$2,634.00

(b) The results are not at all sensitive to the level for the shortage penalty. The order quantity is identical for all levels of p_S. This might be explained by the lumpiness of the demand probability distribution, for which the cutoff level in cumulative probability is the same, even though the computed ratio will change slightly as p_S does.

16-40 (a) Yes, the optimal solution appears somewhat sensitive to p_S.

	A	B	C	D	E
3	Case	p_S	Q^*	r^*	$TEC(Q^*)$
4	1	0.15	11,147	4,347	$10,494
5	2	0.20	10,876	4,890	$10,765
6	3	0.25	10,770	5,174	$10,944
7	4	0.30	10,708	5,367	$11,075
8	5	0.35	10,660	5,511	$11,171

(b) Yes, the optimal solution appears somewhat sensitive to h.

	A	B	C	D	E
3	Case	p_S	Q^*	r^*	$TEC(Q^*)$
4	1	0.18	11,290	5,237	$10,374
5	2	0.19	11,019	5,205	$10,663
6	3	0.20	10,770	5,174	$10,944
7	4	0.21	10,540	5,144	$11,218
8	5	0.22	10,327	5,115	$11,486

17-1

	(a)	(b)	(c)	(d)
L	4	2	.67	1.33
W	.20	.25	.34	3.33
L_q	3.2	1.33	.27	.76
W_q	.16	17	13	1.90
	.8	.67	4	.57

17-5 (a) .20 (b) 66.67%; 2 hour

17-10 $34

17-11 (a) (1) .0923 hour (2) .0606 hour
(b) (1) 528.38 (2) 521.82
One machinist clerk is cheapest.

17-15 (a) 5 checkers; 1.11 minutes
(b) .290 minute
(c) $56.66 for $S = 5$; $61.74 for $S = 6$

17-18 $L_q = .2725$, $L = .7725$, $W_q = .545$ minute, $W = 1.545$ minutes

17-20 (a)

n	P_n
0	.271
1	.217
2	.173
3	.139
4	.111
5	.089

(b) $L = 1.868$, $L_q = 1.139$, $W_q = .31$ hour, $W = .51$ hour
(c) $L = 4$, $L_q = 3.2$, $W_q = .8$ hour, $W = 1$ hour

17-21 (a)

n	P_n
0	.0367
1	.0918
2	.1835
3	.2753
4	.2753
5	.1376

(b) $L_q = 2.11$, $L = 3.07$, $W_q = 1.09$ days, $W = 1.59$ days
(c) $L_q = .5$, $L = 1$, $W_q = .5$ day, $W = 1$ day

17-26 (a) $P[T \geq 1] = 0.606531$
(b) $\Pr[T \geq 1] = 0.367879$
(c) $\Pr[T \leq .5] = 0.22120$
(d) $\Pr[X = 5] = 0.17547$

17-34 (a) The minimum number of checkers is $S = 5$. The corresponding customer waiting time is $W_q = 1.1082$ minutes.
(b) $W_q = 0.2848$ minutes
(c) The hourly costs associated with 5 and 6 checkers are $68.65 and $61.71 so 5 checkers yields the minimum cost solution.

17-38 NUMBER OF SERVERS

M	5	6	7	8	Thousands
P_0	0.0367	0.0121	0.0034	0.0009	0.50000
L	3.0734	4.0242	5.0069	6.0017	1.00000
W	1.5952	2.0367	2.5121	3.0034	1.00000
L_q	2.1101	3.0363	4.0103	5.0026	0.50000
W_q	1.0952	1.5367	2.0121	2.5034	0.50000

17-39 $L = 0.75$, $W = 0.015$, $L_q = 0.25$, $W_q = 0.005$, $r = 0.5$

17-41

	AF	AG	AH	AI	AJ	AK	AL	AM	AN	AO	AP	AQ
1	Optimal Number of Servers, S*											
2												
3							μ					
4	λ	25	26	27	28	29	30	31	32	33	34	35
5	15	3	3	3	3	3	3	3	3	3	3	3
6	16	3	3	3	3	3	3	3	3	3	3	3
7	17	3	3	3	3	3	3	3	3	3	3	3
8	18	3	3	3	3	3	3	3	3	3	3	3
9	19	3	3	3	3	3	3	3	3	3	3	3
10	20	3	3	3	3	3	3	3	3	3	3	3
11	21	3	3	3	3	3	3	3	3	3	3	3
12	22	3	3	3	3	3	3	3	3	3	3	3
13	23	4	3	3	3	3	3	3	3	3	3	3
15	24	4	4	3	3	3	3	3	3	3	3	3
16	25	4	4	4	3	3	3	3	3	3	3	3
17												
18												
19							Probability					
20	t(sec)	0.5	0.6	0.7	0.8	0.85	0.9	0.925	0.95	0.975	0.99	
21	1	2	2	2	2	3	3	3	3	4	4	
22	5	2	2	2	2	3	3	3	3	4	4	
23	10	2	2	2	2	2	3	3	3	4	4	
24	15	2	2	2	2	2	3	3	3	3	4	
25	20	2	2	2	2	2	3	3	3	3	4	
26	25	2	2	2	2	2	3	3	3	3	4	
27	30	2	2	2	2	2	3	3	3	3	4	
28	35	2	2	2	2	2	3	3	3	3	4	
29	40	2	2	2	2	2	3	3	3	3	4	
30	50	2	2	2	2	2	2	3	3	3	4	
31	60	2	2	2	2	2	2	3	3	3	4	

17-42 (a) geometric distribution   (b) No

17-45 (a) normal distribution   (b) beta general
(c) exponential gives reasonable t

18-2 $1/\lambda = 13.05$ seconds

18-5 385

18-7 (a) $95.57 \leq \mu \leq 105.49$ minutes
(b) $69.05 \leq \mu \leq 69.35$ inches
(c) $\$11.27 \leq \mu \leq \$12.73$

18-12 $89.142 for one barber; $113.191 for two barbers. Hire the helper.

18-15 (a)

Net Winnings	Probability
−$1	20/36
1	14/36
2	1/36
3	1/36

(c) −$.09

18-18 (a) $Q^* = 500$

		Avg Net Cost	
Part	Q	r	Per Period
(b)	500	50	$205.72
(c) (1)	100	100	$214.32
(c) (2)	200	100	$216.44
(c) (3)	500	100	$213.14

18-23 (a, b) Answers will vary. One person obtained $MSE = 2.86$ (with $\alpha = .10$ and $\gamma = .20$) and $MSE = 1.18$ (with $\alpha = .30$ and $\gamma = .20$). Those results resulted in a t value of 2.19 and rejection of the null hypothesis of identical mean MSE's.

18-27 (a, b, c) Answers will vary. One person achieved a string of 12 consecutive heads, 2 strings of 11 tails, one string of 11 heads, and one string each of 10 heads and 10 tails.

18-35 (a) $1,083,471. Answers vary for the remaining parts.

INDEX